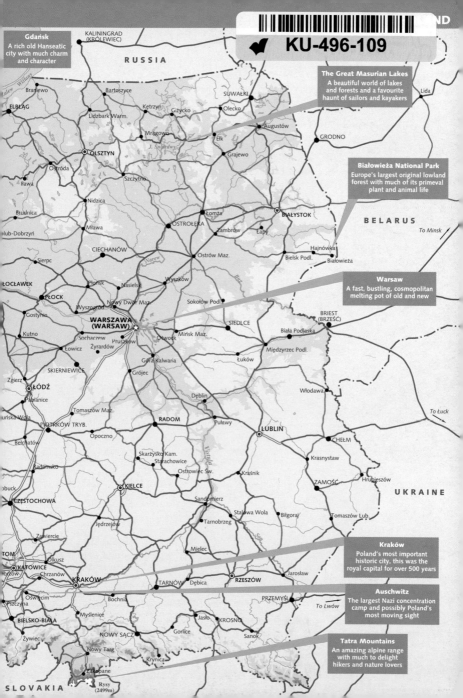

KU-496-109

Gdańsk
A rich old Hanseatic city with much charm and character

KALININGRAD (KRÓLEWIEC)

RUSSIA

Braniewo
Bartoszyce
SUWAŁKI
Lida

ELBLĄG
Ketrzyn
Giżycko
Olecko

Lidzbark Warm.
Mrągowo
Ełk
Augustów

The Great Masurian Lakes
A beautiful world of lakes and forests and a favourite haunt of sailors and kayakers

Ostróda
OLSZTYN
J. Śniardwy
Grajewo
GRODNO

Iława
Szczytno

Brodnica
Nidzica
ŁOMŻA

Białowieża National Park
Europe's largest original lowland forest with much of its primeval plant and animal life

olub-Dobrzyń
Mława
OSTROŁĘKA
Zambrów
Łapy
BIAŁYSTOK
BELARUS

Sierpc
CIECHANÓW
Ostrów Maz.
Narew
To Minsk

ŁOCŁAWEK
Płońsk
Nasielsk
Wyszków
Sokołów Podl.
Bielsk Podl.
Hajnówka
Białowieża

PŁOCK
Nowy Dwór Maz.
Bug

Gostynin
Wyszogród
WARSZAWA (WARSAW)
Mińsk Maz.
SIEDLCE
BRIEST (BRZEŚĆ)

Warsaw
A fast, bustling, cosmopolitan melting pot of old and new

Kutno
Sochaczew
Pruszków
Otwock
Biała Podlaska

Łowicz
Żyrardów
Góra Kalwaria
Łuków
Międzyrzec Podl.

ŁÓDŹ
SKIERNIEWICE
Grójec
To Łuck

Zgierz
Włodawa

Pabianice
Dęblin

uńska Wola
Tomaszów Maz.
RADOM
Puławy
LUBLIN

PIOTRKÓW TRYB.
Opoczno
CHEŁM

Bełchatów
Skarżysko Kam.
Starachowice
Krasnystaw

Radomsko
Ostrowiec Św.
Kraśnik
ZAMOŚĆ
Hrubieszów

obuck
KIELCE
Sandomierz
UKRAINE

CZĘSTOCHOWA
Jędrzejów
Stalowa Wola
Biłgoraj
Tomaszów Lub.

Zawiercie
Tarnobrzeg

TOM
Olkusz
Mielec

KATOWICE
Chrzanów
Kraków
Poland's most important historic city, this was the royal capital for over 500 years

orzów
KRAKÓW
TARNÓW
Dębica
RZESZÓW
Jarosław

Oświęcim
Bochnia
PRZEMYŚL

Pszczyna
Myślenice
Jasło
KROSNO
To Lwów
Auschwitz
The largest Nazi concentration camp and possibly Poland's most moving sight

BIELSKO-BIAŁA
Gorlice
Sanok

Żywiec
NOWY SĄCZ
Tatra Mountains
An amazing alpine range with much to delight hikers and nature lovers

Nowy Targ
Krynica

Zakopane

SLOVAKIA
Rysy (2499m)

Poland
3rd edition – July 1999
First published – February 1993

Published by
Lonely Planet Publications Pty Ltd A.C.N. 005 607 983
192 Burwood Rd, Hawthorn, Victoria 3122, Australia

Lonely Planet Offices
Australia PO Box 617, Hawthorn, Victoria 3122
USA 150 Linden St, Oakland, CA 94607
UK 10a Spring Place, London NW5 3BH
France 1 rue du Dahomey, 75011 Paris

Photographs
All of the images in this guide are available for licensing from
Lonely Planet Images.
email: lpi@lonelyplanet.com.au

Front cover photograph
Countryside chapel for a small congregation, southern Poland
(Krzysztof Dydyński)

ISBN 0 86442 655 0

text & maps © Lonely Planet 1999
photos © photographers as indicated 1999

Printed by Craft Print Pte Ltd, Singapore

Contents – Text

SILESIA 353

WIELKOPOLSKA 420

POMERANIA 454

4 Contents – Text

Contents – Maps

6 Contents – Maps

MAP LEGEND   see back page

MAP INDEX BY CHAPTER BREAKDOWN

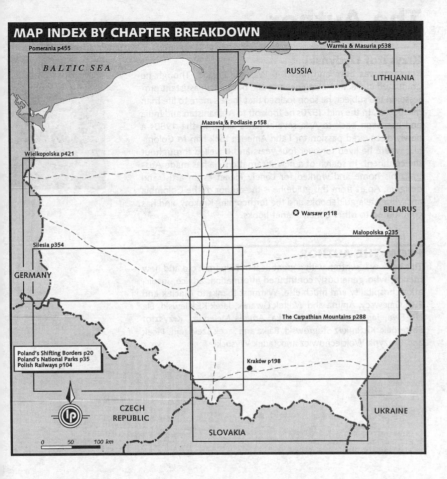

Pomerania p455

Warmia & Masuria p538

BALTIC SEA

RUSSIA

LITHUANIA

Mazovia & Podlasie p158

Wielkopolska p421

Warsaw p118

BELARUS

Małopolska p235

Silesia p354

GERMANY

The Carpathian Mountains p288

Poland's Shifting Borders p20
Poland's National Parks p35
Polish Railways p104

Kraków p198

CZECH
REPUBLIC

UKRAINE

SLOVAKIA

0   50   100 km

The Author

Krzysztof Dydyński

Krzysztof was born and raised in Warsaw, Poland. Though he graduated in electronic engineering and became an assistant professor in the subject, he soon realised that there's more to life than microchips. In the mid-1970s he took off to Afghanistan and India and has been back to Asia several times since. In the 1980s a newly discovered passion for Latin America took him to Colombia, where he lived for over four years and travelled throughout the continent. In search of a new incarnation, he has made Australia his home and worked for Lonely Planet as an artist and designer. Apart from this guide he is the author of the Colombia and Venezuela guidebooks and the forthcoming Kraków, and has contributed to other Lonely Planet books.

FROM THE AUTHOR

This book was written with a great deal of help from old and new friends, who generously contributed information, advice, inspiration, hospitality and much else. Warmest thanks to Maciek and Ewa Gajewscy, Aniuta and Wojtek Gwarek, Jarek Kisielewski, Ela Lis, Ewa, Jaga and Janusz Mączka, Angela Melendro, Krzysztof Pasternak, Kazimierz Stagrowski, Bajka and Jacek Szelegejd, Jacek and Grażyna Wojciechowicz and Tadek Wysocki.

This Book

From the Publisher

This edition of Poland was edited in Lonely Planet's Melbourne office by Shelley Muir with the assistance of Craig MacKenzie. Janet Austin, Carolyn Bain, Rebecca Turner and Liz Filleul helped with proofing. The mapping, design and layout were co-ordinated by Csanád Csutoros, who was assisted by Shahara Ahmed, Adrian Persoglia, Mark Griffiths and Lisa Borg. Piotr Czajkowski produced the colour country map, new illustrations were provided by Kate Nolan, and Guillaume Roux designed the front cover. Photographs were provided by Lonely Planet Images.

Thanks to Liz and Marcel Gaston for guidance, to Matt King for organising the illustrations, to Leonie Mugavin and Quentin Frayne for the Health and Language sections respectively, and to Tim Uden for layout advice and helping 'Polish the book off' (his words). Thanks also to the A-team for everything, and to Piotr for advice on all things Polish.

THANKS

Many thanks to the travellers who used the last edition and wrote to us with helpful hints, advice and interesting anecdotes. Your names appear in the back of this book.

Foreword

ABOUT LONELY PLANET GUIDEBOOKS

The story begins with a classic travel adventure: Tony and Maureen Wheeler's 1972 journey across Europe and Asia to Australia. Useful information about the overland trail did not exist at that time, so Tony and Maureen published the first Lonely Planet guidebook to meet a growing need.

From a kitchen table, then from a tiny office in Melbourne (Australia), Lonely Planet has become the largest independent travel publisher in the world, an international company with offices in Melbourne, Oakland (USA), London (UK) and Paris (France).

Today Lonely Planet guidebooks cover the globe. There is an ever-growing list of books and there's information in a variety of forms and media. Some things haven't changed. The main aim is still to help make it possible for adventurous travellers to get out there – to explore and better understand the world.

At Lonely Planet we believe travellers can make a positive contribution to the countries they visit – if they respect their host communities and spend their money wisely. Since 1986 a percentage of the income from each book has been donated to aid projects and human rights campaigns.

Updates Lonely Planet thoroughly updates each guidebook as often as possible. This usually means there are around two years between editions, although for more unusual or more stable destinations the gap can be longer. Check the imprint page (following the colour map at the beginning of the book) for publication dates.

Between editions up-to-date information is available in two free newsletters – the paper *Planet Talk* and email *Comet* (to subscribe, contact any Lonely Planet office) – and on our Web site at www.lonelyplanet.com. The *Upgrades* section of the Web site covers a number of important and volatile destinations and is regularly updated by Lonely Planet authors. *Scoop* covers news and current affairs relevant to travellers. And, lastly, the *Thorn Tree* bulletin board and *Postcards* section of the site carry unverified, but fascinating, reports from travellers.

Correspondence The process of creating new editions begins with the letters, postcards and emails received from travellers. This correspondence often includes suggestions, criticisms and comments about the current editions. Interesting excerpts are immediately passed on via newsletters and the Web site, and everything goes to our authors to be verified when they're researching on the road. We're keen to get more feedback from organisations or individuals who represent communities visited by travellers.

Lonely Planet gathers information for everyone who's curious about the planet – and especially for those who explore it first-hand. Through guidebooks, phrasebooks, activity guides, maps, literature, newsletters, image library, TV series and Web site we act as an information exchange for a worldwide community of travellers.

Research Authors aim to gather sufficient practical information to enable travellers to make informed choices and to make the mechanics of a journey run smoothly. They also research historical and cultural background to help enrich the travel experience and allow travellers to understand and respond appropriately to cultural and environmental issues.

Authors don't stay in every hotel because that would mean spending a couple of months in each medium-sized city and, no, they don't eat at every restaurant because that would mean stretching belts beyond capacity. They do visit hotels and restaurants to check standards and prices, but feedback based on readers' direct experiences can be very helpful.

Many of our authors work undercover, others aren't so secretive. None of them accept freebies in exchange for positive write-ups. And none of our guidebooks contain any advertising.

Production Authors submit their raw manuscripts and maps to offices in Australia, USA, UK or France. Editors and cartographers – all experienced travellers themselves – then begin the process of assembling the pieces. When the book finally hits the shops, some things are already out of date, we start getting feedback from readers and the process begins again ...

WARNING & REQUEST

Things change – prices go up, schedules change, good places go bad and bad places go bankrupt – nothing stays the same. So, if you find things better or worse, recently opened or long since closed, please tell us and help make the next edition even more accurate and useful. We genuinely value all the feedback we receive. Julie Young coordinates a well travelled team that reads and acknowledges every letter, postcard and email and ensures that every morsel of information finds its way to the appropriate authors, editors and cartographers for verification.

Everyone who writes to us will find their name in the next edition of the appropriate guidebook. They will also receive the latest issue of *Planet Talk*, our quarterly printed newsletter, or *Comet*, our monthly email newsletter. Subscriptions to both newsletters are free. The very best contributions will be rewarded with a free guidebook.

Excerpts from your correspondence may appear in new editions of Lonely Planet guidebooks, the Lonely Planet Web site, *Planet Talk* or *Comet*, so please let us know if you *don't* want your letter published or your name acknowledged.

Send all correspondence to the Lonely Planet office closest to you:

Australia: PO Box 617, Hawthorn, Victoria 3122
USA: 150 Linden St, Oakland, CA 94607
UK: 10A Spring Place, London NW5 3BH
France: 1 rue du Dahomey, 75011 Paris

Or email us at: talk2us@lonelyplanet.com.au

For news, views and updates see our Web site: www.lonelyplanet.com

HOW TO USE A LONELY PLANET GUIDEBOOK

The best way to use a Lonely Planet guidebook is any way you choose. At Lonely Planet we believe the most memorable travel experiences are often those that are unexpected, and the finest discoveries are those you make yourself. Guidebooks are not intended to be used as if they provide a detailed set of infallible instructions!

Contents All Lonely Planet guidebooks follow roughly the same format. The Facts about the Destination chapters or sections give background information ranging from history to weather. Facts for the Visitor gives practical information on issues like visas and health. Getting There & Away gives a brief starting point for researching travel to and from the destination. Getting Around gives an overview of the transport options when you arrive.

The peculiar demands of each destination determine how subsequent chapters are broken up, but some things remain constant. We always start with background, then proceed to sights, places to stay, places to eat, entertainment, getting there and away, and getting around information – in that order.

Heading Hierarchy Lonely Planet headings are used in a strict hierarchical structure that can be visualised as a set of Russian dolls. Each heading (and its following text) is encompassed by any preceding heading that is higher on the hierarchical ladder.

Entry Points We do not assume guidebooks will be read from beginning to end, but that people will dip into them. The traditional entry points are the list of contents and the index. In addition, however, some books have a complete list of maps and an index map illustrating map coverage.

There may also be a colour map that shows highlights. These highlights are dealt with in greater detail in the Facts for the Visitor chapter, along with planning questions and suggested itineraries. Each chapter covering a geographical region usually begins with a locator map and another list of highlights. Once you find something of interest in a list of highlights, turn to the index.

Maps Maps play a crucial role in Lonely Planet guidebooks and include a huge amount of information. A legend is printed on the back page. We seek to have complete consistency between maps and text, and to have every important place in the text captured on a map. Map key numbers usually start in the top left corner.

Although inclusion in a guidebook usually implies a recommendation we cannot list every good place. Exclusion does not necessarily imply criticism. In fact there are a number of reasons why we might exclude a place – sometimes it is simply inappropriate to encourage an influx of travellers.

Introduction

Poland is 1000 years old and many of its towns and cities date back to its early days. They shelter a rich architectural and artistic heritage that has survived all the battles fought on Polish soil over the centuries. A huge amount of damage was done during WWII, but the energy and resources that have gone into the rebuilding are astonishing – the old quarters of Warsaw and Gdańsk are miracles of loving reconstruction. Few cities were lucky enough to have passed through the war without damage, and one of these was the illustrious old royal capital of Kraków – a place not to be missed. Other great historic cities include Toruń, Wrocław and Poznań.

Poland has also a lot to offer outside its cities. The southern border follows mountain ranges, where walkers can enjoy spectacular landscapes and scenery. The other, northern part of the country is skirted by the 500km Baltic coast, with an almost uninterrupted ribbon of white sandy beaches. For those who prefer fresh water, north-eastern Poland offers gently rolling woodland with thousands of lakes, a paradise for yachting and canoeing. There's also an abundance of good, flat cycling country.

For centuries a bridge between East and West, set in the heart of Europe, Poland is still a largely unexplored country that retains much of its traditional way of life. You'll still see horse-drawn ploughs in remote areas, and carts laden with vegetables clogging up tiny back roads on their way to markets. There are villages which look as though the 20th century got lost somewhere down the road. The locals fill their rustic wooden churches to overflowing, and every small country road is dotted with wayside chapels and shrines, usually with fresh flowers. Here is a Poland to be savoured.

Poland has been one of the most cosmopolitan countries in Europe, thanks in

part to its constantly shifting borders. It has incorporated Lithuanians, Ukrainians, Belarusians and Germans, and was a refuge for persecuted minorities – the Jews in particular – from all over the continent. The ethnic homogeneity you see today is quite recent – only 50 years old – and is set against the cultural complexity of Poland's past which has left behind a fascinating architectural mosaic, including Teutonic castles, Italian Renaissance palaces, French baroque country mansions and Eastern Orthodox churches crowned with onion domes.

While some parts of Europe have torn themselves apart in recent years for ethnic, religious or nationalistic reasons, Poland has a unity few other nations in the region can match. Bound together by Catholicism, language, nationality and shared experience, the country has swiftly got on after the collapse of communism, building a better home for its people – an opportunity for westerners to see history in the making.

A reflective land of Chopin and Copernicus, Poland remains reasonably cheap and safe, with hospitable people who welcome visitors. Go there soon, before the country joins the EU, an integration which is likely to affect some of the old ways of life, as well as the prices. Now is a good time to go, Poland having improved its tourist infrastructure and developed into a modern, vibrant and progressive state, yet at the same time maintaining its traditional culture relatively unchanged.

Facts about Poland

HISTORY

Poland has not perished yet
As long as we (Poles) still live.
That which foreign force has seized
We at swordpoint shall retrieve.

The first lines of the Polish national anthem reflect the proud and irrepressible nature of the nation. One of the most patriotic and rebellious of peoples, Poles have had innumerable occasions to defend their freedom and sovereignty throughout more than 1000 turbulent years of history.

Nearly all the historical wrongs and atrocities the world could inflict have been experienced by the Poles. Geographically squeezed between two aggressive powers, Germany and Russia, Poland was repeatedly invaded and fought upon. Its boundaries have shifted east and west as its power waxed and waned, from being the largest country in Europe in the 17th century, to being completely wiped off the map from the end of the 18th century until after WWI. The nation re-emerged at this point, only to be devastated just two decades later in WWII, losing six million people.

Poland changed the course of history in 1989 by becoming the first Eastern European state to break free of communism, proving the truth of Stalin's 1944 comment that fitting communism onto Poland was like putting a saddle on a cow. Since then, the economic, social and psychological changes have been tremendous.

Origins

Some time in the Neolithic period (4000 to 2000 BC), permanent agricultural settlements began to appear in what is now Poland, and trading routes started to crisscross the thick forests which covered the area. In the last millennium BC and the early centuries AD, such diverse groups as Celts, Scythians, Balts, Goths, Huns and numerous Germanic tribes invaded, crossed and occasionally settled in the region. It's almost certain that the Slavs, the ethnic group to which the Poles belong, were among them, though some scholars believe it wasn't until the 6th or 7th century AD that the Slavs arrived from the south-east.

Diverse Slavonic tribes eventually settled various regions between the Baltic Sea and the ridge of the Carpathian Mountains. Toward the mid-10th century, one of these groups, the Polanie (literally, the people of the fields or open country dwellers), who had settled on the banks of the Warta River near present-day Poznań, attained dominance over the region. Their tribal chief, the legendary Piast, managed to unite the scattered groups of the surrounding areas into a single political unit, and gave it the name Polska, or Poland, after the tribe's name. The region was later to become known as Wielkopolska or Great Poland. Its first recorded ruler, Duke Mieszko I, was converted to Christianity in 966. This date is recognised as the formal birth of the Polish state.

The Piast Dynasty (966-1370)

From its dawning, Poland's history has been marked by wars with its neighbours. Sandwiched between two expansive powers, Germany (the Holy Roman Empire in those days) and Russia (then a myriad of principalities dominated by Kievan Rus), Poland was engaged in numerous armed conflicts with one or the other, or with both at the same time.

The first important break with the east came in 988, when Vladimir the Great of Kiev accepted the Byzantine version of Christianity, thereby linking his principality to the Eastern Orthodox Church. The religious divergence between the Orthodox Russians and the Roman Catholic Poles subsequently fuelled cultural and political rivalry which often led to armed struggle.

Duke Mieszko I was a talented leader. He managed to conquer the entire coastal region of Pomorze (Pomerania) and soon thereafter extended his sovereignty to include Śląsk (Silesia) to the south and Małopolska (Little Poland) to the south-east. By the time of his death in 992, the Polish state was established within boundaries similar to those of Poland today, stretching over about 250,000 sq km. The first capital and archbishopric were established in Gniezno. By that time, towns such as Gdańsk, Szczecin, Poznań, Wrocław and Kraków already existed.

The son of Mieszko I, Bolesław Chrobry (Boleslaus the Brave, 992-1025), further enlarged and strengthened the empire. Shortly before his death in 1025 he was crowned the first Polish king by papal bull.

Wars continued unabated; the Germans were constantly invading the north, and expanded over the coastal regions. Due to these pressures, the administrative centre of the country was moved from Great Poland to the less vulnerable Little Poland. By the middle of the 11th century, Kraków was established as the royal seat. During subsequent reigns, Polish boundaries were constantly changing.

Bolesław Krzywousty (Boleslaus the Wry-Mouthed, 1102-38) reconquered Pomerania and temporarily reinforced internal unity, but then, hoping to establish an ideal formula for succession, he divided the kingdom among his sons. This proved to be a disaster: Poland's short-lived unity was lost, and the rivalries and struggles between independent principalities left them all weak and vulnerable to foreign invaders. Enemies were quick to take advantage of the internal chaos.

When pagan Prussians from the region that is now the north-eastern tip of Poland attacked the province of Mazovia in 1226, Duke Konrad of Mazovia called for help from the Teutonic Knights, a Germanic military and religious order which had made its historical mark during the Crusades. Once the knights had subjugated the pagan tribes, they set up a state on the conquered territories that they ruled from their castle at Malbork. They soon became a major European military

power, and after capturing all of northern Poland they controlled most of the Baltic coast, including the port of Gdańsk.

Things were not going much better in southern Poland. In their great 13th century invasion, the Mongols (or Tatars, as they are commonly referred to in Poland) conquered Kiev and most of the Russian principalities, then pushed farther west into Poland. They had devastated much of Little Poland and Silesia by 1241-42, and launched yet another destructive raid in 1259.

Not until 1320 was the Polish crown restored and the state reunified. Under the rule of Kazimierz III Wielki (Casimir III the Great, 1333-70), Poland gradually became a mighty, prosperous state. Kazimierz regained suzerainty over Mazovia, then captured vast areas of Ruthenia (today's Ukraine) and Podolia, thus greatly expanding his monarchy towards the south-east.

Kazimierz Wielki was also an enlightened and energetic ruler on the domestic front.

Kazimierz III Wielki, a tolerant ruler who offered protection to Europe's persecuted Jews

Promoting and instituting reforms, he laid down solid legal, economic, commercial and educational foundations. Over 70 new towns were founded, existing towns expanded rapidly and the royal capital of Kraków flourished. In 1364, one of Europe's first universities was established at Kraków. An extensive network of castles and fortifications was constructed to improve the nation's defences. There is a saying that Kazimierz Wielki 'found Poland built of wood and left it built of masonry'.

The Jagiellonian Dynasty (1382-1572)

Kazimierz Wielki died in 1370 leaving no heir, and the Polish crown passed to his nephew, Louis I of Hungary. On his death in 1382, the Polish succession passed to his 10-year-old daughter Jadwiga, whereas the Hungarians chose her older sister Maria as their queen. The Polish aristocracy, which already enjoyed significant political clout, decided on a dynastic alliance with Lithuania, a vast and still pagan country. Grand Duke Jagiełło of Lithuania married the young Crown Princess Jadwiga, accepted the Catholic faith and assumed the name of Władysław II Jagiełło (1386-1434). This political marriage increased Poland's territory fivefold overnight and formed the Polish-Lithuanian alliance, which would continue through the next four centuries.

Under Jagiełło, Polish territory continued to expand. The king led a series of successful wars, and at the Battle of Grunwald in 1410 the Polish-Lithuanian army defeated the Teutonic Knights, marking the beginning of the order's decline. In the Thirteen Years' War of 1454-66, the Teutonic Order was eventually disbanded and Poland recovered Eastern Pomerania, part of Prussia and the port of Gdańsk, regaining access to the Baltic Sea. For 30 years, the Polish empire extended from the Baltic Sea to the Black Sea and was the largest European state.

It was not to last. Another period of constant invasions began in 1475. This time the main instigators were the Ottomans, the Tatars of Crimea and the tsars of Moscow.

Independently or together, they repeatedly invaded and raided the eastern and southern Polish territories and on one occasion managed to penetrate as far as Kraków.

Despite the wars, the Polish kingdom's power was firmly based. In addition to prospering economically, the country advanced both culturally and spiritually. The early 16th century brought the Renaissance to Poland. The incumbent king, Zygmunt I Stary (Sigismund I the Old, 1506-48), was a great promoter of the arts. The Latin language was gradually supplanted by Polish and a national literature was born. Printing presses came into use and books began to appear. Architecture blossomed; many fine buildings of the period have survived to this day. In 1543, Nicolaus Copernicus (Mikołaj Kopernik) published his immortal work *On the Revolutions of the Celestial Spheres*, which altered the course of astronomy by proposing that the earth moves around the sun.

The next and last king of the Jagiellonian Dynasty, Zygmunt II August (Sigismund II Augustus, 1548-72), continued his father's patronage of arts and culture. Thanks to their inspiring and protective policies, the arts and sciences flourished and the two reigns came to be referred to as Poland's golden age.

The bulk of Poland's population at that time was made up of Poles and Lithuanians, but included significant minorities of Germans, Ruthenians (Ukrainians), Tatars, Armenians and Livonians (Latvians). Jews constituted an important and steadily growing part of the community, and by the end of the 16th century Poland had a larger Jewish population than the rest of Europe combined.

Religious freedom was constitutionally established by the Sejm (or Diet – the Polish parliament) in 1573 and the equality of creeds officially guaranteed. Such diverse faiths as Roman Catholicism, Eastern Orthodoxy, Protestantism, Judaism and Islam were able to coexist relatively peacefully.

On the political front, Poland evolved during the 16th century into a parliamentary monarchy with most of the privileges going to the *szlachta* (gentry or the feudal nobility), who comprised roughly 10% of the population. In contrast, the status of the peasants declined, and they gradually found themselves falling into a state of virtual slavery.

The Royal Republic (1573-1795)

During the reign of Zygmunt August, the threat of Russian expansionism increased. Hoping to strengthen the monarchy, the Sejm convened in Lublin in 1569 and unified Poland and Lithuania into a single state. It also made Warsaw the seat of the Sejm's future debates. Since there was no heir apparent to the throne, it also established a system of royal succession based on direct voting in popular elections by the nobility, who would all come to Warsaw with their servants, horses, tents etc to vote. In the absence of a serious Polish contender, a foreign candidate would be considered.

The experiment proved disastrous. For each royal election, foreign powers promoted their candidates by bargaining and bribing voters. During the period of the Royal Republic, Poland was ruled by 11 kings, only four of whom were native Poles.

The first elected king, Henri de Valois, retreated to France after only a year on the Polish throne. His successor, Stefan Batory (Stephen Bathory, 1576-86), prince of Transylvania, was fortunately a much wiser choice. Batory, together with his gifted commander and chancellor Jan Zamoyski, conducted a series of successful battles against Tsar Ivan the Terrible.

After Batory's premature death, the crown was offered to the Swede Zygmunt III Waza (Sigismund III Vasa, 1587-1632), the first of three kings of Poland of the Vasa dynasty. Five years later Zygmunt also inherited the Swedish throne. As ruler of both countries, he tried to establish a Polish-Swedish alliance. This drew strong opposition in Sweden on the basis of religious differences, and the king, a devout Catholic, was dethroned by the predominantly Protestant (Lutheran) Swedes. The subsequent Swedish-Polish war caused Poland to lose part of Livonia (today Latvia and southern Estonia).

Meanwhile, on the eastern front, Polish troops were fighting the Russian army, eventually capturing vast new frontier provinces and giving Poland its greatest ever territorial extent. In effect, Zygmunt Waza ruled over an area of roughly one million sq km, or more than three times the size of present-day Poland. However, he is probably better remembered for moving the Polish capital from Kraków to Warsaw between 1596 and 1609.

Economically, Poland was still a wealthy power serving as the granary of Europe, but the beginning of the 17th century was the turning point. From then on, the Royal Republic gradually declined in almost every way. The main source of further misfortune lay not in foreign aggression but in domestic policies that undermined the country from within. Ironically, it was all done in the name of the freedom, liberty and equality of which the Poles have always been so proud.

The economic and political power of the szlachta grew dangerously throughout the 17th century. The nobility not only divided most of the country into huge estates, which they distributed among themselves, but also usurped political privileges which significantly reduced governmental authority. The most ill-fated move was the introduction of the *liberum veto*: assuming the equality of each voter, no bill introduced to the Sejm could be adopted without a unanimous vote. In other words, each member of the Sejm had a veto over every bill. The height of this utopian concept was the rule that a single veto was sufficient to dissolve the Sejm at any time and to subject all law passed during the previous session to a re-vote during the following convention. This version of democracy (or anarchy, if you prefer) effectively paralysed the Sejm.

The liberum veto was first used in 1652, and later on, particularly in the 18th century, it was applied recklessly. During the 30 year rule of the next-to-last Polish king, August III Wettin, the Sejm only once succeeded in passing any legislation at all. To make things worse, some frustrated nobles judged the Sejm worthless and resorted to their own brand of justice, the armed rebellion.

Meanwhile, foreign invaders were systematically carving up the land. Jan II Kazimierz Waza (John II Casimir Vasa, 1648-68), the last of the Vasa dynasty on the Polish throne, was unable to resist the aggressors – Russians, Tatars, Ukrainians, Cossacks, Ottomans and Swedes – who were moving in on all fronts. The Swedish invasion of 1655-60, known as the Deluge, was particularly disastrous. During the rule of Kazimierz Waza, the country lost over a quarter of its national territory, cities were burned and plundered, the countryside was devastated and the economy destroyed. Of the population of 10 million, four million people succumbed to war, famine and bubonic plague.

The last bright moment in the long decline of the Royal Republic was the reign of Jan III Sobieski (1674-96), a brilliant commander who led several victorious battles against the Ottomans. The most famous of these was the Battle of Vienna in 1683, in which he defeated the Turks and forced their retreat from Europe. Ironically, the victory only strengthened Austria, a country which would later take its turn at invading Poland.

The 18th century saw the agony of the Polish state. By then, Russia had evolved into a mighty, expansive empire which systematically strengthened its grip over Poland. This was somewhat facilitated by the corrupt Polish nobility which, given the disastrous state of affairs at home, was increasingly seeking benefits and favours abroad, principally in Russia. A significant nail in the coffin of Polish independence was the infamous Silent Sejm of 1717, in which Peter the Great succeeded in imposing a protectorate over Poland, effectively allowing Russia to intervene in Poland's internal matters. Although the last Polish king, Stanisław August Poniatowski (1764-95), was a patron of literature and the arts, he was essentially a puppet of the Russian regime. It was only during his reign that the Poles became aware of the severity of their country's situation, with direct inter-

vention in Poland's affairs from Catherine the Great, Empress of Russia.

The Partitions

When anti-Russian rebellion broke out in Poland, Russia entered into treaties with Prussia and Austria, and the three countries agreed to annex three substantial chunks of Poland, amounting to roughly 30% of Polish territory. The Sejm was forced to ratify the partition in 1773.

The First Partition had the effect of a cold shower and led to immediate reforms in the administrative, military and educational spheres. The economy began to recover, and there were new developments in industry. In 1791, a new, fully liberal constitution was passed. It was known as the Constitution of the 3rd of May, and it was the world's second written delineation of government responsibility (the first was that of the USA). It abolished the old machinery of government, including the liberum veto.

Catherine the Great could tolerate no more of this dangerous democracy. Russian troops were sent into Poland, and crushed fierce resistance. The reforms were abolished by force. The Second Partition came in 1793, with Russia and Prussia strengthening their grip by grabbing over half the remaining Polish territory.

In response, patriotic forces under the leadership of Tadeusz Kościuszko, a hero of the American War of Independence, launched an armed rebellion in 1794. The campaign soon gained popular support and the rebels won some early victories, but the Russian troops, stronger and better armed, finally defeated the Polish forces.

This time the three occupying powers decided to eradicate the troublesome nation altogether, and in the Third Partition, effected in 1795, they divided the rest of Poland's territory among themselves. Poland disappeared from the map for the next 123 years.

Under the Partitions (1795-1914)

Despite the partitions, Poland continued to exist as a spiritual and cultural community,

POLAND'S SHIFTING BORDERS

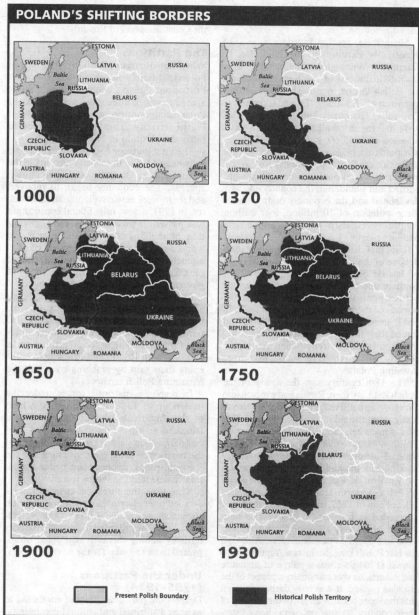

1000

1370

1650

1750

1900

1930

Present Polish Boundary

Historical Polish Territory

and a number of secret nationalist societies were soon created. Since revolutionary France was seen as their major ally in the struggle, some leaders fled to Paris and established their headquarters there.

When Napoleon attacked Prussia in 1806, a Polish popular insurrection broke out in his support as he advanced on Moscow. In 1807, Napoleon created the Duchy of Warsaw, a sovereign Polish state which consisted of former Polish territories which had been annexed by Prussia. However, when Napoleon lost his war with Russia in 1812, Poland was again partitioned.

In 1815, the Congress of Vienna established the Congress Kingdom of Poland, a supposedly autonomous Polish state which nevertheless had the Russian tsar as its king. From its inception, its liberal constitution was violated by Tsar Alexander and his successors.

In response to continuing Russian oppression, several armed uprisings broke out. The most significant were the November Insurrection of 1830 and the January Insurrection of 1863, both of which were crushed by the Russians and followed by harsh repression, executions and deportations to Siberia.

As it became clear that armed protest couldn't succeed, the Polish patriots reconsidered their strategy and advocated 'organic work', a pacifist endeavour to recover the economy, education and culture from the Russians. This change was reflected in the literature and arts, which moved from the visionary political poetry of the Romantics to the more realistic prose of the Positivists.

In the 1870s Russia dramatically stepped up its efforts to eradicate Polish culture, suppressing the Polish language in education, administration and commerce, and replacing it with Russian. Soon after, Prussia imitated the Russians and introduced Germanisation. Only in the Austrian sector (Galicia) were the Poles given any degree of autonomy.

Toward the end of the 19th century, steady economic growth was evident. Political activity was revived and the first political parties were established in the 1890s. On the other hand, this was also a time of mass emigration. Due to the poverty of the rural areas, mainly in Galicia, peasants had no choice but to seek a better life abroad. By the outbreak of WWI about four million out of a total Polish population of 20 to 25 million had emigrated, primarily to the USA.

WWI (1914-18)

WWI broke out in August 1914. On one side were the Central Powers, Austria and Germany (including Prussia); on the other, Russia and its western allies. With Poland's three occupying powers at war, most of the fighting was staged on the territories inhabited by the Poles, resulting in staggering losses of life and livelihood. Since no formal Polish state existed, there was no Polish army to fight for any national cause. Even worse, some two million Poles were conscripted into the Russian, German or Austrian armies, depending on whose territory they lived in, and were obliged to fight one another.

Paradoxically, the war eventually brought about Polish independence. However, it came mostly as a result of a combination of external circumstances rather than through the direct participation of the Poles. After the October Revolution in 1917, Russia, plunged into civil war, no longer had the power to oversee Polish affairs. The final collapse of Austria in October 1918 and the withdrawal of the German army from Warsaw in November brought the opportune moment. Marshal Józef Piłsudski took command of Warsaw on 11 November 1918, declared Polish sovereignty, and usurped power as the head of state. This date is recognised as the day of the founding of the Second Republic, so named to create a symbolic bridge between itself and the Royal Republic which existed before the partitions.

Between the Wars (1918-39)

Poland began its new incarnation in a desperate position. After the war, the country and its economy were in ruins. It's estimated that over one million Poles lost their lives in

WWI. All state institutions – including the army, which hadn't existed for over a century – had to be built up from scratch. Even the borders, which had been obliterated in the partitions, had to be redefined, and they weren't made official until 1923.

The Treaty of Versailles in 1919 awarded Poland the western part of Prussia, thereby providing access to the Baltic Sea. The city of Gdańsk, however, was omitted and became the Free City of Danzig. The rest of Poland's western border was drawn up in a series of plebiscites which resulted in Poland acquiring some significant industrial regions of Upper Silesia.

The eastern boundaries were established when Polish forces led by Piłsudski eventu-ally defeated the Red Army during the Polish-Soviet war (1919-20). The victory brought Poland vast areas of what are now western Ukraine and Belarus.

When Poland's territorial struggle was over, the Second Republic covered nearly 400,000 sq km and was populated by 26 million people. One-third of the population was of non-Polish ethnic background, mainly Jews, Ukrainians, Belarusians and Germans.

Piłsudski retired from political life in 1922, giving way to a series of unstable par-liamentary governments. For the next four years, frequently changing coalition cab-inets struggled to overcome enormous economic and social problems. Although

Marshal Józef Piłsudski – Father of the Second Republic

Marshal Józef Piłsudski is widely admired in Poland, for various reasons. It was he who real-ised the long-awaited dream of a sovereign Poland after WWI, thus becoming the father of national independence. He was also the last great independent Polish leader, a man of authority who commanded respect and contrasted sharply with the subsequent communist puppets. Finally, the Marshal was the last of Poland's rulers who defeated the Russians in battle.

Józef Piłsudski was born in 1867 in the Vilnius region, then part of Poland under Russian occupation. As a teenager, he entered the underground anti-tsarist circles in Vilnius. He was arrested in 1887, sentenced on a fictitious charge of plotting the assassination of the tsar, and sent to a prison in Siberia for five years. Once freed, he returned to Poland and joined the newly founded Polish Socialist Party (PPS) in Warsaw. He was again arrested by the tsarist authorities in 1900 and sent to a jail in St Petersburg but he escaped the following year. He took refuge in Kraków (then under the less oppressive Austrian occupation), which became the base for his anti-tsarist activities until WWI.

In 1908 the PPS, then under the leadership of Piłsudski, began to form paramilitary squads, which in time developed into the Polish Legions, the armed force of the still formally non-existent Poland. During WWI, the legions fought under Piłsudski alongside Germany and Austria against the Russians. However, on the collapse of the tsarist regime in Russia in 1917, the purpose of fighting for the Central Powers was lost, and the legions refused to swear further allegiance to Germany. In response, Piłsudski was imprisoned in Magdeburg, and was released only after Germany's capitulation in November 1918. He came to Warsaw, took power on 11 November and proclaimed Poland's independence.

In an apparent ideological turn against his former revolutionary comrades, Piłsudski launched a massive offensive towards the east in 1919, capturing vast territories which had been Polish before the 18th century partitions. But the Soviet counter-offensive pushed west-ward, and by mid-1920 the Red Army approached Warsaw. In the battle of the city in August

some progress was achieved in the areas of education, agriculture, transport and communications, the overall economic situation remained precarious.

Quite unexpectedly, Piłsudski seized power in a military coup in May 1926, and then held on until his death in 1935. Parliament was gradually phased out. The opposition actively resisted and was occasionally put down, and the army increased its power. Despite the dictatorial regime, political repression had little effect on ordinary people. The economic situation was relatively stable, and cultural and intellectual life prospered.

On the international front, Poland's situation in the 1930s was unenviable. In an attempt to regulate relations with its two inexorably hostile neighbours, Poland signed nonaggression pacts with both the Soviet Union and Germany. Nevertheless, it soon became clear that the pacts didn't offer any real guarantee of safety.

On 23 August 1939, a pact of nonaggression between Germany and the Soviet Union was signed in Moscow by their foreign ministers, Ribbentrop and Molotov. This pact contained a secret protocol defining the prospective partition of Eastern Europe between the two great powers. Stalin and Hitler planned to carve up the Polish state between themselves and divide its citizens as if they were livestock, as others had done before.

(the so-called Miracle on the Vistula), the Polish Army under Piłsudski outmanoeuvred and defeated the Soviets. It may well be that this victory saved the weakened Western Europe, or at least Germany, from the Bolshevik conquest.

After independent Poland was safely back on the map and a modern democratic constitution was adopted in 1921, Piłsudski stepped down in 1922. However, disillusioned with the economic recession and governmental crisis, he re-appeared on the political scene in May 1926. In a classical coup d'état showdown, he marched on Warsaw at the head of the army.

The three-day street fighting which broke out resulted in 400 dead and over 1000 wounded. After the government resigned, the National Assembly elected Piłsudski president. He refused to take the post, though, opting instead for the office of Defence Minister, which he maintained until his death. There are no doubts, though, that it was Piłsudski who ran the country from behind the scenes for a decade, until he died in 1935.

Viewed objectively, Piłsudski is a complex and controversial figure: a fearless patriot and relentless warrior but also a heavy-handed dictator; both ambitious and honourable yet uncompromising and intolerant; a master of strategy with conflicting ideas. However, the Polish perspective seems to be a bit different: despite his obvious faults and dictatorial style, Piłsudski was buried in the crypt of Kraków's Wawel Cathedral among Polish kings, which in itself reflects the degree of national respect and admiration. He continues to be admired today.

WWII (1939-45)

WWII began at dawn on 1 September 1939 with a massive German invasion of Poland. Fighting began in Gdańsk (at that time the Free City of Danzig) when German forces encountered a stubborn handful of Polish resisters at Westerplatte. The battle lasted a week. Simultaneously, another German line stormed Warsaw, which finally surrendered on 28 September. Despite valiant resistance there was simply no hope of withstanding the numerically overwhelming and well armed German forces; the last resistance groups were quelled by early October. Hitler intended to create a Polish puppet state on the newly acquired territory, but since no collaborators could be found, western Poland was directly annexed to Germany while the central regions became the so-called General Government, ruled by the Nazi governor from Kraków.

Winston Churchill observed: 'Poland was the only country which never collaborated with the Nazis in any form and no Polish units fought alongside the German army'.

On 17 September eastern Poland was invaded by the Soviet Union, and by November had been swallowed up. Thus within two months Poland was yet again partitioned. Mass arrests, exile and executions followed in both invaded parts. It's estimated that between one and two million Poles were sent by the Soviets to Siberia, the Soviet Arctic and Kazakhstan in 1939-40.

Soon after the outbreak of the war, a Polish government-in-exile was formed in France under General Władysław Sikorski. It was shifted to London in June 1940. In July 1943 Sikorski died in an aircraft crash at Gibraltar, and Stanisław Mikołajczyk succeeded him as prime minister.

In spring 1940 in Katyń, near Smolensk in Belarus, the Soviets shot and killed some 20,000 Polish prisoners, including nearly 5000 senior army officers. The mass graves were discovered by the Germans in 1943 but the Soviet government denied responsibility and accused the Nazis of the crime. Only in 1990 did the Soviets admit their 'error', without revealing details. In October 1992 the Russian government finally made public secret documents showing that Stalin's Politburo was responsible for the massacre.

The course of the war changed dramatically when Hitler unexpectedly attacked the Soviet Union on 22 June 1941. The Germans pushed the Soviets out of eastern Poland and extended their power deep into Russia. For over three years, the whole of Poland lay under Nazi occupation. Hitler's policy was to eradicate the Polish nation and Germanise the territory. The Polish education system was dismantled, apart from primary schools. Hundreds of thousands of Poles were deported en masse to forced-labour camps in Germany, while others, primarily the intelligentsia, were executed in an attempt to exterminate spiritual and intellectual leadership. Jews, whom Hitler considered an inferior race, were to be eliminated completely. They were at first segregated and confined in ghettos until a more efficient method was applied – the death camps.

The death camps were probably the most horrifying and inhuman chapter of WWII. They were initially established in 1940, and by the following year there was already a large network, with the largest at Oświęcim (Auschwitz). They proved *very* efficient: some five million people were put to death in the gas chambers. Over three million Jews – most of Poland's Jewish population – and roughly one million Poles died in the camps. There was desperate resistance from within the ghettos; the biggest single act of defiance came with the tragic Warsaw Ghetto Uprising which broke out in April 1943.

The Polish national resistance was organised in the cities, and formed and operated the Polish educational, communications and judicial systems. Armed squads were created in 1940 within Poland by the government-in-exile, and later became the Armia Krajowa (AK) or Home Army.

Meanwhile, outside Poland, the warring nations jockeyed for position. Once the Germans had attacked the Soviets, Stalin did an about-face and turned to Poland for help in the war against Germany, promising in exchange to form a Polish army. Diplomatic relations were established with the Polish government-in-exile.

This chumming-up with Stalin elicited mixed feelings in Poland, but at the time it seemed the most pragmatic course of action and certainly the only way to re-establish the Polish armed forces. The army was founded anew late in 1941 under General Władysław Anders but it soon became apparent that the military would have to operate on Soviet terms. Anders tactically removed the majority of his troops to North Africa, where they joined the British fighting forces. The Poles distinguished themselves at Tobruk, Monte Cassino and in other Allied campaigns.

Having failed to control Anders' army, Stalin began to organise a new Polish fighting force in 1943; in order to assure full Soviet control, most of the officers were taken from the Red Army. This army set about liberating German-occupied Poland during the last stage of the war.

As a result of Stalin's efforts to spread communism in Poland, the new Polish communist party, the Polish Workers' Party (PPR), was formed in Warsaw in January 1942. It in turn organised its own military forces, the Armia Ludowa (AL) or People's Army, a counterpart to the already existing noncommunist force, the Armia Krajowa.

Hitler's defeat at Stalingrad in 1943 marked the turning point of the war on the eastern front; from then on the Red Army successfully pushed westwards. After the Soviets liberated the Polish city of Lublin, the pro-communist Polish Committee of National Liberation (PKWN) was installed on 22 July 1944 and assumed the functions of a provisional government. A week later the Red Army reached the outskirts of Warsaw.

Warsaw at that time still remained under Nazi occupation. In a last-ditch attempt to establish an independent Polish administration, the resistance forces decided to gain control of the city before the arrival of the Soviet troops. On 1 August 1944, the orders for a general anti-German uprising, sanctioned by the government-in-exile, were given by General Tadeusz Bór Komo-rowski, then commander of the Home Army. For 63 days the struggle dragged on with unprecedented savagery, but the insurgents were ultimately forced to surrender. Approximately 200,000 Poles were killed in the Warsaw Uprising and all survivors were expelled from the city. Immediately afterwards, on Hitler's order, Warsaw was literally razed street by street to the ground.

During these appalling events, the Red Army, which was sitting just across the Vistula River, didn't lift a finger. Upon learning of the uprising, Stalin halted the offensive and ordered his generals not to intervene or provide assistance in the fighting. Nor were the Soviets to do anything to prevent the destruction that followed. It wasn't until 17 January 1945 that the Soviet army finally marched in to 'liberate' Warsaw, which by that time was little more than a heap of empty ruins.

For the Poles, the Warsaw Uprising was one of the most heroic and simultaneously most tragic engagements of the war. Ironically, the Germans had done the Soviets' work for them by eliminating the best of the Polish nation, the only obstacle standing in the way of a communist takeover of the country.

Through the winter, the Red Army continued its westward advance across Poland, and after a few months reached Berlin. The Nazi Reich capitulated on 8 May 1945.

The impact of the war on Poland was staggering. The country had lost over six million people, about 20% of its prewar population; half of the dead were Jews. The country and its cities lay in ruins; only 15% of Warsaw's buildings had survived. Many Poles who had seen out the war in foreign countries opted not to return to the new political order.

Communist Rule

At the Yalta Conference in February 1945, Roosevelt, Churchill and Stalin decided to leave Poland under Soviet control. They agreed that Poland's eastern frontier would roughly follow the Nazi-Soviet demarcation line of 1939. In effect, the Soviet Union annexed 180,000 sq km of prewar Polish territory. In August 1945 at Potsdam, Allied leaders established Poland's western boundary along the Odra (Oder) and the Nysa (Neisse) rivers, thereby reinstating about 100,000 sq km of Poland's western provinces after centuries of German rule.

The radical boundary changes were followed by population transfers of some 10 million people: Poles were moved into the newly defined Poland while Germans, Ukrainians and Belarusians were resettled outside its boundaries. In the end, 98% of Poland's population was ethnically Polish.

As soon as Poland formally fell under Soviet control, Stalin launched an intensive Sovietisation campaign. Wartime resistance leaders were charged with Nazi collaboration, tried in Moscow and summarily shot or sentenced to arbitrary prison terms. A provisional Polish government was set up in Moscow in June 1945 and then transferred to Warsaw. General elections were postponed until 1947 to allow time for the arrest of prominent Polish political figures by the secret police. Even so, Stanisław Mikołajczyk, the government-in-exile's only representative who returned to Poland, received over 80% of the popular vote. The 'official' figures, however, revealed a majority vote for the communists. The new Sejm elected Bolesław Bierut president; Mikołajczyk, accused of espionage, fled back to England.

In 1948 the Polish United Workers' Party (PZPR), henceforth referred to as 'the Party', was formed to monopolise power. In 1952 a Soviet-style constitution was adopted. The office of president was abolished and effective power passed to the First Secretary of the Party Central Committee. Poland became an affiliate of the Warsaw Pact, the Soviet bloc's version of NATO; and of the Council of Mutual Economic Assistance (Comecon), the communists' equivalent of the European Economic Community.

All commercial and industrial enterprises employing more than 50 workers were nationalised. In a forced march towards industrialisation, priority was given to heavy industry, particularly coal mining and steel manufacturing. Early attempts at agricultural collectivisation were later abandoned and about 80% of cultivated land remained in the hands of individual farmers. In the arts, socialist realism became the dominant style, and was to leave behind an abominable body of painting, sculpture, architecture, literature and music. Meanwhile, the citizenry united to rebuild Polish cities.

Despite all its horrors, Stalinist fanaticism never gained as much influence in Poland as in neighbouring countries and it subsided fairly soon after Stalin's death in 1953. The powers of the secret police were eroded and some concessions were made to popular demands. The press was liberalised and Polish cultural values were resuscitated. In 1956, when Nikita Khrushchev denounced Stalin at the Soviet 20th Party Congress, Bierut died of a heart attack!

In June 1956, a massive industrial strike demanding 'bread and freedom' broke out in Poznań. Tanks rolled in and crushed the revolt, leaving 76 dead and over 900 wounded. Soon afterward, Władysław Gomułka, an ex-political prisoner of the Stalin era, was appointed first secretary of the Party. At first he commanded popular support, primarily because he'd managed to reduce Soviet meddling in Polish affairs and offered some concessions to the Church and peasantry. Later in his term, however, he displayed an increasingly rigid and authoritarian attitude, putting pressure on the Church and intensifying persecution of the intelligentsia. But it was ultimately an economic crisis that brought about his downfall; when he announced official price increases in 1970, a wave of mass strikes erupted in Gdańsk, Gdynia and Szczecin. Again, the violence was put down by force, resulting in 44 deaths. The Party, to save face, ejected Gomułka from office and replaced him with Edward Gierek.

On assuming power, Gierek launched an extensive program of modernisation of the heavy industrial sector. Polish labour, energy and raw materials were cheaper than those in the west, and his strategy was to acquire modern technology abroad which would be paid for from profits made by selling products of the new industry on the international market. Despite some initial growth, however, the poorly conceived factories, inefficiency due to lack of individual worker incentives, the inferior quality of Polish products and, finally, the world market recession of the mid-1970s combined to spell failure for the scheme.

An attempt to raise prices in 1976 incited labour protests, and again workers walked off the job, this time in Radom and Warsaw. Caught in a downward spiral, Gierek took out more foreign loans, but to earn hard currency with which to pay the interest, he was forced to divert consumer goods away from the domestic market and sell them abroad. By 1980 the external debt stood at US$21 billion and the economy had slumped disastrously.

By then, the opposition had grown into a significant force, backed by numerous advisers from the intellectual circles. The election of Karol Wojtyła, the archbishop of Kraków, as Pope John Paul II in 1978 and his triumphal visit to his homeland a year later dramatically increased political ferment. When in July 1980 the government again announced food-price increases, the results were predictable: fervent and well organised strikes and riots broke out and spread like wildfire throughout the country. In August, they paralysed major ports, the Silesia coal mines and the Lenin Shipyard in Gdańsk.

Unlike most previous popular protests, the 1980 strikes were nonviolent: the strikers didn't take to the streets but stayed in their factories. Although the strikes began by demanding wage rises, they very soon took on more general economic and political overtones. Concerted protest by workers and their advisers from the intelligentsia had proved a successful and explosive combination. In contrast, the Party was weak, split and disorganised, and after a decade of mismanagement, the economy was in a state of virtual collapse. The government was no longer in a position to use force against its opponents.

Solidarity

After long-drawn-out negotiations in the Lenin Shipyard in Gdańsk an agreement was eventually reached, and on 31 August 1980 the government was forced to accept most of the strikers' demands. The most significant of these was recognition of the workers' right to organise independent trade unions, and to strike. In return, workers agreed to adhere to the constitution and to accept the Party's power as supreme.

Workers' delegations from around the country convened and founded Solidarność or 'Solidarity', a nation-wide independent and self-governing trade union. Lech Wałęsa, who led the Gdańsk strike, was elected chair. In November, the Solidarity movement, which by then had garnered nearly 10 million members (60% of the workforce), was formally recognised by the government. Amazingly, one million Solidarity members had come from the Party's ranks!

Gierek was ejected from office and his post taken by Stanisław Kania; in October 1981 Kania was replaced by General Wojciech Jaruzelski, who continued to serve as prime minister and minister of defence, posts which he had held prior to his new appointment.

Solidarity had a dramatic effect on the whole of Polish society. After 35 years of restraint, the Poles launched themselves into a spontaneous and chaotic sort of democracy. Wide-ranging debates over the process of reform were led by Solidarity, and the independent press flourished. Such taboo historical subjects as the Stalin-Hitler pact and the Katyń massacre could for the first time be openly discussed.

Not surprisingly, the 10 million Solidarity members represented a wide range of attitudes: from confrontational to conciliatory. By and large, it was Wałęsa's charismatic authority that kept the union on a moderate and balanced course in its struggle to achieve some degree of political harmony with the government.

The government, however, under growing pressure from both the Soviets and local hardliners, became increasingly reluctant to introduce any significant reforms and systematically rejected Solidarity's proposals. This only led to further discontent, and, in the absence of other legal options, strikes became Solidarity's main political weapon. Amid fruitless wrangling, the economic crisis grew more severe. After the unsuccessful talks of November 1981 between the government, Solidarity and the Church, social tensions increased and led swiftly to a political stalemate.

Martial Law & Its Aftermath

When General Jaruzelski appeared unexpectedly on television in the early morning of 13 December 1981 to declare martial law, tanks were already on the streets, army checkpoints had been set up on every corner, and paramilitary squads had been posted to possible trouble spots. Power was placed in the hands of the Military Council of National Salvation (WRON), a group of military officers under the command of Jaruzelski himself.

Solidarity was suspended and all public gatherings, demonstrations and strikes were banned. A night-time curfew was introduced and the principal industrial and communications enterprises were taken over by the army. Telephone conversations and mail were subject to recording and censorship, and the courts were allowed to carry out proceedings virtually without reference to the law, on the pretext of countering 'a threat to public order'. Several thousand people, including most Solidarity leaders and Wałęsa himself, were interned. The spontaneous demonstrations and strikes that followed were crushed, and military rule was effectively imposed all over Poland within two weeks of its declaration.

Whether the coup was a Soviet decision or simply Jaruzelski's attempt to prevent Soviet military intervention, it attained 'its goal: reform was crushed and life in the Soviet bloc returned to the pre-Solidarity norm.

As soon as Jaruzelski became confident in power, he had to turn to the economy, which throughout the period had continued to deteriorate. He increased prices (which was easy under the umbrella of martial law) and the cost of living jumped by over 100% in 1982. He then started to implement economic reforms, but the results were far below expectations. Firstly, the western countries, particularly the USA, imposed economic sanctions in protest against martial law. Secondly, Poland was unable to raise more loans. Lastly, Jaruzelski had no popular support; most Poles were hostile to the government and simply plunged themselves into the inner emigration, as they called it, retreating into their private lives. In October 1982 the government formally dissolved Solidarity and released Wałęsa from detention. Martial law was officially lifted in July 1983.

Solidarity continued underground on a much smaller scale, and enjoyed widespread sympathy and support. In July 1984 a limited amnesty was announced and some members of the political opposition were released from prison. However, further arrests continued, following every public protest, and it was not until 1986 that all political prisoners were freed.

In October 1984 the pro-Solidarity priest Jerzy Popiełuszko was brutally murdered by the security police. The crime aroused popular condemnation, and the funeral was attended by a crowd of over 200,000 people. In an unprecedented public trial the authorities sentenced the perpetrators to prison.

Collapse of Communism

The election of Gorbachev in the Soviet Union in 1985 and his *glasnost* and *perestroika* programs gave an important stimulus to democratic reforms all through Eastern Europe. Again, Poland undertook the role of a guinea pig. Jaruzelski softened his position and become willing to compromise over the democratisation of the system. In April 1989, in the so-called round-table agreements between the government, the opposition and the Church, Solidarity was re-established and the opposition was allowed to stand for parliament. In the consequent semi-free elections in June, Solidarity succeeded in getting an overwhelming majority of its supporters elected to the Senat, the upper house of parliament. However, the communists reserved for themselves 65% of seats in the lower house, the Sejm. Jaruzelski was placed in the presidency as a stabilising guarantor of political changes for both Moscow and the local communists, but the noncommunist prime minister, Tadeusz Mazowiecki, was installed as a result of personal pressure from Wałęsa. This power-sharing deal, with the first noncommunist prime minister in Eastern Europe since WWII, paved the way for the domino-like collapse of communism throughout the Soviet bloc.

The change in power improved Poland's political and economic relations with the west. Diplomatic relations with the Vatican were formally established for the first time since 1945. The Party, losing members and confidence at the speed of light, dissolved itself in January 1990. Despite this political renewal, the economy remained in desperate shape.

In January 1990 the government introduced a package of reforms to change the centrally planned communist system into a free-market economy. The brain behind the radical plan was the finance minister Leszek Balcerowicz. In a shock-therapy transition, all prices were permitted to move freely, subsidies were abolished, the money supply was tightened and the currency was sharply devalued and made fully convertible with western currencies.

Within a few months the economy appeared to have stabilised, food shortages were no longer the norm and the shelves of shops filled up with goods. Meanwhile, however, prices were skyrocketing and unemployment was exploding. During 1990 prices rose by 250% and real incomes dropped by 40%. Not surprisingly, an initial wave of optimism and forbearance was turning into uncertainty and discontent, and the tough austerity measures caused the popularity of the government to decline. By mid-1990 strikes began to occur, though not on the previous scale.

In June 1990 differences over the pace of political reform emerged between Mazowiecki and Wałęsa, leading eventually to open conflict. Wałęsa complained that the government was too slow in removing old communists, the ex-members of the already nonexistent Party, from their political and economic posts. Mazowiecki, on the other hand, wary of political purges during a period of intense hardship, preferred instead to concentrate on the economic program. Solidarity split into two rival factions, leaving the prime minister with most of the intellectual elite on the one side, and the Solidarity leader with the majority of workers and farmers on the other.

This bitter rivalry continued until the presidential elections in November 1990. The first fully free elections were eventually won by Wałęsa. The Third Republic came into being.

Postcommunist Politics

During Wałęsa's statutory five year term in office, Poland witnessed no fewer than five governments with their corresponding five prime ministers, each struggling to put the newborn democracy on wheels and each doing it differently.

After his election, Wałęsa appointed Jan Krzysztof Bielecki, an economist and his former adviser, to serve as prime minister. His cabinet attempted to continue the austere economic policies introduced by the former government but was unable to retain parliamentary support and resigned after a year in office.

The new government under Prime Minister Jan Olszewski was, like its predecessor, plagued by discord, and collapsed after only five months of existence. This period was characterised by constant and fruitless battles between the president and the prime minister, without any major economic or political reforms.

In June 1992, Wałęsa gave his consent to the formation of a government led by Hanna Suchocka of the Democratic Union. An independent and well spoken university professor specialising in constitutional law, she was the nation's first woman prime minister, and became known as the Polish Margaret Thatcher. Suchocka's government managed to command a parliamentary majority, the first to do so during the fractious postcommunist period.

This was not to last. The government was based on a coalition of the majority of those parties which had their roots in the Solidarity movement, which meant that her cabinet embraced just about the entire political spectrum from right to left. The differences were substantial with regard to issues both economic and ideological, such as abortion or the government's relationship with the Catholic Church. On one occasion in June 1993 the government barely survived a vote of no confidence.

The impatient Wałęsa stepped in. Instead of asking another politician to form a government, he decided to dissolve the parliament and call a general election. This was a gross miscalculation. The postcommunist opposition parties accused the parties of the outgoing coalition of mismanagement and indifference to the painful social cost of their radical reforms, and promised a more balanced program offering growth but focused on the people. They succeeded in swaying public opinion and the pendulum swung to the left.

The election resulted in a leftist government based on two parties – the Democratic Left Alliance (SLD) and the Polish Peasant Party (PSL) – both of which had been satellites of the ruling communist party in the pre-1989 era. The two parties commanded almost a two-thirds majority, with 303 seats in the 460-strong Sejm. The new coalition government was headed by PSL leader Waldemar Pawlak, and not by SLD leader Aleksander Kwaśniewski, who enjoyed much greater support, post-communists preferring not to take over so as not to create too much public resentment.

From the beginning, though, the coalition was marked by tensions. It was rather a marriage of convenience, with both leaders, Pawlak and Kwaśniewski, pragmatic and hungry for power. The general direction of transformation to a market economy slowed down, particularly in the area of privatisation and foreign investment.

The continuous problems within the coalition and its running battles with the president spearheaded a change in February 1995, following Wałęsa's threats to dissolve the parliament once again unless Pawlak was replaced by a more pro-reform leader. Kwaśniewski, who was the obvious first choice, chose not to take the position, hoping to enhance his chances in the forthcoming presidential election. The parliament elected Józef Oleksy prime minister.

Oleksy was a former senior communist party official, but vowed to pursue a market economy policy with more determination than his predecessor. However, his declarations didn't materialise and the quarrels with the president continued unabated.

The climate of political wrangling persisted well into the summer of 1995, when the quarrelling factions began to jockey for position in the presidential election due later that year. More than a dozen candidates eventually emerged, including Wałęsa.

Wałęsa's presidential style and his accomplishments were repeatedly questioned by practically all political parties and the majority of the electorate. His quirky behaviour and capricious use of power prompted a slide from the favour he had enjoyed in 1990 to his lowest-ever level of popular support in early 1995, when polls indicated that only 8% of Poles preferred him as president for the next term. Despite this, Wałęsa manoeuvred vigorously towards his goal of another five years in office and, in a miraculous comeback, went close to achieving it.

Recent Developments

The November 1995 election was essentially a duel between the anti-communist folk figure, Wałęsa, and the smooth one-time communist technocrat, Kwaśniewski. They finished nearly neck and neck: Wałęsa with 33% of the vote narrowly behind Kwaśniewski with 35%. As neither collected a clear half of the vote, a second round was held two weeks later. Again, Kwaśniewski won by a narrow margin (51.7% against 48.3%).

Włodzimierz Cimoszewicz, another former communist party official, took the post of prime minister, following Oleksy's stepping down after being accused of collaborating with the KGB. In effect, the postcommunists gained a stranglehold on power, controlling the presidency, government and parliament – a 'red triangle', as Wałęsa warned. Many of the old-time communists were discreetly put back into key political and administrative posts, and they also enjoyed priorities in the economic sector. Yet the social benefits promised in the presidential campaign haven't materialised.

The centre and the right – almost half of the political nation – effectively lost control over the decision-making process. Another loser was the Church, much favoured by Wałęsa during his term in the saddle. The Church didn't fail to caution the faithful against the danger of 'neopaganism' under the new regime.

Two years on, the electorate seems to have realised that the pendulum went too much to the left; the popular mood was reflected in the results of the parliamentary elections of September 1997, won by the alliance of about 40 small Solidarity offshoot parties, the Solidarity Electoral Action (AWS). The alliance formed a coalition with the centrist liberal Freedom Union (UW), pushing ex-communists into opposition. Jerzy Buzek of AWS, a professor in chemistry, became prime minister.

A fully new constitution was finally passed in October 1997, to replace the Soviet-style document in force since 1952 (though it had been amended to correspond with the postcommunist status quo). The new government pushed ahead the privatisation program, and Poland's economic indicators are now among the highest of the Eastern European countries.

On the international front, in March 1999 Poland was finally granted full membership of NATO (along with the Czech Republic and Hungary), on the 50th anniversary of the organisation. The country is also expecting to join the European Union early in the 21st century.

GEOGRAPHY

Poland covers an area of 312,677 sq km. It is approximately as big as the UK and Ireland put together, or less than half the size of Texas. Almost 25 Polands would fit on the Australian continent. The country is roughly square in shape, reaching a maximum of about 680km from west to east and 650km from north to south.

Poland is bordered by the Baltic Sea to the north-west along a 524km coastline; by Germany to the west (along a 460km border); the Czech and Slovak republics to the south (1310km); and Ukraine, Belarus, Lithuania and Russia to the east and north-east (1244km).

A quick glance at the map suggests that Poland is a vast, flat, low-lying plain with mountains only along its southern frontier. A closer look, however, reveals a more complex topography. The really flat part is the wide central belt that stretches from west to east across the middle of the country, comprising the historically defined regions of Wielkopolska (Great Poland), Lower Silesia (Dolny Śląsk), Kujawy, Mazovia (Mazowsze) and Podlasie. This area is Poland's main granary and most of the land is agricultural.

The northern part of Poland, comprising Pomerania (Pomorze), Kashubia (Kaszuby), Warmia and Masuria (Mazury), is varied and gently undulating, relatively well forested and covered by several thousand postglacial lakes, most of which are in Masuria. Poland has over 9000 lakes, more than any other country in Europe except Finland.

Towards the south of the central lowland belt, the terrain rises, forming the uplands of Małopolska (Little Poland) and Upper Silesia (Górny Śląsk). Still farther to the south, along the southern frontier, it concludes in the Sudeten Mountains (Sudety) and the Carpathian Mountains (Karpaty).

The Sudetes, to the west, are 250km long and geologically very old; their highest part, Karkonosze, is topped by Mt Śnieżka (1602m). The Carpathian Mountains, to the east, are fairly young and are made up of several ranges. The highest of these is the

Tatra Mountains (Tatry), the only Alpine-style range in Poland, which is shared with Slovakia to the south. Poland's tallest peak, Mt Rysy (2499m), is in the Tatras.

To the north of the Tatras lies the lower but much larger, densely forested range of the Beskids (Beskidy), with their highest peak, Mt Babia Góra, reaching 1725m. The south-eastern tip of Poland is taken up by the Bieszczady, part of the Carpathians; their tallest peak is Mt Tarnica (1343m).

All Poland's rivers run towards the north and drain into the Baltic Sea. The longest (1047km) is the Vistula (Wisła), which runs through the middle of the country. It is known as the mother river of Poland because it passes through the most historic-ally important cities of Kraków and Warsaw, and its entire basin lies within the country's boundaries.

The second-longest is the Odra (Oder) which forms part of Poland's western border. In July 1997, it caused catastrophic floods (reputedly the largest in the country's history) which cost more than 50 lives and caused damages worth an esti-mated US$2 billion.

CLIMATE

The seasons are clearly differentiated. Spring starts in March and is initially cold and windy, later becoming pleasantly warm and often sunny. Summer, which begins in June, is predominantly warm but hot at times, with plenty of sunshine interlaced with heavy rains. July is the hottest month. Autumn comes in September and is at first warm and usually sunny, turning cold, damp and foggy in November. Winter lasts from December to March and includes shorter or longer periods of snow. High up in the mountains, snow stays well into May. January and February are the coldest months. The temperature sometimes drops below -15°C or even -20°C.

Poland's climate is influenced by a con-tinental climate from the east and a maritime climate from the west. As a result, the weather is changeable, with significant dif-ferences from day to day and from year to

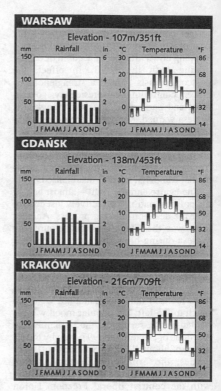

year. Winter one year can be almost without snow, whereas another year heavy snows can paralyse transport for days. Summer is usually warm and sunny but occasionally it can be cold, wet and disappointing.

The average annual rainfall is around 600mm, with the greatest falls in the summer months. The central part of Poland is the driest, receiving about 450mm a year, while the mountains receive much more rain (or snow in winter) – around 1000mm annually.

ECOLOGY & ENVIRONMENT

The communist regime in Poland spent vir-tually nothing on protecting the country's environment. Decades of intensive industri-alisation without even the most elementary protection have turned rivers into sewers and air into smog. It wasn't until 1990, after the regime crumbled, that the Ministry of Environmental Protection was founded and began to develop an environmental policy to try to clean up the mess left by the communists. Today, a decade down the track, Poland's environment is a bit better off yet still in an unenviable state.

Poland has a number of seriously polluted urban and industrial areas (the 'ecological hazard zones'), which account for about 10% of the country's territory. They are a priority of the government's current environmental policy.

Air
Air pollution continues to be one of Poland's most serious problems. The major pollutant is the energy sector, which uses outdated technologies and highly polluting fuels, such as coal and lignite. The situation is worst in large industrial cities, and especially in Upper Silesia, which occupies just 2% of the country's territory but produces about 20% of the sulphur dioxide emissions.

With the sixth highest level of carbon dioxide emissions in Europe, Poland is a significant contributor to global warming. Its goal for 2000 is actually not to diminish emissions but to stabilise them at the (alarmingly high) 1990 level. Poland now receives World Bank assistance to reduce carbon dioxide emissions. Ironically, the main benefactors are the major polluters themselves, the huge, belching plants which have been going bankrupt and closing.

Transportation is currently less of a culprit but a massive rise in the number of cars is likely to worsen the situation in the near future.

Water
Poland's natural water supplies are limited, with the available water per capita figures being among Europe's lowest. At the same time, the use of water in Poland is inefficient, with high per capita consumption. To make matters worse, a great deal of the water available – that received by over half the population – is polluted, largely because

of poor waste water treatment. Poland has upgraded or constructed about 300 waste water treatment plants over the past decade, yet many more are needed. Another aspect of the problem is that virtually all Polish rivers flow into the Baltic Sea, a shallow and tideless body of water with weak circulation, and highly sensitive to pollution.

Waste
Poland is one of Europe's largest sources of industrial waste (mainly from coal mining and heavy industry), and only about 1% of it is treated. Treatment of municipal waste is also minimal, and it virtually all ends up in landfills without sorting.

Nature Conservation
About 22% of the country's territory is currently under some sort of protection (in national or landscape parks or other protected areas), and the goal is to achieve a total of 30%. Remarkably, Poland has succeeded in extending its forested area (mostly by reafforestation) from about 21% of the land just after WWII, to about 28% today. Yet it's still well behind Europe's average of approximately 32%.

A significant part of the forested areas has survived in a remarkably good, natural state, even though the wildlife has decreased. The best-preserved forests, with much of their primeval flora and fauna, are in eastern Poland, mainly along the eastern border, and in the Carpathians, though the latter are endangered by the ski lobby.

Environmental Policies
Although the Ministry of Environmental Protection remains the major player in the environmental management, strategy and conservation field, there are also a number of other government and nongovernment environmental agencies, plus various green groups.

Poland's major goal now is to adjust its internal environmental indicators to comply with EU requirements – a necessary condition for integration with the EU. The process requires a radical improvement of domestic environmental quality by enforcing strict standards in various fields, including air and water pollution, energy and material consumption, waste management, radiation protection and nature conservation. Other related issues are forestry, organic farming and ecotourism.

FLORA & FAUNA

The last ice age ended only about 10,000 years ago in Poland, and depleted the country's vegetation and wildlife, destroying a number of plant and animal species. Consequently, Poland's flora and fauna, like those elsewhere in Europe, are not abundant or extremely diverse.

Forests cover about 28% of Poland's territory. Although some are almost entirely of pine, most are mixed and include, apart from pine, species such as oak, beech, birch, and occasionally larch and fir. In the mountains, the vegetation changes from mixed woods in the lower parts to spruce forests in the uplands and, still farther up, fades into dwarf mountain shrubs and moss.

Poland's fauna numbers some 90 species of mammals, of which the commonest ones include the hare, red deer and wild boar. Wolves and foxes inhabit various regions, but they have been largely decimated. Some elk live in the woods of the far north-east, while occasional brown bears and wildcats can be found in the mountain forests. Several hundred European bison (*Bison bonasus*) live in the Białowieża National Park and some other limited areas. These massive animals once inhabited the continent in large numbers but were brought to the brink of extinction early in the 20th century.

One animal with more than merely symbolic importance is the horse. Poland has a long tradition of breeding Arabian horses, which are much appreciated on world markets. Many important international championships have been won by Polish-bred Arabians. There are a number of stud farms and horse riding is popular.

With some 420 species, birds are better represented than the other fauna and are also more visible. Some of them migrate

The White Stork – A Bird of Good Luck

Everybody knows that storks bring babies. In many countries, including Poland, it is also believed that storks bring good luck. Consequently, they are much loved and attract special attention, and this is particularly true in Poland, which is home to a large population of storks.

Of the 17 stork species that exist, the one seen in Poland is the white stork (*Ciconia ciconia*). It's a fairly large bird, about 1m tall and up to 2m in wingspan, white with black flight feathers, a red bill and long red legs. It is voiceless but can clatter its bill quite loudly.

Poland is home each summer to one in three European white storks, attracting some 30,000 couples every year. The regions where they are most numerous include Masuria and Podlasie in north-eastern Poland. Other European countries with considerable populations of storks are Spain and Ukraine, each with about 15,000 pairs.

Storks come every spring from as far as South Africa to their old nests built years back, or they build new ones. Favourite locations for nests include rooftops of countryside cottages, particularly chimneys, tops of church and castle towers, and posts including phone and power line posts.

The white stork population is diminishing, mostly because of human impact on its habitat. Many storks die by attempting to perch on power lines and towers. In some areas their numbers have dropped drastically, as evidenced by the many abandoned nests. Strong measures are needed to help prevent their extinction.

south in autumn to return in spring. The commonest species are the sparrow, crow, magpie, skylark, nightingale and swallow. Storks, which build their nests on the roofs and chimneys of houses in the countryside, are much loved. In the lake regions, there are plenty of water birds, such as mallards, swans and herons. A small community of cormorants lives in the Masurian Lakes. The eagle, though not very common today, is Poland's national bird and appears in the Polish emblem.

NATIONAL PARKS

As of 1998, Poland had 22 national parks (*parki narodowe*), which covered about 3000 sq km, a mere 0.9% of the country's area. Some new parks are planned for the future. The parks are roughly evenly scattered throughout the country, other than in the Carpathian Mountains where there are six. One Polish national park, Białowieża, is on the UNESCO World Heritage list.

About 85% of the area of all parks is state owned, whereas the remaining 15% is in

POLAND'S NATIONAL PARKS

private hands. The state is gradually acquiring the private land, a process which will take a decade or two to complete. The parks are administered by a special department of the Ministry of Environment; maintenance is financed from the state budget.

No permit is necessary to visit the parks, but most have introduced entry fees (of about US$1), which you pay at the park office or an entry point. Camping in the parks is not allowed except on specified sites.

Apart from the national parks, a network of other, not so strictly preserved, areas called *parki krajobrazowe*, or landscape parks, has been established. As the name suggests, their scenery was the major factor in selecting them and, accordingly, they are usually picturesque. The first landscape park was created in 1976 and today there are already 105 of them. They are found in all regions and together cover about 20,000 sq km, or 6% of the country's area.

There are also the *rezerwaty*, or reserves. These are usually small areas which contain a particular natural feature such as a cluster of old trees, a lake with valuable flora or an interesting rock formation.

GOVERNMENT & POLITICS

Poland is a parliamentary republic. The president is elected in a direct vote for a five-year term as head of state and is empowered to nominate the prime minister.

The parliament consists of two houses, the 460-seat lower house, the Sejm or Diet, and the 100-seat upper house, the Senat or senate. The senate was only created in 1989; before that there was just the one-house parliament based on the Sejm. Both the senate and the president have veto power over the Sejm, but these vetoes can be overridden by a two-thirds majority vote in the Sejm.

Before 1990 the Polish United Workers' Party was constitutionally the leading political force and was guaranteed a majority of seats in the Sejm. Today the Party no longer exists and a myriad of new political parties have appeared on the scene.

Administratively, the country is divided into 16 provinces called *województwa*, which are further split into 373 *powiaty* – 308 rural and 65 urban districts. This division only came into force in 1999, replacing the old 49-province system.

The Polish flag is divided horizontally into two equal belts: white above and red below. The national emblem is a white eagle, which has regained its crown since the fall of communism.

ECONOMY

Bituminous coal has traditionally been Poland's chief mineral resource, with the largest deposits concentrated in Upper Silesia. Coal supplies a large part of the domestic demand for electricity. Poland possesses considerable reserves of sulphur, believed to be among the largest in the world, but large scale exploitation creates daunting ecological problems. Among other mineral resources, there are significant deposits of zinc and lead, and smaller ones of copper and nickel. The country's oil resources are insignificant.

Hydroelectric power is responsible for only a small fraction of electricity production, and the potential is not great. A nuclear reactor based on Soviet technology was started in the early 1980s near Gdańsk but construction was abandoned in 1990.

Approximately half of Poland's territory is arable. Among the main agricultural crops are rye, potatoes, wheat, sugar beet, barley and oats. Over 80% of farmland in Poland, unlike that in the rest of the former communist bloc, remained in the hands of individual farmers even in Soviet times. Collective farms, known as cooperatives, occupied only about 2% of the land.

Many of Poland's huge state-owned factories dating from the period of the postwar rush towards industrialisation are still in operation. Their major products include steel, chemicals (fertilisers, sulphuric acid), industrial machinery and transport equipment (ships, railway cars and motor vehicles). Yet, in a decade since the fall of communism, the situation has changed dramatically. While the old state-owned industries have been falling apart, a plethora of new, mostly small, private enterprises have sprung up.

Today's Poland has the well established foundations of a market economy and a dynamic, new private sector. Trade has shifted towards the west, yet Poland wisely maintains and expands economic links with the countries of the ex-Soviet bloc, to preserve its position as a bridge between west and east.

More than 60% of Poland's GDP is now produced by the private sector, which employs about 60% of the workforce. GDP growth was about 6% in 1997 and is expected to remain similarly high in the coming years. The level of unemployment peaked at 17% in mid-1994, but gradually diminished as the economy recovered, and by the end of 1998 was about 10%.

The huge inflation of the early 1990s dropped to 32% in 1994 and came down below 10% in 1998. Average monthly wages stood at about US$225 at the end of 1993 and reached around US$375 by mid-1998.

POPULATION & PEOPLE

Poland's population in 1998 stood at about 38.5 million. The rate of demographic increase, which was pretty high in the postwar period, has dropped gradually over the last two decades to stabilise at about 0.7%, a figure comparable to those of Western Europe.

There were massive migratory movements in Poland in the aftermath of WWII, and the ethnic composition of the nation is now almost entirely homogeneous. According to the official statistics, Poles make up 98% of the population, Ukrainians and Belarusians about 1%, and the remaining 1% is composed of all other minorities – Jews, Germans, Lithuanians, Tatars, Roma (Gypsies), Lemks, Boyks and a dozen other groups.

Today's ethnic composition differs significantly from that before the war. Poland was for centuries one of the most cosmopolitan countries, and had the largest community of Jews in Europe. Just before the outbreak of WWII they numbered around 3.3 million. Only about 5000 to 10,000 Jews remain in Poland today.

Population density varies considerably throughout the country, with Upper Silesia being the most densely inhabited area while the north-eastern border regions remain the least populated. Over 70% of the country's inhabitants live in towns and cities. Warsaw is by far the largest Polish city (1,650,000), and is followed by Łódź (825,000) and Kraków (750,000). Approximate populations (as of 1998) are given for all cities, towns and major villages described in this book.

According to rough estimates, between five and 10 million Poles live abroad. This is basically the result of two huge migrations, at the beginning of the 20th century and during WWII. Postwar emigration, particularly in the two last decades, has sent additional large numbers of Poles all over the world. The largest Polish émigré community lives in the USA, with the biggest group being in Chicago. Poles joke that Chicago is the second-largest Polish city, as nearly a million of them live there.

EDUCATION

The educational system is well developed and comprehensive at all levels. Education is compulsory between the ages of seven and 18, and the literacy rate stands at 98%. Nearly a fifth of the population have completed secondary and post-secondary education. Education at all levels was free in communist Poland, but this has changed after 1990. School and university programs have been thoroughly revised and adapted to the new Poland.

Private education was almost nonexistent before 1990, only a handful of religious orders having the right to run schools. The only semi-private tertiary facility was KUL, the Lublin Catholic University, supported to a great extent by the Catholic Church.

The law on education has been changed and private schools at all levels have sprung up from nowhere. There are several dozen private higher education facilities, mainly in the areas in high demand, such as business, computer science and languages.

The number of university-level schools has gone up by almost 50% in recent years, mainly because of the introduction of courses which enable people who work to study at the same time. These are provided by both private and public universities. The higher demand for education reflects the situation in the job market, where people who have a degree in certain areas find it much easier to obtain a well paid job.

ARTS
Folk Arts & Crafts

Poland has long and rich traditions in folk arts and crafts, and there are significant regional distinctions. Folk culture is strongest in the mountainous regions, especially in the Podhale at the foot of the Tatras, but other relatively small enclaves such as Kurpie and Łowicz (both in Mazovia) help to keep traditions alive. Naturally, industrialisation and urbanisation increasingly affect traditional customs as a whole. People no longer wear folk dress except for special occasions, and the artefacts they make are mostly for sale as either tourist souvenirs or museum pieces; in any case, not for their original purposes. The growing number of ethnographic museums is an indicator of the decline of traditional folk art; these museums are the best places to see what is left.

One interesting type of ethnographic museum is the *skansen*, or open-air museum, created to preserve traditional rural architecture – see the boxed text.

Yet there's still a lot to see outside the museums and skansens. The Polish rural population is conservative and religious, which means that traditions don't die overnight. The farther off the beaten track you get, the more you'll see. Traditions periodically spring to life around religious feasts and folk festivals, and these events offer the best opportunity to get a feel for how deep the folk roots remain.

Architecture

The earliest dwellings were made of perishable materials, and almost nothing has survived of them. The only important example of early wooden architecture in Poland is the pre-Slavic fortified village in Biskupin, which dates from about 700 BC.

Stone as a construction material was only introduced in Poland with the coming of Christianity in the 10th century. From then on, durable materials – first stone, then brick – were used, and some of that architectural heritage has been preserved to this day.

Generally speaking, Poland has followed the main Western European architectural styles, with some local variations. The first, the Romanesque style, which dominated from approximately the late 10th century to the mid-13th century, used mainly stone and was austere, functional and simple. Round-headed arches, semicircular apses and symmetrical layouts were almost universal. The remnants of the Romanesque style in Poland are few but there are some precious examples, mostly churches.

The Gothic style made its way into Poland in the first half of the 13th century but it was not until the early 14th century that the so-called High Gothic became universally adopted. Elongated, pointed arches and ribbed vaults are characteristic of the style. Brick came into common use instead of stone, and the buildings, particularly churches, tended to reach impressive loftiness and monumental size. Gothic established itself for a long time in Poland and left behind countless churches, castles, town halls and burghers' houses.

In the 16th century a new fashion transplanted from Italy slowly started to supersede Gothic as the dominant style. More delicate and decorative, Renaissance architecture didn't go for verticality and large volume but instead focused on perfect proportions and a handsome visual appearance. In contrast to Gothic, brickwork was almost never allowed to go uncovered. Much attention was paid to detail and decoration, with bas-reliefs, gables, parapets, galleries, round arches and stucco work. There are a number of Renaissance buildings in Poland, though many of them were later 'adorned' by the subsequent architectural fashion, the baroque.

Poland's Skansens

'Skansen' is a Scandinavian word referring to an open-air ethnographic museum. Aimed at preserving the traditional folk culture and architecture, a skansen gathers together a selection of typical, mostly wooden rural buildings such as dwelling houses, barns, churches, mills etc, collected from the region, and often reassembled to look like a natural village. The buildings are furnished and decorated in their original style, incorporating a variety of historical household equipment, tools, crafts and artefacts, giving an insight into our ancestors' lives, work and customs.

The idea of open-air museums emerged in the late 19th century in Scandinavia. Their originator was reputedly the Swedish ethnographer Artur Hazelius, who bought some peasant cottages in 1885, reassembled them on the Djurgården Island in Stockholm and opened them as a museum named 'skansen'. Several similar museums emerged in the following years around Sweden.

It didn't take long for the neighbouring countries to follow the example, with Norway opening its first open-air museum in 1902. By the outbreak of WWI, Norway already had 16 of them, more than a third of Europe's total of 44 open-air museums.

Interest in skansens spread further afield in the interwar period, all over Europe and beyond, including Austria, Germany, the UK and the USA. After WWII, during which many museums were damaged or destroyed, development continued apace, and today there are over 500 open-air museums worldwide. Although a good part of them are in Scandinavia and Central Europe, they now exist on most continents, including Asia, Africa and Australia. The largest existing open-air museum is the Muzeul Satului in Bucharest.

Poland's first skansen was established in 1906 in Wdzydze Kiszewskie, near Gdańsk, and displayed Kashubian folk culture. The next one was founded in 1927 in Nowogród in northern Mazovia, showing traditional Kurpie culture. Both were almost totally destroyed during WWII but were later reconstructed.

There are currently about 35 museums of this kind in Poland, scattered over most regions and featuring distinctive regional traits. They are called museums of folk architecture (*muzeum budownictwa ludowego*), museums of the village (*muzeum wsi*) or ethnographic parks (*park etnograficzny*), but the Scandinavian term 'skansen' is universally applied to all of them.

Most have been established by collecting the buildings from the region, but there are also some small *in situ* skansens, including those in Kluki and Osiek. Skansens usually focus on general aspects of local culture, but there are also some specialist ones, notably the oil industry skansen in Bóbrka and the beekeeping skansen in Swarzędz. Poland's largest skansens include those in Sanok, Ciechanowiec, Lublin, Tokarnia, Nowy Sącz and Dziekanowice. It's hard to list any hard-and-fast 'top 10' but at the very least you shouldn't miss the skansens in Sanok and Nowy Sącz.

Baroque appeared on Polish soil in the 17th century and soon became ubiquitous. A lavish, highly decorative style, it placed a strong imprint on existing architecture by adding its sumptuous décor, which is particularly evident in church interiors and the palaces of rich aristocratic families. The most prominent figure of the baroque period in Poland was Tylman van Gameren, a Dutch architect who settled in Poland and designed countless buildings. In the 18th century baroque culminated in the French-originated rococo, but it didn't make much of a mark on Poland, which by then was swiftly sliding into economic and political chaos.

At the beginning of the 19th century, a more complex phase of architectural development started in Poland which might be characterised as a period of the 'neo', or a general turn back towards the past. This phrase comprised neo-Renaissance, neo-Gothic and even neo-Romanesque styles. The most important of all the 'neo' fashions, though, was neoclassicism, which used ancient Greek and Roman elements as an antidote to the overloaded baroque and rococo opulence. Monumental palaces adorned with columned porticoes were erected in this period, as well as churches that looked like Roman pantheons. Italian architect Antonio Corazzi was very active in Poland in this period, and designed several massive neoclassical buildings, among others the Grand Theatre in Warsaw. Neoclassicism left its strongest mark in Warsaw.

The second half of the 19th century was dominated by eclecticism – the style which profited from all the previous trends – but it didn't produce any architectural gems. More innovative was Art Nouveau, which developed in England, France, Austria and Germany, and made its entrance into Poland (still under partition) at the beginning of the 20th century. It left behind some fresh decorative marks, especially in Kraków and Łódź. After WWI, neoclassicism took over again but lost out to functionalism just before WWII.

The postwar period started with a heroic effort to reconstruct destroyed towns and cities, and the result, given the level of destruction, is really impressive. Meanwhile, one more architectural style, socialist realism, was imposed by the regime. The most spectacular building in this style is the Palace of Culture and Science in Warsaw, a gift from the Soviet Union.

Since the 1960s, Polish architecture has followed more general European styles, though with one important local distinction: almost all major cities are ringed by vast suburbs of anonymous concrete apartment blocks, a sad consequence of massive urbanisation and the lack of imagination of architects. In Poland's defence, it didn't have the necessary cash flow to accommodate aesthetic values. Nor did Poland receive external assistance such as the Marshall Plan, which helped other Western European nations to rebuild after the war. Only after the fall of communism has there been a trend towards the construction of homes on a more human scale.

Painting & Sculpture

Almost nothing is left of Romanesque mural painting but sculpture from this time survives in church portals and tombs. Gothic sculpture reached an outstanding beauty and impeccable realism in countless wooden statues and intricate carved altarpieces, of which the most famous is the work by the German Veit Stoss in St Mary's Church in Kraków. Painting, too, was extremely realistic and reached a high standard. Both forms were almost exclusively religious in character, and most works were anonymous.

Sculpture in the Renaissance period achieved a mastery in the decoration of church chapels and tombs (eg the Wawel Cathedral in Kraków), and bas-reliefs on the façades of houses (such as those in Kazimierz Dolny). Paintings gradually began to depart from religious themes, taking as their subjects members of distinguished families or scenes from their lives.

Baroque was not only a matter of ornate forms and luxuriant decoration – it brought expression and motion to the visual arts. Baroque works are distinguished by dynamic, often dramatic, expression of the figures. Baroque also introduced trompe l'œil wallpainting, which looks three-dimensional. Finally, baroque was extremely generous in the use of gold as an adornment.

Two Italian painters working in Poland distinguished themselves during the reign of Stanisław August Poniatowski, the last Polish king: Marcello Bacciarelli, the king's favourite portraitist, who also produced a set of paintings depicting important moments in Polish history; and Bernardo

Bellotto, commonly known in Poland as Canaletto, who executed a series of paintings which depict with astonishing accuracy Warsaw's major architectural monuments.

As for Polish painters, the first of significance was perhaps Piotr Michałowski (1800-55), whose favourite subject was horses; he also painted numerous portraits.

The second half of the 19th century saw a proliferation of monumental historical paintings. The works of Jan Matejko (1838-93), the greatest artist in this genre, showed the glorious moments of Polish history, presumably in an attempt to strengthen the national spirit during the period of partition. Today, they are the pride of Poland's museums. Other painters of the period who documented Polish history, especially battle scenes, include Józef Brandt (1841-1915) and Wojciech Kossak (1857-1942), the latter particularly remembered as co-creator of the colossal *Panorama Racławicka*, which is on display in Wrocław.

The closing decades of the 19th century saw the development of Impressionism in Europe, but it was met with much reserve by Polish artists. Even though many of the first-rank national painters of the period such as Aleksander Gierymski (1850-1901), Władysław Podkowiński (1866-95), Józef Chełmoński (1849-1914), Leon Wyczółkowski (1852-1936) and Julian Fałat (1853-1929) were in some way or for some periods influenced by the new style, they preferred to express themselves in traditional forms and never completely gave up realism. This is particularly true of their Polish landscapes, an important part of their work.

On the other hand, the revolution in European painting influenced those Polish artists who lived and worked outside Poland, particularly those in Paris. Among them are Olga Boznańska (1865-1940), whose delicate portraits were painted with notable hints of Impressionism, and Tadeusz Makowski (1882-1932), who adopted elements of cubism and developed an individual, easily recognisable style.

The major movement in Polish art and literature between about 1890 and the outbreak of WWI was Młoda Polska or Young Poland, with its centre in Kraków. In the visual arts, the dominant style was the Secesja, highly decorative and characterised by flowing curves and lines, which originated in England, and was known in Austria, Germany and France as Sezessionstil, Jugendstil and Art Nouveau, respectively. (As the last of these terms is most used in English, it has therefore been used in this book regardless of the source of influence.)

The most outstanding figure of the Young Poland movement was Stanisław Wyspiański (1869-1907). A painter, dramatist and poet, he's as much known for his literary achievements as for his pastels. Other artists from that movement include Józef Mehoffer (1869-1946), renowned mainly for his stained-glass designs, and Jacek Malczewski (1854-1929), Poland's best symbolic painter of the era.

The interwar years resulted in a diversity of trends ranging from realism to the avant-garde. The graphic arts began to develop, and colourism, rooted in Paris, attracted some Polish painters, the best known being Jan Cybis (1897-1973).

Stanisław Ignacy Witkiewicz (1885-1939), commonly known as Witkacy, was without doubt the most gifted and exceptional figure of the period. A philosopher, painter, dramatist and photographer, he executed a series of expressionist portraits (the largest collection is in the museum in Słupsk), as well as a number of colourful abstract compositions. Read more about him in the Literature section.

After WWII and up till 1955, the visual arts were dominated by socialist realism, but later they developed with increasing freedom, expanding in a variety of forms, trends and techniques. Among the outstanding figures of the older generation are: Tadeusz Kulisiewicz (1899-1988), who started his career before WWII but reached exceptional mastery in his delicate drawings in the postwar period; Tadeusz Kantor (1915-90), renowned mainly for his famous Cricot 2 Theatre but also very creative in painting, drawing and other experimental forms; Jerzy Nowosielski, whose painting is strongly inspired by the iconography of the Orthodox Church and who has also carried out internal decorations in churches; and Zdzisław Beksiński, considered one of the best contemporary painters Poland has produced, who created a unique, mysterious and striking world of dreams.

Other important postwar painters whose works now adorn museum collections include Jan Tarasin, Leszek Sobocki, Jacek Waltoś, Zbylut Grzywacz, Jerzy Duda-Gracz, Jan Dobkowski, Henryk Waniek and Edward Dwurnik.

Artists who've achieved remarkable success in the graphic arts include Mieczysław Weiman, Janina Kraupe, Antoni Starczewski, Leszek Rózga, Jacek Sienicki, Jan Lebenstein, Józef Gielniak, Andrzej Pietsch, Jacek Gaj, Stanisław Weiman, Krzysztof Skórczewski and Henryk Ożóg.

Among the prominent creators of modern sculpture (including related fields such as assemblages, installations etc) are Bronisław Chromy, Marian Kruczek, Władysław Hasior, Magdalena Abakanowicz, Gustaw Zemła and Adam Myjak.

There's a lot of activity among the younger generation in painting, sculpture and the graphic arts alike. Their works are presented in temporary exhibitions put on by some museums and, particularly, by private commercial art galleries, which also sell them.

Poster Art

Posters in Poland are taken very seriously and since the 1960s have risen to the level of real art, gaining wide international recognition. There is a museum of posters in Warsaw, and plenty of poster exhibitions, from local to international level. Among the great Polish poster artists one cannot avoid mentioning names such as Henryk Tomaszewski, Wiktor Górka, Jan Lenica, Jan Młodożeniec, Franciszek Starowieyski, Roman Cieślewicz and Waldemar Świerzy.

Poster art has found many followers who successfully continue this genre today. The most creative (and arguably most interesting) artists of the younger generation include

Mieczysław Górowski, Jerzy Czerniawski, Wiesław Rosocha, Stasys Eidrigevičius, Wiktor Sadowski, Piotr Młodożeniec, Wiesław Wałkuski, Roman Kalarus, Andrzej Pągowski and Wiesław Grzegorczyk.

Literature

Literature began to develop after the introduction of Christianity in the 10th century, and for nearly half a millennium it consisted mostly of chronicles and political treatises, written almost exclusively in Latin. Not many written records from this period are left; the oldest surviving document is a chronicle from around the 12th century written by Gall Anonim, a foreigner of unknown origin. As for native historians, Jan Długosz (1415-80) was arguably the most outstanding figure and his monumental 12 volume chronicle (in Latin), narrating Polish history from the very beginnings right up till the author's death, is an invaluable source of information concerning events in the country's early history. The oldest text in Polish, the song *Mother of God (Bogurodzica)*, was reputedly written in the 13th century and became the national anthem until the 18th century.

During the Renaissance the Polish language came to be commonly used, and the invention of printing meant that books in Polish became widespread; the first Polish printed text appeared in 1475. In the course of the 16th century Latin came to be completely dominated by the mother tongue and a wide range of Polish-language literature was published, of which the most brilliant was the poetry of Jan Kochanowski (1530-84).

Although the baroque period witnessed a wealth of literary creativity and the subsequent Enlightenment epoch produced some fine poetry by Ignacy Krasicki (1735-1801), it was actually Romanticism that saw Polish poetry really blossom. This was the period when Poland formally didn't exist. Three poets, Adam Mickiewicz (1798-1855), Juliusz Słowacki (1809-49) and Zygmunt Krasiński (1812-59), all working in exile, executed some of the greatest masterpieces of Polish poetry ever written and have since been known to every single Pole. It comes as no surprise that their work is strong in patriotic feelings and prophetic visions. One more noteworthy representative of Romantic poetry, Cyprian Kamil Norwid (1821-83), was not properly recognised until well into the 20th century because of the innovative form and language he used.

In the period of Positivism which followed, it was the prose writers who dominated, and their approach was based on different foundations: in contrast to the Romantic visions, they worked from science, empiricism and realism. The leading writers of this time include Eliza Orzeszkowa (1841-1910), Bolesław Prus (1847-1912) and, particularly, Henryk Sienkiewicz (1846-1916), who was awarded the Nobel Prize in 1905 for *Quo Vadis?* though Poles remember him mostly for his *Trilogy*.

Good times for the novel continued well into the period of Young Poland, with writers such as Stefan Żeromski (1864-1925) and Władysław Reymont (1867-1925), the latter winning another Nobel Prize in literature. For outsiders, however, the literary work of Joseph Conrad (1857-1924) will probably be much better known. Born in Poland as Józef Konrad Korzeniowski, he left the country in 1874 and, after 20 years travelling the world as a sailor, settled in England and dedicated himself to writing (in English).

The period of Young Poland also marked the revival of poetry and saw one of the greatest Polish dramas, *The Wedding (Wesele)* by Stanisław Wyspiański, who also practised painting and many other forms of decorative art.

The interwar period produced several brilliant avant-garde artists who were only understood and appreciated long after WWII. They include Bruno Schulz (1892-1942), Witold Gombrowicz (1904-69) and, the most exceptional and demanding to read, Stanisław Ignacy Witkiewicz, or Witkacy (1885-1939), whose best novel is perhaps *Insatiability (Nienasycenie)*.

An unusual talent in many fields, including painting, literature and photography, Witkacy was the originator of unconventional philosophical concepts, the most notable being the 'theory of pure form', as well as creating the theatre of the absurd long before Ionesco made it famous. Only in the 1960s were Witkacy's plays discovered internationally; they include *Mother (Matka)*, *Cobblers (Szewcy)* and *New Deliverance (Nowe Wyzwolenie)*. He committed suicide soon after the outbreak of WWII as an expression of his belief in 'catastrophism', the disintegration of civilisation.

WWII produced one exceptional talent in the person of Krzysztof Kamil Baczyński (1921-44), who despite his youth created a surprisingly mature poetry. He died fighting as a soldier in the Warsaw Uprising. His verses, Romantic in feel, individual in style and meaningful in content, earned him a permanent place among the best Polish poets of the century.

The postwar period imposed a choice on many writers between selling out to communism and taking a more independent path. Czesław Miłosz, who himself had to solve this moral dilemma and eventually broke with the regime, gives an analysis of the problem in *The Captive Mind (Zniewolony Umysł)*. Miłosz occupies the prime position in Polish postwar literature, and the Nobel Prize awarded to him in 1980 was a recognition of his achievements. He started his career in the 1930s and expresses himself equally brilliantly in poetry and prose, dividing his time between writing, translating and lecturing.

Other internationally known Polish émigrés include Witold Gombrowicz, who started before WWII with *Ferdydurke* but most of whose work, including *The Wedding (Ślub)*, *Operetta (Operetka)* and *Pornography (Pornografia)*, was written during the postwar period; Jerzy Kosiński, known particularly for his novel *The Painted Bird (Malowany Ptak)*; and Sławomir Mrożek, the foremost dramatist who by means of burlesque and satire parodies sociopolitical nonsense.

Wisława Szymborska – 1996 Nobel Prizewinner

Polish postwar literature has twice been awarded the Nobel prize: in 1980 it went to Czesław Miłosz and in 1996 to Wisława Szymborska. While Miłosz, a longtime émigré based in the USA, is familar to international readers due to his extensive literary output and numerous translations, Szymborska is relatively little known outside Poland, or at least she was until 1996.

A poet, translator and literary critic, Szymborska was born in 1923 in the small village of Bnin near Poznań. In 1931 her family moved to Kraków, where she studied Polish literature and sociology at the Jagiellonian University in 1945-48, and where she lives to this day. Her early literary works, which she later disclaimed, were products of a climate of socialist realism, the official artistic doctrine in postwar Poland.

It wasn't until around 1955 that censorship subsided and artists began to create with increasing freedom. Her 1957 collection of poems titled *Calling Out to Yeti (Wołanie Yeti)* was probably Szymborska's first autonomous work. Next was *Salt (Sól)* in 1962. She was a dissident in the 1970s, and later, in the period of martial law and its aftermath, she wrote under a pen name for the local underground press and for the magazine *Kultura* published in Paris by Polish émigrés. She has also translated some French poetry into Polish.

Szymborska's literary output is relatively modest – no more than 10 slim poetry collections, culminating with the 1993 *The End and the Beginning (Koniec i Początek)* – yet it's powerful stuff. The Swedish Academy described her as 'the Mozart of poetry' with 'something of the fury of Beethoven', and awarded her the Nobel prize for 'poetry that with ironic precision allows the historical and biological context to come to light in fragments of human reality'.

The Academy also admitted that 'the stylistic variety in her poetry makes it extremely difficult to translate', which is perhaps one reason why she has been so little known outside Poland. For those interested in sampling her work, a good introduction is the volume titled *View with a Grain of Sand*, from 1995. It's a selection of 100 of Szymborska's poems translated into English, spanning nearly 40 years of her work.

Literary life in Poland has been pretty active since WWII and still has a high profile. One of the most remarkable figures, Tadeusz Konwicki, was initially a follower of official dogma but gradually moved away, which has resulted in two brilliant novels, *A Minor Apocalypse (Mała Apokalipsa)* and *The Polish Complex (Kompleks Polski)*. The work of another judge of Polish reality, Kazimierz Brandys, gives an accurate insight into complex sociopolitical issues, as in his *Warsaw Diary 1977-81 (Pamiętnik Warszawski 1977-81)*.

Polish postwar literature was honoured for a second time with a Nobel Prize in 1996, this time for Wisława Szymborska, a Kraków poet who by the time of the award was little known beyond the boundaries of her motherland. Among other renowned poets are Tadeusz Różewicz (also a playwright), Zbigniew Herbert and Stanisław Barańczak, but a number of younger talents are on their heels.

Stanisław Lem is no doubt Poland's premier science fiction writer, while Ryszard Kapuściński's journalism is internationally known. Kapuściński has always had a good nose for the right place to be in at the right time: he has witnessed 26 coups and revolutions. His books have been translated into 20 languages.

Almost all the authors listed in this section have been translated into English.

Theatre

Early forms of theatre began with the dawn of human development and were related first to pagan, then to Christian, rites. Theatre in the proper sense of the word was born in Poland in the Renaissance period and initially followed the styles of major centres in France and Italy. By the 17th century the first theatre buildings had been erected and original Polish plays were being performed on stage.

In 1765 the first permanent theatre company was founded in Warsaw and its later director, Wojciech Bogusławski, became known as the father of the national theatre. Theatre developed remarkably in this period but was hindered during partition. Only the Kraków and Lviv theatres enjoyed relative freedom, but even they were unable to stage the big national dramas by the great Romantic poets, which could not be performed until the beginning of the 20th century. By the outbreak of WWI, 10 permanent Polish theatres were operating. The interwar period witnessed a lively theatrical scene with the main centre becoming Warsaw, followed by Kraków, Lviv and Vilnius.

It was only after WWII that Polish theatre acquired an international reputation. From the mid-1950s, after socialist realism had been abandoned, theatre erupted with unprecedented strength, and within two decades achieved some remarkable successes. Perhaps the highest international recognition was gained by the Teatr Laboratorium (Laboratory Theatre) created (in 1965) and led by Jerzy Grotowski in Wrocław. This unique experimental theatre, remembered particularly for *Apocalypsis cum Figuris*, was dissolved in 1984, and Grotowski concentrated on conducting theatrical classes abroad until his death in early 1999. Another worldwide success was Tadeusz Kantor's Cricot 2 Theatre of Kraków. Unfortunately, his best creations, *The Dead Class (Umarła Klasa)* and *Wielopole, Wielopole*, will never be seen again; Kantor died in 1990 and the theatre was dissolved a few years later.

Among younger experimental theatres, the most powerful and expressive include the Gardzienice, based in the village of the same name near Lublin, the Teatr Witkacego (Witkacy Theatre) in Zakopane, and the Wierszalin in Białystok.

In the mainstream, the most outstanding theatre company in Kraków is the Teatr Stary (Old Theatre). In Warsaw there are several top-rank theatres, including the Centrum Sztuki Studio (Studio Art Centre), Teatr Polski (Polish Theatre), Teatr Ateneum, Teatr Powszechny and Teatr Współczesny.

Theatre directors to watch out for include Jerzy Jarocki, Andrzej Wajda, Jerzy Grzegorzewski, Kazimierz Dejmek, Krystian Lupa and Maciej Prus. Prominent among other forms of theatre are Wrocławski Teatr Pantomimy (Pantomime Theatre of Wrocław) and Polski Teatr Tańca (Polish Dance Theatre) in Poznań.

Cinema

Though the invention of the cinema is attributed to the Lumière brothers, some sources claim that a Pole, Piotr Lebiedziński, should take some of the credit, having built a film camera in 1893, two years before the movie craze took off.

The first Polish film was shot in 1908, but it was only after WWI that film production began on a larger scale. Until the mid-1930s Polish films were largely banal comedies or adaptations of the more popular novels, and were hardly recognised beyond the country's borders. The biggest Polish contribution to international film in that period was that of the actress Pola Negri, who was born in Poland and made her debut in Polish film before gaining worldwide fame.

During the first 10 years after WWII, Polish cinematography didn't register many significant achievements apart from some semi-documentaries depicting the cruelties of the war. One such remarkable example is *The Last Stage (Ostatni Etap)*, a moving documentary-drama directed by Wanda Jakubowska, an Auschwitz survivor.

The years 1955-63 – the period of the so-called Polish School – were unprecedentedly fruitful, beginning with the debut of Andrzej Wajda. Inspired by literature and often dealing with moral evaluations of the war, the school's common denominator was heroism. A dozen remarkable films were made in that period, including Wajda's famous trilogy: *A Generation (Pokolenie)*, *Canal (Kanał)* and *Ashes and Diamonds (Popiół i Diament)*. Since that period, the tireless Wajda has produced a film every couple of years; three which have gained possibly the widest recognition are *Man of Marble (Człowiek z Marmuru)*, its sequel, *Man of Iron (Człowiek z Żelaza)*, and *Danton*.

In the early 1960s two young talents, Roman Polański and Jerzy Skolimowski, appeared on the scene. The former made only one feature film in Poland, *Knife in the Water (Nóż w Wodzie)*, and then decided to continue his career in the west; the latter shot four films, of which the last, *Hands Up (Ręce do Góry)*, was kept on the shelf for over 10 years, and he left Poland soon after Polański. Whereas Skolimowski's work abroad hasn't resulted in any particular marvels, Polański has made it to the top. His career includes such remarkable films as *Cul-de-Sac*, *Rosemary's Baby*, *Chinatown*, *Macbeth*, *Bitter Moon* and *Death and the Maiden*.

Another ambassador of Polish cinema, Krzysztof Kieślowski, started in 1977 with *Scar (Blizna)* but his first widely acclaimed feature was *Amateur (Amator)*. After several mature films, he undertook the challenge of making the *Decalogue (Dekalog)*, a 10 part TV series which was broadcast all over the world. He then made another noteworthy production, *The Double Life of Veronique*, and confirmed his extraordinary abilities as a film maker with the trilogy *Three Colours: Blue/White/Red*. The last project brought him important international film awards and critics acclaimed him as one of Europe's best directors. He died in March 1996.

Other remarkable directors who started their careers during communist times include Krzysztof Zanussi, Andrzej Żuławski and Agnieszka Holland. The post-communist period has witnessed a rash of young directors but as yet no one of the class of Polański or Wajda.

Poland has produced a number of world-class cinematographers, including Janusz Kamiński, awarded with two Oscars for his work on Steven Spielberg's *Schindler's List* and, more recently, *Saving Private Ryan*. Less known but perhaps no less talented are several other Polish cinematographers responsible for various acclaimed Hollywood productions, including Adam Holender *(Midnight Cowboy)*, Andrzej Bartkowiak *(Verdict, Jade)*, Andrzej Sekuła *(Pulp Fiction)* and Piotr Sobociński *(Marvin's Room, Ransom)*.

Music

Though music has always been an integral part of human life, the first written records mentioning Polish music date only from the Middle Ages. Centred around the Church and the court, it included both vocal and instrumental forms, following mostly western patterns and using the Latin language. Folk music contained more native elements.

The Renaissance marked important developments in Polish musical culture but it was not until the Romantic period that local music reached its peak. The foremost figure was, without doubt, Frédéric Chopin (1810-49), who crystallised the Polish national style, taking his inspiration from folk or court dances and tunes such as the *polonez* (polonaise), *mazurek* (mazurka), *oberek* and *kujawiak*. No one else in the history of Polish music has so creatively used folk rhythms for concert pieces or achieved such international recognition. Chopin has become the very symbol of Polish music.

In Chopin's shade, another eminent composer inspired by folk dances was the creator of Polish national opera, Stanisław Moniuszko (1819-72). Two of his best known operas, *Halka* and *Straszny Dwór*, are staples of the national opera houses. Moniuszko was also the father of Polish solo song; he composed 360 songs to texts by prominent national poets, among them Mickiewicz, and these were known and sung in almost every Polish home.

The Warsaw monument to Frédéric Chopin,
Poland's pre-eminent composer

Also overshadowed by Chopin's fame was the third of Poland's remarkable 19th century composers, Henryk Wieniawski (1835-80), who also was a great violinist.

By the start of the 20th century, Polish artists were starting to make their way onto the world stage. The first to do so were the piano virtuosi Ignacy Paderewski (1860-1941) and Artur Rubinstein (1886-1982), the latter performing almost until his death.

The premier personality in Polish music of the first half of the 20th century was Karol Szymanowski (1882-1937). His best known composition, the ballet *Harnasie*, was influenced by folk music from the Tatra Mountains, which he transformed to produce an original achievement in the contemporary musical idiom.

In the composition of contemporary music, Poland is up there with the world's best. In the 1950s and 1960s a wealth of talents emerged on the musical scene. Among the leading composers are Witold Lutosławski, with his 'perfect' works such

as *Musique Funèbre* or *Jeux Vénitiens*; Tadeusz Baird, who combined the traditional with the experimental; Bogusław Schäffer, representing the avant-garde movement in both music and theatre; and Krzysztof Penderecki, widely known for his monumental dramatic forms such as *Dies Irae*, *Devils of Loudun*, *Ubu Rex*, *Seven Gates of Jerusalem* and *Credo*.

Largely eclipsed by the aforementioned masters, Henryk Górecki was another great talent, developing an original musical language. His Symphony No 3 was written in 1976, but it wasn't until the early 1990s that the second recording of this work hit musical audiences worldwide. The phenomenal success of the Third Symphony shed light on the other, equally remarkable, compositions of Górecki, notably his String Quartets Nos 1 and 2, written for, and exquisitely performed by, the Kronos Quartet.

Another composer whose name has entered international music dictionaries is Zbigniew Preisner, responsible for the music in recent Kieślowski films, including *Decalogue*, *The Double Life of Veronique* and *Three Colours*. His first nonfilm musical piece, *Requiem for my Friend*, dedicated to Kieślowski, had its much celebrated premiere in October 1998.

Folk music is cultivated and propagated by two national song and dance ensembles, Mazowsze and Śląsk, as well as other smaller, mostly amateur bands.

Jazz really took off in the 1950s, at that time underground, around the legendary pianist Krzysztof Komeda, who later composed the music to most of the early Polański films before his tragic death. Komeda inspired and influenced many jazz musicians, such as Michał Urbaniak (violin, sax), Zbigniew Namysłowski (sax) and Tomasz Stańko (trumpet), all of whom became pillars of Polish jazz in the 1960s and remain pretty active today. Urbaniak opted to pursue his career in the USA, and is the best known Polish jazz player on the international scene.

Of the younger generation, Leszek Możdżer (piano) is possibly the biggest revelation to date. Other young jazz talents to watch out for include Piotr Wojtasik (trumpet), Maciej Sikała (sax), Adam Pierończyk (sax), Cazary Konrad (drums), Piotr Rodowicz (bass) and Kuba Stankiewicz (piano).

Poland has 12 philharmonic halls, seven symphony orchestras, nine opera houses and 10 operettas. Seven higher music schools and about 40 secondary music schools contribute to the future development of musical culture.

SOCIETY & CONDUCT

By and large, Poles are more conservative and traditional than westerners and there's a palpable difference between the city and the village. While the way of life in large urban centres increasingly mimics Western European and, especially, North American patterns, the traditional spiritual culture is still very much in evidence in the more remote countryside. Religion plays an important role in this conservatism, the other factor being the still limited and antiquated infrastructure of services and communications. All in all, travelling in some rural areas can be like going back a century in time.

Though it's a risky task to try to draw any general picture of a nation's character, Poles are on the whole friendly and hospitable; there's a traditional saying, 'a guest in the house is God in the house'. If you happen to befriend Polish people, they may be extremely open-handed and generous, reflecting another popular unwritten rule, 'get in debt but show your best'.

Poles are remarkable individuals, each of them with their own solution for any dilemma within the family or the nation, and history proves well enough that there has never been a consensus over crucial national questions. On the other hand, they have an amazing ability to mobilise themselves at critical moments.

Not always realistic, Poles are at times charmingly irrational and romantic. Lovers of jokes and easy-going, they may suddenly turn serious and hot-blooded when it comes to argument.

Poles don't keep as strictly to the clock as people do in the west. You may have to wait a bit until your friend arrives for an appointed meeting in the street or in a café. Likewise, if you are invited for a dinner or a party to someone's home, don't be exactly on time.

When Poles collide with each other on the street they rarely apologise. They're not being rude; it's just the way they do things.

In greetings, Polish men are passionate handshakers. Women, too, often shake hands with men, but the man should wait until the woman extends her hand first. You may often see the traditional polite way of greeting when a man kisses the hand of a woman.

Polish men are also passionate about giving flowers to women. The rose was traditionally the flower reserved for special occasions, but there's no strict rules these days. What does still seem to be largely observed, however, is the superstition of presenting an odd, not even, number of flowers.

RELIGION

Poland is a strongly religious country and over 80% of the population are practising Roman Catholics. Needless to say, the 'Polish pope', John Paul II, has strengthened the position of the Church in his motherland.

Since its introduction in 966, the Catholic Church (Kościół Katolicki) has always been powerful, as it is today. However, in contrast to the present day, for centuries before WWII it had to share power with other creeds, particularly with the Eastern Orthodox Church (Kościół Prawosławny). Poland has always been on the borderline between Rome and Byzantium, and both faiths have been present in Poland for most of its history.

With the Union in Brest (1596), the Polish Orthodox hierarchy split off and accepted the supremacy of the pope in Rome. It became the so-called Uniate Church (Kościół Unicki), often referred to as the Greek-Catholic Church (Kościół Greko-Katolicki). Despite the doctrinal change, the Uniate Church retained its eastern rites, its traditional practices and liturgic language.

After WWII, Poland's borders shifted towards the west, and consequently the Orthodox Church is now present only along a narrow strip on the eastern frontier. Its adherents number less than 1% of the

Poland's Catholic Church Today

A characteristic feature of Poland's current socio-political life is a remarkable expansion of the Catholic Church, which has swiftly filled the vacuum left behind by the communists, claiming land, power and the role of moral arbiter of the nation. Lech Wałęsa himself, when president, was the Church's most prominent supporter, and never went anywhere without a priest at his side.

The interference of the Church in politics notably changed political priorities. In the early 1990s, the crusade against abortion soared to the top of the agenda and pushed economic issues into the background. Abortion had been legalised since 1956 – during the communist era – and was in practice the main form of birth control. Even though only about 10% of the population supported a total ban on abortion, the Church achieved its aim and the parliament duly voted for a ban. An anti-abortion law was introduced in 1993. Moderates did manage to have amendments attached to the law requiring that contraceptives be made available and that Polish schools begin providing sex education for the first time.

The Church has also turned its attention to the rising generation. Voluntary religious education

The 'Polish pope', John Paul II

was introduced in primary schools in 1990 and became mandatory in 1992. Priests have become a new export item: a quarter of all Catholic priests in Europe today are Polish.

Since around 1994, the Church has begun to lose popular support. Ironically, it has become the victim of its own victories. The religious instruction in public schools, the strong anti-abortion law and numerous privileges such as special treatment in the process of granting electronic media licences began to breed resentment among segments of the population, damaging the people's good opinion of the Church.

Perhaps even more ironically, the Church contributed to the 1995 return to power of the former communists, its arch-enemy. It alienated quite a number of voters, who rebelled against the clerical militancy backed by Wałęsa and instead opted for Aleksander. Yet despite losing adherents, the Church remains extremely powerful.

country's population, yet it is the second-largest creed, and the only one of any significance after Catholicism.

The liturgy of the Orthodox Church uses the Old Church Slavonic language, though sermons are usually either in Belarusian or Ukrainian, depending on the ethnic composition of the region. As for their places of worship, Orthodox churches – *cerkwie* (*cerkiew* in the singular) – are recognisable

by their characteristic onion-shaped domes. Inside is the iconostasis, a partition or screen covered with icons, which separates the sanctuary from the main part of the church.

The Uniate Church has an even smaller number of believers, mostly Ukrainians and Lemks scattered throughout the country as a result of the forced resettlement imposed by the communist authorities in the aftermath of WWII. The architecture and decoration of Uniate churches are similar to those of their Orthodox counterparts, and they are also referred to as cerkwie.

One peculiar congregation which originates from the Orthodox Church, the Old Believers, lives in a handful of settlements in north-east Poland. See the Wojnowo section.

Three mosques serve the tiny Muslim population (see the Kruszyniany & Bohoniki section), and a handful of synagogues hold religious services for Jews.

LANGUAGE

Polish belongs to the group of West Slavonic languages, together with Czech, Slovak and Lusatian. Today it's the official language of Poland and is spoken by over 99% of the population.

In medieval Poland, Latin was the lingua franca and the language used by the Crown's state offices, administration and the Church. The Latin alphabet was adapted to write the Polish language, but in order to write down the complex sounds of the Polish tongue a number of consonant clusters and diacritical marks had to be applied. The visual appearance of Polish is pretty fearsome for people outside the Slavonic circle, and it's no doubt a difficult language to master. It has a complicated grammar, with word endings changing depending on case, number and gender, and the rules abound in exceptions.

As for western languages, English and German are the best known in Poland though by no means are they commonly spoken or understood. English is most often heard in larger urban centres among the better educated youth, while German is largely a heritage of prewar territorial divisions and the war itself, and as such is mainly spoken by the older generation, particularly in the regions which were once German. Taking that as a rough rule, you may have some English conversations in major cities, but when travelling in remote parts of Masuria or Silesia, German will be a better tool of communication.

French, traditionally the aristocratic language of the Polish elite, keeps its noble status to some extent, and you may meet people in intellectual circles who speak it fluently.

Lastly, there's Russian, a compulsory language in primary and secondary schools during the communist times. Most Poles who went through the communist educational system know some Russian, or at least understand some of it. Today, with Russian trade-tourism flooding Poland, this language finally becomes helpful in ... bargaining for goods at bazaars.

This said, remember that most ordinary Poles don't speak any other language than Polish. This includes attendants of public services such as shops, post offices, banks, bus and train stations, restaurants and hotels (except for some top-end ones), and you may even encounter language problems at tourist offices. It is also true of phone emergency lines, including police, ambulance and fire brigade.

See the Language chapter near the end of the book for a practical guide to the pronunciation of Polish, and some vocabulary essentials.

Facts for the Visitor

HIGHLIGHTS
Nature
Poland's mountains, lakes and sea coast are superb. The Tatras are the uncontested winners among the mountain ranges, in both height and popularity. Far less known but also magnificent are the Góry Stołowe (Table Mountains) in the Sudetes. The Bieszczady and the Pieniny are quite different though just as picturesque.

There are several lake districts in Poland, of which the Great Masurian Lakes are the largest and most popular. The sea coast has sandy beaches along almost its entire length; one of the most beautiful and least polluted stretches is near Łeba, with its shifting dunes.

The primeval Białowieża Forest on Poland's eastern border is home to the largest remaining herd of European bison, and other wildlife. Each of these environments is distinct and equally worth experiencing.

Historic Towns
Of all Poland's cities, only Kraków has a fully authentic old centre, almost untouched by WWII. The damaged historic cores of Poznań, Toruń and Wrocław have been masterfully restored. The old towns in Gdańsk and Warsaw were destroyed almost totally and rebuilt from scratch, with amazingly good results. All are well worth visiting. Among smaller urban centres, Zamość in south-east Poland is a 16th century Renaissance town.

Museums
Warsaw's National Museum holds Poland's largest art collection, though national museums in Kraków, Wrocław, Poznań and Gdańsk are also extensive and worth visiting. The Modern Art Museum in Łódź houses Poland's largest collection of modern painting, while Płock has the most representative collection of Art Nouveau. The small town of Jędrzejów has a unique set of over 300 sundials, but if icons are what you like, go to Sanok and Przemyśl. The Auschwitz museum at Oświęcim is perhaps the most touching and meaningful.

Anyone interested in traditional rural architecture and crafts should visit some of Poland's *skansens* (open-air museums), in particular those at Sanok and Nowy Sącz.

Castles
There are over 100 castles in Poland of many different kinds. The imposing Malbork castle, one-time seat of the Teutonic Knights, is reputedly the largest surviving medieval castle in Europe. Other remarkable castles built by the knights include those in Lidzbark Warmiński and Kwidzyn.

For hundreds of years the mighty Wawel castle in Kraków sheltered Polish royalty, most of whom are buried in the adjacent cathedral. True castle lovers will also seek out castles in Pieskowa Skała, Baranów Sandomierski, Niedzica, Książ and Gołuchów. All these castles are now museums.

Among ruined castles, the Krzyżtopór in the tiny village of Ujazd is possibly the most impressive, and the charming ruin in Ogrodzieniec is also worth a trip.

Palaces
Warsaw contains Poland's two most magnificent royal palaces: the 17th century Wilanów palace and the 18th century Łazienki palace. In the countryside feudal magnates built splendid Renaissance, baroque and rococo palaces, the best of which include those in Łańcut, Nieborów, Kozłówka, Rogalin and Pszczyna, all open as museums.

Churches
In a country as strongly Catholic as Poland, churches are everywhere from the smallest villages to the largest cities. Kraków alone has several dozen of them. Plenty of old churches are of great historic and often artistic value. It's hard to name highlights here

but any list should include the cathedrals in Kraków, Toruń and Gniezno, St Mary's churches in Kraków and Gdańsk, and the Monastery of Jasna Góra in Częstochowa.

These famous buildings apart, there's a galaxy of other churches, ranging in size from minuscule to colossal, and often of amazing artistic beauty. The region of the Carpathian foothills is dotted with rustic timber Catholic churches and roadside chapels, which deserve in themselves a couple of weeks exploration.

The heritage of the Orthodox and Uniate churches includes over 100 charming wooden churches in the Carpathian Mountains alone, not to mention another hundred scattered along the eastern Polish border.

UNESCO World Heritage List

The list includes eight sites in Poland: the historic quarters of Kraków, Toruń, Warsaw and Zamość, Auschwitz concentration camp, Wieliczka salt mine, Malbork castle and Białowieża National Park.

SUGGESTED ITINERARIES

Your itinerary will depend on an enormous range of factors, including your particular interests, the season, your method of transport and so on, but some very rough guidelines can be given.

The following suggestions have been made assuming you arrive at Warsaw and plan on visiting a reasonable cultural-natural mix of the country, but various options are given to suit personal interests. Regardless of how short your visit is, however, try not to miss Kraków. For more suggestions, see the preceding Highlights section, and the Highlights box at the beginning of each chapter.

One week
Spend one to three days in Warsaw, the rest of the week in Kraków; include a short trip to Auschwitz, and, if time allows, the Tatra Mountains.
Two weeks
To the above, add any of the four following options, depending on your taste:
• the cultural trip to Gdańsk, Malbork and Toruń;
• wildlife watching in Białowieża and Biebrza national parks;
• the pleasant eastern route between Warsaw and Kraków visiting Lublin, Zamość and Sandomierz;
• hiking in the Tatras and the Pieniny.
One month
You'll be able to do most of the options listed above.
Two months
To the above, add Wrocław and the Sudeten Mountains, plus the Beskids and Bieszczady in the Carpathian Mountains – both these ranges provide a good mix of culture and nature; beach-goers might like to relax in some of the Baltic coastal resorts including Łeba and its environs, while lake-lovers may fancy a week or two of kayaking or sailing in Masuria.

PLANNING
When to Go

The tourist season runs roughly from May to September; that is, from mid-spring to early autumn. Its peak is in July and August: these are the months of school and university holidays, and most Polish workers and employees take their annual leave in that period. The Baltic beaches are taken over by swarms of humanity, resorts and spas are invaded by tourists, Masurian lakes are crowded with hundreds of sailing boats, and mountains can hardly be seen for walkers.

In that period, transport becomes more crowded than usual, and can get booked out in advance. Accommodation is harder to find, and sometimes more expensive. Fortunately, a lot of schools, which are empty during the holidays, double as youth hostels, and student dormitories in major cities open as student hostels. To some extent this meets the demand for budget accommodation. Most theatres are closed in July and August.

If you want to escape the crowds, probably the best time to come is either late spring (mid-May to June) or the turn of summer and autumn (September to mid-October), when tourism is under way but not in full flood. These are pleasantly warm periods, ideal for general sightseeing and outdoor activities such as walking, biking, horse riding and canoeing. Many cultural events take place in both these periods.

The rest of the year, from mid-autumn to mid-spring, is colder, darker and perhaps less attractive for visitors. However, this doesn't mean that it's a bad time for visiting city sights and enjoying the cultural life which is not much less active than during the tourist season. Understandably, hiking and other outdoor activities are less prominent in this period, except for skiing in winter. Most camp sites and youth hostels are closed at this time.

The ski season goes from December to March. The Polish mountains are spectacular, but the infrastructure (hotels and chalets, lifts and tows, cable cars, transport) is still not well developed. A handful of existing ski resorts fill beyond their capacity, especially from late December to mid-January. If you plan on skiing in Poland, try to avoid this period or book in advance.

Maps

You don't have to worry about not being able to find maps in Poland. The country produces plenty of maps, and they are generally of good quality, inexpensive and easily available. The situation has improved greatly in recent years. Apart from the state-run map producer, the PPWK, there are now a number of private map publishers.

There's a wide range of general maps of Poland to choose from. You can buy either a single map covering the whole country or a set of four or eight sheets (sold separately) which feature fragments of the country at a larger scale and provide much greater detail. Two different kinds of the book-format *Atlas Samochodowy* (Road Atlas) are available, and they are particularly convenient for motorists. They differ in scale (1:300,000 or 1:250,000) and price (US$10 or US$14, respectively) but both are very accurate and readable, and include sketch maps of major cities, Polish road signs and a full index.

All cities and most large towns have their city maps, which are a good supplement to the maps contained in this book. The maps have a lot of useful information including tram and bus routes, alphabetical lists of streets, post offices, hotels, hospitals, pharmacies etc.

Other very useful maps are the large scale tourist maps (usually between 1:50,000 and 1:75,000) of the most attractive tourist areas. They cover a relatively small sector, a single mountain range or a group of lakes, and are amazingly detailed, showing such tiny features as, for example, the freestanding roadside crosses. These maps show marked hiking routes and practically everything else you might be interested in when trekking, driving, biking etc. They are a must if you plan on walking.

All the maps listed above are easy to buy in the larger urban centres; buy them there, as they may still be hard to come by in the smaller localities. Maps (including city maps) cost somewhere between US$1 and US$2.50 each.

Polish maps are easy to decipher. Most symbols are based on international standards, and they are explained in the key in three foreign languages, English included.

On the city maps, the word for street, *ulica* or its abbreviated version *ul*, is omitted, but *Aleje* or *Aleja*, more often shortened to *Al*, is placed before the names of avenues to distinguish them from streets.

What to Bring

The first and most important rule is to bring as little as possible – a large, heavy backpack can soon become a nightmare. The times of empty shelves in Poland are long over and you can now buy almost everything you might need. Things such as clothes, footwear, toiletries, stationery, sports and camping equipment etc, both locally produced and imported, are easily available in shops and markets, and they can be cheaper than those you've brought along.

When preparing for the trip, concentrate on the most important things, such as a good backpack, comfortable shoes, reliable camera equipment and any medicines you might need. If you plan on hiking, give some thought to trekking gear such as a tent, sleeping bag, waterproof jacket etc. These things are available in Poland but you may prefer bringing your own instead. Disposable gas cartridges for Camping Gaz International stoves can be bought at local sports stores. Winter can be cold, so a good warm jacket is essential at that time of year.

TOURIST OFFICES
Local Tourist Offices

Most larger cities have local tourist offices, which are usually good sources of information and most sell maps and tourist publications.

If you can't find any, try Orbis, Poland's largest travel agency, which runs over 50 top-class hotels and more than 150 travel offices scattered in cities and towns throughout the country. Orbis doesn't focus on providing free information to travellers, yet some of its staff may occasionally help if they're not too busy, and in most offices there's someone who speaks English.

Another possible information source is the Polish Tourists Association (PTTK), the low-budget counterpart to Orbis. It also has an array of accommodation (usually cheap) and a host of offices throughout the country. PTTK was once a very helpful organisation, focusing on outdoor activities such as hiking, sailing, canoeing, cycling and camping. Not much is left of the initial ideals and program of the company which is now just another travel agency. Yet some PTTK offices are well stocked with maps and trekking brochures, can arrange guides, and may provide some information.

Tourist Offices Abroad

Polish tourist offices abroad include:

France
    Office National Polonais de Tourisme
    (☎ 01-47 42 07 42, fax 42 66 35 88)
    49 av. de l'Opéra, 75002 Paris
Germany
    Polnisches Fremdenverkehrsamt
    (☎ 30-210 09 211, fax 210 09 214)
    Marburger Strasse 1, 10789 Berlin

Netherlands
    Pools Informatiebureau voor Toerisme
    (☎ 20-625 35 70, fax 623 09 29)
    Leidsestraat 64, 1017 PD Amsterdam
UK
    Polish National Tourist Office
    (☎ 020-7580 8811, fax 7580 8866)
    1st Floor, Remo House, 310-312 Regent St, London W1R 5AJ
USA
    Polish National Tourist Office
    (☎ 312-236 9013, ☎ 236 9123, fax 236 1125)
    33 North Michigan Ave, Suite 224, Chicago, IL 60601
    (☎ 212-338 9412, fax 338 9283)
    275 Madison Ave, Suite 1711, New York, NY 10016

You can also try offices of the Polish travel agencies, of which Orbis has the widest network. As in Poland, Orbis focuses on selling its services and has package holidays which may include skiing, sailing or horse riding. It can book Orbis hotels and arrange a rental car. As well, it may provide tourist information and have free tourist publications on Poland. Orbis offices abroad appear under the name of either Orbis or Polorbis and include:

France
    Polorbis
    (☎ 01-47 42 07 72, fax 49 24 94 36)
    49 av. de l'Opéra, 75002 Paris
Germany
    Polorbis Reisenternehmen GmbH
    (☎ 221-95 15 34, fax 52 82 77)
    Hohenzollernring 99-101, 50672 Cologne
    (☎ 30-294 13 94, ☎ 294 13 95, fax 294 96 48)
    Warschauer Strasse 5, 10243 Berlin
UK
    Polorbis Travel Ltd
    (☎ 020-7637 4971, ☎ 7580 8028, ☎ 7580 1704, fax 7436 6558)
    82 Mortimer St, London W1N 8HN
USA
    Orbis Polish Travel Bureau
    (☎ 212-867 5011, fax 682 4715)
    342 Madison Ave, New York, NY 10173

VISAS & DOCUMENTS
Passport

Obviously, a valid passport is essential, and it must be stamped with a visa if you need one. Theoretically, the expiry date of your passport shouldn't be less than six months after the date of your departure from Poland. Make sure that your passport has a few blank pages for visas and entry and exit stamps.

Visas

Bilateral conventions allowing visa-free visits have been signed with a number of countries, and by 1998 there were already over 50 countries on the list, including most of Eastern Europe, the Commonwealth of Independent States and the three Baltic republics. Among other countries whose citizens don't need visas for Poland are Argentina, Austria, Belgium, Bolivia, Chile, Costa Rica, Cuba, Cyprus, Denmark, Finland, France, Germany, Greece, Honduras, Iceland, Ireland, Italy, Japan, Liechtenstein, Luxembourg, Malta, Monaco, the Netherlands, Nicaragua, Norway, Portugal, South Korea, Spain, Sweden, Switzerland, Uruguay, the UK and the USA. Stays of up to 90 days are allowed, except for Britons who are allowed to stay in Poland without a visa for up to 180 days.

Nationals of other countries should check with a Polish consulate and apply for a visa if they need one. Canadians, Australians, New Zealanders, South Africans and Israelis still required a visa at the time of writing.

Visas are issued for a period of up to 180 days, and the price is the same regardless of the visa's duration – about US$40 to US$60, varying from country to country. Some consulates may give shorter visas if you apply by mail. You can stay in Poland only within the period specified in the visa, so you need to work out the date of your planned entry when applying. You normally cannot extend your tourist visa in Poland, so ask for a sufficiently long period while applying for your visa at home.

There are also 48-hour transit visas (onward visa required) if you just need to pass through Poland.

Visas are generally issued in a few days, with an express same-day service available in some consulates if you pay 50% more.

Officially from 1 January 1999 all visitors must be able to prove they have the equivalent of at least 500 zł (US$130) or 100 zł (US$25) per day for their stay in Poland. Reduced amounts apply to those under 16: 300 zł (US$80) or 50 zł (US$15) per day; and members of organised tourist groups, youth camps etc: 100 zł (US$25) or 20 zł (US$5) per day.

Travel Insurance

A travel insurance policy to cover theft, loss and medical problems is a good idea. The policies handled by STA or other student travel organisations are usually good value. There is a wide variety of policies available, but always check the small print before buying one.

You may prefer a policy which pays doctors or hospitals directly rather than you having to pay on the spot and claim later. If you have to claim later, make sure you keep all documentation. Some policies ask you to call back (reverse charges) to a centre in your home country where an immediate assessment of your problem is made. Check that the policy covers ambulances or an emergency flight home.

For claims involving loss or theft, you must produce a police report detailing the situation (refer to the Dangers & Annoyances section later in this chapter). You also need proof of the value of any items lost or stolen. Purchase receipts are the best, so if you buy a new camera for your trip, for example, hang onto the receipt.

Driving Licence

If you plan on driving in Poland, make sure you bring your driving licence. Your licence from home will normally be sufficient, but if you want to play absolutely safe, bring an International Driving Licence together with your local one. If you're bringing your own vehicle, car insurance (the so-called Green Card) is required.

Hostel Card

An HI membership card will gain you a 25% discount on youth hostel prices. Bring the card with you, or get one issued in Poland at the provincial branch offices of the Polish Youth Hostel Association (PTSM) in the main cities.

Student Card

If you are a student, bring along your International Student Identity Card (ISIC card). You can also obtain one in Poland if you have your local student card or any document stating that you're a full-time student. The Almatur Student Bureau (which has offices in all major cities) issues ISIC cards for around US$7 (bring a photo). The card gives reductions on museum admissions (normally by 50%), Polferry ferries (20%), LOT domestic flights (10%) and urban transport in Warsaw (50%), plus discounts on international transport tickets. There are no ISIC discounts on domestic trains and buses.

International Health Card

No vaccinations are necessary for Poland, though if you come from an area infected with yellow fever or cholera you may be asked for an International Health Certificate with these inoculations. For your own safety, you are advised to have the vaccination for hepatitis or at least a gamma globulin jab. See Health later in this chapter for more information.

Photocopies

Make copies of your important documents such as passport (data pages plus visas), credit cards, airline tickets, travel insurance policy and travellers cheque receipt slips. Take notes of the serial numbers of your cameras, lenses, camcorder, notebook and any other pieces of high-tech stuff you'll be taking on the trip. Make a list of phone numbers of the emergency assistance services (credit cards, insurance, your bank etc). Keep all this material separate from your passport, money and other valuables. If applicable, it's a good idea to deposit another copy with a travelling companion. Also leave a copy of all these things with someone at home. Slip US$50 or US$100 into an unlikely place to use as an emergency stash.

EMBASSIES & CONSULATES
Polish Embassies & Consulates

Poland has embassies in the capitals of about 90 countries. The consulates are usually at the same address as the embassy. In some countries there are additional consulates in other cities. The list includes:

Australia
(☎ 02-6273 1208)
7 Turrana St, Yarralumla, ACT 2600 (Canberra)
(☎ 02-9363 9816)
10 Trelawney St, Woollahra, NSW 2025 (Sydney)
Belarus
(☎ 172-13 32 60)
Rumiancewa 6, 200034 Minsk
Canada
(☎ 613-789 0468)
443 Daly Av, Ottawa 2, Ont K1N 6H3
(☎ 514-937 9481)
1500 Avenue des Pins Ouest, Montreal, PQ H3G 1B4
(☎ 416-252 5471)
2603 Lakeshore Blvd West, Toronto, Ont M8V 1G5
(☎ 604-688 3530)
1177 West Hastings St, Suite 1600, Vancouver, BC V6E 2K3
Czech Republic
(☎ 2-2422 8722)
Václavské Námestí 49, Nové Mesto, Prague 1
(☎ 69-611 80 74)
ul Blahoslavová 4, 70100 Ostrava 1
France
(☎ 1-45 51 82 22)
5 rue de Talleyrand, 75007 Paris
(☎ 3-20 06 50 30)
45 Boulevard Carnot, 59800 Lille
(☎ 4-78 93 14 85)
79 rue Crillon, 69458 Lyons
Germany
(☎ 221-38 70 13)
Leyboldstrasse 74, 50968 Cologne
(☎ 30-220 25 51)
Unter den Linden 72/74, 10117 Berlin
(☎ 40-631 20 91)
Gründgensstrasse 20, 22309 Hamburg
(☎ 341-585 27 63)
Poetenweg 51, 04155 Leipzig
Japan
(☎ 3-3280 2881)
Oak Homes, 4-5-14, Takanawa, Minato-ku, Tokyo 108
Latvia
(☎ 2-732 16 17)
Elizabetes iela 2, 1340 Riga

Lithuania
   (☎ 2-709 001)
   Smelio gatve 20 A, Vilnius
Netherlands
   (☎ 70-360 28 06)
   Alexanderstraat 25, 2514 JM The Hague
Russia
   (☎ 095-255 0017)
   ulitsa Klimashkina 4, Moscow
   (☎ 812-274 4170)
   ulitsa Sovietskaya 12/14, St Petersburg
   (☎ 0112-274 035)
   ulitsa Kutuzova 43/45, Kaliningrad
Slovakia
   (☎ 7-580 34 18)
   ul Jancova 8, 81102 Bratislava
UK
   (☎ 020-7580 0475)
   73 New Cavendish St, London W1N 7RB
   (☎ 0131-552 0301)
   2 Kinnear Rd, Edinburgh E3H 5PE
Ukraine
   (☎ 44-224 8040)
   vulitsya Yaroslaviv 12, 252034 Kiev
   (☎ 322-760 544)
   vulitsya Ivana Franko 110, Lviv
USA
   (☎ 202-234 3800)
   2640 16th St NW, Washington, DC 20009
   (☎ 312-337 8166)
   1530 North Lake Shore Drive, Chicago, IL 60610
   (☎ 212-889 8360)
   233 Madison Ave, New York, NY 10016
   (☎ 310-442 8500)
   12400 Wilshire Blvd, Suite 555, Los Angeles, CA 90025

Embassies & Consulates in Poland

All countries which maintain diplomatic relations with Poland have their embassies in Warsaw. Consulates are usually at the same address as the embassies, with honorary consulates unable to issue visas. Embassies and consulates (in Warsaw unless otherwise stated) include:

Australia
   (☎ 022-617 60 81, fax 617 67 56)
   ul Estońska 3/5
Belarus
   (☎ 022-617 39 54, fax 617 84 41)
   ul Ateńska 67
   (☎/fax 085-744 66 61, ☎/fax 744 55 01)
   ul Waryńskiego 4, Białystok
   (☎ 058-341 00 26)
   ul Jaśkowa Dolina 50, Gdańsk Wrzeszcz
Canada
   (☎ 022-629 80 51, fax 629 64 57)
   ul Matejki 1/5
Czech Republic
   (☎ 022-628 72 21, fax 629 80 45)
   ul Koszykowa 18
   (☎ 032-51 85 76)
   ul Stalmacha 21, Katowice
France
   (☎ 022-628 84 01)
   ul Piękna 1
   (☎ 012-422 18 64)
   ul Stolarska 15, Kraków
   (☎ 061-851 61 40)
   ul Miełżyńskiego 27, Poznań (honorary)
   (☎ 058-550 32 49)
   ul Kościuszki 16, Sopot (honorary)
   (☎ 071-60 51 31)
   ul Powstańców Śląskich 95, Wrocław (honorary)
Germany
   (☎ 022-617 30 11, fax 617 35 82)
   ul Dąbrowiecka 30
   (☎ 058-341 43 66)
   Al Zwycięstwa 23, Gdańsk Wrzeszcz
   (☎ 012-421 84 73)
   ul Stolarska 7, Kraków
   (☎ 061-852 24 33)
   ul Paderewskiego 7, Poznań (honorary)
   (☎ 091-22 52 12)
   ul Królowej Korony Polskiej 31, Szczecin
   (☎ 071-342 52 52)
   ul Podwale 76, Wrocław
Ireland
   (☎ 022-849 66 55)
   ul Humańska 10
Japan
   (☎ 022-653 94 30, fax 653 94 81)
   Al Jana Pawła II 23
Latvia
   (☎ 022-48 19 47, fax 48 02 01)
   ul Rejtana 15
Lithuania
   (☎ 022-625 34 10, fax 625 34 40)
   Al Szucha 5
   (☎ 087-16 22 73)
   ul Piłsudskiego 28, Sejny
Netherlands
   (☎ 022-849 23 51, fax 849 23 52)
   ul Chocimska 6
   (☎ 058-346 76 18)
   Al Jana Pawła II 20, Gdańsk (honorary)
   (☎ 061-852 78 84)
   ul Gwarna 7, Poznań (honorary)
   (☎ 071-44 49 85)
   Rynek 39/40, Wrocław (honorary)

New Zealand
(☎ 022-645 14 07, fax 645 12 07)
ul Migdałowa 4
Russia
(☎ 022-621 34 53)
ul Belwederska 49
(☎ 058-341 10 88)
ul Batorego 15, Gdańsk Wrzeszcz
(☎ 012-422 83 88)
ul Westerplatte 11, Kraków
(☎ 061-841 75 23)
ul Bukowska 55A, Poznań
(☎ 091-22 48 77)
ul Piotra Skargi 14, Szczecin
Slovakia
(☎ 022-628 40 51, fax 628 40 55)
ul Litewska 6
UK
(☎ 022-628 10 01, fax 621 71 61)
Al Róż 1
(☎ 058-341 43 65)
ul Grunwaldzka 100/102, Gdańsk Wrzeszcz
(honorary)
(☎ 032-206 98 01)
ul PCK 10, Katowice (honorary)
(☎ 061-853 29 19)
ul Kramarska 26, Poznań (honorary)
(☎ 071-44 89 61)
ul Oławska 2, Wrocław (honorary)
Ukraine
(☎ 022-629 34 46)
Al Szucha 7
(☎ 058-346 06 09)
ul Jaśkowa Dolina 44, Gdańsk Wrzeszcz
(☎ 012-656 23 36)
ul Krakowska 41, Kraków
USA
(☎ 022-628 30 41, fax 628 93 26)
Al Ujazdowskie 29/31
(☎ 012-422 14 00)
ul Stolarska 9, Kraków
(☎ 061-851 85 16)
ul Paderewskiego 7, Poznań (honorary)

CUSTOMS

Customs procedures are usually a formality now, on both entering and leaving Poland, and your luggage is likely to pass through with only a cursory glance.

When entering Poland, you're allowed to bring duty-free any articles of personal use required for your travel and stay in Poland. They include clothes, books etc; two still cameras, one cine and one video camera plus accessories; portable self-powered electronic goods such as a personal computer, video recorder, radio set, cassette player and the like, together with accessories; a portable musical instrument; sports and tourist equipment such as a sailboard, kayak (up to 5.5m in length), bicycle, tent, skis etc; and medicines and medical equipment for your own use. You'll rarely be asked to declare these things.

Unlimited amounts of foreign currency and travellers cheques can be brought into the country, but only up to the equivalent of 2000 euros (US$2250) can be taken out by a foreigner without a declaration. If you enter with more than the equivalent of 2000 euros and want to take it all back out of Poland, fill in a currency declaration form upon arrival and have it stamped by customs officials. You can import or export Polish currency, but there's no point in doing so.

As for tobacco and spirits, the duty-free allowance on arrival is up to 250 cigarettes or 50 cigars or 250g of pipe tobacco and up to 2L of alcoholic drinks (not allowed for people aged under 17). Narcotics, naturally, are forbidden and you'd be asking for trouble smuggling them in.

When leaving the country, you may take out free of duty gifts and souvenirs of a total value not exceeding 90 euros (US$100). The export of items manufactured before 9 May 1945 is prohibited, unless you get an authorisation from the Curator of Art Works, which is pretty difficult.

MONEY
Currency

The official Polish currency is the złoty (literally, gold), abbreviated to zł. Złoty is pronounced 'zwo-ti'. It is divided into 100 units called the grosz, abbreviated to gr. New notes and coins were introduced on 1 January 1995, and include five paper bills (10, 20, 50, 100 and 200 złotys) and nine coins (1, 2, 5, 10, 20 and 50 groszy, and 1, 2 and 5 złotys). The bills feature Polish kings, have different sizes and are easily recognisable. The new currency has replaced the old złoty bills and coins, which were withdrawn from circulation on 1 January 1997 and are no longer legal tender.

Exchange Rates

Polish currency is now convertible and easy to change either way. There's no longer a black market in Poland and the official exchange rate roughly represents the currency's actual value. The złoty's rate of depreciation against hard currencies has slowed down significantly over the past few years, to about 10% per year in 1998.

At the time we went to press the approximate rates were:

Country	unit		złoty
Australia	A$1	=	2.54 zł
Canada	C$1	=	2.64 zł
Czech Republic	1Kč	=	0.11 zł
euro	€1	=	4.35 zł
France	1FF	=	0.66 zł
Germany	DM1	=	2.22 zł
Ireland	IR£1	=	5.52 zł
Japan	¥100	=	3.38 zł
Lithuania	1 lita	=	0.99 zł
Netherlands	f1	=	1.97 zł
New Zealand	NZ$1	=	2.14 zł
Russia	R1	=	0.16 zł
Slovakia	Sk1	=	0.10 zł
UK	UK£1	=	6.52 zł
Ukraine	1 hv	=	1.01 zł
USA	US$1	=	3.98 zł

Exchanging Money

An essential question for many travellers is what to bring: cash, travellers cheques or a credit card? Any of the three forms of carrying money is OK in Poland, though it's probably best to bring a combination of the three to allow yourself maximum flexibility. Travelling in Poland is generally safe, so there are no major problems in bringing some hard currency in cash, which is easiest to change. Travellers cheques are safer but harder to change and you get about 2% to 3% less than for cash. Finally, with the recent rash of ATMs, credit cards have become the most convenient option of getting local currency.

Filthy Lucre? Check Your Money

To avoid hassles exchanging currency, one important thing to know before you set off from home is that any banknotes you take to Poland must be in good condition, without any marks or seals. Kantors can refuse to accept banknotes which have numbers written on them in pen or pencil (a common practice of bank cashiers totalling bundles of notes in other countries) even if they are in otherwise perfect condition.

Cash The place to exchange cash in Poland is the *kantor*, the private currency-exchange office. They are ubiquitous; in the centre of the major cities they're on every second block. When you need one you'll probably find one – just ask anybody.

The kantors are either self-contained offices or just desks in the better hotels, travel agencies, train stations, post offices, department stores etc. The farther out from the cities you go, the less numerous they are, but you can be pretty sure that every medium-sized town has at least a few of them. Kantors are usually open on weekdays between roughly 9 am and 6 pm and till around 2 pm on Saturday, but some open longer and a few stay open 24 hours.

Kantors change cash only (no travellers cheques) and accept most of the major world currencies. The most common and thus the most easily changed are US dollars, Deutschmarks and pounds sterling (in that order). Australian dollars and Japanese yen are somewhat exotic to Poles and not all kantors will change them. There's no commission on transaction – you get what is written on the board (every kantor has a board displaying the exchange rates of currencies it changes). The whole operation takes a few seconds and there's no paperwork involved. You don't need to present your passport or fill in any forms.

Kantors buy and sell foreign currencies, and the difference between the buying and selling rates is usually not larger than 2%. Don't forget to change your extra złotys back to hard currency before you leave Poland, but don't leave it to the last minute as exchange offices on the land border crossings and at airports tend to give poor rates, and some may be altogether unwilling to change them back.

Exchange rates differ slightly from city to city and from kantor to kantor (about 1%). Smaller towns may offer up to 2% less, so it's advisable to change money in large urban centres.

Street moneychangers are slowly becoming an extinct species, but some still hang around touristy places. Give them a miss – most are con men. Particularly, beware of moneychangers in Gdańsk.

Travellers Cheques Changing them is not as straightforward as changing cash, and more time-consuming. The usual place to change travellers cheques is a bank, but not all banks handle these transactions. The best known bank which offers this facility is the Bank Polska Kasa Opieki SA, commonly known as the Bank Pekao. It has a dozen offices in Warsaw and branches in all major cities.

Several other banks, including the Bank Gdański, Bank Zachodni, Bank Śląski, Powszechny Bank Kredytowy and Powszechny Bank Gospodarczy, also provide this service, and they too have many regional branches.

Banks in the larger cities are usually open weekdays from 8 am to 5 or 6 pm (some also open on Saturday till 2 pm), but in smaller towns they tend to close earlier. They change most major brands of cheque, of which American Express is the most widely known and accepted.

The exchange rate is roughly similar to, or marginally lower than, that for cash in kantors, but banks charge a commission (*prowizja*) on transactions, which varies from bank to bank (somewhere between 0.5% to 2%). Banks also have a set minimum charge of US$1.50 to US$3. For example, the Bank Pekao commission on

changing cheques into złotys is 1.5% with a minimum charge of US$2.

Some banks also exchange travellers cheques for US cash dollars and the commission is usually lower (eg the Bank Pekao charges 0.5% with a minimum of US$1.25). Once you have US dollars you can go to any kantor and change them into złotys at the usual kantor's rate.

Banks can be crowded and inefficient; you'll probably have to queue a while and then wait until they complete the paperwork. It may take anything from 10 minutes to an hour. You'll need your passport in any transaction. Some provincial banks may insist on seeing the original receipt of purchase of your travellers cheques, and if you don't present it, they can simply refuse to change your cheques. If you have a receipt, bring it with you.

You can also change travellers cheques to złotys (but not to US dollars) in American Express offices, but there are only two offices in Warsaw and one in Kraków. They are efficient, speak English and change most major brands of cheque. Their rates are a bit lower than those of the banks, but they charge no commission, so you may get more złotys for your cheques here than in the bank.

Cash a sufficient amount of travellers cheques in a big city to last until you set foot in another big city before setting off for a trip into remote countryside.

Credit Cards & ATMs Credit cards are increasingly popular for buying goods and services, though their use is still limited to upmarket establishments, mainly in the major cities. Among the most popular cards accepted in Poland are Visa, MasterCard, American Express, Diners Club, Eurocard and Access.

Credit cards are also useful for getting cash advances in banks, and the procedure is faster than changing travellers cheques. The best card to bring is Visa, because it's honoured by the largest number of banks, including the Bank Pekao and all the other banks listed in the previous section. Bank Pekao will also give cash advances on MasterCard.

The first ATMs *(bankomaty)* appeared in 1996 and spread like wildfire. Today almost every office of a major bank has its own bankomat, and there are also a lot of others, strategically placed in key points of the central areas of cities. They accept most major cards, including Visa and Master-Card. The main ATM network in Poland is Euronet which had about 350 ATMs at the time of writing. Euronet ATMs accept 17 types of credit cards.

International Transfers A credit card solves the problem of transferring money, to a large extent, provided you are prepared to carry the credit charge or have someone back at home pay your expenses for you. Be aware of your credit limit.

If you don't have a credit card, you can have money sent to you through some banks, including the Bank Handlowy and the Narodowy Bank Polski. Both have offices in Warsaw and other major cities (check the telephone directory for addresses). Contact the banks for details, then call your sender at home. The transfer may take a while.

If you need money urgently, you can use the Western Union Money Transfer. You will receive the money within 15 minutes from the moment your sender pays it (along with the transaction fee) at any of the 25,000 Western Union agents scattered worldwide. Transaction charges are: US$50 for a transfer of US$1000; US$90 for US$2000; and US$22 for every additional US$500 above US$2000.

Western Union's outlets can be found in all Polish cities and most large towns. Its agents include several major banks, including the Bank Zachodni, Prosper Bank, Powszechny Bank Kredytowy and Bank Depozytowo Kredytowy, and some Orbis offices. Information on locations and conditions can be obtained on the toll-free number ☎ 0800 202 24.

Costs

Though not the bargain it used to be, Poland is still a cheap country for travellers. Just how cheap, of course, depends largely on what degree of comfort you need, what hotel standards you are used to, what kind of food you eat, where you go, how fast you travel and the means of transport you use. If, for example, you are accustomed to rental cars and plush hotels, you can spend just about as much as in the west.

However, if you are a budget traveller, prepared for basic conditions and willing to endure some discomfort on the road, a daily average of around US$30 should be sufficient. This amount would cover accommodation in cheap hotels, food in budget restaurants and moving at a reasonable pace by train or bus, and would still leave you a margin for some cultural events, a few beers and occasional taxis. If you plan on camping or staying in youth hostels, and eating in cheap bistros and other self-services, it's feasible to cut this average down to US$20 per day, without necessarily suffering much pain.

Accommodation, food and transport are the three major items of expenditure. If you are prepared for basic conditions, you shouldn't pay more than US$10 to US$12 per night (on average) for a bed in a hotel. The cost will be lower or the standard better if you travel in a group of two or more.

Food costs vary, though if budget dining is what you are used to, they shouldn't come to more than another US$10 to US$12 per day.

Bus and train, the two means of transport you're most likely to use, are fairly inexpensive in Poland.

Other costs are less significant and won't eat much into your budget. Museum admission fees are usually around US$1 to US$2 (half that price for students), and most museums have one free-entry day during the week (different from place to place). The fees are not listed in this book, unless they considerably exceed US$2. Cultural events (theatre, cinema, music) are still a bargain in Poland. Urban public transport costs next to nothing.

It's important to remember that cities are more expensive than the countryside, with Warsaw the most expensive.

Tipping & Bargaining

In restaurants, service is included in the price so you just pay what is on the bill. Tipping is up to you and there don't seem to be any hard and fast rules about it. In low-priced eateries customers rarely leave a tip; they might, at most, round the total up to the nearest whole figure. In upmarket establishments it's customary to tip 10% of the bill.

Tipping in hotels is essentially restricted to the top-end establishments, which usually have decent room service and porters, who all expect to be tipped. Taxi drivers are normally not tipped, unless you want to reward someone for their effort, help etc.

Bargaining is not common in Poland, and is limited to some informal places such as markets, bazaars, street vendors etc.

POST & COMMUNICATIONS

Postal services are operated by the Poczta Polska, while communications facilities are provided by the Telekomunikacja Polska. Both these companies usually share one office, called the *poczta* (post office), although recently the Telekomunikacja has been opening its own communications-only offices. Yet in most cases you can use the poczta for everything: buying stamps, sending letters, receiving poste restante, placing long-distance calls and sending faxes.

In the large cities there will be a dozen or more post offices, of which the Poczta Główna (main post office) will usually have the widest range of facilities, including poste restante and fax. Larger post offices in the cities are normally open weekdays 8 am to

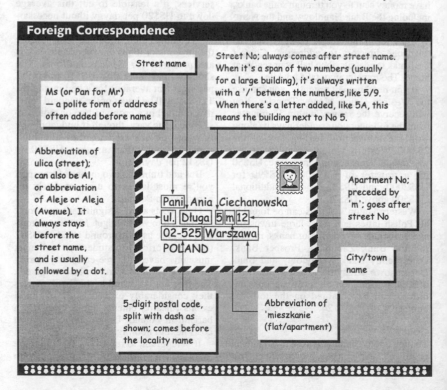

Foreign Correspondence

Street name

Street No; always comes after street name. When it's a span of two numbers (usually for a large building), it's always written with a '/' between the numbers, like 5/9. When there's a letter added, like 5A, this means the building next to No 5.

Ms (or Pan for Mr) — a polite form of address often added before name

Abbreviation of ulica (street); can also be Al, or abbreviation of Aleje or Aleja (Avenue). It always stays before the street name, and is usually followed by a dot.

Apartment No; preceded by 'm'; goes after street No

> Pani Ania Ciechanowska
> ul. Długa 5 m 12
> 02-525 Warszawa
> POLAND

City/town name

5-digit postal code, split with dash as shown; comes before the locality name

Abbreviation of 'mieszkanie' (flat/apartment)

8 pm, and one will usually stay open round the clock. In smaller localities business hours may only be on weekdays till 4 pm and international calls are not always possible.

Sending Mail

Airmail letters sent from Poland take about a week to reach a European destination and up to two weeks if mailed to other continents. The rates for a 20g letter or a postcard are: US$0.40 to Europe, US$0.50 to the USA and Canada, and US$0.60 elsewhere. Packages and parcels are reasonably cheap if sent by surface mail but they can take up to three months to reach their destination. Airmail packages are expensive, with prices comparable to those in Western Europe.

Receiving Mail

Poste restante doesn't seem to be very reliable. If you want mail sent to you, stick to the large cities, such as Warsaw, Kraków and Gdańsk (see these sections for details). Mail is held for 14 working days, then returned to the sender.

American Express customers can receive poste restante mail via the Warsaw and Kraków Amex offices (see those chapters).

Telephone

The Polish telephone system is antiquated and unreliable. Modernisation was minimal until quite recently, and only over the past few years have more adequate telephone exchanges been installed. But it's mainly the lack of lines that hinders development. A Pole still has to wait a few years to get a telephone installed at home (a decade or two ago the wait was at least 10 years!).

Public telephones are few and far between by western standards, and not infrequently out of order. Go to a post office: each should have at least one functioning public phone. Old phones operate on tokens (żetony) which can be bought at the post office. However, these phones have almost disappeared, and may be totally extinct within a few years.

Newly installed telephones only operate on magnetic phonecards. It's well worth buying a phonecard (at the post office) if you think you'll be using public phones from time to time. Cards come in three kinds: a 25 unit card (US$2), a 50 unit card (US$4) and a 100 unit card (US$8). One unit represents one three-minute local call. Cards can be used for domestic and international calls. In 1995 Poland introduced toll-free numbers, which begin with 800, for commercial companies and organisations.

Apart from the regular, cable phone network, there are three cellular phone providers: the analogue Centertel and the digital Era and Plus. All three cover most of Poland's territory. Cellular phone numbers begin with 0501 (Centertel), 0601 (Plus) and 0602 (Era), and don't require dialling of the area code.

Mobile phones are quickly becoming popular, both as a status symbol and a more reliable alternative to the jammed stationary lines and scarce and often inoperable public phones. As of late 1998, there were 1.4 million cellular phones in Poland and the number is expected to triple by the end of 2000.

Intercity direct dialling is possible to almost anywhere in the country. Telephone area codes are listed in this book just below the heading of the relevant town or city.

Phone Number Changes

Telekomunikacja Polska is upgrading the telephone system to a uniform seven-digit system, which should be fully in place by 2000. At the time of writing, the company was midway through the process, involving a massive change of phone numbers. This unfortunately means that some numbers in this book will be already invalid by the time you read this.

Another problem is the administrative revolution; the change from 49 to 16 provinces on 1 January 1999 may affect some area codes. The codes will not be changed in 1999, but they'll probably be adjusted at some later date to correspond to the new administrative boundaries.

They all begin with '0', after which you get another, usually fainter, dial tone; you then dial the rest of the area code and the local phone number.

You can now dial directly to just about anywhere in the world. When dialling direct, a minute will cost around US$0.75 within Europe and US$1.50 anywhere outside Europe. If you place the call through the operator at the post office, the minimum charge is for a three minute call which will cost about US$2.50 within Europe and US$5 elsewhere. Every extra minute costs a third more. For a person-to-person call, add an extra minute's charge.

Collect calls are possible to most major countries. Inquire at any Telekomunikacja Polska office for the toll-free number to the operator in the country you want to call, then call from any public or private telephone. These numbers include:

Australia	☎ 00 800 61 111 61
France	☎ 00 800 33 111 33
Germany	☎ 00 800 49 111 49
UK	☎ 00 800 44 111 44
USA (AT&T)	☎ 00 800 1 1111 11

To call a telephone number in Poland from abroad, dial the international access code of the country you're calling from, the country code for Poland (☎ 48), the area code (drop the initial '0') and the local phone number.

To call abroad from Poland, dial ☎ 00 (the Polish international access code) before the country code of the country you are calling.

Fax

Faxes can be sent from most larger post and communications offices. The service is charged similarly as for phone calls, with a three minute minimum charge applying.

Email & Internet Access

The Internet is becoming popular in Poland (though it's still way behind Western Europe) and there are a number of service providers. Cybercafés that offer public access to the Internet and email have begun to open in the big cities. Other places providing these facilities are computer offices,

software shops and the like. An hour of surfing the Web or emailing normally costs about US$2. Some of the places use quite dated (and accordingly painfully slow) equipment.

INTERNET RESOURCES

There are quite a few Web sites concerning Poland, and the number is swiftly growing. Useful sources of general and tourist information on Poland include:

www.explore-poland.pl
www.polandtour.org
www.infotur.pl
www.insidepoland.pl
www.polishworld.com
www.gopoland.com

If Warsaw is your main interest, check www.bptnet.pl/warsawtour. If you want to keep track of Poland's current political, economical and cultural issues, read *The Warsaw Voice* weekly on www.warsaw voice.com.pl. Also try Lonely Planet's home page on Poland (www.lonelyplanet .com/dest/eur/pol.htm).

BOOKS

You will get far more out of your visit if you read up on the country before you go. There is no shortage of English-language books covering various aspects of Poland as well as translations of the best of Polish writers and poets. There is also a choice of travel guides.

Check with good travel bookshops for tourist guides. For background literature, look for bookshops specialising in Eastern Europe or Poland in particular. They exist in major cities around the world where significant Polish communities live. You can also contact Hippocrene Books (☎ 212-685 4371, fax 779 9338, email contact@hip pocrenebooks.com, www.hippocrenebooks .com), 171 Madison Ave, New York, NY 10016, USA, for its catalogue. It has a variety of books on Poland ranging from guidebooks and dictionaries to translations of Polish literature.

In Poland itself there's an increasing number of foreign-language books about the country. Polish publishers have started to show interest in western tourists, and English and German editions are often printed along with the original Polish version.

Lonely Planet

If you're planning a wider journey than just Poland, consider taking LP's *Eastern Europe*, *Central Europe* or *Europe on a shoestring*, depending on which region you're going to travel around. Also note that LP has individual guidebooks to most European countries, including some of Poland's neighbours. See the back of this book for a complete rundown. Look out also for the new *Kraków* guide, due in 2000.

If you plan to visit several Eastern European countries, the *Eastern Europe Phrasebook* will be useful. It contains essential words and phrases in Polish, Czech, Slovak, Hungarian, Romanian and Bulgarian, together with phonetic transcriptions.

History & Politics

God's Playground: A History of Poland by Norman Davies is one of the best accounts of Polish history. This two volume work is beautifully readable and has at the same time a rare analytical depth, which makes it a perfect key to understanding a thousand years of the Polish nation. The book has also been translated into Polish and is recommended by educational authorities for school students.

The Heart of Europe: A Short History of Poland by Norman Davies is a more condensed account, with a greater emphasis on the 20th century. This is also an excellent work, highly recommended.

Jews in Poland: A Documentary History by Iwo Cyprian Pogonowski provides a comprehensive record of half a millennium of Polish-Jewish relations in Poland.

The theme of the Holocaust has an extensive bibliography. *A Surplus of Memory: Chronicle of the Warsaw Ghetto Uprising* by Yitzhak Zuckerman is a detailed narrative on this heroic act of Jewish resistance. *Mila 18* by Leon Uris is another moving account of the same events.

Primo Levi, an Italian Jew who survived Auschwitz, has contributed several chilling works, including *If this is a Man* and *The Drowned and the Saved*. *My Father's Silence* by Jacob G Rosenberg is an anthology of poetry based on memories from the country of his youth, including the Łódź ghetto and Auschwitz.

Turning to more recent history, *The Polish Revolution: Solidarity 1980-82* by Timothy Garton Ash is an insight into the Solidarity era, a 16 month period which undermined the whole communist system. Entertainingly written, the book explains how it all happened. *The Polish Challenge* by Kevin Ruane documents the same events and is a factual supplement to Garton Ash's book.

Mad Dreams, Saving Graces: Poland, a Nation in Conspiracy by Michael T Kaufman is a trip through the dark times of martial law and the gloomy period up till 1988 – as readable as it's informative.

Unquiet Days: At Home in Poland by Thomas Swick is yet another vivid account of those events, told by an American who lived in Poland during the crucial period of Solidarity and later returned several times.

The Naked President: A Political Life of Lech Wałęsa by Roger Boyes, Eastern Europe correspondent for the *Times*, traces the life of the man who was once the charismatic leader of Solidarity and became a lonely president.

General

The Polish Way: A Thousand-Year History of the Poles and their Culture by Adam Zamoyski is one of the best accounts of the culture of Poland from its birth to the recent past. Fully illustrated and exquisitely written, the book is an excellent introduction to the subject.

Art, Architecture and Design in Poland 966-1990 by Stefan Muthesius is a compact yet comprehensive history of Polish art.

The History of Polish Literature by Czesław Miłosz is an encyclopaedic anthology covering everything from medieval Latin texts to the experimental poetry of today.

It's a good idea to get a copy of a small English-Polish/Polish-English dictionary. Among the best is the one from the well known yellow series published by Langenscheidt, easy to find in large bookshops both in and outside Poland. There are several good Polish phrasebooks around, including the Berlitz, Penguin and Rough Guide ones.

There's a choice of audio systems for language learning which consist of cassettes or CDs plus a textbook. VocabuLearn, Language/30 and Berlitz all have Polish courses. Check what's available in your local library.

NEWSPAPERS & MAGAZINES

Each large city has at least one local newspaper and there are nine papers with country-wide distribution. The *Gazeta Wyborcza* was the first independent daily in postwar Eastern Europe and is now the major national paper, with a circulation of about 460,000. The *Rzeczpospolita* is the main business daily.

Among weekly magazines, the biggest is *Wprost*. The long-lived *Polityka* is still an opinion-forming paper and retains some of its serious, in-depth character. The *Poradnik Domowy* (Home Adviser) is the biggest selling Polish monthly, with a circulation of one million.

Some big foreign magazines – *Elle*, *Burda* and *Playboy* among others – have established themselves on the local market. German publishers have been especially active in flooding Poland with their gossipy weekly and monthly women's magazines.

The major foreign newspapers, including *The Financial Times*, *The Wall Street Journal*, *The International Herald Tribune*, *The Times*, *Le Monde* and *Der Spiegel*, are sold in major cities. Traditionally, *Time* and *Newsweek* have been very widely distributed. The best places to look for foreign publications are EMPiK stores, foreign-language bookshops and newsstands in the lobbies of upmarket hotels.

The major Polish publication in English is *The Warsaw Voice* – a well edited and interesting weekly. It gives a good insight into Polish politics, business and culture, and includes a tourist section which lists local events. It's distributed in top-class hotels, airline offices and embassies, and can be bought from major newsagents (US$1.50). It's hard to find outside large cities.

There has been much development among the English-language tourist magazines, including the useful *Warszawa: What, Where, When* and *Welcome to Warsaw*. Both are practical monthly guides to what's going on in the capital, and both have regional editions covering other cities, including Kraków and Gdańsk. They are available free from major hotels and tourist and airline offices. The *Warsaw Insider* is the most comprehensive what's-on monthly, certainly worth its US$1.25 price. The equally detailed and informative *Krakow Insider*, produced by the same publisher, appears less frequently.

RADIO & TV

The state-run Polish Radio (Polskie Radio) is the main broadcaster. It operates on the AM long and medium-wave bands and on FM, and is received in every corner of the country. In early 1994, two previously local private broadcasters became nationwide networks: the Warsaw-based Radio Zet and the slightly lighter, Kraków-based RFM. Plenty of other private competitors operate locally on FM. Apart from the headline news in English broadcast by some of the private stations, all programs are in Polish.

There are two state-owned, country-wide TV channels: the general program I and the more education and culture-focused program II. Both have commercial advertisements (up to 8% of transmission time), which were previously unknown. Some of the larger cities also have state-owned local programs.

A broadcasting council was created in 1994 to advance private television, and awarded a licence to a country-wide venture called PolSat. However, PolSat lags behind the two state-operated channels.

Meanwhile, individual satellite TV dishes have become hugely popular, allowing Poles to have direct access to western media. Most major hotels have also installed them. Rough estimates indicate that Poland owns more satellite dishes than any other country in Europe except for France and the UK. Experts reckon that every fourth household has either its own dish or access to one.

The indiscriminate installation of dishes and unauthorised reception of diverse broadcasting networks have been under scrutiny, meaning that Poland has entered the era of pay TV. There are already a number of coded cable TV channels and a queue of operators waiting for licences.

VIDEO SYSTEMS

If you want to record or buy video tapes to play back home, you won't get a picture if the image registration system is different. SECAM used to be the standard image registration system in communist Poland, but now the country has turned to PAL, the system used in most of Europe. VHS is the standard format for recording from TV and viewing rented films at home.

PHOTOGRAPHY & VIDEO

Except for the usual restrictions on photographing military, industrial, transport and telecommunications installations, you can take pictures or video of just about anything. Some museums don't allow for photographing inside, or will charge additionally (sometimes a lot) for the permit. Nobody usually minds you taking photos in church interiors, but keep in mind that such places are usually pretty dim and a tripod or a good flash may be necessary.

Skansens are good places for photographing the traditional rural architecture. As for people shots, the best places are regional folk festivals and religious feasts. It's here that you're most likely to see locals decked out in their traditional costumes. Markets, on the other hand, are usually colourless and dull. Needless to say, you should be very discreet in photographing people.

Film & Equipment

Kodak is the most popular, with Fuji and Agfa not far behind. You can buy both slide and negative film in several commonly used speeds. For those who are more demanding, high-quality Ilford B&W film is available as well as Fujichrome professional series film including Velvia and Provia. The prices are comparable to those in Western Europe. For example, a roll of Kodacolor will cost about US$5, Fujichrome 100 will go for around US$7 and Velvia about US$10. These prices are for a roll of 36 exposures and do not include processing. Stock up in major cities; in smaller towns you may be limited to Kodak colour prints.

As for processing, you can easily have your prints done, often within an hour, in any of the numerous photo minilabs. There's also an increasing number of laboratories which handle E6 slide processing.

You can buy Nikon, Canon, Minolta and other popular Japanese cameras, but the choice is limited and the prices are rather high. Bring along your own reliable gear. Getting your camera repaired in Poland can be a problem if you have an uncommon make and any original spare parts are necessary. General mechanical faults can usually be fixed quite easily.

Equipment for both VHS and Video 8 video systems is available, but the variety is limited, and it's expensive.

Poland is sufficiently safe for a tourist to carry a video camera. If you decide to bring a camera, don't forget to bring along a conversion plug to fit electric sockets (two-round-pin type) if you have a different system.

TIME

All of Poland lies within the same time zone, GMT/UTC+1. When it is noon in Warsaw, the time in other cities around the world is:

Auckland	11 pm
Berlin	noon
Hong Kong	7 pm
London	11 am
Los Angeles	3 am
Moscow	2 pm
New York	6 am
Paris	noon

Prague	noon
San Francisco	3 am
Stockholm	noon
Sydney	9 pm
Tokyo	8 pm
Toronto	6 am
Vancouver	3 am

Poland pushes the clocks forward an hour in late March and back again in late September.

A 24 hour clock is applied in Poland for official purposes, including all transport schedules. In everyday conversations, however, people commonly use the 2 x 12 hour system.

ELECTRICITY
Electricity is 220V, 50Hz. Plugs with two round pins are used, the same as in the rest of Continental Europe.

WEIGHTS & MEASURES
Poland uses the metric system. There's a conversion table at the back of this book.

LAUNDRY
Dry cleaners *(pralnia)* exist in the larger cities but are expensive and it will take them several days to clean your clothes. A more expensive express service can cut this time by half. Top-class hotels offer laundry facilities and are faster. Self-service laundrettes are unheard-of so far, and there are still very few which offer service washes.

TOILETS
Self-contained public toilets in the cities are few and far between. If you're really desperate, look for a restaurant. Hotels, museums and train stations are other emergency options. Toilets are labelled 'Toaleta' or simply 'WC'. The gents will be labelled 'Dla Panów' or 'Męski' and/or marked with a triangle (an inverted pyramid), and the ladies will be labelled 'Dla Pań' or 'Damski' and/or marked with a circle.

The use of a public toilet (including those in restaurants and train stations) is almost never free; it costs from US$0.10 to US$0.50, and the price doesn't necessarily reflect the cleanliness of the establishment. Charges are posted on the door and collected by the toilet attendant sitting at the door, who will give you a piece of toilet paper. It's a good idea to carry a roll of paper, though, just in case.

HEALTH
Poland is not the most disease-ridden place on earth, but sanitary conditions still leave much to be desired and heavy pollution contaminates water and air. Medical service and the availability of medications are not as good as in the west.

The public health service is in trouble: public hospital conditions are bad and medical equipment is outdated and insufficient. Private clinics have mushroomed and they are usually better but more expensive.

Travel health depends on your predeparture preparations, your daily health care while travelling and how you handle any medical problem that does develop.

Predeparture Planning
Immunisations While no vaccinations are required for travel to Poland, there are some routine vaccinations that are recommended. You are strongly advised to get vaccinated against hepatitis A or at least have a gamma globulin jab. Hepatitis A vaccine (eg Avaxim, Havrix 1440 or VAQTA) provides long-term immunity (possibly more than 10 years) after an initial injection and a booster at six to 12 months.

Alternatively, an injection of gamma globulin can provide short-term protection against hepatitis A – two to six months, depending on the dose. It is not a vaccine, but a ready-made antibody collected from blood donations. It is reasonably effective and, unlike the vaccine, it is protective immediately, but because it's a blood product, there are long-term safety concerns currently.

Make sure also your vaccinations against tetanus, diphtheria and polio are up to date.

Health Insurance Make sure you have adequate health insurance. See Travel Insurance in the Visas & Documents section for details.

Other Preparations Make sure you're healthy before you start travelling. If you are going on a long trip make sure your teeth are OK. If you wear glasses take a spare pair and your prescription.

Take an adequate supply of any medication required, as it may not be available locally. Taking part of the packaging showing the generic name rather than the brand will make getting replacements easier. A legible prescription or letter from your doctor to show that you legally use the medication is a good idea.

A basic medical kit is always useful, although most items you'll require are readily available.

Water

Tap water is usually safe to drink in Poland but, for reasons of taste, you may prefer to stick to bottled water; it's readily available.

Medical Problems & Treatment

Most minor problems can be solved by a visit to the *apteka* (pharmacy). There's quite a number of them and they have qualified staff, some of whom speak English. They may help you with advice on buying the right medication or even on treating small wounds. Condoms, tampons and syringes are easily available.

In the event of a more serious illness or injury you should seek out a specialised doctor. Your embassy or consulate should be able to advise a good place to go. So can five-star hotels, although they often recommend doctors with five-star prices. This is when that medical insurance really comes in useful.

If you can't find help, just ask anybody for the nearest *przychodnia* (outpatient clinic). These clinics have physicians of various specialities and are the places Poles go when they get ill. Charges are relatively low.

The country-wide emergency phone number for the ambulance service is ☎ 999 but don't expect the operator to speak English. Ask any Pole around to call them for you. See the Language chapter for some basic emergency words and phrases.

Infectious Diseases

Diarrhoea Simple things like a change of water, food or climate can all cause a mild bout of diarrhoea, but a few rushed toilet trips with no other symptoms is not indicative of a major problem.

Dehydration is the main danger with any diarrhoea, and can occur quite quickly in children or the elderly. Under all circumstances fluid replacement (at least equal to the volume being lost) is the most important thing to remember. Weak black tea with a little sugar, soda water, or soft drinks allowed to go flat and diluted 50% with clean water are all good. With severe diarrhoea a rehydrating solution is preferable to replace minerals and salts lost. Commercially available oral rehydration salts (ORS) are very useful; add them to boiled or bottled water. Keep drinking small amounts often. Stick to a bland diet as you recover.

Hepatitis There are several different viruses that cause hepatitis, and they differ in the way that they are transmitted. The symptoms are similar in all forms of the illness, and include fever, chills, headache, fatigue, feelings of weakness and aches and pains, followed by loss of appetite, nausea, vomiting, abdominal pain, dark urine, light-coloured faeces, jaundiced (yellow) skin and yellowing of the whites of the eyes. People who have had hepatitis should avoid alcohol for some time after the illness, as the liver needs time to recover.

Hepatitis A is transmitted by contaminated food and drinking water. You should seek medical advice, but there is not much you can do apart from rest, drink lots of fluids, eat lightly and avoid fatty foods.

HIV & AIDS Infection with the human immunodeficiency virus (HIV) may lead to acquired immune deficiency syndrome (AIDS), which is a fatal disease. Any exposure to blood, blood products or body fluids may put the individual at risk. The disease is often transmitted through sexual contact or dirty needles – vaccinations, acupuncture, tattooing and body piercing can be potentially as dangerous as intravenous drug use.

Fear of HIV infection should never preclude treatment for serious medical conditions.

Bites & Stings

Bee and wasp stings are usually painful rather than dangerous. However, in people who are allergic to them severe breathing difficulties may occur and require urgent medical care. Mosquitoes can drive you almost insane during the late summer months, especially around the Great Masurian Lakes. Most people get used to mosquito bites after a few days as their bodies adjust, and the itching and swelling will be less severe. Calamine lotion or Stingose spray will give relief and ice packs will reduce the pain and swelling.

Ticks

You should check all over your body if you have been walking through a potentially tick-infested area as ticks can cause skin infections and other more serious diseases, including tick-borne encephalitis. You might want to consider a vaccination against tick-borne encephalitis if you plan to do extensive hiking between May and September.

If a tick is found attached, press down around the tick's head with tweezers, grab the head and gently pull upwards. Avoid pulling the rear of the body as this may squeeze the tick's gut contents through the attached mouth parts into the skin, increasing the risk of infection and disease. Smearing chemicals on the tick will not make it let go and is not recommended.

WOMEN TRAVELLERS

Travel for women in Poland is pretty much hassle-free except for occasional encounters with the drunk local males. Harassment of this kind is not usually dangerous, but can be annoying. Steer clear of the drunks and avoid places considered male territory, particularly cheap drink bars.

On the other hand, a woman travelling alone, especially in remote rural areas, may expect to receive more help, hospitality and generosity from the locals than would a man on his own.

GAY & LESBIAN TRAVELLERS

Homosexuality isn't illegal in Poland, but the overwhelmingly Catholic society tends to both deny and suppress it. For many Poles, particularly in the more traditional, rural communities, sexual attraction to members of the same sex is still very much a perversion. To be openly gay in Poland can often limit vocational and social opportunities and may cause family ostracism. Consequently, few gays, and still fewer lesbians, want to voice their attitudes in a family or workplace forum, opting instead for pursuing their lifestyles with discretion.

The Polish gay and lesbian movement is still very much underground and pretty faint. Warsaw has the largest gay and lesbian community and the most open gay life, and therefore is the best place to make contacts and get to know what's going on – get as much information here as you can, because elsewhere in Poland it can be difficult.

The two gay organisations, Lambda and Rainbow, share one office in Warsaw at ul Czerniakowska 178 m 16. Call them on ☎ 022-628 52 22 on weekdays between 6 and 9 pm; there may be someone around speaking English. You can also email them at lambdawa@free.bolbox.pl. They meet regularly on Friday and there are some meetings on other weekdays.

DISABLED TRAVELLERS

Poland offers very little to people with disabilities. Wheelchair ramps are available only at a few upmarket hotels and restaurants, and public transport will be a challenge for anyone with mobility problems. Hardly any office, museum or bank provides special facilities for disabled travellers, and wheelchair-accessible toilets are few and far between. Only quite recently has there been some more determined development of the infrastructure for handicapped people.

Organisations

Disabled travellers in the USA might like to contact the Society for the Advancement of Travel for the Handicapped (☎ 212-447 SATH, fax 725 8253), 347 Fifth Ave, Suite 610, New York, NY 10016. In the UK, a useful contact is the Royal Association for Disability & Rehabilitation (☎ 020-7242 3882), 25 Mortimer St, London W1N 8AB. You may also be interested in picking up *Nothing Ventured: Disabled People Travel the World* (Rough Guides), which provides helpful general advice.

SENIOR TRAVELLERS

There are very few discounts for senior Poles and still fewer for senior visitors. Senior travellers (both nationals and foreigners) can expect a 20% reduction on LOT domestic flights and the Baltic ferries but that's about it. So far, there are no discounts for senior citizens on train and bus fares, accommodation rates, cinema and theatre tickets etc, though this may be slowly changing in the future. Legally, senior Poles get discounts on admission fees for museums and other sights, but this doesn't apply to foreigners.

TRAVEL WITH CHILDREN

Few foreigners travel with children in Poland, but if you do plan on taking along your offspring, there are no particular problems. Children enjoy privileges on local transport, accommodation and entertainment. Age limits for particular freebies or discounts vary from place to place, but are not often rigidly enforced. Basic supplies are easily available in the cities. There are quite a few shops devoted to kids' clothes, shoes and toys, and you can buy disposable nappies (diapers) and baby food in supermarkets and pharmacies. For general suggestions on how to make a trip with kids easier, pick up the current edition of Lonely Planet's *Travel with Children*.

DANGERS & ANNOYANCES

Poland is a relatively safe country to travel in, even though there has been a steady in-crease in crime since the fall of communism; you should keep your eyes open and use common sense. The problems mostly occur in big cities, with Warsaw being perhaps the least safe place in Poland. Take care when walking alone at night, particularly in the centre and the Praga suburb, and be alert at Warsaw central train station, the favourite playground for thieves and pickpockets. Other large cities appear to be quieter, but keep your wits about you. By and large, the smaller the town, the safer it is.

Don't venture into rundown areas, dubious-looking suburbs and desolate parks, especially after dark. Use taxis if you feel uncertain about an area. Watch out for groups of suspicious male characters hanging around markets, shady bars and bus and train stations, and stay away from them. Stay at a safe distance from dogs. Poles are keen on big dogs, many of which roam without leads and not all are muzzled. Some are bigger and uglier than others.

Keep a sharp eye on your pockets and your bag in crowded places such as markets or city buses and trams. Beware of short-changing at train stations, taxis, restaurants etc. Always have some smaller bills in order to make change more easily. Hotels are in general safe, though it's better not to leave valuables in your room; in most places you can deposit them at the reception desk.

Theft from cars is becoming a plague these days – refer to the Car & Motorcycle section

---

Emergency

The nationwide toll-free 24 hour emergency phone numbers include:

Police	☎ 997
Fire Brigade	☎ 998
Ambulance	☎ 999
Roadside Assistance	☎ 981, ☎ 9637

Don't expect the attendants of any of these services to speak English, so try to get a local to call on your behalf.

in the Getting Around chapter for information. Pirate or 'mafia' taxis are a problem in Warsaw and some other large cities – see Taxi in the Getting Around chapter. Theft and robbery in trains has also been on the increase – see Train in the Getting There & Away and Getting Around chapters.

If your passport, valuables and/or other belongings are lost or stolen, report it to the police. They will give you a copy of the statement which serves as a temporary identity document; if you have insurance, you'll need to present the statement to your insurer in order to make a claim. English-speaking police are rare, so it's best to take along an interpreter if you can. Don't expect your things to be found, for the police are unlikely to do anything. They earn next to nothing and can be rather cynical about a 'rich' foreigner complaining about losing a few dollars.

Heavy drinking is a way of life in Poland and drunks may at times be disturbing. Poles smoke a lot and so far there has been little serious anti-tobacco campaigning. Polish cigarettes are of low quality and the smoke they produce is hardly tolerable for anyone unused to them, let alone a nonsmoker.

Slow and impolite service in shops, offices and restaurants is slowly being eradicated by the competitive market economy, though you can still occasionally experience it. Cheating is not common but there are some areas, especially those connected with foreign tourism, where you should be alert.

Since WWII Poland has been ethnically an almost entirely homogeneous nation and Poles, particularly those living in rural areas, had little contact with foreigners. That's why travellers looking racially different, eg of African or Asian background, may attract some stares from the locals. In most cases, this is just a curiosity, without any hostility in mind. On the other hand, there have been some acts of racism in the cities, though it's still not a social problem by any definition.

LEGAL MATTERS

Foreigners in Poland, as elsewhere, are subject to the laws of the host country.

While your embassy or consulate is the best stop in any emergency, bear in mind that there are some things it cannot do for you, like getting local laws or regulations waived because you're a foreigner, investigating a crime, providing legal advice or representation in civil or criminal cases, getting you out of jail, and lending you money.

A consul can, however, issue emergency passports, contact relatives and friends, advise on how to transfer funds, provide lists of reliable local doctors, lawyers and interpreters, and visit you if you've been arrested or jailed.

BUSINESS HOURS

Most grocery shops are open on weekdays from 7 or 8 am to 6 or 7 pm and half a day on Saturday. Delicatessens and supermarkets usually stay open longer, until 8 or 9 pm, and there's at least one food shop in every major town and every district of the city which is open 24 hours. All such night shops have a section selling beer, wine and spirits, which is what keeps them going. General stores (selling clothing, books, stationery, household appliances, photo and sports stuff etc) normally open at 10 or 11 am and close at 6 or 7 pm (at 2 or 3 pm on Saturday). The office working day is theoretically eight hours long, Monday to Friday, and there's usually no lunch-time break.

Consider this as a rough guide only; hours can vary considerably from shop to shop (or office to office) and from the city to the village.

The opening hours of museums and other tourist sights vary greatly. The overwhelming majority of museums are open on Sunday but closed on Monday; most of them also stay closed on the day following a public holiday. Most museums close one or two hours earlier in the off season. Museums usually cease selling tickets half an hour before their official closing time.

Churches are a still bigger puzzle. The major churches in the main cities are often open all day long. On the other hand, rural churches in small villages will almost always be locked except during Mass, which may be only on Sunday morning. In these cases, you'll have to look for the local priest (who usually lives in a house next to the church) who might (or might not) open the church for you.

PUBLIC HOLIDAYS

Official public holidays in Poland include New Year (1 January), Easter Monday (March or April), Labour Day (1 May), Constitution Day (3 May), Corpus Christi (May or June), Assumption Day (15 August), All Saints' Day (1 November), Independence Day (11 November), and Christmas (25 and 26 December).

SPECIAL EVENTS

You can assume that at least every day there are a couple of special events going on somewhere in Poland. Apart from well established national or international festivals of film, theatre and music, there are plenty of small local feasts, fairs, contests, meetings, competitions etc, some of which involve local folklore. Many take place in May/June and September/ October. Add to this a lot of religious celebrations.

Cultural Events

Among the classical music highlights, you should be in Łańcut in May for the Old Music Festival, in Warsaw in June/July for the Mozart Festival, in Kraków in August for the Music in Old Kraków Festival, and in Wrocław in September for Wratislavia Cantans with its oratorios and cantatas.

The best of contemporary music is presented at the Warsaw Autumn International Festival in September. If you are a jazz fan there's nothing better than the Warsaw Summer Jazz Days in June and the Jazz Jamboree, also in Warsaw, in late October.

Major theatre festivals take place in Warsaw (January), Kalisz (May), Toruń (May/June) and Poznań (June). Film comes to the fore in Kraków (May/June), Gdynia (September), Warsaw (October) and Toruń (November/December).

For traditional music, the last week of June in Kazimierz Dolny is a must if you want to listen to genuine folk bands and singers from all over the country, but if you are interested in international folk songs and dances of highlanders, you should try to be in Zakopane in late August. Kraków hosts the prestigious Jewish Culture Festival in June.

Major events on Poland's cultural calendar include:

January
Warsaw Theatre Meetings in Warsaw

February
Shanties – Festival of Sailors' Songs in Kraków

April
Poznań Musical Spring – Festival of Polish Contemporary Music in Poznań
Stanisław Moniuszko International Vocal Competition in Warsaw
Organ Music Days in Kraków

April/May
Warsaw Ballet Days in Warsaw

May
Gaude Mater – International Festival of Religious Music in Częstochowa
Kalisz Theatre Meetings in Kalisz
Jazz on the Oder River – International Jazz Festival in Wrocław
Old Music Festival in Łańcut
International Festival of Orthodox Church Music in Hajnówka
Probaltica – Music & Art Festival of Baltic States in Toruń
International Book Fair in Warsaw
Jazz Fair Festival in Poznań

May/June
Contact – International Theatre Festival in Toruń
Łódź Ballet Meetings in Łódź
International Short Film Festival in Kraków

June
International Folk Bands Meeting in Toruń
Jewish Culture Festival in Kraków
Traditional Folk Dance Competition in Rzeszów
Stanisław Moniuszko International Music Festival in Kudowa-Zdrój
Warsaw Summer Jazz Days in Warsaw
Malta – International Theatre Festival in Poznań
Festival of Folk Bands & Singers in Kazimierz Dolny
Festival of Polish Song in Opole

June/July
Mozart Festival in Warsaw
Zamość Theatre Summer in Zamość
International Festival of Choir Music in Międzyzdroje

June-September
Festival of Organ & Chamber Music in Kamień Pomorski

July
FAMA – Student Art Festival in Świnoujście
Solo-Duo-Trio – International Small Jazz Form Festival in Kraków
International Festival of Street Theatre in Jelenia Góra & Kraków
Piknik Country – International Country Music Festival in Mrągowo

August
International Song Festival in Sopot
Music in Old Kraków – International Festival of Old Music in Kraków
Tatra Autumn – International Festival of Mountain Folklore in Zakopane
Romane Dywesa – International Festival of Gipsy Bands in Gorzów Wielkopolski

September
Wratislavia Cantans – International Oratorio & Cantata Festival in Wrocław
Jan Kiepura Festival of Songs & Arias in Krynica
Festival of Piano Music in Słupsk
Festival of Polish Feature Film in Gdynia
Warsaw Autumn – International Festival of Contemporary Music in Warsaw
International Meetings of Jazz Vocalists in Zamość

October
Chopin International Piano Competition in Warsaw, every five years (the next one will be in 2000)
Warsaw Film Festival in Warsaw
Festival of Puppet Theatres in Opole
Jazz Jamboree – International Jazz Festival in Warsaw

November
All Saints' Day Jazz Festival in Kraków
Wieniawski International Violin Competition in Poznań, every five years (the next one will be in 2001)
International Festival of Poetry in Poznań

November/December
International Piano Jazz Festival in Kalisz
Camerimage – International Film Photography Festival in Toruń

You'll find further information on some of these events in the main text of the book. Check the dates when you come as some festivals can move to neighbouring months.

Catholic Events

Given the strong Catholic character of the nation, religious feasts are much celebrated, especially among the more traditional rural population. The Church calendar is marked by two major cycles which culminate in Christmas and Easter, and both cycles include set periods before and after the proper ceremonies take place. There are also a number of feast days devoted to particular saints, of whom the Virgin Mary is the most widely celebrated.

Christmas The Christmas cycle begins with Advent (*Adwent*), a four-week-long period preceding Christmas, which is characterised by the preparation of Nativity scenes in churches. Kraków is particularly notable for this; a competition is held there and the winning examples are rewarded.

As for Christmas (*Boże Narodzenie*) itself, Christmas Eve (*Wigilia*) is the day most celebrated in Polish homes, culminating in a solemn supper which traditionally should start when the first star appears in the sky. It's then that the family shares holy bread (*opłatek*), wishing each other all the best for the future. Then the proper supper begins. This will usually consist of 12 courses, including some of the best of traditional Polish cuisine. An extra seat and a place setting are left prepared for an unexpected guest. Kids will find their gifts under the Christmas tree (*choinka*), or sometimes they will be handed out by Santa Claus (*Święty Mikołaj*) – a disguised family member or neighbour.

In the more traditional rural homes there will still be much magic and witchcraft involved in the ceremony, the forms differing from region to region. It's believed that animals speak with human voices on that one night, and that at midnight the water in wells turns into wine.

After the supper is finished, the family will set off for the church for the specially celebrated Christmas Mass *(Pasterka)* at midnight. The service is held by almost all churches, and all are packed.

Christmas Day proper (25 December) is, like the previous day, essentially a family day, with Mass, eating and relaxing. This time of relaxation continues for the remaining days of the year. The real action begins on New Year's Eve *(Sylwester)*, with a variety of formal balls and private parties, principally among urban communities.

On 6 January comes Epiphany *(Dzień Trzech Króli)*, marked by carol singers, usually armed with a small portable crib or other religious images, who go in groups from door to door. On this day people have a piece of chalk consecrated in church, then use it to write 'K+M+B' (the initials of the three Magi) on their entrance doors, to assure Heaven's care over the home.

Easter Every bit as important as Christmas, Easter *(Wielkanoc)* is a movable feast falling on the Sunday past the first full moon after 21 March (any time between 22 March and 25 April). It is preceded by Lent *(Wielki Post)*, the season of fasting and penitence which begins on Ash Wednesday *(Środa Popielcowa)*, 40 weekdays prior to Easter Day.

Holy Week *(Wielki Tydzień)* begins with Palm Sunday *(Niedziela Palmowa)*, a reminder of the triumphal entry of Christ into Jerusalem, where he was welcomed with date-palm branches. Today the most common substitutes are willow branches overspread with white catkins. However, there are still some villages, notably Rabka, Tokarnia (near Rabka) and Łyse (in the Kurpie region), where the tradition is taken quite seriously: the 'palms' made there are elaborate works of art, sometimes nearly 10m high.

Palm Sunday also marks the beginning of the famous ceremony in Kalwaria Zebrzydowska which reaches its zenith on Maundy Thursday *(Wielki Czwartek)* and Good Friday *(Wielki Piątek)* when a Passion play is performed, re-enacting the last days of the life of Christ. In a blend of religious rite and popular theatre, local amateur actors take the roles of Roman soldiers, apostles, Jewish priests and Christ himself, and circle 20-odd Calvary chapels representing the stages of the Way of the Cross, accompanied by a crowd of pilgrims and spectators.

On Good Friday people visit the Holy Sepulchres set up in churches, while on Holy Saturday *(Wielka Sobota)* the faithful go to church with baskets filled with food such as bread, sausage, cake and eggs to have them blessed. The eggs are particularly characteristic for Easter as they are decoratively painted, sometimes with very elaborate patterns. Inspired by this tradition, the eggs are also made commercially of wood, painted and sold as souvenirs.

Easter Day *(Niedziela Wielkanocna)* begins with Mass, usually accompanied by a procession, after which the faithful come back home to have a solemn breakfast, when the consecrated food is eaten. Before breakfast, family members share eggs while wishing each other the best.

Easter Monday *(Lany Poniedziałek)* is when people sprinkle each other with water, which can mean anything from a symbolic drop of eau de Cologne to a bucket of water over the head, or even a dousing from a fire engine.

Pentecost *(Zielone Święta)* falls on the 50th day after Easter Day (hence its name), and a further 10 days on comes Corpus Christi *(Boże Ciało)*. The latter is characterised by processions held all over the country, of which the best known and most colourful is that in Łowicz.

Other Feasts Among the Marian feasts, the most important is the Assumption *(Święto Wniebowzięcia NMP)* on 15 August, celebrated in many places throughout Poland but nowhere as elaborately as in the Monastery of Jasna Góra in Częstochowa, where pilgrims from all corners of the country arrive on that very day, sometimes after a journey of several days on foot.

All Saints' Day *(Dzień Wszystkich Świętych)* on 1 November is a time of remembrance and prayers for the souls of the dead. On no other day do cemeteries witness so many people leaving flowers, wreaths and candles on the graves of their relatives, and they look most spectacular at night. The celebrations continue to a lesser extent on the following day.

ACTIVITIES
Hiking
This is probably the most popular of outdoor activities, and not without reason. Thousands of kilometres of marked trails run through the most attractive areas of the countryside, particularly in the mountains. Trails are usually well marked and easy to follow and don't present great difficulties even for beginners. The most popular hiking routes are those in the Tatra Mountains but there are many other amazing trails in the Pieniny, the Bieszczady and the Karkonosze, to list just a few.

Cycling
This is another way of getting closer to the country. Having your own two wheels gives you an opportunity to explore remote areas rarely visited by tourists. Don't worry about the state of the roads – they are usually in acceptable shape – and most of the country is comfortably flat for biking. Bike-rental businesses are finally opening in some touristy areas, including Zakopane.

Kayaking
Though the main rivers are pretty polluted, there are still some almost virgin regions which offer fabulous conditions for kayakers. The Krutynia and Czarna Hańcza rivers, both in Masuria, have some of the best kayaking in the country (see the Olsztyn and Augustów sections for details).

Sailing
The Masurian lakes are ideal for sailing and get crowded with hundreds of boats in summer. It's possible to hire sailing boats in Giżycko, Mikołajki (see these sections) and several other Masurian resorts. Some travel agencies organise sailing holidays.

Sea sailing is less common in Poland. There are not many seagoing yachts, and many of them belong to yachting associations. Only a handful are privately owned. Foreign yachts, on the other hand, are visiting Polish ports more and more often, thus opening up new ways of reaching the country.

Windsurfing
This is becoming popular along the Baltic coast, with the main centre in the Gulf of Gdańsk between Władysławowo and Chałupy (see the Hel Peninsula section for details).

Rafting
Probably the only rafting trip you will be able to find is the well organised tourist run down the Dunajec River. The Dunajec Gorge section has all the details.

Horse Riding
Horse riding is popular in Poland and there are a lot of stud farms. Many of them have riding courses for beginners and will rent horses to experienced riders. Orbis has package tours called 'Holidays in the Saddle', which are week-long cross-country group rides, and they can be arranged in Orbis offices abroad.

Caving
There are over 1000 caves of various kinds in Poland, most of which are found in the Kraków-Częstochowa Upland and in the Tatra Mountains. However, only a handful of caves are adapted for ordinary tourists and open to all. The most spectacular of these are arguably the Bear's Cave near Kłodzko and the Paradise Cave near Kielce, both detailed in the book.

Skiing
Skiing is fairly popular and is mostly concentrated in the Carpathians. Zakopane at the foot of the Tatra Mountains is Poland's No 1 ski centre, and the second is probably Szczyrk in the Beskid Śląski. There are plenty of other, smaller ski resorts though their facilities are usually more modest.

Hang-Gliding & Paragliding

These are relatively new sports but are developing fast, particularly in the mountain regions, which offer the best conditions. There are several centres (in Bielsko-Biała and Zakopane, among others) which provide equipment and training.

Gliding

Several gliding centres (including the ones in Leszno, Jelenia Góra, Nowy Targ and Grudziądz) are now open to glider pilots from abroad, and offer equipment, professional assistance, flights, training and accommodation.

LANGUAGE COURSES

Courses on Polish language are available in most major cities. See the Warsaw, Kraków and Gdańsk sections for further information.

WORK

Travellers hoping to find paid work on the spot in Poland will probably be disappointed. First of all, to work legally you need a work visa, and getting one involves a complex and lengthy paperwork procedure. Secondly, wages are low in Poland (an average monthly salary is about US$375), so unless you are a highly qualified specialist in some area it's not a great deal. Lastly, forget about casual manual jobs as there are armies of 'tourists' from beyond Poland's eastern border, and most will be eager to work for much less than you would ever expect to be paid.

Qualified English teachers have perhaps the best chance of getting a job, yet it's not that easy. Try the English-teaching institutions, linguistic departments at universities, and private language schools. If you don't have a bona fide teaching credential, you may still try to organise some informal arrangements, like for example giving private language lessons.

ACCOMMODATION

The choice of lodgings has grown and diversified considerably over the past few years. Unfortunately, prices have risen as well and in many cases have skyrocketed. This trend is expected to continue in the near future: you'll have a wider choice but you'll pay more.

The standard of accommodation varies a great deal and there's no consistent relationship between quality and price. Some hotels ask a fairly reasonable price for a good, clean room while others demand twice as much for a scruffy, dingy cell. Budget accommodation is still cheap but its standard usually ranges from bad to awful.

Warsaw is the most expensive place to stay, followed by Kraków, Poznań and other major cities. The farther away from the big cities you go, the cheaper. The summer resorts, particularly those on the Baltic coast, on the Masurian Lakes and in the mountains, have higher prices in the high season. Similarly, the mountain ski centres put their prices up in winter. Since 1990 the price of accommodation has been the same for foreigners as for Poles, except in youth hostels, which have a slightly higher tariff for travellers from abroad.

Accommodation listed in the Places to Stay sections of this book is ordered according to price, from the bottom to the top. Where sections are broken down into price brackets, the budget accommodation includes anything costing less than about US$20 a double; the mid-range bracket covers hotels priced from approximately US$20 to US$40 a double, and anything over US$40 is considered top-end. Warsaw and Kraków have higher price brackets – see these chapters for details.

Room prices are usually displayed at the reception desk. You are most likely to find listings there for a *pokój 1-osobowy* (single room) and a *pokój 2-osobowy*, accompanied by some of the following descriptions:

bez łazienki – without bath
z łazienką – with bath (toilet, shower and basin)
z prysznicem or *z natryskiem* – with shower (but usually no toilet)
z umywalką – with basin (but nothing else)

There will usually be some other entries, including:

apartament – suite
opłata za dodatkowe łóżko – charge for an extra bed
opłata za pobyt psa – charge for a dog
opłata za telewizor – charge for a TV set

The prices normally include VAT, so you just pay what is written, unless indicated otherwise.

Camping

Poland has over 500 official camping and bivouac sites registered at the Polish Federation of Camping & Caravanning. They are distributed throughout the country, and can be found in all the major cities (usually on the outskirts), in many towns and in the countryside, particularly in attractive tourist areas.

About 40% of them are authentic camping grounds as understood by this term in the west. They are fenced around and lit, and have electricity, running water, showers, kitchen and caravan facilities. They often have cabins, though it may be hard to come by one in July and August. They are identified by numbers and sometimes by names as well.

The remaining 60% are bivouac sites, or just open grounds for camping, usually equipped with toilets but not much more. The *Campingi w Polsce* map available in large bookshops has details of registered camping and bivouac sites.

Over recent years, a number of private camp sites have sprung up all over Poland. They range from small back gardens with a bath in the owner's house to large grounds with bungalows, cafés, shops, bike and boat rental etc. These sites are not included on the camping map.

Only a handful of camp sites are open year-round; most are open from May to September, but some run only from June to August. The opening and closing dates given here are a rough guide only: they may open and close earlier or later in the season, depending on the weather, flow of tourists etc.

Camping usually costs around US$2 to US$3 per person plus another US$2 to US$3 for the tent. Cabins, where available, go for US$4 to US$8 per person, though in most cases you will have to take the whole room, which may sometimes be a double but is more often a triple or quad.

Youth Hostels

Polish youth hostels *(schroniska młodzieżowe)* are operated by the Polskie Towarzystwo Schronisk Młodzieżowych (PTSM), a member of Hostelling International. PTSM has its main office in Warsaw and branch offices in all provincial capitals. Founded in 1926, PTSM was the world's third youth hostel organisation (after Germany and Switzerland) and managed to operate throughout the period of communist rule as the only such institution in Eastern Europe. What's more, the network expanded during those days to nearly 1000 youth hostels, more than any other country in the world!

By 1998, there were about 550 hostels, including about 125 all-year hostels and 425 seasonal ones open in July and August only. They are distributed more or less uniformly throughout the country, and there's at least one in every major city. PTSM publishes the *Informator PTSM*, a guidebook containing the full list of youth hostels in Poland. It's updated biennially and is available in the central and regional offices and in some of the major youth hostels.

The all-year hostels are more reliable and have more facilities, including showers, a

The symbol you'll see on Polish youth hostels

place to cook and a dining room. Unfortunately, most are in pretty poor shape. Only a handful of hostels have good, modern facilities and enough showers to cope with the number of guests.

The seasonal hostels are usually installed in schools, while the pupils are off for their holidays. These schools are in no way adapted to being hostels – they hardly ever have showers or kitchens, and hot water is a rare occurrence. The only thing done to turn them into hostels is the replacement of the class desks with beds.

The seasonal hostels are highly unreliable; only about 75% of them will actually be open at any one time, while the remaining ones can be under renovation, or simply stay closed without so much as a notice on the door. The situation can change from year to year, and the hostels which are closed one year may open the next and vice versa.

Many previously strict hostel rules have been relaxed or abandoned. Youth hostels are now open to all, members and non-members alike, and there is no age limit. Curfew is 10 pm, but some hostel staff may be flexible about this. Some hostels may admit both sexes in one dorm – not bad for a Catholic country. Almost all hostels are closed between 10 am and 5 pm. Checking-in time is usually until 9 or 10 pm, but this varies from place to place. In some minor seasonal hostels the staff can simply close early and go home. It's therefore wise to check in as soon after 5 pm as possible.

Hostels cost some US$3 to US$7 (depending on the hostel's category) per bed in a dorm for Poles, and about US$1 more for foreigners. Singles and doubles, if there are any, cost about 20% to 50% more. The youth hostel card gives a 25% discount off these prices for nationals and, in some places, for foreigners. If you think you'll be using youth hostels regularly, bring along a membership card or buy one at any branch office of the PTSM in Poland. If you don't have your own bed sheets or a sleeping bag, the staff will provide sheets for about US$1.25 (not available in some seasonal hostels).

Youth hostels are the cheapest form of accommodation after camping, but do be prepared for basic conditions. Given the low prices, hostels are popular with travellers and are often full. A particularly busy time is early-May to mid-June when hostels are crowded with Polish school groups.

Youth hostels are marked with a green triangle with the PTSM logo inside, placed over the entrance door.

PTTK Hostels & Mountain Refuges

Over several decades PTTK has managed to build up an extensive array of its own hostels, called Dom Turysty or Dom Wycieczkowy. They are aimed at budget travellers, providing a simple shelter for the night. They are in areas attractive to tourists, in cities, towns, villages and the countryside, often excellently situated.

PTTK hostels rarely have singles, but always have a good choice of three and four-bed rooms, usually with shared facilities, where you can often take just a bed, not the whole room, and which will cost between US$5 and US$10. There's often a budget cafeteria or a restaurant on the premises. Some of the PTTK hostels, particularly those in the large cities, are now under private management and are more expensive.

PTTK also runs an array of mountain refuges (*schroniska górskie*) which are an essential resource for trekkers. They are often wonderfully located and are charming buildings in themselves. Conditions are usually simple but you don't pay much and the atmosphere can be great. They also serve cheap hot meals. The more isolated refuges are obliged to take in all comers, regardless of how crowded they get, which means that in the high season (summer and/or winter) it can be sometimes hard to find even a space on the floor. Refuges are open all year though you'd better check at the nearest regional PTTK office before setting off.

Student Hostels

These are the hostels set up in student dormitories during the summer holiday period (July to mid-September) when students are away on holiday. In each major university city there are at least a few student dorms, some of which are open as student hostels in summer, and the picture may change from year to year.

Each year the Almatur student agency runs one dorm in each of Warsaw, Gdańsk, Kraków and Poznań. Accommodation costs US$18/28 a single/double for students and a dollar more for nonstudents. To use these hostels you need an Almatur voucher, which can be bought from Almatur offices.

Many other student dorms open in summer as hostels and run independently. They don't need vouchers, take in all comers and are usually cheaper than the Almatur hostels, though their standards can be lower.

Hotels

This is the most voluminous category and is growing fast. It is also the most diverse group, encompassing an immense variety of old and new places ranging from ultra-basic to extra-plush.

The old-generation hotels, dating from before the Berlin Wall went down, were split into classes and given from one to five stars, intended to reflect their quality and price. The rudimentary one-star places are mostly confined to the smaller provincial towns, whereas the upmarket five-star establishments, monopolised by Orbis, dot the central areas of big cities.

The arrival of the market economy has changed the picture altogether. On the one hand, plenty of small, mostly private hotels have sprung up. Many of them cater to the middle-priced market, thus nicely filling the gap between PTTK and Orbis. On the other hand, various international hotel chains have arrived to provide luxury for those who were not satisfied with Orbis' services. Lastly, various state-run lodging networks, previously accessible to only a few, have now opened to all. The latter category includes the sports and workers' hotels (detailed in the following sections), both of which fall into the bottom price bracket.

Most hotels have single and double rooms, and some also offer triples. As a rule, single rooms work out proportionally more expensive than the doubles. A double usually costs only 20% to 40% more than a single. Taking a triple between three people gives a further saving as it is likely to cost only slightly more than a double. Rooms with private bath can be considerably more expensive than those with shared facilities.

If possible, check the room before accepting. Don't be fooled by the hotel reception areas, which may look great in contrast to the rest of the establishment. If you ask to see a room, you can be pretty sure that they won't give you the worst one, which might happen otherwise.

Workers' Hotels During the postwar industrial development, large factories and other enterprises had to provide lodging facilities for their workers, many of whom came from other regions. An extensive network of workers' dormitories had been built up over the communist period, each dorm exclusively for the employees of a given company. Most of these places are now open to the general public.

You'll find these hotels mostly in the cities, particularly industrial ones. They are almost always large, hardly inspiring blocks, often a long way from the city centre. They are called Hotel Pracowniczy or Hotel Robotniczy, though most have disguised themselves under a proper name. Their standards are usually low, but so is the price, US$5 to US$10 per bed in a double, triple or quad. Singles are rare, as are private baths. They are just about the cheapest hotels you can find and, judging by their facilities, they might well be classified as hostels. Many workers' hostels are invaded by visitors from the east.

Sports Hotels Sports hotels were built within sports centres in order to create facilities for local and visiting teams. For a long time, most of them accepted sportsmen/women only but now almost all are open to the general public. In many aspects they are similar to the PTTK hostels and workers' hotels: they seldom have singles, offer mostly shared facilities and you can usually pay just for the beds you are using in a room if you don't mind strangers. By and large, they are marginally better than workers' hotels and charge a little more (US$6 to US$12 per head). They, too, are often located well away from the town or city centre, usually next to the local stadium. Most commonly, they are called Hotel Sportowy, Hotel OSiR or Hotel MOSiR, and some of them run camp sites in summer.

Orbis & Other Luxury Hotels Orbis runs the largest hotel chain in Poland – 55 hotels with a total of over 10,000 rooms. They are found in most of the major cities and smaller places of tourist interest. Focusing on moneyed tourists and business people from abroad as well as the more affluent Poles, Orbis hotels keep their prices high. They range from US$40 to US$80 for a single and US$60 to US$120 for a double, or even more in some establishments in Warsaw, Kraków and Wrocław. Most of the Orbis hotels are classified as four or five-star, and they range from good to very good, though some of the provincial outlets are of rather more average quality.

Until recently a monopolist of hotel luxury, Orbis now faces increasing competition from various joint ventures with international hotel chains, which have moved in to build some even ritzier venues, so far mostly in Warsaw. Predictably, the prices are rather unaffordable for average travellers, but guests can enjoy most of the luxuries they'd find in top-class hotels in the west.

All these hotels are easy to book from abroad, either in Orbis offices or through the respective hotel chains, and payment can be made by credit card.

Holiday Homes

In popular holiday areas such as the mountains or the coast, you'll come across workers' holiday homes, known to Poles as Domy Wczasowe or Domy Wypoczynkowe. In the communist times, these large homes either served the employees of a company or were directed centrally by the FWP (Workers' Holiday Fund), but were off limits to individual tourists. Today they welcome everybody. Most are open in summer only, but some run year-round. They tend to be pretty full in July and August, but it's relatively easy to get a room in June or September. Their standard varies but on the whole it's not bad, and prices are usually reasonable. Almost all have their own canteens, where they serve meals for guests and sometimes for nonguests as well. Full board is usually optional but in some homes it can be compulsory.

Pensions

Also concentrated in the attractive summertime resorts, pensions or *pensjonaty* are small, privately run houses that provide bed and board (half or full). They prefer you to stay for a while, but if they have vacancies they may accommodate you for a night or two. As a rule, pensions are clean, comfortable and friendly, and prices are not astronomic – roughly around US$20/30 for a single/double. Some of them focus directly on westerners, particularly Germans, and may have higher prices and display them in Deutschmarks.

Motels

An expanding category, motels are useful for those travelling by car. They are often well outside the cities, sometimes completely on their own amid forests. There's a variety of motels in Poland, of which the most numerous group are the *zajazdy* or, loosely translated, roadside inns. They focus more on food than on lodging, but almost always there are some rooms for guests at reasonable prices. They differ in quality and style and it's best just to watch out on the road and try one you like.

Private Rooms

In some major cities, you'll find an agency, usually called the Biuro Zakwaterowania or the Biuro Kwater Prywatnych, which arranges accommodation in private homes. The rooms on offer are mostly singles/doubles and cost around US$15/25 (US$18/30 in Warsaw and Kraków). The staff in the office show you what's available, you then decide, pay and go to the address they give you. The most important thing is to choose the right location, taking into consideration both distance and transport. Some places are a hell of a long way from the centre and you'd do far better paying more for a central hotel and saving hours travelling on public transport.

During the high season, there will probably be some people hanging around outside the office offering accommodation, often at lower prices (and open to bargaining) than those in the office. If you decide to deal with them, check exactly where the place is before committing yourself.

Private rooms are a lottery: you don't know what sort of room you'll get or who your hosts will happen to be. It's therefore a good idea to take the room for a night or two and then extend if you decide to stay longer.

In popular holiday resorts, you'll find plenty of signs at the entrances to private homes saying *pokoje* (rooms) or *noclegi* (lodging), which indicate where to knock and ask for a room. They are usually cheaper than in the cities – US$6 to US$10 a head in most cases.

Agrotourist Accommodation

Known as *kwatery agroturystyczne*, this refers to accommodation in farms, country houses and cottages, where owners rent some of their rooms to tourists. They normally can also provide meals if requested, and sometimes offer other facilities such as horse riding, angling, canoes, bikes etc. In most cases, rooms are simple and rarely have private baths, but prices are reasonable – usually between US$5 and US$10 per bed.

The owners of these places are affiliated to the agrotourist associations (*stowarzyszenia agroturystyczne*), which have 36 regional offices around the country, and a central office in Warsaw.

This is the most dynamically growing accommodation sector in the country. In 1995 agrotourism was hardly heard of; by the time of writing, there were a thousand farms providing such accommodation scattered all over the country. There may be twice as many by the time you read this.

Agrotourist lodging can be an interesting proposition for those who want to relax a while somewhere in the countryside, enjoying the slow beat of life, local folklore and traditions and healthy regional food, all for a reasonable price. It can also be just an alternative accommodation for those who have their own means of transport and can easily roam along the back roads and rural areas.

This accommodation is not included throughout this book, but information is pretty easy to get. Contact the central Warsaw office, the Polska Federacja Turystyki Wiejskiej (☎ 22-827 51 56), ul Jasna 15, which can provide details country-wide. Outside Warsaw, inquire at the local tourist office, which will either give you the relevant information or direct you to the regional agrotourist association office. Most offices have published their regional catalogues, and a general catalogue was in preparation at the time of writing.

FOOD

Poland was for centuries a cosmopolitan country and its food has been influenced by various cuisines. Jewish, Lithuanian, Belarusian, Ukrainian, Russian, Hungarian and German traditions have all made their mark. Polish food is hearty and filling, with thick soups and sauces, abundant in potatoes and dumplings, rich in meat but not in vegetables.

Poland's most internationally known dishes are *bigos* (sauerkraut with a variety of meats), *pierogi* (ravioli-like dumplings stuffed with cottage cheese or minced meat or cabbage and wild mushrooms) and *barszcz* (red beetroot soup, originating from Russian

Bring on the Bigos

If there's one genuine traditional Polish dish, it's bigos. It's made of sauerkraut, fresh chopped cabbage and a variety of meats including pork, beef, game, sausage and bacon. All this is cooked on a very low flame for several hours and put aside to be reheated a few times, a process which allegedly enhances its flavour. The whole operation takes a couple of days but the effect can be impressive – a well cooked, several-days-old bigos is mouthwatering. Everybody has their own mysterious recipe as far as the ingredients, spices and cooking time are concerned and you will never find two identical dishes.

Because it's so time-consuming, bigos doesn't often appear on a restaurant menu and the dish you encounter under this name in cheap bars and other seedy eateries is a very far cry from the real thing. The best place to try bigos is a private home and if you ever happen to get such an invitation, don't miss it. Bring along a bottle of good clear vodka; bigos tastes most delicious when it's washed down.

borsch). Favourite Polish ingredients and herbs include dill, marjoram, caraway seeds and wild mushrooms.

Eating Habits

Poles start off their day with breakfast (*śniadanie*) which is roughly similar to its western counterpart and may include bread and butter (*chleb z masłem*), cheese (*ser*), ham (*szynka*), sausage (*kiełbasa*), and tea (*herbata*) or coffee with milk (*kawa z mlekiem*). Eggs (*jajka*) are fairly popular and can be served soft-boiled (*na miękko*), hard-boiled (*na twardo*), fried (*sadzone*) or scrambled (*jajecznica*).

The most important and substantial meal of the day, the *obiad*, is normally eaten somewhere between 2 and 5 pm. It's usually prepared at home, but those who don't cook have it in the workplace canteen (*stołówka*) or in a cafeteria. Obiad has no direct equivalent in English: judging by its contents, it's closer to western dinner, but the timing is probably nearer to lunch.

The third meal is supper (*kolacja*). The time and contents vary greatly: occasionally it can be nearly as substantial as the obiad; more often it's similar to breakfast, or even as light as just a croissant and a glass of tea.

When beginning a meal, whether in a restaurant or at home, it's good manners to wish your fellow diners *smacznego*, or 'bon appétit'. When drinking a toast, the Polish equivalent of 'cheers' is *na zdrowie* (literally, to the health).

Places to Eat

The old places from the half-century of centralised planning have mostly closed down or been taken over by new managers or owners, while hundreds of new places have proliferated and more spring up every day. Although eating outlets in Poland are still some way behind those of the western world in number and variety, the development over the past decade has been enormous.

Following is an outline of the main types of eating establishments. Note that in Poland, the word 'bar' is used to describe a variety of gastronomic venues, not only those for drinking as traditionally understood by the term in the west.

Restaurants A restaurant (*restauracja*) is the main place for a meal with table service. They range from unpretentious cheap eateries where you can have a filling meal for less than US$5 all the way up to luxurious establishments that may leave a sizable hole in your wallet. The former class is mostly to be found in smaller towns and the back streets of city suburbs, while the latter kind is almost exclusively confined to the largest cities. On the whole, local restaurants are still cheap by western standards, though the gap is slowly diminishing, particularly so in the highest price bracket.

Within a decade since the death of communism, Polish restaurants have made a remarkable transformation of their style, service and menu, though the provinces are much slower to change than the big urban centres. Ethnic cuisine, which was almost nonexistent in communist Poland, is now courageously making an appearance on the scene. Warsaw has the widest selection of ethnic restaurants, but they are quickly spreading throughout the other main cities.

Restaurants generally open around 9 or 10 am (usually with a breakfast menu) or about noon. Closing time varies greatly from place to place and from city to province. In smaller towns it may be pretty hard to find somewhere to eat after 8 pm, whereas in big cities there are always places which stay open until 11 pm or midnight.

Milk Bars A Polish milk bar *(bar mleczny)* is a no-frills self-service cafeteria which serves mostly vegetarian dishes at ultra-low prices. The 'milk' part of the name reflects the fact that a good part of the menu is based on dairy products. You can fill yourself up for about US$2.

Milk bars were created to provide cheap food for the less affluent, and were subsidised by the state. The free-market economy forced many to close, but a number have survived by introducing meat dishes, upgrading standards and raising their prices. They are no longer genuine milk bars but remain budget places to eat. They wisely left most of their vegetarian fare (including some Polish specialities) on the menu, and the cost of this hasn't gone up too much.

There are still some archetypal milk bars that have somehow managed to survive in virtually unchanged form and remain extremely cheap. In some of these, however, the food quality may not be worth even this bargain price. These soup kitchens may become extinct over the next few years.

Milk bars open around 7 to 8 am and close at 6 to 8 pm (earlier on Saturday); only a handful are open on Sunday. The menu is posted on the wall. You choose,

then pay the cashier who gives you a receipt which you hand to the person dispensing the food. Once you've finished your meal, carry your dirty dishes to a designated place, as you'll see others doing. Milk bars are popular and there are usually lines to the counter, but they move quickly. Smoking is not permitted and no alcoholic beverages are served.

Cafés A café *(kawiarnia)* in communist Poland was more a meeting place than an eating place. They offered coffee, tea, sweets and a choice of drinks, but hardly anything more substantial. Now most cafés have introduced a meal menu, which may be a competitive alternative to some restaurants. Generally speaking, the borderline between a café and a restaurant is becoming blurred.

Cafés tend to open around 10 am and close at any time between 9 and 11 pm. Almost all cafés are smokers' territory and, given Polish smoking habits, the atmosphere can be really dense.

On the other hand, there has also been a development in the opposite direction, such as the chain named Sklep z Kawą Pożegnanie z Afryką (Farewell to Africa Coffee Shop). They are small shop-cum-cafés that sell and serve nothing but coffee. They offer 30-odd kinds of coffee, all prepared on request in sophisticated coffee makers. They are all nonsmoking places. Born in Kraków, the chain has about 20 outlets in most major cities.

Cocktail Bars In contrast to cocktail bars in the west, those in Poland don't serve alcohol. They are places which offer milk shakes (in Polish, 'cocktails', hence the name), ice cream, cakes, pastries, coffee, tea and soft drinks, and if this is what you are after, they are usually the best places around. Until recently almost all came under the Hortex label, but now they are adopting new names. They are open between roughly 9 am and 8 pm and are nonsmoking.

Other Places With the move towards capitalism, there has been a dramatic development on the gastronomic scene. A constellation of western-style eating outlets – almost nonexistent in communist Poland – such as bistros, snack bars, pizza houses, salad bars and fast-food joints have sprung up to serve things which were previously uncommon or unobtainable. Most of the big international fast-food chains, including McDonald's, Burger King, KFC and Pizza Hut, have already conquered Polish cities, and a myriad of Polish imitations have also settled in.

For some reasons, pizzerias have found a particularly fertile soil and settled in in astonishing numbers. Be warned though: not all pizzas are what you normally associate with this term. Some establishments think that any round pancake covered with a thick layer of tomato sauce (ketchup) is a pizza. Curiously, many Poles share this idea. Fortunately, there are heaps of pizza houses that cook pizza more reminiscent of its Italian parent.

A good number of the old drab restaurants have either closed down or been revamped, and the pavements have filled with food stalls and open-air café-bars. The prices have obviously gone up in the process, but you now have a decent choice, can eat and drink till late, and it's all still cheaper than in the west.

Menus

In low-priced provincial restaurants, menus are usually typed daily, sometimes on as many carbon copies as can be squeezed into the typewriter. If the menu is in printed form, as is the norm in upmarket restaurants, the management will include on it every imaginable dish they might hope to serve some day, but only those which are followed by a price will actually be available.

The menus of most of the top-class restaurants are in Polish with English and/or German translations, but don't expect foreign-language listings in cheaper eateries, nor waiters speaking anything but Polish. This section of the book aims to help you to decipher Polish menus and at the same time to introduce you to some Polish specialities.

The menu is usually split into several sections, under a selection of the following headings:

Specjalność Zakładu – Speciality of the house; it's usually a good bet
Przekąski or Zakąski – Starters and buffet meals
Zupy – Soups
Dania Drugie – Main courses, usually split into *dania mięsne* (meat dishes), *dania rybne* (fish dishes), *dania z drobiu* or simply *drób* (poultry), *dania z dziczyzny* or *dziczyzna* (game) and *dania jarskie* (vegetarian dishes)
Dodatki – Accompaniments to main courses; may include salads unless these appear separately under the heading *surówki*
Desery – Desserts
Napoje – Drinks, often divided into *gorące* (hot) and *zimne* (cold)

The name of the dish in the menu is accompanied by its price and weight (or other quantity), the latter being as important a piece of information as the former. The weight of a portion of some dishes such as fish or poultry is hard to determine beforehand so the price is given for either 100g or 1kg. Don't expect them, however, to cut 100g of fish for you: if you're not precise when ordering, they'll most probably serve you the whole fish, which will weigh and cost much more. To avoid surprises in the bill *(rachunek)*, study the menu carefully and make things clear to the waiter.

Starters & Buffet Meals

Starters and buffet meals have traditionally been the favourite (and sometimes the only) accompaniment to a glass or a bottle of vodka. The most popular include:

befsztyk tatarski or simply *tatar* – raw minced beef accompanied by chopped onion, raw egg yolk and often by chopped dill cucumber; eat it only in reputable restaurants
jajko w majonezie – hard-boiled egg in mayonnaise
karp w galarecie – jellied carp
łosoś wędzony – smoked salmon
nóżki w galarecie – jellied pigs' knuckles
sałatka jarzynowa – vegetable salad commonly known as Russian salad

śledź w oleju – herring in oil accompanied by chopped onion
śledź w śmietanie – herring in sour cream
węgorz wędzony – smoked eel

Soups

Soup *(zupa)* is an essential part of a meal, not just a starter, and for most Poles the *obiad* without soup is unthinkable. Polish soups are usually rich and substantial and some of them can be a filling meal in themselves. The average menu will include some of the following:

barszcz czerwony – beetroot broth, the most typical Polish soup; can be served clear *(barszcz czysty)*, with tiny ravioli-type dumplings stuffed with meat *(barszcz z uszkami)*, or accompanied by a hot pastry filled with meat *(barszcz z pasztecikiem)*
żurek – another Polish speciality: rye-flour soup thickened with sour cream; most likely to be served with hard-boiled egg *(z jajkiem)*, with sausage *(z kiełbasą)* or both, and sometimes accompanied by potatoes
flaki – seasoned tripe cooked in bouillon with vegetables; increasingly popular on menus
chłodnik – cold beetroot soup with sour cream and fresh vegetables; originally Lithuanian but widespread in Poland; served in summer only
botwinka – another summertime soup, but this one is hot and made from the stems and leaves of baby beetroots; often includes a hard-boiled egg
grochówka – pea soup, sometimes served with croutons *(z grzankami)*
kapuśniak – sauerkraut soup with potatoes
kartoflanka or *zupa ziemniaczana* – potato soup
krupnik – a thick barley soup containing a variety of vegetables and occasionally small chunks of meat
rosół – beef or chicken bouillon, usually served with noodles *(z makaronem)*
(zupa) grzybowa – mushroom soup
(zupa) jarzynowa – mixed vegetable soup
(zupa) ogórkowa – dill cucumber soup, usually with potatoes and other vegetables
(zupa) pomidorowa – tomato soup, usually served with either noodles *(z makaronem)* or rice *(z ryżem)*
(zupa) szczawiowa – sorrel soup, most likely to appear with hard-boiled egg

Main Courses

A Pole doesn't usually consider a dish a serious meal if it comes without a piece of meat *(mięso)*. The most commonly consumed meat is pork *(wieprzowina)*, followed by beef *(wołowina)* and veal *(cielęcina)*. Chicken is pretty popular but game and fish tend to be linked to upmarket or specialised restaurants.

One important thing to remember is that the price of the main course in the menu doesn't usually include accompaniments such as potatoes, chips, salads etc. You'll find them listed separately under the *dodatki* section, and then have to tally up the price of the components to get the complete cost of the dish. Only when all these items are listed together is the price which follows for the whole plate of food.

Pork, Beef & Veal These are the staple of every restaurant, from rock bottom to the very top. Among the commonest dishes are the following:

kotlet schabowy – a fried pork cutlet coated in breadcrumbs, flour and egg, found on every menu; the name sometimes bears the addition *panierowany* to distinguish it from the less common *sauté* version
kotlet mielony – a minced-meat cutlet fried in a similar coat to the kotlet schabowy; it mostly appear in cheap restaurants and the contents can be suspicious; Poles nickname it 'a review of the week' – avoid it
pieczeń wołowa/wieprzowa – roast beef/pork
golonka – boiled pigs' knuckle served with horse-radish; a favourite dish for many Poles
gołąbki – cabbage leaves stuffed with minced beef and rice; or occasionally with mushrooms
schab pieczony – roast loin of pork seasoned with prunes and herbs
sztuka mięsa – boiled beef with horseradish
polędwica pieczona – roast fillet of beef
rumsztyk – rump steak
befsztyk – beef steak: if you see the words *po an-gielsku* (literally, in English style), it will be rare; if you want medium, ask for *średnio wysmażony*; if you want well done, ask for *dobrze wysmażony*
bryzol – grilled beef steak
stek – steak; in obscure restaurants you may find it made of minced meat
gulasz – goulash; can be served either as a main course or a soup; originally Hungarian
zraz zawijany – stewed beef rolls stuffed with mushrooms and/or bacon and served in sour cream sauce

Fish Fish dishes don't abound on the menus of average restaurants, but there are places in big cities which specialise in fish. The most common sea fish is cod *(dorsz)*; of the freshwater varieties, you're most likely to encounter carp *(karp)* and trout *(pstrąg)*. Seafood is rare and to be found only in top-end establishments at high prices.

Poultry The most common bird on the table is chicken *(kurczak)*, which is usually roasted or grilled and is more or less the same as all over the world. A more innovative chicken dish is the *kotlet de Volaille*, or chicken fried in breadcrumbs and egg, but don't go for it in basic restaurants. The up-market places will probably also have duck *(kaczka)*, turkey *(indyk)* and goose *(gęś)*, almost always roasted; duck is often stuffed with apples *(kaczka z jabłkami)*.

Game Although game is no longer common in the country's forests, you may still have a chance to eat some. The animals which you're most likely to find on menus are wild boar *(dzik)*, hare *(zając)*, pheasant *(bażant)*, roe-deer *(sarna)* and, occasionally, the European bison *(żubr)*.

Vegetarian Dishes A vegetarian *(jarosz/ jaroszka)* won't starve in Poland – the cheapest place to look is a milk bar, but many of the new restaurants and bistros will have some vegetarian dishes. On the whole, vegetarian food is cheaper than meat; it's varied and usually well prepared. The specialities include:

knedle – dumplings stuffed with plums or apples
kopytka – Polish gnocchi; noodles made from flour and boiled potatoes
leniwe pierogi – boiled noodles served with cottage cheese
naleśniki – crêpes; fried pancakes, most commonly with cottage cheese *(z serem)* or jam *(z dżemem)*, served with sour cream and sugar
pierogi – dumplings made from noodle dough, stuffed and boiled; the most popular are those with cottage cheese *(z serem)*, with blueberries *(z jagodami)*, with cabbage and wild mushrooms *(z kapustą i grzybami)* and – though not for vegetarians – with minced meat *(z mięsem)*

placki ziemniaczane – fried pancakes made from grated raw potatoes with egg and flour, and served with sour cream *(ze śmietaną)* or sugar *(z cukrem)*; a more sophisticated version, called the *placek po węgiersku* ('in Hungarian style') – again, not for vegetarians – consists of a large potato pancake served with goulash
pyzy – ball-shaped steamed dumplings made of potato flour
fasolka po bretońsku – baked beans in tomato sauce

The distinction between meat dishes and vegetarian food is sometimes blurred in Poland. *Fasolka po bretońsku*, for example, may come with lumps of meat floating amongst the beans, while dumplings may be served with a meat-based gravy.

Accompaniments & Salads Potatoes *(ziemniaki)* are the most common accompaniment to the main course and they are usually boiled or mashed. Chips *(frytki)* are readily available but they can be hardly acceptable in cheaper greasy-spoon eateries. Rice *(ryż)* is not common; instead, watch out for *kasza gryczana*, steamed buckwheat groats, which go perfectly with some dishes, especially with *zrazy*.

A couple of other hot side dishes can make your meal richer and more substantial. Here are some suggestions:

pieczarki z patelni – fried mushrooms
marchewka z groszkiem – boiled carrots with green peas
fasolka szparagowa – green beans, boiled and served with fried breadcrumbs

Salads *(surówki* or *sałatki)* can come as a light dish in their own right or as a side dish to the main course. The latter variety includes:

mizeria ze śmietaną – sliced fresh cucumbers in sour cream
ogórek kiszony – dill cucumber
sałatka z pomidorów – tomato salad, most likely to be served with onion
surówka z kiszonej kapusty – sauerkraut, sometimes with apple and onion
ćwikła z chrzanem – boiled and grated beetroot with horseradish

Desserts

Some of the common desserts include:

budyń – milk pudding
lody – ice cream
melba – ice cream with whipped cream and fruit
galaretka – jelly
ciastko – pastry, cake

DRINKS
Nonalcoholic Drinks

Tea & Coffee Poles are passionate tea drinkers; they seem to consume it with each meal and still more in between. Tea *(herbata)* is served in a glass, rarely in a cup, and is never drunk with milk. Instead, a slice of lemon is a fairly popular addition, plus a lot of sugar. In a milk bar, you will often get tea already sweetened, sometimes a virtual syrup; in restaurants you usually get a glass of boiling water and a tea bag on the side.

Coffee *(kawa)* is another popular drink, and here too the Polish way of preparing it probably differs from what you are used to. The most common form is *kawa parzona*, a concoction made by putting a couple of teaspoons of ground coffee directly into a glass and topping it with boiling water. An increasing number of cafés serve espresso coffee *(kawa z ekspresu)* and cappuccino.

Soft Drinks Coke, Pepsi and other soft drinks, either bottled or canned, are readily available everywhere. Mineral water *(woda mineralna)* comes from springs in different parts of the country, and is good and cheap.

Alcoholic Drinks

Beer Polish beer *(piwo)* comes in a number of local brands, the best of which include Żywiec, Okocim and EB. Beer is readily available in shops, cafés, bars, pubs and restaurants – virtually everywhere. Depending on the class of the establishment, a half-litre bottle of Polish beer will cost anything from US$1 to around US$2.50. Not all cheap establishments serve it cold, so ask for *zimne piwo* (cold beer) when ordering.

The fashion for all things western has brought pubs to Poland; they first appeared around 1990 in Warsaw and spread like wildfire to other cities and further on out into the provinces. Warsaw already has a hundred of them and is closely followed by Kraków. Many pubs tend to mimic their English/Irish/Scottish siblings, including the brands of beer on offer. A draught Guinness or a bottled Heineken will be served to you for roughly the same price as at home. Today, the name 'pub' is used indiscriminately to label just about any place which has a few tables and serves beer.

Wine Poland doesn't have much of a wine tradition, and consumption is limited. The country doesn't produce wine *(wino)*, apart from a suspicious alcoholic liquid made on the basis of apples and who knows what else, nicknamed by Poles *wino-wino* or *bełt* and consumed by those on the dark margins of society who either can't afford or can't find a bottle of vodka.

Imported wines have traditionally come from the ex-eastern bloc, mostly from Hungary and Bulgaria, and if you're not too fussy they are acceptable and cheap. Western wines, particularly French, German and Spanish, are increasingly available in shops and restaurants, though some of them are fairly expensive. Pay attention to the price on the menu, which may be for a glass, not a bottle.

A traditional Polish beverage is *miód pitny*, or mead. Like wine, it's obtained by fermentation – though not of grape juice, but of malt in honeyed water.

Spirits Vodka *(wódka)* is by far the No 1 Polish brew and is consumed in astonishing quantities. Commonly associated with Russia, vodka is as much the Polish national drink as it is Russian, and the Poles claim it was invented here. Vodka has always been ubiquitous and abundant, and a product of the first necessity. You can take it for granted that there's at least one emergency bottle in every Polish home and that it will appear on the table as soon as a visitor arrives. Moreover, it's supposed to be emptied before the guest leaves. In restaurants, too, drinking vodka is an important part of life, sometimes

A Vodka 'How-To'

Some basic information about vodka may be useful. To begin with, forget about using vodka in cocktails. In Poland vodka is drunk neat, not diluted or mixed, in glasses usually of 50mL but ranging from 25 to 100mL. Regardless of the size of the glass, though, it's drunk in one gulp, or *do dna* ('to the bottom'), as Poles say. A chunk of herring in oil or other accompaniment, or a sip of mineral water, is consumed just after drinking to give some relief to the throat, and the glasses are immediately refilled for the next drink. As you might expect, at such a rate you won't be able to keep up with your fellow drinkers for long, and will soon end up well out of touch with the real world. Go easy and either miss a few turns or sip your drink in stages. Though this seems to be beyond comprehension to a 'normal' Polish drinker, you, as a foreigner and guest, will be treated with due indulgence. Whatever you do, don't try to outdrink a Pole. *Na Zdrowie* (Cheers)!

virtually the only activity, and you may be shocked by the style and speed in which vodka is absorbed by human beings.

These days drinking habits in the cities are changing, with Poles increasingly turning to beer instead of vodka. Yet, as soon as you go to a small town and enter the only local restaurant, you'll see those same tipsy folk debating jovially over bottles of vodka. Old habits die hard.

Polish vodka comes in a number of colours and flavours. Clear vodka is not, as is commonly thought in the west, the only species of the family. Though it does form the basic 'fuel' for Polish drinkers, there's a variety of other kinds, from very sweet to extra dry, including *myśliwska* (vodka flavoured with juniper berries), *wiśniówka* (flavoured with cherries), *żubrówka* ('bison vodka', flavoured with grass from the Białowieża forest on which the bison feed)

and *jarzębiak* (flavoured with rowanberry). Other notable spirits include *krupnik* (honey liqueur), *śliwowica* (plum brandy), *winiak* (grape brandy) and *Goldwasser* (thick liqueur with flakes of gold). Finally, there's *bimber* – home-made spirit, which ranges in quality from very poor to excellent.

A half-litre bottle of vodka costs US$5 to US$8 in a shop, but in restaurants it can double or even triple in price. Clear vodka should be served well chilled though this does not always happen in lower-class establishments. Coloured vodkas don't need much cooling and some are best drunk at room temperature.

There are plenty of situations that revolve around a bottle of vodka and you're likely to have invitations or opportunities to share one. Drinking with friends in their homes is fine, but use your common sense and be careful with people you meet by chance in obscure places.

Shabby vodka 'drinkeries' are best avoided, especially by women. It's not because there's any danger (though flying glasses are never safe!) but rather because of the overflowing effusiveness of Polish drinkers, which grows in direct proportion to the level of alcohol in their blood and can soon become unbearable, even if motivated by genuine goodwill.

These traditional watering holes are steadily disappearing, along with their usual clients, the old-generation seasoned drinkers. They've already gone from the city centres, to be immediately replaced by younger, smarter establishments – pubs, of course – serving beers to the new generation of Poles.

ENTERTAINMENT

Cinemas run the usual western fare with several months' delay. The majority come from the USA while the number of Polish films is minimal. All films are screened with original soundtrack and Polish subtitles. The entrance fee is around US$4 to US$6.

Polish theatre has long been well known both locally and abroad and it continues to fly high. Language is obviously an obstacle for foreigners, but nonetheless theatre buffs may want to try some of the best theatres if only to see the acting. Some plays are based more on the visual than on language and these are particularly recommended for non-Polish speakers. Productions range from Greek drama to recent avant-garde with room for great classics from Shakespeare to Beckett. Local authors are well represented, with a particular focus on ones who were officially forbidden during the communist era.

Theatres run usually one show nightly from Tuesday to Sunday; Monday is their day off. Almost all theatres close in July and August as the actors go on holiday. At US$5 to US$10, tickets are a bargain.

Opera is another tempting option though only the largest cities have proper opera houses. You'll probably find the best productions in Warsaw and Łódź and they're definitely worth the money – about US$15 at most.

For classical music, the Filharmonia Narodowa (National Philharmonic) is the place to head for. Almost all larger cities have their philharmonic halls, and concerts are usually held on Friday and Saturday, for next to nothing. You might occasionally come upon some of the greatest virtuosi, both national and international. The repertoire ranges from medieval music to the latest works from the pillars of Polish contemporary music, though most of the fare ranges somewhere between Bach and Stravinsky.

Polish jazz stands on a good European level, and the big international jazz names visit the country quite frequently. Warsaw and Kraków have the liveliest jazz life.

Nightlife is centred on bars, pubs, nightclubs and discos, all of which are in good supply, and all may occasionally have live music.

SPECTATOR SPORTS

Soccer (football) is Poland's most popular spectator sport. The country had quite a strong national team in the 1970s, but its fortunes have since risen and fallen (the latter more often than not). Yet, the matches of the national league invariably fill the stadiums.

Soccer apart, there doesn't seem to be any particular sport that drives the nation crazy. Cycling is reasonably popular in some circles, as is basketball. Poland has had some international successes in athletics, and occasionally kayaking and rowing, and was once strong in boxing, wrestling and fencing.

Recently, tennis and skiing are becoming popular, as both spectator and participator sports, though Poland has no international stars in either. With a few racetracks in the country, including ones in Warsaw and Sopot, horse racing has its small group of devotees.

Interestingly, some of the hugely popular sports in some western countries, including cricket, baseball and golf, are almost unknown in Poland.

SHOPPING

For local handicrafts, try Cepelia shops, which exist in all large cities. The most common Polish crafts include paper cutouts, woodcarving, tapestries, embroidery, paintings on glass, pottery and hand-painted wooden boxes and chests.

Amber is typically Polish. It's a fossil resin of vegetable origin, which appears in a variety of colours from pale yellow to reddish brown. You can buy amber necklaces in Cepelia shops, but if you want it in a more artistic form, look for jewellery shops or commercial art galleries. Prices vary enormously with the quality of the amber, and even more with the level of craftwork. Possibly the best choice of amber jewellery is in Gdańsk.

Polish contemporary painting, original prints and sculpture are renowned internationally and sold by private commercial art galleries. The galleries in Warsaw and Kraków have the biggest and most representative choice. Polish posters are among the world's best – a tempting souvenir. The best selection of them is, again, in Warsaw and Kraków.

The main seller of old art and antiques is a state-owned chain of shops called Desa.

Some of these shops also have the work of contemporary artists. Large Desa shops may have an amazing variety of old jewellery, watches, furniture and whatever else you could imagine. Remember that it's officially forbidden to export any item manufactured before 9 May 1945, works of art and books included.

Poland publishes quite an assortment of well edited and lavishly illustrated coffee-table books about the country, many of which are also available in English and German. Check the large bookshops of the main cities.

Polish music (pop, folk, jazz, classical and contemporary) is now commonly produced on CD and is increasingly easy to buy. Polish CDs cost about US$10 to US$15; imported CDs are US$15 to US$20. Cassettes are easier to find and much cheaper than CDs, but avoid buying them from street stalls as they are of dubious quality.

Getting There & Away

Poland is certainly not the world's major tourist destination, but sitting in the middle of Europe it does have plenty of air and overland transport links with the rest of the continent. It is also relatively well connected by air, both directly and indirectly, with the rest of the world.

There are sizable Polish communities living abroad (USA, Canada, Australia, UK, France, Germany) and their own Polish-run travel agents will be happy to sell you tickets. Not only are they familiar with all possible routes to the motherland, but they may also offer attractive deals.

AIR
Airports & Airlines
Poland's major international hub is Warsaw, but other large cities, including Gdańsk, Ka-

towice, Kraków, Poznań and Wrocław, also handle international flights. Poland is serviced by most major European carriers, including Air France, Alitalia, British Airways, KLM, Sabena and SAS, plus the national carrier LOT Polish Airlines.

LOT links Warsaw with most major European cities, and outside Europe has direct flights to/from Bangkok, Beijing, Chicago, Istanbul, New York, Tel Aviv and Toronto. LOT no longer operates noisy, vibrating Russian IL-62 'flying cigars'; it now flies smoothly on Boeings, and has a remarkably young fleet. However, despite its modern stock and friendly in-flight service, LOT doesn't always run on time. Keep this in mind if you have connections with other carriers, and allow sufficient time between flights.

Furthermore, LOT is no longer cheap. It is operating in the same free market as other airlines and is now just one more competitor; it can be cheaper on some routes but more expensive on others. It may work out cheaper to fly to Poland with one of the major European carriers, most of which call at Warsaw.

Fares vary greatly depending on what route you're flying and what time of the year it is. Poland's high season (and that of Europe in general) is in summer and a short period around Christmas, with the rest of the year being quieter and cheaper. Expect the lowest prices in February to March and October to November.

Buying Tickets
Air tickets bought from travel agents are generally cheaper than those bought directly from an airline, even if they cover the same route and have similar conditions or restrictions. How much you save largely depends on where you buy. In some countries or cities there is a big trade in budget tickets; in others, the discount-ticket market is limited, and the prices are not very attractive.

It is always worth putting aside a few hours to research the current state of the

> ## WARNING
>
> The information in this chapter is particularly vulnerable to change: prices for international travel are volatile, routes are introduced and cancelled, schedules change, special deals come and go, and rules and visa requirements are amended. Airlines and governments seem to take a perverse pleasure in making price structures and regulations as complicated as possible. You should check directly with the airline or a travel agent to make sure you understand how a fare (and ticket you may buy) works. In addition, the travel industry is highly competitive and there are many lurks and perks.
>
> The upshot of this is that you should get opinions, quotes and advice from as many airlines and travel agents as possible before you part with your hard-earned cash. The details given in this chapter should be regarded as pointers and are not a substitute for your own careful, up-to-date research.

market. Start early: some of the cheapest tickets have to be bought well in advance, and some popular flights sell out early. Talk to other recent travellers – this may stop you making some common mistakes. Look at ads in newspapers and magazines (including the Polish press published in your country), consult reference books and watch for special offers. Read the Air Travel Glossary to get familiar with the basic terms. Then phone round travel agents for bargains.

If you are travelling from the UK or the USA, you will probably find that the cheapest flights are being advertised by obscure bucket shops (known as consolidators in the USA) whose names haven't yet reached the telephone directory. Many such firms are honest and solvent, but there are a few rogues who will take your money, disappear, and reopen somewhere else a month or two later under a new name. If you feel suspicious about a firm, go somewhere else.

You may decide to pay a bit more than the rock-bottom fare by opting for the safety of a better-known travel agent. Firms such as STA Travel, who have offices worldwide, Council Travel in the USA or Travel CUTS in Canada offer good prices to most destinations and are not going to disappear overnight, leaving you clutching a receipt for a nonexistent ticket.

When buying a ticket to Poland, check where Poles buy their tickets. Poles have immense stamina and they'll usually shop around until they get the cheapest deal in town. Where? You can bet your grandmother's rocking chair that it will be a Polish agent – not for any patriotic reason, but because Polish agents have the same stamina in bargain-hunting around the airlines.

Polish travel agents are usually too small to advertise in major papers but they will have ads in the local Polish press. But don't rely exclusively on them; check other bucket shops, and compare prices and conditions.

Once you have your ticket, write its number down, together with the flight number and other details (or make a photocopy of it), and keep the copy separate from the original. This will help you get a replacement if the ticket is lost or stolen.

If you come to Poland without an onward ticket and want to fly back, keep in mind that the country isn't a mecca for people in search of budget flights, though an increasing number of local travel agencies try to offer competitive fares. Warsaw has the largest number of agencies and is possibly the best place to shop around. The *Gazeta Wyborcza*'s weekend travel section has ads placed by most major operators. Of course, you could probably do better in Berlin, Amsterdam or London, but you'll have to add the cost of getting there and your expenses while shopping around and waiting for a reservation.

Travellers with Special Needs

If you have special needs of any sort – you've broken a leg, you're vegetarian, travelling in a wheelchair, taking a baby or terrified of flying – you should let the airline know as soon as possible so that they can make appropriate arrangements. You should remind them of your needs when you reconfirm your booking (at least 72 hours before departure) and again when you check in at the airport. It may be worth ringing around the airlines before you make your booking to find out how they can handle your particular requirements.

Airports and airlines can be surprisingly helpful, but they do need advance warning. Most international airports will provide escorts from the check-in desk to the plane when needed, and there should be ramps, lifts, and accessible toilets and phones. Aircraft toilets, on the other hand, are likely to present a problem; travellers should discuss this with the airline at an early stage and, if necessary, with their doctor.

Children under two years of age travel for 10% of the standard fare (or free on some airlines), as long as they don't occupy a seat. They don't get a baggage allowance either. 'Skycots' should be provided by the airline if requested in advance; these are capable of carrying a child weighing up to about 10kg. Children between two and 12 years of age can usually occupy a seat for

Air Travel Glossary

Baggage Allowance This will be written on your ticket and usually includes one 20kg item to go in the hold, plus one item of hand luggage.

Bucket Shops These are unbonded travel agencies specialising in discounted airline tickets.

Bumped Just because you have a confirmed seat doesn't mean you're going to get on the plane (see Overbooking).

Cancellation Penalties If you have to cancel or change a discounted ticket, there are often heavy penalties involved; insurance can sometimes be taken out against these penalties. Some airlines impose penalties on regular tickets as well, particularly against 'no-show' passengers.

Check-In Airlines ask you to check in a certain time ahead of the flight departure (usually one to two hours on international flights). If you fail to check in on time and the flight is overbooked, the airline can cancel your booking and give your seat to somebody else.

Confirmation Having a ticket written out with the flight and date you want doesn't mean you have a seat until the agent has checked with the airline that your status is 'OK' or confirmed. Meanwhile you could just be 'on request'.

Courier Fares Businesses often need to send urgent documents or freight securely and quickly. Courier companies hire people to accompany the package through customs and, in return, offer a discount ticket which is sometimes a phenomenal bargain. In effect, what the companies do is ship their freight as your luggage on regular commercial flights. This is a legitimate operation, but there are two shortcomings – the short turnaround time of the ticket (usually not longer than a month) and the limitation on your luggage allowance. You may have to surrender all your allowance and take only carry-on luggage.

Full Fares Airlines traditionally offer 1st class (coded F), business class (coded J) and economy class (coded Y) tickets. These days there are so many promotional and discounted fares available that few passengers pay full economy fare.

ITX An ITX, or 'independent inclusive tour excursion', is often available on tickets to popular holiday destinations. Officially it's a package deal combined with hotel accommodation, but many agents will sell you one of these for the flight only and give you phoney hotel vouchers in the unlikely event that you're challenged at the airport.

Lost Tickets If you lose your airline ticket an airline will usually treat it like a travellers cheque and, after inquiries, issue you with another one. Legally, however, an airline is entitled to treat it like cash and if you lose it then it's gone forever. Take good care of your tickets.

MCO An MCO, or 'miscellaneous charge order', is a voucher that looks like an airline ticket but carries no destination or date. It can be exchanged through any International Association of Travel Agents (IATA) airline for a ticket on a specific flight. It's a useful alternative to an onward ticket in those countries that demand one, and is more flexible than an ordinary ticket if you're unsure of your route.

No-Shows No-shows are passengers who fail to show up for their flight. Full-fare passengers who fail to turn up are sometimes entitled to travel on a later flight. The rest are penalised (see Cancellation Penalties).

On Request This is an unconfirmed booking for a flight.

Air Travel Glossary

Onward Tickets An entry requirement for many countries is that you have a ticket out of the country. If you're unsure of your next move, the easiest solution is to buy the cheapest onward ticket to a neighbouring country or a ticket from a reliable airline which can later be refunded if you do not use it.

Open Jaw Tickets These are return tickets where you fly out to one place but return from another. If available, this can save you backtracking to your arrival point.

Overbooking Airlines hate to fly empty seats and since every flight has some passengers who fail to show up, airlines often book more passengers than they have seats. Usually excess passengers make up for the no-shows, but occasionally somebody gets bumped. Guess who it is most likely to be? The passengers who check in late.

Point-to-Point Tickets These are discount tickets that can be bought on some routes in return for passengers waiving their rights to a stopover.

Promotional Fares These are officially discounted fares, available from travel agencies or direct from the airline.

Reconfirmation At least 72 hours prior to departure time of an onward or return flight, you must contact the airline and 'reconfirm' that you intend to be on the flight. If you don't do this the airline can delete your name from the passenger list and you could lose your seat.

Restrictions Discounted tickets often have various restrictions on them – such as needing to be paid for in advance and incurring a penalty to be altered. Others are restrictions on the minimum and maximum period you must be away, such as a minimum of 14 days or a maximum of one year.

Round-the-World Tickets RTW tickets give you a limited period (usually a year) in which to circumnavigate the globe. You can go anywhere the carrying airlines go, as long as you don't backtrack. The number of stopovers or total number of separate flights is decided before you set off and they usually cost a bit more than a basic return flight.

Stand-by This is a discounted ticket where you only fly if there is a seat free at the last moment. Stand-by fares are usually available only on domestic routes.

Travel Agencies Travel agencies vary widely and you should choose one that suits your needs. Some simply handle tours, while full-services agencies handle everything from tours and tickets to car rental and hotel bookings. If all you want is a ticket at the lowest possible price, then go to an agency specialising in discounted tickets.

Transferred Tickets Airline tickets cannot be transferred from one person to another. Travellers sometimes try to sell the return half of their ticket, but officials can ask you to prove that you are the person named on the ticket. This is less likely to happen on domestic flights, but on an international flight tickets are compared with passports.

Travel Periods Ticket prices vary with the time of year. There is a low (off-peak) season and a high (peak) season, and often a low-shoulder season and a high-shoulder season as well. Usually the fare depends on your outward flight – if you depart in the high season and return in the low season, you pay the high-season fare.

half to two-thirds of the full fare, and do get a baggage allowance. Pushchairs (strollers) can often be taken aboard as hand luggage.

Departure Tax

The airport tax is US$10 for international departures from Warsaw, and around US$8 for departures from other Polish airports servicing international flights. You don't pay the tax at the airport itself, as it is automatically added to the price of your air ticket when you buy it.

The USA

Getting from the USA to Poland is easy though not particularly cheap. Though there are direct, nonstop flights from New York to Warsaw operated by LOT, they are not necessarily the cheapest. Agents often use indirect connections with other carriers such as British Airways, SAS, KLM, Sabena or Air France. Not only may these work out cheaper, but they can also be more attractive in other ways: you are usually allowed to break the journey in Western Europe for the same price or a little extra – a great bonus if you want to visit London, Paris or Amsterdam.

Two of the reputable discount travel agencies in the USA are STA Travel and Council Travel. Although they both specialise in student travel, they also offer discount tickets to nonstudents of all ages. Contact their national head offices to ask about prices, find an office near you or purchase tickets by mail.

Council Travel
   (☎ 1800 226 8624, ☎ 212-822 2700, www .counciltravel.com) 205 East 42nd St, New York, NY 10017
STA Travel
   (☎ 1800 781 4040, ☎ 310-824 1574, www .statravel.com) 920 Westwood Blvd, Los Angeles, CA 90024

STA Travel has offices in Los Angeles, San Diego, San Francisco, Berkeley, Boston, Cambridge and New York. Council Travel has offices in all these cities and in 20 others around the country.

There's a sizable Polish community living in the States, and Polish travel agents specialising in trips to Poland are in good supply, especially in Chicago and New York. They mostly cater for Poles and offer a variety of services ranging from flight tickets originating from either end to package tours. New York is the major centre of the ticketing business as it has the busiest flight links with Europe, including Warsaw. Most Polish agents are based in Greenpoint (in Brooklyn), the 'Polish' suburb, but there are also some in Manhattan. They include:

Fregata Travel
   (☎ 212-541 5707, fax 262 3220) 250 West 57th St, Suite 1211, New York, NY 10107
P&F Travel
   (☎ 718-937 1998 or toll-free ☎ 1800 822 3063, fax 937 2425) 3423 Steinway, Astoria, New York, NY 11101
TWK Travel
   (☎ 212-686 3493, ☎ 686 3496, fax 686 3502) 347 Fifth Ave, Suite 505, New York, NY 10016

The weekend editions of the Polish daily newspaper *Nowy Dziennik* have ads from everyone. Most agents will sell tickets for flights originating in other major US cities, and send them to you. Some agents (including TWK) can also sell you a one-way ticket from Poland to the USA and Canada and deliver it to you in Poland.

Fares depend on a maze of conditions such as the period of the ticket's validity, the season, terms of purchase, restrictions on returning the ticket, possibility of breaking the journey or changing the booking or route etc. As a rough guide, here are some of the cheapest fares (high season):

Route	One way (US$)	Return (US$)
New York-Warsaw	400	600
Miami-Warsaw	550	800
Los Angeles-Warsaw	600	900

If money is more of a concern to you than comfort or time, the cheapest way is to fly with any of several hotly competing airlines to one of the main European destinations such as London or Amsterdam, and then continue overland by bus eastwards. Also check the airfare to Berlin, which may be a reasonable compromise; Berlin is just 100km from the Polish border and 6½ hours by train from Warsaw.

Australia

Australia and Poland are a hell of a long way apart. The distance between Sydney and Warsaw is over 17,000km – nearly half the circumference of the earth. The journey will take at least 20 hours in the air, not to mention stopovers on the way. It won't be the cheapest trip of your life.

There are no direct scheduled flights between Australia and Poland, so any journey will involve a change of flight and, possibly, of carrier as well. There are two popular ways to fly to Poland: via Bangkok from where you use LOT services; and via a major Western European city, from where you continue to Warsaw on another flight. Both options work out roughly similar in price (the former can be slightly cheaper) and may or may not include an overnight stop depending on the connection.

LOT flies three times a week between Warsaw and Bangkok and has arrangements with other carriers, principally Qantas, which take passengers to and from various Australian cities. The return fare from Sydney/Melbourne to Warsaw will cost somewhere between A$1600 and A$2200, depending on the season, and around A$100 to A$200 less out of Perth. A one-way ticket should cost A$1000 to A$1200, or a bit less from Perth.

These flights are popular among Poles living in Australia and tend to fill up fast, particularly during the northern summer, so book well in advance.

You can also fly via Western Europe with one of the major European carriers such as British Airways, Lufthansa or KLM, to London, Frankfurt or Amsterdam respectively. From there a return trip to Warsaw is covered by the same airline or one of its associates. The prices of such

tickets are roughly comparable with each other and marginally higher than those of LOT: say, between A$1700 and A$2300. Any reputable agent should be able to put together such a route and even add a couple of other ports of call if you need any.

There are a number of Polish travel agencies in Australia. Magna Carta Travel is possibly the largest, with offices in Sydney, Melbourne and other major Australian cities. Others operate locally but can be marginally cheaper. The addresses of LOT airlines and some Polish agencies are:

LOT Polish Airlines
  (☎ 02-9299 3700) 44 Market St, Sydney, NSW 2000
  (☎ 03-9920 3874) 310 King St, Melbourne, Vic 3000
All Tours & Travel
  (☎ 02-9356 4155) 17 Bayswater Rd, Kings Cross, NSW 2011
Magna Carta Travel
  (☎ 02-9746 9964) 1 Albert Rd, Strathfield, NSW 2135
  (☎ 03-9523 6981) 387 Glenhuntly Rd, El-sternwick, Vic 3185
Mekina Travel
  (☎ 03-9663 4022) 5th floor, 277 Flinders Lane, Melbourne, Vic 3000
Orbis Express
  (☎ 02-9737 8099) 296 Parramatta Rd, Auburn, NSW 2144
Tatra Travel
  (☎ 03-9576 2444) 8 Glenferrie Rd, Malvern, Vic 3144

Don't miss checking what deals STA Travel can offer. It has offices all over Australia, including Adelaide, Brisbane, Cairns, Canberra, Darwin, Melbourne, Perth, Sydney and Townsville. Flight Centres International, with offices in most major Australian cities, may also offer good deals.

The UK

The London-Warsaw route is operated once daily by both British Airways and LOT, with several more LOT flights in summer. There are also direct weekly London-Gdańsk and London-Kraków flights all year long (with an additional flight in summer), both routes being serviced by LOT. Finally,

LOT has Manchester-Warsaw flights in summer.

Regular one-way fares on all these flights are not cheap at all, so don't even bother to ask for them. More interestingly, both carriers offer a three month Apex fare, but at about £300 for the London-Warsaw return trip, it's still quite expensive.

Fortunately, the travel market is very busy in London and there are countless agents competing to offer the 'cheapest price'. Poland is not a best seller but it does appear on the agents' menus. Pick up the Sunday edition of local papers or, better still, *Time Out* magazine, where you should find some bargains. STA Travel, Council Travel and Usit Campus may offer competitive deals for both students and nonstudents. The London offices of the three agencies are:

STA Travel
(☎ 020-7937 9962) 74 Old Brompton Rd, London, SW7 3LQ
(☎ 020-7465 0484) 117 Euston Rd, London NW1 2SX
Council Travel
(☎ 020-7437 7767) 28A Poland St, London W1
Usit Campus
(☎ 020-7730 3402) 52 Grosvenor Gardens, London SW1 0AG

As elsewhere, it's worthwhile checking the Polish-run agents. These include:

Fregata Travel
(☎ 020-7734 5101, ☎ 7451 7000) 100 Dean St, London W1
(☎ 0161-226 7227) 117A Withington Rd, Manchester M16
New Millennium
(☎ 0121-711 2232) 20 Hill St, Solihull, Birmingham B91 3TB
Polish Travel Centre
(☎ 020-8741 5541) 246 King St, London W6 0RF
Polorbis
(☎ 020-7636 2217) 82 Mortimer St, London W1
Tazab Travel
(☎ 020-7373 1186) 273 Old Brompton Rd, London SW5
Travelines
(☎ 020-8748 9609) 246A King St, Hammersmith, London W6 0RA
(☎ 020-7828 9008) Victoria Station

Expect a London-Warsaw return ticket to cost between £170 and £230, but it will be cheaper if you are under the age of 26. You may also check for cheap flights to Berlin, continuing overland by train (a three hour trip to Poznań or a bit more than six hours to Warsaw).

Continental Europe

There are a number of flights to Warsaw from all major European capitals, with both LOT and western carriers, but regular one-way fares are far from attractive. As from London, cheaper Apex fares are available and travel agents can beat the price down further. As a pointer, the fare from Paris is roughly comparable to that from London, and that from Amsterdam only marginally cheaper. The closer to Poland you are, the more attractive the train and coach become as they guarantee a considerable saving over the cost of an airfare.

Some of the major local weekend papers have travel ads and it's a good idea to ring around. Orbis offices (see Tourist Offices in the Facts for the Visitor chapter for some addresses and phone numbers) either sell tickets or will tell you where to buy one. Some of the agents listed later in this chapter will also sell air tickets.

TRAIN

Quite a number of international trains link Poland with other European countries. On the whole, train travel is not cheap and, on longer routes, the price of an ordinary train ticket can be almost as much as that of a discounted airfare.

Fortunately, there's a choice of special train tickets and rail passes, including the InterRail pass, which gives European residents under 26 years of age unlimited 2nd class travel for a month on most of the state railways of Western and Central Europe (including Poland), and Eurotrain, which gives under-26s a substantial discount off the ordinary fare. Tickets are valid for two months and allow for unlimited stops en route.

US and Canadian residents can learn more about European rail travel from Germanrail

(☎ 212-308 3100), 747 3rd Ave, New York, NY; or French National Railways (☎ 1800 848 7245 toll-free in the USA), 230 Westchester Ave, White Plains, NY 10604.

International trains to Poland, as well as those to other Central European countries, have recently become notorious for theft. Keep a grip on your bags, particularly on the Berlin-Warsaw overnight trains. See Train in the Getting Around chapter for more advice on security.

The UK

From London, you can travel to Warsaw via either the Channel Tunnel or Ostend. The ordinary return fares in high season are around £290 and £220 respectively (£230 and £170 in low season). People under 26 can get a Eurotrain return fare to Warsaw for around £160 and a one month InterRail pass for £250. Both ordinary and Eurotrain tickets are valid for two months and you can break the journey as many times as you wish. Tickets can be bought from British Rail ticket offices or travel centres. Agencies that specialise in travel to Poland, such as Fregata and the Polish Travel Centre (see the earlier Air section for the full list), may offer cheaper fares.

Germany

A number of German cities are linked by train (direct or indirect) with the major Polish cities. Direct connections with Warsaw include Berlin, Dresden, Cologne, Frankfurt/Main and Leipzig. There are also direct trains between Berlin and Gdańsk (via Szczecin), and Berlin and Kraków (via Wrocław).

The Warsaw-Berlin route (via Frankfurt/Oder and Poznań) is serviced by several trains a day, including two Euro-City express trains which cover the 569km distance in 6½ hours.

Czech Republic & Austria

Trains between Prague and Warsaw (three a day) travel via either Wrocław (740km, 12 hours) or Katowice (10 hours). Between Wrocław and Prague (339km), you have four trains a day and the journey takes about seven hours. There's also a train between Prague and Kraków (via Katowice).

Two trains per day travel between Vienna and Warsaw (753km, 11 hours) via Brand Katowice.

Slovakia & Hungary

There are two trains daily between Budapest and Warsaw (837km, 12 hours) via Bratislava and Katowice. These trains are routed through a short stretch of the Czech Republic, so make sure you have a Czech transit visa if required.

A different route through Košice in eastern Slovakia is followed by the train between Budapest and Kraków (598km, 12 hours).

Ukraine, Belarus, Lithuania & Russia

Warsaw has direct train links with Kiev in Ukraine, Minsk and Hrodna in Belarus, Vilnius in Lithuania, and Moscow and St Petersburg in Russia. These trains only have sleeping cars and you'll be automatically sold a sleeper when buying your ticket.

Remember that you need transit visas for the countries you will be passing en route. The Warsaw-Vilnius-St Petersburg rail line, for example, passes via Hrodna in Belarus, and the Belarusian border guards come aboard and slap unsuspecting tourists with a US$30 Belarusian transit visa fee. According to recent reports, they no longer issue transit visas but put you on the next train back to where you've just come from. Be warned. You may avoid this by taking a bus from Poland directly to Lithuania. Also note that a Belarusian transit visa doesn't allow you to break the journey in Hrodna, even just to look around for a few hours before continuing the trip.

BUS

Bus is the cheapest means of public transport to Poland from most of Europe. There are a few reputable international bus companies servicing Poland, of which Eurolines is possibly the best known. It's a consortium of coach lines with offices all over Europe.

Its coaches are comfortable, air-conditioned and often as fast as the train. Eurolines also has flexible two-month 'Euro Explorer' itineraries with unlimited stopovers en route.

Apart from the western bus carriers, there are also a number of bus companies run by Polish émigrés. These mostly cater to the Polish communities scattered over Europe and are cheaper, though their standards vary.

In recent years there's been a revolution in this business in Poland, with countless small private operators offering services from Warsaw and other Polish cities to anywhere in Europe from Madrid to Istanbul. In every Polish city you'll see ads for cheap bus tickets to the main European destinations. These can be of interest if you've come to Poland without a return ticket and want to move on or go back home.

Most coach companies will give a 10% discount to people aged under 26 and senior citizens, and children will usually get still bigger reductions.

The UK

Quite a few bus companies operate services between the UK and Poland. They include big international companies (eg Eurolines), British-based carriers run by Polish émigrés (eg White Eagle Lines) and Polish companies that call at the UK (eg Pekaes Bus).

Eurolines (☎ 0990 143219), 4 Cardiff Rd, Luton LU1 1PP, runs buses from London to Warsaw (via Ostend, Brussels and Poznań) and to Kraków (the same route as far as Poznań, and then via Wrocław and Katowice). The frequency of the service varies depending on the season: it's daily in summer and twice weekly the rest of the year. The fare for each route is around £70 one way and £110 return. Tickets are available from any National Express office and a number of travel agents.

White Eagle Lines (☎ 020-7244 0054, fax 7244 0145), 200 Earls Court Rd, London SW5 9QF, operates three routes, all originating in London: to Warsaw (via Poznań and Łódź), to Gdańsk (via Szczecin and Koszalin) and to Kraków (via Wrocław and Katowice). The one-way fares range

from £45 to £60, depending on the season, and return fares from £65 to £90. White Eagle Lines' partner in Poland, Eurotrans, has two offices in Warsaw: at ul Emilii Plater 49 (☎/fax 620 99 78), and at Al Jerozolimskie 63 (☎ 628 62 53, fax 621 07 88).

Information about other bus carriers is available from the Polish expatriate-run agencies, some of which operate their own buses. Their addresses are listed in the Air section earlier in this chapter.

Western Europe

As mentioned previously, Eurolines operates an extensive coach network all around Europe and maintains plenty of offices, many of which are located at bus terminals in the major cities. Eurolines outlets include:

Amsterdam
  (☎ 20-560 87 87) Amstel Coach Station, Julianaplein 5, 1097 DN
Berlin
  (☎ 30-860 0960) Bayern Express, Mannheimerstrasse 33-34
Brussels
  (☎ 2-217 00 25) 50 Place de Brouckere
Paris
  (☎ 1-49 72 51 51) Gare Routière Internationale, Av du Général de Gaulle, 93541 Bagnolet Cedex
  (☎ 1-43 54 11 99) 55 rue Saint-Jacques, 75005
Vienna
  (☎ 1-712 04 53) Blaguss Reisen, Bahnhof Wien-mitte, Top 7, Landstrasser Hauptstrasse 1b, A-1030

Apart from Eurolines, plenty of Polish companies operate buses which run to and fro across the border to most mainland European destinations (servicing altogether over 200 cities). Standards, reliability and comfort vary, but on the whole are not bad. Most buses are of a modern generation, and are equipped with air-conditioning, toilet and video. Information and booking are available from Orbis/Polorbis bureaus (see Tourist Offices in the Facts for the Visitor chapter) or from travel agencies run by Polish émigrés.

As a rough guide only, the major destinations, average one-way and return fares from Warsaw and journey times are as follows:

To	One way (US$)	Return (US$)	Time (hours)
Amsterdam	80	125	21
Brussels	80	125	22
Cologne	65	100	20
Frankfurt	60	95	19
Hamburg	50	80	16
Munich	65	100	21
Paris	90	140	27
Rome	100	160	28

Hungary

There are a few buses a week between Budapest and Kraków (US$32, 10 hours).

Ukraine, Belarus & Lithuania

The Polish PKS bus company runs daily buses from Warsaw to Lviv (US$17), Minsk (US$21) and Vilnius (US$19). These routes shouldn't normally take more than 12 hours, though the actual time depends on traffic lines at the border and customs. There are also regular buses between Przemyśl and Lviv (US$5, three hours), and one bus a day between Suwałki and Vilnius (US$6, 5½ hours).

CAR & MOTORCYCLE

Travelling by car or motorcycle, you'll pass the frontier via one of the designated road border crossings. Following is the list of road border crossings open 24 hours. The localities listed are the settlements on the Polish side of the border and you can find them on road maps. Some of these crossings are off limits to buses.

German border (from north to south): Lubieszyn, Kołbaskowo, Krajnik Dolny, Osinów Dolny, Kostrzyn, Słubice, Świecko, Gubin, Olszyna, Łęknica, Zgorzelec, Sieniawka
Czech border (west to east): Porajów, Zawidów, Jakuszyce, Lubawka, Kudowa-Słone, Boboszów, Głuchołazy, Pietrowice, Chałupki, Cieszyn
Slovak border (west to east): Chyżne, Chochołów, Łysa Polana, Niedzica, Piwniczna, Konieczna, Barwinek

Ukrainian border (south to north): Medyka, Hrebenne, Dorohusk, Zosin
Belarusian border (south to north): Terespol, Kuźnica Białostocka
Lithuanian border (east to west): Ogrodniki, Budzisko
Russian border (east to west): Bezledy, Gronowo

Travellers bringing their vehicles to Poland need their driving licence, vehicle registration and insurance policy. Normally your domestic licence will do, but it's advisable to bring an International Driving Permit as well. If you're arriving in someone else's car, avoid potential headaches by carrying a notarised letter from the owner saying you're allowed to drive it.

A certificate of insurance, commonly known as a Green Card, is available from your insurer. If you haven't already bought it at home, you'll be required to buy one at the border from the PZM office. PZM, the Polish Motoring Association, has offices at most road border crossings.

Read the Car & Motorcycle section in the Getting Around chapter for more about driving in Poland, local traffic rules, compulsory car accessories, fuel etc.

SEA

Poland has a regular ferry service to/from Denmark and Sweden, operated by the Unity Line, Stena Line and Polferries. The Unity Line covers the Świnoujście-Ystad route (daily, US$55, nine hours). The Stena Line runs between Gdynia and Karlskrona (six days a week, US$55, 11 hours). Polferries services the Świnoujście-Copenhagen route (five times a week, US$65, 10 hours), the Świnoujście-Malmö route (daily, US$65, nine hours), and the Gdańsk-Oxelösund and Gdańsk-Nynäshamn routes (several days a week, US$70, 18 hours either). All routes operate year-round.

The prices given are the deck fares, which normally don't need to be booked. Cabins of different classes are available and reservations are recommended in summer. Book early, but don't pay until you're sure you'll be going: there may be hefty cancellation fees. You can bring along your car (it will cost roughly 150% of the deck fare) but book in advance. Bicycles go free. A return ticket costs about 20% less than two singles and is valid for six months. Students and senior citizens get a 20% discount. There's a variety of other discounts for families, larger parties, groups plus car etc, which vary from route to route. Any travel agent in Scandinavia will have tickets; in Poland inquire at an Orbis office.

ORGANISED TOURS

A number of tours to Poland can be arranged from abroad. Orbis, traditionally the major operator, is still some distance ahead of the other Polish companies based abroad. It offers a choice of packages, usually one to two weeks long, from sightseeing in historic cities to skiing or horse riding holidays. Some Orbis addresses are listed under Tourist Offices in the Facts for the Visitor chapter. Travel agencies run by Polish émigrés (addresses throughout this chapter) also have a selection of packages to Poland. Some of the other US and Britain-based tour operators which include Poland in their programs are specified in the following sections. Also see Organised Tours in the Getting Around chapter for what can be organised from within Poland.

The USA

Affordable Poland (☎ 1800 801 1055), 1600 Saratoga Ave, Suite 609, San Jose, California 95129, specialises exclusively in Poland. The agency has standard and deluxe tours covering Poland's highlights, and offers a range of independent packages, so you can build your own tour and explore destinations of your choice at your own pace. Its other services include local sightseeing trips, car rentals, private tours and transfers.

American Travel Abroad (AMTA) organises tours with fixed dates around Poland and Central Europe. The agency has two offices in the USA: (☎ 212-586 5230 or toll-free ☎ 1800 228 0877, fax 581 7925) 250 West 57th St, New York, NY 10107; and (☎ 773-725 9500 or toll-free ☎ 1800 342 5315, fax 725 8089) 4801 West Peterson Ave, Chicago,

IL 60646. AMTA has its main office in Warsaw (see that chapter for address).

The American-International Homestays (☎ 1800 876 2048), PO Box 1754, Nederland, CO 80466, organises multi-city tours with accommodation in private homes, known as homestays. The 17 day Prague-Budapest-Kraków program costs around US$2500 from New York. The company also arranges B&B accommodation.

Walking Softly Adventures (☎ 503-788 9017 or toll-free ☎ 1888 743 0723, fax 788-0463), PO Box 86 273, Portland, OR 97 286, organises hiking, canoeing and biking tours to Poland's national parks and other off-the-beaten-track areas.

The UK

Martin Randall Travel (☎ 020-8742 3355), 10 Barley Mow Passage, Chiswick, London W4 4PH, has tours to Poland, including a 10 day 'Monasteries, Mansions and Country Towns' tour, which covers Warsaw, Kraków and the south and east of the country; and the Amber Route, which goes to Gdańsk and the Baltic Coast.

Exodus Expeditions (☎ 020-8675 5550), 9 Weir Rd, London SW12 0LT, has a 14 day 'Historic Poland' tour, which includes Warsaw, Gdańsk, Poznań, the Masurian Lakes and Białowieża National Park. Exodus also offers a 14 day hiking trip in the Tatras and Beskids, with accommodation in mountain refuges. Either tour costs around £750.

Bike Events (☎ 01225-480 130, ☎ 310 858), PO Box 75, Bath, Avon BA1 1BX, runs a two week bicycle trek from Kraków to Budapest via the Tatras and Slovakia (£800 from London), plus other Central Europe trips.

World Expeditions (☎ 01628-74174, fax 74312), 8 College Rise, Maidenhead, Berks SL6 6BP, organises two-week trekking and rafting tours in the Polish and Slovak Tatras, plus B&B in Kraków and Prague, for £730 from London.

Poland Tours (☎ 01784-247 286), 22 West View, Bedfont, MIDDX TW14 8PP, offers cheap 10-day packages in Polish mountain resorts.

Getting Around

AIR

LOT Polish Airlines, the country's commercial carrier, services both international and domestic routes. Within the country, it has regular flights from Warsaw to Gdańsk, Katowice, Kraków, Poznań, Rzeszów, Szczecin and Wrocław. There are no direct flights between these cities; all must go via Warsaw, and connections aren't always convenient. On domestic routes, LOT uses French-Italian new-generation ATR 72 turbo aircraft.

From late March to late October, there are theoretically at least two scheduled flights a day from Warsaw to each of the above destinations except Rzeszów, which is serviced by only four flights a week. In the remainder of the year, there are fewer flights, usually one or two per day, and a couple per week to Rzeszów. In practice, however, there may be still fewer flights: occupancy is low, sometimes very low, and cancellation or suspension of LOT flights is a fact of life.

The regular one-way fare on any of the direct flights to/from Warsaw is around US$140, except for Szczecin (US$170). Any combined flight via Warsaw (eg Szczecin-Kraków or Gdańsk-Wrocław) will cost around US$175. Tickets can be booked and bought at any LOT and Orbis office, and from some travel agencies.

Senior citizens over 60 years of age pay 80% of the full fare on all domestic flights. Foreign students holding an ISIC card get a 10% discount. There are attractive stand-by fares (about 25% of the regular fare) for young people below 20 and students below 26; tickets have to be bought right before scheduled departure. There are also some promotional fares on some flights in some periods (eg early or late flights, selected weekend flights etc); they can be just a third of the ordinary fares and are applicable to everybody.

Most airports are a manageable distance – between 10 and 20km – from city centres and are linked to them by public transport. Only Szczecin and Katowice airports are farther out. You must check in at least 30 minutes before departure. Have your passport at hand: you'll be asked to show it. There's no airport tax on domestic flights.

You probably won't be flying a lot in Poland. First, it's expensive compared with taking the train; second, it doesn't save much time except on long, across-country routes.

TRAIN

Trains will be your main means of transport around the country, especially when travelling long distances. Trains in Poland are still relatively inexpensive, pretty reliable and usually run on time. They are normally not overcrowded, except for occasional peaks in July and August.

Railways are administered by the Polskie Koleje Państwowe (Polish State Railways), commonly known by the abbreviation PKP. With over 27,000km of lines, the railway network is fairly extensive and covers most places you might wish to go to. Most of the important lines have been electrified and steam has virtually disappeared save for a handful of narrow-gauge lines. Predictably, the network covers less of the mountainous parts of Poland, and trains are slower there.

Types of Train

There are three main types of train: express, fast and ordinary. The express train (*pociąg ekspresowy* or *ekspres*) is the fastest and the most comfortable of them. These trains only stop at major cities. They cover long intercity routes and carry only bookable seats; you can't travel standing if all the seats are sold out. Express trains tend to run in the morning or evening, rather than overnight. Their average speed is 80 to 100km/h.

A more luxurious version of the express train, the InterCity train, came into operation in the early 1990s. InterCity trains are even faster and more comfortable than regular express trains, and a light meal is included

POLISH RAILWAYS

in the price. These trains run on some major routes out of Warsaw and they don't stop en route at all. The main destinations (along with distances and approximate travelling times) include: Gdańsk (333km, three hours 20 minutes), Katowice (303km, two hours 40 minutes), Kraków (297km, two hours 35 minutes), Poznań (311km, three hours 10 minutes) and Szczecin (525km, five hours 40 minutes).

The fast train (pociąg pospieszny) stops at more intermediate stations. Usually not all carriages require booking; some will take passengers regardless of how crowded they get. At an average speed of between 60 and 80km/h, fast trains are still a convenient way to get around the country and are one-third cheaper than express trains. They often travel at night, and if the distance justifies it they carry couchettes (kuszetki) or sleepers (miejsca sypialne) – a good way to avoid hotel costs and reach your destination early in the morning. Book as soon as you decide to go, as there are usually only a couple of sleeping cars and beds tend to run out fast.

An ordinary or local train *(pociąg osobowy)* is far slower as it stops at every single station along the way. These trains mostly cover shorter distances, but they do run on long routes as well. You can assume that their average speed will be between 30 and 40km/h. They are less comfortable than express or fast trains and don't require reservations. It's OK to travel a short distance, but a longer journey can be tiring and is not recommended.

Almost all trains carry two classes: 2nd class *(druga klasa)*, and 1st class *(pierwsza klasa)*, which is 50% more expensive. The carriages of long-distance trains are usually divided into compartments: the 1st class compartments have six seats, while the 2nd class ones contain eight seats. Smoking is allowed in some compartments and the part of the corridor facing them, but many Poles are chain smokers and a journey in such company is almost unbearable. It's better to book a seat in a nonsmoking compartment and go into the smoking corridor if you wish to smoke.

The 2nd class couchette compartments have six beds, three to a side; the 1st class compartments have four beds, two to a side. Sleepers also come in both 2nd and 1st class; the former sleep three to a compartment, the latter only two, and both have a washbasin, sheets and blankets.

Train Stations

Most larger train stations are purpose-built and of a reasonable standard. They have a range of facilities, including waiting rooms, snack bars, newsstands, left-luggage rooms and toilets. The biggest stations in the major cities may also have a restaurant, a kantor (money exchange office) and a post office. In some small villages, on the other hand, the station can be just a sort of shed without facilities except for a ticket window, which will be open for a short time before trains arrive. If there's more than one train station in a city, the main one is identified by the name 'Główny' and is the one which handles

most of the traffic and usually the only one to operate express trains.

Some train stations – even major ones – are poorly marked, and, unless you're familiar with the route, it's easy to miss your stop. If in doubt, asking fellow passengers is probably the best plan of action.

All large stations have left-luggage rooms *(przechowalnia bagażu)*, which are usually open round the clock. You can store your luggage there for up to 10 days. There's a low basic daily storage charge per item (about US$0.50), plus 1% of the declared value of the luggage as insurance. These cloakrooms seem to be secure. One thing to remember is that they usually close once or twice a day for an hour or so. The times of these breaks are displayed over the counter. If you've put your baggage in storage, be sure to arrive at least half an hour before your departure time to allow time for some queuing and paperwork. You pay the charge when you pick your luggage up, not when you deposit it.

Timetables

Train timetables *(rozkład jazdy)* are displayed in all stations, with departures *(odjazdy)* usually on yellow boards and arrivals *(przyjazdy)* usually on white ones.

The ordinary trains are marked in black print, fast trains in red, and if you spot an additional 'Ex', this means an express train. InterCity trains are identified by the letters 'IC'. The letter 'R' in a square indicates a train with compulsory seat reservation. There will be some letters and/or numbers following the departure time; always check them in the key below. They usually say that the train runs *(kursuje)* or doesn't run *(nie kursuje)* in particular periods or days. The timetables also indicate which platform *(peron)* the train departs from.

Tickets

Since most of the large stations have been computerised, buying tickets *(bilety)* is now less of a hassle than it used to be, but queuing is still a way of life. Be at the station at least half an hour before the departure time of your train and make sure you are queuing at the right ticket window. As cashiers rarely speak English, the easiest way of buying a ticket is to have all relevant details written down on a piece of paper. These should include the destination, the departure time and the class (pierwsza klasa or druga klasa). If seat reservation is compulsory on your train, you'll automatically be sold a reserved seat ticket *(miejscówka)*; if it's optional, you must state whether you want a miejscówka or not.

If you are forced to get on a train without a ticket, you can buy one directly from the conductor for a small supplement, but you should find him/her right away. If the conductor finds you first, you'll be fined for travelling without a ticket.

Couchettes and sleepers can be booked at special counters at the larger stations; it's advisable to reserve them in advance. Advance tickets for journeys of over 100km, couchettes and sleepers can also be bought at Orbis offices, which is usually quicker.

Fares

Fast-train tickets are 50% dearer than those for ordinary trains, and an express train costs 33% more than a fast train (ie twice as much as an ordinary train). First class is 50% more expensive than 2nd class. Following are approximate prices of 2nd class tickets.

Distance (km)	Ordinary (US$)	Fast (US$)	Express (US$)
50	1.80	2.70	3.60
100	3.10	4.65	6.20
150	4.00	6.00	8.00
200	4.60	6.90	9.20
250	5.10	7.65	10.20
300	5.60	8.40	11.20
350	6.00	9.00	12.00
400	6.30	9.45	12.60
450	6.50	9.75	13.00
500	6.70	10.05	13.40

A reserved seat ticket costs an additional US$2 (US$3 on IC trains) regardless of distance. A 2nd/1st class couchette costs an additional US$11/14, while a sleeper costs an additional US$21/32.

The approximate fares on InterCity trains (including the compulsory seat reservation) from Warsaw to any one of Gdańsk, Katowice, Kraków and Poznań are US$17/24 in 2nd/1st class, and those to Szczecin are US$19/27.

There are no discounts for ISIC card holders on domestic trains, even though there are reduced fares for Polish students.

Rail Passes

The Eurotrain Explorer pass is available to people under 26 years of age, ISIC card holders, teachers and their spouses and children. Individual Explorer passes for Poland, Hungary, the Czech and Slovak republics and several other countries allow for a week's unlimited 2nd class travel within the respective country. You must buy these passes outside the country where they are to be used.

You may also be interested in the internal Polrail Pass offered by PKP, which allows for unlimited travel on the entire domestic rail network. The pass comes in durations of eight days (US$65/95 2nd/1st class), 15 days (US$75/110), 21 days (US$85/130) and 30 days (US$110/160). Persons aged under 26 years on the first day of travel can buy a 'Junior' pass for about 25% less. Seat reservation fees are included. The pass is available from North American travel agencies through Rail Europe or Orbis/Polorbis offices abroad (see Tourist Offices in the Facts for the Visitor chapter), and it also can be bought in Poland.

Security

Theft on international trains is becoming a problem, mainly on the Berlin-Warsaw trains, which are notorious for gangs of thieves who unlock compartments and rob the valuables of the sleeping passengers. There have been some recent reports of armed assaults in these trains. Most cases of theft occur between the German/Polish border and Poznań. You should also be on guard in the Berlin-Kraków and Prague-Warsaw trains, though theft here hasn't reached alarming proportions so far.

Some travellers have been robbed at knifepoint in slow local trains while sitting by themselves in a compartment. They were easy prey for robbers, who could do their job inconspicuously, then get off at the next tiny station and disappear without a trace. Don't sit in a cabin alone; join other passengers.

Watch your luggage and your pockets closely when you are getting on or off the train, as these are the most convenient moments for muggers to distract your attention. Warsaw central train station is the favourite playground for robbers, and is therefore a place in which to exercise particular care.

BUS

Buses are often more convenient than trains over a short distance. On longer routes, too, you may sometimes find a bus better and faster when, for instance, the train route involves a long detour. You'll often travel by bus in the mountains, where trains are slow and few. Ordinary buses on short routes are cheaper than the 2nd class of ordinary trains.

Most bus transport is operated by the state bus company, Państwowa Komunikacja Samochodowa, or PKS. The total network of bus routes is much more comprehensive than that of trains, and buses go to almost all villages which are accessible by road. The frequency of service varies a great deal: on the main routes there may be a bus leaving every quarter of an hour or so, whereas some small, remote villages may be visited by only one bus per day. Except for a handful of long-distance buses which travel by night, the vast majority of buses run during the day, sometimes starting very early in the morning.

Unlike PKP, which monopolises the whole train service, PKS is experiencing increasing competition. There are a number of small private operators which run vans, minibuses and buses on regional routes, mostly short-distance. The biggest competitor, though, is Polski Express, a joint venture

with Eurolines National Express based in Britain. It runs several major long-distance routes out of Warsaw, including Białystok, Gdańsk (via Ostróda and Elbląg), Kraków (via Radom and Kielce or Łódź and Katowice), Rzeszów (via Puławy and Lublin) and Szczecin (via Płock, Toruń and Bydgoszcz). It is faster and more comfortable than PKS, and costs much the same.

Types of Bus

There are two types of PKS bus service. The ordinary or local buses (autobusy zwykłe) stop at all stops on the route and their average speed hardly exceeds 35 km/h. The standard of these buses leaves a little to be desired. Their departure and arrival times are written in black on timetable boards. The fast buses (autobusy pospieszne), marked in red, cover mainly long-distance routes and run as fast as 45 to 55km/h. As a rule, they take only as many passengers as they have seats. Their standard tends to be better than that of the ordinary buses.

Bus Terminals

The PKS bus terminal (dworzec autobusowy PKS) is usually found alongside the train station. Save for the large terminals in the major cities, bus terminals don't normally provide a left-luggage service and have few other facilities. They are closed at night. Polski Express uses PKS terminals at most but not all cities.

Timetables

Timetables are posted on boards either inside or outside PKS bus-terminal buildings. There are also notice boards on all bus stops along the route (if vandals haven't damaged or removed them). The timetable of departures (odjazdy) lists destinations (kierunek), the places passed en route (przez) and departure times.

Keep in mind that there may be more buses to the particular town you want to go to than those which are mentioned in the destination column of the timetable under the town's name. You therefore need to check whether your town doesn't appear in the przez (via) column on the way to more distant destinations.

Also check any additional symbols which accompany the departure time, which can mean that the bus runs only on certain days or in certain seasons. They're explained in the key at the end of the timetable.

Tickets

The only place to buy PKS tickets is the terminal itself; Orbis doesn't handle this service. Tickets on long routes serviced by fast buses can be bought up to 30 days in advance but those for short, local routes are only available the same day.

Tickets are numbered, and buying one at the counter at the terminal assures you of a seat. If you get on the bus somewhere along the route, you buy the ticket directly from the driver and you won't necessarily have a seat.

Tickets for Polski Express buses can be bought at the terminals where they arrive/depart from (PKS or the company's own), and from major Orbis offices.

Fares

The approximate fares for ordinary and fast PKS buses are as follows:

Distance (km)	Ordinary (US$)	Fast (US$)
20	0.75	1.00
40	1.30	1.60
60	1.75	2.25
80	2.20	2.90
100	2.75	3.50
120	3.20	4.10
140	3.70	4.70
160	4.20	5.20
180	4.70	5.80
200	5.20	6.40
220	5.70	6.90
240	6.20	7.40

Polski Express may be an interesting alternative to both PKS bus and PKP train on some of its long-distance routes. Following are some of its destinations out of Warsaw:

	Distance (km)	Fare (US$)	Time (hrs)	No (daily)
Białystok	188	5.75	3½	3
Bydgoszcz	255	8.75	4½	14
Gdańsk	339	10.00	5¾	2
Lublin	161	6.00	3	7
Łódź	134	5.00	2½	7
Rzeszów	303	10.00	6¼	1
Toruń	209	7.50	3¾	14

Students below 26 (ISIC cards accepted) and senior citizens over 60 get a 30% discount on all fares from Tuesday to Thursday.

CAR & MOTORCYCLE

Travelling with your own vehicle is a far more comfortable way to visit Poland than by using the public trains and buses. The biggest bonus, though, is the opportunity to get far away from the cities, exploring obscure villages and distant countryside, stopping on the way when you wish. With the relatively low price of petrol and the reasonable roads, travelling by car in Poland really does have lots of advantages.

The *Atlas Samochodowy*, the book-format road map of Poland, is helpful. Two kinds are available, differing in format and scale (1:250,000 or 1:300,000). Apart from the detailed maps, they both contain a full index of localities, sketch maps of major towns and cities complete with locations of filling stations, and a table of the traffic signs used in Poland.

Roads

Poland has a dense network of sealed roads that total 220,000km. The massive increase in traffic over recent years, along with extreme climatic conditions, have led to deterioration in road surfaces, with some in better shape than others.

There are only a few motorways in the proper sense of the word, but an array of two and four-lane highways crisscross the country; some of these roads can be quite crowded. Secondary roads are narrower but they usually carry less traffic and are OK

Road Distances (km)

	Białystok	Bydgoszcz	Częstochowa	Gdańsk	Katowice	Kielce	Kraków	Lublin	Łódź	Olsztyn	Opole	Poznań	Rzeszów	Szczecin	Toruń	Warsaw	Wrocław	Zielona Góra
Białystok	---																	
Bydgoszcz	389	---																
Częstochowa	410	316	---															
Gdańsk	379	167	470	---														
Katowice	485	391	75	545	---													
Kielce	363	348	124	483	156	---												
Kraków	477	430	114	565	75	114	---											
Lublin	260	421	288	500	323	167	269	---										
Łódź	322	205	121	340	196	143	220	242	---									
Olsztyn	223	217	404	156	479	394	500	370	281	---								
Opole	507	318	98	485	113	220	182	382	244	452	---							
Poznań	491	129	289	296	335	354	403	465	212	323	261	---						
Rzeszów	430	516	272	642	244	163	165	170	306	516	347	517	---					
Szczecin	656	267	520	348	561	585	634	683	446	484	459	234	751	---				
Toruń	347	46	289	181	364	307	384	375	159	172	312	151	470	313	---			
Warsaw	188	255	222	339	297	181	295	161	134	213	319	310	303	524	209	---		
Wrocław	532	265	176	432	199	221	268	428	204	442	86	178	433	371	279	344	---	
Zielona Góra	601	259	328	411	356	422	427	542	303	453	245	130	585	214	281	413	157	---

for leisurely travel. The sealed minor roads, which are even narrower, are also often in acceptable condition, though driving is harder work as they tend to twist and turn, are not so well signposted and pass through every single village along the way.

In 1995, the government approved the construction of a new system of motorways. The project includes four major freeways (Gdańsk-Toruń-Łódź-Częstochowa-Katowice-Gorzyce; Świecko-Poznań-Warsaw-Terespol; Szczecin-Zielona Góra-Legnica-Lubawka; and Zgorzelec-Wrocław-Opole-Katowice-Kraków-Medyka), and is due to be completed by 2010. The combined length of the roads will be 2600km and the project is expected to cost about US$15 billion.

Road Rules

As in the rest of continental Europe, you drive on the right-hand side of the road in Poland. Also as in most countries, traffic coming from the right has priority unless indicated otherwise by signs. Driving rules and traffic signs are similar to those in the west, although with some local variations.

Unless signs state otherwise, cars and motorcycles can be parked on pavements, as long as a minimum 1.5m-wide walkway is left for pedestrians. Parking in the opposite direction to the flow of traffic is allowed. Some traffic signs that may be unfamiliar to Britons and non-European visitors include:

Blue disc with red border and red slash: no parking on the road, but you still can park on the pavement; if the sign is accompanied by a white board below saying 'dotyczy również chodnika' or 'dotyczy także chodnika' ('it also refers to the pavement'), you can't park on either the road or the pavement
Blue disc with red border and crossed red slashes: no stopping

White disc with red border: no vehicles allowed
Red disc with horizontal white line: no entry
Yellow triangle (point down) with red border: give way to crossing or merging traffic
Yellow diamond with white border: you have right of way; a black slash through it means you no longer have right of way

The permitted blood alcohol level is 0.02%, so it's best not to drink at all before driving. Seat belts must be worn by the driver and front-seat passengers at all times. From October to February, car and motorbike lights must be on at all times while driving, even during a sunny day. Cars must be equipped with a first-aid kit, a left-hand outside rear mirror and a red warning triangle which has to be placed behind the car in the event of accident or breakdown. Motorcyclists should remember that both rider and passenger must wear crash helmets.

Traffic signs may override the general rules and sometimes they impose ridiculously low speed limits. Don't ignore them, however, as these are favourite spots for the police's well hidden radar speed traps.

Following are the maximum speed limits on Polish roads:

60km/h (37mph) for all vehicles throughout built-up areas

80km/h (50mph) for all vehicles pulling caravans or trailers outside built-up areas, motorways included

90km/h (56mph) for cars and motorbikes on roads outside built-up areas

100km/h (62mph) for cars and motorbikes on two-lane express highways

110km/h (69mph) for cars and motorbikes on four-lane express highways

130km/h (81mph) for cars and motorbikes on motorways

On the approach roads into towns and villages there are signs bearing the name of the locality. If the background of the sign is green there's no need to reduce speed, unless the road signs state otherwise. If the background of the sign is white you must reduce speed to 60km/h, even though the area doesn't exactly look built-up but rather a bucolic countryside. Police speed traps often hide in such places. The same sign with a diagonal line through it marks the end of the 'built-up' area. There's a nice custom of flashing lights which drivers use to warn oncoming vehicles of a radar trap ahead.

In the cities, be careful with trams, especially if you haven't been used to driving alongside them before. Special care should be taken when crossing the tramway, particularly while turning left and on roundabouts; in both cases you have to give way to trams. If you see a tram halting at a stop in the middle of the street, you are obliged to stop behind it and let all passengers get off and on. However, if there's a pedestrian island, you don't have to stop.

Petrol

Petrol is now readily available at hundreds of petrol stations, which have mushroomed throughout Poland. They sell several kinds and grades of petrol, including 94 octane leaded (US$0.60 per litre), 95 octane unleaded (US$0.60), 98 octane unleaded (US$0.65) and diesel (US$0.50). A 25% rise in petrol prices is planned for 1999. The

'Detour' road sign

price of fuel is roughly the same all over Poland. As yet, few petrol stations accept credit cards, but this is likely to change.

Virtually all petrol stations have adopted a self-service system, which was almost unknown previously. Air and water are usually available, as well as oil, lubricants and basic spare parts such as light bulbs, fuses etc. An increasing number of new stations also offer food. Many stations located along main roads and in the large cities are open round the clock.

Rental

Avis, Budget, Hertz and other international agencies are now well represented in Poland, and there are also plenty of local operators. Most rental vehicles are European makes, such as Peugeot, Renault, Opel, Fiat, VW, BMW, Audi, Mercedes and Volvo.

One-way rentals within Poland are possible with most companies (usually for an additional fee), but most will insist on keeping the car within Poland. In any case, no company is likely to allow you to take their car beyond the eastern border.

Rental agencies will require you to produce your passport, a driver's licence held for at least one year, and a credit card. You need to be at least 21 or 23 years of age to rent a car, although renting some cars, particularly luxury models and 4WDs, may require a higher age.

Car rental is not cheap in Poland – the prices are comparable to, or even higher than, full-price rental in western Europe – and there are seldom any promotional discounts. As a rough guide only, economy models offered by reputable companies begin at around US$60 a day plus US$0.35/km, or US$100 daily with unlimited mileage. Add US$10 to US$30 (depending on the model) a day for compulsory insurance. All car rental companies have discount rates if you are going to use the car for a longer time, a week being the usual minimum period. The local operators are cheaper, but their cars and rental conditions may leave something to be desired.

It's usually cheaper to prebook your car from abroad rather than to front up at an agency inside Poland. Furthermore, this will ensure that you have the car you need upon arrival in Poland; otherwise you may wait for a few days or, sometimes, a few weeks.

It would be cheaper to rent a car in the west, say in Berlin, and drive it into Poland, but few rental companies will allow you to take their car to the east.

When renting a car, read the contract carefully before signing it. Pay close attention to any theft clause, as it may load a large percentage of any loss onto the hirer. Check the car carefully before you drive off.

It's next to impossible to hire a motorcycle in Poland.

Bringing Your Own Vehicle

An increasing number of western tourists, mainly Germans, bring their own vehicles with them into Poland. There are no special formalities: all you need at the border is your passport with a valid visa if necessary, your driving licence and vehicle insurance for Poland (the so-called Green Card). If your insurance isn't valid for Poland you must buy an additional policy at the border. The car registration number will be entered in your passport. A nationality plate or sticker has to be displayed on the back of the car.

If you come from outside Europe and plan on travelling in Poland (and/or other European countries) for quite a while, it may be worth buying a second-hand car somewhere in the west, then selling it after the trip. It's best to sell the car in the country where you bought it, to avoid lengthy registration procedures.

If you decide to bring your own vehicle to Poland, remember that life will be easier for you if it's not brand-new or a fancy recent model. A more modest vehicle won't draw crowds of curious peasants – or gangs of thieves in large cities. The shabbier your car looks, the better. Don't wash it too often.

There's a pretty widespread network of garages that specialise in fixing western cars (though not many for motorcycles), but they mostly deal with older, traditional models with mechanical technology. The more electronics and computer-controlled bits your car has, the more problems you'll face having something fixed if it goes wrong. These parts can be ordered for you, but they'll usually take a while to arrive, and you'll pay inflated western prices.

Security & Hazards

Bring along a good insurance policy from a reliable company for both the car and your possessions. Car theft is well established in Poland, with several gangs operating in the large cities. Some of them cooperate with Russians in smuggling stolen vehicles across the eastern border, never to be seen again.

Even if the car itself doesn't get stolen, you might lose some of its accessories, most likely the radio/cassette player, as well as any personal belongings you've left inside. Hide your gear, if you must leave it inside; try to make the car look empty. Preferably, take your luggage to the hotel you stay in. If possible, always park your car in a guarded car park (parking strzeżony). If your hotel doesn't have its own, the staff will tell you where the nearest one is, probably within walking distance. The cost per night shouldn't be more than US$5.

In the cities, it may be more convenient and safer to leave your vehicle in a secure place (eg your hotel car park), and get around by taxi or public transport.

Drive carefully on country roads, particularly at night. There are still a lot of horse-drawn carts on Polish roads, and the farther off the main routes you wander, the more carts, tractors and other agricultural machinery you'll encounter. They are lit poorly or not at all. The same applies to bicycles – you'll hardly ever see a properly lit bike. Pedestrians are another problem, drunks staggering along the middle of the road being the biggest danger.

BICYCLE

Poland is not a bad place for cycling. Most of the country is fairly flat, so riding is easy and any ordinary bike is OK. If you plan on travelling in the mountainous southern regions, you'll do better with a multispeed bike. Camping equipment isn't essential, as hotels and hostels are usually no more than an easy day's ride apart, but carrying your own camping gear does give you more flexibility.

Major roads can carry pretty heavy traffic and are best avoided. Instead, you can easily plan your route along secondary and other minor roads, which are usually much less crowded and in fair shape. You'll thus have a chance to see villages and small towns which are bypassed by main arteries. Stock up with detailed tourist maps, which feature all minor roads, specifying which are sealed and which are not, and also show waymarked walking trails. Some of these trails are easily travelled by bike, which gives you still more itinerary options.

On a less optimistic note, the standard of driving in Poland may not exactly be what you've been used to at home. Some vehicles may drive along the middle of the road and fail to move over for you. The number of upmarket western cars has soared in recent years (Poland is believed to have Europe's largest population of Mercedes outside Germany), and some drivers may relentlessly overtake anything in their path – particularly cyclists – regardless of oncoming traffic. Note that in Poland cyclists are not allowed to ride two abreast.

Cities are not pleasant for cyclists, as separate bike tracks are almost nonexistent, and some car drivers are not particularly polite to cyclists. Furthermore, city roads are often in poor shape, and cobbled streets are not uncommon.

Hotel staff will usually let you put your bike indoors for the night, sometimes in your room; it's often better to leave it in the hotel during the day as well, and get around city sights on foot or by public transport. Bikes, especially western ones, are attractive to thieves, so it's a good idea to carry a solid lock and chain, for the frame and both wheels, and always use them when you leave the bike outdoors, even if only for a moment.

Lake Morskie Oko in the Tatra Mountains

Traditional religious celebrations in Zakopane

Old poster column at Wilanów's Poster Museum

Popular art on wheels, Polish-style.

Richly decorated Bernardine church in Kalisz

Traditional costumes, Corpus Christi celebrations in Łowicz

Pole-ish stork

If you want to skip part of Poland to visit another region, you can take your bike on the train. Some long-distance trains include a freight carriage. If this is the case, you should normally take your bike to the railway luggage office, fill out a tag and pay a small fee. They will then load the bike and drop it off at your destination. It's a good idea to strip the bike of anything easily removable and keep an eye out to be sure they've actually loaded it on your train. You could also take your bike straight to the freight carriage (which is usually attached at the front or the rear of the train), but this can be hard to do at intermediate stations where the train may only stop for a few minutes. Collect the bike as soon as you arrive.

Bikes are not allowed on express trains or on those that take reservations, since these trains don't carry baggage cars. Many ordinary trains don't have baggage cars either, but you can try to take the bike into the passenger car with you as some Poles do. Check at the baggage window in the station before you do so. Buses don't normally take bikes.

Cycling shops and repair centres are popping up in Warsaw and other cities, and in some of the major tourist resorts. You can now buy various makes of western bikes and some popular spare parts – at western prices, of course. For rural riding, you should carry all essential spare parts, for it's unlikely there'll be a bike shop around. In particular, spare nuts and bolts should be carried. Given the jolting from Poland's numerous cobbled roads, cyclists should check their bikes frequently.

Bike-rental outlets are still few and far between. They seldom offer anything other than ordinary Polish bikes, and their condition may leave a bit to be desired.

HITCHING

Hitchhiking (autostop) is never entirely safe anywhere in the world. Travellers who decide to hitch should understand that they are taking a small but potentially serious risk. Those who choose to hitch will be safer if they travel in pairs, and let someone know where they are planning to go.

That said, hitching does take place in Poland, though it's not very popular. Car drivers rarely stop to pick up hitchhikers, and large commercial vehicles (which are easier to wave down) expect to be paid the equivalent of a bus fare.

BOAT

Poland has a long coastline and lots of rivers and canals, but the passenger-boat service is pretty limited and operates only in summer. There are no regular boats running along the main rivers or along the coast. Several cities, including Szczecin, Gdańsk, Toruń, Wrocław and Kraków, have local river cruises in summer, and a few coastal ports (Kołobrzeg and Gdańsk) offer sea excursions.

On the Masurian lakes, excursion boats run in summer between Giżycko, Mikołajki, Węgorzewo and Ruciane-Nida. Tourist boats are also available in the Augustów area where they ply a part of the Augustów Canal. The most unusual canal trip is the full-day cruise along the Elbląg-Ostróda Canal. There is also a spectacular raft trip through the Dunajec Gorge in the Pieniny Mountains.

LOCAL TRANSPORT
Bus, Tram & Trolleybus

Most cities have both buses (autobus) and trams (tramwaj), and some also have trolleybuses (trolejbus). Public transport operates from around 5 am to 11 pm and may be crowded during the rush hours. The largest cities also have night-time services, on either bus or tram. Timetables are usually posted at stops, but don't rely too much on their accuracy.

In most cities there's a flat-rate fare for local transport so the duration of the ride and the distance make no difference. If you change vehicles, however, you need another ticket. The ordinary fare is around US$0.40. In some cities there are also the so-called fast buses (autobus pospieszny), which ignore minor stops and cost twice the ordinary fare. Night services are still more expensive. An ISIC card gives a 50% discount in Warsaw only.

Each piece of bulky luggage (legally anything measuring more than 60 x 40 x 20cm) is an additional ordinary fare.

There are no conductors on board; you buy tickets beforehand and punch or stamp them upon boarding in one of the little machines installed near the doors. You can buy tickets from Ruch kiosks or, in some cities, from street stalls around the central stops, recognisable by the bilety (tickets) boards they display. Buy a bunch of them at once if you are going to use public transport. Buy enough tickets on Saturday morning to last you until Monday, as few kiosks are open on Sunday. Tickets purchased in one city cannot be used in another. Make sure you punch the correct ticket value – you may have to punch one or both ends of the ticket or, on fast buses, a couple of tickets; ask other passengers if in doubt.

The plain-clothed ticket inspectors control tickets more often today than they did before and foreign backpackers are their favourite targets. These inspectors tend to be officious, dogged and singularly unpleasant to deal with.

If you are caught without a ticket, it's best to pay the fine straight away. Never give an inspector your passport, even if they threaten you with police intervention if you don't.

Taxi

Taxis are easily available and not too expensive by western standards. As a rough guide, a 5km taxi trip will cost around US$3, and a 10km ride shouldn't cost more than US$5. Taxi fares are 50% higher at night (10 pm to 6 am) and outside the city limits. The number of passengers (usually up to four) and the amount of luggage don't affect the fare.

There are plenty of taxi companies, including the once monopolist state-run Radio Taxi (☎ 919), which is the largest and operates in most cities. Taxis are recognisable by large boards on the roof with the company's name and its phone number. There are also pirate taxis (called by Poles the 'mafia'), which usually have just a small 'taxi' label on the roof without any name or phone number. Mafia taxis are a plague in Warsaw and are now spreading to some other large cities, principally Kraków and Łódź. They are mostly to be found at major tourist haunts such as airports, top-class hotels and important tourist sights. They tend to overcharge up to several times the normal fare and should be avoided at all costs.

Taxis can be waved down on the street, but it's much easier to go to a taxi stand (postój taksówek) where you'll almost always find a line of them. There are plenty of such stands and everybody will tell you where the nearest one is. Taxis can also be ordered by phone, and there's usually no extra charge for this service. Taxis should normally arrive within 10 minutes unless you request one at a specified time later on.

Taxis have meters, but due to constant inflation some meters may not be adjusted to the current tariff. In this case the fare shown on the meter has to be multiplied by a factor which should be displayed in the taxi. The factor may vary from city to city and from taxi to taxi depending on when the last adjustment was made.

When you get into a taxi, make sure the driver turns on the meter. Also check whether the meter has been switched to the proper rate: '1' identifies the daytime rate, and '2' is the night rate. A typical drivers' scam for foreigners is to drop the flag to the higher night rate during the daytime.

Remember to carry smaller bills, so you'll be able to pay the right fare. If you don't, it's virtually impossible to get change back from the driver who's intent on charging you more. It's always a good idea to find out beforehand how much the right fare should be by asking the hotel staff or an attendant at the airport.

ORGANISED TOURS

For tours organised from outside Poland, see Organised Tours in the Getting There & Away chapter. Included below are tours organised in Poland by Polish agencies and you'll normally arrange them after coming to Poland. See the relevant regional sections for further information about the agencies, their tours, prices etc.

City tours are organised by several companies in Warsaw and Kraków. The same agencies offer various regional tours.

Jewish tourism is run by some specialised operators, including Our Roots in Warsaw and Jarden in Kraków.

Almatur (with its offices in Poland's larger cities, including Warsaw, Kraków, Gdańsk and Wrocław) offers two-week sailing, kayaking and horse riding holidays in July and August. These trips are intended mainly for students and are priced very reasonably.

Mazury travel agency in Olsztyn runs regular 10-day kayak tours along the Kru-tynia River from late June to mid-August. Similar kayak trips along Czarna Hańcza River are available from several agencies in Augustów. Various operators in Masuria (principally in Giżycko and Mikołajki) handle yacht rental.

Some new-generation 'green' tour operators, including Kampio in Warsaw, Bird Service Tours in Białystok and Eko-Tourist in Kraków, organise nature tours (birdwatching, kayaking, biking etc) in out-of-the-way areas. It may be a good idea to contact them before you set off from home to see what their programs and schedules are.

PTTK (with its offices in most major cities) can provide foreign-language guides for city and country trips.

Warsaw

• pop 1,650,000 ☎ 022

The capital of Poland, Warsaw (Warszawa in Polish, pronounced 'Vah-shah-vah') is set roughly in the centre of the country and is twice as populous as the nation's second-largest city, Łódź. Its size and status make it the major focus of political, scientific and educational life.

Annihilated during WWII then emerging like a phoenix from the ashes, Warsaw is essentially a postwar city. Its handful of historic precincts have been meticulously reconstructed, but most of its urban landscape is modern, including everything from dull products of the Stalin era to more creative accomplishments of recent years. The war also changed Warsaw's social structure; vast numbers of its citizens perished and the city was repopulated with new-comers, thus weakening its centuries-old cultural traditions.

A decade after the fall of communism, Warsaw has turned into a thrilling, busy city swiftly catching up with the west. It's Poland's most cosmopolitan, dynamic and progressive urban centre, dotted with luxury hotels, elegant shops and diverse services. Whether you are interested in theatre, good food, shopping, museums or bazaars, you will find more to choose from here than in any other Polish city.

In a way, Warsaw epitomises the Polish nation. It's a blend of old and new, in both appearance and spirit – respecting tradition but racing towards the future. Warsaw is an interesting layered cake which will take several days to digest.

Highlights

- Admire the Old Town, the historic core meticulously rebuilt from scratch
- Stroll through the charming park and palace complex of Łazienki
- Explore Wilanów, another lovely park and palace complex
- Discover a treasure trove of art at the National Museum
- Visit the Royal Castle to learn how kings once lived
- Treat yourself to an evening of opera at the Grand Theatre
- Browse around the gigantic bazaar at the 10th Anniversary Stadium

Warsaw p118
Central Warsaw p122
Warsaw – Old Town & Around p128

HISTORY

By Polish standards, Warsaw is a young city. When other towns such as Kraków, Poznań, Wrocław or Gdańsk were about to celebrate their quincentenaries, the present-day capital was just beginning to emerge from obscurity in the middle of the Mazovian forests.

Though traces of settlement in the area date from the 10th century, it was not until the beginning of the 14th century that the dukes of Mazovia built a stronghold on the site where the Royal Castle stands today, thus giving birth to a township. Like most medieval Polish towns, it was planned on a grid around a central square and surrounded with fortified walls. In 1413 the dukes made Warsaw their seat, and it began to develop more quickly. By then, the New Town had begun to emerge to the north outside the Old Town's walls. In 1526, after the last duke died without an heir, Warsaw and the whole of Mazovia came under the direct rule of the king in Kraków.

The turning point for Warsaw came in 1569, when the Sejm, which had convened in Lublin, unified Poland and Lithuania and voted to make Warsaw the seat of the Sejm's debates, because of its central position. Four years later, Warsaw also became the seat of royal elections, though kings continued to reside in Kraków. The final ennoblement came in 1596 when King Zygmunt III Waza decided to move the capital from Kraków to Warsaw. Reasons of state apart, the king seemed to have a personal motivation for the change – Warsaw was closer to Sweden, his motherland.

Like the rest of Poland, Warsaw fell prey to the Swedish invasion of 1655-60. The city suffered considerable damage, but soon recovered and continued to develop. Paradoxically, the 18th century – a period of catastrophic decline for the Polish state – witnessed Warsaw's greatest ever prosperity. It was then that a wealth of splendid palaces and a number of churches and monasteries were erected. Cultural and artistic life flourished, particularly during the reign of the last Polish king, Stanisław August Poniatowski. In 1791, the first constitution in Europe was signed in Warsaw. By then, the city had 120,000 inhabitants.

When Poland was partitioned in 1795, Warsaw found itself under Prussian domination and was reduced to the status of a provincial town. It became a capital once more in 1807 when Napoleon created the Duchy of Warsaw, and it continued as capital of the Congress Kingdom of Poland. In 1830, however, Poland fell under Russian rule and remained so till WWI broke out.

Steady urban development and industrialisation took place in the second half of the

Warsaw in the 16th century, a thriving town on the Vistula River which became the nation's capital

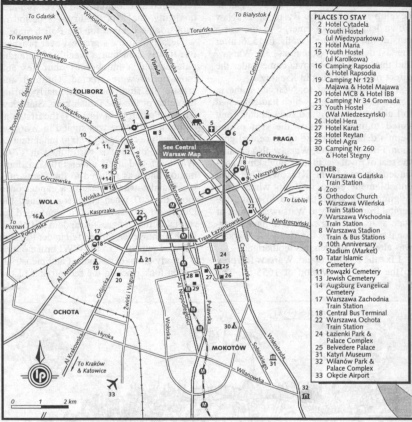

WARSAW

PLACES TO STAY
2 Hotel Cytadela
3 Youth Hostel
   (ul Miedzyparkowa)
12 Hotel Maria
15 Youth Hostel
   (ul Karolkowa)
16 Camping Rapsodia
   & Hotel Rapsodia
19 Camping Nr 123
   Majawa & Hotel Majawa
20 Hotel MCB & Hotel IBB
21 Camping Nr 34 Gromada
23 Youth Hostel
   (Wał Miedzeszyński)
26 Hotel Hera
27 Hotel Karat
28 Hotel Reytan
29 Hotel Agra
30 Camping Nr 260
   & Hotel Stegny

OTHER
1 Warszawa Gdańska
   Train Station
4 Zoo
5 Orthodox Church
6 Warszawa Wileńska
   Train Station
7 Warszawa Wschodnia
   Train Station
8 Warszawa Stadion
   Train & Bus Stations
9 10th Anniversary
   Stadium (Market)
10 Tatar Islamic
   Cemetery
11 Powązki Cemetery
13 Jewish Cemetery
14 Augsburg Evangelical
   Cemetery
17 Warszawa Zachodnia
   Train Station
18 Central Bus Terminal
22 Warszawa Ochota
   Train Station
24 Łazienki Park &
   Palace Complex
25 Belvedere Palace
31 Katyń Museum
32 Wilanów Park &
   Palace Complex
33 Okęcie Airport

19th century. A railway linking Warsaw with Vienna and St Petersburg was built. By 1900, there were 690,000 people living in Warsaw.

After WWI Warsaw was reinstated as the capital of independent Poland and within 20 years made considerable advances in the fields of industry, education, science and culture. The population increased from about 750,000 in 1918 to nearly 1.3 million in 1939. About 350,000 of the latter figure were Jews, who had traditionally made up a significant part of Warsaw's community.

Nazi bombs began to fall on 1 September 1939 and a week later the city was besieged. Despite brave resistance, Warsaw was finally forced to capitulate on 28 September. This, however, turned out to be only the beginning of the tragedy. The five-year Nazi occupation, marked by constant arrests, executions and deportations, triggered two acts of heroic armed resistance, both cruelly crushed.

The first was the Ghetto Uprising in April 1943, when heavily outnumbered and almost unarmed Jews who had been imprisoned in the city's ghetto fought fiercely for almost a month against massive Nazi forces. The victorious Nazis reduced the Jewish quarter to rubble.

The second and larger Warsaw Uprising aimed to liberate the capital and set up an independent government before the arrival of the Red Army (which was already on the opposite bank of the Vistula River). Street fighting began on 1 August 1944, but after 63 days the insurgents were forced to capitulate. For the next three months the Nazis methodically razed Warsaw to the ground. Only on 17 January 1945 did the Soviet army cross the river to 'liberate' the city.

According to postwar estimates, about 85% of Warsaw's buildings were destroyed and 700,000 people, over half of the city's prewar population, perished. No other Polish city suffered such immense loss of life or such devastation in the war. Given the level of destruction, there were even suggestions that the capital should move elsewhere.

After some consideration it was decided to rebuild parts of the prewar urban fabric. According to the plan, the most valuable historic monuments, most notably the Old Town, would be restored to their previous appearance based on the original drawings, which had survived the war. With the help of the citizenry, this gigantic task was carried out for over a decade and the result is truly spectacular.

Apart from historic monuments, the authorities had to build from scratch a whole new city capable of providing housing and services to its inhabitants. This communist legacy is less impressive. The city centre was until recently a blend of bunker-like Stalinist structures and equally boring edifices of a later era, while the outer suburbs, home to the majority of Warsaw's inhabitants, were composed almost exclusively of anonymous prefabricated concrete blocks.

With the arrival of the market economy, the face of Warsaw is changing rapidly. Newly constructed steel-and-glass towers are increasingly breaking the monotony of the grey landscape, shop windows are catching the eye with innovative designs and colour, and the city outskirts are steadily filling up with villas and family houses on a more human scale than the monstrous slabs of yesterday.

ORIENTATION

The city is divided by the Vistula (Wisła) River into two very different parts. The western, left-bank sector is much larger and includes the city centre proper and, to the north, the Old Town, the historic nucleus of Warsaw. Almost all tourist attractions, as well as the lion's share of tourist facilities, are on this side of the river. The eastern right-bank part of Warsaw, the suburb of Praga, has no major sights and sees few tourists.

The main focus of tourist interest is the Old Town area. To the south stretches the new city centre with the monstrous Palace of Culture and Science; this is not a place to go for historic monuments but for the bustling commercial atmosphere of contemporary Warsaw. A few kilometres south-east is the beautiful Łazienki park and palace, linked to the Old Town by the 4km-long Royal Way. Many tourist sights are along this route. Another attraction is Wilanów palace, on the southern outskirts of the city.

Finding your way around is relatively easy. The major inconvenience is that budget and mid-range accommodation is scattered over the city centre and beyond without a clearly defined 'hotel area', but cooperative tourist offices (including the ones at the airport and train station) are likely to find somewhere for you to crash.

If you arrive by air at Okęcie airport, urban bus No 175 and the AirportCity bus will take you to the centre, passing the youth hostel and a good number of hotels. Coming by train, you arrive at the central train station right in the city centre. When arriving by bus at the central bus terminal, you can get to the city centre by the commuter train from the adjoining Warszawa Zachodnia station or by urban bus. By whichever means you come, consider buying a city map, available from newsagents and tourist offices, or rely on one in the publications distributed free of charge (see Tourist Publications in the following section).

If you come by your own means of transport, just follow the signs saying 'Centrum'. Should you have any doubts, simply steer towards the spire of the giant Palace of Culture and Science, which marks the city centre.

INFORMATION
Tourist Offices
The city tourist office (☎ 94 31, fax 826 30 53), Plac Powstańców Warszawy 2, is open weekdays 8 am to 8 pm, Saturday 9 am to 5 pm, Sunday 9 am to 3 pm. It has outlets at the Okęcie airport (arrival hall), in the Rotunda PKO BP on the corner of ul Marszałkowska and Al Jerozolimskie, and in the Historical Museum of Warsaw at the Old Town Square.

Another tourist office (☎ 524 51 84, ☎/fax 654 24 47) is at the Warsaw central train station (ticket counters level), and is open daily 9 am to 7 pm (May to August till 8 pm on weekdays). It's also city-run but is independent of the above listed office.

The private tourist office (☎ 635 18 81), Plac Zamkowy 1/13 opposite the Royal Castle, is open weekdays 9 am to 6 pm, Saturday 10 am to 6 pm, Sunday 11 am to 6 pm (perhaps daily till 8 pm in July and August). It runs a tourist bookshop there.

All three tourist offices are knowledgeable and helpful, and all speak English. They all can find and book a hotel or hostel for you.

Tourist Publications
Pick up a copy of the free monthly magazines *Warszawa: What, Where, When* and *Welcome to Warsaw* at the tourist offices or at luxury hotels. Both include a map of central Warsaw and current information about tourist facilities. The best, however, is the comprehensive monthly *Warsaw Insider* (US$1.25), which also comes with the map of the central area. You may also want to buy the weekly *Warsaw Voice* (US$1.50) to know what's happening in local politics.

A booklet listing youth hostels in Poland is available (US$1.50) from Polskie Towarzystwo Schronisk Młodzieżowych (PTSM; ☎ 849 81 28, ☎ 849 83 54) at ul Chocimska 28, 4th floor, room 426 (open weekdays 8 am to 3 pm).

Foreign Embassies & Consulates
These are listed under Embassies & Consulates in the Facts for the Visitor chapter.

Money
Kantors are everywhere; in the city centre, you will find a kantor on every second block. Some of them work 24 hours, but they lower the exchange rate at night, so try to plan ahead and avoid large night-time transactions.

Travellers cheques are probably best changed at the American Express office (☎ 635 20 02) at ul Krakowskie Przedmieście 11 (open weekdays 9 am to 6 pm), which exchanges its own cheques as well as those of other major banks and charges no commission. The staff speak English and there are no crowds, unlike in the banks. It's here that you report the loss or theft of Amex cheques and apply for a refund. A poste restante service is also available – see the following section.

There's also an Amex outlet (☎ 630 69 52) in the Hotel Marriott, open weekdays 8 am to 8 pm, weekends 10 am to 6 pm. It changes travellers cheques but doesn't have poste restante service.

The Bank Pekao has a dozen offices in the city, including those at Plac Bankowy 2, ul Mazowiecka 14, ul Czackiego 21/23, ul Grójecka 1/3 and Al Jerozolimskie 65/79. The bank changes travellers cheques into cash dollars or złotys, whichever you prefer. You can also get cash advances on Visa and MasterCard here, either from the cashier or the bank's ATM. There has also been a rash of ATMs installed, independent of the banks, around the city centre.

Western Union Money Transfer (general information on ☎ 636 56 88 or toll-free ☎ 0800 20 224) can be found at a number of locations, including Plac Konstytucji 4, ul Krakowskie Przedmieście 55 and ul Marszałkowska 142.

Post & Communications

Warsaw has over 100 post offices, the main one being at ul Świętokrzyska 31/33. It's open 8 am to 8 pm for mail and round the clock for telephones. You can also send faxes from here. If you're going to send parcels abroad, there is a packing service and you don't have to worry about customs. This main post office (as well as most other post offices around the city) also has the reasonably cheap but unreliable EMS-Pocztex courier service.

Poste restante is at window No 12. If you want letters sent to you, the address is c/o Poste Restante, Poczta Główna, ul Świętokrzyska 31/33, 00-001 Warszawa 1. The mail is kept for 14 working days.

Amex card holders can also receive poste restante mail through the American Express office. Letters should be sent c/o American Express Travel, Dom Bez Kantów, ul Krakowskie Przedmieście 11, 00-068 Warszawa. Mail is kept for three months.

Warsaw has both six and seven-digit phone numbers; the former are being gradually converted to seven digits, usually by adding a digit at the beginning. Public telephones are still few and far between and many are out of order. Almost all public phones these days only operate on magnetic phonecards.

Email & Internet Access

Places providing email and Internet facilities include the PDI (☎ 622 66 11) at ul Nowogrodzka 12 m 29; Ośrodek Kultury Ochoty (☎ 822 48 70, ☎ 823 97 81) at ul Grójecka 75; and the pricey Cyberia (☎ 828 14 47) at ul Krakowskie Przedmieście 4/6.

The Telekomunikacja Polska offers email and Internet access at the company's three offices: ul Twarda 54 (☎ 0800 20 822), ul Targowa 33/35 (☎ 0800 20 828) and ul Wólczyńska 14 (☎ 0800 20 888). This is a promotional, free service but you should book up to a week in advance. The British Council (☎ 628 74 01), Al Jero-

zolimskie 59, provides free Internet access (but not email).

Travel Agencies

Orbis is the largest agency, with offices all over town, including ones at ul Bracka 16 (☎ 827 72 65), ul Marszałkowska 142 (☎ 827 08 75), ul Świętokrzyska 20 (☎ 826 20 16) and Plac Konstytucji 4 (☎ 629 92 01). It sells transportation tickets (air, train, ferry and Polski Express bus). It may be faster to buy your train tickets here than at the central train station.

Student travel is handled by Almatur (☎ 826 35 12, ☎ 826 26 39), ul Kopernika 23. It operates summertime student hostels and organises inexpensive sailing, kayaking and horse riding summer holidays. It also sells international air, bus and ferry tickets, and may have attractive discounts for students and people under 26 years. The Almatur outlet at ul Kopernika 8/18 (☎ 828 53 07) issues ISIC cards (US$7).

Trakt (☎ 827 80 68) at ul Kredytowa 6 offers guides in several major languages, English included (US$90 per group for any period up to five hours plus US$15 for each extra hour). The private tourist office at Plac Zamkowy 1/13 can arrange foreign-language guides for marginally less.

Our Roots (☎ 620 05 56), ul Twarda 6, next to the Nożyk Synagogue, is the Jewish travel bureau. The agency stocks some guidebooks and general publications referring to Jewish issues, and offers tours around Jewish monuments in Warsaw and beyond.

Bookshops

Some of the widest selection of maps and guidebooks (including Lonely Planet guidebooks) can be found in the Sklep Podróżnika (☎ 822 54 87) at ul Kaliska 8/10.

The American Bookstore (☎ 660 56 37), ul Koszykowa 55, is one of the best places for English-language publications, including contemporary and classic literature, coffee table books, specialist fare and magazines. It also has most Lonely Planet titles.

Other places for English-language stuff include Co Liber (☎ 828 05 88) at Plac

WARSAW

CENTRAL WARSAW

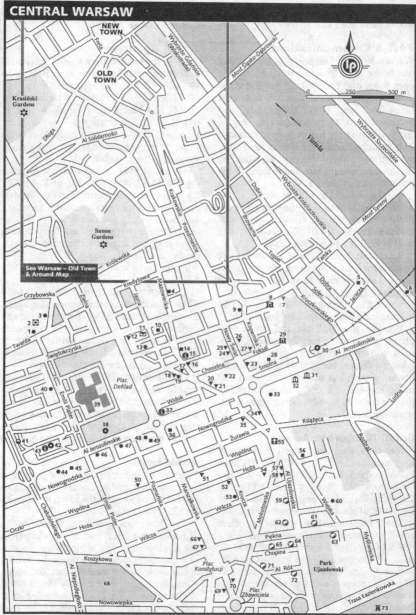

CENTRAL WARSAW

PLACES TO STAY
4   Hotel Mazowiecki
5   Hotel Belfer
6   Hotel na Wodzie
10   Hotel Warszawa
14   Dom Chłopa
28   Youth Hostel
36   Hotel Forum
45   Marriott Hotel
48   Hotel Polonia
49   Hotel Metropol
56   Sheraton Hotel

PLACES TO EAT
7   Salad Bar Tukan
12   Hortex
16   Wedel
17   Grill Bar Zgoda
18   Bar Krokiecik
19   Restauracja Chmielna
20   Między Nami
21   Bar Restauracyjny Expresso
22   Restauracja Polska
23   Bar Sandwicz
24   Café Blikle
25   Bar Mleczny Familijny
26   Restauracja Pacyfik
27   Tam Tam
34   Bar Mleczny Szwajcarski

35   Batida
50   Warsaw Tortilla Factory
51   Restauracja Mekong
52   Bar Mleczny Bambino
54   Restauracja Adler
57   Café Ejlat
58   Restauracja Klub Aktora
66   Bar Mleczny Złota Kurka
67   Hortex
69   Suparom Thai
70   Restauracja Maharaja

OTHER
1   Our Roots Jewish Travel
     Agency
2   Nożyk Synagogue
3   Jewish Theatre
8   Ostrogski Palace & Chopin
     Museum
9   Almatur Student Travel
     Agency
11   Main Post Office
13   Philharmonic Hall
15   Tourist Office
29   Zamoyski Palace
30   Warszawa Powiśle Train
     Station
31   Polish Army Museum
32   National Museum

33   Former Communist Party
     Headquarters
37   Tourist Office
38   Warszawa Śródmieście Train
     Station
39   Palace of Culture & Science
40   Akwarium Jazz Club
41   Polski Express Bus Stop
42   Warsaw Central Train Station
43   Tourist Office
44   LOT Office
46   British Council
47   Fotoplastikon
53   Biuro Kwater Prywatnych
     Syrena Univel (Private Rooms)
55   St Alexander's Church
59   Bulgarian Embassy
60   Parliament House
61   Canadian Embassy
62   US Embassy
63   French Embassy
64   Hungarian Embassy
65   Romanian Embassy
68   Warsaw University of
     Technology
71   Czech Embassy
72   UK Embassy
73   Ujazdów Castle & Centre of
     Contemporary Art

Bankowy 4, MIT (☎ 827 48 52) at ul Nowy Świat 61, Odeon (☎ 622 59 32) at ul Hoża 19, and Bookland (☎ 625 41 46) at Al Jerozolimskie 61.

The Księgarnia MDM (☎ 628 60 89), ul Koszykowa 34/50, just off Plac Konstytucji, houses IPS (International Publishing Service) on the 1st floor, featuring a reasonable choice of specialist publications (law, medicine, psychology etc) plus a fair number of coffee-table books.

The best bookshop with French-language literature is the Marianne (☎ 826 62 71), in the French Institute at ul Senatorska 38. It also has a decent selection of the French press. The only place carrying Spanish-language publications is the Elite (☎ 658 49 02) at ul Tarczyńska 1.

Foreign newspapers and magazines are available from some larger newsagencies, or you can try the foyers of the top-class hotels. The widest selection, however, is to be found in EMPiK stores at ul Nowy Świat 15/17 (☎ 827 06 50) and ul Marszałkowska 116/122 (☎ 827 82 96).

Cultural Centres

All of the foreign cultural centres have their own libraries with a selection of books and press from their country.

Austrian Institute of Culture
    (☎ 620 96 20) ul Próżna 8
British Council
    (☎ 628 74 01) Al Jerozolimskie 59
Cervantes Institute (Spanish)
    (☎ 622 54 19) ul Myśliwiecka 4
Goethe Institute (German)
    (☎ 656 60 50) Palace of Culture and Science
French Institute
    (☎ 827 76 40) ul Senatorska 38
Italian Institute of Culture
    (☎ 826 62 88) ul Foksal 11
Russian Culture and Information Centre
    (☎ 827 76 21) ul Foksal 10

Laundry

Alba laundry at ul Karmelicka 17, on the corner of ul Anielewicza (open weekdays 9 am to 5 pm, Saturday 9 am to 1 pm), charges US$6 to wash and dry up to 6kg. You're asked to call ☎ 831 73 17 a couple of days ahead to make a reservation. Bring your own detergent or buy some in the laundry.

Medical Services

There's a wide network of pharmacies in Warsaw; ask for an *apteka*. There are always several of them that stay open all night; a list is given in the *Gazeta Wyborcza* daily (Supermarket section).

If you happen to get sick, look for an outpatient clinic *(przychodnia)*. There are plenty of them and you can get general information on ☎ 827 89 62 (business hours, English sometimes spoken). If possible, ring your embassy for recommendations.

One of the best (but most expensive) places to try is the American Medical Center (☎ 622 04 89, ☎/fax 622 04 97, emergency 24 hour mobile ☎ 0602 24 30 24), ul Wilcza 23 m 29. This small private clinic has English-speaking staff that handle some services in-house; if they can't, they will refer you to other providers.

Also reliable is the CM Medical Center (☎ 621 06 46, ☎ 630 51 15, fax 630 50 48), in the Hotel Marriott building (3rd floor). It has English-speaking specialist doctors, does pathology tests and makes house calls. It's open weekdays 7 am to 9 pm, Saturday 8 am to 8 pm, Sunday 9 am to 1 pm.

The Danish company Falck (☎ 96 75), ul Szczęśliwicka 34 (staffed with English-speaking attendants), has no clinic but will provide free information on where to go in case of emergency. It has its own 24 hour ambulance service and makes house calls. Falck has branch offices in Gdańsk, Kraków, Poznań and Szczecin, contactable on the same local number ☎ 96 75 in each city.

For dental treatment try the Austria Dent Center (☎ 654 21 16, ☎ 821 31 84), ul Żelazna 54. It's open weekdays 9 am to 9 pm, Saturday 9 am to 1 pm.

If you need hospital treatment, the private Damian Hospital (☎ 644 33 13), ul Wałbrzyska 46, is a reputable institution. An alternative choice is the Hospital of the Ministry of Health and Social Welfare (☎ 621 31 76), ul Emilii Plater 18.

The city ambulance service can be contacted on ☎ 999 and ☎ 628 24 24, but don't count on them speaking English. Alternatively, you can use Falck's ambulance service.

Avoid drinking Warsaw's tap water. Its quality is so bad that half the city's population doesn't drink it either, opting instead for Oligocene water taken from wells several hundred metres deep. This water has undergone centuries of natural filtration and is drinkable without any treatment. There are about 150 wells in Warsaw, 50 of which are accessible to the public. City dwellers carrying water home from them in bottles, buckets, jerry cans etc is a typical Warsaw street scene. Bottled water is easily available from shops and supermarkets.

Emergency

See the Emergency section in the Facts for the Visitor chapter.

Dangers & Annoyances

Warsaw is perhaps the least safe Polish city, so you should take precautions while strolling about streets at night, and watch your possessions on public transport and in other crowded places. Beware of the 'mafia' taxis (see the Taxi section later in this chapter), and be on guard in and around the central train station (see Train in the Getting Around chapter and later in this chapter).

ROYAL CASTLE & AROUND

Like most visitors, you'll probably start your sightseeing from the Old Town area or, more precisely, from the **Castle Square** (Plac Zamkowy), which is the main southern gateway to the Old Town. The square got its present shape in the 19th century when the fortified walls were pulled down. Remnants of the fortifications, most notably a 14th century Gothic bridge on the western edge of the square, were excavated and restored.

In the centre of the square stands the 22m-high **Monument to Sigismund III Vasa** (Kolumna Zygmunta III Wazy), the king who moved the capital from Kraków to Warsaw. It's the second-oldest secular monument in Poland (after Gdańsk's Neptune), erected by the king's son in 1644. The bronze statue, once gilded, represents the king in a coronation cloak over a suit of armour, a sabre and a cross in his hands. The column was knocked down during WWII, but the statue survived and was placed on a new column four years after the war.

The eastern side of the square is occupied by the **Royal Castle** (Zamek Królewski). Its history goes back to the 14th century, when a wooden stronghold was built by the dukes of Mazovia and later rebuilt in brick. Greatly extended when the capital was moved to Warsaw, the castle became the seat of the king and the Sejm and remained so till the fall of the Republic in 1795. It

then served the tsars for over 100 years, and in 1918 became the residence of the president of Poland. After the Warsaw Uprising in 1944, the castle was blown up by the Nazis and virtually nothing was left.

It was not until 1971 that reconstruction work began, and by 1984 the splendid baroque castle stood again as if nothing had happened. It's now a museum, and some of its 300 rooms can be visited. The interior is crammed with works of art as it was two centuries ago.

You visit some rooms on the ground floor, but it's the great and king's apartments on the upper level that really demonstrate the castle's splendour. The **Ballroom** there is the largest and most impressive of all the castle's chambers. Built in the 1740s, it had many uses, serving as an audience room, concert hall and a place for important court meetings. The enormous ceiling painting, *The Dissolution of Chaos*,

The lavishly decorated rooms of Warsaw's Royal Castle display a wealth of artworks

is a postwar reconstruction of a work by Marcello Bacciarelli.

Next to the Ballroom is a magnificent **Knight's Hall** adorned with six large paintings by Bacciarelli, which depict important events in Polish history. The **Marble Room** to one side boasts 22 portraits of Polish kings, from Bolesław Chrobry to Stanisław August Poniatowski, who himself ordered the collection. In the same area is the lavishly decorated **Throne Room**.

Another of the castle's highlights is the **Canaletto Room** with 23 paintings by Bernardo Bellotto (who used the name of his famous uncle and therefore is commonly known in Poland as Canaletto). Bellotto (1721-80) documented with amazing detail the best of Warsaw's architecture of the time. These paintings, which survived the war, were of great help in reconstructing the city's historic monuments.

You'll also see a collection of paintings by Jan Matejko, including one of his most famous works, *The Constitution of the 3rd of May*, the act itself having been proclaimed from the castle in 1791.

From mid-May to mid-September the castle-museum is open daily 10 am to 6 pm (Sunday and Monday from 11 am). The remaining part of the year it opens daily 10 am to 3 pm except Monday. There are two routes of the castle interior taken by guided tours. Route 1 includes the ground-floor rooms, the parliament chambers and Matejko's paintings, and costs US$3 (half that for students). Route 2 covers most of the castle's highlights, principally the great and king's apartments, for US$4 (US$2 for students). The tour ticket allows you to visit other rooms and exhibitions not included in the two routes – don't miss the castle's cellars.

Guided tours in English and other major languages are available for US$14 extra per group; call in advance on ☎ 657 21 78, though English and German-speaking guides can usually be obtained at short notice or even on the spot.

Entry is free on Sunday, but come early as plenty of people take advantage of this and the number of tickets is limited. Visitors go round the castle rooms on their own on combined routes 1 and 2, and there's no guide service on that day. The detailed captions in Polish and English are a good help, and you can also buy a glossy guidebook on the castle published in several major languages.

OLD TOWN

Warsaw's Old Town (Stare Miasto) was rebuilt from the foundations up on what, after the war, was nothing but a heap of rubble. Official records put the level of the quarter's destruction at 90%. The monumental reconstruction took place between 1949 and 1963 and aimed to restore the town to its 17th and 18th centuries appearance, eliminating all accretions from later periods. There's now not a single building in the area that looks younger than 200 years. Every authentic architectural fragment found among the ruins was incorporated in the restoration. UNESCO's decision to include Warsaw's Old Town on the World Heritage list is proof of its value and recognition of the work done by Polish restorers.

Entering the Old Town from the Plac Zamkowy through ul Świętojańska, historically its main artery, you soon come to **St John's Cathedral** (Katedra Św Jana). The oldest of Warsaw's churches, it was built at the beginning of the 15th century on the site of a wooden church, and subsequently remodelled several times. Razed during WWII, it regained its Gothic shape with the postwar reconstruction, except for the façade, which is a new design in the original style. Roofed in by a gracious Gothic vault, the interior is modestly decorated; only a couple of tombstones survived out of about 200. Look for the red-marble Renaissance tomb of the last Mazovian dukes, which is in the right-hand aisle. Go downstairs to the crypt (the entrance is from the left-hand aisle) to see more tombstones, including that of the Nobel Prizewinning writer Henryk Sienkiewicz. The cathedral can be visited daily 10 am to 6 pm (Sunday from 2 pm).

Just next to the cathedral stands the **Jesuit Church** (Kościół Jezuitów), which has the highest tower in the Old Town but nothing special to see inside. Nearby, on ul Piwna, is the third and last church in the Old Town, **St Martin's Church** (Kościół Św Marcina).

The **Old Town Square** (Rynek Starego Miasta) is the loveliest square in Warsaw and one of the most amazing in Poland. If you had been here in 1945 you would have seen a sea of rubble with the walls of two houses (Nos 34 and 36) sticking up out of it. Today the Rynek is a fine blend of Renaissance and baroque with Gothic and neoclassical elements. There used to be a town hall in the middle of the square but it was pulled down in 1817 and never rebuilt.

The Rynek is harmonious if diverse in style and decoration and, more importantly, doesn't give the impression of being a replica. It's alive and atmospheric, particularly in summer, when it fills up with a dozen open-air cafés and stalls selling paintings and drawings. Have a good look at the architectural detail of the façades.

The **Historical Museum of Warsaw** (Muzeum Historyczne Warszawy) occupies the entire northern side of the Rynek (enter through No 42). In 60 rooms on four storeys, you'll find an extensive collection which illustrates the history of Warsaw from its beginnings until the present day. Documents, maps, drawings, paintings, armour, crafts and other Varsoviana, all displayed in period interiors, make this one of the city's most charming museums. Don't miss a startling documentary, screened a few times daily, about the destruction and reconstruction of the city; the English version is usually at noon. The museum is open Tuesday and Thursday noon to 6 pm, Wednesday and Friday 10 am to 3 pm, and Saturday and Sunday 10.30 am to 4 pm.

The **Museum of Literature** (Muzeum Literatury) at Rynek Starego Miasta 20 deals with the history of Polish literature, and also organises exhibitions dedicated to foreign writers. Its displays are unorthodox and imaginative. It's open Monday, Tuesday and Friday 10 am to 3 pm, Wednesday and Thursday 11 am to 6 pm and Sunday 11 am to 5 pm.

From the Rynek it's worth strolling about the neighbouring streets. Wander to the picturesque, triangular Kanonia Square behind the cathedral, which until the 19th century served as a church graveyard. Note the gallery at the southern end, which once gave Poland's kings direct access from the castle to the cathedral. Go to the viewpoint on ul Brzozowa which looks over the Vistula, then continue north along this street and return to the Rynek through a long, narrow stone stairway, the Kamienne Schodki (Stone Steps). Don't miss visiting the Zapiecek Art Gallery, just south of the Rynek, which often holds interesting exhibitions of modern art.

Going north along ul Nowomiejska you'll get to the **Barbican** (Barbakan), a powerful, semicircular Gothic structure topped with a decorative Renaissance parapet, built on a bridge over a moat as a reinforcement of the medieval fortifications. It was partially dismantled in the 19th century, but reconstructed after the war, giving more authenticity and atmosphere to the Old Town; today the Barbican is a summertime art gallery.

NEW TOWN

The New Town (Nowe Miasto) was founded at the end of the 14th century, not long after the Old Town, and in 1408 was granted a ducal privilege which allowed it to have its own jurisdiction and administration. Since then, there have been two towns half a kilometre apart, each with its own main square, town hall and parish church. The New Town was inhabited mostly by people of lower social standing. Consequently, its buildings were simpler and made of wood and there were never fortifications like those around the prosperous Old Town.

Just outside the Barbican, to the left, stands the **Church of the Holy Spirit** (Kościół Św Ducha), a double-towered baroque building which, like all those in the area, was almost totally destroyed in 1944 and reconstructed after the war. Don't expect much original interior decoration in any church in the New Town.

A bit farther down the street, on the opposite side, stands **St Hyacinthus' Church**

WARSAW – OLD TOWN & AROUND

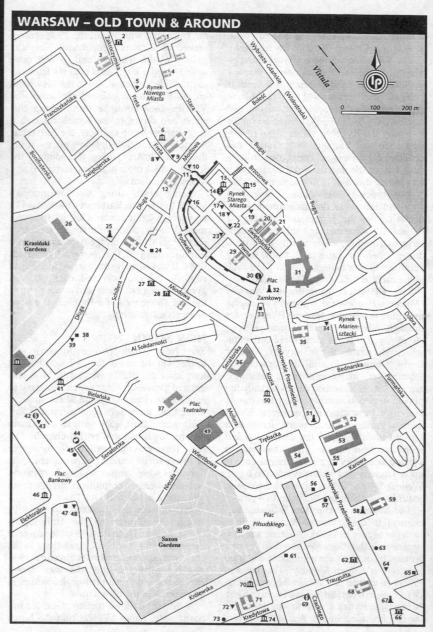

WARSAW

PLACES TO STAY

24	Bursa Szkolnictwa Artystycznego
33	Dom Literatury
38	Pokoje Gościnne Federacja Metalowcy
47	Hotel Saski
55	Hotel Bristol
56	Hotel Europejski
61	Hotel Victoria
65	Hotel Harenda

PLACES TO EAT

5	Restauracja Ekologiczna Nove Miasto
8	Restauracja pod Samsonem
9	Sklep z Kawą Pożegnanie z Afryką
10	Bar pod Barbakanem
16	Restauracja Maharaja Thai
17	Restauracja Fukier
18	Dom Restauracyjny Gessler
19	Restauracja Bazyliszek; Restauracja Fisherman
22	Restauracja Zapiecek
23	Restauracja Kmicic
34	Restauracja Bliss
39	Restauracja Tay-Ho
43	Salad Bar Tukan
48	Restauracja der Elefant
64	Bar Mleczny Uniwersytecki
72	Salad Bar Tukan

OTHER

1	Church of the Visitation of the Virgin
2	Sapieha Palace
3	Franciscan Church
4	Church of the Nuns of the Holy Sacrament
6	Maria Skłodowska-Curie Museum
7	St Hyacinthus' Church
11	Barbican
12	Church of the Holy Spirit
13	Historical Museum of Warsaw
14	Tourist Office
15	Museum of Literature
20	Jesuit Church
21	St John's Cathedral
25	Monument to the Warsaw Uprising
26	Krasiński Palace
27	Archbishop's Palace
28	Pac Palace
29	St Martin's Church
30	Tourist Office
31	Royal Castle
32	Monument to Sigismund III Vasa
35	St Anne's Church
36	Primate's Palace
37	Town Hall
40	Archaeological Museum
41	Museum of Independence

42	Bank Pekao
44	Belgian Embassy
45	French Institute
46	Museum of European Painting
49	Grand Theatre
50	Museum of Caricature
51	Monument to Adam Mickiewicz
52	Carmelite Church
53	Radziwiłł Palace
54	Potocki Palace
57	American Express Office
58	Monument to Cardinal Wyszyński
59	Church of the Nuns of the Visitation
60	Tomb of the Unknown Soldier
62	Czapski Palace (Academy of Fine Arts)
63	Warsaw University
66	Staszic Palace
67	Monument to Nicolaus Copernicus
68	Holy Cross Church
69	Bank Pekao
70	Zachęta Modern Art Gallery
71	Evangelical Church
73	Trakt Guide Service
74	Ethnographic Museum

(Kościół Św Jacka), the largest in the area. Look for the Kotowski Chapel in its left-hand aisle, the work of the most prominent architect of the baroque period in Poland, Tylman van Gameren. Dutch by birth, he settled in Poland and designed countless churches, palaces and the like all over the country.

The house at ul Freta 16 was the family home of Marie Curie, discoverer of radium and polonium and double Nobel Prizewinner, for physics in 1903 and chemistry in 1911. The **Museum of Maria Skłodowska-Curie** has a modest exhibition of the life and work of this distinguished scientist, who was born here in 1867 but spent her adult life in France. It is open Tuesday to Saturday 10 am to 4 pm, Sunday 10 am to 2 pm.

Continue along ul Freta to the **New Town Square** (Rynek Nowego Miasta). Like its Old Town counterpart, this square boasted a town hall, but it was pulled down at the beginning of the 19th century. A cast-iron well marks the place where the town hall once stood.

The **Church of the Nuns of the Holy Sacrament** (Kościół Sakramentek) at the eastern side of the square is another Tylman van Gameren design. Laid out on the plan of a Greek cross and topped by a dome on an octagonal drum, the church was an exquisite example of baroque sacral architecture, with a richly decorated interior. During the 1944 uprising the church was used as a hospital, and several hundred people died inside it when it was bombed.

Marie Curie – Discoverer of Radium & Polonium

One of the major contributors to modern physics, Marie Curie laid the foundations for radiography, nuclear physics and cancer therapy. This Polish-born French physicist won numerous awards and distinctions, including two Nobel Prizes. Determined, tireless and compassionate, she paid the highest price for her scientific work – her life. Albert Einstein, her friend, once wrote that 'she was the only person that had not been corrupted by fame'. She is the first (and so far the only) female of merit buried (in 1995) in the crypt of the famous Panthéon of Paris, among such luminaries as Voltaire, Émile Zola and Victor Hugo.

Born in 1867 in Warsaw (then under Russian partition) into a family of Polish teachers, Maria Skłodowska lived here for the first 24 years of her life. She completed her education at a local state lyceum with a gold medal, by which time she had developed a strong fascination for science and had decided to pursue a scientific career. Under Russian rule, however, women were not allowed to enter institutions of higher education.

Therefore, Skłodowska went to Paris in 1891 to study. Living a humble, almost Spartan, life, she studied physics and mathematics at the Sorbonne, earning degrees in both subjects. In 1895 she married French physical chemist Pierre Curie (1859-1906), and their scientific partnership proved to be extremely fruitful, even though their living conditions were deplorable. Their laboratory was not much more than a barn.

Their investigation of the radiation of uranium ore resulted in the discovery in 1898 of two new radioactive chemical elements, polonium (named after Marie's motherland) and radium. In 1903, they both, together with Henri Becquerel, were awarded the Nobel Prize for physics, for the discovery of natural radioactivity.

After Pierre's tragic death in a traffic accident in 1906, Marie devoted all her energy to the research work they had begun together. She succeeded him as lecturer and head of the physics department at the Sorbonne – the first woman ever to teach in this 650-year-old university.

Just north of the square is the **Church of the Visitation of the Virgin Mary** (Kościół Nawiedzenia NMP). Built in the 15th century as the parish church of the New Town, it was later enlarged several times and got a freestanding belfry in 1581. Its interior has some fine Gothic vaulting.

One block to the west, the **Franciscan Church** (Kościół Franciszkanów) is the only New Town church with any original furnishing, notably the 18th century baroque side altars (the high altar is a replica). Across the street is the mighty **Sapieha Palace** (Pałac Sapiehów), one of dozens of aristocratic palaces in Warsaw. It's now a school.

AROUND THE OLD TOWN

The route suggested below will allow you to see some of the sights to the west and south-west of the Old Town. All are within easy walking distance and are shown on the Warsaw – Old Town & Around map.

Take ul Długa off the Barbican to the corner of ul Bonifraterska, where you'll find the **Monument to the Warsaw Uprising** (Pomnik Powstania Warszawskiego). Only in the late 1980s did the government pay tribute to the heroes of one of the most heroic and tragic acts in the nation's history. The monument was unveiled on 1 August 1989 on the 45th anniversary of the uprising.

Slightly farther west on the opposite side of ul Bonifraterska is the large **Krasiński Palace** (Pałac Krasińskich), considered one of the most splendid baroque palaces in Warsaw. Designed by the ubiquitous Tylman van Gameren, the palace was built

Two years later she became titular professor and in 1911 was awarded the Nobel Prize for chemistry, for the isolation of pure radium.

Marie Curie was instrumental in founding the Radium Institute in Paris in 1914, which later became a universal centre for nuclear physics and chemistry. She directed its physicochemical department and continued to be active in the scientific field. She also helped establish the Radium Institute in Warsaw in 1932, in the country of her birth, with which she always maintained close links. She died in a sanatorium in southern France in 1934 of leukaemia caused by prolonged exposure to radiation. By that time she was almost blind, her fingers burnt with 'her dear radium'.

Marie Curie's contribution to science is enormous, and her Nobel Prize record confirms this. She was the first woman ever to be awarded a Nobel Prize and the first person to be awarded twice. She is also the only woman to date with two Nobel Prizes in science; the only other scientists in the world with two Nobel Prizes are US physicist John Bardeen and English biochemist Frederick Sanger.

Her example inspired scientists of a younger generation, including her own daughter Irène who, with her husband, physicist Jean-Frédéric Joliot-Curie, conducted experiments which led to the discovery of artificial radioactivity. This earned them the Nobel Prize for chemistry in 1935 – only the second in history for a female scientist, the first having been won by Irène's mother. And like her mother, Irène also died of leukaemia.

---

between 1677 and 1683, and though it was later remodelled several times, the postwar reconstruction gave it back its original décor. An elaborate triangular tympanum on the front façade is worth a closer look, as is the other tympanum on the garden elevation. The garden itself, also designed by van Gameren, was reputedly one of the most fashionable in the city, but not much of the original layout remains.

Turn back and continue south-west along ul Długa to the former **Arsenal** (Arsenał), a massive 17th century building which now houses the **Archaeological Museum** (Muzeum Archeologiczne), open weekdays 9 am to 4 pm and Sunday 10 am to 4 pm. The rather uninspiring permanent exhibition on the prehistory of Poland is periodically enlivened by temporary displays.

A short walk south-east will bring you to the Radziwiłł Palace, which houses the **Museum of Independence** (Muzeum Niepodległości), established here after the previous tenant, the Lenin Museum, closed in 1990. The museum stages temporary exhibitions related to Poland's struggles for independence. It's open Tuesday to Friday 10 am to 5 pm, Saturday and Sunday 10 am to 3 pm.

The nearby blue skyscraper marks Plac Bankowy (Bank Square). Its western side is lined by two massive neoclassical palaces, now the seat of the city municipal authorities. At the southern end of the square is the building of the former stock exchange and the Bank of Poland. It's now home to the John Paul II Collection of the Carroll-Porczyński Foundation, otherwise known as the **Museum of European Painting** (Muzeum Malarstwa Europejskiego). Here you'll find works by some of the best European painters, including Cranach, Rubens, Velázquez, Goya, Renoir, Sisley, Van Gogh and Chirico. There's controversy about the authenticity of some canvases, though. The core of the collection was originally assembled by the Carrol-Porczyński family of Polish émigrés and donated to the Church – that's why the pope's name is included in the name of the museum and his portraits adorn the collection. The museum is open 10 am to 4 pm except Monday.

Cross the square and take ul Senatorska to Plac Teatralny (Theatre Square), bordered on the south by the colossal **Grand Theatre** (Teatr Wielki). This neoclassical edifice, thought to be the largest theatre building in Europe, was designed by Antonio Corazzi and erected in 1825-33. After it was burnt out during the war, only the façade was restored; the rest was reshaped to suit modern needs. Inside is an opera auditorium capable of seating 1900 spectators, and two smaller stages. Opposite the theatre is the **Town Hall** (Ratusz), rebuilt in 1997 to its pre-WWII shape.

From Plac Teatralny, proceed along ul Senatorska towards the Old Town. The right-hand side of the street is dominated by the **Primate's Palace** (Pałac Prymasowski), yet another neoclassical folly, adorned with a colonnaded portico and semicircular wings. If you still have an appetite for palaces, take ul Miodowa to the left where, 400m along, you'll find no less than seven of them. The largest is the **Pac Palace** (Pałac Paca), now the Ministry of Health. Next to it stands the **Archbishop's Palace** (Pałac Arcybiskupi), the present-day seat of the Primate of Poland, Cardinal Józef Glemp, and where Pope John Paul II stays while visiting his homeland.

ALONG THE ROYAL WAY

The Royal Way (Trakt Królewski) refers to a 4km-long route from the Royal Castle to Łazienki Palace, the royal summer residence. The route follows Krakowskie Przedmieście, Nowy Świat and Aleje Ujazdowskie, and includes a good number of sights on or near the Way. It's best to do the whole stretch on foot and allow a full day for sightseeing. The time you need will depend largely on how long you spend in museums.

Beginning from the Castle Square, the first stop is **St Anne's Church** (Kościół Św Anny), just a few steps south. One of the most attractive city churches, it was erected in 1454 but burnt down by the Swedes and rebuilt in the 1660s in baroque style. Further alterations gave it a neoclassical façade, while the freestanding belfry acquired a neo-Renaissance form. The interior is more consistent stylistically, and is mostly baroque. The church miraculously escaped major damage in the war and boasts original 18th century trompe l'œil painting on the vault, and an 18th century high altar, pulpit and organ. You can go up to the terrace on top of the freestanding belfry, for a good view over the Castle Square.

Continuing south, you'll pass the **Monument to Adam Mickiewicz**, the most renowned Polish Romantic poet, just before reaching the former **Carmelite Church** (Kościół Karmelitów). This church, too, escaped the ravages of war and, like St Anne's, has its 18th century fittings, including the high altar designed by Tylman van Gameren.

A short detour along ul Kozia will bring you to the **Museum of Caricature** (Muzeum Karykatury), open Tuesday to Sunday 11 am to 5 pm. It has a collection of some 15,000 original works by Polish and foreign caricaturists plus satirical and humorous books, magazines etc.

Next along the Royal Way, two grand palaces face each other on opposite sides of the street. To the west stands the baroque **Potocki Palace** (Pałac Potockich), now the headquarters of the Ministry of Culture and Art, its courtyard guarded by two wrought-iron gates. The Guardhouse (Kordegarda) is a gallery of modern art, worth a visit. To the east, the even larger, neoclassical **Radziwiłł Palace** (Pałac Radziwiłłów) is the Polish equivalent of the White House. The palace is guarded by four stone lions, reinforced by an equestrian **Statue of Prince Józef Poniatowski**, sword in hand, in the palace forecourt. The prince was the nephew of the last Polish king, Stanisław August, and commander in chief of the Polish army of the Duchy of Warsaw created by Napoleon. The 1832 statue, clearly based on antique models, is the work of Danish sculptor Bertel Thorvaldsen.

From here, if you walk between two neo-Renaissance style hotels, the Europejski (1877) and the Bristol (1901), you'll arrive at the **Church of the Nuns of the Visitation** (Kościół Wizytek), with its elegant baroque façade. The highlight of its interior is an ebony tabernacle (1654), lavishly ornamented with silver, at the high altar. Also note the boat-shaped rococo pulpit (1760), looking as if it's sailing in particularly heavy weather.

In front of the church stands the **Monument to Cardinal Stefan Wyszyński**, unveiled in 1987. The Primate of Poland for three decades (1951-81) and a tireless defender of human rights during the communist regime, he came to be known as the 'Primate of the Millennium'.

At this point it's worth taking a short detour off the Royal Way. Take ul Królewska, which opens onto Plac Piłsudskiego (Piłsudski Square) with the **Tomb of the Unknown Soldier** (Grób Nieznanego Żołnierza) on its western side. In the 18th century the mighty Saxon Palace (Pałac Saski) here served the king as a residence, with the magnificent French-style **Saxon Gardens** (Ogród Saski) stretching behind it. The tomb is actually the only surviving fragment of the former palace, while the gardens were turned into an English landscape park in the 19th century. The only reminder of the original layout is the central path shaded by old chestnut trees. Be at the tomb on Sunday at noon when the ceremonial changing of the guard is held. The Piłsudski Square soon will change its appearance quite dramatically; the task of producing a new design was offered to brilliant English architect Norman Foster.

South of the tomb across ul Królewska is the big **Zachęta Modern Art Gallery** (open 10 am to 6 pm except Monday), the leading venue for temporary exhibitions, where you'll always find something interesting.

To the south is the 18th century **Evangelical Church**. A circular edifice topped with the largest dome in Warsaw, the church is renowned for its good acoustics and is the venue for a variety of concerts.

Across the street is the **Ethnographic Museum** (Muzeum Etnograficzne), which provides an insight into Polish folklore and crafts. It also has a collection of tribal art from Africa, Oceania and Latin America. It's open Tuesday, Thursday and Friday 9 am to 4 pm, Wednesday 11 am to 6 pm, and Saturday and Sunday 10 am to 5 pm. Just around the corner from the museum, at ul Mazowiecka 11A, is the art gallery of the Polish Artists Association, the Dom Artysty Plastyka.

If you follow ul Traugutta eastwards you'll return to the Royal Way next to the late baroque **Czapski Palace** (Pałac Czapskich), today the home of the Academy of Fine Arts.

Directly opposite the academy, behind a decorative entry gate with the Polish eagle on top, is **Warsaw University** (Uniwersytet Warszawski), which occupies a whole complex of buildings. The oldest one (1634) is the **Kazimierz Palace** (Pałac Kazimierzowski) at the far eastern end of the campus, now the office of the rector. Since its founding in 1816, Warsaw University has always been a focus for independent political thinking – a child unloved first by tsars and later by communist governments. In the postwar period, most student protests started here. It's also pretty active culturally – go onto the campus to see what's happening.

Because it's so close to the university, the **Holy Cross Church** (Kościół Św Krzyża) has witnessed more student demonstrations and tear gas than any other church in Poland. Earlier, during the Warsaw Uprising, it was the site of heavy fighting between the insurgents and the Nazis. It was seriously damaged, but some original baroque altarpieces have survived and adorn its interior; the high altar is a replica of the original made in 1700. Note the epitaph to Frédéric Chopin on the second pillar on the left-hand side of the nave. It covers an urn with the composer's heart, brought from Paris after Chopin's death and placed here in accordance with his will.

The southern end of Krakowskie Przedmieście is bordered by the **Staszic Palace** (Pałac Staszica), designed by Antonio Corazzi (also responsible for the Grand Theatre) and built in the 1820s for the Society of Friends of Sciences. Following that tradition, the palace is today the headquarters of the Polish Academy of Sciences.

A contemplative figure sitting on a plinth in front of the palace is the **Monument to Nicolaus Copernicus** (Pomnik Mikołaja Kopernika), the great Polish astronomer who, as Poles often say, 'stopped the sun and moved the earth'. The statue is another of Bertel Thorvaldsen's works, unveiled in 1830. During WWII, the Nazis replaced the Polish plaque with a German one and later took the whole statue away for scrap. It was found after the war on a scrap heap in Silesia, and was returned to its site.

At this point, Krakowskie Przedmieście turns into the much narrower Nowy Świat (literally, New World). In the 19th century and up till WWII it was the main shopping street, with fashionable cafés occupying the houses' ground floors. Though the destruction of 1944 was almost total, the reconstruction here was as meticulous as in the Old Town and gave the street back its 19th century neoclassical appearance, characterised by an unusual stylistic unity. Architecture apart, it's also one of the busiest commercial streets in the city, lined with shops, boutiques, bookshops and cafés.

When strolling down Nowy Świat, take a short detour east into ul Ordynacka, which will lead you to the **Ostrogski Palace**. Placed on a high fortified platform on the Vistula escarpment, the small baroque palace (again, designed by Tylman van Gameren) is today

the seat of the Chopin Society, which runs recitals and chamber music concerts in a lovely concert hall inside. There is also a small **Chopin Museum** (closed Tuesday) related to the artist's life and work.

Another detour from Nowy Świat is ul Foksal; at the end of this cul-de-sac is the **Zamoyski Palace**, a handsome building which holds the Foksal Art Gallery in a side wing. At the back of the palace, a fragment of a landscaped park has been preserved.

Back on the Royal Way, proceeding south, you'll soon get to the junction with the busy Al Jerozolimskie. The large, squat block in front of you is the former headquarters of the Polish Communist Party (Dom Partii), today the seat of the Polish stock exchange.

A little farther east towards the Vistula is the massive building of the **National Museum** (Muzeum Narodowe). Don't miss it – there's a treasure house of art, from ancient to contemporary, inside. The ancient art includes Roman, Greek, and Egyptian pieces, plus a collection of over 60 frescoes from an early Christian cathedral in Pharos, Sudan. These date from between the 8th and 12th centuries, and were discovered by a Polish archaeological team. At the far end of the exhibition hall, hidden behind the frescoed slabs, is a display of amazing Coptic crosses (ask the attendants to let you in if this part is closed).

Polish medieval art is a strong aspect of the museum. There is an excellent selection of religious painting and, more notably, sculpture from all over Poland, including some of the best Gothic altarpieces you'll see anywhere in the country.

The upper floors are given over to Polish painting from the 16th century until today, and it's one of the most representative selections in Poland, with almost all the big names. There's also a collection of European painting, including French, Italian, German, Flemish and Dutch works, mainly from the 16th to the 18th centuries.

Apart from permanent exhibitions, there are usually temporary shows. The museum is open Tuesday, Wednesday and Friday

10 am to 4 pm, Thursday noon to 5 pm, and Saturday and Sunday 10 am to 5 pm.

The **Polish Army Museum** (Muzeum Wojska Polskiego), next door in the same building, presents the history of the Polish army from the beginning of the state until WWII. There's also a small collection of old weapons from Asia, Africa and Australia. Heavy armour, tanks and fighter planes used by the Polish Army during WWII are displayed in the park adjoining the museum building. The museum is open Wednesday to Sunday 10 am to 4 pm.

Return to Nowy Świat and follow it south to Plac Trzech Krzyży (Three Crosses Square) to have a look over the 19th century **St Alexander's Church** (Kościół Św Aleksandra), modelled on the Roman Pantheon, in the middle of the square.

From here, the Royal Way leads down Aleje Ujazdowskie, a pleasant avenue bordered by old mansions, embassies and parks. An oasis of greenery close to the city centre, the area has long been popular with the locals for a stroll or a rest.

Go down Aleje Ujazdowskie and turn left just past a busy motorway, Trasa Łazienkowska. There, surrounded by trees, stands the **Ujazdów Castle** (Zamek Ujazdowski), a stately, square building adorned with four corner towers. Erected in the 1620s for King Zygmunt III Waza as his summer residence, it was destroyed during the war and rebuilt to house the **Centre of Contemporary Art**. Various temporary exhibitions are held in the castle and can be visited from 11 am to 5 pm except Monday.

Nearby to the south are the **Botanical Gardens** (Ogród Botaniczny), established in 1818, and 400m farther down Al Ujazdowskie is the 18th century **Belvedere Palace**. It changed owners and appearance several times before becoming the residence of the presidents after WWI, as it was until 1994. It now shelters an exhibition dedicated to Marshal Piłsudski (who was one of the palace's residents). Advance booking (☎ 849 48 39) is necessary. Between the Botanical Gardens and the Belvedere stretches Łazienki Park.

ŁAZIENKI

A former summer residence of King Stanisław August Poniatowski, Łazienki is a park-and-palace complex, one of the most beautiful in the country. Once a hunting ground attached to the Ujazdów Castle, the area was acquired by the king in 1776 and within a short time transformed into a splendid park complete with a palace, an amphitheatre and a number of buildings scattered around. Despite various ups and downs the complex has retained its original shape and architecture and is a good place for a leisurely stroll.

The park can be entered (free of charge) until sunset from different sides but the most popular ways in are from Al Ujazdowskie. The **Chopin Monument** (Pomnik Chopina), just behind the middle entrance, was unveiled in 1926 and is the latest addition to the park's historic structures. Open-air Chopin concerts are held here on summer Sundays, invariably drawing crowds of music lovers and casual passers-by.

Wandering down the hill into the park, you'll come upon the **water tower** (wodozbiór), a circular structure which served to collect underground water for distribution, through wooden pipes, to the palace and its fountain. It's today a commercial art gallery.

The nearby glazed building with a front garden guarded by lions is the **Old Orangery** (Stara Pomarańczarnia). It houses a gallery of Polish sculpture and a court theatre *(teatr dworski)*, one of the few theatres of its type in Europe which preserved its authentic 18th century décor. The orangery is open 9.30 am to 3 pm except Monday.

Continue downhill to the **Little White House** (Biały Domek), the first building erected in the park (1776) and a temporary residence of the king until the proper palace was built. This square wood-and-plaster structure, with four identical façades, has retained most of its 18th century interior decoration.

From here, the King's Promenade (Promenada Królewska) will take you directly to the **Palace upon the Water** (Pałac na

Wodzie), the residence of the king. Like most other Łazienki buildings, the palace was designed by the court architect Domenico Merlini. It was constructed on an islet in the middle of an elongated lake, using an existing bathhouse (in Polish, *łazienki*, hence the name of the whole complex) which had been built on this site 100 years before by the former owners. A fine neoclassical palace was decorated and crammed with *objets d'art*. Not long after, the king had to abdicate and the building has never been inhabited since. During WWII, the Nazis set the palace alight, partly destroying the 1st floor, but they didn't manage to blow it up as they had planned. Renovated and refurbished, the palace is open as a museum (9.30 am to 4 pm except Monday). While visiting it, note the rooms adapted from the former baths, the Bacchus Room lined with Dutch tiles, and the Bathroom decorated with bas-reliefs. An English-speaking guide can be arranged if you call in advance on ☎ 625 79 44 (US$10 per group for a 45 minute palace tour).

The **Myślewice Palace** (Pałac Myślewicki), a few paces east, survived the war unscathed, which is why it has even more authentic if more modest interiors. In the same area is the **Museum of Hunting and Horsemanship** (Muzeum Łowiectwa i Jeździectwa), open 10 am to 4 pm except Monday.

The **Amphitheatre** (Amfiteatr) has been constructed on the bank of the lake in such a way that its stage is on the islet separated by a narrow channel, thus allowing part of the action to take place on the water. Plays are occasionally performed here in summer.

There's a dozen other buildings and pavilions within the grounds, including the **New Orangery** (Nowa Pomarańczarnia) farther south, which houses the posh Belvedere restaurant.

WILANÓW

On the city limits, 6km south of Łazienki, is another park-and-palace complex, Wilanów ('Vee-lah-noof'). It served as the royal summer residence for Jan III Sobieski, remembered for his victory over the Turks in the Battle of Vienna in 1683.

The king acquired the land in 1677 for his rural residence, calling it in Italian *'villa nuova'* (which is where the Polish name came from), and within 20 years managed to transform the existing simple manor house into a splendid Italian baroque villa. After the king's death, Wilanów changed hands several times, with each new owner extending and remodelling it. The palace grew considerably (the side wings, for example, date from after the king's time), acquiring a range of styles from baroque to neoclassical. During WWII, the Nazis plundered it, but the building itself didn't suffer major damage. Most of the furnishings and art were retrieved after the war, and after a decade-long restoration the palace regained its former splendour. It is now open to the public.

There's a lot to see in the **palace**. You proceed through dozens of rooms fitted out with period furniture and decoration in various styles. The two-storey Grand Entrance Hall is perhaps the highlight, though several other chambers, such as the Grand Dining Room, are also superb. Some of the upper-floor rooms accommodate the **Gallery of Polish Portraits**, featuring a collection from the 16th to 19th centuries. Note the so-called coffin portraits – a very Polish feature – which are images of noble persons painted just after their death, usually by any artist at hand. Executed on a piece of tin plate, these portraits were then attached to the coffin during the funeral, personifying the deceased, and removed before burial.

The palace museum is open 9.30 am to 2.30 pm, except Tuesday and the day following public holidays. Saturday, Sunday and holidays are days exclusively for individual visitors; other days are essentially for prebooked groups, but it's often possible to join one. All visitors join guided tours in Polish, which begin every 15 minutes and cost US$3 (US$2 for students). In summer, come early and be prepared to queue. Guided tours in English, French and German are available, for US$40 for a group of up to 10 people. There are short descriptions of the rooms' contents in English and French. If you want to know more about the site, brochures in English and other major languages are available at a small shop in the palace's wing. Thursday is a free-entry, no-guided day but come early as a limited number of visitors are allowed.

The side gate beside the northern wing of the palace leads to the **gardens** and **parks** (open 10 am till sunset), which, like the palace itself, include a variety of styles. The central part is taken by a manicured, two level baroque Italian garden, which extends from the back façade of the palace down to the lake. South of it is the Anglo-Chinese park, and in the northern part of the grounds is the English landscape park. Don't miss an intriguing 17th century sundial with a figure of Chronos, the god of time, on the garden façade of the palace.

The **Orangery** (Oranżeria), off the northern wing of the palace, serves as an exhibition hall and has decorative art and sculpture from the 16th to 19th centuries. It's open 10 am to 3.30 pm.

Just outside the main gateway to the palace grounds is the **Poster Museum** (Muzeum Plakatu), the only institution of its kind in Poland and probably one of the few in the world. It displays just what it says – posters – and the exhibits are changed regularly. It's open Tuesday to Friday 10 am to 4 pm, Saturday and Sunday 10 am to 5 pm. The International Poster Biennial (established in 1966) is held here for a few summer months in even-numbered years.

To get to Wilanów from the city centre, take bus No 180 from ul Marszałkowska, or bus No 116 from anywhere on the Royal Way.

If you take a trip to Wilanów, you can visit the **Katyń Museum** (Muzeum Katyńskie) en route. Opened in 1993, the museum reveals details of the massacre of Polish officers and intellectuals by the Soviets in 1940 at Katyń and two other camps. The moving exhibition includes maps, photographs, documents, letters, press cuttings, personal belongings unearthed during the exhumations, and family memorabilia. Video documentaries can be watched on request. Unfortunately, all the captions and video commentaries are in Polish.

The museum has been set in the casemates of a brick fort built in 1883, at ul Powsińska 13 in the Sadyba district. It's about 2km from Wilanów towards the city centre. Bus No 180 passes this way. The museum is open Wednesday to Sunday 10 am to 4 pm, and also has an outdoor exhibition of heavy armoury, including tanks, guns etc.

NEW CITY CENTRE

The new centre is almost entirely a postwar creature and has few significant tourist attractions. Chaotic, crowded and flooded with cars parked virtually everywhere, it's essentially a shopping area, with trade going on both indoors and outdoors.

The focal point is the **Palace of Culture and Science** (Pałac Kultury i Nauki), a blackened edifice which is hard to miss as it's the largest and tallest city building. A gift of friendship from the Soviet Union to the Polish nation, the palace was built in the early 1950s and briefly named after Stalin. The monster has attracted countless nicknames and insults, from 'the Russian wedding cake' to 'the vertical barracks'.

There's a viewing terrace on the 30th floor (115m up) which gives a bird's-eye view of the city. Poles often joke that this is the best view of the city because it's the only one which doesn't include the Palace of Culture itself! The viewpoint is open 9 am to 5 pm (Sunday from 10 am). Enter the palace through the main entrance from ul Marszałkowska. Continue straight ahead up the stairs and you'll find the ticket office on your left.

Back at ground level, go to the **Fotoplastikon** (☎ 625 35 52) at Al Jerozolimskie 51. This is reputedly the last working example in Europe of a once popular apparatus. It's a great revolving drum; 22 people can sit around it and look through individual eyepieces at 3D photos dating from the beginning of the 20th century, some in colour. It is amazingly lifelike. There's a

The Palace of Culture and Science – A Defiant Monster

'That enormous, spired building has inspired fear, hatred, and magical horror. A monument to arrogance, a statue to slavery, a stone layer cake of abomination. But now it is only a large, upended barracks, corroded by fungus and mildew, an old chalet forgotten at some Central European crossroad.'

Tadeusz Konwicki (from *A Minor Apocalypse*)

Stalin, it seems, must have been envious of New York's famous skyscrapers. Just after WWII, he ordered eight palace-like high-rise towers to be built in Moscow, apparently as counterparts of the Chrysler and Empire State buildings and the like. He altered his plan at the last minute, however, and decided that the eighth tower would be built in Warsaw, presumably to show a Soviet presence on the Vistula. Interestingly, it was the largest and highest 'palace' of the lot.

The building was erected in 1952-55 right in Warsaw's centre, using 40 million bricks. It stands on a vast 30 hectare square, Plac Defilad, reputedly Europe's largest, created for the palace by indiscriminately bulldozing the partly ruined central sector. The sandstone monster occupies an area of 3.32 hectares and has 3288 rooms. It shelters a huge congress hall for 3000 people, three theatres, a swimming pool and a museum; the upper floors house offices. At 231m, it was Europe's second-highest building when erected, and the highest in Poland.

A solitary giant amid ruins, the palace aroused mixed feelings from the moment of its construction. Predictably, it was fêted by official propaganda and hated by most of the city's residents. No one could remain indifferent, for the palace was visible from almost any point in the city and beyond. And it looked clearly out of place.

The Stalinist city planners put height limits on any constructions around the palace, so that it would remain a dominant landmark. It wasn't until the 1980s that the first skyscrapers went up in the area. The Marriott Hotel, erected in 1989, was the nearest competitor, yet at 140m it was still a long way behind.

Once communism collapsed and the borders opened, Warsaw experienced an avalanche of 'tourist-traders' from beyond the eastern frontier, who – irony of ironies – chose the Plac Defilad as their trading ground. The square became a huge Russian bazaar, with the blackened palace overlooking the action. No longer a dead piece of Russian architecture, it was now alive, surrounded with its people, language, merchandise and atmosphere.

Meanwhile, Poles discussed what to do with the 'wedding cake' colossus, and ideas ranged from pulling it down to turning it into a communist skansen. An international competition was held in 1992; the winning design (from 300-odd entries) proposed constructing a ring of high-rise buildings around the palace, vaguely suggesting a crown, to make the palace less conspicuous, yet still visible. The project immediately attracted a storm of criticism from virtually everyone, including architects, historians, business lobbies, local government and the public.

Years have passed and nothing has happened. One reason is that the city authorities apparently didn't want to go ahead with the highly controversial project. Meanwhile a more prosaic reason has appeared – the unsolved issue of the real estate titles of the pre-WWII landowners. Nobody had been able to challenge the Stalinist bulldozers, but now, in the new regime, the legitimate owners and their descendants began to claim their land and rights. So until this is resolved, you can enjoy an unobstructed view of the palace from every side and just about any perspective – something you can't say about the Chrysler or Empire State buildings. Nearly 50 years after its construction, it is still Poland's highest building. And it still remains distinctly alien.

varied selection of programs, and special performances are available upon request. Each 20 minute session (US$1) consists of 48 stereoscopic pictures. This family-run business has been operating here since 1901. It's open weekdays from noon to 5 pm, Saturday 11 am to 2 pm.

To get a feel for today's Warsaw, wander through the busy commercial area to the east of the Palace of Culture, behind the large Centrum department stores, or set off south along ul Marszałkowska. The early postwar architecture which lines this major thoroughfare reaches its peak at Plac Konstytucji, another showpiece of socialist realism adorned with huge stone candelabras.

FORMER JEWISH DISTRICT

The vast area of the Mirów and Muranów districts stretching to the north-west of the Palace of Culture was once inhabited predominantly by Jews. During WWII the Nazis established a ghetto there and after crushing the 1943 Ghetto Uprising razed the quarter to the ground. Few remnants of the Jewish legacy are left.

A five minute walk north-west of the Palace of Culture, right behind the Jewish Theatre, is the Nożyk Synagogue. Built in 1902 in neo-Romanesque style and named after its founder, it was the only one of Warsaw's synagogues to survive WWII, albeit in a sorry state. It was restored and today is open for religious services. It can be visited on Thursday between 10 am and 3 pm.

Some of the important places related to the ghetto's history have been included in the Memorial Route to the Struggle and Martyrdom of the Jews 1940-43. The route begins at the Monument to the Heroes of the Ghetto and goes along ul Zamenhofa and ul Stawki to the Umschlagplatz Wall Monument (which marks the point from which Jews were deported to the death camps). The route, which takes 15 minutes to complete, is marked by black granite blocks commemorating events and people from those tragic days. A large museum of Polish Jewry is to be built in the area.

CEMETERIES

Warsaw has plenty of graveyards of various denominations, of which the oldest ones are grouped in the Wola district, about 3km north-west of the centre. There are four cemeteries here next to each other, which give a good idea of the religious and cultural diversity of Warsaw's past.

The largest and most significant for Poles is the Catholic Powązki Cemetery (Cmentarz Powązkowski), consecrated in 1792. The final resting place of many prominent Poles (including composers Henryk Wieniawski and Stanisław Moniuszko), the 45 hectare graveyard boasts some amazingly ornate old tombstones, intricate sepulchral chapels and mausoleums. It's open daily from 7 am till dusk and the entrance is from ul Powązkowska. Be sure to visit the cemetery on All Saints' Day (1 November) if you happen to be in Warsaw then. Thousands of lit candles on the graves make an impressive sight, especially in the evening (the cemetery is open longer on this day).

North-west of the Powązki is the tiny Tatar Islamic Cemetery (Muzułmański Cmentarz Tatarski). The entrance is from ul Tatarska, and the cemetery is open daily from 9 am to 4 pm except Thursday. It was founded in 1867 to house the remains of local Muslims, mostly Polish Tatars who settled in Warsaw. Most of the 19th century tombstones were destroyed by German tanks in WWII, but enough of them remain to show the effects of Russification on the Mazovia region. Inscriptions are in Cyrillic, with or without the usual Arabic phrases on the head of the slab. The section with the 20th century graves is largely intact, and shows the role the Tatars had in Polish military life up until WWII. Many graves are of military men who were important in the organisation of Poland's cavalry during the interwar years, and who fought in 1939. The Arabic calligraphy engraved on these slabs is quite beautiful. Of interest is the number of Polish surnames and Islamic given names, or Tatar family names with Polish given names, showing the degree to which this ethnic group had become assimilated.

Just south of the Powązki, and almost as large, is the **Jewish Cemetery** (Cmentarz Żydowski). Founded in 1806, it suffered little during the war and still boasts over 100,000 tombstones – the largest collection of its kind in Europe. However, since almost the whole of Warsaw's Jewish community (over 300,000 people) perished in the war, and the communist authorities took no responsibility for the cemetery's preservation, it stayed largely neglected for over 40 years and many tombstones are dilapidated. Yet there's a wealth of remarkable examples, some topping the graves of eminent Polish Jews, including Ludwik Zamenhof, the creator of Esperanto. The cemetery is open from 10 am to 3 pm except Friday and Saturday. The entrance gate is at ul Okopowa 49/51; you can get a detailed guide to the tombs there.

Just south of here, on ul Młynarska, is the small **Augsburg Evangelical Cemetery** (Cmentarz Ewangelicko-Augsburgski). A visit to this tranquil, tree-shaded Lutheran graveyard (open daily) will illustrate the social status of the German minority in the Warsaw area during the Partition years. The graves date back to the late 18th century, but most are from the 19th and early 20th. Most of the people buried here belonged to the learned professions or the merchant class; many tombs of the latter are opulently lavish. The inscriptions and the spelling of the surnames indicate the degree to which many of these expatriates had become Polonised. An odd reminder of Russian occupation is a large sepulchre in the form of an Orthodox church and with Cyrillic inscriptions.

PRAGA

Praga is the part of Warsaw which lies on the right bank of the Vistula. Founded in the 15th century, Praga gradually developed from the original village and was incorporated into Warsaw in 1791. By the outbreak of WWII, it was a large, working-class suburb. As it was not directly involved in the battles of 1944, Praga didn't suffer much damage and retained some of its prewar architecture and atmosphere. However,

since it had no architectural marvels in the first place, there's not much to see. If you decide to set foot in Praga, the most interesting area lies just across the Vistula from the Old Town. It's a short trip by any tram heading east over the Śląsko-Dąbrowski Bridge, or a 15 minute walk.

Past the bridge are the **Zoological Gardens** (Ogród Zoologiczny), established in 1928. The zoo stretches north behind a park and has some 2000 animals representing 280 species from around the world. Farther down Al Solidarności, at the intersection with ul Targowa, is the **Orthodox Church** (Cerkiew Prawosławna), topped with five onion-shaped domes. Built in the 1860s in Russo-Byzantine style, it retains its original interior decoration. The way to see it is to coincide your visit with the Mass (weekdays at 9 am, Sunday at 10 am). This is one of two Orthodox churches functioning in Warsaw (the other one is in the Wola district).

The striking **Monument to the Brotherhood of Arms** (Pomnik Braterstwa Broni), across the street from the church, was erected just after the war in gratitude to the Red Army (which, ironically, was stationed here for several months in 1944 passively observing the tragic events on the other bank of the Vistula). This is one of the last surviving examples of the socialist-realist craze and may be taken down.

LANGUAGE COURSES

There's quite a choice if you want to learn or practise Polish. The 'Polonicum' Institute of Polish Language and Culture for Foreigners (☎/fax 826 54 16) at the Warsaw University, ul Krakowskie Przedmieście 26/28, has the longest tradition. It runs a one year extensive course (six or nine hours a week) and a one month intensive course in August (four hours a day). Polonicum's courses are the cheapest you'll find (about US$4.50 per hour), but the groups may be large (up to 15 students) and the methods seem to be quite traditional.

Private schools which have appeared on the market over recent years are usually more flexible about clients' needs and may apply more modern techniques, but they are more expensive. Warsaw's major private schools include:

Berlitz
  (☎ 624 96 50, fax 624 96 87) ul Elektoralna 26
IKO
  (☎ 826 31 08, fax 828 52 68) ul Nowy Świat 26
Linguae Mundi
  (☎ 654 22 18, fax 654 22 19) ul Złota 61
Meritum
  (☎ 625 46 64, fax 628 19 05) ul Nowogrodzka 21
Schola Polonica
  (☎ 625 26 52, fax 625 08 17) ul Jaracza 3 m 19

They all have a choice of extensive or intensive courses to suit your language level (costing roughly US$6 to US$12 per hour) and can provide teachers for individual classes/courses (about US$12 to US$18 per hour). Note that the 'hour' actually means a 45 minute lesson. Some schools may be able to provide inexpensive accommodation with a Polish family, organise courses in tourist resorts in the mountains or on the coast, arrange tours etc.

Contact the schools in advance for details, but even if you turn up without warning, many will try to snap you up, before a competitor does.

ORGANISED TOURS

Mazurkas Travel (☎/fax 629 18 78, ☎/fax 629 12 49), in the lobby of the Hotel Forum at ul Nowogrodzka 24/26, is Warsaw's major tour operator. It offers tours in the city (US$25 per person) and beyond, including trips to Kraków and Gdańsk. Weco-Travel (☎ 658 17 59, fax 658 18 48), ul Chmielna 132/134, office 408, also offers regular city tours, covering and costing much the same. American Travel Abroad (☎ 825 61 62, fax 825 30 74), ul Armii Ludowej 12, runs tours around Poland's highlights such as Kraków and Gdańsk.

Kampio (☎ 823 70 70, fax 823 71 44, kampio@it.com.pl), ul Maszynowa 9 m 2, focuses on ecotourism, organising kayaking, biking and birdwatching trips to out-of-the-way areas. Kayak trips along the Drawa and Czarna Hańcza rivers and birdwatching in Białowieża and Biebrza national parks are on the tour list.

See the Travel Agencies section earlier in this chapter for tours organised by Almatur and Our Roots.

SPECIAL EVENTS

Warsaw hosts a number of important cultural events. January witnesses the Warsaw Theatre Meetings, a fortnight-long presentation of recent productions by some of the best theatre companies from all over the country – a good opportunity to get an idea of what's new on the Polish scene.

The Witold Lutosławski International Composers Competition is organised by the National Philharmonic in February. The Stanisław Moniuszko International Vocal Competition is held for one week in late April. Founded just a few years ago, both these events are still modest.

Warsaw Ballet Days takes place in the Grand Theatre at the end of April and beginning of May. This week-long event usually includes invited international ballet groups.

The International Book Fair has been held annually in May for over 40 years in the Palace of Culture and Science. May also sees the 10 day International Festival of Sacred Music.

The Mozart Festival, organised by the Warsaw Chamber Opera in June and July, is a young but increasingly important and popular cultural event. If features a presentation of all Mozart's major works.

The second half of June brings the four day Warsaw Summer Jazz Days to town. It's worth checking the program if you're a jazz fan, as there may be some leading international musicians taking part.

The Festival of Organ Music, which goes from July to mid-September, offers quite a different kind of music and atmosphere. It includes organ recitals in the cathedral every Sunday at 4 pm.

With a tradition nearly 40 years old, the 'Warsaw Autumn' International Festival of

Contemporary Music, held for 10 days in September, is the city's pride and offers a chance to hear the world's best avant-garde music, including new works by major Polish composers.

The much-acclaimed Chopin International Piano Competition takes place every five years in October (the next one is in 2000). Also in October, there's the Warsaw Film Festival.

The 'Jazz Jamboree' International Jazz Festival is one of the most prestigious festivals in Europe and has already played host to most of the jazz greats, from Dizzy Gillespie to Miles Davis and Wynton Marsalis. It takes place in late October and lasts four days.

PLACES TO STAY

Warsaw is the most expensive Polish city to stay in. It has an increasing collection of up-market hotels, whereas cheaper places are not that numerous. Furthermore, the latter are scattered throughout the city, sometimes a long way from the centre, and there isn't any obvious 'budget hotel area' to head for upon arrival. If you don't book in advance try to arrive in the city reasonably early in the day, in order to track down a room. The city tourist offices (including the two convenient outlets at the airport and the central train station) will help you to find and book somewhere free of charge. The private office at Plac Zamkowy will also help but will charge a US$1.50 service fee per person.

Places to Stay – Budget

If your budget is up to about US$25 a double per night, you have a choice between youth hostels, camp sites (most of which have bungalows and/or budget all-year hotels), student hostels and private rooms. There are very few other hostels or hotels falling into this price bracket.

Camping Warsaw has several camping grounds. The largest, most central and most popular among westerners is *Camping Nr 34 Gromada* (☎ 825 43 91, ul Żwirki i Wigury 32) in the Ochota suburb. It's open May to September and has budget cabins

and a large pavilion with hotel-style rooms. The place is friendly, helpful and clean, but it may close down in 1999 – check for news when you arrive. The camping ground is accessible from the airport on bus Nos 175 and 188, and from the central train station on bus Nos 136 and 175.

In the same suburb, close to the central bus terminal, is the smaller *Camping Nr 123 Majawa* (☎ 823 37 48, ul Bitwy Warszawskiej 1920r 15/17). It has all-year heated cabins (US$20/30 a double without/with bath) and the all-year *Hotel Majawa* (US$30/38/44 a double/triple/quad without bath).

Camping Nr 260 (☎ 842 27 68, ul Inspektowa 1), in the Stegny suburb on the way to Wilanów, is open from mid-May to mid-September. It has no shade and no cabins, but there is the all-year *Hotel Stegny* in the grounds where triple rooms without bath cost US$30.

Camping Rapsodia (☎ 634 41 64, ul Fort Wola 22) in the Wola suburb is open June to September, and it also has an all-year facility, *Hotel Rapsodia* (US$15/20 a double/triple without bath, US$30/34 with bath).

Youth Hostels There are two all-year youth hostels, far too few for a capital city and insufficient for the needs of tourists. Neither is particularly good or large and both are often full.

The 110-bed *youth hostel* (☎ 827 89 52, ul Smolna 30), close to the National Museum, is accessible by bus No 175 from the airport and by any eastbound tram from the train station. It has large dormitories and charges about US$7 per person. Curfew is at 11 pm. You can buy an HI membership card here (US$10) if you don't have one.

The other all-year *youth hostel* (☎ 632 88 29, ul Karolkowa 53A) is 2km west of the train station in the Wola suburb and is accessible by tram No 24 (there's no direct transport from the airport). The hostel has some smaller rooms that afford more privacy.

There are also two seasonal youth hostels, but they are smaller and more basic. The *youth hostel* (☎ 831 17 66, ul Między-

parkowa 4/6), on the northern outskirts of the New Town, is open 1 April to 31 October. You can get there from both the train station and the airport by bus No 175. The other *youth hostel (☎ 617 88 51, Wał Miedzeszyński 397)* is on the eastern side of the Vistula close to the Trasa Łazienkowska (the main west-east city motorway). It's open 15 April to 15 October. Take bus No 501 from the train station, or bus No 188 from the airport.

Student Hostels The tourist offices may know which student dorms are open as hostels (normally from early July to mid-September). Of those that have opened each summer over the past few years, you could try *Dom Studenta Nr 1 (☎ 668 63 07)* and *Dom Studenta Nr 2 (☎ 822 24 07)* in two large blocks next to one another at ul Żwirki i Wigury 95/99; *Dom Studenta (☎ 822 18 69, ul Spiska 16)*; *Hermes (☎ 849 67 22, ul Madalińskiego 6/8)*; *Grosik (☎ 849 23 02, ul Madalińskiego 31/33)*; and *Sabinki (☎ 646 32 00, Al Niepodległości 147)*. Any of these will cost US$8 to US$10 per bed in doubles or triples with shared facilities.

Private Rooms The Biuro Kwater Prywatnych Syrena Univel (☎ 628 75 40) can arrange accommodation in private rooms. Its address is ul Krucza 17 (open Monday to Saturday 9 am to 7 pm, Sunday to 5 pm). Try to get there reasonably early in the day, as there may be not much to choose from later. The rooms are in the central districts and cost US$17/25 a single/double.

Other Hostels & Hotels The *Bursa Szkolnictwa Artystycznego (☎ 635 79 05, ☎ 635 41 74, ul Miodowa 24A)* is an art school dorm which opens to all in July and August (it may also have some vacancies on weekends in other months). At US$10 per person in double or triple rooms with shared facilities, it's possibly the cheapest place to stay in the immediate vicinity of the Old Town, and it's clean and quiet. The entrance is from ul Kilińskiego.

Another budget place close to the Old Town is the small *Pokoje Gościnne Federacja Metalowcy (☎ 831 40 21, ul Długa 29)*. It costs US$14/22/34 a single/double/quad without bath – it's hard to find a cheaper hotel in central Warsaw.

Hotel na Wodzie (☎ 628 58 83) is in two boats, *Anita* and *Aldona*, anchored to the Vistula shore between the railway and Poniatowski bridges. It operates from around April to November and offers single/double cabins without bath for US$20/25.

Places to Stay – Mid-Range

This section includes hotels which cost between US$25 and US$50 a double. There are not that many central hotels in this price bracket and they tend to fill up fast. The hotels farther from the city centre are more likely to have vacancies.

The ideally located *Dom Literatury (☎ 635 04 04, ☎/fax 828 39 20, ul Krakowskie Przedmieście 87)* is just opposite the Royal Castle. It's not a regular hotel, but it rents out rooms without bath (six doubles and one triple) on its top floor for about US$23 per person. Most rooms provide a superb view over the Castle Square.

A few blocks south-west is the palace-like *Hotel Saski (☎ 620 46 11, fax 620 11 15, Plac Bankowy 1)*. The building was designed by Antonio Corazzi (the same architect who designed the Grand Theatre) and built in 1826-28. It was damaged during the war but the original façade survived. The rooms don't have private baths, but what on earth would you expect for US$33/44 a single/double, with breakfast, at such a central location. The rooms facing the interior courtyard are the quietest.

Hotel Mazowiecki (☎ 682 20 69, ul Mazowiecka 10) is a former army dorm once reserved for military officers but now open to everyone. Rooms with shared facilities cost US$32/44/50 a single/double/triple.

All other mid-range hotels are some distance from the centre. *Hotel Belfer (☎ 625 26 00, Wybrzeże Kościuszkowskie 31/33)* is on the Vistula bank. This large former teachers' hotel has singles/doubles without bath at

US$27/36 and singles/doubles/ triples with bath and breakfast at US$38/52/62. Rooms on the upper floors provide good views.

South of the city centre, in the Mokotów district, you can try *Hotel Hera* (☎ *41 13 08, ul Belwederska 26/30)*, south of the Łazienki park. It costs US$25/34 a single/double without bath, US$50/62 with own bath, breakfast included.

Hotel Agra (☎ *849 38 81, ul Falęcka 9/11)* is also in Mokotów, and has singles/doubles/triples for US$34/38/50. The bath is shared between two adjacent rooms.

Hotel MCB (☎ *668 50 17, ☎/fax 658 28 71, ul Trojdena 4)*, in a quiet location in Ochota, is the hotel of the International Centre of Biocybernetics, but is open to all. Comfortable singles/doubles with bath cost US$35/48, breakfast included. In the same complex of buildings is another scholarly facility, *Hotel IBB* (☎ *658 47 94, fax 658 47 89, ul Pawińskiego 5A)*. It offers similar standards for much the same. Both are small and often full.

Places to Stay – Top End

This section includes hotels which cost more than about US$50 a double, but if you really need luxury be prepared to pay somewhere from US$100 upward. Orbis and Syrena own some of the best locations, but many of their hotels date from the early communist days and completely lack style. Yet they are affordable, which cannot be said about the newest and poshest establishments. Most hotels listed here serve breakfast, which is included in the room price, and have their own restaurants.

Hotel Polonia (☎ *628 72 41, fax 628 66 22, Al Jerozolimskie 45)* is a short walk from the central train station. One of Warsaw's oldest hotels, operating since 1913, its old-fashioned style is particularly evident in its restaurant. It's not a posh place but not terribly expensive either: US$40/60 a single/double without bath, US$60/90 with own bath. Rooms facing the street are pretty noisy.

Just round the corner is the newer if unstylish *Hotel Metropol* (☎ *629 40 01, fax*

625 30 14, ul Marszałkowska 99A), which offers marginally better standards for US$75/100 a single/double with bath.

The refurbished *Hotel Harenda* (☎/fax *826 26 25, ul Krakowskie Przedmieście 4/6)* is conveniently located and has singles/doubles with bath for US$50/75.

The unexciting *Dom Chłopa* (☎ *827 92 51, fax 625 21 40, Plac Powstańców Warszawy 2)* is also well located. Rooms go for US$75/90 with bath. The nearby *Hotel Warszawa* (☎/fax *827 14 72,* (☎/fax *827 18 73, Plac Powstańców Warszawy 9)* costs marginally more.

With the coming of the market economy, new hotels began to open, some of which now offer satisfactory standards for less than their older siblings listed above.

Hotel Maria (☎ *838 40 62, fax 838 38 40, Al Jana Pawła II 71)* is a small hotel with a family atmosphere and a good restaurant. At US$70 a double, breakfast included, it's usually booked out, despite an unattractive location.

Hotel Cytadela (☎ *687 72 36,* ☎/fax *687 77 15, Krajewskiego 3/5)*, a 10 minute walk north-west of the New Town, is also good value. This army-run hotel opened in 1993 and costs US$60/80 a double/triple with bath. Another reasonable choice is the small *Hotel Karat* (☎ *601 44 11, fax 849 52 94, ul Słoneczna 37)* in Mokotów, which offers singles/doubles for US$75/100. Also in Mokotów is the new *Hotel Reytan* (☎ *646 31 66, fax 646 29 89, ul Rejtana 6)*, charging US$60/80.

For a splurge, you have half a dozen luxury hotels, including the classy old-style *Hotel Bristol* (☎ *625 25 25, fax 625 25 77, ul Krakowskie Przedmieście 42/44)*. Originally built in 1901, it reopened in 1993 after a US$36 million renovation. Rooms begin at US$200/250 a single/double.

Other top-end options include *Hotel Victoria* (☎ *657 80 11, fax 657 80 57, ul Królewska 11)*; the *Marriott Hotel* (☎ *630 63 06, fax 830 03 11, Al Jerozolimskie 65/79)*; and the *Sheraton Hotel* (☎ *657 61 00, fax 657 62 00, ul Prusa 2)*. They all have fine restaurants.

Palace of Culture and Science, Warsaw

Cafés in the Old Town Square, Warsaw

Monument to the heroes of the tragic Warsaw Uprising, Old Town, Warsaw

Tomb of Political Prisoners (L), and Katyń Tomb (R) on All Saints' Day, Powazki Cemetery, Warsaw

Decoration inside the grand Wilanów palace, Warsaw

PLACES TO EAT

Warsaw has a wider range of eating places than any other Polish city, in every price bracket. The capital has some of Poland's classiest restaurants, and is the only city which offers a fair variety of ethnic cuisines.

A characteristic feature of present-day Warsaw is a virtual explosion of small, modern bistros, pizzerias, snack bars and fast-food outlets, which have replaced the old drab, run-down places. The big international chains, including McDonald's, Pizza Hut, Burger King and KFC, have all arrived and can be found at various locations. You'll also find a spectacular proliferation of pubs, which have spread like wildfire since the fall of communism.

Another trait of the capital is the profusion of ethnic restaurants. Oddly enough, despite having such long and deeply rooted Jewish, Lithuanian, Ukrainian, Belarusian and Russian traditions, Warsaw ignores their cuisines almost totally. Instead, a variety of restaurants serving culturally exotic food – from Greek and Spanish to Syrian and Japanese – have opened. Most numerous among them are Chinese and Vietnamese eateries.

This section is divided by price range. The budget section includes milk bars, bistros and other cheap eateries where a filling meal should cost below US$6. The mid-range section covers restaurants where an average meal will cost between US$7 and US$15, and anything above that is considered top end.

You can assume that most upmarket restaurants will accept credit cards. Most of these places have foreign-language menus; if the menu is only in Polish, see the Food section in the Facts for the Visitor chapter for help. Check the prices of drinks before ordering – in some posh restaurants they can be extraordinarily expensive.

Places to Eat – Budget

Genuinely cheap restaurants aren't common in the Old Town (this is, after all, the most touristy spot in town), but there's a reasonable supply of fast-food outlets, snack bars and cafés to let you get around without starving. *Bar pod Barbakanem* (*ul Mostowa 27/29*), next to the Barbican, is the only milk bar in the area which has successfully survived the fall of the Iron Curtain and continues to serve cheap, unpretentious food.

There are three surviving milk bars along the Royal Way. *Bar Mleczny Uniwersytecki* (*ul Krakowskie Przedmieście 20*), next to Warsaw University, is invariably packed with students – a sign that it's not a bad place to eat. Some 500m south, *Bar Mleczny Familijny* (*ul Nowy Świat 39*) also provides big helpings for little money. Another 500m south is *Bar Mleczny Szwajcarski* (*ul Nowy Świat 5*). There are some other very cheap places in the area, including *Bar Kubuś* (*ul Ordynacka 13*) which does home-cooked meals.

The new *Bar Sandwicz* (*ul Nowy Świat 28*) has some popular Polish fare and a choice of salads, and you can put together an appetising meal for less than US$5. Next gate to the south from here, at the back of the building, is the tiny *Bar Cô Tú*, which does Vietnamese food for roughly US$3 per average main course. *Palacsinta* (*ul Nowy Świat 27*) is also at the back of the building. This tiny basement place has a choice of crêpes, plus some salads and *pierogi*.

Salad Bar Tukan (*Plac Bankowy 2*), in the blue skyscraper, offers one of the better selections of salads in town. It's not that cheap, but you can still organise a meal below US$6, unless you are very hungry. Tukan has several other outlets around the city, including at ul Tamka 37 and ul Kredytowa 2.

Of the surviving milk bars in the new city centre, you have *Bar Mleczny Bambino* (*ul Krucza 21*) and *Bar Mleczny Złota Kurka* (*ul Marszałkowska 55/73*).

The self-service *Bar Krokiecik* (*ul Zgoda 1*) is deservedly popular thanks to its hearty, cheap dishes, some of which are vegetarian. The *Grill Bar Zgoda* (*ul Zgoda 4*) across the street is a bit more expensive but worth it.

Restauracja Chmielna, on the corner of ul Zgoda and ul Chmielna, focuses on chicken dishes but there are also pork and beef plates, spaghetti, *pierogi* etc, all of which are well prepared and cheap. Start off your meal with the garlic soup.

The nearby *Między Nami (ul Bracka 20)* has good salads, pasta and sandwiches, plus a vegetarian set lunch on weekdays (US$4, different each day). The place is popular with local youth. There's no sign over the door; look for the Gauloises Blondes awnings.

Next door is the simple *Bar Restauracyjny Expresso (ul Bracka 18)*, a sort of milk bar which serves straightforward Polish fare at proletarian prices. Another good place is the nearby *Batida* (see Cafés later in this chapter).

The *Warsaw Tortilla Factory (ul Wspólna 62)* is the cheapest and most authentic Mexican restaurant in town.

There's a cluster of white-and-red plastic cabins on both the east and west sides of Plac Konstytucji. Some of them are run by Vietnamese, and serve everything from spring rolls to sweet-and-sour pork. You can get a plastic plate of tasty Asian food for US$2. Take away or eat at one of the tables beside the cabins.

Similar Vietnamese cabin eateries have sprung up at other busy locations in central Warsaw and beyond, including at ul Marszałkowska between ul Świętokrzyska and ul Królewska. Here, you can also find half a dozen cabins that serve simple, very cheap Middle Eastern meals.

Places to Eat – Mid-Range

Restauracja pod Samsonem (☎ 831 17 88, ul Freta 3/5), in the New Town, is one of the best inexpensive restaurants in the area. The interior is rather simple, but the food – a mix of Polish and Jewish cuisine – is decent and tasty.

Restauracja Ekologiczna Nove Miasto (☎ 831 43 79, Rynek Nowego Miasta 13/15) is the first natural-food restaurant in town. In bright, cheery surroundings it serves vegetarian dishes plus a variety of salads, reputedly prepared from organically grown vegetables.

Restauracja Zapiecek (☎ 831 56 93, ul Piwna 34/36) is among the more affordable restaurants in the vicinity of the Old Town

Square. The food – essentially Polish with some German influences – is OK and the interior is agreeable. Directly opposite, *Restauracja Kmicic (☎ 635 31 21, ul Piwna 27)* cooks traditional Polish food which may not be absolutely top-notch but neither are the prices.

Restauracja der Elefant (☎ 620 46 11, Plac Bankowy 1), round the corner from the Hotel Saski, offers a choice of well prepared grilled meats, hot-served camembert, crumbed seafood and the like, plus plenty of drinks.

Tam Tam (☎ 828 26 22, ul Foksal 18) is Warsaw's first African restaurant, and has immediately become one of the trendiest places in town. The food is not purely African but is good and reasonable.

Restauracja Adler (☎ 628 73 84, ul Mokotowska 69) serves copious plates of hearty Polish and Bavarian food (plus good salads) in a cosy, warm interior (or at outdoor tables in summer).

Restauracja Klub Aktora (☎ 628 93 66, Al Ujazdowskie 45), once an exclusive actors' club, now welcomes everybody for reliable Polish food, including a no-nonsense set three-course lunch. Next door, *Café Ejlat (☎ 628 54 72)* is one of the very few places in town which offers Jewish cuisine.

Qchnia Artystów (☎ 625 76 27, Al Ujazdowskie 6), in the Ujazdów Castle which houses the Centre of Contemporary Art, has, predictably, an artistic touch to it which makes it one of the more original restaurants. The interior is arranged in – as the owners say – 'postmodernist' style, and there's an arty atmosphere The menu – an artistic creation in itself – includes a choice of vegetarian dishes, including excellent salads.

South of the centre, *Café Brama (ul Marszałkowska 8)* has become a trendy youth haunt thanks to the tasty food (salads, spaghetti, ciabatta, sandwiches), good prices and general atmosphere. Outdoor seating is available in summer.

Restauracja Flik (☎ 849 44 34, ul Puławska 43), farther south in Mokotów, combines wonderful cooking, reasonable prices and an enjoyable setting. The focus is on Polish food, and the US$13 lunch buffet is excellent value. Book a couple of days ahead.

A variety of Asian restaurants have settled in the Old Town area, and may be an alternative if you're tired of Polish food. *Restauracja Maharaja Thai* (☎ 635 25 01, *ul Szeroki Dunaj 13*) is Poland's first Thai eatery. *Restauracja Bliss* (☎ 826 32 10, *ul Boczna 3*), Mariensztat Square, is a reliable and pretty authentic Chinese venture. *Restauracja Tay-Ho* (☎ 635 38 88, *ul Długa 29*) also does Chinese food.

On the Royal Way, try *Restauracja Pacyfik* (☎ 826 46 77, *ul Nowy Świat 42*). It's off the street – enter the gate and you'll see it. There are excellent Chinese/Vietnamese dishes (120 to choose from) at good prices.

There are also some Oriental restaurants in the new city centre. For Chinese food, try *Restauracja Mekong* (☎ 621 18 81, *ul Wspólna 35*), while *Restauracja Maharaja* (☎ 621 13 92, *ul Marszałkowska 34/50*) is the place to go for spicy Indian dishes. Diagonally across the street, *Suparom Thai* (☎ 627 18 88, *ul Marszałkowska 45*) is one of the very few Thai eateries.

Places to Eat – Top End

There's an extensive and swiftly growing array of upmarket restaurants all over the Old Town and the surrounding area, and here you'll find some of Warsaw's finest eateries serving traditional Polish and ethnic food. They are not cheap, though. Larger parties are advised to make reservations in summer, particularly for dinner.

Restauracja Fukier (☎ 831 10 13, *Rynek Starego Miasta 27*) is one of the highlights of Warsaw's gastronomic scene. It offers a creative menu, based on old Polish cuisine enriched with French and Spanish elements, served in beautifully arranged surroundings. It has one of the loveliest restaurant interiors in town. Reservations are essential.

The *Restauracja Bazyliszek* (☎ 831 18 41, *Rynek Starego Miasta 3/9, 1st floor*) is one of the better known restaurants in town, and maintains high standards. It serves traditional Polish food (including game) in appropriately old-fashioned surroundings.

It has recently opened a posh fish and seafood outpost next door, *Restauracja Fisherman* (☎ 831 38 50).

Dom Restauracyjny Gessler (☎ 831 44 27, *Rynek Starego Miasta 21/21A, 1st floor*) is another top-notch eatery on the square, noted for its fine food, style and atmosphere. Even more attractive is the cellar, which has been transformed into an amazing traditional country inn serving typical food. Don't miss going there if only to have a look around.

Hotel Bristol's US$36 Sunday brunch (from 12.30 to 4 pm) is superb with unlimited champagne and a buffet that includes smoked salmon, caviar, salads, cheeses, meats, several main dishes, sweets and coffee. Reservations are required a couple of days in advance. You may also be interested in the hotel's *Restauracja Malinowa*, one of the most luxurious establishments in town, serving Polish and French food.

Restauracja Polska (☎ 826 38 77, *ul Nowy Świat 21*) is in the ZAR Gallery building, 100m back from the street – enter gate No 21 and walk straight ahead until you see it on your right. This elegant basement place specialises in traditional Polish cuisine, and the food tastes as if it was cooked by your mum – excellent value.

Restauracja Belvedere (☎ 41 48 06) in the glazed New Orangery in Łazienki Park has a fabulous setting. The tables are scattered around the interior amid lush greenery, and you'll feel as though you are in an exotic garden. The fare, which combines elements of Polish, French and Italian cuisines, is prepared in the manner of *nouvelle cuisine*, so portions are small. It's all exquisite but quite pricey.

The Hotel Marriott has some of the finest eating places around. Its *Parmizzano's* serves arguably the finest authentic Italian food in town, and the *Chicago Grill* has steaks made from imported US beef. The third Marriott venue, *Lila Weneda* (☎ 630 51 76), stages daily (except Sunday) buffets at lunch (US$18) and dinner (US$25) with a different theme – Polish, Greek, Mexican, Asian, Russian – each night of the week, plus Sunday brunch (US$30) with live music and unlimited sparkling wine and Polish beer.

Cafés

Some of the best coffees in town are served in the *Sklep z Kawą Pożegnanie z Afryką (ul Freta 4/6)*. This tiny coffee shop, one of about 20 similar places scattered around Poland's major cities, offers nothing but coffee – but what coffee!

This said, there are cafés all over the Old Town and beyond. In summer, a dozen open-air cafés spring up on the Old Town Square alone. These are all pretty standard places which offer diverse fare, including a variety of alcoholic and nonalcoholic drinks, pastries, ice creams, snacks and even some more substantial meals.

Café Blikle (ul Nowy Świat 33) is a landmark of the Royal Way. This reopened café complements the Blikle cake shop next door. Both began operating here in the 1870s, and gained a reputation for cooking the best doughnuts *(pączki)* in town. Both original establishments were destroyed in 1945, and only the cake shop reopened after the war. Ihe café was only re-established in 1994. It has, of course, the famous doughnuts and a range of other pastries, but its menu goes far beyond that, offering set breakfasts (Polish, French, English, Viennese, Russian and American), light lunches, salads, ice creams, milk shakes, coffee etc. It's a good port of call and the food is not expensive. It's open from 7.30 am to 11 pm.

Café Bristol in the hotel of the same name has a refined interior in a Viennese style – an appropriate setting for a great coffee, a snack (delicious salad with salmon and shrimp sandwiches) or some cakes and pastries. This is obviously not a rock-bottom place, but neither a snack nor a pastry will make a noticeable dent in your wallet.

For much cheaper pastries and cakes, as well as yoghurt desserts, milk shakes, ice creams and the like, try either of the central *Hortex* outlets, at ul Świętokrzyska 35 or Plac Konstytucji 7. Both are two-storey places with waiter service upstairs.

Wedel (ul Szpitalna 8), on the corner of ul Górskiego adjacent to the Wedel chocolate shop, is the place for a cup of hot chocolate and chocolate waffles.

Batida (ul Nowogrodzka 1/3) is a bakery which does some of the best French bread and pastries in town. The adjacent café serves these goods (including delicious croissants) along with excellent espresso, a choice of tasty salads and several hot meals.

ENTERTAINMENT

Warsaw has much cultural fare to offer in the evening, particularly classical music, opera and theatre. When it comes to nightlife, most entertainment is confined to bars, pubs and discos and has somewhat less artistic content to it.

Museums, art galleries, theatre performances and cinema shows are listed in local papers, including *Gazeta Wyborcza*. Its Friday edition has the comprehensive *Co Jest Grane* section on cultural events. The city cultural monthly *IKS* has detailed listings of museums, art galleries, cinemas, theatres, musical events and festivals. Posters are a good source of information too, so keep your eyes open.

As for some English-language help, the *Warsaw Insider* monthly provides good information on cultural events as well as on bars, pubs and other nightspots. Also check the entertainment columns of the *Warsaw Voice*.

The Kasy Teatralne ZASP at Al Jerozolimskie 25 (☎ 621 94 54, ☎ 621 93 83) is the central office selling tickets for most of the city's theatres, opera, musical events and visiting shows. The office is open weekdays 11 am to 6 pm and Saturday 11 am to 2 pm. You can book by phone, but you have to come to the office later anyway, to pay and pick up your tickets. Tickets can also be bought directly from the theatres, which open their ticket windows during the day.

Cinema

There are about 35 cinemas in Warsaw, most of which are in the greater central area. About three-quarters of the films that are shown are US productions, which arrive in Poland within a few months to a year of their release at home. The remaining quarter is mainly Western European films garnished with occasional productions from Australia, New Zealand and some developing countries. Polish films are infrequently screened, as are Russian films, which accounted for up to half the fare during the communist era.

The *Iluzjon Filmoteki Narodowej* (☎ 48 33 33, ul Narbutta 50A) is Warsaw's main art cinema and it's worth checking what's on here. Other cinemas which tend to screen more thought-provoking films include *Kino Agrafka (Plac Żelaznej Bramy 2)*, *Kino Foksal (ul Foksal 3/5)*, *Cinema Paradiso (Al Solidarności 62)*, *Kino Kultura (ul Krakowskie Przedmieście 21/23)* and *Kino Muranów (ul Andersa 1)*.

Almost all foreign films (except for children's films) have original soundtracks and Polish subtitles. Cinema tickets cost about US$4 to US$6.

Theatre

Polish theatre has long had a high profile and continues to do so despite economic problems. Warsaw has about 20 theatres, some of which are among the best in the country. The leading playhouses include the *Centrum Sztuki Studio* (☎ 620 21 02) in the Palace of Culture, the *Teatr Ateneum* (☎ 625 24 21, ul Jaracza 2), and the *Teatr Powszechny* (☎ 18 48 19, ul Zamoyskiego 20). Most theatres close in July and August for their annual holidays.

The *Teatr Żydowski (Jewish Theatre;* ☎ 620 62 81, Plac Grzybowski 12/16) derives inspiration from Jewish culture and traditions, and some of its productions are performed in Yiddish (with Polish and English translations provided through headphones).

Opera & Ballet

The main setting for opera and ballet performances is the *Teatr Wielki* (Grand Theatre). It stages operas from the international repertoire and some by Polish composers, mainly Moniuszko. Tickets can be bought from the box office (open 9 am to 7 pm) or booked by phone (☎ 826 32 88). Advance booking is recommended.

The *Opera Kameralna (Chamber Opera; Al Solidarności 76B)* performs operas in a more intimate but splendid setting. The box office (☎ 831 22 40) is open weekdays 10 am to 2 pm and 4 to 6 pm.

Classical Music

The *Filharmonia Narodowa (National Philharmonic; ul Jasna 5)* has a concert hall (enter from ul Sienkiewicza 10) and a chamber hall (enter from ul Moniuszki 5). Regular concerts are held in both halls, usually on Friday and Saturday, by the brilliant Warsaw Orchestra and visiting ensembles. The ticket office (☎ 826 72 81) is open 10 am to 2 pm and 3 to 7 pm.

The *Akademia Muzyczna (Music High School; ul Okólnik 2)* has its own concert hall on the premises, where student presentations take place. The *Chopin Society* organises piano recitals year-round in its headquarters, the Ostrogski Palace (☎ 827 54 71, ul Okólnik 1).

Piano recitals are also held next to the Chopin monument in Łazienki park every Sunday from May to September, and in Żelazowa Wola, Chopin's birthplace, 53km from Warsaw (see the Mazovia & Podlasie chapter).

The Evangelical Church, situated at ul Kredytowa 4 (Plac Małachowskiego), opposite the Ethnographic Museum, hosts some musical events, including chamber concerts and organ recitals. Chamber concerts are also staged in summer in the Old Orangery in Łazienki park.

Jazz

Akwarium (☎ 620 50 72, ul Emilii Plater 49) near the Palace of Culture, is so far the only regular jazz club in the capital. Live jazz is performed nightly, weekdays 8.30 to 11 pm, Friday and Saturday till 3 am. There's a cover charge of US$1 to US$6 (depending on the day) except for Wednesday night jam sessions, which are free.

Akwarium is going to move, probably in 1999, so check when you arrive.

Akwarium apart, there's not much jazz around. Some student clubs (see the following section for locations) devote one day per week to jazz except during student holidays from July to September; for example, *Riviera Remont* has live jazz every Thursday. *Pub Harenda* (☎ 826 29 00, ul Krakowskie Przedmieście 4/6) may have jazz concerts in its cellar, as can *Jazz Club Rynek* (☎ 831 23 75, Rynek Starego Miasta 2). Also, some pubs host jazz groups. In July and August, there are free open-air jazz concerts in the Old Town Square, every Saturday at 7 pm.

Jazz buffs might want to contact the PSJ office (Polish Jazz Association; ☎ 827 83 71) at ul Chmielna 20.

Student Clubs & Discos

The main student clubs in Warsaw include: *Riviera Remont* (☎ 825 74 97, ul Waryńskiego 12); *Stodoła* (☎ 825 60 31, ul Batorego 10); *Park* (☎ 825 71 99, ul Niepodległości 196); *Proxima* (☎ 822 87 02, ul Żwirki i Wigury 99); and *Medyk* (☎ 628 33 76, ul Oczki 5/7). In the summer holiday period, all the clubs run discos several days a week or even nightly, with occasional live bands. A student card will get you in cheaply.

Ground Zero (☎ 625 43 80, ul Wspólna 62) is one of Warsaw's hippest discos (Wednesday to Saturday), and is becoming popular with foreigners. *Scena* (☎ 625 35 10, Al Armii Ludowej 3/5) is a bar/disco frequented by local artist and journalist types. You may also want to check out the techno disco *Blue Velvet* (☎ 828 11 03, ul Krakowskie Przedmieście 5). *Tam Tam* (☎ 828 26 22, Foksal 18) is a new 'in' disco with an African touch in music, food and clientele. All these places are more upmarket than student clubs.

Bars & Pubs

Warsaw is flooded with bars and pubs these days. *The Irish Pub* (ul Miodowa 3) is one of the popular drinking haunts in the Old

Town area, and stages live music most nights (Irish, folk, country etc).

If you prefer something more local, go to *Pub pod Baryłką* (ul Garbarska 5/7) on the Mariensztat Square. It's a Polish pub offering over 20 kinds of Polish beers – a good testing ground for visiting beer connoisseurs.

John Bull Pub (ul Jezuicka 4) was one of the first pubs to open in Warsaw and perhaps the first genuine English watering hole to cross the Iron Curtain. It's elegant, comfortable and expensive. There's another outlet at ul Zielna 37.

Pub Harenda (ul Krakowskie Przedmieście 4/6) next to Hotel Harenda is a trendy and lively spot and is open longer than most other places of this kind.

Other pubs you might want to try include *Morgan's* (ul Okólnik 1) – enter from ul Tamka; the new, modern *Zanzi Bar* (ul Wierzbowa 9/11); and the *Grand Kredens* (Al Jerozolimskie 111).

Pub B-40 has an unusual location and clientele. It's in one of the pillars of the Poniatowski bridge (on the eastern, Praga side of the Vistula) and is a haunt of rockers and other black-clad characters.

Winiarnia pod Kuchcikiem (ul Nowy Świat 64) is a cosy basement wine bar that also has a choice of beer brands and food.

Gay & Lesbian Venues

Warsaw's gay and lesbian haunts include Friday discos at *Restauracja Rudawka* (ul Elbląska 53); *Koźla Pub* (ul Koźla 10/12); Friday and Saturday discos at *Paradise Pub* (ul Wawelska 5) in the Skra Stadium grounds; *Sauna Galla* (ul Ptasia 2); and *Kawiarnia Galeria Między Nami* (ul Bracka 20).

SHOPPING

Warsaw's shopping scene has changed enormously over the past decade and is now lively, colourful and varied. Much trading has moved out of the shops and onto the street. The shops themselves are now better stocked and the assistants are more polite than they used to be. Supermarkets tend to follow western trends in style, products on offer and prices, and the old gloomy, run-down establishments are disappearing.

Markets

Some streets and squares are virtual bazaars these days, with traders selling their goods from plastic sheets, folding beds or makeshift stalls. There are, however, some proper markets.

The most central is the market at Plac Defilad, just at the foot of the majestic Palace of Culture. In the early 1990s the square was occupied by 'tourist traders' from beyond the eastern frontier (and was commonly re-ferred to as the 'Russian bazaar') but the city authorities have moved them on. There is now a virtual city of kiosks operated by Polish small traders selling food, clothing, electrical goods and the like. It's a good place to go to if you urgently need a pair of jeans or sneakers and cannot buy them on a corner closer to your hotel.

Cheaper and much bigger is the bazaar on the outer slopes of the main city stadium, the Stadion Dziesięciolecia, overlooking the Vistula from the Praga side. With over 3000 regular stalls, plus a constellation of part-time and casual vendors, it's thought to be the largest bazaar in Eastern Europe, and it's growing! Many more permanent stalls have been constructed around the stadium over the past few years. There is now a plethora of stalls and port-a-cabins providing basic food and dubious entertainment. It's a town within a town. Its average daily turnover is thought to be around US$2 million.

Most of the Russian traders from Plac Defilad moved here and now occupy the rim of the stadium, accompanied by Mon-golians, Romanians and other international operators. The market is arguably the cheapest place to buy clothing, toiletries, kitchen appliances etc. It's a good place to get a feel for Warsaw. The bazaar is open daily till around noon; it's busiest on Satur-day and Sunday.

A good place to look for photo equip-ment and film is the Giełda Foto, a photo market which operates every Sunday from 10 am to 2 pm in the Stodoła student club at ul Batorego 10. There's always an amazing variety of cameras and accessories on offer ranging from prewar to the newest equipment, and people from other cities come here to buy and sell photo gear. Film can be bought here more cheaply than in shops. If you are a camera buff it's worth coming even if only to have a look.

There's also a Sunday bric-a-brac and an-tiques bazaar on ul Obozowa at the far end of the suburb of Wola.

Crafts

There's an extensive chain of Cepelia shops, which include outlets at Rynek Starego Miasta 10 ('Dom Sztuki Ludowej'), ul Nowy Świat 35, ul Krucza 6/14, ul Krucza 23/31, Chmielna 8, Plac Konstytucji 2 and 5 (two shops), and ul Marszałkowska 99/101 opposite Hotel Forum.

Antiques

Antiques are sold by Desa outlets and by a variety of small antique shops, most of which are in the Old Town and along the Royal Way. Among the best Desa stores are those at ul Nowy Świat 51 (on the corner of ul Warecka) and at ul Marszał-kowska 34/50 (near Plac Zbawiciela); both have a range of old furniture, silverware, watches, paintings etc. Kosmos at Al Ujaz-dowskie 16, Antiqua at ul Freta 21 in the New Town and Lamus at ul Nowomiejska 7 in the Old Town all have a variety of old books, prints and maps.

Note that it's officially forbidden to export works of art created before 1945.

Contemporary Art

If you are serious about buying Polish modern art, shop around in Warsaw and Kraków, as the choice is limited and rather unpredictable elsewhere.

There are plenty of commercial art gal-leries in Warsaw though their standard varies greatly. The galleries nestling in the lobbies of top-class hotels are predictably targeted at hotel guests – moneyed tourists who are not necessarily connoisseurs – so they tend to have a plentiful supply of genteel daubs.

Zapiecek, in the heart of the Old Town at ul Zapiecek 1, is one of the most prestigious city showrooms and offers good-quality works of art for sale. Galeria Art, ul Krakowskie Przedmieście 17 (near the corner of ul Trębacka), often has interesting prints and paintings, and Galeria Nowy Świat, ul Nowy Świat 23, is not bad for ceramics, jewellery and painting. Piotr Nowicki Gallery, ul Nowy Świat 26 (enter through the gate and you'll see it), may have interesting jewellery and original prints.

However, if you are after original prints, the Galeria Grafiki i Plakatu, ul Hoża 40, has unquestionably the best selection in Poland. It also has a good choice of posters, or try the Galeria Plakatu, Rynek Starego Miasta 23.

Books & Records

There's an increasing number of well edited coffee-table books (in English) about Polish art, architecture and nature – nice souvenirs to take home. The Galeria Plakatu (Poster Gallery), Rynek Starego Miasta 23, is a good point to start looking for such books. You'll find more bookshops around the Old Town as well as along the Royal Way. The city's largest EMPiK stores, at ul Nowy Świat 15/17 and ul Marszałkowska 116/122, have good collections of such books.

The best of Polish classical and contemporary music has been transferred to CD and there are an increasing number of shops selling them. The Księgarnia Muzyczna Przy Operze, ul Moliera 8 beside the Grand Theatre, and Księgarnia Muzyczna Odeon, ul Hoża 19, both stock reasonable selections of national composers from Chopin to Penderecki, and also have some Polish jazz.

The EMPiK stores listed above have big music sections packed with CDs and cassettes. Also check CMR Digital at Al Jerozolimskie 2 opposite the National Museum, and Planet Music at ul Mokotowska 17 (Plac Zbawiciela), both of which have a wide choice.

You may also want to try the Giełda Płyt, or the CD market, which is held every Tuesday from 2 to 5 pm at Palladium cinema, ul Złota 7/9. There's always a crowd of both sellers and buyers. Both brand-new and second-hand discs are on sale, from rare oldies to the newest hits. Popular music is the main fare, with only a little classical, folk or jazz. Prices are lower than in shops and are usually a matter of negotiation.

GETTING THERE & AWAY
Air
Airport Okęcie airport is on the southern outskirts of the city, at the southern end of ul Żwirki i Wigury (the only access road), 10km from the centre. It's the only commercial airport in the city, and it's named after the suburb in which it is located. All domestic and international flights arrive and depart from here.

The small but functional terminal has international arrivals on the ground level and departures upstairs. The domestic section occupies a small separate part of the same building.

The international section houses the tourist office (on the arrivals level), which has good information, sells city maps and can help to find a place to stay. A few ATMs on the same level accept some major credit cards, including Visa and MasterCard. The Orbis office charges very high fees for its services and has a kantor that gives extremely low rates. It's best to go upstairs to the Powszechny Bank Kredytowy which exchanges cash and travellers cheques at the best rates in the terminal. However, these are not the best rates in town so it's advisable to change only a small amount, enough to get to the city where any of the numerous kantors will pay you more for your cash. By the same token, if you are leaving Poland from here, you should change your extra złotys back to a hard currency in the city, not at the airport. Also take note that the duty-free shops are beyond passport control, and there are no exchange facilities there.

The arrivals level houses several car rental companies, a left-luggage room and a newsagency – the place to buy public transport tickets. Buses and taxis depart from this level.

Flights You'll find information about domestic routes and fares in the Air section of the Getting Around chapter. Tickets can be booked and bought from the main LOT office in the building of the Marriott Hotel at Al Jerozolimskie 65/79, or from any Orbis office and many other travel agencies.

LOT and foreign carriers link Warsaw with Europe and beyond. Pick up the LOT timetable, which lists international flights to/from Poland on the airlines that land here, along with domestic flights.

Train

Warsaw has several train stations, of which Warszawa Centralna, or Warsaw central station, opposite the Marriott Hotel in the city centre, handles the overwhelming majority of traffic including all international trains. When you arrive, get off the train quickly as the central station is not the terminus.

The station includes a spacious main hall on street level (which houses ticket counters, a post office, newsagency, the helpful tourist office, an ATM, snack bars etc) and a subterranean level with tracks and platforms, right underneath the hall. On an intermediate level between the hall and the platforms is an extensive array of passageways. Here you'll find more fast-food outlets, half a dozen kantors (one of which is open 24 hours), a left-luggage office (open 7 am to 9 pm), lockers (almost always occupied), several Ruch kiosks (for city transport tickets and city maps), a bookshop (well stocked with regional and city maps from all over the country) and plenty of shops selling food, clothing etc. The taxi stand is also on this level, right outside the station on its northern side.

Watch your belongings closely on all levels, and particularly in the passageways which are usually crowded. Be alert on platforms and while boarding the train – pickpocketing and theft are on the increase here.

Warsaw central station is Poland's busiest railway junction, from where trains run to just about every corner of the country. Read the section in this book that deals with your destination and assume that there are roughly the same number of trains in the opposite direction. Refer to the Train section in the Getting Around chapter for details on InterCity trains originating from Warsaw.

International destinations include Berlin, Bratislava, Brussels, Bucharest, Budapest, Cologne, Dresden, Frankfurt/Main, Hrodna, Kiev, Leipzig, Minsk, Moscow, Prague, St Petersburg, Vienna and Vilnius. Refer to the Land section of the Getting There & Away chapter.

Both domestic and international train tickets are available either directly from the counters at the station or from any Orbis office. Some travel agencies also sell international train tickets.

Buying tickets at the central station can be hell even when all 16 windows are open (all 16 now sell all types of tickets). During the day, the long lines may sometimes keep you queuing for an hour or more. Although fewer windows open in the evening and at night, the queues are shorter and the service is quicker. It may be worthwhile buying your ticket at this time. No English is spoken, so write down your requests on paper – refer to the Train section in the Getting Around chapter for details. In that section you will also find information about types of trains and fares.

Other major train stations include Warszawa Zachodnia (West Warsaw), next to the central bus terminal; Warszawa Gdańska, in the northern sector of the city, on the Gdańsk route; and Warszawa Wschodnia (East Warsaw), in the suburb of Praga. Warszawa Śródmieście station, about 200m east of Warsaw central, handles local trains.

Bus

Warsaw has two PKS bus terminals. The Dworzec Centralny PKS (the central bus terminal) operates all domestic buses which head towards the south and west. The terminal is west of the city centre, adjoining Warszawa Zachodnia train station. To get there from the centre, take the commuter train from Warszawa Śródmieście station (two stops).

The Dworzec PKS Stadion (Stadium bus terminal), behind the main city stadium, adjoining the Warszawa Stadion train station (and also easily accessible by commuter train from Warszawa Śródmieście), handles all domestic bus traffic to the north, east and south-east. Bus tickets are sold at the respective terminals.

The Polski Express bus company (refer to the Bus section in the Getting Around chapter) runs its coaches from Okęcie airport. They all call (and can be boarded) at the carrier's bus stop on Al Jana Pawła II, next to the central train station. Tickets for Polski Express routes are available from either of its offices and from selected Orbis outlets, but they cannot be bought at PKS terminals. Information about their services can be obtained on ☎ 620 03 30.

Using PKS services, you might be interested in taking the bus if you're going to Płock, Kazimierz Dolny, Hajnówka (for Białowieża) and some of the Masurian destinations (Ruciane-Nida, Mikołajki and Giżycko). Otherwise it's perhaps more convenient to travel by train. With Polski Express, you may consider travelling by bus to such destinations as Białystok, Lublin, Rzeszów, Łódź, Płock, Toruń, Bydgoszcz, Ostróda and Elbląg. All these cities are serviced by train, but bus travel will be cheaper, and in most cases is almost as fast as the train.

International buses are operated by a few dozen bus companies and depart from either the central PKS bus terminal or Warsaw central train station. Tickets are available from the companies' offices, selected Orbis offices, Almatur and a number of other travel agencies. Shop around, as the carriers and prices vary. A wide range of options for travel to Western Europe is offered by Anna Travel (☎ 825 53 89) at Warsaw central train station and the Bus Travel Center (☎ 628 62 53) at Al Jerozolimskie 63. The 'Turystyka' section of the Saturday edition of *Gazeta Wyborcza* lists most of the bus companies along with their routes, schedules, bus standards, fares and details of where to buy tickets. PKS has daily departures to Vilnius (US$19), Minsk (US$21) and Lviv (US$17). For more information on international routes, see the Land section in the Getting There & Away chapter.

GETTING AROUND
To/From the Airport

The cheapest way of getting from the airport to the city (and vice versa) is by bus No 175, which will take you right into the centre and up to the Old Town, passing en route Warsaw central train station and the youth hostel at ul Smolna. Watch your bags and pockets closely all the way – this line has become a favourite playground for thieves. Don't forget to buy tickets for yourself and your luggage at the airport's newsagency, and to punch them in one of the ticket machines upon boarding the bus.

The next cheapest option is the AirportCity special bus which goes to the Bristol and Europejski hotels, calling at Warsaw central train station. The bus runs from 6 am to 11 pm, every 20 minutes on weekdays and every 30 minutes on weekends. The fare of US$2 (US$1 for students) covers luggage and is paid directly to the driver.

Don't even think about taking taxis from the stand in front of the arrivals hall – they are operated by 'mafia' drivers who will try to charge an astronomical fare (see Local Transport in the Getting Around chapter).

Bus & Tram

There are about 30 tram routes and over 100 bus routes, which are clearly marked on city maps (tram routes in red, bus routes in blue) and at the stops.

Public transport operates from about 5 am to about 11 pm. After 11 pm several night bus lines link major suburbs to the city centre. The night 'terminal' is at ul

Emilii Plater next to the Palace of Culture, from where buses depart every half-hour.

Warsaw's public transport is frequent and cheap. The fare is a flat US$0.40 (US$1.20 on night buses) for either bus or tram, regardless of distance. Students below 26 years of age with an ISIC card pay half the fare in Warsaw (there are as yet no ISIC student concessions in other cities). Bulky luggage (according to the regulations, any that exceeds 60 x 40 x 20cm) costs an extra, ordinary fare. Daily, weekly and monthly passes are available from the Dział Sprzedaży Biletów office, ul Senatorska 37.

There are no conductors on board; you buy a ticket beforehand from Ruch kiosks, then board the tram or bus and punch the ticket (on the side without a metal strip) in one of the small machines inside. Inspections are not unusual and fines are high: US$25 for travel without a validated ticket and US$10 for luggage. There's a new breed of tough and rude plain-clothes inspectors, who literally hunt for foreign tourists.

Watch out for pickpockets on crowded city buses and trams (especially bus No 175 and trams running along Al Jerozolimskie). Some are highly skilled and can easily zip open a bag you thought was in front of you. Don't become separated from your companion by people reaching between you to grab hold of the handrail. The pleasant-looking young man who says hello may only be trying to distract you.

Metro

The construction of a metro consisting of a single north-south line began in 1983, and half of the line, from the southern suburb of Ursynów (Kabaty station) to the Palace of Culture and Science (Centrum station), is in operation. Plans are to open Ratusz station next to Plac Bankowy by the year 2000, and to finish the remaining part of the northern stretch up to Młociny by 2004.

The 12.5km bit in operation includes 12 stations and is serviced by 14 trains which run every eight minutes (every four minutes in rush hours). The Kabaty-Centrum ride takes 20 minutes.

Yellow signs with a big red letter 'M' indicate the entrances to metro stations. Every station has a public toilet and there are lifts for disabled passengers. You use the same tickets as on trams and buses (US$0.40); the differences are that you punch them on the opposite side (where there's a metal strip), and do so at the entrance to the platform, not in the train itself.

Car & Motorcycle

The condition of Warsaw's road surfaces is disgraceful. Streets are full of potholes – some more dangerous than others – so driving demands constant attention and may become very trying. The city transport authorities estimate that 70% of the road surface needs repair or replacement. However, there are no funds for it.

The local government plans to introduce paid parking on central streets. At the time of writing, you could park free almost anywhere, on the road or on the pavement. See how the locals park their cars and follow their lead. For security, try to park your car in a guarded car park (*parking strzeżony*). There are some in central Warsaw, including one on ul Parkingowa behind Hotel Forum.

Car Rental Warsaw has more than 20 car rental operators. Most companies need advance booking, sometimes as far ahead as one week. The major international companies such as Avis, Budget or Hertz are pricey and rarely offer any discounts. It's probably cheaper to arrange rental through the company office at home before your trip. Polish operators tend to be cheaper, sometimes considerably so. Among them, you can try the Local Rent a Car (☎ 657 81 81, fax 826 11 11) and the Ann Rent a Car (☎ 650 32 62, fax 650 32 63).

Car Problems PZM operates a 24 hour road breakdown service (*pomoc drogowa*) from its office at ul Kaszubska 2 (☎ 981, ☎ 9637). A host of private operators advertise in the

WARSAW

local press and you'll find their ads under the *autoholowanie* heading in the *Gazeta Wyborcza* and *Życie Warszawy* papers.

Taxi

Taxis in Warsaw are easily available and not very expensive by western standards. There are about 20 taxi companies, including Radio Taxi (☎ 919), Super Taxi (☎ 96 22), Lux Taxi (☎ 96 66) and Sawa Taxi (☎ 644 44 44), all of which are pretty reliable. All are recognisable by big signs on top of the car with their name and phone number.

The daytime charge (from 6 am to 10 pm) is US$1.20 for the first kilometre plus US$0.50 per each additional kilometre; night-time fares are US$1.20 and US$0.70, respectively. Most taxis in Warsaw now have their meters adjusted to the appropriate tariff, so you just pay what the meter

says. When you board a taxi, make sure the meter is turned on in your presence, which ensures you don't have the previous passenger's fare added to yours.

Taxis can be waved down on the street, but it's much easier to walk to the nearest taxi stand, which are plentiful. You can also order a taxi by phone and there's no extra charge for this service.

Beware of taxis parked in front of luxury hotels, at the airport, the Warsaw central train station, the Rotunda (on the corner of ul Marszałkowska and Al Jerozolimskie), at Plac Zamkowy and in the vicinity of tourist sights. Many are so-called 'mafia' taxis, whose drivers insist on absurd fares, up to six times the normal fare (see Local Transport in the Getting Around chapter). The local authorities are trying to eradicate the cab mafia, but so far with little success.

Mazovia & Podlasie

Mazovia (Mazowsze in Polish, pronounced 'Mah-zov-sheh') was incorporated into Poland in the early days of Piast rule. It became of central importance to the Crown when two Polish kings, Władysław Herman and Bolesław Krzywousty, had their seat in the Mazovian town of Płock (1079-1138). When the latter divided the country between his sons, Mazovia became one of several rival principalities. Kazimierz Wielki regained suzerainty over the region, though it was ruled by Mazovian dukes until the last of the line died without an heir in 1526. Mazovia again came to the fore in 1596 when Poland's capital was transferred from Kraków to Warsaw.

Despite its political role, however, it was never a rich region – its soil being infertile – so it was not densely populated. Old Mazovian towns are few and far between. Nonetheless, there are some attractions in the region which are well worth exploring. Some sights can be conveniently visited on day trips from Warsaw (the Kampinos National Park, Żelazowa Wola, Sromów, Łowicz, Nieborów and Arkadia), while others are probably better seen on the way to other regions, unless you have your own transport.

To the east of Mazovia, stretching along the Polish-Belarusian border, lies the Podlasie plain. Culturally quite different but geographically similar, it's usually tacked onto Mazovia in studies of Poland.

Highlights

- Experience the colourful Corpus Christi procession in Łowicz
- Wander through the aristocratic palace in Nieborów
- Reflect on the memorial at the Nazi death camp in Treblinka
- Relive history at the skansen in Ciechanowiec
- Go birdwatching in Biebrza National Park
- Explore the unique Białowieża National Park

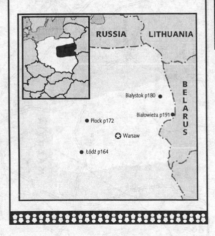

Western Mazovia

KAMPINOS NATIONAL PARK
☎ 022

The Kampinos National Park (Kampinoski Park Narodowy or, as it's popularly called, the Puszcza Kampinoska) begins just outside Warsaw's north-western administrative boundaries and stretches west for about 40km. Occupying an area of 357 sq km, it's one of the largest national parks in Poland. About 75% of its area is covered by forest, mainly pine and oak. The park has wooded dunes up to 30m high, and some barely accessible swamps and bogs, which shelter much of its animal life.

Elk live in the park but are hard to spot; you are more likely to see other animals such as hares, foxes, deer and occasionally wild boar. Among birds, there are black storks, cranes, herons and marsh harriers.

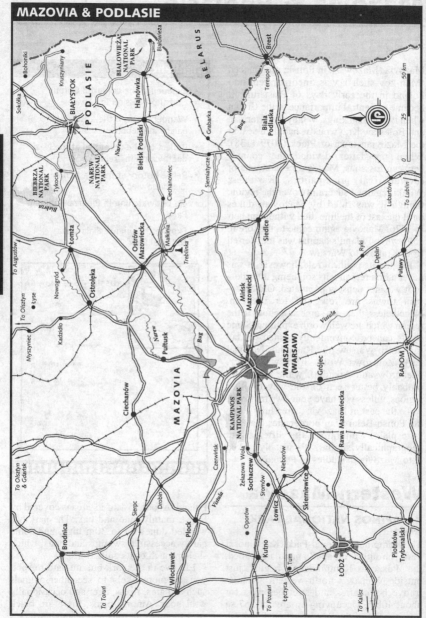

MAZOVIA & PODLASIE

Orientation

The park is popular among hikers from the capital. There are about 300km of marked walking trails running through the most attractive parts of the park, and some trails are good for cycling as well. The eastern part of the park, closer to the city, is more favoured by walkers as it's easily accessible by public transport from the city. The western part is much less visited, though it also provides a variety of one-day routes. For those who want to spend longer in the forest, there are two long trails, marked in red and green, which cross the whole length of the park from east to west. Both start from Dziekanów Leśny on the eastern edge of the park and wind westwards, crossing each other several times on the way. The red trail (54km) ends in Brochów, and the green one (51km) in Żelazowa Wola.

If you plan on hiking in the park, buy a copy of the detailed *Kampinoski Park Narodowy* map (scale 1:50,000), readily available in Warsaw.

Places to Stay & Eat

There are no hotels in the park but you can camp in several bivouac sites designated for camping. There's a small summer *youth hostel* (☎ 725 80 34) in the hamlet of Łubiec, in the central part of the park, and the *Domki Turystyczne* (☎ 725 00 13, ul Padlewskiego 1) in the village of Kampinos, on the southern edge of the park.

Getting There & Away

There are buses from Warsaw to towns and villages on the outskirts of the park and within its borders. The most popular jumping-off point for walks in the eastern part of the park is the village of Truskaw. Warsaw suburban bus No 708 goes there from Plac Wilsona in the Żoliborz district. Alternatively, you can take bus No 701, also from Plac Wilsona, to Dąbrowa Leśna, but this is a less convenient starting point.

If you plan on hiking in the western part of the park, perhaps the best point to start from is Kampinos. 41km from Warsaw, serviced by PKS buses from Warsaw's central bus station.

ŻELAZOWA WOLA

Żelazowa Wola ('Zheh-lah-zo-vah Vo-lah') is a tiny village 53km west of Warsaw, on the edge of the Kampinos National Park. It owes its fame to Frédéric Chopin, who was born here on 22 February 1810. The house where the event took place has been renovated and furnished in the style of the composer's era, and is now a **museum**. The exhibition is modest and doesn't include much of Chopin's original memorabilia, but the tranquillity and charm of the place – the house itself and a park around it – make for a pleasant stop. The museum and the park are open daily, except Monday, 9.30 am to 5.30 pm (October to April till 4 pm). The combined ticket to the museum and the park costs US$2; the park-only ticket costs US$0.70. Students pay half.

The major attraction of the place is the Sunday **piano recitals**, often performed by top-rank virtuosi. These are held from the first Sunday of May to the last Sunday before 17 October, the anniversary of Chopin's death (in Paris in 1849). There are usually two concerts, up to an hour long, on each Sunday, at 11 am and 3 pm. The music is played in the parlour while the audience is seated on the terrace in front of the house. There's no fee for these recitals other than the park-only entrance ticket. Check the times and program in Warsaw (in the tourist offices or the Chopin Society in the Ostrogski Palace) before setting off.

There's a *restaurant* opposite the entrance to the park in Żelazowa Wola but nowhere to stay for the night. The nearest accommodation is in Sochaczew, 6km away.

Getting There & Away

There are two ways of getting to Żelazowa Wola from Warsaw. One is to take a train from Warszawa Śródmieście station to Sochaczew. From there, catch the local urban bus No 6, which goes every hour or two to Żelazowa Wola (6km), or take a taxi.

The other way is to go directly by bus: there are one or two morning buses from the Warsaw central bus terminal to the village of Kamion, which go via Leszno and Kampinos and will drop you off at Żelazowa Wola.

Several travel agencies in Warsaw lay on organised tours for the Sunday concerts – a more comfortable but more expensive option.

ŁOWICZ
- **pop 32,000**   ☎ **046**

After its founding in the 12th century, Łowicz ('Wo-vich') was for over 600 years the seat of the archbishops of Gniezno, the supreme church authority in Poland. Consequently the town has a number of churches and other ecclesiastical buildings, including the massive collegiate church overlooking the central square. Apart from these singular religious structures, however, the town's historical character has been largely lost.

Łowicz has also become well known as a centre for folk arts and crafts of the region. However, this isn't particularly evident either, other than in the local museum or during the elaborate celebrations of Corpus Christi.

Information
The tourist office (☎ 837 32 69) is at Stary Rynek 3 (the main square). The café in the Łowicki Ośrodek Kultury (☎ 837 39 31), ul Pijarska 1 just off the square, provides Internet access. The Bank Pekao, ul Długa 27, exchanges travellers cheques and has a useful ATM, but if all you want is to change cash, there are a couple of kantors on the Stary Rynek.

Things to See
The **Regional Museum**, on the main square, is in the old missionary college, which was designed by prolific Dutch architect Tylman van Gameren and built at the end of the 17th century. The best-preserved part of the college's interior is the former priests' chapel, with its vault decorated with baroque frescoes (1695) by Italian artist Michelangelo

Palloni. The chapel is part of the museum and houses the baroque art section.

The historical section (1st floor) is devoted to the archaeology of the region and the history of Łowicz. The ethnographic section (2nd floor) boasts a fine collection of local folk costumes, decorated wooden furniture, coloured paper cut-outs, painted Easter eggs, pottery and woodcarving.

In the back garden of the museum are two old farmsteads from the surrounding area, complete with original furnishings, implements and decoration.

The museum is open 10 am to 4 pm, except Monday and the day following public holidays. It may be open an hour longer on Sunday and holidays in summer.

Among churches, the most interesting is the vast 15th century **collegiate church** (Kolegiata), just across the main square from the museum. Originally Gothic, it underwent several remodellings and reflects a mishmash of styles including Renaissance, baroque and rococo. Twelve archbishops of Gniezno and primates of Poland are buried in the church.

Corpus Christi
The main religious event of Łowicz is Corpus Christi (on a Thursday in May or June), during which a procession circles the main square and the collegiate church, with most of its participants dressed in traditional costumes. Arguably the most solemnly celebrated Corpus Christi in the country, this is the best time to come to Łowicz to see the brightly coloured and embroidered dresses and get a taste of the Catholic fervour of the Polish countryside. The procession starts about noon and takes roughly two hours to do the whole loop.

Places to Stay & Eat
The cheapest is the summer *youth hostel* (☎ *837 37 03, ul Grunwaldzka 9*), in a primary school next to the Warsaw-Poznań highway, 1.5km north of the main square. It only opens from 1 July to 20 August.

More convenient and reliable is the *Centrum Uczelniane* (☎ *837 44 67, ul*

Sienkiewicza 1), 100m south of the Rynek. This student centre rents out rooms from July to September (US$18/24 a single/double without bath) and has a self-service cafeteria which serves a few cheap meals.

The cheapest all-year accommodation is *Hotel Aneta (☎ 837 52 43, ul Powstańców 1863r 12)*, about 1.5km south of the centre. This workers' dorm of the Syntex factory provides basic doubles/triples without bath for US$10/15, and doubles with bath for US$18.

Hotel Zacisze (☎ 837 33 26, ☎/fax 837 62 44, ul Kaliska 5), a few hundred metres south of the Rynek, is far better than anything listed above. It costs US$30/34/36 a single/double/triple with private bath and breakfast, and has its own restaurant, reputedly the best in town.

The new *Hotel Akademicki (☎ 0602 67 51 83, ul Warszawska 9A)*, near the train station, is also good value at US$30 for a double or triple, and also has some more comfortable suites.

Finally, you have *Zajazd Łowicki (☎ 837 41 64)*, which sits on the ever-busy intersection of the Warsaw, Poznań and Łódź highways, on the north-western outskirts of town, 2km from the centre. It's not a tranquil or attractive place to stay (US$32/35 a double/triple with bath), but it has a 24 hour restaurant, which may be useful for hungry passing motorists.

Getting There & Away

The bus and train stations are side by side, a five minute walk east from the main square. There are regular trains to Warsaw (82km), Łódź (63km) and Kutno (45km). There are also regular buses to Łódź (52km) and several daily to Płock (58km). For Arkadia (5km) and Nieborów (10km), take any bus heading for Bolimów or Skierniewice via Bolimów.

NIEBORÓW

• pop 1500   ☎ 046

The small village of Nieborów ('Nyeh-bo-roof'), 10km south-east of Łowicz, is noted for its magnificent palace. Designed by Tylman van Gameren for Cardinal Radziejowski, the archbishop of Gniezno and Primate of Poland residing in Łowicz, the baroque palace was built in the last decade of the 17th century. Shortly afterwards, a French garden was laid out directly behind the palace.

After changing hands several times, the palace was eventually bought by Prince Michał Hieronim Radziwiłł in 1774. He and his wife Helena lavishly crammed it with valuable furniture and works of art, including paintings and antique sculptures, and an imposing library.

The English-style informal landscaped park, designed by Szymon Bogumił Zug, was laid out next to the old baroque garden. A majolica factory, the only one in Poland at the time, was established on the grounds in 1881 and operated on and off until 1906.

In the 1920s the palace underwent its last important transformation when a mansard storey was added to the building. The palace remained in the possession of the Radziwiłł family right up till WWII, after which, fortunately undamaged, it was taken over by the state and converted into a museum.

Things to See

The **palace museum** occupies over a half of the building's rooms. Part of the ground floor features Roman sculpture and pieces of bas-relief, most of which date from the first centuries AD. You then go upstairs by an unusual staircase clad, both walls and ceiling, with ornamental Dutch tiles dating from around 1770.

The whole 1st floor was restored and furnished according to the original style and contains a wealth of *objets d'art*. Note the tiled stoves, each one different, made in the local majolica factory, and also don't miss the two late 17th century globes in the library, the work of Venetian geographer Vincenzo Coronelli.

The **French garden** on the southern side of the palace, with a wide central avenue lined with old lime trees, is dotted with sculptures, statues, tombstones, sarcophagi, pillars, columns and other stone fragments dating from various periods. Many of them were brought from the Arkadia park (see the following section). The **English land-scape park**, complete with a stream, lake and a couple of ponds, is to the west of the garden, behind an L-shaped reservoir.

From mid-January to mid-November, the museum is open daily, except Monday and the day following public holidays, from 10 am to 4 pm (May to August it closes at 6 pm weekdays). Both the garden and the park can be visited from 10 am till dusk (except Monday).

Places to Stay & Eat

There's a *café* in the palace complex which serves light meals and is all that day trippers to Nieborów will need. It's closed on Monday, as are the palace and park themselves. If you plan an overnight stay, there are no hotels in Nieborów, only a youth hostel and a camp site.

The July-August *youth hostel* (☎ 838 56 94) is in a local school, 1.5km north of the palace on the road towards Bednary. The *Camping Nr 77* (☎ 838 56 92) is west of the palace park, off the Skierniewice road (a 10 minute walk from the park's main gate). It tends to open early in May and close some time in October. It has 20 cabins, each containing two triple rooms and a bath. The room costs US$20, but if there are not many guests they may charge you only for the beds you're occupying. You can also pitch your own tent. There is a snack bar in the grounds, which also offers some meals.

Getting There & Away

There are no direct buses to/from Warsaw (80km), but about six buses daily run to Łowicz (10km), from where hourly trains will take you on to Warsaw. An alternative way to get to Warsaw is by walking to Bednary (4km), where the Łowicz-Warsaw trains stop. See the following section for more about transport.

ARKADIA

Laid out by Princess Helena Radziwiłł, the lady of the Nieborów palace, this romantic park was, in the words of its creator, to be an 'idyllic land of peace and happiness'.

The design of Arkadia was a product of new philosophical and aesthetic trends that had emerged in the second half of the 18th century in Western Europe, originally in Britain and France. Taking their inspiration from the traditions of the classical world and the Middle Ages, the authors of the new philosophy called for a return to the past and to nature.

These fashionable ideas did not take long to inspire the leisured women of the foremost Polish clans, including the Czartoryski, Lubomirski, Ogiński and Radziwiłł families. They all rushed to create their own parks in the closing decades of the 18th century. Of these, Arkadia was probably the most original and unusual.

Begun around 1780, the park was developed, enlarged and improved until the death of the princess in 1821. During her frequent foreign travels, she collected and sent home decorative elements, tombstones and statues, fragments of antique sculptures and rare and exotic works of art. She also brought to Arkadia architectural details from the collegiate church and the ruined castle in Łowicz. All these bits and pieces were then fitted into the park's design, either as freestanding elements or incorporated into buildings (most evident in the Archpriest's Sanctuary, an amazingly haphazard composition).

In the first stage, up till 1800, Szymon Bogumił Zug, the court architect of King Stanisław August Poniatowski, was the chief designer of the park. Most of the structures built during that period have survived in better or worse shape to this day. After 1800, a new architect of Italian origin, Enrico Ittar, introduced innovative and bold solutions and, returning to a Roman vision, built the Amphitheatre (patterned upon the theatre of Pompeii), the Roman Circus and the Tomb of Illusions. Unfortunately, almost nothing of his work survives.

After the princess's death, the park fell into decay. Most of the works of art have been taken to Nieborów's palace and can be admired today either in its museum or the garden, and the abandoned buildings fell gradually into ruin. After WWII, some restoration work was carried out but not completed, and only recently a further conservation program has begun; it will be a while before the work is finished. Meanwhile, the air of decay adds to the romantic atmosphere of the place.

Discover for yourself the charm of the pavilions, temples and other structures, by wandering at your leisure amid tall trees and abandoned bits and pieces of carved stone, some of them 2000 years old. Look for curious details, read the peculiar inscriptions, and feel the poetry of the ruins and tombs. The park is open daily, except Monday, from 10 am till dusk, unless the caretaker feels like closing down earlier.

Getting There & Away
Arkadia is conveniently accessible from Warsaw. Take a train to Łowicz (departing roughly every hour from Warszawa Śródmieście station), get off at the obscure station of Mysłaków (the last one before reaching Łowicz) and walk seven minutes to the park. Note that fast trains don't stop in Mysłaków.

There are five or six buses daily passing through Arkadia on their way to Łowicz (5km) and, in the opposite direction, to Nieborów (5km).

It's hard to 'do' Łowicz, Arkadia and Nieborów within a one day round trip from Warsaw. If you exclude Łowicz, it's relatively easy. Probably the best way to do it is to go by train to Arkadia (as described above) and to check the bus schedule to Nieborów before visiting the park. If there is a bus due, take it and visit Arkadia on your way back. When you arrive at Nieborów, again, first check when the buses return to Arkadia (they go through to Łowicz). Alternatively, you can try to hitch.

SROMÓW
Sromów ('Sro-moof') is a small, unremarkable village 10km north-east of Łowicz, which you can hardly find even on detailed,

large scale maps. Yet it does have one great attraction – the private **Crafts Museum** (Muzeum Ludowe) founded by skilled artisan and passionate crafts collector Julian Brzozowski.

Set in a garden full of gnomes and other models, the museum is housed in three buildings, two of which feature animated tableaux of historic scenes and village life – a country wedding, a pageant of kings, a Corpus Christi procession, the four seasons on the farm etc. The figures are all carved from wood and painstakingly painted and costumed. The animation, with synchronised music, is by concealed rods and shafts driven by electric motors. All this is the result of 40 years of work by Mr Brzozowski and his family. Although a little kitsch, it is unique and fascinating.

Other exhibits include paper cut-outs, regional costumes, folk paintings, decorated wooden chests and embroidery. The third building houses a collection of about 20 old horse carts and carriages assembled by the owner from the people living in the surrounding villages.

The museum is on the village's main road, and is open daily. If it's locked, inquire at Mr Brzozowski's house across the road from the museum, and he or someone else will open it and guide you around.

Getting There & Away
Sromów is 7km from Łowicz along the main highway to Warsaw, then 2km north along the side road towards Rybno, and finally 1km west to the village itself. Sporadic buses from Łowicz to Rybno will let you off at the second turn-off, 1km from the museum. The museum is signposted in Polish and German from the main Łowicz-Warsaw highway. Motorists could easily visit the museum in conjunction with Nieborów palace, only 10 minutes drive away.

ŁÓDŹ
- **pop 825,000**   ☎ 042
Łódź ('Woodge') is a young city, but after rapid industrial development it has surpassed

ŁÓDŹ

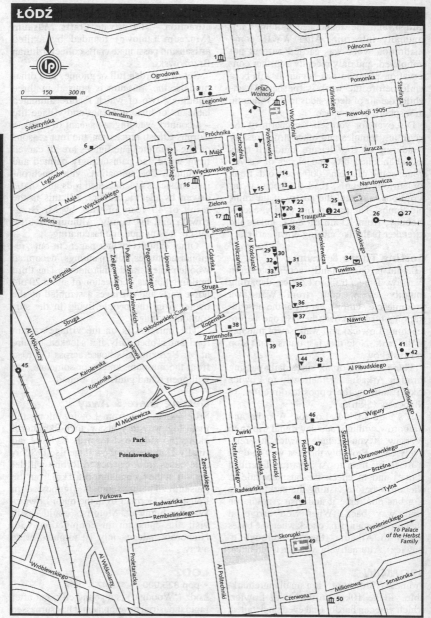

0 150 300 m

ŁÓDŹ

PLACES TO STAY
3 Youth Hostel
6 Hotel Garnizonowy
11 Hotel Polonia
23 Hotel Savoy
25 Hotel Centrum
28 Hotel Grand
38 Youth Hostel
39 Hotel Światowid
43 Hotel Dosko
46 Pensjonat Déjà Vu

PLACES TO EAT
8 Bar Bistro Jędrek
14 Steakhouse Ramzes
15 Jadłodajnia Dietetyczna
19 Steak House Kanion
20 Restauracja BeRoKo
22 Bar Kaskada

30 Restauracja Chińska Złota Kaczka
31 Restauracja u Plastyków
33 Sphinx
35 Restauracja Esplanada
36 Kawiarnia & Cocktail Bar Hortex
40 Blikle
42 Billa Supermarket
44 Restauracja Ha Long

OTHER
1 Historical Museum of Łódź
2 Teatr Powszechny
4 British Council
5 Museum of Ethnography & Archaeology
7 Internet Klub
9 Teatr Nowy
10 Teatr Wielki (Grand Theatre)

12 Teatr im Stefana Jaracza
13 EMPiK
16 Museum of Art
17 City Art Gallery
18 Mesa Computers (Cybercafé)
21 Orbis
24 Tourist Office & Cultural Information Centre
26 Łódź Fabryczna Train Station
27 Central Bus Terminal
29 Irish Pub
32 EMPiK
34 Main Post Office
37 PDI (Cybercafé)
41 Pactor ATK (Cybercafé)
45 Łódź Kaliska Train Station
47 Bank Pekao
48 State Philharmonic
49 Cathedral
50 Textile Museum

MAZOVIA & PODLASIE

much older towns and is today Poland's largest urban centre after Warsaw. Although the first account of its existence dates from the 14th century, it remained an obscure settlement until the beginning of the 19th century. In the 1820s the government of the Congress Kingdom of Poland embarked on a program to industrialise the country, and Łódź was selected to be a new textile centre. It subsequently underwent an unprecedented economic boom.

Enterprising industrialists – Jews, Germans and Poles alike – rushed in to build textile mills, closely followed by workers flooding into the city. The arrival of the steam engine in 1838 and the abolition of customs barriers to Russia in 1850 were two milestones in the city's growth. Opulent palaces of the mill owners mushroomed, as did drab proletarian suburbs. By the outbreak of WWI, Łódź had grown a thousandfold, reaching a population of half a million.

After WWI the city's growth slowed, mainly because of the loss of the huge eastern market, but industrial sectors such as machinery and chemistry continued to expand. In the 1930s ethnic Poles made up only half the population; the rest were mostly Jews and Germans. Having escaped major destruction during WWII, Łódź continued as Poland's textile capital – the Polish Manchester – responsible for nearly half of Poland's textile production, though this figure has dropped over recent years.

Łódź is also the Polish Hollywood. As a result of a film school and film studios being established here, the city became the national centre for cinematography. Most of the great figures of Polish cinema, such as Polański, Skolimowski, Wajda and Kieślowski, started out in Łódź.

At first sight, Łódź looks sprawling, grubby and unpleasant; however, this is only half the picture. Although there isn't a single city building older than 200 years, there is an enormous wealth of 19th century architecture, including the mill owners' residences, in an extraordinary hotchpotch of styles. Look for some amazing examples of Art Nouveau, for which Łódź is known nationally.

Information

Tourist Office The Wojewódzki Ośrodek Informacji Turystycznej (☎ 633 71 69, fax 633 99 02), ul Traugutta 18, is the city's main tourist office, open weekdays 8.15 am to 4.15 pm, Saturday 10 am to 2 pm. It's well run and the staff are helpful and knowledgeable. The cultural information centre is also there (see Entertainment later in this section). Pick up a free copy of *Welcome to Łódź*, a practical tourist magazine.

Money There are plenty of kantors along ul Piotrkowska and in the adjacent streets. There are also several useful ATMs, including at ul Piotrkowska 81 and 126. Travellers cheques can be exchanged in the Bank Pekao offices at ul Piotrkowska 212/214 and 288, which also handle Visa and MasterCard cash advances.

Email & Internet Access There are quite a number of places providing access to the Internet and email, including Internet Klub (☎ 666 35 54) at ul Gdańska 31, Pactor ATK (☎ 676 20 84) at ul Kilińskiego 122/128 (in the building of the Billa supermarket), Mesa Computers (☎ 630 57 03) at Al Kościuszki 1 and PDI (☎ 630 21 94) at ul Piotrkowska 118.

Bookshops The Księgarnia Oxpol (☎ 630 20 13), ul Piotrkowska 63, has possibly the best choice of English-language publications. For foreign press, check the two central EMPiKs, at ul Piotrkowska 81 and ul Narutowicza 8/10.

Things to See
Łódź developed around ul Piotrkowska, its 4km main north-south axis. It is in this area that most of the surviving 19th century architecture can be seen. Most museums, too, are on or near this artery, and in some cases they are installed in old palaces (one in an old mill).

The **Historical Museum of Łódź** (Muzeum Historii Miasta Łodzi), ul Ogrodowa 15, is located in the palace of the Poznański family, who were among the wealthiest Jewish clans in the city. The palace is most impressive, especially its spectacular dining hall. The museum features exhibitions dedicated to Łódź's famous citizens, including pianist Artur

Rubinstein and writer Jerzy Kosiński. Both were of Jewish origin born in Łódź. The museum is open 10 am to 2 pm (on Wednesday 2 to 6 pm); closed Monday.

The **Museum of Ethnography and Archaeology** is at Plac Wolności 14. The archaeological section has finds from central Poland from the Stone Age to the Middle Ages. The changing ethnographic exhibitions feature crafts from various regions of Poland. The museum is open Tuesday, Thursday and Friday 10 am to 5 pm, Wednesday 9 am to 4 pm, Saturday 9 am to 3 pm, and Sunday 10 am to 3 pm.

The **Museum of Art** (Muzeum Sztuki), ul Więckowskiego 36, boasts an extensive collection of 20th century Polish and international paintings, including many by contemporary artists. There are works by Picasso, Chagall and Ernst (not always on display). The museum is open Tuesday 10 am to 5 pm, Wednesday and Friday 11 am to 5 pm, Thursday noon to 7 pm, and Saturday and Sunday 10 am to 4 pm.

Nearby at ul Wólczańska 31/33 is the **City Art Gallery** (Miejska Galeria Sztuki) in the old residence of Kindermann, a German industrialist. There are temporary exhibitions so you never know what you will see, but the building itself is well worth a look. Built in 1903, it is a handsome Art Nouveau villa.

At the far southern end of ul Piotrkowska is the **Textile Museum** (Centralne Muzeum Włókiennictwa). Accommodated inside one of the oldest mills, dating from the 1830s, it houses a collection of textile machinery ranging from the early looms to contemporary devices (ground floor). Fabrics, clothing and other objects related to the industry are on the 1st floor. The two upper floors have temporary exhibitions. The museum is open Tuesday and Saturday 10 am to 4 pm, Wednesday and Friday 9 am to 5 pm, Thursday 10 am to 5 pm, and Sunday 10 am to 3 pm. Tram Nos 6 and 19 from Plac Wolności will let you off at the door.

The **Księży Młyn**, the former residence of the Herbst family, is at ul Przędzalniana 72, 1.5km east of the Textile Museum (a 20 minute walk along ul Tymienieckiego). The building (from 1875) is now a museum and shows how the barons of industry lived in Łódź up till WWII. Although the owners fled abroad, taking all the furnishings and works of art with them, the interior has been restored and furnished like the original. The museum is open Tuesday 10 am to 5 pm, Wednesday and Friday noon to 5 pm, Thursday noon to 7 pm, and Saturday and Sunday 11 am to 4 pm.

Łódź's **Jewish Cemetery** was founded in 1892 to provide a final resting place for members of the large and steadily growing Jewish community. Covering an area of about 40 hectares, this is the largest Jewish graveyard in Europe. There are around 68,000 surviving tombstones, some of which are very beautiful. The cemetery is open 9 am to 3 pm except Saturday. There's a small entry fee. You'll need a head cover to get in. The cemetery is about 3km north-east of the centre. Three tram lines will take you there from the centre: No 1 from ul Kilińskiego, No 15 from Plac Wolności, and No 19 from Al Kościuszki.

Special Events

The Festival of Theatre Schools takes place in April. It's a presentation of the most remarkable productions by students of the major theatre schools in Poland.

The Łódź Ballet Meetings is a ballet festival which includes both Polish and foreign groups. Performances are staged in the Grand Theatre, and the event runs for two weeks over May/June of every odd year.

The International Artistic Textile Triennial gathers together a collection of artistic creations involving textiles. The main exhibition is in the Textile Museum from early June to late October, and is accompanied by other displays in the private art galleries. The 10th Triennial will be held in 2001.

Mediaschool, or the International Film and Television Schools' Festival, is held every October and displays film achievements by students from all over the world.

In December, there's the modest Łódź Theatre Meetings, featuring productions by Polish amateur theatres.

Places to Stay

As in most large cities, hotels in Łódź are relatively expensive for what they offer – particularly in the middle and upper price brackets where many hotels are poor or, at best, average value. The tourist office keeps an eye on local accommodation and prices, and may help to find a room if asked.

Places to Stay – Budget

Łódź has two camping grounds. The all-year *Camping Nr 167 Na Rogach* (☎ 659 70 13, ul Łupkowa 10/16) is about 5km north-east of the city centre on the Łowicz road. It's accessible by bus No 60 from ul Narutowicza near Łódź Fabryczna train station. Heated cabins are US$18/30 a double without/with bath.

Camping Stawy Jana (☎ 646 15 51, ul Rzgowska 247) is 5km south of the centre on the Piotrków Trybunalski road. Take tram No 4 from ul Kilińskiego near Łódź Fabryczna station to the end of the line and continue walking south the remaining 500m. This camp site also has budget all-year cabins.

The city has two youth hostels, both centrally located and both open year-round. The better *youth hostel* (☎ 633 03 65, ul Legionów 27) has 78 beds distributed in singles, doubles, triples and small dorms (maximum of six beds). The other *youth hostel* (☎ 636 65 99, ul Zamenhofa 13) is open Thursday to Monday only unless booked in advance by groups. Both hostels are roughly midway between Łódź Fabryczna and Łódź Kaliska train stations, within a 15 minute walk of either station.

Next in terms of price is *Hotel Szpitala im Kopernika* (☎ 681 15 77, ul Paderewskiego 13), 3km south of the centre but easily accessible by bus No 57 from Łódź Fabryczna station. This small hospital hostel costs US$11/15/22 a single/double/triple with shared facilities.

More convenient is *Hotel Garnizonowy* (☎ 633 80 23, ul Legionów 81). This former army dorm lacks style but is close to the city centre and costs US$18/25 a double/triple without bath.

Places to Stay – Mid-Range

Don't expect luxuries in any of the hotels listed in this section; they are actually quite simple. The centrally located *Hotel Dosko* (☎ *636 04 28, Al Piłsudskiego 8*) is a former workers' dormitory. It occupies the top three floors of a 16-storey tower, and provides good views over the city centre. Beds in doubles, triples or quads without bath cost US$12 each.

Hotel Argo (☎ *655 34 94, ul Łagiewnicka 54*), about 1.5km north of Plac Wolności, is also a former workers' dorm. Singles/doubles/triples with shared facilities cost US$13/26/30.

Hotel Polonia (☎ *632 87 73, fax 633 18 96, ul Narutowicza 38*) is a bit run-down and rather poor value at US$26/38 a single/double without bath, US$40/60 with bath.

Places to Stay – Top End

The cheapest central option in this bracket is *Hotel Savoy* (☎ *632 93 60, fax 632 93 68, ul Traugutta 6*), a five minute walk west from the Łódź Fabryczna station. Singles with bath range between US$30 and US$45 while doubles are US$55 to US$65. Breakfast is included in the price.

The old-style, Orbis-run *Hotel Grand* (☎ *633 99 20, fax 633 78 76, ul Piotrkowska 72*) is the city's oldest existing hotel. Opened in 1888 at the peak of the textile boom, it was for a long time the city's top hotel, with such distinctive guests as Pablo Casals and Isadora Duncan. Today it doesn't fly so high, but nonetheless is still comfortable and stylish, costing around US$65 to US$90 a single and US$100 to US$120 a double, breakfast included.

Hotel Grand's modern competitors include *Hotel Światowid* (☎ *636 36 37, fax 636 52 91, Al Kościuszki 68*), and *Hotel Centrum* (☎ *632 86 40, fax 636 96 50, ul Kilińskiego 59/63*). They both are marginally cheaper than the Grand. Both are in dull high-rise blocks from the mid-1970s, though their rooms have been revamped; the Centrum offers slightly better standards.

Far more stylish is the small *Pensjonat Déjà Vu* (☎ *636 20 60, fax 636 70 83, ul Wigury 4*). Set in a fine villa dating from 1925, and preserving its style and internal decoration, the hotel offers just four spacious double rooms with bath for US$70 each, breakfast included. Advance booking is essential.

Places to Eat

The city's main culinary artery is ul Piotrkowska and its environs. There's still an array of the milk bar-style places in central Łódź, which provide some of the cheapest meals in town. The best of these include *Bar Kaskada* (*ul Narutowicza 7/9*) and *Jadłodajnia Dietetyczna* (*ul Zielona 5*).

A bit more expensive but still very reasonable are some of the new bistros and restaurants that have sprung up along ul Piotrkowska, including *Bar Bistro Jędrek* at No 15, *Steakhouse Ramzes* at No 40, *Steak House Kanion* at No 56, *Restauracja BeRoKo* at No 64 and *Sphinx* at No 93. The last listed is the best value; it has two other outlets farther down ul Piotrkowska, at Nos 175A and 270. The Vietnamese *Restauracja Ha Long* (*ul Piotrkowska 152*) is one of the cheapest Oriental eateries.

Up the price ladder, Łódź has quite a choice of new, decent restaurants, of which *Restauracja Esplanada* (☎ *630 59 89, ul Piotrkowska 100*) is arguably the trendiest these days. It serves respectable Polish food in fine stylish surroundings, with good service, prices to match and live music on some evenings.

Cheaper and less formal is the charming basement *Restauracja u Plastyków* (☎ *636 93 95, ul Piotrkowska 86*). Decorated in a folksy Polish countryside style, it offers hearty, traditional food at good prices.

The rash of attractive new places is overshadowing some of the established venues, including perhaps the city's most famous establishment, *Restauracja Malinowa*, in the Hotel Grand. It offers satisfactory, if a bit uninventive and expensive, Polish cooking in its grandiose dining hall.

Restauracja Chińska Złota Kaczka (☎ *632 22 61, ul Piotrkowska 79*) is the oldest Chinese restaurant in Łódź, and continues to serve good food, mostly of the Beijing variety, in its nonsmoking surroundings.

The *Kawiarnia & Cocktail Bar Hortex* *(ul Piotrkowska 106)* is the place for pastries, cream cakes, milk shakes, ice creams, coffee etc. The famous Blikle's (doughnuts) and a good espresso can be found at the *Blikle* outlet *(ul Piotrkowska 128)*.

Entertainment

Cultural Events With a philharmonic hall, an opera house and eight theatres, Łódź has fairly diverse cultural and artistic offerings. The Ośrodek Informacji Kulturalnej (Culture Information Centre), sharing premises with the tourist office (same phone number and opening hours), is the best place to find out what's on. It also sells tickets for some shows.

The city publishes a good cultural monthly, *Kalejdoskop*, which details (in Polish) what's going on in local theatres, cinemas, art galleries and museums. It can be bought from Ruch kiosks and the culture centre for US$0.50.

The main venue for opera and ballet is *Teatr Wielki (Grand Theatre;* ☎ 633 77 77) at Plac Dąbrowskiego. *Teatr Muzyczny (Music Theatre;* ☎ 678 19 68, ul Północna 47/51) stages mostly operetta and musicals. The most respectable drama theatres include *Teatr im Stefana Jaracza (*☎ 632 66 18, ul Jaracza 27), Teatr Powszechny (*☎ 633 50 36, ul Legionów 21), and Teatr Nowy (*☎ 636 68 47, ul Zachodnia 93).

As for classical music, the *Państwowa Filharmonia (State Philharmonic;* ☎ 637 14 82, ul Piotrkowska 243) gives regular concerts on Friday and on some other days of the week.

Łódź has a dozen commercial *cinemas* screening the same fare as elsewhere in the country. For something more thought-provoking, check out the Łódzki Dom Kultury (City Cultural Centre) at ul Traugutta 18, which runs its own art cinema with an often interesting program.

Bars, Pubs & Discos There has been an explosion of pubs appearing over recent years – there's now around 100 of them (possibly the third-largest number after Warsaw and Kraków). Many are hidden in the backyards of ul Piotrkowska.

The basement *Irish Pub (ul Piotrkowska 77)* is one of the oldest and still among the best. *Pub Fabryka (ul Piotrkowska 80)*, in an old mill hall across the street, is another very trendy drinking hole. It's well off the street in one of the backyards – ask around how to get there or simply follow the crowds.

The *Piotrkowska Klub 97 (ul Piotrkowska 97)* is easily recognisable by its unique, double-level outdoor drinking area. Inside, it's an enjoyable place and serves some budget light meals. Also pleasant and popular with locals is *Pub Łódź Kaliska (ul Piotrkowska 102)*. In the same backyard, *West Side* is the hippest disco in town.

Getting There & Away

Train The city has two main train stations: Łódź Kaliska to the west of the centre and Łódź Fabryczna to the east. They are not directly linked by rail, so trains for different destinations depart from either one or the other station (in some cases, from both).

Łódź Kaliska handles trains to Wrocław (263km, three daily), Poznań (251km, three daily) and Łowicz (63km, nine daily). You'll also use this station when going to Toruń, Bydgoszcz, Kalisz and Gdańsk.

For Warsaw (138km), it's better to take the train from Łódź Fabryczna (about 10 daily) rather than from Łódź Kaliska (three and they take longer). Also use Łódź Fabryczna for Kraków (two). Four trains daily to Katowice (237km) via Częstochowa (151km) run from Łódź Fabryczna.

Bus The PKS bus terminal is next to the Łódź Fabryczna train station. There are eight fast buses daily to Kielce (143km), eight to Radom (137km) and 10 to Płock (104km). Polski Express runs seven buses a day to Warsaw (134km), and three to Kraków (271km) via Częstochowa (121km) and Katowice (196km).

There is an international bus service to major western destinations, including

London, Hamburg, Frankfurt and Paris. For details contact Europol (☎ 632 97 12) at ul Próchnika 1, Atas (☎ 632 48 71) at ul Piotrkowska 77, Orbis (☎ 636 08 88) at ul Piotrkowska 68, and Almatur (☎ 637 11 22) at ul Piotrkowska 59. The tourist office may direct you to other useful travel agencies.

ŁĘCZYCA & TUM
• pop 17,000 & 500

Set amid the marshes in the valley of the Bzura River, Łęczyca ('Wen-chi-tsah') is an ordinary small town with a 1500-year history. It began in the 6th century when a stronghold was built 2km east of the present town site. By the 10th century a Benedictine abbey was established, and one of the first Christian churches in Poland was built. In the 12th century a monumental Romanesque collegiate church replaced the former one, and the settlement expanded. It was burnt down by the Teutonic Knights in the early 14th century, and the town was then moved to its present location, where a castle and defensive walls were erected.

During the next two centuries Łęczyca prospered, becoming the regional centre and the seat of numerous ecclesiastical synods. Later on, however, thanks to wars, fires and plagues, the town lost its importance. In the 19th century the defensive walls and most of the castle were sold for building material. The surviving part of the castle was restored after WWII and turned into a museum.

The original site of the town grew into an independent village and was named Tum. The stronghold fell into ruin but the collegiate church was rebuilt. It was burnt twice thereafter, by the Swedes in 1705 and the Germans in 1939, but each time reconstructed. Today it is a fine example of Romanesque architecture.

Things to See
Łęczyca The focus of interest here is the **museum** set in the castle tower. There are modest archaeological and historical collections, and a larger ethnographic section with regional artefacts including textiles,

basketry, pottery, paper cut-outs and woodcarving. You can climb to the top of the tower, from where you can see the church in Tum. There is a display of wooden figures carved by local artists in the courtyard of the castle. The museum is open Tuesday to Friday 10 am to 4 pm, Saturday and Sunday 10 am to 3 pm.

The mid-17th century **Bernardine Church** is a two minute walk from the Rynek. It has a rococo interior with a frescoed vault from the 18th century.

Tum Although rebuilt several times, the **collegiate church** has essentially preserved its original 12th century form. It's a fair-sized defensive construction with two circular and two square towers, and two semicircular apses on each end, all built from granite and sandstone. The interior retains Romanesque features but is influenced by later Gothic remodellings, especially in the aisles. The Romanesque portal in the porch (the entrance to the church) is one of the finest in Poland. From the same period are the fragments of the frescoes in the western apse. If the church is locked, get the keys from the priest's house, 100m east of the church, on the opposite side of the road.

The remains of the original stronghold are visible about 400m to the south-west from the church but it's just a grass-covered hill.

Places to Stay & Eat
Zajazd Senator in Łęczyca, on the Łódź road, is the only place to stay. It has three doubles with bath (US$24) and one quad (US$28). You can eat in its restaurant, or use *Karczma Boruty* near the castle. There are a couple of more basic restaurants in the town.

Getting There & Away
The train station is on the southern outskirts of Łęczyca. Several trains daily run north to Kutno (24km) and south to Łódź (44km).

The bus terminal is near the castle. There are plenty of buses to Łódź (35km), and several to Kutno (25km). To Tum (2.5km), take any bus to Leśmierz (three daily) or to Łódź via Leśmierz (four more), or walk.

OPORÓW

Lying off the main tourist routes, the village of Oporów ('O-po-roof') is rarely visited, even though it may be worth a detour for its Gothic castle. Although it's a fairly small and not particularly elaborate construction, this is one of the few castles in Poland that have survived in almost their original form. It's entirely surrounded by a moat and a fine park (open 8 am to 6 pm).

The fortified residence was built in the mid-15th century for Władysław Oporowski, the archbishop of Gniezno. Though it changed owners several times during its history, it underwent only a few alterations. The more important changes are the 17th century wooden ceilings on the 1st floor, covered with Renaissance decoration, the enlargement of the windows and the construction of the terrace at the entrance.

Restored after WWII, today it houses a museum featuring a collection of furniture, paintings, weapons and other objects dating from the 15th to the 19th century. The majority of the exhibits are not directly connected with the castle's history – they were acquired from old palaces and residences of the region. There are some really fine objects such as a 15th century Gothic table and an extraordinary Renaissance tiled stove from the beginning of the 17th century. The museum is open 10 am to 3.30 pm except Monday.

Getting There & Away

Unless you have your own transport, the most convenient starting point in the area is Kutno, 15km from Oporów. There are buses between Kutno and Oporów running every hour or two. Kutno has frequent bus or train transport to/from Warsaw, Łowicz, Płock, Łódź and Poznań.

PŁOCK

• pop 130,000   ☎ 024

Perched on a cliff high over the Vistula, Płock ('Pwotsk') still evokes its illustrious past, its skyline being marked with half a dozen old church towers. One of the oldest settlements in Poland, it was the residence of kings between 1079 and 1138 and the first Mazovian town to get its municipal charter (in 1237). A castle and fortified walls were built in the 14th century and the town developed until the 16th century as a wealthy trading centre.

An omen of disasters to come was the flooding of the Vistula in 1532, when half the castle and part of the defensive walls slid into the river. The wars, fires and plagues which tormented the town during the following centuries brought its prosperity to an end. Płock never regained its former glory and failed to develop into a major city.

After WWII the new regime made Płock an industrial centre by building a large oil refinery and a petrochemical plant just 2km north of the historic centre. This altered the town's character and brought heavy pollution. While local authorities focused their attention on the city's industries, the old town was for a long time largely neglected. This has finally changed in recent years. There has been much restoration work and parts of the quarter have recovered their former appearance. This, together with some museums and the cathedral, makes the city a worthwhile stop on the tourist path.

Information

Tourist Office The Centrum Informacji Turystycznej (☎ 262 94 97) is in room No 15 in the Hotel Petropol, Al Jachowicza 49, and is open weekdays 7.30 am to 3.30 pm.

Money The Bank Pekao at ul Kwiatka 6, and the Powszechny Bank Gospodarczy at ul Kolegialna 14A and on the corner of Al Jachowicza and ul Kochanowskiego, all handle travellers cheque transactions and have useful ATMs. Kantors can be found at several locations throughout the centre, mostly on ul Tumska and adjacent streets.

Things to See

The only substantial vestiges of the original Gothic castle are its two brick towers: the

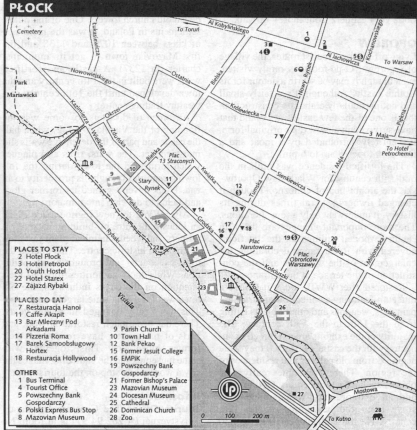

PŁOCK

PLACES TO STAY
2 Hotel Płock
3 Hotel Petropol
20 Youth Hostel
22 Hotel Starex
27 Zajazd Rybaki

PLACES TO EAT
7 Restauracja Hanoi
11 Caffe Akapit
13 Bar Mleczny Pod
    Arkadami
14 Pizzeria Roma
17 Barek Samoobsługowy
    Hortex
18 Restauracja Hollywood

OTHER
1 Bus Terminal
4 Tourist Office
5 Powszechny Bank
   Gospodarczy
6 Polski Express Bus Stop
8 Mazovian Museum

9 Parish Church
10 Town Hall
12 Bank Pekao
15 Former Jesuit College
16 EMPiK
19 Powszechny Bank
    Gospodarczy
21 Former Bishop's Palace
23 Mazovian Museum
24 Diocesan Museum
25 Cathedral
26 Dominican Church
28 Zoo

0   100   200 m

Clock Tower (Wieża Zegarowa) and the Noblemen's Tower (Wieża Szlachecka). The adjoining 16th century Benedictine abbey has been extensively reconstructed and houses the **Mazovian Museum** (Muzeum Mazowieckie). It features exhibits on the history of the town and the castle, and the Art Nouveau (Secesja) exhibition. It's Poland's best Art Nouveau collection, and includes furniture, painting, sculpture, glass, ceramics, everyday utensils etc, from Poland and beyond. The museum is open Tuesday to Friday 9 am to 3 pm, Saturday and Sunday 9 am to 4 pm (October to mid-May closed Tuesday).

The mighty **cathedral**, facing the museum, was built in the 12th century, and although it lost its original Romanesque character during numerous transformations, it remains an imposing structure dominating the area. Note the sculptured main doors made of bronze – they're a copy of the original 12th century doors, commissioned by the local bishops. These doors disappeared in mysterious circumstances and reappeared in Novgorod, Russia, where they can be found now.

The interior, topped with a Renaissance dome added in the mid-16th century, boasts a number of tombstones and altarpieces from various periods. The wall paintings date from the early 20th century and have a certain Art Nouveau feel.

The royal chapel (at the back of the left aisle) holds the sarcophagi of two Polish kings, Władysław Herman and his son Bolesław Krzywousty, who lived in Płock during their reigns.

Next to the cathedral is the **Diocesan Museum** (Muzeum Diecezjalne) with a collection of paintings, religious art and folk woodcarving. The museum is open from April to September from Wednesday to Saturday 10 am to 3 pm and Sunday 11 am to 4 pm; from October to March it closes two hours earlier.

Beyond the castle is the former **Bishops' Palace** (Pałac Biskupi), originally built in the 16th century but extended and remodelled on various occasions as the bishops grew in power.

To the north-west of the palace stretches what was once a medieval town. Although the street layout has been preserved largely unmodified, the architecture has changed a lot over the centuries. Today it's the neoclassical style that is the most noticeable, particularly on the façades of the houses lining ul Grodzka, the old town's thoroughfare. Have a look at the building of the **Jesuit College** (Kolegium Jezuickie) on ul Małachowskiego. Founded in 1180, this is the oldest established school in Poland. The building was reshaped anew with every passing epoch, the last time in 1843 by Antonio Corazzi, when it adopted a neoclassical form.

Stary Rynek, the old market square, was the heart of the 14th century township. The tall trees on the square give a refreshing air to the 18th and 19th century renovated houses standing around it. The Rynek's western side is occupied by the neoclassical **town hall** (Ratusz), built in the 1820s

after an old Gothic town hall, once in the middle of the square, was pulled down in 1816.

Just south of the town hall stands the mid-14th century **parish church**. It was originally twice its present length but suffered in the 18th century when the Vistula caused a slide at the edge of the clifftop. The church was reconstructed in the style of the day at a reduced size, but it lost its Gothic features.

To the west are two large 19th century granaries, recently fully restored. One of them houses a registry, while the other granary is an outlet of the **Mazovian Museum** and features ethnographic and folk art collections plus temporary exhibitions. It's open 9 am to 3 pm except Tuesday (October to mid-May it's also closed Monday).

You can return to the cathedral by the path skirting the clifftop – a pleasant walk providing wide panoramic views over the Vistula all the way along. Continuing farther down the riverside park you'll get to the picturesquely located **zoo** (open daily 9 am till dusk), which has about 2000 animals belonging to 280 species, including Poland's largest snake collection.

Places to Stay

The *youth hostel* (☎ 262 38 17, ul Kolegialna 19) is open July to September. It has dilapidated but cheap two and three-bed cabins in its back garden.

The cheapest all-year accommodation is *Hotel Płock* (☎ 262 93 93, Al Jachowicza 38), next to the bus terminal, which costs US$25/30 a single/double with private bath.

More stylish is *Zajazd Rybaki* (☎ 264 56 58, ul Mostowa 5/7), near the bridge over the Vistula. It's a 19th century country mansion which served as an inn before the bridge was built, when transport was by boat. Restored and refurbished, it provides decent accommodation for US$45/50/60 a single/double/triple, and has a good though not cheap restaurant.

The spectacularly situated *Hotel Starex* (☎ 262 40 61, ul Piekarska 1) has opened after thorough refurbishing and now offers reasonable standards for about US$45/60/70 a single/double/triple. Rooms facing the river provide great views, as does the hotel restaurant.

Less spectacular (and without great vistas) is *Hotel Petrochemia* (☎ *262 40 33, ul 3 Maja 33)*, 1km east of the centre. Located in a revamped apartment block, atmospheric it is not. It's only marginally cheaper than the Starex.

The Orbis-run *Hotel Petropol* (☎ *262 44 51, fax 262 44 50, Al Jachowicza 49)* is the best hotel in town, though it's not stylish either. It costs US$60/90 a single/double, breakfast included.

Places to Eat

Płock's main eating artery is its popular pedestrian mall, ul Tumska. The cheapest here is the very basic *Bar Mleczny Pod Arkadami (ul Tumska 5)*, a surviving milk bar. Slightly better is *Barek Samoobsługowy Hortex*, a few paces away. Among several new Oriental budget eateries, *Restauracja Hanoi (ul Tumska 13)* is arguably the best. You can also try the more expensive *Restauracja Hollywood (ul Tumska 8)*, which despite its name serves Indian food, complemented by several Polish dishes.

In the old town area, you can kill your hunger in the rather basic *Pizzeria Roma (ul Grodzka 13)*, or you might try *Caffe Akapit (Stary Rynek 27)*.

Płock's upmarket eating establishments include the restaurants in *Zajazd Rybaki*, *Hotel Starex* and *Hotel Petropol*.

Getting There & Away

The train station is nearly 2km north-east of the centre. There are no direct trains to Toruń and only one to Warsaw.

The bus terminal is conveniently located in the city centre. There are regular PKS buses to Warsaw (111km) and to Toruń (103km). Polski Express also plies these routes, with hourly departures to each destination. This service is faster and more comfortable, and is approximately the same price as PKS.

SIERPC
- pop 20,000   ☎ 024

If you are interested in traditional rural architecture, you might want to travel via Sierpc ('Shehrpts'), a town in north-western Mazovia. It has a **skansen** (Muzeum Wsi Mazowieckiej), 3km west of town on the Lipno road. Buses ply this route regularly and can let you off near the entrance.

A typical north Mazovian village of a dozen farms was reproduced in the grounds using old buildings collected from the region. As in most skansens, the cottages have traditional furnishings, implements and decoration, and can be visited. The skansen is open daily, except Monday, May to September 10 am to 5 pm, the rest of the year to 3 pm.

Motel Mega (☎ *275 15 63, ul Pułaskiego 34/36)* is probably the only place to stay overnight in town, for US$28/40 a double without/with bath.

CZERWIŃSK
- pop 1700

Set on the bank of the Vistula off the Warsaw-Płock road, the small village of Czerwińsk ('Chehr-vinsk') boasts a Romanesque **church**. The stone basilica, perched on a cliff overlooking the river, was built in 1129-48, and is one of the oldest examples of Romanesque architecture in Poland. Though it has been remodelled several times, the main structure, complete with its twin towers, is close to the original.

Inside, frescoes were found and uncovered in the 1950s; the oldest ones, from the beginning of the 13th century, can be seen at the head of the right-hand aisle. Note also the Romanesque portal at the entrance to the church from the vestibule. The church is usually locked, but someone from the monastery at the back will open it for you and show you around.

If you have more time, walk down to the village and stroll around the streets to see some nice old wooden houses.

The church is 1km off the main road where buses pass regularly on their way to Płock (48km) and Warsaw (63km).

Northern & Eastern Mazovia

PUŁTUSK
- pop 19,000   ☎ 023

With a history going back to the 10th century, Pułtusk is one of the oldest towns of Mazovia. It enjoyed its golden age in the 15th and 16th centuries when it was the residence of the bishops of Płock and an important trade and cultural centre. Later on, however, serious fires devastated the town several times, as did repeated invasions, for Pułtusk often found itself at the centre of conflict. In 1806 Napoleon's army fought one of its toughest battles here in the campaign against Russia, and in 1944 Pułtusk was in the front line for several months and 80% of its buildings were destroyed.

Things to See
The town's historic core, set on an island, is laid out around a 400m-long cobbled Rynek, the longest old market square in the country. In its middle stands the 15th century brick tower of the town hall, today a regional museum (open Tuesday to Saturday 10 am to 4 pm, Sunday to 2 pm), which features the history of the town and archaeology of the region, plus temporary exhibitions.

The northern end of the square is bordered by the collegiate church (kolegiata). Erected in the 1440s, the church received a Renaissance touch a century later. Its interior, crammed with a dozen baroque altars, has Renaissance stucco decoration on the nave's vault but the aisles have retained their original Gothic features. Note the 16th century wall paintings in the chapel at the head of the right-hand aisle. The freestanding bell tower was built in 1507 but largely remodelled in neoclassical style in the 1780s.

At the opposite end of the square stands the castle. Built in the late 14th century as an abode for bishops, it was rebuilt several times in later periods. It's now a plush hotel and conference centre. A small Renaissance church in front of the hotel was initially the castle's chapel.

Places to Stay & Eat
Pułtusk boasts one of the region's best hotels, *Dom Polonii* (☎ 692 90 00, fax 692 05 24), in the castle. Literally, the Polonia Home (Polonia is a general term referring to all Poles living abroad), the hotel mainly serves Polish emigrants but is open to the general public. Good singles/doubles/triples with bath cost US$70/85/100, breakfast included. It also has cheaper rooms in a few other buildings, starting at US$30/35 a single/double without breakfast. There are two restaurants in the castle that offer a good traditional Polish menu, as well as a café and a nightclub. The hotel also offers other facilities, including a tennis court, horses, kayaks and rowing boats.

Pułtusk has some cheaper accommodation, including the simple *Zajazd na Skarpie Zawimex* (☎ 692 05 23, ul Kolejowa 19) near the bus terminal (US$18/30 a double/quad), and *Hotel Baltazar* (☎ 692 04 75) on ul Baltazara off the Ostrołęka road (US$30/35 a double/triple).

Getting There & Away
Pułtusk lies on the route from Warsaw to the Great Masurian Lakes. There's no railway in town, but bus transport is busy, including half-hourly buses to Warsaw (60km).

KADZIDŁO
- pop 2000   ☎ 029

The village of Kadzidło ('Kah-dzee-dwo') is one of the craft centres of the Kurpie, the far northern Mazovian borderlands comprising the Puszcza Zielona, or Green Forest. Its inhabitants, the Kurpie, have developed their own culture recognisable by their style of dress, music and decoration of their houses. Perhaps the best known are their paper cut-outs and weaving. Unfortunately, the traditions are slowly becoming extinct.

Things to See
The Zagroda Kurpiowska is a small open-air museum comprising an old wooden

Kurpie house furnished and decorated in traditional local style, plus a few outbuildings. It's on the outskirts of the village towards Ostrołęka. Note that a more extensive display of Kurpie architecture is in Nowogród – see the following section.

In the village centre, you can visit the craft cooperative **Kurpianka** (open weekdays), to see locals at work weaving rugs, bedspreads and tablecloths on their old looms.

Special Events

On Corpus Christi, locals in Kadzidło and some other Kurpie villages deck themselves out in traditional costumes and take part in a solemn procession. In Łyse, a village 17km north-east of Kadzidło, a competition for Easter 'palms' is held on Palm Sunday. Some specimens are 8m tall. In Myszyniec, a small town 19km north of Kadzidło, the Pentecost Monday is celebrated with a procession of women in folkloric costumes, after the Mass around noon.

Places to Stay & Eat

There's not much except for a summer *youth hostel* (☎ 761 80 82), halfway between the museum and the cooperative, and a squalid restaurant diagonally opposite the cooperative.

Getting There & Away

Buses run regularly south to Ostrołęka (21km) and north to Myszyniec (19km); you catch them in front of the cooperative.

NOWOGRÓD

• pop 2000   ☎ 086

Nowogród ('No-vo-groot') is a small town on the Narew River, on the eastern edge of the Puszcza Zielona. It was one of the early strongholds of the Mazovian dukes and traditionally the centre of the Kurpie region. It had its ups and downs during its long history, but the darkest days came with WWII. During the Nazi offensive of September 1939 the town literally ceased to exist. Slowly rebuilt after the war, it's now just another small place, which probably wouldn't warrant a visit if not for its skansen.

Kurpie Skansen

Founded here in 1927, the Skansen Kurpiowski is the second-oldest museum of its kind in Poland. Like the rest of the town, it was completely destroyed during the war and rebuilt from scratch. It's not, however, a replica; most of the buildings are 19th century pieces of rural wooden architecture collected from all over the Kurpie region, dismantled, brought to the skansen and re-assembled.

There are about 30 buildings including cottages, barns, granaries and mills, and some are open for visits. Although they are mostly small and modest – reflecting the living standards in this relatively poor region – the architectural detail is often fine and elaborate, revealing high levels of skill. A collection of charming beehives, including old hollow tree trunks, suggests that honey must have been important to the Kurpie.

The skansen is spectacularly located on a steep bank of the Narew, which gives it an additional charm and provides a good vista over the river. It's open from April to October only, Tuesday to Friday 9 am to 4 pm, Saturday and Sunday 10 am to 5 pm.

Places to Stay & Eat

The *youth hostel* (☎ 17 65 17), in the school two blocks south of the Rynek, is open in July and August. The *skansen* (☎ 17 55 62) offers accommodation in a small cottage in the grounds (for up to four people) for US$8 per person. Otherwise, you have the decent *Hotel Zbyszko* (☎ 17 55 18, ul Obrońców Nowogrodu 2), 2km from the town centre, off the Olsztyn road. It provides neat singles/doubles/triples with bath and breakfast for US$26/36/48 and has its own restaurant – the only eating place in town to speak of.

Getting There & Away

Buses run regularly to Łomża (16km) and several times a day to Myszyniec (42km). To other destinations, transport is sporadic. The bus stop is on the Rynek, a few minutes walk from the skansen.

TREBLINKA

Treblinka is a small village set amid forests about 100km north-east of Warsaw, yet the name is known to every Pole and Jew, for it was here that the Nazis operated their second-largest extermination camp after Auschwitz. Initially, a penal camp was established here by the Nazis and named after the nearby village. The camp came into being in summer 1941 and operated until July 1944. More than 20,000 inmates, mainly Poles, passed through it; half of them died of starvation or torture, or were shot.

In July 1942, the Nazis set up a second camp 2km north of the existing one. Known as Treblinka II, this was strictly a death camp destined to exterminate Jews. It had 13 gas chambers where the victims were gassed with exhaust fumes. There were no crematoria, as the Germans anticipated that they wouldn't cope with the number of bodies; the dead were placed directly on specially constructed open-air grates, doused with a flammable liquid and burned. The fire and smoke continued day and night.

On average, about five to six thousand people were murdered daily, but this rose to 17,000 victims a day during the camp's 'heyday'. During its 16 month operation, over 800,000 Jews from 10 European countries were murdered in Treblinka II. The camp was closed in November 1943, the gas chambers and barracks demolished and the whole area reforested. Nothing has remained, except the ashes of nearly a million people.

Things to See

Today Treblinka is a memorial site, with a monument erected on the site of each camp to commemorate its victims. Access is from the north by a short road that branches off the Małkinia-Siedlce road and leads to the car park. A shelter built beside this houses the ticket office and a display of photographs. The ticket counter is open daily; in summer 9 am to 7 pm and for the rest of the year till dusk.

It's a 10 minute walk from the car park to the memorial of Treblinka II. The path leads through woods until you reach the mock-up train station, an artistic vision created on the site where the transports of Jews arrived. The central monument, with an inscription saying 'Never Again', is a few hundred metres to the east, clearly visible from the 'station'. It stands on the site where gas chambers were located. Around it is a vast symbolic cemetery in the form of a forest of rocks – 17,000 of them – representing the daily 'output' of the camp. It's one of the most impressive memorials of its kind and will probably live long in your memory.

You'll see the other monument 2km south, on the site where the penal camp once was. The road paved with massive cobblestones – the 'black road' – will take you there. Here, too, there's a cemetery, but this one consists of the usual Christian crosses. Unlike the death camp, here some remains of the camp have been preserved, including the foundations and floor slabs of the demolished barracks.

Getting There & Away

Unless you have your own wheels, Treblinka is not that easy to get to by public transport. Consequently, there aren't many visitors, which only adds to the poignancy of the place.

The usual jumping-off point is the village of Małkinia, a busy railway hub on the Warsaw-Białystok line. The Treblinka memorial site is 8km south by the road to Siedlce (don't be misled by Treblinka village, which is only 4km down this road). Half a dozen buses a day from Małkinia go along this road, and they will let you off at the turn-off to Treblinka, just a five minute walk to the car park. Alternatively, take a train going from Małkinia to Siedlce or farther on, and get off at the Wólka-Okrąglik station. From here, walk back along the road until you see a sign pointing left to the memorial.

CIECHANOWIEC
• pop 4700 ☎ 086

The small old town of Ciechanowiec ('Cheh-hah-no-vyets'), on the borderland between

MAZOVIA & PODLASIE

Mazovia and Podlasie, has a good museum, worth visiting if you are in the area.

Museum of Agriculture

The Muzeum Rolnictwa at ul Pałacowa 5 has been established on the grounds of a former estate, consisting of an early 19th century palace, stables, coach-house and a couple of other buildings, all surrounded by a park. The buildings have been turned into exhibition halls and the park now holds a skansen, with a good range of wooden architecture from Mazovia and Podlasie. The collection includes dwellings representing different social classes, from simple peasant cottages to manor houses of the nobility, and has a variety of granaries, barns and mills. There's a 19th century water mill in perfect working order, and two dozen old beehives.

You'll be guided through the skansen, visiting several interiors. You'll also be shown exhibitions featuring old agricultural machinery, archaic tractors, primitive steam engines, peasants' horse-drawn carts, rudimentary tools and so on. There's also a small botanical exhibition. The tour takes about two hours.

From May to September, the museum is open weekdays 8 am to 4 pm, Saturday and Sunday 9 am to 6 pm; from October to April it's open daily 9 am to 4 pm. English and German-speaking guides (US$7 an hour per group) may be available on the spot but if you want to be sure book in advance on ☎ 77 13 28.

Places to Stay & Eat

The *museum* (☎ 77 13 28) offers accommodation, about 50 beds altogether, distributed in the palace and several other buildings on the grounds. They include some attractive places, such as the hunting lodge from 1858 and even the water mill, both of which are part of the skansen's collection! Most rooms have only shared facilities, but some, including those in the palace, do have their own baths. The price varies slightly depending on where you are staying, from about US$6 to US$8 per person. Bookings can be made by phone.

Alternatively, you can stay at *Ośrodek OSiR* (☎ 77 11 32, ul Stadion 1), which has rudimentary cabins (summer only) and hotel-style rooms open year-round (US$12 a double with bath).

Of the few eating options, the best is *Restauracja Astoria* on the town's main square, Plac 3 Maja.

Getting There & Away

The bus station is a few minutes walk from the museum. There are six buses daily to Białystok (84 or 100km depending on the route), Bielsk Podlaski (48km), Siemiatycze (38km) and Łomża (60km), and two fast buses in the morning directly to Warsaw (138km). Trains don't call at Ciechanowiec.

Podlasie

Podlasie (literally, the land close to the forest) owes its name to the vicinity of the Białowieża Forest. Its core has been made the Białowieża National Park and is the best known tourist sight of the region. There's much more to see here, however.

Stretching along the border of Poland and Belarus, Podlasie ('Pod-lah-sheh') has for centuries been influenced by these two cultures. With its blend of west and east, Catholicism and Orthodoxy, at times you will feel as if you're travelling in another country. The farther off the main track you go, the more onion-shaped domes of Orthodox churches you'll see and the more Belarusian language you'll hear.

The Tatars settled in Podlasie in the 17th century, giving the region a Muslim touch, and their legacy survives to this day (see the Kruszyniany & Bohoniki section later in this chapter). There were also Jews living here and they too have left traces of their presence (see the Tykocin section later in this chapter).

Other attractions of the region include the recently created national parks of the Biebrza and Narew rivers. They both protect extensive lowland marshes of the river valleys. Refer to the appropriate sections for details.

Except for the Białowieża National Park, Podlasie is not a touristy area and seldom sees foreign visitors. The only city is Białystok; everything else, particularly the countryside, seems to be half asleep, enjoying the unhurried life of bygone days, as it has for centuries.

BIAŁYSTOK
• pop 280,000   ☎ 085
Founded in the 16th century, Białystok ('Byah-wi-stok') really began to develop in the mid-18th century, when Jan Klemens Branicki, the commander of the armed forces and owner of vast estates including the town, established his residence here and built a palace. A century later the town received a new impetus from the textile industry, and eventually became Poland's largest textile centre after Łódź.

During the textile booms, Białystok attracted an ethnic mosaic of entrepreneurs, including Poles, Jews, Russians, Belarusians and Germans, and simultaneously drew in a sizable urban proletariat. The town grew in a spontaneous and chaotic manner (still visible today) and by the outbreak of WWI had some 80,000 inhabitants and over 250 textile factories.

In 1920, during the Polish-Soviet war, the Bolsheviks installed a provisional communist government in the Branicki palace, but it didn't survive a month. Its leaders, Julian Marchlewski and Feliks Dzierżyński, called for the formation of a Polish Soviet Republic.

WWII was not kind to Białystok. The Nazis murdered half of the city's population, including almost all the Jews, destroyed most of the industrial base and razed the central district. Postwar reconstruction concentrated on tangible issues such as the recovery of industry, infrastructure and state administration, together with the provision of basic necessities. Historical and aesthetic values receded into the background, as you can see today.

Białystok doesn't have many great attractions and is not a prime tourist destination. However, the mix of Polish and Belarusian cultures gives it a special feel not found in other Polish cities. Białystok is also the obvious starting point for excursions to Tykocin, Kruszyniany and Bohoniki (see the relevant sections).

Information
Tourist Office The Centrum Informacji Turystycznej (☎/fax 745 46 00), ul Piękna 3, is open weekdays 9 am to 5 pm, and (July and August only) Saturday 10 am to 2 pm.

Money The Bank Pekao has its branch offices at ul Sienkiewicza 40 and Al Piłsudskiego 11. Other useful banks include the Bank Gdański at Al Piłsudskiego 13, Powszechny Bank Kredytowy at Rynek Kościuszki 7, and Powszechny Bank Gospodarczy at ul Słonimska 2. Kantors are easy to find throughout the centre, and there are also some ATMs.

Post & Communications The main post office is on ul Warszawska 10, but there are several more central offices, including at ul Lipowa 32 and at Rynek Kościuszki 13.

Email & Internet Access There are several Internet facilities, including the Jard (☎ 742 07 74) at ul Lipowa 37.

Things to See
Most attractions are along the city's main thoroughfare, ul Lipowa. Starting from its western end, **St Roch's Church** (Kościół Św Rocha), overlooking the centre, was built between 1927 and 1940. The octagonal interior, covered with a glass dome, is not as spacious as you might expect when looking from a distance at this apparently large church with its 80m tower.

Walking eastward, you get to **St Nicholas' Orthodox Church** (Cerkiew Św Mikołaja). Built in neoclassical style in the mid-19th century, it has an iconostasis from that period, but the frescoes, copied from a Kiev church, date from the early 1900s. Mass is held daily at 9 am, but if you'd like to listen to the choir come on Sunday. The religious shop in the building opposite the

BIAŁYSTOK

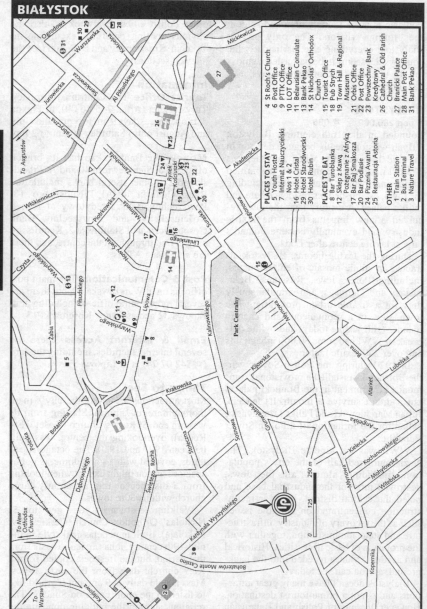

PLACES TO STAY
5 Youth Hostel
7 Internat Nauczycielski
Nos 1 & 2
16 Hotel Cristal
29 Hotel Starodworski
30 Hotel Rubin

PLACES TO EAT
8 Bar Turoblanka
12 Sklep z Kawą
Pożegnanie z Afryką
17 Bar Raj Smakosza
20 Bar Podlasie
24 Pizzeria Avanti
25 Restauracja Astoria

OTHER
1 Train Station
2 Bus Terminal
3 Nature Travel
4 St Roch's Church
6 Post Office
9 PTTK Office
10 LOT Office
11 Belarusian Consulate
13 Bank Pekao
14 St Nicholas' Orthodox
Church
15 Tourist Office
18 Pub Strych
19 Town Hall & Regional
Museum
21 Orbis Office
22 Post Office
23 Powszechny Bank
Kredytowy
26 Cathedral & Old Parish
Church
27 Branicki Palace
28 Main Post Office
31 Bank Pekao

church's entrance has CDs with Orthodox Church music.

One block east of the church is a triangular Rynek. The 18th century **town hall** in the middle was reconstructed from scratch after the war and is now home to the **regional museum** (open 10 am to 5 pm except Monday). The Polish painting section includes important names such as Boznańska, Malczewski, Chełmoński, Gierymski and Witkacy, and the archaeological display gives an insight into the mysterious Jatzvingian culture, which occupied the region north of Białystok until the 13th century (read about the Jatzvingians in the Warmia & Masuria chapter).

A bit farther east is a strange merger of two churches: a small 17th century **old parish church** and, attached to it, a huge mock-Gothic **cathedral**. The latter was constructed at the beginning of this century as an 'extension' of the former, the only way to bypass the tsarist bureaucracy which officially forbade Poles to build Catholic churches.

In the park across the street stands the **Branicki Palace** (Pałac Branickich). Eminent in Polish political life, Branicki was a contender for the Polish crown, but after Stanisław August Poniatowski was elected, Branicki left the court, moved to Białystok and set about building a residence which would rival the king's in importance and luxury. The mighty, horseshoe-shaped baroque palace that was erected used to be referred to as the Versailles of the North.

Though the palace was burnt down in 1944 by the retreating Nazis, a careful reconstruction has restored it to its original 18th century shape. Today it's the seat of the Academy of Medicine. You can't go in but you're not missing much – the interior has been modernised. The park around is open to all and consists of two distinct parts: the formal French garden and the English landscaped park.

Outside the central area, it's worth seeing the **new Orthodox church** at ul Antoniuk Fabryczny 13, 3km north-west of the centre (bus No 5 from ul Lipowa in the centre will let you off nearby). Begun in the early 1980s, the construction of this monumental building, the largest Orthodox church in Poland, is complete, though the interior still needs some work.

The architects took the best of the traditional forms, added modern shapes and lines, and produced a truly impressive church. The huge central onion-shaped dome is topped with a large cross (weighing 1500kg) symbolising Christ, while 12 smaller crosses represent the apostles. The spacious interior boasts a spectacular main iconostasis and another smaller one to one side, and a giant chandelier may already be in place by the time you read this. The church is locked, except for Sunday Mass, but the priest in the house behind the church may open it for you.

There's a new **skansen** (Białostockie Muzeum Wsi) in the village of Jurowce, 5km north of Białystok on the Augustów road (bus No 102 from Rynek Kościuszki goes there). It features a collection of old timber buildings representing traditional architecture of the region.

Organised Tours

Białystok has two useful travel agencies focusing on nature trips and adventure tourism. Bird Service Tours (☎/fax 661 67 68, bird@alfa.nask.bialystok.pl, www.travel.com.pl/tas/birdtour), at ul Popiełuszki 105, is one of Poland's best specialists in birdwatching tours. It organises trips through eastern Poland, including the Białowieża and Biebrza national parks. It also offers week-long bicycle tours in the region, providing accommodation and food and detailed trip instructions allowing you to travel on your own, at your own pace.

Bird Service Tours organises the Polish Bird Festival, held annually in the second week of May. This is a holiday package which covers eight nights accommodation in an optimal birdwatching location, half board and information. Its other services include bike rental and guides.

Nature Travel (☎ 744 45 62, fax 744 45 34, nattrav@alf.optinet.pl), at ul Wyszyńskiego 2/1, essentially targets the German-language market, offering a choice of biking tours around the region and beyond. The trips combine natural and cultural attractions, including city sightseeing, and range in length from one to two weeks. Sailing, kayaking and birdwatching tours are also available. The agency also rents bicycles, kayaks, tents etc, and can provide guides.

Both agencies usually have their tours fully booked and sold a long time in advance. Make inquiries well ahead, preferably from your home country.

Places to Stay

Camping Nr 212 Gromada (☎ 651 16 57, ☎/fax 651 17 01, Al Jana Pawła II 77) is in a forested area 4km west of the city centre on the Warsaw road, just behind Hotel Leśny.

The all-year *youth hostel* (☎ 652 42 50, ul Piłsudskiego 7B) is in an old timber house, within easy walking distance of the train station and the centre. It's tucked away from the street behind the building at No 7, and is oddly set between dull apartment blocks. It can sleep about 50 guests, all in bunk beds in large dormitories.

The next cheapest place in the city centre is probably the *Internat Wojewódzkiego Ośrodka Metodycznego*, also called the Internat Nauczycielski. There are three of them: Nos 1 and 2 (☎ 742 59 09, ul Lipowa 41), next to each other, off the street – enter gate No 43 and you'll see them; and No 3 (☎ 732 36 64, ul Sienkiewicza 86). All offer reasonable room standards, though with shared facilities, and charge US$7 per person in doubles, triples or quads.

The partially restored *Hotel Rubin* (☎ 677 23 35, ul Warszawska 7) costs US$20/25 a double/triple without bath, twice as much with bath. Appreciably better and more pleasant is the small *Hotel Starodworski* (☎ 653 74 18, ul Warszawska 7A) next door. Run by a friendly Macedonian couple, the place costs US$30/50/60 a single/double/triple with bath and breakfast.

The very central *Hotel Cristal* (☎ 742 50 61, fax 742 58 00, ul Lipowa 3) has finally had a much-needed revamping and is now

one of the best places in town. It costs US$60/70 a single/double with bath and breakfast; 20% cheaper on weekends.

Another centrally located top-end option is the new *Hotel Gołębiewski* (☎ 743 54 35, fax 653 73 77, ul Pałacowa 7), which offers decent facilities, including a swimming pool and sauna, for US$70/100, and it too has weekend discounts.

There are a dozen more hotels farther out from the centre, including some budget workers' dorms. The tourist office has a complete list and may help you to find accommodation.

Places to Eat

Bar Podlasie (Rynek Kościuszki 15) is a sort of a modernised milk bar which serves acceptable meals at ultra-low prices. *Bar Raj Smakosza (ul Malmeda 1)* is slightly more expensive, but a bit more agreeable. *Bar Turoblanka (ul Lipowa 37)* is another acceptable budget place for a straightforward meal (the sign in the window says Bar Jard).

Bar Wegetariański Ananda (ul Warszawska 30), behind Hotel Gołębiewski, is a charming place that offers vegie food at very reasonable prices. *Pizzeria Avanti (ul Sienkiewicza 3)* has much more than just pizzas, including a salad bar, and isn't expensive either. Across the street, *Restauracja Astoria* is a more formal place for lunch or dinner.

Most better hotels have their own eating facilities, of which the restaurants in *Hotel Cristal* and *Hotel Gołębiewski* are the best though the most expensive.

The place for a cup of coffee (36 kinds to choose from) is *Sklep z Kawą Pożegnanie z Afryką (ul Częstochowska 6)*.

Entertainment

Białystok has a useful what's-on magazine, *BIK*, which lists museums, theatre, music and other events.

The *Towarzystwo Wierszalin* theatre, established in 1991, has swiftly gained recognition both at home and abroad, and won some important international awards, including ones at the Edinburgh Theatre Festival in 1993 and 1994. The theatre travels a lot and is hard to find in town; inquire at the tourist office. The *Teatr Lalek (ul Kalinowskiego 1)* is one of Poland's best puppet theatres. The *Filharmonia Białostocka (ul Podleśna 2)* has concerts on Friday and sometimes on other days as well.

The *Kawiarnia Odeon Jazz Club (ul Akademicka 10/1)* features live jazz and blues.

If all you need is a beer or two, there's quite a collection of watering holes in the centre, including *Pub Strych (Rynek Kościuszki 22)*.

Getting There & Away

The bus and train stations are adjacent to each other, about 1km west of the central area. You can walk to the centre in 15 minutes or get there by bus No 10.

Train Trains to Warsaw (184km) and Sokółka (41km) leave regularly throughout the day, and there are a couple of departures to Olsztyn (250km) and Gdańsk (429km).

International trains to Vilnius in Lithuania (241km) and St Petersburg in Russia (948km) stop at Białystok. If you plan on taking this route, check in advance whether you need a Belarusian transit visa, because the railway cuts through a short stretch of Belarus, passing through Hrodna.

Bus About 14 buses daily run north to Augustów (91km), of which half continue up to Suwałki (122km). There are only two buses directly to Białowieża (85 or 98km), at 6.30 am and 3 pm. Alternatively, go by any of the frequent buses to Hajnówka (66km), then continue by another bus to Białowieża. Buses to Tykocin (27 or 38km) run roughly every hour. For connections to Kruszyniany (56km) and Bohoniki (46km), see the Kruszyniany & Bohoniki section later in this chapter.

Polski Express operates three coaches a day to Warsaw (188km). They run the distance in 3½ hours (only marginally longer than the fast train) and cost US$5.75 (cheaper than 2nd class in the fast train).

On the international routes, there are four departures a day to Hrodna (US$8, three hours), two to Minsk (US$20, nine hours) and one to Vilnius (US$15, eight hours).

TYKOCIN
• **pop 2100**   ☎ 085

Tykocin ('Ti-ko-cheen') came into being in the 13th century as one of the strongholds of the Mazovian dukes. Its real growth began in the 15th century and was further accelerated after the town became the property of King Zygmunt August in 1543. It was during this period that Jews started to settle in Tykocin, their community growing rapidly to define the town's character for the next four centuries.

Located on the Warsaw-Vilnius trade route and enjoying numerous royal privileges, Tykocin developed into the commercial centre of the region, to be surpassed by Białystok only at the end of the 18th century. This marked the turning point of Tykocin's fortunes and from that time the town gradually slid into decline. During WWII it lost all its Jews – half of the town's population – and in 1950 it was deprived of its town charter to become an ordinary village. It recovered its charter in 1994, but otherwise nothing has changed; it remains a small, sleepy place, where nothing is apparently going on. Yet several surviving historic buildings are evidence of the town's illustrious past.

Things to See

The star of the Tykocin sights is the **synagogue**, one of the best preserved buildings of its kind in Poland. It dominates the western part of the village, which was traditionally inhabited by Jews. This sober-looking edifice erected in 1642 was used for religious services right up till WWII. Renovated after the war, it has been turned into the **Jewish Museum**, open 10 am to 5 pm except Monday. The interior, with a massive Bimah in the centre and an elaborate Aron Kodesh (the Holy Ark where the

MAZOVIA & PODLASIE

Torah scrolls are kept) in the eastern wall, has preserved many of the original wall paintings including Hebraic inscriptions. The exhibition features Talmudic books, liturgical equipment and other objects related to religious ritual.

The **Talmudic house** right behind the synagogue houses a **regional museum** displaying paintings of the local artist Zygmunt Bujnowski, plus objects related to the town's history. There are also temporary exhibitions.

At the opposite end of the village stands the 18th century baroque **Holy Trinity Church** (Kościół Św Trójcy). With two symmetrical towers linked to the main building by arcaded galleries, the whole façade is a little like a palace. It has a typical baroque and rococo interior.

The church overlooks the spacious **Rynek** (called Plac Czanieckiego), lined with old wooden houses, some of which are over 200 years old. In the middle of the square stands the **monument to Stefan Czarniecki**, a national hero who distinguished himself in battles against the Swedes. The statue, from the 1760s, is one of the oldest secular monuments in Poland.

Places to Stay & Eat

Apart from the summer *youth hostel (☎ 718 16 85, ul Kochanowskiego 1)*, open in July and August in the local school, and a few private rooms rented out by the locals (inquire in the museum), there's nowhere to stay in town. The only place to eat is *Restauracja Tejsza*, in the basement of the Talmudic house (enter from the back). It serves inexpensive local and Jewish dishes.

Getting There & Away

There are about 20 buses daily between Tykocin and Białystok. They either take a short cut via Siekierki (27km) or go by the main road via Stare Jeżewo (38km). If you don't plan on returning to Białystok and want to head west, take any bus to Stare Jeżewo (8km), from where there's regular transport to Łomża, Zambrów and farther on. Stare Jeżewo is also the jumping-off

point for Kurowo in the Narew Landscape Park (see that section for further details). In Tykocin, buses stop at Stary Rynek, a square 100m from the synagogue.

BIEBRZA NATIONAL PARK
☎ 086

The Biebrza National Park (Biebrzański Park Narodowy) came into being in 1994 and, with its area of about 592 sq km, is Poland's largest park. It embraces the basin of the Biebrza River ('Byehb-zhah') along almost its entire course of more than 100km, from its source next to the Belarusian border to its mouth at the Narew River.

The Biebrza Valley is Central Europe's largest natural bog area. The varied landscape consists of river sprawls, peat bogs, marshes and damp forests. Typical local flora includes numerous species of moss, reed-grass and plenty of medicinal herbs. The fauna is rich and diverse and features a variety of mammals such as wolf, wild boar, fox, roe deer, otter and beaver. The king of the park, however, is the elk; there are about 500 specimens living in the valley and they're relatively easy to spot.

With a total of about 270 species (more than half of all species recorded in Poland), birds are particularly well represented, and the park has become a favourite destination for birdwatchers. You'll find storks, cranes, hawks, curlews, snipes, ruffs, egrets, harriers, crakes, sandpipers, owls, shrikes and at least half a dozen species of warblers. Among some less common varieties are the great snipe, the white-winged black tern and the aquatic warbler.

Orientation

The park can be broadly divided into three geographical entities corresponding to three stretches of the Biebrza River's course. The northern part, in the upper course of the river, known as the Northern Basin (Basen Północny), is the smallest and least visited area of the park.

The Middle Basin (Basen Środkowy), stretching along the river's middle course, is wide and features a combination of wet forests and boglands. The showpiece here is the Red Marsh (Czerwone Bagno), a strict nature reserve encompassing a wet alder forest inhabited by about 400 elk.

The Southern Basin (Basen Południowy) is equally extensive, but here most of the terrain is taken up by marshes and peat bogs. The river here reaches a width of up to 35m before it flows into the Narew. This basin is possibly the best for birdwatching, as it's the favourite habitat of many species, including two of the park's highlights – the great snipe and the aquatic warbler.

Information

The place to visit before any exploration of the park is the visitors information office (☎/fax 72 06 20, ☎/fax 72 06 21) at the park's headquarters in Osowiec. The helpful English-speaking staff will provide information about the park and its facilities. They'll give you details of where to stay and eat (or to buy food), and will advise on the best watching spots for different bird species and tell you how to get there. They can provide a guide (US$10 an hour per group which is negotiable), and rent rowing boats (US$2 an hour or US$10 a day) and kayaks (US$1 or US$6, respectively).

The office is stocked with maps and brochures on the park, some of which are in English. A helpful map for birdwatchers is the *Bagna Biebrzańskie* (Biebrza Marshes) map at 1:50,000 scale. It consists of two sheets featuring the Middle and Southern basins. The map shows the birdwatching sites for different species and briefly describes, in Polish, English and German, the most common species. Buy this map beforehand in a big city, as it can be unavailable in the office. Another useful publication is the 1:120,000 scale *Biebrzański Park Narodowy* map, which comes with a detailed description of natural conditions in Polish, English and German. This map is usually available in the office.

The office is open weekdays 7.30 am to 3.30 pm and, in summer, Saturday and Sunday 7.30 am to 7.30 pm. You pay the admission fee to the park here – US$0.70 (US$0.35 for students) per day.

If you can't get to the office during opening hours, go to the Karczma Wygoda, a roadside inn by the car park near the camp site in Osowiec, 1km from the park's office. It's open daily 9 am to 10 pm and sells park entry tickets, stocks maps and publications and provides information.

Exploring the Park

Despite its overall marshy character, large parts of the park can be explored relatively easily on foot. About 200km of signposted trails have been tracked through the park's most interesting areas, including nearly 50km through the Red Marsh alone. Dykes, boulders and dunes among the bogs provide access to some splendid birdwatching sites. Several viewing towers on the edge of the marshland allow for a more general panorama of the park.

Another way of exploring the park is by boat. The principal water route in the park goes from the town of Lipsk downstream along the Biebrza to the village of Wizna. This 139km stretch can be paddled at a leisurely pace in seven to nine days. Bivouac sites along the rivers allow for overnight stops and food is available in towns on the way. The visitors office in Osowiec can provide kayaks and canoes, plus maps and information. You can also take the boat or kayak for just a few hours or a day and sail part of the route; the staff will tell you which part to go to.

Biebrza River is part of another canoe route which leads from the town of Rajgród along the Jegrznia, Ełk, Biebrza and Narew rivers down to Łomża. The route is about 130km long and can be done in a week. Group kayak trips are organised by PTTK in Łomża, ul Wojska Polskiego 1 (☎ 16 47 18).

Places to Stay

There are several bivouac sites within the park and more outside its boundaries. The three most strategically located sites are in Osowiec (2km from the office), Grzędy (a gateway to the Red Marsh) and Barwik (close to the great snipe's habitat). All three are accessible by road and have car parks. You'll pay about US$1 per person a night to pitch your tent. There are also five rooms (for up to 16 people) in the hunting lodge in Grzędy (US$7 per person).

The nearest hotels to the park are in Goniądz, Mońki and Rajgród. Youth hostels in the region include ones in Goniądz, Grajewo, Osowiec and Wizna; all are open in July and August only.

Getting There & Away
Osowiec sits on the railway between Białystok (58km) and Ełk (46km), with trains in each direction going every two to three hours. The park office is 200m from Osowiec station.

Other regional destinations can be reached by bus, but the service is infrequent. Having your own transport is a huge advantage, as you can easily access most of the park's major attractions.

NAREW NATIONAL PARK
The Narew ('Nah-ref') National Park (Narwiański Park Narodowy) is another marshland nature reserve, just as interesting as the Biebrza park, though of a slightly different character. The park protects the unusual stretch of the Narew River. Nicknamed the 'Polish Amazon', the river here splits into dozens of channels which spread across a 2km-wide valley, forming a constellation of swampy islets in between. This is said to be the last place of its kind in Central Europe.

The park encompasses an area of about 73 sq km, 25% of which is bog and a further 3% water. Predictably, the most abundant flora and fauna species are those accustomed to aquatic conditions, including the omnipresent white and yellow water lilies. Among mammals, the beaver is the most characteristic inhabitant, numbering at least 250 individuals living in about 70 lodges. The area is a favourite ground for birds, with as many as 200 species identified in the park, including about 150 species that breed here.

Orientation
The park lies some 20km west of Białystok, to the south of the Białystok-Warsaw highway. The most interesting area is the north-western part of the park, where the watery labyrinth of channels is most extensive.

The best way to get a taste of the marshland is by boat. While paddling along narrow, snaking canals and ponds, you'll enjoy the lush, green carpets formed by the flora and will spot many birds living here. The water is so crystal clear that you can see fish and plants to a depth of 2m.

The array of the river's arms is so complex and extensive that you may tour around for hours without passing through the same channel twice. The best time for a birdwatching trip is either early morning or late afternoon, when the water birds are most active.

The two major starting points for exploration of the park are Kurowo and Waniewo. Both are just tiny villages sitting on the riverbank a mere 4km apart as the crow flies. Both provide accommodation and boats.

Kurowo
Kurowo sits on the left (western) bank of the Narew, somewhat in the middle of nowhere. It's connected to the outer world only by a rough road, which rarely sees a passing car. The central point of this tiny hamlet is a late 19th century country mansion surrounded by a 10 hectare park. The building houses the headquarters of the Narew National Park (☎ 085-718 14 17), a small museum related to the park, and accommodation for visitors. There are just four double rooms with shared facilities for US$12 each. There's no restaurant so bring your own food. Two rowing boats can be hired; kayaks may be available by the time you read this.

Waniewo
Waniewo, farther south, is larger and looks more prosperous, and has a sealed access road linking it to civilisation. Midway along

its main street is the office of 'Sołtys' (village administrator), where you'll find Eugeniusz Sokół (☎ 086-76 47 80), the local tour operator who speaks English and German. As well as offering accommodation (US$15/20 a single/double with bath), he runs boat excursions around the nearby Narew channels (US$7 per person for a two hour trip). The trips are in small fishing boats powered by a long wooden pole.

Getting There & Away

There's no public transport to either Kurowo or Waniewo, so you'll have a bit of a walk. The distance depends on which village you're going to, where you're coming from, and which way you walk.

The usual starting point for Kurowo is the village of Stare Jeżewo on the Warsaw-Białystok highway, 28km west of Białystok. It's frequently serviced by buses from Białystok and Tykocin, and there are also some buses passing through from Warsaw and Łomża.

From Stare Jeżewo, walk 500m south on the road to Sokoły, until you get to an unsigned crossroad. Take the sealed side road to the left for 3km until you reach a T-junction where the seal ends. Take the road to the right (south) for another 1km until you see a large brick granary where the road divides. Take the left-hand fork for the last 1km to Kurowo. It all takes a bit over an hour, and it's a pleasant walk through a bucolic landscape.

From Kurowo, you can walk to Waniewo by the red-signed trail. It leads along an unsealed country road for the first 2km, then goes on the sealed road towards Łapy for another 3km, and finally branches off to the left to Waniewo, 1km away.

Another way of getting to both Waniewo and Kurowo is from the south, from the Łupianka-Pszczółczyn road, but it's serviced by only two or three buses a day from Białystok. For Waniewo, get off at the Waniewo bus stop, and walk about 1km to the village. For Kurowo, get off in the village of Pszczółczyn and walk the remaining 3km to the park's headquarters.

If you have your own transport, the best place to start is Stare Jeżewo, and it's easy to get to both villages. For Kurowo, follow the walking route as described above. For Waniewo, take the road heading south in the direction of Sokoły. When you've covered 4km, take the side road branching off to the left to Pszczółczyn (1.5km from the turn-off), go through the village (a lot of turnings) and then after another 5km turn left down the side road to Waniewo, which is 1km ahead.

KRUSZYNIANY & BOHONIKI

These two tiny villages, next to the Belarusian border to the east of Białystok, are remarkable for their timber mosques, the only ones surviving in Poland. They were built by the Muslim Tatars, who settled here at the end of the 17th century.

Kruszyniany

Spreading for over 2km along the road, Kruszyniany looks much larger than it really is. The **mosque**, hidden in a cluster of trees back from the main road, is in the central part of the village. It is an 18th century rustic wooden construction, in many ways similar to old timber Christian churches. Its modest interior, made entirely from pine, is divided into two rooms, the smaller one designed for women, who are not allowed into the main prayer hall. The latter, with carpets covering the floor, has a small recess in the wall, the mihrab, in the direction of Mecca. Next to it is the mimbar, a sort of pulpit from which the imam says prayers. The painted texts hanging on the walls, the muhirs, are verses from the Koran.

The mosque is used for worship only a few times a year, and on the most solemn holy days there may not be enough room inside for all the congregation. At other times it's locked, but go to house No 57, next to the mosque on the same side of the road; the family living there, one of the few remaining families descended from the Tatars, may open it for you. Be properly dressed (no bare legs) and take off your shoes before entering the prayer hall.

The Tatars of Poland

The Tatars were a fierce, nomadic Mongol tribe from central Asia who first invaded Poland in 1241. They overran and devastated most of Silesia and Małopolska, the royal city of Kraków included. Although they eventually withdrew to Asia, some of them remained in Poland and Lithuania in search of a new home.

Not long after, a new danger appeared in the north, where the Teutonic Knights began expanding swiftly southwards taking Polish territory. In 1410 at Grunwald, Jagiełło inflicted a decisive defeat; interestingly, in this battle a small unit of Tatar horsemen fought alongside the Polish-Lithuanian forces. From that time the numbers of Tatar settlers grew, and so did their participation in battles in defence of their adopted homeland. By the 17th century, they had several cavalry formations reinforcing Polish troops in the wars which were particularly frequent at that time.

In 1683, after the victory over the Turks at the battle of Vienna, King Jan Sobieski granted land in the eastern strip of Poland to those who had fought under the Polish flag. The Tatars founded new settlements here and built their mosques. Of all these villages, Kruszyniany and Bohoniki are the ones that have preserved some of the Tatar inheritance, though apart from their mosques and cemeteries not much else remains. The original population either integrated or left, and there are only a few families living here today that are true descendants of the Tatars.

Of a total of some 3000 people of Tatar origin in Poland, the majority found homes in larger cities such as Warsaw, Gdańsk and Szczecin. Nonetheless, they flock together in Kruszyniany and Bohoniki for important holy days, as Poland's only mosques are here (apart from one recently built in Gdańsk). And they usually end up here at the local Tatar graveyards, two of only three still in use in the country (the other is in Warsaw).

The Mizar, or **Muslim cemetery**, is in the patch of woodland 300m beyond the mosque. The recent gravestones are Christian in style, showing the extent of cultural assimilation that has taken place, and are on the edge of the graveyard, well weeded. Don't stop here, however. Go into the wood, where you'll find fine old examples hidden in the undergrowth. Some of them are inscribed in Russian, a legacy of tsarist times.

Today the population of Kruszyniany, like that of the whole region, is predominantly Belarusian, so it comes as no surprise that there's an **Orthodox church** in the village. Unfortunately, after the charming old wooden cerkiew went up in flames in the 1980s, a modern concrete building was erected on the site. There are interesting old tombstones in the surrounding cemetery, some of them topped with decorative wrought-iron crosses.

Bohoniki

This village is smaller and so is its **mosque**. Generally, the interior is quite similar in its decoration and atmosphere to that of Kruszyniany. It, too, can be visited and the keys are kept at house No 24, 50m from the mosque.

The **Muslim cemetery** is about 1km north of the mosque. Walk to the outskirts of the village then turn left up to a small forested area. As in Kruszyniany, the old tombstones have been overgrown by bushes and grass.

Places to Stay & Eat

There's nothing in Bohoniki and only a sort of shabby bar in Kruszyniany. In the vicinity, there's a summer youth hostel (ul Szkolna 10) and a basic restaurant in

Krynki, and two hotels in Sokółka (ul Mickiewicza 2 and ul Wodna 20) along with a few places to eat.

Getting There & Away

The two villages are 37km apart, each about 50km from Białystok. If you plan on visiting only one village, go to Kruszyniany. A visit to both in one day from Białystok is fairly easy but would involve an early start, several changes of bus and a bit of a walk. There are no direct buses from Białystok to Bohoniki, and only a couple to Kruszyniany.

The best way to do the trip is to go first to Kruszyniany, either on the morning direct bus or with a change in Krynki. After visiting the village take a bus to Sokółka, but if there's no bus on its way, go to Krynki and change, as there are more buses from there. Get off at Drahle Skrzyżowanie, the last stop before arriving at Sokółka, and walk 4km east along the side road to Bohoniki. There's virtually no traffic on this road and only a couple of buses. If you're lucky, you might catch the afternoon bus from Bohoniki to Sokółka, but if not, walk the same way back to the main road, where frequent buses to Sokółka run until around 8 pm. There's no problem getting back from Sokółka to Białystok as trains leave regularly till about 10 pm.

HAJNÓWKA

- pop 25,000   ☎ 085

Set on the edge of the Białowieża Forest, Hajnówka ('Hahy-noof-kah') is its only gateway and an obligatory transit point for all tourists heading for the Białowieża National Park. The town was founded in the 18th century as a guard post to protect the Białowieża Forest from intruders. The forest was exclusively used by the Polish kings for hunting, and later by the tsars. Early this century, when the tsars were busy with domestic problems, the exploitation of the forest began in earnest, which is how the town came to grow.

Today, Hajnówka is a local centre for the timber industry, and has a mixed, half Polish and half Belarusian population. In the surrounding countryside however, the Belarusians predominate. The town has just one major sight – the Orthodox church – but this single building may warrant breaking your journey.

Information

The tourist office (☎/fax 682 27 85) is at ul 3 Maja 37. There are two banks in town (PBK and PKO BP) which change travellers cheques and service credit cards.

Orthodox Church

This is without question one of the most beautiful modern Orthodox churches in Poland. Begun in the early 1970s and fully completed two decades later, the irregular structure, covered by an undulating roof, supports two slender towers, the main one 50m high. The bold, unconventional design, the work of Polish architect Aleksander Grygorowicz, has resulted in a powerful and impressive building.

Its creators have also done a good job inside. The icons and frescoes were painted by a Greek artist whereas the stained-glass windows came from a Kraków workshop. Look for the chandelier and the iconostasis.

One of the priests in the house next to the church is likely to show you around the church if you turn up between 9 am and 5 pm, though they prefer the afternoon hours. It's a good idea to coincide with Mass (Sunday at 10 am, weekdays at 8 am), as there's a good choir.

Special Events

The church is the scene for the International Festival of Orthodox Music, which takes place annually in May and attracts a score of choirs from all over the world. The week-long event is organised by the local cultural centre, the Hajnowski Dom Kultury (☎ 682 32 03), ul Białostocka 2, just a few steps from the church.

Places to Stay & Eat

On the budget side, you can choose between *Dom Wycieczkowy PTTK* (☎ 682 23 29, ul Parkowa 8), and *Dom Nauczyciela ZNP*

(☎ 682 25 85, ul Piłsudskiego 6). Appreciably better is the new *Hotel Orzechowski* (☎ 682 27 58, fax 682 23 94, ul Piłsudskiego 14). It costs US$35/45/60 a single/double/triple with bath and breakfast, and also has a reasonable restaurant. The *youth hostel* (☎ 682 24 05, ul Wróblewskiego 16) opens in July and August in a local school.

Entertainment

Pop into *Bar u Wołodzi*, ul 3 Maja 34A next to the market, for a beer amid a bizarre collection of communist memorabilia. Ask to be let into the VIP room, where you can put on any of the dozens of Soviet uniforms and take as many snaps as you wish.

Getting There & Away

The train station is about 1km south of the Orthodox church and you'll see the characteristic onion-shaped dome from the platform – just head in that direction. Halfway to the church you'll come across the bus terminal.

There are about a dozen buses daily to Białowieża. They go by two routes, either directly (20km) or via Budy (25km); both these trips go through the splendid forest and are spectacular. Trains to Białowieża have been suspended due to the poor shape of the rail lines, but PKP has put its own buses (five a day) on this route. They depart from the train station.

There are only a couple of trains to Białystok (76km) but buses ply this route fairly regularly. One train (214km) and one bus (233km) daily go straight to Warsaw. The train from Warsaw departs around 3 pm to reach Hajnówka at about 8 pm. The PKP bus waits in Hajnówka train station to take passengers on to Białowieża.

BIAŁOWIEŻA NATIONAL PARK
☎ 085

Lying on Poland's border with Belarus, the Białowieża National Park (Białowieski Park Narodowy) is the oldest national park in the country and the only Polish one included on UNESCO's World Heritage list. The park is a small section of a vast forest known as the Puszcza Białowieska, or Białowieża Forest ('Byah-wo-vyeh-zhah').

Today encompassing about 1200 sq km, distributed roughly evenly between Poland and Belarus, the puszcza was once an immense and barely accessible forest stretching for hundreds of kilometres. In the 15th century it became a private hunting ground for the Polish monarchs and continued to be so for the tsars in the 19th century after Poland's partition. During WWI the Germans exploited it intensively, cutting some five million cubic metres of timber, and depleting animal life. The inevitable gradual colonisation and exploitation of its margins has also diminished the forest area and altered the ecosystem. Even so, this vast forest, protected for so long by the royal guards, has kept its centre largely untouched. It's the largest original lowland forest in Europe, and retains much of its primeval landscape and plant and animal life.

Soon after WWI the central part of the puszcza was made a nature reserve, and in 1932 it was formally converted into a national park. The total area of the park is 53 sq km, of which nearly 90% is completely protected, making it the largest strictly conserved forest in Europe.

The park is relatively flat, in parts swampy, and covered with mixed forest, with oak, hornbeam, spruce and pine being the predominant species. Trees reach spectacular sizes uncommon elsewhere, with spruce 50m high and oak trunks 2m in diameter. Some of the oak trees are more than 500 years old.

The forest is home to a variety of animals. There are about 120 species of birds including owls, cranes, storks, hazelhens and nine species of woodpecker. Among the mammals are elk, stag, roe deer, wild boar, lynx, wolf, beaver and the uncontested king of the puszcza, the bison.

Orientation

The starting point for all excursions in the area is the village of Białowieża, which lies 1km south of the national park. The village has accommodation, food and several travel

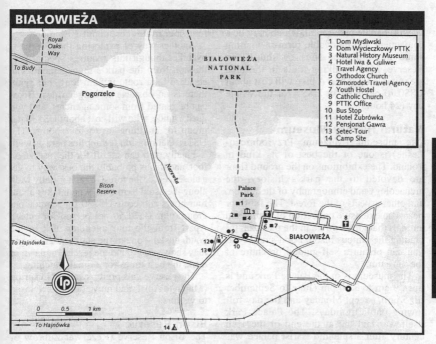

BIAŁOWIEŻA

1 Dom Myśliwski
2 Dom Wycieczkowy PTTK
3 Natural History Museum
4 Hotel Iwa & Guliwer Travel Agency
5 Orthodox Church
6 Zimorodek Travel Agency
7 Youth Hostel
8 Catholic Church
9 PTTK Office
10 Bus Stop
11 Hotel Żubrówka
12 Pensjonat Gawra
13 Setec-Tour
14 Camp Site

MAZOVIA & PODLASIE

agencies, whom you'll need if you want to visit the park.

Coming by bus from Hajnówka, you can get off at the entrance to the Palace Park (Park Pałacowy) next to the unused train station at the western end of the village. You'll find five hotels within a five minute walk from the bus stop (three in the park and two on the main access road). If you plan on staying in the youth hostel, continue by bus to the next stop, opposite the Orthodox church.

Once you've found a place to stay, check the travel agents about visiting the strict nature reserve. Do this soon after your arrival, as all visits must be accompanied by a guide, and it may take a while to arrange one or to collect a group to share the costs. If you have some time before your tour, visit the museum, which will introduce you to the local habitat and its wildlife.

Information

Money There are no kantors in Białowieża, so even though foreign currency is accepted in some places, it's better to come prepared. The nearest place to change money is in Hajnówka.

Travel Agencies There are half a dozen agencies in the village, plus some independent guides. The major operators include PTTK (☎ 681 22 95) at the entrance to the Palace Park; Setec-Tour (☎/fax 681 26 64) at ul Olgi Gabiec 8; Guliwer (☎/fax 681 23 66) in the Hotel Iwa; and Zimorodek (☎ 681 26 09) at ul Waszkiewicza 2.

Their main focus of attention is the strict nature reserve. There are various options for visiting the reserve. See the Strict Nature Reserve section for details. The agencies also offer trips to other attractions in the area.

PTTK and Zimorodek (and Pensjonat Gawra) handle bike rental, which may be a convenient and enjoyable form of visiting some more distant sites eg the Bison Reserve. Many walking trails in the area are suitable for bikes. A bike will cost about US$0.70 per hour or US$7 for the whole day (24 hours).

Natural History Museum

The museum (Muzeum Przyrodniczo-Leśne) is one of the best of its kind in Poland. The exhibitions on the ground floor are devoted to the park's history, the archaeology and ethnography of the region, and other aspects of the forest. The 1st floor boasts an extensive collection of plants and animals that grow or live in the puszcza, including the famous bison. For a small cost, you can obtain a self-guided brochure of the museum.

The museum is in the Palace Park and is open 9 am to 3.30 pm (June to September till 5 pm), except Monday and the day following public holidays. The Palace Park itself was laid out at the end of the 19th century after a splendid tsarist palace was built in 1894. The palace was destroyed by the Nazis during WWII.

Strict Nature Reserve

The strict nature reserve (Rezerwat Ścisły) incorporates almost the whole area of the national park and can only be entered with a guide. Visits can be organised through any of the travel agencies, which can provide English-speaking guides (as well as German and occasionally French).

The most comfortable way to visit the reserve is by horse-drawn cart. Eleven carts are allowed daily into the reserve; five are run by PTTK. The standard tour takes about 2½ hours, but four-hour routes including some more remote areas are also available. The cart takes four people and costs about US$25 for a regular tour. A foreign-language guide will cost another US$25 per group. Add to it a US$1.50 admission fee per person to the reserve (half price for students). In effect, it comes to about US$14 per person if the cart is fully occupied. The four-hour routes cost about 20% more.

Another way of exploring the reserve is by bike, though this requires special permission from the park's management. The standard bike route is 8km long, but again there is no obstacle to longer rides. Bikes can be rented from some agencies, and you need a guide, who will cost about US$30 per group for anything up to four hours. The US$1.50 admission fee applies here as well.

Finally, you can set off for the reserve on foot, and this is probably the best way to get a close feel for the forest. You normally walk along the usual 8km trail, which takes about four hours and costs US$30 for a guide per group (plus US$1.50 per person for entry). Apart from the tour agencies, ask in the youth hostel – one of the staff is a guide and may show you around the reserve at dawn or dusk, the best times for animal-watching.

The reserve gets pretty swampy in spring (March to April) and may at times be closed to visitors.

Bison Reserve

The Bison Reserve (Rezerwat Żubrów or Rezerwat Pokazowy Zwierząt) is a sort of zoo where the animals typical of the puszcza, including bison, elk, wild boar, stag and roe deer, are kept in large enclosures. You can also see the żubroń, a cross between a bison and cow, which has been bred in Białowieża so successfully that the progeny are even larger than the bison itself, reaching weights of up to 1200kg.

Another peculiarity is the tarpan *(Equus caballus gmelini)*, a small, stumpy, mouse-coloured horse with a dark stripe running along its back from head to tail. The tarpan is a Polish cousin of the wild horse *(Equus ferus silvestris)* which once populated the Ukrainian steppes but became extinct in the 19th century. The horse you see is the product of selective breeding in the 1930s, which preserved the creature's original traits. Today, the main breeding centre is in Popielno in Masuria.

The reserve is 3km west of the Palace Park (by road it's 5.5km). You can get there

Traditional rural home in eastern Poland

Tykocin's 17th century synagogue, now a Jewish museum

Memorial at the site of the Treblinka death camp

Inside Oporów's 15th century Gothic castle

Countryside landscape, central Poland

Domes atop the Orthodox church in Hajnówka

The Bison – Back from the Brink

The European bison (*Bison bonasus*), in Polish *żubr*, is the biggest European mammal, its weight occasionally exceeding 1000kg. These large cattle, which live for as long as 25 years, look pretty clumsy but can move at 50km/h when they need to.

Bison were once found all over the continent, but the increasing exploitation of forests in western Europe began to push them eastwards. In the 19th century the last few hundred bison lived in freedom in the Białowieża Forest. In 1916 there were still 150 of them here but three years later they were totally wiped out. By then, there were only about 50 animals of the species kept in zoos throughout the world.

It was in Białowieża that an attempt to prevent the extinction of the bison began in 1929, by bringing several animals from zoos and breeding them in their natural habitat. The result is that today there are about 250 bison living in freedom in the Białowieża Forest alone and about 350 more have been sent to a dozen other places in Poland. Many bison from Białowieża have been distributed among European zoos and forests, and their total current population is estimated at about 2500.

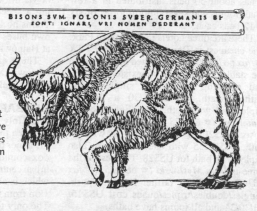

BISONS SVM, POLONIS SVBER, GERMANIS BI SONT: IGNARI, VRI NOMEN DEDERANT

The European bison (engraving from a book published in 1556)

on foot by the green or yellow-marked trails, both starting from the PTTK office, or by the trail called Żebra Żubra (Bison's Ribs). Buses to Hajnówka which go down the main road (not via Budy) will let you off at the Białowieża Skrzyżowanie bus stop, a 10 minute walk from the reserve. You can also get there by horse-drawn cart – ask in the travel agencies for details. The opening hours of the reserve are the same as those of the museum.

The Royal Oaks Way

Some 3km north of the Bison Reserve is the Royal Oaks Way (Szlak Dębów Królewskich), a path traced among a score of ancient oak trees, some over four centuries old. Each of the trees is named after a Lithuanian or Polish monarch. To get there, take the blue trail from Białowieża or the yellow trail from the Bison Reserve. If you take a cart to the Bison Reserve, you can visit the Oaks on the same trip.

Białowieża Village

Apart from the natural attractions, you might like to stroll about the village of Białowieża. This sleepy little place, which today has some 2500 inhabitants (70% of whom are Belarusians), still has some of its 19th century wooden houses. Near the Palace Park is the late 19th century Orthodox church, which features a rare ceramic iconostasis.

Places to Stay

Białowieża has quite a choice of accommodation options and nothing is expensive. Apart from the places listed here there are some rooms rented out by locals in their homes – inquire at travel agencies.

The cheapest is the friendly all-year *youth hostel* (☎/fax 681 25 60, ul Waszkiewicza 6), which is hidden behind a mustard-coloured wooden school building. It has about 50 beds distributed in a few small rooms and several dormitories of six to 12 beds each.

There are three hotels in the Palace Park. The cheapest is *Dom Wycieczkowy PTTK* (☎/fax 681 25 05), established in what were the stables of the now nonexistent palace, and charging US$9/16 a single/double without bath, US$20/25/30 a double/triple/quad with bath. The slightly better *Hotel Iwa* (☎ 681 23 85, ☎/fax 681 22 60) costs US$20/24 doubles/quads without bath, US$24/35 with bath. There are also triples with bath for US$28. The best of the three is *Dom Myśliwski* (☎ 681 25 84, fax 681 23 23), a bit farther into the park. Singles/doubles/triples/quads cost US$15/23/30/34 and all rooms have baths.

Hotel Żubrówka (☎ 681 23 03, ☎/fax 681 25 70, ul Olgi Gabiec 6) offers doubles/triples with bath for US$20/24, and doubles without bath for US$15. Just behind it is the pleasant *Pensjonat Gawra* (☎ 681 28 04), which costs US$15/22 a double/triple without bath, US$18/25 with bath. The Pensjonat also runs a simple *camp site* in Grudki, 2km south-west of the village.

Places to Eat

The restaurant of *Hotel Iwa* serves inexpensive, tasty meals and has a choice of game. You can eat nearly everything you've seen in the bison reserve, including wild boar, roe deer, elk and occasionally bison. The restaurant opens at 8 am and is the only place for a reasonably early breakfast.

The restaurant of *Hotel Żubrówka* is not bad either, but it doesn't have much game and doesn't open till later in the day. *Dom*

Wycieczkowy PTTK has its own bistro, but the choice is more limited.

Getting There & Away

The only gateway to Białowieża from anywhere in Poland is Hajnówka. You have to go through it and, more often than not, change your bus or train.

About a dozen PKS buses daily run to Hajnówka, either via the main road (20km) or via the village of Budy (25km), providing a spectacular trip through the forest. Trains no longer operate, but PKP runs its own buses instead, which will deposit you at Hajnówka's train station.

There are only two direct buses from Białowieża to Białystok (82 or 98km) and two to Bielsk Podlaski (46km).

GRABARKA

The Holy Mountain in Grabarka hardly means a thing to the average Pole, yet it's the major place of pilgrimage for the Orthodox community. Remote from important urban centres and main roads, the mountain, which is actually a small forested hill, lies 1km from the obscure village of Grabarka. The only town of any size in the region is Siemiatycze, 9km west by a rough track.

A convent and a church are hidden among woods at the top, the church being the destination of the pilgrims. It was once a simple wooden structure, but after it went up in flames in 1990, a new brick building was built, similar in shape to the previous one. The most striking thing is that the church is surrounded by a forest of 10,000 to 20,000 crosses of different sizes ranging from 5cm miniatures to structures several metres tall.

The story of the crosses goes back to 1710, when an epidemic of cholera broke out in the region and decimated the population. Amid this utter despair, a mysterious sign came from the heavens which indicated that a cross should be built and carried to a nearby hill. Those who reached the top escaped death, and soon afterwards the epidemic disappeared. The hill became a miraculous site and the thanksgiving church was erected. Since then people have been carrying crosses up there to place alongside the first one.

In the aftermath of WWII, a convent was established in Grabarka to gather all the nuns scattered throughout the country from the five convents that had existed before the war. Since then Grabarka has become the largest Orthodox pilgrimage centre in Poland.

Transfiguration

The biggest feast is the Spas, or the day of Transfiguration of the Saviour, on 19 August. The ceremony begins the day before at 6 pm and continues with Masses and prayers throughout the night, culminating at 10 am in the Great Liturgy, celebrated by the metropolitan of the Orthodox Church in Poland. Up to 30,000 people come annually from all over the country to participate.

Before climbing the Holy Mountain, the pilgrims perform ritual ablutions in the stream at the foot of the hill and drink water from the holy well, which supposedly has miraculous properties. The more fervent of them fill large bottles with the wonderworking liquid to take back home to prevent misfortune or heal the ill. Those who bring crosses have them blessed before adding them to the spectacular collection.

On this night, the surrounding forest turns into a vast car park and camp site, with cars and tents filling the spaces between the trees. Yet, despite this wave of modernity, the older, more traditional generation comes on foot without any camping gear and keeps watch all night. The light of the familiar thin candles adds to the mysterious atmosphere.

If you wish to come on this magical night, you have the same options – to pitch your tent or to stay awake. Naturally, the commercial community is well represented with stalls selling food and drink and a variety of religious goods. There's also a selection of Orthodox music on cassettes and CDs.

Getting There & Away

Transport is basically by train, the Sycze station being a short walk from the hill. Trains run regularly to/from Siedlce (63km) and semi-regularly to/from Hajnówka (58km). There is only one train directly to/from Warsaw (156km) and Lublin (202km), and three trains to/from Białystok (106km).

From the Sycze train platform, it's a little over a kilometre to the Holy Mountain. There is nothing to indicate the direction but the yellow trail heading south will get you there. If you are coming from Hajnówka, go left from the platform down the road. From there the road veers right, but follow the track straight into the forest – you'll find the trail and signs as you go.

Only one or two buses link Grabarka to Siemiatycze (9km) and it's better not to rely on them at the time of the celebrations.

Kraków

• **pop 750,000** ☎ **012**

The royal capital for half a millennium, Kraków has witnessed and absorbed more of Poland's history than any other city in the country. Moreover, unlike most other Polish cities, it came through the last war unscathed, so it has retained much of this history, guarded in its walls, works of art and traditions. The postwar period seems to have had little impact as the tallest structures on Kraków's skyline are not skyscrapers but the spires of old churches.

No other city in Poland has so many historic buildings and monuments, and nowhere else will you encounter such a vast collection of works of art (2.3 million). In appreciation of the town's exceptional historic and artistic values, in 1978 UNESCO included the centre of Kraków on its first World Heritage list.

Yet there's more to see than ancient walls. Kraków is alive and vibrant with the past and present mingling harmoniously. The continuity of its traditions has created its own peculiar atmosphere, and countless legends have added their aura. Kraków is a city with character and soul.

Kraków has traditionally been one of the major centres of Polish culture, and its cultural status remains very high. Many leading figures of contemporary arts and culture – Wajda, Polański and Penderecki, to name just a few – are associated with Kraków. The two Nobel Prizewinners in literature, Czesław Miłosz (1980) and Wisława Szymborska (1996), live here. The city also gave the world its first Polish pope.

Kraków's population is the best educated in Poland. With its renowned Jagiellonian University (over 600 years old) and 12 other institutions of higher education, it has over 70,000 students, a tenth of the city's population.

Give yourself at least several days or even a full week for Kraków. This is not a place to rush through. The longer you stay, the more captivating you'll find it.

Highlights

- Stroll around the magnificent Main Market Square

- Admire Veit Stoss' Gothic altarpiece in St Mary's Church

- View Leonardo da Vinci's *Lady with the Ermine* in the Czartoryski Museum

- Visit Wawel castle and cathedral, possibly Poland's most important historic sights

- Take in an evening of live *klezmer* music in Ariel Café

- Marvel at the labyrinthine 700-year-old salt mine in Wieliczka

- Soak up the atmosphere of the fabulous cellar-vaulted pubs

RUSSIA

Greater Kraków p198
Kraków – Old Town & Wawel p204
Kraków – Kazimierz p214

CZECH REPUBLIC

SLOVAKIA

HISTORY

The first traces of the town's existence date from around the 7th century. In the 8th and

9th centuries Kraków was one of the main settlements of the Vistulans or Wiślanie, the tribe which several centuries earlier had spread around the region known as Little Poland or Małopolska. The earliest written record of Kraków dates from 965, when an Arabian traveller and merchant of Jewish descent, Ibrahim ibn Yaqub from Cordova, visited the town and mentioned it as a large trade centre called Krakwa.

In 1000 the bishopric of Kraków was established, and in 1038 Kraków became the capital of the Piast kingdom. The Wawel castle and several churches were built in the 11th century and the town, initially centred around the Wawel hill, grew in size and power.

In 1241 the Tatars overran Kraków and burned down the town, which was mostly made of timber. In 1257 the new town's centre was designed on a grid pattern, with a market square in the middle. Brick and stone largely replaced wood, and Gothic became the dominant architectural style. Fortifications were gradually built.

Good times came with the reign of King Kazimierz Wielki, a generous patron of art and scholarship. In 1364 he founded the Kraków Academy (later renamed the Jagiel-lonian University), the second university in central Europe after Prague's. Nicolaus Copernicus, who would later develop his heliocentric theory, studied here in the 1490s.

Kraków's economic and cultural expansion reached its peak in the 16th century. The Renaissance period, Poland's golden age, saw the city flourish as never before. The medieval Wawel castle gave way to a mighty palace, learning and science prospered, and the population passed the 30,000 mark.

It was not to last, however. The transfer of the capital to Warsaw in 1596-1609 brought an end to Kraków's good fortune. Though the city remained the place of coronations and burials, the king and the court resided in Warsaw and political and cultural life was centred there. The Swedish invasion of 1655 did a lot of damage, and the 18th century, with its numerous invasions, accelerated the decline. By the end of the century the city population had dropped to 10,000. Following the final Third Partition of Poland, Kraków fell under Austrian rule.

Austria proved to be the least oppressive of the three occupants, and the city enjoyed a reasonable and steadily increasing cultural and political freedom. By the closing

KRAKÓW

Kraków and Kazimierz in the late 15th century: they were separate walled cities until the 1820s

GREATER KRAKÓW

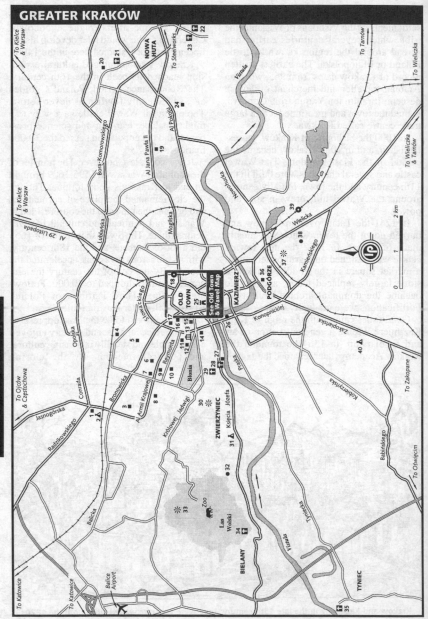

GREATER KRAKÓW

PLACES TO STAY		17	Dom Wycieczkowy		23	St Bartholomew's Church
1	Motel Krak		Chałupnik		25	Wawel
2	Camping Nr 45 Krak	19	Letni Hotel AWF		26	Centre of Japanese Art &
3	Youth Hostel (ul	20	Schronisko Turystyczne			Technology 'Manggha'
	Szablowskiego)		Wagabunda		28	Church of the
4	Schronisko Turystyczne Ekspres	24	Hotel Czyżyny			Premonstratensian Nuns
5	Strawberry Hostel	27	Youth Hostel (ul Kościuszki)		29	Holy Saviour's Church
6	Bydgoska Student Hostel	31	Camping Nr 46 Smok		30	Kościuszko Mound
7	Piast Student Hostel	36	Hotel Korona		32	Polonia Institute
8	Hotel Krakowiak	40	Camping Nr 171 Krakowianka		33	Piłsudski Mound
9	Nawojka Student Hostel				34	Church & Hermitage of the
10	Hotel Wisła	**OTHER**				Camaldolese Monks
11	Youth Hostel (ul Oleandry)	13	Gallery of 20th Century		35	Benedictine Abbey
12	Żaczek Student Hostel		Polish Painting		37	Krakus Mound
14	Hotel Cracovia	18	Kraków Główny Train Station		38	Former Płaszów
15	Hotel Fortuna	21	Church of Our Lady of Poland			Concentration Camp
16	Hotel Logos	22	Cistercian Abbey		39	Kraków Płaszów Train Station

decades of the 19th century it had become the major centre of Polish culture and the spiritual capital of the formally nonexistent country, a focus for intellectual life and theatre. The avant-garde artistic and literary movement known as Młoda Polska or Young Poland was born here in the 1890s. It was also here that a national independence movement originated, which later produced the Polish Legions under the command of Józef Piłsudski.

After Poland's independence was restored in 1918, Warsaw took over most political and administrative functions but Kraków retained much of its status as a cultural and artistic centre. By the outbreak of WWII the city had 260,000 inhabitants, 70,000 of whom were Jews.

During the war, Kraków, like all other Polish cities, witnessed the silent departures of Jews who were never to be seen again. The city was thoroughly looted by Nazis but didn't experience major combat and bombing. As such, Kraków is virtually the only large Polish city that has its old architecture almost intact.

After the liberation, the communist government was quick to present the city with a huge steelworks at Nowa Huta, just a few miles away from the historic quarter, in an attempt to break the traditional intellectual and religious framework of the city. The social engineering proved less successful than its unanticipated by-product – ecological disaster. Monuments which had somehow survived Tatars, Swedes and Nazis plus numerous natural misfortunes are now gradually and methodically being eaten away by acid rain and toxic gas.

With Nowa Huta and other new suburbs, Kraków trebled in size after the war to become the country's third-largest city after Warsaw and Łódź. However, the historic core has changed little and continues to be the political, administrative and cultural centre.

ORIENTATION

The great thing about Kraków is that almost all you need is at hand, conveniently squeezed into the compact area of the Old Town. Even consulates, which normally prefer quiet locations outside central areas, have gathered right in the heart of the historic quarter.

The Old Town, about 800m wide and 1200m long, has the Main Market Square in the middle, and is encircled by the green park of the Planty, which was once a moat. On the southern tip of the Old Town sits the Wawel castle, and farther south stretches the district of Kazimierz.

KRAKÓW

The bus and train stations – where you're most likely to arrive – are next to each other on the north-eastern rim of the Old Town. The tourist office is right opposite the train station and nearly 10 hotels are within a 500m radius. Rynek Główny, the heart of the city, is a 10 minute walk from the station.

INFORMATION
Tourist Offices

The Centrum Informacji Turystycznej KART or the city's state-run tourist information centre (☎ 422 04 71, ☎ 422 60 91) is at ul Pawia 8 opposite the train station. The office is open weekdays 8 am to 4 pm (from June to September till 6 pm and also Saturday 9 am to 1 pm).

Two private travel agencies have their own tourist information desks. The Dexter tourist office (☎ 421 77 06, ☎ 421 30 51, fax 421 30 36), strategically located in the Cloth Hall in the middle of the Rynek Główny, is open weekdays 9 am to 6 pm, Saturday 9 am to 1 pm. The Jordan tourist office (☎ 939) closed down its information outlet at ul Floriańska 37 just before we went to press, but it should open in another central location. Inquire at the company's travel branch (☎ 421 21 25) at ul Długa 9, or call ☎ 939.

Kraków also has a knowledgeable Cultural Information Centre – refer to the Entertainment section later in this chapter.

Tourist Publications

Kraków has the most comprehensive guidebook coverage of all Polish cities. A number of locally produced guidebooks to Kraków have been published in English and German, with some of them in other languages including French. They mostly feature descriptions of the city's attractions, often supplemented with attractive photographic material, while practical information seems to be of a lower priority. Most larger bookshops have a selection of these guidebooks.

Watch out for two free monthly tourist magazines: *Welcome to Cracow* and *Kraków: What, Where, When*. They can be picked up from tourist offices, some upmarket hotels, travel agencies etc. The best magazine on the city is *Krakow Insider*, which has just about all the practical information you would possibly need, and is particularly comprehensive about where to eat and drink. But it may be hard to track down.

Money

Cash can easily be exchanged in any of the numerous kantors scattered throughout Old Town. Some trade on Sunday, but the rates are usually poorer then; change enough money on Saturday to last you until Monday.

Change your travellers cheques at the American Express counter (☎ 422 91 80) in the Orbis office at Rynek Główny 41 (open weekdays 8 am to 6 pm, Saturday 8.30 am to 1 pm), which charges no commission. You can also change cheques in Bank Pekao at Rynek Główny 31, but it charges commission.

Cash advances on Visa and MasterCard are obtainable at Bank Pekao, either from the cashier inside or the ATM outside, and there are many more ATMs throughout the central area.

Post & Communications

The main post office at ul Westerplatte 20 has poste restante. Mail should be addressed c/o Poste Restante, Poczta Główna, ul Westerplatte 20, 31-045 Kraków 1, Poland, and can be collected at window No 1. The mail is kept for 14 working days only. Amex customers may use the services of Kraków's Amex office, in which case mail should be addressed c/o Poste Restante, American Express Travel, Rynek Główny 41, 31-013 Kraków, Poland. Mail is kept here for a month.

There's a telephone centre next to the main post office (open 24 hours), or you can use the more central phone office at Rynek Główny 19 (open till 10 pm). There's also a post/phone office (that has a 24 hour telephone service) at ul Lubicz 4, opposite the central train station.

Email & Internet Access

The oldest and best known place in town is the Cyber Café u Luisa (☎ 421 80 92), set in a spectacular vaulted cellar at Rynek Główny 13. Yet, it has painfully slow connections, so if speed is more important than the ambience try one of the following:

Cyber Net Café
　(☎ 421 89 64) Plac Matejki 5
InterCafe Virtual World
　(☎ 267 63 57) ul Konopnickiej 11
Kompit
　(☎ 632 18 96) ul Batorego 20
Looz Internet Café
　(☎ 422 37 97) ul Mikołajska 11

Travel Agencies

A number of travel agencies operate tours in and around Kraków – see Organised Tours later in this chapter for details.

Bookshops

For English-language literature check out the English Book Centre (☎ 422 62 00) at Plac Matejki 5 and Inter Book (☎ 632 10 08) at ul Karmelicka 27. The Księgarnia Edukator (☎ 421 53 17) in the French Institute at ul Św Jana 15 has the best selection of books in French. The Księgarnia Odeon (☎ 422 24 47) at Rynek Główny 5 and the Księgarnia Znak (☎ 422 45 48) at Sławkowska 1 have modest selections of both French and English books.

The widest choice of publications related to Jewish issues is to be found at the Jarden Jewish Bookshop (☎ 421 71 66) at ul Szeroka 2 in Kazimierz.

Some of the best selection of regional and city maps is in Sklep Podróżnika at ul Jagiellońska 6 (☎ 429 14 85) and ul Szujskiego 2 (☎ 421 89 22); the latter is perhaps the only place in Kraków which sells Lonely Planet guidebooks.

Cultural Centres

Foreign cultural centres in Kraków include:

Center for Jewish Culture
　(☎ 423 55 95, ☎ 423 55 87, fax 423 50 34) ul Meiselsa 17

Centre of Japanese Art and Technology 'Manggha'
　(☎ 267 09 82, ☎ 267 37 53, fax 267 40 79) ul Konopnickiej 26
French Institute
　(☎ 422 09 82) ul Św Jana 15
Goethe Institute (German)
　(☎ 22 69 02, ☎ 422 69 46) Rynek Główny 20
International Culture Centre
　(☎ 421 86 01, fax 421 85 71) Rynek Główny 25
Italian Institute of Culture
　(☎ 421 89 46) ul Grodzka 49

The Centre of Japanese Art and Technology 'Manggha' was the idea of Polish film director Andrzej Wajda, who donated for this purpose the whole of the US$340,000 prize money he received from the City of Kyoto in 1987. The building was designed by well known Japanese architect Arata Isozaki, and the centre was opened in 1994.

Its main aim is to exhibit a valuable collection of old Japanese weapons, ceramics, fabrics and woodcuts. Numbering a few thousand pieces, this unique collection was assembled by Feliks Manggha Jasieński, an avid traveller and visionary writer, but since his death in 1926 it had been exhibited only occasionally. Part of the collection is finally on permanent display. The centre has a multi-functional high-tech auditorium where events presenting Japanese culture (film, theatre, traditional music) are held.

The International Culture Centre (Międzynarodowe Centrum Kultury) focuses on the issues of cultural heritage and its protection. The centre's activities include seminars, conferences (open to the public), exhibitions, publications and educational programs. The centre operates a gallery (1st floor) staging exhibitions presenting some of the prominent events of central European art from the late 19th and early 20th centuries.

Medical Services

Pharmacies are everywhere – the city has more than 130 of them. You will find three pharmacies on Rynek Główny alone, at Nos

KRAKÓW

13, 42 and 45, and more in the adjacent streets.

Profimed (☎ 421 79 97) at Rynek Główny 6 has private specialists. Dent America (☎ 421 89 48) at Plac Szczepański 3 is a Polish-American dental clinic. Falck (☎ 96 75), ul Racławicka 26, attends house calls and has its own ambulance service. The US consulate department of citizen services (☎ 422 12 94) has a list of recommended doctors speaking English. The city ambulance emergency phone number is ☎ 999.

OLD TOWN

The Old Town developed gradually throughout the centuries. Its plan was drawn up in 1257 after the Tatar invasions, and has survived more or less in its original form. The construction of the fortifications began in the 13th century, and it took almost two centuries to envelop the town with a powerful, 3km-long chain of double defensive walls complete with 47 towers and seven main entrance gates plus a wide moat.

With the development of military technology, the system lost its defensive capability and, apart from a small section to the north, was eventually demolished at the beginning of the 19th century. The moat was filled up and a ring-shaped park, the Planty, was laid out on the site, surrounding the Old Town with parkland – a pleasant place to rest after seeing the sights.

The Old Town has plenty of historical monuments, enough to keep you exploring for at least several days. There are a dozen museums and nearly 20 old churches here, not to mention scores of other important sights.

Noble, harmonious and elegant, Kraków's Old Town has a unique atmosphere, felt as much in its busy street life during the day, as in its majestic silence late at night. Except for some enclaves, the sector is car-free so you can stroll undisturbed. Kraków is best explored casually and randomly, savouring its architectural details and the old-time air, and dropping into art galleries, trendy boutiques and cosy cafés and bars along the way.

Main Market Square

Measuring 200 x 200m, Kraków's Main Market Square (Rynek Główny) is the largest medieval town square in Poland and reputedly in all of Europe. It's considered to be one of the finest urban designs of its kind. Its layout was drawn up in 1257 and has been retained to this day, though the buildings have changed over the centuries. Today most of them look neoclassical, but don't let the façades confuse you – the basic structures are older, sometimes considerably so, as can be seen in their doorways, architectural details and interiors. Their cellars date from medieval times.

When strolling around the Rynek, pop into the Krzysztofory Palace (No 35) at the northern corner, which is home to the **Historical Museum of Kraków** (Muzeum Historyczne Krakowa). It features a bit of everything including old clocks, armour, paintings, *szopki* or Nativity scenes, and the costume of the Lajkonik (see Special Events later in this chapter). The museum is open on Wednesday, Friday, Saturday and Sunday 9 am to 3.30 pm, and on Thursday 11 am to 6 pm.

In the past, the square was the marketplace and was crammed with vendors' stalls and houses. All that went in the 19th century, leaving behind three important buildings of which the largest is the centrally positioned **Cloth Hall** (Sukiennice). It was originally a 14th century construction, designed as a centre for the cloth trade, but was gutted by fire in 1555 and rebuilt in Renaissance style. In the late 19th century arcades were added, giving the hall a more decorative appearance. The ground floor continues to be a trading centre, now for crafts and souvenirs, while the upper floor has been taken over by the **Gallery of 19th Century Polish Painting** (open Tuesday, Wednesday, Friday, Saturday and Sunday 10 am to 3.30 pm and Thursday noon to 5.30 pm). It displays works by important painters of the period, including Józef Chełmoński, Jacek Malczewski, Aleksander Gierymski and the leader of monumental historic painting, Jan Matejko.

The gallery is a branch of the National Museum, which has several other outlets in the city, including the Matejko House, the Czartoryski Museum, the Szołajski House, the Wyspiański Museum and the Gallery of 20th Century Polish Painting. All these are described separately in the following sections. On the entrance door of each branch you'll find a board displaying opening hours of all branches. Take good note of them, as they may have changed from when this was written. The National Museum offers special US$5 tickets (US$3.50 for students) which warrant admission to all the permanent exhibitions of all its branches at any time. The ticket is cheaper than a total of individual admission fees, and you can buy it at any of the branch museums.

The **Town Hall Tower** (Wieża Ratuszowa) next to the Cloth Hall is all that is left of the 15th century town hall dismantled in the 1820s. It has been extensively renovated over the past years and may be open again to visitors in summer, as it was before restoration.

In the southern corner of the square is the small, domed **St Adalbert's Church** (Kościół Św Wojciecha). One of the oldest churches in the town, its origins date from the 10th century. You can see the original foundations in the basement, where a small exhibition also presents archaeological finds excavated from the Rynek.

A few steps north from the church is the **Statue of Adam Mickiewicz** surrounded by four allegorical figures: the Motherland, Learning, Poetry and Valour. It's here that the szopki competition is held in early December.

The flower stalls just to the north of the statue have reputedly been trading on this site from time immemorial. This area is also the 'pasture' for Kraków's population of pigeons, thought to be the second-largest in Europe after that of Venice.

St Mary's Church

Overlooking the square from the east is St Mary's Church (Kościół Mariacki). The first church on this site was built in the 1220s and, typically for the period, was 'oriented' – that is, its presbytery pointed east. Following its destruction during the Tatar raids the construction of a mighty basilica started, using the foundations of the previous church. That's why the church stands at an angle to the square.

The facade is dominated by two unequal towers. The lower one, 69m high and topped by a Renaissance dome, serves as a bell tower and holds five bells, while the taller one, 81m high, has traditionally been the city's property and functioned as a watchtower. It's topped with a spire surrounded by turrets – a good example of medieval craftsmanship – and in 1666 was given a 350kg gilded crown, about 2.5m in diameter. The gilded ball higher up is said to contain the written history of the city.

Every hour the *hejnał* is played on a trumpet from the higher tower to the four quarters of the world in turn. Today a musical symbol of the city, this simple melody, based on five notes only, was played in medieval times as a warning call. Intriguingly, it breaks off abruptly in mid-bar. Legend links it to the Tatar invasions; when the watchman on duty spotted the enemy and sounded the alarm, a Tatar arrow pierced his throat in mid-phrase. The tune has stayed this way thereafter. The hejnał is broadcast on Polish Radio every day at noon.

The main church entrance, through a baroque porch added to the façade in the 1750s, is used by the faithful only; tourists enter through the side door, where a small admission fee is charged. The dim interior is illuminated by stained-glass windows. Those in the chancel are originals dating from the late 14th century, while on the opposite side of the church, above the organ loft, you'll see Art Nouveau work by Stanisław Wyspiański and Józef Mehoffer. The wall paintings designed by Jan Matejko harmonise with the medieval architecture and make an appropriate background for the grand high altar, which is acclaimed as the greatest masterpiece of Gothic art in Poland.

KRAKÓW – OLD TOWN & WAWEL

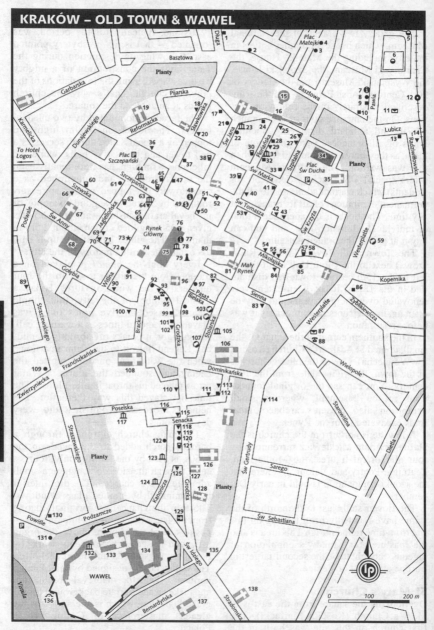

0   100   200 m

KRAKÓW – OLD TOWN & WAWEL

PLACES TO STAY
1 Pokoje Gościnne Jordan
9 Hotel Warszawski
10 Hotel Polonia
13 Hotel Europejski
17 Hotel Francuski
24 Hotel Polski
28 Dom Gościnny UJ
32 Hotel Pokoje Gościnne SARPu
33 Hotel Pollera
37 Grand Hotel
41 Hotel Elektor
47 Hotel Saski
58 Hotel Wit Stwosz
86 Dom Turysty PTTK
99 Dom Polonii
101 Hotel Rezydent
112 Hotel Wawel-Tourist
130 Pensjonat i Restauracja
Rycerska
135 Hotel Royal

PLACES TO EAT
14 Restauracja pod Wieżyczką
18 Restauracja Cyrano de Bergerac
20 Kuchnia Staropolska u Babci
Maliny
25 McDonald's
26 Jadłodajnia Sąsiedzi
27 Różowy Słoń
29 Jama Michalika
36 Jadłodajnia Jak u Mamy
40 Bar Mleczny Dworzanin
42 Café Larousse
43 Jadłodajnia Bistro Stop
50 Pizzeria Grace
51 Grill Aladyn
52 Kawiarnia Camelot
53 Sklep z Kawą Pożegnanie z
Afryką
54 Restauracja u Szkota
55 Jadłodajnia u Górala
56 Jadłodajnia u Stasi & Pizzeria
Cyklop
64 Restauracja Tetmajerowska
66 Kawiarnia u Zalipianek
69 Jadłodajnia Kuchcik
70 Pizzeria Grace
71 Salad Bar Chimera
82 Różowy Słoń
83 Pizzeria Grace
84 Herbaciarnia Słodka Dziurka

89 Różowy Słoń
90 Herbaciarnia Gołębnik
93 Restauracja Wentzl
95 Ristorante da Pietro
100 Chimera II
102 Akropolis Grill
110 Restauracja pod Aniołami
111 Taco Mexicano
113 Restauracja Korsykańska Paese
114 Bar Wegetariański Vega
115 Bar Mleczny pod Temidą
116 Caffeteria pod Błękitnym Kotem
118 Marhaba Grill
119 Bar Grodzki
125 Pizza Hut

OTHER
2 LOT Office
3 Cyber Net Café
4 English Book Centre
5 Bus No 208 to Airport &
Minibuses to Wieliczka
6 Central Bus Terminal
7 KART Tourist Office
8 Waweltur (Private Rooms)
11 Post Office
12 Kraków Główny Train Station
15 Barbican
16 Florian Gate
19 Church of the Reformed
Franciscans
21 Piwnica pod Wyrwigroszem
22 French Institute
23 Czartoryski Museum
30 Piwnica pod Złotą Pipą
31 Matejko House
34 Słowacki Theatre
35 Church of the Holy Cross
38 Pub pod Papugami
39 Pub pod Jemiołą
44 Szołajski House
45 Free Pub
46 Pub u Kacpra
48 Cultural Information Centre
49 American Express & Orbis
Offices
57 Black Gallery
59 Russian Consulate
60 Klub Kulturalny
61 Stary Teatr (Old Theatre)
62 Sklep Podróżnika & Piwnica
pod Ogródkiem

63 Historical Museum of Kraków
65 Bank Pekao
67 St Anne's Church
68 Collegium Maius
72 Piwnica pod Baranami
73 Police Station
74 Town Hall Tower
75 Cloth Hall
76 Public Toilet
77 Dexter Tourist Office
78 Gallery of 19th Century
Polish Painting
79 Statue of Adam Mickiewicz
80 St Mary's Church
81 St Barbara's Church
85 Looz Internet Café
87 Main Post Office
88 Main Telecommunication
Office
91 International Culture Centre
92 Goethe Institute
94 Telecommunication Office
96 St Adalbert's Church
97 Klub pod Jaszczurami
98 Klub u Luisa
103 German Consulate
104 US Consulate
105 Poster Gallery
106 Dominican Church
107 French Consulate
108 Franciscan Church
109 Philharmonic Hall
117 Archaeological Museum
120 Italian Institute of Culture
121 Pub Prohibicja
122 Cricoteka
123 Wyspiański Museum
124 Archdiocesan Museum
126 Church of SS Peter & Paul
127 St Andrew's Church
128 St Martin's Church
129 St Giles' Church
131 Wędrowiec Travel Agency
132 Wawel Cathedral Museum
133 Wawel Cathedral
134 Wawel Castle
136 Dragon's Cave
137 Bernardine Church
138 St Paul's Church

KRAKÓW

The altarpiece is a pentaptych (like a triptych, but consisting of a central panel and two pairs of side wings), intricately carved in limewood, painted and gilded. The main scene represents the Dormition of the Virgin while the wings portray scenes from the life of Christ and the Virgin. The altarpiece is topped with the Coronation of the

Virgin and, on both sides, the statues of the patron saints of Poland, St Stanislaus and St Adalbert.

About 13m high and 11m wide, the pentaptych is the largest piece of medieval art of its kind. It took 12 years for its maker, the Nuremberg sculptor Veit Stoss (known to Poles as Wit Stwosz), to complete this monumental work before it was solemnly consecrated and revealed in 1489.

The pentaptych is opened daily at 11.50 am and closed after the evening Mass, except for Saturday when it's left open for the Sunday morning Mass. The altarpiece apart, don't miss the stone crucifix on the baroque altar in the head of the right-hand aisle, another work by Veit Stoss, and the still larger crucifix placed on the rood screen, attributed to pupils of the master.

To the south of the church is the small, charming **St Mary's Square** (Plac Mariacki) which until the early 19th century was a parish cemetery. The 14th century **St Barbara's Church** (Kościół Św Barbary) bordering the square on the east was the cemetery chapel. Next to its entrance, there's an open chapel featuring stone sculptures of Christ and three apostles, also attributed to the Stoss school.

A passage adjoining the church will take you onto the **Little Market Square** (Mały Rynek) which was once the second-largest marketplace in town and traded mainly in meat.

North of the Market Square

The area to the north of Rynek Główny is noted for its regular chessboard layout. Its main commercial street, ul Floriańska, is part of the traditional Royal Way which leads from the Barbican to the Wawel castle. A suggested walking tour might take in the following attractions, in the order listed.

Church of the Holy Cross Undistinguished from the outside, the small 15th century Church of the Holy Cross (Kościół Św Krzyża) deserves a visit for its Gothic vaulting, one of the most beautiful in the

city. An unusual design with the palm-like vault supported on a single central column, it was constructed in 1528 and recently thoroughly renovated.

Florian Gate The Florian Gate (Brama Floriańska) is the only one of the original seven gates which was not dismantled during the 19th century 'modernisation'. It was built around 1300, although the top is a later addition. The adjoining walls together with two towers have also been left and today host an outdoor art gallery, where you are able to buy the finest kitsch in town.

Barbican The most intriguing remnant of the medieval fortifications, the Barbican (Barbakan) is a powerful, circular brick bastion adorned with seven turrets. There are 130 loopholes in its 3m-thick walls. This curious piece of defensive art was built around 1498 as an additional protection of the Florian Gate and was once connected with it by a narrow passage running over a moat. It's one of the very few surviving structures of its kind in Europe, the largest and perhaps the most beautiful.

Matejko House Ulica Floriańska is the liveliest street of the Old Town and in it you'll find Matejko House (Dom Matejki). Here for the 20 most fruitful years of his life (1873-93) lived and worked Jan Matejko, the uncontested leader of national historical painting, renowned for his powerful canvases documenting Polish history. Today it's a museum (open Tuesday to Thursday, Saturday and Sunday 10 am to 3.30 pm, Friday noon to 5.30 pm) displaying memorabilia of the artist and some of his paintings and drawings (his larger paintings are in the Cloth Hall gallery). The house itself is a 16th century structure, but was remodelled according to a design by Matejko himself.

Czartoryski Museum The Czartoryski Museum (Muzeum Czartoryskich) at ul Św Jana 19 is one of the best in town. Originally established in Puławy by Princess

Izabela Czartoryska as the first historical museum in Poland, the collection was secretly moved to Paris after the November Insurrection of 1830 (in which the family was implicated) and some 50 years later brought to Kraków. The collection experienced another 'excursion' during WWII when the Nazis seized it and took it to Germany, and not all the exhibits were recovered. Even so, there's a lot to see, including Greek, Egyptian and Etruscan ancient art, Oriental armour, artistic handicrafts from Europe and Asia, and old European painting, mainly Italian, Dutch and Flemish. The star pieces of the collection are Leonardo da Vinci's *Lady with the Ermine* (about 1485) and Rembrandt's *Landscape with the Good Samaritan*, also known as the *Landscape before a Storm* (1638). The museum's opening hours are the same as for Matejko House.

Church of the Reformed Franciscans
The rather ordinary 17th century Church of the Reformed Franciscans (Kościół Reformatów) on ul Reformacka is renowned for its crypt, which holds coffins, each one containing a mummified body. The striking thing about it is that no particular embalming procedure has been applied; the bodies were just laid to rest here. The crypt has a unique microclimate which allows the bodies to mummify naturally. It is closed to the public to maintain its special atmospheric conditions.

Szołajski House
A largish, palace-like building at Plac Szczepański 9, the Szołajski House (Kamienica Szołajskich) is a branch of the National Museum which features an extensive collection of religious painting and sculpture from the 14th to 16th centuries. Collected from churches in the region and in Kraków itself, it's one of the best selections of late Gothic and early Renaissance altarpieces and Madonnas in the country. The showpiece is the *Madonna of Krużlowa*, the carved and painted statue of the Virgin Mary and Child from around 1400, considered the best of its kind in

The Madonna of Krużlowa is a highlight of the Szołajski House collection

Poland. The museum was closed for renovation when this book was researched but may have reopened by the time you arrive.

West of the Market Square
A good part of this sector was once inhabited by Jews, who were moved out when the Kraków Academy was founded here in 1364. Since then it has traditionally been the university quarter, which still has its own particular atmosphere during the academic year. Apart from the two major sights listed below, it's worth looking over the other university buildings.

Collegium Maius
The Collegium Maius at ul Jagiellońska 15, built as part of the Kraków Academy, is the oldest surviving university building in Poland, and one of the best examples of 15th century Gothic

KRAKÓW

architecture in the city. It has a magnificent arcaded courtyard, but what is still more interesting is the university collection kept inside.

You proceed through a number of historic interiors where you'll find rare 16th century astronomic instruments, supposedly used by Copernicus, a bizarre alchemy room, old rectors' sceptres and, the highlight of the show, the oldest existing globe (from about 1510) to have the American continent marked on it. You will also visit an impressive Aula, a hall with an original Renaissance ceiling, crammed with portraits of kings, benefactors and professors of the university. It was here that Pope John Paul II and Czesław Miłosz received honorary doctorates.

The museum is open weekdays 11 am to 2.30 pm, Saturday 11 am to 1.30 pm. All visits are guided in groups; tours begin every half-hour and there's usually one tour daily in English. Tours in French and German can be arranged on request. In summer it's advisable to reserve in advance, either personally in the museum office (2nd floor) or by phone (☎ 422 05 49). The courtyard is open 7 am till dusk and can be entered free of charge.

St Anne's Church

Just round the corner from the Collegium Maius, on ul Św Anny, is the baroque St Anne's Church (Kościół Św Anny). Designed by the omnipresent Tylman van Gameren, and built in the late 17th century as a university church, it was long the site of inaugurations of the academic year, doctoral promotions, and a resting place for many eminent university professors. A spacious, bright interior fitted out with fine furnishings, gravestones and epitaphs, and embellished with superb stucco work and murals – all stylistically homogeneous – puts the church among the best examples of baroque.

South of the Market Square

The southern part of the Old Town has no regular layout. This elongated area, steadily narrowing southwards, links the Old Town with the Wawel. The main artery is ul Grodzka, dotted with several churches, while the parallel ul Kanonicza is perhaps the most picturesque of Kraków's streets.

Franciscan Church

The mighty Kościół Franciszkanów was erected in the second half of the 13th century but repeatedly rebuilt and refurnished after at least four fires, the last and the most destructive being in 1850 when almost all the interior was burnt out. Of the present decorations, the most interesting are the Art Nouveau stained-glass windows in the chancel and above the organ loft, the latter regarded as among the greatest in Poland. All were designed by Stanisław Wyspiański, who also executed most of the murals in the presbytery and the transept.

Adjoining the church from the south is the monastery which suffered less damage and still has its original Gothic cloister complete with fragments of the 15th century frescoes. There's also a valuable collection of portraits of Kraków's bishops in the cloister. The entrance to the cloister is from the transept of the church or its right-hand chapel.

Dominican Church

The equally powerful Kościół Dominikanów at the opposite end of the square was also built in the 13th century and badly damaged in the 1850 fire, though its side chapels, dating mainly from the 16th and 17th centuries, have been preserved in reasonably good shape. Monumental neo-Gothic confessionals and stalls are a later adornment. Read the information (in English and German) about the church, displayed in the neo-Gothic porch, and note the original 14th century portal at the main entrance to the church.

The monastery, just behind the northern wall of the church, is accessible through the side door next to the sacristy. The cloister there has retained its Gothic shape pretty well and boasts a number of fine epitaphs, tombs and paintings.

Archaeological Museum

The Muzeum Archeologiczne at ul Poselska 3 presents

Małopolska's history from the Palaeolithic period till the early Middle Ages. It's a comprehensive exhibition, with lots of background information on the boards – pity it's in Polish only. It's open Monday to Wednesday 9 am to 2 pm, Thursday 1 to 4 pm, and Sunday 11 am to 2 pm.

Wyspiański Museum Dedicated to one of Kraków's most beloved sons and the key figure of the Młoda Polska (Young Poland) movement, the Muzeum Wyspiańskiego, ul Kanonicza 9, shows how many diverse branches of art Stanisław Wyspiański explored. A painter, poet and playwright, he was also a designer, particularly renowned for his stained-glass designs, some of which are in the exhibition.

His most unusual proposal, though, was the 'Acropolis', a project to reconstruct the Wawel as a political, religious and cultural centre. Have a close look at the model made according to his design – an amazing mix of epochs and styles, a Greek amphitheatre and a Roman circus included. Wyspiański's vision has never been realised. Later calculations proved that the hill wouldn't support so many buildings squeezed onto its top.

The museum is open on Tuesday, Wednesday, Friday, Saturday and Sunday 10 am to 3.30 pm, and Thursday 10 am to 4.30 pm.

Church of SS Peter & Paul The first baroque building in Kraków, the Church of SS Peter and Paul (Kościół Św Piotra i Pawła) was erected by the Jesuits who were brought to the city in the 1580s to fight the Reformation. Designed on the Latin cross layout and topped with a large dome, the church has a pretty sober interior, apart from some stucco decoration on the vault. The figures of the Twelve Apostles standing on columns in front of the church are copies of the 18th century statues.

St Andrew's Church Built towards the end of the 11th century, St Andrew's Church (Kościół Św Andrzeja) is one of Kraków's oldest and has preserved much of its austere Romanesque stone exterior. As soon as you enter, though, you're in a totally different world; its small interior was subjected to a radical baroque overhaul in the 18th century.

Archdiocesan Museum Opened in 1994, the Muzeum Archidiecezjalne, located in two 14th century stone houses at ul Kanonicza 19 and 21, presents collections of sacred art borrowed from the treasuries of various churches in Kraków and the region. On permanent exhibition is the room where Karol Wojtyła (today's Pope John Paul II) lived in 1951-58, complete with furniture and belongings, including his skis. The museum is open Tuesday to Saturday 10 am to 3 pm.

WAWEL

The very symbol of Poland, the Wawel ('Vah-vel') is saturated with Polish history as no other place in the country. It was the seat of the kings for over 500 years from the early days of the Polish state, and even after the centre of power moved to Warsaw, it retained much of its symbolic, almost magical power. Today a silent guardian of a millennium of national history, the Wawel is possibly the most visited sight in Poland.

A lane leads up the Wawel hill from the end of ul Kanonicza. Past the equestrian statue of Tadeusz Kościuszko, it turns left leading to the front of the cathedral. There are several buildings surrounding a vast, open central square, but the cathedral and the castle are the places to be visited.

Reserve at least three hours if you want anything more than just a general glance over the place. Note the different opening hours of the cathedral and the castle exhibitions (see the following two sections). In summer, come early as there may be long queues for tickets later. Avoid weekends, when the Wawel is literally besieged by visitors. Bicycles are not allowed on the Wawel hill and there's nowhere to store them at the entrance.

Guide services in Polish, English, German and French are available upon request. The guides' office (☎ 422 16 97) is in the entrance hall to the Royal Chambers exhibition in the castle. There's a separate guide company (☎ 422 09 04) at the entrance to the Wawel hill, opposite the statue of Kościuszko. A foreign-language guide will cost about US$30 per group of up to nine people for a tour around the cathedral and all the exhibitions in the castle (all the admission fees extra). It takes about three hours altogether. You can also take a guide for the cathedral-only tour, for a particular castle exhibition or for any combination of your choice.

Cathedral

The national temple, the Wawel royal cathedral has witnessed most of the royal coronations and funerals and is the last resting place for most of the Polish monarchs. Many outstanding artists had a hand in the gradual creation of the cathedral, and it is embellished with a wealth of magnificent works of art and craft. It's both an extraordinary artistic achievement and Poland's spiritual sanctuary.

The building you see is the third church on this site, erected in 1320-64. The original cathedral was founded around 1020 by the first Polish king, Bolesław Chrobry, and was replaced with a considerably larger Romanesque construction some 100 years later. It was completely burnt down in 1305 and only a crypt, known as St Leonard's Crypt, has survived.

The present cathedral is a Gothic structure but in the course of time chapels were built all round it. Before you enter, note the massive iron door and, hanging on a chain to the left, prehistoric animal bones. They are believed to have magical powers; as long as they are here, the cathedral will remain too. The bones were excavated on the grounds at the beginning of the 20th century.

Once inside, you'll immediately get lost amid a maze of sarcophagi, tombstones and altarpieces scattered throughout the nave, chancel and ambulatory. Among a score of chapels, the showpiece is the Sigismund Chapel (Kaplica Zygmuntowska) on the southern wall, often referred to as 'the most beautiful Renaissance chapel north of the Alps'. From the outside, it's easily recognised by its gilded dome. Another highlight is the **Holy Cross Chapel** (Kaplica Świętokrzyska) in the south-western corner of the church, distinguished by the unique 1470 Byzantine frescoes and a marble sarcophagus from 1492 by Veit Stoss.

Right in the middle of the church stands the laboriously decorated baroque **Shrine of St Stanislaus** (Mauzoleum Św Stanisława), dedicated to the bishop of Kraków who was canonised in 1253 to become the patron saint of Poland (see the Kazimierz section later in this chapter). The silver coffin, adorned with 12 relief scenes from the saint's life, was made in Gdańsk around 1670; the ornamented baldachin over it is about 50 years older.

Ascend the **Sigismund Tower** (accessible through the sacristy) to see the Sigismund Bell, popularly called 'Zygmunt'. Cast in 1520, it's 2m high and 2.5m in diameter, and weighs 11 tonnes, making it the largest bell in Poland. Its clapper weighs 350kg, and eight strong people are needed to ring the bell, which happens only on the most important church holidays and for significant state events.

Back down in the church, go downstairs (from the left-hand aisle) to the **Poets' Crypt** where two great Romantic poets, Adam Mickiewicz and Juliusz Słowacki, are buried.

Farther towards the back of the church in the same aisle you'll find the entrance to the **Royal Crypts** (Krypty Królewskie) where, apart from kings, several national heroes including Tadeusz Kościuszko and Józef Piłsudski are buried. The first thing you'll pass will be St Leonard's Crypt, the only remnant of the 12th century Romanesque cathedral. Make sure to visit the Royal Crypts at the end of your cathedral tour, as the exit is outside the cathedral.

Diagonally opposite is the **Cathedral Museum** (Muzeum Katedralne), which holds historical and religious objects from the cathedral. There are plenty of exhibits but not a single crown. They were all stolen from the treasury by the Prussians in 1795 and reputedly melted. Each crown could easily contain 1kg of pure gold, not to mention the artistic value.

The cathedral can be visited from 9 am to 3 pm, but on Sunday and holidays Mass is held in the morning and visits are only from noon to 3 pm. From May to September, the opening hours are extended up till 5.30 pm. The ticket office is diagonally opposite the cathedral entrance. The Cathedral Museum is open 10 am to 3 pm, except Monday.

Castle

The political and cultural centre of Poland until the early 17th century, the Wawel royal castle is, like the cathedral, a symbol of Poland's national identity.

The original small residence was built in the early 11th century by King Bolesław Chrobry, beside the chapel dedicated to the Virgin Mary (known as the Rotunda of SS Felix and Adauctus). King Kazimierz Wielki turned it into a formidable Gothic castle. It was burnt down in 1499, and King Zygmunt Stary commissioned a new residence. Within 30 years a splendid Renaissance palace, designed by Italian architects, had been built. Despite further extensions and alterations, the Renaissance structure, complete with a spacious arcaded courtyard, has been preserved to this day.

Repeatedly sacked and devastated by Swedes and Prussians, the castle was occupied after the last Partition by the Austrians, who intended to make Wawel a citadel. A fancy plan to rebuild the royal seat included turning the castle into barracks, and the cathedral into a garrison church, moving the royal tombs elsewhere.

The Austrians succeed in realising some of their projects. They turned the royal kitchen and the coach house into a military hospital, and razed two churches standing at the outer courtyard (that's why the square is today so conspicuously plain) to make room for a parade ground. During the work, they stumbled upon a perfectly preserved pre-Romanesque Rotunda of SS Felix and Adauctus and pulled down a good part of it.

They also enveloped the whole hill with a new ring of massive brick walls, largely ruining the original Gothic fortifications.

Only in 1918 was the castle recovered by Poles and the restoration work began. It was continued after WWII and succeeded in recovering a good deal of the castle's earlier external form and its interior decoration.

The castle is now a museum containing five separate sections in different parts of the building. The ticket office is in the passage leading to the castle's inner courtyard. You buy tickets here to all the castle's exhibitions, except the Lost Wawel.

The **Royal Chambers** (Komnaty Królewskie) are the largest and most impressive exhibition and you should head there first; the entrance is in the south-eastern corner of the courtyard. Proceeding through the chambers on the two upper floors of the castle, restored in their original Renaissance and early baroque style and crammed with works of art, you'll have an idea how the royalty once lived.

The most valuable items are the magnificent tapestries. The collection, largely formed by King Zygmunt August, once numbered 356 pieces but only 136 survive. Even so, this is probably the largest collection of its kind in Europe.

The Royal Chambers are open Tuesday to Saturday 9.30 am to 3 pm (on Friday until 4 pm), and Sunday 10 am to 3 pm. From May to September, they are open a half-hour longer from Tuesday to Friday. Entry costs US$3 (US$1.50 for students).

Another gem of the castle is the collection of sumptuous embroidered 17th century Turkish tents captured after the Battle of Vienna, displayed along with a variety of old Persian carpets, Chinese ceramics and other Oriental objects at the **Exhibition of Oriental Art** (Wystawa Sztuki Wschodniej). As we went to press the exhibition was closed for restoration.

The **Crown Treasury** (Skarbiec Koronny), housed in vaulted Gothic rooms surviving from the 14th century castle, is in the northeastern part of the castle, on the ground floor. The most famous object here is the

13th century Szczerbiec or Jagged Sword which was used at all Polish coronations from 1320 onwards. The adjacent **Armoury** (Zbrojownia) has a collection of old weapons from various epochs (mainly from the 15th to 17th centuries) as well as replicas of the banners of the Teutonic Knights captured at the battle of Grunwald in 1410.

The Treasury and Armoury are open on the same days and hours as the Royal Chambers, and the joint admission ticket costs another US$3 (US$1.50 for students).

The **Lost Wawel** (Wawel Zaginiony) exhibition is installed in the old royal kitchen. Apart from the remnants of the late 10th century Rotunda of SS Felix and Adauctus, reputedly the first church in Poland, you can see various archaeological finds as well as models of the previous Wawel buildings.

The entrance to the exhibition is from the outer side of the castle; leave the inner courtyard through the gateway and turn left. The Lost Wawel is open daily, except Tuesday, 9.30 am to 3 pm; entrance costs US$1.50 (US$0.75).

Free entry day to all the castle exhibitions (but not the cathedral) is Wednesday (June to September) and Sunday (other months). The number of visitors per day is limited, so you should be early for your free tickets, especially in summer.

Dragon's Cave

You can complete your Wawel trip with a visit to the Dragon's Cave (Smocza Jama), former home of the legendary Wawel Dragon (Smok Wawelski). The entrance to the cave is next to the Thieves' Tower

Kraków's Dragon

According to legend, once upon a time there lived a powerful prince, Krak or Krakus, who built a castle on a hill named Wawel on the banks of the Vistula and founded a town named after himself. It would have been paradise if not for a dragon living in a cave underneath the castle. This fearsome and ever-hungry creature decimated cattle and sheep, and was not averse to human beings, especially pretty maidens.

The wise prince ordered a sheep's hide to

Kraków's Dragon (woodcut by Sebastian Münster, in *Cosmographia*, 1550)

be filled with sulphur, which was set alight and hurled into the cave. The voracious beast devoured the bait in one gulp, only then feeling the sulphur burning in its stomach. The dragon rushed to the river, and drank and drank and finally exploded, giving the citizens a spectacular fireworks display. The town was saved. The dragon has become the symbol of the city, immortalised in countless images, and a sculpture has been placed where the beast once lived.

(Baszta Złodziejska) at the western edge of the hill. From here you'll get a good panorama over the Vistula and the suburbs farther to the west, including the Centre of Japanese Art on the opposite bank of the river, and the Kościuszko Mound far away on the horizon.

You descend 135 steps to the cave, then walk some 70m through its interior and emerge onto the bank of the Vistula next to the fire-spitting bronze dragon, the work of renowned contemporary sculptor Bronisław Chromy. The cave is open daily May to September 10 am to 5 pm.

KAZIMIERZ

Today one of Kraków's inner suburbs located within walking distance south-east of the Wawel, Kazimierz was for a long time an independent town with its own municipal charter and laws. The town was founded in 1335 by King Kazimierz Wielki (hence its name) and swiftly developed thanks to numerous privileges granted by the king. It soon had its own town hall and a market square almost as large as that of Kraków, and two huge churches were built. The town was encircled with defensive walls and by the end of the 14th century it had become the most important and wealthiest city of Małopolska after Kraków.

Jews began to appear in Kraków as early as the 12th century. Their numbers grew quickly from the 1330s when, amid the increasing religious persecution of Jews in the rest of Europe, King Kazimierz offered them shelter in Poland. Their community in Kraków soon became strong enough to be the focus of conflict, and in 1494 King Jan Olbracht (John Albert) expelled them from the city. It was then that the Jews came to Kazimierz, where they settled in a relatively small prescribed area north-east of the Christian quarter, and the two sectors were separated by a wall.

The subsequent history of Kazimierz was punctuated by fires, floods and plagues, with the Jewish and Christian communities living side by side, confined to their own sectors. The Jewish quarter became home to Jews fleeing persecution from all corners of Europe, and it grew particularly quickly, gradually determining the character of the whole town.

At the end of the 18th century Kazimierz was administratively incorporated into Kraków and in the 1820s the walls were pulled down. At the outbreak of WWII Kazimierz was a predominantly Jewish quarter, with a distinctive culture and colour.

Of about 70,000 Jews in Kraków in 1939, only a few hundred survived the war. The current Jewish population in the city is estimated at around 150.

Western Kazimierz

The western part of Kazimierz was traditionally Catholic until the 19th century, when many Jews settled here and altered its character.

Beginning from the Wawel hill, walk south along the river bank. Shortly past the bridge you'll find the **Pauline Church** (Kościół Paulinów), commonly known to Poles as the Skałka (the Rock) due to its location, for it was once on a rocky cliff. The present mid-18th century baroque church is already the third building on the site, previously occupied by a Romanesque rotunda and later a Gothic church.

The place is associated with Bishop Stanisław (Stanislaus), whose shrine you've probably already seen in the Wawel cathedral. In 1079 the bishop was condemned to death by King Bolesław Śmiały (Boleslaus the Bold), for joining the opposition to the king and excommunicating him. According to legend, the king himself carried out the sentence by beheading the bishop. The murder not only got the bishop canonised as patron saint of Poland, but it also cast a curse on the royal line. The first victim was the executioner himself who was forced into exile. Successive kings made penitential pilgrimages to the Skałka church and a sumptuous mausoleum to the saint was erected in the very centre of the Wawel Cathedral, but the curse continued to hang over the throne. It was believed, for example, that no king named Stanisław

KRAKÓW

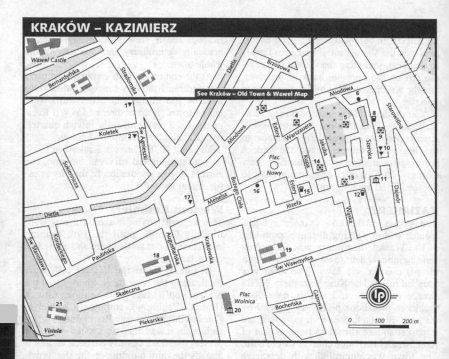

KRAKÓW – KAZIMIERZ

could be buried in the Wawel crypt, and indeed two Polish monarchs bearing this name, Stanisław Leszczyński and Stanisław August Poniatowski, were buried elsewhere.

The church is not particularly remarkable, but the memory of the saint lives on. You can even see the tree trunk (on the altar to the left) believed to be the one on which the king performed the crime. The body is supposed to have been dumped into the pond in front of the church; a sculpture of St Stanislaus was later placed here.

The cult of the saint has turned the place into something of a national pantheon. The crypt underneath the church shelters the tombs of some eminent Poles including medieval historian Jan Długosz, composer Karol Szymanowski, and painters Jacek Malczewski and Stanisław Wyspiański.

On the Sunday following 8 May (the saint's feast day), a well attended proces-

sion, with almost all the episcopate present, leaves the Wawel for the Skałka church.

Take ul Skałeczna eastwards to **St Catherine's Church** (Kościół Św Katarzyny). One of the most monumental churches in the city and possibly the one which has best retained its original Gothic shape, it was founded in 1363 and completed some 50 years later. A large, richly decorated stone Gothic porch on the southern wall was added in the 1420s. The church was once on the corner of Kazimierz's market square but the area was built up in the 19th century.

The lofty and spacious whitewashed interior is austere and hardly decorated save for the singularly imposing 17th century gilded high altar. Adjoining the church are two chapels, each with a palm-like vault supported on a single central column. The monastery cloister features Gothic wall paintings.

Continue east on ul Skałeczna, turn right into ul Krakowska, and you'll see the former **town hall** of Kazimierz in front of you. Built in the late 14th century in the middle of a vast market square (Plac Wolnica is all that's left), it was significantly extended in the 16th century, at which time it acquired its Renaissance appearance. The **Ethnographic Museum** (Muzeum Etnograficzne) installed here after WWII has one of the largest collections in Poland but only a small part of it is on display. The permanent exhibition features the interiors of traditional peasant houses faithfully reconstructed (ground floor), folk costumes from all over Poland, particularly the southern regions (1st floor), and folk painting and woodcarving, mostly religious (2nd floor). The museum is open on Monday 10 am to 6 pm, Wednesday to Friday to 3 pm, and Saturday and Sunday to 2 pm.

In the north-eastern corner of Plac Wolnica is the **Corpus Christi Church** (Kościół Bożego Ciała). Founded in 1340, it was the first church in Kazimierz and for a long time the parish church. Its interior has been almost totally fitted out with baroque furnishings, including the high altar, massive stalls in the chancel and a boat-shaped pulpit. Note the only surviving early 15th century stained-glass window in the presbytery.

Jewish Quarter

A tiny area of about 300 x 300m north-east of Corpus Christi Church, the Jewish sector of Kazimierz became over the centuries a centre of Jewish culture as nowhere else in the country. In WWII, the Jews were slaughtered by the Nazis and with them disappeared all the folklore, life and atmosphere of the quarter. Today only the architecture reveals that this was the Jewish town. Miraculously, most of the synagogues survived the war in better or worse shape, but only two of them continue to function as places of worship, and two more were turned into museums; others serve different purposes and you can only see their exteriors.

During communist rule, Kazimierz was largely a forgotten place on Kraków's map, partly because the government didn't want to touch the sensitive Jewish question. In the early 1990s, the suburb slowly made its way onto the pages of tourist publications, yet its grubby appearance, along with the rather limited interest of Poles in the Jewish legacy, didn't help much to promote it. Then came Steven Spielberg's film *Schindler's List* and all changed overnight.

Actually, Kazimierz was not the main setting for the film – most of the events portrayed in it took place in the Płaszów death camp, the Podgórze ghetto and Schindler's factory, all of which were farther to the south-east, beyond the Vistula. Yet the film turned the world's attention to Kraków's Jewry as a whole, and since Kazimierz is the only substantial visual relic of Jewish heritage, it has benefited the most. 'Schindler's Tourism' now draws in crowds of visitors – Poles and foreigners alike – to the place which hardly saw any tourists before. Isn't it a bitter irony that a couple of hours on screen can mean more than half a millennium of history?

KRAKÓW

As a result of the state's long-lived neglect, the quarter still looks dilapidated, except for some of its small enclaves which have been restored and revitalised by private entrepreneurs. A more comprehensive development program is hindered by limited funds and, particularly, unsettled titles of real estate once belonging to Jews.

Beginning your tour from the Corpus Christi Church, walk north and then eastward along ul Józefa (historically the main entry to the Jewish town) to **Izaak's Synagogue** at ul Kupa 18. Kraków's largest synagogue, built in 1640-44, it's today open to the public as a museum. You can see the remains of the original stucco and wall-painting decoration, and watch two short historic documentaries about Kraków's Jewry. The place is open 9 am to 7 pm daily, except Saturday and Jewish holidays.

One block east is the **Old Synagogue** (Stara Synagoga). The name refers to the fact that this is the oldest Jewish religious building in Poland, dating back to the end of the 15th century. Damaged by fire in 1557, it was reconstructed in Renaissance style by the Italian architect Matteo Gucci. It was plundered and partly destroyed by the Nazis, but later restored to its previous form and today houses the **Museum of History and Culture of Kraków Jewry**. The prayer hall with a reconstructed bimah (raised platform at the centre of the synagogue where the Torah is read) in the middle and the original aron kodesh (the niche where Torah scrolls are kept) in the eastern wall, houses an exhibition of liturgical objects related to Jewish culture. On the upper floor you can see an exhibition of Jewish painting and photographic records depicting Jewish martyrdom during WWII.

The museum is open on Wednesday, Thursday, Saturday and Sunday 9 am to 3 pm and Friday 11 am to 6 pm. It's closed on the first Saturday and Sunday of each month, in which case it opens on the following Monday and Tuesday 9 am to 3 pm.

To the north of the Old Synagogue stretches ul Szeroka, the central street of the Jewish quarter. Short and wide, it looks more like an elongated square than a street, now packed with tourist coaches and cars. Near its northern end is the **Remu'h Synagogue**. This is the smallest synagogue in Kazimierz and one of two open for religious services (the other one, the Tempel Synagogue, is only irregularly active). Established in 1553 by a rich merchant, Israel Isserles, but associated with his son Rabbi Moses Isserles, a philosopher and scholar, the synagogue is open to visitors weekdays 9 am to 4 pm.

Just behind the synagogue is the **Remu'h Cemetery**. Founded at the same time as the synagogue itself, it was closed for burials in the early 19th century, when a new, larger cemetery was established. During WWII Nazis razed the tombstones to the ground. However, during postwar conservation work, workers discovered some old tombstones under the layer of earth. Further systematic work uncovered about 700 gravestones, some of them outstanding Renaissance examples four centuries old. It seems that the Jews themselves buried the stones to avoid their desecration by the foreign armies which repeatedly invaded Kraków in the 18th century. Most tombstones have already been meticulously restored, making up one of the best preserved Renaissance Jewish cemeteries anywhere in Europe. The tombstone of Rabbi Moses, dating from 1572, is right behind the synagogue. You can recognise it by the stones placed on top in an expression of respect.

The much larger **New Jewish Cemetery** is at ul Miodowa 55, just past the railway bridge. It was established around 1800 and is the only current burial place for Jews in Kraków. Its size gives an idea of how large the Jewish population must have been. There are still several thousand surviving tombstones – the oldest dating from the 1840s – some of which are of great beauty. In contrast to the manicured Remu'h cemetery, the newer one is largely unkempt, which makes it an eerie sight. Don't be misled by the locked gate; the entrance to the cemetery is through the building you'll see to your right.

You can return to the Old Town by tram No 3, 13 or 43 from ul Starowiślna, or just walk. However, you may be interested in exploring the tragic Jewish history of WWII. The easiest way to do this is by taking the 'Schindler's List tour', which is run by the Jarden Jewish Bookshop at ul Szeroka 2. You can also do this tour on your own; the bookshop sells a brochure of the same title which describes it in English and German. The tour covers the former Jewish ghetto, Schindler's factory and Płaszów death camp.

ZWIERZYNIEC & AROUND

If you've done your sightseeing in the Old Town and Kazimierz, and want to see something outside the city centre, the suburb of Zwierzyniec ('Zvyeh-zhi-nyets') is perhaps the best place to go. Its prime attraction is the Kościuszko Mound, but you'll pass some interesting places on the way there.

Gallery of 20th Century Polish Painting

A branch of the National Museum, the gallery is housed in a large building called the New Building (Nowy Gmach) at Al 3 Maja 1, opposite the Hotel Cracovia. It has an extensive collection of Polish painting (and some sculpture) covering the period from 1890 to the present. There are several stained-glass designs (including the ones for Wawel Cathedral) by Stanisław Wyspiański, and a good selection of Witkacy's paintings. Jacek Malczewski and Olga Boznańska are both well represented. Of the postwar artists, note the works by Tadeusz Kantor, Jerzy Nowosielski and Władysław Hasior, to name just a few. The gallery is open on Wednesday noon to 5.30 pm, and Thursday to Sunday 10 am to 3.30 pm.

Błonia

West of the gallery, Błonia is the largest green area near the city centre. Once a marsh, it was drained and is today an extensive meadow, the venue for a variety of activities and events from parachute competitions to the Masses celebrated by Pope John Paul II during his visits to his motherland. You may find a circus or a fair there,

or sometimes just grazing cows, the beneficiaries of a 14th century privilege granted by King Kazimierz Wielki to the local peasants, and honoured to this day.

Churches of Zwierzyniec

The three churches of Zwierzyniec are a stone's throw from each other, close to the Vistula. The Church and Convent of the Premonstratensian Nuns (Kościół i Klasztor Norbertanek), a large fortified complex right on the river bank, dates from the 12th century but its present appearance is the result of numerous changes and extensions which continued well into the 17th century.

Up the hill stands the wooden St Margaret's Chapel (Kaplica Św Małgorzaty) and opposite is the Holy Saviour's Church (Kościół Św Salwatora). The latter is one of Kraków's oldest churches; excavations have shown that the first building was erected here in the 10th century, and some fragments of the original structure can be seen.

Despite their historic significance, these churches are not artistically fascinating enough to deserve a special trip. However, if you pass the area when heading farther west, to the Kościuszko Mound or Bielany, you might have a look.

Kościuszko Mound

Kraków is exceptional among Polish cities in having 'mounds'. These are cone-shaped hills of earth erected by human hands, of which the two oldest, the Kopiec Krakusa in Podgórze and Kopiec Wandy in Nowa Huta, are both approximately 15m high and date back to about the 7th century. Little is known about what they were raised for.

Continuing the tradition, the third mound was built in the early 1820s, but here the purpose was absolutely clear – to pay tribute to Tadeusz Kościuszko. A national hero, Kościuszko first distinguished himself in the American War of Independence before returning to Poland to lead the nationwide insurrection of 1794 aimed at saving Poland's sovereignty, which nonetheless was lost a year later. A defender of liberty and independence – two values which Poles hold deep in their hearts – Kościuszko has always been highly respected.

The mound was raised with the enthusiastic participation of thousands of volunteers, and eventually reached a height of 34m. It commands a spectacular view over the city and is now a major tourist attraction. The entrance is through a small neo-Gothic chapel which holds a mini-museum displaying memorabilia related to Kościuszko. The museum and mound are open 10 am to 5 pm (in summer till dusk). The large brick fortification at the mound's foothill is a fortress built by the Austrians in the 1840s (now a hotel).

Bus No 100 will take you (every 1½ hours or so) directly to the mound from Plac Matejki opposite the Barbican. Otherwise you can walk all the way via Błonia or take tram No 1, 2, 6 or 21 to the end of the line in Zwierzyniec and then continue on foot along the tree-shaded, car-free Al Waszyngtona (a 20 minute walk).

From the mound, you might want to go farther west to Bielany. Again, you can walk the whole stretch, or take a bus from ul Księcia Józefa. It's worth including the Polonia Institute in this trip (see Language Courses later in this chapter).

KRAKÓW OUTSKIRTS
Bielany

The suburb of Bielany is a popular Sunday picnic area for Cracovians thanks to the beautiful Las Wolski (Wolski Forest). Its southern part facing the Vistula, referred to as Srebrna Góra (Silver Mountain), is topped with the mighty **Church and Hermitage of the Camaldolese Monks** (Kościół i Erem Kamedułów). The order was brought to Poland from Italy in 1603 and in the course of time founded a dozen monasteries scattered throughout the country; today only two survive (the other is in Masuria). Apart from in Poland and their native Italy where four hermitages still exist, the Camaldolese can only be found at two places in Colombia.

An order with very strict monastic rules, it attracts curiosity – and a few ironic smiles – for its 'Memento Mori' motto ('remember you must die'), and for the way of life of its members. The monks live in seclusion in hermitages and contact each other only during prayers, and some have no contact with the outer world at all. They are vegetarian and have solitary meals in their 'homes', with only five common meals a year. There's no TV or radio, and living conditions are austere. The hermits don't sleep in coffins as rumoured, but they do keep the skulls of their predecessors in the hermitages. Though they presumably think about death constantly, they seem in no hurry to meet it and many monks reach the age of 80 or 90.

Bielany was the first of the Camaldolese seats in Poland; a church and a score of hermitages were built between 1603 and 1642 and the whole complex was walled in. Not much has changed since. The place is spectacularly located and can be visited.

You approach it through a long walled alley that leads to the main gate. Once inside, you come face to face with the massive white limestone façade of the church, 50m high and 40m wide. A spacious, single-nave interior is covered by a barrel-shaped vault and lined on both sides with ornate chapels, some of which are adorned with paintings by the famous Tommaso Dolabella. The simple tomb slab of the founder, Mikołaj Wolski, is placed just behind the entrance so that the faithful have to walk over it – a gesture of humility. His portrait hangs on the wall above the tomb.

Underneath the presbytery of the church is a large chapel used for prayers and, to its right, the crypt of the hermits. Bodies are placed into niches without coffins and then sealed. Latin inscriptions state the age of the deceased and the period spent in the hermitage. The niches are opened after 80 years and the remains moved to a place of permanent rest. It's then that the hermits take the skulls to keep them in their shelters.

In the garden behind the church are 15 or so surviving hermitages where several monks live (others live in the building next to the church), but the area is off-limits to tourists. You may occasionally see hermits in the church, wearing fine cream gowns.

Men can visit the church and the crypt any day from 8 to 11 am and 3 to 5 pm (till 4 pm in autumn and winter), but women are allowed inside only on major holidays. There are 12 such days during the year: 7 February, 25 March, Easter Sunday, Sunday and Monday of the Pentecost, Corpus Christi, 19 June, the Sunday after 19 June, 15 August, 8 September, 8 December and 25 December. These days apart, both men and women can enter the church to take part in two Sunday Masses (at 7 and 10 am), though this obviously limits the visit to the church only.

The hermitage is 7km west of the city centre. Take tram No 1, 2, 6 or 21 to the end of the line in Zwierzyniec and change for any westbound bus except No 100. The bus will let you off at the foot of Srebrna Góra, from where it's a 10 minute walk up the hill to the church.

After visiting the church you can either come back the same way or walk north 20 minutes through the forest to the **Zoological Gardens** (Ogród Zoologiczny). About 1km farther north you'll find the **Piłsudski Mound** (Kopiec Piłsudskiego), the youngest and largest of the four city mounds, erected in honour of the marshal after his death in 1935. Bus No 134 from the zoo will bring you back to the city (get off at the Hotel Cracovia).

Tyniec

A distant suburb of Kraków, about 10km south-west of the centre, Tyniec is the site of the **Benedictine Abbey** (Klasztor Benedyktynów) perched on a cliff above the Vistula. The Benedictines were brought to Poland in the second half of the 11th century, and it was in Tyniec that they established their first home. The original Romanesque church and the monastery were destroyed and rebuilt several times. Today, the church is essentially a baroque building though the stone foundations and the lower parts of the walls, partly uncovered, show its earlier origins.

You enter the complex through a pair of defensive gates, resembling the entrance to a castle, and find yourself in a large courtyard. At its far end stands an octagonal wooden pavilion which protects a stone well dating from 1620.

The monastery cannot be visited but the church is open to all. Behind a sober façade, the dark interior is fitted out with a mix of baroque and rococo furnishings. The organ is plain but has a beautiful tone, and concerts are held here in summer. Check the current program with the cultural information centre and try to make your trip coincide with a concert – a much more attractive bet than just visiting the building. To get to the abbey take bus No 112 from Rynek Dębnicki, 1km south from the Hotel Cracovia. In summer, occasional boats leave from the wharf near the Wawel and take you right to the foot of the abbey.

Nowa Huta

The youngest and largest of Kraków's suburbs, Nowa Huta is a result of the postwar rush towards industrialisation. In the early 1950s a gigantic steelworks, complete with a new dormitory town for the workforce, was built 10km east of the city centre. The steel mill accounts for nearly half the nation's iron and steel output and the suburb has become a vast urban sprawl populated by over 200,000 people.

The complex was deliberately placed by the authorities to give a 'healthy' working-class and industrial injection to the strong aristocratic, cultural and religious traditions of the city. Other, more rational reasons counted less. It was not seen as important, for example, that Kraków had neither ores nor coal deposits and that virtually all raw materials had to be transported from often distant locations. Nor did it matter that the site boasted one of the most fertile soils in the region, or that construction of the complex would destroy villages dating back to the early Middle Ages.

The communist dream didn't materialise exactly as planned. Nowa Huta hasn't in fact threatened the deep traditional roots of

KRAKÓW

the city. Worse, it actually became a threat to its creators, with strikes breaking out as frequently as anywhere else, paving the way for the eventual fall of communism. The steelworks did, however, affect the city in another way; it brought catastrophic environmental pollution which has threatened people's health, the natural environment and the city's historical monuments.

Despite increasing awareness of environmental issues, the plant is still working in top gear, even though it's unprofitable. A new industrial management aims to cut production and reduce the workforce, but it will take a while.

Tours to the steelworks can be organised through the local PTTK office (☎ 643 79 05). They can provide guides (US$20), but you need your own means of transport to get around this huge place. You can also arrange this tour through a travel agency (see the Organised Tours section).

Even if you are not interested in the steelworks, you might still want to visit the suburb. Nowa Huta is a shock after the medieval streets of the Old Town. Tram Nos 4, 5, 10, 15 from the central train station will deposit you at different points of the suburb. It doesn't matter where you start your sightseeing as the landscape varies little throughout the district, and you should have a city map handy so as not to get lost. Some locals fantasise about transferring the Warsaw Palace of Culture out here, making the suburb a perfect *skansen* of Stalinist architecture (architecture?). It would also provide a landmark while you navigate this grey concrete desert.

In the north-western part of the suburb, on ul Obrońców Krzyża, you'll find the **Church of Our Lady of Poland**, known commonly as the **Arka**. This interesting though rather heavy, boat-shaped construction was the first new church permitted in Nowa Huta after WWII, and was completed in 1977. Until that year, the inhabitants used the two historic churches which somehow escaped the avalanche of concrete. They are both on the south-eastern outskirts of Nowa Huta, in the Mogiła

suburb, and are worth a visit if you are in the area. The small, timber, shingled **St Bartholomew's Church** (Kościół Św Bartłomieja) on ul Klasztorna reputedly dates from the 14th century though it acquired its present form in the 1760s. It's open only for the Sunday religious service.

Just across the street is the **Cistercian Abbey** (Opactwo Cystersów), which consists of a church and a monastery with a large garden behind. The Cistercians came to Poland in 1140 and founded their first monastery in Jędrzejów. They later established several other abbeys throughout the country, including this one in Mogiła.

If you arrive at the monastery in the afternoon, one of the monks may guide you around the grounds, including the monastery's Gothic-vaulted cloister with fragments of preserved Renaissance wall paintings. He will then lead you through to the church (note the excellent 13th century portal) to show you its interesting interior – a balanced mix of Gothic, Renaissance and baroque furnishings and decoration.

Wieliczka

Just outside the administrative boundaries of Kraków, 15km south-east of the city centre, Wieliczka ('Vyeh-lee-chkah') is famous for its **salt mine** (kopalnia soli), which has been operating uninterrupted for at least 700 years – the oldest Polish industrial enterprise in continuous operation.

The mine is renowned for the preservative qualities of its microclimate, as well as for its health-giving properties. An underground sanatorium has been established at a depth of 211m, where chronic allergic diseases are treated.

The mine has a labyrinth of tunnels, about 300km of them, distributed over nine levels, the deepest being 327m underground. Part of the mine is open to the public as a museum, and it's a fascinating trip. The Wieliczka mine is on UNESCO's World Heritage list.

You visit three upper levels of the mine, from 64 to 135m below the ground, walking through an eerie world of pits and chambers, all hewn out by hand from solid salt. Some have been made into chapels, with altarpieces and figures included, others are adorned with statues and monuments – all carved of salt – and there are even underground lakes.

The highlight is the ornamented **Chapel of the Blessed Kinga** (Kaplica Błogosławionej Kingi), which is actually a fair-sized church measuring 54 x 17m and 12m high. Every single element here, from chandeliers to altarpieces, is of salt. It took over 30 years (1895-1927) to complete this underground temple, and about 20,000 tonnes of rock salt had to be removed. Occasional Masses and concerts are held here.

The mine is open daily, from 16 April to 15 October from 7.30 am to 6.30 pm, and the rest of the year 8 am to 4 pm. All visitors are guided in groups; the tour takes about two hours and costs US$7 (US$3.50 for students under 25 years). You have about 2km to walk through the mine – wear comfortable shoes. The temperature in the mine is 14°C. In summer, when the mine is often overrun by visitors, tours start every five minutes or so, but in winter tours depart every half-hour to an hour, when enough tourists have turned up.

Tours are in Polish, but from June to September there are English-language tours a few times a day (at the time of writing they started at 10 am, 12.30 and 3 pm, but there may be more – check beforehand with the tourist offices or call the mine on ☎ 278 73 02). Alternatively, you can hire an English guide (US$45 per group plus US$5 entry ticket per person). English-language brochures are available at the souvenir kiosk by the mine entrance.

There's a **museum** accommodated in 16 worked-out chambers on the 3rd level of the mine, where the tour ends. It features a collection of objects related to the mine (captions are in Polish only). You need a separate ticket (US$3, US$1.50 for students) if you want to visit it. From here a lift takes you back up to the outer world.

There's another **museum** in Wieliczka, in the local castle near the mine (open daily 8 am to 2.30 pm), which has exhibits on the archaeology and history of the region, and a collection of some 200 old saltcellars.

The easiest way of getting to Wieliczka from Kraków's centre is by Lux-Bus minibus – they depart frequently all day long from near the bus terminal, and will let you off close to the mine (US$0.70). There are also trains from the Kraków Główny station, but they run irregularly and will leave you farther away from the mine.

LANGUAGE COURSES

The most reputable institute in this matter is the Instytut Polonijny Uniwersytetu Jagiellońskiego (Polonia Institute of the Jagiellonian University; ☎ 429 76 32, fax 429 93 51) at ul Jodłowa 13. The institute conducts a variety of lectures on Polish issues (history, culture, literature etc) throughout the year, and regular one and two-semester classes of Polish language (US$1700 per semester).

In July and August, the institute runs the Szkoła Letnia Kultury i Języka Polskiego (Summer School of Polish Language and Culture). The school offers a choice of three/four/six-week language courses, conducted on eight levels, from 'survival' to 'native speaker', and provides accommodation and board. The courses cost, depending on length, US$830/ 1110/1440 respectively, including bed and full board. Contact the school well in advance for details. From September to June, the school has its office at ul Garbarska 7A, 31-131 Kraków (☎ 421 36 92, fax 422 77 01, plschool@jetta.if.uj .edu.pl). In July and August, it's at ul Piastowska 47, 30-067 Kraków (☎ 637 96 76, fax 637 96 63).

Even if you're not interested in the courses, you may want to visit the institute grounds at ul Jodłowa 13 in the suburb of Przegorzały 5km west of the city centre. The showpiece here is a mock-Renaissance castle spectacularly set on the high cliff overlooking the Vistula River. It was built by the Germans during WWII as a sanatorium for Nazi officers. It now houses a restaurant (Kurdish cuisine) and a café, the

KRAKÓW

terraces of which provide a fabulous view over the Vistula meandering below. On a clear day, you can occasionally spot the peaks of the Tatras 100km to the south. The student compound is in the woods beyond the castle.

Kraków has several other language schools, which are not as renowned but cheaper and more flexible to the tourists' needs. If they're not running a course when you arrive they can arrange teachers for individual classes (US$14 to US$18 an hour). The schools include:

Berlitz
  (☎ 632 90 75, fax 632 90 73) Al Słowackiego 64
Mały Rynek
  (☎/fax 422 78 57) Mały Rynek 3
Poliglota
  (☎ 421 81 28) Plac Szczepański 3
Prolog
  (☎/fax 422 72 28) ul Kościuszki 24

ORGANISED TOURS

Three travel agencies – Orbis (☎ 422 40 35) at Rynek Główny 41, Jan-Pol (☎ 421 42 06) in the Dom Turysty PTTK at ul Westerplatte 15/16 and Intercrac (☎ 422 58 40) in the Dom Polonii at Rynek Główny 14 – jointly operate a set program of tours in and outside Kraków. They include city centre sightseeing by coach (US$20), the traces of Jewish culture (US$20), the Wieliczka salt mine (US$27) and the Auschwitz-Birkenau death camps (US$25). Students get 25% discount on the Wieliczka and Auschwitz tours. Contact any of the three operators for their free 'Cracow Tours' brochure with full descriptions.

A roughly similar program of tours (costing much the same) is offered by the Point travel agency operating from its offices in the Hotel Continental (☎ 423 78 94) at Al Armii Krajowej 11, and in the Hotel Ibis (☎ 421 84 33) at ul Przy Rondzie 2. These tours can also be booked and paid for in several central hotels, including the Royal, Saski and Logos.

The Jarden Jewish Bookshop (☎ 421 71 66) at ul Szeroka 2 in Kazimierz's Jewish quarter is the best known agency offering a choice of tours discovering Jewish heritage, including its showpiece – the Schindler's List tour. This two hour tour, which includes the film's locations and other sites related to local Jewry, is conducted daily in summer (at other times on request) in a car or minibus and costs US$14 per person. Alternatively, buy the *Schindler's List* guidebook (US$2) in the bookshop, and set off for the tour on your own.

All the tours listed above are conducted in English; selected tours have German-speaking guides, and some may be conducted in French if requested. Note that even the cheapest tour won't be really cheap. Unless you specifically want some comfort and a foreign-language guide, it will cost you at most a third of the price to do any of these tours independently.

Some hotels, including Grand Hotel (☎ 421 72 55) and Hotel Polonia (☎ 422 12 33), arrange taxi trips on demand to Auschwitz (US$75 per taxi for up to four people) and to other destinations.

Wędrowiec (☎ 421 89 08), in the kiosk at the car park on ul Powiśle at the foot of the Wawel, has guides speaking major western languages, who can show you around the city (US$50 per group for up to five hours).

Almatur student agency (☎ 422 46 68) at ul Grodzka 2 offers hiking, kayaking, horse riding, sailing etc holidays in summer. It also issues ISIC student cards.

Eko-Tourist travel agency (☎ 422 88 63, fax 423 16 97, eko-tour@interkom.pl) at ul Radziwiłłowska 21 was the first of Kraków's few operators that deal with ecological tourism. It organises tours to national parks and caters for people with particular interests (birdwatching, rock climbing, cycling, canoeing). Contact the agency in advance for its English-language catalogue. If you write to it, add the '31-026' postcode before 'Kraków'.

SPECIAL EVENTS

Kraków has one of the richest cycles of annual events in Poland, and there's almost always something going on. The Cultural

Information Centre (see Entertainment later in this chapter) will give you full details.

The Festival of Sailors' Songs 'Shanties' takes place in February. With a tradition of over 30 years, the Organ Music Festival in April gives a chance to listen to organ recitals taking place in several city churches.

May sees the Student Song Festival, an event organised annually since the mid-1960s. Some concerts are staged on the Main Market Square. In the same month is the Juvenalia, a student carnival, when students get symbolic keys to the town's gates and 'take power' over the city for four days and three nights, with street dancing, fancy dress parades, masquerades and lots of fun. The Polish and International Short Film Festivals take place in May/June.

Seven days after Corpus Christi (a Thursday in May or June), a colourful pageant headed by the Lajkonik, a funny figure disguised as a Tatar riding a horse, sets off from the Premonstratensian Convent in the suburb of Zwierzyniec for the Rynek Główny. The ceremony dates back to the Tatar invasions of the 13th century. Legend has it that the leader of the local raftsmen defeated a Tatar khan, then put the khan's clothes on and triumphantly rode into the city. The garments used in the show were designed by Stanisław Wyspiański and you can see the originals in the Historical Museum of Kraków.

The week-long Jewish Culture Festival in June features a variety of activities including theatre, film, concerts and art exhibitions. It's reputedly the only festival of its kind in Europe.

From late June to late August, the Tyniec organ recitals are held every Sunday in the Benedictine Abbey in Tyniec. There are also organ recitals in July and August in St Mary's Church.

The highlights of July include the International Festival of Street Theatre, taking place on the Main Market Square, and the Kraków Jazz Festival.

The most important musical event of August is the Music in Old Kraków International Festival, which features a series of concerts of old music, presented in the philharmonic hall and the city churches. August also sees the Old Jazz in Kraków Festival, and there's another jazz event, the All Souls' Day Jazz Festival in early November.

On the first Thursday of December, a szopki competition is held on the main square beside the statue of Adam Mickiewicz and invariably attracts crowds of spectators. A sort of Nativity scene, but very different from those elsewhere in the world, the Cracovian szopki are elaborate compositions, usually in a church-like form, made in astonishing detail from cardboard, wood, tinfoil and the like, and sometimes even mechanised. The prizewinning examples are on display till mid-February at a special exhibition in the Historical Museum of

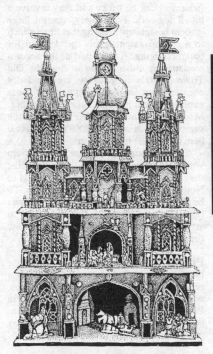

A typical Kraków *szopki*, an amazingly intricate Nativity scene

KRAKÓW

Kraków. You can see some of the old Nativity scenes in the Ethnographic Museum.

Note that there are some important events near Kraków, particularly the famous Passion play on Maundy Thursday and Good Friday during Easter week in Kalwaria Zebrzydowska (see the Carpathian Mountains chapter for details).

In the year 2000 Kraków will be a 'European City of Culture' (along with Avignon, Bergen, Bologne, Brussels, Helsinki, Prague, Reykjavik and Santiago de Compostela) – expect plenty of events. Spirituality is the main theme chosen by Kraków for its Festival 2000.

PLACES TO STAY

Kraków is Poland's premier tourist destination, so finding a bed in the high season (summer) can be tricky and may involve a bit of legwork. Fortunately, several large student hostels open during that time, which to a certain extent meets the demand for budget lodging. A good part of the accommodation is either within or near the Old Town. Hotels in Kraków are generally cheaper than in Warsaw, but a bit more expensive than in other large Polish cities. Most hotels increase their rates for the summer season by 10 to 20% (prices listed here are for the high season).

All these tourist offices are likely to help you find somewhere to stay. If all else fails, they know about some workers' hostels in Nowa Huta which almost never fill up. To be absolutely sure of not ending up in Nowa Huta, book in advance. Otherwise, try to arrive at the city reasonably early to allow time for possible hotel hunting.

Places to Stay – Budget

Despite its touristy status, Kraków has a relatively good supply of budget places, which are reasonably good value, unlike in Warsaw. Included in this section are places to stay where you normally shouldn't pay more than around US$25 per double.

Camping Kraków has several camping grounds, none close to the centre but all linked to it by relatively frequent public transport.

Camping Nr 46 Smok (☎ 421 02 55, ul Kamedulska 18) is 4km west of the centre and 1km beyond the Kościuszko Mound. It's Kraków's only camping ground operating year-round. It's small, quiet and pleasantly located. From Kraków Główny train station, take tram No 2 to the end of the line in Zwierzyniec and change for any westbound bus except No 100.

Camping Nr 171 Krakowianka (☎ 266 41 91, ul Żywiecka Boczna 4) on the road to Zakopane, 6km south of the centre, is open May to September. It's good and clean and the only one which has cabins (US$35 for a six-bed cabin). There's also a budget all-year hotel there (US$30 for a triple without bath). You can get there from the train station by tram No 19 or bus No 119.

Camping Nr 45 Krak (☎ 637 21 22, ul Radzikowskiego 99) is next to Motel Krak on the Katowice road, about 5km north-west of the centre. Take bus No 238 from the station. It's the city's largest, best equipped and most expensive camping ground and is open from mid-May to mid-September. Traffic noise can be considerable.

Youth Hostels Kraków has two all-year youth hostels, both west of the Old Town. The closer to the centre is the *youth hostel* (☎ 633 88 22, fax 633 89 20, ul Oleandry 4) 2km from the train station. Take tram No 15 and get off just past the Hotel Cracovia. From the hostel, it's only a 10 minute walk to the Old Town. With 360 beds, this is the largest youth hostel in the country but it's nonetheless often full. It has some doubles, triples and quads, but if anything is available it's more likely to be a bed in a large dormitory. Unlike most other hostels, its reception desk is open during the day. The curfew is 11 pm.

The other *youth hostel* (☎ 422 19 51, ul Kościuszki 88) is in Zwierzyniec, 1km farther south-west. Set in part of a former convent overlooking the Vistula, it's a nicer place to stay and less invaded by tourists, but it has only 110 beds and also fills up

Open-air café and art gallery, Kraków

Busker performing on the streets of Kraków

Passion play actors, Kalwaria Zebrzydowska

Art Nouveau window, Franciscan church, Kraków

Church of SS Peter and Paul, Kraków

Elegant façades overlooking the main market square in Kraków

quickly. Take tram No 2 from the train station to the end of the line.

There's also a July-August *youth hostel* (☎ 637 24 41, ul Szablowskiego 1C) 4km north-west of the Old Town. Tram No 4 from the station will let you off nearby. It's the least convenient hostel, but possibly least patronised by travellers. Check by phone for vacancies before you go. The hostel may open for longer than just these two months.

Student Hostels There are a number of student dorms operating as student hostels each summer (July to mid-September, approximately), and the picture may change from year to year. Tourist offices tend to keep track of them, so ask which ones are currently open. They are most likely to include the four hostels of the Jagiellonian University: the closest to the centre *Żaczek* (☎ 633 54 77, Al 3 Maja 5) just round the corner from the Oleandry youth hostel; *Nawojka* (☎ 633 52 05, ul Reymonta 11) 2km west of the centre; the nearby *Bydgoska* (☎ 637 44 33, ul Bydgoska 19); and *Piast* (☎ 637 49 33, ul Piastowska 47) a little farther to the west. Any of these will cost around US$18/24 a double without/with bath, and all have a limited number of rooms available year-round.

Letni Hotel AWF (☎ 648 02 07, Al Jana Pawła II 82) is 4km east of the station, midway to Nowa Huta, and can be easily reached by the frequent trams Nos 4, 5, 10 and 44, and the A bus. This large 320-bed hostel has singles/doubles with bath for US$16/24 and its own cafeteria serving inexpensive meals.

Other Hostels There are a dozen other hostels scattered throughout the city. The all-year *Schronisko Turystyczne Ekspres* (☎ 633 88 62, ul Wrocławska 91) 2km north-west of the centre is a cross between a private guesthouse and a youth hostel. Unlike youth hostels it doesn't close during the day and has no curfew. It has 80 beds distributed in doubles (US$7 per person) and six-bed dorms (US$6). Advance reservation is essential – there may be no vacancies for a month ahead. Bus No 130 from the train station goes there; get off at the fifth stop.

Strawberry Hostel (☎ 636 15 00, ul Racławicka 9), not far from the Ekspres, only opens in July and August, and costs US$24/35 a double/triple. *Dom Wycieczkowy Chałupnik* (☎ 633 75 01, ul Kochanowskiego 12) is within a short walking distance from the Old Town and costs US$14/18 a single/double with shared facilities.

There are some budget hostels in the outer suburbs, including Nowa Huta. By and large they are not particularly inspiring (nor is the area), but can provide shelter if nothing else is available. You can try, for example, *Hotel Czyżyny* (☎ 644 98 24, ul Centralna 32) which charges US$20/35 a double/quad, or the slightly cheaper *Schronisko Turystyczne Wagabunda* (☎ 643 02 22, Osiedle Złotej Jesieni 15C). The tourist offices know more places like these.

Private Rooms Waweltur (☎ 422 19 21, ☎ 422 16 40) at ul Pawia 8, next door to the KART tourist office, arranges accommodation in private rooms for US$18/27 a single/double. Rooms are scattered around the city so check the location carefully before deciding. The office is open weekdays 8 am to 8 pm and Saturday 8 am to 2 pm. You can book by phone but only until noon.

You may also be offered a private room by someone on the street outside. The tourist offices don't recommend these services, but if you decide to use them, ask to see the location on the map first, and pay only after you have seen the room.

Places to Stay – Mid-Range
This section includes places where a double room costs between US$25 and US$50. Most of the places listed here offer a choice of rooms with or without bath, but only the latter option will usually allow you to keep your budget below US$50 a night. Breakfast is not included in the price, unless specified otherwise.

There are three affordable hotels near the main train station. **Hotel Warszawski** (☎ 422 06 22, ul Pawia 6) costs about US$36/50/65 a single/double/triple without bath, US$50/60/75 with bath. The more appealing **Hotel Polonia** (☎ 422 12 33, ul Basztowa 25), just around the corner from the Warszawski, is marginally more expensive. **Hotel Europejski** (☎ 423 25 10, ul Lubicz 5) has been revamped and is now the nicest of the three. It costs much the same as Hotel Polonia. All three are often full and fairly noisy; choose a room at the back.

Hotel Saski (☎ 421 42 22, fax 421 48 30, ul Sławkowska 3) is ideally located in a historic townhouse just off Rynek Główny. It costs US$35/45/55 for singles/doubles/triples without bath, US$55/75/85 with bath – good value so close to the main square. Note the century-old lift, still in working order.

Hotel Pokoje Gościnne SARPu (☎ 429 17 78, fax 422 75 40, ul Floriańska 39) is also a good place to stay, if you are lucky enough to get a room there. This former architects' dormitory offers six double rooms only, for US$50 each. Two adjacent rooms share one bath, cooking stove and fridge. The place is on the top (4th) floor of the building.

The big, ugly and crowded **Dom Turysty PTTK** (☎ 422 95 66, ul Westerplatte 15/1) just 500m south of the train station costs US$36/50/65 for singles/doubles/triples without bath, US$48/60/85 with bath (all including breakfast). There are no longer eight-bed budget dorms. The cheap cafeteria on the premises (open 7 am to 10 pm) is actually the only place around for a cheap, early breakfast. The hotel also has a left-luggage room – useful if you don't get a bed here and have to look elsewhere.

You might also try **Hotel Wawel-Tourist** (☎ 422 67 65, ul Poselska 22) which has doubles without/with bath for US$44/60. Better still, check the small **Pensjonat i Restauracja Rycerska** (☎ 422 60 82, fax 422 33 99, Plac Na Groblach 22) at the foot of the Wawel, which offers doubles without/with bath for US$35/50, breakfast

included. On the opposite, northern edge of the Old Town, you have the reasonable **Pokoje Gościnne Jordan** (☎ 421 21 25, fax 422 82 26, ul Długa 9) which costs US$30/50 a single/double with bath and breakfast.

All the above listed hotels are in the centre, but if nothing can be found there, you'll probably have to try some less appealing options farther afield and commute. The sports **Hotel Korona** (☎ 656 15 66, ul Kalwaryjska 9/15) in Podgórze, 2km south of the Old Town (take tram No 10 from the train station), costs US$30/38/50 for a single/double/triple with bath.

Another sports accommodation, **Hotel Wisła** (☎/fax 633 49 22, ul Reymonta 22) 2km west of the Old Town costs US$28/36 for a single/double with bath, but seldom has vacancies. Bus No 139 or 208, or tram No 15 from the train station will let you off nearby. Another 1km farther west, **Hotel Krakowiak** (☎ 637 73 04, fax 637 73 25, Al Armii Krajowej 9) is even cheaper at US$28/32 a single/double. Use the same bus lines as to the Wisła.

Places to Stay – Top End

There are a dozen upmarket options in the Old Town, which is certainly Kraków's most atmospheric area in which to stay. The prices listed include breakfast.

Dom Gościnny UJ (*Jagiellonian University Guest House;* ☎/fax 421 12 25, ul Floriańska 49) is a good (but often full) place. This small hotel has just five singles (US$55) and seven doubles (US$85). Rooms are spacious, quiet and clean, and have large beds, a desk, telephone and private bath.

Just round the corner, **Hotel Polski** (☎/fax 422 11 44, ☎/fax 422 14 26, ul Pijarska 17) is a fair compromise between price and value, with singles/doubles with bath for US$65/95. Another affordable option, **Hotel Royal** (☎ 421 35 00, fax 421 58 57, ul Św Gertrudy 26/29) near the Wawel castle has a 'budget' section rated at US$40/70 a single/double, and a more comfortable part for US$60/110. You may also check the reasonable **Hotel Pollera** (☎ 422 10 44, fax 422 13 89, ul Szpitalna 30) which has a choice of singles/doubles/triples with bath for US$60/70/80, and some cheaper rooms with shower only (toilet outside). The two stained-glass windows you'll see in the main staircase are designed by Wyspiański.

You couldn't ask for a more central location than **Dom Polonii** (☎ 422 61 58, fax 422 63 41, Rynek Główny 14). It has just two doubles (US$60 each) and one double suite (US$110). Nearby is the new **Hotel Rezydent** (☎ 429 54 95, fax 429 55 76, ul Grodzka 9) which has suites to sleep two/three guests for US$120/140 – good value. Another brand new place, **Hotel Wit Stwosz** (☎ 429 60 26, fax 429 61 39, ul Mikołajska 28) is also good value at US$80/110 a double/triple.

There are two reasonable places just west of the Old Town: **Hotel Logos** (☎ 632 33 33, fax 632 42 10, ul Szujskiego 5) which charges US$60/80 a single/double, and **Hotel Fortuna** (☎ 422 31 43, fax 411 08 06, ul Czapskich 5) at US$50/75.

If money is not a problem, you have a choice of posh hotels in the Old Town, including **Hotel Francuski** (☎/fax 422 51 22, ☎/fax 422 52 70, ul Pijarska 13) which charges US$130/180 a single/double), **Grand Hotel** (☎ 421 72 55, fax 421 83 60, ul Sławkowska 5/7) at US$165/190, and **Hotel Elektor** (☎ 421 80 25, fax 421 86 89, ul Szpitalna 28) at US$150/260.

There are more upmarket hotels outside the city centre; the tourist offices will give you information if you need it.

PLACES TO EAT

By Polish standards, Kraków is a food paradise – the Old Town is tightly packed with gastronomic venues, reputedly 300 of them – catering for every pocket from rock bottom to top-notch. Privatisation has eliminated most of the old proletarian eateries, with many excellent places popping up in their place offering superior fare at affordable prices. Don't miss trying the *obwarzanki*, ring-shaped pretzels powdered with poppy seeds, a local speciality sold by pushcart vendors.

Places to Eat – Budget

There are still some milk bars around the centre, but Kraków has an excellent alternative to them, called the *jadłodajnia*. These small places offer hearty Polish meals tasting as if they were cooked at home, and you can be perfectly full for US$3 to US$5. They close early, usually around 6 to 7 pm, earlier on Saturday. Only a few open on Sunday.

One of the oldest and best known of these is the legendary **Jadłodajnia u Stasi** (ul Mikołajska 16) just off Mały Rynek, deservedly popular among the locals for its delicious cheap food, particularly a variety of the *pierogi*, for which they are famous. The place is open weekdays from 12.45 pm until 'the meals run out', which usually happens at around 4 pm though the most attractive dishes run out much earlier. The jadłodajnia is off the street so enter the gate, head for the backyard and join the queue – which may give some indication of the popularity of the place.

If the queue is too long for you, try **Jadłodajnia u Górala** (ul Mikołajska 14) next door, which is also besieged at lunchtime. Other places of a similar kind include **Jadłodajnia Sąsiedzi** (ul Szpitalna 40), **Kuchnia Staropolska u Babci Maliny** (ul Sławkowska 17) which is in the basement of the building of the Polska Akademia Umiejętności, **Jadłodajnia Kuchcik** (ul Jagiellońska 12), **Bar Grodzki** (ul Grodzka 47), **Jadłodajnia Bistro Stop** (ul Św Tomasza 24) and **Jadłodajnia Jak u Mamy** (ul Św Tomasza 2).

You also have **Jadłodajnia Oleandry** (ul Oleandry 1) in the building of the Rotunda Student Club (useful if you are staying in the Oleandry youth hostel), and the tiny five table budget eatery named **Restauracja pod Wieżyczką** (ul Radziwiłłowska 35) near the train station.

Among the milk bars, good central establishments include **Bar Mleczny pod Temidą** (ul Grodzka 43) and **Bar Mleczny**

KRAKÓW

Dworzanin (ul Floriańska 19). *Bar Wegetariański Vega (ul Św Gertrudy 7)* is one of the best budget vegie places, serving tasty *pierogi*, crêpes, salads etc.

When looking for a cheap eatery, don't overlook places called 'café', which may be good budget places to eat. For example, the folksy *Kawiarnia u Zalipianek (ul Szewska 24)* offers a choice of popular dishes, as does the pleasant *Caffeteria pod Błękitnym Kotem (ul Poselska 9)*.

Różowy Słoń (Pink Elephant; ul Straszewskiego 24) quickly gained popularity thanks to a varied menu (including salads, spaghetti, *pierogi*, *barszcz* and 20-odd flavours of crêpes) and low prices. It now has two other central outlets, at ul Sienna 1 and ul Szpitalna 38.

Another recommended place, *Salad Bar Chimera (ul Św Anny 3)* is in an attractive cellar consisting of several vaults, each with its own atmosphere. In summer, a garden is open at the back of the building. On offer is an amazing array of fresh, good, cheap salads. Encouraged by the success, there's now *Chimera II (ul Gołębia 2)*, which serves budget Georgian food in similarly amazing vaults, and has live Georgian music on some evenings.

Taco Mexicano (ul Poselska 20) brings a Mexican breeze to town. Opened in 1993, the place quickly became popular among locals and visitors, for its pretty authentic food at low prices. You, too, can have your enchiladas, burritos and tacos and wash them down with café carajillo.

Bar Hoang Hai (ul Stradomska 13), a few paces south of the Wawel, is arguably the best budget Vietnamese eatery in town. A short walk farther south is *Restauracja Ganges (ul Krakowska 7)*, Kraków's first (and so far only) Indian kitchen, and it too is very moderately priced.

Given the abundance and diversity of cheap places to eat, *McDonald's (ul Floriańska 55)* wouldn't seemingly deserve a mention, but it does. It occupies spacious, two-storey premises, the lower level being in medieval cellars. Locals joke that this is probably the most original Big Mac,

serving the ultimate icon of modern junk culture in 600-year-old brick vaults.

Much the same applies to *Pizza Hut (Plac Św Marii Magdaleny)*. The ground level is pleasant enough to classify this place as above average for Pizza Huts, but do go downstairs to the cellars – they're amazing! It's also opened a small takeaway outlet round the corner at ul Grodzka 57, where it sells pizzas by the portion – convenient if you just want a small snack while tramping around.

Among other pizza houses, arguably the best joints include *Pizzeria Cyklop (ul Mikołajska 16)* which is the only one with a wood-burning brick oven, and *Pizzeria Grace* at its three central locations: ul Św Anny 7, ul Sienna 17 and ul Św Jana 1.

Places to Eat – Mid-Range

Restauracja Chłopskie Jadło (☎ 421 85 20, ul Św Agnieszki 1), a short walk south of Wawel, looks like a rustic country inn somewhere at the crossroads in medieval Poland, and serves traditional Polish 'peasant grub', as its name says. Live folk music on some evenings adds to the atmosphere. It's one of Kraków's most unusual culinary adventures, and at very reasonable prices; don't miss this opportunity.

Restauracja Korsykańska Paese (☎ 421 62 73, ul Poselska 24) offers Corsican and some mainland French cuisine, including very fine seafood. The food is good, the prices acceptable and the interior bright and cheerful. Not without reason, the place is often packed solid.

Ristorante da Pietro (☎ 422 32 79, Rynek Główny 17) serves, you guessed it, Italian food. The menu is extensive, the service satisfactory, and the spacious cellar setting gives it an additional asset. Despite its prime location and elegant look, the prices are very acceptable.

Several Mediterranean and Middle Eastern restaurants have popped up over recent years, including *Akropolis Grill (ul Grodzka 9)*, *Grill Aladyn (ul Św Jana 3)* and *Marhaba Grill (ul Grodzka 45)*. A hearty, copious plate in any of these won't cost more than around US$7.

For Jewish food, go to *Café Ariel* (☎ 421 38 70, ul Szeroka 17) or *Café Ariel* (☎ 421 79 20, ul Szeroka 18). It's not a mistake; these two independent businesses, next to one another in Kazimierz, are in a fierce legal battle over the right to the name. Both serve traditional Jewish dishes, cakes and desserts, and a hearty kosher beer. Their cosy, intimate interiors are furnished in a manner reminiscent of the 19th century. In the evening, both cafés have live performances of Jewish, Roma and Russian folk songs (US$5 admission to either).

Reputedly the best Chinese eatery in town (also serving Vietnamese fare) is *Restauracja A Dong* (☎ 656 48 72, ul Brodzińskiego 3), south across the Vistula from Kazimierz.

Places to Eat – Top End

Restauracja pod Aniołami (☎ 421 39 99, ul Grodzka 35) offers excellent typical Polish food in some of the most amazing surroundings. It's in fantastic vaulted cellars, beautifully decorated with traditional household implements and old crafts. It's easily one of the best options for that special dinner in the city.

Another marvellous place, the new *Restauracja Cyrano de Bergerac* (☎ 411 72 88, ul Sławkowska 26), serves the best French food for hundreds of miles around in one of the city's loveliest cellars. It's not a budget eatery, but still far better value than most upmarket establishments.

Cheaper is *Restauracja u Szkota* (☎ 422 15 70, ul Mikołajska 4) which also enjoys a lovely cellar location. It occupies three cosy vaults while the fourth has been made into a captivating bar. Despite its name (Scottish Restaurant), the cuisine is essentially Polish, but the choice is wide, service quick and prices reasonable. Good Irish cider and possibly the longest list of whisky varieties in town are the restaurant's other strong points.

One of Kraków's famous eateries, *Restauracja Wentzl* (☎ 429 57 12, Rynek Główny 19) reopened recently after decades out of business. Although set in fabulous Gothic cellars, the place has been decorated in a striking modern style and even has a rotating dance floor. It does fine European cuisine at high prices.

Another local icon, *Restauracja Tetmajerowska* (☎ 422 06 31, Rynek Główny 34) is one of the city's most formal and expensive eateries. Accumulating its fame for over a century, it serves both international and Polish dishes in an elegant, 1st floor historic interior topped with a beamed wooden ceiling and a fine mural running around the walls. The food is consistently good, but is it really worth the prices?

Cafés

Kraków has traditionally had a wealth of cafés, a good number of them located in historic buildings and their medieval cellars. Until recently they focused on coffee and sweets and were predominantly meeting places rather than eating places. Now most have introduced food menus, and some have even changed their sign, replacing 'Café' with 'Restaurant'. And they have all extended their once pretty limited drink repertoire. In effect, the distinction between a café, a restaurant and a bar is becoming blurred.

Kraków's most famous café is the legendary *Jama Michalika* (*ul Floriańska 45*). Established in 1895, it was traditionally a hang-out for painters, writers and all sorts of artists. Decorated with works of art of the time, it gives the impression of a small *fin-de-siècle* museum. It's nonsmoking – one of the few such cafés in the city.

For the best choice of coffee in town, go to *Sklep z Kawą Pożegnanie z Afryką* (*Coffee Shop Farewell to Africa; ul Św Tomasza 21*). It is a nonsmoking shop-cum-café which sells about 70 kinds of coffee, half of which can be drunk inside at the tables. Coffee is prepared in sophisticated coffee makers and spring water is used, not tap water which is pretty bad in Kraków.

Smokers can try *Café Larousse* (*ul Św Tomasza 22*) which is just a block away.

KRAKÓW

Papered in leaves from a Larousse dictionary (hence its name), this tiny place of only four tables (predictably often full) serves a choice of exotic coffees. Alternatively, go to the charming, bohemian *Kawiarnia Camelot (ul Św Tomasza 17)*.

For a cup of good tea, choose between *Herbaciarnia Słodka Dziurka (ul Mikołajska 5)* and *Herbaciarnia Gołębnik (ul Gołębia 5)*.

ENTERTAINMENT

Kraków has a lively cultural life, particularly in the theatre, music and visual arts, and there are numerous annual festivals. The Centrum Informacji Kulturalnej (Cultural Information Centre; ☎ 421 77 87, fax 421 77 31) at ul Św Jana 2 just off the main square will provide detailed information on what's on. It publishes a comprehensive Polish/English monthly magazine, *Karnet*, listing cultural events, and sells tickets for some of them. The office is open weekdays 10 am to 7 pm, Saturday 11 am to 7 pm.

The two leading local papers, *Gazeta Krakowska* and *Gazeta Wyborcza*, list programs of cinemas, theatres, concerts etc. The Friday edition of the latter has a more comprehensive what's-on section that include museums, art galleries and outdoor activities. Posters are an important source of information as well, so keep your eyes open when strolling about the streets.

Cinema

Kraków has about 16 movie houses, half of them in the centre. The cinemas that may have some art movies on their program include *Kino Mikro (ul Lea 5)*, *Kino Paradox (Krowoderska 8)* and the cinema club in the *Rotunda Student Club (ul Oleandry 1)*.

Theatre

Established in 1955, the avant-garde Cricot 2 is Kraków's best known theatre outside the national borders, but it was dissolved after its creator and director, Tadeusz Kantor, died in 1990. Theatre buffs may be interested in visiting the Cricoteka (☎ 422

83 32) at ul Kanonicza 5, the centre which documents his works.

In the mainstream, the *Stary Teatr* (Old Theatre) is the best-known city theatre and has attracted the cream of the city's actors. There's the main stage (☎ 422 40 40, ul Jagiellońska 1) and two small stages (☎ 421 19 98, ul Starowiślna 21 and ☎ 421 59 76, ul Sławkowska 14).

Teatr im Słowackiego (Słowacki Theatre; ☎ 422 45 75, Plac Św Ducha 1) focuses on Polish classics and large scale productions. This large and opulent building, a historical monument in itself, was patterned on the Paris Opera and built in 1893. It was totally renovated in 1991 and its interior is spectacular. Opera and ballet performances are also staged here, as there's no proper opera house in Kraków.

Teatr STU (☎ 422 27 44, Al Krasińskiego 16) started in the 1970s as an 'angry', politically involved, avant-garde student theatre and was immediately successful. Today it no longer deserves any of those adjectives, but nonetheless it's a solid professional troupe.

There are a dozen or so other theatres in the city, some of which may have interesting shows. Tickets can be bought directly from the theatres.

Classical Music

The *Filharmonia* (☎ 422 09 58, ul Zwierzyniecka 1) is home to one of the best orchestras in the country. Concerts are held on Friday and Saturday and irregularly on other days, and the ticket office opens weekdays 2 to 7 pm and Saturday one hour before the concerts. Occasionally, concerts are presented in the Collegium Novum of the Jagiellonian University at ul Gołębia 24.

Cabaret

Piwnica pod Baranami is a legendary cabaret operating uninterruptedly since 1956 and acclaimed as the best in the country. It continues despite the death (in 1997) of its long-time spearhead, Piotr Skrzynecki. You may not grasp the finer points of the political satire, but the music, settings, movement and general atmosphere cut across linguistic boundaries. Performances are usually held on Saturday night in the cellar at Rynek Główny 27. Tickets can be bought in WOK (☎ 421 25 00, Rynek Główny 25) weekdays from noon to 5 pm, but they are hard to come by, so book as soon as they go on sale.

Other renowned local cabarets include *Loch Camelot (ul Św Tomasza 17)* which performs in the Kawiarnia Camelot, and *Jama Michalika (ul Floriańska 45)* in the café of the same name.

Jazz

The main jazz outlets include *Jazz Club u Muniaka* (☎ 422 84 48, ul Floriańska 3), *Harris Piano Jazz Bar* (☎ 421 57 41, Rynek Główny 28), *Piwnica pod Wyrwigroszem* (☎ 421 29 94, ul Św Jana 30) and *Café Sukiennice* (☎ 422 24 68) in the Cloth Hall. Live jazz is usually presented from Thursday to Saturday. Other places to check include *Klub pod Jaszczurami (Rynek Główny 8)*, *Klub u Luisa (Rynek Główny 13)*, *Rotunda Student Club* (☎ 634 34 12, ul Oleandry 1) on Tuesday, *Pub Parawan (ul Józefa 25)* on Friday, and *Jazz Club Kornet (Al Krasińskiego 19)* on Wednesday and Friday.

Discos

Popular haunts include *Equinox* (☎ 421 17 71, ul Sławkowska 13/15), *Disco pod Baranami* (☎ 423 07 32, Rynek Główny 27), *Klub pod Papugami* (☎ 422 08 06, ul Szpitalna 1) and *Klub Pasja* (☎ 423 04 83, ul Szewska 5). All operate nightly, with the usual exception of Monday. Most student clubs run discos on Friday and Saturday nights. Try *Klub Rotunda* (☎ 633 35 38, ul Oleandry 1) or *Klub pod Przewiązką* (☎ 637 45 02, ul Bydgoska 19B).

Bars & Pubs

There are more than 50 of these in the Old Town alone. Some offer snacks but most serve just drinks, mainly beer. Many are in vaulted cellars, often very attractive. All are smoking venues, so in some places those

sensitive to cigarette smoke might find an oxygen mask essential. Some pubs are open till midnight, but many don't close until the wee hours of the morning.

Here are a few, just to help you start your exploration: *Piwnica pod Złotą Pipą (ul Floriańska 30)*, *Black Gallery (ul Mikołajska 24)*, *Klub Kulturalny (ul Szewska 25)*, *Pub pod Papugami (ul Św Jana 18)*, *Free Pub (ul Sławkowska 4)*, *Pub u Kacpra (ul Sławkowska 2)*, *Piwnica pod Ogródkiem (ul Jagiellońska 6)*, *Pub Prohibicja (ul Grodzka 51)* and *Pub pod Jemiołą (ul Floriańska 20)*. Should you need a good watering hole in Kazimierz, try *Pub Parawan (ul Józefa 25)*, *Singer Club (ul Estery 20)*, or *Ptaszyl (ul Szeroka 10)*.

Hotel Elektor boasts exquisite medieval cellars, which now house a classy wine bar. Its selection of French and Rhine wines is among the best in town, though it's probably not a proposition for backpackers.

SHOPPING
Crafts

There are several Cepelia shops scattered around the central area, but the obvious place to go is the Cloth Hall in the middle of the main square, where several dozen stands sell every imaginable Polish craft. Some of them sell jewellery, particularly of semiprecious stones and amber set in silver, which may be good value.

If you need shoes or sandals, go to the tiny shop at ul Grodzka 28, which sells some amazing handmade models called Trek.

Antiques

Kraków has several Desa antique shops and they are good though not cheap. They're at ul Grodzka 8, ul Sławkowska 4, ul Mikołajska 10, ul Stolarska 17 and ul Floriańska 13, among others. The Antykwariat at ul Sławkowska 10 (on the corner of ul Św Tomasza) has a variety of old books, prints, maps, drawings and etchings.

In the summer season, an antique and bric-a-brac fair is held for one weekend a month at the main square. For the rest of the

KRAKÓW

year, it's every second and fourth Saturday of the month at ul Siemiradzkiego 13.

Contemporary Art

Kraków is a good place to get an insight into what's currently happening in Polish art and, if you wish, to buy some. There are at least a score of commercial art galleries in town including some considered to be among Poland's best.

Among the most reputable art galleries are the Starmach Gallery at Rynek Główny 45 and ul Węgierska 5 (painting, mostly avant-garde), the Stawski Gallery at ul Miodowa 15 (painting), the Rostworowski Gallery at ul Św Jana 20 (painting and sculpture), and the Jan Fejkiel Gallery at ul Grodzka 25 (best prints in town).

For a bit of fun, visit the Jan Mleczko Gallery at ul Św Jana 14, which displays and sells comic drawings by one of the most popular Polish satirical cartoonists.

Without any doubt, the best choice of posters is to be found at the Galeria Plakatu (Poster Gallery) at ul Stolarska 8/10. Here you'll find works by Poland's most prominent poster makers, and they're worth having a look at even if you don't plan to buy.

Books & Records

Several bookshops on the Rynek have a good choice of coffee-table books on Poland including some alluring photographic accounts of Kraków (English versions available). The best selection of books referring to Jewish issues can be found at the Jarden Jewish Bookshop at ul Szeroka 2 in Kazimierz.

For Polish music CDs, try the Księgarnia Muzyczna Kurant at Rynek Główny 36, Music Corner at Rynek Główny 13 and the Salon Muzyczny at ul Senacka 6. Jazz Compact at Rynek Główny 28 has the best selection of jazz to be found anywhere in the country, including Polish jazz.

GETTING THERE & AWAY
Air

The airport is in Balice, about 12km west of the city, and is accessible by bus No 208 from just north of the PKS bus terminal and by the more frequent bus No 152 from the bus stop across the street from Hotel Europejski. A taxi between the airport and the city centre shouldn't cost more than US$10. The LOT office (☎ 411 67 00) at ul Basztowa 15 deals with tickets and reservations.

Within Poland, the only flights are to Warsaw, but you can get there much more cheaply, centre-to-centre, by train in 2½ hours. LOT has direct flights between Kraków and Frankfurt/Main, London, Paris, Rome, Vienna and Zurich.

Train

The central train station, Kraków Główny, on the north-eastern outskirts of the Old Town, handles all international and most domestic rail traffic. The only other station of any significance is Kraków Płaszów, 4km south-east of the city centre, which operates some trains that don't call at Kraków Główny. Local trains between the two stations run roughly every half-hour. All trains listed in this section depart from the central station.

There are two morning, two afternoon and one evening InterCity trains to Warsaw (297km) and the trip takes about 2½ hours. There are also several express and fast trains to Warsaw which take a bit longer.

To Częstochowa (132km), there are two morning fast trains as well as several evening trains, but with the latter you'll arrive pretty late. Trains to Katowice (78km) run frequently, and there's also good transport farther on to Wrocław (268km), with perhaps a dozen departures a day. Several trains run daily to Zakopane (147km) but it's much faster by bus.

There are plenty of trains daily to Tarnów (78km) which pass through Bośnia (a gateway to Nowy Wiśnicz). A dozen or so of these trains continue to Rzeszów (158km).

To Oświęcim (65km), you have a couple of trains early in the morning and then nothing till the afternoon. There are more trains to Oświęcim from Kraków Płaszów station, though they don't depart regularly either; check the bus schedule before going to Płaszów.

Internationally, there's one or two direct trains daily to Berlin, Bratislava, Bucharest, Budapest, Dresden, Frankfurt/Main, Kiev, Leipzig, Odessa, Prague and Vienna.

Tickets and couchettes can be booked directly from Kraków Główny station or at the Orbis office at Rynek Główny 41.

Bus

The PKS bus terminal is next to Kraków Główny train station. Travel by bus is particularly advisable to Zakopane (104km) as it's considerably shorter and faster than by train. Fast PKS buses go there every hour (US$3.50, 2½ hours). A private company runs nine buses a day to Zakopane, which are faster and cheaper (US$3); tickets are available from Waweltur at ul Pawia 8. Buy your ticket a day or two in advance.

There are two convenient morning departures to Częstochowa (114km), nine buses a day to Oświęcim (64km), one to Lublin (269km), two to Zamość (318km) and eight to Cieszyn (Czech border, 121km). You can also go by bus to Kalwaria Zebrzydowska (33km) and Ojców (26km). To other destinations, it is better to go by train. Tickets are available directly from the bus station.

There are plenty of international bus routes originating in Kraków, going to Amsterdam (US$80), Berlin (US$40), Budapest (US$32), London (US$90), Munich (US$70), Paris (US$90), Prague (US$40), Rome (US$80), Vienna (US$28) and lots of other destinations. Information and tickets are available from a number of travel agencies throughout the town, including Sindbad (☎ 421 02 40) in the bus terminal itself.

GETTING AROUND

Most tourist attractions are in the Old Town or within easy walking distance, so you won't need buses or trams unless you're staying outside the centre. Should you need a taxi, some of the better known companies include Radio Taxi (☎ 919), Tele Taxi (☎ 962), Wawel Taxi (☎ 96 66), Royal Taxi (☎ 96 23) and Express Taxi (☎ 96 29).

If you're travelling by car, note that the Old Town is closed to traffic except for access to two guarded car parks on Plac Szczepański and Plac Św Ducha – the best places to leave your vehicle (US$2 per hour), if you are lucky enough to find space there. If not, use one of the guarded car parks in the surrounding area. Parking on the streets in the belt around the Old Town area requires special tickets (*karta postojowa*) which you buy in a Ruch kiosk, mark with the correct month, day and time, and then display on your windscreen.

AROUND KRAKÓW

Kraków is a convenient jumping-off point for various day trips to nearby places of interest, of which the Ojców National Park and Oświęcim (Auschwitz-Birkenau death camps) are two obvious destinations. Kalwaria Zebrzydowska is one more example, especially if you happen to be here during Easter. You could also consider Nowy Wiśnicz and Dębno if you are not heading farther east. You'll find all these places detailed elsewhere in this book.

Małopolska

Małopolska (literally, Little Poland) is in south-eastern Poland with Mazovia to the north and the Carpathian Mountains to the south. Historically, together with Wielkopolska (Great Poland), it was the cradle of the Polish state. Settled by Slavs from the early Middle Ages, Małopolska became of prime importance after the capital was moved to Kraków in 1038. As the royal province, the region enjoyed the special attention of the kings, who built a fine array of castles to protect it. It was always one of the most 'Polish' regions of the country, and retains much of that flavour to this day.

It is a land of softly rolling hills and green valleys, sprinkled with villages and towns, and much of it still bears a bucolic air of bygone times. You'll see people working the fields as they have for centuries, and long wooden horse carts on the roads.

Geographically speaking, Małopolska encompasses the Małopolska Upland and its two bordering areas – the Kraków-Częstochowa Upland to the west and the valley of the upper Vistula to the south and east. The Lublin Upland, which is similar in both geography and history, is generally included in Małopolska as well.

The Kraków-Częstochowa Upland

The Kraków-Częstochowa Upland (Wyżyna Krakowsko-Częstochowska) is a very picturesque belt of land, roughly 20 to 40km wide, that stretches for over 100km from Kraków to Częstochowa. It was formed of limestone some 150 million years ago in the Jurassic period (the name comes from the Jura mountains in France, and this Polish upland region is also popularly known as the Jura).

Highlights

- Make a pilgrimage to Jasna Góra in Częstochowa, Poland's national shrine

- Check out the unique Sundial Museum in Jędrzejów

- Stroll about the fantastic ruin of Krzyżtopór castle in Ujazd

- Explore the lethargic old town of Sandomierz

- Visit the extraordinary Chapel of the Holy Trinity in Lublin Castle

- See Kozłówka's sumptuous palace and the stunning socialist-realist gallery

- Wander around the lovely Renaissance town of Zamość

BELARUS

Lublin p262
Lublin – Old Town p264
Kazimierz Dolny p272
Chełm p276
Kielce p244
Świętokrzyski National Park p250
Zamość p281
Częstochowa p240
Sandomierz p254
UKRAINE

Erosion of the upland has left behind a variety of rock forms, taking the shapes of freestanding pillars, clubs, gates etc, or forming cliffs. They are popular with rock climbers. There are also between 500 and 1000 caves, the overwhelming majority of

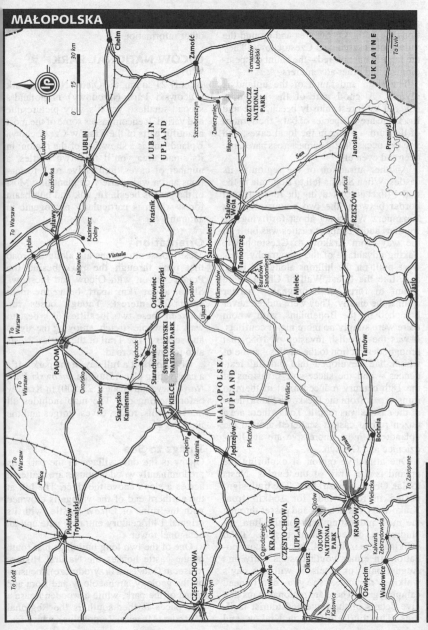

all those in Poland. The largest concentrations are in the Ojców area and around the village of Olsztyn near Częstochowa. They are largely unexplored – the haunt of speleologists and other adventurers.

The flora and fauna of the upland is diverse. A good part of the region is covered by forest, mostly beech, pine and fir. There are 17 species of bat – the symbol of the Jura – living in the local caves, and you can occasionally come across hares, roe deer and even elk.

Another attraction of the region is its castles. When Silesia fell to Bohemia in the mid-14th century, leaving the Jura a natural border between the two countries, King Kazimierz Wielki set about fortifying the frontier, and a chain of castles was built all the way from Kraków to Częstochowa. Taking advantage of the topography, they were built on the hilltops along the ridge and, like the Great Wall of China, were meant to form an impregnable barrier against the enemy. They were indeed never breached by the Bohemians, with whom there were simply no more major conflicts. It was the Swedish invasion of 1655 that brought destruction to the castles – some of which had developed into palatial residences – and the successive invasions of the 18th century reduced most of them to ruins. Apart from the Pieskowa Skała, none of the castles was rebuilt. Today there are a dozen ruined castles scattered around the upland; the most impressive are at Ogrodzieniec and Olsztyn.

One attractive option of exploring the upland is the Trail of the Eagles' Nests (Szlak Orlich Gniazd) hike. The trail, signposted in red, winds for 164km from Kraków to Częstochowa and passes through the most interesting parts of the Jura, including a dozen ruined castles. Total walking time is about 42 hours. Accommodation, in either youth hostels (July and August only) or hotels, is within a day's walking distance, so you don't need camping gear. There are regional maps that give details of the route and tourist facilities. The tourist offices in Kraków and Częstochowa should have these maps and other information.

OJCÓW NATIONAL PARK
☎ 012

At only 21 sq km, the Ojców National Park (Ojcowski Park Narodowy) is Poland's second-smallest, yet it's very picturesque and varied. It encompasses some of the most beautiful parts of the Kraków-Częstochowa Upland, and is a showcase of the region: in its small area you'll find two castles, a number of caves, impressive rock formations and a wide variety of plant life. Most of the park is beech, fir, oak and hornbeam forest which is particularly photogenic in autumn.

Orientation

Most tourist attractions are along the road that runs through the park beside the Prądnik River, with Ojców and Pieskowa Skała, about 7km apart, being the main points of interest. Though buses run between these two localities, it's best to walk the whole stretch, enjoying the sights and scenery. The Trail of the Eagles' Nests also follows this road.

Give yourself a full day in the park – it's a captivating place. Buy the *Ojcowski Park Narodowy* map (scale 1:22,500) in Kraków before setting off. The map includes all marked trails, rocks, caves, gorges and the like.

Things to See

Ojców is the only village in the park. Its predominantly wooden houses are scattered across a slope above the river. The hill at the northern end of the village is crowned with the ruins of **Ojców Castle**, with its original 14th century entrance gate and an octagonal tower.

One of the two long buildings just south of the castle houses the **Natural History Museum** (Muzeum Przyrodnicze), focusing on the geology, archaeology and flora and fauna of the park, while a wooden house a few paces farther south is the **Regional Museum** (Muzeum Regionalne), which features the history and ethnography of the place.

The black trail which heads southwards from Ojców Castle takes you in half an hour to the **Łokietek Cave** (Jaskinia Łokietka). About 250m long, it consists of one small and two large chambers, but it doesn't have the characteristic calcium formations such as stalactites and stalagmites. It is artificially lit and is open May to October 9 am to 4 pm (longer in summer); guided tours take about half an hour.

Possibly more interesting and larger is the **Wierzchowska Górna Cave**, in the village of Wierzchowie outside the park boundaries, 5km south-west of Ojców; the yellow trail will take you there. It's the longest cave so far discovered in the whole region – 1km long – and about 370m of its length can be visited. It's open at similar times as the Łokietek Cave. The 50-minute tours begin on the hour. The temperature inside is 7.5°C year-round.

Two other caves are also open to the public: the **Dark Cave** (Jaskinia Ciemna), close to Ojców and easily reached by the green trail, and the **Bat Cave** (Jaskinia Nietoperzowa), farther away and accessible by the blue trail.

About 200m north of Ojców Castle is the **Chapel upon the Water** (Kaplica na Wodzie), positioned above the river bed where it was rebuilt from the former public baths. The chapel is open only for religious services on Sunday morning.

In the hamlet of Grodzisko about 2km to the north the road divides: take the left-hand fork skirting the river and look for the red trail that branches off the road to the right and heads uphill. It will take you to the small baroque **Church of the Blessed Salomea**, erected in the 17th century on the site of the former convent of Poor Clares. The stone wall encircling the church is adorned with statues representing Salomea and her family. Behind the church is an unusual carved stone elephant (1686) supporting an obelisk on its back.

Follow the red trail, which will bring you back down to the road. Walk along it for

several more kilometres to an 18m-tall limestone pillar known as **Hercules' Club** (Maczuga Herkulesa). A short distance beyond it is the **Pieskowa Skała Castle**. The castle was erected in the 14th century but the mighty fortress you see is the result of extensive rebuilding in the 16th century. It's the best-preserved castle in the upland and the only one with more than bare walls: it houses a museum.

You first enter a large outer courtyard which is accessible free of charge daily 8 am to 8 pm. From here you get to the arcaded inner courtyard and the museum (open 10 am to 3 pm, except Monday). On display is European art from the Middle Ages to the mid-19th century, including furniture, tapestries, sculpture, painting and ceramics.

There's a restaurant-café in the outer courtyard of the castle, a good place to finish your sightseeing with a beer, coffee or something more substantial – the trout is recommended. In summer they open the terrace on the roof, providing a good view over the castle and the surrounding forest.

Places to Stay & Eat

Local people in Ojców rent out rooms in their homes but it can be hard to get one on summer weekends. The rooms can be arranged through the Ojcowianin travel agency (☎ 389 20 89) in the building of the regional museum. The PTTK office (☎ 389 20 36), in the same building, also handles private rooms.

Dom Wycieczkowy Zosia (☎ 389 20 08) in Złota Góra, 1km west of Ojców Castle, is open in summer. Some 500m farther up the road is *Camping Złota Góra* (which has tents with beds) and *Zajazd* restaurant, both open May to September. There's also a couple of restaurants in Ojców.

With your own transport, you can stay at either *Zajazd Krystyna* (☎ 419 30 02) in Bębło or *Zajazd Orle Gniazdo* (☎ 419 10 37) in Biały Kościół. Both these motels are located on the Kraków-Olkusz road, 2km south-west of the park, and both have restaurants.

Getting There & Away

There are about eight buses daily from Kraków to Ojców (22km), some of which continue up to Pieskowa Skała. Fewer buses run at weekends.

From Pieskowa Skała, you can take a bus back to Kraków (29km), or continue to Olkusz (16km) and from there farther north to Ogrodzieniec and Częstochowa. The bus stop is at the foot of the castle.

OGRODZIENIEC
• pop 4500

Perched on top of the highest hill of the whole upland (504m), the fairy-tale ruin of the Ogrodzieniec **castle** is among the most picturesque in the country. Using natural rock for the foundations and some parts of the walls – a feature typical of castles in the region – the fortress was built during the reign of King Kazimierz Wielki but enlarged and remodelled in the mid-16th century. The owner at the time, the wealthy Kraków banker Seweryn Boner, employed the best Italian masters from the royal court, who turned the Gothic castle into a Renaissance residence said to be almost as splendid as the Wawel itself.

The castle fell prey to the Swedes in 1655 and never regained its grandeur; the last owners abandoned it in the 1810s, and since then the ruin has been untouched. It's now a tourist sight, open from 15 April to 15 November, 9 am till dusk.

The castle is in the small village of Podzamcze, 2km east of Ogrodzieniec; the two places are linked by fairly frequent local buses. Ogrodzieniec lies on the Zawiercie-Olkusz road and buses run regularly between these towns. From Zawiercie, you can continue north on one of the frequent trains to Częstochowa, while buses from Olkusz can take you to Pieskowa Skała, Ojców or directly to Kraków.

CZĘSTOCHOWA
• pop 260,000   ☎ 034

Częstochowa (pronounced 'Chen-sto-ho-vah') is the spiritual heart of Poland and the country's national shrine. It owes its fame to the miraculous icon of the Black Madonna, kept in Jasna Góra (Bright Mountain) Monastery, which has been pulling in pilgrims from all corners of the country and beyond for centuries. Today, Częstochowa attracts some of the largest pilgrimages in the world (local sources put it fifth, after Varanasi, Mecca, Lourdes and Rome). Tourists and the faithful alike flock in large numbers throughout the year, with significant peaks on Marian feasts, particularly on the day of the Assumption on 15 August. You too are likely to find yourself drawn to the city, whether through devotion or curiosity.

Though the earliest document mentioning Częstochowa's existence dates from 1220, the town's development really began with the arrival of the Paulite Order from Hungary in 1382. The monks founded a monastery atop a hill known as Jasna Góra. The monastery probably would not have gained its exceptional fame if not for a painting of the Virgin Mary, commonly referred to as the Black Madonna, which was presented in 1384 to the order and soon began to attract crowds of believers, thanks to numerous miracles attributed to the image.

Growing in wealth and importance, the monastery was gradually extended and turned into a fortress surrounded by stout defensive walls with massive bastions. It was one of the few places in the country to withstand the Swedish sieges of 1655-56, the miracle naturally being attributed to the Black Madonna and contributing to still larger floods of pilgrims. Interestingly, before the siege the Madonna had been transferred to Silesia for safekeeping, yet she was still able to save the monastery.

The town of Częstochowa grew as a centre providing facilities for the pilgrims visiting the monastery. In the second half of the 19th century, the construction of the Warsaw-Vienna railway line stimulated the development of commerce and industry. By the outbreak of WWII the city had 140,000 inhabitants.

After the war, in an attempt to overshadow its religious status, the communists

The Black Madonna of Częstochowa

The Black Madonna is a painting on a wooden panel measuring 122 x 82cm that depicts the Virgin Mary with the Christ child. The picture looks like a Byzantine icon, but it's not known when and where the original was created: the time of its creation is put somewhere between the 6th and 14th centuries, and theories of its provenance range from Byzantium and Red Ruthenia to Italy and Hungary. What is known is that the icon was damaged in 1430 by the Hussites, who slashed the face of the Madonna and broke the panel. The picture was repainted afterwards in a workshop in Kraków, but the scars on the face of the Virgin Mary were left as a reminder of the sacrilege.

In 1717 the Black Madonna was crowned 'Queen of Poland' in a ceremony attended by 200,000 of the faithful. Since then the image has traditionally been dressed with richly ornamented robes and crowned, and these days the Madonna has a wardrobe of robes and crowns which are changed on special occasions.

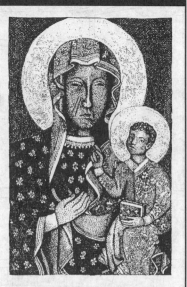

intensified the development of industry. Today Częstochowa has a large steelworks and a number of other factories complete with a forest of smoky chimneys. Amid them, however, the tower of the Paulite monastery still proudly overlooks the city, showing pilgrims the way to the end of their journey.

Orientation

The main thoroughfare in the city centre is Al Najświętszej Marii Panny (referred to in addresses as Al NMP), a wide, tree-lined avenue with the Monastery of Jasna Góra at its western end and St Sigismund's Church (Kościół Św Zygmunta) at the eastern end. The train and bus stations are just south of the eastern part of Al NMP, 20 minutes walk from the monastery. Most places to stay are near the monastery, whereas many places to eat are either on or just off Al NMP.

Information

Tourist Office The Centrum Informacji Turystycznej (☎ 324 13 60, ☎/fax 324 34 12), Al NMP 65, is open weekdays 9 am to 6 pm, Saturday 10 am to 6 pm, Sunday (15 April to 15 October) 10 am to 6 pm. It's well stocked with maps from all over the country.

Money You'll find several kantors and ATMs on Al NMP. The Bank Pekao at ul Kopernika 19 changes travellers cheques and gives cash advances on Visa and MasterCard.

Email & Internet Access The Centrum Internetowe (☎ 366 48 13) is on the top floor of Dom Handlowy Seka at Al NMP 12D (open daily till 10 pm).

Monastery of Jasna Góra

A vibrant symbol of Catholicism in a secular sea, the monastery retains the appearance of

MAŁOPOLSKA

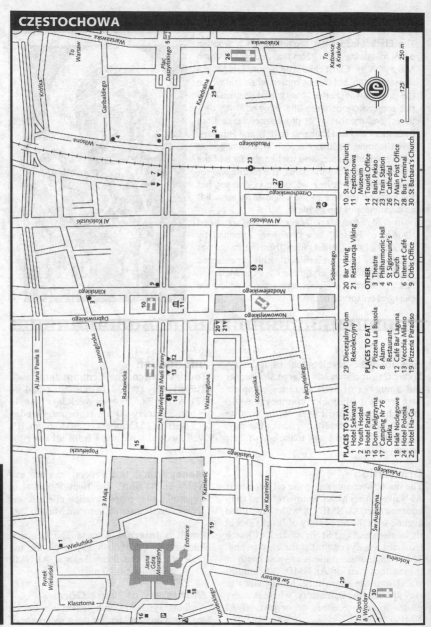

CZĘSTOCHOWA

PLACES TO STAY
1 Hotel Sekwana
2 Youth Hostel
15 Hotel Patria
16 Dom Pielgrzyma
17 Camping Nr 76 Oleńka
18 Hale Noclegowe
24 Hotel Polonia
25 Hotel Ha-Ga

PLACES TO EAT
7 Pizzeria La Bussola
8 Alamo Restaurant
13 Café Bar Laguna
19 Pizzeria Paradiso

20 Bar Viking
21 Restauracja Viking

OTHER
3 Theatre
4 Philharmonic Hall
5 St Sigismund's Church
6 Internet Café
9 Orbis Office
10 St James' Church
11 Częstochowa Museum
14 Tourist Office
22 Bank Pekao
23 Train Station
26 Cathedral
27 Main Post Office
28 Bus Terminal
30 St Barbara's Church

29 Diecezjalny Dom Rekolekcyjny

MAŁOPOLSKA

a fortress. It's on the top of a hill west of the city centre and is clearly recognisable from a distance by its slender tower. The main entrance is from the southern side through four successive gates. There's also a gate from the western side.

Inside the walls are a number of buildings including a chapel, a church, the monastery and three museums. The **Chapel of the Miraculous Picture** (Kaplica Cudownego Obrazu) is the oldest part of the whole complex and, as its name suggests, is where the Black Madonna is kept. The picture is placed on the high altar and covered with a silver screen at night and from noon to 1 pm (1 to 2 pm on Saturday, Sunday and public holidays). It may be difficult to get close to the picture as the chapel is invariably packed with pilgrims.

The **basilica** (bazylika) adjoining the chapel to the south was initially a single-nave Gothic construction. Its present shape dates from the 17th century and the interior has opulent baroque furnishings and decoration.

On the opposite, northern side of the chapel is the monastery, where you can visit the 17th century **Knights' Hall** (Sala Rycerska) on the 1st floor. The hall boasts a series of nine paintings that depict major events from the monastery's history, including the Hussite raid of 1430 and the Swedish siege of 1655. An exact copy of the Black Madonna, not embellished with robes, is placed in the corner of the hall, allowing for a closer inspection of the icon.

The monastery's **600th Anniversary Museum** (Muzeum Sześćsetlecia), on the western side of the complex, displays liturgical vessels and vestments, old musical instruments, painted scenes from monastic life and portraits of the founders and superiors, plus a number of votive offerings including Lech Wałęsa's 1983 Nobel Peace Prize. Next door, the **arsenal** (arsenał) contains a variety of old weapons and one of the robes for the Madonna.

The **treasury** (skarbiec) is above the sacristy and displays votive offerings presented by the faithful. Among a variety of exhibits you'll find old reliquaries, monstrances,

home altars, drawings by Matejko and yet another robe for the Madonna. The opening hours of all three museums are 9 am to 5 pm.

To complete your visit, climb up the **tower** (wieża). It has been destroyed and rebuilt several times and the present one only dates from 1906. Over 106m high, it's the tallest church tower in Poland. Note the crow with a loaf of bread on the very top. The tower houses a set of 36 bells which play a Marian melody every quarter of an hour. The tower is open daily from April to November 8 am to 4 pm.

Other City Attractions

The monastery is obviously Częstochowa's drawcard, but if you've got a leisurely itinerary, you may want to visit other sights. **St Barbara's Church** (Kościół Św Barbary), about 1km south of the monastery, was built in the 17th century on the spot where the Hussites were thought to have slashed the icon and thrown it away. The monks who found the panel wanted to clean the mud off it, and a spring miraculously bubbled from the ground. The spring exists to this day in the chapel behind the church and the water is supposed to have health-giving properties. The painting on the vault of the chapel depicts the story.

The **Częstochowa Museum** (open daily 11 am to 6 pm except Monday), in the late neoclassical town hall dating from 1828 at Plac Biegańskiego, features an ethnographic collection and modern Polish paintings, plus some temporary exhibitions. Opposite the town hall is **St James' Church** (Kościół Św Jakuba), built by the tsarist regime in the 1870s as an Orthodox church. When Poland's independence was achieved in 1918, it was turned into a Catholic church and the typical Orthodox 'onion' domes were removed from the roof, to quite an awkward effect.

The **cathedral** at Plac Jana Pawła II, one block east of the train station, is a monumental, mock-Gothic structure built in 1901-27, although its towers were only completed in 1997. One of the largest

MAŁOPOLSKA

churches in Poland (100m long), its interior has little decoration to catch your eye.

Olsztyn Castle

A visit to the Olsztyn castle, 11km east of Częstochowa, is a refreshing trip out of the city. The castle is in ruins, but what a charming ruin it is. A firework and laser show is organised here in September. You can get to Olsztyn by city bus No 58 or 67 from ul Piłsudskiego opposite the train station. Alternatively, you can walk along the Trail of the Eagles' Nests, which starts from Plac Daszyńskiego and leads via Olsztyn up to Kraków.

Special Events

The major Marian feasts at Jasna Góra are 3 May, 16 July, 15 August, 26 August, 8 September, 12 September and 8 December, and on these days the monastery is packed with pilgrims. The celebration of Assumption (15 August) is particularly important, with pilgrims from all over Poland travelling to Jasna Góra on foot. The Warsaw pilgrims leave the capital on 6 August every year for the 250km trip. Up to 250,000 of the faithful can flock to the monastery for this feast.

On a more artistic front, the city's main event is the 'Gaude Mater' International Festival of Religious Music, held in May.

Places to Stay

Bear in mind that Częstochowa gets lots of pilgrims, so finding a place to stay, especially a cheap one, may not be easy – particularly on and around Marian feast days; avoid these periods or make a day trip to the city.

The all-year *Camping Nr 76 Oleńka* (☎ 324 74 95, *ul Oleńki 10/30*), near the monastery, is clean and good. It has bungalows containing rooms of different sizes, with a total capacity of 80 guests. Rooms are US$5/10 a single/double without bath, US$23/30/37 for three/four/five people with bath, or you can pitch your tent for US$2 per person. There's an inexpensive snack bar on the grounds.

The *youth hostel* (☎ 324 31 21, *ul Jasnogórska 84/90*) is also close to the monastery, but it's open only in July and August and has modest facilities.

Some of the cheapest accommodation is provided by the Church-run *Hale Noclegowe* (☎ 365 66 88 ext 224, *ul Klasztorna 1*), just next to the monastery. You pay US$3.50 per head in a four to nine-bed dorm with shared facilities and cold water only, and there's a 10 pm curfew. The place operates April to October only.

The Church's better lodging facility is *Dom Pielgrzyma (Pilgrim's Home; ☎ 324 70 11, fax 365 18 70)*, right behind the monastery. This large hostel has singles/doubles/triples with bath for US$15/18/25, or you can pay US$5 for a bed in a quad without bath. The door closes at 10 pm. There's a cheap cafeteria on the premises. *Diecezjalny Dom Rekolekcyjny* (☎ 324 11 77, *ul Św Barbary 43*), a 10 minute walk south of the monastery, offers similar conditions and also has a curfew.

A much better place to stay in the monastery area is the small *Hotel Sekwana* (☎ 324 89 54, ☎/fax 324 63 67, *ul Wieluńska 24*), which costs US$40/60 a single/double with bath. It has a pleasant and reasonably priced French restaurant – good value.

The top-end option in this area is the Orbis-run *Hotel Patria* (☎ 324 70 01, fax 324 63 32, *ul Popiełuszki 2*). Like most Orbis stock, it's hardly an inspiring place but provides a certain level of comfort for US$90/120, breakfast included.

There are a few hotels close to the train station, including the basic *Hotel Ha-Ga* (☎ 324 61 73, *ul Katedralna 9*). It has singles/doubles/triples/quads with shared facilities for US$13/15/18/20 and rooms with bath for US$18/22/25/28. Better is *Hotel Polonia* (☎ 324 23 88, *ul Piłsudskiego 9*), also called Centralny, opposite the station. It has been renovated and now costs US$33/40/50/60 with bath and breakfast.

Places to Eat

In the monastery area, apart from the above-mentioned cafeteria of *Dom Pielgrzyma* and the *Bar Oleńka* at the camping ground, there's a line of budget fast-food outlets on ul 7 Kamienic, including the pleasant *Pizzeria Paradiso*. If you need somewhere more upmarket, the best option is possibly the restaurant of *Hotel Sekwana*.

There are also quite a number of inexpensive eateries along Al NMP, including *Café Bar Laguna (Al NMP 57)*, *Alamo Restaurant (Al NMP 16)*, and *Pizzeria La Bussola* next door. Some of the best ice cream and cappuccinos in town can be found at *Vecchia Milano (Al NMP 59)*.

The upmarket *Restauracja Viking (ul Nowowiejskiego 10)* is one of the best places to eat in the centre. Just round the corner is the good and cheap *Bar Viking*, which has an outdoor eating area in summer.

Getting There & Away

Train The new train station handles half a dozen fast trains to Warsaw (235km) and about the same number of fast trains to Kraków (132km). Łódź (153km) is serviced by half a dozen trains daily and there are a couple of trains running to Opole (95km) and Wrocław (177km). Trains to Katowice (86km) run every hour or so, from where there are connections to Kraków and Wrocław.

Bus The bus terminal is close to the central train station and operates plenty of buses in the region. You may use it if going to Jędrzejów (93km) or Opole (98km). There are also infrequent buses to Ogrodzieniec (59km), but it's faster to take any of the frequent trains to Katowice, get off in Zawiercie and change for a bus.

The Małopolska Upland

Occupying a large area skirted by the Vistula and Pilica rivers, the Małopolska Upland (Wyżyna Małopolska) culminates in the Holy Cross Mountains (Góry Świętokrzyskie), at the foot of which sits Kielce, the main urban centre of the region. The upland offers a fair number of varied attractions, including castles, churches, museums and wide stretches of beautiful landscape.

KIELCE
* **pop 215,000**   ☎ 041

Kielce ('Kyel-tseh') does not have many tourist attractions, but it lies close to a fine mountain range (see the Świętokrzyski National Park section) and might be a stopover before or after visiting the park. There are also some interesting places in Kielce's vicinity (see the Around Kielce section).

The city itself, set in a valley amid gentle hills, consists of a relatively compact centre with predominantly 19th century architecture, and a ring of postwar suburbs perched on the surrounding slopes.

Information

The tourist office (☎/fax 344 62 40) is in the building of the Kielce Cultural Centre at Plac Moniuszki 2B (enter from ul Winnicka). It's open weekdays 8 am to 5 pm.

Travellers cheques can be changed at the Bank Pekao at ul Sienkiewicza 18, which also gives advances on Visa and MasterCard and has an ATM. For changing cash, there are several kantors on ul Sienkiewicza.

Things to See

The most important city sight is the **Bishops' Palace** (Pałac Biskupi) at Plac Zamkowy, a sumptuous 17th century baroque structure reflecting Kraków's wealth and prosperity. Yes, Kraków – because Kielce and its surroundings were the property of the Kraków bishops from the 12th century up to 1789, and they built the palace as one of their seats.

Today, the two-storey building is part of the national museum where you can see authentic interiors from the 17th and 18th centuries (upper floor). Of unique value are the three elaborate plafonds (ornamented ceilings) of around 1641, painted in the workshop of the Venetian Tommaso Dolabella. The whole clan of Kraków bishops looks indifferently down on you from the

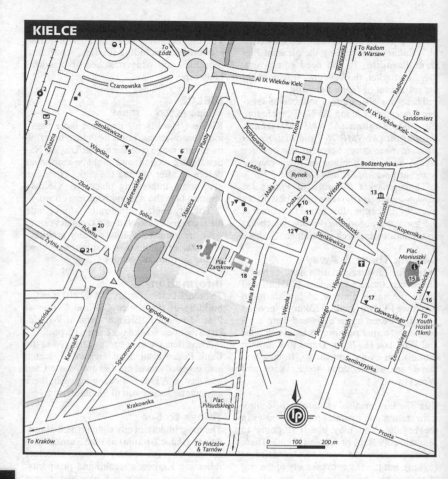

KIELCE

murals in their former dining hall, the largest room in the palace: the upper strip was painted in the 1640s, the lower one added two centuries later.

The ground floor houses a gallery of Polish painting from the 17th century to WWII. The collection includes works by Wyspiański, Boznańska, Makowski, Witkacy, Malczewski, Chełmoński, Kossak and Gierymski. The palace is open 9 am to 4 pm except Monday.

The **cathedral** facing the palace was originally Romanesque, but the present-day building dates from the 17th century and has been altered several times since then; the interior reflects these transformations, though baroque decoration predominates.

Two blocks north, at Rynek 3/5, is another branch of the **national museum** (open 9 am to 4 pm except Monday and Wednesday). It features permanent ethnographic and archaeologic sections plus temporary exhibitions.

Nearby to the east, at ul Kościuszki 11, is the **Toy Museum** (Muzeum Zabawkarstwa),

KIELCE

PLACES TO STAY
4   Hotel Łysogóry
8   Hotel Bristol
20 Hotel Elita

PLACES TO EAT
5   Restauracja Bravo
6   Bar Rybex
7   Piwnica pod Feniksem
10 Bar Łasuch
12 Bar Mleczny Smak
16 Restauracja Winnica
17 Jadłodajnia Bartosz

OTHER
1   Bus Terminal
2   Train Station
3   Post Office
9   National Museum
11 Bank Pekao
13 Toy Museum
14 Tourist Office
15 Kielce Cultural Centre
18 Cathedral
19 Bishop's Palace (National Museum)
21 Bus No 31 & Minibus Stops to Paradise Cave

open 10 am to 5 pm except Monday. It's the only toy museum in Poland, apart from a private collection in Karpacz.

Places to Stay

The all-year, 60-bed *youth hostel* (☎ 342 37 35, ul Szymanowskiego 5) is a 15 minute walk east of the city centre. Another budget place near the centre, the basic *Hotel Pracowniczy PUSB* (☎ 345 51 50, ul Urzędnicza 13) is about 1km south-west of the train station.

There are a few hotels in the centre but they don't seem to be great value. *Hotel Łysogóry* (☎ 366 25 11, fax 366 29 48, ul Sienkiewicza 78) is conveniently located opposite the train station but it can be noisy if you're in a front room. Singles/doubles/ triples without bath cost US$40/50/55, while rooms with bath are about US$65/80/85, breakfast included.

You might prefer to try *Hotel Bristol* (☎ 368 24 66, fax 366 30 65, ul Sienkiewicza 21); its rooms all have baths and cost

US$45/60/65 with breakfast. The best central option is the small *Hotel Elita* (☎ 344 17 64, fax 344 33 37, ul Równa 4A), which costs US$50/90/110 with bath and breakfast.

Out of town, you can stay at *Zajazd Raj* (see Paradise Cave in the Around Kielce section).

Places to Eat

There is quite a choice of budget eateries in the centre, including *Jadłodajnia Bartosz* (ul Głowackiego 1), *Bar Mleczny Smak* (ul Sienkiewicza 13), *Bar Łasuch* (ul Duża 9) and *Bar Rybex* (ul Sienkiewicza 52). *Restauracja Bravo* (ul Sienkiewicza 57) is also cheap and good.

For somewhere a little more upmarket, try *Piwnica pod Feniksem* (ul Sienkiewicza 25), whose speciality is tatar (raw minced beef), or *Restauracja Winnica* (ul Winnicka 4), which has some Ukrainian dishes.

Getting There & Away

Train The train station is in the centre, at the western end of ul Sienkiewicza. Two dozen trains run daily to Radom (85km) and half of them continue on to Warsaw (187km). There are six trains daily to Kraków (132km), six to Lublin (213km), four to Częstochowa (113km) and six to Katowice (173km).

Bus The UFO-shaped bus terminal, close to the train station, is pretty well organised. There are seven fast buses daily to Łódź (143km) and seven to Kraków (114km). Five buses go daily to Święty Krzyż (32km), and six to Sandomierz (90km). For Święta Katarzyna (21km), take a bus going to Bodzentyn or Starachowice; for Nowa Słupia (36km), a bus to Ostrowiec Świętokrzyski; and for Tokarnia (20km), the Jędrzejów bus via Chęciny.

AROUND KIELCE
☎ 041
Paradise Cave

Discovered in 1964, the Jaskinia Raj (Paradise Cave) is one of the better caves in Poland (the best one is arguably the Bear's

MAŁOPOLSKA

Cave in the Sudeten Mountains – see the Kletno section in the Silesia chapter). Although relatively small – only 8m high at its highest point – the cave has a couple of spectacular chambers ornamented with stalactites, stalagmites and columns.

A house at the entrance to the cave serves as a ticket office, a café and a museum. Some finds from the cave which are on display in the museum show that it was once used by animals and primitive humans as a shelter. You enter the cave and do a 150m-long loop through its chambers. All visits are guided (in Polish only) in groups of up to 15 people; the tour takes around half an hour and costs US$3. The cave is open April to November, 10 am to 5 pm except Monday. No photography is allowed inside.

The cave has become the major tourist attraction of the region and, obviously, must be 'done' by all school excursions, with the result that at times (particularly in May and June) little room is left for individual tourists. Owing to environmental factors, a limited number of people are allowed inside each day, so some days may be fully booked out. In order to be assured of a tour, book in advance on ☎ 346 55 18. Bring warm clothes, as the temperature inside the cave is only 9°C year-round.

The cave is 1km off the Kraków road, about 10km from central Kielce. You can get close on city bus No 31, which runs through to Chęciny every half-hour (every hour on Sunday). It departs from the corner of ul Żytnia and ul Paderewskiego. Ask to be let off at the bus stop just before the turn-off to the cave; the next bus stop is a long way off. There are also private minibuses departing from the same place as buses, as soon as they fill up with passengers.

Zajazd Raj (☎ *346 51 27*), near the cave beside the car park, offers rooms for US$18/24/32 a single/double/triple, and has a restaurant which serves cheap meals.

Chęciny

Chęciny, a small town at the foot of a hill topped by a ruined **castle**, is another popular spot near Kielce. The town was once a large mining centre due to its rich copper and lead deposits, and its 14th century castle was an important strategic point frequently visited by kings. Today the castle is just a ruin providing nice views of the town, which has preserved some of its old buildings including a couple of churches and a synagogue. Bus No 31 from Kielce (15km) can bring you here.

Tokarnia

The village of Tokarnia has a **skansen** (Muzeum Wsi Kieleckiej), which was established in the 1970s and is developing steadily. With an area of 80 hectares (including 20 of woodland), it's one of Poland's largest open-air museums, and it aims to be one of the best. There are plans to build a sort of small town complete with a rynek and a church in the future.

So far, one-third of the planned 80 structures have been completed, including their interiors. A number of fine implements have been collected, some of them quite amazing (note the huge barrels carved out of a single tree trunk). Give yourself about two hours to see it all at a leisurely pace.

The skansen is open April to September 10 am to 5 pm, October 10 am to 4 pm; on Monday and the day following public holidays it's closed. It can also be visited from November to March, on weekdays only, 10 am to 2 pm, but the interiors are locked in that period. In summer, a café opens in the house at the entrance to the skansen.

The skansen is on the Kielce-Kraków road, 20km from Kielce; buses ply this route roughly every hour. Coming from Kielce, take the bus to Jędrzejów via Chęciny. Get off at the bus stop in the village of Tokarnia and walk for 10 minutes up the road to the skansen's entrance.

JĘDRZEJÓW

• pop 18,000   ☎ 041

The pride of Jędrzejów ('Yend-zheh-yoof') is its **Sundial Museum** (Muzeum Zegarów Słonecznych), which has over 300 specimens, reputedly the world's third-largest sundial collection after Oxford and

Chicago. Among the exhibits are the 16th and 17th century pocket sundials made of ivory that are adjustable depending on the latitude; two intricate instruments capable of measuring time to within half a minute; and a range of sundials from the Far East. Strangest of all is the 18th century apparatus equipped with a cannon which used to fire at noon. The oldest instrument in the collection, dating from 1524, was designed for measuring time at night from the position of the stars. The museum also has an extensive gnomonics (the science of sundials) library, old clocks and watches, furniture and household implements.

The museum is in two old houses at Rynek 7/8 and is open from 16 April to 15 October 8 am to 4 pm; in the remaining part of the year 8 am to 3 pm; on Monday and the day following public holidays it's closed. All visitors are guided in groups; 50-minute tours begin on the hour. The last tour departs one hour before closing time.

Church buffs might be interested in visiting the **Cistercian Abbey** (Opactwo Cystersów) on the western outskirts of town, 2km from the Rynek on ul 11 Listopada (the road to Katowice). Founded in 1140, this was the first Cistercian abbey in Poland. For the Poles, the place is associated with Wincenty Kadłubek (1161-1223), Kraków's bishop and the first known Polish chronicler, author of *Chronica Polonorum*. He spent the last years of his life in the monastery and was buried here.

The original Romanesque church was repeatedly modified, most recently in the 18th century, when the twin towers were added to the façade and the interior acquired its baroque décor. The stucco walls resemble marble, and the rich interior decoration includes illusionistic wall paintings on the vault, opulent altarpieces, stalls in the presbytery, a gilded tabernacle in the high altar and a splendid organ – all dating from the 18th century. Kadłubek's remains repose in a small 17th century baroque coffin in the side chapel off the left-hand aisle. The monastery adjoining the church has a courtyard lined with 15th century Gothic cloisters.

Places to Stay & Eat

The only regular accommodation is provided by *Hotel Zacisze* (☎ 286 18 26, Al Piłsudskiego 4). It's a large, uninspiring block, 800m west of the Rynek along ul 11 Listopada, and it has its own restaurant. Singles/doubles/quads with shared facilities cost US$8/14/20. There are more places to eat in the town centre.

Getting There & Away

The bus and train stations are next to each other, 2km west of the Rynek and linked to it by urban buses. Since Jędrzejów lies on the Kraków-Kielce highway and railway line, there's sufficient transport to either destination and you shouldn't have to wait more than an hour for a bus or train.

An attractive way to get to Pińczów and Wiślica is by the Ekspres Ponidzie narrow-gauge tourist train which operates on weekends and public holidays from May to September.

PIŃCZÓW

- **pop 12,000** ☎ 041

Pińczów ('Peen-choof') was founded in the 15th century, and its past is certainly more glorious than its present. The town developed around the stone workshops established by visiting Italian artists, Santi Gucci being the most eminent among them. Taking advantage of the local limestone quarries, a variety of stonework including portals, altarpieces and tombstones were carved here and distributed to churches all over Poland. The Reformation had one of its strongest bastions here in the mid-16th century, though Pińczów later became the property of the bishops of Kraków and Catholicism came back to the region.

Pińczów had a large Jewish population. After their first arrival in the 16th century, Jews grew steadily in number to make up over 60% of the town's population by the 18th century. With this proportion maintained right up to the outbreak of WWII, it was one of the most Jewish towns in Poland.

MAŁOPOLSKA

Things to See

The town was destroyed by the Nazis and there's not much historic architecture left, but you might want to have a glance if you're in the region. The **parish church** on the Rynek is a 15th century construction, but its interior furnishings, including the high altar, side chapels, pulpit and organ, all date from the mid-18th century. The adjoining building, once the Paulite monastery, houses the **Regional Museum**, which has a somewhat random collection of objects to do with the archaeology and history of the town. It's open Wednesday and Thursday 9 am to 4 pm, and Friday to Sunday 10 am to 3 pm.

About 150m east of the Rynek, at ul Klasztorna 8, the 17th century **synagogue** is located. A massive building, now falling into disrepair, it's the only important remnant of the Jewish past. Another 150m to the east, the former **Reformate Church** (Kościół Poreformacki) has some fine stucco work inside.

To the north, the town is dominated by two hills. On top of one stands **St Anne's Chapel** (Kaplica Św Anny), designed by Santi Gucci and erected around 1600. The other hill was once topped by a large 15th century castle, said to have been one of the most splendid in Poland, but it was pulled down in the 19th century and virtually nothing is left.

Places to Stay & Eat

Dom Wycieczkowy MOSiR (☎ 357 20 44, *ul Pałęki 26*) on the lake shore, 500m south-west of the Rynek, offers basic singles/doubles/triples without bath for US$8/14/18. A camp site and cabins open in summer. There are some simple places to eat in town, including *Restauracja Manhattan (ul Krótka 3)*, a short block west of the Rynek.

Getting There & Away

The bus terminal is 500m south of the Rynek. Buses to Kielce (37km) and Busko-Zdrój (16km) run roughly every hour, and there are also several departures daily to Wiślica (31km) and Jędrzejów (28km).

There's no standard-gauge railway in Pińczów, but the narrow-gauge tourist train can take you to Jędrzejów and Wiślica (weekends and public holidays from May to September).

WIŚLICA

• pop 700

An obscure village way off tourist tracks and major urban centres, Wiślica ('Veesh-lee-tsah') caused a stir among historians in the 1960s following the archaeological excavations which led to the discovery of three churches built before the existing 14th century collegiate church. Beside the oldest one, built in the 10th century, a baptismal font was found, which to everybody's surprise dates from the 9th century. The find made Wiślica the earliest Christian site so far discovered in Poland, active a century before the baptism of Duke Mieszko in Gniezno in 966. Some scholars believe that Wiślica was one of the most important settlements of the Vistulans, in the same league as Kraków. However, there isn't enough information to be sure about this.

Things to See

The **collegiate church** (kolegiata) on the eastern side of the Rynek is a late Gothic building founded around 1350 by King Kazimierz Wielki. The carved stone plaque commemorating the act of foundation, placed over the southern entrance to the church, shows the king offering a model of the church to the Virgin Mary, accompanied by the bishop of Kraków.

Inside the church, the most striking feature is the unusual two-naved interior with three massive columns placed right across the middle of the church, supporting an exquisite palm-like vaulting. The fragments of the frescoes in the presbytery, dating from the 1390s, display clear Byzantine influences, while the high altar boasts a stone statue of the Madonna, an anonymous work from the late 13th century.

The remnants of two previous churches are underneath but are off limits to tourists. However, you can see the remains of the earliest church, the **St Nicholas Church** (Kościół Św Mikołaja), and the famous **font** (misa chrzcielna); they are protected by a small pavilion right behind the presbytery of the collegiate church. Just to the south of the church stands the **Długosz House** (Dom Długosza), built for the great medieval historian Jan Długosz in 1460.

The wave of enthusiasm over the discoveries led to the founding of a **museum** in the village, but there's more in the way of reading matter (in Polish only) than actual finds. The most interesting exhibit is the replica of a large decorative gypsum slab from the floor of the 12th century church; the original is *in situ* in the basement of the collegiate church. The museum is off the upper side of the Rynek and is open 8 am to 4 pm except Sunday and Monday.

There's nowhere in Wiślica to stay, and the only restaurant to speak of is *Zajazd Kasztelański*, 500m from the Rynek on the Busko-Zdrój road.

Getting There & Away

Wiślica is relatively well serviced by buses, with several departures daily to Kraków (72km), Pińczów (31km), Kazimierza Wielka (21km) and Busko-Zdrój (14km). The main bus stop is on the Rynek. From May to September, the narrow-gauge tourist train runs to Pińczów and on to Jędrzejów (on weekends and public holidays only).

ŚWIĘTOKRZYSKI NATIONAL PARK
☎ 041

The Góry Świętokrzyskie (Holy Cross Mountains) run for 70km east-west across the Małopolska Upland. This is Poland's oldest mountainous geological formation, and consequently the lowest, due to gradual erosion for over 300 million years. The highest peak is just 612m, and the whole outcrop is more a collection of gently rolling wooded hills than mountains in the real sense of the word. The region retains some of its primeval nature, and a national park has been set up to protect the best of what is left.

The Świętokrzyski National Park ('Shvyen-to-kzhis-kee') has taken under protection the highest, 15km-long central range, known as the Łysogóry, or Bald Mountains. It has a peak at each end: Mt Łysica (612m) in the west and Mt Łysa Góra (595m) in the east. Between them is a belt of forest, mostly fir and beech, which covers almost all the 60 sq km of the park. Watch out for the unusual *gołoborza*: heaps of broken quartzite rock on parts of the northern slopes below the two peaks.

Apart from these natural attractions, there's the Święty Krzyż abbey and a museum on top of Mt Łysa Góra, and another museum at the foothill village of Nowa Słupia. The mountains make a pleasant half or full-day trip.

Orientation

The park is about 20km east of Kielce. You can get there by bus from the city to three different access points: the village of Święta Katarzyna on the western end, at the foot of Mt Łysica; the Święty Krzyż abbey on the top of Mt Łysa Góra; and the village of Nowa Słupia, 2km east from Święty Krzyż.

If you're not enthusiastic about walking, it's best to go by bus directly to Święty Krzyż, visit the place, then go down to Nowa Słupia to see the museum and take a bus back to Kielce or wherever else you want to go.

If you plan on hiking, there's an 18km marked trail between Święta Katarzyna and Nowa Słupia, via Święty Krzyż. It's best to set off from Nowa Słupia, as there are museums here and in nearby Święty Krzyż; if you started from the opposite end of the trail, you would have to get moving early to reach the museums before they close. The following description includes the whole route from Nowa Słupia to Święta Katarzyna.

Nowa Słupia

The village of Nowa Słupia is known for its **Museum of Ancient Metallurgy** (Muzeum Starożytnego Hutnictwa Świętokrzyskiego), on the road to Święty Krzyż, open

MAŁOPOLSKA

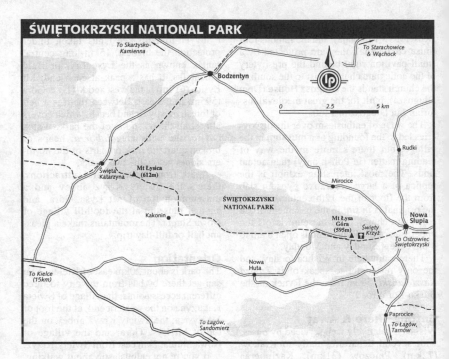

ŚWIĘTOKRZYSKI NATIONAL PARK

To Skarżysko-Kamienna

To Starachowice & Wąchock

Bodzentyn

0   2.5   5 km

Rudki

Święta Katarzyna

Mt Łysica (612m)

Mirocice

ŚWIĘTOKRZYSKI NATIONAL PARK

Kakonin

Mt Łysa Góra (595m)

Święty Krzyż

Nowa Słupia

To Ostrowiec Świętokrzyski

Nowa Huta

To Kielce (15km)

Paprocice

To Łagów, Sandomierz

To Łagów, Tarnów

---

9 am to 4 pm except Monday. The museum has been established on the site where primitive smelting furnaces, or *dymarki*, dating from the 2nd century AD, were unearthed in 1955. A huge number of furnaces have been found in the surrounding area, indicating that the region was an important ancient metallurgical centre, the largest so far discovered in Europe.

From the museum, a 2km path called King Way (Droga Królewska) leads up to Święty Krzyż; by car, it's a 16km detour.

There's an all-year *youth hostel* (☎ 317 70 16) next to the museum, as well as *Zespół Domków Turystycznych Pod Skałką* (☎ 317 70 85) a few paces away, which offers cheap cabins and a camping ground from May to September.

Buses from Nowa Słupia can take you to Kielce (36km) and to Starachowice (the route to Wąchock). For Sandomierz, you

have to change buses in either Ostrowiec Świętokrzyski or Łagów.

Święty Krzyż

Giving its name to the mountains, Święty Krzyż, or Holy Cross, is a **Benedictine abbey** built on top of Mt Łysa Góra in the early 12th century, on the site of a pagan place of worship which existed here in the 8th and 9th centuries. The abbey was rebuilt several times and the present-day church is a product of the late 18th century with a mainly neoclassical interior. The monastery has retained more of its original shape and you can visit its Gothic vaulted cloister and a small missionary collection kept inside (open weekdays 10 am to 4 pm).

The **Natural History Museum** (Muzeum Przyrodniczo-Leśne) is on the western side of the abbey facing a huge TV mast, and focuses on the geology and the plant and animal life of the park. It is open 10 am to 4 pm (November to March 9 am to 3 pm) except Monday and the day following public holidays. The entrance to the museum is from the western side of the complex.

The gołoborze is just past the TV mast to the right; a short side path will lead you there.

From Święty Krzyż you can take the bus straight to Kielce (32km, every three hours) or walk along the red trail to Święta Katarzyna.

The Trail

The 16km trail from Święty Krzyż to Święta Katarzyna provides an easy four hour walk in the park. The trail follows the road for the first 2km, then branches off and runs west along the edge of the forest for about 9km. It then enters the woods, ascends the peak of Mt Łysica and winds down for 2km to Święta Katarzyna.

Święta Katarzyna

This small village has no particular attractions. The Bernardine convent founded here in the 15th century was rebuilt after a fire in the mid-19th century; it's not worth the effort to be allowed inside.

Buses go regularly to Kielce (21km), or you can stay in either the all-year *youth hostel* (☎ 311 22 06) or *Dom Wycieczkowy PTTK* (☎ 311 21 11); the latter has a budget restaurant.

UJAZD

• pop 600

The small village of Ujazd ('Oo-yahst') is known for **Krzyżtopór**, an enormous castle whose ruins dominate the area. Designed by Italian architect Lorenzo Muretto (Wawrzyniec Senes to the Poles) for the governor of the Sandomierz province, Krzysztof Ossoliński, this monumental building was erected between 1631 and 1644 and was definitely not intended to be an average castle.

Built inside massive stone walls with bastions at the five corners, this mannerist palace embodied the structure of the calendar. It had four towers symbolising the four seasons and 12 big halls, one for each month. Exactly 52 rooms were built, one for each week in the year, and 365 windows. The designer didn't forget to provide an additional window which was only to be used during the leap year, and walled up the rest of the time.

An extensive system of cellars was built; some of them were used as stables for the owner's 370 white stallions, and equipped with mirrors and black-marble mangers. The octagonal dining hall had a huge crystal aquarium built into its ceiling.

Ossoliński didn't enjoy his home for long; he died in 1645, a year after the castle had been completed. Only 10 years later, the Swedes did significant damage to the castle, and took away some of the most precious treasures. Though the subsequent owners lived in part of the castle till 1770, it was only a shadow of its former self and swiftly declined thereafter.

After WWII, plans to transform the castle into a military school were discussed but rejected and the ruins were left to their fate for four decades. In the early 1990s, restoration work started, aiming to rebuild the castle and perhaps make it into a hotel, but the plan was abandoned. So, until a new program is launched, all you can see is a formidable ruin – there's hardly another one like it in Poland.

Miraculously, the entrance gate still proudly bears the two massive stone symbols of the castle – the Krzyż, or Cross, representing the religious devotion of the owner, and the Topór, or Axe, the coat of arms of the Ossoliński family, both still in good condition.

Don't miss this place: the longer you stay, the more it grows on you. The castle is way off the beaten track so it doesn't get many tourists, particularly on weekdays. It is open daily till late and you can wander about on your own.

Places to Stay & Eat

A small barracks was built opposite the ruin's entrance to provide accommodation for the workers, but since the reconstruction program was stopped, most of the building is used as a basic *hostel* for tourists (US$3 a person). If you have a tent, you can camp at the foot of the castle or in its courtyard – an idyllic location. There doesn't seem to be anywhere to eat, except for a *kiosk* where you can buy some basic food and drink.

Getting There & Away
Ujazd lies on a side road and has no direct transport links with the major cities of the region. The only points of access are Opatów (16km) or Klimontów (13km), which are linked with Ujazd by several buses daily and also have onward transport to Sandomierz and Kielce.

SANDOMIERZ
• pop 27,000   ☎ 015
Sandomierz is one of the most pleasant towns in Małopolska. Overlooking the Vistula from a 40m hill, it preserves the yesteryear lethargy typical of old country towns, and shelters some fine historic buildings, remnants of its illustrious past. Both its atmosphere and architecture make a visit worthwhile.

It's not exactly clear when the town sprang to life, but at the end of the 11th century the chronicler Gall Anonim classified Sandomierz along with Kraków and Wrocław as *sedes regni principales*, or major settlements of the realm. Destroyed by Tatar raids in 1259, the town was moved uphill to its present location and fortified in the 14th century. A busy river port and trade centre on the Kraków-Kiev route, Sandomierz prospered until the mid-17th century. Its glory came to an abrupt end with the Swedish Deluge, after which the town never really revived. By the outbreak of WWII it numbered 10,000 inhabitants, not many more than three centuries earlier.

The town came through the war unscathed and preserved its historic architecture intact, but ironically it nearly lost the lot in the 1960s when the soft loess soils on which Sandomierz sits began a dangerous slide

down into the river. A rescue operation was launched, and the city was again 'fortified', this time with substantial injections of concrete and steel into the slopes. Today, safe and restored, the town still proudly boasts its historic gems.

Information
Tourist Office The tourist office is in the Galeria Zapole premises at ul Opatowska 17. It's open weekdays 9 am to 5 pm, and may also open on summer weekends.

Money There are only a couple of kantors in the Old Town, including one at the post office on the Rynek. The Kredyt Bank a few doors south also changes cash and may pay better than the kantor. There are also a few kantors on ul Mickiewicza close to the corner of ul 11 Listopada, about 1km northwest of the Old Town. At the time of writing, there were no ATMs in the Old Town, and the only one in Sandomierz was in the Bank Depozytowo Kredytowy at ul Kościuszki 4.

Things to See
The 14th century **Opatów Gate** (Brama Opatowska) is the main entrance to the Old Town and the only surviving gate of the four that were built as part of the fortification system. The decorative Renaissance parapets were added in the 16th century. You can go to the top (open daily 10 am to 5.30 pm) to look around, but the view of the Old Town is not that good.

The 18th century **synagogue** on ul Żydowska retains the remains of its decoration on the inside, but it houses the town's registry and cannot be visited.

The sloping **Rynek** is lined with houses dating from different periods, some of which were built after the war. In the 16th century all the houses had arcades. Today only two of them, those at Nos 10 and 27, still have their arcades.

Right in the middle stands the **town hall**, the oldest building on the Rynek. Its main Gothic structure was adorned with decorative parapets and a tower in the Renaissance period. Its ground floor houses a small **museum** of the town's history (open Tuesday to Sunday 9 am to 4 pm) featuring a fine model of what the town looked like three centuries ago.

One of the town's star attractions is the **Underground Tourist Route** (Podziemna Trasa Turystyczna), which leads through a chain of 30-odd cellars beneath the houses around the Rynek. Built mostly during the boom times in the 15th and 16th centuries, these storage cellars gradually fell into disuse and were abandoned when trade declined. Dug out of soft soil and lacking proper reinforcements, they effectively undermined the city and contributed to the postwar near-disaster. In the complex restoration program carried out in 1964-77 they were restored and linked together to ensure the safety of the town and provide yet another tourist attraction.

The entrance to the cellars is from ul Oleśnickich, just off the Rynek, and you finish the tour in the town hall. The route is open 10 am to 5 pm except Monday (till 3 pm from November to March). It can only be visited on a guided tour in Polish; these leave approximately every hour.

From the Rynek, take ul Mariacka to the **cathedral**. Built in the 1360s, this massive church has preserved much of its Gothic exterior, apart from the baroque façade added in the 17th century. The baroque took hold more strongly inside the building,

though some of the earlier decoration has survived, notably the Russo-Byzantine frescoes in the chancel. One of the few examples of such frescoes in Poland, they were painted in the 1420s but later whitewashed, and only revealed and restored at the beginning of the 20th century.

A series of 12 large paintings on the side walls of the church gives a bizarre insight into all imaginable methods of torture and other horrors, and you could easily spend an hour examining the details. This early 18th century *Martyrologium Romanum* is the work of Karol de Prevot. The paintings symbolise the 12 months of the year. Next to each scene of torture on each painting is the ordinal number which represents the day of the month. Legend has it that you need only find the month and the day on which you were born, and you'll discover how you're going to die.

Prevot was also responsible for another four similarly macabre paintings on the back wall under a sumptuous baroque organ. These pictures depict scenes from the town's history, including the Tatar massacre of 1259 and the blowing up of the castle by the Swedes in 1656. The cathedral is open to visitors Tuesday to Saturday 10 am to 2 pm and 3 to 5 pm, Sunday and public holidays 3 to 5 pm. Next to the cathedral, at ul Katedralna 5, is the modest **Museum of Literature** (Muzeum Literatury), open Tuesday to Sunday 9 am to 4 pm.

Sandomierz in its late 16th century heyday was a prosperous port and trade centre

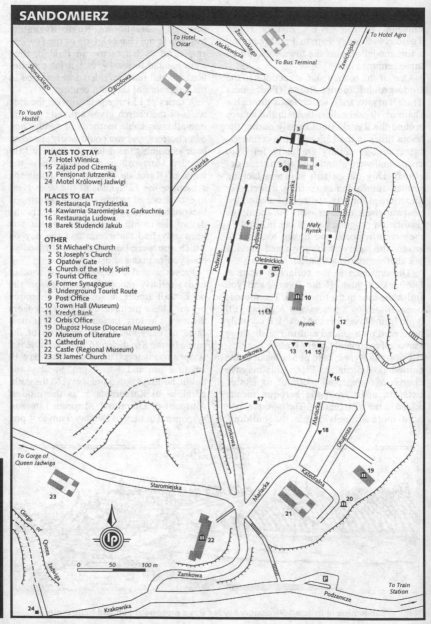

SANDOMIERZ

PLACES TO STAY
7 Hotel Winnica
15 Zajazd pod Ciżemką
17 Pensjonat Jutrzenka
24 Motel Królowej Jadwigi

PLACES TO EAT
13 Restauracja Trzydziestka
14 Kawiarnia Staromiejska z Garkuchnią
16 Restauracja Ludowa
18 Barek Studencki Jakub

OTHER
1 St Michael's Church
2 St Joseph's Church
3 Opatów Gate
4 Church of the Holy Spirit
5 Tourist Office
6 Former Synagogue
8 Underground Tourist Route
9 Post Office
10 Town Hall (Museum)
11 Kredyt Bank
12 Orbis Office
19 Długosz House (Diocesan Museum)
20 Museum of Literature
21 Cathedral
22 Castle (Regional Museum)
23 St James' Church

To Hotel Oscar
Mickiewicza
Żeromskiego
To Hotel Agro
To Bus Terminal
Zawichojska
Słowackiego
Ogrodowa
To Youth Hostel
Tatarska
Opatowska
Sokolnickiego
Mały Rynek
Podwale
Żydowska
Oleśnickich
Rynek
Zamkowa
Mariacka
Staromiejska
To Gorge of Queen Jadwiga
Gorge of Queen Jadwiga
Długosza
Katedralna
Mariacka
Zamkowa
To Train Station
Podzamcze
Krakowska

0   50   100 m

MAŁOPOLSKA

Nearby is the Długosz House built for the medieval historian in 1476. Inside, the **Diocesan Museum** (Muzeum Diecezjalne) features furniture, tapestries, ceramics, crafts and archaeological artefacts, and a collection of religious art. The museum is open Tuesday to Saturday 9 am to 4 pm (to noon November to March), Sunday and public holidays 1.30 to 4 pm (to 3 pm November to March).

The **castle**, a few steps downhill from the cathedral, was built in the 14th century on the site of a previous wooden stronghold and gradually extended during the next three centuries. It now accommodates the **Regional Museum** (Muzeum Okręgowe), featuring small ethnographic and art collections, and the old castle kitchen. It's open Tuesday to Friday 9 am to 4 pm, Saturday 9 am to 3 pm and Sunday 10 am to 2 pm.

St James' Church (Kościół Św Jakuba), on ul Staromiejska west of the castle, is the oldest monument in town. Dating from the 1230s, it's believed to be the first brick church in Poland and is particularly renowned for its Romanesque portal. The church retains the austere exterior typical of the period, but the interior has been radically modernised and looks pretty dull with its contemporary high altar, pews and chandeliers. Among the few historic objects left is the sarcophagus in the presbytery, carved in 1676 out of a single oak trunk. The church is open for visitors 9 am to 12.30 pm and 3 to 5.30 pm (on Sunday and public holidays from 11 am). The belfry beside the church holds two of the oldest bells in Poland, cast in 1314 and 1389. They can only be heard on very special occasions.

Continue up ul Staromiejska as far as St Paul's Church and turn left downhill into the **Gorge of Queen Jadwiga** (Wąwóz Królowej Jadwigi), the best of the gorges around the town. It will lead you down to ul Krakowska, or you can take the first path to the left and back to St James' Church.

Places to Stay

The *youth hostel* (☎ 832 26 52, ul Krępianki 6), in a school a 10 minute walk

west from the Old Town, is open only from 1 July to 25 August. The tourist office may arrange a *private room*.

There are a few small places to stay in the Old Town. The cheapest is *Pensjonat Jutrzenka* (☎ 832 22 19, ul Zamkowa 1), midway between the Rynek and the castle. It has only four rooms with shared facilities: two doubles (US$18 each), a triple (US$20) and a quad (US$28).

Hotel Winnica (☎ 832 31 30, Mały Rynek 2) also has rooms with shared facilities only, which cost US$15/21/26/30 a single/double/triple/quad.

Zajazd pod Ciżemką (☎ 832 36 68, Rynek 27) was undergoing thorough refurbishing when this book was researched, and is expected to be a decent central option. By the time you read this, there may be another good place, *Motel Królowej Jadwigi* (☎ 832 29 88, ul Krakowska 24), already in operation. Both these places will offer baths.

Another place with baths is *Hotel Oscar* (☎ 832 11 44, ul Mickiewicza 17A, 2nd floor), a 10 minute walk north-west of the Old Town, diagonally opposite the police station. It has singles/doubles with bath for US$28/34.

If you cannot find anywhere cheap in the centre, check *Hotel Agro* (☎ 832 34 00, ul Mokoszyńska 3), off the Lublin road about 2km north-east of the Old Town. Neither the location nor the standards are terribly good here, but you can get a bed in a double or triple without bath for US$9. Bus No 10, 15 or 16 from the Brama Opatowska can drop you off near the hotel.

Places to Eat

Some of the cheapest meals in town are served at *Barek Studencki Jakub* (ul Mariacka 9). There are a few cafés and restaurants on and just off the Rynek. Try, for example, *Kawiarnia Staromiejska z Garkuchnią* (Rynek 28) or *Restauracja Trzydziestka* (Rynek 30), both of which are pleasant and serve reasonable food. Cheaper are the basic *Restauracja Ludowa* (ul Mariacka 5) and *Restauracja Winnica*

MAŁOPOLSKA

(Mały Rynek 2). **Restauracja pod Ciżemką** *(Rynek 27)* may be the best choice around the Rynek, when it opens. As yet the best food in town is served at **Motel Królowej Jadwigi** *(ul Krakowska 24)*.

Getting There & Away

Train The train station is 3km south of the Old Town, on the other side of the Vistula, and is served by the city buses to/from Brama Opatowska.

Three fast trains run daily to Warsaw (243km). There is also one train to Kielce (143km) and two to Przemyśl (153km).

Bus The bus terminal is better located but it's still 1.5km north-west of the Old Town; frequent urban buses go there from Brama Opatowska.

There are a dozen fast buses to Warsaw (248km), which cost roughly the same as the train. To Zamość (138km), only one bus runs daily at around 4 pm.

Buses to Tarnobrzeg (14km) depart roughly every half-hour but suburban bus No 11 from Brama Opatowska is more convenient, and just as frequent. From Tarnobrzeg, frequent buses will take you on to Baranów Sandomierski (another 14km).

For Ujazd (39km), you have to go to Klimontów (buses roughly every hour) and change there. The staff at the terminal can work out the connection.

BARANÓW SANDOMIERSKI
• pop 1500   ☎ 015

The village of Baranów Sandomierski lies on the edge of an area where huge sulphur deposits were discovered in the 1950s. Its fame, however, is based on its **castle** rather than sulphur. The castle was built at the end of the 16th century for the Leszczyński family, the owners of large estates in Wielkopolska including the Gołuchów castle. The castle was encircled with powerful fortifications but they were dismantled in the 19th century. The whole is thought to have been designed by talented Italian architect Santi Gucci, responsible for many other projects in Poland.

Under the Lubomirski family, the enlargement of the western wing was carried out by Tylman van Gameren in the late 17th century. Although the castle suffered two major fires in the 19th century, it was refurbished both times and was inhabited almost continuously until WWII. Damaged during the war, it was handed over to the care of the Siarkopol, a state-owned sulphur enterprise, which has restored it and maintains it today.

The castle is considered one of the most beautiful Renaissance residences in Poland. Set in a pleasant, well kept park, it has four corner towers and a lovely arcaded courtyard. The two-storeyed arcades, with their slender columns supporting graceful arches, are very Italianesque. Look at the fanciful masks on the column plinths, at the vault decoration, and the superb carved-stone portals.

Some of the castle's original rooms, complete with period furnishings, paintings and decoration, are open to visitors. The former chapel on the west side of the building is used for temporary exhibitions.

Another exhibition, a reminder of the castle's patron, is in the basement and shows the achievements of the sulphur industry; unless you're a sulphur fanatic, you won't find it much fun, although it's worth seeing a few archaeological finds that are exhibited there as well. They include the remains of the Gothic stronghold discovered after WWII during the process of the castle's restoration. All the exhibitions are open 9 am to 3 pm (on Sunday until 4 pm), except Monday and the day following public holidays.

Places to Stay & Eat

Hotel przy Zamku (☎/fax 811 80 39, ☎/fax 811 80 40), in the building just to the west of the castle, was being renovated at the time of writing but should have reopened by the time you read this. It is likely to be a pleasant and quiet place to stay at midrange prices.

You can also stay in the *castle (☎/fax 811 80 39, ☎/fax 811 80 40)* itself: one side of it has been modified to provide plush accommodation in historic interiors for US$80/120 a single/double. There's a budget *café* in the basement of the castle.

Zajazd Wisła, a roadside hotel on the Tarnobrzeg road, about 1km from Baranów, has doubles with bath for US$30 and a restaurant. The *youth hostel (☎ 811 80 04, ul Kościuszki 6)* in Baranów's primary school is open from 1 July to 25 August.

Getting There & Away

The train station is well out of the village so it's much more convenient to travel by bus; the bus stop is close to the Rynek, a 10 minute walk from the castle.

There's no direct transport to Sandomierz (28km) but frequent buses run to Tarnobrzeg (14km), where you catch another, equally frequent bus. Some of the buses to Tarnobrzeg depart from the entrance to the castle.

There are four fast buses to Kraków (190km); the last one passes through just before 1 pm. All Kraków-bound buses go via Tarnów (104km). Four buses a day run to Warsaw (223km) and one (around noon) to Zamość (143km). There are also two buses a day to Zakopane via Tarnów and Nowy Sącz.

WĄCHOCK
- **pop 3100**   ☎ 047

The small town of Wąchock ('Von-hotsk') is home to the **Cistercian Abbey** (Opactwo Cystersów). It was founded in 1179 as one of the numerous seats of the then expanding order, and within a century the church and the monastery were erected. Though both buildings underwent various changes, extensions and additions in the course of time, parts of the original structure have been preserved to this day intact, and are some of the most important examples of medieval architecture in Poland.

The church today is crammed with baroque and rococo furnishings and has several layers of wall painting, the last dating from the 19th century. Despite this disguise, you can easily recognise the original features of the structure, particularly

the vaulting, whose style is on the borderline between late Romanesque and early Gothic.

The adjacent monastery looks like a palace these days, the result of 16th century alterations. The cloister around the square courtyard was rebuilt in the 17th century, becoming higher in the process, but plaster has been removed from some parts of the walls to show the original sandstone blocks. Of particular interest are the 13th century vaulted refectory, the fraternity room with its vault supported on a central column, and the monastery's highlight – the chapter house. A splendid stone vault supported on four pillars with delicately carved capitals, all beautifully proportioned and perfectly preserved, makes it one of the best Romanesque interiors to be found in the country.

The abbey can be visited daily 9 am to noon and 2 to 5 pm (on Sunday and public holidays 2 to 5 pm only).

The abbey is close to the Rynek, where all buses stop. There's a good bus service to Kielce (44km) but only a couple of buses go to Radom (40km); to get there, take any bus to Skarżysko Kamienna (18km), where you'll have far more transport options by both train and bus. If heading south-east to Ujazd or Sandomierz, take the urban bus to Starachowice (5km) and change there.

SZYDŁOWIEC
- **pop 13,000**   ☎ 048

Szydłowiec ('Shid-wo-viets'), on the Kielce-Radom highway, is an old town which got its municipal charter in 1470. It passed through the hands of some great aristocratic families, including the Sapieha and Radziwiłł, who made it a prosperous urban centre. Just before WWII, 70% of its population was Jewish. The town has some important sights, justifying a visit.

Things to See

The **town hall**, in the middle of the Rynek, is a handsome, castle-like structure complete with towers and decorative parapets, recently whitewashed all over. Built in the early 17th century, it's a good example of Polish Renaissance architecture.

The **church**, shaded by tall trees on the southern side of the Rynek, dates from the end of the 15th century and its interior is living proof of its age. The original details include the wooden high altar, the polyptych in the presbytery, the panelled ceiling under the organ loft – all from the beginning of the 16th century – and, most striking of all, the flat wooden ceiling of the nave made and decorated in 1509. The bell tower beside the church is just as old.

A five minute walk north-west of the Rynek is a large 16th century **castle** encircled by a moat. It was rebuilt a century later but since then not much has changed. Its interior still shelters the original chapel and some of the old decoration (off limits to tourists), but its major attraction is the **Museum of Polish Folk Musical Instruments** (Muzeum Polskich Ludowych Instrumentów Muzycznych), the only one of its kind in the country. It's open 9 am to 3 pm except Monday (on Saturday 10 am to 5 pm).

The town has a singularly impressive **Jewish cemetery**, one of the largest in Poland. Actually, what you see today is a quarter of the original graveyard – it was four times larger when founded in 1788 and right up to WWII. Over 2000 tombstones, mostly from the 19th century (the oldest dating from 1831), stand amid trees and undergrowth untouched for decades. In order to get there, take ul Kilińskiego eastwards from the Rynek, turn left onto ul Kościuszki (the road to Radom) and after 250m turn right into ul Spółdzielcza. The cemetery is just 100m ahead.

Places to Stay & Eat

Other than the all-year *youth hostel (☎ 17 13 74, ul Kilińskiego 2)*, there is nowhere to stay in town. The hostel has doubles, triples and quads, with a total capacity for 30 guests. Reception is open 6 to 9 pm.

The most pleasant place to eat and drink in town is *Piwnica Szydłowiecka*, in the cellars of the town hall. It serves hearty meals plus drinks, including coffee and beer.

Getting There & Away

The bus terminal is a 10 minute walk north from the Rynek. There are plenty of buses to Radom (31km), passing Orońsko on their way. Only a few buses go straight to Kielce (44km); if you don't want to wait, take a half-hourly bus to Skarżysko Kamienna and continue on another bus, also frequent.

The train station is 5km east of town – not worth the trip.

OROŃSKO
- **pop 1200**   ☎ 048

A small roadside village near Radom, Orońsko is home to the **Centre of Polish Sculpture** (Centrum Rzeźby Polskiej). Established in the grounds of a 19th century estate complete with a palace, chapel, orangery, granary and coach house, all surrounded by a landscaped park, the centre is a workshop for sculptors, providing them with facilities to work, and exhibiting modern Polish sculpture.

A spacious exhibition hall was constructed in 1993 to present changing displays of some of Poland's best contemporary artists. Temporary exhibitions are also held in the orangery and outbuildings. Some of the sculptures have been scattered around the park to make a pleasant outdoor display. Additionally, you can visit the palace; it has been left in late 19th century style, as it was when the remarkable Polish painter Józef Brandt (1841-1915) lived and worked here.

The indoor exhibitions and the palace are open Tuesday to Friday 9 am to 3 pm, Saturday and Sunday 10 am to 4 pm; the park is open daily till dusk.

Places to Stay & Eat

Rebuilt from a former granary, the small *hotel (☎ 362 19 16)* offers neat rooms, all with bath. The singles/doubles/triples are US$13/18/22. Occasionally, when there are no sculptors staying in the centre, you may be allowed to stay in their dorms, paying just US$3 a bed. The reception desk is open Monday and Tuesday 7 am to 3 pm, Wednesday to Friday 7 am to 10 pm, and Saturday and Sunday 10 am to 5 pm.

The centre's kitchen can provide meals for guests if requested, but you should let them know in advance. The hotel's *café* serves drinks and snacks.

Getting There & Away

Orońsko lies on the Kielce-Radom highway and the bus service is frequent (no railway at all). To Radom (17km), you can go either on the Radom urban bus K or the PKS bus coming through from Szydłowiec. The same buses will let you off close to Radom's skansen (roughly halfway to Radom; ask the driver). To Szydłowiec (14km), PKS buses run every hour or so. There are no direct buses to Kielce (58km); you must change in Skarżysko Kamienna.

RADOM

• pop 235,000   ☎ 048

Radom is a large industrial centre 100km south of Warsaw. Although it developed into a strong fortified town during the reign of King Kazimierz Wielki, little of its historical character is left.

Today Radom is an uninspiring city, with few attractions to show tourists. You might want to look around if passing this way, but even so, it would probably be more pleasant to stay the night in Orońsko than in Radom itself.

Things to See

The Miasto Kazimierzowskie, or the historic town founded by Kazimierz Wielki in the mid-14th century, preserves its layout but not its urban fabric. Possibly the best reminder of those times is the Gothic **parish church**, built in the 1360s.

One block west is the Rynek, today lined with a hotchpotch of buildings, mostly from the 19th century. On its southern side is the overpriced **Regional Museum** (Muzeum Okręgowe), which features a small permanent archaeological collection plus some temporary exhibitions.

East of the old quarter is Radom's new centre, along its main nerve, the 1km-long ul Żeromskiego. Partly closed to the traffic, the street boasts some 19th century neo-classical houses. Near its western end is the late Gothic **Bernardine Church**.

The most interesting city sight is the **skansen** (Muzeum Wsi Radomskiej). It's at ul Szydłowiecka 30, on the south-western outskirts of the city, 9km outside the centre and 1km off the Kielce road. Urban bus Nos 5, 14, 17, E and K from different points of the central area will let you off nearby.

The skansen features examples of traditional rural architecture brought together from all over the region. It has five charming windmills and a cluster of over 100 beehives. A couple of peasants' cottages have been furnished in the original style while other timber houses display exhibitions on local folklore.

From April to October, the skansen is open Tuesday to Friday 9 am to 4 pm, and on Saturday and Sunday 10 am to 6 pm. From November to March, it opens Tuesday to Friday 10 am to 3 pm. There's a café in one of the windmills; in summer, tables are placed outside.

Places to Stay & Eat

Radom has two all-year *youth hostels*, both some distance from the centre. Try the better one (☎ *331 10 06, ul Batalionów Chłopskich 16*), with checking-in time between 6 and 8 pm. If it's full, call the other one (☎ *405 60, ul Miła 18*).

The cheapest central option is probably *Hotel Garnizonowy Iskra* (☎ *362 84 33, ul Planty 4*), opposite the train station, which has doubles without/with bath for US$23/28. Alternatively, you could try *Hotel Karina* (☎ *365 57 69, Al Wojska Polskiego 11*), where singles/doubles with bath and breakfast cost US$24/28. Take bus No 2 from the train station.

Hotel TM (☎/fax 363 27 08, ☎/fax 363 35 53, ul Focha 12) is the best place to stay in the city centre. It costs US$60 a double with bath and breakfast, and has its own restaurant which is good and reasonably priced.

Getting There & Away

The train and bus stations are next to each other, a 15 minute walk south from the

MAŁOPOLSKA

central city mall, ul Żeromskiego. A dozen trains and two dozen buses run to Warsaw (102km). To Lublin (105km) and Puławy (58km), take the bus (seven daily), while to Kielce (85km) it's best to go by train (at least 15 daily). Buses to Szydłowiec (31km) run roughly every hour; the same buses, as well as the urban bus K, will take you to Orońsko (17km).

The Lublin Upland

The Lublin Upland (Wyżyna Lubelska) stretches to the east of the Vistula and San rivers, up to the Ukrainian border. The upland is largely unspoilt, the only city of any size being Lublin. The closer to the eastern border you get, the stronger the Eastern Orthodox influence. Having private transport is useful for exploring more remote areas. Otherwise, you'll probably visit the three important historic towns and the showpieces of the region – Lublin, Kazimierz Dolny and Zamość – and perhaps some of their environs.

LUBLIN
• pop 355,000   ☎ 081

Lublin has always been one of Poland's most important cities. Interestingly, it often seemed to take the lead at crucial historical moments when the country's fate hung in the balance. In 1569 the so-called Lublin Union was signed here, uniting Poland and Lithuania into a single political entity, thus creating the largest European state of the time. In November 1918, the last days of WWI, it was in Lublin that the first government of independent Poland was formed, which soon handed power over to Józef Piłsudski. It was here again that the provisional communist government was installed by the Soviets during the last stages of WWII, in July 1944. Lublin is also considered by some to be the cradle of Solidarity; the avalanche of strikes that in 1980 spread like wildfire throughout Poland and eventually led to the Gdańsk agreements began in Lublin.

Somehow, however, Lublin usually came in second best, a poorer cousin of more illustrious, progressive or simply nicer towns. Even today, when most of the great historical cities have their old quarters beautifully restored or rebuilt, Lublin is still grimly struggling with the task of restoration, and it will be a while before it's completed.

History

Lublin came to life as an outpost protecting Poland from the east, against repeated raids by Tatars, Lithuanians and Ruthenians. In the 12th century, a stronghold was built on the site where the castle stands today. In 1317 Lublin received a municipal charter and soon after the castle and fortified walls were built by Kazimierz Wielki. When the Polish kingdom expanded towards the south-east, the town became an important trading centre and continued to develop. In 1578 the Crown Tribunal, the highest law court of Małopolska, was established here. By the end of the 16th century the population passed the 10,000 mark and the town prospered.

The glorious times ended here. As elsewhere, from the mid-17th century Lublin slid into decline. It revived before WWI, and in 1918 the Lublin Catholic University (commonly known as KUL) was founded. It managed to operate throughout the period of communist rule. Right up until the collapse of communism in 1989, it was the only private university in Eastern Europe.

A Jewish community developed in Lublin in the mid-14th century, and grew so rapidly that some 200 years later the town had the third-largest Jewish population in Poland after Kraków and Lviv. In the mid-18th century Jews formed half of the city's inhabitants, and just before WWII about 30%. Over three dozen synagogues and four Jewish graveyards existed. A visit to the Majdanek death camp will help you to understand what happened later.

Since WWII Lublin has expanded threefold and today it is the largest and most important industrial and educational centre in eastern Poland. Vast, anonymous suburbs and factories have been built all around the historic city.

Luckily, Lublin didn't experience significant wartime damage, so its Old Town has retained much of its historic architectural fabric. However, the early postwar restoration was superficial, and the quarter looks dilapidated and untidy. A more thorough program is currently under way, but it's progressing painfully slowly.

Orientation

Lublin is a fairly big city but as usual you should aim for the centre. Coming by bus you arrive right in the city centre, while the train deposits you, less conveniently, 2km south of the town's heart.

The centre consists of the Old Town, where you'll do most of your sightseeing, and the New Town stretching to the west along its main thoroughfare, ul Krakowskie Przedmieście, where the tourist office is located.

Information

Tourist Office The tourist office (☎ 532 44 12) at ul Krakowskie Przedmieście 78 (open weekdays 9 am to 5 pm, Saturday 10 am to 2 pm) sells maps and is generally helpful.

Money The Bank Pekao at ul Królewska 1, facing the Kraków Gate, changes travellers cheques and gives cash advances on Visa and MasterCard. Bank Depozytowo Kredytowy and Bank Przemysłowo Handlowy, both on ul Krakowskie Przedmieście, handle travellers cheques and Visa card transactions. Plenty of kantors line ul Krakowskie Przedmieście and adjacent streets, and you'll also find several ATMs there.

Email & Internet Access The InterCafé (☎ 743 64 06) is in the basement at ul Graniczna 10.

Old Town

The Old Town (Stare Miasto) is so small and compact that it takes less than an hour to get to know its narrow, winding streets. It's a bit

dilapidated and soulless, as there are few of the shops, cafés, restaurants and other commercial outlets that normally give life and atmosphere to a town. Most streets are unlit and deserted after 8 or 9 pm, and may be positively dangerous. Avoid strolling at night around the area; this also applies to the vicinity of the castle and the bus terminal.

The **Rynek**, built on an irregular plan, is lined with burghers' houses. In the 19th century most of them still had Renaissance parapets and ornamentation but almost all are gone. Instead, third storeys were added here and there, and the façades were newly decorated. With the exception of house No 12 with its preserved Renaissance bas-reliefs, all that you see around you is essentially the work of the 19th and 20th centuries, with the neoclassical style a dominant feature.

In the middle of the Rynek is the **Old Town Hall** (Stary Ratusz), which from 1578 was the seat of the royal tribunal. The oversized neoclassical building you see today is the 1781 work by Domenico Merlini, who was otherwise a good architect, noted for designing the Łazienki Palace in Warsaw. In the splendid cellars of the building is the **Museum of the Crown Tribunal** (Muzeum Trybunału Koronnego), open Wednesday to Saturday 9 am to 4 pm, and Sunday 9 am to 5 pm. Enter from the southern side.

The Old Town was once surrounded by fortified walls, of which the only significant remnant is the **Kraków Gate** (Brama Krakowska). Built in Gothic style, it received an octagonal Renaissance superstructure in the 16th century and a baroque topping in 1782 – you can clearly distinguish these three parts of the tower. Inside, the **Historical Museum of Lublin** (Muzeum Historii Miasta Lublina), open Wednesday to Saturday 9 am to 4 pm, Sunday 9 am to 5 pm, contains old documents, maps, photographs and so on, which refer to the town. More interesting, perhaps, is the view from the top.

A much better view, however, is from the top of the nearby **Trinitarian Tower** (Wieża Trynitarska), which houses the

LUBLIN

Podzamcze

To Zamość

To Lubartów

To Puławy & Warsaw

Al Tysiąclecia

Al Tysiąclecia

Lubartowska

Grodzka

Wodopojna

Królewska

See Lublin – Old Town Map

Al Unii Lubelskiej

Wyszyńskiego

Bernardyńska

Zamojska

To Train Station

Al Zygmuntowskie

26

To Train Station

Ruska

Dolna Panny Marii

Narutowicza

Niecała

Radziwiłłowska

Plac
Litewski

Krakowskie Przedmieście

3 Maja

Chmielna

Ogrodowa

Spokojna

Chopina

Niecała

15

14

5
12 13

16
17

10
11

9

8

7 6

Narutowicza

Górna

Granicza

19

18

Okopowa

Chopina

Lipowa

Nadbystrzycka

Al Piłsudskiego

20

Leszczyńskiego

Ogród Saski

Al Racławickie

Długosza

Popiełuszki

Skłodowskiej-Curie

Radziszewskiego

21

6

5

22

3

23

Obrońców Pokoju

Weteranów

Akademicka

Rauszego

Głęboka

Cemetery

Sowińskiego

24

25

To Puławy
& Warsaw

MAŁOPOLSKA

0   125   250 m

LUBLIN

PLACES TO STAY
1 Motel PZM
2 Hotel Pracowniczy LPBP
3 Youth Hostel
6 Hotel Unia
20 Hotel Victoria
22 Dom Nauczyciela
25 Hotel Studenta Zaocznego UMCS
26 Hotel Bystrzyca

PLACES TO EAT
4 Karczma Słupska
9 Restauracja Resursa
11 Bar Uniwersalny Ludowy
14 Bar Turystyczny
17 Klub Hades

OTHER
5 Lublin Catholic University (KUL)
7 Tourist Office
8 Bank Przemysłowo Handlowy
10 Bank Depozytowo Kredytowy
12 Main Post Office
13 Telecommunication Centre.3
15 Osterwa Theatre
16 Kawiarnia Artystyczna
18 Orbis Office
19 Internet Café
21 Philharmonic Hall & Musical Theatre
23 Marie Curie University (UMSC)
24 Chatka Żaka

Archdiocesan Museum (Muzeum Archiecezjalne), open 10 am to 5 pm except Monday, May to October only.

The square in front of the tower is where the Jesuit monastery stood until the Jesuits were expelled in 1773 and the monastery dismantled. What is left is the former Jesuit Church, dating from the end of the 16th century but largely remodelled later and turned into the **cathedral**. Its neoclassical façade is a bit arid, but go inside to see the baroque frescoes painted all over the walls and vault in the 1750s. These trompe l'œil wall paintings, which look three-dimensional and make the interior seem more spacious, are the work of Moravian artist Józef Majer. Visit the acoustic chapel (kaplica akustyczna), so called because two people standing in opposite corners can whisper and still be heard. Behind the chapel is the treasury (skarbiec), where you can inspect trompe l'œil frescoes by Majer in more detail (those in the chapel are reproductions). Both the chapel and the treasury are open 10 am to 2 pm and 3 to 5 pm, except Monday. The entrance is through the far end of the right-hand aisle of the cathedral.

From the cathedral, pass through the Trinitarian Tower and walk to the **Dominican Church** (Kościół Dominikanów), possibly the finest religious building in the Old Town. Though the church was founded by King Kazimierz Wielki in 1342, it was burnt down twice, rebuilt in Renaissance style and most of its internal fittings later replaced by baroque decoration. It was here that the Lublin Union was signed in 1569. There are some interesting chapels inside the church, including one at the head of the right-hand aisle. On the opposite side of this aisle, near the entrance door, is a large historical painting by an unknown artist around 1740. It depicts the 1719 fire of the city. The church is open only for Mass, in the morning and evening; times are displayed next to the entrance.

Castle

Built atop a hill just north-east of the Old Town, the original 14th century castle was destroyed (apart from its tower and chapel), and what you see today is actually a neo-Gothic prison established in the 1820s and functioning until 1944. During the Nazi occupation, over 100,000 people passed through this building, to be deported later to the death camps.

Most of the edifice is now occupied by the extensive **Lublin Museum** (open Wednesday to Saturday 9 am to 4 pm, Sunday 9 am to 5 pm), which contains several sections including archaeology, ethnography, decorative art, arms, coins and painting. The ethnographic section features fine woodcarving, pottery, basketry, paper cut-outs, Nativity scenes and traditional costumes from the region. The Polish painting section covers works from the 18th century to the present and has several big names including Jacek Malczewski,

LUBLIN – OLD TOWN

PLACES TO STAY
8 Archidiecezjalny Dom Rekolekcyjny
14 Wojewódzki Ośrodek Metodyczny

PLACES TO EAT
6 Kawiarnia Szeroka 28
12 Oberża Artystyczna Złoty Osioł
16 Piwnica u Biesów
17 Bar Staromiejski
22 Bar pod Basztą

OTHER
1 Main Bus Terminal & Hotel PKS
2 Chapel of the Holy Trinity
3 Castle & Lublin Museum
4 Synagogue
5 Grodzka Gate
7 St Adalbert's Church
9 Carmelite Church
10 Memorial to the Jewish Victims
11 Post Office
13 Dominican Church
15 Old Town Hall & Museum of the Crown Tribunal
18 Kraków Gate & Historical Museum of Lublin
19 New Town Hall
20 Church of the Holy Spirit
21 Bank Pekao
23 Trinitarian Tower & Archdiocesan Museum
24 Cathedral
25 Bernardine Church

To Train Station

Witkacy and Tadeusz Kantor, plus two important works by Jan Matejko: the giant *Lublin Union of 1569* and the smaller *Admission of the Jews to Poland in 1096*. The archaeological section has a collection of ceramics from the region, from about 3000 BC to the early centuries AD.

Adjoining the eastern end of the castle is the 14th century **Chapel of the Holy Trinity** (Kaplica Św Trójcy). Its beautiful Gothic vault is supported on a single pillar standing in the middle of the square nave. Its interior is entirely covered with amazing Russo-Byzantine frescoes painted in the 1410s, considered the finest medieval wall paintings in Poland. It's a real gem – don't miss it.

The frescoes were commissioned by King Władysław Jagiełło, who apparently preferred eastern iconography over western style. The frescoes were later plastered over and only discovered in 1897. The complex restoration took (with some breaks) exactly 100 years. The chapel is open for visitors within the museum opening hours.

Majdanek

Majdanek, 4km south-east of Lublin, was one of the largest death camps in Europe. Established in autumn 1941, the camp operated till liberation in July 1944, and during that period some 360,000 people, representing 51 nationalities from 26 countries, were exterminated. Jews were the dominant group – some 100,000 perished here.

Barracks, guard towers and long lines of formerly electrified double barbed wire remain as they were 50 years ago, and you don't need much imagination to feel the horror of those days. What is more difficult to imagine is how people could have sunk to such depths of inhumanity. There is a sobering exhibition, and a small cinema shows documentaries.

Near the road, in front of the camp, is a large monument to the victims of Majdanek, while at the rear of the camp is a domed mausoleum holding their ashes. Both memorials are impressive.

The museum is open daily 8 am to 5 pm except Monday (October to April till 3 pm). Entrance is free. The building at the entrance houses a café, the cinema and a bookshop selling publications about the site, including useful, concise brochures (in English, German and French) with a map and description of the camp. To get to the camp from the Old Town, take trolleybus No 156 from ul Królewska near the Bank Pekao. From Al Racławickie and ul Lipowa, catch trolleybus No 153 or 158.

Jewish Relics

The first census of 1550 recorded 840 Jews in Lublin. In 1939, just before WWII, there were 42,830 Jews, about 8000 of whom survived the war. Today there are at most two dozen Jews living in the city.

The only surviving **synagogue** (of the 38 which functioned before WWII) is at ul Lubartowska 8. It's in an early 20th century building, similar to many others on this street, without any apparent features of a synagogue. The synagogue occupies the 1st floor of the building, as it did before the war. Religious services are now sporadic.

There's a modest exhibition of old photographs, books in Hebrew and ritual objects, which can be visited on Sunday from 1 to 3 pm. Enter the gate from the street and you'll find the door leading upstairs to the synagogue on your right in the passageway.

The **old Jewish cemetery** was established in the first half of the 16th century and today has 30-odd readable tombstones. The oldest of these dates from 1641 and is the oldest Jewish tombstone in Poland in its original location. The graveyard occupies a wooded hill between ul Sienna and ul Kalinowszczyzna, a short walk north-east from the castle. It is surrounded with a high brick wall so you cannot see anything from the outside, and the gate is locked. Contact Józef Honig at his flat at ul Dembowskiego 4 apt 17 (☎ 747 86 76), 200m north of the cemetery; he has the keys and will show you around (leave a donation).

The **new Jewish cemetery** was founded in 1828, and about 52,000 Jews were buried here until 1942. The cemetery was devastated by the Nazis and there are no tombs except for a few very damaged ones. In 1991 a modern concrete mausoleum was erected behind the entrance, and it houses a small museum dedicated to the history of the Lublin Jewry. The new graveyard is on ul Walecznych, a 10 minute walk north from the old one. The graveyard and the museum can be visited daily at any time during daylight – there is a 24 hour guard on duty.

If you are interested in the Jewish legacy of Lublin and the region, buy the English-language brochure titled *The Traces of Monuments of Jewish Culture in the Lublin Region* by Andrzej Trzciński, available from the tourist office-shop. The practical information is pretty much out of date, but the description of the sights is correct and detailed.

Skansen

Lublin has an interesting skansen, about 5km west of the city centre, on the Warsaw road. Covering an undulating terrain of 25 hectares, it has half a dozen old farmsteads with fully equipped interiors, open to visitors. It all looks like a natural traditional village. There's also a fine manor house, a windmill and a carved timber gate of 1903 designed by Stanisław Witkiewicz (refer to the Zakopane section in the Carpathian Mountains chapter).

The skansen is open April to October, Tuesday to Saturday 10 am to 5 pm, Sunday 10 am to 6 pm. The ticket office closes an hour earlier. The guide will show you around, opening the interiors one by one as your group proceeds. To get to the skansen from the centre, take bus No 18 from ul Krakowskie Przedmieście anywhere west of Plac Litewski.

Places to Stay

Lublin has quite a choice of places to stay and many of them are fairly inexpensive. The other side of the coin is that most are pretty ordinary and some distance from the centre, involving the use of public transport or at least a long walk.

Places to Stay – Budget

Camping There are three camping grounds in the city; all have bungalows and are open May to September, and all are pretty far out. The closest one is *Camping Nr 91 Na Sławinku* (☎ 741 22 31, ul Sławinkowska 46), about 5km west of the centre, close to the skansen (bus No 18 from the bus terminal, bus No 20 from the train station).

The other two camping grounds are both on an artificial lake, the Zalew Zemborzycki, about 8km south of the centre. *Camping Nr 65 Marina* (☎ 744 10 70, ul Krężnicka 6) is accessible by bus No 8 from ul Narutowicza opposite the Osterwa Theatre in the centre. From the main train station, take bus No 17, 20, 21 or 27 to the Stadion Sygnał and change for bus No 25. *Camping Nr 35 Dąbrowa* (☎ 744 08 31, ul Nad Zalewem 12) is right across the lake from the Marina, but a long way around. There's no direct public transport from either the centre or the train station.

Hostels & Hotels The all-year, 80-bed *youth hostel* (☎ 533 06 28, ul Długosza 6)

is 2km west of the Old Town (take trolleybus No 150 from the train station, bus Nos 5, 10, 18, 31 and 57 from the bus terminal). Just a five minute walk south of the youth hostel is *Dom Nauczyciela* (☎ 533 82 85, ul Akademicka 4), a clean and cheap teachers' hostel, costing US$12/18 a single/double without bath. It's often full.

There are two budget places to stay in the Old Town, but it's hard to find a vacancy there. The 28-bed *Wojewódzki Ośrodek Metodyczny* (☎ 743 61 33, ul Dominikańska 5) charges US$9 per person in a four or five-bed dorm with bath. You have more chance of getting shelter at *Archidiecezjalny Dom Rekolekcyjny* (☎ 532 41 38, ul Podwale 15). Two to seven-bed dorms (some with bath) cost US$7 per person, and you can get budget meals on the premises. Behave like a Good Samaritan – this is a Catholic Church institution.

The simple *Motel PZM* (☎ 533 42 32, ul Prusa 8) is nothing special but it's within walking distance of the Old Town. Singles/doubles without bath cost US$12/ 20, or US$26/28 with bath.

Some student dorms near the Almatur office (☎ 533 32 37, ul Langiewicza 10) open as *student hostels* in summer. The office may have some information about that; otherwise inquire at the tourist office. More reliable student accommodation is at the all-year *Hotel Studenta Zaocznego UMCS* (☎ 525 10 81, ul Sowińskiego 17). It offers singles/doubles/triples for US$20/23/ 26. One bathroom is shared by two adjacent rooms.

If you can't find anything in any of the above, you'll probably have to resort to lodging offered by workers' hotels. There are several of these unsavoury options, all located in drab blocks, scattered throughout the city. Their main clientele are visitors from across the eastern border who worry less about the standard than the price. The most central of these is *Hotel Pracowniczy LPBP* (☎ 747 44 07, ul Podzamcze 7), 500m north-east of the bus terminal. A double/triple/quad with shared facilities costs US$12/14/16. Bus Nos 17 and 33 from the train station area will drop you off at the hotel's door.

If you're arriving late or tired by train, you can try the basic *Hotel Piast* (☎ *532 16 46, ul Pocztowa 2*), next to the train station. Singles/doubles/triples with shared facilities cost US$13/17/23, or you can pay US$7 a bed in a four or five-bed dorm. Similarly, if you're coming by bus, there's a convenient but basic *Hotel PKS* (☎ *747 87 01, Al Tysiąclecia 6*) in the bus terminal. It costs US$12/18/24.

Places to Stay – Mid-Range & Top End

Hotel Bystrzyca (☎ *532 30 03, Al Zygmuntowskie 4*), 1km north of the train station (a 10 minute walk), is the former sports dorm. It costs US$20/27/32; one bathroom is shared by two rooms. The quiet *Hotel Garnizonowy* (☎ *533 05 36, ul Spadochroniarzy 7*), 3km west of the Old Town, has neat rooms with bath for US$34/40/44.

Better and more convenient is *Hotel Victoria* (☎ *532 70 11, fax 532 90 26, ul Narutowicza 58/60*), which has fairly comfortable if noisy singles/doubles with bath for US$65/100.

The best place in town is the Orbis-run *Hotel Unia* (☎ *533 20 61, fax 533 35 01, Al Racławickie 12*), 1.5km west of the Old Town. It costs about US$120/140, breakfast included (weekend rates are about 20% lower). Like most Orbis joints, it's overpriced, but in Lublin it doesn't have to worry about this as it has no competitors.

Places to Eat

There are still a few milk bars, including *Bar Staromiejski* (*ul Jezuicka 1*) next to the Kraków Gate, and *Bar Turystyczny* (*ul Krakowskie Przedmieście 29*). Both are basic. Better places for a budget lunch include *Bar Uniwersalny Ludowy* (*ul Krakowskie Przedmieście 60*) and *Bar pod Basztą* (*ul Królewska 6*).

If you are staying in the youth hostel, you can eat in the nearby *Karczma Słupska* (*Al Racławickie 22*), which has acceptably cheap food.

There are finally some interesting eating establishments in the Old Town, which until recently was almost a culinary ghost town. *Oberża Artystyczna Złoty Osioł* (*ul Grodzka 5A*) has a pleasant interior and a cosy inner garden, and serves hearty food and drinks. The newer *Kawiarnia Szeroka 28* (*ul Grodzka 21*) also has much artistic charm and some good food. A little cheaper is another charming place, *Piwnica u Biesów* (*Rynek 18*), in the cellar (enter through the best doorway on the square). It is essentially a drinking establishment but it has a reasonable food menu.

For a more upmarket lunch or dinner (but probably less atmosphere), you may consider *Restauracja Resursa* (*Krakowskie Przedmieście 68*) or *Klub Hades* (*ul Peowiaków 12*) in the basement of a large building of the Cultural Centre (Dom Kultury). The club has a restaurant, open noon till 3 am, and an adjacent bar with pool tables. Access to both is restricted to club members, but the manager will probably let you in.

Entertainment

The major local daily paper, the *Kurier Lubelski*, has listings of what's on. The tourist office may also help.

For classical music, check the program of *Filharmonia Lubelska* (*ul Skłodowskiej-Curie 5*) at its huge, brand-new hall. The *Teatr Muzyczny* also stages operettas and a variety of musical events in the hall. The main city venue for drama is *Teatr im Osterwy* (*ul Narutowicza 17*), featuring mostly classical plays with some emphasis on national drama.

Theatre buffs may be interested in the experimental *Gardzienice Theatre*, one of the most outstanding companies currently performing in Poland. Each of its productions is a whirl of sights and sounds performed barefoot by candlelight with reckless energy and at breakneck speed, accompanied by music and singing by the actors themselves. Established in 1977 in the small village of Gardzienice, 28km south-east of Lublin, the theatre is based and performs there, but has an office (☎ 532 98 40, ☎ 532 96 37) in Lublin at ul Grodzka 5A. Getting to see this company is not easy. It is often abroad and, when at home, only performs on weekends, to an audience small enough to be packed into its tiny theatre. You need to book well in advance.

As for lighter fare, Kawiarnia Artystyczna of *Klub Hades* has live music (rock, jazz etc) and discos on Friday. The club organises the three day Hades Jazz Festival in late October.

Chatka Żaka (ul Radziszewskiego 16) is the student club of the Marie Curie University, which has cultural events on some days. Behind the Chatka is a popular student disco, the *Art-Bis-Club*.

Getting There & Away

Train The main train station, Lublin Główny, is linked to the Old Town by trolleybus No 160 and several buses including Nos 13 and 17. There are at least half a dozen fast trains daily to Warsaw (175km), Radom (128km) and Kielce (213km), and two fast trains to Kraków (345km). Tickets can be bought directly from the station or from the Orbis office at ul Narutowicza 33A. Ordinary trains to Chełm (75km) depart every one or two hours.

Bus The central bus terminal, Dworzec Główny PKS, is at the foot of the castle near the Old Town and handles most of the traffic. Buses to Kazimierz Dolny (44km) run every hour or so (look for the Puławy bus via Nałęczów and Kazimierz). To Zamość (89km), PKS buses run every half-hour, and there are also private minibuses departing every 20 minutes from just behind the terminal.

There are three buses daily to Sandomierz (110km) – look for the Tarnobrzeg bus in the timetable. Buses to Chełm (68km) run approximately every other hour. Every morning a fast bus goes directly to Kraków (269km). A Polski Express bus goes to Warsaw every other hour.

There are two morning buses to Kozłówka (38km), and then nothing until

about 3 pm. They are hard to find in the timetable – ask at the information counter.

Four buses a day to Przemyśl (185km) depart from the south terminal next to the train station.

KOZŁÓWKA

The hamlet of Kozłówka ('Koz-woof-kah'), 38km north of Lublin, is famous for its magnificent late baroque palace. Built in the mid-18th century, the residence was acquired by the wealthy Zamoyski family in 1799. The palace was then extended and remodelled and its interior fitted out in sumptuous pseudo-rococo style. The new owner's collection of 1000 paintings proved difficult to accommodate, and pictures were placed on every available bit of wall, bathrooms included.

Things to See

Much of the palace's original decoration has been preserved and can be seen in the **palace museum**. You will be guided around the opulent rooms fitted out with period furnishings, ceramic stoves, crystal mirrors etc. The most striking feature is the paintings, each one complete with its own distinct ornate frame. The pictures date mostly from the 17th to 19th centuries (the oldest is from 1672) and aren't necessarily valuable pieces of art; many are copies. Yet the sheer quantity – about 360 on display – makes for a very unusual sight.

Kozłówka is also known country-wide for its unique **socialist-realist gallery**, displayed in one of the palace's side wings. Socialist realism originated in the 1920s in the Soviet Union and became the only accepted style in the visual arts, architecture and literature by the mid-1930s. After WWII, it spread widely throughout the countries of the eastern bloc including Poland, where it came to be the official artistic doctrine until 1954. A huge body of paintings, sculptures, monuments, poems and songs was produced, but later on, when the Stalinist lunacy subsided, these works of 'art' were discreetly removed from public view and put into the confines of warehouses. Kozłówka was one of the major recipients.

Today it's all back on the walls and pedestals, but as museum pieces. You will find here the whole pantheon of beloved comrades, including Stalin, Lenin, Marx and Mao Zedong, plus most Polish revolutionary communist leaders. There's also a collection of paintings depicting everyday scenes from communist life – a typical theme of the style. The canvases are tightly packed all over the walls – a bizarre bridge to the Zamoyski painting collection in the palace.

The palace is open April to November, on Tuesday, Thursday and Friday 10 am to 4 pm, and on Wednesday, Saturday and Sunday 10 am to 5 pm. Weekdays are normally intended for prebooked excursions, but individual tourists can usually tag along with one of the groups. On weekends, individual visitors have priority.

All visits to the palace are guided in groups which depart on the hour and take 45 minutes, but there may be more tours if there is a demand. The socialist-realist gallery can be visited individually, before or after the palace tour, as you wish. To round off your visit, take a stroll about the garden and park stretching behind the palace. Watch out for a huge statue of Bolesław Bierut standing among the trees near the palace. There's a café beside the gallery.

Getting There & Away

The usual departure point for Kozłówka is Lublin – see that section for transport details. Returning to Lublin, there are buses in the afternoon roughly every hour, or you can hang around the car park for a lift with any of the motorised visitors. There are also four buses a day to Puławy.

PUŁAWY
- **pop 55,000**   ☎ 081

Puławy ('Poo-wah-vi') reached its golden age at the end of the 18th century when the Czartoryski family, one of the big aristocratic Polish clans, made it an important centre of political, cultural and intellectual life. Prince Adam Kazimierz Czartoryski and his

wife Izabela accumulated a large library and a collection of works of art, and surrounded themselves with artists and writers.

After the failure of the November Insurrection of 1830, which was strongly backed by the Czartoryskis, the whole estate was confiscated by the tsar, and the family had to flee the country. The art collection was secretly moved to Paris. In the 1870s it was brought back to Poland, but to Kraków, not Puławy, and today it constitutes the core of the Kraków Czartoryski Museum.

After WWII a huge nitrate combine was built near Puławy and the town has become a badly polluted industrial centre.

Information

There's no genuine tourist office in Puławy. If in need, try the PTTK office (☎ 886 47 56) at ul Czartoryskich 8A, at the entrance to the Czartoryski park-and-palace complex.

The Bank Pekao is at Al Królewska 11A, close to the Czartoryski palace. There are several kantors in the centre, including a few on ul Piłsudskiego.

Things to See

The **Czartoryski palace**, designed by the ubiquitous Tylman van Gameren and erected in 1676-79, was later altered quite substantially and eventually ended up as a sober, late neoclassical building. Now the home of an agricultural research institute, it is not a tourist sight but nobody will pay attention if you have a discreet look inside. Enter through the main central door, turn to the right and go up the staircase to the 1st floor to see the only two rooms worth a glimpse, the music hall and the Gothic hall.

The **landscape park** that surrounds the palace is more attractive. Founded in the late 18th century by Princess Izabela, it is a typical romantic park of the era (similar to the Arkadia park in Mazovia) and incorporates several pavilions and buildings. The Temple of the Sybil (Świątynia Sybilli) and the Gothic House (Domek Gotycki) both date from the early 19th century and are used as exhibition grounds from May to October (open 10 am to 4 pm except

Monday). A map of the park showing the location of important sights is displayed at the entrance.

The **regional museum** at ul Czartoryskich 6A, 200m north of the palace, features ethnographic and archaeological exhibits, plus temporary displays, some of which are related to the Czartoryski family. It is open 10 am to 2 pm except Monday.

Some 200m to the west, on ul Piłsudskiego, is the **Czartoryski chapel**, modelled on the Roman Pantheon and built in 1801-03. The circular, domed interior has lost its original furnishings and decoration. Today it's a parish church.

Places to Stay & Eat

Puławy has quite a choice of accommodation, and you might need to use some of it if you can't find anywhere to stay in Kazimierz Dolny; otherwise you probably won't be interested in hanging around the town for long.

The cheapest option is the all-year *youth hostel* (☎ 886 33 67, ul Włostowicka 27), 2km out of the centre on the Kazimierz Dolny road. Don't come back into the centre if you're heading for Kazimierz – catch the bus near the entrance of the hostel.

Wojewódzki Ośrodek Metodyczny (☎ 887 42 77, ul Kołłątaja 1), opposite the Czartoryski chapel, has singles with bath for US$18 and doubles without bath for US$22. Just behind it is *Motel PZM* (☎ 887 42 01, ul Piłsudskiego 15), which has doubles with shower (but toilet outside) for US$20. Better value is *Hotel Wisła* (☎ 886 27 37, ul Wróblewskiego 1), in the centre, which offers airy doubles/triples with bath for US$24/30, and has its own restaurant.

The renovated *Dom Turysty PTTK* (☎ 887 40 48, ul Rybacka 7) beside the Vistula River, 1km west of the centre, now costs US$32/44/50 for singles/doubles/triples with bath and breakfast. You'll pay much the same at *Centrum Szkoleniowo-Kongresowe Instytutu Uprawy, Nawożenia i Gleboznawstwa* (☎/fax 887 73 06, Al Królewska 17), 200m from the palace. Marginally cheaper is the central *Hotel Izabella*

(☎ 886 30 41, fax 887 99 89, ul Lubelska 1). All three have their own restaurants.

If all you need is a straightforward lunch, go to the *Bufet* in the basement of the Urząd Rejonowy, a brick building opposite the palace, which serves cheap, tasty meals until 3.30 pm on weekdays.

Getting There & Away

Train The town has two train stations: Puławy and Puławy Miasto. The latter is the main one and is closer to the centre, yet it's still nearly 2km north-east of the central area. It is serviced by city buses; otherwise use taxis.

At least one train per hour leaves for Lublin (50km) but it's more convenient to travel by bus, which goes centre-to-centre. Trains to Warsaw (125km) run roughly every other hour. For Kraków (294km), there is only one morning and one evening train, but several fast trains go to Radom (78km) and on to Kielce (157km), from where the transport to Kraków is regular.

Bus The PKS bus terminal is close to the centre and is pretty busy. PKS buses to Lublin (47km) depart every half-hour, but the service to Warsaw (127km) is less frequent. Both these destinations are also serviced by Polski Express, with seven departures a day to each. There are half a dozen PKS buses to Radom (58km), four to Łódź (193km) and one to Zamość (136km). There are also three morning buses to Lubartów which will let you off at Kozłówka.

For Kazimierz Dolny (13km), PKS buses leave at least every hour, but you should also check the schedule of suburban bus No 12 in front of the terminal and take the one that goes first. Do the same if you head for Janowiec (choosing between PKS and city bus No 17).

KAZIMIERZ DOLNY
• pop 4000   ☎ 081

Set on the bank of the Vistula at the foot of wooded hills, Kazimierz Dolny is a small, picturesque town with much charm and atmosphere. It has some fine historic architecture, good museums and attractive countryside. For many years Kazimierz has attracted artists and intellectuals, and you will almost always see painters with their easels here.

Kazimierz has become a fashionable weekend and holiday spot for tourists, mainly from Warsaw, which gives it a noticeable split personality – from a quiet, sleepy, old-fashioned village on weekdays and off season, it turns into a hive of activity on summer weekends.

History
The formal founding of the town is attributed to King Kazimierz Wielki (hence its name), who in the 14th century gave it a municipal charter with numerous privileges attached, and built the castle. The town was called Dolny (lower), to distinguish it from upriver Kazimierz, today part of Kraków.

The town soon became a port and commercial centre. Merchandise from the whole region, principally grain and salt, was shipped down to Gdańsk and farther on for export. Kazimierz enjoyed particularly good times between the mid-16th and mid-17th centuries. A large port, a number of splendid burghers' mansions and nearly 50 granaries were built in that period, and the population passed the 2500 mark by 1630.

The Swedish Deluge, then the Northern War and the cholera epidemic of 1708, brought an end to the town's prosperity, and the displacement of the Vistula bed farther towards the west, away from the town, accelerated its economic decline. By the 19th century, Puławy overshadowed Kazimierz as both a trade and a cultural centre. A small scale revival as a tourist spot began at the end of the 19th century, but then came WWI and WWII, both of which caused serious damage to Kazimierz. After the war, a development plan aimed at preserving the town in line with its historical character was approved, and many old buildings have since been restored.

The history of Kazimierz, like that of the whole region, is intimately linked with Jewish culture. From the town's beginnings, Jews formed an important and expanding part of the community, becoming the majority during the 19th century. Before WWII they formed over half the town's population, but only a handful survived the war. About 3000 Jews from Kazimierz and its environs ended their lives in the Nazi death camps.

Information
The PTTK office (☎ 81 00 46) at Rynek 27 has information about the town and sells brochures and maps. From May to September, the office is open weekdays 8 am to 6 pm, Saturday 10 am to 5.30 pm. For the rest of the year it closes at 3.30 pm on weekdays and 2 pm on Saturday.

There are no banks in town; the nearest are in Puławy. There's just one kantor, in the post office building at ul Tyszkiewicza 2.

Things to See
The **Rynek**, with an old wooden well in the middle, is lined with merchants' houses, of which the finest are the two arcaded **Houses of the Przybyła Brothers** (Kamienice Przybyłów). Built in 1615, both of them have rich Renaissance façade decoration with bas-relief figures of the owners' patron saints, St Nicholas and St Christopher, and are topped by ornamented parapets. Also on the Rynek are the baroque-style **Gdańsk House** (Kamienica Gdańska) from 1795, and several characteristic arcaded houses with wooden-tiled roofs, dating from the 18th and 19th centuries.

There's another fine historic building, the 1630 **House of the Celej Family** (Kamienica Celejowska), at ul Senatorska 17. It shelters the **Town Museum** (Muzeum Kazimierza Dolnego) which features paintings of Kazimierz and its surroundings. Also here (temporarily) is the **Museum of Goldsmithery** (Muzeum Sztuki Złotniczej), which has a collection of gold and silverwork, including Judaic cult silverware and jewellery, mostly from the 17th to 19th centuries. From October to April, the museums are open 10 am to 3 pm; from

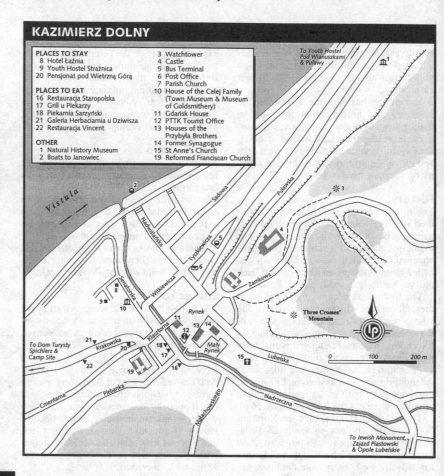

KAZIMIERZ DOLNY

PLACES TO STAY
8 Hotel Łaźnia
9 Youth Hostel Strażnica
20 Pensjonat pod Wietrzną Górą

PLACES TO EAT
16 Restauracja Staropolska
17 Grill u Piekarzy
18 Piekarnia Sarzyński
21 Galeria Herbaciarnia u Dziwisza
22 Restauracja Vincent

OTHER
1 Natural History Museum
2 Boats to Janowiec
3 Watchtower
4 Castle
5 Bus Terminal
6 Post Office
7 Parish Church
10 House of the Celej Family
   (Town Museum & Museum
   of Goldsmithery)
11 Gdańsk House
12 PTTK Tourist Office
13 Houses of the
   Przybyła Brothers
14 Former Synagogue
15 St Anne's Church
19 Reformed Franciscan Church

MAŁOPOLSKA

May to September they close at 4 pm. They
are closed on Monday and the day following public holidays.

Set on the nearby hill is the **Reformed
Franciscan Church** (Kościół Reformatów).
It was built at the end of the 16th century
but lost its original style with subsequent
baroque and neoclassical decorations. Its
courtyard offers a nice view over the town.

The Gothic **parish church** on the opposite
side of the Rynek was built in the mid-14th
century but was remodelled when the Re-

naissance style flooded Poland. Of particular
interest in its interior is the ornate carved
organ from 1620, which sounds as good as it
looks; organ recitals are held here. Also note
the Renaissance stalls in the chancel and the
stucco decoration of the nave's vault, a
classic example of the so-called Lublin-
Renaissance style, typical of the whole
region. Looking up, don't miss the unusual
chandelier featuring the stag's antlers.

Up ul Zamkowa is the **castle** or, more
precisely, what is left of it. Built in the 14th

century, it was partly destroyed by the Swedes, and later gradually fell into ruin. Only fragments of the walls remain.

The **watchtower**, 200m up the hill, was built a century before the castle as a part of the wooden fortifications, which no longer exist. It's 20m high and its walls are 4m thick at the base. For security, the entrance was built 6m above the ground and access was by ladders, but wooden stairs were later built. There's a panoramic view once you reach the top.

Don't go down the same way to the Rynek; take the path to the left leading to **Three Crosses' Mountain** (Góra Trzech Krzyży). The crosses were erected in the early 18th century to commemorate the plague that decimated the town's population. The view over the town is even better than from the watchtower. The path down will lead you directly to the parish church and on to the Rynek.

Have a glimpse at the 18th century **synagogue** on ul Lubelska, rebuilt after the war and turned into a cinema. Just behind it is the reconstructed wooden building which used to house the Jewish butchers' stalls. This area was once the Jewish quarter but not much is left of it.

Perhaps the most moving reminder of the Jewish legacy is the **Jewish monument** raised in 1984 in homage to the Jews murdered in Kazimierz during WWII. It's a large concrete wall covered by several hundred tombstones and tombstone fragments from the old cemetery, which was just behind the wall. There are still some finely carved tombstones *in situ*, worth looking around. The monument is a little over 1km from the Rynek, on the road to Opole Lubelskie.

On the opposite side of town, on the Puławy road, is the **Natural History Museum** (Muzeum Przyrodnicze), open the same hours as the two other museums. It is housed in a large, finely restored granary dating from 1591, and has mineralogy and flora and fauna sections. When you get to the top floor, look up at the intricate wooden structure supporting the roof – an exquisite example of 16th century engineering. The massive beams have been joined by wooden pegs only – no nails were used.

Only a few **granaries** have survived out of a total of nearly 50. Most were built in the 16th and 17th centuries, during a boom in the grain trade. Apart from the one listed above and its neighbour just 50m away, there's a good example on ul Krakowska, which is now a hotel (Dom Turysty Spichlerz).

Hiking

The area around Kazimierz has been decreed the Kazimierz Landscape Park (Kazimierski Park Krajobrazowy). Many walking trails are traced in the countryside, and in places they wind through the gorges which are a feature of the region.

There are three easy short trails known as *szlaki spacerowe* (walking routes) signposted in yellow, green and red, and three significantly longer treks called *szlaki turystyczne* (tourist routes) marked in blue, green and red. Almost all these routes originate in the Rynek. The tourist office sells maps of the park, which have trails marked on them.

Special Events

The highly acclaimed Festival of Folk Bands and Singers takes place during the last week of June, from Friday to Sunday. Concerts are held on the Mały Rynek, while the main Rynek fills up with handicraft stalls. The festival offers an opportunity to listen to kinds of music you rarely hear nowadays. Dozens of amateur groups perform, ranging from soloists to large choirs, and they all wear the traditional costumes of their regions.

Kazimierz also hosts a relaxing Film and Art Festival in August, with classical music concerts, art exhibitions and outdoor film shows.

Places to Stay & Eat

Kazimierz has plenty of places to stay, yet you might face some problems on summer

MAŁOPOLSKA

weekends. At the budget end, there are two all-year youth hostels: the good *Pod Wianuszkami* (☎ 81 03 27, ul Puławska 64) on the Puławy road about 1.5km from the Rynek, and the very central but more basic *Strażnica* (☎ 81 04 27, ul Senatorska 23A) in the building of the fire brigade station.

Camping Nr 36 (☎ 81 00 36) behind Dom Turysty Spichlerz is open May to September. It has no cabins. The PTTK office on Rynek arranges accommodation in *private rooms* (US$6 to US$8 per person).

Hotel-type accommodation includes *Zajazd Piastowski* (☎ 81 03 51, ul Słoneczna 3) at US$20/28/36 a single/ double/triple, *Hotel Łaźnia* (☎ 81 02 98, ul Senatorska 21) at US$34/48/58 and *Dom Turysty Spichlerz* (☎ 81 00 36, ul Krakowska 61) at US$48 a double.

Alternatively, try the small *Pensjonat pod Wietrzną Górą* (☎ 81 05 43, ul Krakowska 1) at US$18 per person. All four have reasonable restaurants, and there are more places to stay and eat around the town.

Several cafés on and around the Rynek serve simple meals. The bakery *Piekarnia Sarzyński* (ul Nadrzeczna 6) has delicious rolls and bread, including some unusual bread in the shape of roosters, crayfish and other animals. Next door is *Grill u Piekarzy* which serves budget meals. The nearby *Restauracja Staropolska* (ul Nadrzeczna 14) has good food and copious portions, though its prices have gone up.

Galeria Herbaciarnia u Dziwisza (ul Krakowska 6) is a charming, cosy place recommended for good tea (80-odd flavours to choose from). Diagonally opposite is perhaps the best eatery in town, *Restauracja Vincent* (ul Krakowska 11/13).

Getting There & Away

Kazimierz can be conveniently visited as a stop on your Lublin-Warsaw route, or as a day trip from Lublin. There's no railway in Kazimierz but the bus service is OK.

Bus The PKS bus terminal is a two minute walk from the Rynek and has a service to Puławy (13km) every half-hour or so. The similarly frequent Puławy urban bus No 12 can take you directly to the Puławy train station. Buses to Lublin (44km) go roughly every hour, taking nearly two hours to get there. There are about five fast buses daily straight to Warsaw (140km), taking 3½ hours, or go to Puławy and change for the train.

Boat A pleasure boat to Janowiec, on the opposite side of the Vistula, runs in summer if there are passengers interested – ask at the wharf at the end of ul Nadwiślańska.

There's also a car/passenger ferry from May to September. Its departure point is a 10 minute walk west of the camp site.

JANOWIEC
- pop 1000   ☎ 081

The village of Janowiec ('Yah-no-vyets'), 2km upstream on the other side of the Vistula from Kazimierz Dolny, is known for its **castle**. Built at the beginning of the 16th century by the Firlej family and gradually extended during the next century by the subsequent owners, the Tarło and Lubomirski families, it grew to have over 100 rooms and became one of the largest and most splendid castles in Poland. Many prominent architects, including Santi Gucci and Tylman van Gameren, had a hand in the castle's development.

The castle went into decline in the 19th century and was largely destroyed during WWI and WWII. It was the only private castle in Poland under communist rule until its owner donated it to the state in 1975. By then, it was a genuine ruin.

While it's still a ruin, much has changed over recent years. Intensive work has been going on and has given the castle back some of its rooms and portions of the walls, complete with vaults, arcades and external painted decoration. The latter is possibly its most striking feature; the walls have been painted with horizontal white and red strips and grotesque human figures. It all looks like a modern-art joke, but reputedly isn't; historians say that's how the original castle was adorned.

Some of the restored rooms house an exhibition related to the castle's history. Other rooms, still under reconstruction, are destined to be a hotel and café, which may already be in operation by the time you read this.

In the park beside the castle is a **manor house** from the 1760s, fitted out with period furnishings and decoration. It's open as a **museum**, giving an insight into how Polish nobility once lived. Among the outbuildings surrounding the manor is an old two-storey granary, which has an interesting **ethnographic exhibition** that features old fishing boats, ceramics, tools and household implements.

All the exhibitions (including that in the castle) are open daily 10 am to 3 pm except Monday (May to September till 5 pm).

It's also worth going downhill to the village of Janowiec, at the foot of the castle, to visit its mid-14th century Gothic **parish church**, extensively rebuilt in Renaissance style in the 1530s. Inside is the tomb of the Firlej family, carved in the workshop of Santi Gucci in 1586-87.

Places to Stay & Eat

There are seven double rooms with bath in the *manor house* (☎ 881 52 28), rented out for US$8 a head. As previously mentioned, hotel rooms in the *castle* may be ready by 1999. For a meal, go to the *Karczma Czarna Dama* at the village's Rynek.

Getting There & Away

You can visit Janowiec from Kazimierz Dolny, by pleasure boat or ferry. Alternatively, there is a regular service from/to Puławy (13km) by urban bus No 17 and PKS buses.

CHEŁM

- **pop 69,000**   ☎ 082

Chełm ('Helm') is a mid-sized town about 70km east of Lublin, not far from the Ukrainian border. It's way off the popular tourist tracks, but it doesn't take much effort to include it in your Lublin-Zamość route.

Chełm was founded in the 10th century and, like most towns along the eastern border, it shifted between the Polish Piast crown and the Kievan duchy on various occasions. King Kazimierz Wielki eventually got hold of the area in 1366 and Władysław Jagiełło established a bishopric here some 50 years later.

At about that time Jews began to settle in the town, and the multi-ethnic community relied for its economic development on rich deposits of chalk; Chełm sits on a layer of almost pure chalk 800m thick. The Jewish population swiftly grew in strength and number – by the end of the 18th century they accounted for 60% of the town's population. At that time there were 49 houses lining the market square, and 47 of them belonged to Jews.

As happened elsewhere in the country, Chełm's good times ended in the 17th century – the period of wars, ravages and Poland's general decline. The town suffered from the invading armies of, consecutively, Cossacks, Muscovites, Swedes and Transylvanians. Most of the buildings fell into ruin and, consequently, the current urban fabric features few architectural monuments older than 300 years. Later came the Partitions, and Chełm fell under first Austrian then Russian occupation.

It wasn't until WWI that the town began to recover as part of independent Poland, only to experience the horrors of WWII two decades later, including the mass execution of Jews, whose population had grown by that time to about 17,000.

Information

The Ośrodek Informacji Turystycznej (☎ 565 36 67, fax 565 41 85), ul Lubelska 20, is open weekdays 8 am to 4 pm, and Saturday 9 am to 2 pm.

The Bank Pekao is at ul I Armii WP 41, but there's a more central ATM in the Bank Spółdzielczy at ul Lwowska 11. Kantors are in reasonable supply but they may give lower rates than you'll get in Lublin.

The Internet Café Dobrex (☎ 565 42 69) is at ul Kopernika 3.

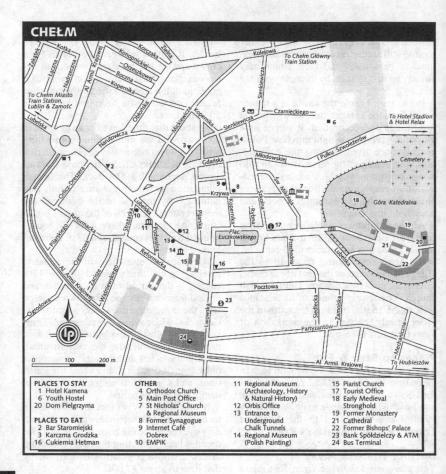

CHEŁM

PLACES TO STAY
1 Hotel Kamena
6 Youth Hostel
20 Dom Pielgrzyma

PLACES TO EAT
2 Bar Staromiejski
3 Karczma Grodzka
16 Cukiernia Hetman

OTHER
4 Orthodox Church
5 Main Post Office
7 St Nicholas' Church & Regional Museum
8 Former Synagogue
9 Internet Café Dobrex
10 EMPiK

11 Regional Museum (Archaeology, History & Natural History)
12 Orbis Office
13 Entrance to Underground Chalk Tunnels
14 Regional Museum (Polish Painting)

15 Piarist Church
17 Tourist Office
18 Early Medieval Stronghold
19 Former Monastery
21 Cathedral
22 Former Bishops' Palace
23 Bank Spółdzielczy & ATM
24 Bus Terminal

Things to See

Chełm lies on a plain with a conspicuous hill called the Góra Katedralna (Cathedral Mountain) right in the middle. The first settlement and stronghold were on top of the mountain. Nothing is left of this apart from a distinctly recognisable man-made elevation.

Today, the hill is crowned with a large **cathedral** surrounded by a complex of religious buildings that were once a bishops' palace and a monastery. The cathedral is a late baroque basilica, remodelled from a Uniate church built here in the mid-18th century. The interior is sober and lacks much decoration, except for the silver antependium at the high altar, which shows Polish knights paying homage to Our Lady of Chełm. The picture of the lady herself overlooks the altar. It's a replica; the original hasn't survived.

Far more impressive is the former **Piarist Church** (Kościół Pijarski), next to the Rynek (called Plac Łuczkowskiego). This

MAŁOPOLSKA

twin-towered late baroque church was built on an oval plan in the mid-18th century. Once you enter through the massive ornamented doors, you'll find yourself enveloped in a colourful interior, with wall paintings covering every square centimetre of the walls and vaults. This trompe l'œil decoration was executed in 1758 by Józef Mayer, the same artist who embellished Lublin's cathedral. The furnishing is remarkably homogeneous: the high altar (note the ornate frame with the picture of Our Lady of Chełm – another copy), pulpit, organ and side altars are all in rococo style. Today it's the parish church.

The former monastery next door (ul Lubelska 55) houses the Regional Museum (Muzeum Okręgowe), which features a collection of modern Polish painting. It is open Tuesday to Friday 10 am to 4 pm, and Saturday and Sunday 11 am to 3 pm. The museum has two other outlets (open the same hours). The branch at ul Lubelska 57 has sections on archaeology, history and natural history. The other one, in the St Nicholas' Chapel at ul Św Mikołaja 4, stages temporary exhibitions. Concerts of classical music are held here at times.

Chełm's star attraction is its underground chalk tunnels (Podziemia Kredowe), an array of the old chalk passages hewn out by hand about 12m below ground level. Reputedly the world's only underground chalk mine, it started in medieval times, and by the 16th century was known nationally for the excellent quality of the local chalk. By 1939 a multilevel labyrinth of corridors grew to a total length of 15km. They effectively undermined the town and became a real danger. Following the collapse of a building and part of a street in 1965, the mine was closed and the voids were silted up, except for an 1800m stretch which was strengthened and opened as a tourist attraction.

The entrance to the tunnels is at ul Lubelska 55A near the Piarist Church. All visits are guided (in Polish only) in groups. Tours normally depart at 11 am and 1 and 4 pm, but there may be more tours (departing on the hour), especially on Saturday and Sunday when more visitors come. Information is available on ☎ 565 25 30. The tour takes about 45 minutes and costs US$2. The temperature down in the tunnels is 9°C year-round, so come prepared.

Of the scarce relics of the Jewish legacy, you may want to have a look at the synagogue of 1914, on the corner of ul Kopernika and ul Krzywa. It now houses a café and a bank. A few steps north, on Plac Kościuszki, is the neoclassical Orthodox church built under tsarist rule in the mid-19th century. Services are held on Sunday morning.

Places to Stay

There's not many options, but then there doesn't seem to be much demand for accommodation, as tourists in town are few and far between.

The all-year *youth hostel* (☎ 564 00 22, ul Czarnieckiego 8) is conveniently located in the centre, but it only has dorms, to sleep five to 14 people. An interesting budget option might be *Dom Pielgrzyma* (☎ 565 36 56), behind the cathedral, which has two singles, one double and two dorms, all with bath, for US$4 per person regardless of where you sleep.

There are some inexpensive places farther away from the centre. *Hotel Stadion* (☎ 563 02 86, ul I Pułku Szwoleżerów 15A) is next to the city stadium, beyond the Góra Katedralna. It charges US$7 per bed in triples and quads without bath, and US$10 in doubles and triples with bath. Some 500m farther east is *Hotel Relax* (☎ 563 10 23, ul 11 Listopada 2). It costs US$20/25/30 for doubles/triples/quads without bath.

The central *Hotel Kamena* (☎ 565 64 01, fax 565 64 00, Al Armii Krajowej 50), is the best place in town, with singles/doubles with bath and breakfast for US$40/60.

Places to Eat

The cheapest is the very basic *Bar Staromiejski* (ul Lubelska 68), an old-fashioned milk bar. There are several better places in the centre, such as the inexpensive

Karczma Grodzka (ul Gdańska 11). The restaurant of *Hotel Kamena* is the town's top offering and prices are quite acceptable. *Cukiernia Hetman (ul Lwowska),* off the Rynek, is the place for pastries and coffee in a nonsmoking environment.

Getting There & Away

Train The town has two train stations: Chełm Miasto 1km west of the Old Town, and Chełm Główny 2km to the north-east. Both are serviced by urban buses. Trains to Lublin (75km) run every hour or two. There are three fast trains to Warsaw. Two fast trains a day to Kiev stop at Chełm.

Bus The bus terminal is on ul Lwowska just 300m south of the Rynek. Buses to Lublin (68km) depart roughly every two hours, and there are half a dozen buses a day to Zamość (62km). Two fast buses daily go straight to Warsaw (229km).

ZAMOŚĆ

* pop 66,000   ☎ 084

The Pearl of the Renaissance, the Padua of the North, the Town of Arcades – that's how local tourist brochures refer to Zamość ('Zah-moshch'). The copywriters may seem a bit over-enthusiastic about the place, but nonetheless this is not your average town. Designed in its entirety four centuries ago, Zamość was built in one go in the middle of the Lublin Upland, and there it stands today, relatively unchanged. With more than 100 architectural monuments of historical and artistic value, Zamość's Old Town was included on the World Heritage list by UNESCO in 1992.

The brain behind the plan, Jan Zamoyski (1542-1605), chancellor and commander in chief of the Crown, intended to create a perfect city which would at the same time be a great cultural and trading centre and an impregnable fortress. Having studied in Padua, Zamoyski – like virtually all the Polish aristocracy of the period – was looking for artistic inspiration and models in Italy, not in neighbouring Russia. For his great plan, he commissioned an Italian architect from Padua, Bernardo Morando, who followed the best Italian theories of urban planning in putting Zamoyski's ideas into practice.

The whole project started in 1580 and within 11 years there were already 217 houses built and only 26 plots still empty. Soon afterwards most of the great public buildings, including the palace, church, town hall and university, were completed, and the city was encircled with a formidable system of fortifications.

The experiment proved as successful as its founder hoped. The location of the town on the crossroads of the Lublin-Lviv and Kraków-Kiev trading routes attracted foreign merchants including Armenians, Jews, Greeks, Germans, Scots and Italians, who came to settle here. Its academy, founded in 1594 as the third institution of higher education in Poland, after Kraków and Vilnius, soon became one of the main centres of learning.

The first military test of the fortress came in 1648 with the Cossack raid, and the city passed it effortlessly. The town's defensive capabilities were confirmed during the Swedish invasion of 1656, when Zamość was one of only three Polish cities to withstand the Swedish siege (Częstochowa and Gdańsk were the other two).

During the partitions, Zamość fell first to Austria but later came under tsarist rule. In the 1820s the Russians further fortified the town, at considerable aesthetic cost. It was then that many of the previously splendid buildings (the palace, academy and the town hall among others) were adapted for military purposes and accordingly were given a uniform, barracks-like appearance. Much of the Renaissance decoration was destroyed during that period and replaced with a dry neoclassical overlay.

The Russian efforts proved more successful in depriving the city of its beauty than anything on the military front. The increasing development of weapons and techniques of war from the mid-19th century reduced the defensive importance of the fortress. The defences were aban-

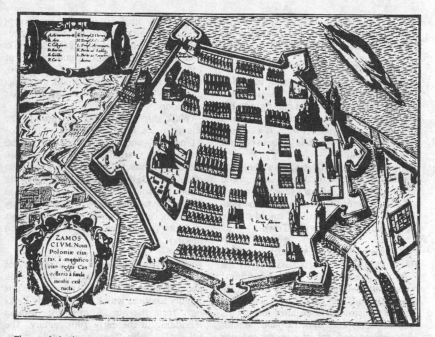

The newly built city of Zamość in about 1605; its fortifications withstood all attacks for 200 years

doned in 1866 and partly dismantled soon afterwards.

During WWII Zamość, renamed by the Germans 'Himmlerstadt', became the centre of Nazi colonisation, the first of its kind on Polish territory. After the brutal expulsion of the Polish population, Germans settled in their place to create what Hitler planned would become the eastern bulwark of the Third Reich. However, they had to flee before the Red Army and fortunately didn't manage to destroy the city.

A thorough restoration plan, aimed at bringing back the Renaissance look of the town, was launched in 1963 and initially progressed swiftly; parts of the Old Town, notably the Rynek, have been renovated. Yet the project bogged down in the 1990s and many buildings in the backstreets are still awaiting repair. Even worse, the program is taking so long that some of the already restored houses are once again in urgent need of plastering or painting. Let's hope help comes soon – it might give some credibility to the superlatives used in the tourist brochures.

Information

Tourist Office The staff in the Zamojski Ośrodek Informacji Turystycznej (☎ 639 22 92; ☎/fax 627 08 13) in the town hall on Rynek Wielki are helpful and knowledgeable. From May to September, it's open weekdays 7.30 am to 5 pm, Saturday and Sunday 9 am to 2 pm; in other months, weekdays only 7.30 am to 3.30 pm.

Money The Bank Pekao at ul Grodzka 2 (which has an ATM) changes travellers cheques and gives advances on Visa and

MAŁOPOLSKA

MasterCard. It also changes cash, as do several central kantors, but rates may be lower than in large cities.

Things to See

Zamość is one of those towns in which strolling at random is more fun than walking map in hand from one sight to the next. The Old Town is a car-free area and only 600m long by 400m wide. It's centred around the square, which is likely to be your first destination.

The original fortifications were altered beyond recognition by the Russians; those on the eastern side of town survived in part, including one of the bastions, and the position of the rest can still be traced by the mound surrounding the Old Town.

Old Town Square Measuring 100 x 100m, the spectacular Renaissance Rynek Wielki is lined with old arcaded burghers' houses, the whole dominated by a lofty **town hall**, built into the northern side of the square. Constructed soon after the town's foundation, it was extended around the mid-17th century and got its curving exterior stairway in 1768.

Each side of the Rynek has eight houses (except for the northern one where half the space is taken by the town hall) and each is bisected by streets designed as the two main axes of the town: one running west-east from the palace to the most important bastion, and the other one oriented north-south, linking three market squares. Zamoyski didn't want the town hall to compete with his palace and interrupt the view, and that's why it doesn't sit, as is usual, in the middle of the square.

Originally, all the houses had decorative parapets on their tops but these were removed in the 1820s; only those on the northern side have been restored. These are the most beautiful houses in the square, and probably always were. As they once belonged to Armenian merchants, you will find some Oriental motifs on their façades.

Two of these houses, Nos 24 and 26, now shelter the **Regional Museum** (Muzeum Okręgowe), open 10 am to 4 pm, except Monday. The collection includes archaeological finds and portraits of the Zamoyski family, and there's also a good model of fortified Zamość from the end of the 17th century. Note the original wooden ceilings and wall decoration around the windows and doors.

Walk through the arcades around the square to see some fine doorways (eg Nos 21 and 25) and the stucco work on the vaults in the vestibules (eg No 10). Go into the old pharmacy of 1609 (No 2) and the BWA Art Gallery (No 14). If you walk round the square outside the arcades you can see the façades (eg No 5, where an army officer once lived, which explains the busts of Minerva and Hercules and the weapon motifs).

Around the Old Town Just south-west of the Rynek is the **collegiate church**. It took about 40 years (1587-1628) to complete this mighty basilica, which unfortunately looks ugly from the outside after the ill-fated rebuilding in the early 19th century. The original Lublin-Renaissance-style vault, some good stone and stucco work, and the unusual arcaded organ loft can be seen inside. In the high altar is the rococo silver tabernacle of 1745. The Zamoyski chapel at the head of the right-hand aisle shelters the tomb of the founder. The stairs next to the chapel will take you down to the family crypt (for a nominal entry fee).

Back outside the church, you can go up to the top of the freestanding **bell tower** for a panoramic view, though the terrace is not high enough to provide a good vista over the Old Town and the Rynek. The original tower was made of timber and went up in flames. The present one was built in 1755-75. There are three bells inside, of which the largest, named Jan after the founder, weighs 4300kg and is over three centuries old.

Behind the church is the former vicarage from the 1610s, known as the Infułatka, with its splendid ornate doorway. It leads to the **Religious Museum** (Muzeum Sakralne) which features a collection of religious art

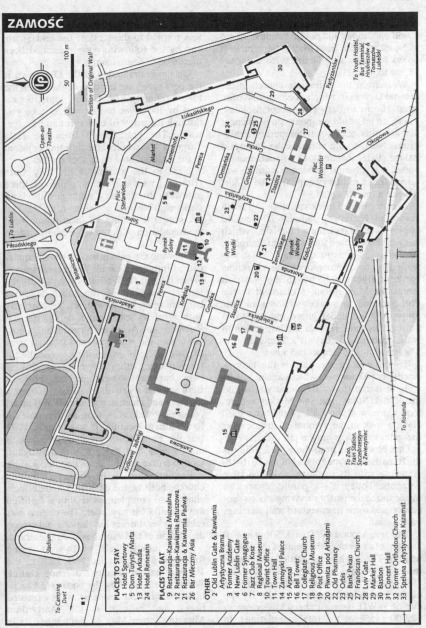

ZAMOŚĆ

PLACES TO STAY
1 Hotel Sportowy
5 Dom Turysty Marta
13 Hotel Arkadia
24 Hotel Renesans

PLACES TO EAT
9 Restauracja-Kawiarnia Muzealna
12 Restauracja-Kawiarnia Ratuszowa
21 Restauracja & Kawiarnia Padwa
26 Bar Mleczny Asia

OTHER
2 Old Lublin Gate & Kawiarnia Artystyczna Brama
3 Former Academy
4 New Lublin Gate
6 Former Synagogue
7 Jazz Club Kosz
8 Regional Museum
10 Tourist Office
11 Town Hall
14 Zamoyski Palace
15 Arsenal
16 Bell Tower
17 Collegiate Church
18 Religious Museum
19 Post Office
20 Piwnica pod Arkadami
22 Old Pharmacy
23 Orbis
25 Bank Pekao
27 Franciscan Church
28 Lviv Gate
29 Market Hall
30 Bastion
31 Concert Hall
32 Former Orthodox Church
33 Speluna Artystyczna Kazamat

accumulated by the church. It's open year-round on Sunday and public holidays 10 am to 1 pm. As well, from May to September it opens Monday and Thursday to Saturday 11 am to 4 pm.

West from the collegiate church is the **arsenal** (arsenał), which is now a museum, open 10 am to 3.30 pm except Monday. There's a lot of old weaponry on permanent display plus occasional temporary exhibitions. Next, to the north, is the **Zamoyski Palace** (Pałac Zamoyskich), which was reputedly a splendid residence until it was turned into a military hospital in the 1830s. It's not a tourist sight.

A partly ruined brick structure just north across ul Królowej Jadwigi is the **Old Lublin Gate** (Stara Brama Lubelska), which has never been used for its original purpose. Just after its construction in 1588 it was walled up to commemorate the victorious battle at Byczyna in which the Austrian Archduke Maximilian, a claimant to the Polish throne, was taken prisoner and triumphantly led under guard into the town through the gate. He was the last person to walk through. Today it's home to the Theatre Cultural Centre and a bar.

To the east of the gate is the famous **Academy** (Akademia) which, again, lost its style in tsarist times. Behind it you'll find the Rynek Solny, the Salt Market Square. You are now at the back of the town hall. Have a look at the symbol of justice over the gate; there was once a jail inside.

One block east from the Rynek Solny is the Renaissance **synagogue** built in 1610-18, complete with its reconstructed decorative parapets. Today it's a public library; go inside to see the partly surviving stucco decoration and some fragments of wall paintings on the vault.

The area around the Rynek Solny and ul Zamenhofa was once the heart of the Jewish quarter. The Jews were granted permission to settle in Zamość in 1588, and by the mid-19th century they accounted for about 60% of the town's population of 4000. By the eve of WWII their numbers had grown to 12,000 (45% of the total population). In 1941 they were moved to the ghetto that was formed to the west of the Old Town, and by the following year most had been murdered in death camps.

On the eastern edge of the Old Town is the best surviving **bastion** of the seven the town originally had. Guided tours, organised by the town tourist office, take you through the array of underground passageways. The entrance is from the Hala Targowa Nadszaniec, the building adjacent to the bastion, now an indoor market.

Next to the market is the **Lviv Gate** (Brama Lwowska). It was one of three gateways to the city and, despite later changes, it has retained some of its original decoration including an inscription about the foundation of the town (from its eastern side).

Opposite the gate is the massive **Franciscan Church** (Kościół Franciszkanów). When built in 1637-65, it was reputedly the largest and one of the most beautiful baroque churches in Poland, yet virtually nothing of its splendour is left. After the Partitions, the Austrians turned it into a hospital; then the Russians used it as an arms depot until 1840, when they remodelled it for barracks, pulling down its magnificent twin baroque towers in the process. Between the wars, the building housed a museum and cinema, and after WWII an art college moved in as soon as the museum found a new location. It wasn't until 1994 that the Franciscans eventually reclaimed the building and made it a church again, though so far there's almost no decoration.

Farther south is the former **Orthodox church**, built in the 1620s by Greek merchants and complemented with a fortified tower half a century later. The church was rebuilt several times but the original stucco decoration of the vault has been preserved.

A 10 minute walk south-west is the **Rotunda**, a ring-shaped fort built in the 1820s as part of the city's defence. During WWII it was used by the Nazis for executions (8000 local residents were executed here), and now it is the **Martyrdom Museum**, open May to September daily

9 am to 5 pm (October to April 10 am to 4 pm). It's more a shrine than a museum, with tombs and ever-fresh flowers.

Zamość has a small zoo, which features popular local species and some exotic attractions, including monkeys and tigers. It's on ul Szczebrzeska opposite the train station, and is open daily 9 am till dusk.

Special Events

There are two annual jazz festivals in town: the Jazz on the Borderlands in June and the International Meeting of Jazz Vocalists in September. Both events are organised by, and take place at, Jazz Club Kosz at ul Zamenhofa 3 (entrance from the back of the building). The club stages unscheduled jazz concerts and jam sessions if somebody turns up in town.

The Zamość Theatre Summer takes place from mid-June to mid-July with open-air performances on the Rynek Wielki in front of the town hall.

Places to Stay

Camping Duet (☎ 639 24 99, ul Królowej Jadwigi 14), 1km west of the Old Town, charges US$2 per person to camp. It has all-year bungalows (US$14/20/28/34 a single/double/triple/quad with bath), a snack bar and tennis courts. A covered swimming pool is being built.

The July-August *youth hostel (☎ 627 91 25, ul Zamoyskiego 4)* is in a school, about 1.5km east of the Old Town, not far from the bus terminal.

The cheapest place to stay in the Old Town is the simple *Dom Turysty Marta (☎ 639 26 39, ul Zamenhofa 11)*, costing US$6 per person in two to eight-bed dorms with shared facilities. More comfortable is the modern *Hotel Renesans (☎ 639 20 01, ul Grecka 6)*, which offers singles/doubles with bath for US$44/62.

Hotel Sportowy (☎ 638 60 11, ul Królowej Jadwigi 8), in the sports centre, is a 10 minute walk from the Rynek. Singles/doubles/triples/quads with bath cost US$20/26/28/32, or a five or six-bed dorm costs US$8 a bed, without bath.

The brand-new *Hotel Arkadia (☎ 638 65 07, Rynek Wielki 9)* is the best and most central place in town. It has just four rooms: two doubles (US$50 each), one triple (US$60) and one suite (US$85). The triple and suite overlook the Rynek.

There are also several less convenient hotels farther away from the centre; the tourist office will give you information.

Places to Eat

For a simple cheap meal, go to *Bar Mleczny Asia (ul Staszica 10)*. Several cafés, most of which are on the Rynek, serve the usual set of popular dishes such as flaki, barszcz, sausage etc. *Restauracja-Kawiarnia Ratuszowa* in the town hall has reasonable food at low prices.

Of the more decent places for lunch or dinner, try *Restauracja-Kawiarnia Muzealna* in a cellar next to the regional museum, the basement *Restauracja Padwa (ul Staszica 23)* at the Rynek, or the 1st floor *Restauracja Arkadia* in the hotel of the same name.

Entertainment

For a drink or two, try either of the 'artistic' bars, both located in the old fortifications: *Speluna Artystyczna Kazamat (ul Bazyliańska 36)* or *Kawiarnia Artystyczna Brama* in the Old Lublin Gate. You can also check *Piwnica pod Arkadami (ul Staszica 25)* at the Rynek, a cellar bar-café with pool tables.

Getting There & Away

The tourist office will inform you about the train and bus schedules, and Orbis at ul Grodzka 18 books and sells train tickets.

Train The train station is about 1km southwest of the Old Town; walk or take the city bus. There are several slow trains to Lublin (118km) but give them a miss – they take a long, roundabout route. It's much faster to go by bus, and you will arrive in the centre of Lublin.

Three ordinary trains go directly to Warsaw (293km), but they take over six

MAŁOPOLSKA

hours to get there. It's faster to go by bus or take a special PKP bus (departing from the train station) to Lublin at 5 am which goes to Lublin train station and meets the express train to Warsaw at 7 am. The whole trip takes four hours. There's a convenient morning fast train to Kraków, which takes six hours, or you can take the morning Kraków PKS bus.

Bus The bus terminal is 2km east of the centre; frequent city buses link it with the Old Town. Buses to Lublin (89km), either fast or ordinary ones, run roughly every half-hour till about 6 pm, and there are also plenty of private minibuses, which are cheaper. There are two morning buses to Rzeszów (148km), passing Łańcut on the way, and one to Przemyśl (148km). One morning fast bus goes directly to Kraków (318km), one to Sandomierz (157km) and four to Warsaw (247km).

SZCZEBRZESZYN
* pop 5500   ☎ 084

The name of this town is familiar to almost every Pole for its weird spelling, which has earned it a place in the most popular Polish tongue-twister: *W Szczebrzeszynie chrząszcz brzmi w trzcinie* (In Szczebrzeszyn the cockchafer buzzes in the weeds). Yet few people would be able to tell you anything about the town itself or point out its location on the map.

Szczebrzeszyn ('Shcheb-zheh-shin') is a small town 21km west of Zamość on the road to Biłgoraj. It received its municipal charter as early as 1388, but it didn't really develop a great deal until Jan Zamoyski of Zamość took the whole region into his possession in 1589. The first half of the 17th century was a period of rapid urban growth in the town, reflected in the construction of two mighty churches and a synagogue. After a short period of prosperity, however, the town fell prey to repeated forays by foreign armies, including Cossacks (1648), Swedes (1656) and Turks (1672). In the 19th century Szczebrzeszyn became the major centre of the anti-tsarist movement in

the region. Today it's a sleepy little place which still boasts some important relics of its heyday – justifying a stop if you are travelling this route, or perhaps a return trip out of Zamość.

Things to See
St Catherine's Church (Kościół Św Katarzyny) is possibly the most spectacular edifice in town. Built in 1620-38 in typical Lublin-Renaissance style, it was roughly modelled on Zamość's collegiate church. Past the decorative Renaissance doorway you will find yourself in a spacious interior topped by a fine vault and decorated with stucco work and wall paintings.

St Nicholas' Church (Kościół Św Mikołaja) was built in 1620 but was plundered and partly destroyed by the Cossacks in 1648. It's more modest than St Catherine's church, yet it's still a fine piece of Lublin-Renaissance architecture, with good stucco work on the vault. It's now the parish church.

The town has a large **synagogue**, now the local cultural centre. Built in late Renaissance style at the beginning of the 17th century, it was damaged by the Cossacks and then reconstructed to serve the Jewish community until WWII; by then they numbered 3200 people. Burnt out by the Nazis, it was renovated in the early 1960s. Go inside to see the partly preserved stucco work and the original stone Holy Ark, the niche in the eastern wall where the Torah was kept.

Some 100m up the hill is the **Orthodox church** (cerkiew), converted from a former Catholic church. The interior boasts wall paintings from about 1620.

About 200m farther up the hill is the **Jewish cemetery**, one of the most abandoned you will see in Poland. There are still about 400 tombstones, some of them with exquisite decoration, but many fallen over. The oldest tombs date from the early 1700s, but most are from the 19th and early 20th centuries; some retain traces of polychromy.

Places to Stay & Eat

Zajazd pod Bażantem (☎ 682 12 97, ul Zwierzyniecka 19A) has singles/doubles with bath for US$12/24 and triples/quads without bath for US$25/28, and provides simple meals. Between 1 July to 25 August you can also try the *youth hostel (☎ 682 11 06)* in the local primary school.

Getting There & Away

The PKS bus terminal is just 100m from the main square. Buses to Zamość (21km) go every half-hour or so, and there are about half a dozen buses a day to Biłgoraj (32km), all of which pass through Zwierzyniec (11km).

The train station is in Brody, 2km south of the town on the road to Zwierzyniec, but there are barely enough trains to justify the trip.

ZWIERZYNIEC
• **pop 3800**   ☎ 084

Zwierzyniec ('Zvyeh-zhi-nyets'), 11km south of Szczebrzeszyn, appeared on the map at the end of the 16th century, when Jan Zamoyski created a game reserve in the area (see the following Roztocze National Park section). Soon afterwards the family's summer residence was established here. This consisted of a palatial larch-wood villa (reputedly designed by Bernardo Morando, the man responsible for the Zamość project) and a spacious park. Later a chapel was built on an island on the lake opposite the palace. Meanwhile, a hamlet grew around the residence, eventually developing into a small town. The palace itself was pulled down in 1833.

Things to See

Today Zwierzyniec is essentially the gateway to the Roztocze National Park, housing the park's headquarters and the **Natural History Museum** (Muzeum Przyrodnicze) related to the park. Located in a stylish building inspired by an old manor house, the museum is open daily 10 am to 5 pm except Monday, (November to February 9 am to 4 pm). It's at ul Plażowa 3 on the southern edge of the town, a 10 minute walk from the bus stop.

The only significant structure left of Zamoyski's residential complex is the chapel. Known as the **Chapel upon the Water** (Kaplica na Wodzie), this beautiful, small baroque church enjoys a spectacular location. It sits on one of the four tiny islets on the small lake named the Staw Kościelny (Church Pond), and is linked to the mainland by a bridge. The lake is halfway between the bus stop and the museum.

Places to Stay & Eat

Hotel Jodła (☎ 687 20 12, ul Parkowa 3A), near the bus stop, is in a fine, stylish villa. It offers accommodation in doubles, triples and quads; you pay US$8/12 per bed in rooms without/with private bath. There's a café but meals are available only if requested in advance.

The basic *Camping Echo (☎ 687 23 14, ul Biłgorajska 3)* is open from early May to early October. It has cheap cabins with three and six-bed rooms and a snack bar serving light meals.

There's also the summer *youth hostel (☎ 687 21 42, ul Partyzantów 3)* in the local school, open from 1 July to 25 August.

Getting There & Away

The bus stop is on ul Zamojska, in the centre of the town. There's a large town map posted beside it, which has the tourist attractions and facilities marked on it. Buses to Zamość (32km) pass somewhat regularly, and there are infrequent buses to more distant destinations, including Sandomierz and Rzeszów. The train station is about 1km east of town.

ROZTOCZE NATIONAL PARK

Declared a national park in 1974, the Roztoczański Park Narodowy covers an area of 79 sq km to the south and east of Zwierzyniec. The site was actually a nature reserve for over 350 years as part of the estates owned by the Zamoyski family until WWII. Following the purchase of a vast stretch of land complete with six towns, 149 villages and about 1600 sq km of forest in 1589, Jan Zamoyski created an enclosed game reserve named Zwierzyniec (hence the name of the town). A remarkable achievement at that time, this was not a hunting ground but a protected area where various species of animals roamed in relative freedom. It was here that the world's last specimens of the original tarpan (see Białowieża National Park in the Mazovia & Podlasie chapter) were kept in the 19th century, until they were given away to the locals when the estate fell into disarray under tsarist rule.

Today's national park includes much of Zamoyski's original reserve. Occupying undulating terrain, 93% of which is covered with forest, the park retains much of its primeval character, with rich and varied flora and fauna. The park is crossed from east to west by the Wieprz, one of the least polluted rivers in the region.

The forest features an interesting mix of plant species typical of the valley as well as of the mountain. A product of different soil types, topography, climate and water sources, it contains a wide variety of trees, including fir, spruce, pine, beech, sycamore, hornbeam, oak, elm and lime. Fir trees in the park reach heights of up to 50m – the tallest in Poland – and beech trees are not much shorter.

The park's fauna is just as diverse. Almost all species of forest animals, including stag, roe deer, boar, fox, marten and badger, live here, and elk, wolves and lynxes show up from time to time. In 1969 beavers were reintroduced, and in 1982 a refuge for tarpans was created.

There are approximately 190 bird species, about 130 of which nest regularly in the park. There is also a rich world of insects, the beetles alone numbering approximately 2000 different species.

Walking Trails

The normal starting point for walks in the park is the town of Zwierzyniec, or more specifically the museum (see the preceding Zwierzyniec section). Here you can buy booklets and maps on the park, and the staff can provide further information. You pay a US$0.50 entrance fee to the park. Tarpans can be seen beyond the museum – ask the staff to point out where they are.

The most popular walking path begins from the museum and goes south up to the top of the Bukowa Góra (Beech Mountain) at 306m (a 75m ascent). Just 1.5km long, the path (which is actually a former palace's park lane) gives a good idea of the park's different forest habitats, passing from pine to fir to beech woods at 500m intervals.

Halfway to the top, you can take a side path branching off to the west and walk 1km to the Piaseczna Góra (298m). You can then return the same way, or descend to the east and walk along a dirt road to the Stawy Echo (Echo Ponds), frequented by a variety of avifauna.

The Bukowa Góra is one of five strict nature reserves in the park; the other four are farther east. There are three longer trails, called tourist trails, crossing different parts of the park and providing access to selected areas; they are marked on tourist maps.

The Carpathian Mountains

The Carpathian Mountains (Karpaty in Polish) are the highest and largest mountain system in Central Europe, stretching like a huge sausage from southern Poland to central Romania. The Polish portion of the Carpathians occupies a 50 to 70km-wide belt along the southern border from Upper Silesia to Ukraine.

Geographically, the Polish Carpathians are made up of rugged mountain ranges that run east-west along the frontier, and a vast stretch of undulating terrain to the north, known as the Pogórze Karpackie, or the Carpathian Foothills. This chapter deals with all the territory lying south of the Kraków-Tarnów-Rzeszów-Przemyśl road.

This is one of the most attractive regions for tourists. Not only is it largely unspoilt, with wooded hills and mountains (predictably a favourite haunt for hikers), but its culture and rural architecture have preserved more of their traditional forms than those of other regions. Travelling around you'll still see plenty of old-style timber houses and rustic shingled churches as well as hundreds of tiny roadside chapels and shrines dotting every winding country lane. Here is a Poland to be savoured.

This is also the traditional homeland of two interesting ethnic minorities, the Boyks and the Lemks.

The Carpathian Foothills

The Carpathian Foothills are a green hilly belt sloping from the true mountains in the south to the valleys of the Vistula and San rivers to the north. Except for Kalwaria Zebrzydowska, which is usually a round trip from Kraków, most sights of the region are located along the Kraków-Tarnów-Rzeszów-Przemyśl road (and are ordered thus, west-east, in this chapter).

Highlights

- Watch the mysterious Passion play at Easter in Kalwaria Zebrzydowska
- Visit the Łańcut palace with its fabulous art collection
- Examine the splendid icon collection and perhaps Poland's best skansen at Sanok
- Go for a relaxing hike in the Bieszczady
- Tour around the charming timber Catholic, Orthodox and Uniate churches scattered about the region
- Explore Nowy Sącz's lovely skansen
- Take a walk through the picturesque Pieniny and an enjoyable raft trip down the Dunajec Gorge
- Hike among the dramatic alpine scenery of the Tatra mountains

KALWARIA ZEBRZYDOWSKA
- **pop 4500**   ☎ 033

One of Poland's major pilgrimage destinations, Kalwaria Zebrzydowska (pronounced

THE CARPATHIAN MOUNTAINS

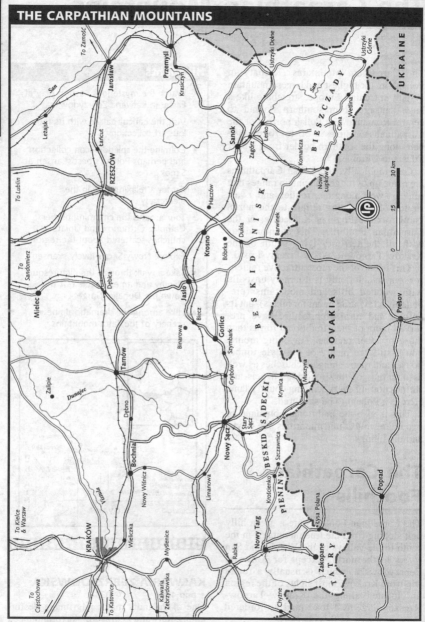

Interior of the 15th century parish church in Szydłowiec

From the kitsch to the classy: handicrafts at a Kazimierz Dolny craft market

Rustic windmill at Lublin's open-air museum

Old granaries at Kazimierz Dolny

Ogrodzieniec's once-splendid castle, spectacularly sited on a hilltop

'Kahl-vah-ryah Zeb-zhi-dov-skah') is set amid hills about 30km south-west of Kraków. The town owes its existence and subsequent fame to the squire of Kraków, Mikołaj Zebrzydowski, who in 1600 commissioned the church and monastery for the Bernardine Order. Having seen the resemblance of the area to the site of Jerusalem, he set about creating a place of worship similar to that in the Holy City. By 1617, 24 chapels were built over the surrounding hills, some of which looked as though they'd been brought directly from the mother city. As the place attracted growing numbers of pilgrims, more chapels were erected, eventually reaching 40.

The **church** was gradually enlarged and today it's a massive edifice. Its baroque high altar boasts a silver figure of the Virgin, but the holiest image inside is a miraculous painting of the Virgin in the Zebrzydowski Chapel, to the left of the high altar. Legend has it that the eyes of the Virgin shed tears in 1641, and from that time miracles happened. Pilgrims flock to Kalwaria on all Marian holy days, particularly from 13 to 15 August, when processions around the chapels are held.

However, what has really made Kalwaria famous are the **Passion plays** which have been held here since the 17th century during Holy Week (Easter). This blend of religious ceremony and local theatre, re-enacting the most crucial days of Christ's life, is performed by local peasants and monks who play the parts of Jesus, the apostles, Roman legionaries etc, during a two-day-long procession.

The procession sets off early afternoon on Maundy Thursday and goes on till dusk, covering half of the circuit round the chapels. It starts again at about 6 am the next morning (Good Friday) and ends at roughly 2 pm. The procession calls at about two dozen chapels, with a shorter or longer stop and a sermon in most of them. The play that is performed along the way often becomes such a realistic spectacle that some of the more vigorous pilgrims have been known to rush in to rescue Jesus from the hands of his oppressors.

The time of the year adds a dramatic touch to the ceremony, especially when Easter falls early, at the end of winter. The weather is unpredictable then, with snow or rain possible at any time and mud almost guaranteed over large stretches on the route. It sometimes gets bitterly cold, especially when you are moving slowly around the chapels for most of the day.

If your visit coincides with one of the two big religious events you'll find Kalwaria flooded with people; at other times it's a peaceful place.

Once in Kalwaria, you might also want to visit the village of **Lanckorona**, 5km from Kalwaria, for its spectacular setting on the slope of a cone-shaped mountain, fine old villas in varying states of decay, a sloping Rynek lined with timber-shingled, single-storey houses and a general air of absolute lethargy.

Another possible place to visit from Kalwaria is **Wadowice**, 14km to the west. It's a rather unattractive industrial town, whose name has become known to every Pole for one reason: it was here that Karol Wojtyła, today Pope John Paul II, was born in 1920. The house where he lived as a child, just off the Rynek, is now a museum.

Places to Stay

Accommodation is scarce, and forget about it during the celebrations. One of the very few options in Kalwaria is the simple *Hotel Kalwarianka*, popularly called the Hotel Stadion (☎ 76 64 92, ul Mickiewicza 16), next to the stadium, which costs US$9/12/15/18 a single/double/triple/quad without bath.

There are a couple of places in Lanckorona, including the all-year *youth hostel* (☎ 76 35 89, ul Kazimierza Wielkiego 1) just off the Rynek (the reception desk closes at 8 pm), and *Hotel Korona* (☎ 76 64 01, ul Krakowska 513), which costs US$7 per person.

Getting There & Away

There's fairly regular bus transport from Kraków to Kalwaria (33km), and some of the buses continue on to Wadowice. Trains also pass Kalwaria on their way to Zakopane.

NOWY WIŚNICZ

- **pop 2500**   ☎ 014

The little town of Nowy Wiśnicz ('No-vi Veesh-neech'), just south of Bochnia, has reached the pages of tourist guidebooks thanks to its castle. This well proportioned, early baroque building with graceful corner towers surrounded by massive pentagonal fortifications was designed by Italian architect Matteo Trapola for one of the most powerful men in Poland at the time, Stanisław Lubomirski (1583-1649). It was built in 1615-21 using the foundations and parts of the walls of a 14th century stronghold which previously stood on this site. The new castle was reputedly very well prepared to defend itself from enemies – it had food and ammunition to withstand a siege for three years.

As soon as the castle was completed, Lubomirski commissioned the same architect to build the monastery for the Discalced Carmelites. Equally splendid and similarly fortified, the monastery was erected between 1622 and 1635 half a kilometre up the hill from the castle, and the two structures were connected by an underground passage. By the time of the monastery's completion, the energetic Lubomirski was already rebuilding his newly acquired possession, the palace in Łańcut.

Neither the castle nor the monastery enjoyed their beauty and splendour for long. Despite its defensive capabilities, the castle surrendered to the Swedes in 1655 in exchange for the promise that they would not destroy it. They indeed kept their word, but nonetheless thoroughly plundered the interior, taking away some 150 wagonloads of treasure. After a series of further misfortunes, the castle was eventually consumed by a fire in 1831, which left it in ruins. Only after WWII was restoration undertaken, and this is still going on. The exterior has already been renovated, but there is still a long way to go on the inside.

The monastery and the church haven't had a glorious history either. After the Carmelites were expelled in the 1780s, the monastery was turned into a prison and remains so to this day. It's designed for particularly dangerous common criminals and is among the best guarded in the country. The church was totally destroyed by the Nazis in 1944.

Things to See

The **castle** is a 10 minute walk uphill from the town's centre and, despite the work in progress, can be visited. You can view its courtyard and rooms on the two upper floors including the domed chapel, a large hall with a splendid ornate ceiling, and a huge ballroom measuring 30 x 9m and 9m high. There's also the sarcophagus of Stanisław Lubomirski and a small exhibition displaying three models of the castle from different periods and photographic documentation of the post-war reconstruction.

The castle is open year-round weekdays 9 am to 2 pm. From May to October, it is also open on Saturday 11 am to 3 pm, and on Sunday and public holidays noon to 6 pm. All visitors must join a group tour, so you may have to wait a while for the next tour to depart.

The road up the hill from the castle goes to the prison. Halfway along you'll find a fine wooden house called Koryznówka in which Jan Matejko was once a frequent guest. Today it's a modest **museum** (open Wednesday to Sunday 10 am to 2 pm) with some memorabilia of this most famous Polish history painter.

In the town centre, near the Rynek, you can visit the **parish church**, also the work of Trapola.

Places to Stay & Eat

Hotel Podzamcze (☎ 612 88 25), next to the castle, offers basic accommodation in triples and quads with shared facilities, charging US$7 per head. It has its own café, but it's better to eat in *Bufet Kmita* by the prison's gate. There are also a few basic eating outlets in the town's centre, includ-

Jan Matejko's monumental paintings documented great moments of Polish history

ing *Restauracja Hetmańska* on the corner of the Rynek.

The best place to stay in the area is the small *Pensjonat Atlas* (☎ 612 91 25), on the road to Bochnia, about 2.5km from Nowy Wiśnicz. It has neat singles/doubles/triples with bath for US$25/30/35. Optional breakfast is US$4.

The castle management plans to open a hotel for 20 guests and a restaurant in the castle's outbuildings. This seems to be rather an upmarket proposition.

Getting There & Away

Nowy Wiśnicz is well serviced from Bochnia (7km) by either hourly suburban Bochnia bus No 12, or the PKS buses running every quarter of an hour or so. Bochnia is on the main Kraków-Tarnów route, with frequent buses and trains to both destinations.

DĘBNO
• pop 1200   ☎ 014

Halfway between Bochnia and Tarnów is the small village of Dębno. Though little known and rarely visited, the **castle** that stands here is a good example of a small defensive residence. It was built in the 1470s on the foundations of a previous knights' stronghold, and extended gradually until the 1630s. It was plundered several times since, but the stone and brick structure came through without major damage. The postwar restoration work took more than three decades and the result is admirable: the castle looks much as it would have done 350 years ago.

The castle consists of four two-storey buildings joined at the corners to form a small, rectangular courtyard, all surrounded by a moat and ponds, now dry. The structure is adorned with fine corner towers, oriels, bay windows and doorways, which have survived almost intact.

The castle is a **museum** today and you can visit a good part of the interior including the cellars. The rooms have been refurnished and have some exhibitions (weapons, paintings, the castle's history). Its small size gives you the refreshing feeling that you are visiting a modest private home, the only two larger rooms being the knights' room and the concert room, the latter serving for occasional piano recitals.

The castle is open Tuesday and Thursday 10 am to 5 pm, Wednesday and Friday 9 am to 3 pm, Saturday 11 am to 3 pm, and Sunday 11 am to 5 pm (till 3 pm from October to April). In January and February, the castle is closed on Saturday and Sunday. Concise English booklets about the site are available at the ticket desk.

Places to Stay & Eat

There's nowhere to stay nearby, but there are a few places to eat, including *Restauracja pod Jesionami* at the turn-off to the castle, and *Restauracja Agawa*, 1km down the road toward Tarnów.

Getting There & Away

The castle is an easy stopover on the Kraków-Tarnów highway. There are regular buses on this road, which will let you off at the village's centre, from which the castle is just a five minute walk.

TARNÓW

- **pop 120,000**　☎ 014

Tarnów ('Tar-noof') is an important regional industrial centre, yet you wouldn't notice this while strolling about its pleasant, finely restored Old Town. The city has some attractions and can be a worthwhile stop if you are travelling around the region.

The city map reveals the familiar layout – an oval centre with a large square in its middle – suggesting that the town was planned in medieval times. Tarnów is indeed an old city, its roots going back to the 12th century, with its municipal charter granted in 1330. Developing as a trade centre on the busy Kraków-Kiev route, the town enjoyed particularly good times in the Renaissance period, and a branch of the Kraków Academy was opened here.

Not uncommonly for the region, Tarnów had a sizable Jewish community, which by the 19th century accounted for half the city's population. Of 20,000 Jews living here in 1939, only a handful survived the war.

Today the city is considered to be one of the major centres of the Polish Gypsies. However, Gypsies (or Roma, as they call themselves) never settled in Poland in such numbers as they did elsewhere in Europe, say in Spain or Romania, and their total current population in the whole country is thought to be no more than about 15,000, and only a small proportion of these live in the Tarnów area. Before WWII there were over 50,000 Roma in Poland but the Nazis treated them the same way as they treated the Jews. Of a total of a million Roma living in Europe before the war, the Nazis exterminated over half.

Information

As yet, there's no tourist office in Tarnów. Try the PTTK office (☎ 27 55 23) at ul Żydowska 20 or some of the travel agencies.

The Bank Pekao at Plac Kazimierza Wielkiego 3A doesn't change travellers cheques, nor has it an ATM. The nearest useful ATM (Euronet) is at Plac Sobieskiego 6, while travellers cheques can be cashed in the Bank Przemysłowo Handlowy at ul Wałowa 10 (note the ornate façade of the building) or in another branch of the Bank Pekao at Plac Kościuszki 4. Kantors are easy to find in the central area.

Things to See

The **Rynek** retains some of its former appearance. The **town hall** in the middle is a familiar combination of Gothic walls and a tower, with Renaissance parapets topping the roof. The Renaissance doorway at the southern side leads to the **Regional Museum** (Muzeum Okręgowe), open Tuesday and Thursday 10 am to 5 pm, Wednesday and Friday 9 am to 3 pm, and Saturday and Sunday 10 am to 2 pm. It features a collection of historic paintings, armoury, furniture, glass and ceramics. The museum's extension, in the arcaded houses on the northern side of the square, has temporary exhibitions.

The **cathedral**, just off the Rynek, dates from the 14th century but it was thoroughly remodelled in the 1890s, eventually mutating into a neo-Gothic edifice. The interior shelters several Renaissance and baroque tombs, of which two in the chancel are among the largest in the country. Also of interest are the 15th century stalls under the choir loft and two original stone portals – at the southern and western porches – both dating from the early 16th century.

Right behind the cathedral, in a lovely house from 1524, is the **Diocesan Museum** (Muzeum Diecezjalne) with a good collection of Gothic sacred art, including some marvellous Madonnas and altarpieces, and an extensive display of folk and religious painting on glass, reputedly the best in the country. The museum is open Tuesday to Saturday 10 am to 3 pm, Sunday and public holidays 9 am to 2 pm.

The area east of the Rynek was traditionally inhabited by Jews, but not much original architecture has survived. Of the 17th century **synagogue** off ul Żydowska, only the brick bimah is left. Perhaps a more moving sign of the Jewish legacy is the **Jewish Cemetery** (Cmentarz Żydowski),

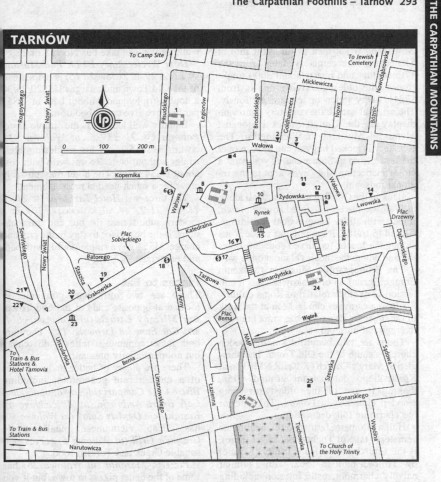

TARNÓW

To Camp Site
To Jewish Cemetery

Mickiewicza
Nowodąbrowska

Rogoyskiego
Nowy Świat
Piłsudskiego
Legionów
Brodzińskiego
Goldhammera
Nowa
Bożnic

1

Wałowa

2
3

4

Kopernika

5

8
9
11
12
13
14
Lwowska
Plac Drzewny

6
10
Żydowska
Szeroka
Dąbrowskiego

Wałowa
Rynek
15

Katedralna
16
Plac Sobieskiego
Sowińskiego
Nowy Świat
Batorego
Stuzka
Krakowska
18
17
Targowa
Bernardyńska
24

19

21
20
23
Św. Anny
Plac Bema
Wątok
NMP

22

Urszulańska
Bema
Limanowskiego
Łazienna
Szewska
25
26
Sądowa
Konarskiego
Wspólna
Tuchowska

To Train & Bus Stations & Hotel Tarnovia

To Train & Bus Stations

Narutowicza
To Church of the Holy Trinity

0   100   200 m

TARNÓW

PLACES TO STAY
4	Hotel Polonia
12	Dom Wycieczkowy PTTK Pod Murami
25	Youth Hostel

PLACES TO EAT
2	Pizzeria Maranto
3	Restauracja Ognisty Smok
7	Granada Grill
14	Bar Sam

16	Restauracja Bella Italia
19	Bistro Cafe Campari
20	Restauracja Bristol
21	Bar Mleczny Łasuch
22	Cafe Bistro Ambrozja

OTHER
1	Church of the Holy Cross
5	Tomb of the Unknown Soldier
6	Bank Przemysłowo Handlowy

8	Diocesan Museum
9	Cathedral
10	Regional Museum
11	Former Synagogue
13	PTTK Office
15	Town Hall & Regional Museum
17	Bank Pekao
18	Euronet ATM
23	Ethnographic Museum
24	Bernardine Church
26	St Mary's Church

which is a short walk north along ul Nowodąbrowska, then to the right into ul Słoneczna. The cemetery dates from the 17th century and boasts about 3000 tombstones (the oldest surviving one is from 1734), many fallen or leaning perilously. The original gate to the cemetery is now on display at the United States Holocaust Memorial Museum in Washington. The cemetery is locked but you can look in over the fence from ul Słoneczna. If you want a closer inspection, the key is kept in the regional museum.

Back in the Old Town, have a stroll along ul Wałowa, the best restored street in town, lined with fine neoclassical buildings. Closed to traffic, it's a popular rendezvous among the locals. Its curved course follows the line where the medieval moat once was.

The **Ethnographic Museum** (Muzeum Etnograficzne) on ul Krakowska has a collection of exhibits related to Roma culture. Six Roma caravans can be seen at the back of the museum. It's open the same hours as the regional museum.

There are two beautiful small wooden churches south of the Old Town. The shingled **St Mary's Church** (Kościół NMP) on ul Konarskiego dates from around 1458, making it one of the oldest surviving wooden churches in Poland. The interior has charming folk decoration.

Half a kilometre farther south, behind the cemetery (take ul Tuchowska to get there), is the **Church of the Holy Trinity** (Kościół Św Trójcy), built in 1562, with a similar naively charming rustic interior including an early baroque high altar.

Places to Stay

Camping Nr 202 (☎ 21 51 24) is 1km north of the Old Town on ul Piłsudskiego. Open June to September, it has simple, cheap cabins (US$14/18/20 a double/triple/quad).

The all-year *youth hostel* (☎ 21 69 16, ul Konarskiego 17), a five minute walk south from the Rynek, is simple but clean and well run. It only has large dormitories (for 12 and 16 people) where a bed will cost foreigners US$6. You need to check in before

8 pm. From the station it's a 20 minute walk, or you can take bus No 1, 8 or 25.

Dom Wycieczkowy PTTK Pod Murami (☎ 21 62 29, ul Żydowska 16) is in the heart of the Old Town and charges US$20/25/30 a double/triple/quad without bath or US$7 per bed in a five or six-bed dorm.

Equally well located is the simple *Hotel Polonia* (☎ 21 33 36, ul Wałowa 21), costing US$15/24/28 for singles/doubles/triples without bath. Rooms with bath cost about US$4 more. The hotel may possibly close for a much-needed refurbishment.

The three-star *Hotel Tarnovia* (☎ 21 26 71, fax 21 27 44, ul Kościuszki 10), in a modern suburb near the bus and train stations, is the best place to stay in the city and charges US$40/55 a single/double with bath and breakfast.

Places to Eat

There are two milk bars conveniently located at opposite ends of the Old Town: *Bar Mleczny Łasuch* (ul Sowińskiego 4) and *Bar Sam* (ul Lwowska 12). They are both intact communist relics – dirt cheap but not particularly pleasant.

There are plenty of better budget places of a more recent generation, including *Bistro Cafe Campari* (ul Krakowska 3) and *Cafe Bistro Ambrozja* (ul Mościckiego 6). *Restauracja Ognisty Smok* (ul Wałowa 30) has cheap Vietnamese meals, while *Granada Grill* (ul Wałowa 5) serves reasonable Greek and Turkish food.

Pizzeria Maranto (ul Wałowa 26) has some of the better pizzas in town, but if you want something more Italian, try *Restauracja Bella Italia* (Rynek 5), which is reasonably priced and also has Polish food.

Restauracja Bristol on ul Krakowska is an intact survivor of the old days. Today it doesn't have a large clientele, yet the food is still acceptable and the prices fairly low. Possibly a better option, though, is the restaurant of *Hotel Tarnovia*.

Getting There & Away

The train and bus stations are next to each other, south-west of the centre. It's a 20 minute walk to the Old Town, or you can take bus No 2, 9, 35, 37 or 41.

Train Trains to Kraków (78km) run every hour or so; get off in Bochnia if you plan on visiting the Nowy Wiśnicz castle. There are regular departures to Rzeszów (80km) and Nowy Sącz (89km), and several trains to Warsaw (396km).

Bus There are frequent buses west to Kraków (86km) and regular departures south-east to Jasło (58km) and Krosno (83km). One morning bus goes to Zamość (238km). For Sandomierz (104km), take any of the Tarnobrzeg buses which depart every other hour, and then change; there's frequent transport between Tarnobrzeg and Sandomierz.

ZALIPIE
• **pop 800**
The village of Zalipie has been known as a centre of folk painting for almost a century, since its inhabitants started to decorate their houses with colourful floral designs. Actually, they used to adorn everything possible: their cottages, barns, wells, stoves, tools and furniture. The best-known painter was Felicja Curyłowa (1904-74), and after her death a museum opened on her farm. The House of Women Painters (Dom Malarek) was established in 1978 to serve as a centre for the village's artists. A contest for the best decorated house has been held annually since 1948.

The tradition of painted houses seems to have weakened since the early 1990s, and the local museum was closed for a long period but is now open again. If you find it locked, ask for the keys in the house across the road.

The contest is still going, just after Corpus Christi (Friday to Sunday), but it's not a tourist event. It's better to visit Zalipie after the contest rather than before, as you'll see fresh paintings. However, don't expect every house to be painted over – there are perhaps a dozen decorated cottages in the whole village.

There are only a few buses daily from Tarnów (31km), and the village spreads over a large area with decorated houses few and far between. It's useful to have your own transport, and better still if you find a guide (the Dom Malarek doesn't have any) to take you round the most interesting examples. The management of the ethnographic museum in Tarnów may have some current information about Zalipie.

RZESZÓW
• **pop 160,000   ☎ 017**
The chief city of south-eastern Poland, Rzeszów ('Zheh-shoof') started life in the 13th century as an obscure Ruthenian settlement. When in the mid-14th century Kazimierz Wielki captured vast territories of Ruthenia, the town became Polish and acquired its present name. It grew rapidly in the 16th century when Mikołaj Spytek Ligęza, the local ruler, commissioned a castle and a church, and built fortifications. It later fell into the hands of the powerful Lubomirski clan but this couldn't save the town from the subsequent gradual decline experienced by the whole of Poland.

After WWII the new government tried to revive the region and crammed the city with industry and new residential suburbs. The hurried building program increased the size of the town but with little aesthetic consideration. Fortunately, a handful of surviving historic buildings have been restored to their original form, which may be a reason to visit if you are passing this way.

Information
Tourist Office The Centrum Informacji Turystycznej (☎ 852 46 12, ☎/fax 852 46 11), ul Asnyka 6, is open weekdays 9.30 am to 5 pm, Saturday 9 am to 2 pm.

Money The Bank Pekao at Al Ciepliń-skiego 1 opposite the Hotel Rzeszów will change travellers cheques, give advances on Visa and MasterCard, and also has a useful ATM. There are two Euronet ATMs closer to the centre, at Al Piłsudskiego 34 and

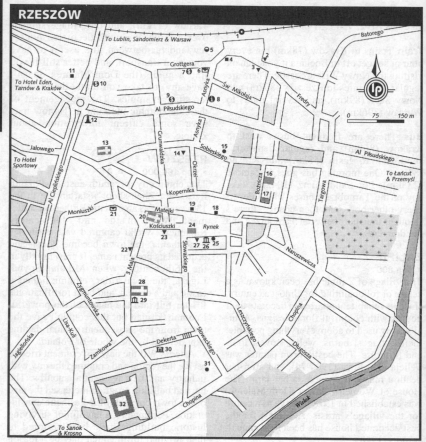

RZESZÓW

ul Grottgera 10. Cash can be exchanged in one of the kantors around the centre.

Things to See

Most of the **Rynek** has been restored over recent years, though it will still be a while before the remaining part is completed. In the middle of the square is a monument to Tadeusz Kościuszko. The 16th century **town hall**, in the corner of the Rynek, was wholly remodelled a century ago in pseudo-Gothic style and looks a bit like a wedding cake. The **Ethnographic Museum** (Muzeum Etnograficzne) at Rynek 6 has folk costumes and woodcarvings from the region on permanent display and puts on occasional temporary shows. It's open daily 9 am to 2 pm except Monday and Saturday.

The nearby **parish church** dates from the 15th century, but only the chancel with its Gothic vault has survived from that period. The church was largely reconstructed in the 1750s, and most of the fittings come from this time. Note the interesting Renaissance

RZESZÓW

PLACES TO STAY		23	Restauracja Rzeszowska	15	LOT Office
4	Hotel Polonia	27	Restauracja Ksania	16	New Town Synagogue
11	Hotel Rzeszów			17	Old Town Synagogue
18	Dom Polonii & Restauracja	**OTHER**		20	Parish Church
	Wspólnota	1	Train Station	21	Main Post Office
19	Youth Hostel	5	Bus Terminal	24	Town Hall
		6	Post Office	25	Orbis Office
PLACES TO EAT		7	Euronet ATM	26	Ethnographic Museum
2	Bar u Wojciecha	8	Tourist Office	28	Piarist Church
3	Bar Powszechny	9	Euronet ATM	29	Regional Museum
14	Restauracja	10	Bank Pekao	30	Lubomirski Palace
	Bohema	12	Communist Monument	31	Philharmonic Hall
22	Restauracja Śródmiejska	13	Bernardine Church	32	Castle

tombs at the left (northern) side of the chancel.

About 200m south on ul 3 Maja is the **Piarist Church** (Kościół Pijarów), built in the mid-17th century and still with its original Lublin Renaissance vault embellished with fine stucco work by Jan Falconi. The baroque character of the façade is the result of the 1706 remodelling by Tylman van Gameren.

Next door, in the former Piarist monastery at ul 3 Maja 19, is the **Regional Museum** (Muzeum Okręgowe). It has permanent exhibitions featuring Polish painting from the 18th to 20th centuries, glass and faïence, and the history of the region. A bonus attraction is the surviving 17th century frescoed vaults. It's open Tuesday and Friday 10 am to 5 pm, Wednesday and Thursday to 3 pm, and Sunday to 2 pm.

A short walk south, on ul Dekerta, is the early 18th century baroque **Lubomirski Palace**, also the work of Tylman van Gameren, today home to the Academy of Music.

Nearby to the south-west stands the **castle**. Begun at the end of the 16th century, the building has changed a lot since then but the entrance tower and the bastions have retained their original shape. From the 19th century until 1981 the castle served as a jail, its inmates including political prisoners. It has recently been solidly renovated

and looks like new. Today it houses the law court.

Return north to the **Bernardine Church** (Kościół Bernardynów), built for Ligęza as his mausoleum. There are life-size alabaster effigies of his family in the side walls of the chancel. In the gilded chapel to the right is the early 16th century statue of the Virgin Mary to whom numerous miracles have been attributed; intriguing wall paintings on both sides depict a hundred people who were cured.

Go eastwards to ul Bożnicza where two synagogues stand close to each other. Though less attractive from the outside, the 18th century **New Town Synagogue** (Synagoga Nowomiejska) has more to offer as it holds an art gallery. Note the entrance to its café on the 1st floor, the work of the contemporary sculptor Marian Kruczek. The 17th century **Old Town Synagogue** (Synagoga Staromiejska) now houses the city's registry and a centre for studies on the history of local Jews.

Places to Stay

The all-year *youth hostel* (☎ 853 44 30, Rynek 25) is the cheapest and most central option – right on the main square.

Hotel Sportowy (☎ 853 40 77, ul Jałowego 23A), located in a sports complex a 10 minute walk west of the Rynek, is a good budget choice. It has quiet doubles without/with bath for US$14/22.

Poorer value is the central *Hotel Polonia* (☎ 852 03 12, ul Grottgera 16) opposite the train station. It has been revamped and the rooms now have private showers, yet toilets are down the corridor. Singles/doubles/triples cost US$28/35/44.

Hotel Eden (☎ 852 56 83, ul Krakowska 150) is a student hostel operating year-round and offering reasonable standards, but it's a long way from the centre – take the westbound bus No 1 from Al Piłsudskiego. You pay US$7 per head in a triple or quad without bath, and US$11 in a double or triple with bath.

For somewhere small and pleasant in the centre, try *Dom Polonii* (☎ 62 14 52, Rynek 19), which has just one single room for US$30 and two double suites for US$60 each.

Possibly the best facilities in town are provided by *Hotel Rzeszów* (☎ 852 34 41, fax 853 33 89, Al Cieplińskiego 2), in a drab building. If you take a front room (US$50/75 a single/double with bath), you'll have a good view from your window of the huge monument erected 'in memory of the heroes of the revolutionary struggles for the People's Poland', a legacy of the communist fantasy, but now a dilemma for the authorities.

Places to Eat

There are two very cheap places near the train station: *Bar u Wojciecha* (Plac Kilińskiego 6) and the more pleasant *Bar Powszechny* (ul Grottgera 28) across the street. You'll find more simple, small eateries in the Rynek area, including the front, budget section of *Restauracja Śródmiejska* (ul 3 Maja 8).

Restauracja Bohema (ul Okrzei 7) serves the usual Polish fare at reasonable prices. The new, attractive *Restauracja Ksania* (Rynek 4) offers similarly priced meals.

Slightly more expensive is *Restauracja Wspólnota* (Rynek 19) in the cellar of Dom Polonii. *Restauracja Rzeszowska* (ul Kościuszki 9) has a salad bar and is yet another good central option.

Getting There & Away

The train and bus stations are next to each other and only about 500m from the Rynek. Rzeszów is an important transport hub and there are a lot of buses and trains in all directions. The airport is in Jasionka, 11km north of the city, accessible by bus No 14 from Al Piłsudskiego.

Air From late March to late October, there are five flights a week to Warsaw, Rzeszów's only direct air link. In the remaining period, there may be only a few flights per week. The LOT office (☎ 62 03 47) at Plac Ofiar Getta 6 will book and sell tickets.

Train There are at least two dozen trains daily to Przemyśl (87km) and almost the same number to Tarnów (80km). A dozen trains a day leave for Kraków (158km) and eight for Jasło (71km). Two night trains run daily to Sandomierz (84km). To Warsaw (326km), there are two morning express trains and one evening fast train. There's also one train to Lviv which continues to Kiev.

Bus PKS buses leave regularly throughout the day to Sanok (76km), Krosno (59km), Przemyśl (84km) and Lublin (170km). Six buses go daily to Ustrzyki Dolne (116km) and one of them continues up to Ustrzyki Górne (163km). There are two fast buses to Zamość (163km). Buses to Łańcut (17km) run roughly every half an hour and are more convenient than trains, as they deposit you near the palace.

Polski Express runs one bus a day to Warsaw (303km, US$10, 6¼ hours), going via Lublin and Puławy. Tickets can be bought from Orbis.

ŁAŃCUT

• pop 17,000   ☎ 017

Łańcut ('Wahyn-tsoot') is famous for its palace, which is arguably the best-known aristocratic home to be found anywhere in Poland. It's one of the largest residences of its kind and holds an extensive and diverse collection of art.

The building started life in the 15th century as a castle and is still often referred to as such; it was Stanisław Lubomirski who made it a palace worthy of the name. Soon after he had successfully completed his beautiful Nowy Wiśnicz castle, he came into possession of the large property of Łańcut and commissioned Matteo Trapola to design a new home even more spectacular than the old one. The palace was built in 1629-41 and surrounded with a system of fortifications laid out in the shape of a five-pointed star, modelled on the latest Italian theories of the day.

Some 150 years later the fortifications were partly demolished while the palace itself was reshaped in rococo and neoclassical style. The last important alteration, executed at the end of the 19th century, gave the building its neo-baroque façades, basically the form which survives today.

A fabulous collection of art was accumulated here, and the last private owner, Alfred Potocki, was regarded as one of the richest men in prewar Poland. Shortly before the arrival of the Red Army in July 1944, he loaded 11 railway carriages with the most valuable objects and fled with the collection to Liechtenstein.

Things to See

Just after WWII, the palace was taken over by the state and opened as a **palace museum**, which suggests that there must have been enough works of art left to put on display. The collection has systematically been enlarged and supplemented, and today it conveys the impression of being perhaps bigger than before the war. In fact the rooms are so crammed that it's virtually impossible to take it all in on one visit.

You'll see the whole 1st floor and the western side of the ground floor, altogether about 50 rooms. In the carefully restored original interiors – representing various styles and periods – you'll find heaps of paintings, sculptures and *objets d'art* of all sorts. The 18th century theatre (reshaped later), the ballroom, and the dining room with a table that seats 80 people are among

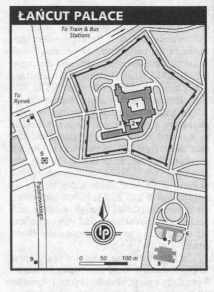

ŁAŃCUT PALACE

1 Palace
2 Restauracja Zamkowa
3 Hotel Zamkowy
4 Ticket Office
5 Synagogue
6 Exhibition of Icons
7 Souvenir Shop
8 Carriages
9 Pensjonat Pałacyk

the highlights. Brochures in English are available, for more information.

The palace is surrounded by a well kept **park** which extends east behind the fortress. However, before taking a leisurely stroll (which you can do until dusk) go and see Potocki's collection of 55 **carriages**, in the coach house, south of the castle. A further 70 old horse-drawn vehicles have been acquired by the museum since WWII, making this one of the largest collections of its kind.

The stable opposite holds over a thousand **icons**, from the 15th century onwards. This is essentially a storage facility and

THE CARPATHIAN MOUNTAINS

only a small portion is on display, but there are some real gems among them.

The ticket office is by the western entrance to the park. You buy one combined ticket to the palace museum and carriages (US$3, US$1.50 for students) and a separate ticket to see the icon collection (US$0.50). The office also sells tourist brochures.

The palace is visited in groups accompanied by a guide (guide service in Polish is included in the ticket's price), and the tour takes from 1½ to two hours. Guides speaking English, French and German are available for US$24 per group (plus tickets). Book your guide a day or two in advance on ☎ 225 23 38. In summer, there are many individual foreign visitors and package bus excursions, and you can often tag along with one of the groups and share costs.

The palace, carriages and icons are open from 1 February to 30 November 10 am to 3 pm daily except Monday. From 1 April to 30 September, they open at 9 am and close at 4 pm on Sunday. The closing hours listed are the time when the last tour departs but don't go on it, as you'll have only 45 minutes to rush around everything. The park is open from 7 am till dusk.

Just west outside the palace park is the **synagogue**. Built in the 1760s, it has retained much of its decoration and is today a museum. It's open 15 June to 30 September 10 am to 4 pm except Monday, and entry costs US$0.50. In other months (except December and January) it can be opened on request for the equivalent of 25 tickets.

A long way from the palace, opposite the train station, is the large Polmos distillery, which houses the **Distillery Museum** (Muzeum Gorzelnictwa), the only one of its kind in Poland. So far, the museum only opens for VIPs (and the visits include tastings of the delicious, locally made spirits), but there are plans to open it to the general public.

Special Events
In May, the Old Music Festival is held in Łańcut for two weeks, with chamber music concerts performed in the palace's ball-room. The festival has gained a high reputation and, given the limited capacity of the auditorium, tickets run out fast. The palace is closed to visitors during the festival.

Places to Stay & Eat
Hotel Zamkowy (☎ 225 26 71, ☎ 225 26 72) in the palace is simple but perfectly OK and cheap: US$14/20 for doubles/triples without bath, US$30/40 with bath. *Restauracja Zamkowa* across the small courtyard is similar: acceptable food at reasonable prices. It's open 9 am to 9 pm. The hotel and restaurant are almost permanently full in July and August. On summer weekends you might wait a long time for a table.

Another pleasant place to stay in Łańcut is *Pensjonat Pałacyk* (☎ 225 20 43, ☎ 225 43 56, ul Paderewskiego 18), about 200m south of the synagogue. Set in a small palace-like mansion, it has five doubles with bath for US$25 to US$30 and a quad for US$35. It also has a restaurant, perhaps the best eatery in town.

Dom Wycieczkowy PTTK (☎ 225 45 12, ul Dominikańska 1), in the former Dominican monastery just off Łańcut's Rynek, offers simple rooms without bath to sleep from two to 10 people. You pay US$7 per head in a double, US$6 in a triple or quad, and US$5 in a larger room. There's the small *Restauracja Zabytkowa* on the premises, or you can eat in *Caffé Antico* across the Rynek, which serves Greek and Italian food including pizzas.

Getting There & Away
The bus terminal is half a kilometre north-east of the palace while the train station is about 2km north; it's therefore more convenient to arrive and depart by bus.

Buses and trains to Rzeszów (17km) run roughly every half an hour, and to Przemyśl (67km) every hour or two. Three buses a day go to Zamość (157km).

PRZEMYŚL
• pop 70,000   ☎ 016

Founded in the 10th century on terrain long fought over by Poland and Ruthenia,

Przemyśl ('Pzheh-mishl') changed hands several times before being annexed by the Polish Crown in 1340. It experienced its golden period in the 16th century, and declined afterwards. During the Partitions it fell under Austrian administration.

Around 1850 the Austrians began to fortify Przemyśl. This work continued right up till the outbreak of WWI, producing one of the largest fortresses in Europe, perhaps the second-biggest after Verdun. It consisted of a double ring of earth ramparts, including a 15km-long inner circle and an outer girdle three times longer, with over 60 forts placed at strategic points. This formidable system played an important role during the war but nevertheless the garrison had to surrender to the Russians in 1915 for lack of provisions.

At the end of WWII, only 60% of Przemyśl's buildings were left. The major historic monuments in the Old Town were restored, while new districts sprang up on the opposite, northern side of the San River.

Information

Tourist Office The Ośrodek Informacji Turystycznej (☎/fax 678 73 09) is in the Clock Tower at ul Władycze 3. From June to September, it's open weekdays 8 am to 6 pm, and Saturday 10 am to 2 pm. Outside this period, it opens weekdays 8 am to 4 pm.

Money The Bank Pekao at ul Jagiellońska 7 and the Bank Depozytowo Kredytowy at ul Mickiewicza 6 opposite the train station both handle travellers cheque transactions and have useful ATMs. There are several kantors in the centre, though their exchange rates may be relatively poor. You are likely to get more złotys for your dollars in Rzeszów – change there if you're coming from that direction.

Things to See

Perched on a hillside and dominated by four mighty churches, the Old Town is a picturesque place. Most of the architectural fabric dates from the 19th century, a product of the extensive urbanisation by the

Austrians. The grassy sloping **Rynek** has preserved some of its older arcaded houses, mostly on its southern and northern sides.

The **Franciscan Church** (Kościół Franciszkański), just off the Rynek, was built in 1754-78 in the late baroque style but its monumental façade was remade later. The church has an amazing interior with florid baroque decoration of both the altars and vault.

Just up the hill behind it stands the former **Jesuit Church** (Kościół Pojezuicki). Built in 1627-59, it was used as an army depot by the Austrians until they decided to pull it down altogether. Happily they changed their mind and, after some revamping, made it a garrison church. It's also a baroque construction, and has its original façade. The church has recently been handed over to the Uniate congregation (see the following paragraphs). All the Catholic fittings, including the massive black marble high altar, have been removed and replaced with decoration related to the Eastern rite, principally the heavily gilded iconostasis.

The adjacent former Jesuit college now shelters the **Archdiocesan Museum** (Muzeum Archidiecezjalne), which contains religious art. It's open daily May to October 10 am to noon and 1 to 3 pm.

Up the hill is one more house of worship, the **Carmelite Church** (Kościół Karmelitów). It looks a bit odd, with its massive Byzantine dome sitting atop an otherwise handsome Renaissance building. The church epitomises the sometimes uneasy coexistence of the Roman Catholic and Uniate communities in the city.

Designed by the Italian architect Galeazzo Appiani (who also built the Krasiczyn castle – see the following section), the church and the adjacent monastery were built for the Carmelites. Following their expulsion in 1784, the Austrian authorities handed the church over to the Uniates. It was then that the timbered dome was added and the baroque black marble high altar replaced with an iconostasis. The church served as a Uniate cathedral until the end of

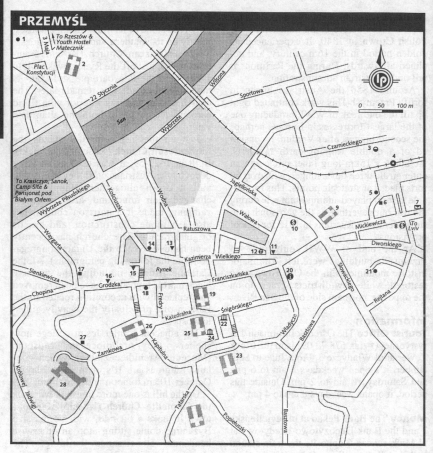

PRZEMYŚL

0   50   100 m

WWII, after which the new government gave it back to the Carmelites.

With the political changes of the past decade, the Uniates came out of the closet to reclaim the church, and the religious conflict rose to quite a serious level by 1991. The quarrel was eventually settled by the pope himself, who gave the Uniates the former Jesuit church, while the Carmelites retained their original church. The city's current Uniate congregation is about 2500.

The building has preserved some of its original features, including the main doorway and stucco work on the vaulting. Note the large wooden pulpit in the shape of a boat complete with mast, sail and rigging.

A few steps down from the church is the **Regional Museum** (Muzeum Ziemi Przemyskiej), which displays an excellent selection of about 90 Ruthenian icons (of over 500 pieces in the museum's collection assembled from the region). You'll also come across the ethnographic and archaeo-

PLACES TO STAY		OTHER		14	Klub Niedźwiadek
6	Dom Wycieczkowy	1	Former Synagogue	18	PTTK Office
	Przemysław	2	Church of the Holy Trinity	19	Franciscan Church
17	Dom Wycieczkowy PTTK	3	Bus Terminal	20	Tourist Office (Clock Tower)
	Podzamcze	4	Train Station	21	Former Synagogue (Public
27	Hotel pod Basztą	5	Orbis Office		Library)
		7	Main Post Office	22	Regional Museum
PLACES TO EAT		8	Bank Depozytowo	23	Carmelite Church
11	Bar Rubin		Kredytowy	24	Archdiocesan Museum
13	Pizzeria Margherita	9	Reformed Franciscan Church	25	Jesuit Church
15	Pub Wyrwigrosz	10	Bank Pekao	26	Cathedral
16	Kasyno Wojskowe	12	Public Toilet	28	Castle

logical galleries. The museum is open 10 am to 2 pm except Monday and the day after public holidays (on Tuesday and Friday 10.30 am to 5.30 pm).

A short walk west along ul Katedralna is the **cathedral** with its 71m-high freestanding bell tower. Originally a Gothic building (still visible in the vault in the chancel), the church was remodelled on various occasions and is now predominantly baroque.

Continue up the same street to the **castle**, or rather what is left of it. Built by Kazimierz Wielki in the 1340s, it mutated into a Renaissance building two centuries later when it got its four corner towers. Two of them have been repaired along with one side of the castle. A local theatre, the Teatr Fredreum, and a café now occupy the restored rooms. One of the towers is open to visitors (April to September 10 am to 6 pm, other months until 4 pm, closed Monday) and provides a sweeping view over the new districts of the city beyond the San River. The view over the Old Town is unfortunately obscured by trees.

Possibly a better panorama will be seen from the top of the **Clock Tower** (Wieża Zegarowa), on ul Władycze, when it opens. Built in 1775-77, this solitary baroque structure was used from 1905 to 1983 as a watchtower by the local fire brigade. Now it's in the hands of the regional museum, and will house some exhibitions. The tourist office is here.

Those interested in war strategy may want to check out the famous **fortifications**.

However, as these were mostly earth ramparts, they are overgrown with grass and bushes and now resemble natural rather than artificial bulwarks. If you want to see what's left, perhaps the best places to go are Siedliska and Bolestraszyce. The tourist office can give you information about the sites and transport details. The PTTK office (☎ 678 32 74) at ul Grodzka 1 can provide guides.

The only significant relics of the Jewish legacy are two synagogues, both dating from the late 19th century, renovated after the war and given other uses. One is off the Plac Konstytucji on the northern side of the San River; the other (now the public library) is on ul Biblioteczna near the train station.

Don't miss the castle in Krasiczyn, 10km west of Przemyśl (see the following section).

Places to Stay

Przemyśl has quite a choice of budget accommodation, yet you may occasionally have problems in finding somewhere, as these places are frequented by the 'tourists' from beyond the eastern frontier, just 14km away.

Camping Nr 233 Zamek (☎ 678 56 42, Wybrzeże Piłsudskiego 8A) has all-year cabins, where doubles/triples/quads with bath cost US$20/24/28. Additionally, cheaper seasonal cabins without bath are available from 15 May to late September;

you pay US$5 per bed. You can also pitch your own tent.

The good *Youth Hostel Matecznik* (☎ *670 61 45, ul Lelewela 6*) is open all year and costs between US$4 and US$7 per bed depending on the room. It's not ideally located – a 15 minute walk to the Old Town – but frequent city buses ply this route.

There are two simple places conveniently located in the Old Town close to the castle. The basic *Dom Wycieczkowy PTTK Podzamcze* (☎ *678 53 74, ul Waygarta 3*) has rooms with bunks and shared facilities only. You pay US$6/5/4 for a bed in a double/triple or quad/large dorm. The nearby *Hotel pod Basztą* (☎ *678 82 68, ul Królowej Jadwigi 4*) has no private facilities either but is better. It offers one single (US$13), three doubles (US$17) and two triples (US$24).

There are a few budget places close to the train station but the area is less attractive and farther away from the Old Town. The ultra-basic *Dom Wycieczkowy Przemysław* (☎ *678 90 31, ul Sowińskiego 4*), just opposite the station, is one of the favourite shelters among visitors from the east. Singles/doubles/triples/quads without bath cost US$10/14/19/24.

A bit better is *Hotel Sportowy*, popularly called the Hala (☎ *678 38 49, ul Mickiewicza 30*), a 10 minute walk east from the station, away from the Old Town. Doubles/triples/quads without bath go for US$16/21/26, while singles/doubles/triples with bath cost US$18/22/27.

Some 200m farther east is *Hotel Krokus* (☎ *678 51 27, ul Mickiewicza 47*), which provides reasonable standards in rooms with bath for US$20/28/34/40 a single/double/triple/quad.

Marginally better is *Pensjonat pod Białym Orłem* (☎ *678 61 07, ul Sanocka 13*), about 1km west of the Old Town – follow the extension of Wybrzeże Piłsudskiego. It offers doubles/triples with bath and breakfast for US$35/45.

Hotel Marko (☎ *678 92 72, ul Lwowska 36A*), 3km east of the centre, on the road to Medyka on the border, is arguably the best of the lot. The rooms are small but have

their own bath and satellite TV and cost US$45/55/65 a single/double/triple with breakfast.

Places to Eat

Pizzeria Margherita (Rynek 4) serves inexpensive pizzas, spaghetti and risotto. Enter from the side street. Diagonally across the Rynek is *Pub Wyrwigrosz*, which has an outdoor eating/drinking area in summer. The wicker chairs make this a comfortable place to sit and enjoy a coffee, beer or a meal from a small selection of Polish, Mexican and Chinese dishes. Round the corner is the drab but very cheap *Kasyno Wojskowe (ul Grodzka 8)*.

Possibly the best place to eat in town is *Bar Rubin (ul Kazimierza Wielkiego 19)*. It's a small, friendly, fast family restaurant serving hearty Polish food, including *pierogi* and *barszcz*, at very affordable prices. There are only six tables, so you may have to wait a few minutes in the mid-afternoon, but it's worth it.

Entertainment

The café-bar *Klub Niedźwiadek (Rynek 1)* may have occasional live music, mostly jazz.

Getting There & Away

The train and bus stations are next to each other, on the north-eastern edge of the centre.

Train Frequent trains run to Rzeszów (87km), and there are at least half a dozen fast trains and two express trains a day to Kraków (245km). Two express and two fast trains go daily to Warsaw (414km), and two trains to Lublin (241km). International trains to Lviv, Odessa and Kiev pass via Przemyśl. There are no longer trains to Ustrzyki Dolne.

Have a look at the station building, a neo-baroque piece of architecture, now a historic monument. Built in 1895, it retains some of its decoration, both inside and out.

Bus At least five buses daily run to Sanok (63km) and three to Ustrzyki Dolne

(77km). There are about 10 fast buses a day to Rzeszów (84km). One fast bus leaves (around 2 pm) for Zamość (148km).

The development of 'tourism' across the border is clearly reflected in the transport – half a dozen buses daily go to/from Lviv (95km, US$5, three hours), and are packed with salespeople.

KRASICZYN
• pop 1000   ☎ 016

No one would notice the small village of Krasiczyn ('Krah-shee-chin') if not for its castle, a late Renaissance construction acclaimed as one of the finest of its kind in the country. It's in a spacious landscaped park abounding with a variety of trees and shrubs.

The castle was designed by an Italian, Galleazzo Appiani, and built between 1592 and 1618 for the rich Krasicki family. Despite numerous wars and fires it didn't suffer any major damage and has somehow retained most of its original shape. Extensive restoration began in the 1960s but almost stopped in the early 1990s, leaving the work incomplete. By 1998 the castle was probably in worse shape than a decade earlier.

The castle is more or less square, built around a spacious, partly arcaded courtyard, with four different cylindrical corner towers. They were supposed to reflect the social order of the period and were named (clockwise from the south-western corner) after God, the pope, the king and the nobility. The God tower, topped with a dome, houses a chapel. The fifth, square tower, in the middle of the western side, served as the main entrance to the castle and is accessible by a long arcaded bridge over a wide moat.

Although the restoration is unfinished, tourists can visit the courtyard and three of the corner towers in summer. Visits are in groups with a guide, which depart a few times a day (at 9.30 am, 11.30 am and 2 pm at the time of writing). Even if you don't take the tour, a view of the castle from the outside and a walk around the park (open daily 10 am till dusk except Monday) are perhaps enough to justify a return trip from Przemyśl or a stop if you are passing through.

Places to Stay & Eat

The all-year *Hotel Zamkowy* (☎ 671 83 21, ☎/fax 671 83 16) next to the castle offers good singles/doubles/triples with bath for US$40/50/80, plus suites from US$60 to US$150. Discount weekend rates may be available out of the summer season. The hotel has its own restaurant (for guests only) and a budget snack bar (open to all).

Getting There & Away

The castle is a short round-trip from Przemyśl (10km) on one of the regular suburban (No 40) or PKS buses. You can continue from Krasiczyn to Sanok (55km, four buses daily) or Ustrzyki Dolne (67km, three buses).

The Bieszczady

The Bieszczady ('Byesh-chah-di') is a wild, scantily populated mountain region of thick forests and open meadows. It's in the far south-eastern corner of Poland, sandwiched between the Ukrainian and Slovakian borders. Largely unspoilt and unpolluted, it's one of the most attractive areas in the country. As tourist facilities are modest, roads sparse and public transport limited, the Bieszczady retains its relative isolation and makes for an off-the-beaten-track destination. It's popular with nature lovers and hikers, but large scale tourism hasn't yet arrived.

In geographical terms, the Bieszczady is a mountain system running east-west for some 60km along Poland's southern frontier, and lower hills to the north, referred to as the Przedgórze Bieszczadzkie, or the foothills. In practical terms, the Bieszczady is the whole area to the south-east of the Nowy Łupków-Zagórz-Ustrzyki Dolne railway line, up to the national borders: approximately 2100 sq km, about 60% of which is forest, largely fir and beech. Trees grow only to an altitude of about 1200m, above which you find the *połoniny*, the steppe-like pastures that are particularly lush in June.

The highest and most spectacular part has been declared the Bieszczady National Park

THE BIESZCZADY

(Bieszczadzki Park Narodowy), and at 271 sq km it's Poland's third-largest national park after Biebrza and Kampinos. The highest peak is Mt Tarnica (1346m).

The region was once much more densely populated than it is today – and not by Poles, but by the ethnic groups known as the Boyks and the Lemks. See the boxed text for details of them. Today, the most evident survivors of their tragic history are the *cerkwie*, or Orthodox or Uniate churches. These dilapidated wooden buildings still dot the countryside and add to the region's natural beauty. When hiking on remote trails, especially along the Ukrainian border, you'll find many traces of destroyed villages, including ruined houses and orchards. Visit the skansen in Sanok, which has some good examples of Boyk and Lemk architecture.

SANOK

● pop 42,000 ☎ 013

For the average Pole, Sanok brings to mind the *Autosan* – the locally produced bus. It's

The Boyks & the Lemks – Variations on a Theme

The Bieszczady, as well as the Beskid Niski and Beskid Sądecki farther west, were settled from about the 13th century by various nomadic groups migrating from the south and east. Most notable among them were the Wołosi from the Balkans and the Rusini from Ruthenia. Living in the same areas and intermarrying for centuries, they slowly developed into two distinct ethnic groups known as the Bojkowie and Łemkowie. The Bojkowie, or the Boyks, inhabited the eastern part of the Bieszczady, roughly east of Cisna, while the Łemkowie, or the Lemks, populated the mountainous regions stretching from the western Bieszczady up to the Beskid Sądecki. The two groups had much in common culturally, though there were noticeable differences in their dialects, dress and architecture. They shared the Orthodox creed with their Ukrainian neighbours.

After the Union of Brest in 1596, most Lemks and Boyks turned to the Uniate Church, which accepted the supremacy of Rome but retained the old Eastern rites and religious practices. From the end of the 19th century, however, the Roman Catholic hierarchy slowly but systematically imposed Latin rites. In response, many locals opted for a return to the Orthodox Church. By WWII both creeds were practised in the region, coexisting with varying degrees of harmony and conflict. By that time the total population of Boyks and Lemks was estimated at 200,000 to 300,000. The ethnic Poles were a minority in the region and consequently the Roman Catholic Church was insignificant.

All this changed dramatically in the aftermath of WWII when the borders were moved and the new government was installed. Not everyone was satisfied with the new status quo and some of its opponents didn't lay down their arms. One such armed faction was the Ukrainian Resistance Army, known to the Poles as UPA, which operated in the Bieszczady. Civil war continued in the region for almost two years. Eventually, in order to destroy the rebel base, the government decided to expel the inhabitants of all the villages in the region and resettle the whole area. In the so-called Operation Vistula (Operacja Wisła) in 1947, most of the population was brutally deported either to the Soviet Union or to the northern and western Polish territories just regained from Germany. Ironically, the main victims of the action were the Boyks and the Lemks, who had little to do with the conflict apart from the fact that they happened to live there. Moreover, Lemks were also deported from areas farther west where there was no partisan activity.

Their villages were abandoned or destroyed, and those that survived were resettled with new inhabitants from other regions. Only some 20,000 Lemks were left in the whole region, and very few Boyks.

the major type used in intercity and urban transport throughout the country. The bus factory along with several other plants make the town an important regional industrial centre. Don't let this put you off, however. Sanok has some important attractions well worth visiting.

Information
Tourist Office In the absence of a municipal tourist office, the PTTK office (☎ 463

21 71, ☎/fax 463 25 12), ul 3 Maja 2, performs this role. It's open weekdays 8 am to 4 pm.

Money The Bank Pekao at ul Mickiewicza 29 and the Bank Depozytowo Kredytowy at ul Kościuszki 4 both change travellers cheques and have ATMs. There are half a dozen kantors on ul Kościuszki in the vicinity of the latter bank, and others elsewhere in the centre.

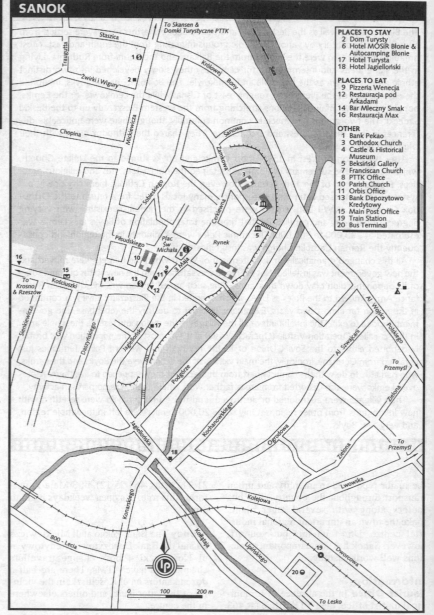

SANOK

To Skansen &
Domki Turystyczne PTTK

PLACES TO STAY
2 Dom Turysty
6 Hotel MOSiR Błonie &
Autocamping Błonie
17 Hotel Turysta
18 Hotel Jagielloński

PLACES TO EAT
9 Pizzeria Wenecja
12 Restauracja pod
Arkadami
14 Bar Mleczny Smak
16 Restauracja Max

OTHER
1 Bank Pekao
3 Orthodox Church
4 Castle & Historical
Museum
5 Beksiński Gallery
7 Franciscan Church
8 PTTK Office
10 Parish Church
11 Orbis Office
13 Bank Depozytowo
Kredytowy
15 Main Post Office
19 Train Station
20 Bus Terminal

Staszica

Trauguetta

Żwirki i Wigury

Królowej Bony

San

Mickiewicza

Chopina

Zamkowa

Sanowa

Sobieskiego

Cerkiewna

Piłsudskiego

Plac
Św
Michała

Rynek

3 Maja

Kościuszki

To
Krosno
& Rzeszów

Sienkiewicza

Grzki

Daszyńskiego

Jagiellońska

Podgórze

Jagiellońska

Al. Wojska Polskiego

Al. Szwajcarii

To
Przemyśl

Zielona

To
Przemyśl

Kochanowskiego

Ogrodowa

Zielona

Lwowska

Konarskiego

Kolejowa

Upińskiego

800 - Lecia

Kolejala

Dworcowa

To Lesko

0   100   200 m

Things to See

One of the star attractions of the town is the **Historical Museum** (Muzeum Historyczne) in the castle. However, the castle was in the process of being thoroughly revamped at the time of writing, and only a limited part of its collection was on display. Most of the work is expected to conclude by 1999, and the exhibitions (including archaeology, weaponry and painting) should return to the restored interiors.

The museum's highlight is a 700-piece collection of Ruthenian icons, one of the best in Poland. They date from the 15th to 18th centuries and should be displayed in roughly chronological order, as before, so you can study the evolution of the style: the pure, somewhat unreal early images gradually giving way to the greater realism of later icons showing the Roman Catholic influence. Most icons were acquired after WWII from abandoned Uniate churches. If you are particularly interested in icons, note that there are also collections in Przemyśl, Łańcut and Nowy Sącz.

Some totally different paintings can be seen in the **Beksiński Gallery**, diagonally opposite the castle. The gallery features the works of Zdzisław Beksiński, one of Poland's most remarkable contemporary painters, who was born and lived in Sanok. The collection consists of 40-odd paintings and drawings, including some of his best works. Yet it's too small and patchy to be representative of the work of this visionary artist who produced hundreds of excellent paintings, many of which have gone abroad. The gallery is open daily 9 am to 3 pm (from 11 am on Monday). From mid-June to mid-September the opening hours are extended till 5 pm (on Monday till 3 pm). The gallery may move to the castle after it's restored.

Another place you shouldn't miss is the **skansen** (Muzeum Budownictwa Ludowego), 1.5km north of the centre. One of Poland's best open-air museums, it has so far gathered about 100 traditional buildings from the south-east of the country and provides an insight into the culture of the Boyks and Lemks. Among the buildings, there are three beautiful wooden churches, an inn, a school and even a fire brigade station.

The skansen is open daily, in April 9 am to 4 pm, May to October 8 am to 6 pm, and November to March 9 am to 2 pm. Visits are in guided groups of up to 20 people (in Polish), and the tour takes nearly two hours. In summer, there may be some English-speaking guides – inquire at the ticket office, or preferably call in advance on ☎ 463 16 72. They cost US$10 per group, in addition to the entry ticket of US$1.50 paid by each visitor. You can buy a leaflet in English with a short description of selected objects. There's a café at the entrance serving the usual fare of snacks and light dishes. Bus No 1 or 3 from the Rynek will let you off by the bridge leading across the San River to the skansen.

Of the town's churches, the oldest (built in the 1630s) is the **Franciscan Church** but it was reshaped several times after its construction. In the left-side altar is the venerated painting of the Virgin Mary. The neo-Romanesque **parish church** dating from 1874-86 has Art Nouveau wall paintings. The neoclassical **Orthodox church** was built in 1784 and initially served the Uniate congregation; it's open for Sunday Masses at 10.30 am and 5 pm, but can be opened on request for visitors – inquire at the neighbouring building.

Places to Stay

There is a 60-bed summer *youth hostel* (☎ 463 09 25, ul Konarskiego 10). Another very cheap seasonal place is *Domki Turystyczne PTTK* (☎ 463 28 18) in Biała Góra close to the skansen. This collection of a dozen basic tent-like bungalows is open June to September. A bed in a two/five-bed room will cost US$5/4.

Dom Turysty (☎ 463 10 13, ☎/fax 463 14 39, ul Mickiewicza 29) is a large PTTK hostel. It was in disastrous shape but is now being renovated. Refurbished doubles with bath are US$32, or you can go for an unrefurbished single/double with bath for

US$12/18, but make sure to inspect the room before you decide.

Hotel Turysta (☎/fax 463 09 22, ul Jagiellońska 13) is better and more central, and costs US$20/24/30 a single/double/triple with bath.

Hotel MOSiR Błonie (☎ 463 02 57, ☎/fax 463 14 93, Al Wojska Polskiego 1), in the sports centre, is still better value for money – it costs US$18/23/28 a single/double/triple with bath, or you can pay US$7 a bed in a four or five-bed dorm. From June to August they open an additional building, where beds in dorms without bath cost US$4. During this period, they also run *Autocamping Błonie* on the grounds.

The best place in town is *Hotel Jagielloński* (☎/fax 463 12 08, ul Jagiellońska 49), which costs US$18/24/30 for a neat, spacious single/double/triple with bath.

Places to Eat

Some of the cheapest food in town is at the basic *Bar Mleczny Smak* (ul Mickiewicza 4). The restaurant in *Dom Turysty* is also very cheap. If pizza is what you're after, try *Pizzeria Wenecja* (ul 3 Maja 16).

Among the better places, *Restauracja Max* (ul Kościuszki 34) has a simple interior but the food is OK and reasonably priced. Marginally more expensive is the basement *Restauracja pod Arkadami* (ul Grzegorza 2). Another place in this league is the restaurant of *Hotel Jagielloński*.

Getting There & Away

The train and bus stations are next to each other, a bit over 1km south of the centre.

Two trains a day run to Warsaw (460km) and two to Kraków (244km). A dozen ordinary trains go to Jasło (62km) via Krosno.

There's regular bus transport to Rzeszów (76km) and Lesko (15km). About 10 buses daily run to Ustrzyki Dolne (40km) and half of them continue up to Ustrzyki Górne (87km). There are several buses to Cisna (54km) and Wetlina (73km) plus additional buses in summer. A couple of buses go to Komańcza (38km). Four fast buses go directly to Kraków (205km) and one to Warsaw (379km).

AROUND SANOK
Icon Trail

The environs of Sanok are sprinkled with small villages, many of which still boast old Orthodox or Uniate churches, a reminder of the prewar ethnic and religious fabric of the region. In 1993, an idea to include some of the churches into a tourist route emerged, and by 1998 a walking trail, called the Szlak Ikon (Icon Trail), was traced and marked. It's a 70km loop path which begins and ends in Sanok and winds along the San River valley north of the city. The net walking time is about 15 hours.

The route includes about 10 churches, most of which are charming small timber structures typical of the region. Most date from the 18th and 19th centuries, but en route you'll also see the oldest Orthodox timber church in Poland, in Ulucz, built in 1510. You can visit all the churches on the way; arrangements have been made with each church's host to let the visitors in and show them around. A small donation will be appreciated.

A large board in front of Sanok's castle has the route's sketch map and general description (in Polish). Inquire at Sanok's PTTK office for further information. A brochure with the trail's description should be published by 1999. It is likely to include details of where to ask to have the church opened for you. If not, be sure to ask about it. Also inquire about accommodation and eating options along the route.

Czerteż

Czerteż is a small village 5km north-west of Sanok on the Rzeszów road. It has a beautiful wooden Uniate church from 1772 with the original iconostasis. It's not included in the Icon Trail, but it's one of the best churches in the region and is certainly worth a short trip. Sanok urban buses will drop you nearby. The church is hidden in the cluster of tall trees behind an agricultural cooperative. It can be visited under the same arrangements as the churches on the Icon Trail. The PTTK office can provide further information.

LESKO
- pop 6500   ☎ 013

Founded in the 15th century, Lesko had a mixed Polish-Ruthenian population, a reflection of the region's history. From the 16th century onwards, a lot of Jews arrived, initially from Spain, trying to escape the Inquisition. Their migration continued to such an extent that by the 18th century Jews made up half of the town's population.

WWII and the years that followed changed the ethnic picture altogether. The Jews were slaughtered by the Nazis, the Ukrainians were defeated by the Polish military and the Lemks were deported. The town was rebuilt, and without having developed any significant industry, is now a small tourist centre, a stopover on the way south into the Bieszczady. It's a pleasant and convenient place to begin your mountain travels, much more so than Ustrzyki Dolne to the east.

Information
There's no tourist office here; you can try the PTTK office in the old synagogue, open weekdays 8 am to 3 pm. A large town map, posted on a board next to the town hall, is useful for orientation.

Things to See
Lesko is notable for its Jewish heritage. The 17th century **synagogue**, just off the Rynek, has a Spanish flavour and its tower is a sure sign that it was once part of the town's defensive system. The interior houses an art gallery but little of its original decoration has survived. At the front is what looks like a row of small houses built on to the main structure; these served as a prayer hall for women (they now house the PTTK office).

Follow the street that goes downhill from the synagogue and you'll see stairs on the right leading up to the old **Jewish cemetery**. Several hundred gravestones, the oldest ones dating back to the 16th century, are

scattered amid trees and high grass. Some of them have amazingly rich decoration. Left in total isolation, in different stages of decay, they're a very impressive sight.

Go back to the Rynek, passing the 19th century **town hall** in the middle, and head 200m north to the **parish church**. It was built in 1539 and its exterior still retains many Gothic features. The freestanding baroque bell tower was added in 1725. At that time the church's interior got its baroque overlay, including the high altar and ornate pulpit.

Lesko has a **castle** – it's on the Sanok road 200m downhill from the Rynek. Built at the beginning of the 16th century, it lost most of its original form with extensive neoclassical alterations. Postwar restoration converted it into a hotel.

Places to Stay & Eat
Camping Nad Sanem (☎ 469 66 89, ☎ 469 69 91), open May to September, is on the riverside beneath the castle. It has a dozen bungalows with rooms of different sizes (US$5 per head), an area where you can pitch your tent and a basic restaurant.

The cheapest all-year place is the youth hostel which is now called *Baza Noclegowa Bartek* (☎ 469 62 69) and is run by the local agricultural school. It's basic and run-down, and often packed with school excursions or hiking groups in summer. The hostel is on the outskirts of Lesko on the Sanok road, over 1km from the town's centre, but it's a short walk from the bus terminal. The place is difficult to find as there are no signs. Watch for a basketball court next to the road – a mustard-coloured building behind it is the hostel.

Diagonally opposite the bus terminal is the simple 80-bed *Hotel Relax* (☎ 469 85 73, ul Piłsudskiego 3), which charges US$14 for a double and US$5 for a bed in a triple or quad, without bath.

Some 200m up the road towards the town's centre, just behind the petrol station, is the basic *Motel Fux* (☎ 469 80 81), open May to September. It has doubles/triples without bath for US$12/18. If things are slow, you can just pay US$6 for your bed. At the time of writing, a new building was going up next to the petrol station, intended to improve on the old one.

Far better and more convenient is *Pensjonat Zamek* (☎ 469 62 68, fax 469 68 78, ul Piłsudskiego 7) in the castle. It was a holiday centre for miners but now is a regular hotel open all year. It charges US$20/35/50 a single/double/triple with bath.

Lesko hasn't progressed much on the culinary front. There are half a dozen basic eateries on or near the Rynek, but nothing worth particular mention.

Getting There & Away

There's no railway in Lesko. The bus terminal is on ul Piłsudskiego (the road to Sanok), about 1km from the Rynek. It's convenient to all the places to stay listed above.

There are plenty of buses to Sanok (15km), a dozen of which continue to Krosno (55km). About 10 buses daily run to Rzeszów (91km) and one goes directly to Kraków (220km).

For the Bieszczady, there are several buses daily to Cisna (39km), and some wind up as far as Wetlina (58km). Three or four buses to Ustrzyki Górne (72km) go via Ustrzyki Dolne. In summer, there are a couple of extra buses to each of these destinations.

USTRZYKI DOLNE
• pop 10,000   ☎ 013

An uninspiring town in the south-eastern corner of Poland, Ustrzyki Dolne ('Oost-zhi-kee') is really only an overnight stop for those heading south into the Bieszczady. There's nothing much to see or do here except the **Natural History Museum** (Muzeum Przyrodnicze), at ul Bełska 7 just off the Rynek, which is a good introduction to the geology, flora and fauna of the Bieszczady National Park. It's open Tuesday to Saturday 9 am to 5 pm, and in July and August also on Sunday 9 am to 2 pm.

If you plan on independent trekking up to the mountains, Ustrzyki Dolne is the last re-

liable place to stock up on a decent range of provisions and exchange money. Farther south, food supplies are poor.

Information

Tourist Office The PTTK office (☎ 461 14 15) at Rynek 14 (2nd floor) is open weekdays from 7.30 am to 1 pm, but don't count too much on finding information on the region.

Money There are only a few kantors, one of which is in the Dom Handlowy Halicz, a shopping centre 100m east of the Rynek. The Bank PKO and Bank Spółdzielczy will also change cash but they won't probably touch your travellers cheques or credit cards.

Places to Stay & Eat

There are half a dozen places to stay, but they all may well be packed in July and August. Off season, some places close down altogether and the rest are usually half or totally empty.

The most reliable place is probably the all-year *Hotel Bieszczadzki* (☎ 461 10 71, Rynek 19), a 10 minute walk west along the main road from the train and bus stations. It has doubles/triples/quads without bath for US$14/20/26 and doubles/triples with bath for US$25/30. There's a cheap restaurant on the premises.

Just off the Rynek is the basic *Hotel Strwiąż* (☎ 461 14 68 ul Sikorskiego 1), which charges US$6 per bed in a double or triple without bath. *Jadłodajnia Kuchcik*, behind the local government office, 100m east of the Hotel Strwiąż, serves budget meals.

In the northern suburb, high on the mountain slope is the large *Dom Wycieczkowy Laworta* (☎ 461 11 78, ul Nadgórna 12). This 170-bed hostel is a 10 minute walk uphill from the stations. It costs US$10/14/20/24 a single/double/triple/quad, all with bath. Its restaurant serves set meals.

Getting There & Away

The train and bus stations are in one building. You won't get far by train (trains to

Przemyśl and on to Warsaw no longer operate, and there are only a few to Zagórz and Jasło), but bus traffic is reasonable. A dozen buses run daily to Sanok (40km) and pass Lesko (25km) on the way. Five buses (several more in summer) go daily to Ustrzyki Górne (47km). Most come through from Przemyśl or Sanok.

USTRZYKI DOLNE TO USTRZYKI GÓRNE

This 50km-long scenic route winds south along river valleys through woody hills and arrives in the heart of the Bieszczady. If you have your own transport, you can do this trip at your own pace, stopping to see old Orthodox and Uniate churches, the only visible reminders of the Boyks who lived here until WWII. Without your own transport, this is more difficult and, above all, time-consuming, as buses are infrequent.

The churches of the Boyks are more modest and simpler than those of the Lemks, and usually don't have the characteristic onion domes. The surviving examples date mostly from the 18th and 19th centuries, and after the war they were practically all either taken over by the Roman Catholics or left in ruins. The Uniate rite, once dominant, is no longer practised in the region as there are simply no worshippers. The churches listed below are all former wooden *cerkwie* and some of them retain their original interior decoration.

They are all locked except during Mass, which is usually only on Sunday morning. It's often not possible to get inside at other times, as the priests arrive only for Mass, covering several churches en route, and nobody else has keys. If you have a particular interest in the interiors, it's best to arrange with the priest to go with him on a Sunday trip, visiting several in a row.

Beginning from Ustrzyki Dolne and going south, the first good example is in **Równia**, a bit off the main road. The early 18th century church complete with its wooden-tiled roof is in many ways typical of the Boyks' architecture, and well preserved. The interior is very modest. You can go to Równia by bus, or take the blue trail starting from the Rynek in Ustrzyki Dolne – it's up to an hour's walk each way.

Back on the main road, the 19th century church in **Hoszów** is on the outskirts of the village and well hidden in the trees – look out to your left after you pass the village. In **Rabe**, 4km farther south, the church was restored and its roof covered with tin instead of timber. You can see part of the old iconostasis through the small windows in the main door. Directly across the road is a budget place to stay.

A small rustic church in **Żłobek**, 3km south along the road, looks fine from outside but no longer has its original internal decoration. The *Zajazd przy Kominku* next door offers budget accommodation and meals.

The cerkiew in **Czarna Górna** was built in 1830 but later remodelled. If you want to see its 19th century iconostasis, ask the priest in the house opposite the church. There's a *youth hostel* in the local school, open from 1 July to 25 August, and a basic *restaurant* on the main road.

Two more churches require a 6km side trip to the east (sporadic buses from Czarna Górna). The church in **Bystre**, erected in 1911, is probably the largest in the whole region and is in itself an impressive piece of architecture, quite different from most of the others. It is no longer used for religious services and has nothing inside. In nearby **Michniowiec**, the much older church lost its original interior after parts of its former iconostasis were redistributed and some 'folksy' wall paintings added, perhaps to give more of a Roman Catholic feel. If you want to see this curiosity, the elderly woman living in the cottage downhill from the church has the keys.

Back on the main road again, and 15km farther south, you come across the last church, in **Smolnik**. One kilometre past the village, the church sits on the hill some distance from the road and is accessible by a footpath. In the nearby hamlet of Stuposiany, 2km south, there's a seasonal *youth hostel*.

At this point you enter the Bieszczady mountains proper, and this can be seen and felt – there are fewer people and houses, and steeper and greener hills around you.

USTRZYKI GÓRNE
- **pop 500**   **☎ 013**

Ustrzyki Górne is a string of houses loosely scattered along the road rather than a village in the proper sense of the word, yet it's Bieszczady's major hiking base. Thanks to its location in the heart of these beautiful mountains (now a national park), the place has long attracted trekkers curious for something new and prepared for difficult conditions.

Since the Bieszczady loop road was built in 1955-62, the mountains have become more accessible and fashionable. The region has begun to change but the process is slow. It's still remote country and Ustrzyki Górne is a good example – there are a few rudimentary places to stay and eat, a shop and not much else. The village springs to life in summer, then sinks into a deep sleep for most of the rest of the year, only stirring a little in winter when the cross-country skiers come.

Places to Stay & Eat
Camping Nr 150 PTTK (☎ 461 10 36 ext 41), in the northern part of the village, is open May to September. It has old cabins without bath (US$6 a bed in a triple) and new cabins with bath (US$10 in a double). You can camp in your own tent and facilities for caravans are provided.

The old, all-year PTTK hostel, *Schronisko Kremenaros* (mobile ☎ 090 68 37 89), is in the last house of the village on the Cisna road. It's basic but the staff are friendly and the atmosphere good. A bed costs US$4 to US$6, depending on the dorm's size, plus US$1 if you need bed linen. If the dorms are full, you can sleep on the floor for US$2.50. Their *Bar Kremenaros* has a very short menu but the food is cheap and OK.

Another year-round budget option is *Hotel Biały* (☎ 461 10 36 ext 50), run by the management of the Bieszczady National Park. It is on a side road, about 500m from the turn-off next to the shop. It has slightly better standards than the Kremenaros and costs US$5 a bed (US$1.25 extra for bed linen) in a four or five-bed dorm.

Significantly better than anything else around is the new PTTK-run *Hotel Górski* (☎ 461 10 36 ext 104), at the end of the village, on the Ustrzyki Dolne road. It has 54 rooms – singles, doubles, triples and quads – all clean, comfortable and modern, and all have their own baths. You pay US$20 per bed in July and August, US$15 in other months. The hotel has a large and well run restaurant with reasonable prices, though much higher than the Kremenaros.

Apart from the two all-year PTTK eateries listed above, more places open in summer along the main road.

Getting There & Away
There are four buses to Ustrzyki Dolne (47km), two to Krosno (117km) and one to Rzeszów (163km). A couple more buses run in July and August to the above destinations, as well as a few buses to Wetlina (15km) and Cisna (34km).

WETLINA
Wetlina is another popular jumping-off spot for hiking in the Bieszczady. In many ways it's similar to Ustrzyki Górne – it also has a choice of simple places to sleep and eat, and attracts a similar genre of people.

Places to Stay & Eat
Like in Ustrzyki Górne, PTTK operates the old, cheap *Schronisko PTTK* and the new *Hotel Górski* (mobile ☎ 090 26 93 86), and both have restaurants. Hotel Górski has doubles and triples with bath (US$13 a bed), bungalows (US$7 a bed) and a camp site.

The 50-bed *youth hostel*, across the road from the Schronisko, is open year-round, and there are several more places to stay, including *Zajazd pod Połoniną*. In summer, a number of places to eat open along the main road.

Getting There & Away

Wetlina is accessible from Sanok (73km) and Lesko (58km) by a few buses a day all year round. A few buses per day run in summer east to Ustrzyki Górne (15km).

HIKING IN THE BIESZCZADY

The Bieszczady is one of the best places in Poland to go hiking. The region is beautiful and easy to walk, and you don't need a tent or cooking equipment, as hostels and mountain refuges are a day's walk apart and provide food. The main area for trekking is the national park, with Ustrzyki Górne and Wetlina being the most popular starting points. You can also use Cisna as a base (see the following section).

Once in the mountains, things become easier than you might expect. There are plenty of well marked trails giving a good choice of shorter and longer walks. All three jumping-off points have PTTK hostels and the friendly staff can give you information. All have boards depicting marked trails complete with walking times, uphill and downhill, on all routes. The mountain refuges will put you up for the night and feed you regardless of how crowded they get. In July and August the floor will most likely be your bed, as these places are pretty small. Take a sleeping bag with you.

Get a copy of the *Bieszczady* map (scale 1:75,000) which covers the whole region, not just the national park. The map is also helpful if you plan to explore the region using private transport. Though the map is usually available in the region, buy it beforehand in one of the larger towns or cities, just in case.

CISNA

Cisna sits on the borderland between the territories once inhabited by Boyks to the east and Lemks to the west. The region was quite densely populated before WWII. Today Cisna and its environs have no more than 1000 inhabitants, yet it's still the largest village in the central part of the Bieszczady. The village is not attractive in itself but it has a choice of accommodation and can therefore be used as a base for hiking. It is also the place from which to take the narrow-gauge tourist train.

Places to Stay & Eat

Schronisko Turystyczne Okrąglik, centrally located on the crossroads, operates most of the year. It has simple doubles, triples and quads with shared facilities, and charges US$4 per bed (US$1 extra for bedsheets).

A 10 minute walk north-west, off the Sanok road, is the large all-year *Hotel Wołosań*. It's the best place in Cisna, offering decent doubles/triples with bath for US$16/24. It also has the best eatery around, *Restauracja Partyja*.

Another 10 minute walk uphill along the steep dirt track is the beautifully located all-year *Bacówka Pod Honiem (mobile ☎ 090 31 29 81)*, the PTTK mountain refuge. It's basic, friendly and cheap and will let you sleep on the floor if all the rooms are taken. Its snack bar serves simple meals.

There's also the *youth hostel* in the local school, open in July and August.

Getting There & Away

Train The narrow-gauge train known as Kolejka Leśna (Forest Train) was built for transporting timber and had its main station in Majdan, 2km west of Cisna. The first stretch of the railway between Majdan and Nowy Łupków was built at the end of the 19th century and subsequently extended north to Rzepedź and east to Moczarne beyond Wetlina. The train on the Majdan-Rzepedź route was used until 1993 for the transport of timber. Additionally, a tourist train was put into operation on this line in summer. Though the trip lost some of its charm after steam was replaced by diesel in 1980, it was still a spectacular ride.

Both the freight and tourist trains were suspended in 1993 due to the dangerous condition of the railway. After several seasons out of operation, in summer 1998 the tourist train was shifted to the 12km stretch from Majdan to Przysłup (midway between Cisna and Wetlina). At the time we went to press it was unclear which route (if any) the train would ply in 1999. Check when you come.

Bus Several buses run daily to Sanok (57km) and Wetlina (19km). There are more seasonal buses in summer, including a few to Ustrzyki Górne (34km).

KOMAŃCZA
* pop 600   ☎ 013

A village nestled in the valley between the Bieszczady and Beskid Niski, Komańcza is yet another base for hikers, though not as popular as Ustrzyki Górne, Wetlina or Cisna. However, it offers something different: as it somehow escaped Operation Vistula in 1947, there's more of an ethnic and religious mix here than elsewhere in the region. There's a sizable community of Lemks living in the village and around, and the old Uniate and Orthodox rites have not been pushed out by Catholicism.

Things to See
Small as Komańcza is, it boasts three churches – Uniate, Orthodox and Roman Catholic – and all three are in use. The oldest is a beautiful wooden **Orthodox church** from 1805, tucked away on the outskirts of the village, on the Dukla road. It's only open for Sunday morning Mass and attracts a small congregation.

On the other hand, the Uniates make up half of the village's population. In the early 1990s, they built a fair-sized if not architecturally impressive **Uniate church** in the centre of the village.

The **Roman Catholic church**, a modest wooden structure, was built in the early 1950s for the newly settled worshippers of the creed, which was virtually nonexistent in the region before WWII. The church is opposite the train station on the road to Sanok.

Continuing north along this road for about 1km and taking a narrow track which branches off to the left under the railway bridge, you'll get to the **Convent of the Nazarene Sisters**. Known to Poles as the

site of the house arrest (in 1955-56) of Cardinal Stefan Wyszyński, Primate of Poland until his death in 1981, this pleasant wooden building is now a sort of shrine, though there's nothing special to look at inside.

Places to Stay & Eat
The all-year *Schronisko PTTK Podkowiata* (☎ 462 52 11 ext 13), next to the convent, is a pleasant though basic budget place to stay. It costs US$5 a bed and serves simple hot meals. In summer it also operates cabins.

Two kilometres from Komańcza on the Dukla road (1km beyond the Orthodox church), the *petrol station* (☎ 462 52 11 ext 57) has five basic cabins without bath (no showers at all), costing just US$6 a double.

Otherwise, you have a *youth hostel* in Komańcza (open 1 July to 25 August), a summer *camp site*, and five *agrotourist farms*. There are also some simple eating facilities.

Getting There & Away
The standard-gauge railway links Komańcza with Zagórz via Rzepedź, with four trains daily in each direction. From Zagórz, you have frequent bus transport to Sanok and Lesko.

There are half a dozen buses to Sanok (49km). One bus goes daily to Cisna (30km) and there is also sporadic transport to Dukla (42km).

AROUND KOMAŃCZA
Avid church visitors would not want to miss some fine Uniate and Orthodox churches scattered around the Komańcza region. You'll find three good examples of these churches around the village of Rzepedź, 5km north of Komańcza, on the Sanok road. The first one is in **Rzepedź** itself, 1km west of the main road. This wooden structure, dating from 1824, with the bell tower in front of the entrance, is today the Uniate church. The people living in the two-storey house downhill from the church may have the keys.

Similar in shape, though nicer, is the church in **Turzańsk**, 1.5km east of Rzepedź. Topped with graceful onion domes and with a freestanding belfry, the church was built in 1838 and has preserved its internal decoration complete with the rococo iconostasis. The only way to see it, though, seems to be to turn up at Sunday Mass at 9 am. Today the church serves the Orthodox community.

One more cerkiew, also following the Orthodox rite, is in the village of **Szczawne**, 3km north of Rzepedź by the main road, just before crossing the railway track. Watch out to the left as it's well hidden in a cluster of trees. Masses are held every other Sunday.

The Beskid Niski

The Beskid Niski (literally, the Low Beskid) is a mountain range that runs for about 85km west-east along the Slovakian frontier. It's bordered on the west by the Beskid Sądecki and on the east by the Bieszczady. As its name suggests, it is not a high outcrop, its highest point not exceeding 1000m. Made up of gently undulating and densely forested hills, the Beskid Niski is easier for walking than its taller neighbours. It's perhaps less spectacular than the Bieszczady, but its attraction lies in dozens of small Orthodox and Uniate churches, most of which are in the western half of the region.

KROSNO
• pop 51,000 ☎ 013
Founded in the 14th century and prospering during the Renaissance – even referred to as 'little Kraków' – Krosno, like the rest of Poland, slid into decay later on. It revived in the mid-19th century with the development of the oil industry in the region and since then has slowly grown to become a regional petroleum centre. Krosno is also well known for its glassworks.

Today it is a rather ordinary town with a tiny historic core perched on a hill, a remnant of its glorious past. There are some interesting sights nearby, notably the church in Haczów and the skansen in Bóbrka.

Information
The tourist office (☎/fax 432 77 07) is at ul Pużaka 49, close to the train station, and is open weekdays 8 am to 4 pm.

The Bank Pekao is pretty far from the centre, at ul Bieszczadzka 5, but you can try the Bank Depozytowo Kredytowy at ul Powstańców Warszawskich 3 or the Bank Śląski at Rynek 8. There are several kantors in the Old Town.

Things to See
The Old Town is the focal point for the visitor. The spacious **Rynek** has retained some of its former appearance, notably in the houses fronted by wide arcaded passageways that line the south and half of the north side of the square.

A few steps east of the Rynek is the large 15th century **Franciscan Church** (Kościół Franciszkanów), today filled with neo-Gothic furnishings. The showpiece here is the Oświęcim Family Chapel (Kaplica Oświęcimów), just to the left as you enter the church. Built in 1647 by the Italian architect Wincenty Petroni, and embellished with stucco work by another Italian master, Jan Falconi, the chapel has been preserved with virtually no changes to this day and is considered one of the best early baroque chapels in the country.

Another massive brick structure, the **parish church**, is 100m north-west of the Rynek. Built in the 15th century, it was almost entirely consumed by fire in 1638 – only the chancel survived – and reconstructed in an altered style. In contrast to its quite sober exterior, the church's interior is exuberant. The powerful gilded high altar is 350 years old, as is the elaborate pulpit. The organ looks a bit more modest, yet it's acclaimed for its excellent sound, reputedly the best in the region.

The solid freestanding **bell tower** next to the church, dating from the time of the church's reconstruction, houses three bells;

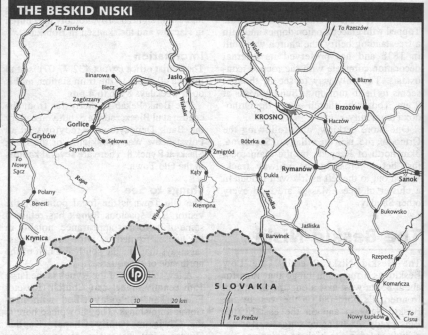

THE BESKID NISKI

the 2.5-tonne Urban cast in 1639 is one of the largest in Poland.

One block north-west of the bell tower, at ul Piłsudskiego 16, is the **Regional Museum** (Muzeum Okręgowe), installed in the 15th century former Bishops' Palace. It has the usual historical, archaeological and art sections but the highlight is an extensive collection of decorative old kerosene lamps. From May to mid-October, the museum is open Tuesday to Sunday 10 am to 5 pm; the rest of the year it closes at 3 pm.

Directly opposite is the **Craft Museum** (Muzeum Rzemiosła), featuring old objects of everyday use and tools and workshops used to manufacture them. It's open daily 9 am to 3 pm except Monday.

Places to Stay

Krosno doesn't have a great accommodation selection. There are few places anywhere near the centre and almost nothing with private baths.

The July-August *youth hostel* (☎ 432 10 09, ul Konopnickiej 5) is 2km north-west of the centre. The cheapest all-year place to stay is the basic *Hotel Resbud* (☎ 432 19 54, ul Okulickiego 16), in the industrial suburb 1km west of the train station. This workers' hostel costs US$8/10/15 a single/double/triple without bath.

Most central is probably *Hotel Elenai* (☎ 436 43 34, ul Łukasiewicza 3), 500m south-west of the Old Town. It offers singles/doubles/triples with shared facilities for US$22/25/36. *Pensjonat Śnieżka* (☎ 432 34 49, ul Lewakowskiego 22), near the train station, has no private facilities either, and is even more expensive at US$30/40 a double/triple.

The only place around with private baths is the small *Motel Scorpion* (☎ 432 39 90, *ul Podkarpacka 38)*, next to the petrol station, 4km out of the centre on the Rzeszów road. It has just one single (US$30), three doubles (US$40) and one triple (US$50).

Hotel Nafta-Krosno (☎ 432 20 11, ul Lwowska 21), a bit over 1km from the centre on the Sanok road, was being refurbished at the time of writing, but promises to be the city's top-end accommodation.

Places to Eat

There are some inexpensive places in the centre, including the *Tawerna (ul Słowackiego 16)* and *Pizzeria Wenecja (ul Słowackiego 2)*.

Upmarket places in the Old Town include the cellar restaurant *Piwnica Wójtowska (Rynek 7)*, and the *Pałac Club (ul Piłsudskiego 16)*, in the building of the regional museum.

Getting There & Away

The train and bus stations are next to each other, 1.5km west of the Old Town; it's a 15 minute walk to the centre, or you can take the urban bus.

Most trains cover the Zagórz-Jasło route which can be used for Sanok but not much else. There are two trains a day to Warsaw and two to Kraków.

Bus traffic is busier and will take you all around the region. There are a dozen buses eastwards to Sanok (40km), of which four continue to Ustrzyki Dolne (83km) and one goes as far as Ustrzyki Górne (130km). A dozen fast buses depart daily to Kraków (165km), and even more buses go to Rzeszów (59km). To the south, there are around 15 buses a day to Dukla (21km) and about 10 to Bóbrka (10km). Buses to Haczów (13km) depart roughly every hour (in the timetable, watch out for the Brzozów buses via Haczów).

HACZÓW

The village of Haczów ('Hah-choof'), 13km east of Krosno, has one of the largest timber Gothic churches in Europe. Built around the mid-15th century on the site of a previous church founded by Władysław Jagiełło in 1388, it is also one of the oldest timber churches in Poland. What's more, it has beautiful interior wall paintings, dating from approximately 1494. Only discovered in 1955, they have been partly restored. The main altar and other old furnishings are still in bits and pieces scattered inside the church. Some objects, including the singularly impressive pietà from around 1400, are now in the new church, built in 1935-39 right next to the old one.

The priest, who lives in the house diagonally opposite the church, can open it for you if you turn up at a reasonable time of day. Avoid Sundays, when the priest is busy with several Masses in the new church (don't miss seeing the pietà).

There's another excellent old timber church in Blizne, 5km north of Brzozów.

Getting There & Away

You shouldn't wait more than one hour for a bus to Krosno. They go either via Krościenko or Miejsce Piastowe, and both are OK. Buses to Brzozów (15km) run regularly throughout the day.

Haczów's lovely pietà resides in the village's new church

THE CARPATHIAN MOUNTAINS

BÓBRKA
- **pop 800**   ☎ 013

The small village of Bóbrka, 10km south of Krosno, is the cradle of the oil industry. It has an interesting open-air museum, worth visiting if you want to learn where and how the world's big oil business was born.

Natural oil was known in the region for centuries: it oozed to the earth's surface out of crannies in the rock and was used by the locals for domestic and medicinal purposes. However, it was in 1854 in Bóbrka that Ignacy Łukasiewicz sank possibly the world's first oil well, giving birth to commercial oil exploitation. More shafts were immediately sunk, followed by the opening of primitive refineries. The region prospered, reaching its peak before WWI. Later, when larger deposits were discovered elsewhere, the importance of the local oil fields diminished. Rudimentary exploitation continues, and you'll spot the odd oil derrick while travelling around the region.

In 1962 a **skansen** (Muzeum Przemysłu Naftowego) was established in Bóbrka. Unlike most other skansens, this one doesn't feature peasant architecture but the oil industry. It's based on a group of early oil wells, complemented by their old drilling derricks and other machinery collected elsewhere. The first surviving oil shaft from 1860, Franek, can be seen with oil still bubbling inside. The other shaft nearby, Janina, is over 100 years old and still used commercially.

The building which once was Łukasiewicz's office now shelters a small museum. The collection of kerosene lamps includes decorative and industrial examples. Note the original map of the Bóbrka oil field with the shafts marked on it; the deepest went down as far as 319m. A copy of the lamp invented by Łukasiewicz can also be seen. The lamp, constructed in 1853, was first used in the Lviv hospital to light a surgical operation. Łukasiewicz also invented a method of refining oil.

The skansen is open May to September 9 am to 5 pm, other months till 3 pm; closed Monday and the day after public holidays.

Place to Stay & Eat
The 30-bed *youth hostel* (☎ *431 30 97*) in the local school of the village is open year-round (it may be closed in winter – check in advance). Bring some food with you as there's nowhere to eat out.

Getting There & Away
The usual jumping-off point for Bóbrka is Krosno. There are about 10 buses daily (fewer on weekends) to the village of Bóbrka. The skansen is 2km away, linked by road but not by buses. This road leads through the forest and makes a pleasant walk (take the left-hand branch when the road divides halfway). Alternatively, take a bus from Krosno to Kobylany or Makowiska (at least a dozen daily), get off in Równe Skrzyżowanie and walk 600m uphill to the skansen. One or two buses from Równe run south to Dukla, or you can walk 1.5km east to the main road where the buses to Dukla pass by every hour.

DUKLA
- **pop 2200**   ☎ 013

Dukla is close to the Dukla Pass (Przełęcz Dukielska), the lowest and most easily accessible passage over the Western Carpathians. In the 16th century this strategic location brought prosperity to the town, which became a centre of the wine trade on the route from Hungary. In autumn 1944, on the other hand, the town's position led to its destruction after one of the fiercest mountain battles of WWII was fought nearby, in which the combined Soviet and Czechoslovak armies crushed the German defence, leaving over 100,000 soldiers dead.

Dukla has some attractions and can also be a starting point for hikes in the Beskid Niski. The town sits on the easternmost route to Slovakia; the border is 17km to the south, on the Dukla Pass.

Things to See
Dukla's large **Rynek**, with its squat town hall in the middle, feels rather oddly like a model, especially when it's deserted late in

Cheese made from sheep's milk, a specialty of the Tatra Mountains region

Wooden tombs at the old cemetery, Zakopane

Beware of ghosts: Niedzica castle, Pieniny

Baroque castle in Nowy Wiśnicz

KRZYSZTOF DYDYŃSKI

Old Catholic church, Sanok open-air museum

KRZYSZTOF DYDYŃSKI

Dilapidated Orthodox church in the Bieszczady

KRZYSZTOF DYDYŃSKI

Leaning gravestones at the old Jewish cemetery in Lesko, Bieszczady Mountains

the afternoon. Nearby, on the other side of the Krosno road, is the mighty **parish church** built in 1764-65, a good example of late baroque architecture with a warm pastel rococo interior.

Diagonally opposite the church, the **museum** is in an 18th century palace. It has a permanent display related to the battle of 1944 and some temporary exhibitions. In the palace park, there are some heavy weapons from WWII. From May to September the museum is open 10 am to 5 pm, the rest of the year it closes at 3 pm; on Monday it's closed.

About 200m north along the Krosno road is the **Bernardine Church**, another baroque-rococo affair, roughly similar to, though more modest than, the parish church.

Places to Stay & Eat

The basic *Dom Wycieczkowy PTTK (✆ 433 00 46, Rynek 25)* costs US$20 a double with bath and US$5 a bed in a dorm without bath. Its restaurant downstairs has some short-order dishes, and there are a couple of other basic eateries around.

The *youth hostel (✆ 433 00 28, ul Kościuszki 11)*, in the school, opens from 1 July to 25 August.

In Lipowica, 1.5km south of Dukla, there's the small, all-year *Zajazd Rysieńka (✆ 433 00 82)*, which has a few rooms and can provide meals. The place is neat and comfortable, and costs US$10 per person. Buses to Barwinek will drop you nearby; otherwise take a taxi or just walk.

Getting There & Away

There are regular buses north to Krosno (21km) and several buses south to Barwinek (16km) near the border. Crossing the border is fast and easy, but get rid of złotys in Barwinek's kantor – it will be hard to trade them in Svidnik or Bardejov in Slovakia. Along this road you'll see some tanks, planes and other machinery preserved from the battle of 1944.

Only one seasonal bus from Dukla runs the backwoods route to Komańcza (42km) and on to Cisna (72km), which is a con-venient short cut to the Bieszczady. Westwards, one bus daily plies the Dukla-Gorlice road (43km).

BIECZ
* **pop 4800**　　✆ 013

One of the oldest settlements in Poland, Biecz ('Byech') was for a long time a busy commercial centre benefiting from the trading route heading south over the Carpathians to Hungary. In the 17th century its prosperity came to an end and Biecz found itself in the doldrums, left only with its memories. This sleepy atmosphere seems to have remained to this day and, combined with some important historic monuments and a good museum, makes the town worth hanging around in for a while.

Things to See

The town's landmark is the **town hall** in the Rynek or, more precisely, its overgrown 40m-high octagonal **tower**, looking a bit like a lighthouse. It was built in 1569-81, although the top is a later, baroque addition. It still retains some of the original Renaissance decoration, including the unusual 24 hour clock face on its eastern side.

West of the Rynek is a monumental **parish church**. This mighty Gothic brick structure, evidence of former wealth but now looking too large for the town's needs, dates from the late 15th/early 16th centuries. Inside, the chancel holds most of the church's treasures, most notably the late Renaissance Flemish high altar and the massive stalls, both from the early 17th century. Less conspicuous but worthy of attention is a gilded woodcarving depicting the genealogical tree of the Virgin Mary, standing to the side of the high altar. Further up, on the rood beam, is an impressive crucifix from 1639.

The church is only open for visits immediately before or after Mass. There are several Masses on Sunday, but on weekdays they are only held early in the morning and late in the afternoon.

Biecz has a good **museum** accommodated in two 16th century buildings, both close to the church. The one at ul Węgierska 2 holds the complete contents of an ancient pharmacy including its laboratory, musical instruments, traditional household utensils and equipment from old craft workshops. The other part of the museum, at ul Kromera 1, has more historical exhibits on the town's past.

The museum is open Tuesday to Saturday 8 am to 3 pm; from May to September it also opens on Sunday 9 am to 2 pm. On Monday and the day following public holidays it's closed.

Places to Stay & Eat

There are only two places to stay in Biecz, and both are good value. *Hotel Restauracja Grodzka* (☎ 447 11 21, ul Kazimierza Wielkiego 35) is on the Krosno road, a 10 minute walk from the Rynek and close to the train station. It has doubles without/with bath for US$14/18 and double suites for US$25. There's also a restaurant here which is OK and not expensive. About 300m east along the road is the marginally cheaper *Restauracja Manhattan* (ul Kazimierza Wielkiego 53). However, the most pleasant place to eat is *Restauracja u Becza*, at the western side of the Rynek.

The other place to stay is the 60-bed all-year *youth hostel* (☎ 447 18 29, ul Parkowa 1), in a large school building up the hill from the Grodzka. The entrance is at the back; walk round the building on the right-hand side and ring the bell at the back door. The hostel is on the top floor and has only doubles and quads, so it provides more privacy than most. It's one of the best hostels you'll come across in the country.

Getting There & Away

There's no bus terminal in Biecz; all buses pass through and stop on the Rynek. Transport eastwards to Jasło (18km) is frequent but only a few buses continue to Krosno (43km). Plenty of buses, both the PKS and No 1 suburban buses, run to Gorlice (15km). A couple of buses daily go to Nowy Sącz (56km), Nowy Targ (132km) and Zakopane (156km).

The very sleepy train station, 1km west of the centre, handles an infrequent service to Jasło and two trains a day to Kraków (164km).

BINAROWA

The village of Binarowa, 5km north-west of Biecz, has a beautiful wooden Catholic church. Built around 1500, its interior is entirely covered with paintings which have remained in remarkably good shape. Those on the ceiling were executed shortly after the church's construction, while the wall decoration, in quite a different style, dates from the mid-17th century. Though the church is open only for Masses (early in the morning on weekdays, all morning till noon on Sunday) the priest who lives in the house behind it will probably open it for you.

Binarowa is accessible by buses from Gorlice via Biecz. They go every hour or so on weekday, less frequently on weekends.

GORLICE
* pop 32,000   ☎ 018

Gorlice, together with Bóbrka, shares the honours of being the cradle of the Polish oil industry. In 1853, in the local chemist's shop, Ignacy Łukasiewicz obtained paraffin from crude oil. Gorlice was also the site of the great 1915 battle fought for 126 days, which ended with the Austrians breaking through the Russian Carpathian front, leaving 20,000 dead.

Gorlice has little to show tourists but the region to the south was once Lemk land and still shelters some amazing old Orthodox and Uniate churches. It is a major transportation hub for this area, and the helpful tourist office can provide information.

It can be used as a starting point for hiking into the Beskid Niski. Two marked trails, blue and green, wind south-east from the town up the mountains, joining the main west-east red trail which crosses the range.

Information

The Gorlickie Centrum Informacji (☎ 353 50 91), ul Legionów 3, is open weekdays 8 am to 6 pm, Saturday 9 am to 2 pm.

The Bank Pekao is at ul Legionów 12, and there are a few kantors in the centre.

The Internet Caffe Minix (☎ 353 69 71 ext 12) is at ul Biecka 12 near the bus terminal.

Things to See

The regional museum is in an 18th century house at ul Wąska 7 just off the Rynek. It has exhibitions on Lemk ethnography, the oil industry and the Gorlice battle of 1915. It's open Tuesday to Friday 9 am to 4 pm, and Saturday 10 am to 2 pm. From May to September it also opens on Sunday 10 am to 2 pm.

Gorlice claims to have the world's first street kerosene lamp. It's attached to the chapel topped by a figure of a contemplating Christ, on the corner of ul Kościuszki and ul Węgierska, a short walk south from the centre.

Places to Stay

There are three places right in the town's centre. The cheapest, *Dom Nauczyciela* (☎ 353 52 31, ul Wróblewskiego 10), 100m from the Rynek, costs US$6 a bed in simple doubles without bath. Reception may not open until 3 pm.

Next door is *Dwór Karwacjanów* (☎ 353 56 18, ul Wróblewskiego 10A), a fine old mansion whose roots reputedly go back to 1417. Extensively renovated, the Dwór now houses the BWA Art Gallery, a café, and six double rooms without bath on the top floor (US$15 each). The rooms are expected to be equipped with baths in the near future, which will affect the prices.

The small *Hotel Maxbud* (☎ 352 16 28, ☎ 353 61 73, ul Legionów 6D) is the top central option, costing US$30 for a double with bath and breakfast.

If you can't find a room in the centre, try the *Hotel Lipsk* (☎ 352 27 60, ul Szopena 43), in a large olive-coloured apartment block over 2km from the centre on the Krosno road. It's unattractive and nothing special for US$24/28 a double/triple without bath, but this means there's more chance of a vacancy.

The summer *youth hostel* (☎ 353 57 46, ul Wyszyńskiego 16) is even less conveniently located on the outskirts of town.

Places to Eat

The central *Bar Bistro (ul Łukasiewicza 3)* is possibly the best budget place around – ask for the grochówka wojskowa and placek po węgiersku. For somewhere with table service, try *Restauracja Bankietowa (ul 3 Maja 10)* or *Restauracja Biesiadna (ul Piłsudskiego 6)*, both very central and reasonable.

Getting There & Away

Train Gorlice has no train station in the true sense of the word. The main railway track is 5km north, through the village of Zagórzany which is linked with Gorlice by a shuttle train, running back and forth every two or three hours. From Zagórzany, there's transport to Jasło, and two trains a day to Kraków.

Bus Bus transport is much better. Six fast buses go to Kraków (140km) and double that number to Nowy Sącz (41km). Nowy Targ (117km) is serviced by at least five buses daily, as is Krosno (57km). For Biecz (15km), buses run every half an hour or so.

There's also a reasonable service southwards to Łosie, Ujście Gorlickie, Hańczowa and Wysowa, plus occasional buses to Izby, Kwiatoń, Smerekowiec and Gładyszów. Each of these villages has an old Orthodox or Uniate church.

The bus terminal is next to the shuttle train station, a 10 minute walk from the centre.

SĘKOWA

Sitting in the prewar ethnic borderland between the Poles and the Lemks, Sękowa was one of the southernmost outposts of Roman Catholicism. Farther south, the Orthodox and Uniate faith predominated and you won't find old Catholic churches beyond this point.

The small wooden church in Sękowa is one of the most beautiful examples of timber architecture in Poland. The main part of the building dates back to the 1520s, though the bell tower and the *soboty*, which look like verandahs around the church, were added in the 17th century. The soboty – the word means 'Saturdays' – were built to shelter churchgoers from distant villages arriving late on Saturday night in time for early Sunday morning Mass. You will see many soboty on churches in the region.

The church passed through particularly hard times during WWI when the Austro-Hungarian army took part of it away to reinforce the trenches and for firewood, but careful reconstruction has restored its gracious outline. The interior lacks some furnishings but it's worth seeing anyway – the nuns who live in the house next to the church will give you the key. The wall painting hasn't survived apart from small fragments in the chancel.

Getting There & Away

Getting to the church from Gorlice is easy. Take suburban bus No 6 (to Ropica), No 7 (to Owczary) or No 17 (to Sękowa), get off in Siary and continue in the same direction for 50m until the road divides. Take the left-hand fork, cross the bridge 300m ahead and you'll see the church to your right.

SZYMBARK
• pop 3000   ☎ 018

A scattering of houses spread over 3km along the Gorlice-Grybów road – that's Szymbark. You'd hardly notice you were passing through it if not for the road signs with the village's name. Roughly halfway through stands a large modern church of no particular charm and it's here that the buses stop.

The old peasant cottages in the orchard next to the church constitute the **skansen** (Ośrodek Budownictwa Ludowego). It's still young and small, but nonetheless has some curiosities, the best being a fortified castle-like manor house from the 16th century adorned with characteristic Renaissance parapets. It has been partly renovated but is off-limits to visitors. Of a dozen old

timber houses in the grounds, some have been furnished and decorated inside and can be visited. Two tiny windmills complete the collection. From May to September, the skansen is open 9 am to 4 pm except Monday. During the rest of the year it's open weekdays 9 am to 3 pm.

On the opposite side of the large church from the skansen stands a small wooden church from 1782, today unused and locked.

Places to Stay & Eat

Across the road from the skansen, there's the simple *Pensjonat Perełka* (☎ 351 30 11) in an 80-year-old timber villa. You can stay overnight for US$7 a bed in a double, triple or quad with shared facilities. Meals can be provided if requested in advance.

Half a kilometre from the skansen towards Gorlice is *Restauracja Watra* (☎ 351 30 19), which serves reasonable food and has six double rooms with bath for US$20 each.

Getting There & Away

The buses on the main east-west road run regularly throughout the day to both Gorlice (7km) and Nowy Sącz (34km).

HIKING IN THE BESKID NISKI

There are two main trails winding through the whole length of the range. The trail marked blue originates in Grybów, goes south-east to the border and winds eastwards all along the frontier to bring you eventually to Nowy Łupków near Komańcza. The red trail begins in Krynica, crosses the blue trail around Hańczowa, continues east along the northern slopes of the Beskid, and arrives at Komańcza. Both these trails head farther east into the Bieszczady.

You need four to six days to do the whole of the Beskid Niski on either of these routes, but there are other trails as well as a number of rough roads that link the two main trails.

About a dozen youth hostels scattered in small villages throughout the region provide shelter but most are open only in July and August. If you plan on more ambitious trekking, camping gear is recommended. You can buy some elementary supplies in the villages you pass but you're better off stocking up on the essentials before you start.

The major starting points for the Beskid Niski are Krynica, Grybów and Gorlice from the western side; Komańcza and Sanok from the east; and Krosno, Dukla and Barwinek for the central part. Most of these places are described in separate sections in this chapter.

The *Beskid Niski i Pogórze* map (scale 1:125,000) will give you all the information you need for hiking. It's usually available in larger cities, but not always in the region itself. The map is also very useful for those exploring the region using private transport.

The Beskid Sądecki

Lying south of Nowy Sącz, the Beskid Sądecki ('Son-dets-kee') is yet another attractive mountain range where you can hike, sightsee or simply have a rest in one of the mountain spas, the most popular being Krynica. The mountains are easily accessible from Nowy Sącz by two roads that head south along the river valleys, joining up to form a convenient loop; public transport is good on this route.

The Beskid Sądecki consists of two ranges, the Pasmo Jaworzyny and the Pasmo Radziejowej, separated by the valley of the Poprad River. There are a number of peaks over 1000m, the highest being Mt Radziejowa (1262m). It's good hiking country and you don't need a tent or cooking gear as mountain refuges dot the trails.

The Beskid Sądecki was the westernmost territory populated by the Lemks, and a dozen of their charming rustic churches survive, particularly around Krynica and Muszyna. The *Beskid Sądecki* map (scale 1:75,000) is helpful for both hikers and cerkiew-seekers.

NOWY SĄCZ
- **pop 82,000**   ☎ 018

Founded in 1292 and fortified in the 1350s by King Kazimierz Wielki, Nowy Sącz ('No-vi Sonch') developed rapidly until the 16th century thanks to its strategic position on trading crossroads. Between 1430 and 1480 the town was the centre of the renowned Sącz school (Szkoła Sądecka) of painting. The works of art created here in that period now adorn a number of collections, including that of the royal seat of Wawel in Kraków.

As elsewhere, the 17th century decline gave way to a partial revival at the close of the 19th century. Nowy Sącz grew considerably after WWII, and its historic district has been largely restored over recent years. It's a pleasant place and has some attractions, notably a good museum and a skansen. The town has an array of hotels and restaurants and as such can be a good base for further exploration.

Information
Tourist Office The Centrum Informacji Turystycznej (☎ 444 18 38, ☎/fax 443 55 97), ul Piotra Skargi 2, just off the Rynek, is open weekdays 9 am to 5 pm, Saturday 9 am to 2 pm.

Money The Bank Pekao at ul Jagiellońska 50A (which changes travellers cheques and gives advances on Visa and MasterCard) is outside the centre, but it has a useful ATM at ul Jagiellońska 15 near the Rynek. Even more central is the Euronet ATM at Rynek 6, and there are several kantors around.

Email & Internet Access The Cafe Internet (☎ 444 26 55) is at Rynek 5 (the entrance is from ul Wazów). It's open daily till 10 pm.

Things to See
At 160 x 120m, the **Rynek** is one of the largest in Poland and is lined on all sides with a harmonious collection of old houses. The eclectic **town hall**, plonked in the middle in 1897, is quite large but it

THE BESKID SĄDECKI

fortunately doesn't look oversized on this spacious square.

St Margaret's Church (Kościół Św Małgorzaty), a block east of the Rynek, is the oldest church in town, dating from the 17th century, yet it has undergone many additions and changes. The eclectic interior goes from Gothic to contemporary. A largish Renaissance high altar has a small 15th century image of Christ at its centre, recalling the Byzantine influence.

The building just to the south of the church is the **Regional Museum** (Muzeum Okręgowe); the entrance is from ul Lwowska 3. The ground floor features an assortment of paintings, woodcarvings and crafts from the 14th to 19th centuries. On the 1st floor, you'll find works of religious folk art collected from rural churches, domestic altars and roadside chapels of the region. The woodcarvings and paintings on

show are mostly the work of anonymous local artists from the 18th to the early 20th centuries.

Next comes the collection of icons from the 15th to 18th centuries, a sign of the Lemks' presence. As this region was the westernmost outpost of the Orthodox church, the Roman Catholic influence is noticeable, particularly in the icons dating from the 17th century on. The iconostasis on display is not a single complete specimen; it was assembled from icons brought from different places.

The museum is open Tuesday to Thursday 10 am to 3 pm, Friday 10 am to 5.30 pm, and Saturday and Sunday 9 am to 2.30 pm. There are captions in English and German. A useful brochure in English and German is available.

Two blocks north of the Rynek, at ul Joselewicza 12, is the former **synagogue**, built in the first half of the 18th century in baroque style but remodelled in the 1920s. Partly destroyed in WWII, it was restored and now houses an art gallery presenting changing exhibitions plus a small permanent display of Jewish memorabilia. It's open the same hours as the museum except it's closed Tuesday.

The remains of the **Royal Castle** (Zamek Królewski), built by King Kazimierz Wielki in the 1350s, are 100m farther north. The castle often hosted Polish kings but after a fire in 1616 and subsequent misfortunes of nature it never revived.

A five minute walk further north on ul Rybacka is the **Jewish cemetery**. Predictably, it's a sad sight: a couple of hundred destroyed tombstones amid overgrown grass. This can be seen from over the fence but if you want a closer inspection, the keys to the cemetery gate are kept in the house at ul Rybacka 3 (1st floor), directly opposite the gate.

Fans of churches may want to visit **St Casimir's Church** (Kościół Św Kazimierza) on the corner of ul Kościuszki and ul Długosza. This neo-Gothic building was erected in 1908-12. The interior decoration is largely the 1920s work of Jan Bukowski, who produced colourful Art Nouveau wall paintings, the pulpit and the neo-Gothic triptych in the high altar. A set of 14 ceramic stations of the Way of the Cross is a work from 1957 by Władysław Hasior.

The latest addition to the city churches is the large **St Mary's Church** (Kościół Matki Bożej Niepokalanej) on the corner of ul Królowej Jadwigi and Al Piłsudskiego, 2km south-east of the Old Town. Opened in 1992, it's a bold futuristic design, although its interior is rather disappointing.

The **skansen** (Sądecki Park Etnograficzny) is one of the best open-air museums in the country. It's about 3.5km south-east of the centre (1.5km beyond St Mary's Church). The infrequent urban bus Nos 14 and 15 go there from the train station, passing the bus terminal on their way and skirting the edge of the central area.

The skansen gives an insight into the typical rural architecture of the region. The buildings of several ethnic cultures from the Carpathian Mountains and the foothills are displayed in groups. About 50 buildings of various kinds have so far been assembled, of which a dozen can be visited. The interiors have all been carefully decorated, furnished and filled with household implements. The collection is steadily growing and future plans include a Catholic church; an Orthodox church has recently been re-assembled.

The skansen is open May to September 10 am to 5 pm, and in other months 10 am to 2 pm. On Monday and the day following public holidays it's closed. Visits are in groups guided in Polish. You can buy a booklet in English or German which describes the skansen's contents.

Places to Stay

The town has a reasonable array of lodgings and it's usually easy to find somewhere to stay. The other side of the coin is that only one hotel is in the Old Town, while all the rest are a fair way out.

The cheapest is the all-year *youth hostel* (☎ 442 38 97, Al Batorego 72), close to the train station. It mostly has large dormitories (45 beds in all) and is often full in spring and summer.

The next cheapest is probably *Hotel Nauczycielski* (☎ 443 56 90, ul Długosza 61) in the Dom Studenta, near the bus terminal. This student/teacher dorm is essentially open to the public in July and August, but there are a few rooms available year-round. Doubles with bath cost US$17 and quads without bath go for US$4 per bed.

Zajazd Sądecki (☎ 443 67 17, ul Królowej Jadwigi 67), opposite St Mary's Church, has simple doubles/triples with bath for US$20/24 and its own restaurant.

If it's full, cross the river to *Hotel PTTK* (☎ 441 50 12, ul Jamnicka 2), which costs US$18/20 a double/triple without bath, US$20/34 a double/quad with bath. From May to September, *Camping Nr 87* opens in the grounds behind the hotel. There are

NOWY SĄCZ

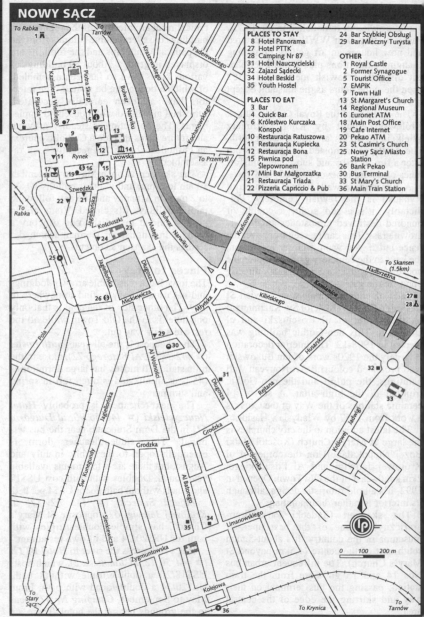

PLACES TO STAY
8 Hotel Panorama
27 Hotel PTTK
28 Camping Nr 87
31 Hotel Nauczycielski
32 Zajazd Sądecki
34 Hotel Beskid
35 Youth Hostel

PLACES TO EAT
3 Bar
4 Quick Bar
6 Królestwo Kurczaka Konspol
10 Restauracja Ratuszowa
11 Restauracja Kupiecka
12 Restauracja Bona
15 Piwnica pod Ślepowronem
17 Mini Bar Małgorzatka
21 Restauracja Triada
22 Pizzeria Capriccio & Pub
24 Bar Szybkiej Obsługi
29 Bar Mleczny Turysta

OTHER
1 Royal Castle
2 Former Synagogue
5 Tourist Office
7 EMPiK
9 Town Hall
13 St Margaret's Church
14 Regional Museum
16 Euronet ATM
18 Main Post Office
19 Cafe Internet
20 Pekao ATM
23 St Casimir's Church
25 Nowy Sącz Miasto Station
26 Bank Pekao
30 Bus Terminal
33 St Mary's Church
36 Main Train Station

no cabins, just a space to pitch a tent, and there is also a small snack bar.

If you want to stay in the Old Town, *Hotel Panorama (☎ 443 71 10, fax 443 71 45, ul Romanowskiego 4A)* is the only central option. It offers singles/doubles/triples with bath for US$25/38/44 and has a reasonable restaurant.

At the top of the scale is the Orbis-run *Hotel Beskid (☎ 443 57 70, fax 443 51 44, ul Limanowskiego 1)*, 300m from the train station but a long walk to the centre (take a bus). Singles/doubles with bath go for around US$50/75 including breakfast. Discount weekend rates may be available.

Places to Eat

Budget eating is not a problem whatsoever. Arguably the best cheap place is *Mini Bar Małgorzatka (ul Dunajewskiego 8)*, a tiny four-table business just off the Rynek. No smoke, no beer, but hearty Polish food, including delicious *golonka*, for next to nothing. Warmly recommended.

Other places for a simple cheap meal include *Bar Szybkiej Obsługi (ul Jagiellońska 31)*, *Bar (ul Franciszkańska 7)* and *Quick Bar (ul Piotra Skargi 4)*. The pleasant basement *Piwnica pod Ślepowronem (ul Jagiellońska 1)* also provides inexpensive food, as does the rather ordinary *Restauracja Triada (ul Szwedzka 1)*. If you're arriving in town hungry by bus, there's the basic *Bar Mleczny Turysta (ul Staszica 7)* next to the bus terminal. If you're after chicken, *Królestwo Kurczaka Konspol (Rynek 23)* offers a variety of cheap chicken dishes.

Among restaurants, *Restauracja Bona (Rynek 28)* has Italian cuisine at reasonable prices. *Restauracja Kupiecka (Rynek 10)*, set in a beautiful cellar, offers European cuisine. It's not that cheap but is one of the best places in town. Also check *Restauracja Ratuszowa* in the cellar vaults of the town hall. It was just about to open as we went to press and was expected to serve quality Polish fare.

Don't miss going to *Pizzeria Capriccio & Pub (ul Szewska 3)*, lodged in fabulous vaults – enter from ul Wąsowiczów 2. The place is popular with locals, has good background music and atmosphere, and is as good for a budget pizza, salad or fish as it is for an espresso, beer or a stronger drink.

Getting There & Away

Train The main train station is over 2km south of the Old Town but urban buses run frequently between the two. There are some trains to Kraków (167km) but buses are more useful. Trains to Krynica (61km) go regularly throughout the day and pass Stary Sącz (7km) on their way. There's a reasonable service to Tarnów (89km), with trains departing every hour or two. One early morning express train goes to Warsaw, and there's another express train in the afternoon, plus a fast train in the evening. The train to Budapest passes via Nowy Sącz around midnight.

The Nowy Sącz Miasto station is close to the centre but trains (six a day) only go from here to Chabówka (halfway along the Kraków-Zakopane route).

Bus The bus terminal is midway between the city centre and the train station. Buses to Kraków (99km) and Krynica (34km) depart every half an hour or so and are much faster than the trains. There's a regular service to Gorlice (41km), Szczawnica (48km) and Zakopane (100 or 116km depending on the route). Frequent PKS and urban buses run to Stary Sącz (8km).

STARY SĄCZ
* pop 8500   ☎ 018

The oldest town in the region, Stary Sącz ('Stah-ri Sonch') owes its existence to Princess Kinga (1234-92), the wife of King Bolesław Wstydliwy (Boleslaus the Shy), who in the 1270s founded here the convent of the Poor Clares (Klasztor Klarysek). After the king's death Kinga entered the convent, where she lived for the last 13 years of her life, becoming its first abbess. This, together with various charity acts and donations she made to the town, gave birth to the cult of the Blessed Kinga which spread through the region. The name Kinga is ubiquitous in the town.

On the secular front, the town's position on the trade route between Kraków and Buda (now Budapest) made it a busy commercial centre, though it gradually lost out to its younger but more progressive sister, Nowy Sącz. Today there's no comparison between the two: Stary Sącz is just a small satellite town. However, it has preserved much of its old atmosphere and architecture.

Things to See

There are not many genuine cobbled market squares left in Poland but the **Rynek** in Stary Sącz is definitely one of them. A solitary cluster of trees in its centre shades an old well. The town hall that was once here burnt down in 1795. The neat houses lining the square are almost all one-storey buildings. The oldest, No 6, dates from the 17th century and now holds the **regional museum**. Its collection of objects related to the town is reminiscent of a charming antique shop. In summer the museum is open Tuesday to Saturday 9.30 am to 5 pm, Sunday 10 am to 1 pm; in the rest of the year it closes at 1 pm.

Enter the gate at Rynek 21 and note the decoration on the vault above your head. Then walk to the backyard to see a dilapidated house guarded by folksy figures. Until 1990 this was a centre for local naive artists, complete with a folk art gallery. It was run by Józef Raczek, an amateur painter, sculptor and writer, but since his death the house has gradually fallen into ruin. Hopefully, you'll still be able to see some of the decoration left in this unique place.

The **parish church**, one block south of the Rynek, dates from the town's beginnings but has been changed considerably and is now a textbook example of unbridled baroque, with its five large florid altars fitted into the small interior. The elaborate pulpit, organ and, particularly, the unique stalls under the choir loft, complete the decoration. Also note the crucifix at the top of the arch leading to the chancel.

Equally splendid is the **Church of the Poor Clares** (Kościół Klarysek), a short walk east. Surrounded by a high defensive wall, this was the birthplace and nucleus of the town. Originally a Gothic building, completed in 1332, this church also ended up with opulent baroque fittings. The traces of its creator are clearly visible: the baroque frescoes in the nave depict scenes from the life of the Blessed Kinga, and her chapel (in front of you as you enter the church) boasts a 1470 statue of her on the altar. On the opposite wall, the pulpit from 1671 is without doubt an extraordinary piece of art.

Places to Stay & Eat

The only year-round accommodation to be found is *Zajazd Szałas* (☎ 446 00 77, ul Jana Pawła II), 1.5km outside the town on the Nowy Sącz road. It has two doubles (US$12), one triple (US$18) and one quad (US$24). The restaurant downstairs serves inexpensive meals.

Just behind is the basic *Camping Nr 62* (☎ 446 11 97), open June to September. It has tent spaces, a collection of dilapidated bungalows (US$10/14 a double/triple) and a snack bar.

The only place to stay in the town proper is the *youth hostel* (☎ 446 05 84, ul Kazimierza Wielkiego 14), open 2 July to 25 August in the school next to the parish church.

The most pleasant place to eat in town is *Restauracja Marysieńka (Rynek 12)*, on the 1st floor of the tallest house in the square. If the weather is fine, the balcony is the right place to grab a table and enjoy a vista over the square while having some of the simple, cheap dishes from the menu. Otherwise, try *Restauracja Staromiejska*, also on the Rynek; the food is OK but the place is pretty dull.

Getting There & Away

Train The train station is a 15 minute walk east from the centre and has a regular service south to Krynica (54km) and north to Nowy Sącz (7km). Several trains daily to Kraków (174km) and Tarnów (96km) depart mostly in the afternoon and evening.

Bus Buses stop in the Rynek. A continuous service to Nowy Sącz (8km) is provided by both the PKS and several lines of urban buses (Nos 8, 9, 10, 11, 24 and 43). About nine buses run daily to Szczawnica (48km) and six to Zakopane (100km); all come from Nowy Sącz.

KRYNICA
• **pop 13,000**   ☎ **018**
Set in attractive countryside amid the wooded hills of the Beskid Sądecki, Krynica ('Kri-nee-tsah') is possibly Poland's most popular mountain health resort. Though the healing properties of the local mineral springs had been known for centuries, the town only really began to develop in the 1850s. By the end of the century it was already a fashionable hang-out for the artistic and intellectual elite, and continued to be so right up till WWII. Splendid villas and pensions were built in that period, blending into the wooded landscape. Development continued after the war but priorities shifted towards the needs of the working class rather than artists. Massive holiday homes and sanatoria came to occupy the slopes of surrounding hills, some of them less sympathetic to their environment.

Information
Tourist Office Information is provided by the Jaworzyna tourist bureau (☎ 471 56 54, ☎/fax 471 55 13), ul Piłsudskiego 8. The office is open weekdays 8 am to 8 pm, Saturday 8 am to 4 pm. In the summer and winter high seasons it closes later on Saturday and also opens on Sunday.

Money There are still no useful ATMs in town and the three local banks may not want to touch your credit cards or travellers cheques. On the other hand, they will probably exchange your cash, as will the two kantors: at ul Piłsudskiego 9 and in the post office at ul Zdrojowa 1.

Things to See & Do
About 20 mineral springs are exploited and roughly half of them feed the public **pump**

rooms where, for a token fee, the waters can be tried by anybody. The main pump room, the Pijalnia Główna, is in a large modern building on Al Nowotarskiego, the central pedestrian promenade (called *deptak*) where the life of the town is concentrated. There are a number of different waters to choose from in the Pijalnia and displays list the chemical composition of each. By far the heaviest, as you'll notice, is the Zuber, which has over 21g of soluble solid components per litre – a record for all liquids of that type in Europe. It won't be the best tasting brew you've ever tried, and it smells appalling.

You'll need your own drinking vessel; a bottle or a plastic cup will do, but if you want to follow local style, buy one of a striking collection of small porcelain tankards from downstairs in the Pijalnia or in the shops nearby. Local practice also is to drink the water slowly while walking up and down the promenade. If you want to kill the taste, there's a good supply of places serving beer, coffee etc.

On a more cultural front, there's the interesting **Nikifor Museum** (Muzeum Nikifora) at Bulwary Dietla 19, just west of the promenade. The museum contains about 100 works by Nikifor (1895-1968), possibly the best-known Polish naive painter. Lemk by origin, he produced hundreds of watercolours and drawings and is referred to as the Matejko of Krynica, the town of his birth. There are also various temporary exhibitions. The museum is open Tuesday to Saturday 10 am to 1 pm and 2 to 5 pm, Sunday 10 am to 4 pm.

You can take a short trip on the **funicular** up to the top of the Góra Parkowa (741m); the bottom station is near the northern end of the promenade. The car departs every half-hour (more often in high season) till late. The ascent of 142m takes less than three minutes. You can walk down or take the funicular back.

A longer trip can be taken by the recently built, modern **cable car.** Finished in 1997, the Austrian-made cable car system consists of 55 six-person cars that run from the bottom station in the Czarny Potok Valley (about 5km from Krynica's centre) up to the top of Mt Jaworzyna (1114m). The route is 2210m long and you climb 465m in seven minutes (US$4 return).

Places to Stay

Krynica has lots of holiday homes, hotels and pensions – approximately 90 in all – and there are also plenty of private rooms waiting for tourists. Like all resorts of this sort, the supply of accommodation changes notably throughout the year, peaking in summer, particularly in July and August, and in winter, mostly in January and February. The prices fluctuate depending on the season, weather, annual events etc, and are sometimes negotiable in the off-season.

Many places – particularly holiday homes, but also some pensions – will insist on you paying for full board, not just a bed, which can be convenient and cheaper than dining out, but you may not always want it.

It's best to start off at the Jaworzyna office, which deals with accommodation as well as tourist information. The staff will help you find and book a place – they claim they won't leave anybody on the street no matter how busy the season might be.

Expect to pay somewhere between US$6 and US$12 per bed in most places with shared facilities, US$10 to US$20 with baths. Add another US$10 to US$20 for full board.

Jaworzyna also arranges private rooms (US$7 to US$10 per person), though in the high season few owners will be interested in travellers intending to stay just a night or two (less hassle in the off-season).

Among the places that offer accommodation for less than US$10 per person in a double or triple room are *Pensjonat Adria* (☎ 471 34 15, ul Zielona 15), *Hotel Mimoza* (☎ 471 34 31, ul Świdzińskiego 1), *Pensjonat Pamela* (☎ 471 21 18, ul Zdrojowa 16) and *Pensjonat Promień* (☎ 471 57 88, ul Słoneczna 11).

Among the better options, you may try *Pensjonat Irys* (☎ 471 21 55, ul Piękna 3), *Pensjonat Witoldówka* (☎ 471 55 77, Bulwary Dietla 10) or *Hotel Rapsodia*

(☎ 471 27 85, ul Ebersa 5). None of these will make a huge dent in your wallet.

Places to Eat

The culinary scene is also volatile. In the high season heaps of eating establishments open, including dining rooms and cafés in holiday homes and pensions, and small bistros and snack bars along the central streets.

Of the more permanent eateries, you may try *Restauracja pod Zieloną Górką* (ul Nowotarskiego 5), *Restauracja Koncertowa* (ul Piłsudskiego 76), *Restauracja Cichy Kącik* (ul Sądecka 2), *Restauracja Czarny Kot* (Stara Droga 28) or *Restauracja Rapsodia* (ul Ebersa 5). There's also a restaurant on the Góra Parkowa at the upper station of the funicular.

Getting There & Away

The train and bus stations are next to each other in the southern part of the town; it's a 10 minute walk to the promenade from here.

Train There's a regular service to Nowy Sącz (61km) by a roundabout but pleasant route via Muszyna and Stary Sącz. Half a dozen trains continue to Tarnów (150km) and some of these go up to Kraków (228km).

Bus Buses to Nowy Sącz (34km) take a different, much shorter route to the train and run every half-hour to hour. The buses to Grybów (25km) depart regularly, passing through Berest and Polany. There are plenty of buses (both PKS and suburban) south to Muszyna (11km) via Powroźnik, and a fairly regular service to Mochnaczka, Tylicz and Muszynka (see the following section).

AROUND KRYNICA
☎ 018

Krynica is a good base for hiking into the surrounding countryside, with its beautiful wooded valleys, hills and charming small villages. Some of these, once populated by the Lemks, have their old churches preserved to this day. An essential aid for exploring the region (whether you're interested in hiking or in churches) is the *Beskid Sądecki* map (scale 1:75,000), which is readily available.

Churches

Most of the churches are accessible by bus. All those listed below were originally the Uniate churches of the Lemks, but were taken over by the Roman Catholics after WWII. All are wooden structures, characteristic of the region.

To the north of Krynica, on the road to Grybów, there are good cerkwie in **Berest** and **Polany**, both with some of the old interior fittings including the iconostasis. Buses ply this route every hour or so and you shouldn't have problems in coming back to Krynica or continuing to Grybów, from where there's frequent transport west to Nowy Sącz or east to Szymbark and Gorlice.

The loop via Mochnaczka, Tylicz and Powroźnik is a particularly interesting trip. The 1846 church in **Mochnaczka Niżna** still has its old iconostasis, although it's disfigured by a central altar with the Black Madonna. More attractive is the old small cerkiew, 600m down the road towards Tylicz on the other side. Built in 1787, it holds a beautiful tiny iconostasis complete with original icons. If you find the church locked, ask the nuns living in the nearby house. There are several buses daily from Krynica to Mochnaczka but take an early one if you want to continue along the route.

The next village, **Tylicz**, boasts two churches, a Catholic one and the Uniate cerkiew. The latter is only used for funerals. The priest is not eager to open the churches for visitors but in July and August he runs a guided tour around their interiors (Monday at 10 am, at the time of writing). Call ☎ 471 13 10 for information on current times.

From Tylicz, a spectacular road skirts the Muszyna River valley to **Powroźnik** which features yet another cerkiew. This one is the oldest in the region (1643) and the best known. The exterior is beautiful, and inside

is an 18th century iconostasis (unfortunately the central panel has been removed to make space for the Roman Catholic altar) and several older icons on the side walls. The sacristy (the door to the left of the high altar) still holds the remnants of wall paintings from the 1640s. The church can only be visited just before or after Masses which are held on Sunday at 7 and 11 am, and once a day on weekdays: on Wednesday and Friday at 6 pm; and on the remaining days at 6.30 am.

If you have your own means of transport, you can include Muszynka and Wojkowa in your loop, both of which have old churches (bus transport is infrequent on these side roads). St Mary's Church in Krynica (the town's main church) displays the times of religious services in all churches in the region, which could help you plan your trip.

Hiking

Two marked trails, green and red, go westward from Krynica up to the top of Mt Jaworzyna (1114m). It's two to three hours to walk there by either trail (or you can also get there faster by cable car). Up there, you'll get a panoramic view, and may even spot the Tatras on some clear days. There's a PTTK refuge (☎ 471 54 09) just below the summit where you can stay overnight (in good doubles or cheap dorms) and eat, or you can go back down to Krynica the same day. You can also continue on the red trail west to Hala Łabowska (2½ hours from Mt Jaworzyna) where you'll find another PTTK refuge (☎ 442 07 80) providing cheap beds and food. The red trail continues west to Rytro (five hours). This route, leading mostly through the forest along the ridge of the main chain of the Beskid Sądecki, is spectacular and easy, and because of the accommodation on the way you can travel light. From Rytro, you can go back to Krynica by train or bus.

MUSZYNA

• pop 5000   ☎ 018

Much smaller than Krynica, Muszyna is also geared to tourism. Here, too, mineral springs have been discovered and exploited and a number of sanatoria have sprung up. There's a small local **museum** in the old inn, which displays artefacts and old household implements collected from the region. Otherwise, Muszyna has no sights worth mentioning, though it can be a convenient starting point for trips into the surrounding region (see the following section), which is every bit as interesting as the area around Krynica.

Information
The Vector travel agency (☎ 471 40 77), Rynek 32, can provide tourist information, help in finding accommodation, organise a tour and find an English-speaking guide. The office is open Monday to Saturday 8 am to 6 pm, and (in summer only) on Sunday 8 am to 3 pm.

Places to Stay
There are perhaps as many as 30 holiday homes in the area and plenty of private rooms. It's best to go directly to the Vector agency instead of going hotel-hunting on your own.

Ośrodek Wczasowy Kraśniczanka (☎ 471 42 25, ul Piłsudskiego), 800m south of the Rynek, is one of the cheapest options.

Another budget place is *Ośrodek Wczasowy Eda,* off the road to Złockie. Contact Jan Tokarz (☎ 471 45 64), ul Nowa 15, to arrange accommodation in Eda, or he can also provide you with a private room.

There are some options in Złockie, 3km north of Muszyna, including the good *Ośrodek Wczasowo Sanatoryjny Geofizyk* (☎ 471 41 83).

Getting There & Away
Muszyna is on the Nowy Sącz-Krynica railway line and trains go regularly to either destination. Buses to Krynica (11km) run frequently, and there's also an adequate service to Nowy Sącz (52km).

AROUND MUSZYNA
Having belonged to the bishops of Kraków for nearly 500 years (from 1288 to 1772),

Muszyna was traditionally a Polish town so, not surprisingly, it has a Catholic church but not a cerkiew. But the surrounding villages were populated predominantly by Lemks, whose wooden Uniate churches still dot the region; there are at least five within 5km of Muszyna.

Three of them are north of the town, in **Szczawnik, Złockie** and **Jastrzębik**. All three were built in the 19th century – the 1860s one in Złockie being the youngest and different in style – and each boasts the original iconostasis. Krynica suburban buses go via Muszyna to these villages several times a day and can shorten the walk.

Two more wooden churches, in **Milik** and **Andrzejówka**, are west of Muszyna, and have their original iconostases; you can get there by the regular buses or trains heading for Nowy Sącz. In Andrzejówka, ask for the key in the mustard-coloured house 50m down the road from the church; in Milik, the priest lives in the house at the foot of the cerkiew.

Two **hiking trails** originate in Muszyna and wind north up the mountains. The green one will take you to Mt Jaworzyna (1114m), while the yellow one goes to the peak of Mt Pusta Wielka (1061m). You can get to either in three to four hours, then continue to Krynica, Żegiestów or Rytro – the *Beskid Sądecki* map has all the details.

The Pieniny

The Pieniny, the mountain range between the Beskid Sądecki and the Tatras, is famous for the raft trip down the spectacular Dunajec Gorge, which has become one of Poland's major tourist highlights. Yet there's much more to see and do here. Walkers won't be disappointed with the hiking paths, which offer more dramatic vistas than the Beskid Sądecki or Bieszczady, while lovers of architecture will find here some amazing old wooden Catholic churches. There's also a picturesque mountain castle in Niedzica, or you can just take it easy in the pleasant spa resort of Szczawnica.

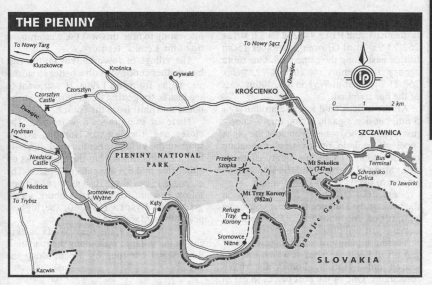

THE PIENINY

To Nowy Targ
Kluszkowce
Krośnica
Grywałd
To Nowy Sącz
KROŚCIENKO
Czorsztyn Castle
Czorsztyn
Dunajec
To Frydman
SZCZAWNICA
Niedzica Castle
PIENINY NATIONAL PARK
Przełęcz Szopka
Mt Sokolica (747m)
Bus Terminal
Schronisko Orlica
To Jaworki
Niedzica
To Trybsz
Sromowce Wyżne
Kąty
Mt Trzy Korony (982m)
Refuge Trzy Korony
Dunajec Gorge
Sromowce Niżne
Kacwin
SLOVAKIA
0   1   2 km

The Pieniny consists of three separate ranges divided by the Dunajec River, the whole chain stretching east-west for about 35km. The highest and most popular is the central range topped with Mt Trzy Korony (Three Crowns, 982m), overlooking the Dunajec Gorge. Almost all this area is now the Pieniny National Park (Pieniński Park Narodowy). To the east, behind the Dunajec River, lies the Małe Pieniny (Small Pieniny), while to the west extends the Pieniny Spiskie. The latter outcrop is the lowest and the least spectacular, though the region around it, known as the Spisz, is an interesting blend of Polish and Slovakian cultures.

SZCZAWNICA
- pop 7200   ☎ 018

Szczawnica ('Shchahv-nee-tsah') is the major tourist centre in the region. Picturesquely located along the Grajcarek River, the town has developed into a popular summer resort, and its mineral springs have made it an important spa. It's also the finishing point for Dunajec Gorge raft trips.

The town spreads over 4km along the main road, ul Główna, and is divided into two suburbs, the Niżna (Lower) to the west and Wyżna (Upper) to the east, with the bus terminal between the two. A good part of the tourist and spa facilities are in the upper part, which also boasts most of the fine old timber houses.

Szczawnica is a good starting point for hiking in the Pieniny or the Beskid Sądecki. Three trails originate from the town and two more begin from Jaworki, 8km east.

Places to Stay & Eat
Accommodation in Szczawnica is the same affair as in many other mountain resorts: plentiful, cheap and highly varied depending on the season. There are few all-year regular hotels but there are a number of small pensions and holiday homes (most only open in summer), and plenty of locals rent out rooms in their homes to tourists.

Travel agencies which arrange accommodation include Orbis (☎ 262 22 57, ☎/fax 262 22 37) at ul Główna 32, 150m east of the bus terminal; Podhale (☎ 262 23 70,

☎/fax 262 27 27) at ul Główna 20, 150m further east; and PTTK (☎ 262 23 32, ☎/fax 262 22 95) at ul Główna 1, another 150m further east along the same road. One more agency, the Pieniny (☎ 262 14 79, ☎/fax 262 21 74), is at ul Wygon 4A, 400m west of the bus terminal.

All the offices tend to close around 4 or 5 pm, but don't panic if you arrive later – just ask for a bed where you spot the signs 'noclegi', 'pokoje' or 'kwatery', indicating private rooms. There are plenty of these signs along ul Główna and the side streets. Expect to pay US$5 to US$10 a bed.

Schronisko Orlica (☎ 262 22 45) is on the bank of the Dunajec River: if you come by raft you end your trip 500m from the hostel – just walk back along the shore.

There are plenty of small eateries on or just off ul Główna, most of which trade in season only. Holiday homes also have restaurants. One of the best places to eat in town is *Restauracja B & M* near PTTK.

Getting There & Away

Buses to Nowy Targ (38km) and to Jaworki (8km) depart roughly every hour. There are also regular buses to Nowy Sącz (48km) which pass via Stary Sącz (40km). Five fast buses daily run straight to Kraków (118km).

For the Dunajec Gorge, take a bus (four daily in season) to Sromowce Niżne and get off in Kąty (21km) – the driver will set you down at the right place. There are also private minibuses which depart when full from ul Główna, midway between PTTK and Podhale. Also, check the PTTK, which organises tours if it can assemble 10 or more people; this may work out much the same price that you'd pay if doing the trip on your own.

SZLACHTOWA & JAWORKI

East of Szczawnica, the road winds 5km along a picturesque valley to the village of Szlachtowa, which has a Uniate church. Built in the early 20th century on the site of the former wooden church, it was taken over after WWII by the Roman Catholics but still has its original iconostasis. While the church is not particularly inspiring, it's interesting to note this was the westernmost tip of the Lemks' territory.

The village of Jaworki 3km farther east has another cerkiew, with a better iconostasis, dating from the 1790s. If you want to see inside, try getting the key from the third house downhill from the church.

There are two gorges near Jaworki. The closer one, the Wąwóz Homole, is just south of the village, near the road. It's only half a kilometre long but the high rocks on either side make it a spectacular place. The green trail goes along its bottom, and if you follow it south for about 1½ hours, you'll get to Mt Wysoka (1050m), the highest peak of the Małe Pieniny.

The other gorge, the Biała Woda, is 2km east of the village; walk along the road until it ends and continue by a path along the stream.

KROŚCIENKO

- **pop 4500**   ☎ 018

A small old town (founded in 1348) at the northern foot of the Pieniny, Krościenko is today a local holiday resort that fills with tourists in summer. Rich mineral springs were discovered in the 19th century, but the town didn't exploit them and the title of spa went to nearby Szczawnica, which did take advantage of the curative waters. With time Szczawnica overshadowed Krościenko in popularity, but Krościenko remains No 1 as a hiking base for the Pieniny.

While in town, you can drop into the local church to see the surviving fragments of 15th century frescoes depicting scenes from the life of Christ, and look over the pleasant Rynek in front of the church.

Information

The tourist office (☎ 262 33 04) at Rynek 32 is open weekdays 8 am to 4 pm (May to September till 6 pm and also on Saturday and Sunday 11 am to 4 pm).

Places to Stay & Eat

There are half a dozen small pensions, including *Pensjonat Granit* (☎ 262 57 07, ul

Jagiellońska 70), **Pensjonat Leśnik** (☎ 262 30 22, ul Jagiellońska 102), **Pensjonat Hanka** (☎ 262 32 98, ul Jagiellońska 55) and **Pensjonat u Gerwazego** (☎ 262 34 52, ul Zdrojowa 23) across the river.

None of the above will cost more than US$10 per bed, but if you need somewhere cheaper, the PTTK office (☎ 262 30 59) at ul Jagiellońska 28, right in the centre, has a list of private rooms for rent, at around US$5 to US$7 per head. If you arrive after 3 pm (the time they close the office) or on Saturday or Sunday, just look for signs that read 'noclegi' or 'kwatery' outside the houses.

There are several restaurants in town that will keep you going. The best is **Karczma u Walusia**, 800m from the Rynek along the Nowy Targ road. Their specialities include the *żurek po pieninsku*, the *placki po góralsku* and the *placki po hajducku*.

Getting There & Away

Lying on the Nowy Sącz-Nowy Targ route, Krościenko has a regular bus service to both these destinations. To Szczawnica (5km), buses run every 20 minutes or so. Four buses go daily to Sromowce Niżne (21km), which is the way to the raft wharf in Kąty (16km), and there are also private minibuses to Kąty in summer. You can also walk to Kąty (see the following section). Five fast buses run directly to Zakopane. Krościenko's main bus stop is at the Rynek.

HIKING IN THE PIENINY

Almost all hiking concentrates on the central Pieniny range, a compact area of 10 x 4km declared a national park. Trails are well marked and short and no trekking equipment is necessary. There are three starting points on the outskirts of the park, all providing accommodation and food. The most popular is Krościenko at the northern edge, then Szczawnica on the eastern rim and Sromowce Niżne to the south. Buy the *Pieniński Park Narodowy* map (scale 1:22,500), which shows all hiking routes.

Most walkers start from Krościenko. They follow the yellow trail as far as the pass, the Przełęcz Szopka, then switch to the blue trail branching off to the left and head up to the top of Mt Trzy Korony (982m), the highest summit of the central range. The reward of this two hour walk is a breathtaking view all around with a panorama of the Tatras, 35km to the southwest, if the weather is clear. You are now about 520m above the level of the Dunajec River which runs just below you.

Another excellent view, particularly over the gorge itself, is from Mt Sokolica (747m), 2km east as the crow flies from Mt Trzy Korony, or a 1½ hour walk along the blue trail. From Mt Sokolica, you can go back down to Krościenko by the green trail, or to Szczawnica by the blue one, in less than an hour to either.

If you plan on taking the raft trip through the Dunajec Gorge, you can hike all the way to Kąty. There are several ways of getting there and the map mentioned shows all of them. The shortest way is to take the blue trail heading west from the Przełęcz Szopka and winding up along the ridge. After 30 to 40 minutes, watch for the red trail branching off to the left (south) and leading downhill. It will take you directly to the wharf in about half an hour.

Alternatively, take the yellow trail descending south from the Przełęcz Szopka into a gorge. In half an hour or so you'll get to the beautifully located PTTK refuge. You can stay here for the night, leaving rafting for the next day, or continue 1km downhill to the village of Sromowce Niżne (where there is a basic camp site and some locals rent out private rooms) and go by bus (nine daily) or foot to Kąty (5km).

DUNAJEC GORGE
☎ 018

The Dunajec Gorge (Przełom Dunajca) is a spectacular stretch of the Dunajec ('Doonah-yets') River, which snakes for about 8km between steep cliffs, some of which are over 300m high. The river is narrow, in one instance funnelling through a 12m-wide bottleneck, and changes constantly from majestically quiet, deep stretches to shallow mountain rapids.

The place has been a tourist attraction since the mid-19th century, when primitive rafts did the honours for the guests of the Szczawnica spa. Today the raft trip through the gorge attracts some 200,000 people annually, not counting the canoeists who struggle with the elements in their own kayaks. This is not a white-water experience: the rapids are gentle and you won't get wet.

The raft itself is a set of five narrow, 6m-long, coffin-like canoes lashed together with rope. Until the 1960s they were genuine dugouts but now they are made of spruce planks. The raft takes 10 passengers and is steered by two raftsmen, each armed with a long pole and usually decked out in embroidered folk costume.

The raft wharf (Przystań Flisacka; ☎ 262 97 21, fax 262 97 93) where the trip begins is in Kąty, and after a 15km journey you disembark in Szczawnica. The trip takes two to three hours, depending on the level of the river, and costs US$8 per head. If you want to go down on your own, you pay the full fare of US$80 per raft. Some rafts go farther downriver to Krościenko (US$10).

There are about 250 rafts in operation and they depart as soon as 10 passengers are ready to go. In general you won't have to wait long to get on the raft.

The season is from 1 May to 31 October though both dates can change if it snows. From May to August the rafts operate 8.30 am to 5 pm, in September 8.30 am to 4 pm, and in October 9 am to 2 pm. There may also be some trips in early November if the weather is fine. The trips may be suspended occasionally for a day or two when the river level is high.

Places to Stay & Eat

The nearest places to stay around Kąty are in Niedzica, 5km west (see The Spisz section) and in Sromowce Niżne 5km east (see the Hiking in the Pieniny section). In Szczawnica, where the trip ends, there are heaps of places to stay (see earlier in this chapter). There's a simple *snack bar* at the wharf in Kąty.

Getting There & Away

Kąty is serviced by five buses daily from Nowy Targ (33km) and four from Szczawnica (21km). There are also a seasonal private minibus service from Szczawnica and Krościenko, and two PKS buses a day from Zakopane. Another way of getting to Kąty is to hike from Krościenko or Szczawnica (see the previous section). Travel agencies in Kraków, Zakopane, Szczawnica, Krynica and other touristy places in the region organise tours.

If you have private transport, you either have to leave your vehicle in Kąty and come back for it after completing the raft trip in Szczawnica, or (perhaps a better option) you can drive to Szczawnica and leave your vehicle there, so you'll have it as soon as you complete the trip. There are car parks in both Kąty and Szczawnica, and the raft operator provides a bus service between the two locations.

THE SPISZ
☎ 018

The Spisz ('Speesh') is the hilly region stretching across the Polish-Slovakian border between the Pieniny and the eastern Tatras. Its Polish portion – about 170 sq km – is bordered on the west and north by the Białka and Dunajec rivers, and on the other sides by the national frontier. In the northern part of the region is a gentle east-west mountain range, the Pieniny Spiskie. See the Tatra Mountains, Podhale & Spisz map, a few pages ahead, for general orientation.

For centuries and until 1920, the whole area was outside the Polish borders, ruled for most of the time by Hungary but populated by Slovaks. Some of their cultural heritage, reflected in their buildings, costumes and language, has survived to this day and is maintained by the Slovak minority living in the area.

Despite its proximity to some major tourist destinations (eg Zakopane, the Dunajec Gorge or Szczawnica), the Spisz feels distinctly remote with its own lethargic atmosphere. There's almost no accommodation or eating facilities and transport is infrequent. Consequently, the Spisz sees few tourists, even though it has some attractions including a good castle and several fine old churches. If you decide to explore the region, get a copy of the *Tatry i Podhale* map (scale 1:75,000), which covers the Spisz.

Niedzica

Niedzica, at the easternmost edge of the Spisz, is known for its **castle**. Perched on a rocky hill above the Dunajec reservoir, this is one of the best mountain castles in the country and the Spisz's most visited tourist sight. It was built in the first half of the 14th century as one of the Hungarian border strongholds and was extended in the early 1600s. Since then it has altered little and has retained its graceful Renaissance shape.

The castle shelters a **museum** featuring small collections on the archaeology, history and ethnography of the region. You'll also get fine views over the surrounding area, including the reservoir of a hydroelectric project, just at the foot of the castle. From May to September the castle is open daily 9 am to 5 pm; the rest of the year 9 am to 4 pm except Monday. Visitors are taken around in groups. Brochures in English and German are available, providing a concise description of the castle and its history.

Places to Stay & Eat There's the all-year hotel in the *castle* (☎ 262 94 89, ☎ 262 94 73, fax 262 94 80) offering doubles/triples with bath (US$34/40) and two triple suites (US$70). Meals can be provided if requested in advance. A few snack bars open in the tourist season near the castle's entrance.

The castle's management also operates the *Celnica*, a fine timber house built in the local style, 200m up the road from the castle. It has one single (US$25), two doubles (US$35) and two suites (US$40), all with bath. Opposite the Celnica is *Wojskowy Dom Wypoczynkowy*, which has cheap bungalows and a camping ground, open May to September.

Farther away are the small *Pensjonat Pieniny* (☎ 262 94 08, ul 3 Maja 12) in the village of Niedzica, 2km south of the castle, and *Hotel Pieniny* (☎ 262 93 83, ul Kanada 38), halfway between the village and the castle. Both are budget options.

Getting There & Away There are half a dozen buses a day from Nowy Targ (25km) to the Niedzica castle. The village of Niedzica is better serviced from Nowy Targ, with about 10 buses per day, but not all go via the castle. When buying your ticket, make sure to specify 'Niedzica-Zamek' (castle). Bus links between the castle and other towns in the region are sporadic.

Around the Spisz

Minuscule as they are, almost all Spisz villages boast a church, some of which are lovely. Together with the overall unhurried atmosphere, these are the major attractions of the region. Unless you have your own transport, moving around may be time-consuming. If you can't manage detours, the best route to take is the Niedzica-Trybsz road, going east-west right across the middle of the Spisz. Buses ply this road fairly regularly and it's also here that two of the region's finest churches are located.

One of them is in Łapsze Wyżne. Built in the 1760s, it has a rococo interior including three ornate altars and the pulpit. Also note the illusionistic altar on the left-hand wall. The priest in the house opposite the church may open it for you.

Completely different is the 1576 small shingled church in Trybsz, standing beside a new one. Inside, the whole length of the walls and the ceiling are covered with fantastic naive paintings depicting saints and biblical scenes, all done in 1647. The mountain landscape on the ceiling is regarded as the oldest painted panorama of the Tatras, and note the smiling Christ. The rococo pulpit is a fine addition to the painted decoration. To see all this, get the keys from house No 27 across the road from the church.

From Trybsz, there are about 10 buses daily to Nowy Targ from where there's frequent transport to Zakopane. Otherwise, get to Białka Tatrzańska and go to Zakopane by the more interesting road via Bukowina Tatrzańska.

KROŚCIENKO TO NOWY TARG

Krościenko is linked to Nowy Targ (described in The Tatras section) by a good 30km road, and you can easily do this route in one go in one of the frequent buses. However, with more time, it's well worth stopping en route to see the old wooden Catholic churches in the villages you pass by, and the Czorsztyn castle a bit off the road.

Grywałd

Going westward from Krościenko, the first village on the route (1km north of the main road, actually) is Grywałd, which has a small and quite amazing rustic **church**. To see inside, ask the priest living in the house just north of the church. The original wall paintings from 1618 adorn a good part of the walls and the ceiling. The central panel of the Gothic triptych in the high altar has been covered by a painting of the Virgin and Child, the infant looking anything but an infant. All the charming internal decoration was done by amateur folk artists.

Czorsztyn

A farther 3km west along the main road, in the village of Krośnica, a side road branches off south to Kąty and then Sromowce Niżne. This road will take you to the village of Czorsztyn, 2km from the turn-off. Only two buses per day from Nowy Targ and two from Szczawnica call at Czorsztyn, but you can take any Sromowce bus which will drop you off 500m away.

The village was built in the 1990s to accommodate the residents of old Czorsztyn, farther west, now flooded by the waters of the hydroelectric scheme. The picturesque ruin of the **Czorsztyn castle**, the Polish counterpart to the Hungarian Niedzica stronghold, is 2km west of the village (no public transport). It is open for visitors May to September, daily 9 am to 6 pm. In other months it's open 10 am to 3 pm except

Monday. There's a small exhibition featuring the castle's history plus a fine view over the Dunajec valley and the Tatras.

Dębno Podhalańskie

The **church** in the village of Dębno Podhalańskie is one of the oldest and most highly rated timber churches in Poland. It was built in the 1490s on the site of a former church and, like most others, the larch-wood construction was put together without a single nail. The paintings that cover all the ceiling and most of the walls date from around 1500 and have not been renovated since; despite that, the colours are still brilliant.

A triptych from the late 15th century adorns the high altar, whereas the crucifix that stands on the rood beam dates from 1380 and was probably transferred from the previous church. There are some antique objects on the side walls, including an intriguing wooden tabernacle from the 14th century.

Another curiosity is a small musical instrument, a sort of primitive dulcimer from the 15th century, which is used during Mass instead of the bell. The seemingly illogical thing about it is that the thicker the bars, the higher the notes they produce.

The church can be visited weekdays 8 am to noon and 2 to 5 pm (till 4 pm in autumn and winter), Saturday 8 am to noon. The priest living just across the road takes visitors through. He will wait until about 10 people turn up, so you may have to wait as well. Brief brochures (in English and German) about the church may be available.

If you want to stay longer in the village, the *youth hostel* opens between 2 July and 25 August in the local school.

Harklowa

Harklowa, 3km west of Dębno, also has a timber Gothic **church**, similar to that in Dębno but larger. They were built in the same period and had almost identical wall paintings, but Harklowa was unlucky; in the 19th century its nave was remodelled and a chapel added to one side. Original wall paintings were removed and today can only be seen in the porch under the bell tower. The interior (except for the porch) was repainted in 1932 in complex patterns of rich blues, greens, yellows and reds, and makes a colourful accompaniment for the florid baroque altars. The priest in the house next door may open it for you.

Łopuszna

Another 3km to the west, the **church** in Łopuszna is a very similar, shingled construction dating from 1504. The high altar boasts a triptych from 1460 and has two baroque side altars. The original wall paintings haven't survived and the current ones were made in 1935.

Just west of the church is an old farmstead, recently partly renovated. Its core is a manor house from around 1790 whose interior has been arranged in the original style and is now a **museum** (open 10 am to 4 pm except Monday and Tuesday).

The Tatras

The Tatras are the highest range of the Carpathians and the only alpine type, with towering peaks and steep rocky sides dropping hundreds of metres to icy lakes. There are no glaciers in the Tatras but patches of snow remain all year. Winters are long, summers short and the weather erratic.

Typically, the vegetation changes with altitude, from mixed forest in the lower parts (below 1200m) to evergreen spruce woods higher up (to 1500m), then to dwarf mountain shrubs and highland pastures (up to 2300m) and finally moss. The wildlife is similarly stratified, with deer, roe deer and wildcats living in the lower forests, and the marmot and chamois in the upper parts.

The whole range, roughly 60km long and 15km wide, stretches across the Polish-Slovakian border. A quarter of it is Polish territory and was declared the Tatra National Park (Tatrzański Park Narodowy), encompassing about 212 sq km. The Polish

Tatras boast a score or more peaks exceeding 2000m, the highest of which is Mt Rysy (2499m).

To the north, at the foot of the Tatras, lies the Podhale region, its hills and valleys extending from Zakopane to Nowy Targ. The Podhale, dotted with small villages populated by the *górale* (literally, highlanders), is one of the few Polish regions where old folk traditions are still largely observed in everyday life.

NOWY TARG
- pop 34,000   ☎ 018

One of the oldest settlements at the foot of the Tatras, Nowy Targ started life around the 13th century, but in 1784 it was almost entirely consumed by fire and little of its old architecture has survived. Comfortably sitting in the fork of the Czarny (Black) and Biały (White) Dunajec rivers, today it is a busy commercial town and a transport hub on the crossroads between the Tatras, Gorce, Pieniny, Spisz and Orawa. Nowy Targ is also known as a gliding centre; the airfield is on the south-eastern outskirts of the town.

The town is a possible jumping-off point for the surrounding countryside, eg for hiking in the Gorce or exploring the Spisz region, though accommodation offerings are poor. You'll find far wider lodging options in Zakopane and Szczawnica.

Information
There's no tourist office to speak of. The Bank Pekao is at Al Tysiąclecia 44 and has an ATM. The Bank Przemysłowo Handlowy is at Rynek 4. There are several kantors in the central area.

Things to See
The town hall on the Rynek shelters the **Regional Museum** (Muzeum Podhalańskie) featuring local folk art. It's open on weekdays 9 am to 2 pm.

One block north of the Rynek is **St Catherine's Church** (Kościół Św Katarzyny), built in the mid-14th century (the presbytery still has Gothic features) but extensively reformed in the early 1600s.

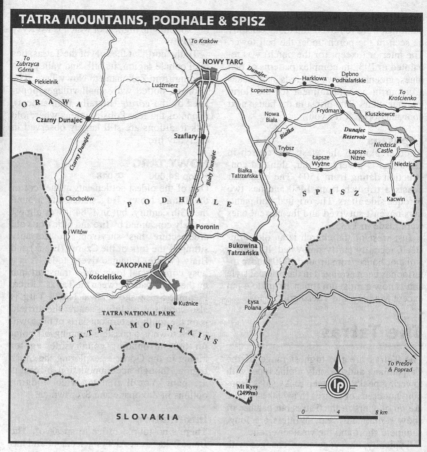

TATRA MOUNTAINS, PODHALE & SPISZ

The interior boasts the usual baroque overlay.

Farther north, beyond the Czarny Dunajec River, is the cemetery. At its entrance is the 16th century shingled **St Anne's Church** (Kościół Św Anny). The interior, embellished with wall paintings from 1866, shelters a baroque high altar. The church is only open for Sunday services, at 10.30 am and 4 pm.

The town's best-known attraction is the **Thursday market**, which has traditionally been held here for over half a millennium, following the king's privilege granted in 1487. However, since mass-produced consumer goods have become the dominant fare in recent years, the market has lost much of its former character and atmosphere. It has also acquired an 'international' flavour, provided by Russian/Ukrainian vendors and Slovak bargain seekers. If you're thinking about buying hand-knitted sweaters, typical hats or other handicrafts, you'll find more in Zakopane. The market is held on the Plac Targowy, a few blocks east of the Rynek. These days, an equally big market is also held on the same square on Saturday. Watch your belongings closely.

If you happen to be in town on 15 August (the Assumption), don't miss the small village of **Ludźmierz**, 5km from Nowy Targ, where the holy statue of the Virgin Mary in the local church attracts crowds of the górale, most of them wearing traditional costumes.

Places to Stay & Eat
Hotel Limba (☎ 266 70 64, ul Sokoła 8), one block west of the Rynek, is pretty basic. It costs US$18/24 for doubles/triples without bath, US$28/34 with bath.

Klub Sportowy Gorce (☎ 266 26 61, Al Tysiąclecia 74), a few blocks south of the Rynek, is cheaper although also far from posh. Doubles/triples without bath cost US$13/18 and singles/doubles with bath are US$14/18. The Klub also has three heated cabins, where a bed costs US$6.

The *youth hostel* (☎ 266 56 51, Osiedle Na Skarpie 11) is in school No 6, 1km west of the train station (3km west of the centre on the Ludźmierz road). Theoretically, it's open from 2 July to 25 August.

The best and most central place in town is *Hotel Podhalanka* (☎ 266 63 66, Rynek 39). It has spacious rooms with bath for US$30/40/50/60 a single/double/triple/ quad, breakfast included. Enter from ul Szaflarska.

There are several fast-food options on the Rynek, but you're better off trying *Restauracja Kaprys* (ul Sokoła 3), which serves solid, inexpensive meals – good value.

Getting There & Away
The bus terminal is on the western edge of the central area of Nowy Targ, a 10 minute walk from the Rynek; the train station is 1km south-west of the bus station, on the town's outskirts.

All the Kraków-Zakopane traffic passes through the town and the route is pretty busy. Trains and buses to Zakopane (24km)

run frequently. To Kraków, it's much faster to go by bus (80km) as the trains take the long way around (126km).

Buses to Szczawnica (38km) run roughly every hour. There are six or seven buses daily to Zubrzyca Górna (42km) if you want to visit the skansen there. There are three morning buses to the Niedzica castle, going via the village of Niedzica. Three buses daily go to the border crossing at Łysa Polana (37km), and five to Kąty (33km), where the raft trips through the Dunajec Gorge begin.

ZAKOPANE
• pop 30,000   ☎ 018

Nestled at the foot of the Tatras, Zakopane is the most famous mountain resort in Poland and the winter sports capital. The town attracts a couple of million tourists a year, with peaks in summer and winter. Though Zakopane is essentially a base for either skiing or hiking in the Tatras, the town itself is an enjoyable enough place to hang around in for a while, and it has lots of tourist facilities.

Zakopane came to life in the 17th century, but only in the second half of the 19th century did it become something more than a mountain post, attracting tourists and artists alike. At the time of the Young Poland movement (late 19th century), the town became popular with artists, many of whom came to settle and work here. The best known of these are the composer Karol Szymanowski and the writer and painter Witkacy. The father of the latter, Stanisław Witkiewicz (1851-1915), was inspired by the traditional local architecture and created the 'Zakopane style'; some of the buildings he designed stand to this day.

The town grew at a much faster pace in the interwar period, and shortly before WWII the cableway and the funicular railway were built, today the prime tourist attractions. Development continued after the war but fortunately the town is still reasonably small and hasn't acquired many of the concrete blocks typical of most urban centres in Poland. Apart from a few central streets, Zakopane feels more like a large village rather than a town, its mainly villa-type houses set informally in their own gardens.

In 1998, Zakopane's attention was centred on its bid to host the 2006 Winter Olympic Games. However, there has been vocal opposition among local environmental circles, claiming that the Tatra National Park, where some of the events are planned to take place, would be irreparably damaged.

Orientation
Zakopane sits at an altitude of 800 to 1000m at the foot of Mt Giewont. The bus and train stations are adjacent in the north-east part of town. It's a 10 minute walk down ul Kościuszki to the town's heart, the pedestrian mall of Krupówki, always jammed with trendy tourists.

The funicular to Mt Gubałówka is just off the north-western end of Krupówki. The cable car to Mt Kasprowy Wierch is at Kuźnice, 3km to the south-east.

Information
Tourist Office The helpful Centrum Informacji Turystycznej (☎/fax 201 22 11, ☎/fax 206 60 51), ul Kościuszki 17, is open daily 7 am to 9 pm.

Money The Bank Pekao at ul Gimnazjalna 1 behind the bus terminal changes most major brands of travellers cheques and pays złoty advances on Visa and MasterCard. Bank Przemysłowo Handlowy at ul Krupówki 19 opposite Hotel Gazda changes cheques and accepts Visa card. As for cash, kantors dot ul Krupówki every 50m or so, and there are also a few ATMs.

Email & Internet Access The Internet Café is on the 1st floor of the Morskie Oko gastronomic complex at ul Krupówki 30.

Travel Agencies Centrum Przewodnictwa Tatrzańskiego (Tatra Guide Centre; ☎ 206 37 99) at ul Chałubińskiego 44 and the Biuro Usług Turystycznych PTTK (☎ 201

58 48) at ul Krupówki 12 can arrange mountain guides speaking English and German, but advance notice is necessary. The cost depends on the difficulty of the hike or climb: from about US$40 to US$100 a day per group.

Another useful address for arranging a mountain guide is Barbara and Arek Gąsienica-Józkowy (☎/fax 206 63 43) at Bulwary Słowackiego 7, who also do rock and ice climbing and paragliding.

Orbis (☎ 201 50 51), ul Krupówki 22, sells domestic and international train tickets, arranges accommodation in private houses and selected holiday homes and organises tours. Teresa (☎ 201 43 01) at ul Kościuszki 7 specialises in international bus tickets.

Other useful travel agencies include Trip (☎ 201 59 47) at ul Zamoyskiego 1 (international bus tickets, tours); Tatry (☎ 201 43 43) at ul Chramcówki 35 just off the train station (private rooms, tours); Giewont (☎ 206 35 66) at ul Kościuszki 4 (private rooms, tours); Fregata (☎ 201 33 07) at ul Krupówki 81B (international tickets) and Kozica (☎ 201 32 77) at ul Jagiellońska 1 right behind the Bar FIS (private rooms, tickets).

Many of these and other agencies will have tours to the Dunajec Gorge (US$15 to US$18 per person) and other popular regional tourist destinations.

Bookshops You'll find the best choice of maps and guidebooks on the Tatras and various other mountain regions at Księgarnia Górska, on the 1st floor of Dom Turysty PTTK.

Things to See
You will probably start your sightseeing in Krupówki, the trendy central mall. The mall is lined with restaurants, cafés, boutiques and souvenir shops. After wandering up and down once or twice you'll have a bit of a feel for the local atmosphere. Krupówki is the place to be, and some tourists seem to do nothing but parade up and down this mall for hours.

Your first stop might be the **Tatra Museum** (Muzeum Tatrzańskie), ul Krupówki 10, close to the lower end of the mall. It has several sections including history, ethnography, geology and flora and fauna and is thus a good introduction to the region; open 9 am to 4 pm except Monday.

A little down ul Krupówki, on the opposite side of the street, is the large stone neo-Romanesque **parish church**, which looks as though it has been imported from a completely different culture. It was built at the end of the 19th century when the much smaller **old parish church** couldn't cope any longer with the numbers of worshippers. The latter, 100m away on ul Kościeliska, is a rustic wooden construction dating from 1847. It has charming folksy decorations inside.

The **stone chapel** standing beside it is about 30 years older and is in fact the first place of worship and the oldest surviving building in Zakopane. Just behind it is the **old cemetery** with a number of amazing wooden tombs.

Continue west along ul Kościeliska to the **Villa Koliba**, the first design (1892) of Witkiewicz in the Zakopane style. It now accommodates the **Museum of Zakopane Style** (Muzeum Stylu Zakopiańskiego), open Wednesday to Sunday 9 am to 4 pm.

Some 500m south-east, on ul Kasprusie, is the **Villa Atma**, once the home of Karol Szymanowski, today a **museum** (open from 10 am to 4 pm except Monday) dedicated to the composer. Summer piano recitals are held here.

Don't miss the **Władysław Hasior Art Gallery**, displaying striking assemblages by this contemporary avant-garde artist, who is also closely associated with Zakopane. The gallery is off ul Jagiellońska 18B near the train station, and is open Wednesday to Saturday 11 am to 6 pm, Sunday 9 am to 3 pm.

A 20 minute walk south of here, next to the roundabout called Rondo, is the **Tatra National Park Museum** (Muzeum TPN) with an exhibition on the natural history of the park. It's open Tuesday to Saturday 9 am to 2 pm.

A short walk east up the hill will lead you to the **Villa pod Jedlami**, another splendid house in the Zakopane style (the interior cannot be visited). Perhaps Witkiewicz's greatest achievement is the **Jaszczurówka Chapel**, about 1.5km farther east on the road to Morskie Oko.

Funicular to Mt Gubałówka

Mt Gubałówka (1120m) offers an excellent view over the Tatras and is a favourite destination for those tourists who don't feel like exercising their legs too much. The funicular, built in 1938, provides comfortable access to the top. It covers the 1388m-long route in less than five minutes, climbing 300m (US$3 return). In summer, it operates every 10 minutes from 7.30 am to 9 pm. It tends to close from around 20 April to 15 May and from 15 to 31 October.

Cable Car to Mt Kasprowy Wierch

Since it opened in 1935, the cable-car trip from Kuźnice to the summit of Mt Kasprowy Wierch (1985m) – where you can stand with one foot in Poland and the other in Slovakia – has become almost a must for tourists to Poland. The route is 4290m long with an intermediate station midway at Mt Myślenickie Turnie (1352m). The one-way journey, ascending 936m, takes 20 minutes.

The trip is an easy way to see the real mountains: you'll have splendid views from the car during the journey itself and from the top, clouds permitting. Many people don't come back by cable car but walk. There are several marked trails from Mt Kasprowy Wierch that can take you either back to Kuźnice or to other parts of the Tatras. The most intrepid hikers walk the ridges all the way across to Morskie Oko Lake via Pięć Stawów, a strenuous hike taking a full day in good weather. You can eat at the restaurant at the top before setting off.

The cable car normally operates from about mid-December to mid-May and from early June to late October (this is a rough guide only). In midsummer, it runs from

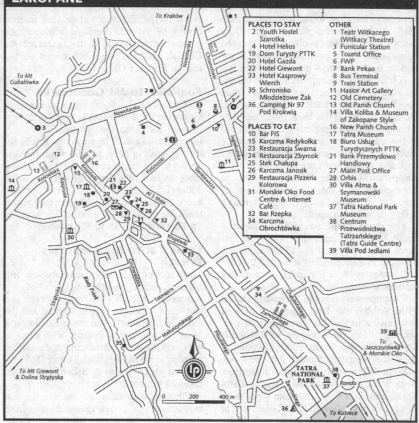

ZAKOPANE

PLACES TO STAY
2 Youth Hostel Szarotka
4 Hotel Helios
19 Dom Turysty PTTK
20 Hotel Gazda
22 Hotel Giewont
33 Hotel Kasprowy Wierch
35 Schronisko Młodzieżowe Żak
36 Camping Nr 97 Pod Krokwią

PLACES TO EAT
10 Bar FIS
15 Karczma Redykołka
23 Restauracja Swarna
24 Restauracja Zbyrcok
25 Stek Chałupa
26 Karczma Janosik
29 Restauracja Pizzeria Kolorowa
31 Morskie Oko Food Centre & Internet Café
32 Bar Rzepka
34 Karczma Obrochtówka

OTHER
1 Teatr Witkacego (Witkacy Theatre)
3 Funicular Station
5 Tourist Office
6 FWP
7 Bank Pekao
8 Bus Terminal
9 Train Station
11 Hasior Art Gallery
12 Old Cemetery
13 Old Parish Church
14 Villa Koliba & Museum of Zakopane Style
16 New Parish Church
17 Tatra Museum
18 Biuro Usług Turystycznych PTTK
21 Bank Przemysłowo Handlowy
27 Main Post Office
28 Orbis
30 Villa Atma & Szymanowski Museum
37 Tatra National Park Museum
38 Centrum Przewodnictwa Tatrzańskiego (Tatra Guide Centre)
39 Villa Pod Jedlami

7.30 am to 6 pm; in winter, it runs from 7.30 am to 4 pm.

The one-way/return ticket costs US$5/7. If you buy a return, your trip back is automatically reserved two hours after departure time. In other words, you have one hour and 40 minutes at the top. Tickets can be bought at the Kuźnice cableway station (for the same day only). You can also buy them in advance from Orbis and some other travel agencies, but normally only if you purchase some of their services. At peak

tourist times (both summer and winter), tickets run out fast and there are usually long lines in Kuźnice; you should get there early. PKS buses go to Kuźnice frequently from the bus terminal, and there are also private minibuses that park in front of the Bar FIS.

Special Events

The International Festival of Mountain Folklore in late August is the town's leading cultural event. In July, a series of concerts presenting music by Karol Szymanowski is held in the Villa Atma.

Places to Stay

Zakopane has heaps of places to stay and, except for occasional peaks, finding a bed is no problem. Even if hotels and hostels are full, there will generally be some private rooms around – in fact, private rooms provide some of the cheapest and best accommodation in town.

As with all seasonal resorts, accommodation prices in Zakopane fluctuate (sometimes considerably) between high and low seasons, peaking in late December, January and February, and then in July and August. Prices given are for the high season.

Camping The all-year *Camping Nr 97 Pod Krokwią* (☎ 201 22 56) on ul Żeromskiego has large heated bungalows, each containing several double and triple rooms. They cost US$10 per person in July and August (less in other months), but they are often full in that period. To get to the camping grounds from the bus/train stations, take any bus to Kuźnice or Jaszczurówka and get off at Rondo.

Zakopane has several more camping grounds, including the all-year *Camping Nr 160 Harenda* (☎ 206 84 06) on the Kraków road, the summer *Camping za Strugiem* (☎ 201 45 66, ul Za Strugiem 39), *Camping u Daniela* (☎ 206 12 96) in Oberconiówka, and *Auto Camping Nr 252 Comfort* (☎ 201 49 42, ul Kaszelewskiego 7) on the Kościelisko road.

Youth Hostels Zakopane has the year-round *Youth Hostel Szarotka* (☎ 206 62 03, ul Nowotarska 45), a 10 minute walk from both the centre and the stations. With some 250 beds (mostly in eight to 12-bed dorms), this is one of the largest hostels in the country, yet it can still get packed solid. It's frequently used by school excursion groups – expect large kiddie brigades at most times of year. Sadly, the toilets and showers cannot cope with such numbers of people.

The all-year *Schronisko Młodzieżowe Żak* (☎ 201 57 06, ul Marusarzówny 15) is in a quiet, verdant south-western suburb of the town. Run by Almatur, it's not a regular PTSM youth hostel, but it works on similar principles and costs much the same. It has seven small dorms (US$5 a bed) and two doubles (US$6 a bed); bed linen is US$1.50 extra if needed. The place is well run and friendly, and it may be easier to find a bed here than in the Szarotka.

Other Hostels The very central 460-bed *Dom Turysty PTTK* (☎ 206 32 07, ☎ 206 32 81, ul Zaruskiego 5) has heaps of rooms of different sizes, mostly dormitories. Doubles/triples with bath cost US$32/40, rooms with shower only go for US$26/36, and those without bath are US$24/30. You can stay in a dorm with four beds (US$8 per head), eight beds (US$6) or 28 beds (US$5). Like the Szarotka, the place can often be swamped with excited crowds of preteens. There's an 11 pm curfew.

Private Rooms The business of private rooms for hire is flourishing in Zakopane. It is run by the tourist office and most travel agencies, including Orbis, PTTK, Tatry and Kozica (see the Information section earlier). In the peak season, they probably won't want to fix up accommodation for a period shorter than three nights, but in the off season, this shouldn't apply. You can expect a bed in a double room to cost US$6 to US$10 in the peak season. Check the location before deciding.

In the high season, there are usually quite a few locals hanging around the bus and train stations, who approach arriving passengers to offer them rooms in their homes. The prices given upfront are sometimes absurdly inflated (particularly for foreigners), but can be swiftly negotiated down to the normal level. As a rule, you shouldn't pay more than when renting a room through an agency. Again, check the location first before setting off for the place.

Many locals don't bother to wait for arriving buses or trains, but simply put boards reading 'pokoje', 'noclegi' or 'zimmer frei' outside their homes. You'll find many such signs, and a number of 'pensjonat' (pensions), which may offer better facilities, but are usually more expensive and may insist on selling a bed-and-board package.

Holiday Homes There are plenty of holiday homes in Zakopane. These days, most of them are open to the general public, renting rooms either directly or through travel agencies. The major agent is FWP (☎ 201 27 63), which has its office in the DW Podhale at ul Kościuszki 19. It's open weekdays 8 am to 5 pm, and in the busy season also on Saturday.

The office rents rooms in 11 FWP holiday homes scattered around the town. Rooms range from doubles to quads, some with baths. You can take just a room or room with board (three meals). As a rough guide, in July and August a bed in rooms without/with bath will cost US$10/18; in the off season US$6/10. Add US$10 for full board. One-night stays are OK.

Hotels Given the abundance of private rooms and holiday homes, plus other cheap options, few travellers bother to look for a hotel, which are more expensive and aren't always good value. However, if you need one, there are a number of them, including several central establishments: *Hotel Gazda* (☎ 201 50 11, fax 201 53 30, ul Zaruskiego 2), the Orbis-run *Hotel Giewont* (☎ 201 20 11, fax 201 20 15, ul Kościuszki 1), *Hotel Kasprowy Wierch* (☎/fax 201 27 38, ul Krupówki 50B), and *Hotel Helios* (☎ 20 138 08, ☎/fax 201 36 36, ul Słoneczna 2A). Any of these will cost around US$50/70 (US$40/60 off season).

Places to Eat

The central mall, ul Krupówki, boasts heaps of eateries, everything from hamburger stands to well appointed establishments. Eating cheaply is not a problem in Zakopane – the proliferation of small fast-food outlets around the town is astonishing, and there are also plenty of informal places in private homes in the back streets, displaying boards saying 'obiady domowe' (home-cooked lunches).

Among the cheapest places are the basic *Bar Mleczny* (ul Krupówki 1), *Bar Rzepka* (ul Krupówki 43), *Bistro Grota* (ul Kościuszki 5), and the *Bufet* in the building of the Urząd Miasta (local government headquarters) at ul Kościuszki 13. Slightly more expensive is *Restauracja Świarna* (ul Kościuszki 4). If you arrive hungry by bus or train, the large, drab *Bar FIS* can be an emergency option.

The folksy *Stek Chałupa* (ul Krupówki 33) has popular Polish dishes at low prices. Opposite, the pleasant *Restauracja Pizzeria Kolorowa* has been totally revamped, and serves more than pizza. *Morskie Oko*, a few steps up the mall, is a large food centre, with a vast restaurant in the basement.

There's a fair choice of reasonable restaurants serving typical food, most of which are decorated accordingly and even have waiters decked out in regional costumes. From north to south, you have *Karczma Redykołka* (ul Krupówki 2), *Restauracja Zbyrcok* (ul Krupówki 29), *Karczma Janosik* (ul Krupówki 35) and, probably the best of its kind, *Karczma Obrochtówka* (ul Kraszewskiego 10A).

Don't miss trying the smoked sheep's-milk cheese sold at street stands all along ul Krupówki.

Entertainment

The *Teatr Witkacego* (Witkacy Theatre; ul Chramcówki 15) is one of the best theatres in Poland.

Getting There & Away

Most regional routes are covered by bus, while the train is useful mainly for long-distance travel – to Warsaw, for example.

Train There are several trains to Kraków (147km) but buses are faster and run more frequently. One train daily (two in season) runs to Warsaw (439km). Tickets are available from the station or from Orbis at ul Krupówki 22.

Bus The PKS fast buses run to Kraków (104km) every hour; the trip costs US$3.50 and takes 2½ hours. There are also nine buses a day to Kraków operated by a private company (departing from ul Kościuszki 19). They are cheaper (US$3) and a bit faster than PKS. Tickets are available from the office next to Kozica travel agency. There are several PKS buses daily to Nowy Sącz and single buses to Tarnów, Przemyśl, Rzeszów and Krynica. PKS has introduced a useful direct bus to Kąty (for the Dunajec raft trip).

In the region around Zakopane, bus transport is relatively frequent. PKS buses can take you to the foot of the Kościeliska and Chochołowska valleys as well as to Polana Palenica near the Lake Morskie Oko. There are also private minibuses which ply the most popular tourist routes, leaving from in front of Bar FIS.

There are a couple of buses per week to Budapest (US$16, nine hours), and a daily morning bus to Poprad in Slovakia (US$3), where you can catch the express train to Prague, departing around 11 am and arriving about 6.30 pm.

You can also take any of the Polana Palenica PKS buses or private minibuses, get off at Łysa Polana (22km), cross the border on foot and continue by bus (regular transport) to Tatranská Lomnica (30km). Southbound this route is easy but northbound you could find the Polana Palenica bus to Zakopane crowded with day-trippers from Morskie Oko (in which case you should consider hitching, as taxi drivers want 20 times the bus fare).

Getting Around

Cycling can be an attractive and convenient means of visiting the Zakopane region. There are several companies renting bikes, including the Sport Shop & Service (☎ 201 58 71) at ul Krupówki 52A, and the Wypożyczalnia Sukces (☎ 201 48 44) at ul Sienkiewicza 39 (which also rents out skis). Expect a bike to cost US$2 per hour (with a possible three hour minimum charge), and US$12 per day.

HIKING IN THE TATRAS

With a huge variety of walking trails, the Tatras are ideal for walks. No other area in Poland is so densely crisscrossed with hiking paths and nowhere else will you find such a diversity of landscapes.

Before you go, get a map – the *Tatrzański Park Narodowy* map (scale 1:25,000) published by Sygnatura is probably the best one. It shows all the trails in the area, complete with the walking times uphill and downhill.

The Tatras are beautiful in every season, and there is no one time when they are at their best. If you don't like crowds, it's better to avoid July and August, when they may be literally overrun by tourists. Late spring and early autumn seem to be the best times for visits. Theoretically at least, you can expect better weather in autumn (September to October) when the rainfall is lower than in spring.

Like all alpine mountains, the Tatras can be dangerous, particularly during the snowy period, roughly from November to May. Use common sense and go easy. Remember that the weather can be tricky, with snow or rain, thunderstorms, fog, strong wind etc occurring frequently and unpredictably. Bring good footwear, warm clothing and rain gear.

Around Zakopane

If you just want to go for a short walk, there are several picturesque small valleys south of Zakopane, the **Dolina Strążyska** being arguably the nicest. You can come back the same way or transfer by the black trail to either of the neighbouring valleys, the Dolina Małej Łąki to the west or the Dolina Białego to the east, and then return.

You can also continue from the Strążyska by the red trail to **Mt Giewont** (1909m, 3½ hours from Zakopane), and then walk down the blue trail to Kuźnice in two hours.

West Tatras

There are two long and beautiful valleys, the **Dolina Chochołowska** and the **Dolina Kościeliska**, in the western part of the park,

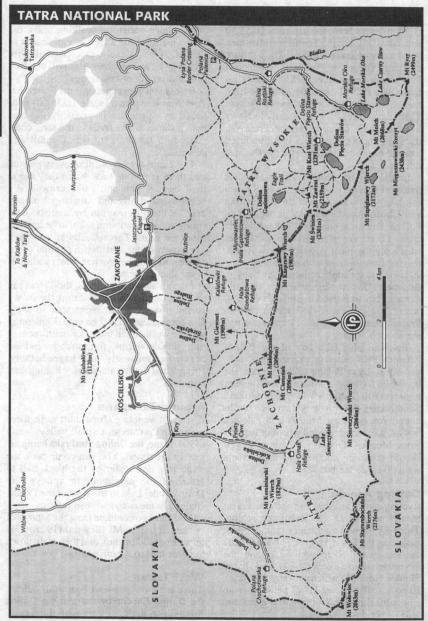

TATRA NATIONAL PARK

known as the Tatry Zachodnie (West Tatras). You can switch from one to the other, either by the black trail called the Ścieżka nad Reglami, or by the more demanding yellow trail higher up, via the Iwaniacka Przełęcz, a pass at 1459m. Visit the **Jaskinia Mroźna** (Frosty Cave) in the Kościeliska valley, the only cave in the Tatras open as a tourist sight (May to October 9 am to 4 pm).

Each valley has a mountain refuge if you want to eat or stay overnight. The valleys are serviced by PKS buses and private minibuses from Zakopane.

High Tatras

The Tatry Wysokie (High Tatras), in the south-eastern part of the park, offer quite different scenery: it's a land of bare granite peaks with alpine lakes at their feet. An easy way of getting close is to take the cable car to **Mt Kasprowy Wierch**, from where you can head eastwards along the red trail to Mt Świnica (2301m), and on to the Zawrat pass (2½ hours from Mt Kasprowy). It's a spectacular walk along the ridge. From Zawrat you can descend either north to the Dolina Gąsienicowa along the blue trail and back to Zakopane, or south (also by the blue trail) to the wonderful **Dolina Pięciu Stawów** (Five Lakes' Valley) where you'll find a mountain refuge (1¼ hours from Zawrat).

The most adventurous and breathtaking route is the **Orla Perć** (Eagle Trail): the red path from Zawrat will take you east over the rocky ridge to the Krzyżne pass (six to seven hours), from where you can either descend north to the Dolina Gąsienicowa or south to the Dolina Pięciu Stawów to the afore-mentioned refuge (1½ hours from Krzyżne). You can descend at several other points from the Orla Perć if you feel like shortening the trek.

The Eagle Trail is difficult and shouldn't be undertaken by inexperienced trekkers. The terrain is such that chains, foot holes and ladders have been put in place to help you – great if you're into that but a bit daunting to some people.

The blue trail heading west from the refuge will bring you to Lake Morskie Oko (see the following section), 1½ hours from the refuge. You can then go back to Zakopane by bus, or challenge the highest peak in the Polish Tatras, **Mt Rysy** (2499m). In return for your four hour climb from Morskie Oko, you will get a view of over 100 peaks and a dozen lakes. This trek is also difficult, and is only recommended for people with trekking experience.

Lake Morskie Oko The emerald-green Lake Morskie Oko (Eye of the Sea), acclaimed as being among the loveliest in the Tatras, is the most popular tourist destination in this part of Poland. You can get there on foot from the Dolina Pięciu Stawów as described above, but the lake is easier to get to by road from Zakopane. As the trip involves little walking, it's extremely popular with tourists of all ages and is done by every second visitor to Zakopane. Hence, the lake is swamped with people in the high season, particularly in July and August. Try to avoid these months, but do come – this really is one of the most amazing corners of the Tatras.

PKS buses from Zakopane depart for the lake regularly, as do private minibuses from across the road from the bus terminal. They all go as far as the car park at the Polana Palenica (US$1.25, 30 minutes). The 9km road continues uphill to the lake, but cars, bikes and buses are allowed no farther. You can walk the distance in two hours (it isn't steep and the scenery is beautiful), or a horse-drawn carriage will bring you to Włosienica, 2km from the lake. Between the car park and Włosienica, the road climbs 339m.

Horse-drawn carriages leave as soon as they collect about 15 people. The trip takes about 1¼ hours uphill and costs US$7; downhill takes 45 minutes and costs US$5. In summer, carriages go up until about 4 or 5 pm and return up to around 8 pm. In winter, transport is by horse-drawn four-seater sledges, which are more expensive than the carriages.

From the carriage stop at Włosienica, it's a 20 minute walk to the lake shore. The Morskie Oko mountain refuge at the lakeside serves hearty *bigos* and drinks. A stone walking path circles the lake (45 minutes). You can climb to the upper lake, Czarny Staw, in half an hour. The trail continues steeply up to the top of Mt Rysy (see the previous section).

Places to Stay & Eat

Camping is not allowed in the park but there are eight PTTK mountain refuges (see the map for locations) which provide simple accommodation, costing around US$5 to US$8 per person in a dorm or US$20 to US$25 per double room. Most refuges are pretty small and fill up fast. In both midsummer and midwinter they are invariably packed far beyond capacity. No one is ever turned away, though you may have to crash on the bare floor if all the beds are taken. Don't arrive too late and bring along your own bed mat and sleeping bag.

All refuges serve simple hot meals, but their kitchens and dining rooms close early, in some places at 7 pm, so get there at a reasonable time if you want to eat something after your hiking. Hot water is usually available free of charge – you may want to bring along some tea bags, as many Polish hikers do. The refuges are open year-round but some may be temporarily closed for repairs, usually in November. Before you set off, check the current situation at the PTTK office in Zakopane.

The easiest refuge to get to from Zakopane is the large and decent *Kalatówki Refuge* (84 beds, US$15 per person, breakfast included), a 30 minute walk from the Kuźnice cable-car station. Half an hour beyond Kalatówki on the trail to Giewont is the *Hala Kondratowa Refuge* (20 beds). For location and atmosphere it's great, but note the small size.

Hikers wishing to traverse the park might begin at the *Dolina Roztoki Refuge* (96 beds), accessible via the Morskie Oko bus. An early start from Zakopane, however, would allow you to visit Morskie Oko in the morning and either stay at the *Morskie Oko Refuge* or continue through to the *Dolina Pięciu Stawów Refuge* (70 beds). This is the highest (1700m) and most scenically located refuge in the Polish Tatras. A leisurely day's walk north-west of Pięć Stawów is the *Murowaniec Hala Gąsienicowa Refuge* (100 beds), from which you can return to Zakopane. The last three refuges are the most crowded ones.

In the western part of the park are the *Hala Ornak Refuge* (75 beds) and *Polana Chochołowska Refuge* (161 beds), connected by a trail.

Silesia

Occupying the whole of south-western Poland, Silesia (Śląsk in Polish; pronounced 'Slonsk') is made up of three geographically quite distinct regions. Its eastern part is the Silesian Upland (Wyżyna Śląska), or Upper Silesia (Górny Śląsk). This relatively small area is Poland's most industrialised and densely populated region.

To the north-west lies the Silesian Lowland (Nizina Śląska), known as Lower Silesia (Dolny Śląsk), which stretches along the Odra River for over 300km. The main city, Wrocław, is also the main tourist attraction of the region.

The lowland is bordered on the south-west by the Sudetes (Sudety), a mountain range running along the Czech border. This is probably the most interesting area for travellers, for both its natural beauty and its picturesque towns.

Silesia has had a chequered history. The region was settled gradually during the second half of the 1st millennium AD by Slavonic tribes known collectively as the Ślężanie or Silesians. It became part of Poland during the rule of Duke Mieszko I shortly before the year 1000. When Poland split into principalities in the 12th century, Silesia was divided into independent duchies ruled by Silesian Piasts, a branch of the first Polish dynasty.

During the second quarter of the 14th century the region was gradually annexed by Bohemia. In 1526 it fell under Habsburg administration, and in 1741 it passed to Prussia. Part of Upper Silesia returned to Poland after WWI but the rest of the region, including the whole of Lower Silesia, joined Poland only in the aftermath of WWII. The Germans were repatriated into the new Germany soon after the end of the war, and their place was taken by Poles resettled from Poland's eastern provinces lost to the Soviet Union. Traces of this complex history can be detected in the local architecture, the people and the atmosphere.

Upper Silesia

Upper Silesia occupies only about 2% of Poland's territory, yet it's home to over 10% of the country's population. It's the nation's main centre of heavy industry thanks to large deposits of coal. The bulk of

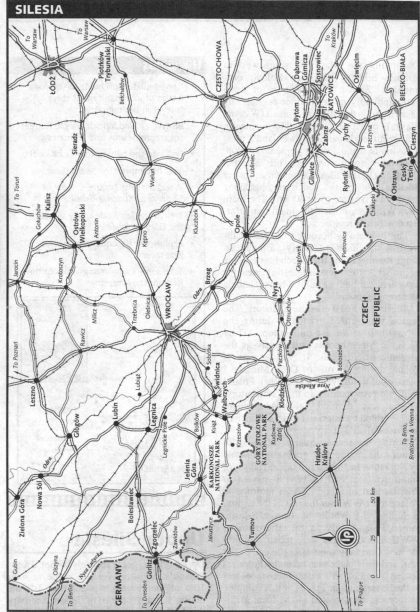

SILESIA

the industry – principally coal and steel – is concentrated in the central part of the upland, around the city of Katowice.

Though the beginnings of mining date from the 12th century, the region really developed in the 19th century under Prussian rule. After WWI, following a plebiscite, Upper Silesia was cut in two. Its eastern part returned to Poland, while the west remained in German hands. After WWII, the whole region came under Polish administration and became the nation's industrial heartland.

Today, the heart of Upper Silesia is an agglomeration of mines, steelworks and other industries squeezed in between the cities, making it the most densely urbanised area in Central Europe, and the most polluted. The area was named Black Silesia after the coal, but ironically the name came to suit other aspects of the environment.

KATOWICE

- **pop 355,000**   ☎ 032

Katowice ('Kah-to-vee-tseh') is the centre of the so-called Upper Silesian Industrial District (Górnośląski Okręg Przemysłowy). The GOP contains 14 cities and a number of neighbouring towns, which merge to form one vast conurbation with a population of over three million. It includes over 50 coal mines, 16 steelworks and various chemical and machinery factories. It's one of the biggest industrial centres in Europe, and one of the most outdated.

Historically, Katowice is the product of the 19th century industrial boom, but it only became a city in the interwar period. After WWII, on the wave of the Stalinist craze, the city was renamed Stalinogród, but the name was dropped soon after its namesake died. Katowice has few significant historical monuments, though like any city of its size it's a considerable commercial and cultural centre, with several theatres and museums.

Information

There's been no tourist office in the city since 1995, though there are plans to open one at some stage.

Useful banks include the Bank Pekao at ul Św Jana 5, the Powszechny Bank Gospodarczy at ul Warszawska 8 and the Wielkopolski Bank Kredytowy at ul Wita Stwosza 2. They all have ATMs and, additionally, there are a number of Euronet ATMs around the central area including one in the main hall of the train station. Kantors are plentiful.

Things to See

If you start your tour from the **Rynek**, you may be disappointed, as Katowice's central square is not lined with historic burghers' houses but with drab postwar blocks. It's a showpiece of the early Gierek style – this is the term Poles sarcastically give to the architecture of the brisk period of apparent prosperity in the early 1970s, when Gierek's government took out hefty loans from the west to make Poland a 'second Japan'.

Just north of the Rynek, at Al Korfantego 3, is the **Silesian Museum** (Muzeum Śląskie), which features a collection of Polish paintings from 1800 till WWII, plus various temporary exhibitions. It's open Tuesday to Friday 10 am to 5 pm, Saturday and Sunday 11 am to 4 pm.

A 10 minute walk south from the Rynek is the **Cathedral of Christ the King** (Katedra Chrystusa Króla), a massive sandstone structure erected in 1927-55. It's one of the biggest churches built in Poland. Its spacious interior is topped with a large dome, but apart from colourful stained-glass windows it's fairly plain and scarcely decorated.

Right behind the cathedral is the **Archdiocesan Museum** (enter from ul Wita Stwosza 16). Its collection of sacral art from the late 14th century on includes some beautiful Gothic altarpieces and Madonnas. It's open Tuesday and Thursday 2 to 6 pm, and Sunday 2 to 5 pm.

About 1.5km farther to the south-west, in the Park Kościuszki, is the charming, timber-shingled **St Michael's Church** (Kościół Św Michała), dating from 1510. It was brought here from the Upper Silesian village of Syrynia and reassembled in 1939.

SILESIA

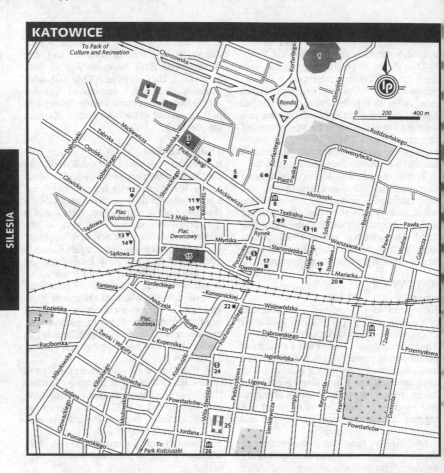

KATOWICE

PLACES TO STAY
2 Youth Hostel
5 Hotel Silesia
7 Hotel Katowice
17 Hotel Centralny
20 Hotel Śląski
22 Hotel Polonia

PLACES TO EAT
10 Bar Filipek
11 Bar pod 7
13 Restauracja u Kolumba
14 Restauracja A Dong
19 Restauracja Le France

OTHER
1 'Flying Saucer' Sports Hall
3 Bus Terminal
4 EMPiK
6 Orbis Office
8 Silesian Museum
9 Silesian Theatre
12 Silesian Philharmonic
15 Train Station
16 Bank Pekao
18 Powszechny Bank Gospodarczy
21 Historical Museum of Katowice
23 Jewish Cemetery
24 Wielkopolski Bank Kredytowy
25 Cathedral of Christ the King
26 Archdiocesan Museum

Katowice has the best-preserved **Jewish Cemetery** (Cmentarz Żydowski) in the region. Established in 1869, it's divided into two parts, of which the front one is older. Amid trees and thick undergrowth are several hundred tombstones, many of which are in remarkably good shape. Inscriptions on most older tombstones are in Hebrew and German, while those on the younger ones are in Hebrew and Polish – a reflection of the city's chequered history. The graveyard is at ul Kozielska 16, 500m south-west of the train station. It's open 8 am to 5 pm except Saturday (on Friday till noon). If you want to take photos, you have to go first to the Gmina Żydowska at ul Młyńska 13 and ask for a permit.

The **Park of Culture and Recreation** (Wojewódzki Park Kultury i Wypoczynku) is possibly Katowice's most popular attraction (though administratively it belongs to the neighbouring city of Chorzów). This vast park, over five sq km, is the conurbation's major recreation area. It includes a stadium, zoo, amusement grounds, planetarium and an interesting **skansen** (Górnośląski Park Etnograficzny). The park is about 3km north-west of Katowice's centre; several bus and tram lines going to Chorzów will take you there.

Places to Stay

Camping Nr 215 (☎ 255 53 88, ul Murckowska 6) is 2.5km south-east of the centre in the Dolina Trzech Stawów (Valley of Three Ponds). It's open May to September and has cabins.

The good, 50-bed *youth hostel (☎ 59 64 87, ul Sokolska 26)* is open all year. It's a 10 minute walk north of the train station.

Hotel Uniwersytecki (☎ 255 44 17, ul Paderewskiego 32), 1.5km east of the centre, is a student dorm which offers plenty of budget beds in summer holidays (US$14 a double without bath). It also has better all-year rooms (US$35/55 a double without/with bath). Another all-year student facility, *Hotel AWF (☎ 51 02 25, ul Mikołowska 72C)*, 1.5km south-west of the centre, has doubles and triples without bath

for US$18 each, and doubles with bath for US$35.

There are several central hotels within a short walk of the train station. They include *Hotel Centralny (☎ 253 90 41, ul Dworcowa 9)*, 300m east of the station; *Hotel Śląski (☎ 253 70 11, ul Mariacka 15)*, a farther 300m eastwards; and *Hotel Polonia (☎ 51 40 51, ul Kochanowskiego 3)*, 200m south of Centralny. Any of these will cost about US$30/45 a single/double without bath and US$35/50 with bath. None is anything special or great value.

The upmarket options in the centre include *Hotel Katowice (☎ 58 82 81, Al Korfantego 9)* for US$75/120 a single/double, and *Hotel Silesia (☎ 59 62 11, ul Piotra Skargi 2)* for US$110/130. Both are overpriced.

Places to Eat

The 200m-long pedestrian ul Stawowa, just north of the train station, is packed with eating outlets, including two good and cheap places for straightforward Polish food: *Bar pod 7* at No 7, and *Bar Filipek* at No 9.

For a more substantial lunch or dinner, you might try the basement *Restauracja u Kolumba (☎ 253 04 02, Plac Wolności 12A)*, with an unusually long menu of mostly Polish food, the French *Restauracja Le France (☎ 253 77 37, ul Mariacka 6)* for all those escargots and frog legs, at a price of course, and *Restauracja A Dong (☎ 59 89 28, ul Matejki 3)*, possibly the best Chinese/Vietnamese eatery in town.

Getting There & Away

Air The airport is in Pyrzowice, 33km north of Katowice. The LOT office (☎ 206 24 60), Al Korfantego 36, takes bookings and sells tickets. Orbis (☎ 58 72 81), Al Korfantego 2, does the same.

Train Trains are the main means of transport in the area. The train station is in the city centre and there are plenty of trains in all directions, including Oświęcim (33km), Pszczyna (36km), Kraków (78km), Opole

(98km), Wrocław (180km), Częstochowa (86km) and Warsaw (303km). International destinations include Berlin, Frankfurt, Prague and Vienna.

Bus The PKS bus terminal is on ul Piotra Skargi, 500m north of the train station, and handles buses around the region and beyond. International PKS connections include Bratislava (US$11), Budapest (US$20) and Lviv (US$15).

Polski Express buses depart from the front of the Orbis office at Al Korfantago 2. There are three buses a day to Kraków and three to Warsaw via Częstochowa and Łódź.

OŚWIĘCIM
- **pop 45,000** ☎ 033

Oświęcim ('Osh-vyen-cheem') is a medium-sized industrial town about 30km south of Katowice and 60km west of Kraków. The Polish name may be unfamiliar to outsiders, but the German one – Auschwitz – is not: the largest Nazi concentration camp was here. This is the scene of the largest experiment in genocide in the history of humankind and the world's largest cemetery. It is possibly the most moving sight in Poland.

The Auschwitz camp was established in April 1940 in the prewar Polish army barracks on the outskirts of Oświęcim. It was originally destined to hold Polish political prisoners but it eventually came to be a gigantic centre for the extermination of European Jews. For this purpose, in 1941-42 the much larger Birkenau (Brzezinka) camp, also referred to as Auschwitz II, was built 2km west of Auschwitz, and followed by another one in Monowitz (Monowice), several kilometres to the west of the town. About 40 smaller camps, branches of Auschwitz, were subsequently established all over the region. This death factory eliminated some 1.5 to two million people of 27 nationalities, about 85 to 90% of whom were Jews. The name Auschwitz is commonly used for the whole Auschwitz-Birkenau complex, both of which are open to the public.

Auschwitz
Auschwitz was only partially destroyed by the fleeing Nazis, and many of the original buildings stand to this day as a bleak testament to the camp's history. A dozen of the 30 surviving prison blocks now house a museum; some blocks stage general exhibitions, while others are dedicated to victims from particular countries which lost citizens at Auschwitz.

During the communist era, the museum was conceived as an anti-fascist exhibition – the fact that most of the victims were Jewish was played down, and undue prominence was given to the 75,000 Polish Catholics killed here. This approach has changed; block No 27, dedicated to the 'suffering and struggle of the Jews', now presents Auschwitz more correctly as a place of martyrdom of European Jewry.

From the visitors centre in the entrance building, you enter the barbed-wire encampment through the gate with the cynical inscription 'Arbeit Macht Frei' (Work Makes Free), then visit exhibitions in the prison blocks and finally see the gas chamber and crematorium. You don't need

The grim entrance to Auschwitz, scene of unprecedented inhumanity

much imagination to take in what happened here.

A 15 minute documentary about the liberation of the camp by Soviet troops on 27 January 1945 is screened in the cinema in the visitors centre every half-hour, and a few times a day it is shown with a foreign-language soundtrack (English, French or German). Before you set off for the camp check with the information desk at the visitors centre for screening times of the different versions – although the film's message is clear in any language.

The museum opens daily at 8 am and closes at 7 pm in June, July and August; at 6 pm in May and September; at 5 pm in April and October; at 4 pm in March and November; and at 3 pm in December, January and February. Admission is free; there's a US$0.50 fee to enter the cinema. Photos, film and video are permitted free of charge throughout the camp. Anyone under 13 is advised by the museum management not to visit the camp, but the final decision is left to the accompanying adults. There's a cheap, self-service Bar Smak by the entrance, facing the car park. There's also a kantor, a left-luggage room and several bookshops stocked with publications about the place.

Get a copy of a small brochure (available in a number of languages, including Polish, English, French and German) which is quite enough to get you round the grounds. Tours in English and German are organised daily at 11.30 am (US$4 per person). Otherwise you can hire a foreign-language guide for your party at the information desk; they cost US$40 for Auschwitz-Birkenau (three hours).

From 15 April to late October, there is a special bus from Auschwitz to Birkenau (US$0.40). It departs hourly, 10.30 am to 4.30 pm, from outside the entrance to the visitors centre, opposite Bar Smak. Alternatively, you can walk (2km) or take a taxi.

Birkenau

It was actually at Birkenau, not Auschwitz, that the extermination of large numbers of Jews took place. Vast (175 hectares), purpose-built and 'efficient', the camp had over 300 prison barracks and four huge gas chambers complete with crematoria. Each gas chamber accommodated 2000 people and there were electric lifts to raise the bodies to the ovens. The camp could hold 200,000 inmates at a time.

Though much of Birkenau was destroyed by the retreating Nazis, the size of the place, fenced off with long lines of barbed wire and watchtowers stretching almost as far as the eye can see, will give you some idea of the scale of the crime. Don't miss going to the top of the entrance gate-tower for the view. Some of the surviving barracks are open to visitors.

At the back of the complex is the monument to the dead, flanked on each side by the sinister remains of gas chambers. In the far north-western corner of the compound is a pond into which the ashes of the victims were dumped. It is still a distinctive grey colour – a chilling sight.

In many ways, Birkenau is an even more shocking sight than Auschwitz. It has the same opening hours as Auschwitz and entry is free. Make sure to leave enough time (at least an hour) to walk around the camp – it is really vast.

There are no buses from Birkenau to the train station; walk (2km) or go by taxi. Alternatively, take the same special bus back to Auschwitz (departing 11 am to 5 pm on the hour) and change there for one of the frequent buses to the station.

Places to Stay & Eat

For most visitors, the Auschwitz-Birkenau camp is a day trip, in most cases from Kraków, and *Bar Smak*, mentioned previously, probably has all you need to keep you going. However, if you want to linger longer, Oświęcim has a choice of places to stay and eat.

The Catholic Church-built *Centrum Dialogu i Modlitwy (Centre of Dialogue and Prayer; ☎ 43 10 00, fax 43 10 01, ul Św Maksymiliana Kolbe 1)*, 700m south-west of the Auschwitz camp, provides comfortable

SILESIA

OŚWIĘCIM

1 Train Station
2 Hotel Glob
3 Międzynarodowy Dom
   Spotkań Młodzieży
4 Auschwitz Museum
   Visitors' Centre
5 Bar Smak
6 Centrum Dialogu i Modlitwy

0   250   500 m

To Katowice
To Kraków Główny Station via Trzebinia
To Kraków
To Katowice
To Kraków Płaszów Station via Skawina
CENTRE
To Bus Terminal
Dąbrowskiego
Rynek
Birkenau Camp
Konopnickiej
Konarskiego
Jagiełły
Powstańców Śląskich
Prusa
Łukowa
Chodniki
Legionów
Garbarska
Dworcowa
Wyzwolenia
Obozowa
Orłowskiego
Więźniów Oświęcimia
Leszczyńskiej
Maksymiliana Kolbego
Soła
Legionów
Auschwitz Camp
To Czechowice-Dziedzice
To Pszczyna & Rybnik
To Bielsko Biała

---

and quiet accommodation in rooms of two to 10 beds (most with bath) and a restaurant. Bed and breakfast costs US$20 (US$15 for students). You can also camp here (US$6 per person).

Another good place is **Międzynarodowy Dom Spotkań Młodzieży** (*International Meeting House for Youth;* ☎ *43 21 07, fax 43 23 77, ul Legionów 11*), 1km east of the train station. Built in 1986 by the Germans, the place essentially provides lodging for groups coming for longer stays but will take anyone

if there are vacancies. Singles/doubles/quads with bath cost US$18/25/34; students pay US$12/20/27, respectively. Inexpensive meals are served in the dining room on the premises. Camping is also possible here.

Hotel Glob (☎ *43 06 32,* ☎/*fax 43 06 43, ul Powstańców Śląskich 16*), outside the train station, has decent (if noisy) singles/doubles with bath for US$25/36 and its own restaurant.

Hotel Olimpijski (☎ *42 38 41, fax 47 41 94, ul Chemików 2A*) is diagonally opposite the bus terminal. It has singles/doubles with bath for US$28/34, breakfast included, and also has its own restaurant.

Getting There & Away

For most tourists, the jumping-off point for Oświęcim is Kraków, from where you can come by train or bus, or take a tour. Many tours to the camp are organised from Kraków (see that chapter for details), though even the cheapest tour will cost you four or five times more than you'd spend taking public transport.

There are a few early morning trains from Kraków Główny station via Trzebinia (65km) but then nothing till around 3 pm. More trains depart from Kraków Płaszów station via Skawina (also 65km), though they are not very regular either. Frequent urban buses (Nos 24 to 29) run from Oświęcim train station to Auschwitz camp (1.7km), but none to Birkenau camp (2km).

Possibly a better means of transport is bus. There are about 10 buses per day from Kraków to Oświęcim (64km); they pass by Oświęcim train station and Auschwitz museum before reaching the terminal on the far eastern outskirts of the town. Don't miss the Auschwitz stop, otherwise you'll have to backtrack 4km by local bus No 2 or 3, both of which are infrequent.

To get back to Kraków, check the schedule of trains at the Oświęcim train station and that of buses at the bus stop across the street from the station, and take whichever passes through first. Better still, take note of these schedules upon arrival in town and plan your visit accordingly.

If Katowice is your starting point for Oświęcim, there are frequent trains between the two (33km).

If you want to go to Pszczyna from Oświęcim, take the train to Czechowice-Dziedzice (21km, regular departures) and change there for another one (8km, also frequent); or go directly by bus (25km), though there are only a couple a day.

You can also go from Oświęcim direct to Zakopane. The train takes four hours, leaving Oświęcim around 4 pm. The fast bus leaves Oświęcim at 1.30 pm and takes about three hours.

International trains stop in Oświęcim. There's one train a day each to Bratislava, Prague and Vienna.

PSZCZYNA
- **pop 35,000** ☎ 032

In heavily industrialised and urbanised Upper Silesia, Pszczyna comes as a surprise, for it feels like a small market town surrounded by wooded countryside. And it has the best palace-and-park complex in Silesia.

Pszczyna ('Pshchi-nah') is one of the oldest towns in the region, its origins going back to the 11th century when it was a Piast settlement. It came under the rule of the Opole dukes following the division of the kingdom, but later changed hands several times. In 1847 it became the property of the Hochberg family, powerful Prussian magnates and the owners of huge estates which they ruled from the Książ castle near Wałbrzych. In the last months of WWI, Pszczyna was the cradle of the first of three consecutive Silesian uprisings, in which Polish peasants took up arms and demanded that the region be incorporated into Poland. Their wishes were granted in 1921, following a plebiscite held by the League of Nations.

Information

There's no tourist office here; you may try the PTTK office (☎ 210 25 30) at Rynek 3. Travellers cheques can be cashed in the Bank Śląski on the Rynek. A Euronet ATM is in the Hydrobudowa Śląsk building opposite the bus terminal.

Things to See

The elongated **Rynek** is lined with old burghers' houses dating mostly from the 18th and 19th centuries. On its northern side is the Protestant church and, next to it, the town hall, both remodelled early this century. Behind the town hall is the 14th century parish church, much changed later.

Just west of the Rynek is the town's prime attraction, the **castle**. Its origins date from

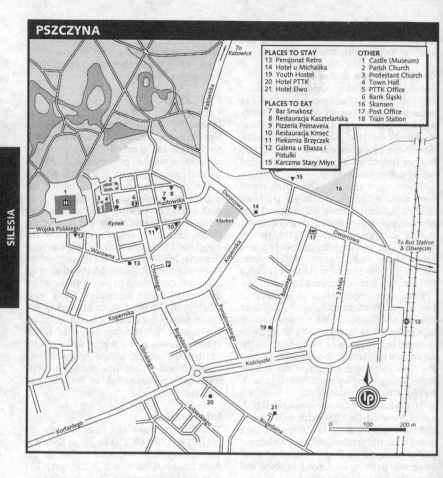

PSZCZYNA

PLACES TO STAY
13 Pensjonat Retro
14 Hotel u Michalika
19 Youth Hostel
20 Hotel PTTK
21 Hotel Elwo

PLACES TO EAT
7   Bar Smakosz
8   Restauracja Kasztelańska
9   Pizzeria Primavera
10 Restauracja Kmieć
11 Piekarnia Brzęczek
12 Galeria u Eliasza i Pistulki
15 Karczma Stary Młyn

OTHER
1   Castle (Museum)
2   Parish Church
3   Protestant Church
4   Town Hall
5   PTTK Office
6   Bank Śląski
16 Skansen
17 Post Office
18 Train Station

the 12th century, when the Opole dukes built a hunting lodge here, but the building has been enlarged and remodelled several times, most recently at the end of the 19th century. The simple medieval castle gradually became a magnificent palace, incorporating various styles from Gothic to neoclassical. The Hochbergs, who owned it until 1945, furnished their home according to their status (they were believed to be among the richest families in Europe), and embellished it with numerous works of art.

After WWII the palace – which had been plundered but not destroyed – was taken over by the state, restored and turned into a museum. The furnished and decorated interiors, representing different periods of the castle's existence, feature some splendid rooms, such as the Mirror Hall; chamber music concerts are held here occasionally. Some of the palace's rooms shelter exhibitions, including the collection of armoury on the ground floor and hunting trophies on the 2nd floor.

The museum is open from February to mid-December, on Wednesday 9 am to 4 pm, Thursday and Friday 9 am to 3 pm, Saturday 10 am to 3 pm, and Sunday 10 am to 4 pm. From April to October it is also open Tuesday 11 am to 3 pm. In July and August visits on Saturday are extended till 4 pm and on Sunday till 6 pm. All visits are guided (in Polish); the last tour begins an hour before closing time. You can buy a guidebook (in English and German) on the castle's history and the museum's contents.

Right behind the castle is an extensive, 84 hectare English-style **park**. With its lakes, streams, arched bridges, pavilions and a variety of exotic trees and shrubs, it's regarded as the most picturesque landscape park in Silesia.

A five minute walk east of the Rynek is a small **skansen** (open March to November 10 am to 3 pm except Monday), which features several old timber houses collected from the region.

Places to Stay

Hotel PTTK (☎ *210 38 33, ul Bogedaina 16)*, south of the Rynek, is in a former prison building which operated from 1902 to 1975. After thorough remodelling (taking 15 years), it now offers simple singles/doubles without bath for US$13/24 and doubles with bath for US$28. There's also triples/quads for US$8/7 a bed.

Hotel Elwo (☎ *210 38 93, ul Bogedaina 23)*, a little farther down the street, has singles with bath for US$18 and doubles without bath for US$15.

The unreliable *youth hostel* (☎ *210 34 08, ul Batorego 26)* may be open from 5 July to 25 August, in a local school.

Appreciably better than anything above is the new *Hotel u Michalika* (☎ *210 13 88, ☎ 210 13 55, ul Dworcowa 11)*. It has singles/doubles with bath and breakfast for US$40/50 and its own restaurant.

Also decent is the small *Pensjonat Retro* (☎/fax *210 22 45, ☎/fax 210 12 63, ul Warowna 31)*, which has singles/doubles/ triples for US$35/60/70, breakfast included, and its own restaurant.

Places to Eat

For cheap eats, try the basic *Bar Smakosz* or *Pizzeria Primavera* (which has a salad bar), both of which are on the local mall, ul Piastowska. *Piekarnia Brzęczek (ul Piekarska 4)* has beautiful, fresh bread, pastries and espresso, and is a good place for breakfast or a snack. There are a few cafés on the Rynek, of which *Galeria u Eliasza i Pistulki (Rynek 21)* is perhaps the most pleasant and is open till late.

For something more substantial, try *Restauracja Kasztelańska (ul Bednarska 3)*, *Restauracja Kmieć (ul Piekarska 10)*, *Restauracja Retro* in the pensjonat or *Restauracja u Michalika. Karczma Stary Młyn*, lodged in an old wooden house, next to the skansen, is slightly cheaper.

Getting There & Away

The bus and train stations are to the east of the centre, 200m apart. Trains to Katowice (36km) run roughly every hour. To Oświęcim, take any of the frequent Żywiec or Bielsko-Biała trains to Czechowice-Dziedzice (8km) and change for one to Oświęcim (21km). There are only two buses to Oświęcim (25km), and both continue to Kraków. If you want to get to Kraków and there's no bus due, go by train to Katowice, from where trains go to Kraków every hour or so. There's just one direct train between Pszczyna and Kraków.

Wrocław

• **pop 645,000   ☎ 071**

Wrocław ('Vrots-wahf'), on the Odra River in the middle of Lower Silesia, is the major industrial, commercial, educational and cultural centre for the whole of south-western Poland. It's the provincial capital and Poland's fourth-largest city after Warsaw, Łódź and Kraków.

After six centuries in foreign hands – Bohemian, Austrian and Prussian – Wrocław only returned to Poland in the aftermath of WWII. The city has preserved some of these different historic layers overlapping each other, which makes an interesting architectural and cultural mosaic. The city has a magnificent old market square, a number of good museums and a memorable cluster of churches by the river, plus a developed tourist infrastructure. Wrocław is also a lively cultural centre, with five theatres, an opera house, a concert hall, several festivals, and a large student community based in 13 institutions of higher education.

A bonus attraction is the city's location on the Odra banks, with its 12 islands, 112 bridges and large park stretches along the river. Ironically, this location saw the city suffer serious damage in the catastrophic flood of July 1997. The flood waters damaged about 80 important historic monuments in the city (including several centuries-old churches and the opera house), as well as apartment blocks, houses, roads, bridges and parks. Miraculously, the Old Town area escaped major harm.

HISTORY

Wrocław was originally founded on the island of Ostrów Tumski – which is no longer an island since an arm of the Odra was filled in during the 19th century. The first recorded Polish ruler, Duke Mieszko I, brought the town, together with most of Silesia, into the Polish state. It must have already been a fair-sized stronghold by the year 1000, as it was chosen as one of Piast Poland's three bishoprics, along with Kraków and Kołobrzeg, all three being ruled from the archbishopric in Gniezno.

During the period of division in the 12th and 13th centuries, Wrocław was the capital of one of the principalities of the Silesian Piasts. Like most settlements in southern Poland, the town was burned down by the Tatars, and a short time later the town centre was moved to the left bank of the river and laid out on the chessboard plan which survives to this day. It was surrounded by defensive walls, and though they have gone, their position can be seen on the map, running along Grodzka, Nowy Świat, Kazimierza Wielkiego, Janickiego and Kraińskiego streets.

Wrocław continued to grow under Bohemian administration (1335-1526), reaching perhaps the height of its prosperity in the 15th century, and maintaining trade and cultural links with the Polish Crown. This speedy development led to the construction of new fortifications at the beginning of the 16th century, and the wide moat of the Fosa Miejska shows where they once were.

The Habsburgs, who ruled the city for the next two centuries, were less tolerant of the Polish and Czech communities, and things got even worse after 1741 when Wrocław fell into the hands of Prussia and was increasingly Germanised for the subsequent two centuries; its name was changed to Breslau.

In the last stages of WWII, the city was besieged by the Red Army for nearly three months, the Nazis defending their last bastion to the end. During the battle, 70% of the city was razed to the ground. Of the prewar population of over 600,000 (mainly German), most were evacuated before the siege and those who were left either died or fled with the retreating German army.

A handful of Germans who remained were expelled to Germany, and the ruined city was resettled with people from Poland's prewar eastern regions, mostly from Lviv, which had been lost to the Soviet Union.

The restoration of the ruins was painful and difficult, and continued well into the 1980s. There's a lot of postwar concrete, but the most important historic buildings have been faithfully reconstructed. Only in the late 1980s did the city surpass its prewar population level.

ORIENTATION

The train and bus stations are near to each other 1km south of the Old Town. Hotels are conveniently close to the city centre and the train station, and almost all major tourist attractions are within walking distance in the central area.

The addresses of the buildings around the edge of the central square are given as

Rynek, while the block in the middle of the square is referred to in addresses as Rynek-Ratusz.

INFORMATION
Tourist Office
The municipal tourist office (☎ 44 31 11, fax 44 29 62) at Rynek 14 is open weekdays 9 am to 5 pm, Saturday 10 am to 2 pm. Pick up the practical *Welcome to Wrocław* free magazine. If the tourist office doesn't have it, try a travel agency or upmarket hotel.

Money
The Bank Pekao at ul Oławska 2 changes travellers cheques and gives advances on Visa and MasterCard. Bank Zachodni is useful for those with travellers cheques and a Visa card; it can be found at several locations, including ul Ofiar Oświęcimskich 41/43 and Rynek 9/11. For changing cash, there are plenty of kantors throughout the central area, including two or three in the train station which trade 24 hours a day. There are also a number of ATMs in the centre, including Euronet outlets in Orbis at Rynek 29 and in Topaz jewellers at ul Świdnicka 30/32.

Email & Internet Access
The Internet Café is at ul Świdnicka 19 (2nd floor).

Travel Agencies
The Orbis office (☎ 343 26 65) is at Rynek 29. PTTK at Rynek-Ratusz 11/12 (☎ 343 03 44, ☎ 343 83 56) can arrange foreign-language guides, but it usually needs to be notified well in advance. Almatur (☎ 44 47 28) at ul Kościuszki 34 sells ISIC cards and international transportation tickets for students and nonstudents.

Bookshops
English-language books are available from PolAnglo at ul Szczytnicka 28, the bookshop of the English Department of Wrocław University at ul Kuźnicza 22, Columbus at ul Kuźnicza 57/58 and the bookstore at ul Więzienna 16.

The best place for maps of Polish cities and regions is the Księgarnia Firmowa PPWK at ul Oławska 2, just off the Rynek. EMPiK at Plac Kościuszki 21/23 has the widest choice of foreign-language papers and magazines.

RYNEK
At 173 x 208m, the Rynek is the second-largest old market square in the country, surpassed only by that in Kraków. A large area in the middle is occupied by a block of buildings so big that it incorporates three internal streets. Recently wholly refurbished, the Rynek is lively and architecturally mixed; the most immediately conspicuous building is the town hall on the southern side of the central block.

Town Hall
This is certainly one of the most beautiful old city halls in Poland. The main structure took almost two centuries (1327-1504) to complete, and work on the tower and decoration continued for another century. Since then, it hasn't changed much; amazingly, it came through WWII without major damage.

The eastern façade, looking like a group of three different buildings, reflects the stages of the town hall's development. The northern segment, with its austere early Gothic features, is the oldest, while the southern part is the most recent and shows elements of the early Renaissance style. The central and most impressive section is topped by an ornamented triangular roof adorned with pinnacles – a favourite cover picture for local tourist brochures. The astronomical clock, made of larch wood, was incorporated in 1580.

The intriguing decorative post in front of the façade is the **whipping post** (pręgierz), marking the site where public floggings were carried out in medieval times. It's an exact replica of the 1492 original which stood here until WWII.

The southern façade of the town hall, dating from the early 16th century, is the most elaborate, with bay windows, carved stone figures and two elaborate friezes.

SILESIA

SILESIA

WROCŁAW

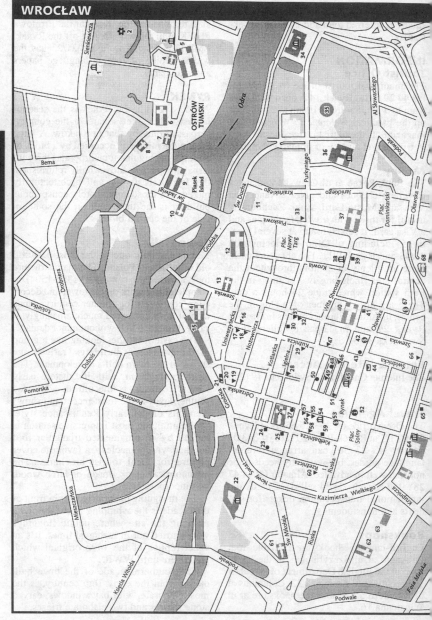

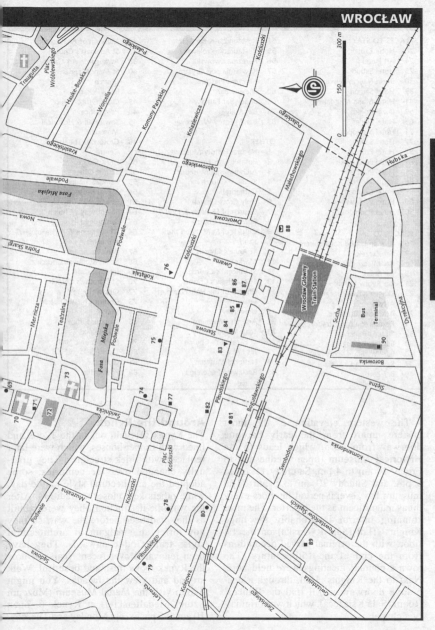

WROCŁAW

SILESIA

Wrocław Główny Train Station

WROCŁAW

PLACES TO STAY
20   Hotel Zaułek
24   Art Hotel
25   Hotel Exbud
30   Bursa Nauczycielska
39   Hotel Saigon
41   Hotel Maria Magdalena
59   Dwór Polski
65   Hotel Mirles
71   Hotel Monopol
77   Hotel Savoy
82   Hotel Polonia
84   Hotel Europejski
85   Hotel Piast
86   Youth Hostel
87   Hotel Grand
89   Hotel Wrocław
90   Hotel Podróżnik

PLACES TO EAT
16   Kawiarnia pod Kalamburem
17   Bar Żaczek
18   Bar Mleczny Miś
19   Bar Smak
21   Bar Rybny Karpik
28   Sklep z Kawą Pożegnanie z Afryką
29   Academia Brasserie
31   Restauracja Magistracka
32   Pizzeria Rancho
33   Bar Jacek i Agatka
46   Bar Wegetariański Vega
47   Restauracja La Scala
49   Bar Zorba

51   Restauracja & Bar Spiż
55   Restauracja Królewska
56   Karczma Lwowska
57   Kawiarnia pod Gryfami
58   Karczma Piastów
60   Mexico Bar
66   Snack Bar Fantasy
76   Bar Mały
83   Bar Mleczny Wzorcowy

OTHER
1   Natural History Museum
2   Botanic Gardens
3   Archdiosesan Museum
4   St Giles' Church
5   Cathedral
6   Holy Cross Church
7   Church of SS Peter & Paul
8   St Martin's Church
9   Church of St Mary on the Sand
10   St Anne's Church
11   Market Hall
12   St Vincent's Church
13   St Matthew's Church
14   Church of the Holy Name of Jesus
15   University
22   Arsenał (Museum)
23   Teatr Współczesny
26   St Elizabeth's Church
27   Jaś i Małgosia
34   National Museum
35   Racławice Panorama

36   Museum of Architecture
37   St Adalbert's Church
38   Awangarda Art Gallery
40   St Mary Magdalene's Church
42   Bank Pekao
43   Orbis Office
44   Post Office
45   Town Hall & Historical Museum
48   Grotowski Theatre Centre
50   PTTK Office
52   Tourist Office
53   Bank Zachodni
54   Medal Museum
61   St Barbara's Church
62   St Anthony's Church
63   Synagogue
64   Ethnographic & Archaeological Museums
67   Bank Zachodni
68   St Christopher's Church
69   Internet Café
70   St Dorothy's Church
72   Opera House
73   Corpus Christi Church
74   EMPiK
75   Almatur Office
78   LOT Office
79   Philharmonic Hall
80   Teatr Polski
81   Operetta
88   Post Office

The western elevation is the most austere, apart from the early baroque doorway from 1615, which leads to the **Historical Museum** (open Wednesday to Friday 10 am to 4 pm, Saturday 11 am to 5 pm, and Sunday 10 am to 6 pm). The museum has several period interiors every bit as magnificent as the exterior. The most stunning interior is probably the huge Knights' Hall (Sala Rycerska) on the 1st floor, with the original carved decorations from the end of the 15th century. The town's council meetings were held here. Next to the Knights' Hall, through a decorative doorway, you'll find the Princes' Room (Sala Książęca), which was originally a chapel.

Around the Rynek

The Rynek was laid out in the 1240s and lined with timber houses, which were later replaced with brick structures. They gradually changed over the centuries; some adopted the architectural style of the day, while others kept closer to tradition. After the wartime destruction, they were rebuilt as they had been before the war, so they now offer an amalgam of architectural styles from Gothic onwards. They have been renovated over recent years, so now the Rynek looks fresh and beautiful. Walk around and view the façades. You might like to visit the **Medal Museum** (Muzeum Sztuki Medalierskiej) at Rynek 6, open 10 am to 5 pm except Monday and Tuesday.

In the north-western corner of the Rynek are two intriguing houses called **Jaś i Małgosia**, or Hansel and Gretel, linked with a baroque gate from 1728, which once led to the church cemetery. Just behind them is the monumental brick **St Elizabeth's Church** (Kościół Św Elżbiety) with its 83m-high tower – you can go to the top for a good view. This Gothic church went up in flames in 1975 in suspicious circumstances, and much of the furnishing, including the organ, was lost. Repairs are now finished, and it's open again for the faithful and visitors.

The south-western corner of the Rynek spills into **Plac Solny**, or Salt Square. As its name suggests, the square was the site of the salt trade, a business which was carried on for over five centuries until 1815, when the last stalls were closed down. Nowadays, mostly flowers are on sale.

AROUND THE OLD TOWN

If you are on a tight schedule, concentrate on the areas north and east of the Rynek, where the most important historical monuments and best museums are. With more time to spend, you might visit the southern and western parts of the city centre too, where you'll find several more old churches and a couple of museums.

One block east of the Rynek is **St Mary Magdalene's Church** (Kościół Św Marii Magdaleny), a mighty Gothic brick building constructed during the city's heyday in the 14th century. Its showpiece is a splendid Romanesque portal from around 1280, regarded as one of the best of its kind in Poland. The portal originally adorned the Benedictine Abbey in Ołbin, now one of Wrocław's northern inner suburbs, but was moved here in 1546 and incorporated in the southern external wall after the abbey was demolished. The tympanum is on display in the National Museum.

One block east along ul Wita Stwosza is the **Awangarda Art Gallery**, housed in a historic palatial building, which has temporary exhibitions of modern art.

About 100m farther east is the single-naved Dominican **St Adalbert's Church**

(Kościół Św Wojciecha), another largish Gothic structure. The highlight of its interior is the baroque chapel adjoining the southern transept, with its alabaster sarcophagus of the Blessed Czesław, founder of the monastery.

A few steps east is the former Bernardine church and monastery, which provide a splendid setting for the **Museum of Architecture** (Muzeum Architektury), open Wednesday to Saturday 10 am to 3.30 pm, Sunday 10 am to 5 pm. The collection features stone sculptures and stained-glass windows from various historic buildings of the region. The oldest exhibit, a Romanesque tympanum, dates from 1165.

Racławice Panorama

A cylindrical building in the park behind the museum shelters Wrocław's most visited sight, the *Racławice Panorama* (Panorama Racławicka). It's a canvas painting 15m high and 114m long – about half the area of a soccer field – and weighing 3500kg. It is wrapped around the internal walls of the rotunda in the form of an unbroken circle and is viewed from an elevated central balcony.

The picture shows the battle of Racławice (a village about 40km north-east of Kraków) fought on 4 April 1794 between the Polish insurrectionist peasant army, led by Tadeusz Kościuszko, and Russian troops. One of the last attempts to defend Poland's independence, the battle was won by the Poles, but seven months later the nationwide insurrection was crushed by the tsarist army and the Third Partition was effected. Poland formally ceased to exist until WWI, yet the battle lived in the hearts of Poles as the most glorious engagement of the rebellion.

One hundred years later, a group of patriots in Lviv set about commemorating the battle and the idea of the panorama emerged. The project successfully got through the Austrian bureaucracy.

The painting is essentially the work of two artists, Jan Styka and Wojciech Kossak, with the help of seven painters commissioned for background scenes and details. They completed the monumental canvas in an amazingly short time – nine months and two days – while a specially designed rotunda was erected. The picture became one of Lviv's favourite attractions and was on display until 1944, when a bomb hit the building and seriously damaged the canvas.

After the war the painting, along with most of Lviv's legacy, was moved to Wrocław, but as it depicted a defeat of the Russians – Poland's official friend and liberator – the new authorities were reluctant to put it on display. The rolled-up picture was kept in storage for 35 years. Only in 1980, after the Solidarity movement had brought the beginnings of democracy, was the decision taken to renovate the canvas and put it on public view. The work took five years and was regarded as the most difficult conservation operation of its kind in Poland.

The Panorama is normally open 9 am to 4 pm except Monday, but hours are extended if there's the demand. Entry costs US$5 (US$3 for students). The tour takes about 30 minutes, moving around the balcony to inspect each scene in turn while a recorded commentary provides you with explanations. Foreign-language versions including English, German and French are available; ask for headphones in your language from the stand at the balcony.

Buy your ticket early, as the place tends to be overrun by tourists, including endless school excursions. You may have some time to spare before your tour, which you can spend in the waiting room watching videos of the painting's restoration or visiting the exhibition in the 'small rotunda', just behind the ticket office, which features a model of the battlefield and the uniforms of forces engaged in the battle.

National Museum

If you have more time you can visit the National Museum (Muzeum Narodowe), just a few minutes walk to the east, open 10 am to 4 pm except Monday. If you have a ticket for the Panorama, you are entitled to a free visit to the museum on that day; otherwise it costs US$1.50.

The museum's medieval Silesian art section is one of the highlights of the collection. Old stone sculpture is displayed in the central ground-floor hall, and the exhibits include the Romanesque tympanum from the portal of St Mary Magdalene's Church, depicting the Dormition of the Virgin Mary. Medieval wooden sculpture is on the 1st floor and features some powerful Gothic triptychs and statues of saints. Also on this floor are European paintings from the 15th to 19th centuries.

The 2nd floor has Polish art, mainly painting, from the 17th century to the present. The collection covers most of the big names, including Malczewski, Wyspiański, Witkacy and Matejko. Among contemporary artists, Nowosielski, Hasior and Brzozowski are particularly well represented. Wrocław's collection of modern Polish painting is considered one of the best in the country.

University Quarter

The quarter occupies the northern part of the Old Town, between the riverfront and ul Uniwersytecka. Coming from the museum, the first important historic building you'll see will be the Gothic **St Vincent's Church** (Kościół Św Wincentego), originally a Romanesque basilica founded before 1240. The largest church in the city after the cathedral, it was completely burned out in 1945 and reconstruction work has only recently been completed. The church has still no decoration inside and is not used.

St Matthew's Church (Kościół Św Macieja), a bit farther west, is also Gothic though the Romanesque portal in the porch indicates its earlier origins.

The baroque **Church of the Holy Name of Jesus** (Kościół Najświętszego Imienia Jezus) was built in the 1690s on the site of the former Piast castle. The spacious, lofty interior is adorned with fine illusionistic frescoes on its vault and crammed with ornate fittings.

The monumental building adjoining the church is the **university**. It was founded by

Emperor Leopold I in 1702 as the Jesuit Academy and was built in 1728-42. Enter the central gate and go up to the 1st floor to see the **Aula Leopoldinum**. Embellished with elaborate stucco work, sculptures, paintings and a trompe l'œil ceiling fresco, it's the best baroque interior in the city. It's used for special university ceremonies but at other times can be visited between 10 am and 3.30 pm except Wednesday. Classical music concerts are occasionally held here. The slightly more modest **Oratorium Marianum**, on the ground floor, is open for visitors Friday to Sunday 10 am to 3.30 pm.

West & South of the Old Town

A five minute walk west along ul Grodzka will take you to the **Arsenal** (Arsenał), the most significant remnant of the 15th century fortifications. Appropriately, it now houses a museum of old weapons (open Tuesday, Thursday and Friday 10 am to 4 pm, Saturday 11 am to 4 pm, Sunday 10 am to 5 pm).

The nearby **St Barbara's Church** (Kościół Św Barbary) was built in the 13th century, initially as a cemetery chapel, but it was expanded and turned into a three-naved church in the late Gothic period. After WWII it was handed over to the Orthodox community, and the interior was redecorated for the Eastern rite. The iconostasis and frescoes are the design of contemporary Kraków painter Jerzy Nowosielski.

A short walk south-east from the church will take you to the large, recently renovated **synagogue**, one of the very few relics of the Jewish legacy.

Nearby is the **Ethnographic Museum**, open 10 am to 4 pm except Monday. A good part of the collection features old artefacts and household implements brought from the east by postwar settlers.

The **Archaeological Museum** in the same building (open Wednesday to Friday 10 am to 4 pm, Saturday and Sunday 10 am to 5 pm) displays the usual collection of archaeological finds, emphasising the Polish and Slavic roots of the region.

One block south-east is **St Dorothy's Church** (Kościół Św Doroty), another massive Gothic affair. It was founded in 1351 to commemorate the meeting between Polish King Kazimierz Wielki and his Bohemian counterpart, Charles IV, at which it was agreed to leave Silesia in Bohemia's hands. The lofty, whitewashed interior is filled with large baroque altars, and there's a sizable rococo tomb in the right-hand (southern) aisle.

To the south of the church is the Monopol, Wrocław's oldest hotel, and facing it, the neoclassical Opera House.

OSTRÓW TUMSKI & PIASEK ISLAND

Once an island, Ostrów Tumski was the cradle of Wrocław. It was here that the Ślężanie tribe built its stronghold in the 7th or 8th century. After the town was incorporated into the Polish state and a bishopric established in 1000, the first Wrocław church was built here and was followed by other ecclesiastical buildings which gradually expanded onto the neighbouring island, the Piasek (literally, the Sand). Towards the 13th century the centre of the town moved to the left bank of the Odra, but Ostrów retained its role as the seat of the church authorities. In the course of time a number of churches, monasteries and other religious buildings were constructed on both islands, and despite all further misfortunes, many of them are still standing today, giving a distinctive, markedly ecclesiastical character to the district.

Piasek Island is just north-east of the Old Town, over the Most Piaskowy (Piasek Bridge). The main monument here is the **Church of St Mary on the Sand** (Kościół NMP na Piasku), a lofty 14th century building which dominates this tiny islet. The church was badly damaged during WWII but carefully reconstructed, including its magnificent ribbed vault.

Almost all the prewar fitments were burned out and the old triptychs you see inside have been collected from other Silesian churches. The Romanesque tympanum

SILESIA

in the right-hand aisle is the only remnant of the first church built on this site in the 12th century. There's a mechanised *szopka* (Nativity scene) in the first chapel to the right.

The bridge behind the church will put you on Ostrów Tumski. The small 15th century **Church of SS Peter and Paul** (Kościół Św Piotra i Pawła) to your left has a fine Gothic vault supported by a single central column. It's open only for Masses in the morning and evening. The entrance is through the adjoining building, a former orphanage.

Opposite is the much larger **Holy Cross Church** (Kościół Św Krzyża), built between 1288 and 1350. There are actually two churches inside the building, one on top of the other. The lower one, which was once the crypt of the Wrocław Piasts, was given to the Uniate community after WWII.

The monumental, two-towered structure farther east is the **cathedral**. This three-aisled Gothic basilica, 100m long, was built between the 13th and 15th centuries and was the fourth church on this site. Seriously damaged during WWII, it was reconstructed in its previous Gothic form, and its dim interior was refurbished with a variety of works of art collected from other churches. The high altar boasts a triptych from 1522 depicting the Dormition of the Virgin Mary, attributed to the school of Veit Stoss. There's an interesting Gothic Marian Chapel (Kaplica Mariacka) right behind the altar, and two ornate baroque chapels on either side. Access to the chapels is via the right-hand aisle.

Directly north of the cathedral is the little **St Giles' Church** (Kościół Św Idziego). Built in 1218-30, this is the oldest surviving church in Wrocław, and has an original Romanesque doorway at the entrance.

A few steps east is the **Archdiocesan Museum** (Muzeum Archidiecezjalne), open 9 am to 3 pm except Monday. It has a collection of Silesian sacred art, including some exquisite Gothic altarpieces, plus temporary exhibitions.

The green area to the north is the **Botanic Gardens** (Ogród Botaniczny), and at their far northern end is the **Natural History Museum** (Muzeum Przyrodnicze), open 10 am to 3 pm except Monday.

EASTERN SUBURBS

There are some attractions in the eastern districts. Take tram No 2 or 10 from Plac Dominikański in the centre (or from behind the cathedral), and go to the **zoo** on ul Wróblewskiego. With about 3000 animals representing over 500 species, this is the largest zoo in Poland and supposedly the best. It's also Poland's oldest zoo, founded in 1865. It's open daily 9 am to 4 pm (longer in summer).

Across the street from the zoo is the **Centenary Hall** (Hala Ludowa), a huge, round auditorium capable of accommodating 6000 people. It was designed by the German architect Max Berg, and built in 1913 to commemorate Napoleon's defeat in 1813. The hall is topped with a huge dome, 65m in diameter, regarded as a great achievement in its day. Today it's a place for large scale performances, exhibitions and sporting events. At other times it is locked, but the guards may let you in to have a look.

The 96m-high steel **spire** (iglica) in front of the entrance was built in 1948 on the occasion of the Exhibition of the Regained Territories.

Behind the hall is the **Park Szczytnicki**, Wrocław's oldest and largest wooded area, encompassing 112 hectares. A short walk north along the pergola will bring you to a small Japanese Garden (seriously damaged by the 1997 flood), while farther east is a fine 16th century larch church, brought here from the Opole region and reassembled in 1914. Temporary exhibitions are held in the church in summer.

At the north-eastern end of the park is a large sports complex with an Olympic stadium, all built before WWII in the expectation of holding the Olympic Games in 1940. Tram No 9, 12 or 17 will take you back to the city centre.

SPECIAL EVENTS

Wrocław's major annual events include the Musica Polonica Nova Contemporary

Music Festival in February, the Jazz on the Odra International Festival in May and the Wratislavia Cantans Oratorio and Cantata Festival in September.

PLACES TO STAY

Wrocław has a reasonable choice of accommodation. Many hotels are either near the train station or the Old Town, and these are the most convenient places to stay. Predictably, they tend to fill up first, so you may occasionally have to stay outside the centre, particularly if you arrive late. If this is the case, check for vacancies in the central area the following morning.

Places to Stay – Budget

Wrocław has two camping grounds and both have bungalows. The all-year *Camping Nr 267 Ślęża* (☎ 343 44 42, ul Na Grobli 16/18) is on the bank of the Odra 2km east of the Old Town. There's no urban transport all the way there; get to Plac Wróblewskiego (tram No 4 from the train station) and walk 1km eastwards.

Camping Nr 117 Olimpijski (☎ 348 46 51, ul Paderewskiego 35), near the Olympic stadium in Park Szczytnicki, is about 4km east of the city centre – take tram No 9 or 17 from the train station. It's open May to September and has more cabins than the other camping ground.

One of Wrocław's two all-year *youth hostels* (☎ 343 88 56, ul Kołłątaja 20) is near the train station. It's small (47 beds) and hardly ever has vacancies in summer. If anything is available, it is most likely to be a bed in the 22-bed dorm.

The other, larger *youth hostel* (☎ 345 73 96, ☎/fax 345 73 99, ul Kiełczowska 43) is in the distant suburb of Psie Pole, about 10km north-east of the station. Bus N can take you there from its terminus on ul Sucha between the train station and bus terminal.

The *Bursa Nauczycielska* (☎ 44 37 81, ul Kotlarska 42) is a teachers' hostel, ideally located just a block north-east of the Rynek. It costs US$14/24 for a single/double or US$8/7 for a bed in a triple/quad. Rooms don't have baths, but they are clean, well

kept and quiet. The location, standard and prices make the Bursa possibly the best budget place in town.

Another teachers' hostel, *Dom Nauczyciela* (☎ 22 92 68, ul Nauczycielska 2), is 1.5km east of the Old Town, 300m past Most Grunwaldzki. It has singles/doubles with shared facilities for US$12/18, or you can just pay US$6 for a bed in a triple or quad.

Some student dorms open in summer as *student hostels*, but this changes from year to year. The tourist office may know which ones are currently open.

Odra Tourist (☎ 343 00 37), at Hotel Piast at ul Piłsudskiego 98 diagonally opposite the train station, arranges *private rooms* for about US$12/18 a single/double. Check the location and transport details before committing yourself.

Places to Stay – Mid-Range

The noisy *Hotel Piast* (☎ 343 00 33, ul Piłsudskiego 98) is the cheapest hotel in the vicinity of the station but it's hardly inspiring. It costs US$15/27/33/40 a single/double/triple/quad without bath.

The equally noisy *Hotel Grand* (☎ 343 60 71, ul Piłsudskiego 100/102) is just across the street. Grand it is not, but it's still a bit better than the Piast. It has singles/doubles without bath for US$24/34 and with bath for US$38/55, breakfast included.

Appreciably quieter is *Hotel Savoy* (☎ 40 32 19, ☎ 344 30 71, Plac Kościuszki 19), within easy walking distance from the station. Singles/doubles/triples with bath cost US$30/40/50. It's good value and, predictably, is often full.

You can also try *Hotel Podróżnik* (☎/fax 73 28 45, ul Sucha 1) on the 1st floor of the bus terminal. Simple doubles/triples/quads with bath cost US$30/38/48.

There are a few affordable hotels in the Old Town area, of which *Hotel Mirles* (☎ 341 08 73, ul Kazimierza Wielkiego 45) is one of the cheapest. It has just three doubles (US$30) and two triples (US$42), but it's little known, so you have some chance of getting in. Baths are shared.

Places to Stay – Top End

Near the train station, you can stay at *Hotel Europejski* (☎ *343 10 71, fax 44 34 33, ul Piłsudskiego 88*), which has rooms with bath for US$80/90 a single/double, breakfast included. One block west, *Hotel Polonia* (☎ *343 10 21, fax 44 73 10, ul Piłsudskiego 66*) offers and charges pretty much the same as the Europejski. Neither is great value and both suffer from heavy traffic noise on ul Piłsudskiego; try for a room at the back.

In the Old Town, the cheapest in this price bracket is *Hotel Saigon* (☎ *44 28 81, fax 343 30 37, ul Wita Stwosza 22/23*), three blocks east of the Rynek. Its rooms have baths and cost about US$52/58 a single/double.

Better is the small *Hotel Zaułek* (☎ *40 29 45, ☎/fax 40 29 47, ul Odrzańska 18A*), a short walk north of the Rynek. It has only six singles (US$75) and six doubles (US$85); breakfast is included in the price.

Of the five Orbis outlets in the city, the stylish *Hotel Monopol* (☎ *343 70 41, fax 343 51 03, ul Modrzejewskiej 2*), beside the Opera House, is the cheapest and most colourful. Rooms go for US$40/65 a single/double without bath and US$65/100 with bath, breakfast included. Operating since 1892, the Monopol is the city's oldest hotel. Hitler stayed here whenever he visited Breslau (Wrocław's German name) and addressed the crowds from the balcony.

There are two new upmarket places just one block from the Rynek: the modern *Hotel Exbud* (☎ *341 09 16, ☎/fax 72 36 49, ul Kiełbaśnicza 24*), and the old-style *Art Hotel* (☎ *342 42 49, fax 342 39 29, ul Kiełbaśnicza 20*). Nearby is another stylish place, *Dwór Polski* (☎/fax *72 34 15, ☎/fax 72 34 19, ul Kiełbaśnicza 2*), in a finely restored historic building. Expect a single/double in any of the three to cost roughly US$100/120, and all offer some more comfortable (and expensive) suites.

Possibly the plushest central option is the new *Hotel Maria Magdalena* (☎ *341 08 98, fax 341 09 20, ul Św Marii Magdaleny 2*). It costs around US$120/150 a single/double.

It's unlikely that none of the above will be able to accommodate you, but if this happens, try the uninspiring Orbis-run *Hotel Wrocław* (☎ *61 46 51, fax 61 66 17, ul Powstańców Śląskich 7*), 1km west of the train station, which hardly ever fills its 600 beds with guests willing to pay US$120/140 a single/double.

PLACES TO EAT

Budget eating is no problem in Wrocław. The array of milk bars includes *Bar Mleczny Wzorcowy* (*ul Piłsudskiego 86*), near the train station; the basic *Bar Mleczny Miś* (*ul Kuźnicza 43/45*), in the university area; and the best and most central *Bar Wegetariański Vega*, in the central block of the Rynek, next to the town hall.

There are a number of other cheap places, mostly of the newer generation, scattered throughout the Old Town area. *Snack Bar Fantasy* (*ul Świdnicka 8*) is a large self-service cafeteria serving meals (not only snacks) from 11 am to 10 pm. *Bar Smak* (*ul Odrzańska 17*) is open from 9 am to 8 pm (entrance from ul Nożownicza). Other budget eateries include *Bar Jacek i Agatka* (*Plac Nowy Targ 27*), *Bar Żaczek* (*ul Kuźnicza 43/45*) and *Bar Mały* on the corner of ul Kołłątaja and ul Kościuszki.

Bar Rybny Karpik on the corner of ul Grodzka and ul Odrzańska serves cheap fish. *Bar Zorba*, right in the middle of the block in the centre of the Rynek, grills souvlaki and other common Greek dishes. The small *Mexico Bar* (*ul Rzeźnicza 34*) offers simple but pretty authentic Mexican food at budget prices.

The cosy *Pizzeria Rancho* (*ul Szewska 59*) does inexpensive pizza. Next door, the elegant, well appointed *Restauracja Magistracka* (☎ *343 37 51*) has fine Polish and international food at upmarket prices. Cheaper is *Academia Brasserie* (☎ *343 45 29, ul Kuźnicza 65/66*), which serves hearty crêpes, salads, sandwiches and some unsophisticated French-style dishes.

The posh *Restauracja Królewska* (King Restaurant), in the gastronomic complex of Dwór Polski (*Polish Court;* ☎ *72 48 96,*

Rynek 5), is one of Wrocław's top spots for traditional Polish cuisine in a historic interior. The more informal *Karczma Piastów* (Piast Inn), at the back of the same complex, also has Polish food and is cheaper. *Restauracja La Scala (☎ 72 53 94, Rynek 38)* is possibly the best Italian eatery around. The enjoyable *Karczma Lwowska (☎ 343 98 87, Rynek 4, upstairs)* brings some fine Lviv cuisine to town and an often wonderful atmosphere.

The best choice of aromatic coffees is served in *Sklep z Kawą Pożegnanie z Afryką (ul Igielna 16)* one block north of the Rynek. Typically for the chain, it's a nonsmoking venue.

With its Art Nouveau decoration and an arty atmosphere, *Kawiarnia pod Kalamburem (ul Kuźnicza 29A)* is one of the most charming cafés in town. A short menu of light dishes is available at lunch time. Also pop into another stylish café, *Kawiarnia pod Gryfami (Rynek 2)* in the lofty historic Griffin House.

ENTERTAINMENT

Wrocław is an important cultural centre, and there's much cultural activity year-round. Local papers have listings of what's on, or pick up the detailed, free cultural monthly, *Co Jest Grane.* It's in Polish only, but some of the contents can be deciphered. The tourist office may provide more information.

Theatre

Wrocław is internationally known for the avant-garde *Teatr Laboratorium* (Laboratory Theatre) of Jerzy Grotowski, created in the early 1960s and dissolved 20 years later after its founder moved to Italy and established a theatre research centre in Pontedera.

In 1990 the *Grotowski Theatre Centre (☎ 343 42 67)* was founded in the theatre's former home at Rynek-Ratusz 27, which has documentaries on the Laboratory Theatre and can present them on request. It also invites various experimental groups, occasionally from abroad, to give performances in its small theatre.

Today, the main ambassador for Wrocław theatre is the *Wrocławski Teatr Pantomimy* created by Henryk Tomaszewski. The theatre is usually on tour somewhere. Try to see it if it is in town – check with the tourist office for news.

Teatr Polski (ul Zapolskiej 3) is the major mainstream city venue, staging classic Polish and foreign drama, while *Teatr Współczesny (ul Rzeźnicza 12)* tends more towards contemporary productions.

Opera & Classical Music

The *Opera House* is at ul Świdnicka 35, but was damaged in the floods of summer 1997 and performances are held elsewhere, including at the Hala Ludowa. The *Operetta* is at ul Piłsudskiego 72. Concerts of classical music are held usually on Friday in the *Filharmonia (Philharmonic Hall; ul Piłsudskiego 19).*

Jazz

The basement *Klub Muzyczny Jazzgot (ul Rzeźnicza 11)* is one of the very few places which stages live jazz. Also check out *Czarny Salon (Rynek-Ratusz 24).*

Bars & Pubs

The *Irish Pub (Plac Solny 5)* is rather expensive, but has live music on some nights. One of the cheapest watering holes is the open-air *Kalogródek* on the corner of ul Uniwersytecka and ul Kuźnicza, an informal place with an amphitheatre-like patio. The new *Pub Szkocki Haggis (ul Świdnicka 39)* has an unusually extensive whisky selection. The *Koniec Wieku,* behind the Hala Targowa (Market Hall), is a pleasant wine bar with a vaguely bohemian atmosphere. It has a good variety of wines and is often packed with students and academics.

Wrocław's most unusual drinking spot is probably *Restauracja & Bar Spiż (Rynek-Ratusz 9),* a subterranean, German-style restaurant-cum-bar beside the town hall, which serves beer straight from its own brewery. The restaurant is upmarket but a mug of its rich brew in the adjacent wood-panelled bar should fit into almost anyone's budget and belly, and you can see brass vats used in the production process behind the buffet. There's a beer garden in summer on the square outside.

GETTING THERE & AWAY

Air

The airport in Strachowice, 10km west of the city centre, is accessible by bus No 106 from the Wrocław Świebodzki train station, a 10 minute walk west of the Rynek. There are direct connections with Warsaw (four times a day), Frankfurt/Main (daily), Copenhagen (daily) and Vienna (four days a week). The LOT office (☎ 343 17 44) at ul Piłsudskiego 36 and Orbis (☎ 343 26 65) at Rynek 29 reserve seats and sell tickets.

Train

The main train station, Wrocław Główny, was built in 1856 and is a historical monument in itself. Trains are plentiful and can take you to most places in the region and beyond.

Fast trains to Katowice (190km) depart every hour or two and pass via Brzeg (42km) and Opole (82km) on their way. Many of them continue to Kraków (268km). There are at least half a dozen fast trains plus three express trains to Warsaw (385km) and some call at Łódź (242km) en route. Wrocław also has regular train links with Poznań (165km), Wałbrzych (70km), Jelenia Góra (126km), Legnica (66km), Zielona Góra (156km) and Kłodzko (96km).

International destinations include Berlin, Budapest, Dresden, Frankfurt/Main, Kiev and Prague.

Bus

The bus terminal is on ul Sucha, just south of the train station. You probably won't need a bus to get out of Wrocław, except to Trzebnica (24km) and Bolków (79km), where trains don't go, and Sobótka (34km), Świdnica (53km) and Nysa (83km), to which buses are more frequent than trains.

There are a number of international bus routes to places including Prague and plenty of cities in Western Europe. Tickets are available from Virgo (☎ 67 54 11, ☎ 67 73 77) at the terminal itself, Orbis, Almatur and other travel agencies.

Around Wrocław

TRZEBNICA

• **pop 12,000**   ☎ 071

A small town 24km north of Wrocław, Trzebnica ('Tzheb-nee-tsah') is noted for its former Cistercian Abbey (Opactwo Cysterskie). The order was brought to Poland in 1140 and established its first monastery in Jędrzejów, from where it swiftly expanded and set up nearly 40 abbeys all over the country. Among other places, the order had monasteries in Kraków, Gdańsk, Pelplin, Wąchock, Krzeszów, Henryków and Lubiąż, most of which are described in the appropriate sections of this book. Trzebnica was the site of the first Cistercian convent in Poland.

The convent was founded in 1202 by Princess Jadwiga (Hedwig), the wife of the Duke of Wrocław, Henryk Brodaty (Henry the Bearded). After the duke's death, she entered the abbey and lived an ascetic life to the end of her days. Only 24 years later, in 1267, she was canonised and the abbey church where she had been buried has become a destination for pilgrims. She is regarded as the patron saint of Silesia.

Things to See

The church is thought to be one of the first brick buildings of its kind in Poland. Though it was rebuilt in later periods, the structure has preserved much of its initial austere Romanesque shape and, more importantly, still boasts two original portals. The one next to the main entrance, unfortunately partly hidden behind the baroque tower added in the 1780s, is particularly fine thanks to its tympanum from the 1220s, which depicts King David on his throne playing the harp to Queen Bathsheba.

Once inside, you are surrounded by ornate baroque decoration, including a lavishly ornamented high altar. At its foot is the very modest black-marble tomb of Henryk Brodaty.

The showpiece of the interior is **St Hedwig's Chapel** (Kaplica Św Jadwigi), to the right of the chancel. It was built soon after the canonisation of the princess, and the graceful, ribbed Gothic vault has been preserved unchanged from that time, though the decoration dates from a later epoch. Its central feature is the large tomb of St Hedwig, an elaborate work in marble and alabaster created in stages between 1680 and 1750. Beside the sarcophagus is the entrance to the three-naved crypt downstairs, the oldest part of the church.

The **convent** next to the church was reshaped and extended to monumental proportions in the early 18th century but, since the order was abolished in 1810, it is no longer a Cistercian abbey. The lion's share of the building has been taken over by a hospital. The only feature worth viewing is the gorgeous baroque doorway on the northern façade, just beside the church.

Places to Stay

There are several options for the night, of which the cheapest is *Ośrodek OSiR (☎ 312 07 47, ul Leśna 2)*. It features a camp site, seasonal cabins without bath (US$14/20 a double/triple) and all-year rooms without bath (US$18/25 a double/triple).

If you want a private bath, try *Hotel pod Platanami (☎ 312 09 80, ul Kilińskiego 2)*, which costs US$24/30 a double/triple. Alternatively, there's the unnamed *Hotel (☎ 312 16 87, ul Obornicka 14)*, which costs much the same.

Getting There & Away

Buses from Wrocław to Trzebnica run frequently and will let you off near the church. Trains no longer ply this route.

LUBIĄŻ

The small village of Lubiąż ('Loobyonsh'), about 50km north-west of Wrocław, also owes its fame to the Cistercians. It boasts a gigantic **Cistercian Abbey** (Opactwo Cystersów), one of Europe's largest monastic complexes. Founded in 1175, the modest original abbey was gradually extended as the order grew, but was also destroyed on several occasions – by Hussites in 1432 and Swedes in 1642, among others. After the Thirty Years' War the monastery recovered and entered a period of prosperity, and it was then that a magnificent baroque complex was built – the work taking almost a century and finishing in 1739. It has a 223m-wide façade and 365 rooms. A team of distinguished artists, including the famous painter Michael Willmann, was commissioned for the monumental project.

In 1810 the abbey was closed down, and the buildings were subsequently occupied and devastated by a bizarre range of tenants: it was a horse stud, mental hospital, arsenal, Nazi military plant (during WWII), Soviet army hospital (1945-48), and finally a storehouse for the state book publisher. The postwar renovation was minimal and a large part of the complex is still unused.

It wasn't until 1991 that a Polish-German foundation took things in hand in order to restore the abbey. A few rooms have already been renovated and are open to the public (July to September daily 9 am to 6 pm, the remaining part of the year 10 am to 3 pm). The showpiece is the huge, 15m-high Knights' Hall (Sala Książęca) with its opulent baroque decoration from the 1730s.

The work on further interiors, including the refectory and library, is in progress, but the mighty church and adjoining chapel will probably take longer to be restored. As yet they have no decoration apart from some surviving portals and fragments of frescoes by Willmann. The crypt beneath the church reputedly holds 98 mummified bodies, including that of Willmann himself, but cannot be visited.

Lubiąż lies off the main roads, and bus transport is infrequent, with only one bus daily to/from Legnica (28km) and several to/from Wrocław (51km). There's no railway here.

SOBÓTKA & MT ŚLĘŻA
- pop 6600   ☎ 071

About 35km south-west of Wrocław, the solitary, forested, cone-shaped Mt Ślęża rises from an open plain to a height of 718m, about 500m above the surrounding plain. Mt Ślęża was one of the holy places of an ancient pagan tribe which, as in many other places around the world, used to set up its cult sites atop the mountains. It's not known for sure who they were – Celts, Scythians or one of the pre-Slavic tribes – though we do know that a centre of worship existed here from at least the 5th century BC till the 11th century AD, when it was overtaken by Christianity. The summit was circled by a stone wall marking off the sanctuary where rituals were held, and the remains of these ramparts survive to this day. Mysterious statues were carved out of granite, and several of them, in better or worse shape, are still scattered over the mountain's slopes.

At the northern foot of the mountain is the small town of Sobótka, a starting point for the hike to the top. The town's Rynek is dominated by the massive parish church, originally Romanesque but repeatedly remodelled later. Nearby to the west is another church, St Anne, and beside it is one of the stone statues, known as the Mushroom (Grzyb).

A few hundred metres south of the Rynek, at ul Św Jakuba 18, is the small local museum (open Wednesday to Sunday 9 am to 4 pm) recognisable by a fine Renaissance doorway from 1568. The museum displays some of the finds of archaeological excavations in the region.

Proceed south along the same street for 300m and take ul Żymierskiego turning off to the right (west) and going uphill. About 500m on, you'll pass another stone statue, called the Monk (Mnich), perhaps the finest and best preserved of all. Another 500m up the road, you'll get to a hostel, the Schronisko pod Wieżycą. The yellow trail from the hostel will take you up Mt Ślęża in about an hour; you'll find two more statues on the way, and a tall TV mast and a 19th century church at the top.

Places to Stay & Eat
The simple *Dom Wycieczkowy Niedźwiadek* (☎ *16 22 52, Rynek 8*) has rooms with shared facilities but is cheap – US$12/14/16 for a double/triple/quad or US$5 per bed in a large dorm. It has a budget restaurant.

The better *Hotel pod Misiem* (☎ *16 20 35, fax 16 20 34, ul Mickiewicza 7/9*), just off the Rynek, can put you up for the night for US$30/35 a double/triple with bath, and it also has its own restaurant.

The previously mentioned *Schronisko pod Wieżycą* (☎ *16 28 57*), at the foot of Mt Ślęża, offers singles/doubles/triples/quads with shared facilities for US$10/13/15/20, and it also provides hot meals.

Possibly the most attractive accommodation around is at *Hotel Zamek Górka* (☎/fax *16 21 33*), a fairy-tale castle in Górka, a distant suburb of Sobótka, 3km west of the Rynek off the road to Świdnica. The hotel has triples and quads without bath (you pay US$10 per bed) and more comfortable doubles/triples with bath for US$28/35, plus its own restaurant.

Getting There & Away
Sobótka is easily accessible by bus and train from Wrocław (32km) and Świdnica (21km). Buses are more frequent and will deposit you in the town centre next to St Anne's Church.

Lower Silesia

A fertile lowland extending along the upper and middle course of the Odra River, Lower Silesia (Dolny Śląsk) was settled relatively early on, and is full of old towns and villages. In July 1997, Lower Silesia was hit by a violent flood when the Odra burst its banks. The disaster caused the death of over 50 people and damages worth an estimated US$2 billion.

Apart from Wrocław and its environs (detailed in the previous sections), there are no great tourist destinations in Lower Silesia, though some places harbour interesting sights which warrant a stop. They have been organised in this section following the route downstream along the Odra.

OPOLE
- pop 131,000   ☎ 077

Set halfway between Katowice and Wrocław, Opole lies on the border of Upper and Lower Silesia, and there's no consensus as to which region it belongs. Most locals don't feel part of either, but rather of their own Opolan Silesia (Śląsk Opolski). The region is known for an active German minority, which is well represented in local government.

Opole has already passed its first millennium. The first stronghold was built in the 9th century, initially on Pasieka Island. In the 13th century the town became the capital of a principality, and it was ruled by a line of the Silesian Piasts until 1532, even though from 1327 it was part of Bohemia. Later on, Opole fell subsequently to Austria, then to Prussia, and after significant destruction during WWII returned to Poland in 1945. Today it's a fairly large regional industrial centre.

For most Poles, Opole is known for its Festival of Polish Song, which has taken place annually in late June for over 30 years and is broadcast nationwide on TV. On these days the city sees crowds of visitors; the rest of the year few tourists bother to come here to explore its few attractions.

Information
There's no tourist office in town. Useful banks include the Bank Pekao at ul Osmańczyka 15 and the Bank Zachodni at ul Ozimska 6, and both have ATMs. Additionally, there's a Euronet ATM in Orbis at ul Krakowska 31. Kantors are easy to find in the centre. There's an Internet Café (☎ 453 03 71) at ul Krakowska 1 (enter from ul Św Wojciecha).

Things to See
The **Rynek** was badly damaged during WWII but remarkably well rebuilt. The houses which line the square make up a coherent baroque-rococo composition.

However, the oversized town hall in the middle looks as if it had been imported from another cultural sphere. It was patterned on the Palazzo Vecchio in Florence and built in the 1930s.

The **Franciscan Church** (Kościół Franciszkanów), off the southern corner of the Rynek, was built around 1330, but the interior was reshaped later on various occasions. It boasts an ornate high altar, 18th century organ, and domed Renaissance chapel in the left-hand aisle, separated by a fine late 16th century wrought-iron grille.

The highlight of the church is the **Piast Chapel**. The entrance is from the right-hand aisle through a doorway with a tympanum. The Gothic-vaulted chapel houses a pair of massive double tombs of the local dukes, carved in sandstone in the 1380s. They were originally painted but the colour has almost disappeared. The central panel of the triptych (made only in 1958) in the chapel's altar shows two dukes presenting St Anne with models of churches, the local one and that in Częstochowa.

Adjoining the church is the **monastery**, whose cloister is adorned with fragments of plaster with the original wall paintings from the Piast Chapel. Downstairs, in the crypt where the Opole dukes were buried, are several simple wooden coffins. One of the tombs bears an *al secco* painting of the Crucifixion from around 1320, unfortunately seriously harmed by the 1997 flood. The entrance to the monastery is from Plac Wolności 2. It's open for visitors 10.15 to 11.30 am and 2 to 4.30 pm.

Two blocks east of the Rynek, the former Jesuit college on ul Św Wojciecha houses the **Regional Museum** (Muzeum Śląska Opolskiego). The permanent display features the prehistory and history of the region and city, and there are always temporary exhibitions. The museum is open Tuesday to Friday 9 am to 3 pm, Saturday 10 am to 3 pm, and Sunday from noon to 5 pm.

The Gothic **cathedral**, a short walk north of the Rynek, now features mostly baroque furnishing. The chapel in the right-hand aisle shelters the 1532 red-marble tombstone

SILESIA

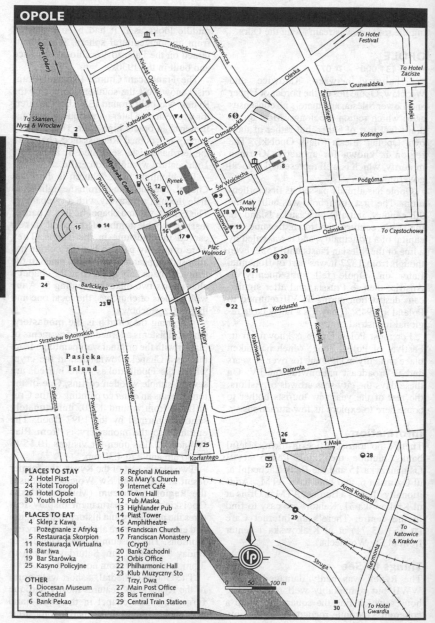

OPOLE

PLACES TO STAY
2 Hotel Piast
24 Hotel Toropol
26 Hotel Opole
30 Youth Hostel

PLACES TO EAT
4 Sklep z Kawą
   Pożegnanie z Afryką
5 Restauracja Skorpion
11 Restauracja Wirtualna
18 Bar Iwa
19 Bar Starówka
25 Kasyno Policyjne

OTHER
1 Diocesan Museum
3 Cathedral
6 Bank Pekao

7 Regional Museum
8 St Mary's Church
9 Internet Café
10 Town Hall
12 Pub Maska
13 Highlander Pub
14 Piast Tower
15 Amphitheatre
16 Franciscan Church
17 Franciscan Monastery
    (Crypt)
20 Bank Zachodni
21 Orbis Office
22 Philharmonic Hall
23 Klub Muzyczny Sto
    Trzy, Dwa
27 Main Post Office
28 Bus Terminal
29 Central Train Station

0   50   100 m

of the last of the Opole dukes. The only surviving Gothic triptych of the 26 that the church once had is also in this chapel.

A bit farther north, the **Diocesan Museum** (Muzeum Diecezjalne), ul Kominka 1A, boasts sacred sculpture collected from the region. It's open Tuesday and Thursday 10 am till noon and 2 to 5 pm, and the first Sunday of the month from 2 to 5 pm.

The only vestige of the dukes' castle is its 42m-tall **Piast Tower** (Wieża Piastowska). Built in the 13th century on Pasieka Island, the castle was pulled down in the 1920s to make room for office buildings. The tower, which miraculously escaped 'modernisation', sticks up oddly from behind the drab blocks. You can climb to the top (from 9.30 am to 5 pm except Monday) for a panoramic view over the city.

Opole has a good **skansen** (Muzeum Wsi Opolskiej). Located in the Bierkowice suburb at ul Wrocławska 174, 5km west of the centre, and accessible by urban bus No 5 or 19, the skansen has a variety of rural architecture from the region. The shingled church of 1613, the water mill of 1832 and a couple of large granaries are among the showpieces. Several houses are fully furnished and decorated, and can be visited. The skansen is open from 15 April to 15 October 10 am to 5 pm except Monday. The rest of the year you can enter the grounds on weekdays 9 am to 2 pm, but the buildings stay locked.

Places to Stay

A good budget bet is *Hotel Toropol* (☎ 453 78 83, ul Barlickiego 13). Well located on the 2nd floor of a freestanding building next to the amphitheatre (where the festival is held) on the quiet Pasieka Island, it's only a five minute walk from the Rynek and 10 minutes from the train station. Its triples cost US$22 each. Unfortunately, they are full up with groups most of the time.

You have more chance of getting a room at *Hotel Zacisze* (☎ 453 95 53, ☎ 454 23 04, ul Grunwaldzka 28), within reasonable walking distance of both the Rynek (10 minutes) and the station (15 minutes).

Small singles/doubles/triples without bath go for US$18/28/38.

A less attractive option is *Hotel Gwardia* (☎ 454 55 76, ul Kowalska 2) south of the station. While it's a 10 minute walk from the station it's twice that distance from the centre. It has doubles with bath (US$35) and five-bed dorms sold by the bed (US$6). The *youth hostel* (☎ 453 33 52, ul Struga 16) midway between the station and the Gwardia opens from 2 July to 25 August.

Far better than anything above is *Hotel Festival* (☎/fax 455 60 11, ul Oleska 86) about 2km north-east of the centre. Decent, spacious singles/doubles with bath cost US$65/80, breakfast included.

The strategically sited *Hotel Opole* (☎ 453 86 51, fax 453 60 75, ul Krakowska 59) facing the train station has recently been renovated and now costs US$75/100 a single/double with breakfast.

Hotel Piast (☎ 454 97 10, fax 454 97 17, ul Piastowska 1) is attractively located on the northern tip of Pasieka Island, but is noisy due to heavy traffic, especially if you take a room facing the street. The standards, on the other hand, are high, as are the rates – US$90/100 a single/double.

Places to Eat

For a cheap meal, try *Bar Starówka* (ul Krakowska 17), a sort of upgraded milk bar near the Rynek. Better and only marginally more expensive is *Bar Iwa* (Mały Rynek 17). In the train station area, you have the dirt-cheap *Kasyno Policyjne* (ul Korfantego 4) – the police station canteen.

Restauracja Skorpion (ul Książąt Opolskich 2/6) was a hit when it opened several years ago. It's still a charming place though the food quality has diminished.

Better is *Restauracja Wirtualna* (Rynek 2), with international dishes. A curiosity of the place are dishes from the menu of the *Titanic*, reputably prepared according to original recipes. They are expensive, but the originals probably weren't cheap either.

Other upmarket options include the restaurants of *Hotel Piast* and *Hotel Opole* (the latter was still being refurbished as we went to press).

Entertainment

For a drink, there's the amazing *Pub Maska (Rynek 4)*. The **Highlander Pub** *(ul Szpitalna 3)* is an alternative. You can also try **Klub Muzyczny Sto Trzy, Dwa** on ul Niedziałkowskiego, which has a pleasant outdoor drinking area in summer, and stages live music at times.

Getting There & Away

The train station and bus terminal face each other, not far south of the Old Town; you can walk to the Rynek in 10 minutes.

Train Opole is on the Katowice-Wrocław railway line and transport to both these destinations (98 and 82km, respectively) is frequent. Most to the former continue on to Kraków (176km) There are also several trains a day to Częstochowa (95km), as well as morning and late afternoon express trains to Warsaw (325km).

Bus Few buses go to Wrocław and Brzeg, but you can easily get there by train. Buses, on the other hand, go regularly to Nysa (53km) and Kłodzko (108km), a route which is not well serviced by trains.

BRZEG

- **pop 40,000**   ☎ **077**

A quiet, medium-sized town midway between Opole and Wrocław, Brzeg ('Bzhek') was founded in 1248 and became the capital of yet another Silesian Piast principality, the Duchy of Legnica-Brzeg. The princes initially set themselves up in Legnica but spent more and more of their time in Brzeg, which gradually took over many of the capital's functions.

During the town's heyday in the 16th century the existing Gothic castle was greatly extended and became a splendid Renaissance residence, modelled on Kraków's royal palace; it was even referred to as the 'Silesian Wawel'. In 1675 the last duke of the family died, marking the end of the Piast

dynasty in Poland, and the town came under direct Habsburg rule and became known as Brieg. A century later, Prussia turned the town into a massive fortress, which nonetheless was seized by Napoleon, and the fortifications were later pulled down. In their place, a ring of parks was established, which now surrounds the historic core of the town, the ponds being the remains of the moat.

The town, like the whole region, was defended fiercely by the Germans in 1945, and half of its buildings were destroyed. The most important monuments have been reconstructed, and for these, principally the castle, it's worth breaking your journey for a couple of hours.

Information

There's no tourist office as such. The PTTK office (☎ 16 21 00), Rynek 4, may answer some questions. The Bank Pekao is at Rynek 9 and the Bank Zachodni at ul Powstańców Śląskich 6; both will cash travellers cheques and have ATMs.

Things to See

Coming from the station, you enter the Old Town by ul Długa. The monumental 14th century **St Nicholas' Church** (Kościół Św Mikołaja) to your right was partially burned down during WWII and the twin towers were reconstructed – as you can tell from the different colour of the brick. The interior, whitewashed throughout, is sober, apart from the burghers' epitaphs in the side walls.

The Rynek was partly ruined during the war and looks a bit plain, mainly because of the substantial amount of postwar architecture. Yet the Renaissance **town hall**, from the 1570s, was restored to a form close to the original.

Two blocks west by ul Chopina is the large building of the former **Piast College** (Gimnazjum Piastowskie), founded in 1564 and famous throughout Silesia. The building was badly damaged during the war and much altered in reconstruction; only the Renaissance doorway was returned to its previous form.

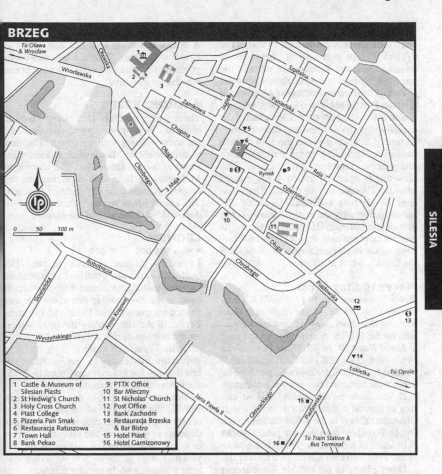

BRZEG

To Oława
& Wrocław

Wrocławska

Oławska

Szpitalna

Zamkowa

Jagiełły

Panieńska

Chopina

Długa

Chrobrego

3 Maja

▼5
▼6
7
8
9
Rynek
Reja

Dzierżona

▼10

11

Długa

Chrobrego

Robotnicza

Piastowska

Słowiańska

Armii Krajowej

12

13

Wyszyńskiego

▼14

Łokietka
To Opole

Jana Pawła II

Głowackiego

Piaskowa

15 ■

16 ■
To Train Station &
Bus Terminal

0   50   100 m

1 Castle & Museum of Silesian Piasts	9 PTTK Office
2 St Hedwig's Church	10 Bar Mleczny
3 Holy Cross Church	11 St Nicholas' Church
4 Piast College	12 Post Office
5 Pizzeria Pan Smak	13 Bank Zachodni
6 Restauracja Ratuszowa	14 Restauracja Brzeska & Bar Bistro
7 Town Hall	15 Hotel Piast
8 Bank Pekao	16 Hotel Garnizonowy

SILESIA

A few steps to the north is the **Holy Cross Church** (Kościół Św Krzyża) built in the 1730s for the Jesuits. Its ample, single-naved interior is decorated in exuberant baroque style throughout, including the trompe l'oeil painted vault.

Undoubtedly the pride of the town is the **castle**, next to the church. There was already a stronghold here in the 13th century, but it was turned into a large Renaissance palace by Duke Jerzy II (George II). The richly decorated façade (circa 1552) of the central three-storey gateway gives some idea of the palace's former splendour. Immediately above the archway are the stone figures of Duke Jerzy and his wife Barbara. Farther up, the two-tier frieze depicts 24 busts of the Piast kings and princes, from the first legendary Piast to the father of Jerzy II, Duke Fryderyk II (Frederick II). In the middle of the balustrade at the top is the coat of arms of King Zygmunt August, with the Jagiellonian eagle at the centre.

The gate leads to a spacious arcaded courtyard, vaguely reminiscent of that of the Wawel except that one of the sides is missing. Note the Renaissance portals; the one at the main gate is particularly elaborate.

Part of the interior houses the **Museum of Silesian Piasts** (Muzeum Piastów Śląskich), which traces the history of Silesia under the dynasty. The rooms upstairs shelter a collection of Silesian art from the 15th to 18th centuries, including some extraordinary altarpieces, retables and statues. The museum is open 10 am to 4 pm except Monday (Wednesday to 6 pm). The adjacent St Hedwig's Church (Kościół Św Jadwigi), formerly the castle's chapel, is not part of the museum. If you want to see its interior (and the only one of the dukes' sarcophagi on display), it's open to the faithful for Sunday Mass at 10 am.

Places to Stay & Eat

Hotel Garnizonowy (☎ 11 76 27, ul Piastowska 20), close to the bus and train stations, has simple singles/doubles without bath for US$10/18. About 100m up the road is *Hotel Piast* (☎ 16 20 27, ul Piastowska 14), which costs US$18/24 a single/double without bath, US$25/32/40 a single/double/triple with bath, and has its own restaurant.

If you have private transport, you can stay at *Zajazd u Rybiorza* (☎ 16 34 73) at Obwodnica, next to the petrol station on the Opole-Wrocław road, which passes about 2km south of Brzeg. It costs much the same as the Piast and also has its own restaurant.

Other places to eat include *Restauracja Ratuszowa* in the basement of the town hall, and *Restauracja Brzeska* (ul Piastowska 15C). There's the very cheap *Bar Mleczny* (ul Długa 41), but better inexpensive meals are served at *Bar Bistro* adjacent to the Brzeska restaurant. Also reasonably cheap is *Pizzeria Pan Smak* at the Rynek, with a modest salad bar.

Getting There & Away

The train and bus stations are opposite each other, 1km south of the Old Town. Trains run regularly every hour or two west to Wrocław (42km) and east to Opole (40km). A dozen fast trains continue east as far as Kraków (216km). Several trains and buses go south to Nysa (48km or 53km); choose whichever goes first.

AROUND BRZEG

There are several interesting Gothic churches in nearby villages, distinguished for their original wall paintings. The best examples are in Małujowice, Krzyżowice, Pogorzela and Strzelniki. The church in Małujowice, 5km west of Brzeg, is the largest, with amazing 15th century frescoes. The hourly urban bus No 3 from Brzeg will deposit you at the gate of the church.

LEGNICA

• pop 108,000   ☎ 076

Legnica's origins go back to the 10th century, but it wasn't until the 13th century that its real development began when it became the co-capital of one of the Silesian Piast principalities, the Duchy of Legnica-Brzeg. In the 16th century the town – then under Bohemian rule – saw good times as an active centre of culture, with the first university established in Silesia. After the last duke of the Piast dynasty died in 1675, the town fell to the Habsburgs, and in 1741 to the Prussians. Badly damaged during WWII, the city revived as an industrial centre following the discovery of copper deposits in the region. For tourists, Legnica is not a particularly fascinating place, but you may want to see its few surviving historic buildings while passing this way.

Information

The municipal tourist office (☎ 851 22 80) is at Rynek 29 (open weekdays 9 am to 5 pm). The Bank Pekao is at ul Wrocławska 26/28, 500m south of the train station, while the Bank Zachodni is at ul Gwarna 4A, 200m west of the Rynek. Both banks have ATMs and will cash travellers cheques.

Things to See

From the bus terminal, head south over a footbridge and then along ul Skarbowa to

St Mary's Church (Kościół Mariacki), one of the oldest in Silesia but refurbished in mock-Gothic style in the 19th century. It's used today by the small Protestant community for infrequent services (Sunday only), and doubles as a stage for cultural events, such as organ and chamber music concerts.

Proceeding south-west by ul Najświętszej Marii Panny you'll get to the **Church of SS Peter and Paul** (Kościół Św Piotra i Pawła). This also underwent a neo-Gothic metamorphosis, but its two original Gothic doorways survive. The one on the northern side has a splendid tympanum depicting the Adoration of the Magi. The interior has the usual hotchpotch of furnishings, of which the oldest piece, the bas-reliefed bronze baptismal font (in the chapel off the left aisle), dates from the late 13th century and is reputedly the oldest metal font in Poland.

The **Rynek** is lined with ordinary modern buildings. The baroque **town hall** and a row of eight small arcaded houses known as the **herring stalls** (kramy śledziowe) are just about the only historic buildings on the square.

Just north of the Rynek is the **Museum of Copper** (Muzeum Miedzi), open Wednesday to Sunday 11 am to 4.30 pm. It focuses on the history of the town and the copper industry in the region, and also features temporary exhibitions.

Across the street from the museum is the baroque **St John's Church** (Kościół Św Jana). The chapel off the right-hand wall is actually the presbytery of the former Gothic church, set at right angles to the current one. The chapel is the mausoleum of the Legnica Piasts and houses their tombs. It can be visited weekdays 11 am to 4 pm; buy your ticket in the museum and they will open the chapel for you.

Back towards the station along ul Partyzantów, you'll pass the **castle**. Built in the 13th century, it was rebuilt in Gothic style (two brick towers from that period survive), then thoroughly modernised in the 1530s for a Renaissance residence, and again in 1835, when the noted German architect Karl Friedrich Schinkel gave it a neoclas-

sical look. Enter the main gate embellished with a Renaissance portal, the only significant remnant of the 16th century renovation. A pavilion in the middle of the courtyard shelters the foundations of the 13th century Romanesque chapel built here along with the original brick and stone castle by Henryk Brodaty. It's often closed, but you can look through the windows.

Places to Stay

There's not much to choose from. At the budget end is the all-year *youth hostel* (☎ 862 54 12, ul Jordana 17), a 10 minute walk east from the centre and about the same distance from the station.

Next up the price ladder comes *Dom Wycieczkowy* (☎ 862 00 10, ul Kominka 7), 500m north-west of the Rynek, which offers simple but acceptable singles/doubles/triples without bath for US$10/14/18. It also has some doubles with bath for US$18. For a similar price you can stay at *Hotel Narol* (☎ 866 95 78, ul Gliwicka 1), a former workers' dorm within a short walking distance from the station, but it has no rooms with baths.

At the top is *Hotel Cuprum* (☎ 862 80 41, fax 862 85 44, ul Skarbowa 7) diagonally opposite the bus station. It has rooms of varying standards (all with bath) costing about US$30 to US$55 a single and US$55 to US$85 a double, breakfast included.

Places to Eat

For somewhere really cheap try the basic *Bar Mleczny Ekspres* (ul Dworcowa 8), right opposite the train station. Better and not much more expensive is *Pizza Pub Fantazja* (ul Wrocławska 6), a short walk south, which apart from pizza has the usual Polish fare of *pierogi*, *bigos* and the like.

In the Rynek area, you have *Restauracja Adria* (Rynek 27), but first check out *Restauracja Tivoli* (ul Złotoryjska 21), which is reputedly better and even marginally cheaper – good value. Alternatively, dine in the reliable but more expensive restaurant of *Hotel Cuprum*.

Getting There & Away

The train and bus stations are next to each other on the north-eastern edge of the city and both offer frequent services to Wrocław (75km). To other destinations such as Jelenia Góra (61km), Świdnica (56km) and Kłodzko (126km), take the bus. One bus a day (weekdays) departs for Lubiąż (30km). There are two trains daily to Warsaw. Trains to Frankfurt (one a day), Leipzig (one) and Dresden (three) stop in Legnica.

LEGNICKIE POLE

- pop 2000   ☎ 076

A small village 11km south-east of Legnica, Legnickie Pole (literally, the Legnica Field; 'Leg-neets-kyeh Po-leh') was the site of a great battle in 1241, in which Silesian troops under the command of Duke Henryk Pobożny (Henry the Pious) were defeated by the Tatars. The duke himself was killed and beheaded. The Tatars stuck the head on a spear and proceeded to Legnica but didn't manage to take the town. The duke's body was identified by his wife, Princess Anna, thanks to the fact that he had six toes on his left foot; this was confirmed in the 19th century when his tomb was opened.

Henryk's mother, Princess Hedwig (Księżna Jadwiga, the saint from Trzebnica), built a small commemorative chapel on the site of his decapitation, which was later replaced by a Gothic church. The church now shelters the **Museum of the Legnica Battle** (Muzeum Bitwy Legnickiej), open Wednesday to Sunday 11 am to 5 pm. The modest exhibition features a hypothetical model of the battle (commentary in German available) and some related objects, including a copy of the duke's tomb (the original is in the National Museum in Wrocław).

Across the road from the museum is the former Benedictine Abbey. Its central part is occupied by **St Hedwig's Church** (Kościół Św Jadwigi), a masterpiece of baroque art designed by Austrian architect Kilian Ignaz Dientzenhofer and built in the 1730s. Past the elaborate doorway you'll find yourself in a beautifully proportioned,

bright and harmonious interior, with the splendid frescoes on the vault, the work of Bavarian painter Cosmas Damian Asam. The fresco over the organ loft shows Princess Anna with the body of her husband after the battle, as does the painting on the high altar.

The church is locked except for religious services (it serves as a parish church), but ask in the museum and they will either give you the key or show you round once a few more tourists have arrived.

Places to Stay & Eat

The only all-year place to stay is *Motel Legnickie Pole* (☎ 858 20 94), which costs US$20/25 a double/triple without bath, US$28 a double with bath. It has a simple restaurant. In summer, you can also stay at *Camping Nr 234*, equipped with bungalows and open June to September.

Getting There & Away

There's a regular PKS service from Legnica, with buses every hour or two. There's also private minibuses, leaving from next to Legnica's bus terminal.

ZIELONA GÓRA

- pop 116,000   ☎ 068

If you are coming to Poland overland from Germany, Zielona Góra on the north-western edge of Silesia may be your first stop on Polish soil. The town has no notable historical monuments, but it's an inviting place with a pleasant centre and a choice of accommodation.

The town was founded by the Silesian Piasts. It was part of the Głogów Duchy, one of the numerous regional principalities, before it passed to the Habsburgs in the 16th century and to Prussia two centuries later. Unlike most other Silesian towns, Zielona Góra came through the 1945 offensive with minimal damage, which is why prewar architecture is so well represented, giving the town a refreshingly stylish appearance.

Zielona Góra is Poland's only wine producer. The tradition goes back to the 14th century, but the climate is less than ideal

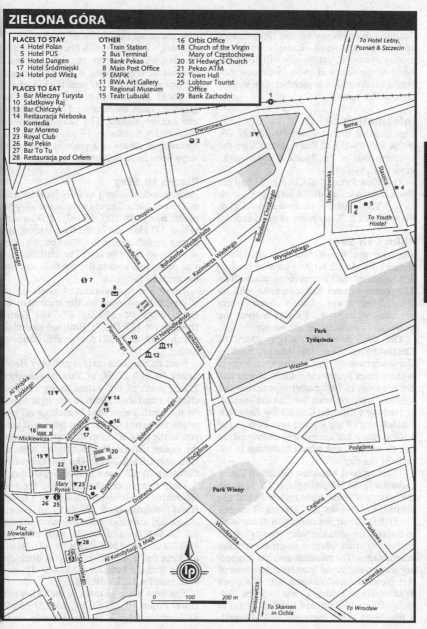

ZIELONA GÓRA

PLACES TO STAY
4 Hotel Polan
5 Hotel PUS
6 Hotel Dangen
17 Hotel Śródmiejski
24 Hotel pod Wieżą

PLACES TO EAT
3 Bar Mleczny Turysta
10 Sałatkowy Raj
13 Bar Chińczyk
14 Restauracja Nieboska
   Komedia
19 Bar Moreno
23 Royal Club
26 Bar Pekin
27 Bar To Tu
28 Restauracja pod Orłem

OTHER
1 Train Station
2 Bus Terminal
7 Bank Pekao
8 Main Post Office
9 EMPiK
11 BWA Art Gallery
12 Regional Museum
15 Teatr Lubuski

16 Orbis Office
18 Church of the Virgin
   Mary of Częstochowa
20 St Hedwig's Church
21 Pekao ATM
22 Town Hall
25 Lubtour Tourist
   Office
29 Bank Zachodni

To Hotel Leśny,
Poznań & Szczecin

To Youth
Hostel

To Hotel Leśny

Park
Tysiąclecia

Park
Winny

Plac
Słowiański

0   100   200 m

To Skansen
in Ochla

To Wrocław

SILESIA

and business was never very profitable. It declined dramatically in the 19th century and never recovered. Today's output is merely symbolic, yet the city still holds the Feast of the Grape Harvest (Święto Winobrania) at the end of September, as it has for almost 150 years.

Information

The Lubtour tourist office (☎ 320 27 00, ☎/fax 325 59 42), ul Pod Filarami 1 on the southern side of the Rynek is open weekdays 8 am to 4 pm.

The Bank Pekao at ul Chopina 21 and the Bank Zachodni at ul Sikorskiego 9 both have ATMs. There's a convenient ATM at Stary Rynek 6. Kantors are in good supply.

Things to See

The renovated **Rynek** (formally called Stary Rynek), lined with brightly painted houses, is a pleasant and harmonious place. The 17th century **town hall**, complete with its slim 54m tower, hasn't been over-modernised in spite of changes over the years, and fits nicely on the square.

The **Church of the Virgin Mary of Częstochowa** (Kościół Matki Boskiej Częstochowskiej), just north of the Rynek, is the former Protestant church, as you can deduce from its half-timbered structure and the two-tiered galleries that line the interior. **St Hedwig's Church** (Kościół Św Jadwigi), a block east of the Rynek, was built in the 13th century but completely destroyed by fire three times and rebuilt each time in the style of the day.

The **Regional Museum** (Muzeum Ziemi Lubuskiej), Al Niepodległości 15, features the history of wine in the region and an exhibition of works by Marian Kruczek (1927-83), the largest collection of his work in Poland. He used everyday objects – from buttons to spark plugs – to create striking assemblages. The museum also has temporary displays of items from its collections of Art Nouveau and modern art. It's open Wednesday to Friday 11 am to 5 pm, Saturday 10 am to 3 pm and Sunday 10 am to 4 pm. Next to the museum, at Al Niepod-

ległości 19, is the **BWA Art Gallery** which runs changing exhibitions of modern art.

There's a **skansen** in Ochla, 7km south of the city, serviced by the regular bus No 27 (get off before arriving at the village; ask the driver to let you off near the entrance). Of about 20 buildings reassembled on the grounds, some are furnished and decorated and can be visited. The skansen is open Wednesday to Sunday 10 am to 3 pm (on Saturday it closes at 2 pm). In summer it stays open an hour longer.

Places to Stay

Accommodation isn't usually hard to find in Zielona Góra. The cheapest is the all-year *youth hostel* (☎ 327 08 40, ul Wyspiańskiego 57) 1km east of the train station, but it may be full in summer. Reception closes at 9 pm, so don't be late. The staff may let you pitch your tent in the grounds and use the hostel's facilities.

There are two workers' hostels on ul Wyspiańskiego close to the train station: *Hotel PUS* (☎ 320 21 97) and *Hotel Dangen* (☎ 327 19 17). Both are basic but cheap – about US$12 a double without bath.

Next on the price scale is probably *Hotel Leśny* (☎ 320 27 94, ul Sulechowska 39), 1.5km north of the station along ul Sulechowska and then 500m to the right (east) on the small forest road branching off opposite the petrol station. Bus No 1 will take you to the turn-off from the station or from the centre. Singles/doubles/triples without bath cost US$18/24/28. The hotel operates *Camping Nr 52*, open May to September.

More convenient than all these are two affordable hotels right in the town's heart. *Hotel Śródmiejski* (☎ 325 44 71, ul Żeromskiego 23) has singles/doubles without bath for US$18/28, and rooms with bath for US$25/38. *Hotel pod Wieżą* (☎ 327 10 91, ul Kopernika 2) offers singles/doubles/triples without bath for US$24/34/38, and with bath for US$30/40/48.

The best place in town is the Orbis-run *Hotel Polan* (☎ 327 00 91, fax 327 18 59, ul Staszica 9A). It is significantly more expensive than the rest, costing US$60/90 a single/double, breakfast included.

Places to Eat

At the rock-bottom end, there's the basic *Bar Mleczny Turysta* opposite the train station. Good budget places to eat in the centre include *Bar Moreno (ul Mariacka 7)*, *Bar To Tu (Plac Pocztowy 17)* and *Kasyno pod Wieżą (ul Kopernika 2)*. You also have *Sałatkowy Raj (ul Pieniężnego 20)*, a cosy salad bar, and two cheap Oriental outlets: *Bar Pekin (ul Sobieskiego 4)* and *Bar Chińczyk (ul Kupiecka 40)*.

Among some more upmarket central establishments, try the *Royal Club (Stary Rynek 2)*, *Restauracja Nieboska Komedia (Al Niepodległości 3)* or *Restauracja pod Orłem (ul Sikorskiego 4)*.

Getting There & Away

Train The train station is about 1km northeast of the city centre and linked to it by several urban bus lines. There are seven trains daily to Wrocław (153km), three to Kraków (411km), four to Szczecin (207km) and six to Poznań (139km). Only one train runs daily to Legnica (115km) and two to Jelenia Góra (172km). There's one morning express train and one night fast train to Warsaw (445km). The Kraków-Berlin train calls at Zielona Góra.

Bus The bus terminal is 200m west of the train station and operates plenty of buses in the region. You can take the bus instead of the train to Poznań (130km) and Wrocław (157km), with six fast buses to each destination. There are four fast buses to Jelenia Góra (148km), a more convenient way of getting there than by train.

The Sudeten Mountains

The Sudeten Mountains (Sudety in Polish) run for over 250km along the Czech-Polish border. The highest part of this old and eroded chain is the Karkonosze, reaching a maximum height of 1602m at Mt Śnieżka. Though the Sudetes don't offer much alpine scenery, they are amazingly varied and heavily cloaked in forest, and boast spectacular geological formations such as the Góry Stołowe (literally, the Table Mountains).

To the north, the Sudetes gradually decline into a belt of gently rolling foothills known as the Przedgórze Sudeckie. This area is more densely populated, and many of the towns and villages in the region still boast some of their centuries-old buildings. This section of the book covers both the mountains proper and the foothills; the information is organised from east to west.

The Sudetes and their foothills are well known for minerals and gem stones. This is Poland's richest region in precious and semiprecious stones, and reputedly holds just about every jewel except for diamond. You can find agate, amethyst, quartz, tourmaline, opal, chrysoprase, serpentine, morion and nephrite here, to name a few.

While the variety is impressive, the quantity is rather modest. In most cases the size of the deposits is too small to be worth processing. But gem collectors will be in their element here, with the numerous old quarries (mostly no longer in use).

NYSA

- **pop 49,000**   ☎ 077

Nysa ('Ni-sah') was for centuries one of the most important religious and cultural centres in Silesia. In the 17th century it became a seat of the Catholic bishops, in flight from newly Protestant Wrocław. The bishops soon made Nysa a powerful bastion of the Counter-Reformation, so strong that it came to be known as the Silesian Rome. A number of churches were built in that time, some of which still survive.

Nysa experienced the pain of WWII with particular severity – 80% of its buildings were destroyed during the fierce battles of 1945, and it had to be rebuilt almost from the ground up. The reconstruction leaves a lot to be desired in aesthetic terms, yet amid

SILESIA

the usual communist-style urban fabric there are a few surviving historic buildings.

Information

The PTTK office (☎ 33 41 71) at ul Bracka 4, off the Rynek, is just about the only source of information. It's open weekdays 9 am to 4 pm.

The Bank Pekao is at Plac Kilińskiego 2. There are several kantors in the centre.

Things to See

The vast **Rynek** shows the extent of the war damage. Only the southern side of the square is anything like the way it used to be, with its restored houses originally dating from the 16th century. The freestanding building facing them is the 1604 **Town Weigh-House** (Dom Wagi Miejskiej), which retains fragments of 19th century wall painting on its side wall. Just round the corner, on ul Bracka, there are a few more historic houses and a 1701 baroque fountain.

The northern side of the Rynek is occupied by the large stone **cathedral** with a fine double doorway. It was built in the 1420s and remodelled after the fire of 1542, but it hasn't changed much since then. Its interior is not crammed with the usual baroque furnishings and looks distinctly sober and noble, its loftiness being the most arresting feature. On closer inspection, however, you'll see that its side chapels (18 in all) boast a wealth of tombstones, funeral monuments and epitaphs, which together make up the largest collection of funerary sculpture in any Silesian church.

Most of the church's interior is off limits, except during Mass (8 am and 6 pm). If you can't coincide with these times, ask the nuns in the adjacent building to switch off the alarm system.

The construction of the cathedral's freestanding **bell tower** began 50 years after the church and it was supposed to be over 100m high. Despite 40 years work it only ever reached half that height, and as a result looks quite odd.

To the east of the cathedral, on ul Jarosława, is the 17th century **Bishops'** **Palace** (Pałac Biskupi), whose spacious interior is occupied by the **museum** (open Tuesday to Friday 9 am to 3 pm, Saturday and Sunday 10 am to 3 pm). The collection related to the town's history includes exhibits ranging from archaeological finds to the photos documenting war damage, plus a model of the town in its heyday. The museum also features European paintings from the 15th to the 19th century, mostly from the Flemish and Dutch schools.

Facing the palace is the **Bishops' Residence** (Dwór Biskupi), which has been rebuilt so extensively that its original style has completely disappeared. To the south, of this the 17th century **Jesuit Church** (Kościół Jezuitów) has some interior stucco decoration and wall paintings, and the former Jesuit college farther south is now a school.

More interesting is the mighty twin-towered **Church of SS Peter and Paul** (Kościół Św Piotra i Pawła), built in the 1720s for the Hospitallers of the Holy Sepulchre. It has one of Silesia's best baroque interiors, complete with an opulent high altar, organ and trompe l'œil wall paintings. The church is locked except for services (8 am or 6 pm on weekdays and 10 am on Sunday).

The only significant vestiges of the medieval defences are two 14th century brick towers: the **Ziębice Tower** (Wieża Ziębicka) on ul Krzywoustego (you can go to the top from May to August), and the **Wrocław Tower** (Wieża Wrocławska) on ul Wrocławska.

Places to Stay

The cheapest shelter is the well positioned, all-year *youth hostel* (☎ 33 37 31, ul Bohaterów Warszawy 7). It occupies the top floor of a large school (enter from the back) and is pretty reliable.

Hotel Garnizonowy (☎ 32 26 99, ul Kościuszki 4), just north across the river, is simple but acceptable and cheap – US$10/17/20 a single/double/triple without bath, US$27 a double with bath. Another budget option is the uninspiring *Hotel Budowlani*

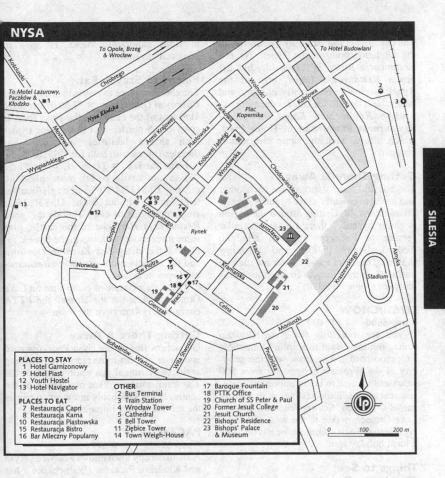

NYSA

PLACES TO STAY
1 Hotel Garnizonowy
9 Hotel Piast
12 Youth Hostel
13 Hotel Navigator

PLACES TO EAT
7 Restauracja Capri
8 Restauracja Kama
10 Restauracja Piastowska
15 Restauracja Bistro
16 Bar Mleczny Popularny

OTHER
2 Bus Terminal
3 Train Station
4 Wrocław Tower
5 Cathedral
6 Bell Tower
11 Ziębice Tower
14 Town Weigh-House

17 Baroque Fountain
18 PTTK Office
19 Church of SS Peter & Paul
20 Former Jesuit College
21 Jesuit Church
22 Bishops' Residence
23 Bishops' Palace & Museum

(☎ 33 37 51, ul Słowiańska 21), even cheaper (US$9/15/20) but less convenient, in a suburb 1km north of the centre.

The most central place is **Hotel Piast** (☎ 33 40 84, fax 33 40 86, ul Krzywoustego 14), but it's not cheap – US$40/50/70 for singles/doubles/triples with bath, breakfast included.

None of the above, however, can compete with **Hotel Navigator** (☎ 33 41 70, ul Wyspiańskiego 11). Set in a spacious old mansion owned and run by a friendly German-speaking couple, the place is full of antiques and has a family atmosphere. There are a dozen rooms, some of which have baths, and the price is around US$25 to US$45 for singles, US$35 to US$60 for doubles, all including breakfast.

Motel Lazurowy (☎ 33 40 76) is on the Kłodzko road near Lake Nyskie, about 3.5km west of Nysa, and costs US$15/25 a single/double with bath. Urban bus No 2 from the centre or the train station goes there.

SILESIA

Places to Eat

The cheapest is **Bar Mleczny Popularny** in the southern corner of the Rynek. Nearby **Restauracja Bistro** is reasonable, but the newer **Restauracja Capri**, also at the Rynek, seems to be slightly cheaper and better. Next door to the latter is the more expensive **Restauracja Kama**, or go to **Restauracja Piastowska** at Hotel Piast, which offers much the same fare and is cheaper.

Getting There & Away

The bus and train stations face each other and are conveniently close to the Rynek, a 10 minute walk. Getting around the region is easier by bus – there's a fairly regular service to Paczków (26km), Kłodzko (55km), Opole (53km) and Wrocław (83km). Trains are less frequent but may be useful when travelling to Brzeg (four trains daily) or Opole (six daily).

OTMUCHÓW

* pop 5500   ☎ 077

If you are travelling the Nysa-Kłodzko route, you may want to stop in Otmuchów ('Ot-moo-hoof'). The town was the property of the Wrocław bishops for over 500 years and it came to be an important ecclesiastical centre. Some vestiges of its history can still be seen. Set between two lakes – Lake Otmuchowskie to the west and Lake Nyskie to the east – Otmuchów has become a local holiday spot.

Things to See

The sloping Rynek retains little of its former character apart from the 16th century **town hall**, which has a Renaissance tower and a lovely double **sundial** built in 1575 around the corner of two walls. The baroque **parish church**, overlooking the Rynek, was built at the end of the 17th century and most of its internal decoration, including frescoes by Dankwart and paintings by Willmann, dates from that period.

Just south of the church, atop the hill, stands a massive **castle**, erected in the 13th century but much extended and remodelled

later. It's now a hotel, but its tower, which provides panoramic views, is open to nonguests in summer.

Places to Stay & Eat

The cheapest place to stay is the basic **Hotel Cukrowni Otmuchów** (☎ 31 50 01 ext 220), 1km east of the centre on the Nysa road. It costs US$5 per head in doubles or triples with shared facilities, and also has doubles/triples with bath for US$18/25.

Hotel Zamek (☎ 31 46 91, ☎/fax 31 51 48) in the castle is far more pleasant, costing US$18/24/30/36 a single/double/triple/quad without bath, US$30/35 a single/double with bath. There's the good **Restauracja Herbowa** in the castle, plus some more modest options in the Rynek, including the cheap **Bar Kuchnia Domowa** and the slightly more expensive **Restauracja Capri** next door.

There are a couple of camp sites on Lake Otmuchowskie, but the closest, the **PTTK camp site**, is 4km from the town.

Getting There & Away

Otmuchów lies on the Nysa-Paczków road and buses ply this route regularly, stopping at the bus terminal just south of the castle. The train station is 2km north-west of the centre, but it's probably not worth a trip as the service is very infrequent.

PACZKÓW

* pop 8500   ☎ 077

A small, sleepy town midway between Nysa and Kłodzko, Paczków ('Pah-chkoof') has one of the most complete medieval fortifications in the country. Within the walls, the tiny Old Town has managed to retain some of its old appearance.

Information

The Eden travel agency at Rynek 14 may answer some queries. The Bank Zachodni at Rynek 11 has a useful ATM.

Things to See

The oval ring of the **defensive walls** was built around 1350 and surrounded by a

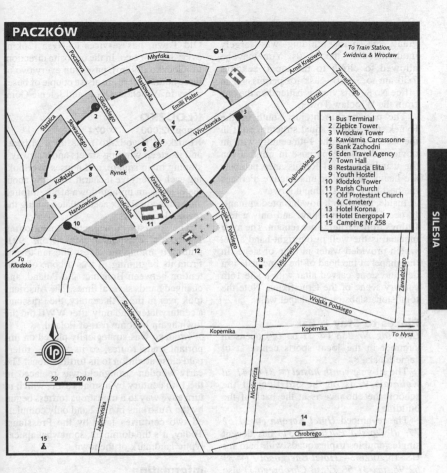

PACZKÓW

1	Bus Terminal
2	Ziębice Tower
3	Wrocław Tower
4	Kawiarnia Carcassonne
5	Bank Zachodni
6	Eden Travel Agency
7	Town Hall
8	Restauracja Elita
9	Youth Hostel
10	Kłodzko Tower
11	Parish Church
12	Old Protestant Church & Cemetery
13	Hotel Korona
14	Hotel Energopol 7
15	Camping Nr 258

SILESIA

moat. This system protected the town for a time, but when firearms arrived in the 15th century, an additional, external ring of defences was erected outside the moat (it was eventually pulled down in the 19th century). The original walls were fortunately retained and, as the town escaped major destruction during WWII, they still encircle the historic quarter. They were initially about 9m high for the whole of their 1200m length and had a wooden gallery for guards just below the top.

Four gateways were built, complete with towers and drawbridges (three towers are still in place), and there were 24 semicircular towers built into the walls themselves (19 have survived though most are incomplete). The best way to see the system is to walk along the walls, inside or outside. The oldest of the three main towers, the 14th century **Wrocław Tower**, can be climbed – it's open 10 am to 5 pm in summer.

The **Rynek** occupies a good part of the Old Town. The **town hall** was built in the mid-16th century but only its tower is original; the main building was largely modernised in the 1820s. You may be allowed to climb to the top (weekdays 7.30 am to 3 pm) – ask for permission in office No 8. This view is better than the one from the Wrocław Tower.

The **parish church**, just south of the Rynek, is a sturdy, squat structure built in the second half of the 14th century with an obvious defensive purpose in mind. Even the usually graceful Renaissance parapets are heavy and rather unattractive. Perhaps the best bit is the Gothic doorway.

Inside, the church now has predominantly neo-Gothic furnishing, and only a few fittings from earlier times remain. The most unusual is the well in the right-hand aisle, which provided water in time of siege. In the chapel at the head of the same aisle is a delicate stone-carved altar with a late 16th century scene of the Crucifixion. Note the tombstone slabs on the chapel walls.

Places to Stay & Eat

Camping Nr 258 (☎ *31 65 09*) opens in summer in the local sports centre at ul Jagiellońska 8.

The all-year *youth hostel* (☎ *31 64 41, ul Kołłątaja 9*) is on the 3rd floor of the school; the entrance is at the back of the building.

The revamped *Hotel Korona* (☎ *31 62 77, ul Wojska Polskiego 31*) has decent singles/doubles/triples/quads with bath for US$15/20/28/34. *Hotel Energopol 7* (☎ *31 62 98, fax 31 68 77, ul Chrobrego 1*) also provides reasonable standards and is cheaper: singles/doubles/triples with bath cost US$13/17/20. It has its own restaurant. There are also a few simple places to eat in the Rynek, including *Restauracja Elita* and *Kawiarnia Carcassonne*.

Getting There & Away

Train The train station, a long way to the north-east, doesn't have much to offer: one train daily to Jelenia Góra (131km) and Kłodzko (33km), and several to Nysa (27km).

Bus The bus terminal, on the edge of the Old Town, has services to Nysa (26km) every hour or two. In the opposite direction, to Kłodzko (29km), buses run every two or three hours. There are also a couple of buses a day to Wrocław, Opole and Jelenia Góra.

KŁODZKO

• pop 32,000   ☎ 074

Kłodzko ('Kwodz-ko') sits on a hillside, and its steep winding streets and stairways, sloping main square, and houses overlooking each other give it charm. Strolling about the place is an up-and-down affair, through an architectural mix accumulated during the town's long history.

The first document mentioning Kłodzko's existence dates from 981, putting it among the oldest Silesian towns. From its beginning, it was a bone of contention between Bohemia and Poland, and changed hands several times. The Austrians took over in the 17th century, the Prussians a century later, and only after WWII did the town again become part of Poland.

Kłodzko was strategically placed on important trade routes, so its various rulers paid close attention to its fortifications. The early wooden stronghold was replaced in the 14th century by a stone castle, which in turn gave way to a monstrous fortress begun by the Austrians in 1662 and only completed two centuries later by the Prussians. Today, it's the dominant, somewhat apocalyptic landmark of the town.

Information

The PTTK office (☎ 67 37 40), ul Wita Stwosza 1, just off the Rynek, may provide information. It's open weekdays 8 am to 4 pm, and (in summer only) Saturday 9 am to 2 pm.

The Bank Pekao on the Rynek and the Bank Zachodni at ul Kościuszki 7 both have ATMs.

Things to See

You'll probably enter the Old Town over the **Gothic Bridge** (Most Gotycki). Built of stone in the 1390s, it was originally part of the town's fortifications but later lost its defensive function and was adorned with statues of the saints.

A short walk uphill is the **Rynek**. Its northern side is a recent addition, built on what was for a long time a grassy slope left after the previous houses had been demolished to make space for the expanding fortress. The **town hall** was built 100 years ago after its predecessor had gone up in flames; nothing but the Renaissance tower survived. Several houses in the Rynek have preserved their Renaissance and baroque décor.

The **Regional Museum** (Muzeum Ziemi Kłodzkiej), ul Łukasiewicza 4, has a display relating to the history of the town and the region. The top floor features a collection of old clocks, some of which are working; their ticking provides unusual background 'music' to the exhibition. The museum is open Tuesday 10 am to 3 pm, Wednesday to Friday 10 am to 5 pm, Saturday and Sunday 11 am to 5 pm.

The nearby **parish church** is the most imposing religious building in town. It took almost 150 years before the massive Gothic structure was eventually completed in 1490, and the overall shape hasn't changed much since. Inside, however, changes continued for at least another 250 years. The altars, pulpit, pews, organ and 11 monumental confessionals all blaze with florid baroque. Even the Gothic vaulting, usually left plain, has been sumptuously decorated. Organ recitals are held in the church from time to time – inquire at the PTTK office or in the local cultural centre, Kłodzki Ośrodek Kultury, at Plac Jagiełły 1 (which organises the recitals).

A few steps down the stairs from the church is the entrance to the **Underground Tourist Route** (Podziemna Trasa Turystyczna), similar to that in Sandomierz. The 600m route uses some of the medieval cellars that were hollowed out for storage under most of the Old Town. Later on, when trade slumped, most of the cellars were abandoned. The town was reminded of their existence when houses began falling down

for no apparent reason. In the late 1950s a complex conservation program started and the combined work of speleologists, miners and builders led to the restoration of the cellars, which were linked to form the underground route. It's open daily 9 am to 5 pm and you can walk the whole length in 10 minutes; the exit is at the foot of the fortress (you can do the route in reverse).

In the **fortress** (open daily 9 am to 4 pm, May to September till 5 pm) you have more underground legwork to do, though of a different kind. Here you'll visit the network of defensive tunnels, which are less comfortable to walk through.

Altogether 40km of **tunnels** were drilled around the fortress, essentially for two purposes. Those under the fortifications were principally for communication, shelter and storage; the others ran up to 500m away from the fortress and were designed to destroy the enemy's artillery. They were divided into sectors, stuffed with gunpowder and when the enemy happened to move their guns directly above a particular sector, it was blown up. This bizarre minefield was initiated in 1743 by a Dutch engineer, and by 1807 an immense labyrinth of tunnels had been built, to good effect – Napoleon's army didn't manage to take the fortress.

Part of the underground network is open to tourists. Guided 40-minute tours begin on the hour. You walk 1km or so, and some of the passageways are so low that you have to bend double. The average temperature is about 7°C and the humidity almost 100%. The corridors are now lit but the soldiers had to work here in complete darkness; the only source of light at that time was open flame, which was a little bit risky with all that gunpowder lying around.

After completing your underground trip, you can go to the top of the fortress for a bird's-eye view of the town. There are also three exhibitions in the grounds: old firebrigade vehicles, contemporary glass from a local factory, and bits and pieces of old stone sculptures (mostly tombstones) collected from historic buildings around the region.

SILESIA

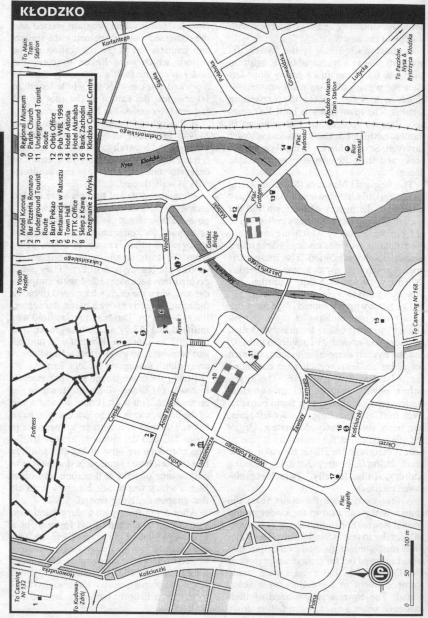

KŁODZKO

1 Motel Korona
2 Bar Pizzeria Romano
3 Underground Tourist
  Route
4 Bank Pekao
5 Restauracja w Ratuszu
6 PTTK Office
7 Sklep z Kawą
8 Pożegnanie z Afryką

9 Regional Museum
10 Parish Church
11 Underground Tourist
   Route
12 Orbis Office
13 Pub WBL 1998
14 Hotel Astoria
15 Hotel Marhaba
16 Bank Zachodni
17 Kłodzko Cultural Centre

Places to Stay

There are two camp sites in town. *Camping Nr 132* (☎ 67 30 31, *ul Nowy Świat 1*) is 1km north of the centre; the other one, *Camping Nr 168* (☎ 67 24 25), is in the opposite direction, in the sports centre on ul Kusocińskiego, 1km south of the Old Town. Apart from their seasonal camping grounds (open May to September), both operate year-round hostels (around US$15 for a double) and bungalows in summer, and both have basic restaurants.

The all-year *youth hostel* (☎ 67 25 24, *ul Nadrzeczna 5*), 1km north of the Rynek, offers 53 cheap beds in doubles, triples and larger dorms.

There are no posh hotels in town and, accordingly, nothing is very expensive. *Hotel Astoria* (☎ 67 30 35, *Plac Jedności 1*), opposite the bus and train stations, has singles/doubles/triples with bath for US$20/30/40. *Hotel Marhaba* (☎ 67 40 70, *ul Daszyńskiego 16*), a five minute walk from the Astoria, has similar prices and standards. *Motel Korona* (☎ 67 37 37, *ul Noworudzka 1*) offers doubles with bath for US$30. Urban bus Nos 2, 3 and 5 from the station can take you there, but it's only a 10 minute walk.

Places to Eat

There are some unpretentious budget eateries around the centre, including *Bar Pizzeria Romano* (*ul Armii Krajowej 14*), which apart from its pizzas has a choice of Polish dishes.

Better food in finer surroundings is available at cosy *Kawiarnia Muzealna* (*ul Łukasiewicza 4*) in the museum. You could also try *Restauracja w Ratuszu* in the town hall, but it's more expensive.

All the places to stay mentioned above (except for the youth hostel) have their own dining facilities. The restaurant at *Hotel Marhaba* specialises in Tunisian cuisine and is perhaps the most interesting option of the lot.

The best place for a cup of coffee is, predictably, *Sklep z Kawą Pożegnanie z Afryką* by the Gothic bridge, while *Pub* *WBL 1998* (*Plac Grottgera 8*) is a good place for a glass of beer.

Getting There & Away

Train Kłodzko has two train stations. The centrally located Kłodzko Miasto station handles mostly regional services, including trains to Bystrzyca Kłodzka (16km) and Wrocław (96km), plus a couple of trains to Warsaw. You have more long-distance trains from the main Kłodzko Główne station, 2km north. Take either bus No 5 or the train which shuttles between the two stations every hour or two. Orbis (☎ 67 27 75), Plac Grottgera 1, sells train tickets.

Bus The bus terminal, next to the Kłodzko Miasto train station, is the transport hub of the region. Buses to Duszniki-Zdrój (23km), Kudowa-Zdrój (37km), Lądek-Zdrój (23km) and Bystrzyca Kłodzka (16km) run roughly every hour. There's also a regular service to Wrocław (87km). There are no buses to Kletno; take the bus to Bolesławów (only one in the morning), get off in Stara Morawa and walk 5km to the Bear's Cave.

The Czech Republic There are two road border crossings in the region, both open 24 hours for pedestrians and vehicles. One is at Kudowa-Zdrój (Poland)/Náchod (Czech Republic), 37km due west of Kłodzko on the way to Prague. The other one is at Boboszów/Králíky, 40km due south of Kłodzko on the Brno road.

One bus daily goes from Kłodzko to Náchod across the border (US$3). It departs weekdays at 8 am, and at 7 am on Saturday. It goes through the three spa towns of Polanica-Zdrój, Duszniki-Zdrój and Kudowa-Zdrój, stopping in each of them.

There are no buses direct to the Czech Republic via Boboszów. Take the bus to Boboszów (leaving at 6 am weekdays only) and walk across the border 2km to Králíky, from where you have onward transport. There are more buses to Boboszów from Bystrzyca Kłodzka.

BYSTRZYCA KŁODZKA
- pop 12,000 ☎ 074

South of Kłodzko, Bystrzyca Kłodzka ('Bist-zhee-tsah') is the second-largest town in the region. Perched on a hill above the Nysa Kłodzka River, it is also a picturesque place. Since the 13th century, when it was founded, the town has been destroyed and rebuilt several times, but it survived WWII virtually unscathed. It doesn't seem to have seen much fresh paint since and looks pretty shabby, though it's perhaps still worth a glance.

Things to See

The houses lining the **Rynek** are a blend of styles of different epochs, including some fine Renaissance and baroque examples. Note the elaborate baroque monument standing in the western part of the square. The octagonal Renaissance tower of the **town hall**, in the middle of the square, gives

the place an unusual, slightly Spanish feel. The tower, built in 1567, is the only really old part of the building, which assumed its current appearance in the 19th century.

In the 14th century, the town was surrounded by fortified walls, some of which are still in place. The most substantial structures include the **Water Gate** (Brama Wodna) just south of the Rynek, and the **Kłodzko Tower** (Wieża Kłodzka) on the opposite side of the Old Town; the latter has access to the top from where there's a good panoramic view.

The nearby **Knights' Tower** (Wieża Rycerska) was reshaped in the 19th century and turned into the belfry of a Protestant church which had been built alongside. After WWII the church was occupied by a **Philumenistic Museum** (Muzeum Filumenistyczne) related to the match industry. A display of old cigarette lighters and matchbox labels from various countries forms the core of the

KRZYSZTOF DYDYŃSKI

The hillside town of Bystrzyca Kłodzka, with its Renaissance town hall tower on the skyline

museum's collection, which can be viewed from 9 am to 4 pm except Monday. On the square in front of the museum stands the old whipping post *(pręgierz)* from 1556; the Latin inscription on its top reads 'God punishes the impious'.

The **parish church** sits at the highest point of the Old Town, one block north-west of the Rynek. It has an unusual double-naved interior with a row of six Gothic columns running right across the middle.

There's a good view of the Old Town from the bridge over the Nysa River on the Międzylesie road, just off the Old Town's walls. A wider vista can be viewed from the swimming pool *(basen)*, a 10 minute walk from the bridge.

Places to Stay

The basic *Hotel Piast (☎ 11 03 22, ul Okrzei 26)* is on the edge of the Old Town. It costs US$8/12 a single/double without bath, and has some doubles/triples with bath for US$18/22. Beds in triples and quads go for US$4.

Hotel Energetyk (☎ 11 15 54, ul Strażacka 28), on the Polanica-Zdrój road, about 1km from the centre, is the former workers' dorm. It costs US$7 per person in a double or triple without bath.

Places to Eat

For a cheap and tasty meal go to *Bistro Kasyno (ul Słowackiego 8)*, the police canteen, round the corner from the bus terminal. Of the few undistinguished restaurants in town, *Restauracja Regionalna (Rynek 5)* is probably the safest choice.

Getting There & Away

The train station is just east of the Old Town; several trains daily go from here to Kłodzko (16km), Międzylesie (18km) and Wrocław (112km). You can also get to Kłodzko by bus; it goes every hour from the terminal 200m north of the parish church. There are also reasonable bus connections to Międzygórze (13km), Polanica-Zdrój (18km) and Lądek-Zdrój (22km), and a few buses to Boboszów (24km). From early May to mid-October, one morning bus goes to Kletno (38km).

MIĘDZYGÓRZE

• pop 700   ☎ 074

Small as it is, Międzygórze ('Myen-dzi-goo-zheh') is one of the most charming mountain resorts in the region. Beautifully set in a deep valley surrounded by forested mountains, it is also architecturally one of the loveliest. Its splendid (albeit run-down) villas dating from the late 19th/early 20th century look as if they have been brought from the Tyrol. The finest are on ul Sanatoryjna which heads north up the hill from the village centre. They are now used as holiday homes and will accommodate individual tourists.

Międzygórze boasts the highest waterfall in the Sudetes (27m high). It's on the western edge of the village and there are paths all around, so you can see it from various angles including from a bridge right above.

Hiking

Międzygórze's countryside is attractive for hikers. North-west of the village is Mt Igliczna (845m), with a small baroque church on top, and a PTTK refuge, Maria Śnieżna. You can get there by any of three different routes – the trails waymarked red, green or yellow – in about an hour.

There are at least five longer trails originating in or passing through the village. The most popular is the hike to the top of Mt Śnieżnik (1425m), the highest peak in the region. It will take about three hours to get there by the red trail, and if you don't want to come back the same day, there's a PTTK refuge, Na Śnieżniku, half an hour before you reach the top. Take candles – there's no electricity there. If you plan on hiking in the area, get a copy of the *Ziemia Kłodzka* map (scale 1:90,000).

Places to Stay & Eat

Accommodation shouldn't be a problem. Some of the *holiday homes* are controlled by the Centralna Recepcja or a central reception

SILESIA

office (☎ 13 51 09, ☎/fax 13 51 07) which does all the paperwork, charges the room fee (about US$7/10 per person in rooms without/with bath) and then gives you keys to the house. The office is at ul Sanatoryjna 2 in the centre and is open daily from 7 am to 9 pm, or even longer in summer.

There are other accommodation options, including pensions, hotels and private rooms. *Hotel Złoty Róg (☎ 13 51 25, ul Wojska Polskiego 3)*, opposite the church, charges US$5 a person in simple rooms without bath, and has a cheap restaurant. Better standards are provided by *Hotel nad Wodospadem (☎ 13 51 20, ☎/fax 13 51 92, ul Wojska Polskiego 12)*, at the western end of the village, next to the waterfall. It costs US$18/22 for doubles/triples with bath. It also has its own *restaurant*, possibly the best place to eat in the village.

Getting There & Away

The best connection is to Bystrzyca Kłodzka (13km), with buses running every couple of hours or so. Some of them continue to Kłodzko (29km).

For the Bear's Cave, take the ski trail marked black that goes east from the village along a rough road, and switch to the yellow one leading north. You should get to the cave in two hours.

KLETNO
- **pop 300**   ☎ 074

Kletno is a tiny 'one-street' hamlet stretching along the road for over 3km. Its fame, however, is greater than its size would suggest, for Poland's most beautiful cave is near here. It was discovered accidentally in 1966 during marble quarrying. Bones of the cave bear, which lived here during the last ice age, were found and gave the place its name – the Jaskinia Niedźwiedzia, or the **Bear's Cave**. Today five species of bats plus some insects inhabit the cave.

A small 400m section of the 3km labyrinthine corridors and chambers, with stalactites and stalagmites, was opened in 1977. You enter the cave through a pavilion which houses a snack bar and a small exhib-ition focusing on the cave's history. The humidity inside the cave is nearly 100% and the temperature 6°C all year – so come pre-pared.

The cave is open February to April 10 am to 5.40 pm, May to August 9 am to 4.40 pm, and September to November 10 am to 5.40 pm. It's closed on Monday and Thursday. Visits are by tours (in Polish only), in groups of up to 15 people. The tour takes about 40 minutes and costs US$4 (US$2.50 for students). The cave is popular and may be swamped with school excursions, especially in late spring/early summer. It's recommended to call the cave management in advance on ☎ 14 12 50 to check the situation and book if necessary.

There's an all-year *youth hostel* at the lower end of Kletno, 4km down the road from the cave.

Getting There & Away

There's one seasonal bus (May to mid-October) from Bystrzyca Kłodzka to Kletno (38km) via Lądek-Zdrój and Stronie Śląskie. The bus terminates at the upper end of Kletno, at the tourist car park (a stall sells snacks here in summer), about 1.5km below the cave.

There are no direct buses from Kłodzko to Kletno. If you don't mind walking, you can easily get by bus to Stronie Śląskie (regular transport) and walk 9km to the cave by the yellow trail (2½ hours). If this is too much for you, take the bus to Bolesławów (one morning departure only), get off at Stara Morawa and walk the re-maining 5km.

You can also get to the cave by walking from Międzygórze (see that section for details).

LĄDEK-ZDRÓJ
- **pop 7000**   ☎ 074

Lądek-Zdrój ('Lon-dek Zdroo-y') sits at the foot of the Góry Złote (Golden Mountains) on the eastern edge of the Kłodzko Valley. It's one of the oldest spas in Poland (*zdrój* means spa). The earliest records of local mineral springs date back to the 13th

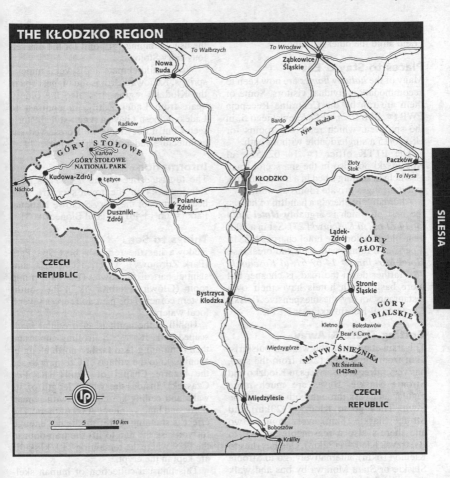

THE KŁODZKO REGION

To Wałbrzych

To Wrocław

Nowa Ruda

Ząbkowice Śląskie

Radków

Bardo

Nysa Kłodzka

Wambierzyce

GÓRY STOŁOWE

Karłów

GÓRY STOŁOWE NATIONAL PARK

KŁODZKO

Paczków

Złoty Stok

To Nysa

Kudowa-Zdrój

Łężyce

Nachod

Polanica-Zdrój

Lądek-Zdrój

GÓRY ZŁOTE

Duszniki-Zdrój

CZECH REPUBLIC

Zieleniec

Stronie Śląskie

GÓRY BIALSKIE

Bystrzyca Kłodzka

Kletno

Bolesławów

Bear's Cave

Międzygórze

MASYW ŚNIEŻNIKA

Mt Śnieżnik (1425m)

CZECH REPUBLIC

Międzylesie

0   5   10 km

Boboszów

Králíky

SILESIA

century, and by the end of the 15th century the first bathing facilities were built. Later on Lądek acquired competitors at the other end of the valley, such as Duszniki and Kudowa, but it continued to develop and today it's an important spa.

Things to See

The town consists of two distinct parts. Its western sector is a typical old market town complete with the familiar **Rynek**. Two sides of the square are relatively well pre-served and feature some fine 17th and 18th century baroque houses. The town hall was rebuilt in the 19th century and lost much of its grace.

The eastern half of the town, 1km away, is the spa proper, which is where tourists gather. Many of the sanatoria and holiday homes date from the postwar period, though older buildings can still be found. Of those, the most impressive is the **Wojciech** of 1678, reminiscent of a Turkish bath. With substantial neo-baroque decoration added in the 19th century, it looks extravagantly grand amid the other buildings.

Places to Stay & Eat

Many of the *holiday homes* are now keen to accommodate individual visitors. Some of them are run by the Centralna Recepcja FWP (☎ 14 62 72), ul Paderewskiego 5, in the spa area, which rents out rooms for US$10/15 a single/double without bath.

The PTTK office (☎ 14 62 55), ul Kościuszki 36, also in the spa sector, may also help in finding a bed in a holiday home, and it arranges private rooms as well.

Alternatively, there's a handful of hotels, the best of which is arguably *Hotel Lido* (☎ *14 71 65, ul Kościuszki 23*). Set in a 100-year-old mansion, the hotel charges US$15 a person in rooms with bath and breakfast. *Hotel Mir-Jan* (☎ *14 67 61, ul Kościuszki 78*), farther down the road, is cheaper but more basic. Both hotels have their own restaurants, or try the inexpensive *Polska Chata* on ul Kościuszki near PTTK.

Getting There & Away

The train station, on the western outskirts, 1km from the Rynek (2km from the spa), has very infrequent services to Kłodzko and Stronie Śląskie. Buses are much more regular and pass through both parts of the town. They go to Kłodzko (23km) and Stronie Śląskie (8km) every hour or two and there's also a reasonable service to Bystrzyca Kłodzka (22km). One bus runs to Kletno (16km); alternatively, go to Stronie Śląskie or Stara Morawa by bus and walk the remaining distance to the cave.

KUDOWA-ZDRÓJ
- **pop 11,000**   ☎ 074

There are three popular spas west of Kłodzko: Polanica-Zdrój, Duszniki-Zdrój and Kudowa-Zdrój. The closest, Polanica, is the youngest and perhaps least attractive. The next one, Duszniki, has some historic sights (including the Rynek, the Church of SS Peter and Paul, and the old paper mill, now the Museum of the Paper Industry). Finally, the last resort, Kudowa, is possibly the most pleasant and popular, and it's also the usual jumping-off point for the marvellous Góry Stołowe.

With a mild climate and several mineral springs, Kudowa-Zdrój is the biggest spa in the Kłodzko region. It's also the oldest, apart from Lądek-Zdrój. In contrast to Lądek, it doesn't have a rynek-style historic sector but it does have well preserved spa architecture and a pleasant spa park.

Information

The tourist office (☎ 66 13 87) is at ul Zdrojowa 44 in the town's centre. The headquarters of the Góry Stołowe National Park (☎ 66 13 46) are at ul Słoneczna 31.

Things to See

Kudowa has the region's best **Spa Park** (Park Zdrojowy), which occupies a substantial part of the town. The **main pump room** (Główna Pijalnia) is in the southeastern corner of the park and serves several local waters.

Uphill to the north is an irregular landscaped park. It's worth strolling about and then continuing 1km farther north along ul Moniuszki to the village of Czermna to see the bizarre **Chapel of Skulls** (Kaplica Czaszek). Inside, the whole length of its walls and ceiling are covered with human skulls and bones – about 3000 of them. The effect is stunning, but if this is not enough for you, ask the nun to lift the trap-door in the floor where the remaining 21,000 skulls are kept in the crypt.

This unusual collection of human skeletons was initiated in 1776 by the local parish priest, Tomasek, a Czech by origin. Within 18 years, he and the grave-digger Langer, succeeded in accumulating about 25,000 human remains. The cholera epidemic and numerous wars contributed greatly in obtaining such an impressive quantity of material. In the glass case to the left of the altar, you can admire the skulls of the authors of the enterprise. The chapel is open daily (except Monday in the off-season) 10 am to 1 pm and 2 to 5 pm (on Sunday 2 to 5 pm only).

Places to Stay & Eat

Like most resorts of this sort, Kudowa has extensive accommodation, including six hotels, a dozen holiday homes, another dozen pensions and a number of private rooms. The tourist office is likely to inform you about the options, and the PTTK office (☎ 66 11 62), ul Zdrojowa 42A, may help in booking. It also deals with private rooms, which are among the cheapest places in town (about US$5 to US$8 per head).

As for hotels, one of the cheapest is *Hotel Sportowy* (☎ 66 17 08, *ul Łąkowa 12*), 1km south of the centre (just off the road heading to the Czech border). It charges US$18 for doubles with toilet and handbasin, and runs a *camp site* in the grounds in summer. Among the best places are *Hotel Kosmos* (☎ 66 15 11, *ul Buczka 8A*) and *Hotel Gwarek* (☎ 66 18 90, *ul Słowackiego 10*). All three hotels have their own eating facilities.

Pensions include *Pensjonat Kaprys* (☎ 66 16 63, *ul Sikorskiego 2*), *Pensjonat Lucyna* (☎ 66 15 70, *ul Okrzei 6*), *Pensjonat Małgosia* (☎ 66 16 13, *ul Mickiewicza 6*) and *Pensjonat Scallano* (☎ 66 18 67, *ul Sikorskiego 6*). All are reasonably cheap.

Getting There & Away

Train The train station (the terminus of the line) is a long way south of the town and isn't much use unless you want to go a good distance, eg to Warsaw (two trains daily). To Kłodzko and Wrocław it's better to go by bus.

Bus Buses depart from ul 1 Maja in the town's centre. There's frequent transport to Kłodzko (34km) and regular services throughout the day to Wrocław (124km). There are three buses daily to Wałbrzych (94km).

For the Góry Stołowe National Park, there are half a dozen buses a day to Karłów, which pass by the turn-off to Błędne Skały. In the high season, there are also private minibuses.

One morning bus daily (except Sunday) comes through from Kłodzko and goes across the Czech border to Náchod (see the Kłodzko section). Alternatively, go by local bus (or walk) to the border (3km), cross it on foot to Náchod, 2km behind the frontier, from where there are onward buses and trains.

GÓRY STOŁOWE

The Góry Stołowe (literally, the Table Mountains; 'Goo-ri Sto-wo-veh') are among the most spectacular ranges of all the Sudetes. Lying roughly 10km north-east of Kudowa-Zdrój, they are almost as flat-topped as their name suggests. However, from the main plateau rise smaller 'tables' which are the remnants of the eroded upper layer of the mountains. Fantastic rock formations are scattered on the tops of these 'islands', as well as all over the main plateau. This magical landscape was created when soft sandstone, the dominant material of the formation, was eroded, leaving harder rocks behind. Lush vegetation adds more colour to the rocks.

In 1994 the whole area became the Góry Stołowe National Park (Park Narodowy Gór Stołowych) which covers 63 sq km. The highlights of the park are the Szczeliniec Wielki and the Błędne Skały.

Information

The park's headquarters in Kudowa-Zdrój can provide information. Whether you hike in the mountains or explore them by car, the *Góry Stołowe* map (scale 1:60,000) is a great help. It has all the walking routes and the important rocks individually marked as well as detailed plans of the Szczeliniec and the Błędne Skały. If you can't get this map, buy a copy of the more general *Ziemia Kłodzka* map (scale 1:90,000), which covers the Góry Stołowe but in less detail.

Szczeliniec Wielki

The Szczeliniec Wielki is the highest outcrop of the whole range (919m). From a distance, it looks like a high plateau adorned with pinnacles, rising abruptly from fields and forests. The most popular way to the top is from Karłów, a small village about 1km south of the plateau from where a short road leads to the foothills. You then ascend 682 stone steps (built in 1790) to a PTTK hostel on the top – it takes about half an hour to get there. The hostel is not for overnight stays; it's only used during the day as a café.

From the hostel, a trail skirts the cliff (excellent views) before turning inland. The 'Long Steps' take you down to the 'Devils' Kitchen' from where, after passing 'Hell' and 'Purgatory', you go up to 'Heaven', which is another viewpoint. Whatever the nicknames say, however, it feels as though you are wandering through the ruins of a mysterious ancient castle, the rocks appearing to be artificially shaped into enormous geometrical blocks.

The trail continues to two more viewpoints on the opposite side of the plateau and winds back to the hostel, passing a string of rocks formed in a wild array of shapes.

The whole loop takes about an hour, including scenic stops. You can visit the place at any time; in summer a ticket desk opens and charges a small admission fee.

Błędne Skały

Some 4km west as the crow flies, the Błędne Skały (literally, the Erratic Boulders) are another impressive sight. These are hundreds of monstrous boulders in vaguely geometric shapes that make a vast stone labyrinth. A trail runs between the rocks, which are so close together in places that you'll find you have to squeeze through sideways.

An hour is enough to do the loop, stopping to take pictures. As in Szczeliniec, a small entrance fee is charged in summer and there's a café by the entrance, but you can visit the place whenever you wish. Some adventurous trekkers come here in the middle of winter and dig their way through snow which in places can be chest-deep.

The Błędne Skały are 3.5km off the Kudowa-Karłów road, linked to it by a narrow, paved side road (there's no public transport). The turn-off is 7km from Kudowa (6km from Karłów). There is a red hiking trail between the Szczeliniec and the Błędne Skały.

Places to Stay & Eat

The usual jumping-off point is Kudowa-Zdrój, but you can stay and eat closer to the mountains. Karłów, the closest village to Szczeliniec, has several places to stay and eat, including the cheap *Hotel Karłów* and *Restauracja pod Mamutem*. Numerous stalls open in summer and serve fast food. Nearby to the north of Szczeliniec, in the village of Pasterka, there's a friendly *PTTK hostel* which is open all year and provides simple meals.

Getting There & Away

The Table Mountains cover a fairly small area, and a day trip is enough for visiting the two highlights. There are half a dozen buses a day from Kudowa-Zdrój to Karłów (13km), though some of these buses run in summer only and not on weekends. They go along the Road of the Hundred Bends, which snakes spectacularly through the forest and has virtually no straight sections. There are also private minibuses from Kudowa to the Table Mountains; they pick up passengers at the bus terminal.

A private means of transport is a great bonus. You can drive or ride to within a short distance of the attractions and, additionally, enjoy the Road of the Hundred Bends at your own pace.

WAMBIERZYCE

A small village at the north-eastern foot of the Table Mountains, Wambierzyce ('Vahm-byeh-zhi-tseh') is an important pilgrimage site and one of the oldest. Legend has it that in 1218 a blind peasant recovered his sight after praying to a statue of the Virgin Mary, which had been placed in a hollow lime-tree trunk. A wooden chapel was built on the site of the miracle and later replaced with a church. The fame of the place spread, and a large, two-towered basilica was erected in 1695-1711, but it collapsed shortly after its completion, except for its façade. Immediately afterwards a new sanctuary was built using the surviving Renaissance façade, and that's the church which stands to this day, more or less unchanged.

The largest numbers of pilgrims arrive on 8 July, 15 August and 8 September, and on the nearest Sunday to those dates.

Things to See

A wide flight of 33 steps (Christ was 33 when he was crucified) leads to the 50m-wide façade of the **church**, its palatial appearance emphasised by the absence of towers. The side entrance takes you into the square cloister running around the church, which is lined with chapels and Stations of the Cross, and adorned with paintings and votive offerings.

The church proper, in the centre of the complex, is laid out on two ellipses, with the main one being the nave and the other the chancel, each topped with a painted dome. The baroque décor includes an elaborate pulpit and four side altars. In the presbytery behind an ornamental grille of 1725, the florid high altar displays the miraculous miniature figure (only 28cm high) of the Virgin Mary with Child.

The eastern part of the village and the surrounding hills are dotted with chapels, gates, grottoes, sculptures etc, representing the **Stations of the Cross**. The Calvary, established in the late 17th century, was modelled on the one in Jerusalem and was subsequently developed to include 79 stations.

East of the church, on ul Objazdowa, is the **Szopka**, a set of mechanised Nativity scenes (open 10 am to 1 pm and 2 to 4 pm except Monday). The main scene, representing Jesus' birth in Bethlehem, includes 800 tiny figurines (all carved of limewood), 300 of which can move. Other scenes portray the Crucifixion, the Last Supper and the Massacre of the Innocents. The Szopka was made by local artist Longinus Wittig (1824-95); it took him 28 years.

Places to Stay & Eat

There's the basic *Hotel Turystyczny* on the main square, which has its own restaurant downstairs, and there are a few more simple places to eat around.

Getting There & Away

There are several buses from Kłodzko, Polanica-Zdrój and Nowa Ruda. Wambierzyce is not on a railway line.

WAŁBRZYCH
* **pop 140,000** ☎ **074**

The largest city of Lower Silesia after Wrocław, Wałbrzych ('Vahlb-zhihk') is an important industrial and mining centre. It's a heavily polluted city with few tourist attractions. If you are passing through, you may want to have a look at the arcaded baroque houses in the Rynek, the neoclassical church nearby and the regional museum at ul 1 Maja 9 with its geology and porcelain collections. However, the major tourist sight is the Książ castle (see the following section) on the northern outskirts of the city.

If you need more information, the tourist office (☎ 220 00) is at Rynek 9. If staying overnight, the cheapest placc is the all-year *youth hostel* (☎ 779 42, ul Marconiego 1), while at the top you have *Hotel Sudety* (☎ 774 31, ul Parkowa 15), and there are several options in between. Being the main city in the region, Wałbrzych has good transport connections by both train and bus.

KSIĄŻ
☎ **074**

With its 415 rooms, Książ ('Ksyonsh') is the largest **castle** in Silesia. It was built in the late 13th century by the Silesian Piast Prince Bolko I of Świdnica but continuously enlarged and remodelled until well into the 20th century. It's thus an amalgam of styles from Romanesque onwards.

During WWII Hitler planned to use the castle as one of his shelters and a huge bunker was hewn out of the rock directly beneath the courtyard. Predictably, the castle itself was stripped of its valuable art collection. The Soviets used it as a barracks until 1949, after which it was more or less abandoned for 20 years. Finally, the authorities set about restoring it and turned it into a museum (open May to September, Tuesday to Friday 10 am to 5 pm, Saturday and Sunday 10 am to 6 pm; in April and October it closes one hour earlier; and from November to March it opens Tuesday to Sunday 10 am to 3 pm).

Approaching the castle from the car park, you will pass near the **viewpoint**; it's just to the left past a large, decorative, freestanding gate. Seen from the lookout, the castle, majestically perched on a steep hill amid lush woods, looks pretty impressive. Its central portion with three massive arcades is the oldest. The eastern part (to the right) is an 18th century baroque addition, while the western segment with two corner towers was only built in 1908-23, in neo-Renaissance style. At about the same time the top of the main **tower** was added; it's open to visitors.

The castle's showpiece is the **Maximilian Hall**, built in the first half of the 18th century. It's the largest room in the castle and the only one restored to its original form, including the painted ceiling (1733) which depicts mythological scenes.

The 12 terraced **gardens** on the slopes around the castle were laid out gradually as the medieval fortifications were dismantled, from the 17th century on.

A five minute walk east of the castle is a **stud farm** (☎ 242 94), once the castle stables, which can be visited. It offers riding holidays and hires horses.

Places to Stay & Eat

Some of the outbuildings in the castle complex accommodate *Hotel Książ* (☎ 43 27 98). There are some budget doubles with shared facilities for US$14, but most rooms have private bath and cost US$17 to US$40 a single, US$27 to US$55 a double. There's a reasonably priced *restaurant* in the castle and a couple of *snack bars* in the car park.

Getting There & Away

The castle is right on the northern administrative boundaries of Wałbrzych, about 8km from the centre. You can get to it from Wałbrzych by the hourly No 8 city bus which takes you to the entrance. Alterna-tively, bus No 31 plies the Wałbrzych-Świdnica route every 20 minutes (every half-hour on Sunday), and will let you off on the main road near the car park, a 10 minute walk to the castle.

ŚWIDNICA
• **pop 65,000**   ☎ **074**

The second-wealthiest medieval town of Silesia after Wrocław, Świdnica ('Shveed-nee-tsah') was founded in the 12th century, and in 1290 became the capital of yet another of the myriad Silesian Piast principalities, the Duchy of Świdnica-Jawor. Unlike its neighbours, it didn't accept the sovereignty of Bohemia and only fell under its rule after the local Piast line died out in 1392. The Duchy of Świdnica-Jawor was one of the most powerful and largest, thanks essentially to its two gifted rulers: Bolko I, who founded it, and his grandson Bolko II, who significantly extended it.

The capital itself was a flourishing commercial centre, well known for its beer, which was served on the tables of Prague, Buda and Kraków. With 6000 inhabitants and 1000 houses by the end of the 14th century, it was one of the largest Polish towns, though in administrative terms it was by then part of Bohemia.

The town's heyday continued right up to the outbreak of the Thirty Years' War (1618-48). By 1648 the population of Świdnica had dropped to 200, the lowest in its history. It has never managed to become a city, remaining one of the many towns of its size in Silesia, way behind its former rival Wrocław. Świdnica escaped major damage in WWII and has some important historic buildings. It's an agreeable place for a short stop, and certainly a more pleasant jumping-off point for Książ castle than Wałbrzych.

Things to See

Świdnica's **Rynek** has everything from baroque to postwar architecture, the cumulative effect of rebuilding after successive fires and the damage caused by Austrian, Prussian and Napoleonic sieges. Most of the façades

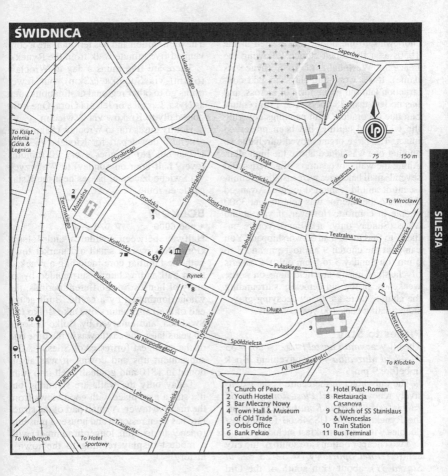

ŚWIDNICA

Map legend:
1 Church of Peace
2 Youth Hostel
3 Bar Mleczny Nowy
4 Town Hall & Museum of Old Trade
5 Orbis Office
6 Bank Pekao
7 Hotel Piast-Roman
8 Restauracja Casanova
9 Church of SS Stanislaus & Wenceslas
10 Train Station
11 Bus Terminal

Map labels: To Książ, Jelenia Góra & Legnica; To Wrocław; To Kłodzko; To Wałbrzych; To Hotel Sportowy; Saperów; Kościelna; Łukasińskiego; Chrobrego; 1 Maja; Konopnickiej; Folwarczna; Muzealna; Żeromskiego; Grodzka; Siostrzana; Franciszkańska; Getta; 1 Maja; Teatralna; Wrocławska; Kotlarska; Bohaterów; Pułaskiego; Rynek; Budowlana; Łukowa; Różana; Długa; Kolejowa; Al Niepodległości; Trybunalska; Spółdzielcza; Al Niepodległości; Westerplatte; Wałbrzyska; Lelewela; Nauczycielska; Traugutta

0   75   150 m

SILESIA

have been thoroughly revamped over recent years, giving the square a pleasant air.

The **town hall** dates from the 1710s, and though well kept it looks a bit squat, lacking its tower which collapsed in 1967. Inside is the **Museum of Old Trade** (Muzeum Dawnego Kupiectwa), open Tuesday to Friday 10 am to 3 pm, Saturday and Sunday 11 am to 5 pm.

The parish **Church of SS Stanislaus and Wenceslas** (Kościół Św Stanisława i Wacława), east of the Rynek, is a massive Gothic stone building whose façade is adorned with four elegant 15th century doorways and an 18m-high window. The tower was completed in 1565 and is 103m high – the tallest in the country after that of the basilica in Częstochowa (106m). The spacious interior has the familiar Gothic structure but, as usual, has been filled with ornate baroque decoration and furnishings. Six huge paintings that hang high up in the nave seem thoroughly at home in this lofty interior.

SILESIA

The **Church of Peace** (Kościół Pokoju), a short walk to the north, was erected in the 1650s as a Protestant church following the Peace of Westphalia of 1648 (hence its name). It's a wood-and-clay shingled construction laid out in the form of a cross, and has no less than 28 doors. The 17th century baroque decoration, with paintings covering the walls and ceiling, has been preserved intact. The large organ proved unreliable so another one was added above the high altar. Along the walls, two storeys of galleries and several small balconies were installed, reminiscent of an old-fashioned theatre. Arranged this way, the interior was able to seat 3500 people in comfort. However, if you attend Mass (Sunday only, at 10 am), you're unlikely to find more than 50 worshippers. You can visit the church 9 am to 1 pm and 3 to 5 pm (on Sunday 3 to 5 pm only). Concerts of classical music are held here on some weekends. In the old cemetery surrounding the church, there are many decaying gravestones dating back 100 years or more.

Places to Stay

The all-year *youth hostel* (☎ 52 04 80, ☎ 53 71 48, ul Muzealna 4) is convenient. Book in before 9 pm.

The only hotel in the centre is the extensively renovated *Hotel Piast-Roman* (☎ 52 13 93, fax 52 30 76, ul Kotlarska 11), just off the Rynek. It costs US$48/60 for singles/doubles with bath, breakfast included.

Two cheaper options are south of the city centre. *Hotel Sportowy* (☎ 52 25 32, ul Śląska 31), about 1km south of the Old Town, offers doubles/triples without bath for US$15/20. Slightly better but less convenient is *Hotel Alex* (☎ 52 54 32, Polna Droga 9), off the Wałbrzych road. It has doubles with shower (but shared toilet) for US$20 and doubles with bath for US$25.

Places to Eat

The restaurant of *Hotel Piast* is a reliable choice. Alternatively, try *Restauracja Casanova*, on the Rynek. For something really cheap, go to *Bar Mleczny Nowy (ul Grodzka 7)*.

Getting There & Away

The train station and bus terminal are a convenient five minute walk from the Rynek.

There are five trains a day to Wrocław (61km) via Sobótka (23km), but fewer trains go to other regional destinations such as Nysa, Legnica or Jelenia Góra. One train goes daily to Kraków via Oświęcim.

Hourly buses run to Wrocław (53km) and several a day depart for Kłodzko (63km). Urban bus No 31 goes every 20 minutes (every half-hour on Sunday) to Wałbrzych via Świebodzice and passes near the Książ castle en route.

BOLKÓW
- **pop 6000**   ☎ 075

Halfway between Świdnica and Jelenia Góra, Bolków is a small old market town with the familiar core including a rynek, a town hall and a church, surrounded by an array of houses from different periods, the whole dominated by a **castle**. Built at the end of the 13th century by Duke Bolko I of Świdnica, and enlarged by Bolko II some 50 years later, the castle was at the time one of the strongest fortresses of Silesia. After subsequent ups and downs, it was abandoned in 1810 and gradually fell into ruin.

Today only the walls are standing, but it's still a nice place with good views from the massive tower. A small part of the structure has been restored and houses a museum (open 9 am to 3 pm, longer in summer) with a modest display relating to the town's history.

Places to Stay & Eat

The *youth hostel* (☎ 741 32 11, ul Księcia Bolka 8) opens from 1 July to 20 August.

Hotel Panorama (☎ 741 34 44, ☎ 741 45 84, ul Mickiewicza 6) is a small private pension with neat singles/doubles without bath for US$10/15 and doubles with shower for US$18. There's a good view over the castle from the windows.

Hotel Bolków (☎ 741 39 95, fax 741 39 96, ul Sienkiewicza 17) offers doubles with bath ranging in standards and price from US$22 to US$40. Its restaurant is good if not the cheapest. For cheaper meals, there are a few basic eateries around the Rynek.

Getting There & Away
The train station is over 1km north-east of the centre but you can get around more easily by bus. From the main bus stop at the edge of the Old Town, buses go to Jelenia Góra (31km), Kamienna Góra (19km), Świdnica (33km) and Wrocław (79km) regularly every hour or two.

KAMIENNA GÓRA
• pop 24,000   ☎ 075

Kamienna Góra is a grubby industrial town 20km south of Bolków. It developed as a textile centre for over 500 years, and the tradition continues. Today it's the most important producer of linen in Lower Silesia.

The **Museum of the Silesian Textile Industry** (Muzeum Tkactwa Dolnośląskiego) at Rynek 11 documents the history of weaving in the region (open 10 am to 4 pm except Monday). You may also want to visit the town's two **churches**, SS Peter and Paul and the former Protestant church. However, the main reason for coming here lies 7km away in Krzeszów (see the following section), for which Kamienna Góra is the gateway.

Places to Stay & Eat
The small private pension *Hotel Pan Tadeusz* (☎ 744 52 27, ul Legnicka 2E), 1km north from the Rynek, has doubles with bath for US$25. Another pension-like facility, *Hotel Krokus* (☎/fax 744 35 14, ul Parkowa 1B), in the centre, costs US$28/38 a single/double with bath and breakfast.

Hotel Karkonosze (☎/fax 744 22 30, ul Jana Pawła II 33), opposite the train station, offers singles/doubles with bath for US$30/40, and also has some rooms without bath for US$20/30; breakfast is included in the price. The hotel has its own restaurant, or you could try the little *Kawiarnia u Leszka* (ul Stara 2), near the Rynek, which has good food, generous portions and reasonable prices.

Getting There & Away
The train and bus stations are next to each other on the western outskirts of the town, a 10 minute walk from the centre. You won't get far by train but buses travel fairly regularly around the region. There are departures every hour or two to Jelenia Góra (38km), Bolków (19km), Wałbrzych (19km) and Krzeszów (7km).

KRZESZÓW
If you plan on visiting just a few of the best baroque churches in Poland, Krzeszów ('Kzheh-shoof') should be included on your list. This obscure village near the Czech border, well off the main roads and tourist routes, has not one but two extraordinary churches.

Krzeszów was founded in 1242 by Princess Anna, the widow of Henryk Pobożny (Henry the Pious), who was killed a year earlier in the Battle of Legnickie Pole. The princess donated the land to the Benedictine order from Bohemia, but the monks showed little interest and in 1289 relinquished the property to Prince Bolko I, the grandson of Henryk. Bolko, the wise ruler of the newly created Duchy of Świdnica-Jawor, granted the land to the Cistercians, who were by then well established in Poland and swiftly expanding. The monks soon built their monastery, and the donor of the land was buried in the newly constructed church in 1301. The church became the mausoleum of the Świdnica-Jawor dukes until the line died out in the late 14th century.

Repeatedly destroyed by various invaders, from the Hussites (1426) to the Swedes (1633), the monastery was systematically rebuilt and extended. At the end of the 17th century a fair-sized church was raised and some 40 years later it was followed by another one, twice the size and even more splendid.

Despite the fact that the Cistercian order was secularised in 1810 and the abbey abandoned for over a century, the two churches survive today virtually unchanged.

Things to See

The older one, **St Joseph's Church** (Kościół Św Józefa), was built in 1690-96. From the outside, the building looks a bit plain, largely because its towers collapsed soon after they were built and were never reconstructed. The interior, in contrast, is impressive, with frescoes covering the whole of the vault, the chancel and 10 side chapels. These wall paintings are the work of Michael Willmann and are considered to be among his greatest achievements. In some 50 scenes, the life of St Joseph is portrayed, with the Holy Trinity on the vault of the chancel. Painted at the end of the 17th century, some of the frescoes are unusually free in their execution, strangely evocative of the Impressionist style of two centuries later. Willmann left his own image on the walls – he is standing at the door of an inn painted on the wall in the right-hand chapel just before the presbytery. Also note the elaborate rococo pulpit and a tiny organ.

The **Church of the Assumption** (Kościół Wniebowzięcia NMP) is much more developed architecturally, and at 118m in length is much bigger. Its twin-towered façade (70m high) is elaborately decorated from top to bottom and rich in detail. You can go up one of the towers for a sweeping view.

The lofty interior is exceptionally coherent stylistically, as the church was built (1728-35) from scratch and not adapted from an earlier structure as was usually the case. Furthermore, all the decoration and furnishings date from the short period of the church's construction and hardly anything was added later. The high altar, with the huge (7 x 3.5m) background painting by Peter Brandl depicting the Assumption of Virgin Mary, displays the miraculous icon of the Madonna, while at the opposite end of the church, the organ is regarded as the most splendid instrument in Silesia. The frescoes on the vault are the bravura work of George Wilhelm Neunhertz, the grandson and pupil of Michael Willmann.

Behind the high altar is the **mausoleum** of the Świdnica Piasts, built as an integral part of the church (but you get in by a sep-arate entrance from the outside). It's in the form of two circular chambers, each topped with a frescoed cupola and linked with a decorative arcade. The mausoleum holds the 14th century tombstones of Prince Bolko I and his grandson Prince Bolko II, while the ashes of the two dukes and other rulers of the line have been deposited in the pillar in between. The frescoes, like those in the church, were executed by Neunhertz and show scenes from the abbey's history.

The abbey occupies the centre of the village, with the main church sitting in the middle of the grounds and the other one just 50m to the north. Between the two churches is the information office, which sells brochures about the place and tickets to the tower and mausoleum (the churches can be visited free of charge from 9 am to 5 pm except during Mass). The monastic building (off limits) beside the larger church is now occupied by the Benedictines, who returned to Krzeszów in 1919.

There's also the **Way of the Cross** in Krzeszów, dating from the beginning of the 18th century, and consisting of a score of chapels scattered over the surrounding countryside to the west of the abbey.

Getting There & Away

The obvious jumping-off point for Krzeszów is Kamienna Góra, 7km away, with buses every hour or two on weekdays, but the service is poorer on weekends.

JELENIA GÓRA
• pop 94,000　☎ 075

Set in a valley surrounded by mountain ranges, Jelenia Góra is a nice place with much historic character. Unlike many other towns in Silesia, it survived WWII pretty much undamaged; and as well as its architectural inheritance, it has the pleasant Cieplice spa (see the following section) at its southern end. Farther south are the Karkonosze Mountains, for which Jelenia Góra is a convenient starting point.

The town was founded in 1108 by King Bolesław Krzywousty (Boleslaus the Wry-Mouthed) as one of his fortified border strongholds, and came under the rule of the powerful Duchy of Świdnica-Jawor. Gold-mining in the region gave way to glass production around the 15th century, but it was weaving that gave the town a solid economic base from the 16th century on, and its high-quality linen was exported all over Europe.

After WWII the city was further industrialised with diverse branches of light industry, but fortunately, that side of business is well away from the historical centre.

Information
Tourist Offices The regional tourist office (☎ 752 51 14, ☎/fax 752 40 54), ul 1 Maja 42, is open weekdays 8 am to 4 pm, Saturday 9 am to 1 pm. The city tourist office (☎ 767 69 25, fax 767 69 35), Plac Ratuszowy 2, is open weekdays 9 am to 6 pm, Saturday and Sunday 10 am to 2 pm. Both are helpful.

Money The Bank Pekao at Plac Wyszyńskiego 35 and Bank Zachodni at ul Bankowa both handle travellers cheque transactions and have useful ATMs. There's also a convenient ATM in the window of the Smok restaurant on the main square.

Things to See
The elongated **Rynek**, formally called Plac Ratuszowy, is lined with a harmonious group of historic houses; their unique charm is due to their ground-floor arcades, providing a covered passageway all around the square. The town hall on the square was built in the 1740s after its predecessor collapsed.

The **parish church**, off the central square, was erected in the 15th century, and the best-preserved relic from that time is the Gothic doorway in the southern entrance. The interior, with its powerful theatrical high altar, boasts mostly baroque furnishing and decoration.

There are two small chapels on ul 1 Maja: **St Anne's Chapel** (Kaplica Św Anny), which started life as a 15th century

defensive gate, and **St Mary's Chapel** (Kaplica NMP), built in 1738 and handed over to the Orthodox community after WWII.

About 100m farther down the street, the massive **Holy Cross Church** (Kościół Św Krzyża) is the most outstanding of the city's ecclesiastical buildings. Designed by a Swede and modelled on St Catherine's Church in Stockholm, it was built in the 1710s for the Lutheran congregation and is thought to be the biggest Protestant church in Silesia (it now serves the Catholic community). The three-storeyed galleries plus the ground floor accommodate 4000 people. The ceiling is embellished with illusionistic baroque paintings of scenes from the Old and New Testaments, while the ornate 1720 organ over the high altar is a magnificent piece of craftwork and sounds as good as it looks.

The city has a good **Regional Museum** (Muzeum Okręgowe), ul Matejki 28, renowned for its extensive collection of glass, dating from medieval times to the present day. Only a small part of the total of 5500 items (the largest collection in Poland) is on display. There are some amazing exhibits, including Art Nouveau pieces from the late 19th/early 20th centuries. One of the rooms has been arranged as a typical peasant cottage interior from the western Sudeten foothills, furnished and decorated as it might have been a century ago. The museum also has a large collection (over 1000 pieces) of old folk paintings on glass but it's not on permanent display. It's open Tuesday, Thursday and Friday 9 am to 3.30 pm, and Wednesday, Saturday and Sunday 9 am to 4.30 pm.

Special Events
The International Festival of Street Theatre is held in July. The Theatre Festival at the end of September has been taking place for over 20 years, and is the best established event in the city. It attracts theatres from all over Poland. Also in September is the International Organ Music Festival in the Holy Cross Church.

SILESIA

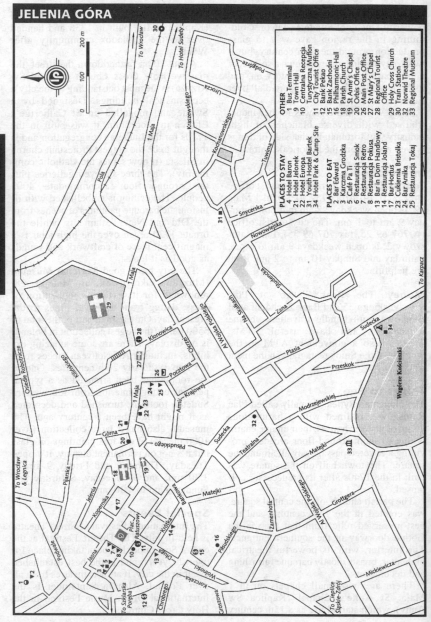

JELENIA GÓRA

0   100   200 m

To Wrocław

To Hotel Sudety

PLACES TO STAY
4   Hotel Baron
21   Hotel Jelonek
22   Hotel Europa
31   Youth Hostel Bartek
34   Hotel Park & Camp Site

PLACES TO EAT
2   Bar Edward
3   Karczma Grodzka
5   Café Pa Ti
6   Restauracja Smok
7   Restauracja Retro
8   Restauracja Pokusa
13   Bar in Dom Handlowy
14   Restauracja Joland
17   Bar Hortus
23   Cukiernia Bristolka
24   Bar Amika
25   Restauracja Tokaj

OTHER
1   Bus Terminal
9   Town Hall
10   Centralna Recepcja
     Turystyczna Muf/on
11   City Tourist Office
12   Bank Pekao
15   Bank Zachodni
16   Philharmonic Hall
18   Parish Church
19   St Anne's Chapel
20   Orbis Office
26   Main Post Office
27   St Mary's Chapel
28   Regional Tourist
     Office
29   Holy Cross Church
30   Train Station
32   Norwid Theatre
33   Regional Museum

Places to Stay

The city tourist office can provide detailed information on lodging options. The Centralna Recepcja Turystyczna Muflon (☎ 752 45 06, ☎/fax 752 31 63) next door can book accommodation for you in the city and the region.

The all-year *Youth Hostel Bartek* (☎ 752 57 46, ul Bartka Zwycięzcy 10) provides the 60 cheapest beds in town.

Among the hotels, one of the cheapest is *Hotel Park* (☎ 752 69 42, ul Sudecka 42), which has doubles/triples with bath for US$20/24. You can camp in its grounds (see the following Cieplice Śląskie-Zdrój section for another camp site).

Hotel Europa (☎ 764 72 31, fax 752 44 95, ul 1 Maja 16/18), in the city centre, has singles/doubles without bath (US$16/25) and with bath (US$30/50).

Cheaper but not as well located is *Hotel Sudety* (☎ 752 93 00, ul Krakowska 20), a five minute walk east of the train station. It costs US$13/22 a single/double without bath, US$24/40 with bath.

There are two charming and stylish small hotels in the centre. *Hotel Baron* (☎/fax 752 53 91, ☎/fax 752 33 51, ul Grodzka 4) is ideally located just off the Rynek. Its spacious singles/doubles/triples with bath cost US$45/60/70. Optional buffet breakfast will add US$7 per head. The newer *Hotel Jelonek* (☎ 764 65 41, ☎/fax 764 72 15, ul 1 Maja 5) is in a fine historic burgher's house. It offers singles/doubles for US$50/65 and more attractive double suites for US$80 to US$100 (choose a room facing the street). Prices are negotiable to some extent and include breakfast.

Less atmospheric is the large 340-bed, Orbis-operated *Hotel Jelenia Góra* (☎ 764 64 81, fax 752 62 69, ul Sudecka 63), which offers singles/doubles/suites for about US$100/120/180.

Places to Eat

Rock-bottom options include *Bar Arnika* (ul Pocztowa 8), *Bar Edward* at the PKS bus terminal, *Bar Hortus* (Plac Ratuszowy 34) and the *bor* on the top floor of Dom Handlowy on the corner of ul Długa and ul Krótka.

The western side of the Rynek is occupied by three restaurants, the *Smok*, *Retro* and *Pokusa*, all of which are OK and popular with visitors. But possibly a better place for a reasonably priced lunch or dinner is *Karczma Grodzka*, next door to Hotel Baron, which serves solid Polish food in beautiful surroundings. On the other side of the same hotel is the more upmarket *Café Pa Ti*, which is also good.

Other acceptable restaurants in the central area include *Restauracja Joland* (ul Krótka 23/24) for Polish cuisine and *Restauracja Tokaj* (ul Pocztowa 6) for Hungarian food.

For dessert, one of the best options is *Cukiernia Bristolka* (ul 1 Maja 18).

Getting There & Away

The train station is about 1km east of the Old Town, a 15 minute walk to the Rynek, while the vast bus terminal is on the northwestern edge of the town centre.

Buses are a better means of getting around the region than trains. Buses to Karpacz (24km), Szklarska Poręba (20km) and Bolków (31km) run every hour or so, and there's also reasonable transport to Kamienna Góra (38km) and Wrocław (117km).

There's a regular train service to Szklarska Poręba (32km) and Wrocław (126km), and a couple daily to Kraków (394km), Zielona Góra (191km) and Warsaw (516km).

There are buses in summer to Prague and Berlin. Contact the bus terminal for information.

CIEPLICE ŚLĄSKIE-ZDRÓJ
☎ 075

As its suffix 'Zdrój' suggests, Cieplice ('Cheh-plee-tseh') is a spa, one of the oldest in the region. The local sulphur hot springs have probably been used for a millennium and the first spa house was established as early as the 13th century. Later on, the town developed as a weaving centre and glass

SILESIA

producer. Only in the late 18th century were the curative properties of the springs recognised, paving the way for the building of the spa infrastructure. Set just 6km from Jelenia Góra, the spa was absorbed by the city in 1976 and is today a suburb within a single administrative area, yet it retains its distinctive atmosphere.

Information
The tourist office (☎ 755 88 44, ☎/fax 755 88 45) is on the central mall, Plac Piastowski 36. It's open weekdays 9 am to 5 pm, Saturday 10 am to 2 pm. In summer, it closes an hour later on weekdays, and also opens on Sunday 10 am to 2 pm.

Things to See
The town's core is made up by a **Spa Park** (Park Zdrojowy) with a **Spa Theatre** (Teatr Zdrojowy) built on its grounds. The theatre holds concerts and opera/operetta performances in summer.

The main mall, Plac Piastowski, is just to the north of the park. Roughly halfway along it stands the monumental **Schaffgotsch Palace**, built in the 1780s as a residence of the long-time owners of the town. These days it houses a high school.

At the western end of the mall is the 18th century **parish church**, the interior of which has baroque furnishings. The painting on the large high altar is by Michael Willmann, and three more canvases under the organ loft come from the same school. Should you wish to try the local waters, the **pump room** (pijalnia) is near the church on ul Ściegiennego and serves water from four of the eight springs that the town exploits.

South of the spa park is the Norwegian Park that holds the **Natural History Museum** (Muzeum Przyrodnicze). Its display of birds and butterflies from all over the world stems from the collection of the Schaffgotsch family, who established the museum in 1876.

Places to Stay & Eat
Hotel Pod Różami (☎ 755 14 53, Plac Piastowski 26) directly opposite the palace is OK as long as you don't need a private bath. It charges about US$10/14/18/20 a single/double/triple/quad, but in season it tends to push prices up and is often full. The best place is *Hotel Cieplice* (☎ 755 10 41, fax 755 13 41, ul Cervi 11), costing US$35/50 a single/double with bath and breakfast. Both hotels have their own restaurants, and there are more places to eat, including the charming *Zajazd pod Złotym Łukiem* behind the tourist office.

There's the good *Camping Słoneczna Polana* (☎ 755 25 66, ul Rataja 9), 1km west of the spa park. Open from 1 May to 30 September, it's run by a friendly Dutch couple, is well equipped with modern facilities and has a snack bar and bungalows. Dutch, English, French and German is spoken, and you can get information about the region.

Getting There & Away
Cieplice is served by frequent urban buses from Jelenia Góra. Bus Nos 4, 6, 7, 9, 13, 14 and 15 will deposit you at either the western or eastern end of Plac Piastowski. If you're heading for Hotel Cieplice, it's best to take bus No 9; for the camp site, take bus No 7 or 15.

KARPACZ
• pop 5600   ☎ 075
There are several mountain resorts along the foothills of the Karkonosze, of which Karpacz and Szklarska Poręba (see the next section in this chapter), on the eastern and western ends of the range, respectively, are the largest and have the best tourist facilities.

Karpacz sits on the slopes of Mt Śnieżka (1602m), the highest peak of the Sudetes. It's one of the most popular mountain resorts in Poland, as much for skiers in winter as for walkers in summer. This large village – it hardly has the appearance of a town – spreads over 3km along a winding road, with houses scattered across the slopes, without any obvious central area.

The eastern, lower part, known as Karpacz Dolny or Lower Karpacz, is more densely populated and has most of the accommodation and places to eat. At the far north-eastern end of this sector is the train station. The western part, the Karpacz Górny or Upper Karpacz, is just a collection of holiday homes. In the middle of the two districts is the bus terminal and Hotel Biały Jar. From this point several marked trails wind up the mountains. About 1km uphill from here is the lower station of the chairlift *(wyciąg krzesełkowy)* to Mt Kopa (1375m).

Information

The Centrum Informacji Turystycznej (☎/fax 761 97 16) is at ul Konstytucji 3 Maja 25A in Lower Karpacz. It's open weekdays 9 am to 4 pm, Saturday and Sunday to 1 pm (it may open one or two hours longer in the summer and winter seasons). The Bank Zachodni, ul Konstytucji 3 Maja 43, has an ATM.

Things to See & Do

Like most resorts of this kind, Karpacz is not a place to look for historical relics, though it does happen to have a curious architectural gem – the **Wang Chapel** (Świątynia Wang), the only Nordic Romanesque building in Poland. It was originally built at the turn of the 12th century on the bank of Lake Wang in southern Norway as one of about 400 of its sort (23 survive to this day).

By the 19th century the church was too small for the local congregation, and was offered for sale, to make way for a larger and better building. It was bought in 1841 by the Prussian King Friedrich Wilhelm IV, carefully dismantled piece by piece and brought to Berlin. It was then transported to Karpacz, meticulously reassembled over a period of two years and consecrated in the presence of the king himself. Not only is it the oldest church in the Sudetes, it's also the most elevated, at an altitude of 886m.

The church is made of hard Norwegian pine and put together without a single nail. It's surrounded by a cloister that helps to keep it warm. Part of the woodcarving is

original and preserved in excellent shape, particularly the carved doorways and the capitals of the pillars. The freestanding stone belfry was added later.

The church is in Upper Karpacz, just off the main road, and can be visited from 9 am to 6 pm (in winter it closes earlier) except for Sunday morning Mass. There is a taped commentary; German and English versions are available for groups of tourists.

Another peculiar sight, the **Museum of Toys** (Muzeum Zabawek), one of only two in Poland (the other is in Kielce), features a private collection of puppets, dolls, teddy bears etc assembled from all over the world by Henryk Tomaszewski, founder and longtime director of Wrocław Pantomime Theatre. It's in a former holiday home in Upper Karpacz, and is open 9 am to 4 pm, except Monday.

Karpacz is a good starting point for hiking (or skiing in winter). The village is bordered on the south by the Karkonosze National Park, an obvious destination for walkers. Most tourists aim for **Mt Śnieżka**, and there are half a dozen different trails leading there. The most popular routes originate from Hotel Biały Jar, and you can get to the top in three to four hours depending on the trail you choose. When planning a trip to Mt Śnieżka, try to include in your route two picturesque post-glacial lakes bordered by rocky cliffs, Wielki Staw and Mały Staw. A couple of trails pass near the lakes.

The fastest and most comfortable way of getting to Mt Śnieżka is by taking the **chairlift** to Mt Kopa, which will take you up 528m in 17 minutes for US$4 (US$5 return). The lift operates from 8 am to 5 pm (stops earlier in winter). From Mt Kopa, you can get to the top of Mt Śnieżka in less than an hour by the trail signposted in black.

Places to Stay & Eat

There's plenty of accommodation in Karpacz and it's easy to find a room, even in the high season. The town offers tourists about 12,000 beds, twice the number of its inhabitants. Apart from about 20 hotels,

SILESIA

there are over 170 holiday homes and pensions, and they all will be eager to put you up for the night. Locals also offer rooms in their homes – look for boards reading 'pokoje', 'noclegi' or 'zimmer frei', the latter demonstrating the increase in German tourism in the region.

In the season (summer or winter), most holiday homes and private houses will cost around US$7 to US$10 per bed in rooms without bath, US$8 to US$15 with bath; off season, it will be 20 to 40% cheaper. Hotels charge more, normally not less than US$30 a double.

The tourist office has a full list of accommodation options. Rooms in private houses and holiday homes can be arranged through some local travel agencies, including Karpacz (☎ 761 95 47) at ul Konstytucji 3 Maja 52, Edi-Tour (☎ 761 88 93) at ul Karkonoska 1 and Sudety (☎ 761 92 82) at ul Konstytucji 3 Maja 31. Zarząd Okręgu FWP (☎ 761 94 59) at ul Obrońców Pokoju 1 can arrange rooms in its holiday homes.

There are two camp sites in Karpacz: *Camping Nr 165 Pod Lipami (☎ 761 88 67, ☎ 761 93 16, ul Konstytucji 3 Maja 8)* near the train station and *Camping Nr 211 Pod Brzozami (☎ 761 91 65, ul Obrońców Pokoju 4)*. Both are open from June to September. The *Youth Hostel Liczyrzepa (☎ 761 92 90, ul Gimnazjalna 9)* is open year-round.

Karpacz's top-end accommodation includes *Hotel Ariston (☎ 761 95 12, ul Piastowska 2A)*, *Hotel Corum (☎ 761 85 33, ul Kościuszki 12)* and *Hotel Karkonosze (☎ 761 82 77, ul Wolna 4)*.

As with accommodation, eating is no problem in Karpacz. A variety of places, ranging from rudimentary roadside stands selling sausages to the dining rooms of holiday homes, open during the tourist season.

Getting There & Away
The train station, on the north-eastern outskirts of the resort, is of marginal interest as there are only two trains to Jelenia Góra. You can get there easily on one of the frequent buses which run along the main road, and you can pick them up at different points of the resort, the Wang Chapel included.

SZKLARSKA PORĘBA
• pop 8000   ☎ 075
Szklarska Poręba ('Shklah-skah Po-ren-bah') is the other major Karkonosze resort, this one being at the foot of Mt Szrenica (1362m). It's also spread wide over the hills, but has a definite centre along ul Jedności Narodowej skirting the Kamienna River. At the lower end of this 500m street is the bus terminal, while off the upper end is the train station.

Information
The local tourist office (☎ 717 24 94, ☎/fax 717 24 49), ul Jedności Narodowej 3, is open weekdays 8 am to 6 pm, Saturday and Sunday 9 am to 7 pm. The Bank Zachodni is at ul Jedności Narodowej 16, and there are half a dozen kantors around the centre.

Things to See & Do
The town has a few small museums, including the **Regional Museum** at ul 11 Listopada 23 and **Mineralogical Museum** at ul Kilińskiego 20, but it's the natural beauty of the region and its activities that attract most visitors. There's a chairlift to **Mt Szrenica** which takes you up 603m and deposits you at the top in about 25 minutes for US$5 (US$6 return). The lower chairlift station is about 1km south of the centre, uphill along ul Turystyczna.

There are several attractions within easy walking distance of Szklarska Poręba. The road to Jelenia Góra winds east in a beautiful valley along the Kamienna River. Some 3km down the road (or along the green trail on the opposite side of the river) you'll get to the 13m-high **Szklarka Waterfall** (Wodospad Szklarki). From here the blue trail heads up to the mountains and you can walk along it to Mt Szrenica in two to three hours.

The road that goes west from Szklarska Poręba to the Czech border in Jakuszyce passes the rocky cliffs called Krucze Skały

Griffin House, Old Town Square, Wrocław

Gothic cathedral in Wrocław

Old Town Square, Wrocław

Clock up some time at Kłodzko's regional museum

Chapel of Skulls near Kudowa-Zdrój

Vault frescoes, St Hedwig's church, Legnickie Pole

Neo-Gothic Church of SS Peter & Paul, Legnica

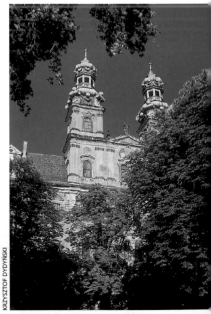

Lubiąż's colossal Cistercian Abbey

(Ravens' Rocks). About 500m farther on, a red trail branches off to the left. It's a 25 minute walk up the hill along this trail to the **Kamieńczyk Waterfall** (Wodospad Kamień-czyka), one of the prettiest and highest (27m) falls in the Sudetes. Continuing for about 1½ hours along the same trail you'll get to Mt Szrenica.

Places to Stay

There are plenty of options, including 10 hotels, 85 holiday homes, 50 pensions and 60 registered private room owners, provid-ing about 10,000 beds in all. The tourist office has all the listings and several local travel agents handle bookings. They include Karkonosze (☎ 717 23 93) at ul 1 Maja 1, Szrenica (☎ 717 22 51) at ul Jedności Naro-dowej 7 and WNT Travel (☎ 717 21 00) at ul Jedności Narodowej 22. Prices are much the same as in Karpacz (see that section).

Camp sites include the central *Camping Pod Mostem (☎ 717 30 62, ul Gimnazjalna 5)*, *Camping Pod Klonem (☎ 717 35 25, ul Armii Krajowej 2)* close to the train station and *Camping Nr 40 Południowy Stok (☎ 717 21 29, ul Batalionów Chłopskich 12)* farther from the centre. The all-year *Youth Hostel Wojtek (☎ 717 21 41, ul Pias-towska 1)* is a long way north-east of the centre.

Among the finer hotels are the stylish *Hotel Weneda (☎ 717 29 57, ul Wzgórze Paderewskiego 12)*, the Disneyland-like *Hotel Las (☎ 717 29 55, ul Turystyczna 8)*, *Hotel Górski Korvita (☎ 717 26 76, ul Par-tyzantów 8)* and *Hotel Olimp (☎ 717 23 42, ul 1 Maja 62)*.

Getting There & Away

Trains and buses run regularly to Jelenia Góra (20km). There are also two trains and two buses daily directly to Wrocław.

For the Czech Republic, take the bus to Jakuszyce (6km) and cross the border to Harrachov, the first Czech village, from where there are regular buses onwards. There are also direct buses (daily except weekends) from Szklarska Poręba to Jablonec and Liberec.

THE KARKONOSZE NATIONAL PARK

The Karkonosze National Park (Karkonos-ki Park Narodowy), just south of Karpacz and Szklarska Poręba, stretches up to the Czech border (which follows all the highest peaks of the Karkonosze). The 56 sq km park is a narrow belt that runs along the frontier for some 25km. On the other side, the Czech counterpart protects the southern part of the outcrop.

The range is divided by the Przełęcz Karkonoska (Karkonosze Pass, 1198m). The highest summit of the eastern section is Mt Śnieżka (1602m), while the western portion is crowned by Mt Wielki Szyszak (1509m).

Up to an altitude of about 1250m the park is predominantly spruce forest. Higher up are dwarf mountain pines and alpine vege-tation, which fade away to leave only mosses on the highest peaks.

Characteristic of the Karkonosze are *kotły*, or cirques – huge hollows carved by glaciers during the ice age and bordered with steep cliffs. There are six cirques on the Polish side of the range; the most spec-tacular are Kocioł Małego Stawu and Kocioł Wielkiego Stawu near Mt Śnieżka, and Śnieżne Kotły at the foot of Mt Wielki Szyszak.

The Karkonosze is known for its harsh climate, with heavy rainfall (snow in winter) and highly variable weather, and strong winds and mists possible at any time. Statistically, the best chances of good weather are in January, February, May and September. Higher up, there's snow on the ground for six months of the year.

The Karkonosze National Park is the most popular hiking territory in the Sudetes. The two main gateways are Karpacz and Szklarska Poręba, from where most tourists ascend Mt Śnieżka and Mt Szrenica, re-spectively. There's a restaurant, a chapel and a meteorological observatory on the top of Mt Śnieżka.

For longer walks, the best idea is to take the red trail that runs right along the ridge between the two peaks, with good views to

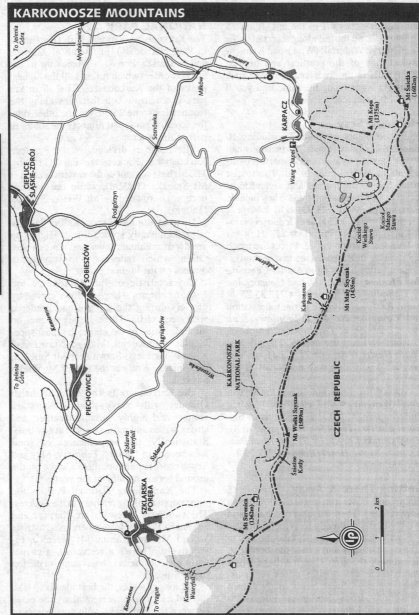

KARKONOSZE MOUNTAINS

SILESIA

To Jelenia Góra

Myslakowice

Lomnica

Milków

KARPACZ

Mt Śnieżka (1602m)

Mt Kopa (1375m)

Sosnówka

CIEPLICE ŚLĄSKIE-ZDRÓJ

Podgórzyn

Wang Chapel

Kocioł Małego Stawu

Kocioł Wielkiego Stawu

SOBIESZÓW

Kamienna

Podgórna

Jagniątków

Karkonosze Pass

Mt Mały Szyszak (1435m)

KARKONOSZE NATIONAL PARK

To Jelenia Góra

PIECHOWICE

Wrzosówka

CZECH REPUBLIC

Szklarka Waterfall

Szklarka

Mt Wielki Szyszak (1509m)

Śnieżne Kotły

SZKLARSKA PORĘBA

Mt Szrenica (1362m)

Kamienna

To Prague

Kamieńczyk Waterfall

2 km

0   1

both sides. The trail also passes along the upper edges of the kotły. You can walk the whole stretch in six to seven hours. If you start early enough, it's possible to do the Karpacz-Szklarska Poręba (or vice versa) trip within a day, preferably by using the chairlift to speed up the initial ascent.

You can break the walk at the Odrodzenie mountain refuge, roughly halfway between the two peaks, or in any other of the half-dozen refuges within the park. The

Samotnia refuge at Kocioł Małego Stawu is possibly the most amazing place of all. You can also shorten the trip by taking one of several trails that branch off downhill from the main red one at different points. Get a copy of the *Karkonoski Park Narodowy* or *Karkonosze* map. They come in different scales, produced by various map publishers. Take warm, waterproof clothes as the weather, as mentioned, is totally unpredictable.

Wielkopolska

Wielkopolska (literally, Great Poland) is the cradle of the Polish state, for it was here that the first recorded ruler, Duke Mieszko I, unified the scattered Slav tribes of the region into a single political unit in the second half of the 10th century. In 966 Mieszko was baptised, and Gniezno, where the event took place, became the capital.

Shortly after, the nearby town of Poznań took on a range of administrative and political functions, and came to be the main seat of Mieszko and his son and successor Bolesław Chrobry (Boleslaus the Brave). The two rulers succeeded in expanding the country's territory to an area not much smaller than that of present-day Poland, eventually taking in the regions of Wielkopolska, Pomerania, Mazovia, Silesia and Małopolska.

Despite the fact that the royal seat moved to Kraków in 1038, Wielkopolska remained an integral part of Poland during its often chequered history, even though it underwent intensive Germanisation under the Prussians during the 19th century Partitions.

Wielkopolska is a vast, flat lowland, and it's not famous for its landscape. It's the architectural legacy of the early Polish nation that is the main attraction for tourists. Moreover, Wielkopolska boasts the 2700-year-old fortified village of Biskupin, the oldest surviving settlement in Poland, which shows that the region was settled by well organised social groups long before the birth of the state.

Poznań is the region's major city and an important tourist centre. From here most visitors set off along the so-called Piast Route (Szlak Piastowski) through the places where Poland was formed.

Poznań

- **pop 580,000**   ☎ **061**

A large industrial centre and the provincial capital, Poznań is also an important historic city and was the de facto capital of Poland in the early years of the state. Most Poles, though, associate the city with the international trade fairs that have taken place regularly since WWI. These days there are two dozen different fairs throughout the year.

As you'd expect, during the fairs accommodation fills up with crowds of businesspeople and visitors, and prices rise. These are not good times for sightseeing. It's best to come at a quieter time, giving

Highlights

- Stroll around Poznań's old town square with its lovely town hall and museums
- Visit the superb cathedral in Gniezno, the cradle of the Polish state
- Look around the 2700-year-old fortified village of Biskupin
- Explore the castle in Gołuchów
- Experience Poland's Catholic fervour at the popular pilgrimage site of Licheń

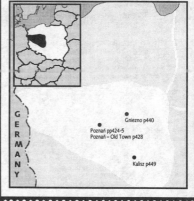

Gniezno p440

Poznań pp424-5
Poznań – Old Town p428

Kalisz p449

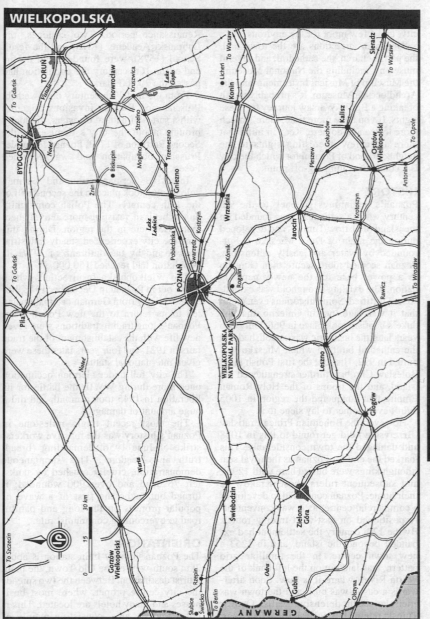

yourself two or three days to explore the city, and a few more for the environs.

The main attractions are the town hall, the parish church, the cathedral, and several museums, including the National Museum, the Museum of Musical Instruments and the Archdiocesan Museum. It's probably worth breaking a Berlin-Warsaw journey for these sights. If you have more time, there's much more to see and do here. Keep in mind that there are a few interesting sights in the neighbourhood of Poznań for which the city is a convenient jumping-off point.

HISTORY

Poznań's beginnings go back to the 9th century when a settlement was founded on the island of Ostrów Tumski, and developed during the reign of Duke Mieszko I. Surrounded by water and easily defensible, Poznań seemed more secure than Gniezno as a power base for the newly baptised nation. The existing stronghold was extended and fortified. Some historians even claim that it was here, not in Gniezno, that the duke's baptism took place in 966. Only two years later the bishopric was established and the cathedral built, in which Mieszko was buried in 992. His son, the first Polish king, Bolesław Chrobry, further strengthened the island, and the troops of the Holy Roman Empire that conquered the region in 1005 didn't even bother to lay siege to it.

However, the Bohemian Prince Bratislav (Brzetysław) did get round to this in 1038 and damaged the town considerably. This marked the end for Poznań as the royal seat (though kings were buried here until 1296), and subsequent rulers chose Kraków as their home. Poznań continued to develop as a commercial centre, as it was conveniently positioned on east-west trading routes. By the 12th century the settlement had expanded beyond the island, and in 1253 a new town centre, in the familiar grid pattern, was laid out on the left bank of the Warta River, where it is now. Soon afterwards a castle was built and the town was encircled with defensive walls. Ostrów Tumski retained its ecclesiastical functions.

Poznań's trade flourished during the Renaissance period. Two colleges, the Lubrański Academy (1518) and the Jesuit School (1578), were founded, and by the end of the 16th century the population had passed the 20,000 mark.

From the mid-17th century on, Swedish, Prussian and Russian invasions, together with a series of natural disasters, gradually brought about the city's demise. In the Second Partition of 1793, Poznań fell under Prussian occupation and was renamed Posen.

Intensive Germanisation and German colonisation took place in the second half of the 19th century. The Polish community dug its heels in, resisting more actively here than elsewhere in the region. During this time the city experienced steady industrial growth and by the outbreak of WWI its population had reached 150,000.

The Wielkopolska Insurrection, which broke out in Poznań in December 1918, liberated the city from German occupation and led to its return to the new Polish state. Poznań's long trading traditions were given new life with the establishment of the trade fairs in 1921, and four years later these were given international status.

The city fell under German occupation once more during WWII; the battle for its liberation in 1945 took a month and did a huge amount of damage.

The most recent tragic milestone in Poznań's history was the massive workers' strike of June 1956, demanding 'bread, truth and freedom'. This spontaneous demonstration, cruelly crushed by tanks, left 76 dead and over 900 wounded; it turned out to be the first of a wave of popular protests on the long and painful road to overcoming communist rule.

ORIENTATION

The Poznań Główny train station is about 2km south-west of the Old Town, the main tourist destination. Between the two spreads the city centre proper, where most businesses and many hotels are located. This is not a touristy area, consisting mainly of postwar concrete plus some monumental public buildings from the Prussian era.

You are most likely to arrive in Poznań at the main train station. It has two exits, to the west and to the north. If you need a private room or plan on staying in the youth hostel on ul Berwińskiego, or want to go by tram to the centre, take the western exit. Otherwise, leave the station through the main northern exit, go straight ahead and take ul Św Marcin to the right which will lead you to the Old Town, past several hotels on the way.

Most tourist sights are either on or near the medieval marketplace, the Stary Rynek. The other important area for visitors is the birthplace of the city, Ostrów Tumski island, 1km east of the Old Town beyond the Warta River.

INFORMATION
Tourist Offices
Poznań has three useful tourist offices. The provincial tourist office (☎ 852 61 56, fax 852 69 64), Stary Rynek 59, is open weekdays 9 am to 5 pm, and Saturday 10 am to 2 pm. The city tourist office (☎ 851 96 45, ☎/fax 851 96 87), ul Ratajczaka 44, is open weekdays 10 am to 7 pm, and Saturday 10 am to 5 pm. The private agency Glob-Tour (☎ 866 06 67), in the main hall of the central train station, is open round the clock. All three offices provide good information, have a selection of maps and tourist publications, and can help you find a room.

Tourist Publications
Poznań has a comprehensive what's-on monthly, *iks* (US$1), containing listings and comments (in Polish) on everything from museums to outdoor activities, plus a useful city map. It's available from Ruch kiosks and the tourist offices. There's also *Welcome to Poznań*, a free tourist magazine. If you can't find it in any of the tourist offices, try the desks of top-class hotels.

Money
Useful banks include Bank Pekao at ul Św Marcin 52/56 and ul Masztalarska 8, Powszechny Bank Kredytowy at Stary Rynek 97/98 and Bank Gdański at ul Paderewskiego 10. Kantors are plentiful throughout the central area, and there are also several ATMs. There's a round-the-clock kantor at the main train station next to Glob-Tour.

Post & Communications
The main post office is at ul Kościuszki 77, near the corner of ul Św Marcin.

Email & Internet Access
The Internet Club (☎ 853 78 18), ul Garncarska 10 m 1, is open Monday to Saturday 10 am to 10 pm.

Bookshops
Omnibus Bookshop, ul Św Marcin 39, is the best for English-language books, and also has some French and German ones. The newsagency at Café Głos, ul Ratajczaka 39, and EMPiK Megastore, ul Ratajczaka 44, have the largest choice of foreign press in town. For maps, check Księgarnia Turystyczna Globtrotter on ul Żydowska just off the Stary Rynek, which is also the only place in town that sells Lonely Planet guidebooks.

OLD TOWN SQUARE
The Stary Rynek, 140 x 140m square, was laid out in 1253 along with the rest of the Old Town. The early timber buildings lining the square gave way to brick burghers' houses, and in the 18th century two palaces were erected (Nos 78 and 91). The middle of the square has gradually changed over the centuries as well, and the buildings that have been accommodated here make up a haphazard collection dating from different periods.

Town Hall
The unquestioned architectural pearl is the town hall, topped with a 61m-high tower. What you see is the second building on this site; it replaced the 13th century Gothic town hall which was entirely consumed by fire in the early 16th century, along with

WIELKOPOLSKA

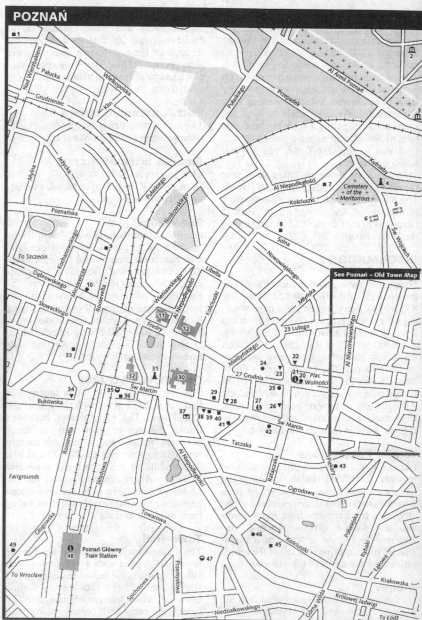

POZNAŃ

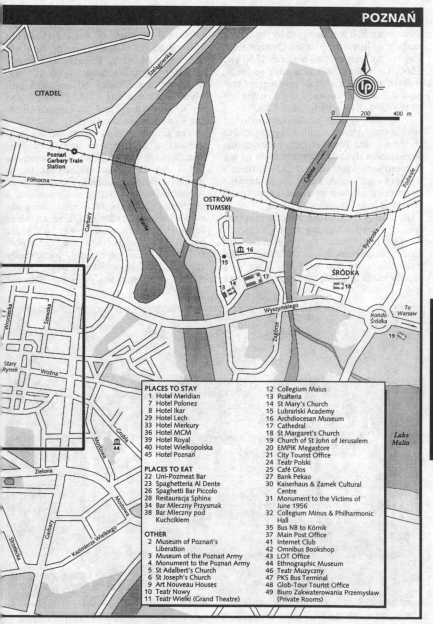

POZNAŃ

CITADEL

Poznań Garbary Train Station

Północna

OSTRÓW TUMSKI

ŚRÓDKA

To Warsaw

Rondo Śródka

Stary Rynek

Woźna

Lake Malta

WIELKOPOLSKA

PLACES TO STAY
1 Hotel Meridian
7 Hotel Polonez
8 Hotel Ikar
29 Hotel Lech
33 Hotel Merkury
36 Hotel MCM
39 Hotel Royal
40 Hotel Wielkopolska
45 Hotel Poznań

PLACES TO EAT
22 Uni-Pozmeat Bar
23 Spaghetteria Al Dente
26 Spaghetti Bar Piccolo
28 Restauracja Sphinx
34 Bar Mleczny Przysmak
38 Bar Mleczny pod Kuchcikiem

OTHER
2 Museum of Poznań's Liberation
3 Museum of the Poznań Army
4 Monument to the Poznań Army
5 St Adalbert's Church
6 St Joseph's Church
9 Art Nouveau Houses
10 Teatr Nowy
11 Teatr Wielki (Grand Theatre)

12 Collegium Maius
13 Psałteria
14 St Mary's Church
15 Lubrański Academy
16 Archdiocesan Museum
17 Cathedral
18 St Margaret's Church
19 Church of St John of Jerusalem
20 EMPiK Megastore
21 City Tourist Office
24 Teatr Polski
25 Café Głos
27 Bank Pekao
30 Kaiserhaus & Zamek Cultural Centre
31 Monument to the Victims of June 1956
32 Collegium Minus & Philharmonic Hall
35 Bus NB to Kórnik
37 Main Post Office
41 Internet Club
42 Omnibus Bookshop
43 LOT Office
44 Ethnographic Museum
46 Teatr Muzyczny
47 PKS Bus Terminal
48 Glob-Tour Tourist Office
49 Biuro Zakwaterowania Przemysław (Private Rooms)

much of the town. The splendid Renaissance town hall was designed by the Italian architect Giovanni Battista Quadro from Lugano and constructed between 1550 and 1560. Only the tower is a later addition, built in the 1780s after its predecessor collapsed. Note the crowned eagle on the top of the spire, with a wingspan of 2m.

The main, eastern façade is embellished with a three-storey arcaded loggia. Above it, the painted frieze depicts kings of the Jagiellonian dynasty. In the middle of the decorative parapet, above the clock, there's a pair of small doors. Every day at noon the doors open and two metal goats appear and butt their horns together 12 times.

In front of the building, near the main entrance, is the **whipping post** (*pręgierz*), once the site of public floggings and also of more serious penalties, as the statue of the executioner on top suggests. This is a replica made in 1925; the original pręgierz

dating from 1535 is on display in the **Historical Museum of Poznań** (Muzeum Historii Miasta Poznania) inside the town hall, open Monday, Tuesday and Friday 10 am to 4 pm, Wednesday noon to 6 pm, Thursday and Sunday 10 am to 3 pm. There's an interesting exhibition relating to the town's history, and the original building's interiors are excellent.

The Gothic vaulted cellars are the only remains of the first town hall. They were initially used for trade but later became a jail. Today they house exhibits relating to medieval Poznań, including fragments of Romanesque and Gothic sculpture and a collection of objects discovered during excavations in the cathedral. Have a look at the model of the town as it was 1000 years ago. You will also find some coffin portraits, a Polish art form particularly common in Wielkopolska. A larger collection of these portraits is in the National

Poznań's tourist hub is its Old Town Square, a mosaic of architecture from medieval to modern

Museum, and there are also some in the cathedral, St Adalbert's Church and the Franciscan Church.

The 1st floor has three splendid rooms, of which the largest, the richly ornamented **Renaissance Hall** (Sala Renesansowa), is a real gem, with the original stucco work and paintings from 1555. The 2nd floor contains more recent exhibits, including some from the Prussian period.

Around the Old Town Square

To the south of the town hall is a row of a dozen small arcaded **Fish Sellers' Houses** (Domki Budnicze). They were built in the 16th century on the site of the fish stalls but were largely destroyed in WWII and reconstructed later.

Directly opposite the houses, on the eastern side of the Rynek, is the **Museum of Musical Instruments** (Muzeum Instrumentów Muzycznych), open Tuesday and Thursday 10 am to 4 pm, Wednesday, Friday and Saturday 9 am to 5 pm, and Sunday 11 am to 4 pm. It has hundreds of instruments, from whistles to concert pianos from the whole of Europe and beyond, dating from the 15th to 20th centuries, and including some intriguing folk specimens.

Behind the town hall is the **Weigh House** (Waga Miejska), a postwar replica of the 16th century building designed by Quadro, which was dismantled in the 19th century. South of it are two large modern structures, strikingly out of harmony with the rest of the old Rynek. Unfortunately, the authorities put these nondescript blocks on the site of the old arsenal and the cloth hall, thus ruining the unity of the square. The one to the east houses the **Wielkopolska Military Museum** (Wielkopolskie Muzeum Wojskowe), open 9 am to 4 pm except Monday. The other building houses the **Modern Art Gallery**, also closed Monday, which has temporary exhibitions, plus a restaurant and a bookshop.

Finally, in the south-western part of the square is the 19th century neoclassical Guardhouse (Odwach) which is now the **Wielkopolska Historical Museum** (Wiel-kopolskie Muzeum Historyczne), open Tuesday to Saturday 10 am to 5 pm, Sunday to 3 pm.

SOUTH-EAST OF THE OLD TOWN SQUARE

Off the south-eastern corner of the Rynek, in the 16th century Górka Palace (Pałac Górków), is the **Archaeological Museum** (Muzeum Archeologiczne), open Tuesday to Friday 10 am to 4 pm, Saturday to 6 pm, Sunday to 3 pm. Before going in, have a look at the fine Renaissance doorway on the building's eastern façade. The museum itself presents the prehistory of the region, from the Stone Age to the early medieval period. You'll also find a copy of the famous bronze doors from the Gniezno cathedral.

A few steps south of the museum is the **Parish Church** (Kościół Farny), originally built for the Jesuits by architects from Italy. After more than 80 years of work (1651-1732), an impressive baroque church was created, with an ornamented façade and a spacious, three-naved interior supported on massive columns and crammed with monumental altars.

Facing the church is the former **Jesuit School** (Szkoła Jezuicka), which was granted a college charter by King Zygmunt Waza, later annulled by the pope when the Kraków Academy protested. Today it's the Ballet School; in summer, plays are occasionally performed in the fine arcaded courtyard of the building.

A five minute walk east from here is the **Ethnographic Museum** (Muzeum Etnograficzne), open Tuesday, Wednesday, Friday and Saturday 10 am to 4 pm, and Sunday to 3 pm. It has a good collection of folk woodcarving, especially the large roadside posts and crosses, and the traditional costumes of the region. The entrance to the museum is from ul Mostowa 7, not from ul Grobla as may be assumed from the map.

WEST OF THE OLD TOWN SQUARE

If you head down ul Franciszkańska from the Rynek you'll come to the **Franciscan**

WIELKOPOLSKA

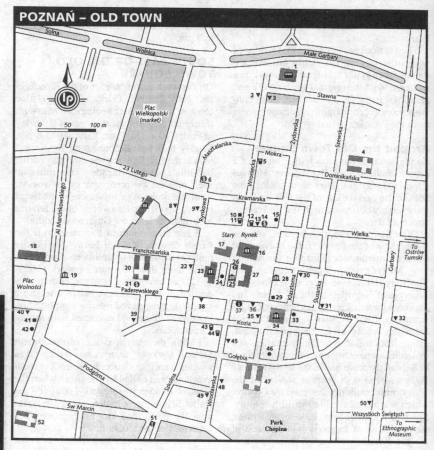

POZNAŃ – OLD TOWN

Church (Kościół Franciszkanów). Built in 1674-1728, it has a complete baroque interior adorned with wall paintings and rich stucco work. Note the Chapel of the Virgin Mary (Kaplica NMP) in the left transept, with an altar carved in oak and a tiny miraculous image of St Mary.

On the hill opposite the church stands the **castle**, or rather what is left of it. The original 13th century castle was repeatedly destroyed and rebuilt. What you see today is the postwar reconstruction of a late 18th century building, hardly looking like a castle at all. It houses the **Museum of Decorative Arts** (Muzeum Sztuk Użytkowych), open the same hours as the Ethnographic Museum. The collection includes furniture, gold and silverware, glass, ceramics, weapons, clocks, watches and sundials from Europe and the Far East; the exhibits date from the 13th century to the present.

Go west to Plac Wolności, one of the main squares of contemporary Poznań. The finest (and oldest) building here is the neo-

POZNAŃ – OLD TOWN

PLACES TO STAY
10 Dom Turysty & Restauracja Turystyczna
29 Dom Polonii
41 Hotel Rzymski

PLACES TO EAT
2 Jadłodajnia w Ramce
3 Pizzeria Tivoli
8 Restauracja Africana
9 Spaghetti Bar Piccolo
13 Avanti pod Koziołkami
22 Bistro Avanti
30 Energia
31 Pizzeria di Trevi
32 Restauracja pod Psem
35 Restauracja Orfeusz
36 Restauracja Stara Ratuszowa
38 Restauracja Chińska Bambus
39 Piwnica Murna
40 Bar Mleczny Apetyt
45 Trattoria Valpolicella

48 Bar Wegetariański
49 Restauracja u Garniewiczów
50 Ristorante Estella

OTHER
1 Swimming Pool (former Synagogue)
4 Dominican Church
5 Yankari Club
6 Bank Pekao
7 Castle & Museum of Decorative Arts
11 Harry's Pub
12 Pub Stara Piwnica
14 Powszechny Bank Kredytowy
15 Księgarnia Turystyczna Globtrotter
16 Town Hall & Historical Museum of Poznań
17 Weigh House
18 Raczyński Library
19 National Museum

20 Franciscan Church
21 Bank Gdański
23 Guardhouse & Wielkopolska Historical Museum
24 Modern Art Gallery
25 Wielkopolska Military Museum
26 Public Toilet
27 Fish Sellers' Houses
28 Museum of Musical Instruments
33 Klub za Kulisami
34 Górka Palace & Archaeological Museum
37 Provincial Tourist Office
42 Orbis Office
43 Tawerna
44 Pub pod Aniołami
46 Jesuit School
47 Parish Church
51 Public Toilet
52 St Martin's Church

---

classical **Raczyński Library** (Biblioteka Raczyńskich), dating from the 1820s. However, the real interest lies inside the less appealing edifice of the **National Museum** (Muzeum Narodowe), where an extensive collection of Polish and European art is displayed in countless rooms.

Polish painting of the last two centuries is represented by almost all the big names, including Jan Matejko, Stanisław Wyspiański and Jacek Malczewski. The museum also has a reasonable selection of Italian, Spanish, Flemish and Dutch painting.

A curiosity worth noticing is the collection of coffin portraits, a prerequisite for the funeral ceremonies of the Polish nobility. They first appeared in the 16th century, and became ubiquitous in the baroque period. The portraits were attached to the coffins to give the impression that the deceased were participating actively in their own funeral. Medieval church woodcarving and painting are displayed in the basement.

The museum is open Wednesday to Saturday 10 am to 4 pm, and Sunday 11 am to 3 pm. The building itself was erected in the early years of the 20th century to serve as the Prussian museum.

There are more examples of Prussian architecture farther to the west, close to the railway track. They include the Grand Theatre, the Collegium Maius, the Collegium Minus and, most massive of all, the neo-Romanesque **Kaiserhaus** built for the German Emperor Wilhelm II. The castle-like building – gloomy and blackened – is today the Zamek Cultural Centre which houses several cultural institutions.

Next to the Kaiserhaus, on Plac Mickiewicza, stands the **Monument to the Victims of June 1956** (Pomnik Poznańskiego Czerwca 1956r), commemorating one of the first mass protests in the communist bloc. The monument was unveiled on 28 June 1981, the 25th anniversary, and the ceremony was attended by over 100,000 people. Past the railway line, you'll find some fine examples of Art Nouveau decoration at ul Roosevelta 4 and 5.

Farther south, a five minute walk from the main train station along ul Głogowska,

WIELKOPOLSKA

is the monument to US president (Thomas) Woodrow Wilson, made in the socialist-realist style. The monument stands at the entrance to the Park Wilsona. Enter it and walk to the **Palm House** (Palmiarnia), at the opposite, northern end. Built in 1910 and occupying an area of over 4000 sq metres and a volume of 44,000 cubic metres, this is one of the biggest greenhouses in Europe. Inside are 19,000 species of tropical and subtropical plants, including reputedly Europe's largest cactus collection and tallest bamboo trees. There's also a collection of exotic fish in the adjacent aquarium. The palm house is open daily, except Monday, 9 am to 3 or 5 pm, depending on the season. German-speaking guides are available (US$8 per group for a 1½ hour tour).

NORTH OF THE OLD TOWN SQUARE

Beginning from the Rynek, walk north along ul Żydowska. Before WWII this sector was populated mainly by Jews. Turn right into ul Dominikańska to look over the former **Dominican Church** (Kościół Podominikański), now belonging to the Jesuits. Built in the mid-13th century, it's the oldest monument on the left bank of the Warta River. It was repeatedly reshaped and redecorated in later periods but the fine early Gothic doorway at the main entrance is still in place.

Continue on ul Żydowska north to the end of the street, where you'll see a large building (from 1907) which was formerly the **synagogue**; now it's … a swimming pool!

Cross the busy thoroughfare and take ul Św Wojciech towards the two churches facing each other on opposite sides of the street. To your right is the 15th century **St Adalbert's Church** (Kościół Św Wojciecha), with its façade combining Gothic and Renaissance styles. Its freestanding wooden belfry from the 16th century is the only substantial historic wooden building in Poznań. Inside the church, the Gothic vaulting is decorated with Art Nouveau wall paintings.

The crypt beneath, open to visitors, has become a mausoleum for the most eminent Poles from Wielkopolska, among them Józef Wybicki, who wrote the lyrics of the national anthem.

During the Christmas period, the mechanised *szopka* (Nativity scene) is open in the church. It includes several dozen movable figures which depict the history of the region from Mieszko I to the present day.

On the opposite side of the street is the early baroque **St Joseph's Church** (Kościół Św Józefa), but there's not much to see inside.

A few steps up the street is the sloping **Cemetery of the Meritorious** (Cmentarz Zasłużonych), the oldest existing cemetery in the city (1810). There are some fine 19th century tombstones. Across the street is the modern **Monument to the Poznań Army** (Pomnik Armii Poznań) dedicated to the local armed force which resisted the German invasion of 1939 for almost two weeks.

Farther north is a large park laid out on what was the massive fortress known as the **Citadel** (Cytadela). It was built by the Prussians in the 1830s on a hill once occupied by vineyards. The fortress was involved in one major battle, when the Germans defended themselves for four weeks in 1945. It was completely destroyed and only a few fragments have survived. Today it's the largest city park, and incorporates two museums (the Museum of Poznań's Liberation and the Museum of the Poznań Army) and cemeteries for Polish, Soviet and British and Commonwealth soldiers, all on the southern slopes of the hill.

OSTRÓW TUMSKI & BEYOND

The island of Ostrów Tumski is where Poznań and with it the Polish state took their first steps. The original 9th century settlement was transformed in the mid-10th century into an oval stronghold surrounded by wood-and-earth ramparts, and an early stone palace was built. Mieszko I added a cathedral and further fortified the township. By the end of the 10th century Poznań was the most powerful stronghold in the country.

A couple of centuries later it spread beyond the island, first to the right, then to the left bank of the river. In the 13th century, when the newly designed town was laid out, Ostrów lost its trade and administrative importance but remained the residence of the Church authorities, which it still is.

Today it's a tiny, quiet ecclesiastical quarter, dominated by a monumental double-towered **cathedral**. Basically Gothic with additions from later periods, most notably the baroque tops of the towers, the cathedral was badly damaged in 1945 and its reconstruction took 11 years. Since not much of the internal furnishing has survived, the present-day decoration has been collected from other churches, mostly from Silesia.

The aisles and the ambulatory are ringed with a dozen chapels containing numerous tombstones. The most famous of these is the **Golden Chapel** (Złota Kaplica) behind the high altar. Dating from the 15th century, it was completely rebuilt in the 1830s as the mausoleum of the first two Polish rulers, Mieszko I and Bolesław Chrobry. Enveloped in Byzantine-style decoration are the double tomb of the two monarchs on the one side and their bronze statues on the other.

The kings' original burial site was the **crypt**, accessible from the back of the left-hand aisle. There, apart from the fragments of what are thought to have been their tombs, you can see the relics of the first pre-Romanesque cathedral from 968 and of the subsequent Romanesque building from the second half of the 11th century.

Opposite the cathedral is **St Mary's Church** (Kościół NMP), built in the mid-15th century and virtually unaltered since then. Its internal decoration, though, is modern. Just behind it is the early 16th century **Psałteria**, which was home to the choristers.

A short walk north of the cathedral is the **Lubrański Academy** (Akademia Lubrańskiego), also known as the Collegium Lubranscianum, the first high school in Poznań (1518). Across the street from it is the **Archdiocesan Museum** (Muzeum Archidiecezjalne), open Monday to Saturday from 9 am to 3 pm, which has a collection of sacred art.

Farther east, past the bridge over the Cybina River (a branch of the Warta), is the microscopic Śródka suburb. It was the main trade centre of Poznań in the 13th century, but gradually lost its significance when the town was moved to its present site. **St Margaret's Church** (Kościół Św Małgorzaty), originally a 14th century structure but much altered later and filled with baroque furnishings, is one of the few remainders of the heyday.

More interesting is the **Church of St John of Jerusalem** (Kościół Św Jana Jerozolimskiego) in the suburb of Komandoria, a five minute walk farther east, behind the Rondo Śródka. The late 12th century building (one of the oldest brick churches in the country) was extended in the Gothic period and later acquired a baroque chapel. The interior is an unusual combination of a nave with a single aisle to one side (both with beautiful Gothic star vaults) plus a chapel on the opposite side. Note the Romanesque doorway in the main western entrance.

South-east of the church is the 70 hectare artificial Lake Malta (Jezioro Maltańskie), and beyond it a zoo.

SPECIAL EVENTS

Poznań's pride are the trade fairs, the main ones taking place in January, June, September and October, but there are two dozen other fairs throughout the year. July, August and December are fair-free months.

Culturally, the major events include the Poznań Musical Spring (contemporary music) in April, the Jazz Fair Festival in May, the Malta International Theatre Festival in late June, and the Wieniawski International Violin Festival which takes place in November every five years (the next one will be in 2001).

St John's Fair (Jarmark Świętojański), which takes place at the Stary Rynek in

June, is a handicraft and antiques fair, but it has been heavily commercialised over recent years.

PLACES TO STAY

Poznań's hotels and private rooms tend to double their prices when the trade fairs are on. During the major fairs all hotel rooms are likely to be fully booked, and private rooms may be scarce and at distant locations. The prices given in this section are for the 'off-fair' periods. All three tourist offices are knowledgeable about the city's lodging options and are likely to help you in finding a bed.

Places to Stay – Budget

Camping Poznań has three camping grounds, and all have cabins. Closest to the centre is the all-year *Camping Nr 155 Malta* (☎ 876 62 03, ul Krańcowa 98), on the north-eastern shore of Lake Malta, 3km east of the Old Town. Bungalows to sleep two/three/five people, all with private bath and kitchenette, cost US$40/70/100.

The two other camping grounds are on the north-western outskirts of the city, each about 10km from the centre. *Camping Nr 111 Strzeszynek* (☎ 848 31 29, ul Koszalińska 15) is in the Strzeszynek suburb. *Camping Nr 30 Baranowo* (☎ 814 28 12) is on Lake Kierskie. Both are open from May to September and have much cheaper cabins than the Malta.

Youth Hostels There are four all-year youth hostels in the city. The closest *youth hostel* (☎ 866 40 40, ul Berwińskiego 2/3) is a 10 minute walk south-west from the train station along ul Głogowska. It's the smallest and the most basic of the lot and fills up fast.

The newest (and best) *youth hostel* (☎ 848 58 36, ul Drzymały 3) is 3km north of the train station (take tram No 11) and 3km from the Old Town (tram No 9).

The two remaining hostels are a long way from the centre. One *youth hostel* (☎ 822 10 63, ul Biskupińska 27) is about 7km north-west in the suburb of Strzeszyn – bus No 60

from ul Solna on the northern edge of the centre will take you there. Another *youth hostel* (☎ 878 84 61, ul Głuszyna 127) is on the southern city limits over 10km from the centre (there's no direct transport).

Other Hostels The tourist offices should know which student dorms open in summer as student hostels. They are likely to include *Jowita* (☎ 866 12 71, ul Zwierzyniecka 7), the *Eskulap* (☎ 867 56 11, ul Przybyszewskiego 39) and *Zbyszko* (☎ 820 16 12, ul Obornicka 80). The tourist offices will also know about several inexpensive workers' hostels, but most are located in the outer suburbs.

Private Rooms Private rooms are run by Biuro Zakwaterowania Przemysław (☎ 866 35 60) at ul Głogowska 16 opposite the train station; it's open weekdays 8 am to 6 pm, Saturday 10 am to 2 pm (longer at fair times). Rooms normally go for US$10/15 a single/double and are almost always available, but at fair times it's US$24/32 and there may be few rooms to choose from.

Glob-Tour arranges private rooms for marginally more.

Places to Stay – Mid-Range

Dom Turysty (☎ 852 88 93, Stary Rynek 91) is in the 1798 former palace (destroyed in 1944 and reconstructed later) on the market square. Enter from ul Wroniecka. It has singles/doubles/triples without bath for US$26/40/45, and singles/doubles with bath for US$36/58. It also has four and five-bed dorms with shared facilities for US$12 a bed. Breakfast is included in the price.

The small *Hotel Royal* (☎ 853 78 84, fax 851 79 31, ul Św Marcin 71), midway between the train station and the Old Town, is tucked away from the street but easy to track down – enter the gate and go straight through to the back. It's simple but affordable – US$18/28/40 without bath, US$20 a single with bath.

An interesting proposition may be *Hotel MCM* (☎ 853 66 69, ul Skośna 1), near the June 1956 Monument, which has beds with magnetic mattresses, reputedly good for your health. Doubles with bath cost US$33.

There are more hotels in this price bracket, but they are farther away from the centre. Check with the tourist offices.

Places to Stay – Top End

Dom Polonii (☎/fax 853 19 61, Stary Rynek 51) is ideally located. It has just two double rooms (one overlooking the Rynek), both with private bath, each costing US$30/50 for single/double occupancy.

Hotel Wielkopolska (☎ 852 76 31, fax 851 54 92, ul Św Marcin 67) doesn't provide great luxuries but is one of the cheapest in this price bracket and well located. It costs US$27/44 without bath, US$35/50 with bath.

There are several other affordable hotels in the central area, including *Hotel Rzymski* (☎ 852 81 21, fax 852 89 83, Al Marcinkowskiego 22) at US$40/60, *Hotel Lech* (☎ 853 01 51, fax 853 08 80, ul Św Marcin 74) at US$45/65 and *Hotel Ikar* (☎ 857 67 05, fax 851 58 67, ul Kościuszki 118) at US$50/80.

Orbis has four hotels here, including *Hotel Merkury* (☎ 855 80 00, fax 855 89 55, ul Roosevelta 20), *Hotel Polonez* (☎ 869 91 41, fax 852 37 62, Al Niepodległości 36) and *Hotel Poznań* (☎ 833 20 81, fax 833 29 61, Plac Andersa 1). They are all nondescript, but provide decent standards. Rooms are around US$70/100, but cost significantly more during fairs.

More recent additions include *Hotel Park* (☎ 879 40 81, fax 877 38 30, ul Majakowskiego 77), on the southern bank of Lake Malta, at US$90/110, and *Hotel Meridian* (☎ 847 15 64, fax 847 34 41, ul Litewska 22) at US$70/100. They both surpass the Orbis stock in quality.

PLACES TO EAT

Poznań has a wide range of eateries for every pocket, including a variety of fast-food outlets and posh restaurants. The majority of the places to eat are in the Old Town and west of it, particularly along ul Św Marcin and ul 27 Grudnia.

Some of the cheapest food in town is in the modernised *Bar Mleczny Apetyt* (Plac Wolności 1). It has delicious *naleśniki*, *pierogi* and *pyzy*. Other central milk bars include *Bar Mleczny Przysmak* (ul Roosevelta 22) and the basic *Bar Mleczny pod Kuchcikiem* (ul Św Marcin 75).

Uni-Pozmeat Bar (Plac Wolności 14) and *Energia* (ul Woźna 21) are slightly more expensive than milk bars but open a bit longer. Vegetarians can try the simple *Bar Wegetariański* (ul Wrocławska 21).

The very cheap and popular *Bistro Avanti* (Stary Rynek 76) serves tasty platefuls of spaghetti (US$1); it has a 24 hour outlet at the main train station. *Spaghetti Bar Piccolo* (ul Rynkowa 1), a few steps north of the Rynek, also does spaghetti and is even cheaper than the Avanti. It also has another outlet at ul Ratajczaka 37. Yet another similar budget place is *Spaghetteria Al Dente* (ul 3 Maja). They all have a modest choice of salads.

For pizza, choose between *Pizzeria Tivoli* (ul Wroniecka 13) and *Pizzeria di Trevi* (ul Wodna 7). *Avanti pod Koziołkami* (Stary Rynek 95) is a salad bar with reasonable choice and prices. *Piwnica Murna* (☎ 851 86 64, ul Murna 3A) is an enjoyable mid-priced grill pub, good for both eating and drinking. *Restauracja Sphinx* (☎ 852 07 02, ul Św Marcin 66/72) serves good-value grilled dishes and popular Middle Eastern fare.

Restauracja Turystyczna (Stary Rynek 91), downstairs from the Dom Turysty (enter from ul Wroniecka), has inexpensive Polish food. *Restauracja pod Psem* (☎ 851 99 70, ul Garbary 54) is more pleasant and the food is better though more expensive. Another agreeable place with an innovative menu and reasonable prices is *Jadłodajnia w Ramce* (☎ 855 75 57, ul Wroniecka 10).

Restauracja Stara Ratuszowa (☎ 851 53 18, Stary Rynek 55) has a café on the ground level and a restaurant and bar in the attractive 16th century cellar, all beautifully decorated with old photos and antiques. The food – mostly Polish fare – is good, though not particularly cheap. Other top-end options include *Restauracja u Gar-niewiczów* (☎ 853 03 82, *ul Wrocławska 18)*, with traditional local food plus some Lithuanian and Ukrainian dishes, and *Restauracja Orfeusz* (☎ 851 98 44, *ul Świętosławska 12)*, with European cuisine.

For a fine Italian meal, choose between *Trattoria Valpolicella* (☎ 855 71 91, *ul Wrocławska 7)* and *Ristorante Estella* (☎ 852 34 10, *ul Garbary 41)*. *Restauracja Chińska Bambus* (☎ 853 06 58, *Stary Rynek 64/65)* is one of the better Chinese eateries in town. African food in appropriate surroundings can be tried in *Restauracja Africana* (☎ 853 08 19, *ul Zamkowa 3)*.

ENTERTAINMENT

Poznań has a reasonable cultural menu. Get a copy of *iks* magazine, to know what's going on. It's in Polish, but you should be able to work a few things out.

Opera & Ballet

Operas are performed at the *Teatr Wielki* (*Grand Theatre;* ☎ 852 82 91, *ul Fredry 9)*. The *Polski Teatr Tańca* (*Polish Dance Theatre;* ☎ 852 42 41)*, one of the best groups of its kind in Poland, performs here as well, if it's in town. Its office is at ul Kozia 4. The *Teatr Muzyczny* (*Musical Theatre;* ☎ 852 17 86, *ul Niezłomnych 1e)*, next to Hotel Poznań, features Broadway-style shows.

Classical Music

The *Filharmonia* (☎ 852 47 08, *ul Św Marcin 81)* runs concerts at least once a week on Fridays, performed by the local symphony orchestra and often by visiting artists. Poznań has Poland's best boys' choir, the *Poznańskie Słowiki* (Poznań Nightingales), which sometimes can be heard here.

Theatre

The main repertory theatres are the *Teatr Polski* (☎ 852 56 27, *ul 27 Grudnia 8/10)* and the *Teatr Nowy* (☎ 848 48 85, *ul Dąbrowskiego 5)*. The former usually has some classics in its repertoire, while the latter tends more towards contemporary productions.

It's also worth checking the *Teatr Ósmego Dnia* (*Theatre of the Eighth Day;* ☎ 852 77 14)*, which started in the 1960s as an avant-garde, politically involved student theatre. Its office at ul Ratajczaka 44 will inform you about the program and sell tickets (weekdays from 11 am to 2 pm).

The *Teatr Biuro Podróży* (*Travel Agency Theatre;* ☎ 852 60 76, *Al Niepodległości 26)* is Poznań's excellent street theatre which has already gained international acclaim.

Zamek Cultural Centre

Located in the Kaiserhaus, the *Centrum Kultury Zamek* (☎ 853 60 81, *ul Św Marcin 80/82)* is an active cultural centre featuring art cinema, several art galleries, concerts (classical, jazz, rock etc) and other events. In summer, concerts are staged in the courtyard of the building.

Pubs & Bars

Harry's Pub (*Stary Rynek 91)* was the first establishment of this sort and is still popular day and night, but these days it faces increasing competition from more atmospheric places, including *Pub Stara Piwnica* just across the street, *Pub pod Aniołami* (*ul Wrocławska 4)*, *Tawerna* (*ul Kozia 4)*, round the corner, and the African-themed *Yankari Club* (*ul Wroniecka 18)*. And don't miss visiting the charming *Klub za Kulisami* (*ul Wodna 24)*.

GETTING THERE & AWAY
Air

Poznań's airport is in the western suburb of Ławica, 7km from the centre and accessible by several bus lines. Direct connections include three flights a day to Warsaw, two to Copenhagen and one to Düsseldorf in Germany. The LOT office (☎ 852 28 47) is at ul Piekary 6.

Train

Poznań is a busy railway hub. There are about 10 trains daily to Warsaw (311km), including the EuroCity and InterCity trains which take just over three hours. Equally frequent are services to Wrocław (165km) and Szczecin (214km), and there are also five fast trains direct to Kraków (398km).

Gdańsk (313km) is serviced by four express and two fast trains, and Toruń (142km) by three fast and four ordinary trains; all pass via Gniezno (51km). Six trains depart daily for Zielona Góra (139km).

Six international trains run daily to Berlin (261km), including two EuroCity trains which take just three hours to get there. There are also direct trains to Budapest, Cologne and Moscow.

Tickets and couchette reservations are handled by the train station or the Orbis office (☎ 852 49 94) at Al Marcinkowskiego 21.

Bus

The PKS bus terminal is a 10 minute walk east of the train station. Buses run half-hourly to Kórnik (20km) and every couple of hours to Rogalin (24 or 31km, depending on the route). You can also get to Kórnik by hourly suburban bus NB from ul Św Marcin near the rail track. Buses to Gniezno (49km) depart every hour or so and go via either Kostrzyn or Pobiedziska; the latter pass Lake Lednica. On longer routes, you may use buses to get to Kalisz (130km) and Zielona Góra (130km), as they run more frequently than trains.

GETTING AROUND

Unlike most other cities, public transport fares depend on how much time the journey takes. Tickets cost US$0.20 for a 10 minute ride, US$0.40 for a half-hour trip, and US$0.80 for a journey up to one hour. Approximate times of rides are posted at bus and tram stops.

Around Poznań

SWARZĘDZ
• pop 26,000 ☎ 061
Swarzędz ('Svah-zhents') is a satellite town of Poznań, 11km east of the city on the Warsaw road. It's widely known as one of Poland's main furniture producers, with a large factory and some 300 small carpentry workshops. Tourists, however, may be more interested in the **skansen** (open-air museum) which was established here in 1963.

The skansen is in a small park squeezed between the busy Poznań-Warsaw highway and the equally busy railway line. It's devoted exclusively to bee-keeping and has the largest and most diverse collection of beehives in Poland – over 200 specimens. They range from simple hollow trunks (the oldest dating from the 14th century) to intriguing basket-like examples woven of straw. There are also beehives carved and painted in the shapes of people, animals, churches, houses, windmills – and even faithful copies of Poznań's town hall and cathedral.

The skansen is open Tuesday to Sunday 8 am to 4 pm (longer in summer). There's a small *hotel (☎ 817 31 47)* in an old hunting lodge in the grounds (US$30 a double with bath, US$10 per person without bath) and a budget bistro.

Frequent city buses go to Swarzędz from Rondo Śródka in Poznań. The skansen is on the right-hand side of the road just before Swarzędz; ask the driver where to get off.

KÓRNIK
• pop 6000 ☎ 061
An uninspiring small town 20km south-east of Poznań, Kórnik has found its way into the tourist brochures thanks to its **castle**. It was built by the powerful Górka family in the 15th century, but changed hands and was much altered in later periods. Its present-day appearance dates from the mid-19th century, when its owner at the time, Tytus Działyński, a fervent patriot and art collector, gave the castle a somewhat eccentric, fortified mock-Gothic character, partly based on a design by German architect Karl Friedrich Schinkel.

The interior was extensively remodelled as well, to provide a plush family home and accommodate the owner's collection. On the 1st floor a spectacular Moorish Hall was created, clearly influenced by the Alhambra in Granada, as a memorable setting for the display of armour and military accessories. The collection was expanded by Tytus' son Jan and his nephew Władysław Zamoyski; the latter donated the castle and its contents to the state in 1924.

The castle luckily survived the war and, miraculously, so did its contents. It is now open as a **museum**. You can wander through its fully furnished and decorated 19th century interiors, some of which have family collections on display. The museum is open March to November, Tuesday to Sunday from 9 am to 3 pm (until 5 pm in summer).

Behind the castle is a large, English-style park known as the **arboretum**, which was laid out during the castle's reconstruction. Numerous exotic species of trees and shrubs were imported from leading European nurseries, and Kórnik was considered to be the best stocked park in the country. Many species were later transplanted to Gołuchów where Jan Działyński was creating his new residence. Today the arboretum is run by a scientific research institute and has some 3000 plant species and varieties. It's open daily from 9 am to 5 pm May to September, to 3 pm the rest of the year.

One more place to visit is the **coach house** (*powozownia*), 150m towards the town centre from the castle, on the opposite side of the road. Three London coaches, brought by Jan Działyński from Paris in 1856, can be seen here.

Getting There & Away

There's frequent bus transport from Poznań to Kórnik (20km). You can either take the PKS bus from the central bus terminal (departing every half-hour or so) or go by suburban bus NB from ul Św Marcin (every hour). Either bus will deposit you at the Rynek in Kórnik, a three minute walk from the castle.

If you plan on continuing to Rogalin (13km), there are about five buses daily (check the timetable before visiting the castle).

ROGALIN

The tiny village of Rogalin, 13km west of Kórnik, was the seat of yet another Polish aristocratic clan, the Raczyński family, who built a **palace** here in the closing decades of the 18th century, and lived in it until WWII. Typically for such country residences of the period, the complex included a garden and park and some outbuildings complete with stables and coach house. Plundered but not damaged during WWII, the complex was taken over by the state and is today a branch of Poznań's National Museum, open Tuesday to Sunday 10 am to 4 pm.

Less visited than Kórnik's castle and quite different in its appearance, the Rogalin palace consists of a massive two-storey baroque central structure and two modest symmetrical wings linked to the main body by curving galleries, forming a giant horseshoe enclosing a vast forecourt. The main house is closed due to snail-pace restoration, but the wings are open and used for temporary displays of some of the Raczyński collection.

Just beyond the left wing is the **Gallery of Painting** (Galeria Obrazów), with a display of Polish and European canvases from the 19th and early 20th centuries. The Polish collection has some first class work, with Jacek Malczewski best represented. The dominant work, though, is Jan Matejko's colossal *Joan of Arc*, which occupies an entire wall of a large exhibition hall.

In the **coach house** by the front courtyard are a dozen old coaches, including Poznań's last horse-drawn cab.

Behind the palace is an unkempt **French garden** with a mound at the far end, which would have provided the owner with a fine view over his home.

West beyond the garden, the **English landscaped park** was laid out in primeval oak forest. Not much of the park's design can be deciphered today, but the ancient oak trees are still there. The three most imposing specimens have been fenced off and baptised with the names Lech, Czech and Rus, after the legendary founders of the Polish, Czech and Russian nations. The largest –

9m in circumference – is Rus, and it also seems to be in the best health, quite in contrast with the health of its country itself.

One more place to see is the **chapel** on the eastern outskirts of the village. It was built in the 1820s to serve as a mausoleum for the family and is a replica of the Roman temple known as Maison Carrée in Nîmes, southern France. The vaulted crypt beneath the church houses several dilapidated tombstones. The priest living in the house behind the church may open it for you.

Getting There & Away
There are several buses from Poznań to Rogalin via either Rogalinek or Kórnik. Buses from Rogalin back to Poznań pass through every couple of hours till late afternoon; check the timetable before visiting the palace and plan accordingly.

WIELKOPOLSKA NATIONAL PARK
☎ 061
Lying just a few kilometres south-west of Poznań's administrative boundaries, the 76 sq km Wielkopolska National Park (Wielkopolski Park Narodowy) is the only park in the region. About 80% of it is forest – pine and oak being the dominant species – and its postglacial lakes give it a certain charm. It's reputedly one of the most interesting stretches of land in Wielkopolska, for its diversity and for the variety of flora and fauna concentrated in its small area.

The park is surrounded by Poznań's expanding satellite towns and suffers from the industrial pollution of the city itself, but, so far, you can walk through the woods and beside the lakes and still feel that you're amid the undisturbed, natural world. It can be a pleasant day away from the city rush.

Getting to the park from Poznań is relatively easy by train or bus, and there are good walks from several different places. If you plan a one day trip, perhaps the best point to start is Osowa Góra (21km from Poznań), deep in the park where the train terminates. The route is serviced by only a couple of trains daily from Poznań. Catch

the one departing early in the morning (the next one is about 2 pm). Once in Osowa Góra, take the red trail which winds westwards; after passing two miniature lakes it reaches Lake Góreckie, the most beautiful body of water in the park. The trail skirts the eastern part of the lake and turns northeast to bring you eventually to the town of Puszczykowo, from where trains can take you back to Poznań. It's about a 14km walk altogether, through what's probably the most attractive area of the park.

If you want to do more walking, there are four more trails to choose from. They cover most of the park and cross each other at several points. Get a copy of the *Wielkopolski Park Narodowy* map (scale 1:35,000), which has all the details.

Places to Stay & Eat
The two small towns of Puszczykowo (with its southern suburb of Puszczykówko) and Mosina provide food and accommodation. They both lie on the eastern edge of the park, 4km apart, on the Poznań-Wrocław railway line (with regular transport in both directions).

The place to stay in Mosina is *Hotel Morena* (☎ 813 27 46, ul Konopnickiej 1) at US$15 per double, which also has a restaurant. In Puszczykowo-Puszczykówko there are two budget options, the *Dom Wycieczkowy Sadyba* (☎ 813 31 28, ul Brzozowa 15) and *Dom Wycieczkowy Pod Kukułką* (☎ 813 38 47, ul Reymonta 17) at US$15 for a double in either. *Hotel Santa Barbara* (☎ 813 32 91, ul Niwka Stara 8) is better at US$30 for doubles with bath. There are several eating options around, including the Santa Barbara.

The Piast Route

The Piast Route (Szlak Piastowski) is a popular tourist route winding from Poznań to Inowrocław. It covers places related to the early centuries of the Polish state, and historic monuments from that period, including the Iron Age village of Biskupin.

WIELKOPOLSKA

LAKE LEDNICA

Lake Lednica, about 30km east of Poznań, is the first important point on the Piast Route. The 7km elongated postglacial lake has four islands, the largest of which, Ostrów Lednicki, was an important defensive and administrative outpost of the early Polish state. There is also a skansen and a museum on the lake shore.

Skansen

The skansen (Wielkopolski Park Etnograficzny) is on the eastern side of the lake, 500m north of the Poznań-Gniezno road, on the southern outskirts of the tiny village of Dziekanowice. Though the open, almost treeless grounds are not attractive, there is a good selection of 19th century rural architecture from Wielkopolska.

About half of a typical village has been re-created so far and several houses can be visited. Just to the south is a manor house and its outbuildings, but they're occupied by the administration and can only be seen from the outside. The skansen is open daily except Monday 9 am to 5 pm mid-April to October; in November, February, March and the first half of April it closes at 3 pm; in December and January it's closed.

Museum

Two kilometres north of the skansen on a sealed road (the signposts along the road will direct you), on the lake shore facing Ostrów Lednicki island, is the Museum of the First Piasts (Muzeum Pierwszych Piastów), which can be easily recognised by its stylised gateway. Among several wooden buildings in the grounds is the oldest windmill in Poland, dating from 1585. Beside it stands an 18th century granary which boasts a display of human remains excavated on the island.

The main exhibition is in the church-like building, which looks like a simplified version of the Church of St John of Jerusalem in Poznań. There are two floors of finds from excavations on and around the island. Among the exhibits, most of which date from the 10th and 11th centuries, are weapons, household items and implements, pottery and ornaments, and a dugout canoe which is one of the very few wooden objects to have survived for almost a millennium. The place has the same opening hours as the skansen and the entrance fee includes a boat trip to the island of Ostrów Lednicki, 175m away, but the boat operates only from mid-April to late October.

Ostrów Lednicki

Excavations have shown that Ostrów Lednicki was one of the major settlements of the first Piasts in the late 10th and early 11th centuries, rivalling Poznań and Gniezno. It was settled as early as the Stone Age, and in the 10th century a stronghold was built here along with a stone palace and a church. Two wooden bridges were constructed to link the island to the western and eastern shores of the lake, and it was over these bridges that the route between Poznań and Gniezno ran. The western bridge was 428m long and its foundations were nearly 12m under water at the deepest point.

The settlement was overrun and destroyed by the Bohemians in 1038, and though the church and the defensive ramparts were rebuilt, the island never regained its previous importance. Between the 12th and 14th centuries a large part of it was used as a graveyard. Some 2000 tombs have been found here, making the site the largest cemetery from that period discovered in central Europe. Some of the finds are on display in the granary in the museum.

On the island you can see what's left of the palace and the church. The foundations and lower parts of the walls are still in place and give a rough idea of how big the complex was. There are some helpful drawings in the museum of what the buildings might have looked like.

Getting There & Away

The lake lies on the Poznań-Gniezno road and there's a fairly regular bus service between the two cities. From whichever end you start, take the bus via Pobiedziska, not via Kostrzyn. If you are coming from

Poznań, you'll see three old windmills on the hill to the left of the road, but don't get off there. Stay on the bus for another 2.5km and get off at the turn-off to Komorowo (the bus stop is just by the turn-off). From here it's only a five minute walk to the skansen. Another 25 minute walk north will bring you to the museum.

GNIEZNO

• pop 71,000   ☎ 061

Gniezno ('Gnyez-no') is commonly considered to be the cradle of the Polish state, for it was probably the major stronghold of the Polanie, and the dispersed tribes of the region were unified from here in the 10th century.

Legend has it that Gniezno was founded by the mythical Lech, the grandson of the legendary Piast and the grandfather of Mieszko I, who while hunting in the area found the nest (*gniazdo*) of a white eagle, giving the town its name and the nation its emblem.

In historical terms, the settlement most likely existed even earlier than the folk story indicates, perhaps since the 7th or 8th century, and it was initially the centre of a pagan cult. Archaeological excavations have shown that by the end of the 8th century Gniezno was already fortified with wood and earth ramparts, and had regular trade links with commercial centres far outside the region.

This early development contributed to the key role that the town played. Duke Mieszko I is thought to have been baptised here in 966, thus raising Poland (at that time the region of Wielkopolska) from obscurity to the rank of Christianised nations. Gniezno was then made the capital of the newborn state.

Historical records from these early days are scarce, and don't show precisely where the capital was, though it's likely that Mieszko favoured Poznań over Gniezno. The first cathedral was, after all, built in Poznań, and the ruler was buried there.

Gniezno came to the fore in the year 1000, when the archbishopric was established here, and its position was further strengthened in 1025 when Bolesław Chrobry was crowned in the local cathedral as the first Polish king. Only 13 years later, the Bohemian invasion devastated the region – Poznań, Gniezno and other strongholds alike – and the seat of power was shifted to the more secure Kraków in Małopolska.

This inevitably deprived the town of its importance, though kings were crowned in Gniezno until the end of the 13th century (but buried in Poznań). The town retained its status as the seat of the Church of Poland, and continues to be the formal ecclesiastical capital, even though archbishops are only occasional guests these days.

Cathedral

Gniezno's pride is its cathedral, a large, double-towered Gothic structure, which looks pretty similar to the one in Poznań. The present church is already the third or fourth building on this site (the first was built in the 970s), and was constructed in the second half of the 14th century after the destruction of the Romanesque cathedral by the Teutonic Knights in 1331. It changed a lot in later periods: chapels sprouted all round it, and the interior was redecorated in successive styles. After considerable damage in WWII, it was rebuilt according to the original Gothic structure.

Inside, the focal point is the elaborate silver **sarcophagus of St Adalbert** (Św Wojciech for the Poles) in the chancel. The baroque coffin, topped with the reclining figure of the saint, is the work of Peter van der Rennen and was made in 1662 in Gdańsk.

St Adalbert was a Bohemian bishop who in 997 passed through Gniezno on a missionary trip to convert the Prussians, a heathen Baltic tribe which inhabited what is now Masuria in north-eastern Poland. The pagans were less than enthusiastic about accepting the new faith and terminated the bishop's efforts by cutting off his head. Bolesław Chrobry recovered the body,

WIELKOPOLSKA

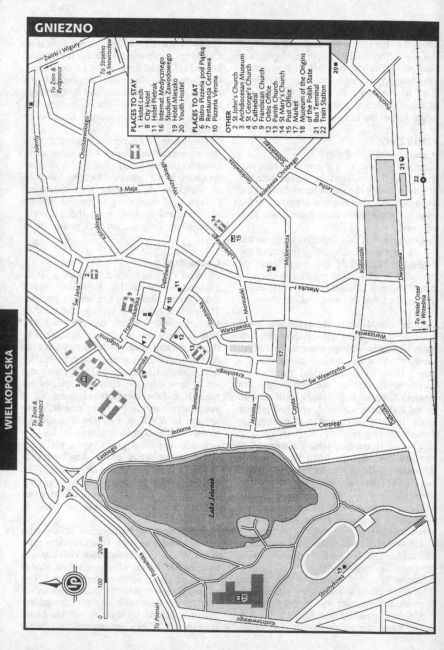

GNIEZNO

PLACES TO STAY
1   Hotel Lech
8   City Hotel
11 Hotel Pietrak
16 Internat Medycznego
    Studium Zawodowego
19 Hotel Mieszko
20 Youth Hostel

PLACES TO EAT
6   Bistro Pizzeria pod Piątką
7   Restauracja Cechowa
10 Pizzeria Verona

OTHER
2   St John's Church
3   Archdiocesan Museum
4   St George's Church
5   Cathedral
9   Franciscan Church
12 Orbis Office
13 Parish Church
14 St Mary's Church
15 Post Office
17 Market
18 Museum of the Origins
    of the Polish State
21 Bus Terminal
22 Train Station

0   100   200 m

To Żnin &
Bydgoszcz

Żwirki i Wigury

To Strzelno
& Inowrocław

Jolenty

Chociszewskiego

To Żnin &
Bydgoszcz

3 Maja

Kilińskiego

Wyszyńskiego

Sienkiewicza

Bolesława Chrobrego

Sobieskiego

Lecha

Pocztowa

Dworcowa

Kościuszki

Lubrańskiego

Dąbrówki

Mickiewicza

Mieszka I

Moniuszki

Warszawska

Warszawska

To Hotel Orzeł
& Września

Św Jana

Franciszkańska

Rynek

Tumska

Podgórna

Łąkiego

Rzeźnicka

Krasickiego

Św Wawrzyńca

Słomianka

Jeziorna

Czysta

Cierpięgi

Dalkoska

Strumykowa

Kostrzewskiego

To Poznań

Pstrażańska

Lake Jelonek

paying its weight in gold, then buried it in Gniezno's cathedral in 999. In the same year, Pope Sylvester canonised the martyr. This contributed to Gniezno's elevation to an archbishopric a year later, and also led to the placing of several important memorials to the saint in the church.

One of these is the red marble **tombstone of St Adalbert**, made around 1480 by Hans Brandt. Unfortunately, it has been moved from the middle of the church to behind the high altar and is almost impossible to see.

Much easier to appreciate are two beautifully carved tombstones on the back wall of the church: to the left is the red marble **tomb of Primate Zbigniew Oleśnicki**, attributed to Veit Stoss; and to the right, the late 15th century bronze **tomb of Archbishop Jakub** from Sienna. Also note an expressive wooden crucifix from around 1440, placed high on the rood beam at the entrance to the chancel.

The most precious possession of the church is the pair of Romanesque **bronze doors** from about 1175, in the back of the right-hand (southern) aisle, at the entrance from the porch. Undeniably one of the best examples of Romanesque art in Europe, the doors depict in bas-relief 18 scenes from the life of St Adalbert. They are ordered chronologically from the bottom side of the left-hand door – where the birth of the saint is portrayed – up to its top and then down the other door to the final scene of the burial in the cathedral.

Framing the doors is the exquisite 15th century **Gothic portal** with the scene of the Last Judgment in its tympanum. In the opposite porch, right across the nave, is another elaborate **Gothic portal**, dating from the same period, this one with the scene of the Crucifixion in its tympanum.

The nearby entrance in the back wall of the church leads downstairs to the **basement** where the relics of the previous Romanesque cathedral can be seen, along with the Gothic tombstones of the bishops.

All along the aisles and the ambulatory are a dozen **chapels** built from the 15th to 18th centuries, and separated from the aisles by decorative wrought-iron screens. There are 17 screens in all, ranging in style from Gothic via Renaissance to baroque, and they reputedly make for the most beautiful collection of its kind gathered in a single church in Poland. Inside the chapels, there are some fine tombstones, altarpieces, paintings and wall decorations – well worth a closer look.

The cathedral is open Monday to Saturday from 10 am to 5 pm, Sunday and holidays from 1.30 to 5.30 pm. You can look around the interior free of charge, except for the bronze doors and the basement, both of which are visited with a guide for a small fee, but with a minimum of US$3 per group for either sight. English or German-speaking guides for the cathedral tour are usually available for US$20 per group. Ask in the office in the porch opposite the bronze doors.

Other Attractions

To the north-east of the cathedral is a group of houses built in the 18th and 19th centuries as residences for the canons and priests. The largest of them, right behind the small St George's Church (Kościół Św Jerzego), has been turned into the **Archdiocesan Museum** (Muzeum Archidiecezji Gnieźnieńskiej), and contains a rich collection of sacral sculpture and painting, liturgical fabrics, coffin portraits and votive offerings. The museum is open Tuesday to Saturday from 10 am to 4 pm.

No other church in Gniezno measures up to the cathedral, but if time permits, you might have a look at the **Franciscan Church** (Kościół Franciszkanów), the **parish church** and **St John's Church** (Kościół Św Jana). The latter is the most interesting, thanks to its 14th century *al secco* wall paintings, which are unfortunately fading away. The church is usually only open for Mass: weekdays at 6 pm, Sunday from 10 am to about 1 pm.

The **Museum of the Origins of the Polish State** (Muzeum Początków Państwa Polskiego) on the opposite side of Lake Jelonek contains archaeological finds, architectural details, documents and works of art, all relating to the development of the Polish nation from pre-Slavic times to the end of the Piast dynasty. The upper floor's rooms are used for temporary exhibitions. The museum is open from 10 am to 5 pm, except Monday and the day following public holidays.

Places to Stay

The all-year *youth hostel* (☎ 426 27 80, *ul Pocztowa 11*) is a five minute walk northeast from the train and bus stations.

The *Internat Medycznego Studium Zawodowego* (☎ 426 34 09, *ul Mieszka I 27*) is a dorm of a medical college, but it rents some rooms to the general public; at US$16 for a neat, ample double room, it's good value. One bath is shared between two adjacent rooms. The Internat is at the back of the corner building of Zespół Szkół Medycznych (Medical School); get there by the gate from either ul Mieszka I or ul Mickiewicza.

Also cheap but more basic and less convenient is *Hotel Orzeł* (☎ 426 49 25, *ul Wrzesińska 25*). It's a former sports dorm in a three-storey building next to the stadium, 800m past the railway track on the Września road. It costs US$10/20/28 a single/double/triple without bath. It has its own restaurant, as simple as the hotel itself.

For somewhere really central, try the *City Hotel* (☎ 425 35 35, *Rynek 15*), which has five double rooms with bath for US$30. Also very central is *Hotel Pietrak* (☎/fax 426 14 97, *ul Chrobrego 3*). Arguably the town's best accommodation, it costs US$40/60/80 with bath and breakfast.

Other options are farther away from the centre and include *Hotel Mieszko* (☎/fax 426 46 25, *ul Strumykowa 2*), in a quiet green area, at US$25/40 a single/double and *Hotel Lech* (☎ 426 23 85, fax 426 12 94, *ul Jolenty 5*) at US$35/50 with breakfast.

If you are travelling between Lake Lednica and Gniezno, you may want to stay in the friendly all-year *youth hostel* (☎ 427 52 99) in Łubowo, 9km west of Gniezno. The hostel is on the main road and is clearly

signposted. Once you're in Łubowo, you might want to visit the fine timber baroque church dating from 1660.

Places to Eat

All the hotels listed above have their own restaurants, with food quality roughly corresponding to the hotel price. The snack bar in *Hotel Pietrak* provides some of the best budget food in town, or you can eat more comfortably in its restaurant.

Apart from the hotel restaurants, there are a number of eating establishments in the centre, including the cheap *Bistro Pizzeria pod Piątką* (*ul Tumska 5*), and the *Pizzeria Verona* (*Rynek 20*). The cosy *Restauracja Cechowa* (*ul Tumska 15*) is among the best in town.

Getting There & Away

The train and bus stations are side by side 1km south-east of the cathedral.

Train Trains run regularly throughout the day to Poznań (51km), and in the opposite direction to Inowrocław (56km), passing via Trzemeszno and Mogilno. There are also several departures daily to Bydgoszcz (102km), Toruń (91km) and Wrocław (216km).

Bus Buses go to Poznań (49km) via Kostrzyn every hour or so, but if you want to stop at Lake Lednica (18km), take the Poznań bus via Pobiedziska (eight daily but fewer on weekdays).

There are three or four morning buses to Żnin via Gąsawa (31km), where you can change for the narrow-gauge train to Biskupin or just walk 2km.

BISKUPIN

Biskupin is a fortified lake village built around 700 BC by a tribe of the Lusatian culture, which at that time lived in central Europe alongside many other groups. The village was accidentally discovered in 1933 and unearthed from beneath a thick layer of turf. It is the only known surviving Iron Age town in Poland, and proves that this region was already inhabited by well organised social groups over 1600 years before the Polish state was born. It has been partially reconstructed to make it more interesting for the casual visitor.

The village was built on a flat island measuring about 180 x 120m, on one of the numerous lakes of the region. It was encircled by an oval, 6m-high barricade consisting of a wooden framework filled with earth and sand. The island's shores were reinforced with a palisade of over 35,000 oak stakes lined up in several rows and driven into the lake bottom to serve as a breakwater and a protection from potential invaders. The only access to the village was through a gateway topped with a watchtower and connected by a 120m bridge to the lake shore.

Within the defensive walls, 13 parallel rows of houses were laid out with streets between them, the whole encircled by a street running inside the ramparts. Over 100 almost identical houses were built for the total population of some 800 to 1000 people.

Farming, livestock breeding and fishing provided a steady, self-sufficient existence for the community, which also maintained trade ties with other settlements in the region and far beyond. Excavations revealed objects from places as distant as Egypt, Italy and the Black Sea coast.

Around 400 BC the village was destroyed, most likely by the Scythians, and it wasn't rebuilt. This was probably because of climatic changes, which were causing the lake's level to rise, making the island uninhabitable. The remains of the village were preserved in mud and silt for 2300 years. Early in the 20th century the water level began to drop and the island re-emerged, eventually turning into a peninsula, as it is today.

The excavations have unearthed a variety of objects belonging to the tribe, including household implements, tools, artefacts and weapons, thus giving a picture of the lifestyle, culture and religion of this ancient society.

Things to See

The Iron Age village together with the land lying between the road and the lake shore form the Archaeological Park (Park Archeologiczny), which is open daily from 9 am to 5 or 6 pm, May to September (closing earlier the rest of the year).

Entering the complex from the road, you find a car park, ticket office, half a dozen budget food outlets, and stalls that sell souvenirs and publications about the place (including some in English).

The Iron Age village lies on the peninsula in the northern end of the park, a five minute walk from the entrance. The gateway, a fragment of the defensive wall and two rows of houses have been reconstructed to give some idea of what the town must have looked like. The interiors of a few houses have been fitted out as they may have been 2700 years ago. From the wharf near the gateway, a tourist boat

KRZYSZTOF DYDYŃSKI

WIELKOPOLSKA

The entrance to Biskupin's Iron Age Village, the earliest known settlement in Poland departs several times a day for a short trip around the lake.

The **museum**, halfway between the peninsula and the park's entrance, shows the finds excavated in and around the village, together with background information about the place and the people. There's a model of the village as it once looked.

Getting There & Away
Bus From the bus stop at the entrance to the Archaeological Park, buses run every hour or two north to Żnin (7km) and south to Gąsawa (2km). There are no direct buses from Biskupin to Gniezno (33km); go to Żnin and change. You may also go via Gąsawa, but there are fewer buses from there to Gniezno than from Żnin.

Narrow-Gauge Train The narrow-gauge tourist train operates from May to September between Żnin and Gąsawa passing Biskupin and Wenecja on the way. There are five trains daily in either direction between around 10 am and 4 pm. In Żnin, the station is alongside the standard-gauge train station; in Gąsawa it's 700m southwest of the Rynek on the Gniezno road. In Biskupin, it's right by the entrance to the park.

WENECJA
Wenecja ('Veh-neh-tsyah'), a small village across the lake from Biskupin, has the **Museum of Narrow-Gauge Railways** (Muzeum Kolei Wąskotorowej), open daily from 9 am to 4 pm (longer in summer). It has old steam locomotives and carriages, some of which house uniforms, tools and other objects related to the railway. A convenient way to visit the museum is to break the Żnin-Biskupin train journey for an hour.

ŻNIN
• **pop 15,000**   ☎ 052
Żnin ('Zhnin') is a stage on your journey to Biskupin rather than a destination in itself. The narrow-gauge train will take you from here to Wenecja and on to Biskupin, and there are also a number of buses. Żnin has

a regular service by either bus or standard-gauge train to/from Gniezno, Bydgoszcz, Toruń and Poznań.

If you have some time to spend here, visit the large brick Gothic tower in the middle of the Rynek, all that's left of the 15th century town hall. The tower houses a museum with an ethnographic collection from the region. The other part of the museum is in the old building on the side of the square.

Places to Stay & Eat
The refurbished *Hotel Basztowy* (☎ 302 00 06), on the corner of the Rynek, costs US$35/45/55 a double/triple/quad with bath and has a reasonable restaurant. Comparable standards are provided by *Hotel Martina* (☎ 302 87 31, ul Mickiewicza 37), 2km from the centre on the Bydgoszcz road. It has fairly good singles/doubles/triples with bath and breakfast for US$20/30/45, and a budget restaurant. Cheaper but more basic is the *Dom Wycieczkowy PTTK* (☎ 302 01 13, ul Szkolna 16), 700m south of the Rynek (US$7 per person in a quad with bath). You can camp in the PTTK grounds. The town has a summer *youth hostel* (☎ 302 04 10, ul Sienkiewicza 1).

TRZEMESZNO
• **pop 8000**   ☎ 052
Trzemeszno ('Tzheh-mesh-no'), 16km east of Gniezno, is an uninspiring regional industrial centre. Few people remember that the first monastery in Poland was founded here, in the closing years of the 10th century. The original church was destroyed by the Bohemians in 1038, and a new Romanesque building went up in the mid-12th century. It was so thoroughly remodelled and enlarged in the baroque period, however, that it's difficult to detect the original features, apart from two Romanesque columns at the back of the nave.

For a casual visitor, though, it's the baroque aspect that will probably be more attractive. The central circular hall, topped with a huge dome, is spacious and bright, and the whole of the vaulting is covered with wall paintings. Note the three paintings in the nave, depicting the death of St Adalbert, the recovery of his body for a ransom in gold, and his funeral. The church is on Plac Kosmowskiego, near the centre.

Places to Stay & Eat

Trzemeszno has a summer *youth hostel* (☎ 315 40 31, ul Wyszyńskiego 3) and two hotels: the simple *Hotel Czeremcha* (☎ 315 43 86), opposite the church (US$14/20 a double without/with bath), and the far better *Hotel Pietrak* (☎/fax 315 44 00, ul Foluska 2), on the eastern fringes of the town (US$40/45 a single/double with bath and breakfast). Both have their own eating facilities, their quality roughly reflecting the hotel rates.

Getting There & Away

The main bus stop is on the central Plac Św Wojciecha, a short walk from the church. Buses run regularly between Gniezno, Mogilno and Strzelno, stopping en route at Trzemeszno. There are trains to Gniezno and Mogilno, but the station is a long way from the centre, on the town's northern outskirts.

MOGILNO
- pop 13,000   ☎ 052

Mogilno, 15km north-east of Trzemeszno, has little for tourists except for the 11th century **Church of St John the Evangelist** (Kościół Św Jana Ewangelisty), one of the largest Romanesque buildings in the region. The church was extensively transformed in later periods and has mostly baroque decorations. The lower parts of the walls and columns have had their plaster removed to reveal the stone blocks of the original structure. Underneath are two Romanesque crypts where some archaeological finds are on display. The church is about 1km south of the town's centre, on the Strzelno road.

Places to Stay & Eat

The as yet unnamed *hotel* (☎ 315 74 94, Rynek 17) next door to the post office has

rather basic doubles/triples/quads with shared facilities for US$14/17/20. Appreciably better is *Hotel Józefina* (☎ 315 71 60, Plac Wolności 4), which offers 10 doubles rated from US$20 to US$35 depending on the standard. It has its own restaurant, probably the best eating place in town. If you happen to be in town between 1 July and 25 August, you can try the *youth hostel* (☎ 315 26 83, ul Piłsudskiego 18).

Getting There & Away

The train and bus stations are at the western end of the town; both provide good transport around the region. To get to the centre from either station, head eastward across the park bordering a lake to Plac Wolności.

STRZELNO
- pop 6000   ☎ 052

Much more interesting than Trzemeszno and Mogilno is Strzelno ('Stzhel-no'), which boasts two of the best Romanesque churches in the region. They are next to each other, about 200m east of the Rynek.

Church of the Holy Trinity

This church (Kościół Św Trójcy), built around 1170, acquired a Gothic vault in the 14th century and a baroque façade four centuries later. The interior has mainly baroque furnishings, including the high altar and a decorative rood beam, which form a remarkably harmonious composition with the whitewashed Gothic vaulting supported on four original Romanesque columns. These columns, revealed only in 1946 during the postwar restoration (they were previously plastered over in the walls which separated the nave from the aisles), are the most precious treasure of the church, particularly the two with elaborate figurative designs. There are 18 figures carved in each column; those on the left-hand column personify vices while those on the right are virtues. Of the other two, one is plain but the other has unusual spiral grooves from top to bottom.

The door at the head of the right-hand aisle leads to St Barbara's Chapel, its fine, palm-like vault resting on yet another delicately carved Romanesque pillar.

Next to the main entrance to the church (to the left as you face the façade) is an arched doorway. Enter it and you'll see on your right a Romanesque portal supported on two carved columns. Its tympanum depicts the scene of the Teaching of Christ. This was once the main entrance to the church. There's another fine Romanesque doorway on the right wall of the church.

St Procopius' Church

This church (Kościół Św Prokopa) was built of red stone a decade or two earlier than its neighbour, and has preserved its austere Romanesque form remarkably well, even though its upper part was rebuilt in brick after its destruction in the 18th century. It has a circular nave, with a square chancel on one side and a tower on the other, the whole adorned with typical semicircular apses on the northern side of the nave. The interior, almost free of decoration, looks admirably authentic. Right by the entrance is the original 12th century font. The church is kept locked; ask the doorkeeper to open it for you. He lives in the building between the two churches – enter it from the back.

Places to Stay & Eat

The *Dom Wycieczkowy Strzelno* (☎ 318 92 37, Plac Daszyńskiego 1) costs US$9/12 per person in doubles or triples without/ with bath. Opposite the hotel is the only restaurant to speak of, the *Restauracja Piastowska*, though it's nothing special. There are a few snack bars on and around the Rynek. The summer *youth hostel (ul Parkowa 10)* is open from 1 July to 25 August.

Getting There & Away

Passenger trains no longer call at Strzelno, but bus transport is reasonable to Inowrocław, Mogilno and some other regional destinations. The bus terminal is at the western end of the town. Walk east from here 500m along ul Kolejowa to Plac Daszyńskiego, a square where the road divides (the above-mentioned hotel and restaurant are here). Take the left-hand fork leading to the Rynek (a five minute walk) and turn right to the churches.

KRUSZWICA

• pop 10,000   ☎ 052

Set on the northern end of the 20km-long Lake Gopło, Kruszwica ('Kroosh-veetsah') existed from at least the 8th century as a fortified village of the Goplanie, one of the Slav tribes living in the area. The Polanie farther to the west and the Goplanie didn't get along particularly well, and the latter group was eventually subjugated. Today Kruszwica is an undistinguished small industrial town which boasts the following two remnants of the Piasts.

Things to See

The early 12th century stone Romanesque **collegiate church** was much altered in later periods but returned more or less to its original form in the course of postwar restoration. The interior fittings include the 12th century baptismal font at the entrance to the chancel. The church is on the northeastern outskirts of the town, a 10 minute walk from the Rynek.

The 32m-high octagonal **Mouse Tower** (Mysia Wieża), near the Rynek, is the only remainder of the 14th century castle built by King Kazimierz Wielki. The name derives from a legend of the evil ruler of the Goplanie, the legendary Popiel, who was eaten here by mice. You can go to the top of the tower (May to September 9 am to 5 or 6 pm) for a view over the town and lake. From the foot of the tower a tourist boat departs several times a day in summer for an hour-long trip around Lake Gopło.

Places to Stay & Eat

Hotel Sportowy Gopło (☎ 351 52 33, ul Poznańska 17), next to the stadium (five minutes from the Rynek), offers acceptable doubles with bath for US$20, and beds in triples or quads with shared facilities for US$7. It has a budget bistro, or you can go for a meal at the *Zajazd u Piasta Kołodzieja* next to the Mouse Tower.

An alternative place to stay is *Hotel w Pałacu* (☎ *351 54 21*) in Kobylniki, a village 1.5km north of Kruszwica on the Inowrocław road. The hotel is in an eclectic Prussian-style brick palace built at the beginning of the 20th century by a German baron. It's pretty run down, yet still good value at US$6/16 per bed in rooms without/with bath. The palace is surrounded by a large wooded park.

Getting There & Away
There is no longer a train service but buses to Inowrocław (15km) run every half-hour, and to Strzelno (15km) every other hour or so. The main bus stop is on the Rynek.

INOWROCŁAW
• pop 80,000   ☎ 052

Inowrocław ('Ee-no-vrots-wahf') is the last (or first) stop on the Piast Route. Its historic monuments probably don't deserve a special journey, but the place is a regional transport hub and you can get to virtually every town on the route from there by bus or train.

From its beginnings in the 12th century, Inowrocław was a busy trading centre and a manufacturer of woollen cloth, as well as a regional nucleus of political power. The discovery of vast salt deposits in the mid-19th century turned the town into an important salt producer. A 140km network of tunnels was hewn out under the city, but this led to catastrophic building collapses and the authorities were forced to close the mines down altogether. Salt also provided the town with a spa, set in a lush spa park 1km west of the Old Town. The town now suffers from pollution, mainly from the chemical industry.

Things to See
The 12th century stone St Mary's Church (Kościół NMP), commonly referred to as the Ruin (Ruina), is on the corner of ul Laubitza and ul Orłowska. It was destroyed almost completely by fire in 1834 and was long left in ruins (hence its nickname). It wasn't until 1901 that the reconstruction gave it back its original Romanesque shape. The sparse interior decoration adds nobility to the severe stone structure.

If you need something more decorative, go to the elephantine neo-Romanesque brick Church of the Annunciation (Kościół Zwiastowania NMP) with its exuberant wall paintings all over the vault, and colourful stained-glass windows. It's just 200m west of the Ruin.

Places to Stay & Eat
The only central place to stay is the overpriced *Hotel Bast* (☎ *357 20 24*, ☎/*fax 357 28 88, ul Królowej Jadwigi 35/37*), with singles/doubles/triples without bath for US$30/50/65 and singles/doubles with bath for US$50/80.

In the spa area, *Hotel Park* (☎ *357 28 03, fax 357 00 11, ul Świętokrzyska 107*) is possibly better value at US$25/35 a single/double without bath, US$40/50 with bath. The basic *Schronisko Turystyczne OSiR* (☎ *357 67 30, ul Wierzbińskiego 9*) nearby charges US$7 per person in three to seven-bed dorms.

Inowrocław has a summer *youth hostel* (☎ *357 72 22, ul Poznańska 345A*), but it's in the distant suburb of Mątwy, 5km south of the centre.

Both listed hotels have their own dining facilities, or you can have your meal in the reasonable *Bar Bistro Aleksandria* (*ul Dworcowa 11*).

Getting There & Away
Train The train station is on the north-western outskirts of the town, on the Bydgoszcz road, 1.5km from the centre, and is serviced by frequent urban buses.

There's a wealth of trains to most major cities including hourly trains to Bydgoszcz (46km) and Toruń (35km), and a regular service to Gdańsk (206km), Poznań (107km) and Wrocław (272km). Trains to Mogilno (26km) and Gniezno (56km) depart every hour or so and several trains to Żnin (38km) give easy access to Biskupin.

WIELKOPOLSKA

Bus The bus terminal is halfway between the train station and the Rynek, a 10 minute walk to either. There are frequent connections to Kruszwica (15km) and Strzelno (20km), which are not well serviced by trains.

South-Eastern Wielkopolska

KALISZ

• pop 107,000   ☎ 062

The main urban centre of south-eastern Wielkopolska, Kalisz ('Kah-leesh') is not a major tourist destination but can be a place to break your journey if you travel in the area. If you decide to stop here you may want to visit the two fine palaces nearby, at Gołuchów and Antonin (detailed in separate sections after Kalisz).

Kalisz has the longest documented history of any town in Poland: it was mentioned by Claudius Ptolemy in his renowned *Geography* of the 2nd century AD as Kalisia, a trading settlement on the Amber Route between the Roman Empire and the Baltic Sea. In about the 9th century a stronghold was built (in the present-day suburb of Zawodzie) and the town continued to develop until the 13th century. Burnt down in 1233, it was rebuilt farther to the north, in its present location.

During the reign of Kazimierz Wielki the town acquired defensive walls with 15 watchtowers and a castle. It continued to grow steadily until the 16th century, from which point it began to decline. A huge fire in 1792 left only the churches standing, and almost all the fortifications were taken down in the early 19th century.

The greatest tragedy, sometimes compared to Warsaw's annihilation in 1944, came in WWI: in August 1914 Kalisz was razed to the ground by the invading Germans. Within a month, the population dropped from 70,000 to 5000 and most buildings lay in ruins, though the churches – as before – miraculously escaped destruction. The town was rebuilt on a new plan, only occasionally following the earlier one. Most of the buildings survived WWII without much damage, but apart from those on the Rynek not many have been renovated.

Information

The Centrum Informacji Turystycznej (☎/fax 764 21 84), ul Garbarska 2, is open weekdays 10 am to 5 pm.

The Bank Pekao, ul Grodzka 7, will exchange travellers cheques and has an ATM. Cash can be easily changed at any of the kantors around the Rynek.

Things to See

The Old Town sits in the angle between the Prosna and Bernardynka rivers, with a dozen small bridges and a pleasant park stretching to the south-east. The best point to begin your sightseeing is possibly the tower of the town hall in the middle of the Rynek; it's open weekdays 9 am to 3 pm.

Kalisz has some good churches. The oldest, **St Nicholas' Church** (Kościół Św Mikołaja), dates from the 13th century and was originally Gothic, but has been modernised several times. The present-day interior is mainly baroque with a vault in Renaissance style. The painting of the Descent from the Cross over the high altar is a copy. The original work, painted in Rubens' workshop about 1617 and donated to the church, was burnt or stolen during a mysterious fire in 1973.

The Gothic **collegiate church** was built in the 14th century, but the main nave collapsed in 1783 and was rebuilt in baroque style; only the presbytery has preserved its original shape. The most valuable item inside is the Gothic triptych from around 1500; once placed on the high altar, it is now in the head of the left-hand aisle. In the opposite aisle, the ornate St Joseph's chapel dates from 1790. Its main altar boasts the painting of the Holy Family, venerated by the faithful thanks to numerous miraculous healings that are said to have happened.

The former **Bernardine Church** (Kościół Pobernardyński), built in 1607 and now

Hunting Palace in Antonin near Kalisz

Renaissance town hall, Old Town Square, Poznań

Summer sunset in Wielkopolska National Park

Moorish Hall within the mock-Gothic castle in Kórnik

Baroque 18th century palace in Rogalin

KALISZ

PLACES TO STAY
17 Hotel Europa

PLACES TO EAT
5 Restauracja
  Piętorko
7 Bar Mleczny
8 Bar Nem-Nam-Khong
18 Restauracja KTW
20 Restauracja Kalmar

OTHER
1 Bernardine Church
2 St Nicholas' Church
3 Bank Pekao

4 Main Post Office
6 Tourist Office
9 EMPiK
10 Town Hall
11 Collegiate Church
12 Jesuit Church
13 Regional Museum
  (Kulisiewicz Gallery)
14 Centre of Culture & Arts
15 Franciscan Church
16 Regional Museum
  (Archaeology &
  Ethnography)
19 Theatre
21 Reformate Church

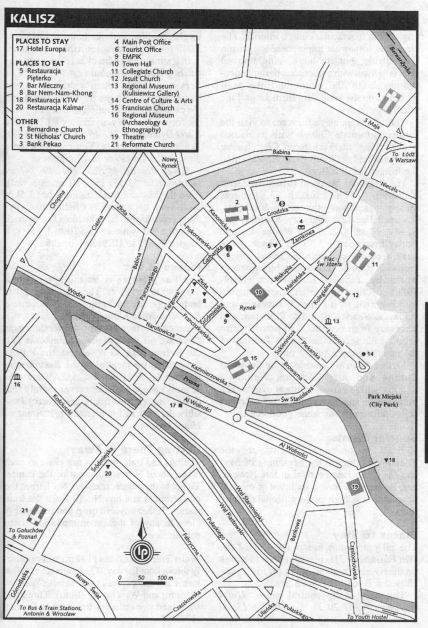

owned by the Jesuits, contains possibly the city's most spectacular church interior. The church is somewhat unprepossessing from the outside, but its large, single-naved interior glows with sumptuous baroque decoration. Both the altars and the wall paintings on the vault date from around the mid-18th century.

Church-lovers may also want to visit the former Reformate Church with its rococo woodcarving, the Franciscan Church near the Rynek and the Jesuit Church adjacent to the former Jesuit college.

The **Regional Museum** (Muzeum Ziemi Kaliskiej), ul Kościuszki 12, features archaeological and ethnographic exhibits. It's open Tuesday, Thursday, Saturday and Sunday 10 am to 2.30 pm, Wednesday and Friday from noon to 5.30 pm. The museum has a separate section in the Jesuit college (entrance from ul Łazienna), which displays works by Tadeusz Kulisiewicz (1899-1988), a Kalisz-born artist, known mainly for his drawings. It's open Wednesday and Friday to Sunday 10 am to 2.30 pm, and Thursday from noon to 5.30 pm. It's also open on the second and fourth Tuesday of the month from 12.30 to 5 pm.

Farther down ul Łazienna is the **Centre of Culture and Arts** (Centrum Kultury i Sztuki), where various cultural events take place, and a small art shop by the entrance sells crafts including some good glass.

Special Events

Kalisz's major annual events are the Theatre Meetings at the beginning of May and the Piano Jazz Festival in late November. Both events have a tradition of over 20 years and rank high on the national cultural map.

Places to Stay

The all-year *youth hostel* (☎ 757 24 04, Wał Piastowski 3) is pleasantly set in a park on the riverbank, about 200m off ul Częstochowska. Book in before 8 pm.

The only really central place, *Hotel Europa* (☎ 767 20 31, fax 767 24 15, Al Wolności 5) has long passed its best days

but it's still not a bad bet at US$14/22 for singles/doubles without bath and US$27/34/40 for singles/doubles/triples with bath.

In a similar price bracket is the undistinguished *Hotel u Bogdana* (☎ 753 08 23, ul Legionów 15/17), set in a drab apartment block midway between the train station and the centre. Another option in this bracket is the former Dom Wycieczkowy PTTK, now *Hotel Dyonizy* (☎ 757 46 50, ul Łódzka 29), 1km east of the centre. You can walk there through the City Park in 15 minutes.

Hotel Prosna (☎/fax 764 49 74, ul Górnośląska 53/55) is a 10 minute walk from the bus and train stations, but 1.5km away from the centre. It's better than anything listed above, but like most Orbis stock it's not good value at US$70 to US$100 a single, US$70 to US$120 a double.

Places to Eat

The *Bar Mleczny* is on the corner of ul Targowa and ul Złota. There are some other budget options, including the Vietnamese *Bar Nem-Nam-Khong* (ul Złota 4).

Among restaurants, try the *Restauracja Pięterko*, off the Rynek (ul Zamkowa 12), the *Restauracja KTW*, across the Prosna River from the theatre, or the *Restauracja Kalmar* (ul Śródmiejska 26). All are reasonably cheap; the latter serves mainly fish dishes. Better restaurants are scarce. Possibly the best in town is the restaurant of *Hotel Prosna*.

Getting There & Away

The bus and train stations are close to each other, about 2km south-west of the centre. To get to the centre, take bus No 1 from the bus terminal and bus No 10 from the train station. Either bus will drop you reasonably close to any of the accommodation listed earlier.

Train Trains to Łódź (113km) run regularly throughout the day. There are several fast trains and one express train to both Warsaw (256km) and Wrocław (130km). Three fast trains and two ordinary trains go to Poznań (138km).

Bus There are eight buses daily to Poznań (130km), and five to Wrocław (121km). The Wrocław buses can drop you off at Antonin (40km). To Gołuchów (22km), take the hourly suburban bus No 12 to Pleszew; it passes through the centre along ul Sukiennicza and ul Kolegialna.

GOŁUCHÓW
- **pop 1200**   ☎ **062**

The small village of Gołuchów ('Go-woo-hoof') boasts a castle looking a bit like those in the Loire Valley in France. It began around 1560 as a small fortified mansion with four octagonal towers at the corners, built by the Leszczyński family. Some 50 years later it was enlarged and re-shaped into a palatial residence in late Renaissance style. Abandoned at the end of the 17th century, it gradually fell into ruins until the Działyński family, the owners of Kórnik (see that section), bought it in 1856. It was completely rebuilt in 1872-85, and it was then that it acquired its French appearance.

The castle's stylistic mutation was essentially the brainchild of Izabela Czartoryska, daughter of the renowned Prince Adam Czartoryski and wife of Jan Działyński. She commissioned the French architect Viollet le Duc, and under his supervision many architectural bits and pieces were brought from abroad, mainly from France and Italy, and incorporated into the building.

Having acquired large numbers of works of art, Izabela crammed them into the castle (or rather the palace, by that stage), which became one of the largest private museums in Europe. During WWII the Nazis stole the works of art but the building itself survived relatively undamaged. Part of the collection was recovered and is now once more on display in the palace.

Things to See

The **castle** doesn't look particularly impressive from the park entrance, but walk around it to discover its charm; the best view is from the northern side. You enter the castle through a decorative 17th century doorway which leads into a graceful arcaded courtyard.

Inside the building is the **museum**. In its numerous rooms, a wealth of furniture, paintings, sculptures, weapons, tapestries, rugs and the like have been collected from Europe and beyond. The highlight is a collection of Greek vases from the 5th century BC. The museum is open Tuesday to Sunday 10 am to 4 pm. Visitors are taken round in groups; tours start every half-hour.

To the south of the castle is the **oficyna**, which looks like a small palace. Initially a distillery, it was considerably extended in 1874 and adapted for a residence. It was here that the owners lived after the castle was turned into a museum. Today the building accommodates the **Museum of Forestry**, which focuses on the history of Polish forestry and the timber industry. There's also a collection of contemporary art connected to forestry, either in subject matter or by means of the material used. The building has its original interior decoration. It's open Tuesday to Sunday 10 am to 3 pm. You can have a cup of coffee in the café in the adjoining building before taking a stroll through the park.

The English-style **park** with several hundred species of trees and shrubs was laid out during the last quarter of the 19th century. Its oldest part is the lime-tree alley planted in 1857. The park is open daily 8 am to 8 pm and entrance is free.

The **Museum of Forest Techniques and Technology**, in the far north of the park, features tools and machinery used in forestry. If it is closed, ring the door bell on the next door to your right.

A dozen **bison** live relatively freely in a large, fenced-off part of the forest, just west of the park. Don't expect them to pose for photos; except at feeding times (around 8 am and 7 pm), you will usually only see them in the distance.

Places to Stay

The summer *camp site* (☎ *761 82 81*) is in the forest by a lake, about 1.5km from Gołuchów towards Kalisz. A bed in a cabin costs around US$5. The small *youth hostel* (☎ *761 70 20)* opens from 1 May to 31 September in the Gołuchów school.

The *Dom Pracy Twórczej* (☎ *761 71 11, ul Borowskiego 2)*, off the Kalisz road, is open year-round and costs US$28 for a reasonable double or triple room with private bath.

Getting There & Away

Suburban bus No 12 goes roughly every hour (on Sunday every two hours) to/from Kalisz (22km). About eight buses daily run to Poznań (108km) and can drop you off in Kórnik (another castle; see the Kórnik section).

ANTONIN

* pop 500   ☎ 062

Today a local weekend/holiday resort, before WWII Antonin was the summer residence of the Radziwiłł family, one of the richest and best known aristocratic clans in Poland. In 1822-24 Prince Antoni Radziwiłł (after whom the place was named) built the Hunting Palace (Pałac Myśliwski). This handsome wooden structure was designed by Karl Friedrich Schinkel, one of the outstanding German architects of the period who was responsible for a number of monumental buildings in Berlin.

The palace is an unusual structure. The main body of the building is a large, octagonal, three-storey hall, called the Chimney Room, with a column in the middle supporting the roof and also functioning as a chimney for the central fireplace. There are four side wings, originally designed as living rooms for the owner and his guests. One such guest, Frédéric Chopin, stayed here twice, giving concerts and composing.

Today the palace is a hotel. Its wings have been converted into hotel rooms and there's a stylish restaurant in the Chimney Room. The palace is surrounded by a forest which offers some pleasant walks; there are several marked trails.

Special Events

In memory of Chopin, piano recitals are held in the palace (normally from mid-June to mid-September, on Sunday at 6 pm). A special bus is laid on for guests from Ostrów Wielkopolski; it departs at 5 pm from the Szkoła Muzyczna (Music School) at ul Wolności 29. There's also a four day Chopin Festival in September.

Places to Stay & Eat

By far the most romantic place is the *Pałac Myśliwski* (☎ *734 81 14, fax 736 16 51)*, which offers singles/doubles/triples with bath for US$28/40/44. You can eat in the restaurant in the Chimney Room. The hotel is open all year. Advance booking is recommended as the palace also caters for conferences, meetings etc.

On the opposite side of the road from the palace is the *Motel Lido* (☎ *734 81 91)*, which has eight double rooms with bath, for US$35, and a restaurant.

Behind the motel is a large lakeside holiday centre, the *Ośrodek Rekreacyjno-Wypoczynkowy Lido* (☎ *734 81 27)*. It features a collection of double and triple cabins with and without bath (US$10 to US$25 per cabin depending on the size and standard), open from May to September. There are also two snack bars on the grounds.

Adjacent to the Ośrodek is the *Camping Nr 26* (☎ *734 81 94)*, open June to September. It also has cabins, or you can pitch your own tent; choose a place as far from the road as possible – the traffic noise can be annoying.

There is a July-August *youth hostel* (☎ *734 81 78)* in Ludwików, 2km west of Antonin.

Getting There & Away

The train station is about 1km from the palace, beyond the lake. Several trains run daily to Poznań (130km). There are no direct trains to Kalisz: you must change in Ostrów Wielkopolski.

There are five buses daily to Wrocław (81km), and five to Kalisz (40km). About eight buses run to Ostrów Wielkopolski (17km); from Ostrów suburban bus No 19 runs regularly to Kalisz.

LICHEŃ

Licheń ('Lee-hen'), a small village 13km north-east of Konin in the centre of Poland, is reputedly Poland's second most visited pilgrimage site after Częstochowa. The pilgrims' destination, a sizable ecclesiastical complex, occupies the village's centre and includes two churches, the Way of the Cross (Golgotha) in the form of a fairy-tale stone fortress, and chapels and statues scattered over the grounds. The place attracts more than a million pilgrims annually, who come to pay tribute to the miraculous image of the Virgin Mary, deposited in the high altar of the main church. But things are changing …

The energetic local priest Eugeniusz Makulski has decided to build a third church as a 'votive offering of the nation for the year 2000', to celebrate two millennia of Christianity. Construction began in 1994 and is due to conclude by 2000. About 500 people work daily on the construction site.

This is not your average church. The gigantic basilica will be the largest church in Poland, seventh largest in Europe and 11th largest in the world. It's 120m long and 77m wide, and its tower will be 128m high. Its 8300 sq metre interior will comfortably house 20,000 faithful. Beneath the main hall is the round Golden Chapel, which is a good-sized church in itself. It was completed in 1996 and is crammed with crystal chandeliers and golden stucco. The floor is of marble imported from all over the world to form a multicoloured design.

The basilica has 60 doors and 365 windows, some of which are 9m tall and have gilded frames. There will be 50 confessionals. The 35m-diameter dome is said to be the world's fifth largest. The basilica will shelter the largest monument to Pope John Paul II – a 9m-tall, 8-tonne bronze statue designed by Kraków sculptor Marian Konieczny.

The design of the church, by Polish architect Barbara Bielecka, is nothing bold, futuristic or stunning, except for the mammoth size of the building. It's a quite traditional, heavy edifice which 'combines the architectural style of the first centuries of Christianity with that of the 19th century'.

The whole project is said to be financed exclusively by the donations of the faithful, collected by the priest for nearly 20 years. He doesn't give the figure, commenting that one shouldn't look into God's pockets. Whatever can be said about the cost, it is enormous. The doors and windows alone cost US$3 million.

Places to Stay & Eat

The Church provides basic accommodation in the sanctuary complex. A bed in a four to six-bed dorm costs US$4. There's also a simple, cheap cafeteria. The locals rent out rooms in their homes as well. As work progresses, there is likely to be some hotel and restaurant development in the vicinity.

Getting There & Away

Konin, a fair-sized town 13km to the south-west, is the jumping-off point for Licheń. The busy Poznań-Warsaw rail line goes through Konin, with frequent connections in both directions. There are hourly buses linking Licheń with Konin.

Pomerania

Pomerania, or Pomorze, stretches along Poland's Baltic coast, from the German frontier in the west to the lower Vistula valley in the east. The region rests on two large urban pillars: Szczecin at its western end and Gdańsk to the east. Between them hangs the coastline and, farther inland, a wide belt of lake country.

Gdańsk is perhaps Poland's most attractive historic city after Kraków, while Szczecin is far less atmospheric. The lower Vistula valley is notable for its castles and the fine Gothic town of Toruń. For those who prefer beaches to castles, there's a long string of seaside resorts along the coast.

Polish history has nowhere been more complex than in the north, where various areas have changed hands on numerous occasions. On balance, the north has spent more time outside the national borders than within them.

The Lower Vistula

The valley of the lower Vistula is a fertile land bisected by the wide, leisurely river. Flat, open and largely occupied by farms, the region is not renowned for its natural charms, nor is the river itself particularly attractive. On the other hand, the area has a rich cultural inheritance, even though much of it was lost in WWII.

The Vistula was an important waterway through which Crown goods were shipped to the Baltic and abroad. In medieval times many trading ports were founded along the Vistula's banks all the way from Toruń down to Gdańsk. But most of these ports were not Polish; the medieval history of the lower Vistula is intimately linked with the German organisation called the Teutonic Order (see the boxed text for details of them). Remnants of the Teutonic Order now comprise some of the most important sights in the region.

Highlights

- Explore the Gothic city of Toruń with its mighty churches
- Wander around the lethargic old town of Chełmno
- See the exuberant 15th century basilica in Pelplin
- Go for a tour of the giant Malbork castle
- Discover the little town of Frombork, the home of Copernicus
- Stroll about the streets of Gdańsk's meticulously reconstructed historic core and visit the colossal St Mary's Church
- View the unique shifting dunes in the Słowiński National Park

BYDGOSZCZ

- **pop 390,000** ☎ 052

On the border of Wielkopolska and Pomerania, Bydgoszcz ('Bid-goshch') is the only place in this area which was outside the territory of the Teutonic Order. Founded in 1346, the town developed unhurriedly as a

POMERANIA

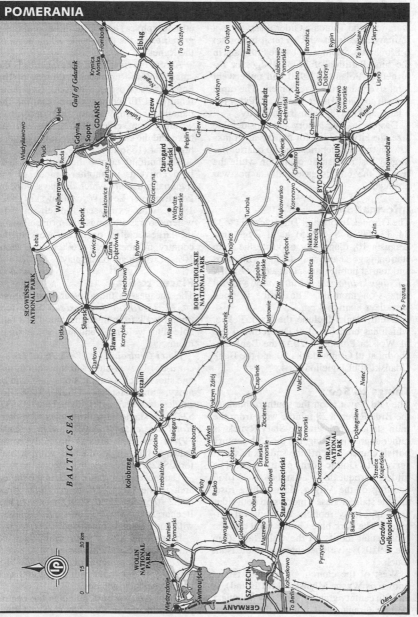

trading centre and beer producer. During the wars with the Teutonic Order it served as a military base from which Polish troops set off for battle. Subjugated by the Prussians in the First Partition of 1773, Bydgoszcz returned to Poland in 1920 and underwent intensive industrial development. The rapid growth continued after WWII, and today it's a large and heavily industrialised city.

Despite its long history and considerable size, the city has little for tourists and ranks low on travel itineraries. Its old quarter has largely lost its historic character, while the rest of the city is essentially a postwar product.

Information

The Ośrodek Informacji Turystycznej (☎ 22 84 32, fax 345 47 85) at ul Zygmunta Augusta 10, diagonally opposite the train station, is good and well stocked with maps and tourist publications. Get a copy of *BIK – Bydgoski Informator Kulturalny*, a useful what's-on monthly. The office is open weekdays 8 am to 4 pm.

Useful banks include the Bank Pekao, which has branches at ul Dworcowa 6 and ul Wojska Polskiego 20A, the Bank Zachodni at ul Grunwaldzka 50 and the Bank Gdański at ul Jagiellońska 4.

Things to See

The Old Town is on the southern bank of the Brda River, a 20 minute walk from the train station. Its heart, the Stary Rynek, is rather unprepossessing, but the 15th century **parish church**, just off the square, has preserved its Gothic form pretty well. The gilded baroque high altar boasts a 1466 painting of the Virgin Mary with a rose, and the stained-glass windows on both sides are supposedly replicas of medieval originals. The dark blue Gothic vault and the ornamental motifs on the walls (added in the 1920s) give the interior a pleasant touch.

West of the church, on a small island known as Wyspa Młyńska (Mill Island), is an 18th century granary, the Biały Spichlerz (White Granary). It houses the **regional museum** featuring the area's history and ethnography. There are three more old **granaries** on the river bank, 100m north of the Rynek.

Across the river from the granaries is the small Gothic-Renaissance **Church of the Poor Clares** (Kościół Klarysek). Its interior features 17th century paintings on the panelled ceiling and a fine decorative wrought-iron screen (1651) between the nave and the chancel with its heavily gilded high altar (1636).

The building next to the church, formerly a convent, is another branch of the **regional museum**, which displays work by Polish painter Leon Wyczółkowski (1852-1936), who expressed himself in oils, watercolours, drawings and prints. This is the largest collection of his work in the country, numbering over 600 pieces, about 10% of which are on display.

Places to Stay

The cheapest is the all-year *youth hostel* (☎ 22 75 70, ul Sowińskiego 5), a five minute walk from the train station. It's reliable and well run, and has some small rooms.

Hotel Centralny (☎ 22 88 76, ul Dworcowa 85) is even closer to the station, just one short block away. It's busy and can be noisy, and charges US$24/40/68 for singles/doubles/quads without bath, US$32/52/75 for singles/doubles/triples with bath. *Hotel Asystenta* (☎ 22 06 31, ul Dworcowa 79) in the same area is probably better value. It has singles/doubles without bath for US$25/30.

The most comfortable place in the station area is the large, 270-room *Hotel Brda* (☎ 22 40 61, fax 22 56 55, ul Dworcowa 94). It charges US$60/90 for singles/doubles with bath, breakfast included.

If you want to stay in the Old Town, the only place is *Hotel Ratuszowy* (☎ 22 88 61, ul Długa 31), which charges US$28/44 a single/double without bath, US$40/60 with bath (breakfast included).

There are two posh hotels in the centre, just north of the Old Town. The Orbis-

The Teutonic Order vs the Polish Crown

The Teutonic Order was a German religious and military organisation founded in the 1190s in Palestine during the Third Crusade. Initially overshadowed by two similar orders, the Templars and the Hospitallers, the Teutonic Knights came to the fore under their fourth Grand Master, Hermann von Salza, when they began spreading into Central Europe. They were backed by German feudal overlords, who saw this as an opportunity for territorial and political expansion to the east.

The order's involvement in Polish affairs began in 1226, when Duke Konrad of Mazovia sought its help against the Prussians, a pagan Baltic tribe which repeatedly invaded and laid waste to the northern provinces of the principality. The duke offered the order a stretch of land north of Toruń in exchange for protection of his duchy and the conversion to Christianity of the troublesome Prussians. The duke hoped to retain sovereignty over the Teutonic territory, but matters soon got out of hand and the agreement turned out to be one of Poland's worst political deals. The subsequent conflict punctuated the history of the two states for 250 years.

The order founded its first strongholds in Chełmno and Toruń, and in following decades expanded swiftly into the surrounding region. Following the loss of their base in Palestine, the knights began the construction of a new fortress in Malbork, into which the Grand Master moved from Venice in 1309. By that time, the order had conquered the region of Gdańsk, including the city itself (1308), and expanded to the east, swallowing up large areas of the Baltic provinces. In other words, the order effectively cut Poland off from the sea. It also solved the problem of converting the native Prussians, in the simplest possible way – by wiping them out. The name of the tribe survived, however; oddly enough, it passed to their exterminators (and descendants thereof), whose ethnic origin was quite different from the original tribe.

Apart from its military power, the order also grew in economic strength, taking advantage of its association with the Hanseatic League, or Hansa. Founded in the second half of the 13th century, the Hansa was an alliance of northern German towns which aimed to protect the trading interests of its members. It was soon joined by most of the ports of the North Sea and the Baltic, and inland cities of northern Europe. By the mid-14th century, the league numbered 100 towns and virtually monopolised north European trade. Many of the order's outposts such as Gdańsk, Toruń and Königsberg entered the league, as well as some major Polish cities including royal Kraków.

The conflict between the order and the Polish Crown intensified throughout the 14th century, culminating in the Battle of Grunwald of 1410, in which Władysław Jagiełło won a decisive victory over the knights. However, he was unable to capture Malbork, which was only seized in 1457 during the Thirteen Years' War (1454-66), presaging the eventual defeat of the order. The 1466 Treaty of Toruń gave Poland the western part of the knights' territory, which became known as Royal Prussia, while the remaining eastern part, Ducal (or East) Prussia, came under Polish rule in 1525, when the order converted to Lutheranism.

POMERANIA

operated *Hotel pod Orłem* (*Under the Eagle;* ☎ 22 18 61, fax 22 89 88, ul Gdańska 14) is the city's landmark. Built in 1896, it has hosted most visiting VIPs. Singles/doubles cost US$100/120 (30% less on weekends), breakfast included.

Completely different is the *City Hotel* (☎ 22 88 41, fax 22 52 66, ul 3 Maja 6). Austrian built, owned and managed, this is a modern place which opened in 1992. It charges much the same as the Pod Orłem.

Places to Eat

The cheapest place in the train station area is *Bar Mleczny Dworcowy (ul Dworcowa 75)*, a genuine milk bar serving tasty food for next to nothing. The nearby *Gospoda przy Kominku (ul Dworcowa 87)* is a reasonable restaurant.

In the Old Town, *Bar Mleczny Kaskada (ul Mostowa 2)*, in a glass-and-steel building just off the Rynek, is the place to go for a cheap meal. Otherwise, check out the inexpensive *Bar Ratuszowy* in Hotel Ratuszowy. You can also have simple budget meals in the new and charming *pub* (still unnamed as we went to press) at Stary Rynek 16, which is a good place to drink as well.

More upmarket places in the centre include *Piwnica Ratuszowa (ul Jezuicka 16)* and *Restauracja Orfeusz (ul Długa 62)*. Arguably the best in town is the old-fashioned restaurant of *Hotel pod Orłem*, which serves reliable Polish and European food. *Restauracja Chopin* in the City Hotel is a serious competitor.

Getting There & Away

The train station is 1.5km north-west of the Old Town, while the bus terminal is 1km east of the historic quarter; urban bus Nos 77 and 104 link the two stations, passing through the centre.

There are plenty of trains and PKS buses; both go frequently to Toruń (51km or 47km, respectively) and Inowrocław (46km or 43km). There are a dozen trains daily to Gdańsk (160km) and three to Warsaw (288km).

Polski Express has hourly buses to Warsaw (255km, US$8.75, 4½ hours) via Toruń and Płock.

TORUŃ
* pop 205,000   ☎ 056

A wealthy Hanseatic port, Toruń retains much of its old charm and character in its narrow streets, mighty churches, vaulted cellars and museums. The city has a well preserved complex of Gothic architecture, which isn't common in this part of Europe. Toruń is also the birthplace of Nicolaus Copernicus (1473-1543). Though the famous astronomer only spent his youth here, the city is very proud of the man who 'stopped the sun and moved the earth'; his name (Mikołaj Kopernik for Poles) is all over town.

In 1997, Toruń's historic core was included on UNESCO's World Heritage list. The city offers a chance to step briefly back in history without a lot of other tourists on your heels. It's certainly well worth coming here.

History

A Slav settlement is known to have existed on this site as early as the 11th century, but Toruń really came to life in 1233 when the Teutonic Knights set about transforming it into one of their early outposts, under the name of Thorn. The knights surrounded the town with a ring of walls and built a castle, and its position on the Vistula accelerated its development. So fast was its growth that the newly arriving merchants and craftspeople had to settle outside the city walls and soon built what became known as the New Town. It had its own square, town hall and church, and was also fortified. In the 1280s Toruń joined the Hanseatic League which gave further impetus to its development.

As the conflict between Poland and the Teutonic Order intensified, the town's internal affairs became explosive. In 1454, in a wave of protest against the economic restrictions imposed by the order, the inhabitants took up arms and destroyed the local castle. By then full-blown war had broken out between the order and Poland (the Thirteen Years' War) which concluded with the Treaty of Toruń in 1466. The treaty returned to Poland a large area of land stretching from Toruń to Gdańsk, and also presaged the military downfall of the Teutonic Order.

The period of prosperity which followed ended with the Swedish wars and since then the town's fortunes have been erratic. Following the Second Partition of Poland in 1793 the city fell under Prussian domination and didn't return to Poland until the

Treaty of Versailles in the aftermath of WWI.

After WWII, which fortunately did relatively little damage to the city, Toruń expanded significantly, with vast new suburbs and industries. However, the medieval quarter was almost unaffected by the expansion and largely retains its old appearance. Much restoration has been carried out in recent decades, though there's still a long way to go.

Orientation

The historic sector of Toruń sits on the northern bank of the Vistula. It is made up of the Old Town (Stare Miasto) to the west and the New Town (Nowe Miasto) to the east. Both towns, originally separated by walls and a moat, developed around market squares, but gradually merged after the walls were taken down in the 15th century. All the major tourist attractions and plenty of accommodation are in this area.

The bus terminal is a five minute walk north of the historic quarter, while the main train station is south across the river, a short bus ride. When coming from the station

over the bridge, you'll get a fine view of the historic district, the impressive silhouette of the cathedral being the dominant landmark.

Information

Tourist Office The friendly and knowledgeable Wojewódzki Ośrodek Informacji Turystycznej (☎ 621 09 31, ☎/fax 621 09 30), ul Piekary 37/39, is open Monday and Saturday 9 am to 4 pm, Tuesday to Friday 9 am to 6 pm and Sunday (May to August only) from 9 am to 1 pm.

Money Bank Pekao at ul Bydgoska 86/88, west of the Old Town, and the Bank Gdański at Wały Sikorskiego 15 exchange travellers cheques, give advances on Visa (Pekao also accepts MasterCard) and have ATMs. There's also a convenient ATM at ul Szeroka 35. Cash can be easily exchanged in any of the numerous kantors in the city centre.

Post & Communications The main post office is at Rynek Staromiejski 15. There's also a post office at the Toruń Główny main train station. As we went to press, the local

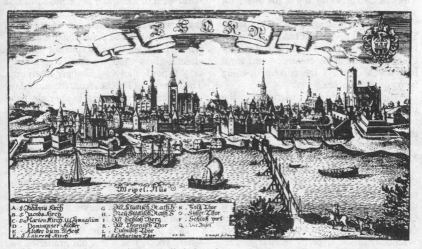

The thriving trading port of Toruń (called Thorn by its German controllers) in the 15th century, showing the city's three main churches and many other structures still visible today

phone numbers were turned into seven-digit numbers, so expect a two-digit prefix before the five-digit numbers listed here.

Old Town

Old Town Square The Old Town Square (Rynek Staromiejski) is the usual starting point for the visitor. The spacious brick building in the middle is the **Old Town Hall** (Ratusz Staromiejski). Erected at the end of the 14th century, it hasn't changed much, save for some Renaissance additions giving a decorative touch to the sober Gothic structure. Apart from serving as the municipal seat, the town hall provided market facilities, but it lost them in the course of internal remodelling in the 19th century. After WWII, it also lost its administrative functions and today most of the building is occupied by the **Regional Museum** (Muzeum Okręgowe).

In the original interiors, you'll find several exhibitions, including a collection of Gothic art (note the amazing stained glass), a display of the work of local craftspeople, a gallery of portraits and a collection of 19th century Polish paintings. You can also go to the top of the tower for a fine panoramic view.

The regional museum is open Tuesday to Sunday 10 am to 4 pm. It has several other branches, all open at similar times, but check the board at the entrance to the town hall which displays the current opening hours of all branches.

A few steps from the entrance to the museum stands the **Statue of Copernicus**, one of the oldest monuments dedicated to the astronomer.

There are several fine buildings lining the Rynek. The most richly decorated is the house at No 35, known as the **House under the Star** (Kamienica pod Gwiazdą). Its ornate baroque appearance is the result of the extensive modernisation of an original Gothic structure. The **Museum of Far Eastern Art** (Muzeum Sztuki Dalekiego Wschodu) inside is pretty modest; nevertheless the interior itself is a fine example of the period, preserved intact. There's an eye-catching spiral wooden staircase dating from 1697, going right up to the top floor; another, made of wrought iron, was added later. Another outstanding mansion is the **Artus Court** (Dwór Artusa) at No 6, which is now a cultural centre. On the western side of the square stands the mid-18th century **Church of the Holy Spirit** (Kościół Św Ducha), which was originally built for the Protestant congregation.

Between the church and the town hall is a small **fountain** (1914) with bronze-cast frogs sitting on its rim and topped with a statue of a boy playing violin, known as Janko Muzykant. Legend has it that a witch once came to the town, but wasn't welcomed by the locals. In revenge, she invoked a curse, and the town was invaded by frogs. The mayor offered a sackful of gold and his daughter to anyone who would rescue the town. A humble peasant boy then appeared and began to play his rustic violin. The frogs, enchanted by the touching melodies, followed him to the woods and the town was saved.

Other Old Town Attractions Just to the north-west of the square is the huge brick **St Mary's Church** (Kościół NMP), erected by the Franciscans at the end of the 13th century. Austere and plain from the outside, it has a lofty, whitewashed interior with tall, stained-glass windows that is pleasantly bright, particularly on a sunny afternoon. The remains of frescoes from the early days of the church can be seen in the right-hand nave. Note the impressive early 15th century Gothic stalls in the presbytery. The organ, placed unusually on a side wall, was added two centuries later.

Behind the church is the **Planetarium** (entrance from ul Franciszkańska 15/21). Installed in an old gas tank, the planetarium has a high-tech auditorium that can seat 160 spectators. Diverse shows are presented several times daily, Tuesday to Sunday.

Take ul Piekary southwards to the end, where you'll find a few old **granaries** and the **Leaning Tower** (Krzywa Wieża) just round the corner. One block east is the

Monastery Gate (Brama Klasztorna), one of three surviving medieval gates.

Walk north along ul Ducha Świętego, passing the **Dyptyk State Art Gallery** (changing displays of contemporary art), and turn right onto ul Kopernika. The fine brick Gothic house to your right is where Copernicus was born. This building and its equally attractive neighbour house the **Museum of Copernicus** (Muzeum Kopernika), which has exhibits related to the great man (including replicas of his astronomical instruments). The museum runs a short audiovisual presentation about Copernicus' times in Toruń, with a model of the town during that period. There are versions in several languages, English included.

One block east of the museum is the largest and most impressive of the city's churches, the **Cathedral of SS John the Baptist and John the Evangelist** (Katedra Św Janów). Work started around 1260 and was only completed at the end of the 15th century, by which time the church dominated the town's skyline. Its massive tower houses Poland's second-largest bell (after the Wawel cathedral in Kraków), the Tuba Dei, which was cast in 1500 and is rung before Mass. On the southern side of the tower, facing the Vistula, is a large 15th century clock; its original face and hand (one only, as was the rule at the time) are still in working order.

Walking into the church with its once white, now blackened, walls and vault is like travelling back centuries in time. If you're lucky enough to come here in the absence of school excursions, the majestic peace of the enormous space will only be disturbed by the murmuring of a handful of elderly women praying.

The combination of the Gothic vaulting high above and the maze of baroque altars and chapels at ground level is unusually harmonious. The walls and vaults were whitewashed by the Protestants, who used the church during the Reformation era and considered the brightly coloured medieval paintings unsuitable. Small fragments have been uncovered and can be seen in the

chancel and the aisles. The most striking mural is the devil's figure high at the back of the right-hand aisle. The work of an unknown artist and dating from 1478, it's a startling monochrome, quite rare at the time.

The high altar, adorned with a Gothic triptych and topped with a crucifix, has as a background a superb stained-glass window in the best medieval style. The last chapel in the right-hand aisle holds the oldest object in the church, the font where Copernicus was baptised. To one side is his epitaph, carved in the 1580s.

A few steps south of the church, at ul Żeglarska 8, is the immaculately renovated former **Bishops' Palace** (Pałac Biskupi), now part of the local university. A bit farther down the street is the plain **Sailors' Gate** (Brama Żeglarska).

The Gothic **House of the Esken Family** (Dom Eskenów), at the back of the church, was converted into a granary in the 19th century and now is a **museum**. There's a small collection of old weapons and a gallery of postwar Polish paintings on permanent display, while other rooms house temporary exhibitions.

At the southern end of ul Mostowa is the third surviving city gate, **Bridge Gate** (Brama Mostowa), where the bridge across the river once was. The 700m-long bridge was built here in 1497-1500 and survived for over three centuries. It was the second-oldest bridge over the Vistula, but the first one, in Kraków, was much shorter. By comparison, the bridge in Warsaw was only built in 1568-73.

From the gate, take ul Podmurna, dotted with several dilapidated granaries. To the east, in a triangle squeezed between the Old and New Towns, is the **castle**, built by the Teutonic Knights. It was destroyed in 1454 and has remained in ruins to this day. The surviving cellars have been cleared out and are now used for some cultural events.

New Town

North of the castle lies the New Town centred around the **New Town Square**

TORUŃ

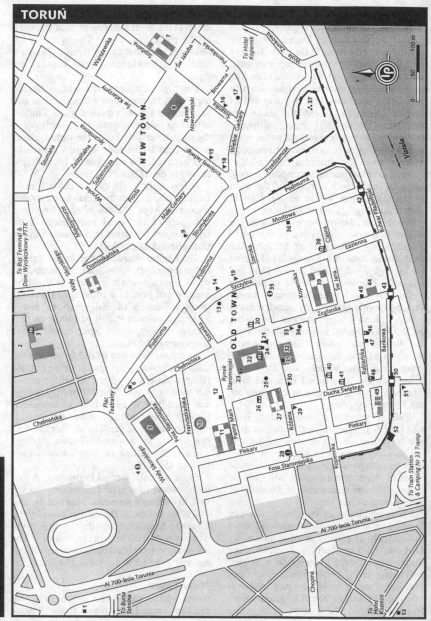

TORUŃ

PLACES TO STAY
1 Hotel Helios
6 Hotel Polonia
12 Hotel Trzy Korony
36 Hotel pod Orłem
45 Zajazd Staropolski
47 Hotel pod Czarną Różą
53 Hotel Wodnik

PLACES TO EAT
9 Restauracja Orientalna Lotus
14 Bar Mleczny Małgośka
15 Restauracja Chińska Shao Lin
16 Grill Bar Landa
18 Restauracja Palomino
19 Ristorante Italiano Staromiejska
29 Bar Mleczny pod Arkadami
30 Pizzeria Bella Italia
33 Alladyn
51 Kawiarnia Flisacza

OTHER
2 Skansen
3 Ethnographic Museum
4 Bank Gdański
5 Teatr im Horzycy
7 St James' Church
8 Former Protestant Church
10 Planetarium
11 St Mary's Church
13 Elana Klub
17 Dyskoteka Blue
20 House Under the Star & Museum of Far Eastern Art
21 Statue of Copernicus
22 Old Town Hall & Regional Museum
23 Public Toilet
24 Piwnica Artystyczna pod Aniołem
25 Fountain
26 Main Post Office

27 Church of the Holy Spirit
28 Tourist Office
31 Sklep Kopernik
32 Artus Court
34 Sklep Firmowy Katarzynka
35 ATM
37 Ruins of the Teutonic Castle
38 House of the Esken Family & Museum
39 Cathedral of SS John the Baptist & John the Evangelist
40 Museum of Copernicus
41 Dyptyk State Art Gallery
42 Bridge Gate
43 Sailors' Gate
44 Former Bishops' Palace
46 Pub Czarna Oberża
48 Pub Koci Ogon
49 Medieval Granaries
50 Monastery Gate
52 Leaning Tower

(Rynek Nowomiejski). It's not as spectacular as its older counterpart nor does it have a town hall. The building in the middle is the former Protestant church erected in the 19th century after the town hall was pulled down. Among the houses which line the Rynek, the best two stand at opposite ends of the south-western side of the square.

St James' Church (Kościół Św Jakuba), just off the eastern corner of the square, dates from the same period as its Old Town brothers. It's also huge, though it's shaped like a basilica and is more elaborate from the outside, thanks to architectural details including a series of pinnacles adorning the rim of the roof. Its interior is filled with mostly baroque furnishings, but Gothic wall paintings have been uncovered in various places, notably under the organ loft. The high altar and the decorative rood-arch both date from the 1730s.

Around the Old & New Towns

The **Ethnographic Museum** (Muzeum Etnograficzne), in a park just to the north of the Old Town, focuses on traditional fishery, with all sorts of implements, boats and nets. In the grounds behind the museum is a good **skansen** (open-air museum), containing examples of the traditional rural architecture of the region and beyond, including two farms, a blacksmith's shop, windmill and watermill. From 1 May to 30 September, the museum and the skansen are open Monday, Wednesday and Friday 9 am to 4 pm, and other days 10 am to 6 pm. In the off season they are open daily 10 am to 4 pm except Monday.

Special Events

Major annual events include the 'Probaltica' Music and Art Festival of Baltic States in May, the 'Contact' International Theatre Festival in May/June, the International Meeting of Folk Bands in June and the 'Camerimage' International Film Photography Festival in late November/early December.

Places to Stay

Toruń has a reasonable array of places to stay and finding a room isn't usually difficult. There's no longer an agency arranging private rooms, but the tourist office should be able to track down a bed.

Places to Stay – Budget

Camping Nr 33 Tramp (☎ 654 71 87, *ul Kujawska 14)*, near the southern end of the bridge, is a five minute walk from the main train station. It operates from mid-May to mid-September and has simple, cheap cabins (US$12/14/16 a double/triple/quad) and hotel-style rooms (US$12/18 a double/triple). There are only shared facilities.

The all-year *youth hostel* (☎ 654 45 80, *ul Św Józefa 22/24)* is 2km north-west of the centre. Bus No 11 links the hostel with the train station and the Old Town. The hostel has five six-bed dorms.

Bursa Szkolna (☎ 267 37, *ul Słowackiego 47/49)*, 1km west of the Old Town, is a school dorm but has some rooms for the general public. It charges US$5 per bed in dorms of four to eight beds with shared facilities. The conditions are simple but acceptable.

Dom Wycieczkowy PTTK (☎ 238 55, *ul Legionów 24)* is a 10 minute walk north of the Old Town (five minutes walk from the bus terminal). Singles/doubles/triples/quads with shared facilities will cost you US$16/20/25/32.

Old *Hotel Trzy Korony* (☎ 260 31, *Rynek Staromiejski 21)* is basic and run-down, yet it's ideally situated. It charges US$17/20/24/28 a single/double/triple/quad without bath. Ask for a room facing the square. The hotel may close for renovation.

Hotel Polonia (☎ 230 28, *Plac Teatralny 5)*, one block north of the square, has better rooms than the Trzy Korony (though also with shared baths) and charges much the same. Another budget central option is *Hotel Kopernik* (☎ 652 25 73, *ul Wola Zamkowa 16)* in the New Town. It charges US$17/20 a single/double without bath, US$28 a double with bath.

Places to Stay – Mid-Range

The central *Hotel pod Orłem* (☎/fax 250 24, *ul Mostowa 17)* has newly refurbished singles/doubles/triples with private bath for US$35/55/70. Another well located place, *Hotel pod Czarną Różą* (☎ 621 96 37, *ul Rabiańska 11)* is pretty simple, though you

may consider it worth US$40/55/70 with bath and breakfast.

Hotel Wodnik (☎ 260 49, ☎/fax 251 14, *Bulwar Filadelfijski 12)*, a short walk west of the Old Town, has singles/doubles with bath for US$36/48.

Possibly better value is the *Hotel Refleks* (☎ 300 15, fax 307 11, *ul Wojska Polskiego 20/24)*, a 10 minute walk north-east of the New Town. In an utterly colourless residential area yet close to the centre, the hotel is clean and quite decent and charges US$30/48 for a room with bath and breakfast.

For a mild splurge consider *Zajazd Staropolski* (☎ 260 60, fax 253 84, *ul Żeglarska 10/14)*, a tasteful small hotel in a fine 14th century townhouse. It charges US$50/80 for rooms with bath, TV and breakfast.

Otherwise you can choose from the two Orbis hotels, both uninspiring modern blocks within walking distance of the Old Town. The cheaper *Hotel Kosmos* (☎ 289 00, fax 213 41, *ul Popiełuszki 2)*, beyond the Hotel Wodnik, charges around US$60/90, with breakfast (20% less on weekends). The renovated *Hotel Helios* (☎ 659 54 16, fax 655 54 29, *ul Kraszewskiego 1/3)* is the most expensive place in town at US$75/110, breakfast included.

Places to Eat

At the budget end, there are two central milk bars: the basic *Bar Mleczny Małgośka* (*ul Szczytna 10/12)* and the better *Bar Mleczny pod Arkadami* (*ul Różana 1)* just off the Old Town Square.

The *Kawiarnia Flisacza* right outside the Monastery Gate has a dozen fish species to choose from and is cheap. The *Grill Bar Landa* (*ul Ślusarska 5)* off the New Town Square offers a choice of salads. *Alladyn* (*ul Żeglarska 27)* does inexpensive Middle Eastern food.

Pizzeria Bella Italia (*Rynek Staromiejski 10)* serves pizza, spaghetti, risotto etc at reasonable prices. *Ristorante Italiano Staromiejska* (☎ 267 25, *ul Szczytna 2/4)*, lodged in a historic house, is a more decent (but more expensive) option for good Italian cuisine.

Restauracja Palomino (☎ 621 09 79, ul Wielkie Garbary 18), on the 1st floor, specialises in grilled meat. The place is open till midnight and has a balcony perfect for a beer session while watching the world go by.

Zajazd Staropolski in the hotel of the same name has decent Polish food at affordable prices – good value.

Central Toruń has two Chinese eateries. *Restauracja Chińska Shao Lin* (☎ 621 08 36, ul Królowej Jadwigi 9) specialises in Shanghai cuisine. *Restauracja Orientalna Lotos* (☎ 621 04 97, ul Strumykowa 16) serves Chinese and Vietnamese fare; it's cheaper than the Shao Lin and nearly as good.

Gingerbread Toruń is famous for its gingerbread *(pierniki)*, which has been produced here since the town was founded. It comes in a variety of shapes, including figures of Copernicus. The places to buy it are *Sklep Firmowy Katarzynka (ul Żeglarska 25)* and *Sklep Kopernik (Rynek Staromiejski 6)* in the Artus Court.

Entertainment
Get a copy of the *Toruńskie Vademecum Kultury*, a useful cultural monthly distributed free by the tourist office.

The neo-baroque *Teatr im Horzycy (Plac Teatralny 1)*, built in 1904, is the main stage for theatre performances. Classical music is presented in *Dwór Artusa (Rynek Staromiejski 6)*.

Lighter fare such as rock, jazz, folk etc can be heard in *Piwnica Artystyczna pod Aniołem* set in a splendid, spacious cellar in the town hall. *Art Café (ul Szeroka 35)* has blues and jazz, while *Elana Klub (ul Szczytna 15/17)* is a jazz venue.

The above-mentioned Piwnica is also one of the most popular drinking haunts among local youth, as are *Pub Czarna Oberża (Black Inn; ul Rabiańska 9)*, which also serves food, and the newer *Pub Koci Ogon (ul Rabiańska 17)*, which has a nonsmoking section.

Among the discos, check out the huge *Central Park (☎ 220 52, Szosa Bydgoska 3)* and *Dyskoteka Blue (☎ 621 07 05, ul Browarna 1)* in the New Town.

Getting There & Away
Train The Toruń Główny main train station is about 2km south of the Old Town, on the opposite side of the Vistula. Bus Nos 22 and 27 link the two. There's also the Toruń Miasto train station, 500m east of the New Town, but not all trains call in here.

It's easy to get around the region as trains to Grudziądz (62km), Bydgoszcz (51km), Inowrocław (35km) and Włocławek (55km) leave at least every other hour. As for longer routes, there are a few departures daily to Malbork (138km), Gdańsk (211km), Łódź (178km), Olsztyn (163km) and Poznań (142km). One express and two fast trains go to Warsaw (237km) in 3½ hours.

Bus The bus terminal, close to the northern edge of the Old Town, handles a regular service to Chełmno (41km), Golub-Dobrzyń (43km), Płock (103km) and Bydgoszcz (47km). Polski Express has a dozen departures daily to Warsaw (209km, US$7.50, 3¾ hours).

GOLUB-DOBRZYŃ
• pop 12,500   ☎ 056

Golub-Dobrzyń, about 40km east of Toruń, was created in 1951 by unifying two settlements on opposite sides of the Drwęca River. Dobrzyń ('Dob-zhin') on the southern bank is newish and not worth a mention, but Golub was founded in the 13th century as a border outpost of the Teutonic Knights and still has their castle.

Castle
Overlooking the town from a hill, the castle consists of a massive Gothic brick base with a more refined Renaissance superstructure added in the 17th century, all extensively restored after WWII. There's a small museum inside which is worth visiting more for the original Gothic interiors than for the modest ethnographic collection.

POMERANIA

Every July the castle hosts the International Knights' Tournament; the program includes re-enactments of medieval jousting.

Places to Stay & Eat

The castle's upper floor houses the **Dom Wycieczkowy PTTK** (☎ 683 24 55), with double rooms for around US$16. This is some of the cheapest 'castle accommodation' in Poland. A pleasant café in the vaulted cellar serves snacks and drinks.

Getting There & Away

The town has a regular bus service to Toruń (39km) and less frequent buses to Grudziądz (52km). The bus stop is at the foot of the castle. The train station is on the opposite side, on the Grudziądz road, and operates several trains daily to Bydgoszcz (83km) and Brodnica (35km).

CHEŁMNO

• **pop 22,000** ☎ **056**

The small town of Chełmno ('Helm-no'), 41km north of Toruń, is a bit of a surprise. Not only does it have almost its entire ring of medieval fortified walls – perhaps the most complete in Poland – but it also boasts half a dozen red-brick Gothic churches and a beautiful town hall.

Chełmno was a Polish settlement existing from the late 10th century, but it really began to develop as the first seat of the Teuonic Knights. They arrived in the late 1220s and immediately began to build a castle, which they completed by 1265. Naming the town Kulm, they initially planned to make it their capital but later opted for Malbork. Chełmno also did well out of the Vistula trade, benefiting from its affiliation to the Hanseatic League.

After the Treaty of Toruń, Chełmno returned to Poland, but despite its royal privileges it didn't shine as brightly as before. The Swedish invasion did considerable damage and a series of wars in the 18th century left the town an unimportant place with some 1600 inhabitants. Though it survived WWII without major damage, it never really revived. Today it's a lethargic town sealed within its walls, as it was six centuries ago.

Information

The Chełmińska Informacja Turystyczna (☎ 686 16 41, ☎/fax 686 21 04) is in the town hall in the middle of the Rynek.

The Bank Gdański at ul Dworcowa 3 will exchange your travellers cheques and cash, and has an ATM.

Things to See

Coming from the bus terminal, you'll enter the Old Town through the **Grudziądz Gate** (Brama Grudziądzka), the only surviving medieval gateway. It was remodelled in the 17th century to incorporate a chapel. Note an expressive pietà in the niche in the gate's eastern façade.

Past the gate, you'll find yourself on a chessboard of streets, with the Rynek at its heart. In the middle stands the graceful Renaissance **town hall**, built around 1570 on the site of the previous Gothic structure and now home to the **Regional Museum** (Muzeum Ziemi Chełmińskiej). It's open Tuesday to Friday 10 am to 4 pm, Saturday 10 am to 3 pm and Sunday 10 am to 1 pm. The collection related to the town is exhibited in the original interiors, of which the courtroom is probably the highlight.

On the back wall of the town hall is the old Chełmno measure, the 4.35m-long *pręt chełmiński*. The entire town was laid out according to this measure, the streets all the same width apart. It is divided into 'feet' a little smaller than an English foot. The town also had its own weights. This unique system was used until the 19th century.

Just off the Rynek is the massive Gothic **parish church**, dating from the late 13th century. The singularly magnificent interior is crammed with ornate baroque and rococo furnishings, including the high altar from 1710, the shell-shaped pulpit, the elaborate three-part organ from 1690 and the numerous altarpieces throughout the nave and aisles. There are also some remnants from previous periods, most notably the

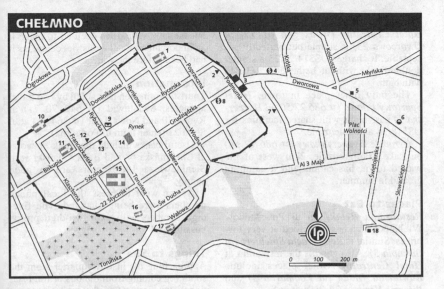

CHEŁMNO

1 Church of SS Peter & Paul
2 Kawiarnia Diada
3 Grudziądz Gate
4 Bank Gdański
5 Hotel Centralny
6 Bus Terminal
7 Restauracja Relaks
8 Kantor
9 Post Office
10 Church of SS John the Baptist & John the Evangelist
11 St James' Church
12 Pizzeria Vezuvio
13 Restauracja Spichlerz
14 Town Hall, Regional Museum & Tourist Office
15 Parish Church
16 St Martin's Church
17 Church of the Holy Spirit
18 Hotel Sportowy Pilawa

Romanesque stone baptismal font and fragments of Gothic frescoes.

The **Church of SS John the Baptist and John the Evangelist** (Kościół Św Jana Chrzciciela i Jana Ewangelisty), in the western end of the Old Town, was built in 1266-1325 next to the castle (which didn't survive) as part of the Cistercian convent. Unusual for its two-level nave, it has a richly gilded high altar and an ornate organ to the side. Underneath the organ is a black-marble tombstone from 1275, one of the oldest in the region. The church is usually closed; enter the gate at ul Dominikańska 40 and ask to be let in.

Other churches are less spectacular and most of them are unused (after all, a town of this size doesn't need six houses of worship). Nevertheless they're worth a look (particularly the Church of SS Peter and Paul) just for their original Gothic structures, all dating from the 13th and 14th centuries.

Finally, you may want to inspect the 2.2km-long **fortified walls**, which are, together with those in Paczków in Silesia, the only examples in Poland to have survived almost in their entirety. There were once 23 defensive towers in the walls and some still exist though they're not all in good shape.

POMERANIA

Places to Stay

Hotel Centralny (☎/fax 686 02 12, ul Dworcowa 23) is simple but perfectly acceptable. It charges US$14/20/25 a single/double/triple without bath, US$22/30/40 with bath.

The only other place in town, *Hotel Sportowy Pilawa (☎ 686 27 50, ul Harcerska 1)* has rooms with shared facilities for US$18/24 a double/triple.

Ośrodek Wypoczynkowy (☎ 686 12 56) on Lake Starogrodzkie, 2km west of the walled town, has cabins and a camping ground in summer.

Places to Eat

Restauracja Relaks on ul Powstańców Wielkopolskich has tasty food at very low prices. Similar is *Restauracja Spichlerz (ul Biskupia 3).* Also good is the restaurant at *Hotel Centralny.* Other places include *Kawiarnia Diada (ul Podmurna 3)* and *Pizzeria Vezuvio (ul Biskupia 6).*

Getting There & Away

Trains no longer come to town but buses leave pretty regularly to Bydgoszcz (49km), Toruń (41km) and Grudziądz (33km).

GRUDZIĄDZ

• pop 105,000   ☎ 056

Some 30km down the Vistula from Chełmno, Grudziądz ('Groo-dzyonts') is a large industrial town circled with nondescript postwar suburbs. The centre is not particularly attractive either, with its ragbag of buildings of various periods, most of which are still awaiting a coat of fresh paint. However, there are some attractions, including a line of gigantic granaries, their size and location making them unique in Poland.

Grudziądz started life as an early Piast settlement. Repeatedly destroyed by the Prussians, it came under the rule of the Teutonic Knights as Graudenz in the 1230s, returning to the Crown in 1454 after an anti-Prussian rebellion. In the First Partition of 1773 it was swallowed by Prussia and went back to Poland once more in the aftermath of WWI.

Grudziądz was badly damaged in 1945 but the new authorities decided to make it an important regional industrial centre, as it had been before the war.

Information

Tourist information is handled by two travel agencies: Światowid (☎ 642 70 71) at Rynek 20 and Nowa Tour (☎ 264 41) at ul Stara 23 (enter from ul Podgórna).

Useful banks include the Bank Pekao at ul Chełmińska 68 and Bank Gdański at ul Sienkiewicza 19. Kantors are in good supply.

As we went to press the local phone numbers were being changed. The five-digit numbers will get a two-digit prefix, possibly '64'.

Things to See

Approaching the historic quarter from the south (eg coming from the bus or train stations) you first get to the **museum** (open Tuesday to Friday 10 am to 3 pm, weekends 10 am to 2 pm). Part of it – contemporary paintings from the region and temporary exhibitions – is in a former Benedictine convent at ul Wodna 3/5. Perhaps more interesting are the sections on local archaeology and history, in two old granaries just to the west.

From the museum, go down to the bank of the Vistula through the 14th century **Water Gate** (Brama Wodna) to see the granaries *(spichrze).* They were built along the whole length of the town's waterfront to provide storage and protect the town from invaders. Begun in the 14th century, they were gradually rebuilt and extended until the 18th century, and some were later turned into apartments by cutting windows in the walls. Decayed as they are, these massive buttressed brick buildings – most of them six storeys high – are an impressive and unusual sight. The best view is from the opposite bank of the Vistula but it's a long walk south and then over the bridge.

If you are not up to this, walk north along the shore and take the first stairs up to the right. They will lead you to the Gothic brick cathedral, which has a well preserved original structure but is a stylistic mishmash inside.

Next to it is a former **Jesuit Church** (Kościół Pojezuicki), built in 1715. Undistinguished from the outside, it has a beautiful mid-18th century baroque high altar and unusual chinoiserie (particularly visible beneath the organ loft), a decorative style almost unused in Polish churches.

One block south is the **Rynek**, the historic centre of the town, lined with houses built mainly at the end of the 19th century. Till the 1850s there was also a town hall in the middle of the square.

Places to Stay & Eat

Camping Nr 134 (☎ 225 81) is 5km south of town on ul Zaleśna, on the shore of Lake Wielkie Rudnickie. It has simple cabins for US$14/18 a triple/quad. The seasonal urban R bus goes there from ul 23 Stycznia in the centre.

The all-year *youth hostel (☎ 202 04)* is in the Bursa Szkolna, a large 11-storey block at ul Hallera 37, 1.5km south of the Old Town.

Another budget place, *Internat Garnizonowy (☎ 293 82)* is at two locations, both away from the centre: No 1 at ul Chełmińska 106 (bus Nos 19 and 20 from the train station) and No 2 at ul Legionów 53 (tram No 1). Both are acceptable and charge US$6 per person in doubles/triples/quads without bath.

The most convenient budget place in town is the basic *Hotel Pomorzanin (☎ 261 41, ul Kwiatowa 28)*, midway between the train station and the Old Town. Doubles/triples without bath cost US$12/18.

One block west is *Hotel u Karola (☎ 260 37, ul Toruńska 28)*, one of the few places in town that has private baths, at US$30/40 for singles/doubles. It also has cheaper rooms without bath (US$17/25). The hotel has its own restaurant, which is reasonable, though nothing out of the ordinary.

Next door, on the corner of ul Marcinkowskiego, is the cheap *Bar Pierożek*, a sort of milk bar.

Another place to stay with private baths is the refurbished *Hotel Adriano (☎ 465 88 98, ul Hallera 4)* next to the cemetery, about 1km south of the train station. Doubles without/with bath cost US$25/42. It too has an acceptable restaurant.

Getting There & Away

The train station is about 1km south-east of the Old Town, a 15 minute walk away. The bus terminal is near the station. Trains run regularly throughout the day south to Toruń (62km) and north to Kwidzyn (38km); most of the latter continue farther north to Malbork. Buses to Bydgoszcz (70km) leave every hour and to Chełmno (33km) every hour or two. There are also infrequent buses to Kwidzyn.

KWIDZYN
* pop 40,000   ☎ 055

About 30km downriver from Grudziądz sits Kwidzyn, another medieval Teutonic stronghold, noted for its castle and cathedral.

Things to See

The square **castle** with a central courtyard was built in the first half of the 14th century. It experienced many ups and downs in subsequent periods and suffered a serious loss in 1798 when the Prussians pulled down two sides (eastern and southern) and the main tower. It passed unscathed through WWII.

After the war, the Polish authorities treated the castle with much more respect than their predecessors, carefully restoring what was left. Most of the building from the cellars up to the 2nd floor is now a **museum** (open from 9 am to 3 pm except Monday), with several sections including medieval sacred art, regional folk crafts and natural history, particularly stuffed birds. Note the fine original interiors of the ground floor and cellars.

The most curious feature of the castle is the unusual tower standing some distance away from the western side and linked to it by a long arcaded bridge. This was the knights' toilet, later serving also as the execution

POMERANIA

ground. You can visit it while wandering around the interior, but it's also worth walking round the outside to see this peculiar construction.

The **cathedral** adjoining the castle from the east is a familiar Gothic brick block-buster which has a somewhat defensive appearance and 19th century tower. Look for the interesting ceramic mosaic from around 1380 in the external wall above the southern porch. The spacious interior supported on massive columns has some 14th century frescoes while the furnishings are a combination of Gothic and neo-Gothic elements.

Places to Stay & Eat

The cheapest place in town, central *Hotel Piastowska* (☎ 279 34 33, ul Braterstwa Narodów 42) is close to the castle. It has doubles without bath for US$16 and a basic restaurant.

Hotel Kaskada (☎ 279 37 31, fax 279 41 96, ul Chopina 42), opposite the train station, charges US$17/34 for doubles without/with bath and also has a simple restaurant.

The best central place, *Hotel Maxim* (☎/fax 279 63 18, ul Słowiańska 10) has just one single (US$60), one double (US$70) and two suites (US$80). Prices include breakfast, and the hotel's restaurant is possibly the best place to eat in town.

Away from the centre, *Hotel Sportowy* (☎ 279 38 66, ul Sportowa 6) is next to the stadium, 1.5km south of the train station on the Grudziądz road. It charges US$28/32 a double/triple. One bath is shared between two adjacent rooms.

Motorists may be interested in *Pensjonat Miłosna* (☎ 279 40 52), 2km past the Sportowy. Set in the woods, this stylish house offers one single (US$20), 10 doubles (US$24) and two triples (US$28). All rooms have TV and bath and its restaurant is good.

Getting There & Away

The bus and train stations are 200m apart, about a 10 minute walk to the castle. Trains

north to Malbork (38km) and south to Grudziądz (38km) go fairly regularly throughout the day. Buses also ply these routes but not so frequently.

There are also five direct trains daily to Toruń (100km) and two buses (no trains) direct to Gdańsk (76km). Travel by train to Gdańsk involves a change in Malbork.

GNIEW

* pop 7200   ☎ 069

Far less known and visited than Kwidzyn, the small town of Gniew ('Gnyef') on the other side of the Vistula also has a castle, which is even more complete than that in Kwidzyn. The town has preserved its original medieval layout complete with the Rynek, church and a chessboard of streets. It's a charming place to pop into for a couple of hours.

Things to See

The first stronghold of the Teutonic Order on the left bank of the Vistula, the **castle** was built in the late 13th century on a square plan and is a massive multistorey brick structure with a deep courtyard. In 1464 it came under Polish rule and remained so until the First Partition of 1773. Predictably, the Prussians remodelled it to accommodate a barracks, jail and ammunition depot. It was seriously burnt out in 1921, except for the 2m-thick walls. Restoration work began only in 1976 and is still in progress.

There's an archaeological exhibition on the ground floor and you can then wander through most of the castle, up to the top floor (good views). It is open in summer from 9 am to 5 pm except Monday.

The **Rynek** is a fine if dilapidated example of the old market square with the central town hall, even though most of the buildings were reshaped on various occasions and their façades don't reveal much of the original features. The monumental **parish church**, off the square, has preserved its Gothic external shape and vaults much better, yet inside it has a combination of baroque and neo-Gothic furnishings.

Places to Stay & Eat

Part of the castle houses a simple hostel called *Dormitorium*, where you pay US$6 in a four or eight-bed dorm.

A largish palatial building next to the castle has been extensively renovated to become the *Hotel Pałac Marysieńki* (☎ 135 25 37, ☎/fax 135 21 62). It provides comfortable accommodation in singles/doubles/triples with bath for US$24/30/40 – good value. Its *Restauracja Husarska* is OK and affordable.

Getting There & Away

There's no train in Gniew but the bus service is satisfactory. The bus terminal is about 200m north-west of the Rynek. There are over a dozen buses daily to Tczew (31km), nine to Gdańsk (65km), four to Grudziądz (48km) and one to Toruń. Buses to Pelplin leave every hour or two.

PELPLIN
* **pop 8500**   ☎ 069

Pelplin, 14km north-west of Gniew, is another small town which hardly ever makes it into tourist brochures, yet it has one of the best churches in Poland. There's nowhere to stay in Pelplin and only a few basic places to eat, but this is not a problem as transport to other areas is readily available.

Things to See

Pelplin's church, which today acts as the cathedral, owes its existence to the Cistercians who came in 1276 and founded their monastery. The construction of the church progressed until the mid-15th century, by which time it reached its monumental proportions. The 80m-long, 11-span basilica is one of the largest historic churches in the country.

The lofty interior, topped with an amazing Gothic vault, is a veritable treasury of sacred art, including 22 altars. The five-tier, 26m-tall late Renaissance high altar (1629-40) is a masterpiece and reputedly the largest timber altar in Central Europe. The baroque organ (1677-79), Gothic stalls

(1450-63) and pulpit (1682) are some of the other showpieces.

The cathedral is open 9 am to 4 pm, but if you find it locked, inquire at the seminary at the back. Visitors are guided around the church and part of the adjacent cloister. The tour takes about an hour (US$0.50), regardless of the number of people in the group. Tours in English, French, German and Italian can sometimes be arranged.

Another attraction is the Diocesan Museum (Muzeum Diecezjalne) at ul Biskupa Dominika 11, 1km west of the cathedral, off the road to Starogard Gdański. It has a collection of religious objects, including paintings, sculptures and manuscripts. The highlight is a Gutenberg Bible, one of 45 worldwide and the only one in Poland. The museum opens Tuesday to Saturday 11 am to 4 pm, Sunday 10 am to 5 pm.

Getting There & Away

The PKP and PKS stations are next to each other on the eastern edge of town, 1km from the church.

Train transport to Gdańsk is fairly regular, with 10 departures during the day. Half a dozen trains go daily to Bydgoszcz and one fast evening train to Toruń.

There are about 15 buses daily to Gniew and regular departures to Tczew and Starogard Gdański, from where you have good transport around the region and beyond.

MALBORK
* **pop 41,000**   ☎ 055

Malbork is famous for its castle. Not only is it the largest castle in the country and one of the oldest, but it's also a splendid example of a classic medieval fortress, with its multiple defensive walls, a labyrinth of rooms and chambers, and some exquisite architectural detail and decoration. In 1997, the castle was included on UNESCO's World Heritage list.

Castle

The castle sits on the bank of the Nogat River, an eastern arm of the Vistula, which was once the main bed of the river. The

POMERANIA

castle's enormous size is what hits you first. The best view of the complex is from the opposite side of the river (you can get there by footbridge), especially in the late afternoon when the brick turns an intense red-brown in the setting sun.

Most of the rooms and chambers of the High and Middle castles are open for visitors, some of them housing exhibitions. The entrance to the complex is from the northern side, through what used to be the only way in. From the main gate, you walk over the drawbridge, then go through five iron-barred doors to the vast courtyard of the Middle Castle (Zamek Średni). On the western side (to your right) is the Grand Master's Palace (Pałac Wielkiego Mistrza) with some splendid interiors. Alongside is the Knights' Hall (Sala Rycerska). Measuring 450 sq metres, it's the largest chamber in the castle. It has preserved its original palm vaulting in a remarkable shape, but the foundations of the building are subsiding. While the rescue work is in progress, it's closed to visitors and may not be open for several years. The building on the opposite side of the courtyard houses exhibitions of the armoury and ceramics.

The Life & Times of the Malbork Castle

The Malbork castle was built by the Teutonic Knights, who named it Marienburg or the 'Fortress of Mary', made it their main seat and ruled their state from Malbork for almost 150 years.

The immense castle took shape in stages. First was the so-called High Castle, which was begun around 1276 and finished within three decades. It was a stronghold to be reckoned with, square with a central courtyard and surrounded by formidable fortifications.

When the capital of the order was moved from Venice to Malbork in 1309 and the castle became the home of the Grand Master, the fortress was expanded considerably, both to cope with its newly acquired functions and to provide adequate security. The Middle Castle was built to the side of the high one and followed by the Lower Castle still farther along. The whole was encircled by three rings of defensive walls and strengthened with dungeons and towers. The castle eventually spread over 21 hectares, making it perhaps the largest fortress built in the Middle Ages.

The castle was only seized in 1457 during the Thirteen Years' War, when the military power of the order had already been eroded, and the Grand Master had to retreat to Königsberg (present-day Kaliningrad in Russia). Malbork then became the residence of Polish kings visiting Pomerania, but from the Swedish invasions onwards it gradually went into decline. After the First Partition, the Prussians turned it into barracks, destroying much of the decoration and dismantling parts which were of no use for their military purposes. They initially planned to take the castle down altogether and use its fabric to build new barracks. Only the enormous cost of the operation prevented the plan from being carried out.

A change in the castle's fortunes came with the 19th century's increasing interest in old monuments. Marienburg was one of the first historic buildings taken under government protection to become a symbol of the glory of medieval Germany. It underwent a thorough restoration from the closing decades of the 19th century until the outbreak of WWI, regaining a shape close to the original. Not for long, however; during WWII, the eastern part of the fortress was shelled and the whole process had to start again, this time with Polish restorers. The bulk of the restoration was finished by the 1970s and the castle looks much the same as it did six centuries ago, dominating the town and the surrounding countryside.

POMERANIA

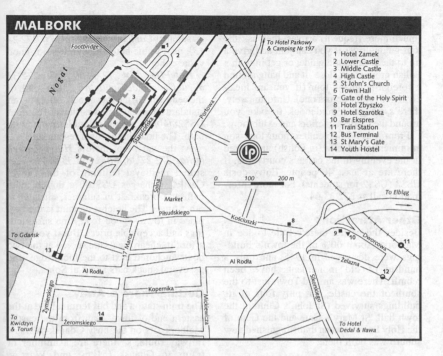

MALBORK

To Hotel Parkowy
& Camping Nr 197

1 Hotel Zamek
2 Lower Castle
3 Middle Castle
4 High Castle
5 St John's Church
6 Town Hall
7 Gate of the Holy Spirit
8 Hotel Zbyszko
9 Hotel Szarotka
10 Bar Ekspres
11 Train Station
12 Bus Terminal
13 St Mary's Gate
14 Youth Hostel

0   100   200 m

Nogat

Footbridge

Portowa

Słona

Sienkiewicza

Market

Piłsudskiego

Kościuszki

To Elbląg

To Gdańsk

17 Marca

6

7

13

Al Rodła

Al Rodła

Kopernika

Zymierskiego

Żeromskiego

Mickiewicza

Dworcowa

Żelazna

Skłonskiego

To Kwidzyn
& Toruń

To Hotel
Dedal & Iława

The tour proceeds south to the **High Castle** (Zamek Wysoki), over another drawbridge and through a gate (note the 1280 doorway ornamented with a trefoil frieze in brick) to a spectacular arcaded courtyard with a well in the middle.

You'll then be taken round numerous rooms on three storeys, including the knights' dormitories, kitchen, bakery, chapterhouse and refectory. Three rooms accommodate an **amber exhibition**. The entrance to the **castle church** is through a beautiful Gothic doorway, known as the Golden Gate. Underneath the church's presbytery is St Anne's Chapel with the Grand Masters' crypt below its floor, both of which are off limits.

Visitors can climb the castle's main square **tower** for a good view over the whole complex and the amazingly flat countryside around. Finally, you'll visit the terraces which run around the High Castle between the castle itself and the fortified walls.

The castle is open daily, except Monday, 9 am to 5 pm May to September (9 am to 3 pm October to April). Visitors go round in groups, which set off as soon as enough people have arrived. The tour (in Polish) costs US$4 per person (US$2.50 for students) and takes up to three hours. Late tours, which leave shortly before closing time, run at breakneck speed and may miss some exhibitions.

German and English-speaking guides are available on request for US$30 per group (plus the US$4 entrance fee per person; US$2.50 for students). You should book in advance (☎ 272 26 77), especially if you are in a large group, but perhaps not for individuals or small parties. The latter have two options: either wait until a tour group that

POMERANIA

speaks English (not very often) or German (much more frequent) arrives, then ask the tour guide/driver if you can join and give a tip to the local castle guide; or get in with a Polish group, then 'lose' it and hang around a foreign-language tour (if you are lucky enough to come across one). Unfortunately, there's no good guidebook to take you around the castle's interiors and exhibitions.

From May to September, hour-long son et lumière spectacles (in Polish) are staged in the evening in the castle's courtyards, if there are at least 40 people. Entry costs US$3 (US$2 for students). For more information call ☎ 272 33 64.

Other Attractions
Besides the castle, there's little to see in Malbork. About 60% of the town's buildings were destroyed in 1945, and only a handful of old monuments have been rebuilt. There was an Old Town just to the south of the castle, but only four of its buildings survived (St John's Church, the town hall, St Mary's Gate and the Gate of the Holy Spirit) and an undistinguished new suburb was built there.

Places to Stay & Eat
The cheapest place to stay is the all-year *youth hostel* (☎ 272 24 08, ul Żeromskiego 45) in the local school. It has a few doubles, but most are dorms sleeping eight or more people.

The next cheapest is *Hotel Szarotka* (☎ 272 36 01, ul Dworcowa 1A), a workers' dorm near the train station which offers basic singles/doubles/triples/quads without bath for US$7/14/19/24. *Bar Ekspres* next door is like a milk bar and serves acceptable meals at low prices.

Hotel Zbyszko (☎ 272 26 40, fax 272 33 95, ul Kościuszki 43) is well located and reasonable value. It charges US$20/26/34 a single/double/triple without bath, US$24/34/44 with bath (breakfast included). The hotel has its own restaurant, which is OK and relatively inexpensive.

Hotel Parkowy (☎ 272 24 13, ul Portowa 1), 1200m north of the castle, is less convenient and overpriced, but you may need its summer *Camping Nr 197* (also ☎ 272 24 13), next to the hotel, though it's not good value either.

Hotel Dedal (☎ 272 68 50, ☎/fax 272 31 37, ul Charles de Gaulle'a 5), 1km south of the centre along the Iława road, offers better standards than any listed earlier and charges US$28/40/48 a single/double/triple with bath. The hotel has its own restaurant.

At the very top, there's *Hotel Zamek* (☎/fax 272 27 38, ☎/fax 272 33 67) in a restored medieval building of the Lower Castle. It charges US$100 a double with bath and breakfast in summer, cheaper at other times. The hotel restaurant is the best place in town – good food, fine surroundings and acceptable prices. But if you can't afford it, cheap meals are served at the two boats anchored next to the footbridge, and at several snack bars along ul Solna.

Getting There & Away
The train station and bus terminal are at the eastern end of town, 1km from the castle. Malbork sits on the busy Gdańsk-Warsaw railway route, so there are a number of trains to Gdańsk (51km) and Warsaw (278km). There are also fairly regular links with Elbląg (29km), Kwidzyn (38km), Grudziądz (76km), Toruń (138km) and Olsztyn (128km). There are buses to Elbląg (33km) and Kwidzyn (39km) and other regional destinations. Coming from Gdańsk, you'll catch a splendid view of the castle; watch out to your right when crossing the Nogat River.

ELBLĄG
• pop 130,000   ☎ 055
One of the earliest strongholds of the Teutonic Knights, Elbląg ('El-blonk') was their first port. At that time the Vistula Lagoon (Zalew Wiślany) extended much farther south than today and the town developed as a maritime port for several centuries.

When Elbląg came under Polish rule after the Toruń Treaty, it became one of the Crown's main gateways to the sea, taking much of the trade from the increasingly independent Gdańsk. It was in Elbląg that the first Polish galleon was built in the 1570s, when King Zygmunt August set about establishing a national navy. Later, the Swedish invasions and the gradual silting up of the waterways eclipsed the town's prosperity, and a partial revival came only with the industrial development of the late 19th century.

WWII turned Elbląg into a heap of rubble, particularly the Old Town. The recovery was hard and long, but it eventually made the town an important industrial centre. Not much of the old architecture has been recreated, but the new centre, currently being constructed, is a fine and innovative design.

The city is a gateway for Frombork and a starting point for the trip along the Elbląg-Ostróda Canal (see the Warmia & Masuria chapter). It's also a jumping-off point for Kaliningrad in Russia.

Information

The tourist office (☎ 232 84 71, ☎/fax 232 73 73), ul 1 Maja 30, is open Monday to Friday 9 am to 5 pm, Saturday 9 am to 1 pm. They may also have information on the Sunday organ recitals in the cathedral at Frombork, if this is on your agenda.

Useful banks include Bank Pekao at ul Hetmańska 3 and Bank Gdański at ul 1 Maja 16. There's no shortage of kantors throughout the centre.

Cyberia (☎ 235 24 95) is a cybercafé in the new shopping centre at ul Hetmańska 5.

Things to See

For a long time after the war, the Old Town area was not much more than a meadow with the scattered remains of old buildings. It wasn't until the arrival of the market economy that work really started on a project combining elements of the old and new, a stylised **New Old Town**. There's still a long way to go, but many buildings have already been put up and the result is interesting. What's more the quarter bustles with city life, with offices, banks, shops and bars springing up around the place.

In the middle of this construction site stands the Gothic **St Nicholas' Church** (Kościół Św Mikołaja), noted for its 95m-high, carefully reconstructed tower. Less care was given to its interior and what was once a Gothic vault is now a flat concrete ceiling. Fortunately, part of the original woodcarving, including several triptychs, escaped war destruction.

Some 200m to the north is **St Mary's Church** (Kościół NMP), another massive Gothic brick temple. It houses a gallery of modern art and it's worth a look if only to see the imposing, spacious interior. A few steps from here stands the only surviving gate of the medieval fortifications, the **Market Gate** (Brama Targowa).

A five minute walk south along the river bank is the **museum** (open Tuesday, Wednesday and Friday 10 am to 4 pm and Thursday, Saturday and Sunday 10 am to 6 pm). Occupying two large buildings, the museum has sections on archaeology and the city's history, plus a photographic record of the town from the 19th century to WWII.

Places to Stay

Camping Nr 61 (☎/fax 232 43 07, ul Panieńska 14) is on the Elbląg River. It's close to the Old Town and about 1km west of the train and bus stations. It's open from May to September and has cabins (US$22 per quad). There is a summer *youth hostel* (☎ 232 56 70, ul Browarna 1).

The only budget place right in the city centre is the simple *Hotel Galeona* (☎ 232 48 08, ul Krótka 5). It charges US$14/17/20 a single/double/triple without bath, US$20/30 a single/double with bath. *Hotel Dworcowy* (☎ 233 80 49, Al Grunwaldzka 49), diagonally opposite the bus terminal, charges US$16/20 a single/double without bath, US$28/42 with bath. It's nothing special but convenient if you are in transit. There are more budget hotels in the city but they are farther away from the centre. The tourist office keeps a list and will help you find one.

Going up the price scale, the small *Hotel Żuławy* (☎ 234 57 11, fax 234 83 38, ul

Królewiecka 126) is 2km north-east of the centre (tram No 2 from the bus and train stations). It charges US$35/45 for rooms with bath and breakfast. The new *Pensjonat Boss* (☎ *232 79 73, fax 232 83 66)* on ul Św Ducha in the Old Town, offers fine and stylish accommodation with bath and breakfast for US$50/70.

At the top end is the large *Hotel Elzam* (☎ *234 81 11, fax 232 40 83, Plac Słowiański 2)*. It charges US$80/100 for rooms with bath and breakfast (cheaper in winter). Before booking in, check out *Hotel ABB Zamech* (☎ *232 40 26, fax 232 46 40)*, round the corner in the same building, which offers almost the same for US$70/90.

Places to Eat
There already are many small eating outlets in the rebuilt Old Town, and more are to come. *Bar Rybny u Bosmana (ul Św Ducha 27)* is a good budget fish eatery, while the *Bar Zagłoba (ul Stary Rynek 11)* has excellent *golonka* (boiled pigs' knuckle served with horseradish) and other Polish staple dishes at low prices. *Restauracja Chińska Mandaryn (ul Św Ducha 8)* brings Oriental flavours to the Old Town, while there are also some pizzerias, cafés and pubs around the place.

For a more formal lunch or dinner, try the *Restauracja Słowiańska (ul Krótka 4)* or the restaurant in the *Hotel Elzam*.

Getting There & Away
Train The train station is 1km south-east of the centre. There are about 20 trains daily to Malbork (29km), six to Frombork (40km), 15 to Gdańsk (80km) and nine to Olsztyn (99km).

Bus The bus terminal is next to the train station and handles regular buses to Gdańsk (61km) and Frombork (51km). Apart from the PKS buses, there are half-hourly private buses to Braniewo via Frombork. In summer, there are hourly buses to Krynica Morska (72km), the most popular seaside resort east of Gdańsk.

Boat Boats for the Elbląg-Ostróda Canal (see that section in the Warmia & Masuria chapter for details) depart from the wharf next to the Old Town. Information and tickets are available at the Camping Nr 61. In the same area are hydrofoils to Krynica Morska (US$8 one way, US$11 return), from mid-June to late August.

A bit farther south is the departure point for hydrofoils to Kaliningrad in Russia. They go from May to September daily at 8 am and return late in the afternoon, leaving you about six hours for visiting the city. Return tickets cost about US$45. You need a Russian visa and a multiple Polish visa for your return. Information and booking in Elbląg are available from Halex (☎ 232 52 70), Orbis (☎ 232 72 42) and Elzam (☎ 232 51 58).

FROMBORK
• pop 2700   ☎ 055
Although Kraków, Toruń and Olsztyn claim close links with Nicolaus Copernicus (1473-1543), it was actually in the tiny coastal town of Frombork that the astronomer spent the latter half of his life and conducted most of the observations and research for his heliocentric theory. By proving that the earth moves round the sun, he changed the course of astronomy, supplanting the old geocentric Ptolemaic system, which placed our planet at the centre of the universe. Copernicus was buried in the local cathedral, though the precise site is unknown.

The town owes its existence to the Warmian bishops (see the boxed text in the Olsztyn Region section of the Warmia & Masuria chapter), who arrived at the end of the 13th century in search of a new base after their previous seat in Braniewo was ravaged by the Prussians. Within a century they had turned a local hill into a fortified ecclesiastical township, dominated by a huge cathedral and known since as Cathedral Hill. At the foot of the hill a town developed, but it lacked defensive walls and was invaded on several occasions. In 1626 Swedish troops plundered the town and

FROMBORK

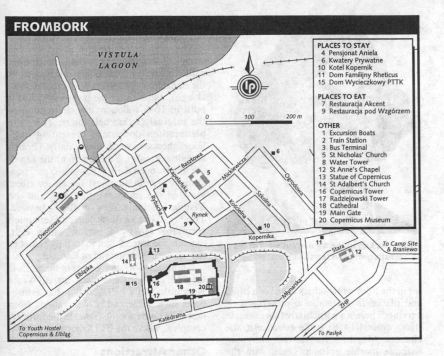

PLACES TO STAY
4 Pensjonat Aniela
6 Kwatery Prywatne
10 Kotel Kopernik
11 Dom Familijny Rheticus
15 Dom Wycieczkowy PTTK

PLACES TO EAT
7 Restauracja Akcent
9 Restauracja pod Wzgórzem

OTHER
1 Excursion Boats
2 Train Station
3 Bus Terminal
5 St Nicholas' Church
8 Water Tower
12 St Anne's Chapel
13 Statue of Copernicus
14 St Adalbert's Church
16 Copernicus Tower
17 Radziejowski Tower
18 Cathedral
19 Main Gate
20 Copernicus Museum

cathedral complex and took most of the valuables, including the cathedral library and the Copernicus collection. The greatest disaster, though, came with WWII, when 80% of the town was destroyed. Today Frombork is a small, sleepy town, still dominated by the cathedral complex, which somehow survived the war unharmed.

Cathedral Hill

The Cathedral Hill (Wzgórze Katedralne) holds all the major attractions. The entrance to the complex is from the southern side through the massive **Main Gate** (Brama Główna).

The **cathedral** (open 9.30 am to 5 pm except Sunday), in the middle of the courtyard, is a monumental brick Gothic construction embellished with a decorated main (western) façade and a slim octagonal tower at each corner. Built from 1329 to

1388, it was, and still is, the largest Warmian church and a model for most other churches put up by the bishops throughout the region.

Inside, the nave and chancel (90m long altogether) are topped with a Gothic star vault and crammed with predominantly baroque altars. The large marble high altar, modelled on the one in Kraków's Wawel cathedral, was made around 1750. Up to that year, a 1504 polyptych stood here, which is now in the left-hand (northern) aisle.

The baroque organ, dating from the 1680s, is a replacement for the one looted by the Swedes in 1626. The organ is noted for its rich tone, best appreciated during the Sunday recitals held in July and August. Ask about these at a tourist office before you set off for Frombork.

Note the large number of tombstones (about 130 in all), some of which are still

POMERANIA

Nicolaus Copernicus carried out most of his astronomical research in Frombork

set in the floor while others have been lifted and placed in the walls to preserve their carving. There's a particularly fine example (from around 1416) at the entrance to the chancel. Also look for the two intriguing baroque marble epitaphs, each with the image of a skeleton and a skull: one is in the northern wall near the chancel, the other on the sixth column between the nave and the southern aisle.

In the south-eastern corner of the courtyard is the **Old Bishops' Palace** (Stary Pałac Biskupi) which now houses the **Copernicus Museum** (Muzeum Kopernika), open 9 am to 4 pm except Monday. On the ground floor are objects discovered during postwar archaeological excavations, while the 1st floor is devoted to the life and work of the astronomer.

Though Copernicus is mainly remembered for his astronomical achievements, his interests extended to many other fields, including medicine, economy and the law. Apart from the early edition of his famous *On the Revolutions of the Celestial Spheres (De Revolutionibus Orbium Coelestium)*, there are others of his treatises and manuscripts, together with astronomical instruments and a copy of Matejko's painting depicting the astronomer at work.

The high tower at the south-western corner of the defensive walls is the former cathedral belfry, commonly referred to as the **Radziejowski Tower** (Wieża Radziejowskiego), named after the bishop who had it built in 1685 following the destruction of the original Gothic bell tower. There's a **planetarium** downstairs presenting half-hour shows several times daily (Polish soundtrack only). You can go to the top of the tower (open daily 9.30 am to 5 pm, possibly longer in summer) for an excellent view of the cathedral, the town and the Vistula Lagoon (Zalew Wiślany) beyond. This vast but shallow lagoon, separated from the sea by a narrow sandy belt, extends for some 90km to its only outlet to the sea near Kaliningrad in Russia.

At the north-western corner of the walls is the 14th century **Copernicus Tower** (Wieża Kopernika). It's believed that the astronomer took some of his observations from here. His home was just outside the fortified complex, where the PTTK hostel is today.

Other Attractions

The 15th century **St Anne's Chapel** (Kaplica Św Anny) on ul Stara east of the cathedral boasts the late 15th century wall painting depicting the Last Judgment, plus exhibitions of religious art and old medicine.

The **water tower** (wieża wodna), across the main road from the cathedral, was built in 1571 as part of one of the first water supply systems in Europe and was used for two centuries to provide Cathedral Hill with water through oak pipes. The water was taken from the Bauda River by a 5km-long canal built for this purpose. You can go to the top of the tower.

Places to Stay & Eat

Camping Nr 12 (☎ 243 73 68, ul Braniewska 12) is at the eastern end of town, on the Braniewo road. It has bungalows costing US$10/15 a double/triple, and a snack bar, and is open from mid-June to early September.

The all-year *Youth Hostel Copernicus* (☎ *243 74 53, ul Elbląska 11)* is 500m west of Cathedral Hill on the Elbląg road. It's good and neat and offers 120 beds for guests. You can camp at the back of the building, which is cheaper than using the camp site.

Dom Wycieczkowy PTTK (☎ *243 72 52)* occupies three buildings just west of the cathedral complex. It has rooms ranging from singles to 10-bed dorms and charges US$7/10 per person in rooms without/with bath. It has its own restaurant which looks shabby but serves acceptable cheap food.

Pensjonat Aniela (☎ *243 78 19, ul Basztowa 2)* offers better standards than PTTK and charges US$8/16 per head in rooms without/with bath. The latter price includes breakfast.

Kwatery Prywatne (☎ *243 77 31, ul Ogrodowa 24)* is a private villa that rents out three double rooms in the basement (US$28, including breakfast).

The upmarket *Hotel Kopernik* (☎ *243 72 85, fax 243 73 00, ul Kościelna 2)* has 32 doubles with bath and TV for US$48 (US$34 for single occupancy), breakfast included.

Another top-end place, *Dom Familijny Rheticus* (☎*/fax 243 78 00, ul Kopernika 10)* offers apartments with kitchen (containing one/two/three rooms) for US$50/75/100.

Apart from the eateries listed here, there's the reasonable *Restauracja Akcent* (*ul Rybacka 4)*, the more basic *Restauracja pod Wzgórzem* in the Rynek, and a few bistros and fast-food outlets.

Getting There & Away

The train and bus stations are next to each other near the waterfront. Trains and buses run to Elbląg (40km or 51km, respectively) every two to three hours; take whichever goes first and change there for Gdańsk or Malbork, though you may prefer to wait for one of the few direct buses to Gdańsk (112km).

There are two or three buses daily to Lidzbark Warmiński (76km), providing an interesting backwoods route to the Great Masurian Lakes.

Just north of the stations is the wharf from which boats go to Krynica Morska several times daily in summer (US$8, 1½ hours).

Gdańsk

* **pop 465,000** ☎ **058**

Gdańsk is the largest city in northern Poland, even if you don't include Sopot and Gdynia, two urban centres which are merging with Gdańsk to form a single metropolis. The whole conurbation, known as the Tri-City (Trójmiasto), spreads for some 35km along the Gulf of Gdańsk (Zatoka Gdańska) and has a population of nearly 800,000.

Gdańsk is the biggest, oldest and by far the most interesting component of the Tri-City. Known as Danzig in German, it was the Hanseatic trading hub of the Teutonic Knights in medieval times, and evolved into the greatest port on the Baltic. Though it owed loyalty to the Polish kings for over 300 years, Poland had no more than nominal suzerainty and at times had to fight even for this. Demographically mostly German, architecturally reminiscent of Flanders rather than Poland, Gdańsk was effectively an independent city-state, yet it controlled most Polish trade. Wealthy, cultured and cosmopolitan, it was a city that forged its own history.

Napoleon was once heard to say that Gdańsk was the key to everything and Hitler seemed to share this opinion when he started WWII here. Not many European cities were devastated on the scale of Gdańsk, and nowhere on the continent was postwar reconstruction so extensive. Admirably – if somewhat surprisingly – the communist regime rebuilt, brick by brick, house by house, and street by street, the historic city from the ashes. Walking around central Gdańsk today is a bit like going back in time to a 16th century town.

Over hundreds of years, many artists and scholars came to Gdańsk from all over

POMERANIA

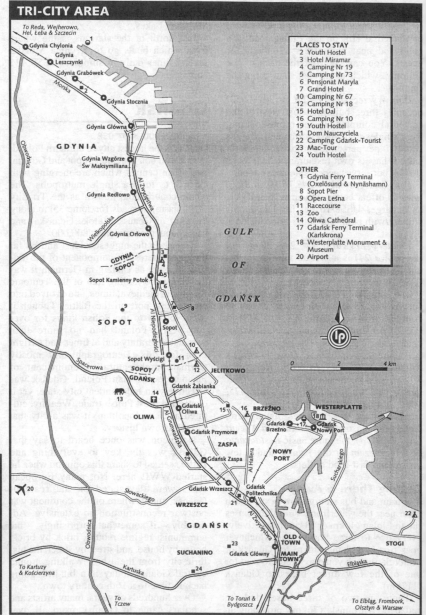

TRI-CITY AREA

To Reda, Wejherowo,
Hel, Łeba & Szczecin

Gdynia Chylonia
Gdynia Leszczynki
Gdynia Grabówek
Morska
Gdynia Stocznia
Gdynia Główna
GDYNIA
Gdynia Wzgórze Św Maksymiliana
Al Zwycięstwa
Gdynia Redłowo
Obwodnica
Wielkopolska
Gdynia Orłowo
GDYNIA
SOPOT
Sopot Kamienny Potok
SOPOT
Al Niepodległości
Spacerowa
Sopot
Sopot Wyścigi
SOPOT
GDYNSK
Gdańsk Żabianka
OLIWA
Gdańsk Oliwa
Gdańsk Przymorze
ZASPA
Gdańsk Zaspa
Słowackiego
Gdańsk Wrzeszcz
Gdańsk Politechnika
WRZESZCZ
Al Grunwaldzka
GDAŃSK
Obwodnica
To Kartuzy & Kościerzyna
SUCHANINO
Gdańsk Główny
Kartuska
To Tczew

JELITKOWO
Al Hallera
Gdańsk Żabianka
BRZEŹNO
Gdańsk Brzeźno
Gdańsk Nowy Port
NOWY PORT
WESTERPLATTE
Al Zwycięstwa
MAIN TOWN
OLD TOWN
STOGI
Elbląska
Sucharskiego
To Elbląg, Frombork, Olsztyn & Warsaw
To Toruń & Bydgoszcz

GULF
OF
GDAŃSK

PLACES TO STAY
2 Youth Hostel
3 Hotel Miramar
4 Camping Nr 19
5 Camping Nr 73
6 Pensjonat Maryla
7 Grand Hotel
10 Camping Nr 67
12 Camping Nr 18
15 Hotel Dal
16 Camping Nr 10
19 Youth Hostel
21 Dom Nauczyciela
22 Camping Gdańsk-Tourist
23 Mac-Tour
24 Youth Hostel

OTHER
1 Gdynia Ferry Terminal (Oxelösund & Nynäshamn)
8 Sopot Pier
9 Opera Leśna
11 Racecourse
13 Zoo
14 Oliwa Cathedral
17 Gdańsk Ferry Terminal (Karlskrona)
18 Westerplatte Monument & Museum
20 Airport

0   2   4 km

POMERANIA

Europe, attracted by its lively cultural and intellectual life. The city also produced its own famous citizens. The astronomer Jan Heweliusz (or Johannes Hevelius, 1611-87), who produced one of the first detailed maps of the moon's surface, was born, lived and worked in Gdańsk. Also born here was Gabriel Daniel Fahrenheit (1686-1736), the inventor of the mercury thermometer whose name lives on, applied to his temperature scale. Gdańsk was also the birthplace of philosopher Arthur Schopenhauer (1788-1860), and writer Günter Grass (born in 1927). Finally, the Solidarity trade union was born in Gdańsk in 1980 and made its contribution to the end of communism a decade later.

Though Gdańsk is known best to outsiders as the home of Solidarity, there are many other reasons to come here. This is a real city with bones and soul – a place to be savoured.

Besides sightseeing in the city centre, your itinerary might include a half-day trip to the suburb of Oliwa and a boat trip to the port and Westerplatte.

Gdynia is probably best done as a half-day visit from Gdańsk, but Sopot can be a destination in itself, particularly if you want to see how the Poles spend their holidays.

HISTORY

There was a fishing village here in the 9th century. It stood on the site of the present Main Town and had a population of around 300. In the closing decades of the 10th century Gdańsk, along with the rest of Pomerania, was annexed to the newborn Polish state and a stronghold was built where the Radunia canal flows into the Motława.

In 997 the Bohemian Bishop Adalbert arrived here from Gniezno and baptised the inhabitants before setting off eastwards on his ill-fated mission to convert the Prussians (see the Gniezno section in the Wielkopolska chapter). The story of his life, *Vita Sancti Adalberti*, written two years later by a monk from Rome, is the first historical document mentioning the town,

under the name of Gyddanyzc. Accordingly, the year 997 in considered as the city's formal birth.

The settlement developed as a port over the next centuries, expanding northwards onto what is today the Old Town. Following Poland's fragmentation in 1138, the region of Gdańsk became an independent principality ruled by a local Slav dynasty, the East Pomeranian dukes. The German community arrived from Lübeck in the early 13th century, when the cosmopolitan character of the town developed, to determine the history of Gdańsk for over seven centuries.

The picture changed considerably after the Teutonic Knights, who were already comfortably established on the Lower Vistula, seized Gdańsk in 1308 and slaughtered the Polish population. Expansive and energetic, the knights swiftly turned Gdańsk into a fully fledged medieval town. A castle was built about 1340, replacing the existing ducal stronghold, and the Main Town was redesigned on a pattern which has survived unchanged to this day. The familiar ring of defensive walls enveloped the town to assure safety.

Joining the Hanseatic League in 1361, Gdańsk soon grew fat on trade and by 1400 had about 10,000 inhabitants. By then the knights had become involved in an armed struggle with Poland; they increased taxes on local merchants and recruited soldiers from the local population to fight their battles. The citizens weren't particularly happy about the order's militarism or its religious goals, so discontent and protests ensued. As in Toruń, tensions exploded in 1454 into a revolt in which the townspeople razed the knights' castle and soon afterwards pledged their loyalty to the Polish monarch. In turn, Gdańsk was rewarded with numerous privileges, including a monopoly on the grain trade and a greater degree of political independence than any other Polish city. The town continued to thrive for the next two centuries.

By the mid-16th century, Gdańsk had come to control three-quarters of Poland's foreign trade and its population reached 40,000. It was the largest Polish city, bigger than royal Kraków. Not only was it the Baltic's greatest port, but it was also the most important trading centre in Central and Eastern Europe. It attracted legions of international traders – Dutch people, Swedes, Scots, Italians and others – who joined the local German-Polish population.

The Reformation arrived in the 1520s, leaving a strong mark on the multinational community, and in 1580 the first academy, known as Athenae Gedanensis, was established. Splendid public buildings and burghers' houses were constructed, making the place reminiscent of northern European ports rather than of inland Polish towns. An outer ring of fortifications was built which, as it turned out, soon proved very useful; Gdańsk was one of the very few Polish cities which withstood the Swedish Deluge of the 1650s. However, since the rest of the country was devastated, the trade on which the town's prosperity stood declined drastically.

Prussia didn't try to seize Gdańsk in the First Partition of 1773, but it did take the area all around, separating the town from what was left of Poland. It imposed trade restrictions on the Vistula and blockaded the city from the sea. Twenty years later, in the Second Partition, Prussia annexed Gdańsk easily, for the port had already been weakened and its population had dropped to 36,000, half of that a century earlier.

The city was besieged in 1807, this time with the Prussians inside while the Napoleonic army, strengthened by Polish regiments, attacked it for two months. After taking it, Napoleon proclaimed it a free city under the supervision of a French governor. Not for long, though. Ironically enough, following Napoleon's retreat from Moscow in 1813, the French and the Poles in their turn were entrenched inside and held the fortress for 10 months against the combined Prussian and Russian troops.

In 1815 the Congress of Vienna gave Gdańsk back to Prussia. In the century that followed, the Polish minority was systematically Germanised, the city's defences

reinforced and there was gradual but steady economic and industrial growth.

The next of the numerous changes in control came in the aftermath of WWI. The Treaty of Versailles gave Poland the so-called Polish Corridor, a strip of land stretching from Toruń to Gdańsk, providing the country with an outlet to the sea. Gdańsk was excluded, however, and made the Free City of Danzig. It became virtually autonomous under the protection of the League of Nations represented by its high commissioner residing in the city. In the first elections to the 120-seat parliament, the Poles gained seven seats, which more or less represented their initial share of power. Step by step, the Germans further increased their control, particularly after Hitler came to power. The shipyard was then used for the production of German warships and the first German submarines.

WWII started in Gdańsk, at dawn on 1 September 1939, when the German battleship *Schleswig-Holstein* fired the first shots over Westerplatte at the port entrance. During the occupation of the city, the Nazis continued to use the local shipyards for building warships (136 were made here), with Poles as forced labour.

The Russians arrived in March 1945; during the fierce battle the city virtually ceased to exist. The destruction of the historic quarter was comparable to that of Warsaw's Old Town – Polish authorities put it at 90%.

The social structure changed drastically after the war. The German majority either perished or fled, and those few who were left were expelled in 1946. Their place was taken by Polish newcomers, mainly from the territories lost to the Soviet Union.

After the initial shock, in 1949 the complex reconstruction of the Main Town began, firstly by removing two million square metres of rubble. The restoration took over 20 years, though work on some interiors continued well into the 1990s. Nowhere else in Europe was such a large area of a historic city reconstructed from the ground up.

In December 1970 a massive strike broke out in the shipyard and was 'pacified' by the authorities as soon as the workers left the gates, leaving 44 dead. This was the second important challenge to the communist regime after Poznań in 1956.

Gdańsk came to the fore again in 1980, when another popular protest paralysed the shipyard. This time, however, it culminated in negotiations with the government and the foundation of Solidarity. The electrician who led the strike and the subsequent talks, Lech Wałęsa, became the first freely elected president in postwar Poland.

ORIENTATION

You're most likely to arrive at the Gdańsk Główny main train station, from where it's just a 10 minute walk to the core of the historic quarter. If you come by bus, you arrive right next to the train station.

Sightseeing in Gdańsk is straightforward, for almost all the major attractions are in the city centre and a short walk apart. Buses and trams operate on the outskirts of the centre but don't go through it.

The city centre consists of three historic districts: the Main Town in the centre (part of it is a pedestrian precinct), the Old Town to the north, and the Old Suburb to the south. To the east of the Main Town, beyond the Stara Motława River, is the fourth integral part of the historic city, Spichlerze (Granary) Island, once crammed with over 300 granaries.

INFORMATION
Tourist Offices

The private Agencja Informacji Turystycznej (☎ 301 93 27), ul Długa 45, opposite the main town hall, is open daily 9 am to 6 pm and is a good source of information. It's well stocked with maps and brochures.

You can also use the helpful municipal tourist office (☎ 301 43 55, ☎/fax 301 66 37), ul Heweliusza 27, on the northern edge of the Old Town; it's open weekdays 8.30 am to 4 pm.

Pick up *Welcome to Gdańsk, Sopot, Gdynia* and *Gdańsk, Gdynia, Sopot: What,* *Where, When,* which are two useful free tourist magazines. If the tourist offices don't have them, try the reception desks of upmarket hotels.

Money

The Bank Pekao is at ul Garncarska 23; the Bank Gdański has offices at several central locations, including Wały Jagiellońskie 14/16, Długi Targ 14/16 and the main train station; Powszechny Bank Kredytowy is at ul Ogarna 116. These and some other banks will exchange most major brands of travellers cheques and give advances on Visa; Bank Pekao will also accept MasterCard. ATMs are easy to find in the centre.

Kantors are plentiful throughout the central area. Ignore the moneychangers who hang around Długi Targ and Długie Pobrzeże and offer foreigners attractive rates. You won't get what you expect!

Post & Communications

The main central post office is at ul Długa 22. Poste restante is in the same building but you enter through the back door from ul Pocztowa. Mail sent here should be addressed: your name, Poste Restante, ul Długa 22/28, 80-801 Gdańsk 50, Poland.

Email & Internet Access

Try Comptrade (☎ 341 47 14) in Gdańsk Wrzeszcz, ul Grunwaldzka 102, 2nd floor, room 34 (open Monday to Friday 10.30 am to 4 pm), or Cybermind in Gdańsk Żabianka, ul Grunwaldzka 613, behind the Bank Gdański (almost on Gdańsk's administrative border with Sopot).

Travel Agencies

Almatur (☎ 301 24 24) at Długi Targ 11 provides its usual services, including ISIC student cards and international transportation tickets.

PTTK (☎ 301 60 96) in the Upland Gate arranges guides speaking English, German and French (US$55 per group for up to five hours plus US$10 for each extra hour).

Orbis (☎ 301 56 31) at ul Heweliusza 22 sells ferry tickets, international and domestic

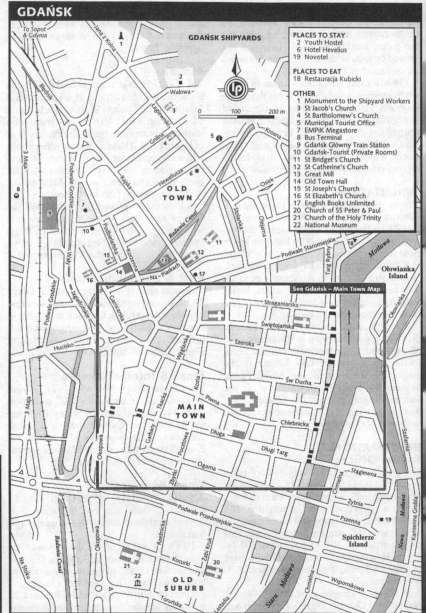

GDAŃSK

GDAŃSK SHIPYARDS

To Sopot & Gdynia

0   100   200 m

PLACES TO STAY
2 Youth Hostel
6 Hotel Hevelius
19 Novotel

PLACES TO EAT
18 Restauracja Kubicki

OTHER
1 Monument to the Shipyard Workers
3 St Jacob's Church
4 St Bartholomew's Church
5 Municipal Tourist Office
7 EMPiK Megastore
8 Bus Terminal
9 Gdańsk Główny Train Station
10 Gdańsk-Tourist (Private Rooms)
11 St Bridget's Church
12 St Catherine's Church
13 Great Mill
14 Old Town Hall
15 St Joseph's Church
16 St Elizabeth's Church
17 English Books Unlimited
20 Church of SS Peter & Paul
21 Church of the Holy Trinity
22 National Museum

OLD TOWN

See Gdańsk – Main Town Map

MAIN TOWN

OLD SUBURB

Ołowianka Island

Spichlerze Island

POMERANIA

train tickets, and international bus tickets. It also organises tours in the city and beyond (Hel, Malbork, Frombork).

The Biuro Turystyki Lauer (☎ 301 16 19), ul Piwna 22/23, organises trips to Kaliningrad in Russia. Transport is by road to Elbląg and then by hydrofoil.

Bookshops

English Books Unlimited (☎ 301 33 73) at ul Podmłyńska 10 has probably the best choice of English-language literature, phrasebooks and dictionaries. Other places to check include the First Book Bank (☎ 346 20 33) at ul Heveliusza 11 and Libri Mundi (☎ 305 15 74) at ul Rajska 1. Some of these bookshops sell English-language newspapers and magazines, but the widest selection (as well as the German and French press) is the EMPiK Megastore across the street from the main train station. There's another, smaller EMPiK at Długi Targ 25/27.

MAIN TOWN

The Main Town (Główne Miasto) is the largest of the three historic quarters. It was always the richest architecturally, and after WWII was the most carefully restored. It now looks much as it did some 300 to 400 years ago, during the times of its greatest prosperity. Prussian accretions of the Partition period were not restored.

The town was laid out in the mid-14th century along a central axis consisting of ul Długa (Long Street) and Długi Targ (Long Market). The latter was designed for trading, which in most inland medieval towns would have taken place in the Rynek or central market square. The axis came to be known as the Royal Way, for it was the thoroughfare through which the Polish kings traditionally paraded during their periodical visits.

Royal Way

Of the three Royal Ways in Poland (Warsaw, Kraków and Gdańsk), the Gdańsk one is the shortest – only 500m long – but it's architecturally perhaps the most refined.

The traditional entry point for kings was the **Upland Gate** (Brama Wyżynna) at the western end of the Royal Way. The gate was built in 1574 as part of the city's new fortifications, which were constructed outside the medieval walls to strengthen the system. It was originally a plain brick structure but the authorities weren't happy with it, and in 1586 they commissioned a Flemish artist, Willem van den Block, to embellish it. It was covered with sandstone slabs and ornamented with three coats of arms: of Prussia (with unicorns), Poland (with angels) and Gdańsk (with lions). You'll find Gdańsk's shield, invariably with heraldic lions, on countless public buildings throughout the city. The gate survived the last war without major damage but is seriously blackened and in urgent need of cleaning.

Just behind the Upland Gate stands a large 15th century construction known as the **Foregate** (Przedbramie). It consists of the Torture House (Katownia) to the west and a high Prison Tower (Wieża Więzienna) to the east, linked to one another by two thick walls called the Neck (Szyja).

When the Upland Gate was built, the Foregate lost its defensive function and was turned into a jail. The Torture House then had an extra storey added as a court room and was topped with decorative Renaissance parapets. A gallows was built on the square to the north, where public executions of condemned foreigners were held. The locals had the 'privilege' of being hanged at the Long Market in front of the Artus Court.

The Foregate was used as a jail till the mid-19th century. It was damaged during WWII and the restoration work which began in 1951 has not yet been fully completed. The building is being turned into a museum where you'll probably be able to see a medieval torture chamber complete with torturers' tools.

To the east is the **Golden Gate** (Złota Brama). Its function was not defensive but symbolic. Designed by Abraham van den Block, the son of the decorator of the Upland Gate, and built in 1612, it's a sort of

POMERANIA

triumphal arch ornamented with a double-storey colonnade and topped with eight allegorical statues. The four figures on the side of the Prison Tower represent Peace, Liberty, Wealth and Fame, for which Gdańsk was always struggling against foreign powers, the Polish kings included. The sculptures on the opposite side symbolise the burghers' virtues: Wisdom, Piety, Justice and Concord. Today's figures are postwar copies of the 1648 originals. The statues and other sculptural details were once richly gilded, which accounts for the name of the gate.

Adjoining the gate to the north is the **Court of the Fraternity of St George** (Dwór Bractwa Św Jerzego), a good example of late Gothic secular architecture, dating from the 1490s. The roof is topped with a 16th century octagonal tower, with St George and the Dragon on the spire (the 1556 original is in Gdańsk's National Museum).

Once you pass the Golden Gate, you are on the gently curving **Long Street** (ul Długa), one of the loveliest streets in Poland, though despite its name it's only 300m long. In 1945 it was just a heap of smoking rubble. Stop at the **Uphagen's House** (Dom Uphagena) to see the restored historic interior.

At the eastern end of the street is the **town hall**, with its tall slim tower, the highest in Gdańsk (81.5m). Look at the pinnacle; there's a life-sized gilded figure of King Zygmunt August on top – he was particularly generous in granting privileges to the city.

The town hall is a fine piece of architecture with Gothic and Renaissance elements. The first building was reputedly put up in the 1330s, but it grew and changed until the end of the 16th century. In 1945 it was almost completely burnt out and the authorities were on the point of demolishing the ruin, which was eventually saved thanks to local protests.

After serving as a municipal seat for over half a millennium, today it houses the **Historical Museum of Gdańsk** (Muzeum Historii Miasta Gdańska), open 10 am to 4 pm (in summer till 5 pm) except Monday. Enter the building by twin flights of balustraded stairs and go through an ornate baroque doorway (1766) topped by the city's coat of arms guarded by two lions which, unusually, are both looking towards the Golden Gate, supposedly awaiting the arrival of the king. The doorway was the final addition to the external decoration of the building.

Inside are several rooms with period decoration, either original or re-created from old drawings, engravings and photographs. The showpiece is the Red Room (Sala Czerwona) in the Dutch Mannerist style from the end of the 16th century, which was once the setting for the Town Council's debates. There's a large, richly carved fireplace (1593) and a marvellous portal (1596) but your eyes will immediately be attracted to the ornamented ceiling, with 25 paintings dominated by the oval centrepiece entitled *The Glorification of the Unity of Gdańsk with Poland*. The painter, Isaac van den Block, yet another member of the Flemish family of artists, incorporated various themes in the painting, from everyday scenes to the panorama of Gdańsk on the top of the triumphal arch. All the decoration of the room is authentic; it was dismantled in 1942 and hidden outside Gdańsk.

The 2nd floor houses exhibitions related to Gdańsk's history, including photos of the destruction of 1945. From this floor you can enter the tower for a great view. To the east, just at your feet, is the **Long Market** (Długi Targ), once the main city market and now the major focus for tourists.

Next to the town hall is the **Neptune Fountain** (Fontana Neptuna), dominated by the sea god, trident in hand. The bronze statue is the work of another Flemish artist, Peter Husen; it was made in 1606-13 and is the oldest secular monument in Poland. In 1634 the fountain was fenced off with a wrought-iron barrier. This is linked to a legend that the Gdańsk vodka, Goldwasser, spurted out of the trident one merry night and Neptune found himself endangered by crowds of drunken locals. A menagerie of

Now Gdańsk's tourist heart, Long Market was the city's major marketplace in earlier days

stone sea creatures was added in the 1750s during the restoration of the fountain.

Behind the fountain is the **Artus Court** (Dwór Artusa), where the wealthy local merchants held their meetings, banquets and general revelries. Built at the end of the 15th century, the court was given its monumental façade by Abraham van den Block in the 1610s. Inside, there's a huge hall, topped with a Gothic vault supported on four slim granite columns. It's open to visitors Tuesday to Saturday 10 am to 5 pm, Sunday 11 am to 5 pm (it closes earlier in the off season).

The undisputed highlight of the court is the giant Renaissance **tiled stove**, standing in the corner of the hall and almost touching the vault. Looking like a five-tier tower, 10.65m high, this is reputedly the highest tiled stove in Europe. It's also amazingly beautiful, with a wealth of decoration in bas-relief and colour portraying rulers, allegorical figures, coats of arms etc. Built in 1546 by Georg Stelzener, the stove survived virtually unchanged until 1943, when the local conservators dismantled the upper part and hid it outside the city. The lower tiers were badly damaged during the 1945

fighting. All fragments were recollected after the war, and after a long and complex restoration, the stove was eventually put together and revealed to the public in 1995. It contains 520 tiles, 437 of which are original.

The nearby 1618 **Golden House** (Złota Kamienica), designed by Johan Voigt, has the richest façade in the city. In the friezes between storeys are 12 elaborately carved scenes interspersed with the busts of famous historical figures, including two Polish kings. The four statues waving to you from the balustrade at the top are Cleopatra, Oedipus, Achilles and Antigone.

The Long Market is flanked from the east by the **Green Gate** (Zielona Brama), marking the end of the Royal Way. It was built in the 1560s on the site of a medieval defensive gate and was supposed to be the residence of the kings. But none of them ever stayed in what turned out to be a cold and uncomfortable place; they preferred the houses nearby, particularly those opposite the Artus Court.

Waterfront

Just behind the Green Gate is the Motława River. There was once a busy quay along

GDAŃSK – MAIN TOWN

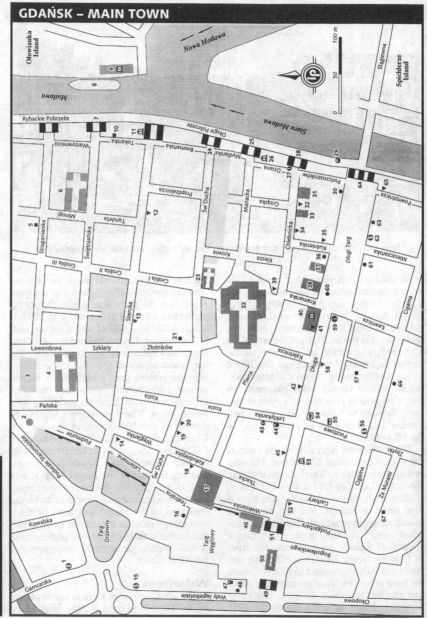

GDAŃSK – MAIN TOWN

here, crowded with hundreds of sailing ships loading and unloading their cargo, which was stored either in the cellars of the burghers' houses in town or in the granaries on the other side of the river, on Granary Island. Today it's a popular tourist promenade lined with cafés, art galleries and souvenir shops.

In medieval times, the parallel east-west streets of the Main Town all had defensive gates at their riverfront ends. Some of them still exist, though most were altered in later periods. Walking north along the Długie Pobrzeże (literally, Long Waterfront), you first get to the **Bread Gate** (Brama Chlebnicka) at the end of ul Chlebnicka. It was built around 1450, still under the Teutonic Order, as shown by the original city coat of arms consisting of two crosses. The crown was added by King Kazimierz Jagiellończyk in 1457, when Gdańsk was incorporated into the kingdom.

Enter the gate and walk a few steps to see the palatial **House under the Angels** (Dom pod Aniołami), also known as the English House (Dom Angielski) after the native country of the merchants who owned it in the 17th century. At that time it was the largest burgher's house in Gdańsk.

At No 14 stands the late Gothic **Schlieff House** of 1520. It's a replica built after the emperor of Prussia, Friedrich Wilhelm III, fell in love with its predecessor in the 1820s and had it taken apart brick by brick and rebuilt in Brandenburg. The original is in Potsdam, near Berlin.

The tiny ul Grząska will take you to **St Mary's Street** (ul Mariacka), the most atmospheric of all the streets in Gdańsk and unique in Poland. It was reconstructed after the war almost from the ground up with the utmost piety on the basis of old documents and illustrations, and every old detail found in the rubble was incorporated. It looks amazingly authentic. It's the only street with a complete row of terraces, which gives it enormous charm, and is a trendy place lined with shops selling amber jewellery.

The street ends at **St Mary's Gate** (Brama Mariacka), similar to the Bread Gate but

POMERANIA

constructed later as you'll see from its coats of arms. Next to it is the fair-sized Renaissance **House of the Naturalists' Society** (Dom Towarzystwa Przyrodniczego) with a tower and a five-storey oriel, unusual in Gdańsk. It now houses the **Archaeological Museum** (Muzeum Archeologiczne), open 10 am to 4 pm except Monday (till 6 pm in summer). The collection stresses the Polish cultural and ethnic roots of the region, and you can go to the top of the tower.

Back on the waterfront and a bit farther north is the modest **Gate of the Holy Spirit** (Brama Św Ducha) and, beyond it, the conspicuous **Gdańsk Crane** (Żuraw Gdański) at the end of Wide Street (ul Szeroka). Built in the mid-15th century as the biggest double-towered gate on the waterfront, it also served to move heavy cargoes directly onto or off the vessels. For this purpose two large wheels – 5m in diameter – were installed as a hoist with a rope wound around the axle; it was put in motion by people 'walking' along the inner circumference of the wheels which formed a treadmill. It could hoist loads of up to 2000kg, making it the biggest crane in medieval Europe. At the beginning of the 17th century another set of wheels was added higher up, for installing masts.

The crane suffered considerably in 1945 but was meticulously rebuilt; it's the only fully restored relic of its kind in the world. It is now part of the **Maritime Museum** (Muzeum Morskie), which has exhibits relating to the history of shipping, plus a collection of shells, corals and other marine life from all over the world. You can also have a look at the hoisting gear of the crane. The modern building next to the crane is an extension of the museum, where traditional rowing and sailing boats from various non-European countries are on display.

The museum continues in three reconstructed granaries just across the Motława, on Ołowianka Island. The museum's boat shuttles between the crane and the island; otherwise it's a 10 minute walk around via the bridge facing the Green Gate. The exhibits, displayed in nine large halls in the granaries, illustrate the history of Polish

seafaring from the earliest times to the present and include models of old sailing warships and ports, a 9th century dugout, navigation instruments, ships' artillery, flags and the like. There's also a score of Swedish bronze cannons from the end of the 16th century, the largest weighing almost 1000kg, recovered from the wrecks of ships that sank in the Gulf of Gdańsk.

Finally, there's the *Sołdek* museum-ship moored in front of the granaries. It was the first freighter built in Gdańsk after WWII (1948); it has now been withdrawn from service and is open to visitors.

All sections of the museum are open from 10 am to 4 pm except Monday and the day following public holidays (daily till 6 pm in summer). Set apart three hours to visit all the sites – there's really a lot to see.

St Mary's Church

Set right in the middle of the Main Town, the Kościół Mariacki (or Kościół NMP) is believed to be the largest old brick church in the world. It's 105m long and 66m wide at the transept, and its massive squat tower is 78m high. Some 25,000 people can be easily accommodated in its half-hectare (5000 sq metre) interior.

The church was begun in 1343 and reached its present gigantic size in 1502. It served as the parish church for the Catholic congregation until the Reformation gale blew into Gdańsk, and it passed to the Protestants in 1572, to be used by them until WWII.

The church didn't escape the destruction of 1945; half of the vault collapsed and the interior was largely burnt out. Fortunately, the most valuable works of art had been removed and hidden before the battle front arrived.

From the outside, the church isn't particularly attractive, and apart from the corner turrets it looks a bit like a huge brick box. Its elephantine size, however, is arresting, and you feel even more ant-like when you enter the building.

Illuminated with natural light passing through 37 large windows – the biggest is

127 sq metres in area – the three-naved, whitewashed interior topped with an intricate Gothic vault is astonishingly bright and spacious. It was originally covered with frescoes, the sparse remains of which are visible in the far right corner. Imagine the impact the church must have made on medieval worshippers.

On first sight, the church looks almost empty, but walk around its 30-odd chapels to discover how many outstanding works of art have been accumulated. In the floor alone, there are about 300 tombstones. In the chapel at the back of the left (northern) aisle is the replica of Memling's *The Last Judgment* – the original is in the National Museum. Note the extraordinary baroque organ.

The high altar boasts a Gothic polyptych from the 1510s, with the Coronation of the Virgin depicted in its central panel. Large as it is, it's a miniature in this vast space. The same applies to the 4m crucifix high up on the rood beam. Directly below it is a lofty wooden sacrarium from 1482, elaborately carved in the shape of a tower.

One object which does stand out, in terms both of size and rarity, is the church's **astronomical clock** placed in the northern transept. It was constructed in the 1460s by Hans Düringer and functioned until 1553. It's claimed that during this time it lost only three minutes. When made, it was the largest clock in the world (14m high). Legend has it that Düringer paid dearly for his masterpiece; his eyes were put out to prevent him from ever creating another clock that might compete with this one. He was probably buried under his clock.

Not only did the clock show the hour, day, month and year but also the phases of the moon, position of the sun and moon in the zodiac cycle and the calendar of the saints. It had six devices allowing figures of saints and the apostles to appear and disappear at certain times, and Adam and Eve rang the bells every hour.

The clock was stored outside Gdańsk during WWII and, after a long and costly renovation and repair, it was put back into work in October 1993. There are still some figures missing (the 12 apostles, among others), but the clock shows the time and displays some of its puppet-theatre abilities. Be there at noon.

Another great attraction of the church is its **tower** or, more precisely, the sweeping bird's-eye view which you get if you can climb 405 steps to the viewing platform. The entrance is from the north-western corner of the church; it's open in summer only.

Royal Chapel

Just to the north of St Mary's Church, and completely overshadowed by the monster, sits the small Royal Chapel (Kaplica Królewska), squeezed between two houses. The only baroque church in old Gdańsk, it was built in 1678-81 to fulfil of the last will of the Primate of Poland of the time, Andrzej Olszowski, which set aside funds for a house of worship for the Catholic minority in what was by then a predominantly Lutheran city. The local clergy felt obliged to respect the Primate's bequest and reluctantly allocated part of the upper floor of St Mary's vicarage to the chapel.

The chapel was designed by famous royal architect Tylman van Gameren. It was built on the 1st floor, though the façade was extended over the whole of the elevation to make the building look bigger and more impressive. Parts of the two adjoining houses were adapted as the chancel and the vestibule, and the nave was topped with a dome, typical of the baroque style and particularly of Gameren. The façade is more attractive than the bare interior. It has the coats of arms of Poland, Lithuania and King Jan Sobieski (the sponsor of the chapel) but, significantly, not that of Gdańsk.

Great Arsenal

To the west of St Mary's Church, ul Piwna (Beer Street) ends at the Great Arsenal (Wielka Zbrojownia). In Gdańsk, even such an apparently prosaic building as an armoury has evolved into an architectural gem. It's the work of Antoon van

The ornately decorated façade of the Great Arsenal in the 17th century

Opberghen, built at the beginning of the 17th century and, like most of Gdańsk's architecture, clearly shows the influence of the Low Countries. The main eastern façade, framed within two side towers, is floridly decorated and guarded by figures of soldiers on the top. Predictably, military motifs predominate, and the city's coat of arms guards the doorways. A small stone structure rather like a well, in the middle of the façade, is the lift which was used for hoisting heavy ammunition from the basement. Above it stands the goddess of warfare, Athena.

The armoury is now home to an indoor market but, even if you are not interested in shopping, walk through to the square on the opposite side, known as the Coal Market (Targ Węglowy) to see the western façade. Though not as heavily ornamented as the other one, it's a fine composition looking like four burghers' houses.

Northern Main Town

The main attraction of this sector is **St Nicholas' Church** (Kościół Św Mikołaja),
one of the oldest in town. It was built by the Dominican Order which arrived from Kraków in 1227, but the church reached its final shape only at the end of the 15th century. Unlike most of the other Gothic churches in the city, this one has unusually rich interior decoration. The magnificent late Renaissance high altar of 1647 first catches the eye, followed by the imposing baroque organ made a century later. Among other highlights are the stalls in the chancel and an ornate baptismal chapel in the right-hand aisle, just as you enter the church. And don't miss the bronze rosary chandelier (1617) with the Virgin and Child carved in wood. It's hanging in the nave in front of the entrance to the chancel.

Just behind the church is the large and bustling **Market Hall** (Hala Targowa), constructed in the late 19th century after the Dominicans were expelled by the Prussian authorities and their monastery standing on this site was pulled down.

In front of the market hall is the tall octagonal **Hyacinthus' Tower** (Baszta Jacek), one of the best-preserved remnants of the medieval fortifications. It was built around 1400 and apart from its defensive role also served as a watchtower.

Some 200m east towards the river stands the massive Gothic **St John's Church** (Kościół Św Jana). It was built during the 14th and 15th centuries on marshy ground and buttresses had to be added to support it. Note the crooked eastern wall. Damaged but not destroyed during the war, it was given a new roof to protect the interior, but at this point work stopped and the church was locked for four decades. The internal decorations were removed; the organ and the pulpit, for instance, now adorn St Mary's Church. Only the monumental stone high altar was left inside, simply because it was too large and heavy to be moved elsewhere. The interior has recently been partly restored and is used as an auditorium for some artistic events.

OLD TOWN

Despite its name, the Old Town (Stare Miasto) was not the cradle of the city. The earliest inhabited site, according to archaeologists, was in what is now the Main Town area. Nonetheless, a settlement existed in the Old Town from the late 10th century and developed in parallel to the Main Town.

Under the Teutonic Order, the two parts merged into a single urban entity, but the Old Town was always poorer and had no defensive system of its own. One other difference was that the Main Town was more 'German' while the Old Town had a larger Polish population. During WWII it suffered as much as its wealthier cousin but, apart from a handful of buildings, mainly churches, it was not rebuilt in its previous shape. Today it's just a little more than an average postwar town, garnished here and there with reconstructed relics. The most interesting area is along the Radunia Canal, between Garncarska and Stolarska streets.

The largest monument of the Old Town is **St Catherine's Church** (Kościół Św Katarzyny), the oldest church in Gdańsk, begun in the 1220s. It was the parish church for the whole town until St Mary's was completed. As is common, the church evolved over centuries and only reached its final shape in the mid-15th century (save for the baroque top to the tower, added in 1634); since then it has remained unchanged. The tower houses the carillon, a set of 37 bells which plays a melody before Mass.

The vaulted Gothic interior was originally covered with frescoes, fragments of which were discovered under a layer of plaster. Some of the old fittings survived the war, having been hidden elsewhere, but much has been lost. Note the huge painting (11m long) depicting the entry of Christ to Jerusalem, placed under the organ loft in the left-hand aisle, and the richly carved enclosure of the baptismal font (1585) in the opposite aisle. The astronomer Jan Heweliusz was buried in the church's chancel and there is an 18th century epitaph above the grave.

Immediately behind St Catherine's Church stands **St Bridget's Church** (Kościół Św Brygidy). This was almost completely destroyed in 1945 and until 1970 only the walls were left standing. Once the authorities set about rebuilding it, it took five years for the whole structure, complete with a perfect Gothic vault and a Renaissance tower, to be returned to its original state. There's almost nothing left of the prewar furnishing and the interior has modern fittings. Wałęsa attended Mass here when he was an unknown electrician in the nearby shipyard. With the wave of strikes in 1980 the church became a strong supporter of the dockyard workers and its priest, Henryk Jankowski, took every opportunity to express their views in his sermons.

The church remains a record of the Solidarity period, with several contemporary craftworks related to the trade union and to modern Polish history in general. You'll find the tombstone of murdered priest Jerzy Popiełuszko, the Katyń epitaph, a collection of crosses from the 1980 and 1988 strikes and a door with bas-reliefs of scenes from Solidarity's history – all in the right-hand (northern) aisle. At the head of the same aisle is a modern altar featuring a picture of the Black Madonna. Note the decorative wrought-iron screen encircling the altar, which depicts the history of the Polish national emblem – the white eagle – from Poland's early days to today.

The peculiar seven-storey building opposite St Catherine's Church is the **Great Mill** (Wielki Młyn). Built around 1350 by the Teutonic Knights, it was the largest mill in medieval Europe, over 40m long and 26m high, and equipped with a set of 18 millstones, each 5m in diameter. The mill operated until 1945 and just before WWII produced 200 tons of flour per day. It might still be working today if not for the war damage. The building was reconstructed but not its machinery. It is now used for offices and shops.

Behind the mill across a small park is the **Old Town Hall** (Ratusz Staromiejski), once the seat of the Old Town council. A Renaissance building, well proportioned and crowned with a high central tower typical of its Flemish provenance, it was designed at the end of the 16th century by Antoon van Opberghen, the architect later responsible for the Great Arsenal. The brick structure is delicately ornamented in stone, including the central doorway and a frieze with the shields of Poland, Prussia and Gdańsk.

The building now houses the Baltic Cultural Centre and an exhibition hall. Go upstairs to see the entrance hall, notable for its rich decoration, partly assembled from old burghers' houses. Note the arcaded stone wall (1560) with three Roman gods in bas-relief. This composition, older than the town hall itself, was moved here from one of the houses in the Main Town. One of the doors leads to the Great Hall, which can also be visited. Concerts are held here – check the program.

The northern part of the Old Town is uninspiring, as it has virtually no old buildings left. Nonetheless, it's worth walking north for 10 minutes to see a document of recent history, the **Monument to the Shipyard Workers** (Pomnik Poległych Stoczniowców), erected in memory of the workers killed in the riots of 1970. Placed in front of the Gdańsk shipyard where Solidarity was born and unveiled on 16 December 1980, 10 years after the massacre, the monument is a set of three 40m-tall steel crosses, with a series of bronze bas-reliefs in their bases. One of the plates contains a fragment of a poem by Czesław Miłosz that reads:

You, who have wronged a simple man,
Bursting into laughter over his suffering,
DO NOT FEEL SAFE. The poet remembers.
You can kill him – another will be born.
Words and deeds will all be written down.

The first monument in a communist regime to commemorate the regime's victims, it immediately became a symbol and landmark of Gdańsk and a must for every visitor.

OLD SUBURB

The Old Suburb (Stare Przedmieście), south of the Main Town, was the product of the expansion of the city between the 15th and 17th centuries. Reduced to rubble in 1945 and rebuilt in the familiar styleless postwar fashion, the suburb has little charm but boasts some important sights.

The most significant of these is the **National Museum** (Muzeum Narodowe) in the well restored vaulted interiors of the former Franciscan Monastery and open Tuesday 11 am to 5 pm, Wednesday to Sunday 9 am to 3 pm. Ranking among the best museums in the country, it contains extensive collections of paintings and woodcarvings, gold and silverware, fabrics and embroidery, porcelain and faïence, wrought iron and furniture. It has the original figure of St George from the spire of the Court of the Fraternity of St George, an assortment of huge, elaborately carved Gdańsk wardrobes (typical of the city from where they were sent all over the country) and several beautiful ceramic tiled stoves.

The 1st floor is given over to paintings, with a section devoted to Dutch and Flemish work. The jewel of the collection is Hans Memling's (1435-94) triptych of the

Last Judgment, one of the earlier works of the artist, dating from 1472-73. You'll also find works by the younger Breughel and Van Dyck, and the beautiful macabre *Hell* by Jacob Swanenburgh, who was the master of the young Rembrandt.

Adjoining the museum from the north, and formerly belonging to the Franciscan monastery, is the **Church of the Holy Trinity** (Kościół Św Trójcy). It was built at the end of the 15th century, when the Gothic style had already reached its late decorative stage, best seen in the elaborate top of the western façade. After St Mary's Church it's the largest in town, with an extremely spacious and lofty whitewashed interior topped with a superb, net-like vault. The chancel was badly damaged during the war and was separated from the nave by a wall to allow for its undisturbed reconstruction. The work has been completed but the two sections haven't yet been joined. Meanwhile, the chancel is used for temporary exhibitions.

In the church proper, the high altar has an assembly of panels from triptychs of different origins, while the filigree late Gothic pulpit from 1541 is topped with a Renaissance canopy. Note the floor paved almost entirely with old tombstones and the spidery baroque chandeliers of the mid-17th century.

To complete your picture of Gdańsk's Gothic churches, have a look at the **Church of SS Peter and Paul** (Kościół Św Piotra i Pawła) a block to the east, with its stepped gable on the tower. Once the parish church of the Old Suburb, it was destroyed in the war and is being reconstructed. You can wander farther south (a 10 minute walk) to see the remnants of old fortifications with the former moat still full of water.

WESTERPLATTE

Westerplatte is a long peninsula at the entrance to the harbour, 7km north of the historic town. When Gdańsk became a free city after WWI, Westerplatte was the Polish tip of the port. It served both trading and military purposes and had a garrison to protect it.

WWII broke out here, when the German battleship *Schleswig-Holstein* began shelling the Polish post. The garrison numbered 182 men and held out for seven days before surrendering. The site has now become a memorial, with some of the ruins left as they were after the bombardment, plus a massive monument put up in memory of the defenders.

One of the barracks buildings is now a **museum** (open daily) where you can see maps of the peninsula in its three incarnations: German resort with beaches (up to WWI); Polish military site (early 1920s to 1939); and docks and parks (postwar). There's also information about the course of the Battle of Westerplatte, including a detailed model with English labels.

Bus No 106 goes to Westerplatte from the main train station (every 40 minutes or so), but a more attractive way to get there is by boat. Boats depart several times daily from the wharf next to the Green Gate. Take the one which includes a visit to the port.

OLIWA

Oliwa, the north-westernmost suburb of Gdańsk, about 9km from the historic city centre, has a fine cathedral set in a quiet park – an enjoyable half-day break after tramping the medieval streets of the Main Town. To get there, take the commuter train from central Gdańsk and get off at Gdańsk Oliwa station, from where it's a 10 minute walk west to the cathedral.

The beginnings of Oliwa go back over 800 years, when the Pomeranian dukes who then ruled Gdańsk invited the Cistercians to settle here in 1186 and granted them land together with privileges, including the revenues of the port of Gdańsk.

The abbey did not have an easy life. The original church dating from around 1200 was burnt out first by the pagan Baltic Prussians, then by the Teutonic Knights. A new Gothic church, built in the mid-14th century, was surrounded by defensive walls, but they didn't save it from further misfortune. When in 1577 the abbots supported King Stefan Batory in his attempts to

POMERANIA

reduce the city's independence, the citizens of Gdańsk burned the church down in revenge. The monks rebuilt their holy home once more, but then the Swedish wars began and the church fell prey to repeated looting, losing its organ and pulpit among other things. The monks' troubles came to an end in 1831, when the Prussian government decided to expel them from the city. The church was given to the local parish and, in 1925, raised to the rank of **cathedral**. It came through the war almost unscathed, and is an important, and unusual, example of ecclesiastical architecture.

The first surprise is its façade, a striking composition of two octagonal brick Gothic towers with a central baroque portion literally squeezed between them. You enter the church by going downstairs, for its floor is more than 1m below the external ground level. The interior looks extraordinarily long, mainly because of the unusual proportions of the building; the nave plus the chancel are 90m long but only 8.3m wide. At the far end of this 'tunnel' is a baroque high altar (1688), while the previous oak-carved Renaissance altar (from 1606) is now in the left-hand transept. Opposite, in the right transept, is the marble tombstone of the Pomeranian dukes (1613), placed on the site where the princes are supposed to have been buried.

The undeniable showpiece of the church is the **organ**. The instrument, begun in 1763 and completed 30 years later, is noted for its fine tone and the mechanised angels which blow trumpets and ring bells when the organ is played. In July and August, recitals take place on Tuesday and Friday evenings, but 20 minute performances are held daily every hour or two between 10 am and 3 or 4 pm (on Sunday in the afternoon only). Check the schedule with the tourist offices before setting off for Oliwa.

Behind the cathedral is the 18th century abbots' palace which now accommodates the **Modern Art Gallery** (Wystawa Sztuki Współczesnej), a branch of the National Museum of Gdańsk. The old granary opposite the palace houses the **Ethnographic Museum** (Muzeum Etnograficzne) with its collection of rural household implements and crafts from the region. Both the museum and the gallery are open from 9 am to 4 pm except Monday.

A **park** with several lakes and a small formal French garden supplies a fine natural setting for the historic complex.

About 1.5km west of the cathedral (a 20 minute walk or take bus No 122) is a small **zoo** (Ogród Zoologiczny), picturesquely sited on the wooded slopes of a valley.

LANGUAGE COURSES

The main facility in the Tri-City area is the Sopocka Szkoła Języka Polskiego (Sopot School of Polish Language; ☎ 550 32 84, fax 550 06 96), Al Niepodległości 763, 81-838 Sopot. It offers scheduled courses on several levels throughout the year and can organise individual programs.

SPECIAL EVENTS

The Dominican Fair (Jarmark Dominikański) is undoubtedly the oldest city event, going back to 1260, when the Dominicans received the papal privilege of holding a fair on the feast day of their saint, 4 August. The fair was initially held on Plac Dominikański, the square next to St Nicholas' Church, but today it takes place on various sites in the Main Town during the first two weeks of August. It's become commercialised over recent years, but there's still a lot of antiques, bric-a-brac and craftworks.

The International Organ Music Festival is held in the Oliwa cathedral, with twice weekly organ recitals from mid-June till the end of August. St Mary's Church is the stage for the International Organ, Choir and Chamber Music Festival (Fridays from June to September). St Nicholas' and St Bridget's churches are also used for organ recitals.

July hosts the Folklore Festival of the People from the North, featuring groups from such exotic locations as Greenland or Kamchatka. Also in this month is the International Street and Open-Air Theatre Festival.

Nearby, Sopot is famous for its International Song Festival, which has been held annually in August for over 30 years. Gdynia hosts the Gdynia Summer Jazz Days in July and the Festival of Polish Feature Films in October.

PLACES TO STAY

Gdańsk doesn't shine in the accommodation department. You can usually easily find somewhere cheap to crash but it will usually involve a bit of commuting. If you are looking for a decent, middle-priced hotel you may be disappointed as there are not many in Gdańsk.

Both tourist offices provide good information about accommodation options. The private tourist office can also find and book a hotel or hostel for a US$1.75 service charge per reservation.

Places to Stay – Budget

Camping Gdańsk has four camping grounds. The nearest to the city centre (about 5.5km to the north-east) is *Camping Gdańsk-Tourist* (☎ 307 39 15, ul Wydmy 1) in the seaside holiday centre in the suburb of Stogi; it's open June to September. Here is possibly Gdańsk's best beach. Tram No 13 from the main train station goes there.

The three remaining camping grounds are open from May to September and all have cabins. *Camping Nr 10* (☎ 343 55 31, ul Hallera 234) in the suburb of Brzeźno is accessible by tram No 13 from the main train station. If you arrive by ferry from Sweden, this is the closest camping ground to the ferry terminal, a short ride on tram No 15.

Camping Nr 18 (☎ 553 27 31, ul Jelitkowska 23) is in the suburb of Jelitkowo. Take tram No 2 or 6 from the main train station. *Camping Nr 69* (☎ 308 07 39, ul Lazurowa 5) in Sobieszewo is about 15km east of the city centre. Take bus No 112 from the train station.

Youth Hostels Gdańsk has three all-year youth hostels. The most convenient is the *youth hostel* (☎ 301 23 13, ul Wałowa 21) a five minute walk north-east from the main train station. Predictably, it's often full, particularly in summer.

The next closest is the *youth hostel* (☎ 302 60 44, ul Kartuska 245B) 3.5km west of the main train station. To get there, take bus No 161, 167 or 174 from ul 3 Maja at the back of the station, or go by tram No 10 or 12 to the end of the line, then walk west along ul Kartuska for about 10 minutes.

The other *youth hostel* (☎ 341 16 60, ul Grunwaldzka 240/244) is in a sports complex next to the soccer field, 6km north-west of Gdańsk's centre. Take the commuter train to Gdańsk Zaspa station and walk north-west for five minutes along ul Grunwaldzka.

Student Hostels From July to September, the *Politechnika Gdańska* opens 10 hostels in its own student dorms, all of which are in Gdańsk Wrzeszcz. A bed in a double or triple will cost US$5 to US$15, depending on the facilities and standards. The hostels' central office (☎ 347 25 47, ☎ 347 25 89, fax 341 44 14) is at ul Wyspiańskiego 7A.

Other Hostels & Hotels There are two budget places conveniently based in the Main Town. *Dom Harcerza* (☎ 301 36 21, ul Za Murami 2/10) has doubles/triples without bath for US$32/36, plus dorms of four/five/six/12 beds costing US$9/7/5/4 per bed (but in summer you have to pay for the whole room).

Hotel Zaułek (☎ 301 41 69, ul Ogarna 107/108) is just 100m from the town hall. It's in the five-storey, freestanding building between ul Długa and ul Ogarna. This former workers' dorm offers basic accommodation for US$17/22/25/28 a single/double/triple/quad or US$6 a bed in a five, six or seven-bed dorm. Again, they may refuse to rent the room by the bed in the high season. In both these places it's pretty hard to find a vacancy during that season anyway.

There are some inexpensive options outside the historic quarter. The closest is probably **Dom Nauczyciela** (☎ 341 55 87, ul Uphagena 28) in Gdańsk Wrzeszcz. It's a teachers' hotel, offering simple singles/doubles/triples/quads without bath for US$15/20/24/28, and singles/doubles with bath for US$33/48. The hotel is close to the Gdańsk Politechnika station.

Private Rooms Gdańsk-Tourist (☎ 301 26 34) at ul Heweliusza 8 near the train station (open daily in summer from 8 am to 7 pm) is the main agency handling private rooms. Singles/ doubles in the central area are US$15/24, while rooms farther out from the centre cost US$12/20. When making your choice, don't worry too much about the distance from the centre – work out how close the place is to the commuter train.

Mac-Tur (☎ 302 41 70) at ul Beethovena 8 in the suburb of Suchanino, 2km west of the main train station (bus No 184 from the front of the station goes there), is a private agency (English spoken) which offers accommodation in private houses, including the house the agency is based in. Bed and a filling breakfast cost US$15.

The private tourist office may have some central private rooms for about US$15 per person.

Places to Stay – Mid-Range & Top End

The old **Hotel Jantar** (☎ 301 27 16, fax 301 35 29, Długi Targ 19) has singles/doubles without bath for US$38/55 and doubles/triples with bath at US$70/80. It's probably not great value for your money in this rather run-down place (which may close for a long needed revamp), but you couldn't ask for a more central location. You may be lucky enough to get a front room, but note that the 1st-floor rooms can be noisy due to the band playing on weekends in the restaurant downstairs.

A better central option is **Dom Aktora** (☎/fax 301 59 01, ul Straganiarska 55/56). It has six small apartments which sleep two/three/four guests for US$65/85/100. It also has its own bistro. Advance booking is essential.

Outside the central area, you can check **Hotel Dal** (☎/fax 556 39 44, ☎/fax 553 29 51, ul Czarny Dwór 4) in the suburb of Przymorze. It has reasonable rooms for US$50/65 a double/triple with bath and breakfast.

Hotel Hevelius (☎ 301 56 31, fax 301 19 22, ul Heweliusza 22) is perhaps the most attractive of the city's four Orbis hotels, especially if you get a room facing south on an upper floor, with good views over old Gdańsk. Rooms go for US$100/130 a single/double with breakfast. The other central Orbis place, the **Novotel** (☎ 301 56 11, fax 301 56 19, ul Pszenna 1), is on Spichlerze Island just east of the Main Town.

If money is not a problem, the classiest place is the new **Hotel Hanza** (☎ 305 34 27, fax 305 33 86) attractively sited on the waterfront next to the Gdańsk Crane. Doubles go for US$150, suites for up to double that price.

PLACES TO EAT

You're not likely to starve in Gdańsk as there's a large number of eateries throughout the centre catering to every budget. As you might expect, fish is better represented here than farther inland, though mainly in the more expensive bracket. Oddly enough for such an important port and cosmopolitan city, ethnic cuisines are almost nonexistent; central Gdańsk has so far just two restaurants serving non-European food (both are Vietnamese).

Ultra-budget dining is provided by two central milk bars: **Bar Mleczny Neptun** (ul Długa 33/34) and the more basic **Bar Mleczny Turystyczny** (ul Węglarska 1/4). There are plenty of other cheap, self-service joints, including **Bar Złoty Kur** (ul Długa 4), **Bar pod Rybą** (Długi Targ 35/38) and **Bar Starówka** on ul Św Ducha.

One of the best places for a tasty, cheap lunch (from noon to 6 pm) is the **Jadłodajnia u Plastyków** (ul Chlebnicka 13/16). The **Bar Bistro** in the Dom Aktora is marginally more expensive but the food is good and worth its price. **La Pasta** (ul Szeroka 32) does reasonable pizzas, pastas and salads.

POMERANIA

Restauracja Kubicki (☎ *301 00 50, ul Wartka 5)*, on the waterfront, has served solid, tasty Polish food at reasonable prices since its founding in 1918, making it Gdańsk's oldest restaurant in continuous operation.

Restauracja Milano (☎ *301 78 47, ul Chlebnicka 4)*, in the shade of St Mary's Church, offers good Italian cuisine at good prices (try the carpaccio).

Pub u Szkota (☎ *301 49 11, ul Chlebnicka 10)*, also called the Scotland Restaurant, is a cosy double-level place combining the functions of a restaurant and bar. Food is good and affordably priced (drinks perhaps not so), it is beautifully decorated and is open till midnight.

Central Gdańsk has several upmarket establishments, of which *Restauracja pod Łososiem* (☎ *301 76 52, ul Szeroka 54)* is probably the classiest and most famous. Founded in 1598, its strong point is fish, particularly the salmon after which the place is named, but it also has some local meat dishes. Its typical drink is Goldwasser, a thick sweet vodka with flakes of gold floating in it. It was produced in its cellars from the end of the 16th century till the outbreak of WWII.

Restauracja Tawerna (☎ *301 41 14, ul Powroźnicza 19/20)*, next to the Green Gate, is popular with westerners for its food and atmosphere. There's a choice of fish and traditional Polish dishes, served in a pleasant, more informal interior than most other upmarket places, but prices are high. The speciality is roasted duck with apples.

Other recommended places for a fine dinner are *Restauracja Gdańska* (☎ *305 76 71, ul Św Ducha 16)* and *Restauracja Hanza* in the hotel of the same name.

Cafés

Kawiarnia Palowa in the basement of the town hall is one of Gdańsk's best known cafés and has a reasonable food menu, which makes it a pleasant, though not cheap, place for lunch.

For good milk shakes, pastries and espresso, head for *Cocktail Bar Capri* (*ul*

Długa 59), diagonally opposite the post office. The nearby *Cukiernia Kaliszczak* (*ul Długa 74)* has good ice cream and excellent *pączki* (doughnuts). The best selection of exotic coffees is at *Sklep z Kawą Pożegnanie z Afryką* (*ul Kołodziejska 4)*.

The photogenic Mariacka Street has several romantic little café-bars, which put tables on their charming front terraces. You'll find more open-air coffee houses and bars on the waterfront, Długie Pobrzeże.

ENTERTAINMENT

The *Opera House and Concert Hall* (*Al Zwycięstwa 15)* are in Gdańsk Wrzeszcz, just off the Gdańsk Politechnika station. The main city theatre is the *Teatr Wybrzeże* (*Targ Węglowy 1)*, next to the Arsenal in the Main Town. There are usually some Polish and foreign classics in the theatre's repertoire.

Klub Żak (*Wały Jagiellońskie 1)*, on the western outskirts of the Main Town, is the leading student club, with its own café, theatre and a bar in the basement. Sadly, by the time we went to press, the club was looking for a new, still unknown, location. Inquire at the tourist offices for news.

The main jazz venue is the *Jazz Club* (*Długi Targ 39/40)*, which has live music on weekends; jazz is also staged at the *Cotton Club* (*ul Złotników 25/29)*.

If all you want is a beer or five, some of the most amazing surroundings in which to linger over a bottle are at the *Latający Holender* (*Wały Jagiellońskie 2/4)*, in the basement of the LOT building; the *Celtic Pub* (*ul Lektykarska 3)*; and the *Irish Pub* in the fabulous vaulted cellar of the old town hall (the last two may have live music).

SHOPPING

Gdańsk is known for amber (see the following boxed text for the story of amber). It's sold either unset or, more often, in silver jewellery, some of which is high quality. Most shops selling amber are on

POMERANIA

Amber – The Baltic Gold

If there's a typical Polish 'precious stone', it's probably amber – with the distinction that amber is not a precious stone at all. It's actually an organic substance, a fossilised tree resin. Different kinds of amber have been found all over the world, including Canada, the USA, Mexico, Sicily, Myanmar, Japan, Tanzania and New Zealand, but the largest deposits have been found along the Baltic shores.

Baltic amber was formed roughly 40 to 60 million years ago, during the subtropical period of the early Cenozoic era. The vast forests of the region (which wasn't a sea by that time) produced thousands of tonnes of resin. Millions of years later the climate cooled and the forests were buried under a thick layer of ice. They surfaced again in a fossilised form with the climatic warming millions of years later. The melting of ice formed the Baltic Sea, which only reached its present size and shape around 6000 BC.

As a result of its complex evolution, amber is not a uniform material but can contain small air bubbles, sand grains, particles of minerals, carbonised wood and cones, insects and fragments of plants. Amber's chemical composition can vary greatly depending on the botanical source, as can its colour – from ivory through various shades of yellow and orange to reddish and brownish tints. The degree of transparency also varies, from perfectly clear to wholly opaque.

The majority of amber is on the Baltic's south-east shores, particularly on the Samland Peninsula in the Kaliningrad Region (between Lithuania and Poland). There are smaller deposits along the Polish, Lithuanian and Latvian coasts, and still smaller ones in other countries bordering the Baltic. The largest amber mine is in Yantarnyi near Kaliningrad; with an annual yield of around 750 tonnes, it produces over two-thirds of the world's amber and over

---

ul Mariacka, Długi Targ and Długie Pobrzeże. Although a selection of amber can also be found in Warsaw, Kraków and other major cities, Gdańsk has the best choice. However, beware of some overpriced jewellery and souvenir shops catering to western visitors.

GETTING THERE & AWAY
Air

The airport is in Rębiechowo, 14km west of Gdańsk. Bus No 110 goes there from the Gdańsk Wrzeszcz train station, or you can take the infrequent bus B from the Gdańsk Główny station. The LOT office (☎ 301 11 61) is at ul Wały Jagiellońskie 2/4, next to the Upland Gate.

The only direct domestic flights are to Warsaw (four times daily but fewer in the off season), while international flights go to Copenhagen (daily), Hamburg (daily) and London (twice a week).

Train

The main train station, Gdańsk Główny, on the western outskirts of the Old Town, handles all incoming and outgoing traffic. Note the station building itself; it's another historic monument which has been restored to its former glory.

Almost all long-distance trains coming from the south go to Gdynia (and usually appear under Gdynia in the timetables). Trains heading south originate not from Gdańsk but from Gdynia. On the other hand, most trains along the coast to western destinations such as Szczecin originate (and terminate) in Gdańsk and stop at Gdynia en route.

Gdańsk is a busy railway junction, with a dozen trains daily to Warsaw (329km), including eight express trains and two InterCity trains (which cover the distance in less than 3½ hours). All these trains go via Malbork (51km) but InterCity trains don't

POMERANIA

90% of Baltic amber. The largest existing lump of Baltic amber, kept in the Natural Museum of Humboldt University in Berlin, weighs 9.75kg and was found on the Polish coast in 1890.

Baltic amber has been collected and traded for 12,000 years or more. It has been found in Egyptian tombs dating from 3200 BC, and in 4000-year-old burial sites near Stonehenge in England. It was carved into a variety of decorative and ritual objects, such as beads, rosaries, amulets and altarpieces. It wasn't until the 1860s that commercial exploitation, by dredging and mining, started; until then amber was collected from the beaches.

Amber has long attracted interest for its delicacy, striking variations of colour and unusual properties, such as generating static electricity when rubbed, or the ability of some pieces to fluoresce. Often believed to hold special mystical powers, amber was named 'elektron' or 'substance of the sun' by the ancient Greeks.

Finds of extinct insects entombed inside, sometimes preserved in an exquisite state, have captured the imagination. They are usually small flies, mosquitoes, beetles or spiders, but butterflies and even lizards have also been found. They make fascinating material for DNA studies and for some (so far) fantasies like the one popularised by Steven Spielberg's film *Jurassic Park*.

Over recent years, amber has become one of the most popular 'stones' in Polish jewellery-making. Manufacturers use 220 to 240 tonnes of amber a year, but only 10 to 20% is collected in Poland (mainly on the shores of the Gulf of Gdańsk); the rest comes from the Kaliningrad Region. About 85% of Polish amber jewellery is exported, earning roughly US$300 million annually. Of all Polish cities, Gdańsk has the longest traditions in amber jewellery.

stop there (express trains do). There are six fast trains daily to Olsztyn (179km), which call at Malbork en route.

If you're travelling to Warsaw or Olsztyn and don't plan on stopping in Malbork, make sure your camera is ready for when you pass the castle at Malbork.

There are two express and three fast trains to Wrocław (478km); they all go through Bydgoszcz (160km) and Poznań (313km). There are also six fast trains to Toruń (211km). Four fast trains leave for Szczecin (374km); one of them continues to Berlin.

Bus

Gdańsk's bus terminal is behind the central train station and you can get there by an underground passageway. You'll find that buses will be handy for several regional destinations which seldom, or never, have trains.

There's one morning bus directly to Frombork (112km). Alternatively, take any of the half-hourly buses to Elbląg (61km), from where you have regular transport to Frombork by both bus and train. Four fast buses daily go to Olsztyn (156km) and four to Lidzbark Warmiński (157km). For Łeba, go to Gdynia, from where four direct buses daily run to Łeba in summer, or take a bus or train to Lębork and change there.

For the Kaszuby region, you have hourly buses to Kartuzy (31km) and Kościerzyna (56km). From July and August there are three direct morning buses to Wdzydze Kiszewskie (72km), which is noted for its skansen.

There are plenty of connections to Western European cities; travel agencies (including Almatur and Orbis) have information and sell tickets. To the east, two PKS buses travel daily to Kaliningrad (US$8, five hours).

POMERANIA

Ferry

Car ferries to Oxelösund and Nynäshamn in Sweden depart from Gdańsk, while those to Karlskrona in Sweden start from Gdynia. Information, booking and tickets can be obtained from the Orbis office at ul Heweliusza 22. Turn to the introductory Getting There & Away chapter for ferry routes and prices.

GETTING AROUND
Commuter Train

A commuter train, known as SKM or Szybka Kolej Miejska (Fast City Train), runs constantly between Gdańsk Główny and Gdynia Główna (21km) from 5 am till midnight, stopping at a dozen intermediate stations, including Sopot. The trains run every five to 10 minutes (not so frequently late in the evening) and the Gdańsk-Gdynia trip takes 35 minutes. You buy tickets in ticket offices in the stations or some Ruch kiosks and validate them in the machines at the platform entrance (not in the train itself).

Tram & Bus

These are slower means of transport than SKM and are advisable only for destinations not connected by the train. They run between around 5 am and 11 pm.

Like Poznań, fares depend on the duration of the journey: US$0.20 for up to a 10 minute trip, US$0.40 for up to a half-hour ride and US$0.60 for an hour's journey. Your ticket doesn't get punched, but are stamped with the date and time you get on.

Boat

From mid-May to late September excursion boats go from Gdańsk's wharf near the Green Gate to Sopot (US$8 one way, US$11 return), Gdynia (US$10 one way, US$15 return) and across the Gulf of Gdańsk to the fishing village of Hel on the Hel Peninsula (US$11 one way, US$15 return). Students pay about two-thirds of the normal fare. The trip to Hel is a nice way to get in a sailing mood and do some sightseeing and beach bathing (see the Hel section later in this chapter). The boat schedule gives you about six hours at Hel.

Boats to Westerplatte run several times daily (hourly in summer) from April to October and include a visit to the port (US$8 return).

Around Gdańsk

SOPOT
• pop 45,000   ☎ 058

Sopot, immediately north of Gdańsk, is one of Poland's most fashionable seaside resorts, though its pulling power has been weakened after the Gulf of Gdańsk was shown to be polluted in the early 1990s.

A fishing village belonging to the Cistercians of Oliwa has existed here since the 13th century, yet Sopot was really discovered by Jean Georges Haffner, a former doctor of the Napoleonic armies, who established sea bathing here in 1823. Soon afterwards spa buildings went up, and a horse-drawn bus service from Gdańsk was introduced. In the course of the following decades an array of fine villas sprang up, some of which still exist.

After WWI, Sopot was attached to the Free City of Danzig and soon boomed, becoming a place where the filthy rich of the day rubbed shoulders. By the outbreak of WWII Sopot was a vibrant resort with 30,000 residents.

In the postwar period, in Polish hands, Sopot was given a generous injection of 'new' architecture which happily hasn't managed to overpower what was built earlier. You can still get some of the feel of the past, even though the guest lists are somewhat different nowadays. One of the last exotic visitors was the Shah of Iran.

Orientation & Information

The tourist office (☎ 551 26 17) is at ul Dworcowa 4 diagonally opposite the train station. A few minutes walk north from here will bring you to ul Bohaterów Monte Cassino, Sopot's attractive pedestrian mall which leads straight down to the 'molo',

Poland's longest pier, built in 1928 and jutting 512m out into the Gulf of Gdańsk. North of the pier is the old-fashioned 1927 Grand Hotel and farther north stretches a long waterfront park. If you wander about the back streets in the centre, you'll find some fine villas from the end of the 19th century.

The western part of Sopot, behind the railway track and the Gdańsk-Gdynia thoroughfare, consists of newer suburbs, which ascend gradually, finally giving way to a wooded hilly area. Here is the Opera Leśna (Opera in the Woods), the amphitheatre that seats 5000 people, where the International Song Festival is held in the second half of August. On the southern outskirts of Sopot is the racecourse established in 1898.

Places to Stay

As with all such resorts, accommodation varies largely in price and quantity between the high and low season. The all-year lodging facilities are supplemented by a variety of pensions and holiday homes in summer. Prices listed below are for the high season which peaks in July and August. In that period, it may be difficult to find accommodation, other than at camp sites or in private rooms – the cheapest option in Sopot as there's no longer a youth hostel.

Sopot has three camping grounds. The largest and best is *Camping Nr 19* (☎ 550 04 45, ul Zamkowa Góra 25), in the northern end of town (a five minute walk from the Kamienny Potok train station). It's open May to September and has bungalows. Close to the south is *Camping Nr 73* (☎ 551 07 25, ul Sępia 41/45), open June to August, which has fewer facilities and no cabins. The third one, *Camping Nr 67* (☎ 551 65 23, ul Bitwy pod Płowcami 69), is in the southern end of Sopot, near the beach. It's far from the commuter train line.

Private rooms are handled by the tourist office. Be prepared to pay about US$10/18/24 a single/double/triple in July and August. During this time, there may be some locals hanging around the office who will offer rooms.

Of the regular all-year hotels, one of the cheapest is *Hotel Miramar* (☎ 550 00 11, ul Zamkowa Góra 25). It charges US$28/34/38 a double/triple/quad without bath, US$36/50 a single/double with bath.

A five minute walk south of Hotel Miramar is *Pensjonat Maryla* (☎ 551 00 34, ul Sępia 22). It's a good, pension-style place which offers singles/doubles with bath for US$35/50. In summer, it hires out cabins in its grounds (US$25/30 a double/quad).

Across the street is the much larger, modern *Sopot Lucky Hotel* (☎ 551 22 25, ul Haffnera 81/85), which has doubles/triples/quads with bath for US$45/60/75.

If you want to stay where the fashionable once flocked to, go to the Orbis-run *Grand Hotel* (☎ 551 00 41, fax 551 61 24, ul Powstańców Warszawy 12/14) by Sopot pier next to the beach. The hotel probably lived up to its name more before the war than it does today, but it's still a plush place to stay. Singles/doubles go for US$90/120.

For somewhere cosier, try the *Villa Hestia* (☎ 550 32 51, ul Władysława IV 3/5), which will charge US$180 a double.

Places to Eat

Apart from a number of all-year eating outlets, plenty of bars, bistros, cafés, open-air restaurants and street stands open in summer throughout the town, particularly in the beach area. Sopot's top-end eateries include *Restauracja Balzac* (ul 3 Maja 7), with top-notch French cuisine; *Restauracja Rozmaryn* (ul Ogrodowa 8), with the best Italian food for miles around; and the restaurant at *Villa Hestia*. Don't miss two amazing artistic creations: the cosy *Błękitny Pudel* (ul Bohaterów Monte Cassino 44) and the spacious *Club Café Nr 5* (ul Bohaterów Monte Cassino 5). Both serve reasonably priced food and plenty of drinks.

Getting There & Away

For details of long-distance trains, see the Gdańsk section, as all trains that service Gdańsk go to Gdynia and stop in Sopot.

POMERANIA

There are commuter trains to Gdańsk (12km) and Gdynia (9km) which run every five to 10 minutes.

Excursion boats, running from mid-May to the end of September, go daily to Gdańsk (US$8), Gdynia (US$5) and Hel (US$9 one way, US$13 return). The landing site is at the pier.

GDYNIA

• pop 255,000 ☎ 058

North of Sopot is the third component of the Tri-City, Gdynia. It has nothing of the historic splendour of Gdańsk, nor of the relaxed beach atmosphere of Sopot. Gdynia is just a busy port city without much style or character.

Gdynia is a young city. Though a fishing village existed as early as the 14th century, it had hardly more than 1000 inhabitants by the outbreak of WWI. In the aftermath of that war, when Gdańsk became the Free City of Danzig and no longer represented Polish interests, the Polish government decided to build a new port in Gdynia to give Poland an outlet to the sea.

With the help of French capital, the construction of the port began in 1923 and 10 years later Gdynia had the largest and most modern port on the Baltic. By 1939 the population of the city had reached 120,000. The port was badly damaged during WWII, but was rebuilt and modernised and is now the base for much of Poland's merchant and fishing fleet.

Orientation & Information

You are most likely to arrive in town at Gdynia Główna main train station. Take ul 10 Lutego to the waterfront where the major tourist attractions are. On the way you'll pass near the tourist office (☎ 621 77 51) at ul 3 Maja 27, the useful Bank Gdański and the main post office.

Things to See

The Southern Pier (Molo Południowe) has most of the sights. Near its tip is the **Oceanographic Museum and Aquarium** (Muzeum Oceanograficzne i Akwarium Morskie), open 10 am to 5 pm except Monday (daily till 7 pm in summer).

Moored on the northern side of the pier are two **museum ships**: the three-masted frigate *Dar Pomorza* (built in Hamburg in 1909) and the WWII destroyer *Błyskawica*. Both are open 10 am to 4 pm except Monday. On the opposite side of the pier is the marina *(basen jachtowy)*.

South of the pier, on Bulwar Nadmorski, is the **Naval Museum** (Muzeum Marynarki Wojennej), which has an open-air display of guns, warplanes, helicopters and rockets. It's open 10 am to 4 pm except Monday.

Behind the museum there is a 52m-high hill called the **Stone Mountain** (Kamienna Góra), which provides views over the city centre and the harbour.

Places to Stay

The all-year *youth hostel* (☎ 627 00 05, ul Morska 108C) is 2km north-west of the centre (get off at the Gdynia Grabówek station).

Private rooms are arranged (at US$13/22 a single/double) by Biuro Zakwaterowań Turus (☎ 621 82 65, ul Starowiejska 47, entrance from ul Dworcowa), opposite the main train station. Minimum stays of three nights are required.

There are a few affordable hotels right in the city centre, including *Hotel Lark* (☎ 621 80 46, ul Starowiejska 1), charging US$22/33/38/42 for a single/double/triple/quad without bath, and *Hotel Neptun* (☎ 626 64 77, ul Jana z Kolna 6), charging US$24/34 a single/double without bath.

You'll find some better options south of the centre near the beach. Of these, *Hotel Antracyt* (☎ 620 65 71, ul Korzeniowskiego 19) is good value at US$36/50/60 for singles/doubles/triples with bath, breakfast and view over the sea. A few steps to the south is *Dom Marynarza* (☎ 622 00 25, Al Piłsudskiego 1), which has spacious rooms for marginally less.

The best place in town is the central *Hotel Gdynia* (☎ 620 66 61, fax 620 86 51, ul Armii Krajowej 22). It charges US$90/110 a single/double.

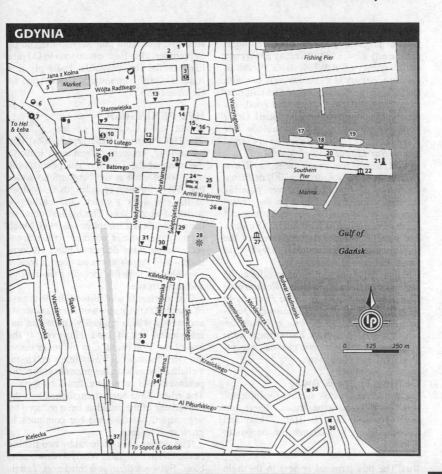

GDYNIA

PLACES TO STAY
2   Hotel Neptun
14 Hotel Lark
25 Hotel Gdynia
35 Hotel Antracyt
36 Dom Marynarza

PLACES TO EAT
1   Restauracja La Gondola
5   Restauracja Jackfish
9   Bistro Prima
13 Bar Uniwersalny
15 Restauracja Szeyk
16 Bistro Kwadrans
20 Restauracja Róża Wiatrów

29 Bar Chata
31 Bar Mleczny Słoneczny
32 Snack Bar Liliput

OTHER
3   Public Toilet
4   Consulates of Finland,
    Norway & Sweden
6   Bus Terminal
7   Gdynia Główna Train Station
8   Biuro Zakwaterowa Turus
10 Bank Gdaski
11 Tourist Office
12 Main Post Office
17 *Błyskawica* Museum Ship

18 Excursion Boats
19 *Dar Pomorza* Museum Ship
21 Monument to Joseph Conrad
22 Oceanographic Museum &
    Aquarium
23 Orbis Office
24 St Mary's Church
26 Teatr Muzyczny
27 Naval Museum
28 Lookout (Stone Mountain)
30 EMPiK
33 LOT office
34 Teatr Miejski
37 Gdynia Wzgórze Św
    Maksymiliana Train Station

POMERANIA

Places to Eat

Gdynia has plenty of eating outlets throughout the city centre. *Bar Mleczny Słoneczny* on the corner of ul Władysława IV and ul Żwirki i Wigury is a genuine milk bar with exclusively vegetarian dishes that cost next to nothing. Efficient, clean and good, it's deservedly popular among the locals. Other good budget eating options include *Bar Uniwersalny (ul Starowiejska 14)* and *Snack Bar Liliput (ul Świętojańska 75)*.

You won't pay much more in *Bistro Kwadrans (Skwer Kościuszki 20)* or *Bistro Prima (ul 3 Maja 21)*. However, possibly the best value is *Bar Chata (ul Świętojańska 49)*, which serves copious portions of home-cooked Polish food for US$3 a dish. For popular Middle Eastern fare, try the inexpensive *Restauracja Szeyk (ul Świętojańska 15)*.

Gdynia also has something to offer at the top end of the scale, including *Restauracja La Gondola (☎ 620 59 23, ul Portowa 8)* with Italian cuisine and *Restauracja Jackfish (☎ 661 75 34, ul Jana z Kolna 55)*, which specialises in fish. *Restauracja Róża Wiatrów* on the southern pier has acceptable food and good views.

Getting There & Away

Train See the Gdańsk section for information on long-distance trains. There are several trains daily to Hel (77km) and Lębork (where you change for the bus to Łeba).

Bus The bus terminal is next to the train station. Regional routes you may be interested in include Hel (78km) and Łeba (89km). Two fast buses run daily to Świnoujście (324km).

Boat Ferries to/from Karlskrona, Sweden, depart from and arrive at the Terminal Promowy, ul Kwiatkowskiego 60, 5km north-west of central Gdynia. Ask about the free bus to the terminal when you book your ticket.

There are excursion boats to Gdańsk (US$10), Sopot (US$5) and Hel (US$8 one way, US$12 return) departing from the southern pier from mid-May to the end of September. One-hour excursions to Gdynia harbour are also available; boats ply this route several times daily from April to October (US$5).

HEL PENINSULA
☎ 058

The Hel Peninsula (Mierzeja Helska) is a 34km-long, crescent-shaped sand bank to the north of the Tri-City. The peninsula is only 300m wide at the base and no wider than 500m for most of its length. Only close to the end does it widen out, reaching a width of about 3km. The highest point of the peninsula is 23m above sea level. Much of the landscape is covered with trees – picturesque, wind-deformed pines predominate – and there's also a number of typical coastal plant varieties including sand sedge and dune thistle.

The peninsula was formed in the course of about 8000 years by western sea currents and winds, which gradually created an uninterrupted belt of sand. However, at the end of the 17th century, as old maps show, the sand bar was cut by six inlets making it a chain of islands. In the present century the peninsula was cut several times by storms. The edges have been strengthened and the movement of the sand has been reduced by vegetation, but the sand bar continues to grow inch by inch.

The peninsula is enclosed by two fishing ports: Hel at its tip and Władysławowo at its base. Between them is a third port, Jastarnia, and three villages: Chałupy, Kuźnica and Jurata. All are tourist resorts during the short summer season (July and August). There's a railway and a good road running the whole length of the peninsula.

All along the northern shore stretch beautiful sandy beaches and, except for small areas around the resorts (which are usually packed with holidaymakers), they are clean and deserted.

The Hel peninsula is easily accessible from the Tri-City by train, bus and boat. The bus and train can take you anywhere you want, while boats sail from Gdańsk, Sopot and Gdynia to Hel. The boat trip is the most popular way of getting the feel of the peninsula.

Hel

Hel is a fishing port whose history is buried in the obscurity of the 9th century. The original village was founded 2km to the north-west from where it is today, not much later than Gdańsk, and benefited from its strategic location at the gateway of the developing port. By the 14th century Hel had a population of over 1200 and was a prosperous fishing port and trading centre.

The town never grew much bigger, however, as it was constantly threatened by storms and the shifting coastline, and was relatively isolated from the mainland because of the lack of overland links. Long belonging to Gdańsk, Hel followed the changes in power and religion of the big city, and, like Gdańsk, fell into decline in the 18th century.

During the Nazi invasion of 1939, Hel was the last place in Poland to surrender; a garrison of some 3000 Polish soldiers defended the town until 2 October. The peninsula became a battlefield once more in 1945, when about 60,000 Germans were caught in a bottleneck by the Red Army and didn't lay down their arms until 9 May; it was the last Polish territory of all to be liberated.

Things to See A dozen 19th century half-timbered fishing houses on the town's main street, ul Wiejska, somehow managed to survive the various battles. The oldest building in the town is the Gothic church from the 1420s, which is now the **Fishing Museum** (Muzeum Rybackie), open 10 am to 4 pm (till 6 pm in summer) except Monday. It features exhibits related to fishing and boat-building techniques, plus a collection of old fishing boats outside. You can go up to the tower for good panoramic views.

The **Fokarium**, a large tank for grey seals, complete with a laboratory and observation

desks, is being built near the museum. The grey seal is the largest and most populous seal species in the Baltic but it's under threat. There are only 3000 seals left, down from 5000 two decades ago.

There's a beautiful 100m-wide beach on the sea coast, 1km north of the town, and a 42m brick **lighthouse**, which is open for visitors in summer.

Places to Stay & Eat *Hotel Riviera* (☎ 675 05 28, ul Wiejska 130) is Hel's top place (US$30 a double with bath), but you can stay for less next door (☎ 675 05 40, ul Wiejska 132), where inexpensive lunches are also served.

Private rooms can be arranged in the PTTK (☎ 675 06 21) at ul Wiejska 78, or directly with owners by asking people around you. The usual price is about US$15 per double room, but you'll probably find that few locals will want to rent out a room for just one night.

The town has a reasonable array of summer bars and small restaurants. The most charming places to eat and drink include *Maszoperia (ul Wiejska 110)* and *Pub Captain Morgan (ul Wiejska 21)*.

Getting There & Away Hel can be reached by road and railway (fairly regular services by both train and bus from Gdynia) and by excursion boat from mid-May to the end of September from Gdańsk, Sopot and Gdynia (see those sections for fares). Note that the return ticket is considerably cheaper than two singles, so buy one if you plan on returning by boat. The boat schedule allows for up to six hours at Hel. There's a small bar aboard where you can get coffee or a beer, and the open deck at the back makes for a pleasant trip (if the weather is fine). The road along the peninsula is now open for private cars all the way to Hel.

Around the Peninsula

Instead of hanging around in Hel, you might like to walk along the beach to **Jurata** (12km) or 2km farther to **Jastarnia** and take the train from there, or stay for the night.

Both are lively holiday resorts and have camp sites, places to eat and an array of holiday homes where you should be able to find a bed.

Farther north-west are two tiny ports, **Kuźnica** and **Chałupy**, which have retained their old atmosphere more than other places on the peninsula. Finally you get back to the base of the peninsula at **Władysławowo**, the largest fishing port and a town of some 13,000 people, with a good wide beach. The town has several accommodation options, two camping grounds and an array of restaurants.

Between Chałupy and Władysławowo, there are six camp sites which have wind-surfing centres, providing equipment and instructors. This is one of the most popular windsurfing areas in Poland.

Some 8km west along the coast from Władysławowo is the **Rozewie Cape** (Przylądek Rozewie), the northernmost tip of Poland. Its 33m-high lighthouse set on a cliff houses a small museum dedicated to the lighthouse business; you can go to the top for sweeping views.

KASHUBIA
☎ 058

The region of Kashubia (Kaszuby in Polish) stretches for 100km to the south-west of Gdańsk. Hilly, well forested and dotted with many post-glacial lakes, it's a picturesque area garnished with small villages where people still seem to live close to nature. There are no cities, towns are few and far between, and large scale industry hasn't arrived, leaving the lakes and rivers virtually unpolluted.

The original inhabitants, the Kashubians, were Slavs, once closely related to the Pomeranians. In contrast to most of the other groups which gradually merged to form one big family of Poles, the Kashubians have managed to retain some of their early ethnic identity, expressed in their distinctive culture, craft, architecture and language.

Far from the main trading routes and important urban centres, they lived as peacefully as frequent wars and shifting borders allowed. What's more, they were not displaced in the aftermath of WWII by the communist regime, which removed most other groups that didn't fit the ethnic picture.

The Kashubian language, still spoken by some of the old generation, is the most distinct dialect of Polish; other Poles have a hard time understanding it. It's thought to derive from the ancient Pomeranian language, which survived in its archaic form but which has assimilated words of foreign origin, mostly German during the Germanisation imposed by the Prussians.

The region between Kartuzy and Kościerzyna is the most diverse topographically, and the highest point of Kashubia, Mt Wieżyca (329m) is here. This is also the most touristy area of Kashubia; an array of tourist facilities have already been built and others are in progress.

Apart from accommodation options in Kartuzy and Kościerzyna (listed in the sections immediately following) you can stay and eat at *Zajazd Burczybas* (☎ 681 26 56) in Dzierżążno; *Zajazd Sobótka* (☎ 681 38 40) in Ręboszewo; *Zajazd Jezioranka* (☎ 684 17 83) in Ostrzyce; *Pensjonat Hubertówka* (☎ 684 38 96) in Szymbark, and *Leśny Dwór* (☎ 684 40 60) in Sulęczyno. Public transport between Kartuzy and Kościerzyna is fairly regular, with buses running every hour or two.

The region south-west of Kościerzyna is not so rugged but more forested and remote. Roads are fewer here, as are buses, and places to stay and eat are scarce. Camping wild and hitching are probably the best way to explore this region, if you are sufficiently adventurous.

Unless you have your own transport – which is particularly useful in exploring Kashubia – you miss out on some of the region by being limited to the irregular bus links, which become less frequent the farther off the track you go. The two major regional destinations detailed below will give a taste of the culture of Kashubia, though less of its natural beauty.

Kartuzy
• **pop 16,000**   ☎ 058

The town of Kartuzy, 30km west of Gdańsk, owes its birth and its name to the Carthusians, the order which was brought here from Bohemia in 1380. Originally founded in 1084 near Grenoble in France, the order was known for its austere monastic rules, its monks living an ascetic life in hermitages and, like another unusual congregation, the Camaldolese (see the Bielany section in the Kraków chapter for details of them), passing their days in the contemplation of death, their motto being 'Memento Mori'.

When they arrived in Kartuzy the monks built a church and, beside it, 18 hermitages laid out in the shape of a horseshoe. The order was dissolved by the Prussians in 1826 and the church is now a parish church. Of the hermitages, only one survives, still standing beside the church as does the refectory on the opposite side. The church is a 10 minute walk west of the bus and train stations across the town's centre.

The **church** seems to be a declaration of the monks' philosophy; the original Gothic brick structure was topped in the 1730s with a baroque roof that looks like a huge coffin. On the outer wall of the chancel there's a sundial and, just beneath it, a skull with the 'Memento Mori' inscription.

The maxim is also tangibly manifested inside, on the clock on the balustrade of the organ loft. Its pendulum is in the form of the angel of death armed with a scythe. The clock is stopped periodically if there's an unusual number of funerals in town and it seems to help.

The interior fittings are mainly baroque, and the richly carved stalls deserve a closer look. There's some unusual cordovan (painting on goat leather) decoration (1685) in the chancel, while the oldest object, the extraordinary Gothic triptych from 1444 (only the central panel survives), is in the right-hand chapel.

Another attraction is the **Kashubian Museum** (Muzeum Kaszubskie), south of the train station near the railway track. It depicts the traditional culture of the region, with everything from curious folk musical instruments and costumes to typical household implements and furniture. Tours in German are available for US$14 per group. The museum is open Tuesday to Friday 8 am to 4 pm, Saturday 8 am to 3 pm and Sunday (but only May to mid-September) 10 am to 2 pm.

There's only one hotel in town, the *Rugan* (☎ 681 16 35, ul 3 Maja 36), charging US$34/45 a double/triple with bath and breakfast, but you can easily leave on one of the hourly buses to Gdańsk (31km).

Wdzydze Kiszewskie
• **pop 1000**   ☎ 058

The small village of Wdzydze Kiszewskie, 16km south of Kościerzyna, boasts an interesting **skansen** (Kaszubski Park Etnograficzny) featuring typical Kashubian architecture. Established in 1906 by the local schoolmaster, this was Poland's first skansen. Pleasantly positioned on the lakeside, it now contains a score of buildings collected from central and southern Kashubia, including cottages, barns, a school, a windmill and an 18th century church used for Sunday Mass. As elsewhere, some of the interiors are fitted with furnishings, implements and decorations, showing how the Kashubians lived a century or two ago. From 15 April to 15 October, the skansen is open 9 am to 4 pm; other times of the year it's open 10 am to 3 pm. It's closed on Monday year-round.

For an overnight stay, there's the *Hotel Niedźwiadek* (☎ 686 60 80), complete with its own restaurant, and a summer *camp site*.

If you are caught for the night in Kościerzyna, the gateway to Wdzydze, you can stay either in the basic *Hotel Pomorski* (☎ 686 22 90, ul Gdańska 15) in the town centre, or in the better *Zajazd Bazuny* (☎ 686 37 98, ul Kościuszki 17), 2km out of town on the Słupsk road.

The village is linked to Kościerzyna by several buses daily. In summer, there are also three direct buses between Wdzydze and Gdańsk.

POMERANIA

Central & Western Pomerania

To the west of Kashubia, the rolling, wooded countryside continues for about 150km; the lakes and forests only thin out as you descend to the Szczecin Lowland (Nizina Szczecińska), some 50km before reaching the Odra River and the border with Germany. Like Kashubia, the area is essentially rural, sparsely populated, with only occasional towns and very little industry. Whether you're travelling by public transport, car or kayak, it's a lovely region to spend some time exploring. Some places, including Szczecinek, Czaplinek and Połczyn Zdrój, have developed into local holiday centres.

Despite its beauty, the lake country hasn't evolved into a popular tourist region, unlike Masuria in the east. What has developed into a prime holiday destination is the coast, which attracts thousands of visitors every summer.

The Polish coastline is predominantly flat and straight, but its dunes, woods and coastal lakes give it a lot of charm. There are sandy beaches along almost the whole length, all the way from Hel to Świnoujście. Two particularly interesting portions of the coast have been made national parks.

The Baltic is considerably colder than the Mediterranean. The water temperature hardly ever goes above 20°C. Sea-bathing is a bit of a challenge except during a midsummer heatwave. On the whole, summers are not as hot on the coast as in central Poland. Conversely, winters are not as cold.

On numerous occasions throughout their history, Central and Western Pomerania (Pomorze Środkowe i Zachodnie) have passed from hand to hand, with the Germans doing the honours for most of the time. The region has been an ethnic melting pot since time immemorial, providing a home for pre-Roman communities and subsequently for various Germanic tribes as they expanded eastwards. Goths from Scandinavia settled here early in the 1st millennium AD and some five centuries later the Slavs arrived from the south and gradually became dominant.

The first Polish monarch, Mieszko I, brought the whole of Pomerania, as far west as the Odra River, into the newborn Poland. However, typically for those early days, real power lay in the hands of the local rulers rather than in those of the king hundreds of kilometres away. For a time, Western Pomerania remained a largely independent dukedom ruled by Pomeranian Slavs. Set on the border between the Holy Roman Empire and Poland, it was influenced by both those cultures and colonised by both Germans (mostly in urban centres) and Poles (in the countryside).

The picture changed by the 14th century, the province gradually turning to the west, politically and economically. At that time Poland was expanding swiftly to the east and was more interested in keeping control of the vast, newly conquered territories stretching almost as far as the Black Sea, rather than in getting into wars with its strong western neighbour over its dubious western fringes. Economically too, Pomerania, and the coast in particular, was far more involved in trading with other western ports in the Hanseatic League than with Poland's inland towns. In 1521 the region formally pledged its loyalty to the Holy Roman Empire.

In 1621 the Swedes, who were by then a significant military power, conquered most of the Pomeranian coast. The Treaty of Westphalia of 1648 awarded them part of Pomerania, which became their strategic stronghold, a base for their devastating war against Poland. The Swedes were eventually forced out in the 1720s and the Brandenburgs (or by then the kingdom of Prussia, created in 1701) regained control over the whole of Central and Western Pomerania, hanging on until the end of WWII. Only then did the region become part of Poland again.

Pomerania was the scene of particularly fierce fighting in 1945, and most of the urban fabric, from Gdańsk to Szczecin, was devastated. Most of the German population – the dominant group in the region – fled west before the Red Army came and all those who stayed were forcibly expelled in the aftermath of the war.

The ruined and deserted land was settled by a completely new population, people who in their turn had lost their homes in prewar Poland's eastern provinces, taken over by the Soviet Union.

ŁEBA
- **pop 4200**   ☎ **059**

Łeba ('Weh-bah') is a small old fishing port which these days is also a popular seaside resort. The wide sandy beach stretches in both directions as far as the eye can see and the water is reputedly the cleanest on the Polish coast. The nearby Słowiński National Park (see that section later in this chapter), with its unusual shifting dunes and relatively undisturbed nature, is well worth exploring. If you're looking to relax at a Baltic beach resort, Łeba is one of the best places to consider.

A settlement known as Old Łeba was founded on the western side of the mouth of the Łeba River, perhaps as early as the 12th century, but a catastrophic storm destroyed it almost completely in 1558. The inhabitants moved to a safer place farther inland on the opposite bank of the river and built a new village. In the course of time, the remains of the original settlement were buried by shifting dunes and the sole reminder of the tragedy is a fragment of the wall of a Gothic church.

Nature was not very kind to the new village either. The maritime trade was paralysed by the silting up of the port, and agriculture was unprofitable since fields were constantly covered by sand. At the end of the 19th century a new port was built and protected with breakwaters while the dunes were forested, slowing down the movement of the sands. This, together with the construction of the road and railway from Lębork, brought gradual economic growth. By then Łeba had also begun to develop as

a seaside resort. Today it's still a large village rather than a town, but it attracts 50 times more visitors than it has permanent inhabitants.

Orientation
The train and bus stations are next to each other in the south-western part of Łeba, two blocks west of ul Kościuszki, the town's main drag. This shopping street runs north to the port, set on a brief stretch of the Łeba River which joins Lake Łebsko to the sea. The river divides Łeba's beach in two. The town is nestled behind the eastern beach: this is also the main resort area. The beach on the western side of the river is less crowded and the broad white sands stretch back 75m to the dunes, making up some of the best beaches on the Baltic coast. The town map is posted outside the train station.

Information
The tourist office (☎/fax 66 25 65) is at ul 11 Listopada 5A, just round the corner from the train station. Cash can be easily exchanged in any of several kantors, including one in the post office, but travellers cheques can be hard to cash.

Places to Stay & Eat
As in most seaside resorts, the lodging and culinary picture varies widely between the high season (July and August) and the rest of the year. Many holiday homes and pensions open their doors in summer; most also have their own eating facilities, apart from countless fish stalls and snack bars that mushroom all around the town. Locals rent out rooms in their homes.

A useful first port of call in town is the Centrum Turystyczne Łeba (☎ 66 22 77) at ul Kościuszki 64, which arranges rooms in private homes, pensions and holiday homes. A bed in high season will cost anywhere between US$7 and US$20, depending on the standard, demand etc. In the off season, prices drop significantly to between US$4 and US$12 per head. The Biuro Wczasów Przymorze (☎ 66 13 60) at ul Dworcowa 1

POMERANIA

diagonally opposite the train station also arranges private rooms.

There are half a dozen camping grounds in Łeba, including *Camping Nr 41 Ambré* (☎ 66 24 72) and *Camping Nr 48 Przymorze* (☎ 66 23 04), next to each other on ul Nadmorska 9 in the resort area; and *Intercamp 84* (☎ 66 22 40), *Camping Nr 21 Leśny* (☎ 66 13 80) and *Camping Nr 145 Rafael* (☎ 66 19 72), all on ul Turystyczna west beyond the Łeba River. Most camping grounds are open June to September and some have their own eating facilities. Bring mosquito repellent, or you might be eaten alive.

Among more permanent accommodation (some operating year-round) are the cheap *Dom Wycieczkowy PTTK* (☎ 66 13 24, ul 1 Maja 6) near the station; *Dom Wczasowy Kowelin* (☎ 66 14 40, ul Nad Ujściem 6); *Zespół Wypoczynkowy Mazowsze* (☎ 66 18 88, ul Nadmorska 15); *Ośrodek Arkun* (☎ 66 24 19, ul Wróblewskiego 11); and *Hotel Wodnik* (☎ 66 15 42, ul Nadmorska 10). The closest to the seashore is the expensive *Hotel Neptun* (☎ 66 14 32, ul Sosnowa 1), which has a terrace overlooking the beach and great views of the sunset.

Of the few all-year restaurants, you can try the *Karczma Słowińska (ul Kościuszki 28)* or the *Restauracja BD*.

Getting There & Away

The usual transit point to/from Łeba is Lębork, a town 29km to the south, where you may need to change bus or train. Trains to Lębork run every three or four hours, and four of them continue on up to Gdynia. Buses ply the Łeba-Lębork route every hour or so. There are two buses direct between Łeba and Gdynia (94km) plus two extra ones in summer.

SŁOWIŃSKI NATIONAL PARK

The 186 sq km Słowiński National Park (Słowiński Park Narodowy) includes the 33km stretch of coast between Łeba and the fishing-tourist village of Rowy, complete with two large lakes to the south, the Łebsko and the Gardno, with their sur-

rounding belts of peatbogs, meadows and woods. The park ('Swo-veen-skee') is named after the Slav tribe of the Slovincians (Słowińcy), a western branch of the Kashubians who once inhabited this part of the coast. In the 19th century there were still several villages populated by the descendants of these aboriginal people. Today they're part of history.

The park contains a diversity of habitats, including forests, lakes, bogs, beaches and dunes. There's also a skansen and a natural history museum, and the lake wildlife is remarkably rich, particularly in birds. The park was included in UNESCO's 1977 list of World Biosphere Reserves.

Shifting Dunes

The most unusual feature of the national park are the shifting dunes (*wydmy ruchome*), which create a genuine desert landscape. They are on the sandbar separating the sea from Lake Łebsko, about 8km west of Łeba. It's actually a 5 sq km ridge of sand 40m high and it's moving. During WWII, Rommel's Afrika Korps trained in this desert and V-1 rockets were fired at England from here.

The phenomenon consists of an accumulation of sand thrown up on the beach by the waves. Dried by wind and sun, the grains of sand are then blown away to form dunes which are steadily moving inland. The 'white mountain' walks at a speed of up to 10m a year, burying everything it meets on its way. The main victim is the forest, which is gradually disappearing under the sand, to reappear several decades later as a field of skeletal trees,˙after the dune has passed.

The dunes are easily reached from Łeba. Take the road west to the hamlet of Rąbka (2.5km), where there's a car park and the gate to the park. Private minibuses ply this road in summer, or you can just walk. The sealed road continues into the park for another 3.5km to the site of the rocket launcher (which didn't survive), from where a wide path goes on through the forest for another 2km to the southern foot

Magnificent architecture, Gdańsk's Main Town

Bustling Long Market, Gdańsk

Shingle-spired St Gertrude's Chapel, Darłowo

Ornamented town hall in Stargard Szczeciński

Medieval, massive & majestic: Malbork Castle is Poland's largest castle

Gothic cathedral in Kołobrzeg

Picturesque corner in Gdańsk's Long Market

SŁOWIŃSKI NATIONAL PARK

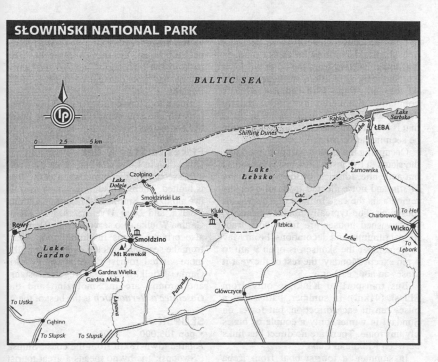

of the dunes, where trees can be seen half-buried in the sand.

No cars or buses are allowed beyond the car park. You can walk to the dunes (70 minutes), take one of the small electric trolleys (US$5 per three people), take a horse-drawn cart (US$14 per five people) or rent a bicycle (US$0.80 per hour) There are also large electric trolleys, but they only go as far as the launcher (US$0.50), so you'll still have 2km to walk to the dunes. You then can climb a vast high dune for a sweeping view of desert, lake, beach, sea and forest. You can walk back to Łeba along the beach, perhaps stopping for a swim – something you can't do in the Sahara!

Lakes

There are four lakes in the park, two large and two small. They are shallow lagoons which were once sea bays, gradually cut off from the sea by a sand bar. With densely overgrown, almost inaccessible marshy shores, they provide a habitat for some 250 species of birds which live here either permanently or seasonally. They include swans, mallard, gulls, geese and grebe, to list but a few. The white-tail eagle, the largest bird found in Poland, with a wingspan of up to 2.5m, nests in the park, though nowadays it's very rare. Large parts of the lake shores have been declared strict reserves, safe from human interference.

About 16km long and 71 sq km in area, Lake Łebsko is the biggest in Pomerania and the third-largest in Poland, after Śniardwy and Mamry in Masuria. It's steadily shrinking as a result of the movement of the dunes, the growth of weeds, and silting.

POMERANIA

Kluki

Set on the south-western shore of Lake Łebsko, Kluki is a tiny hamlet of perhaps 200 souls. Isolated from the outer world, it was where local traditions survived longest. At the end of the 19th century, Kluki's population numbered over 500, mostly descendants of the Slovincians. The little that is left of their material culture can now be seen in the skansen.

Occupying the central part of the village, the **skansen** (Skansen Słowiński) is modest but authentic, for most of the buildings are *in situ* and not collected from all over the region as is the case in most other open-air museums. The typically long, two-family, whitewashed houses are fitted with traditional furniture and decorations. From May to September the skansen is open 9 am to 4 pm except Monday; the rest of the year it closes an hour earlier.

Bus transport to Kluki is only from Słupsk (41km): in summer, half a dozen buses run in each direction, but fewer on Sunday; in winter, only a couple of buses ply this route. There are no direct bus links between Kluki and Łeba.

In summer, a tourist boat from Łeba leaves for the skansen in the morning and returns in the afternoon (US$8 return, no student discounts). You can also get to the skansen on bicycle (rented in Rąbka or Łeba).

If you're feeling fit, you can walk from Łeba, by either the northern (red) or the southern (yellow) route. The red trail goes from Łeba via the shifting dunes to Czołpino (25km). From here, it's 9km by road to Kluki. The yellow trail goes along the southern side of Lake Łebsko and it's 21km to Kluki.

Smołdzino

West of Kluki, outside the park's boundaries, Smołdzino boasts the **Natural History Museum** (Muzeum Przyrodnicze), which features flora and fauna from the park. The park's headquarters are also here.

Just 1km south-west of the village is Mt Rowokół, the highest hill in the area, 115m

above sea level. On its top is a 20m **observation tower**, providing sweeping views over the forest, the lakes and the sea. The path up the hill begins next to the petrol station and you can get to the top in 15 minutes.

Buses to Słupsk (30km) go fairly regularly till late afternoon. There are no buses to Łeba.

Places to Stay & Eat

Other than in Łeba and Słupsk (see the relevant sections), accommodation in the area is limited. There are summer *youth hostels* in Smołdzino, Smołdziński Las and Gardna Wielka, and *Dom Wycieczkowy PTTK* in Gardna Wielka.also serves meals. There are also private rooms in Smołdzino. Apart from the seasonal snack bars in some of the more visited tourist destinations (Kluki, Gardna Wielka), the only regular restaurants around are in Smołdzino and the *Gościniec u Bernackich* is the best of them.

SŁUPSK

• pop 105,000   ☎ 059

A large town 18km from the coast, Słupsk ('Swoopsk') is by no means a great tourist destination, yet it has some attractions, a good tourist office and a choice of places to stay and eat. It can be a jumping-off point for the coast or a stopover on the coastal route.

Słupsk's history is every bit as chequered as that of other Pomeranian settlements. After its birth in the 11th century as a Slav stronghold on the Gdańsk-Szczecin trading route, it came under the rule of the Gdańsk dukes in 1236, then passed into the hands of the Brandenburg margraves in 1307, but later became part of the West Pomeranian Duchy. In 1648 it reverted to the Brandenburgs and remained under Prussian administration until WWII. It was largely destroyed in 1945 and returned to Poland after the war.

Information

The tourist office (☎ 42 07 91, ☎/fax 42 43 26) is at Al Wojska Polskiego 16. It's open

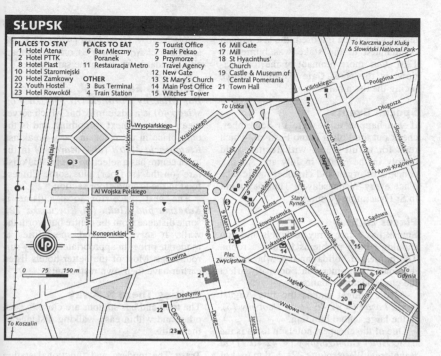

SŁUPSK

PLACES TO STAY	PLACES TO EAT	5 Tourist Office	16 Mill Gate
1 Hotel Atena	6 Bar Mleczny	7 Bank Pekao	17 Mill
2 Hotel PTTK	Poranek	9 Przymorze	18 St Hyacinthus'
8 Hotel Piast	11 Restauracja Metro	Travel Agency	Church
10 Hotel Staromiejski		12 New Gate	19 Castle & Museum of
20 Hotel Zamkowy	OTHER	13 St Mary's Church	Central Pomerania
22 Youth Hostel	3 Bus Terminal	14 Main Post Office	21 Town Hall
23 Hotel Rowokół	4 Train Station	15 Witches' Tower	

Monday to Friday 8 am to 4 pm (till 6 pm in July and August). The Bank Pekao is at ul 9 Marca 6, while kantors are easy to track down in the centre.

Things to See

The most important sight is the 16th century **castle** or, more precisely, the **Museum of Central Pomerania** (Muzeum Pomorza Środkowego) which occupies its interior. Apart from sacral woodcarvings, historic furniture and other exhibits related to the town's history, the museum contains an extensive collection (the best in Poland) of portraits by Stanisław Ignacy Witkiewicz (commonly known as Witkacy). This controversial writer, photographer and painter was one of the foremost figures in interwar Polish art.

The building opposite the castle gate is the 14th century **mill** *(młyn)*, which also served as a granary. Today it's an extension of the museum and houses the regional ethnographical collection. Both sections of the museum are open Wednesday to Sunday 10 am to 4 pm (from June to August also on Monday and Tuesday and for one hour longer).

Next to the mill, the 15th century **St Hyacinthus' Church** (Kościół Św Jacka) has had substantial later alterations and contains a late Renaissance high altar and pulpit, both from 1602. The organ has a fine tone which you can hear if your visit coincides with the summer concerts.

Almost nothing is left of the 15th century fortified walls which once encircled the town. Two survivors, though, are the **Mill Gate** (Brama Młyńska), beside the mill, and the **Witches' Tower** (Baszta Czarownic), a bit farther north. In the 17th century the latter was turned into a jail for women

POMERANIA

suspected of witchcraft, and death sentences were often imposed; the last woman condemned to the stake was burned in 1701. One more remnant of the fortifications is the **New Gate** (Brama Nowa), facing the town hall.

Special Events
If you happen to be here in September, check out the Polish Piano Festival, which runs for a full week, with recitals held mainly in the castle. In July and August, concerts of organ and chamber music take place every Wednesday or Thursday night in St Hyacinthus' Church.

Places to Stay
Słupsk has a fair array of hotels and you shouldn't have problems finding a room. The hordes of holidaymakers who invade the coast in summer don't normally affect the city's accommodation.

At the budget end is the July-August *youth hostel* (☎ 42 46 31, ul Deotymy 15), in the large school building.

One of the cheapest hotels in town is the basic *Hotel Garnizonowy* (☎ 42 40 71, ul Bohaterów Westerplatte 22), 1.5km east of the centre (2.5km from the train station). Urban bus No 11 from the station will take you there. Singles/doubles/triples without bath cost US$10/15/20.

Far more convenient is *Hotel PTTK* (☎ 42 29 02, ul Szarych Szeregów 1), which offers doubles without bath for US$18 and singles/doubles with bath for US$16/22 – this is the cheapest hotel in the central area.

Round the corner is the better *Hotel Atena* (☎ 42 88 14, ul Kilińskiego 7), a former police dorm, which has comfortable rooms with bath for US$27/30. *Hotel Rowokół* (☎ 42 72 11, ul Ogrodowa 5) offers pretty much the same for similar prices.

The refurbished *Hotel Zamkowy* (☎ 42 52 94, ul Dominikańska 4), next to the castle, charges US$30/50 for rooms with bath and breakfast. The central *Hotel Staromiejski* (☎ 42 84 64, fax 42 50 19, ul Jedności Narodowej 4) has singles/doubles/triples with bath and breakfast for US$40/50/60. Nearby, *Hotel Piast* (☎/fax 42 52 86, ul Jedności Narodowej 3) offers comparable standards for much the same price.

Places to Eat
Bar Mleczny Poranek (Al Wojska Polskiego 46) is a basic milk bar which serves meals that cost next to nothing and is the only place in town for an early breakfast. *Restauracja Metro* (ul 9 Marca 3) in the town centre has a selection of classic Polish fare (on the 1st floor) plus some Chinese food in the ground-floor section.

The best place for local cuisine is *Karczma pod Kluką* (ul Kaszubska 22), some distance from the centre but worth the walk. It serves regional specialities at moderate prices in appropriately folksy surroundings. Most of the better hotels listed earlier have their own restaurants.

Getting There & Away
The train and bus stations are close to each other and within easy walking distance of the centre.

Train The modern and functional station has regular services east to Gdańsk (132km) and west to Koszalin (67km); half a dozen trains continue west up to Szczecin (242km). Three trains go straight to Warsaw (461km), with three extras in summer. Two trains daily go to Berlin.

Bus Five or six buses leave daily for Łeba (61km), Gdynia (110km), Koszalin (68km) and Darłowo (48km). Buses to Smołdzino (30km) go regularly throughout the day, some continuing as far as Kluki (41km). For Ustka (18km), take the hourly suburban bus No 20.

International buses go through the city from Gdańsk on their way to Berlin, Hamburg, Cologne and other destinations. Information and tickets are available from Orbis (☎ 42 70 14) on the 1st floor of the train station, Przymorze (☎ 42 27 23) at ul Jedności Narodowej 4 and other travel agencies.

USTKA

• pop 17,500   ☎ 059

A fishing port and the gateway to the sea for Słupsk, Ustka is also a seaside resort which swarms with holidaymakers in summer. It's much bigger than Łeba and has a good tourist infrastructure, but its beaches are narrower and perhaps less attractive (the beach west of town is better and less crowded).

The helpful Biuro Promocji Miasta (☎ 14 60 41, ☎ 14 71 70, fax 14 43 78) is at ul Marynarki Polskiej 87, 100m from the train station. In July and August, the office is open daily 8 am to 8 pm; at other times, it opens Monday to Friday 7.30 am to 3.30 pm. It has good information and can arrange accommodation.

Places to Stay

The tourist office will find you a place to stay in a hotel, pension, holiday home or private house. The cheapest lodging in summer shouldn't cost more than US$8 per person.

There are two summer camp sites in town: *Camping Nr 101 Morski* (☎ 14 47 89) on ul Armii Krajowej at the south-eastern end of the town; and *Camping MOSiR* (☎ 14 55 86, ul Grunwaldzka 33), closer to the sea. Both have cabins.

All-year accommodation includes the *youth hostel* (☎ 14 50 81, ul Jagiellońska 1) in a large school; *Dom Rybaka* (☎ 14 45 26, ul Marynarki Polskiej 31), right in the town centre beside the harbour (US$20/30 a double/triple); and *Pensjonat Sonata* (☎ 14 68 03, ul Armii Krajowej 1), *Hotel Korsarz* (☎ 14 70 84, ul Limanowskiego 1A) and *Zajazd Bałtycki* (☎ 14 40 48) on ul Grunwaldzka. The last three are near Camping Nr 101, quite far from the town centre and the beach, and charge US$35 a double.

Getting There & Away

The only good connections are with Słupsk, 18km to the south. Ustka is the end of the railway line from Słupsk (trains every other hour approximately); the bus service is much more frequent.

DARŁOWO

• pop 16,000   ☎ 094

West of Ustka, the first place on the coast that's larger than a village is Darłowo ('Dar-wo-vo'). Once a prosperous medieval Hanseatic port, Darłowo is one of a handful of towns in Western Pomerania which has retained some of its original character. It still has the familiar chessboard of streets, as laid out in 1312, and several interesting historic buildings.

Darłowo isn't exactly on the coast but is 2.5km inland on the bank of the Wieprza River. The town's gateway to the sea is Darłówko, a waterfront suburb at the mouth of the river. It's a small fishing port which developed as a summer resort around its beaches and has a totally different atmosphere to the main town. Darłówko is linked to Darłowo by local buses which run regularly along both sides of the river.

Things to See

Darłowo The western side of the Rynek is occupied by the **town hall**, a largish baroque building, lacking a tower and fairly sober in decoration except for its original central doorway. Right behind it rises the massive brick **St Mary's Church** (Kościół NMP). Begun in the 1320s and enlarged later, it has preserved its Gothic shape pretty well (particularly the beautiful vaults), even though the fittings date from different periods. Note the wooden baroque pulpit from around 1700, with carved scenes from the life of Christ and of the Last Judgment on the canopy.

A curiosity of the church are three tombs placed in the chapel under the tower. The one made of sandstone holds the ashes of Erik of Pomerania, king of Denmark, Sweden and Norway between 1396 and 1438. After his unwilling abdication, the king went into exile in the castle of Visby on Gotland, from where he commanded corsair raids on the Hansa's ships. Forced to flee, he found a refuge in Darłowo, where he died in 1459. His tombstone, commissioned in 1882 by the Prussian Emperor Wilhelm II, isn't as impressive as the two mid-17th century, richly decorated tin tombs standing on both sides of it.

South of the Rynek is the 14th century **castle**, the best preserved Gothic castle in Central and Western Pomerania. It was the residence of the Pomeranian dukes until the Swedes devastated it during the Thirty Years' War, and the Brandenburgs took it following the Treaty of Westphalia. The dethroned King Erik, the 'last Viking of the Baltic', lived in the castle for the last 10 years of his life and is believed to have hidden his enormous loot here; so far it remains undiscovered.

The castle is now the **Regional Museum** (Muzeum Regionalne), open from 10 am to 3.30 pm except Monday. In the well restored period interiors – an attraction in themselves – you'll find a varied collection including folk woodcarving, portraits of Pomeranian princes, old furniture, sacred art, armour and even some exhibits from the Far East.

Of the town's medieval fortifications, only the **Stone Gate** (Brama Kamienna) survives, which despite its name is made of brick. It's a block north of the Rynek. A few hundred metres beyond it is the marvellous **St Gertrude's Chapel** (Kaplica Św Gertrudy). The most unusual building in town, it is 12-sided and topped with a high, shingled central spire. It has been renovated and looks amazing, but is only open for Mass, at 6 pm on weekdays, with more Masses on Sunday.

Darłówko Darłówko is not a place for historic sights but a pleasant beach resort, packed with tourists in summer. It's cut in two by the Wieprza River, and linked by a pedestrian drawbridge which opens when boats go into or out of the bay, providing a spectacle for tourists. There are two breakwaters leading into the sea at the outlet of the river, which make for an enjoyable walk. At the base of the eastern mole is a lighthouse.

Places to Stay

Predictably, accommodation is highly seasonal, with all-year places scarce and summer lodgings operating mainly in Darłówko. At the budget end, you have private rooms starting from about US$7 per person. They can be arranged through PTTK (☎ 314 30 51) at ul Zielona 3A near the Stone Gate, Jantaria (☎ 314 30 70) at ul Żeromskiego 1, near the train station, or Biuro Turystyczne (☎ 314 20 73) at ul Dorszowa 1 in Darłówko.

Camping Nr 243 (☎ 28 72, ul Conrada 20) is open from June to August in Darłówko, 500m from the beach.

Among the permanent accommodation in Darłowo, there's *Hotel Kubuś* (☎ 314 29 19, Al Wojska Polskiego 63A) and *Hotel Irena* (☎ 314 36 92, Al Wojska Polskiego 64), next to each other and midway between the train station and the Rynek. Expect to pay about US$25 for a reasonable double room with bath in high season.

In Darłówko, you have the simple *Dom Rybaka* (☎ 314 24 19, ul Wschodnia 2) next to the bridge, which charges US$20 a double without bath. There are also a number of small private *pensjonaty* (guesthouses) and locals rent out rooms in their homes – watch out for signs saying 'pokoje' or 'noclegi'.

Places to Eat

There are a few simple places in Darłowo, including the *Bar Rarytas* (ul Powstańców Warszawskich 25). Darłówko, by contrast, is completely packed in summer with snack bars, fish bars, cafés, street food stands etc.

Getting There & Away

The train and bus stations are next to each other in the south-western end of Darłowo, a 10 minute walk from the Rynek.

Buses run regularly to Sławno (21km) and Koszalin (34km) and – less often – to Ustka (38km) and Słupsk (48km). Trains no longer provide passenger service at Darłowo.

KOSZALIN

• pop 113,000   ☎ 094

The largest city on the central coast, halfway between Szczecin and Gdańsk, Koszalin ('Ko-shah-leen') was once a

POMERANIA

wealthy Hanseatic port competing with Kołobrzeg for sea trade. The good times came to an end after its access to the sea through Lake Jamno silted up in the 17th century. WWII reduced the city to one big ruin with little left to be restored. Consequently, Koszalin is a postwar creation that offers few tourist attractions. Yet, if you're travelling along the coast, you'll almost inevitably pass through the city.

Information

The helpful tourist office (☎ 342 73 99, fax 342 43 40) at ul Dworcowa 10 is open weekdays 8 am to 4 pm (till 5 pm in July and August). It's close to the train station. Exit from the station's main door and go straight ahead through a pedestrian underground passageway; the office is to your left as you leave the passageway.

Orbis is opposite the tourist office, while PTTK is 50m east down the street. The Bank Pekao is behind the office, at ul Jana z Kolna 11. The Bank Gdański is at ul 1 Maja 36, one block south of the Rynek.

Things to See

The only historic relic of substance in the centre is the **cathedral** just off the Rynek, which miraculously survived the 1945 shelling. It has finely restored Gothic vaults but otherwise little remains of the old fittings.

The **Regional Museum** (Muzeum Okręgowe) at ul Piłsudskiego 53, about 1.5km north-east of the Rynek, focuses on the region's archaeology and the city history. The other branch of the museum at ul Młyńska 38, 300m north of the Rynek, has sculpture and painting from Gothic to Art Nouveau, plus temporary exhibitions. It also has an ethnographic display in a 200-year-old cottage beside the museum's building. Both sections of the museum are open from 10 am to 4 pm except Monday.

Places to Stay

The all-year *youth hostel* (☎ 342 60 68, ul Gnieźnieńska 3) has four large dorms plus six rooms (doubles to quads). The hostel is about 2km south-east of the train station (1.5km from the Rynek) and is hard to find because of the lack of signs and the confusing address. Walk about 600m down ul Gnieźnieńska from the roundabout (the only roundabout you pass coming from the station), and then 200m to the right into a small street, ul Kwiatowa, until you see a building with a large sign at the top saying 'Zespół Szkół Samochodowych'. It's here. Southbound bus No 13 from near the station will take you to the hostel.

There are also two summer *youth hostels* in Koszalin, at ul Podgórna 55 (☎ 343 07 95) and ul Morska 108 (☎ 343 24 21).

Among the hotels, one of the cheapest is the basic **Hotel PKS** (☎ 342 78 51, ul Zwycięstwa 6) at the bus terminal. It charges US$12/14/16 a single/double/triple without bath. Slightly better is **Hotel Turystyczny** (☎ 342 30 04, ul Głowackiego 7), 800m east of the Rynek. It has doubles/triples with shower (but shared toilets) for US$24/30. **Hotel La Mirage** (☎ 345 13 21, ul Fałata 34) costs much the same but it's farther away from the centre (1.5km north-east of the Rynek).

The best place to stay in town and conveniently close to the station is **Hotel Arka** (☎/fax 342 79 11, ul Zwycięstwa 20/24). It charges US$70/90 a single/double, breakfast included.

Getting There & Away

The train and bus stations are next to each other, 800m west of the Rynek, a 10 minute walk away. There's a fair number of buses to the seaside resorts as well as a regular train service on the Szczecin-Gdańsk route. Trains to Kołobrzeg leave every hour or two and there are five fast trains to Poznań.

KOŁOBRZEG

• pop 48,000   ☎ 094

With 1300 years of history, Kołobrzeg ('Ko-wob-zhek') is one of the oldest settlements in Poland. It goes back to the 7th century, when salt springs were discovered here. Their exploitation was the force behind the town's development. When in

972 it became part of the Polish state, Kołobrzeg was already a well fortified and prosperous township, and as such gained the honour of becoming a seat of the bishopric in 1000. With this, it reached a position in the religious hierarchy equal to that of Kraków and Wrocław. Though in 1125 the seat was moved to Wolin, Kołobrzeg was by then a well developed port, the fish and salt trades keeping it stable for centuries.

A wave of disasters began in the Thirty Years' War when Kołobrzeg was seized by the Swedes. In the aftermath of the war it fell under Brandenburg rule. The margraves set about making the town an impregnable fortress, but their elaborate fortifications didn't help much – Kołobrzeg (or Kolberg, as it was called then) was subsequently captured and destroyed by the Russians in 1761 and by Napoleon's army in 1807. The town recovered slowly, this time as a spa and seaside resort, but the worst was yet to come: in March 1945 the two-week battle over the city left it completely devastated.

Rebuilt, Kołobrzeg is once more a lively town and an important port, though it lacks any sense of history. For tourists, however, it's not history that pulls the hordes into the town, but the beach and the array of holiday homes and sanatoria that have sprung up along the waterfront. This holidaymakers area is separated by the railway track from the town's centre farther inland, where a few remnants of the town's past can be found.

Information

The Centrum Informacji Turystycznej (☎ 352 79 39) is at ul Wojska Polskiego 6C. It's open weekdays 9 am to 3 pm (till 5.30 pm in July and August).

Useful banks include the Bank Pekao at ul Źródlana 5, Powszechny Bank Kredytowy at ul Łopuskiego 6 and Bank Gdański at ul Unii Lubelskiej 33B. All three have ATMs.

Things to See

The 14th century **cathedral** is the most important historic sight in town. Though badly damaged in 1945, it has been rebuilt close to its original form. Its colossal two conjoined towers occupy the whole width of the building, and the façade is a striking composition of windows placed haphazardly – a bizarre folly of its medieval builders and rebuilders.

The five-naved interior is impressively spacious and still retains fragments of old frescoes. The most striking feature, however, is the leaning columns on the right side of the nave, which give the impression that the cathedral is on the point of collapsing. Don't worry – they have been leaning since the 16th century.

Old fittings include three 16th century triptychs and the unique Gothic wooden chandelier from 1523 hanging in the central nave. There are some even older objects such as the bronze baptismal font (1355) featuring the scenes of Jesus Christ's life, a 4m-high, seven-armed candelabra (1327) and the stalls in the chancel (1340).

The **town hall**, just east of the cathedral, is a neo-Gothic structure designed by Karl Friedrich Schinkel and erected in the 1830s after the previous 14th century building was razed by Napoleon's forces in 1807. One of its wings houses a modern art gallery.

The area south of the town hall and the cathedral has been rebuilt as what you might call the **New Old Town** – an interesting architectural design, a blend of old and new, that adds some character to the otherwise gloomy landscape of monstrous tower blocks looming from behind.

If you are interested in military matters, the **Polish Army Museum** (Muzeum Oręża Polskiego) at ul Gierczak 5 covers the history of the Polish army. The other sections of the museum, at ul Armii Krajowej 13, contain some folk woodcarvings and archaeological finds.

In the seaside sector, there are no sights as such; the beach is the attraction. Walk out 200m over the sea on the pier (*molo*), an obligatory trip for all holidaymakers. Nearby to the west, by the harbour, stands the lighthouse; you can climb to its top.

KOŁOBRZEG

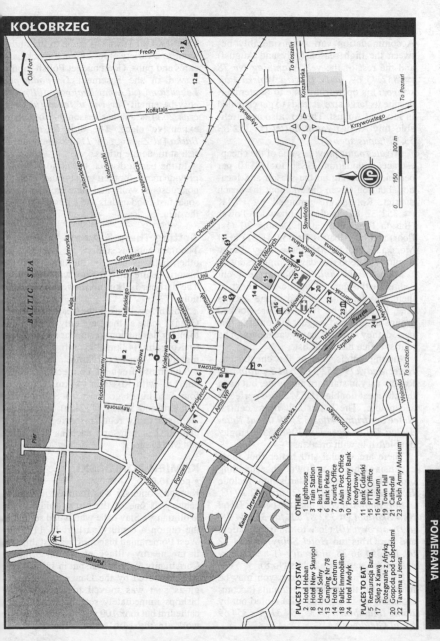

0   150   300 m

PLACES TO STAY
2 Hotel Heban
8 Hotel New Skanpol
12 Hotel Solny
13 Camping Nr 78
14 Hotel Centrum
18 Baltic Immobilien
24 Hotel Medyk

PLACES TO EAT
5 Restauracja Barka
17 Sklep z Kawą
20 Pożegnanie z Afryką
22 Taverna u Jensa

OTHER
1 Lighthouse
3 Train Station
4 Bus Terminal
6 Bank Pekao
7 Tourist Office
9 Main Post Office
10 Powszechny Bank
  Kredytowy
11 Bank Gdański
15 PTTK Office
16 Museum
19 Town Hall
21 Cathedral
23 Polish Army Museum

Places to Stay

Accommodation varies considerably between the high season (July and August) and the rest of the year. *Camping Nr 78* (☎ 352 45 69, *ul IV Dywizji Wojska Polskiego 1*) is open from June to September; despite its large size, it tends to get crowded in July and August. There is also an unreliable July-August *youth hostel* (☎ 352 33 53, *ul Łopuskiego 2*).

Private rooms provide some of the cheapest accommodation, US$5 to US$10 per person, depending on the season and location, but don't even dream about the beach district. Rooms are arranged by PTTK (☎ 352 32 87) in the Gunpowder Tower (Baszta Prochowa) at ul Dubois 20 (1st floor) and by Albatros (☎ 352 41 51) at ul Morska 7A near the lighthouse. They usually require a three to five day minimum stay.

Many of the *holiday homes* rent out rooms to the general public and most of them are pleasantly located in the seaside area. They can be full with pre-booked groups in July and August but outside this period they usually have vacancies. The tourist office has a full list.

Among hotels, one of the cheapest is *Hotel Medyk* (☎ 352 34 50, *ul Szpitalna 7*). Rooms vary in standard and price, but even the cheapest doubles (US$22) are perfectly acceptable. The better and more central *Hotel Centrum* (☎/fax 352 29 05, *ul Katedralna 12*) charges US$30/45/55 a single/double/triple with breakfast.

There are several still better (but more expensive) hotels in town. In ascending order of prices and standards they include *Hotel Heban* (☎ 352 48 41, *fax 352 20 03, ul Borzymowskiego 3*) near the beach; *Hotel New Skanpol* (☎ 352 82 11, *fax 352 44 78, ul Dworcowa 10*) close to the train station; and the Orbis-run *Hotel Solny* (☎ 354 57 00, *fax 354 58 28, ul Fredry 4*), a long way east of the station (take bus No 8).

If you're in a larger party, you may be interested in the central apartments (accommodating up to eight people) rented out by *Baltic Immobilien* (☎ 352 34 31, *fax 354 69 51, ul Giełdowa 8A*).

Places to Eat

The New Old Town has come to life and is home to a variety of restaurants, snack bars, cafés and pubs. Good budget Polish food is served in the basement *Gospoda pod Łabędziami* (*ul Armii Krajowej 30B*). The cosy basement *Taverna u Jensa* (*ul Gierczak 26A*) is another reasonable but more expensive place. The dull *Restauracja Barka* (*ul Zwycięzców 11*) has a choice of fish at moderate prices.

In the beach district, the holiday homes provide meals for their guests (and often for nonguests as well), and there are many seasonal fast-food outlets and cafés throughout the area.

Getting There & Away

The train and bus stations are next to each other, halfway between the beach and the historic centre (a 10 minute walk to either). The harbour is 1km north-west of the stations.

Kołobrzeg lies off the main Szczecin-Gdańsk route so there are only a few trains to either destination. A regular service goes to Koszalin (43km). Two fast trains go nightly to Warsaw (571km).

The most frequent connection (every hour) is with Koszalin (44km). Three or four fast buses go daily to Świnoujście (106km) and Słupsk (112km). In summer there's a fairly regular service to neighbouring beach resorts such as Niechorze and Mrzeżyno.

KAMIEŃ POMORSKI
• pop 10,000   ☎ 091

Kamień Pomorski was founded in the 9th century as one of the strongholds of the Wolinians, a Slav tribe which had settled in the region a century earlier. In 1125 the West Pomeranian bishopric was established in the nearby village of Wolin, bringing Christianity to the locals, but in 1175 Wolin was destroyed by the Danes and the religious seat was moved to Kamień. The bishops immediately set about building a cathedral but took 100 years to complete the work. In the 14th century the town was circled with a ring of fortified walls and a town hall was erected in the Rynek.

Apart from its importance as a religious centre, the town was also a prosperous port and a trading centre – a tempting titbit for aggressive neighbours. The Swedes took it in 1630 and a few decades later it fell under Brandenburg rule. Not until 1945 was the town, which had been flattened as the battle front rolled over it, incorporated into Polish territory.

Facing the same dilemma as elsewhere, the new authorities restored what had partly survived but flooded the rest of the space with the familiar nondescript apartment blocks. Yet it's still worth coming for what remains, particularly the cathedral.

Information

There's no tourist office in Kamień. The Pomorski Bank Kredytowy just off the Rynek changes travellers cheques and cash and has a useful ATM. There are several kantors in town (including one at the post office) but they will probably pay you less than the bank.

Cathedral

Originally a Romanesque building begun in 1176, the church was thoroughly revamped in the 14th century in Gothic style, which has basically survived to this day. Inside, the chancel has retained some of its old fitments, including an impressive triptych on the high altar, thought to derive from the school of Veit Stoss (the maker of the famous triptych in St Mary's Church in Kraków), the oak stalls and a large crucifix hanging from the vault. Up above the altar some of the 13th century wall paintings have survived.

Baroque outfits were added in the second half of the 17th century and include a decorative wrought-iron screen separating the chancel from the nave, the pulpit and the organ. The latter deserves special attention for both its impressive appearance and excellent tone. The Festival of Organ and Chamber Music was started here in 1965 and takes place annually from mid-June to late August, with concerts held every Friday evening. If you can't turn up in Kamień on a Friday, there's a short performance on the organ twice daily, usually at 11 am and 4 pm.

While you're in the church, go up the steps from the left transept to the former treasury, now a small museum, and don't miss the cloister garth *(wirydarz)* – the entrance is through a door from the left-hand aisle. The 1124 baptismal font in the middle of the garth is the cathedral's oldest possession. The old tombstones on the walls of the cloister were moved here in 1890 from the church's floor. You can also go to the top of the tower but there's almost no view from there.

Other Attractions

The Rynek, a three minute walk to the west, is a postwar production apart from its **town hall**, a 14th century Gothic building with the familiar Renaissance additions. Going west you'll get to the massive **Wolin Gate** (Brama Wolińska), the only surviving medieval gate of the original five.

The former **synagogue** (hardly recognisable) on ul Pocztowa is just about the only legacy of the Jewish population. Nearby, tucked away amid trees, stands **St Nicholas' Church** (Kościół Św Mikołaja), built as the hospital's chapel in the 14th century (the tower was added later).

Places to Stay

Camping Nr 147 Fregata (☎ 382 00 76) on the waterfront at the foot of the cathedral is open from June to September. It has no cabins but there's another camp site past the footbridge, which does have cabins (US$20 a quad).

The July-August *youth hostel* (☎ 382 08 41, Plac Katedralny 1) is in a school. The basic *Hotel Żeglarski* (☎ 382 08 17) at the sailing boats' wharf is a cheap alternative to the hostel (US$10/15/17/20 a single/double/triple/quad) but it's often full with pre-teen groups.

Much better is the friendly *Hotel pod Muzami* (☎ 382 22 40, ul Gryfiiów 1), in a

POMERANIA

KAMIEŃ POMORSKI

ZALEW KAMIEŃSKI

Footbridge

Pier

Rynek

Strzelecka

Basztowa

Jagiełły

Pocztowa

Wysockiego

Kopernika

Rejtana

Chrobrego

5-go Marca

Mickiewicza

Kościuszki

Market

Dziwnowska

Dworcowa

Szpitalna

Konopnickiej

Matejki

To Dziwnów

To Kołobrzeg

To Wolin   To Szczecin

0   100   200 m

1 Camping Nr 147 Fregata
2 St Mary's Church
3 Cathedral
4 Hotel Staromiejski
5 Hotel pod Muzami
6 Pomorski Bank Kredytowy
7 Bistro Paulinka
8 Town Hall &
   Kawiarnia Ratuszowa
9 Kantor
10 Wolin Gate
11 Bishops' Palace
12 Youth Hostel
13 Hotel Żeglarski
14 Former Synagogue
15 Post Office
16 Bistro Magellan
17 St Nicholas' Church
18 Bus Terminal
19 Train Station

beautiful old house on the corner of the Rynek. Singles/doubles/triples/quads with bath and breakfast are US$30/ 40/55/65.

The recently revamped *Hotel Staromiejski* (☎ 382 26 44, ul Rybacka 3) now charges US$36/50/65/75 with bath but without breakfast, which is probably poorer value than Pod Muzami.

Places to Eat

The most pleasant place to eat is the inexpensive, cosy *Bar pod Muzami* in the hotel of the same name. Alternatively, try the *Bistro Magellan (ul Wysockiego 5)*, with similar menu and prices. Also good and cheap is the *Bistro Paulinka (ul Strzelecka 1)*. The *Kawiarnia Ratuszowa* in the basement of the town hall on the Rynek has not much to eat but plenty to drink.

Getting There & Away

The train station handles only local traffic and is pretty useless. The bus terminal next to it has regular services (every hour or two)

POMERANIA

to Szczecin (88km), Dziwnów (12km), Międzyzdroje (39km) and Świnoujście (52km). There are also four fast buses daily to Kołobrzeg (67km) and two to Gdynia (via Koszalin and Słupsk).

WOLIN NATIONAL PARK

Set in the far north-western corner of the country, Wolin National Park (Woliński Park Narodowy) occupies the central part of Wolin Island. With a total area of about 50 sq km, it's one of the smaller Polish parks, yet it's picturesque enough to deserve a day or two's walking. See the Wolin Island map.

The park encompasses a coastal moraine left by a glacier, reaching a maximum height of 115m. On its northern edge, the ground drops sharply into the sea, forming a sandy cliff nearly 100m high in places. The cliff is 11km long, the only one of its kind on the Polish coastline, except for the Rozewie area at the opposite end of the coastline, which is lower and less dramatic. To the south, the moraine descends gradually to the Szczecin Lagoon (Zalew Szczeciński).

The park features many lakes. Most (about 10) are on the remote eastern edge of the park, forming a small lakeland. The most beautiful is the horseshoe-shaped Lake Czajcze. The lakeland apart, there's Lake Turkusowe (Turquoise), named after the colour of its water, at the southern end of the park, and the lovely Lake Gardno close to the seashore, next to the Międzyzdroje-Dziwnów road.

Virtually the whole of the park is covered with thick mixed forest, with beech, oak and pine predominating. The flora and fauna is relatively diverse, with a rich bird life. There's a small bison reserve (open June to September from 10 am to 6 pm, except Monday) inside the park, 2km east of the resort of Międzyzdroje. Bison were brought here from Białowieża and some have already been born in the reserve. The last bison living wild in Pomerania were wiped out in the 14th century.

Three marked trails wind into the park from Międzyzdroje. The red trail leads north-east along the shore, then turns inland

to Wisełka and continues through wooded hills to the small village of Kołczewo. The green trail runs east across the middle of the park, skirts the lakeland and also ends in Kołczewo. The blue trail goes to the southern end of the park, passing the Turquoise Lake on the way. It then continues east to the town of Wolin.

All the trails are well marked and easy. Get a copy of the detailed *Woliński Park Narodowy* map (scale 1:30,000). The park's management in Międzyzdroje can provide further information.

MIĘDZYZDROJE

• pop 6000   ☎ 091

Międzyzdroje ('Myen-dziz-dro-yeh') is one of the most popular seaside resorts on the Polish coast. It has good beaches and a sandy coastal cliff just to the east of the town and it's surrounded by forests. The sea here is warmer than on the eastern part of the coast and it's cleaner than around the resort's bigger western neighbour, the port of Świnoujście. Międzyzdroje lives almost entirely off summer tourism and is more or less dead for the rest of the year.

Międzyzdroje hosts the annual International Festival of Choral Music, usually at the end of June and beginning of July.

Natural History Museum

The Natural History Museum (Muzeum Przyrodnicze) features the flora and fauna of Wolin National Park and beyond. There's a good display of stuffed birds, including the white eagle *(Haliaeetus albicilla)*, and an amazing collection of 120 ruffs *(Philomachus pugnax)*, each different, which makes it one of the largest collections of this species in Europe.

Next to the museum building is a large cage with a live white eagle. The bird is a symbol of the park and reputedly a model for Poland's national emblem. With a wingspan of up to 2.5m, this is the largest bird species in the country, but is today threatened with extinction.

The museum is open Monday to Friday 9 am to 3 pm (from May to September open

POMERANIA

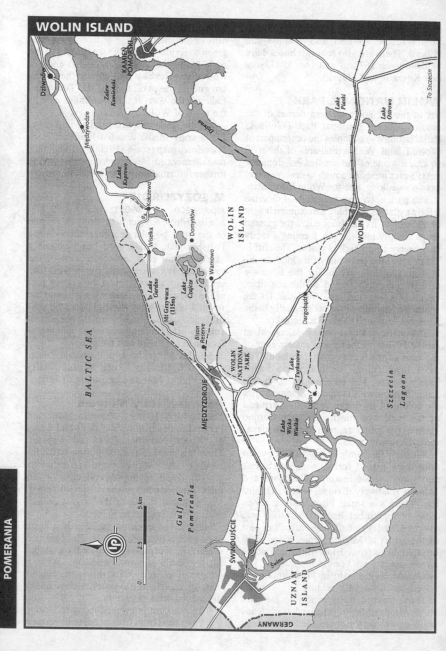

WOLIN ISLAND

KAMIEŃ POMORSKI

Dziwnów

Zalew Kamieński

Międzywodzie

Dziwna

Lake Koprowo

Kołczewo

Wisełka

Domysłów

WOLIN ISLAND

Lake Piaski

Lake Ostrowo

To Szczecin

WOLIN

Warnowo

Lake Czajcze

Mt Grzywacz (115m)

Lake Gardno

Bison Reserve

BALTIC SEA

WOLIN NATIONAL PARK

Dargobądz

Lake Turkusowe

Lubin

Szczecin Lagoon

MIĘDZYZDROJE

Lake Wicko Wielkie

5 km

2.5

0

Gulf of Pomerania

ŚWINOUJŚCIE

Świna

UZNAM ISLAND

GERMANY

Tuesday to Sunday 9 am to 5 pm). The park's headquarters are also here.

Places to Stay & Eat

Międzyzdroje has lots of holiday homes open to all comers. In addition, newly built hotels and pensions have sprung up everywhere and they're advertised on large boards around town. Finally, private rooms can be arranged through half a dozen local travel agencies, including Viking Tour (☎ 328 07 68) at ul Gryfa Pomorskiego 44; Wineta Travel (☎ 328 06 10) at ul Kolejowa 56 opposite the train station; PTTK (☎ 328 04 62) at ul Kolejowa 2; Elmar (☎ 328 21 27) at ul Zwycięstwa 20; and Bałtyk (☎ 328 15 18) at ul Zwycięstwa 9A. Expect a double to cost from US$20 in July and August, and US$15 in the off season.

Camping Nr 24 (☎ 328 02 75, ul Polna 10), in the south-western end of the town, is open from June to September; there are two other camp sites in the same area closer to the beach.

Dom Wycieczkowy PTTK (☎ 328 03 82, ul Kolejowa 2) is one of the cheapest places to stay; it charges about US$12 per bed in rooms without bath in the high season (US$7 at other times). There's another *Dom Wycieczkowy PTTK (☎ 328 09 29, ul Dąbrówki 11)* in the western end of the town, which has rooms with private bath (US$18 per person in high season).

If you fancy a splurge, you're in the right place. Międzyzdroje has one of the best hotels on the coast, the plush *Hotel Amber Baltic (☎ 328 08 00, ☎ 328 10 00, fax 328 10 22)* in the middle of the waterfront promenade. A single/double/suite will cost US$100/140/320, buffet breakfast included. The US$16 buffet dinner (6 to 11 pm) is cheaper than an average three course à la carte meal. The hotel operates the Amber Baltic Golf Club on the Dziwnów road, one of the few golf courses in the country.

Getting There & Away

The train station is at the southern end of town; the main bus stop is on ul Niepodległości opposite the museum.

Międzyzdroje is on the Szczecin-Świnoujście railway line and all trains stop here, providing regular transport to either destination. There are also some trains farther on to Gdynia, Poznań, Wrocław and Warsaw.

Frequent buses run to Świnoujście, but none to Szczecin. Six fast buses go daily to Kołobrzeg and two as far as Gdynia. In summer there are several buses to Kamień Pomorski (42km), but fewer during the rest of the year.

ŚWINOUJŚCIE
- pop 44,000   ☎ 091

The westernmost town on the Polish coast, Świnoujście ('Shvee-nooysh-cheh') is a fairly large fishing and trading port, as well as an important naval base. On the other hand, Świnoujście has developed as a resort around the beach and as a spa thanks to its salt springs, used for over a century to treat a variety of diseases.

The town is a convenient entry/exit point for those travelling between Poland and Scandinavia, with ferry links with Denmark and Sweden. It also has a boat service and an overland border crossing with Germany. Świnoujście is both a bustling seaport and a tourist centre frequented by Poles, Scandinavians and Germans.

Orientation

Świnoujście sits on two islands at the mouth of the Świna River. The eastern part of the town, on the Wolin Island, has the port and transport facilities; here are the bus and train stations and the international ferry wharf from/to Scandinavia. The main part of Świnoujście is across the river (frequent shuttle ferry service), on Uznam Island (Usedom in German). Here are the town centre and, 1km farther north, the beach resort; the two are separated by a belt of parks.

Information

The Centrum Informacji Turystycznej (☎/fax 322 49 99), Plac Słowiański 15, is open Monday to Friday 9 am to 5 pm (daily in summer).

ŚWINOUJŚCIE

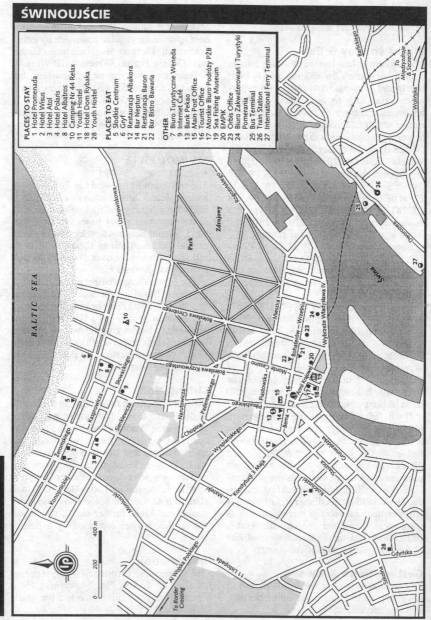

PLACES TO STAY
1 Hotel Promenada
2 Hotel Wisus
3 Hotel Atol
4 Hotel Polaris
8 Hotel Albatros
10 Camping Nr 44 Relax
11 Youth Hostel
18 Hotel Dom Rybaka
28 Youth Hostel

PLACES TO EAT
5 Słodkie Centrum
6 Gryf
12 Restauracja Albakora
14 Bar Neptun
21 Restauracja Baron
22 Bar Bistro Bawaria

OTHER
7 Biuro Turystyczne Weneda
9 Internet Café
13 Bank Pekao
15 Main Post Office
16 Tourist Office
17 Morskie Biuro Podróży P2B
19 Sea Fishing Museum
20 EMPIK
23 Orbis Office
24 Biuro Zakwaterowani i Turystyki
   Pomerania
25 Bus Terminal
26 Train Station
27 International Ferry Terminal

The Bank Pekao, ul Piłsudskiego 4, changes travellers cheques and has an ATM. Cash is easy to exchange at any of the many kantors throughout the centre.

An Internet café (☎ 324 32 00) is in the Klub Garnizonowy Marynarki Wojennej (Navy Club) at ul Piłsudskiego 35A.

Things to See

The beach is, obviously, the major tourist attraction and it's good and wide, though environmentalists might be concerned about pollution from the river and the port. The waterfront resort district is a nice area as well, still retaining a *fin-de-siècle* air with its elegant villas and the main pedestrian promenade.

In the town centre is the **Sea Fishing Museum** (Muzeum Rybołówstwa Morskiego), open Tuesday to Friday 9 am to 4 pm, weekends 10 am to 3 pm. It has collections of sea fauna, fishing equipment and navigation instruments, plus exhibits related to the town's history.

Places to Stay

As in other Baltic beach resorts, the high season is in July and August, and at times it may be difficult to find anywhere to stay other than the camp site. The prices given are for the high season.

The large *Camping Nr 44 Relax* (☎ 321 39 12, ul Słowackiego 5) is excellently located close to the beach. It's open June to September and has bungalows, but you'll need a miracle to get one in July or August.

The all-year *youth hostel* (☎ 327 06 13, ul Gdyńska 26) is far from the beach and there's also a poorer summer *youth hostel* (☎ 321 34 65, ul Kościuszki 11) in the nearby school.

For *private rooms*, inquire at the Biuro Zakwaterowań i Turystyki Pomerania (☎/fax 321 37 66), Wybrzeże Władysława IV 12, opposite the ferry landing. The tourist office also may have some rooms. Be prepared to pay US$8 to US$12 per person. Note that there are almost no private rooms in the beach area; they are mostly in the south-western suburbs.

Many *holiday homes* (almost all are near the beach) accept individual tourists, though most will insist on full board. Prices vary according to demand and standards, but count roughly US$20 to US$25 per bed with three meals, and not much less without. The tourist office has a detailed list of these homes and will help you to find somewhere.

Świnoujście has several all-year hotels. In the centre, the cheapest is the pretty basic *Hotel Dom Rybaka* (☎ 321 29 43, Wybrzeże Władysława IV 22). It charges US$11/20/24 a single/double/triple without bath, US$20/35 a single/double with shower (but without toilet).

In the beach area, budget travellers may try the basic *Hotel Wisus* (☎ 321 58 50, ul Żeromskiego 17), ideally located just off the beach. This Almatur-owned hostel offers about 100 beds arranged mostly in quads and you pay US$12 per bed.

Of the more decent places near the beach, try *Hotel Albatros* (☎ 321 23 35, ul Kasprowicza 2) at US$24/34/50 a single/double/triple with bath. Still better are *Hotel Polaris* (☎/fax 321 24 37, ul Słowackiego 33); *Hotel Atol* (☎/fax 321 38 46, ul Orkana 3); and *Hotel Promenada* (☎ 327 94 18, ul Żeromskiego 20). Any of these will charge US$50 to US$60 for a double with bath and breakfast.

Places to Eat

There are not many all-year restaurants (and these are mostly in the centre), but in summer a lot of seasonal venues open, including bistros, street stalls, bars and nightclubs (mainly in the beach area). There are two budget food centres, *Gryf* and *Słodkie Centrum*, on the beach promenade, ul Żeromskiego. Some holiday homes serve lunch and dinner for nonguests.

One of the popular budget places in the centre is *Bar Neptun* (ul Bema 1). You could try *Bar Bistro Bawaria* (ul Bohaterów Września 51). Better options in the centre include the *Restauracja Albakora* (ul Konstytucji 3 Maja 6) and the *Restauracja Baron* (ul Bohaterów Września 14).

POMERANIA

Getting There & Away

The overland crossing to/from Germany is 2km west of town. The first town on the German side, Ahlbeck, handles bus transport farther into the country. The border is open to pedestrians only (bicycles can go as well), of all nationalities.

Train & Bus The bus and train stations are next to each other on the right (eastern) bank of the Świna River. Passenger ferries shuttle constantly between the town centre and the stations (free, 10 minutes).

Ordinary trains go to Szczecin (116km) via Międzyzdroje (16km) every two or three hours (2¼ hours).

There's one summer fast night train directly to Warsaw (607km) and it has sleeping cars. To Kraków (729km), there are two all-year fast trains; they go via Poznań (301km) and Wrocław (466km). Tickets, sleepers and couchettes are available from the Orbis office (☎ 321 44 11), ul Chrobrego 9.

Buses don't run to Szczecin, but do cover the coast, going as far as Gdynia (two fast buses daily). There's half a dozen buses to Kamień Pomorski (52km), and three or four fast buses to Kołobrzeg (98km); they all go via Międzyzdroje.

Car & Motorcycle If you're travelling by your own transport, you'll be crossing the Dźwina River 7km south of Świnoujście. Expect to wait during the peak season (usually no longer than a couple of hours). Passage for both vehicles and passengers is free.

Boat Świnoujście has many boat services, listed in this section.

To Szczecin The Świnoujście-Szczecin hydrofoil is the fastest and most pleasant (but also most expensive) transport between these two ports; it runs three times daily (US$5/8 weekdays/weekends, one hour).

To Scandinavia Large car ferries run daily to Ystad and Malmö in Sweden and five times a week to Copenhagen. All services operate year-round. Information and tickets are handled by Morskie Biuro Podróży PŻB (☎/fax 322 43 96), ul Armii Krajowej 14A. Refer to the introductory Getting There & Away chapter for general information.

To Germany Boats from Świnoujście go to Ahlbeck, Heringsdorf, Bansin and Sassnitz. Inquire at the Biuro Turystyczne Weneda (☎/fax 327 08 05), ul Żeromskiego 1, in the seaside area, which handles tickets and package trips.

SZCZECIN
- pop 420,000   ☎ 091

Close to the German border, only 130km away from Berlin (and four times that distance from Warsaw), Szczecin ('Shchehchin') is the main urban centre of northwestern Poland and the largest Polish port in terms of tonnage handled. Once Western Pomerania's capital, it has a colourful and stormy history. Most of the remnants of this history, however, were lost in the last war.

History

Szczecin's beginnings go back to the 8th century, when a Slav stronghold was built here. In 967, Mieszko I annexed the town, together with a large chunk of the coast, to the newborn Polish state. Mieszko didn't succeed in holding the region for long nor was he able to Christianise it. It was Bolesław Krzywousty who recaptured the town in 1121 and brought the Catholic faith to the locals. Four years later, he moved the bishopric from Kołobrzeg to nearby Wolin, to have the priests and their gospel at hand.

Krzywousty died in 1138 and the Polish Crown crumbled; Pomerania formally became an independent principality. At that time, though, the Germans were expanding aggressively, and gradually took trade and decisive administrative posts into their hands. In 1181 the Pomeranian Duke Bogusław I paid homage to the Holy Roman Emperor Frederick Barbarossa.

Three years later Denmark attacked and conquered Pomerania, taking control of vast parts of the Baltic coast as far as Estonia. In 1227, the Danes were defeated and forced out, and Szczecin, together with the surrounding region, came back under the rule of the Pomeranian princes, by then strongly dependent on the Brandenburg margraves.

In 1478 Western Pomerania was unified by Duke Bogusław X and Szczecin was chosen as the capital. Since the duke had been brought up at the Polish court and had married the daughter of the Polish King Kazimierz Jagiellończyk, he was keen to seek closer relations with Poland. This led to protests from the Brandenburgs and under pressure Western Pomerania acknowledged its allegiance to its western neighbour in 1521.

The next shift in power came in 1630. This time the Swedes conquered the city and occupied it until the Treaty of Westphalia of 1648 formally assigned it to them. After the Peace of Stockholm of 1720 concluded the Northern War, Sweden sold Szczecin to what was by then the kingdom of Prussia, which held the region until WWII. Under Prussian rule, Szczecin grew considerably, becoming the main port for Berlin, the two cities having been linked by a canal. By the outbreak of WWII the city had about 300,000 inhabitants.

In April 1945 the Red Army arrived on its way to Berlin and 60% of the urban area was left in ruins after the battle. Only 6000 souls remained of the former population, most of the others having fled.

With new inhabitants and new rulers, the battered city started a new life. However, there doesn't seem to have been the same enthusiasm and stamina in recreating the former city as there were in some other big historic centres. Only individual buildings were restored and the rest of the ruins were replaced with the usual postwar creations.

Information

The Centrum Informacji Turystycznej (☎ 434 04 40, ☎/fax 433 84 20) is in a round pavilion at Al Niepodległości 1. It's open weekdays 9.30 am to 5 pm (in June to August also on Saturday 10 am to 2 pm). There's also a tourist office (☎ 489 16 30) in the castle.

The Bank Pekao is at ul Grodzka 9, facing the Plac Orła Białego (White Eagle Square). There are at least three other banks on the same square, some of which will change travellers cheques and accept credit cards. Kantors are plentiful all over the central area; the one at the train station is open round the clock.

Check out the Espol computer shop (☎ 433 65 85), ul Piłsudskiego 23, which had the only email and Internet facility as we went to press.

Things to See

The most sizable city monument is the **Castle of the Pomeranian Princes** (Zamek Książąt Pomorskich). It was originally built in the mid-14th century but only in 1577 did it become a large residence with a square central courtyard. It was further enlarged and remodelled on various occasions. Badly damaged in 1945, the reconstruction gave it a predominantly Renaissance look, as it had been in the late 16th century. You can go to the top of its tower for a view of the town.

The castle now accommodates the opera auditorium, a restaurant and the **Castle Museum** (Muzeum Zamkowe), open 10 am to 4 pm (longer in summer) except Monday. The permanent exhibition on the castle's history includes six spectacular sarcophagi of the Pomeranian princes. They are large tin boxes decorated with a fine engraved ornamentation, made between about 1606 and 1637 by artists from Königsburg. Following the death of the last Pomeranian duke, Bogusław XIV (whose sarcophagus is the most elaborate), the crypt, containing 14 sarcophagi, was walled up and only opened in 1946. The remains of the dukes were deposited in the cathedral, while the best preserved sarcophagi have been restored and are now the highlight of the display.

Various temporary exhibitions are presented in other rooms of the castle. In summer, concerts are held on Sunday at

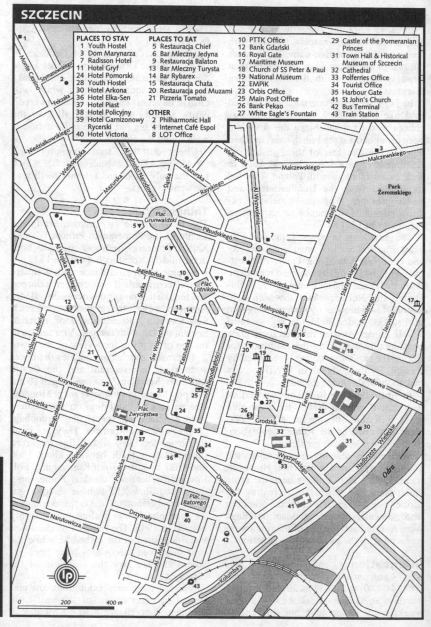

SZCZECIN

PLACES TO STAY
1   Youth Hostel
3   Dom Marynarza
7   Radisson Hotel
11 Hotel Gryf
24 Hotel Pomorski
28 Youth Hostel
30 Hotel Arkona
36 Hotel Elka-Sen
37 Hotel Piast
38 Hotel Policyjny
39 Hotel Garnizonowy
      Rycerski
40 Hotel Victoria

PLACES TO EAT
5   Restauracja Chief
6   Bar Mleczny Jedyna
9   Restauracja Balaton
13 Bar Mleczny Turysta
14 Bar Rybarex
15 Restauracja Chata
20 Restauracja pod Muzami
21 Pizzeria Tomato

OTHER
2   Philharmonic Hall
4   Internet Café Espol
8   LOT Office

10 PTTK Office
12 Bank Gdański
16 Royal Gate
17 Maritime Museum
18 Church of SS Peter & Paul
19 National Museum
22 EMPiK
23 Orbis Office
25 Main Post Office
26 Bank Pekao
27 White Eagle's Fountain

29 Castle of the Pomeranian
      Princes
31 Town Hall & Historical
      Museum of Szczecin
32 Cathedral
33 Polferries Office
34 Tourist Office
35 Harbour Gate
41 St John's Church
42 Bus Terminal
43 Train Station

noon in the courtyard or in the former chapel of the castle, which occupies nearly half the northern side.

A short walk south will bring you to the 15th century Gothic **town hall**, one of the finest buildings in the city. This is the only relic of the Old Town which was razed to the ground in 1945 and never rebuilt. A line of stylised burghers' houses has recently been put up right behind the town hall, in striking contrast to the line of communist blocks opposite.

The town hall houses the interesting **Historical Museum of Szczecin** (Muzeum Historii Miasta Szczecina), open Tuesday and Thursday 10 am to 5 pm, Wednesday and Friday 9 am to 3.30 pm and weekends 10 am to 4 pm.

There are two historic churches nearby. **St John's Church** (Kościół Św Jana), a typical 14th century Gothic building, somehow escaped war destruction. Its interior is refreshingly devoid of decoration and has a perfect vault in the nave, supported on charmingly leaning columns. Vestiges of wall paintings from 1510 can be seen in the right-hand aisle.

The **cathedral** is much larger, if similar in shape, but the interior is now fitted out with mostly modern decoration. On one side of the cathedral is the 15th century vicarage and on the other a huge bell weighing almost six tonnes, dating from 1681.

Two blocks north, at ul Staromłyńska 27, is the **National Museum** (Muzeum Narodowe) – same opening hours as the Historical Museum of Szczecin – in the 18th century palace which formerly served as the Pomeranian parliament. On the ground floor is a collection of religious art, mostly woodcarving from the 14th to 16th centuries, including some beautiful altarpieces. The upper floor is taken up by Polish painting from the 18th to the early 20th century, plus other historical exhibits related to Szczecin and Pomerania.

An extension of the museum, directly across the street, contains changing displays of modern art. Also part of the national museum is the **Maritime Museum** (Muzeum Morskie) on the waterfront at Wały Chrobrego 3. On your way there, you'll pass the **Church of SS Peter and Paul** (Kościół Św Piotra i Pawła); it was founded in 1124 but the present building dates from the end of the 15th century. A recognisably Gothic structure, it has a wooden ceiling with a large plafond in its central part depicting the Holy Trinity.

To round up your city sightseeing, take the boat trip around Szczecin harbour (US$4, one hour). Boats depart several times daily in summer from the Dworzec Morski, the wharf 500m north of the Maritime Museum.

Places to Stay – Budget

Szczecin has the good *Camping Nr 25* (☎/fax 460 11 65, ul Przestrzenna 23), on the shore of Lake Dąbie in Szczecin Dąbie, about 7km south-east of the city centre. If you are coming by train and plan on staying there, get off in Szczecin Dąbie and continue by urban bus No 56, 62 or 79, or walk 2km. The camp site has cabins and is open May to September.

The good all-year *youth hostel* (☎ 22 47 61, fax 423 56 96, ul Monte Cassino 19A) is 2km north-west of the centre – take tram No 3 from either the bus or train stations to Plac Rodła and change for the westbound tram No 1. The hostel is friendly and well run, and has 120 beds reasonably distributed among single and double rooms to 12-bed dorms.

There are also two July-August *youth hostels* in the city: at ul Jodłowa 21 (☎ 352 33 24), 2km west of the centre, and at ul Grodzka 22 (☎ 433 29 24). The latter is basic but perfectly situated halfway between the castle and the cathedral in the city heart.

Szczecin has several student hostels, but they are away from the centre. One of the closest and cheapest is *Dom Studencki Nr 3* (☎ 449 44 17, Al Piastów 26). It has just seven rooms and charges US$11/15 a single/double. Take tram No 4 from the train station. You'll probably find it easier to get in at *Hotel Eskulap* (☎ 482 03 16,

POMERANIA

ul Dunikowskiego 6) which charges US$16/20.

Of the central hotels, probably the cheapest is the run-down *Hotel Pomorski (☎ 433 61 51, ☎ 434 25 02, Plac Brama Portowa 4)*, which charges US$18/22 a double/triple without bath, US$16/24 a single/double with bath. If it's full, or if its standards are not exactly up to your expectations, check several other hotels (listed later) just a few steps away.

Places to Stay – Mid-Range

Hotel Policyjny (☎ 433 77 45, ☎ 451 81 91, Plac Zwycięstwa 1) is a former police dorm, now open to all and discreetly labelled 'Hotel' only so don't be confused. Simple singles/doubles/triples without bath go for US$20/25/30.

Just behind the police hotel, in a gloomy red-brick building, is the army-run *Hotel Garnizonowy Rycerski (☎ 445 24 85, ☎ 488 81 64, ul Potulicka 1/3)*, which offers similar basic standards for much the same. It may be closed for renovation.

Hotel Piast (☎ 433 75 15, ☎ 433 50 71, Plac Zwycięstwa 3) is possibly better, yet more expensive. It charges US$18/28/40 a single/double/triple without bath, US$22/34/45 with bath.

The new *Hotel Elka-Sen (☎ 433 56 04, ul 3 Maja 1A)* offers the best value rooms at US$24/32/38 a single/double/triple with bath and breakfast.

You may also check out the old *Hotel Gryf (☎ 433 45 66, Al Wojska Polskiego 49)*, farther north-west, which is nothing special but affordable at US$25/38 a single/double with bath and breakfast. Appreciably better is *Dom Nauczyciela (☎ 433 04 81, ul Śląska 4)*, at US$40/60 a double/triple with bath and breakfast.

Places to Stay – Top End

Dom Marynarza (☎ 424 00 01, fax 434 45 30, ul Malczewskiego 10/12), 1km north of the centre, has reasonable singles/doubles with bath and breakfast for US$35/50. *Hotel Victoria (☎ 434 38 55, fax 433 73 68, Plac Batorego 2)* charges US$55/70. The hotel is just a three minute walk uphill from the bus terminal and not much more from the train station.

Orbis runs three hotels in the city, including the most central, revamped *Hotel Arkona (☎ 488 04 32, fax 488 02 60, ul Panieńska 10)*, next to the town hall (US$65/80).

Szczecin's poshest option, the *Radisson Hotel (☎ 359 55 95, fax 359 45 94, Plac Rodła 10)* easily surpasses Orbis standards and has prices to match (US$150/180).

Places to Eat

The central milk bars include *Bar Mleczny Jedyna (Al Jedności Narodowej 42)* and *Bar Mleczny Turysta (ul Obrońców Stalingradu 6)*. Next door to the latter is the budget *Bar Rybarex* which serves good fish. *Pizzeria Tomato (Al Wojska Polskiego 10)* has some of the cheapest acceptable pizzas in town. There are plenty of other budget snack bars, bistros and fast-food outlets scattered throughout the city centre and easy to find.

Restauracja Zamkowa (☎ 434 04 48) in the castle occupies three spacious rooms, which makes it possibly the largest eatery in town. It offers solid Polish fare at affordable prices. More expensive is *Restauracja pod Muzami (☎ 434 72 09, Plac Żołnierza Polskiego 2)* near the castle, which also bases its menu on the local cuisine. The most charming place in the area is *Restauracja Chata (☎ 488 73 70, Plac Hołdu Pruskiego 8)*. It serves traditional Polish food in rustic countryside surroundings.

Restauracja Chief (☎ 434 37 65, ul Rayskiego 16) on the corner of Plac Grunwaldzki is a fish restaurant with some of the best fish in town. *Restauracja Balaton (☎ 434 68 73, Plac Lotników 3)* has a selection of Hungarian fare at affordable prices. The posh *Restauracja Pireus (☎ 433 62 30, Plac Batorego 2)*, downstairs from the Hotel Victoria, serves Greek specialities in charming surroundings, but it's not that cheap.

The *Radisson Hotel Szczecin* has three luxurious restaurants serving Polish and international cuisine. None of these will disappoint, though they may upset your wallet.

Entertainment

The *Philharmonic Hall (Plac Armii Krajowej 1)* has regular concerts, usually on Friday. The opera and operetta productions are staged in the castle. The *Teatr Polski (ul Swarożyca 5)* is the main scene for drama performances.

Among night spots, the *Tawerna u Wyszaka*, in the spacious, marvellous cellar of the town hall, operates as a restaurant-cum-bar during the day, but devotes the night to dancing. The trendy *Night Club Tango* occupies the cellars of the Hotel Victoria and has a more affluent clientele, as you can tell from the cars parked outside, and prices are accordingly high. It has disco/live music every night till 5 am.

Getting There & Away

Air Szczecin has two LOT flights daily to Warsaw and weekday SAS flights to Copenhagen. The airport is in Goleniów, about 45km north-east of the city. The LOT office (☎ 433 50 58), ul Wyzwolenia 17, provides information and booking.

Train The main train station, Szczecin Główny, is on the bank of the Odra River, 1km south of the centre. It's pretty busy, so you may prefer to buy tickets at Orbis (☎ 434 26 18), Plac Zwycięstwa 1.

There are a dozen fast trains to Poznań (214km) and five to Gdańsk (374km). There's three express trains to Warsaw (525km), including one InterCity train which covers the distance in 5½ hours. A couple of trains leave daily for Kołobrzeg (138km) and five to Zielona Góra (207km). Trains to Stargard Szczeciński (40km) leave about every 30 minutes, and to Świnoujście (116km) every two or three hours. There are three fast trains daily to Berlin (US$25).

Bus The bus terminal is uphill from the train station and handles regular summer departures to Kamień Pomorski (88km) but fewer buses off season. Buses to Stargard Szczeciński (32km) leave frequently. There are summer buses to beach resorts such as Dziwnów, Pobierowo and Niechorze, but almost nothing to Świnoujście and Międzyzdroje; go there by train.

Two minibuses run daily to Berlin (US$18); contact Orbis for details.

Ferry There are ferries from Świnoujście to Copenhagen (Denmark) and Malmö and Ystad (Sweden). Polferries (☎ 488 09 45), ul Wyszyńskiego 28, and Orbis handle information and booking.

The hydrofoil to Świnoujście runs June to August and has three departures daily (US$5 on weekdays, US$8 on weekends, one hour).

STARGARD SZCZECIŃSKI

• pop 75,000 ☎ 092

Stargard Szczeciński was once a flourishing port and trading centre with reputedly the most elaborate system of fortified walls in Pomerania. So wealthy and prosperous was the town that it even fought with Szczecin for the right to send merchandise down the Odra River to the sea. The fierce competition between the two ports led in 1454 to a virtual war, including regular battles complete with the ransacking and sinking of the enemy's ships. This, however, is history.

Today, Stargard has no port at all and is just a satellite town of Szczecin. It suffered badly in WWII when over 70% of its buildings were destroyed. Now revived, it's a grey urban sprawl with a fair amount of industry.

The Old Town evokes mixed feelings: surrounded by medieval walls, partly preserved, it consists not of the old burghers' houses but of a mass of postwar drab blocks from which a few historic buildings stand out, with the two massive churches dominating. It's worth stopping here for the little that's left.

Things to See

The town's pride is **St Mary's Church** (Kościół Mariacki), a mighty brick construction (one of the largest in Western

Pomerania) begun in 1292 and extended successively until the end of the 15th century; since then, no major alterations have been made to its structure. In contrast to most Gothic churches in the region, this one has rich external decorations of glazed bricks and tiles and three different elaborate doorways. The spacious interior is almost free of the usual baroque additions.

Next to the church is the **Regional Museum** (Muzeum Regionalne), open 10 am to 4 pm except Monday. It has exhibits on local history, archaeology and weights and measures. Adjoining the museum is the **town hall**, the late Gothic building with a beautifully ornamented Renaissance gable.

St John's Church (Kościół Św Jana), on the opposite side of the Old Town, was built in the 15th century but was later changed significantly; it has the highest tower in Western Pomerania (99m) but otherwise is not interesting.

The **fortified walls** were begun in the late 13th century and completed at the beginning of the 16th century, by which time they were 2260m long. Roughly half of that length has survived, complete with several towers and gates. You can walk around the walls – you'll come across three gates and four towers; one of them houses a display of old armour (open the same hours as the museum).

Places to Stay & Eat

Hotel PTTK (☎ 578 31 91, ul Kuśnierzy 5), in a fine old house, charges US$14/18/24 a single/double/triple without bath, US$20/28/36 with bath. If it's full, walk 200m north to a large apartment block, which is now *Hotel Staromiejski* (☎ 577 22 23, ul Spichrzowa 2). It has rooms with shared facilities only for US$19/24/30.

Hotel Inwit (☎ 573 40 24, ul Pierwszej Brygady 1), about 1km west of the bus terminal off the Szczecin road, is slightly better than the above two but more expensive and inconvenient for sightseeing.

One of the cheapest places is *Bar Filipinka* (ul Czarnieckiego 9), 500m west of the museum. Central restaurants include *Restauracja Ratuszowa* (ul Kramarska 1) and *Restauracja Huong Nam* (ul Chrobrego 7A), with reasonable Vietnamese cooking. Both *Hotel Staromiejski* and *Hotel Inwit* have inexpensive restaurants.

Getting There & Away

The train and bus stations are close to each other, 1km west of the Old Town. Urban buses ply this route if you feel lazy.

Transport to/from Szczecin is frequent by both bus (32km) and train (40km). For Świnoujście, take the train (five daily) as buses are scarce. Two trains go daily to Warsaw (via Poznań) and five to Gdańsk; all come through from Szczecin.

Warmia & Masuria

Warmia and Masuria occupy north-eastern Poland, from the lower Vistula valley in the west to the Lithuanian border in the east. The region is gently undulating, forested and not densely populated. There's little industry and consequently pollution is minimal.

Masuria (Mazury in Polish) has a myriad of postglacial lakes – perhaps as many as 3000. Most of them are concentrated in the Great Masurian Lake District (Kraina Wiel-kich Jezior Mazurskich), which is Poland's major destination for yachtspeople and canoeists. Warmia is more remarkable for its cultural heritage rather than lakes. Although its geography is roughly similar to that of Masuria, its history is quite distinct. The only significant urban centre in the whole region is Olsztyn, on the southern edge of Warmia.

Originally the region was inhabited by diverse pagan tribes, of which the non-Slavic Prussians and the Jatzvingians were the major ones. When the region was conquered by the Teutonic Knights in the second half of the 13th century, the native inhabitants were wiped out. Warmia came to Poland in the aftermath of the Toruń Treaty of 1466 but Masuria only paid fealty to the Polish king in 1525. Even then Masuria – known since then as Ducal Prussia – continued in the German sphere of influence, and in the mid-17th century it came under the rule of the Hohenzollerns of Brandenburg. Warmia was annexed to the kingdom of Prussia in the First Partition of 1773 and the whole region stayed this way until WWII (except for a small area around Suwałki, which joined Poland after WWI).

After WWII Stalin arbitrarily defined the Soviet-Polish border by drawing an almost straight east-west line on the map. The area to the south was given to Poland, while the land to north, with the port of Kaliningrad (previously Prussian Königsberg), was taken by the Soviet Union. The Russians

Highlights

- Paddle in a kayak down the lovely Krutynia River
- Take a boat trip along the unique Elbląg-Ostróda Canal
- Visit the Gothic castle in Lidzbark Warmiński
- Explore Święta Lipka, the best baroque church in northern Poland
- Sail around the Great Masurian Lakes
- Enjoy a kayak trip down the Czarna Hańcza River

didn't give this strategic territory to any of the republics but kept it for themselves, even though it is cut off geographically from its motherland by Lithuania, Latvia and Belarus.

The Olsztyn Region

The Olsztyn region covers Warmia and the land to the south of Olsztyn. There are

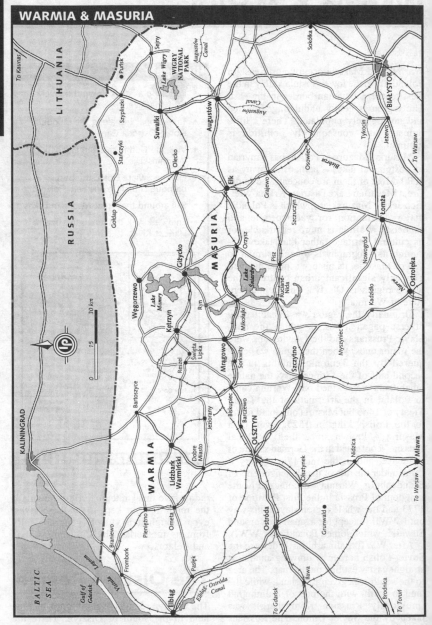

WARMIA & MASURIA

From Knight to Bishop – Warmia's History

Warmia is one of Poland's historically determined regions, sitting in the far north of the country between Pomerania and Masuria. Its name derives from the original inhabitants of this land, the Warmians, who were wiped out by the Teutonic Knights in the 13th century, in much the same manner as other ethnic communities of the region.

Like most of Poland, Warmia has had a turbulent history, but what clearly differentiates it from the other provinces is that for over five centuries it was an ecclesiastical state, largely autonomous of Poland. It was a citadel of Catholicism run by the Warmian bishops.

The Warmian diocese was brought into being by the papal bulls of 1243 as the largest (4250 sq km) of four which were created in the territories conquered by the Teutonic Order. Though administratively within the Teutonic state, the bishops used papal protection to achieve a far-reaching autonomy. Their bishopric extended to the north of Olsztyn up to the present-day national border, and from the Vistula Lagoon in the west to the town of Reszel in the east. It was divided into 10 districts with regional seats in Frombork, Braniewo, Pieniężno, Orneta, Lidzbark Warmiński, Dobre Miasto, Olsztyn, Barczewo, Jeziorany and Reszel.

The first seat of the bishopric was founded around 1250 in Braniewo but was soon destroyed by the Prussians. The seat was then moved to the more defendable Frombork, and in 1350 was transferred to Lidzbark Warmiński, where it stayed for over four centuries.

Following the 1466 Treaty of Toruń, Warmia was incorporated into the kingdom of Poland, but the bishops retained much of their control over internal affairs. The bishopric was not subordinated to the archbishopric of Gniezno but was responsible directly to the pope. When the last Grand Master adopted Protestantism in 1525, Warmia became a bastion of the Counter-Reformation. In 1773 Warmia fell under Prussian rule and it wasn't until WWII that it returned to Poland.

several important architectural monuments in this area (particularly the castle in Lidzbark Warmiński and the church in Święta Lipka), a good skansen in Olsztynek, and the unique Elbląg-Ostróda Canal.

The Teutonic Knights arrived here in the mid-13th century, but it was the Warmian bishops who eventually converted and colonised the region, and controlled it for several centuries. Travelling around the region, you'll still come across relics of the bishops' great days, mostly to be found in their former district seats.

The so-called Copernicus Route (Szlak Kopernikowski) winds through places connected with the astronomer. It includes several Warmian towns with which Copernicus was closely related, among them Olsztyn, Lidzbark Warmiński and Frombork.

OLSZTYN
- pop 170,000   ☎ 089

The history of Olsztyn ('Ol-shtin') has been a successive overlapping of Prussian and Polish influences, as in most of the region. Founded in the 14th century as the southernmost outpost of Warmia, Olsztyn came under Polish control following the Toruń Treaty of 1466. With the First Partition of Poland in 1773, Olsztyn became Prussian (renamed Allenstein) and remained so until WWII. Only in 1945 did the town, 40% of which was destroyed during the war, return to Poland. After massive rebuilding, the city is now the largest and most important urban centre in Warmia and Masuria – though little can be seen of its past.

For travellers, Olsztyn is probably more important as a jumping-off point for, or stopover between, attractions in the region rather than a destination in itself. Though the city has reasonable food and accommodation facilities, you can see its historic sites in a few hours.

Information

Tourist Office The tourist office (☎/fax 527 57 76), in a bookshop at Plac Jana Pawła II 2/3, is open weekdays 9 am to 6 pm, and Saturday 10 am to 4 pm. It sells maps, although a better selection can be found at the Sklep Podróżnika (Traveller's Shop) behind the High Gate.

Money Useful banks include Bank Pekao at ul 1 Maja 10 and Powszechny Bank Kredytowy at ul Mickiewicza 2, and both have their own ATMs. Kantors are easy to find in the centre.

Things to See

The **High Gate**, the usual gateway to the Old Town, is all that remains of the 14th century city walls. Just to the west is the **Museum of Warmia and Masuria** (Muzeum Warmii i Mazur), open 9 am to 4 pm except Monday. It features exhibitions related to the city's and region's past. A block south is the **Rynek** (formally called ul Stare Miasto). It was destroyed during WWII and rebuilt in a style only superficially reverting to the past.

The most important historical building in town is the **castle**, a massive red-brick structure built in the 14th century. It now houses the **Regional Museum** (open 10 am to 4 pm except Monday), which displays works of art from Warmia, including paintings and silverware. Part of the 1st floor is dedicated to Copernicus, who was the administrator of Warmia and lived in the castle for more than three years (1516-20). He also made some of his astronomical observations here, and you can still see the diagram he drew on the cloister wall to record the equinox and thereby calculate the exact length of the year. Models of the instruments he used for his observations, and a copy of the painting by Matejko depicting the master at work, are on display in his

Olsztyn's huge castle served as a home for Copernicus for three years

former living quarters. Note the original crystal-like vaulting of the ceiling.

The **cathedral** dates from the same period, though its huge 60m tower was only added in 1596. Here, too, crystal-like vaults can be seen in the aisles, but the nave is different, having net-like vaulting from the 17th century. Amongst the most remarkable works of art is the 16th century triptych at the head of the left aisle.

Outside the Old Town, there is a **planetarium** (☎ 533 49 51) at Al Piłsudskiego 38, which has shows several times a day except Monday. The **astronomical observatory** (☎ 527 67 03) in the old water tower at ul Żołnierska 13 provides observations of the sun (several times a day except Monday), and of the stars (Tuesday to Friday twice nightly), provided the sky is clear.

Organised Tours

The Mazury travel agency (☎ 527 40 59, fax 527 34 42) in the PTTK office next to the High Gate runs 10-day canoeing tours along the Krutynia Kayak Route (Szlak Kajakowy Krutyni). The 105km route begins from Sorkwity, 50km east of Olsztyn, and goes down the Krutynia River and Lake Bełdany to Ruciane-Nida. The 10-kayak (20-people) tours go daily from late June to mid-August. The US$200 price includes kayak, food, lodging in cabins and a Polish-speaking guide. You can just show up at

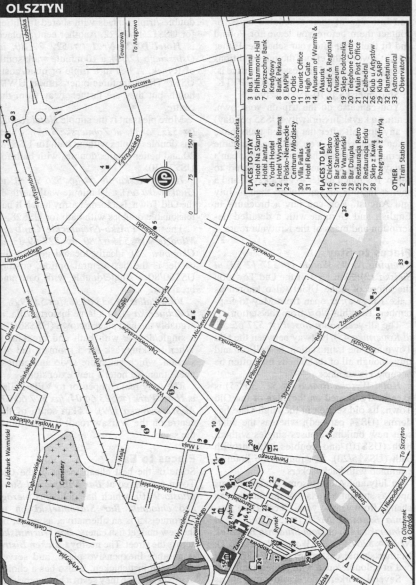

OLSZTYN

PLACES TO STAY
1 Hotel Na Skarpie
4 Hotel Jantar
6 Youth Hostel
12 Hotel Wysoka Brama
24 Polsko-Niemieckie
Centrum Młodzieży
30 Villa Pallas
31 Hotel Relaks

PLACES TO EAT
16 Chicken Bistro
17 Bar Staromiejski
18 Bar Warmiński
23 Bar Dziupla
25 Restauracja Retro
27 Restauracja Eridu
28 Sklep z Kawą
Pożegnanie z Afryką

OTHER
2 Train Station
3 Bus Terminal
5 Philharmonic Hall
7 Powszechny Bank
Kredytowy
8 Bank Pekao
9 EMPiK
10 Orbis
11 Tourist Office
13 High Gate
14 Museum of Warmia &
Masuria
15 Castle & Regional
Museum
19 Sklep Podróżnika
20 Telephone Centre
21 Main Post Office
22 Cathedral
26 Klub u Artystów
29 Klub SARP
32 Planetarium
33 Astronomical
Observatory

0   75   150 m

To Mrągowo

To Lidzbark Warmiński

To Szczytno

To Olsztynek & Ostróda

their Olsztyn office and hope they can fit you into one of their scheduled tours, or contact them before you leave for Poland and fit their tour into your schedule. Either way, it's worth the effort, though conditions are basic. The postal address of the office is: Biuro Podróży Mazury przy OZGT PTTK, ul Staromiejska 1, 10-950 Olsztyn.

You can also do the trip on your own, renting a kayak in Sorkwity (US$5 per day) if any are left after the guided tours have taken their share. You can use the same overnight bases as the tours but you can't always count on them – be prepared to camp. It's much easier to get a kayak and a shelter in June or September, than in July and August. You can buy a brochure in English and German with a detailed description and maps of the Krutynia route.

Places to Stay

Camping Nr 95 Wanda (☎ 527 12 53, ul Sielska 12), 3km west of the Old Town on the shore of Lake Ukiel (also known as Lake Krzywe), is open from May to September. Take bus No 7 from the station.

The all-year *youth hostel* (☎ 527 66 50, ul Kopernika 45), halfway between the Old Town and the train station, is well run and tidy, though all of its 80 beds may often be occupied in summer.

Hotel Wysoka Brama (☎ 527 36 75) is excellently located on the edge of the Old Town. Its old section in the High Gate has dorms (US$4 per bed), whereas the adjacent new building houses singles without bath (US$10) and doubles without/with bath (US$15/20). In summer the hotel is crammed with backpackers.

In July and August, some student dorms open as student hostels, but the picture can change from year to year. Check *Dom Studenta Bratniak No 1* (☎ 527 60 34, ul Żołnierska 14B) or *Dom Studenta Bratniak Nr 3* (☎ 526 65 41, Al Wojska Polskiego 1). Neither should cost more than US$7/5 per bed in a double/quad with shared facilities.

Several workers' dorms now operate as hotels. The closest to the train station is the uninspiring *Hotel Jantar* (☎ 533 54 52, ul

Kętrzyńskiego 5), which offers singles/doubles/triples/quads with shared facilities for US$12/15/18/22. Another central place is *Hotel UWM Nr 1* (☎ 527 27 80, ul Osińskiego 12/13), a 10 minute walk south of Rynek. A bed in a triple or quad costs US$7. There are three other similar UWM hotels but they are farther away from the centre.

More pleasant is the simple *Hotel Relaks* (☎ 527 75 34, ul Żołnierska 13A), which has doubles/triples without bath for US$18/20 and better singles/doubles with bath for US$26/30.

Hotel Na Skarpie (☎/fax 526 93 81, ul Gietkowska 6A), a 10 minute walk north of the Old Town, is a former army hotel. It has reasonable doubles with bath for US$28.

The new *Polsko-Niemieckie Centrum Młodzieży* (☎ 534 07 80, fax 527 69 33, ul Okopowa 25), ideally located next to the castle, is the best central option, costing US$60/80 a single/double with bath and breakfast.

Villa Pallas (☎ 535 01 15, fax 535 99 15, ul Żołnierska 4), in a large historic villa, is arguably the best place in town (US$80/100 a single/double with bath and breakfast). When booking, ask for a room in the old section, which has more style and atmosphere than the hotel's new extension.

The only real competitor to Villa Pallas is *Hotel Park* (☎ 523 66 04, fax 527 60 77, Al Warszawska 119), 3.5km south of the centre on the Warsaw road. It costs much the same.

Places to Eat

Some of the best cheap meals in the Old Town are served at *Bar Dziupla* (ul Stare Miasto 9/10), which has delicious *pierogi* and *chłodnik*. *Bar Staromiejski* on ul Staromiejska is an alternative, as might be the new budget fish eatery, *Bar Warmiński*, across the street. The nearby *Chicken Bistro* is another inexpensive place, and serves more than just chicken. It also has a choice of salads, though they seem a bit overpriced.

Of the Old Town's restaurants, *Restauracja Retro* (ul Okopowa 20), in a fine house, has tasty food at reasonable prices. Better, though more expensive, is the restaurant of *Polsko-Niemieckie Centrum Młodzieży*. Inexpensive Middle Eastern food, including the inevitable falafel, is served at *Restauracja Eridu*.

Both *Villa Pallas* and *Hotel Park* have their own restaurants, which are about the best and most expensive in town.

For a cup of well prepared coffee (30-odd flavours to choose from) go to *Sklep z Kawą Pożegnanie z Afryką (ul Podwale 2)*.

Entertainment
Klub SARP (ul Kołłątaja 14) and *Klub u Artystów (ul Kołłątaja 20)* are among the trendiest places for a drink.

Getting There & Away
The bus and train stations are in one building and are pretty busy. You can walk to the Old Town in 15 minutes or take one of the frequent city buses which drop you off in front of the High Gate.

Train About five fast trains daily leave for Gdańsk (179km) via Elbląg (99km). One express and two fast trains go to Warsaw (233km) all year, and there are a few more trains in summer. There are half a dozen departures daily for Toruń (163km), a route which is not covered by buses.

Bus Buses go every hour to Olsztynek (28km) and every half-hour to Lidzbark Warmiński (46km). There are about eight buses each to Giżycko (104km), Kętrzyn (88km) and Elbląg (95km) daily. Half a dozen fast PKS buses run to Warsaw (213km) year-round, or take the faster Polski Express bus (once per day, US$6, 3¼ hours).

Among international destinations, PKS has daily departures to Kaliningrad (US$6, four hours) and Vilnius (US$11, nine hours).

OLSZTYNEK
• pop 8000   ☎ 089
Olsztynek wouldn't perhaps merit a visit, if not for its open-air museum. Tucked away

on the north-eastern outskirts of town, about 1km from the centre, the **skansen** (Muzeum Budownictwa Ludowego) features about 40 examples of regional timber architecture from Warmia and Masuria, and even has a cluster of Lithuanian houses. There's a variety of peasant cottages complete with outbuildings, various windmills and a thatch-roofed church. A number of buildings have been furnished and decorated inside, and it's been done really well.

The skansen is open daily except Monday, from early May to mid-October 9 am to 4 pm (June to August until 5 pm), when the buildings are open for visits. The rest of the year, it opens 9 am to 3 pm but the houses are locked. There's a small café in one of the old cottages.

The 14th century Protestant **church**, on the town's main square, was rebuilt after WWII damage and is now an exhibition hall displaying mostly crafts. It's open 9 am to 4 pm except Monday.

Places to Stay & Eat
Zajazd Mazurski (☎ 519 28 85), about 1km from the centre on the Gdańsk road, is the only place to stay. It has doubles/quads with bath and breakfast for US$25/40, and its own restaurant, or you can eat in one of a few simple eateries in the town's centre.

Getting There & Away
Train The sleepy railway station is about 1km north-east of the centre but much closer to the skansen. Trains north to Olsztyn (31km) and south to Działdowo (53km) run every hour or two.

Bus The bus terminal is 250m south of the Rynek, but many regional buses call in at the train station. You can go from either to Olsztyn (28km, buses every half an hour or so), Grunwald (19km, five daily) and Ostróda (29km, six daily).

GRUNWALD
Grunwald is hard to find even on detailed maps, yet the name is known to every Pole.

Here, on 15 July 1410, the combined Polish and Lithuanian forces (supported by contingents of Ruthenians and Tatars) under King Władysław Jagiełło defeated the army of the Teutonic Knights. A crucial moment in Polish history, the 10 hours of carnage left the Grand Master of the Teutonic Order, Urlich von Jungingen, dead and his forces decimated. This was reputedly the largest medieval battle in Europe.

The battlefield is an open, gently rolling meadow adorned with three monuments. A small museum (open May to September 8 am to 6 pm) built on the central hill displays period armour, maps, battle banners etc, and its cinema runs films about the battle. The ruin of the chapel erected by the Order a year after the battle, in the place where the Grand Master is supposed to have died, is 500m from the museum.

Frequently visited by Poles, Grunwald is essentially a memorial to this glorious moment in Poland's history. Foreigners may find it less interesting. The shop by the entrance to the battlefield sells brochures in English and German, and the snack bar serves basic food.

There's a bus stop next to the snack bar, from which four or five buses daily go to Olsztynek (18km), Olsztyn (47km) and Ostróda (26km).

OSTRÓDA
- **pop 36,000   ☎ 088**

Ostróda is the starting/finishing point for excursions through the Elbląg-Ostróda Canal, and if you take this trip you're likely to spend a night in town, either before or after the journey. Otherwise there are few reasons to come here.

Places to Stay & Eat
A popular, cheap place to stay is *Dom Wycieczkowy Drwęcki (☎ 46 30 35, ul Mickiewicza 7)*, 500m east of the bus and train stations. It's just 100m from the boat landing site, and costs US$12/16/22/28 a single/double/triple/quad with shared facilities. There's an unpretentious restaurant downstairs.

About 500m north of the Drwęcki is a cinema, the *Kino Świt (☎ 46 27 03, ul Mickiewicza 34A)*, which offers simple singles/doubles/triples for US$10/16/18.

Another 200m north down the same road, there are two budget hotels next to each other at ul Mickiewicza 23: *Hotel Renata (☎ 46 47 06)* and *Hotel Kingston (☎ 46 60 57)*. Either will cost much the same as the cinema.

One of the cheapest options with private bath is *Hotel Falcon (☎ 46 49 41, ul 3 Maja 19A)*, beside the soccer field, at US$20 a double. For somewhere appreciably better, choose between the new *Hotel Ostróda (☎ 46 42 75, ☎/fax 46 42 78, ul Mickiewicza 3)*, next door to the Drwęcki, and *Hotel Park (☎ 46 22 27, fax 46 38 49, ul 3 Maja 21)*, near the Falcon. Either will cost about US$45/65 a single/double with bath and breakfast, and both have their own restaurants. Hotel Park operates a *camping ground* behind its building.

Getting There & Away
The train and bus stations are next to each other, 500m west of the wharf. Trains to Olsztyn (39km) and Iława (30km) run every couple of hours, and there are seven trains daily to Toruń (124km). There are no direct trains to Elbląg or Warsaw (239km), and only two to Gdańsk (150km). If you don't want to wait, go to Iława and change there as it's on the Warsaw-Gdańsk route and trains are frequent.

There's fairly regular bus transport to Olsztyn (42km), Olsztynek (29km), Grunwald (26km) and Elbląg (75km).

From 15 May to 15 September a boat to Elbląg leaves daily at 8 am. See the following section for details.

ELBLĄG-OSTRÓDA CANAL
The 82km Elbląg-Ostróda canal is Poland's longest navigable canal still in use. It's also the most unusual: the canal deals with the 99.5m difference in water levels by means of a system of five slipways; boats are carried across dry land on rail-mounted trolleys.

from the colourful ...

... to the quaint: roadside shrines in rural Poland

Rustic country house in north-east Poland

Tiny wayside chapel

Medieval brick castle in Reszel

KRZYSZTOF DYDYŃSKI

Camaldolese monastery on a peninsula in Lake Wigry

Peaceful country road in north-eastern Poland

Traffic jam at a lock, Masurian lake district

The Elbląg-Ostróda Canal – A Wonder of 19th Century Engineering

The rich forests of the Ostróda region have attracted the merchants of Gdańsk and Elbląg since medieval times, yet the only way of getting timber down to the Baltic was a long water route along the Drwęca and Vistula rivers via Toruń. Engineers considered building a canal as a short cut but the terrain was rugged and too steep for conventional locks.

In 1836 the Prussian engineer Georg Jakob Steenke (1801-82) from Königsberg produced a sophisticated design for an Elbląg-Ostróda canal incorporating slipways but the Prussian authorities rejected the project as unrealistic and too costly. Steenke didn't give up, however, and eventually succeeded in getting an audience with the king of Prussia. Interestingly, the monarch was convinced not by the technical or economic aspects but by the fact that nobody had ever constructed such a system before.

The part of the canal between Elbląg and Miłomłyn, which included all the slipways, was built in 1848-60. The remaining leg to Ostróda was completed by 1872. The canal proved to be reliable and profitable, and cut the distance of the original route along the Drwęca and Vistula almost fivefold. Various extensions were subsequently planned, including one linking the canal with the Great Masurian Lakes 120km to the east, but none were ever built.

The canal was damaged during the 1945 Red Army offensive but was repaired soon after liberation and opened for timber transport in 1946. A year later, the first tourist boat sailed the route. It remains the only canal of its kind in Europe and continues to operate, though no longer for transporting merchandise; it's now a tourist attraction.

The canal follows the course of a chain of six lakes. The largest is the considerably overgrown Lake Drużno near Elbląg, left behind by the Vistula Lagoon, which once extended as far as here.

The five slipways are on a 10km stretch of the northern part of the canal. Each slipway consists of two trolleys tied to a single looped rope, operating on the same principle as a funicular. They are powered by water.

There are also two conventional locks near the southern end of the canal, close to Ostróda, and a side canal leading west to Iława without either locks or slipways.

Boat Trips

From mid-May to late September, pleasure boats sail the main part of the canal between Elbląg and Ostróda. They depart from both towns at 8 am and arrive at the other end at about 7 pm. The trip costs US$22, or US$15 for foreigners under 18 (there are no ISIC student discounts). Bulky luggage

(formally, anything larger than 20 x 40 x 60cm) costs US$3.50 extra, but it's US$7 for a bicycle.

Some boats from Elbląg go only as far as Buczyniec, covering the most interesting part of the canal, including all five slipways. This trip costs US$16 (US$11 for under 18s, US$2 for luggage, US$4 for a bicycle) and takes five hours. The boat operator usually provides return bus transport from Buczyniec to Elbląg (US$3), returning you by 2 pm. This is a comfortable option for anyone not prepared for an 11 hour trip; indeed, the remaining seven hour sail may be monotonous for some. This is also a good solution for motorists who had to leave their vehicles in Elbląg.

The boats, with a capacity of 65 passengers, only run when at least 20 passengers turn up for the trip. You can expect regular daily services in July and August but outside this period there may be some days off. You can ring the wharf a couple of days in advance to find out about the availability of

WARMIA & MASURIA

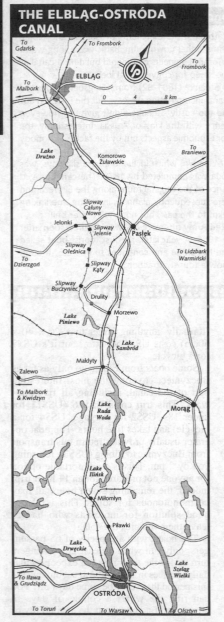

THE ELBLĄG-OSTRÓDA CANAL

tickets and the likelihood of the trip taking place (in Elbląg ☎ 055-232 43 07, in Ostróda ☎ 088-46 38 71). Boats have snack bars, which serve some basic snacks, tea, coffee, beer etc.

If you're not going to take the boat trip but have your own transport and want to see the slipways, it's best to go to Buczyniec between noon and 2 pm, where boats pass on their way north and south. There's a small museum here and you can see the impressive machinery which powers the trolleys. There are two roads leading to Buczyniec, both branching off the Elbląg-Ostróda road: one near Pasłęk, the other one in Morzewo.

DOBRE MIASTO
- **pop 11,000**   ☎ 089

Dobre Miasto, midway along the Olsztyn-Lidzbark Warmiński road, has a good 14th century Gothic church, which might be worth a stop if you're heading this way. Buses ply this route frequently, so you shouldn't have to wait long.

This massive brick blockbuster topped with a tall tower is the largest church in Warmia, after Frombork's cathedral. The predominantly baroque fittings include an exuberantly florid pulpit from 1693 and a baptismal font in the right aisle dating from the same period. The baroque stalls still have the old Gothic steps carved in the shape of lions. The late baroque high altar is patterned upon that of the Frombork cathedral, whereas the altars in the aisles hold Gothic triptychs; the one in the right-hand aisle, from 1430, is particularly beautiful.

The church is only open for Mass. At other times inquire in the Kancelaria Parafialna at the back of the church.

LIDZBARK WARMIŃSKI
- **pop 18,000**   ☎ 089

Forty-odd kilometres north of Olsztyn Lidzbark Warmiński is a peaceful if rather ordinary town. Its past is certainly more glorious than its present: it was the capital of the Warmian bishopric for over four centuries and was reputedly the richest and most cultured town of the region. Not much is left from that time, but the castle alone is enough to justify the trip: it's the best one surviving in Warmia and Masuria.

Lidzbark was a base for the Teutonic Knights' eastward expansion, but when the Warmian diocese was created in 1243, the settlement came under the administration of the bishops. Lidzbark grew at a faster pace after it received a municipal charter in 1308, and in 1350 the bishops chose it as their main residence and the seat of the whole bishopric. A castle and a church were built and the town swiftly became an important religious and cultural centre. Copernicus lived here in 1503-10, serving as a doctor and adviser to his uncle, Bishop Łukasz Watzenrode.

When the Reformation arrived in the 16th century Lidzbark, along with most of the province, became a citadel of Catholicism, and it remained so until the First Partition of 1773, when the Prussians took over the region. Deprived of his office, the last bishop, Ignacy Krasicki, turned to literature, to become Poland's most outstanding man of letters of the period, particularly noted for his sharp social satire.

Information

The Bank Gdański at ul Świętochowskiego 14 opposite the train station will exchange cash and travellers cheques and has an ATM. Cash can also be changed in a few kantors in the centre.

Castle

This mighty red-brick structure adorned with turrets on the corners is the most important sight in Lidzbark. The entrance to the castle is from the south through a palatial, horseshoe-shaped building (known as *przedzamcze*), extensively rebuilt in the 18th century.

The castle was constructed in the second half of the 14th century on a square plan with a central courtyard, the whole surrounded by a moat and fortified walls. In the 16th and 17th centuries residential buildings were added to the southern and northern sides of the castle, but they were pulled down when the bishops' era ended with the Partitions. The castle itself fell into decline and served a variety of purposes, including barracks, storage, hospital and orphanage. Restoration was finally undertaken in the 1920s and within 10 years the building had been more or less returned to its original form. Miraculously, it came through the war unharmed, and today it is easily one of Poland's best preserved medieval castles.

Most of the interior, from the cellars up to the 2nd floor, now houses the **Warmian Museum** (Muzeum Warmińskie), open 9 am to 4 pm except Monday (to 5 pm mid-June to late August). Guides speaking German (but not English) are available for around US$25 per group.

The first thing you'll see is a beautiful **courtyard** with two-storey arcaded galleries all round it. It was constructed in the 1380s and has hardly changed since.

The 1st floor boasts the castle's main chambers, of which the vaulted **Grand Refectory** (Wielki Refektarz) is the largest and most remarkable. The unusual chessboard-style wall paintings date from the end of the 14th century. The exhibition inside features works of medieval art collected from the region, including some charming smiling Madonnas. The adjoining chapel was redecorated in sumptuous rococo style in the mid-18th century.

The top floor contains several exhibitions, including 20th century Polish painting and a collection of icons and other liturgical objects of the Old Believers. They were brought here from Wojnowo (see that section) though they originally came from the main Old Believers' Church in Moscow.

While you're there you should also visit the excellent two-storey vaulted **cellars**, with the old cannons on display. These belonged to the bishops, who had their own small army. At the end of the 16th century, the 'armed forces' of the Warmian diocese numbered about 450 men.

LIDZBARK WARMIŃSKI

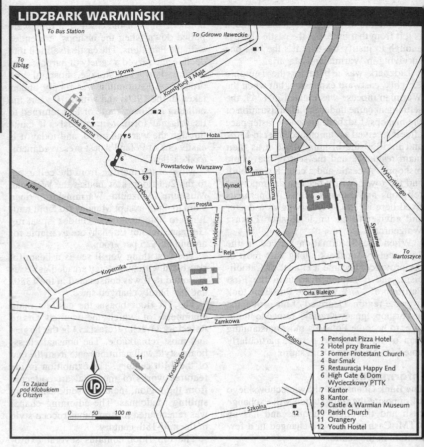

1 Pensjonat Pizza Hotel
2 Hotel przy Bramie
3 Former Protestant Church
4 Bar Smak
5 Restauracja Happy End
6 High Gate & Dom
   Wycieczkowy PTTK
7 Kantor
8 Kantor
9 Castle & Warmian Museum
10 Parish Church
11 Orangery
12 Youth Hostel

Other Attractions

The 15th century **High Gate** (Brama Wysoka) marks the entrance to what once was the Old Town and is now a non-descript postwar suburb. Wrecked in WWII, the historic quarter – regarded as one of the richest and most picturesque in the region – unfortunately hasn't been reconstructed.

Near the gate is the wooden **Protestant church** erected in the 1820s, believed to be based on a design by Karl Friedrich Schinkel. It's now used by the Orthodox community for their infrequent Masses.

At the south end of the Old Town looms the familiar brick **parish church**. Its structure retains much of the original Gothic shape, except for the top of the tower, which was struck by lightning in 1698 and rebuilt in baroque style. The interior is a mishmash of styles from different periods.

In the mid-17th century the bishops laid out the gardens to the south of the church, and built the **Orangery** (Oranżeria). Most of the gardens were turned into a cemetery at the beginning of the 20th century, but the Orangery stands to this day, though it's been altered and is now the local library.

Places to Stay

Dom Wycieczkowy PTTK (☎ 767 25 21), attractively located in the High Gate, has singles/doubles at US$9/14, plus triples, quads and larger dorms where a bed will cost US$4. Still cheaper is the summer *youth hostel* (☎ 767 24 44, ul Szkolna 3), in the building of the Internat (boarding school), south of the Old Town.

Far better than either of the above is *Pensjonat Pizza Hotel* (☎ 767 52 59, ul Konstytucji 3 Maja 26) in a stylish house, north of the Old Town. It offers three doubles sharing one bath (US$24 each) and one double with its own bath (US$36). In the same area, *Hotel przy Bramie* (☎ 767 32 58, ul Konstytucji 3 Maja 18) is the best place to stay in town, at US$45 a double with bath and breakfast.

You can also stay at *Zajazd pod Kłobukiem* (☎ 767 32 92, ul Olsztyńska 4), 2km south-west of the centre on the Olsztyn road, but it's inconvenient unless you have your own transport. It costs US$22/38 for singles/doubles with bath.

Places to Eat

Bar Smak (ul Wysoka Brama 4), close to the High Gate, is passable and cheap (open till 7 pm). Better and more pleasant, but also more expensive, is *Restauracja Happy End* (ul Konstytucji 3 Maja 6) in the same area. You can also eat at *Pensjonat Pizza Hotel*, which has more than just pizza. *Zajazd pod Kłobukiem* has its own restaurant – convenient if you're staying there.

Getting There & Away

The bus terminal is next to the defunct train station, about 500m north-west of the High Gate. Buses to Olsztyn (46km) depart every hour or so and call at Dobre Miasto en route. There are two buses a day to Frombork (75km) and four to Gdańsk (157km). One bus runs eastwards to Kętrzyn (62km)

passing Reszel and Święta Lipka on the way.

RESZEL
* pop 6000   ☎ 089

If you decide to take the backwoods route from Lidzbark east to the Great Masurian Lakes via Kętrzyn, you'll be passing Reszel and Święta Lipka on the way. Both may result in pleasant stops.

Reszel ('Reh-shel') is a small market town which began its life at the end of the 13th century as the easternmost outpost of the Warmian bishopric. A century later it evolved into a small fortified town, complete with a central square, castle and church. It didn't get much bigger, but was a prosperous craft centre before the wars of the 18th century brought about its decline. The town never really recovered, yet its minuscule centre still boasts the original street plan dotted with several historic buildings including the castle. The town has retained some of the lethargic atmosphere of times gone by, and even the clock on the church tower has stopped.

Things to See

Reszel's tiny Old Town, measuring no more than 250 x 250m, is centred around the Rynek with the usual town hall in its middle. One block east is the 14th century brick **castle**, built at the same time as that in Lidzbark and likewise retaining much of its original form, except for the southern side, which was turned into a Protestant church in the 19th century, with a belfry and gable added on top. Today it's an art gallery (open 10 am to 4 pm except Monday) featuring modern art. Go to the top of the castle's massive cylindrical tower for a view over the red-tiled roofs of the Old Town.

The 14th century **parish church** is a large Gothic brick construction with a tall square tower. It was refurnished and redecorated in the 1820s and has a harmonious though not outstanding interior.

A block north of the Rynek, on ul Spichrzowa, is a fine if derelict 18th century half-timbered **granary**. A stone's throw east, at the entrance to the Old Town from Kętrzyn, stands the unusually massive brick **Fishing Bridge** (Most Rybacki), built in the 14th century and only recently closed to traffic.

Places to Stay & Eat

The most attractive place to stay in Reszel is the *castle* (☎ 755 02 16, ☎ 755 01 09). Arranged on the upper floor of the eastern side of the building, unusual double-storey rooms (for up to three people) with bath cost US$34; there's a charming vaulted café on the ground floor, with meals for guests.

Hotel Astra (☎ 755 02 73, ul Krasickiego 6A), a few minutes walk south-west from the bus station, is undistinguished but acceptable and cheap: US$16/25 a double/quad without bath, US$24/32 with bath. The *youth hostel* (☎ 755 00 12, ul Krasickiego 7), in the school, 100m from the Astra, is open in July and August.

There are a few budget snack bars and cafés around the central streets.

Getting There & Away

Trains no longer call at Reszel, but bus transport is OK. The bus terminal is a five minute walk north of the Old Town. There are plenty of buses east to Kętrzyn (19km) and all pass via Święta Lipka (6km). Half a dozen buses daily go to Mrągowo (28km) and roughly the same number to Olsztyn (67km). Two buses run west to Lidzbark Warmiński (43km), and one of them continues to Gdańsk (200km).

ŚWIĘTA LIPKA
☎ 089

The tiny hamlet of Święta Lipka (literally, the Holy Lime Tree; 'Shvyen-tah Leep-kah') was once on the border between Warmia and Ducal Prussia. It boasts the most beautiful baroque church in northern Poland.

The church's origins are linked to a miracle. The story goes that once upon a time there was a prisoner in the Kętrzyn castle sentenced to death. The night before the execution the Virgin Mary unexpectedly appeared and presented the culprit with a

tree trunk out of which to carve her effigy. The resulting figure was so beautiful that the judges took it to be a sign from Heaven and gave the condemned man his freedom. On his way home, he placed the statue on the first lime tree he encountered, as required by the Virgin – which happened to be in Święta Lipka.

Miracles immediately began to occur, and even sheep knelt down while passing the shrine. Pilgrims arrived in increasing numbers; one of them was the last Grand Master of the Teutonic Order, Albrecht von Hohenzollern, who walked here barefoot, six years before deciding to convert to Lutheranism.

Baroque Church

The church was built in 1687-93 and later surrounded by an ample rectangular cloister, with four identical towers housing chapels on the corners. The best artists from Warmia, Königsberg and Vilnius were commissioned for the furnishings and decoration, which were completed by around 1740. Since then the church has hardly changed, either inside or outside, and it is considered one of the purest late baroque churches in the country.

The entrance to the complex is through an elaborate wrought-iron **gateway**. Just behind it, the two-towered cream **façade** holds in its central niche a stone sculpture of the holy lime tree with a statue of the Virgin Mary on top.

Once inside, the visitor is enveloped in colourful and florid but not overwhelming baroque. All the **frescoes** are the work of Maciej Mayer of Lidzbark, and display the then fashionable trompe l'œil images. These are clearly visible both on the vault and the columns; the latter look as if they were carved. Mayer left behind his own image: you can see him in a blue waistcoat with brushes in his hand, in the corner of the vault-painting over the organ.

The three-storey, 19m **high altar**, covering the whole back of the chancel, is carved of walnut and painted to look like marble. Of the three paintings in the altar, the lowest

The splendid baroque church in Święta has attracted pilgrims for over 300 years

one depicts the Virgin Mary of Święta Lipka with the Christ child.

The **pulpit** is ornamented with paintings and sculptures. Directly opposite, across the nave, is the **holy lime tree** topped with the figure of the Virgin Mary, supposed to have been placed on the site where the legendary tree once stood.

The pride of the church is its **organ**, a sumptuously decorated instrument of about 5000 pipes. The work of Johann Jozue Mosengel of Königsberg, it is equipped with a mechanism which puts in motion figures of saints and angels when the organ is played. Short demonstrations are held from May to September several times a day and irregularly the rest of the year. From June to August, organ recitals take place every Friday evening.

The **cloister** surrounding the church is ornamented with frescoes by Mayer. The artist painted the corner chapels (and part of the northern and western cloister) in trompe l'œil style, but died before the work was complete. It was continued by other artists but, as you can see, without the same success.

Święta Lipka is frequently visited by both tourists and pilgrims. The church is open for sightseeing Monday to Saturday 8 am to 6 pm, Sunday 10 to 11 am, noon to 2 pm and 3 to 5 pm. The main religious celebrations fall on the last Sunday of May, and on 11, 14 and 15 August. The PTTK kiosk near the gate can provide English and German-speaking guides (US$14 per group for a tour up to two hours).

Places to Stay & Eat

Dom Pielgrzyma (☎ 755 14 81) in the monastery complex next to the church provides lodgings for pilgrims for about US$5 per head, but it's often full in July and August. Some locals living nearby may have a room or two for rent in their house.

South of Święta Lipka, on the shore of Lake Dejnowa, are two holiday centres (open May to September): *Ośrodek Wypoczynkowy Dejnowo*, 1km from the church, and *Ośrodek Wypoczynkowy Staniewo*, 1.5km farther south. Both have basic cabins and simple eating outlets.

A collection of food stands spring up in summer around the square in front of the church. *Restauracja West* on the road opposite the church is a place for something more substantial and is reasonably priced.

Getting There & Away

Buses to Kętrzyn (13km) and Reszel (6km) run every hour or so. There are several to Olsztyn (73km) and Mrągowo (19km), and a couple to Lidzbark Warmiński (49km).

The Great Masurian Lakes

The Great Masurian Lake District (Kraina Wielkich Jezior Mazurskich), east of

Olsztyn, is a verdant land of rolling hills interspersed with countless lakes, healthy little farms, scattered tracts of forest and small towns. The district is centred around Lake Śniardwy (114 sq km), Poland's largest lake, and Lake Mamry and its adjacent waters (totalling an additional 104 sq km). Over 15% of the area is covered by water and another 30% by forest.

The lakes are well connected by rivers and canals, to form an extensive system of waterways. The whole area has become a prime destination for yachtspeople and canoeists, and is also popular among anglers, hikers, bikers and nature-lovers. Tourists arrive in great numbers in July and August, though after 15 August the crowds begin to thin out.

The main lakeside centres are Giżycko and Mikołajki, with two additional ones, Węgorzewo and Ruciane-Nida, at the northern and southern ends of the lakeland, respectively. They all rent out kayaks and sailing boats, though it may be difficult to get one in July and August.

Getting Around the Lakes

Yachtspeople can sail most of the larger lakes, all the way from Węgorzewo to Ruciane-Nida, which are interconnected and are the district's main waterway system. Kayakers will perhaps prefer more intimate surroundings along side rivers and smaller lakes. The best established and most popular kayak route in the area originates at Sorkwity and follows the Krutynia River and Lake Bełdany to Ruciane-Nida (see Organised Tours in the Olsztyn section). There's also a beautiful kayak route along the Czarna Hańcza River in the Augustów area farther east (see the Augustów section).

If you're not up to sailing or canoeing, you can enjoy the lakes in comfort from the deck of the excursion boats operated by the Masurian Shipping Company. These large boats have an open deck above and a coffee shop below, and can carry backpacks and bicycles.

Theoretically, boats run between Giżycko, Mikołajki and Ruciane-Nida daily from May to September, and to Węgorzewo from June to August. In practice, the service is most reliable from late June to late August. In other times trips can be cancelled if too few passengers turn up. Examples of fares are US$9 from Węgorzewo to Giżycko, US$10 from Giżycko to Mikołajki, and US$9 from Mikołajki to Ruciane-Nida. There are no discounts for foreign students. Schedules are clearly posted at the lake ports.

The detailed Wielkie Jeziora Mazurskie map (scale 1:100,000) is a great help for anyone exploring the region by boat, kayak, bike, car or foot. It shows walking trails, canoeing routes, accommodation options, petrol stations and much more. It's normally available in the region but you're safer buying a copy in a city before you come.

KĘTRZYN
• **pop 31,000**   ☎ **089**

Kętrzyn ('Kent-zhin') might be a stopover if you're wandering around the western fringes of the Great Masurian Lakes. The town has a couple of attractions and is a handy jumping-off point for two of the most spectacular sights in the region: the Wolf's Lair to the east and Święta Lipka to the west.

Kętrzyn was founded in the 14th century by the Teutonic Knights under the name of Rastenburg. Though partially colonised by Poles, it remained Prussian until WWII, after which it became Polish and got its present name. The name derives from Wojciech Kętrzyński (1838-1919), a historian, scholar and patriot who documented the history of the Polish presence in the region.

Things to See

There are still some vestiges of the Teutonic legacy. The mid-14th century brick **castle** was damaged and rebuilt on various occasions; today it houses the local **museum**, open Tuesday to Sunday 9 am to 4 pm (daily 10 am to 5 pm in summer). It has a permanent display dedicated to the town's history, plus temporary exhibitions. It's a five minute walk from the train station westward along ul Dworcowa.

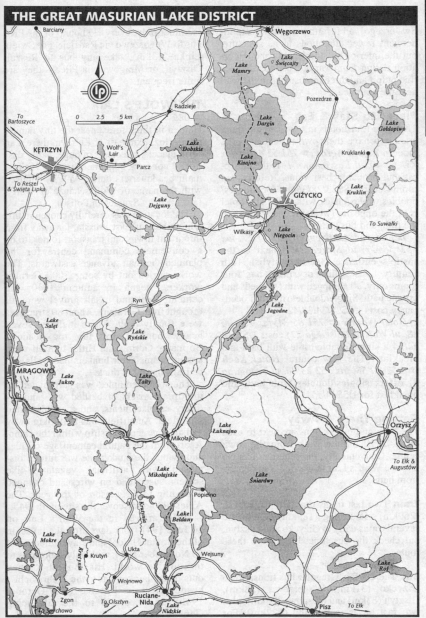

THE GREAT MASURIAN LAKE DISTRICT

The Gothic **St George's Church** (Kościół Św Jerzego), a bit farther up the street, underwent fewer alterations to its structure, but the interior has furnishings and decoration dating from various periods. Note a fine pulpit and three tombstones in the wall near the entrance.

Places to Stay & Eat

There are four hotels in town; all are quite good and have their own restaurants. The modern *Zajazd Agros* (☎ 751 52 41, ☎/fax 751 52 40, ul Kasztanowa 1) is the cheapest and probably best value. Refurbished rooms cost US$23/28/36/44 for singles/doubles/triples/quads with bath. The hotel is at the opposite (western) end of town to the train and bus stations.

Zajazd pod Zamkiem (☎ 752 31 17, fax 752 38 37, ul Struga 3) is next to the castle's entrance. Set in a stylish 19th century house, this cosy place has four rooms only, all equipped with four beds and private bath. Single/double/triple/full occupancy costs US$28/34/38/42.

Hotel Wanda (☎ 751 85 84, fax 751 00 88, ul Wojska Polskiego 27) costs US$30/44/54 a single/double/triple with bath and breakfast. The new central *Hotel Koch* (☎ 752 20 58, fax 752 23 90, ul Traugutta 3) offers singles/doubles with bath and breakfast for US$44/75.

Getting There & Away

The train and bus stations are next to each other, a 10 minute walk from the town centre. Conveniently, the suburban bus No 1 to the Wolf's Lair in Gierłoż also departs from here.

Train Two fast trains run daily to Gdańsk (269km) via Elbląg (189km). .There are several trains daily to Giżycko and Olsztyn, but check the bus timetable too on these routes.

Bus There's fairly regular bus transport to Giżycko (31km), Węgorzewo (38km), Olsztyn (83km) and Mrągowo (25km), plus two fast buses to Suwałki (122km). For Gierłoż (8km), take a suburban bus No 1 (summer only, every 1½ hours) or the PKS bus to Węgorzewo via Radzieje. For Święta Lipka (13km), take any bus to Reszel, Olsztyn, or Mrągowo via Pilec – they are quite frequent.

THE WOLF'S LAIR
☎ 089

Hidden in thick forest near the tiny hamlet of Gierłoż, 8km east of Kętrzyn, there's an eerie place: 18 hectares of huge, partly destroyed concrete bunkers. This was Hitler's main headquarters during WWII, baptised with the name of Wolfsschanze or Wolf's Lair (Wilczy Szaniec in Polish).

The location was carefully chosen in this remote part of East Prussia, far away from important towns and transport routes, to be a convenient command centre for the planned German advance eastwards. The work, carried out by some 3000 German workers, began in autumn 1940; the cement, steel and basalt gravel were all brought from Germany. About 80 structures were finally built, which included seven heavy bunkers for the top leaders: Bormann, Göring and Hitler himself were among them. Their bunkers had walls and ceilings up to 8m thick.

The whole complex was surrounded by multiple barriers of barbed wire and artillery emplacements, and a sophisticated minefield. An airfield was built 5km away and an emergency airstrip within the camp. Apart from the natural camouflage of trees and plants, the bunker site was further disguised with artificial vegetation-like screens suspended on wires and changed according to the season of the year. The Allies did not discover the site until 1945.

Hitler arrived in the Wolf's Lair on 26 June 1941 (four days after the invasion of the Soviet Union) and stayed there until 20 November 1944, with only short trips to the outside world. His longest journey outside the bunker was to the Wehrmacht's headquarters in Ukraine (July-October 1942), to be closer to the advancing German front.

The 'Hit' on Hitler

Hitler used to say that the Wolf's Lair was one of the very few places in Europe where he felt safe. Paradoxically, it was here that an assassination attempt came closest to succeeding. It was organised by a group of pragmatic, high-ranking German officers who considered the continuation of the war to be suicidal, with no real chance of victory. They planned to negotiate peace with the Allies after eliminating Hitler.

The leader of the plot, Claus von Stauffenberg, arrived from Berlin on 20 July 1944 on the pretext of informing Hitler about the newly formed reserve army. A frequent guest at the Wolf's Lair, he enjoyed the confidence of the staff and had no problems entering the bunker complex with a bomb in his briefcase. He placed his briefcase beneath the table a few feet from Hitler and left the meeting to take a pre-arranged phone call from an aide. The explosion killed two members of Hitler's staff and wounded half a dozen others, but Hitler himself suffered only minor injuries and was even able to meet Mussolini, who arrived later the same day. Stauffenberg and some 5000 people involved directly or indirectly in the plot were executed.

Had the outcome of the plot been otherwise, it could have turned the whole course of WWII and the postwar period. A peace treaty between the Germans and the Allies might well have saved the lives of some five million people (including three million Jews) and the devastation of vast parts of Poland and Germany. One can also speculate that the former East Germany and perhaps a good chunk of Eastern Europe might have avoided half a century of Soviet communism.

to be destroyed, should the enemy attempt to seize them. About 10 tonnes of explosives were stuffed into each heavy bunker. The complex was eventually blown up on 24 January 1945 and the Germans retreated. Three days later the Soviets arrived, but the minefield was still efficiently defending the empty ruins. It took a total of 10 years to clear the area of mines; about 55,000 were detected and defused.

Today, you can wander around the gruesome place; it's open daily till dusk. There's a board with a map of the site by the entrance, from which a red marked trail winds around the bunkers. All structures are identified with numbers. Of Hitler's bunker (No 13) only one wall survived, but Göring's 'home' (No 16) is in remarkably good shape. A memorial plate (placed in 1992) marks the location of Stauffenberg's assassination attempt (see the boxed text).

Entry costs US$2, plus another US$2 for the compulsory car park if applicable. English and German-speaking guides are available for about US$15 per 1½ hour tour. Alternatively, you can buy an information booklet (available in English and German).

Places to Stay & Eat

Dom Wycieczkowy (☎ 752 44 29), in the former officers' hostel at the entrance to the complex, has recently been fully refurbished and now costs US$20/30/40 a single/double/triple with bath and breakfast. At the opposite end of the same building is a reasonable restaurant and a bar. Diagonally opposite is a basic *camping ground*, open June to September; check in at the hotel reception.

Getting There & Away

PKS buses between Kętrzyn (8km) and Węgorzewo (30km) stop here several times a day. You can also go to Kętrzyn (in summer only) by suburban bus No 1.

WĘGORZEWO
• pop 12,500   ☎ 087

Set at the northern end of the Great Masurian Lake District, Węgorzewo

As the Red Army approached, Hitler left the Wolf's Lair and the headquarters were evacuated. The army prepared the bunkers

('Ven-go-zheh-vo') is the northernmost lakeside centre for both excursion boats and individual sailors. Less overrun by tourists than its southern cousins Giżycko and Mikołajki, Węgorzewo isn't quite on the lake shore but is linked to Lake Mamry by a 2km river canal.

Sprawling and rather unprepossessing, the town is perhaps not worth a special journey, though you may end up here while sailing or taking the Giżycko-Węgorzewo boat cruise, an attraction in itself. From Węgorzewo you can continue by bus to Gierłoż and farther to the west (eg Lidzbark Warmiński), or east along the northern, rarely used border route to the Suwałki region.

Information

The useful Biuro Informacji Turystycznej (☎/fax 27 40 09, ☎/fax 28 25 78), ul Zamkowa 7, is open in summer weekdays 8 am to 5 pm, weekends to 3 pm. It handles private rooms, yacht charter, kayak tours, horse riding etc.

Places to Stay & Eat

The cheapest central place to stay is *Stanica Wodna PTTK* (☎ 27 24 43, ul Wańkowicza 3), facing the canal. It operates from late May to September and charges US$6 per bed in doubles or triples, but in July and August it's usually filled up with groups.

Another budget option, the *Internat Garnizonowy* (☎ 27 28 82, ul Bema 18), 1km from the centre on the Giżycko road, costs US$10/18/20 a single/double/triple. You may also try *Pensjonat pod Dębami* (☎ 27 22 18, ul Łuczańska 33), another 1km towards Giżycko, which has rooms with bath for US$20/30/40 a double/triple/quad.

Pensjonat Nautic (☎/fax 27 20 80, ul Słowackiego 14) is the best place in town. It has three singles (US$25), three doubles (US$40) and three suites (US$100 to US$160). All rooms have a bath and satellite TV. Add US$6 per person for the optional breakfast. The pensjonat has its own restaurant which is the best place around to eat.

Camping Nr 175 Rusałka (☎ 27 20 49) on Lake Święcajty opens from May to Sep-

tember. With bungalows, pleasant grounds for tents, a restaurant, and boats and kayaks for hire, it's a good place and well run. It's 3km from the town along the Giżycko road plus 1km more to the lake. Infrequent PKS buses go there in season but, if you don't want to wait, take any bus to Giżycko, get off at the turn-off to the camp site and walk the remaining distance.

Getting There & Away

Trains no longer operate here but the bus terminal, 1km north-west of the centre, provides reasonable transport to Giżycko (26km) and to Kętrzyn (38km); buses to Kętrzyn via Radzieje will drop you at the entrance to the Wolf's Lair bunkers. There are several buses to Gołdap (45km), from where you can continue to Stańczyki and Suwałki. Two fast morning buses run directly to Warsaw (278km); book in advance in season.

From July to August, there's an excursion boat to Giżycko (US$9, 2½ hours).

GIŻYCKO
- pop 31,00   ☎ 087

Set on the northern shore of Lake Niegocin, Giżycko ('Ghee-zhits-ko') is the largest lakeside centre in the Great Masurian Lake District. The town started life under the Teutonic Knights but was destroyed on numerous occasions, by Lithuanians, Poles, Swedes, Tatars, Russians and Germans in turn.

Today, Giżycko is a rather ordinary place without much charm or historical character. The town is essentially a transport hub and provision base for holiday homes and watersports centres that have grown up outside the town, and for hordes of holidaymakers who arrive en masse in the short summer season and take to the lakes. You'll find it's a useful springboard from where you can take an excursion boat to Mikołajki or Węgorzewo, or rent a boat.

Information

The tourist office (☎ 28 52 65, ☎/fax 28 57 69) is at ul Warszawska 7 (enter from ul Kętrzyńskiego).

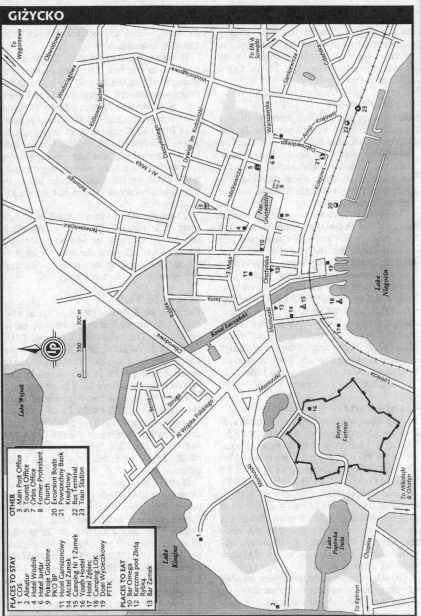

GIŻYCKO

PLACES TO STAY
1 COS
2 Almatur
4 Hotel Wodnik
6 Hotel Jantar
9 Pokoje Gościnne
PKO BP
11 Hotel Garnizonowy
14 Mctel Zamek
15 Camping Nr 1 Zamek
16 Youth Hostel
17 Hotel Zębiec
18 Camping LOK
19 Dom Wycieczkowy
PTTK

PLACES TO EAT
10 Bar Omega
12 Karczma pod Złotą
Rybką
13 Bar Zamek

OTHER
3 Main Post Office
5 Tourist Office
7 Orbis Office
8 Former Protestant
Church
20 Excursion Boats
21 Powszechny Bank
Kredytowy
22 Bus Terminal
23 Train Station

Powszechny Bank Kredytowy at ul Dąbrowskiego 12 near the train station exchanges travellers cheques and gives advances on Visa. There are some kantors in the centre including one in the Orbis office at ul Dąbrowskiego 3.

Boyen Fortress

Named after the Prussian minister of war General Hermann von Boyen, the Boyen Fortress (Twierdza Boyen) was erected in 1844-55 to protect the border with Russia. Since the frontier ran north-south along the 90km string of lakes, the stronghold was strategically placed in the middle, on the isthmus near Giżycko.

The fortress, which consists of several bastions and defensive towers surrounded by a moat, was continually modified and strengthened, and successfully withstood Russian attacks during WWI. In WWII, it was a defensive outpost of the Wolf's Lair and was given up to the Red Army without a fight during the 1945 offensive. The fortifications survived in pretty good shape, though they're slowly being taken over by bushes. There's an amphitheatre and youth hostel here, while some of the old buildings are used as storage rooms. You can wander around freely at any time – the fortress is 1km west of the town centre.

Yacht Charter

Sailing boats are hired out by a number of local operators, including Almatur (☎ 28 59 71) at ul Moniuszki 24; Centrum Mazur (☎ 28 54 38) at Camping Zamek at ul Moniuszki 1; Ośrodek Żeglarski LOK (☎ 28 14 08) at ul Lotnicza 4; PUH Żeglarz (☎ 28 20 84) at ul Kościuszki 1; COS (☎ 28 23 35) at ul Moniuszki 22; and Orbis (☎ 28 51 46) at ul Dąbrowskiego 3. It's a good idea to get a copy of the *Żagle* yachting monthly magazine, in which many yacht-charter operators, from Giżycko and other Masurian yachting centres, advertise.

Giżycko has possibly the largest number of yacht-charter agencies and, accordingly, offers the widest choice of boats, yet your chances of finding anything in July and

August without booking are rather slim. Booking well in advance for this period is virtually essential.

Boats are much easier to find in June (especially in the first half) and September (particularly in the second half). At these times, shop around, as prices and conditions can vary substantially from place to place and bargaining is possible with some agents.

In July and August, expect to pay somewhere between US$25 and US$100 per day for a cabin sailing boat large enough to fit four to five people and equipped with mattresses. Prices are significantly lower in June and September – often half of the in-season prices.

Check the state of the boat and its equipment in detail, and report every deficiency and bit of damage in advance to avoid hassles when returning the boat. Come prepared with cooking equipment, sleeping bag, good rain gear, torch etc.

Places to Stay

Camping Nr 1 Zamek (☎ 28 34 10, ul Moniuszki 1) opens from mid-June to early September. The more basic *Camping LOK* (☎ 28 25 30, ul Lotnicza 4) is a little to the south, on the lakeside. The large, basic *youth hostel* (☎ 28 29 59) in the Boyen Fortress operates from May to September.

The well located but dilapidated *Dom Wycieczkowy PTTK* (☎ 28 29 05, ul Nadbrzeżna 11) costs US$6 per head. It's small and often full in summer. Similarly simple and cheap (US$7 a bed) is *Hotel Zębiec* (☎ 28 25 30, ul Lotnicza 4) in the LOK centre.

Hotel Garnizonowy (☎ 28 14 14, ul Olsztyńska 10A) is better, back off the street behind apartment blocks. Singles/doubles/triples without bath cost US$13/20/28. *Pokoje Gościnne PKO BP* (☎ 28 54 63, Plac Grunwaldzki 11) offers reasonable rooms for US$16/26/32. The small *Motel Zamek* (☎ 28 24 19, ul Moniuszki 1) has doubles with bath for US$32. Locked garage (optional) costs US$5 extra.

From May to September (or longer), you can stay in *COS* (☎ 28 23 35, ul Moniuszki

22), on Lake Kisajno. It's a large sports centre with bungalows and rooms. The latter cost US$32/45/58. Near COS, *Almatur* (☎ *28 59 71, ul Moniuszki 24*) also has a collection of bungalows and buildings, some of which are heated and open year-round.

The central *Hotel Wodnik* (☎ *28 38 72, fax 28 39 58, ul 3 Maja 2*) and the *Hotel Jantar* (☎*/fax 28 54 15, ul Warszawska 10*) are more upmarket options. Either will cost US$40/65 a single/double with bath and breakfast.

Places to Eat
Some of the cheapest meals in town are served in the basic *Bar Omega* (*ul Olsztyńska 4*). Marginally more expensive is *Bar Zamek* (*ul Moniuszki 1*). There are many other budget places throughout the central area.

Karczma pod Złotą Rybką (*ul Olsztyńska 15*) has about the widest choice of fish in town and good prices. Crayfish is available at times. *Motel Zamek*, *Hotel Jantar* and *Hotel Wodnik* have their own restaurants.

Getting There & Away
Train The train station is on the southern edge of town near the lake. Around eight trains run daily to Ełk (47km), Kętrzyn (30km) and Olsztyn (120km), and two fast trains to Gdańsk (299km) and Białystok (151km). Trains to Warsaw (353km) take a roundabout route – it's faster to go by bus.

Bus Just next to the train station, the bus terminal offers a regular service to Węgorzewo (26km) and Mrągowo (41km). Half a dozen buses daily run to Mikołajki (31km), Kętrzyn (31km), Olsztyn (104km) and Suwałki (91km). There's a bus or two to Lidzbark Warmiński (93km), and several fast buses to Warsaw (251km) in summer.

Boat Boats operate from May to September with extra ones in July and August. To the north, you can take a trip to Węgorzewo (US$9, 2½ hours). Southbound, you can either go to Mikołajki (US$10, three hours)

or do a loop on Lake Niegocin (US$5, 1½ hours). The wharf is near the train station.

MIKOŁAJKI
- **pop 4000**   ☎ **087**

Mikołajki ('Mee-ko-wahy-kee') is far smaller than Giżycko but is also an important lakeside centre of the Great Masurian Lakes. It's much more pleasant and has some style, which can be seen and felt in its architecture and scenic location. Perched on picturesque narrows crossed by three bridges, the town has a collection of fine red-roofed houses and a lively waterfront packed with hundreds of yachts in summer. There's much development going on these days, with new pensions, eating places and other tourist facilities mushrooming.

The town is entirely geared to tourism and, like most other resorts of this kind, lives a high-speed life in July and August, takes it easy in June and September, and dies almost completely the rest of the year. As it lies on the main waterway linking Giżycko with Ruciane-Nida, and is the gateway to the vast Lake Śniardwy 3km south-east of the town, yacht traffic and excursion-boat services are very busy here in summer.

Two places within walking distance from Mikołajki, Popielno and the Łuknajno Reserve (detailed in the following sections), might be worth visiting if you're staying in town.

Information
The tourist office (☎/fax 21 68 50) is at Plac Wolności 3, the town's central square.

Several kantors in the centre change cash but there's nowhere to exchange travellers cheques. There's an ATM at Hotel Gołębiewski.

Yacht Charter
The Wioska Żeglarska PZŻ (☎ 21 60 40) at the waterfront has some sailing boats for hire and its staff may know who else has them. Other places include Agencja Sagit (☎ 21 64 70) in Hotel Wałkuski at ul 3 Maja 13A Propeller (☎ 21 69 10) at Plac

Kościelny 1; and Fun (☎ 21 62 77) at ul Kajki 82. See the Giżycko section for more information about yacht charter.

Places to Stay

Plenty of small pensions have sprung up over recent years, and a number of 'zimmer frei' boards appear in summer, indicating rooms available. The language used is the result of the massive increase of German tourism in Mikołajki and throughout the region. Many pensions simply list their prices in Deutschmarks. On the whole, prices are flexible and volatile. Try not to arrive late in the day in midsummer as you could be forced to pay a lot for your room.

The town's main camping ground, *Camping Nr 2 Wagabunda* (☎ 21 60 18, ul Leśna 2), is across the bridge from the centre and a 10 minute walk south-west. In addition to camping space it has plenty of small bungalows varying in standard and price. It's open from May to September.

The July-August *youth hostel* (☎ 21 64 34, ul Łabędzia 1) is in the large school next to the stadium, some 500m from the main square on the Łuknajno road. It's the cheapest place to stay, but it only has large dormitories and facilities are poor. The central *Cinema Quick Bar* (☎ 21 61 60) has several rooms for rent costing US$10 per person.

There are several pensions on ul Kajki, the main street that skirts Lake Mikołajskie, including *Pensjonat Król Sielaw* (☎ 21 63 23) at No 5; *Pensjonat Mikołajki* (☎ 21 63 25) at No 18; *Pensjonat na Skarpie* (☎ 21 64 18) at No 96; and *Pensjonat Wodnik* (☎ 21 61 41) at No 130. Except for the first one, they are all on the lake shore. Expect to pay around US$25/35 a single/double in any of them.

There's another collection of pensions on the town's outskirts on the road to Ruciane-Nida. They include *Pensjonat Iwa* (☎ 21 65 06), *Pensjonat Martyna* (☎ 21 68 85) and *Pensjonat Magda* (☎ 21 68 86). You will find more pensions on the road to Ełk past the train station.

There are two upmarket all-year hotels in the town's centre: *Hotel Mazur* (☎ 21 69 41, fax 21 69 43, Plac Wolności 6) at US$55 a double; and *Hotel Wałkuski* (☎/fax 21 66 28, ul 3 Maja 13) at US$60 to US$90 a double.

The largest and most expensive addition to the local lodging scene is the five-star 440-room *Hotel Gołębiewski* (☎ 21 65 17, fax 21 60 10, ul Mrągowska 34), across the bridge and a short walk to the north-west. Built in 1992, the hotel has three restaurants, a nightclub, indoor swimming pool, sauna, tennis courts, marina and an elderly clientele bused in from Germany. A double in summer costs around US$100. If you are not up to this, you may still be interested in the hotel's recreational facilities, which can be used by nonresidents, including the swimming pool (US$6 for 1½ hours).

Places to Eat

There are plenty of small eating outlets operating in summer in the town's centre and along the waterfront, and it doesn't take long to find somewhere for a pizza, fried fish or a pork chop.

Cinema Quick Bar (Plac Wolności 9) is inexpensive, as is *Bar Dino* next door. *Pensjonat Król Sielaw* has reasonable food. All the upmarket hotels listed above have their own restaurants, with the food prices roughly corresponding to the accommodation rates.

Getting There & Away

Train The sleepy train station is 1km from the centre on the Giżycko road. It handles three trains a day to Ełk and three to Olsztyn.

Bus The bus terminal is in the centre, near the large Protestant church. Buses to Mrągowo (25km) run roughly every hour; change there for Olsztyn or Kętrzyn. Several buses daily go to Giżycko (31km), and there are two buses to Suwałki (122km). Two or three fast buses depart in summer to Warsaw (224km) and are much faster than the trains.

Boat From May to September, boats ply the main routes from Mikołajki to Giżycko (US$10, three hours) and Ruciane (US$9, two hours), the round trip to Lake Śniardwy (US$7, 1½ hours), and combination routes (Mikołajki-Lake Śniardwy-Ruciane (US$10, 2½ hours).

ŁUKNAJNO RESERVE

The shallow 700 hectare Lake Łuknajno, 4km east of Mikołajki, shelters Europe's largest surviving community of wild swans (*Cygnus olor*) and is home to many other birds; 128 species have been recorded here. The 1200 to 2000 swans nest in April and May but stay at the lake all summer. A few observation towers beside the lake make viewing possible.

A rough road from Mikołajki goes to the lake but there's no public transport. Walk 3.5km until you get to a sign which reads 'do wieży widokowej' ('to the viewing tower'), directing you to the left. Continue for 10 minutes along the path through a meadow (can be muddy in spring and after rain) to the tower on the lake shore. Depending on the wind, the swans may be close to the tower or far away on the opposite side of the lake.

POPIELNO

The hamlet of Popielno, on the Śniardwy lake shore about 7km south-east of Mikołajki, is where the Polish Academy of Science has its research station and breeds various species of animals, including the **tarpan**, cousin of a wild horse which died out in the wild at the beginning of the 19th century.

A group of horses with characteristics close to those of the extinct horse were selected in the 1930s near Zamość (the Zamoyski family once had a zoo there – see the Roztocze National Park section in the Małopolska chapter) and bred in Białowieża. After WWII, Popielno took on the task of preserving the species. Today, there are about 500 tarpans in Poland, many of them bred in Popielno. Around 100 horses live here, some of them roaming freely in the surrounding forest while others are kept in large fenced enclosures in the grounds.

The research station also breeds the beaver, and has about 30 of them. There's also a deer farm, about 1km west of the research station.

The station offers modest *rooms* for about US$7 to US$10 per person but they are often full in season. Meals are provided for guests.

Getting There & Away

From Mikołajki, walk 5km south along the western shore of Lake Mikołajskie (follow the red trail), take the decrepit ferry across Lake Bełdany (operating from 7 am to 5 pm, but stopping at 2 pm on Sunday) to the village of Wierzba, and walk 1.5km from there to Popielno.

From Ruciane-Nida, there's a bus to Popielno (14km) around 6 am, and sometimes another one in the afternoon. There are more buses to Wejsuny (6km), from where it's a pleasant two-hour walk to Popielno.

RUCIANE-NIDA
- **pop 6000**   ☎ 087

Ruciane-Nida ('Roo-chah-neh Nee-dah') is the southernmost base for the Great Masurian Lakes. Set on the banks of two lakes, Guzianka Wielka and Nidzkie, the town is surrounded by forest. As the name suggests, it consists of two parts: Ruciane, the holiday resort; and, 2km to the south-west, Nida, a collection of dull apartment blocks around the local paper mill. The two parts are linked by Al Wczasów, which runs through woods and is lined with holiday homes. About 1.5km north of Ruciane is the Śluza Guzianka, the only lock on the Great Masurian Lakes.

Ruciane-Nida is not a great attraction in itself but is a good point to stop on your trans-Masurian journey. From here, excursion boats go north to Mikołajki and south to the beautiful Lake Nidzkie. There are several marked trails originating from Ruciane. You can also use the town as a jumping-off point for exploring the Puszcza

Piska (Pisz Forest), a vast area of thick woodland to the south-east. There are no marked trails there but many dirt tracks and paths crisscross the woods; some are OK for bikes. Ruciane is also a handy starting point for visiting the villages of Wojnowo and Popielno.

Places to Stay
The cheapest place around is *Dom Wycieczkowy PTTK* (☎ 23 10 06, ul Mazurska 14), a 10 minute walk north from the train station towards the Guzianka Lock. It's open year-round and offers beds in doubles/triples/quads for US$7. From June to September it also operates bungalows in the grounds (US$5 per bed).

Farther down the same road are two small pensions, *Pensjonat Janus* (☎ 23 64 50, ul Guzianka 1) and *Pensjonat Bełdan* (☎ 23 10 94, ul Guzianka 10). Both have reasonable doubles/triples with bath for about US$25/30.

Dom Wypoczynkowy FWP Perła Jezior (☎ 23 10 44, ul Wczasów 15) is a large holiday home that offers inexpensive rooms with shared facilities. The nearby *Ośrodek Turystyki Wodnej* (☎ 23 10 12, Al Wczasów 17) has a camp site and cabins, and handles kayak and sailing boat rental.

Places to Eat
There are two popular restaurants in Ruciane, *Restauracja Kormoran* and *Restauracja Warmianka*, next to each other on ul Dworcowa. In summer, a number of places open between the train station and the wharf, and several more on the road to Nida.

Getting There & Away
Train Ruciane lies on the Olsztyn-Ełk railway line and trains to both these destinations go regularly throughout the day. There are also connections to Gdańsk and Warsaw (once a day), plus an additional train to Warsaw in summer.

Bus There are six buses daily to Mrągowo (37km) and three to Mikołajki (22km). All go via Ukta where you can get off for Wojnowo. One or two buses daily go as far east as Suwałki.

An early morning bus goes to Popielno (14km); if you miss it take a bus to Wejsuny (6km) and walk the rest of the way through a beautiful forest.

Boat Excursion boats operate from May to September with additional ones from June to August. Two boats go daily to Mikołajki (US$9, two hours). There's also one boat to Mikołajki which makes a detour to Lake Śniardwy (US$10, 2½ hours). A few boats a day depart for round trips south around Lake Nidzkie (US$4, one hour).

WOJNOWO
The small village of Wojnowo ('Voy-no-vo'), 10km west of Ruciane-Nida, has Poland's only convent of the Starowiercy, or Old Believers, an almost unknown religious congregation, today dying out. The convent is on the shore of Lake Duś, about 1km south of the village. Its church is an unpretentious white-plastered structure and will usually be opened for you if you arrive at any reasonable time. In summer there's generally someone taking care of tourists. The interior is very modest, but there are some fine old icons and a beautiful 18th century chandelier. Behind the church is a tiny cemetery with simple, almost identical wooden crosses on the graves of the nuns.

In the village centre is the small Old Believers' church (*molenna*). The woman living in house No 48, diagonally opposite the church, has keys and will open it for you (leave a small donation). She speaks German and can give you some information about the church. There's no iconostasis inside; the icons are placed on the wall.

Getting There & Away
Wojnowo lies off the main roads and there are only a couple of buses from Ruciane-Nida (10km) which call at the village. If you don't want to wait, take any bus from Ruciane heading to Mikołajki, Mrągowo or Olsztyn, get off in the village of Ukta (7km)

The Old Believers

The Old Believers (Starowiercy or Staroobrzędowcy in Polish) are a religious group which split off after reforms were introduced in the Russian Orthodox Church around the middle of the 17th century. Opting for the traditional rites and rejecting the new order, they were excluded from the Church. Consequently they were condemned by the Moscow synods and by tsarist decree were excluded from the Church and persecuted. Some of them looked for shelter in the far eastern regions of Russia while others emigrated west to Poland and Sweden, to disperse later all over Europe.

In Poland, they initially settled in the Suwałki region, where they founded villages and built houses of worship. Of all those, only a few churches survive today, with a handful of followers spread over several settlements.

In the 1820s, in a new wave of migration from both the Suwałki region and Russia itself, they came to central Masuria. Here, too, they set about founding settlements and building churches, and in Wojnowo they established a monastery. It reached its heyday in the mid-19th century but later went into decline, and in 1884 closed down. The Old Believers' centre in Moscow reacted immediately; a young but enterprising nun was sent to Wojnowo and founded a convent. It developed steadily until WWI and, though it subsequently declined, it somehow managed to survive the turmoil of wars and persecution, and still exists today. There are two nuns currently living in the convent, both over 80 years of age.

The Old Believers reject ecclesiastical hierarchy and their clergy are elected at general meetings. In liturgy, they use the Old Church Slavonic language; all their liturgical and prayer books come from the prewar period. In everyday life, you can still hear old people speaking a strange hybrid of archaic Russian and Polish. They are strongly traditional and follow strict rules. They don't drink tea, coffee or wine, and don't smoke; some even eschew milk. There are still one or two thousand of them in Poland, but their numbers are diminishing.

and walk the remaining 3km south to Wojnowo.

Alternatively, take the bus west to Myszyniec via Spychowo, and ask the driver to set you down at the turn-off to Wojnowo (7km); then walk 1km north to the convent and another 1km to the village.

The Augustów-Suwałki Region

The far north-eastern corner of Poland, called Suwalszczyzna, is noted for its lakeland, but this one is quite different from the Great Masurian Lake District. Here the lakes (about 200 altogether) are smaller but deeper and even more crystal-clear than farther west. At 108m, Lake Hańcza is the deepest lake in the country, and perhaps in the whole Central European lowland. Forests cover only about 20% of the surface, but the terrain is diverse, with steep hills and deep valleys.

Suwalszczyzna is the coldest part of Poland: winter here is long and snow lies on the ground for 100 to 120 days a year. The average January temperature is -6°C, but during the occasional cold snap it may drop to -40°C. Summer is short, though the continental climate makes it pleasantly warm and even hot at times.

To the south, towards Augustów, the terrain becomes flatter and more forested. The area east of Augustów up to the national border is an uninterrupted stretch of woodland, the Augustów Forest (Puszcza

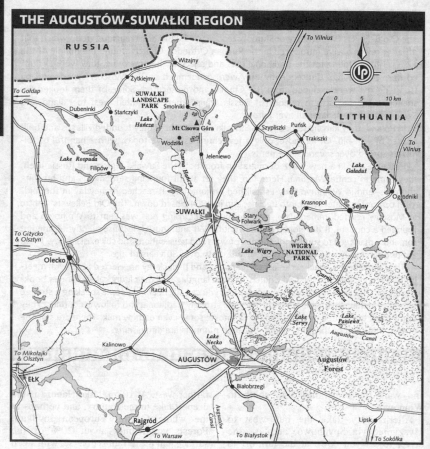

THE AUGUSTÓW-SUWAŁKI REGION

Augustowska), cut in two by the Augustów Canal (Kanał Augustowski).

Despite its natural beauty, the region is far less visited than the Great Masurian Lakes. Yachting is restricted, as the lakes are smaller and not connected by channels, but canoeists will be in their element on the local rivers, which are among the best in the country. Walking and cycling are good too, and the last vestiges of a complex ethnic mix are an added attraction.

The first inhabitants of this land were Jatzvingians (Jaćwingowie). They belonged to the same ethnic and linguistic family as the Prussians, Latvians and Lithuanians, and lived off farming, fishing and breeding livestock. They were also warlike, and a bit of a headache for the Mazovian dukes, as they invaded and ravaged the northern outskirts of the principality and not infrequently made their way farther south. On one occasion, in 1220, they got as far as Kraków. Their total population around that time is estimated to have been about 50,000.

In the second half of the 13th century, the Teutonic Knights expanded eastwards over the region, and by the 1280s they had wiped the tribe out completely, much as they had done earlier to the Prussians.

The region became a bone of contention between the Teutonic Order and Lithuania, and remained in dispute until the 16th century. At that time the territory formally became a Polish dominion but its colonisation was slow. Development was further hindered by the Swedish invasions of the 1650s and the catastrophic plague of 1710.

In the Third Partition of 1795, the region was swallowed by Prussia, and in 1815 it became a part of the Congress Kingdom of Poland, only to be grabbed by Russia after the failure of the November Insurrection of 1830. After WWI Poland took over the territory, not without resistance from Lithuania, but the region remained remote and economically unimportant, and in many ways still is.

Though today the population consists predominantly of Poles (with the exception of a small Lithuanian enclave centred in the village of Puńsk), it was for centuries an ethnic and religious mosaic comprising Poles, Lithuanians, Belarusians, Tatars, Germans, Jews and Russians. Traces of this complex cultural mix can still be found, at least in the local cemeteries.

There are only two important towns in the region, Augustów and Suwałki, which you may use as a base for further exploration. They are notably different from each other and provide access to quite different parts of the region.

AUGUSTÓW
- **pop 30,000** ☎ 087

Augustów ('Ow-goos-toof'), at the southern end of the region, is a small but sprawling town. It was founded in 1557 by King Zygmunt August and named after him. Located on the bank of the Netta River, the border between the Polish Crown and the Grand Duchy of Lithuania until

they were united between 1569 and 1795, the town had trading potential but grew painfully slowly. Even 150 years after its foundation, it had no more than 500 inhabitants. Its development really began in the 19th century after the construction of the Augustów Canal, and was further boosted when the Warsaw-St Petersburg railway was completed in 1862.

The 1944 battle over the region lasted for a couple of months, during which time the town switched from German to Russian hands several times and 70% of it was destroyed. Predictably, there's not much to see of the prewar architecture, nor are there many sights.

What the town itself lacks in terms of special attractions, you'll find in its surroundings. The beautiful Augustów Forest begins just on the eastern outskirts of the town and boasts the spectacular Czarna Hańcza River and the unusual Augustów Canal (see the Around Augustów section). The town is a handy base for these places and has become the most popular waterside centre in this corner of Poland.

Information

Tourist Office The Centrum Informacji Turystycznej Szot (☎ 643 28 83, ☎/fax 643 43 99), ul 3 Maja 39, is open weekdays 9 am to 4 pm (in July and August till 5 pm and also Saturday till 3 pm and Sunday till 1 pm). Apart from providing information, the office organises kayaking trips (see Organised Tours), rents out kayaks and canoes, and arranges private rooms.

Money Cash can be easily exchanged in any of several kantors, eg at the Orbis office on the Rynek. Travellers cheques are cashed at the Bank Przemysłowo Handlowy, the Powszechny Bank Kredytowy and the Bank Zachodni, but only the last one has a useful ATM.

Regional Museum
The most important sight in town, the Muzeum Ziemi Augustowskiej, is at two locations. The main section, featuring an

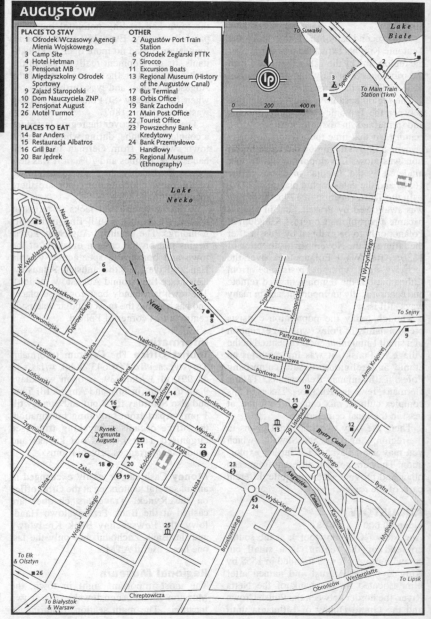

AUGUSTÓW

PLACES TO STAY
1 Ośrodek Wczasowy Agencji Mienia Wojskowego
3 Camp Site
4 Hotel Hetman
5 Pensjonat MB
8 Międzyszkolny Ośrodek Sportowy
9 Zajazd Staropolski
10 Dom Nauczyciela ZNP
12 Pensjonat August
26 Motel Turmot

PLACES TO EAT
14 Bar Anders
15 Restauracja Albatros
16 Grill Bar
20 Bar Jędrek

OTHER
2 Augustów Port Train Station
6 Ośrodek Żeglarski PTTK
7 Sirocco
11 Excursion Boats
13 Regional Museum (History of the Augustów Canal)
17 Bus Terminal
18 Orbis Office
19 Bank Zachodni
21 Main Post Office
22 Tourist Office
23 Powszechny Bank Kredytowy
24 Bank Przemysłowo Handlowy
25 Regional Museum (Ethnography)

ethnographic exhibition, is in the modern public library building on ul Hoża (open 9 am to 4 pm except Monday). The section dedicated to the history of the Augustów Canal is at ul 29 Listopada 5A, and is open in summer only; during the remaining part of the year, it can be opened on request for groups.

Boat Excursions

From May to September, excursion boats ply the surrounding lakes and a part of the Augustów Canal to the east of the town. All trips originate from the wharf (☎ 643 28 81) at ul 29 Listopada 7, and all are return journeys which deposit you back at the wharf.

The shortest trip (US$4, 1½ hours) will take you around the Necko and Rospuda lakes but doesn't go along the canal. More interesting are the cruises farther east along the canal system. The longest is the trip to Lake Gorczyckie (US$13, seven hours); the boat goes through two locks each way. It's scheduled on Wednesday in July and August only.

Organised Tours

The Czarna Hańcza River is the most popular kayaking spot in the region. The river is part of various kayaking routes, organised by several local tour operators including PTTK, Sirocco and Szot.

The Ośrodek Żeglarski PTTK (☎ 643 34 55, ☎/fax 643 38 50), ul Nadrzeczna 70A, was the first agency organising Czarna Hańcza trips, and it still runs tours along the same route. They are designed as a loop, beginning in Augustów and leading along the Augustów Canal as far as Lake Serwy and up to the northern end of this lake. The kayaks are then transported overland to the village of Wysoki Most on the Czarna Hańcza, from where the canoeists follow the river downstream to the Augustów Canal and return by the canal to Augustów.

PTTK runs trips daily from 20 June till mid-August, providing kayaks, accommodation and food along the way in waterside hostels (stanice wodne). The group consists of 24 people (12 kayaks). The trip takes 12

days at a rather leisurely pace and costs around US$220 per person, all-inclusive. Book in advance, though it's sometimes possible to get on a tour at short notice.

Sirocco (☎/fax 643 31 18), ul Zarzecze 5A, is PTTK's partner which runs the waterside hostels. It sells the same tours and can provide a guide speaking English or German, and also can organise other tours on request.

The Szot (which also handles tourist information) is the most flexible. It runs kayaking tours of four, seven and 10 days (US$80, US$140 and US$180 per person, respectively), and also offers one-day trips through arguably the most spectacular bit of the Czarna Hańcza, from Frącki to Rygol (25km). It will cost about US$12 per person in a group of 10.

You can do your own tour, hiring a kayak from any of the three agencies (US$5 per kayak a day). You can have it transported to a place of your choice for US$0.50 per kilometre from Augustów.

There are some less known kayaking routes, including the Rospuda River, from Lake Rospuda down to Augustów (68km), easily done in six days.

Places to Stay

There's a range of all-year hotels and hostels scattered all over the town, which is about 4km long from end to end. Also, plenty of holiday homes open in summer and are eager to accommodate individual tourists whenever they have vacancies. There are no posh hotels in town, and nothing is very expensive. The prices listed are for the high season.

It's perhaps a good idea to call at the Szot tourist office, which will have current information on what's available and can help in finding somewhere. It also handles accommodation in private homes (US$5 to US$8 per person).

Going from north to south, *Hotel Hetman* (☎/fax 644 53 45, ul Sportowa 1), close to the Augustów Port train station, offers acceptable standards for US$36 per double or triple with bath and also has some simpler doubles without bath for US$20. The building itself is a 1939 design by the Polish architect Maciej Nowicki, later co-designer of the United Nations building in New York.

The hotel runs a basic *camp site* opposite the entrance but it doesn't have cabins and the facilities are poor. There are a few primitive bivouac sites a few kilometres farther north on the Suwałki road. They are nicely located on a lake shore but have no sanitary facilities and are practically unattended.

Ośrodek Wczasowy Agencji Mienia Wojskowego (☎ 643 34 94), in a fine location on Lake Białe right behind the Augustów Port train station, charges US$7 per person in fairly good doubles or triples without bath.

Still cheaper but not as good is *Międzyszkolny Ośrodek Sportowy* (☎ 643 32 04, ul Zarzecze 1), which costs US$5 per bed in doubles, triples or quads, and US$4 in larger dorms. Bedsheets are extra.

Zajazd Staropolski (☎ 644 70 73, ul Armii Krajowej 28) doesn't provide great luxuries but is cheap: US$8 to US$10 per person in singles, doubles or triples. The nearby *Pensjonat August* (☎ 643 23 77, ul Piwna 8) looks more like a workers' hostel rather than a pension, but is not expensive either – US$8 a bed in doubles or triples. Appreciably better is the small *Pensjonat MB* (☎/fax 644 67 34, ul Spacerowa 4), which offers doubles/suites for US$30/40.

Dom Nauczyciela ZNP (☎/fax 643 20 21, ul 29 Listopada 9) is next to the wharf. It has reasonable singles/doubles/triples with bath for US$35/45/55, but singles/doubles without bath (US$20/25) are nothing special. All the prices include breakfast.

Motel Turmot (☎ 643 28 67, ☎/fax 643 20 57, ul Mazurska 4) on the town's southern outskirts has doubles without/with bath for US$20/32, and triples without bath for US$26.

Places to Eat

Some of the cheapest meals are served at *Bar Jędrek* (Rynek 8), a basic milk bar.

Grill Bar (Rynek 30) is slightly better and more pleasant, and costs a bit more. The cafeteria at *Dom Nauczyciela ZNP* is another inexpensive option. Possibly the best budget place around is the new *Bar Anders* (ul Mostowa 12D).

Restauracja Albatros (ul Mostowa 3) is arguably the best restaurant in town. Both *Motel Turmot* and *Hotel Hetman* run their own restaurants.

Getting There & Away

Train Augustów has two train stations, but both are a long way from the town centre. The minor Augustów Port station is a more convenient place to get off when you come, as it's closer to some of the hotels, but fast trains don't stop there. It doesn't even have a ticket office, so if you want to buy a ticket you need to go to the main Augustów station, 1km farther east.

There are three fast trains daily to Warsaw (282km). They all go via Sokółka and Białystok and cover the distance in about 4½ hours. The Orbis office at the Rynek will book and sell tickets. There are also four trains a day to Suwałki.

Bus You can get around the region more easily by bus. The bus terminal is on the southern side of the Rynek and handles frequent services (every hour or so) to Białystok (91km), Suwałki (31km) and Ełk (42km). There are four buses directly to Warsaw (243km); all come through from Suwałki and can be full. Five buses a day run to Sejny (43km) and five to Grajewo (42km).

AROUND AUGUSTÓW
Augustów Forest

The Augustów Forest (Puszcza Augustowska) stretches east of Augustów as far as the border with Lithuania and Belarus. At about 1100 sq km, it's Poland's largest continuous forest after the Bory Dolnośląskie in Lower Silesia. It's a remnant of the vast primeval forest which once covered much of this borderland of Poland and Lithuania.

The forest is made up mainly of pine and spruce, with colourful deciduous species such as birch, oak, elm, lime, maple and aspen. The wildlife is rich and diversified, and includes beaver, wild boar, wolves, deer and even some elk. Birds are also well represented and the lakes abound in fish. There are 55 lakes in the forest.

The forest was almost unexplored until the 17th century. Today there are paved roads, dust tracks and paths crisscrossing the woodland, yet large stretches remain almost untouched.

You can explore part of the forest using private transport; roads will take you along the Augustów Canal almost to the border. Many of the rough tracks are perfectly OK for bikes, and on foot you can get almost everywhere except the swamps. The detailed *Puszcza Augustowska* map (scale 1:70,000) shows all the roads, tracks and tourist trails.

Augustów Canal

A remarkable achievement of 19th century hydraulic engineering, the Augustów Canal (Kanał Augustowski) was built by the short-lived Congress Kingdom of Poland. It was intended to provide the country with an alternative outlet to the Baltic, since the lower Vistula was in the hands of the hostile Prussians, who imposed heavy customs barriers on the river trade. The project aimed to connect the tributaries of the Vistula with the Niemen River and to reach the Baltic Sea at the port of Ventspils in Latvia. Despite the roundabout route, this seemed to be the most viable way of getting goods abroad.

The Polish part of the waterway, the Augustów Canal, linking the Biebrza and Niemen rivers, was designed by an army engineer, General Ignacy Prądzyński, and built in an astonishingly short time during 1824-30 (final works continued till 1839). About 7000 people worked daily on the site. It was the largest transport project realised by the Congress Kingdom, and it was an engineering triumph. However, Poland was subjugated by Russia after the November Insurrection of 1830. The Russians were meant to build their part from the town of Kaunas via the Dubissa River up to Ventspils, but the work was never completed.

Linking lakes and stretches of river with artificial channels, the Augustów Canal is a 102km-long waterway (80km within present-day Polish borders). Its route includes 28km of lakes, 34km of canalised rivers and 40km of canal proper. There are 18 locks along the way (14 in Poland) to bridge the 55m change in water level (15m upwards followed by 40m downwards). The canal remains in its original form together with most of its archaic machinery.

The canal begins at the confluence of the Netta and Biebrza rivers and goes 33km north to Augustów through low and swampy meadows, partly using the bed of the Netta. It then continues eastwards through a chain of wooded lakes to the border. This part is the most spectacular.

The whole Polish stretch of the canal is navigable, but tourist boats from Augustów only go as far east as Lake Gorczyckie. By kayak, you can continue to the border, but the locks beyond Lake Gorczyckie are closed.

SUWAŁKI
- **pop 68,000**   ☎ 087

Suwałki ('Soo-vahw-kee') is the largest town in the region, and until 1998 was its provincial capital. In contrast to Augustów, Suwałki is not surrounded by lakes and forests, and is far less visited by travellers. There are no holiday homes here, nor much in the way of tourist facilities. It's just an ordinary town without much to see or do, a gateway to the surrounding countryside rather than a destination in itself.

Suwałki appeared on the map at the end of the 17th century as one of the villages established by the Camaldolese monks from Wigry. Isolated in this remote lakeland at the meeting point of different ethnic groups, its small multinational community grew slowly; at different times it included Jews, Lithuanians, Tatars, Russians and Germans, and there is still a tiny congregation of Old Believers.

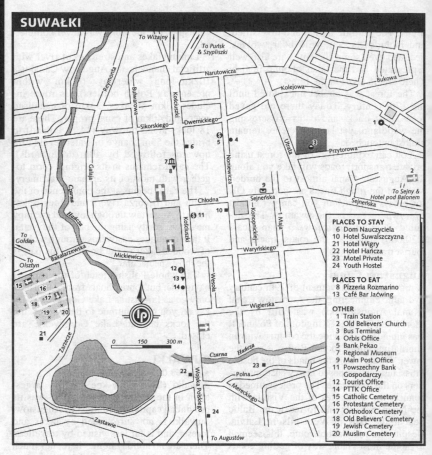

SUWAŁKI

PLACES TO STAY
6 Dom Nauczyciela
10 Hotel Suwalszczyzna
21 Hotel Wigry
22 Hotel Hańcza
23 Motel Private
24 Youth Hostel

PLACES TO EAT
8 Pizzeria Rozmarino
13 Café Bar Jaćwing

OTHER
1 Train Station
2 Old Believers' Church
3 Bus Terminal
4 Orbis Office
5 Bank Pekao
7 Regional Museum
9 Main Post Office
11 Powszechny Bank
  Gospodarczy
12 Tourist Office
14 PTTK Office
15 Catholic Cemetery
16 Protestant Cemetery
17 Orthodox Cemetery
18 Old Believers' Cemetery
19 Jewish Cemetery
20 Muslim Cemetery

Information

Tourist Office The Centrum Informacji Turystycznej (☎ 66 58 72, ☎/fax 66 54 94), is at ul Kościuszki 45, and is open weekdays 8 am to 4 pm (from mid-June to late August till 6 pm and also on Saturday 9 am to 2 pm).

Money Useful banks include the Bank Pekao at ul Noniewicza 95 and the Powszechny Bank Gospodarczy at ul Kościuszki 72, and both have ATMs.

Things to See

The local **cemetery** gives a good picture of the town's ethnic history. It actually consists of several cemeteries where people of different creeds were buried.

There must have been a large Jewish community, judging by the size of their graveyard; in fact, at the beginning of the 20th century they made up half the town's population. Their cemetery was destroyed in WWII and only a memorial stands in the middle, assembled out of fragments of old grave slabs. The tiny Muslim graveyard is the last remnant of the Tatars, but the graves are now hardly recognisable.

At the back of the Orthodox cemetery is the Old Believers' graveyard. A handful of followers still gather on Sunday at 6 am in their church *(molenna)* at ul Sejneńska 37A, on the opposite side of the town. The simple timber church dates from the beginning of the 20th century, but the icons inside are much older. Except during Mass, you have little chance of seeing them.

The main thoroughfare of the town, ul Kościuszki, retains some 19th century neoclassical architecture. Here you'll also find the **Regional Museum** (open Tuesday to Friday 8 am to 4 pm, Saturday and Sunday 10 am to 5 pm), which presents the little that is known of the Jatzvingian culture.

Organised Tours
The PTTK office (☎ 66 59 61, ☎/fax 66 79 47), ul Kościuszki 37, operates 12-day kayak trips down the Czarna Hańcza River. See the Augustów section for details. The office also rents out kayaks (US$5 a day) and will provide information if you want to do the trip on your own.

Places to Stay
For somewhere very cheap and basic, try the summer *youth hostel* (☎ 66 58 78, ul Wojska Polskiego 9). The next cheapest is *Hotel Wigry* (☎ 66 72 20, ul Zarzecze 26), next to the Jewish cemetery. It's simple but acceptable and costs US$14/18 a double/triple without bath. There's also the budget *Hotel pod Balonem* (☎ 66 54 16, ul Sejneńska 80) at US$15/20 a double/triple without bath, but it's a long way from the centre on the Sejny road.

The refurbished *Hotel Hańcza* (☎/fax 66 66 33, ☎/fax 66 66 44, ul Wojska Polskiego 2), near the youth hostel, lacks style but is otherwise perfectly OK and reasonably priced. It costs US$20/25/40 for singles/ doubles/triples with bath and breakfast.

Dom Nauczyciela (☎ 66 69 00, fax 66 60 28, ul Kościuszki 120) isn't significantly better but costs much more: US$40/50/55

with bath and breakfast. The small *Motel Private* (☎/fax 66 53 62, ul Polna 9) is probably better value. It offers just six double rooms, all with bath and satellite TV, for US$40 each. There's a possibility of pitching your tent in the garden.

The central *Hotel Suwalszczyzna* (☎/fax 65 19 00, ☎/fax 65 19 29, ul Noniewicza 71A) is the most recent addition to the local accommodation scene, and just about the best, at US$45/55/65 with bath and breakfast.

Places to Eat
One of the best budget places is *Café Bar Jaćwing* (ul Kościuszki 41). Also good is *Pizzeria Rozmarino* (ul Kościuszki 75), which apart from pizza has pasta and salads. Most hotels have their own eating facilities, and their standards reflect the class of the establishment: the restaurant at *Hotel Hańcza* is OK and inexpensive, the one at *Dom Nauczyciela* seems overpriced, and the one at *Hotel Suwalszczyzna* is perhaps the best in town.

Getting There & Away
The train station is 1.5km north-east of the centre; the bus terminal is a little closer to the central area. Trains are useful mostly for longer journeys, with several departures a day to Białystok and Warsaw. Getting around the region is easier by bus. Buses also ply longer routes: to Gdańsk (one bus daily), Olsztyn (three buses, all via Giżycko) and Warsaw (four). There's one bus a day to Vilnius in Lithuania (US$6, 5½ hours).

AROUND SUWAŁKI
Wigry National Park
☎ 087
The Wigry National Park (Wigierski Park Narodowy) covers the whole of Lake Wigry and a wide, predominantly forested belt of land around it, sprinkled with 50 or so small lakes. At 21 sq km, **Lake Wigry** is the largest lake in the region and one of the deepest, reaching 73m at its deepest point. It's also one of the most beautiful lakes. Its

shoreline is richly indented, forming numerous bays and peninsulas, and there are 15 islands on the lake. The Czarna Hańcza, a favourite among canoeists, flows through the park. The wildlife is diverse, with fish, birds and mammals, and the beaver is the park's emblem.

There is a **monastery** spectacularly located on a peninsula in Lake Wigry. It was built by Camaldolese monks (the monks of 'Memento Mori' – see the Bielany section in the Kraków chapter for more about them) soon after they were brought to Wigry by King Jan Kazimierz in 1667. The whole complex, complete with a church and 17 hermitages, was originally on an island, which was later connected to the shore. In 1795 the Prussians expelled the monks and confiscated the property, which by then covered 300 sq km and included over 30 villages. The monastery has been turned into a hotel, providing an atmospheric base for exploring the park.

There are marked trails throughout the park, which make it possible to visit more remote corners. You can even walk all round Lake Wigry (49km by the green trail), provided you have three days. Three or four lakeside *camp sites* along the trail are located within reasonable day-walking distances. You cannot camp anywhere else inside the park. If you are planning to walk in the park, the *Wigierski Park Narodowy* map (scale 1:46,000) shows the necessary detail.

The most popular access is from the Suwałki-Sejny road, which crosses the northern part of the park. In the village of Stary Folwark, 9km outside Suwałki, is the very basic *Dom Wycieczkowy PTTK* (☎ 67 97 27), where you can stay for around US$4 per head. The hostel operates a *camp site* from June to August on the lake shore. Buses between Suwałki and Stary Folwark run every hour till late.

If you want to go directly to the monastery, take the bus to Wigry (four buses per day in summer). The hotel, *Dom Pracy Twórczej* (☎ 16 42 49, ☎/fax 16 42 48), is open all year and provides meals. You have a choice of staying in the main building (US$40 a double with bath) or in the hermitages (US$25/30 a double/triple with bath).

Pensjonat Dowcień (☎ 16 42 22), on the road to Wigry, is a pleasant alternative, for US$35/40 a double/triple.

Sejny
- **pop 5000**   ☎ 087

Sejny, 30km east of Suwałki, is the last Polish town before the Ogrodniki border crossing to Lithuania, 12km beyond. The town has a Lithuanian consulate (☎ 16 22 73) at ul Piłsudskiego 28, your last chance to get a visa if you need one, though it's recommended to get one earlier.

The town grew around the Dominican monastery which had been founded in 1602 by the monks from Vilnius. The order was expelled by the Prussian authorities in 1804 and never returned, but the pastel silhouette of the **church** still proudly dominates the town from its northern end. It dates from the 1610s, but its façade was thoroughly remodelled 150 years later in the so-called Vilnius baroque style. Its interior has harmonious rococo decoration.

At the opposite, southern end of the town is a large **synagogue**, built by the sizable local Jewish community in the 1880s. During the German occupation it served as a fire station and after the war as a storage room. Today it's an **art gallery** operated by the 'Borderland' Foundation (Fundacja 'Pogranicze') which focuses on the arts and culture of different ethnic and religious traditions from the region. The staff organise concerts and theatre performances, and they also sell various publications on ethnic issues.

If you decide to stay overnight, the only place is *Hotel Skarpa* (☎ 16 20 65, ul Piłsudskiego 13) in the town centre, which has doubles/triples/quads without bath for US$18/22/25, doubles with bath for US$24; the hotel has a restaurant.

There are regular buses to Suwałki (30km), or you may venture north via a remote backwoods route up to Puńsk (25km, about five buses a day).

Puńsk

- **pop 1000**   ☎ 087

Puńsk is a Lithuanian village up near the Lithuanian border at the north-eastern edge of the region. Around 80% of its inhabitants are Lithuanians; they have their own school, cultural centre, folk music ensembles and press. The local parish church holds services in both Polish and Lithuanian.

Generally speaking, Lithuanians are a tiny minority in Poland, their total population estimated at 15,000 at most; the majority of them live in little villages scattered throughout this corner of the country, of which Puńsk is the largest.

Puńsk was on the Polish side of the border in the interwar period as well, but had a quite different ethnic make-up at that time: the majority were Jews (about 300 inhabitants), followed by Lithuanians (200) and a few Poles. Almost nothing is left of the Jewish legacy; their synagogue in the village centre is unrecognisable and the cemetery on the outskirts is in the state in which it was left at the end of the war.

The village has a noticeable eastern feel but otherwise is an ordinary place with no special monuments. You may want to see the Lithuanian **ethnographic museum** on ul Szkolna, close to the petrol station. It's largely the work of one man, Juozas Vaina, who collected most of the exhibits, set up the museum and now works as its curator. You'll probably have to call him at home (☎ 16 11 78) and arrange a visit.

The only place to stay and eat is *Kawiarnia Sodas* (☎ 16 13 15, ul Mickiewicza 17), which has a few rooms (US$10 per person) and serves meals, including some typical Lithuanian dishes.

Puńsk is linked to Suwałki (27km) by half a dozen buses daily and there are marginally fewer to Sejny (25km).

Suwałki Landscape Park

Established in 1976, the 63 sq km Suwałki Landscape Park (Suwalski Park Krajobrazowy) was the first nature reserve of that kind. It covers some of the most picturesque stretches of land in the region north of Suwałki, including 26 lakes (totalling 10% of the park's area) and patches of fine forest (another 24%).

A handy base for exploring the park is the village of Smolniki, 20km north of Suwałki. It's popular with hikers and there are several marked trails passing through the village. The local *youth hostel* (open July and August) will put you up for the night, but check whether it's open before you set off.

The Smolniki neighbourhood is rugged, largely wooded, and dotted with a dozen small lakes, and there are three good viewpoints in the village, which allow you to enjoy some of this landscape. One of the numerous walking options is an hour's walk west to **Lake Hańcza**, the deepest lake in the country (108.5m). With its steep shores, stony bottom and amazing crystal-clear water, it's like a mountain lake.

If you travel between Smolniki and Suwałki, it's worth stopping in Gulbieniszki at the foot of **Mt Cisowa Góra**. This 256m-high hill just off the road is cone-shaped like a volcano and provides a fine view over the surrounding lakes.

The *Suwalski Park Krajobrazowy i Okolice* map (scale 1:50,000) is good for exploring the area. It has all hiking trails marked on it and good sightseeing information in English on the reverse.

Stańczyki

☎ 087

Deep among forested hills close to the northern border, there's a pair of unusual bridges that rise out of the woods. Linking the steep sides of the valley of the Błędzianka River, 36m above water level, these two identical 180m-long constructions were built together just 15m apart.

The bridges were constructed in the 1910s by the Germans, in what was then the territory of East Prussia, as part of the 31km Gołdap-Żytkiejmy railway track destined for the transport of timber. An interesting technique was used: the concrete structure was strengthened with tree trunks sunk into it, thus reducing the steel reinforcement to a minimum. Later, the track was dismantled and the bridges were left behind. These huge, surrealistic sculptures in the middle of nowhere, with their tall pillars supporting wide, elegant classical arches, have the air of a Roman aqueduct.

Zajazd Stańczyki (☎ *15 81 72*), in the hamlet of Stańczyki ('Stahn-chi-kee') near the bridges, offers beds (US$8) in doubles, triples and quads, and has a snack bar which serves simple hot meals. In July and August, the scout camp near the bridges will probably let you pitch your tent and use its facilities. You might also eat in its canteen for next to nothing – talk

to the boss. The student camp Unikat at the foot of the bridges will also let you camp in the grounds, but has few facilities. If you prefer, you can camp virtually anywhere; many independent hikers choose the most romantic spots just under the bridges.

In July and August, there are two buses a day direct from Suwałki to Stańczyki. Alternatively, there's access from the Gołdap-Żytkiejmy road (serviced by about four buses daily in each direction). Get off at the turn-off to Stańczyki and walk 1.5km, and you'll see the bridges on your left. The Zajazd is about 500m farther down the road.

Language

Polish is a western variety of the Slavonic languages found in central and eastern Europe, such as Czech, Russian, Serbian-Croatian, Slovak and Slovene.

Ideally, everyone who wants to travel in Poland should know some basic Polish – the more you know the easier your travel is likely to be and the more you'll get out of your time in the country. This chapter gives pronunciation guidelines and some basic vocabulary to help you get around Poland.

For a more comprehensive guide to the language, a phrasebook and a small dictionary are essential. See the Books section in the Facts for the Visitor chapter for some suggestions.

The Polish Alphabet

Polish letters with diacritical marks are treated as separate letters, and the order of the Polish alphabet is as follows:

a ą b c ć d e ę f g h i j k l ł m n ń o ó p (q) r s ś t u (v) w (x) y z ź ż

The letters q, v and x appear only in words of foreign origin.

Pronunciation

Written Polish is phonetically consistent, which means that the pronunciation of letters or clusters of letters doesn't vary from word to word. The stress almost always goes on the second-last syllable.

Vowels

Polish vowels are pure, consisting of one sound only, and are of roughly even length. Their approximate pronunciation is as follows:

a	as the 'u' in 'cut'
e	as in 'ten'
i	similar to the 'ee' in 'feet' but shorter
o	as in 'not'
u	as in 'put'
y	similar to the 'i' in 'bit'

There are three vowels which are common only to Polish:

ą	a highly nasalised vowel; a cross between the 'awn' in 'lawn' and the 'ong' in 'long'
ę	also highly nasalised; like the 'eng' in 'engage' (where the 'ng' is one sound, not 'n' followed by 'g'); pronounced as e when word-final
ó	the same as Polish u

Consonants

Most Polish consonants are pronounced as in English. However, there are some very fine distinctions between certain consonants in Polish which English speakers may find difficult to produce. The following guide gives approximations only of the correct pronunciation – your best bet is to listen to and learn from native speakers:

c	as the 'ts' in 'its'
ch	similar to 'ch' in the Scottish *loch*
cz	as the 'ch' in 'church'
ć	similar to c but pronounced with the tongue a little further back on the roof of the mouth; pronounced as 'tsi' before vowels
dz	as the 'ds' in 'adds up'
dź	similar to dz but pronounced with the tongue a little further back on the roof of the mouth; pronounced as 'dzi' before vowels
dż	as the 'j' in 'jam'
g	as in 'get'
h	the same as ch
j	as the 'y' in 'yet'
ł	as the 'w' in 'wine'
ń	as the 'ni' in 'onion'; written as 'ni' before vowels
r	always trilled
rz	as the 's' in 'pleasure'

s   as in 'set'
sz   as the 'sh' in 'show'
ś   similar to **s** but not as strident; written as 'si' before vowels
w   as the 'v' in 'van'
ź   similar to **z** but not as strident; written as 'zi' before vowels
ż   the same as **rz**
szcz the most awful-looking cluster; pronounced as the 'shch' in 'fresh cheese'

The following consonants are unvoiced when they are word-final: **b** is pronounced as **p**, **d** as **t**, **g** as **k**, **w** as **f**, **z** as **s** and **rz** as **sz**.

Finally, here's the favourite Polish tongue-twister for you to test your pronunciation skills on: *Chrząszcz brzmi w trzcinie* (The cockchafer buzzes in the weeds).

Greetings & Civilities

Good morning.	*Dzień dobry.*
Good evening.	*Dobry wieczór.*
Hello.	*Cześć.* (informal)
Goodbye.	*Do widzenia.*
Good night.	*Dobranoc.*
Yes.	*Tak.*
No.	*Nie.*
Please.	*Proszę.*
Thank you (very much).	*Dziękuję (bardzo).*
You're welcome.	*Proszę.*
How are you?	*Jak się Pan/ Pani miewa?* (m/f)
Very well, thank you.	*Dziękuję, bardzo dobrze.*
May I?	*Czy mogę?*
Excuse me/ I'm sorry.	*Przepraszam.*
OK.	*Dobrze.*

Basics

I	*ja*
you	*ty*
he/she	*on/ona*
we	*my*
you	*wy*
they	*oni/one*
What?	*Co?*
Where?	*Gdzie?*
When?	*Kiedy?*
Who?	*Kto?*
Why?	*Dlaczego?*
How?	*Jak?*
and	*i*
Mrs/Madam	*Pani*
Mister/Sir	*Pan*

Language Difficulties

Do you speak English?	*Czy Pan/Pani mówi po angielsku?* (m/f)
Does anyone here speak English?	*Czy ktoś tu mówi po angielsku?*
I don't speak Polish.	*Nie mówię po polsku.*
I understand.	*Rozumiem.*
I don't understand.	*Nie rozumiem.*
Please speak more slowly.	*Proszę mówić wolniej.*
Could you repeat that please?	*Proszę to powtórzyć.*
What does it mean?	*Co to znaczy?*
Please write that down.	*Proszę to napisać.*
How do you pronounce it?	*Jak się to wymawia?*

Getting Around

What time does the ... leave/ arrive?	*O której godzinie przychodzi/ odchodzi ...?*
plane	*samolot*
boat	*statek*
bus	*autobus*
train	*pociąg*
tram	*tramwaj*
Where is (the) ...?	*Gdzie jest ...?*
airport	*lotnisko*
train station	*stacja kolejowa*
bus station	*dworzec autobusowy*
bus stop	*przystanek autobusowy*
petrol station	*stacja benzynowa*
Two tickets to ... please.	*Poproszę dwa bilety do ...*
ticket	*bilet*
ticket office	*kasa biletowa*

timetable	*rozkład jazdy*
1st/2nd class	*pierwsza/druga klasa*
next	*następny*
first	*pierwszy*
last	*ostatni*
arrival	*przyjazd*
departure	*odjazd*
left-luggage room	*przechowalnia bagażu*
How can I get to ...?	*Jak się dostać do ...?*
How far is it?	*Jak to daleko stąd?*
Please show me on the map.	*Proszę pokazać mi to na mapie.*
Turn left.	*Proszę skręcić w lewo.*
Turn right.	*Proszę skręcić w prawo.*
Go straight ahead.	*Proszę iść prosto.*
Where can I hire a ...?	*Gdzie mogę wypożyczyć ...?*
car	*samochód*
motorbike	*motocykl*
bicycle	*rower*

Out & About

town, city	*miasto*
village	*wieś*
road	*szosa, droga*
street	*ulica*
city centre	*centrum*
bridge	*most*
castle	*zamek*
cathedral	*katedra*
church	*kościół*
embassy	*ambasada*
monastery	*klasztor*
monument	*pomnik*
museum	*muzeum*
old town	*stare miasto*
old town square	*rynek*
open-air museum	*skansen*
palace	*pałac*
police station	*posterunek policji*
public toilet	*toaleta publiczna*
square	*plac*
synagogue	*synagoga*
town hall	*ratusz*
university	*uniwersytet*

Signs

WEJŚCIE	**ENTRANCE**
WYJŚCIE	**EXIT**
INFORMACJA	**INFORMATION**
OTWARTE	**OPEN**
ZAMKNIĘTE	**CLOSED**
WZBRONIONY	**PROHIBITED**
POSTERUNEK POLICJI	**POLICE STATION**
TOALETY	**TOILETS**
PANOWIE	**MEN**
PANIE	**WOMEN**

beach	*plaża*
cave	*jaskinia*
coast	*wybrzeże*
forest	*las/puszcza*
island	*wyspa*
lake	*jezioro*
mountain	*góra*
river	*rzeka*
valley	*dolina*
waterfall	*wodospad*

Accommodation

Do you have any rooms available?	*Czy są wolne pokoje?*
May I see the room?	*Czy mogę zobaczyć pokój?*
How much is it?	*Ile kosztuje?*
Does it include breakfast?	*Czy śniadanie jest wliczone?*
hotel	*hotel*
youth hostel	*schronisko młodzieżowe*
room	*pokój*
dormitory	*sala zbiorowa*
bathroom	*łazienka*
bed	*łóżko*
key	*klucz*
sheets	*pościel*
shower	*prysznic/natrysk*
toilet	*toaleta*
cheap/expensive	*tani/drogi*
clean/dirty	*czysty/brudny*

LANGUAGE

good/poor, bad	*dobry/niedobry*
noisy/quiet	*głośny/cichy*
hot/cold	*gorący/zimny*

Post & Communications

post office	*poczta*
postcard	*pocztówka*
letter	*list*
parcel	*paczka*
stamp	*znaczek*
air mail	*poczta lotnicza*
registered letter	*list polecony*
letter box	*skrzynka pocztowa*
international call	*rozmowa międzynarodowa*
long distance call	*rozmowa międzymiastowa*
public telephone	*automat telefoniczny*
telephone card	*karta telefoniczna*
token	*żeton*

Money

bank	*bank*
money	*pieniądze*
cash	*gotówka*
travellers cheque	*czek podróżny*
commission	*prowizja*
credit card	*karta kredytowa*
ATM	*bankomat*

Shopping

Do you have ...?	*Czy są ...?*
How much is it?	*Ile to kosztuje?*
I (don't) like it.	*(Nie) podoba mi się.*
shop	*sklep*
shopping centre	*centrum handlowe*
market	*targ/bazar*
pharmacy	*apteka*
price	*cena*
cheap/expensive	*tani/drogi*
big/small	*duży/mały*
many/much	*dużo*
a few	*kilka*
a little	*trochę*
enough	*wystarczy*
more/less	*więcej/mniej*

Food

Only some basic words are given here. See the Food and Drinks sections in the Facts for the Visitor chapter for more terms.

I'm a vegetarian.	*Jestem jaroszem.*
the bill	*rachunek*
cup	*filiżanka*
dish	*danie*
fork	*widelec*
glass	*szklanka*
knife	*nóż*
menu	*jadłospis*
plate	*talerz*
spoon	*łyżka*
teaspoon	*łyżeczka*
bread	*chleb*
butter	*masło*
egg	*jajko*
fish	*ryba*
fruit	*owoce*
ham	*szynka*
meat	*mięso*
milk	*mleko*
pepper	*pieprz*
potatoes	*ziemniaki*
rice	*ryż*
salad	*sałatka, surówka*
salt	*sól*
sandwich	*kanapka*
sausage	*kiełbasa*
sugar	*cukier*
vegetables	*warzywa, jarzyny*
water	*woda*

Time, Dates & Numbers

What is the time?	*Która godzina?*
time	*czas*
now	*teraz*
today	*dzisiaj, dziś*
tonight	*dziś wieczorem*
tomorrow	*jutro*
yesterday	*wczoraj*
this week	*w tym tygodniu*
next week	*w przyszłym tygodniu*
last week	*w zeszłym tygodniu*
morning/afternoon	*rano/popołudnie*
evening/night	*wieczór/noc*

Emergencies

Please call a doctor/the police.
  Proszę wezwać lekarza/policję.
Where is the nearest hospital?
  Gdzie jest najbliższy szpital?
Could you help me please?
  Proszę mi pomóc.
I don't feel well.
  Źle się czuję.
I have a fever.
  Mam gorączkę.
Could I use the telephone?
  Czy mogę skorzystać z telefonu?
I want to contact my embassy.
  *Chcę się skontaktować z moją
  ambasadą.*
Please leave me alone!
  Proszę mnie zostawić!

accident	*wypadek*
ambulance	*karetka pogotowia*
dentist	*dentysta*
doctor	*lekarz*
hospital	*szpital*
medicine	*lek/lekarstwo*
police	*policja*

August	*sierpień*
September	*wrzesień*
October	*październik*
November	*listopad*
December	*grudzień*
summer/autumn	*lato/jesień*
winter/spring	*zima/wiosna*
¼	*jedna czwarta*
½	*jedna druga*
0	*zero*
1	*jeden*
2	*dwa*
3	*trzy*
4	*cztery*
5	*pięć*
6	*sześć*
7	*siedem*
8	*osiem*
9	*dziewięć*
10	*dziesięć*
11	*jedenaście*
12	*dwanaście*
13	*trzynaście*
14	*czternaście*
15	*piętnaście*
16	*szesnaście*
17	*siedemnaście*
18	*osiemnaście*
19	*dziewiętnaście*
20	*dwadzieścia*
21	*dwadzieścia jeden*
22	*dwadzieścia dwa*
30	*trzydzieści*
100	*sto*
1000	*tysiąc*
100,000	*sto tysięcy*
one million	*milion*

midday/midnight	*południe/północ*
sunrise/sunset	*wschód/zachód*
minute/hour	*minuta/godzina*
day/week	*dzień/tydzień*
month/year	*miesiąc/rok*
Monday	*poniedziałek*
Tuesday	*wtorek*
Wednesday	*środa*
Thursday	*czwartek*
Friday	*piątek*
Saturday	*sobota*
Sunday	*niedziela*
January	*styczeń*
February	*luty*
March	*marzec*
April	*kwiecień*
May	*maj*
June	*czerwiec*
July	*lipiec*

1st	*pierwszy*
2nd	*drugi*
3rd	*trzeci*
percent	*procent*
once	*raz*
twice	*dwa razy*
three times	*trzy razy*
often/seldom	*często/rzadko*

Glossary

You may encounter the following terms and abbreviations in your travels throughout Poland. For further Polish terms, see the previous Language chapter, the Food and Drink sections in Facts for the Visitor, and the Getting Around chapter.

Aleja or **Aleje** – avenue, main city street; abbreviated to Al in addresses and on maps
Almatur – the nationwide Student Travel & Tourist Bureau

bankomat – ATM
bar mleczny – milk bar; a sort of self-service basic soup kitchen which serves very cheap, mostly vegetarian dishes
barszcz – beetroot soup; one of Poland's national dishes
basen – swimming pool
bigos – sauerkraut and meat; another national dish
bilet – ticket
biuro turystyczne – travel agency
biuro zakwaterowania – office that arranges private accommodation

Cepelia – a network of shops that sell artefacts made by local artisans
cerkiew – (plural *cerkwie*); an Orthodox or Uniate church
cocktail bar – type of café that serves cakes, pastries, milk shakes, ice creams and other sweets
cukiernia – cake shop

Desa – state-owned chain of old art and antique sellers
dom kultury – cultural centre
dom wczasowy or **dom wypoczynkowy** – holiday home
dom wycieczkowy – term applied to PTTK-run hostels
domek campingowy – cabin, bungalow, chalet

grosz – unit of Polish currency; abbreviated to gr; see also *złoty*

jadłospis – menu

kantor – private currency-exchange office
kasa – ticket office
kawiarnia – café
kino – cinema
kiosk Ruch – newsagency
kolegiata – collegiate church
kościół – church
kościół farny – parish church
księgarnia – bookshop
kwatery agroturystyczne – agrotourist accommodation; increasingly numerous and popular
kwatery prywatne – rooms in private houses rented out to tourists

LOT – Polish Airlines

miejscówka – reserved seat ticket
miód pitny – mead; a traditional Polish beverage obtained by fermentation of malt in honeyed water

na zdrowie! – cheers!; literally, to the health; what Poles say before drinking

odjazdy – departures (on transport schedules)
Orbis – the largest travel/tourist company in Poland
otwarte – open

pensjonat – pension or private guesthouse, usually small
peron – railway platform
piekarnia – bakery
pierogi – dumplings made from noodle dough, stuffed and boiled
PKP (Polskie Koleje Państwowe) – Polish State Railways
PKS (Państwowa Komunikacja Samochodowa) – the state bus company

poczta – post office
Polonia – general term applied to the Polish community living outside Poland
powiat – sub-province; a unit of administrative division
pralnia – dry cleaner
prowizja – the commission banks charge on transactions
przechowalnia bagażu – left-luggage room
przychodnia – outpatient clinic
przyjazdy – arrivals (on transport schedules)
PTSM – Polish Youth Hostel Association
PTTK – Polish Tourists Association
PZM or **PZMot** (Polski Związek Motorowy) – Polish Motoring Association

rachunek – bill or check
rozkład jazdy – transport timetable
Rynek – Old Town Square

schronisko górskie – mountain refuge, usually run by PTTK
schronisko młodzieżowe – youth hostel
Sejm – lower house of Poland's parliament
skansen – open-air museum of traditional architecture
sklep – shop
smacznego – preprandial civility; *bon appétit*
specjalność zakładu – on a menu, speciality of the house

stanica wodna – waterside hostel, usually with boats, kayaks and related facilities
stołówka – canteen; restaurant or cafeteria of a holiday home, hostel etc
szlachta – gentry or feudal nobility in 17th to 18th century Poland

Święty/a – Saint; abbreviated to Św (St)
Święty Mikołaj – Santa Claus

ulgowy (bilet) – reduced or discounted (ticket)
ulica – street; abbreviated to ul in addresses (and placed before the actual name); usually omitted on maps

wódka – vodka; the No 1 Polish brew
województwo – province; unit of administrative division (there are 16 in Poland), further divided into smaller territorial entities called *powiat*

zakaz wstępu – no entry
zamknięte – closed
zdrój – spa
złoty – the unit of Polish currency; abbreviated to zł; divided into 100 units called *grosz*
zniżka studencka – student discount

żeton – token used to make calls from public telephones
żubr – the European bison

Alternative Place Names

E – English   G – German

Brzeg – Brieg (G)
Brzezinka – Birkenau (G)
Bydgoszcz – Bromberg (G)
Bystrzyca Kłodzka – Habelschwerdt (G)
Chełmno – Kulm (G)
Częstochowa – Tschenstochau (G)
Elbląg – Elbing (G)
Frombork – Frauenburg (G)
Gdańsk – Danzig (G)
Gdynia – Gdingen (G)
Giżycko – Lötzen (G)
Gniezno – Gnesen (G)
Grudziądz – Graudenz (G)
Jelenia Góra – Hirschberg (G)
Kalisz – Kalisch (G)
Kamienna Góra – Landeshut (G)
Kamień Pomorski – Cammin (G)
Kartuzy – Karthaus (G)
Katowice – Kattowitz (G)
Kętrzyn – Rastenburg (G)
Kłodzko – Glatz (G)
Kołobrzeg – Kolberg (G)
Koszalin – Köslin (G)
Kościerzyna – Berent (G)
Kraków – Krakau (G) – Cracow (E)
Kwidzyn – Marienwerder (G)
Legnica – Liegnitz (G)
Lidzbark Warmiński – Heilsberg (G)
Lwów – Lemberg (G) – Lviv (E)
Łódź – Lodsch (G)
Malbork – Marienburg (G)
Małopolska – Little Poland (E)

Mazowsze – Mazovia (E)
Mazury – Masuria (E)
Mikołajki – Nikolaiken (G)
Nowy Sącz – Neusandez (G)
Nysa – Neisse (G)
Odra – Oder (G)
Olsztyn – Allenstein (G)
Opole – Oppeln (G)
Ostróda – Osterode (G)
Oświęcim – Auschwitz (G)
Pomorze – Pommern (G) – Pomerania (E)
Poznań – Posen (G)
Pszczyna – Pless (G)
Ruciane-Nida – Rudschanny (G)
Słupsk – Stolp (G)
Sopot – Zoppot (G)
Stębark – Tannenberg (G)
Szczecin – Stettin (G)
Śląsk – Schlesien (G) – Silesia (E)
Świdnica – Schweidnitz (G)
Świnoujście – Swinemünde (G)
Toruń – Thorn (G)
Trzebnica – Trebnitz (G)
Wałbrzych – Waldenburg (G)
Warmia – Ermeland (G)
Warszawa – Warschau (G) – Warsaw (E)
Węgorzewo – Angerburg (G)
Wielkopolska – Great Poland (E)
Wilczy Szaniec – Wolfschanze (G) – Wolf's Lair (E)
Wisła – Weichsel (G) – Vistula (E)
Wrocław – Breslau (G)
Zielona Góra – Grünberg (G)

Acknowledgments

THANKS

Many thanks to the travellers who used the last edition and wrote to us with helpful hints, useful advice and interesting anecdotes:

Solli, Michelle, Beatrice Allen, Mark Allingham, Aaron Alton, Jorgen Alving, Nicholas Anchen, Peter Aspinall, Michelle Austin, Artur Babecki, Stephen Barnard, KBJ & Dr J Belza, Jill Bennett, Ben Bergonzi, Richard Beswick, David N Biacsi, Jordan Blackman, Dennis Blazey, Cilla Bohlund, Jerry Bollfrass, Jill Bowden, Braun, Christopher & Janet Brookes, Jeroen Bruggeman, Trevor Butcher, Steven Butler, Daniel S Byer, Flouis Bylsma, Gill Callaghen, Jeff Kolano Callon, Annelise Carleton, Jason Chapple, Dave Chippendale, Marek Ciennik, Tammy Colebrook, Lisa Collecott, Ian Collier, Delta M Compo, Liam Connolly, Louise Cowcher, Ake Dahllot, Alicia Darvall, Dave Depooter, Barbara Deskiewicz, Kristian Dillenburger, Nick Diouoyniotis, Jeff & Julie Dobslaw, Gavin Doyle, Richard Draper, Paul Drooks, Leon PJ Drysdale, Kelly Duffy, Mavra Dundon, Michael Eckert, Fatima Entckhabi, Gert Eriksson, Natè Espino, Sheila Eustace, Ian Fair, B Filion, Ralph Fitchett, Tracey Ford, Marianne Fuchs, Brandon Furman, Daphne Gallagher, Alisoun Gardner-Medwin, Lyall C Gibb, Traci Gleason, Felix Godwin, Owen Goldfarb, Lynne & David Golding, Arron & Kirsten Goodwin, Ravi Gowda, Chris Greenwood, Owen Groves, Genevieve Guay, Elio Gutierrez, Robert Gwalkoniak, Michael Hall, Beatrice Hebersen & students, Sarah Heckscher, Lorenz A Heinze, Jelka Hopster, Bob Huber, Claudia Hueppmeier, Martin Hula, Marta Huscall, Tomasz Jelen, Pamela Johson, Myrddin Jones, Jay & Stefanie Jordan, Martyn & Nel Kaal, Ann & Alna Keenan, Gavan Kierans, K Klidzia, Christian Knappe, Stefan Korski, Roeland Krul, Hartmut Kuhne, M Kulowski Sr, Mike Kulowski, PM Lajeunesse, Ronald Leganger, Bill Lehman, Manfred Lenzen, Vincent & Susan Lewonski, Jadwiga Lopata, B Mackinnon-Little, M&J Malkiewicz, Thomas Martin, Miguel Herrera Martinez, Irving Massey, K McDowell, John Michasiuk, Fabiano Koich Miguel, Simon Miller, Elzbeta Mitura, Fiona Mooniariech, Stacja Morska, Penny Moyes, Margot Munzer, Jameela Naseem, Nahid Nasscri, Chris Nelson, Pawel Neugebauer, Batek Nitka, Dave Norris, Jane O'Connell, Katarina en Dick Oosthoek, David O'Reyan, RN Paech, Lee Palmer, Alec Parkin, Stephen Paton, Mike Penrith, William Pentony, Dariusz Piotrowski, William D Preston, Sophia Pugsley, Chad Garrett Randl, Anin Rattan, Jack Richards, Simon Rideout, Davina Rippon, Clifford Rogers, Piotr Romanowski, Kang Rong, Magdalena Rybka, Piotr Rybka, Valerie Rzepka, Marcin Sadurski, Gladys Saenz, R Samuelson, Dorota Sarska, Nigel Saynor, Vicki Schwidden, Teresa Scollon, The Secher Family, Oliver Selwyn, Mary Jane Sheffet, Ellen Skarsgard, PJM van der Sloot, Peter Sluijter, George Soranidis, Vicky Southgate, Juldborg Sovik, Phiana Stanley, George Steed, Rudolfvon Stein, Nicole Stewart, Mildred Stone, Sarah Stratton, Bobbie Strich, Ken Swain, Prof Nancy Swanson, Chris Swiderski, Barbara Szczepanik, Deborah Thatcher, Brian Todd, Janet Tomkins, Arto Tuominen, Marek Verhoeven, Carl R Walkanshaw, Malcolm Wallace, Sally Watkins, Katherine Watson, Arnold Watson, Claire Weetman, Frederic Wehowski, Bill Wein, Jan Werbinski, Marek Wesolowski, Ian Wheeler, Jarek Wieczorek, Di Wilson, C Wolf, Piers Wood, Philip G Woodward, C Worrall, Richard J Wyber, Harry Zaski, Arek Zawada, Frans JL Zegers, Carolyn Zukowski

LONELY PLANET

Phrasebooks

L onely Planet phrasebooks are packed with essential words and phrases to help travellers communicate with the locals. With colour tabs for quick reference, an extensive vocabulary and use of script, these handy pocket-sized language guides cover day-to-day travel situations.

- handy pocket-sized books
- easy to understand Pronunciation chapter
- clear & comprehensive Grammar chapter
- romanisation alongside script to allow ease of pronunciation
- script throughout so users can point to phrases for every situation
- full of cultural information and tips for the traveller

'...vital for a real DIY spirit and attitude in language learning'
– Backpacker

'the phrasebooks have good cultural backgrounders and offer solid advice for challenging situations in remote locations'
– San Francisco Examiner

Arabic (Egyptian) • Arabic (Moroccan) • Australian *(Australian English, Aboriginal and Torres Strait languages)* • Baltic States *(Estonian, Latvian, Lithuanian)* • Bengali • Brazilian • Burmese • Cantonese • Central Asia • Central Europe *(Czech, French, German, Hungarian, Italian, Slovak)* • Eastern Europe *(Bulgarian, Czech, Hungarian, Polish, Romanian, Slovak)* • Ethiopian (Amharic) • Fijian • French • German • Greek • Hill Tribes • Hindi/Urdu • Indonesian • Italian • Japanese • Korean • Lao • Latin American Spanish • Malay • Mandarin • Mediterranean Europe *(Albanian, Croatian, Greek, Italian, Macedonian, Maltese, Serbian, Slovene)* • Mongolian • Nepali • Papua New Guinea • Pilipino (Tagalog) • Quechua • Russian • Scandinavian Europe *(Danish, Finnish, Icelandic, Norwegian, Swedish)* • South-East Asia *(Burmese, Indonesian, Khmer, Lao, Malay, Tagalog Pilipino, Thai, Vietnamese)* • Spanish (Castilian) *(also includes Catalan, Galician and Basque)* • Sri Lanka • Swahili • Thai • Tibetan • Turkish • Ukrainian • USA *(US English, Vernacular, Native American languages, Hawaiian)* • Vietnamese • Western Europe *(Basque, Catalan, Dutch, French, German, Greek, Irish)*

Lonely Planet Journeys

J UURNEYS is a unique collection of travel writing – published by the company that understands travel better than anyone else. It is a series for anyone who has ever experienced – or dreamed of – the magical moment when they encountered a strange culture or saw a place for the first time. They are tales to read while you're planning a trip, while you're on the road or while you're in an armchair in front of a fire.

These outstanding titles explore our planet through the eyes of a diverse group of international writers. JOURNEYS books catch the spirit of a place, illuminate a culture, recount a crazy adventure or introduce a fascinating way of life. They always entertain, and always enrich the experience of travel.

MALI BLUES
Traveling to an African Beat
Lieve Joris (translated by Sam Garrett)

Drought, rebel uprisings, ethnic conflict: these are the predominant images of West Africa. But as Lieve Joris travels in Senegal, Mauritania and Mali, she meets survivors, fascinating individuals charting new ways of living between tradition and modernity. With her remarkable gift for drawing out people's stories, Joris brilliantly captures the rhythms of a world that refuses to give in.

THE GATES OF DAMASCUS
Lieve Joris (translated by Sam Garrett)

This best-selling book is a beautifully drawn portrait of day-to-day life in modern Syria. Through her intimate contact with local people, Lieve Joris draws us into the fascinating world that lies behind the gates of Damascus. Hala's husband is a political prisoner, jailed for his opposition to the Assad regime; through the author's friendship with Hala we see how Syrian politics impacts on the lives of ordinary people.

THE OLIVE GROVE
Travels in Greece
Katherine Kizilos

Katherine Kizilos travels to fabled islands, troubled border zones and her family's village deep in the mountains. She vividly evokes breathtaking landscapes, generous people and passionate politics, capturing the complexities of a country she loves.

'beautifully captures the real tensions of Greece' – *Sunday Times*

KINGDOM OF THE FILM STARS
Journey into Jordan
Annie Caulfield

Kingdom of the Film Stars is a travel book and a love story. With honesty and humour, Annie Caulfield writes of travelling in Jordan and falling in love with a Bedouin with film-star looks.

She offers fascinating insights into the country – from the tent life of traditional women to the hustle of downtown Amman – and unpicks tight-woven western myths about the Arab world.

LONELY PLANET

Lonely Planet Travel Atlases

Lonely Planet has long been famous for the number and quality of its guidebook maps. Now we've gone one step further and produced a handy companion series: Lonely Planet travel atlases – maps of a country produced in book form.

Unlike other maps, which look good but lead travellers astray, our travel atlases have been researched on the road by Lonely Planet's experienced team of writers. All details are carefully checked to ensure the atlas corresponds with the equivalent Lonely Planet guidebook.

- full-colour throughout
- maps researched and checked by Lonely Planet authors
- place names correspond with Lonely Planet guidebooks
- no confusing spelling differences
- legend and travelling information in English, French, German, Japanese and Spanish
- size: 230 x 160 mm

Available now: Chile & Easter Island • Egypt • India & Bangladesh • Israel & the Palestinian Territories • Jordan, Syria & Lebanon • Kenya • Laos • Portugal • South Africa, Lesotho & Swaziland • Thailand • Turkey • Vietnam • Zimbabwe, Botswana & Namibia

---

Lonely Planet TV Series & Videos

Lonely Planet travel guides have been brought to life on television screens around the world. Like our guides, the programs are based on the joy of independent travel, and look honestly at some of the most exciting, picturesque and frustrating places in the world. Each show is presented by one of three travellers from Australia, England or the USA and combines an innovative mixture of video, Super-8 film, atmospheric soundscapes and original music.

Videos of each episode – containing additional footage not shown on television – are available from good book and video shops, but the availability of individual videos varies with regional screening schedules.

Video destinations include: Alaska • American Rockies • Australia – The South-East • Baja California & the Copper Canyon • Brazil • Central Asia • Chile & Easter Island • Corsica, Sicily & Sardinia – The Mediterranean Islands • East Africa (Tanzania & Zanzibar) • Ecuador & the Galapagos Islands • Greenland & Iceland • Indonesia • Israel & the Sinai Desert • Jamaica • Japan • La Ruta Maya • Morocco • New York • North India • Pacific Islands (Fiji, Solomon Islands & Vanuatu) • South India • South West China • Turkey • Vietnam • West Africa • Zimbabwe, Botswana & Namibia

The Lonely Planet TV series is produced by: Pilot Productions
The Old Studio
18 Middle Row
London W10 5AT, UK

LONELY PLANET

Lonely Planet On-line
www.lonelyplanet.com *or* AOL keyword: lp

Whether you've just begun planning your next trip, or you're chasing down specific info on currency regulations or visa requirements, check out Lonely Planet On-line for up-to-the minute travel information.

As well as mini guides to more than 250 destinations, you'll find maps, photos, travel news, health and visa updates, travel advisories, and discussion of the ecological and political issues you need to be aware of as you travel. You'll also find timely upgrades to popular guidebooks which you can print out and stick in the back of your book.

There's also an on-line travellers' forum where you can share your experience of life on the road, meet travel companions and ask other travellers for their recommendations and advice.

And of course we have a complete and up-to-date list of all Lonely Planet travel products including travel guides, diving and snorkeling guides, phrasebooks, atlases, travel literature and videos, and a simple on-line ordering facility if you can't find the book you want elsewhere.

Lonely Planet Diving & Snorkeling Guides

Known for indispensible guidebooks to destinations all over the world, Lonely Planet's Pisces Books are the most popular series of diving and snorkeling titles available.

There are three series: **Diving & Snorkeling Guides**, **Shipwreck Diving** series and **Dive Into History**. Full colour throughout, the **Diving & Snorkeling Guides** combine quality photographs with detailed descriptions of the best dive sites for each location, giving divers a glimpse of what they can expect both on land and in water. The **Dive Into History** series is perfect for the adventure diver or armchair traveller. The **Shipwreck Diving** series provides all the details for exploring the most interesting wrecks in the Atlantic and Pacific oceans. The list also includes underwater ature and technical guides.

LONELY PLANET

Guides by Region

Lonely Planet is known worldwide for publishing practical, reliable and no-nonsense travel information in our guides and on our Web site. The Lonely Planet list covers just about every accessible part of the world. Currently there are nine series: travel guides, shoestring guides, walking guides, city guides, phrasebooks, audio packs, travel atlases, diving and snorkeling guides and travel literature.

AFRICA Africa – the South ● Africa on a shoestring ● Arabic (Egyptian) phrasebook ● Arabic (Moroccan) phrasebook ● Cairo ● Cape Town ● Central Africa ● East Africa ● Egypt ● Egypt travel atlas ● Ethiopian (Amharic) phrasebook ● The Gambia & Senegal ● Kenya ● Kenya travel atlas ● Malawi, Mozambique & Zambia ● Morocco ● North Africa ● South Africa, Lesotho & Swaziland ● South Africa, Lesotho & Swaziland travel atlas ● Swahili phrasebook ● Trekking in East Africa ● Tunisia ● West Africa ● Zimbabwe, Botswana & Namibia ● Zimbabwe, Botswana & Namibia travel atlas
Travel Literature: The Rainbird: A Central African Journey ● Songs to an African Sunset: A Zimbabwean Story ● Mali Blues: Traveling to an African Beat

AUSTRALIA & THE PACIFIC Australia ● Australian phrasebook ● Bushwalking in Australia ● Bushwalking in Papua New Guinea ● Fiji ● Fijian phrasebook ● Islands of Australia's Great Barrier Reef ● Melbourne ● Micronesia ● New Caledonia ● New South Wales & the ACT ● New Zealand ● Northern Territory ● Outback Australia ● Papua New Guinea ● Papua New Guinea (Pidgin) phrasebook ● Queensland ● Rarotonga & the Cook Islands ● Samoa ● Solomon Islands ● South Australia ● Sydney ● Tahiti & French Polynesia ● Tasmania ● Tonga ● Tramping in New Zealand ● Vanuatu ● Victoria ● Western Australia
Travel Literature: Islands in the Clouds ● Sean & David's Long Drive

CENTRAL AMERICA & THE CARIBBEAN Bahamas and Turks & Caicos ● Barcelona ● Bermuda ● Central America on a shoestring ● Costa Rica ● Cuba ● Dominican Republic & Haiti ● Eastern Caribbean ● Guatemala, Belize & Yucatán: La Ruta Maya ● Jamaica ● Mexico ● Mexico City ● Panama
Travel Literature: Green Dreams: Travels in Central America

EUROPE Amsterdam ● Andalucía ● Austria ● Baltic States phrasebook ● Berlin ● Britain ● British phrasebook ● Central Europe ● Central Europe phrasebook ● Croatia ● Czech & Slovak Republics ● Denmark ● Dublin ● Eastern Europe ● Eastern Europe phrasebook ● Edinburgh ● Estonia, Latvia & Lithuania ● Europe ● Finland ● France ● French phrasebook ● Germany ● German phrasebook ● Greece ● Greek phrasebook ● Hungary ● Iceland, Greenland & the Faroe Islands ● Ireland ● Italian phrasebook ● Italy ● Lisbon ● London ● Mediterranean Europe ● Mediterranean Europe phrasebook ● Paris ● Poland ● Portugal ● Portugal travel atlas ● Prague ● Provence & the Côte D'Azur ● Romania & Moldova ● Russia, Ukraine & Belarus ● Russian phrasebook ● Scandinavian & Baltic Europe ● Scandinavian Europe phrasebook ● Scotland ● Slovenia ● Spain ● Spanish phrasebook ● St Petersburg ● Switzerland ● Trekking in Spain ● Ukrainian phrasebook ● Vienna ● Walking in Britain ● Walking in Italy ● Walking in Ireland ● Walking in Switzerland ● Western Europe ● Western Europe phrasebook
Travel Literature: The Olive Grove: Travels in Greece

INDIAN SUBCONTINENT Bangladesh ● Bengali phrasebook ● Bhutan ● Delhi ● Goa ● Hindi/Urdu phrasebook ● India ● India & Bangladesh travel atlas ● Indian Himalaya ● Karakoram Highway ● Nepal ● Nepali phrasebook ● Pakistan ● Rajasthan ● South India ● Sri Lanka ● Sri Lanka phrasebook ● Trekking in the Indian Himalaya ● Trekking in the Karakoram & Hindukush ● Trekking in the Nepal Himalaya
Travel Literature: In Rajasthan ● Shopping for Buddhas

LONELY PLANET

Mail Order

Lonely Planet products are distributed worldwide. They are also available by mail order from Lonely Planet, so if you have difficulty finding a title please write to us. North and South American residents should write to 150 Linden St, Oakland, CA 94607, USA; European and African residents should write to 10a Spring Place, London NW5 3BH, UK; and residents of other countries to PO Box 617, Hawthorn, Victoria 3122, Australia.

ISLANDS OF THE INDIAN OCEAN Madagascar & Comoros • Maldives • Mauritius, Réunion & Seychelles

MIDDLE EAST & CENTRAL ASIA Arab Gulf States • Central Asia • Central Asia phrasebook • Iran • Israel & the Palestinian Territories • Israel & the Palestinian Territories travel atlas • Istanbul • Jerusalem • Jordan & Syria • Jordan, Syria & Lebanon travel atlas • Lebanon • Middle East on a shoestring • Turkey • Turkish phrasebook • Turkey travel atlas • Yemen
Travel Literature: The Gates of Damascus • Kingdom of the Film Stars: Journey into Jordan

NORTH AMERICA Alaska • Backpacking in Alaska • Baja California • California & Nevada • Canada • Florida • Hawaii • Honolulu • Los Angeles • Miami • New England USA • New Orleans • New York City • New York, New Jersey & Pennsylvania • Pacific Northwest USA • Rocky Mountain States • San Francisco • Seattle • Southwest USA • USA • USA phrasebook • Vancouver • Washington, DC & the Capital Region
Travel Literature: Drive Thru America

NORTH-EAST ASIA Beijing • Cantonese phrasebook • China • Hong Kong • Hong Kong, Macau & Guangzhou • Japan • Japanese phrasebook • Japanese audio pack • Korea • Korean phrasebook • Kyoto • Mandarin phrasebook • Mongolia • Mongolian phrasebook • North-East Asia on a shoestring • Seoul • South-West China • Taiwan • Tibet • Tibetan phrasebook • Tokyo
Travel Literature: Lost Japan

SOUTH AMERICA Argentina, Uruguay & Paraguay • Bolivia • Brazil • Brazilian phrasebook • Buenos Aires • Chile & Easter Island • Chile & Easter Island travel atlas • Colombia • Ecuador & the Galapagos Islands • Latin American Spanish phrasebook • Peru • Quechua phrasebook • Rio de Janeiro • South America on a shoestring • Trekking in the Patagonian Andes • Venezuela
Travel Literature: Full Circle: A South American Journey

SOUTH-EAST ASIA Bali & Lombok • Bangkok • Burmese phrasebook • Cambodia • Hill Tribes phrasebook • Ho Chi Minh City • Indonesia • Indonesian phrasebook • Indonesian audio pack • Jakarta • Java • Laos • Lao phrasebook • Laos travel atlas • Malay phrasebook • Malaysia, Singapore & Brunei • Myanmar (Burma) • Philippines • Pilipino (Tagalog) phrasebook • Singapore • South-East Asia on a shoestring • South-East Asia phrasebook • Thailand • Thailand's Islands & Beaches • Thailand travel atlas • Thai phrasebook • Thai audio pack • Vietnam • Vietnamese phrasebook • Vietnam travel atlas

ALSO AVAILABLE: Antarctica • Brief Encounters: Stories of Love, Sex & Travel • Chasing Rickshaws • Not the Only Planet: Travel Stories from Science Fiction • Travel with Children • Traveller's Tales

LONELY PLANET

FREE Lonely Planet Newsletters

W e love hearing from you and think you'd like to hear from us.

Planet Talk

Our FREE quarterly printed newsletter is full of tips from travellers and anecdotes from Lonely Planet guidebook authors. Every issue is packed with up-to-date travel news and advice, and includes:

- a postcard from Lonely Planet co-founder Tony Wheeler
- a swag of mail from travellers
- a look at life on the road through the eyes of a Lonely Planet author
- topical health advice
- prizes for the best travel yarn
- news about forthcoming Lonely Planet events
- a complete list of Lonely Planet books and other titles

To join our mailing list, residents of the UK, Europe and Africa can email us at go@lonelyplanet.co.uk; residents of North and South America can email us at info@lonelyplanet.com; the rest of the world can email us at talk2us@lonelyplanet.com.au, or contact any Lonely Planet office.

Comet

O ur FREE monthly email newsletter brings you all the latest travel news, features, interviews, competitions, destination ideas, travellers' tips & tales, Q&As, raging debates and related links. Find out what's new on the Lonely Planet Web site and which books are about to hit the shelves.

Subscribe from your desktop: www.lonelyplanet.com/comet

Index

Text

Bold indicates maps.
Italics indicates boxed text.

D

Bold indicates maps.
Italics indicates boxed text.

Bold indicates maps.
Italics indicates boxed text.

Boxed Text

MAP LEGEND

BOUNDARIES

▬▪▬▪▬▪▬ International
▬▪▪▬▪▪▬ State
▬ ▬ ▬ ▬ Disputed

HYDROGRAPHY

Coastline
/. River, Creek
Lake
Intermittent Lake
Salt Lake
Canal
◎ ⟿ Spring, Rapids
Waterfalls
Swamp

ROUTES & TRANSPORT

Freeway
Highway
Major Road
Minor Road
Unsealed Road
City Freeway
City Highway
City Road
City Street, Lane

Pedestrian Mall
Tunnel
Train Route & Station
Metro & Station
Tramway
Cable Car or Chairlift
Walking Track
Walking Tour
Ferry Route

AREA FEATURES

Building
✿ Park, Gardens
Cemetery

Market
Beach, Desert
Urban Area

MAP SYMBOLS

✈	Airport		←	One Way Street
	Ancient or City Wall		▣	Parking
∴	Archaeological Site		)(	Pass
⊖	Bank		★	Police Station
⋒	Beach		✉	Post Office
⊼	Castle or Fort		❖	Shopping Centre
⌒	Cave		🏛	Stately Home
✚	Church		▭	Swimming Pool
	Cliff or Escarpment		✡	Synagogue
○	Embassy		☎	Telephone
⊕	Hospital		⊙	Toilet
☪	Mosque		❶	Tourist Information
▲	Mountain or Hill		⊖	Transport
🏛	Museum		🐘	Zoo

✪ **CAPITAL** National Capital
◉ **CAPITAL** State Capital
● **CITY** City
● **Town** Town
● **Village** Village
○ Point of Interest

■ Place to Stay
Å Camping Ground
ᴔ Caravan Park
⌂ Hut or Chalet
▼ Place to Eat
▯ Pub or Bar

Note: not all symbols displayed above appear in this book

LONELY PLANET OFFICES

Australia
PO Box 617, Hawthorn, Victoria 3122
☎ (03) 9819 1877 fax (03) 9819 6459
email: talk2us@lonelyplanet.com.au

USA
150 Linden St, Oakland, CA 94607
☎ (510) 893 8555 TOLL FREE: 800 275 8555
fax (510) 893 8572
email: info@lonelyplanet.com

UK
10a Spring Place, London NW5 3BH
☎ (020) 7428 4800 fax (020) 7428 4828
email: go@lonelyplanet.co.uk

France
1 rue du Dahomey, 75011 Paris
☎ 01 55 25 33 00 fax 01 55 25 33 01
email: bip@lonelyplanet.fr
minitel: 3615 lonelyplanet *(1,29 F TTC/min)*

World Wide Web: www.lonelyplanet.com *or* **AOL keyword: lp**
Lonely Planet Images: lpi@lonelyplanet.com.au